Solaris 9 Operating Environment Reference

Janice Winsor

Sun Microsystems Press
A Prentice Hall Title

Printed in the United States of America

10 9 8 7 6 5 4 3 2 1

ISBN 0-13-100701-7

Sun Microsystems Press
A Prentice Hall Title

PREFACE

The *Solaris 9 Operating Environment Reference* is your complete guide to all of the manual pages in Section 1, "User Commands," of the online reference documentation (except the FMLI commands).

All documentation references within this guide are to the official Solaris documentation. To access Sun Microsystems, Inc. documentation online, see

`http://docs.sun.com.`

Audience

This book is for any user of the Solaris Operating Environment who needs to refer to any of the Section 1 User Commands in the online manual pages for quick reference or for more detailed information.

Conventions Used in This Book

The following table shows the typographic conventions used in this book.

Typeface or Symbol	Description
`courier`	Indicates a command, file name, object name, method, argument, JavaScript keyword, HTML tag, file content, or code excerpt.
`courier italics`	Indicates a variable that you should replace with a valid value.

Typeface or Symbol	Description
`courier`	Indicates text that you type.
italics	Indicates definitions, emphasis, or a book title.

Icons

New!

Within this reference, any material that is new or revised in the Solaris 8 or 9 release is marked with a "New!" icon in the margin.

The list of commands in the `Intro` manual page in Chapter I is marked with asterisks to show commands that are changed or revised in the Solaris 7 release. Commands new in the Solaris 8 and Solaris 9 releases are marked with the "New!" icon in the margin.

Any command introduced in the Solaris 8 release is marked with a "New!" icon in the margin next to the command name. Any additional changes made in the Solaris 9 release are marked with a "New!" icon next to the new material.

How This Book Is Organized

The Introduction chapter provides a quick reference to the contents of this book by functional grouping. The commands are grouped alphabetically within their installation package categories. Within the "Core Solaris (Usr)" category, the commands are grouped by function.

The Introduction chapter also provides a list of commands added in the Solaris 8 and Solaris 9 releases along with a list of commands that were removed from each release.

This book is a dictionary-style alphabetic reference to the A through Z commands.

ACKNOWLEDGMENTS

Sun Microsystems Press would like to acknowledge the following people for their contributions to the *Solaris 9 Operating Environment Reference.*

Gordon Marler for his excellent technical input and many examples. Gordon unpacked his first Sun workstation in 1987 and has been fascinated by UNIX ever since. He has worked as a UNIX System Administrator and Architect in Texas, Washington state, and New York City for various firms in the pharmaceutical, telecommunications, and financial fields, as well as a government contract here and there. He is currently a UNIX System Administrator for a global financial service institution and lives in New Jersey.

Peter H. Gregory, author of *Solaris Security* and *Sun Certified System Administrator for Solaris 8 Study Guide,* for organizing Gordon's help as a technical reviewer.

Bill Lane, Sun Microsystems, Inc., for enabling me to participate in the Solaris 9 Beta program and to Larissa Brown, Miguel Ulloa, and Beauty Shields, for help with administrative details.

The following members of the Solaris 9 Beta team, listed in alphabetical order, who were instrumental in answering questions and responding to my Solaris 9 Beta problem reports: Leanne Berger, Kevin Brown, Jim Carleton, Suzanne Chapple, Tom Hardesty, Vladimir Juric, Brian Pryor, Sharon Sam, Devesh Shah, Mike Wahlberg, and Ed Wetmore.

Linda Gallops, SQA Product Engineering, Sun Microsystems, Inc., for technical help.

The author would like to acknowledge the following people for their contributions to this book.

All individuals at Sun Microsystems, Inc., who contributed to the Section 1 manual pages.

Michael Alread of Sun Microsystems Press; Greg Doench of Prentice Hall; and Rachel Borden, formerly of Sun Microsystems Press, for their ongoing support and friendship.

Mary Lou Nohr for editing this manuscript with her usual skill and tact.

Wil Mara of Prentice Hall for help with troubleshooting pesky font problems.

Kathleen M. Caren of Prentice Hall for production support.

CONTENTS

E

K

L

M

O

P

T

INTRODUCTION

This book is your complete alphabetic reference to all (except the FMLI commands) of the manual pages in Section 1 of the online reference documentation for the Solaris 9 release. Refer to the *Solaris 8 System Administrator's Reference* by Janice Winsor—published by Sun Microsystems Press and Prentice Hall—for information about the commands in Section 1M.

This chapter provides a quick reference to the contents of this book by functional grouping. The commands are grouped alphabetically within their installation package categories. Within the "Core Solaris (Usr)" category, the commands are grouped by function.

Commands new in the Solaris 8 and Solaris 9 releases are marked with a "New" icon in the margin. See "Commands New in Solaris 8 Releases" on page 22 and "Commands Removed from Solaris 8 Releases" on page 23 for changes in the Solaris 8 releases. See "Commands New in the Solaris 9 Release" on page 24 and "Commands Removed from the Solaris 9 Release" on page 24 for changes in the Solaris 9 release. New package names in the Solaris 9 release are marked with a "New" icon in the margin, and commands that have been moved between packages are noted in the description for the moved command.

Netscape Communicator (NSCPcom)

netscape	Start Netscape Communicator for Solaris.

Audio Applications (SUNWauda)

audioconvert	Convert audio file formats.
audioplay	Play audio files.
audiorecord	Record an audio file.

New!   `mixerctl`   Audio mixer control command-line application.

ABI Application Certification Tools (SUNWapct)

New!   `appcert`   Examine application-level products for unstable use of Solaris interfaces.

Utility for Writing to CD-R/RW Discs (SUNWcdrw)

New!   `cdrw`   CD read and write.

New! Basic IP Commands (Usr) (SUNWbip)

`ftp`   File transfer program. Moved from SUNWcsu in the Solaris 9 release.

CCS Tools Bundled with SunOS (SUNWbtool)

`ar`	Maintain portable archive or library.
`dis`	Object code disassembler.
`dump`	Dump selected parts of an object file.
`elfdump`	Dump selected parts of an object file.
`gprof`	Display call-graph profile data.
`lex`	Generate programs for lexical tasks.
`lorder`	Find ordering relation for an object or library archive.
`mcs`	Manipulate the comment section of an object file.
`nm`	Print name list of an object file.
`prof`	Display profile data.
`ranlib`	Convert archives to random libraries.
`size`	Print section sizes in bytes of object files.
`strip`	Strip symbol table, debugging, and line-number information from an object file.
`symorder`	Rearrange a list of symbols.
`tsort`	Topological sort.
`unifdef`	Resolve and remove `ifdef`ed lines from C program source.
`yacc`	Yet another compiler-compiler.

CPU Performance Counter Libraries and Utilities (SUNWcpcu, SUNWcpcux)

New!   `cputrack`   Monitor process and LWP behavior with CPU performance counters.

Core Solaris (Usr) (SUNWcsu)

Archiving Commands

cpio	Copy file archives in and out.
eject	Eject media such as CD-ROM and diskette from drive.
fdformat	Format diskette or PCMCIA memory card.
mt	Magnetic tape control.
pax	Portable archive interchange.
rmformat	Removable rewritable media format command.
tar	Create tape archives and add or extract files.
unzip	List, test, and extract compressed files from a ZIP archive.
zip	Package and compress (archive) files.
zipinfo	List detailed information about a ZIP archive.

Communication Commands

login	Sign on to the system.
mail, rmail	Read mail or send mail to users.
mailcompat	Provide compatibility for Solaris mailbox.
mailx, mail, Mail	
	Interactive message processing system.
mconnect	Connect to SMTP mail server socket.
mesg	Permit or deny messages.
rsh, remsh, remote_shell	
	Remote shell.
tip	Connect to remote system.
vacation	Reply to mail automatically.
write	Write to another user.

Device Allocation

allocate	Device allocation.
deallocate	Device deallocation.
list_devices	List allocatable devices.

Extended Attribute Commands

runat	Execute command in extended attribute namespace.

File Management Commands

cat	Concatenate and display files.

`cd, chdir, pushd, popd, dirs`

              Change working directory.

`chgrp`   Change file group ownership.

`chmod`   Change the permissions mode of a file.

`chown`   Change file ownership.

`cksum`   Write file checksums and sizes.

`cmp`   Compare two files.

`cp`   Copy files.

`crypt`   Encrypt or decrypt a file.

`file`   Determine file type.

`getfacl`   Display discretionary file information.

`head`   Display first few lines of files.

`kill`   Terminate or signal processes.

`ln`   Make hard or symbolic links to files.

`ls`   List contents of directory.

`mkdir`   Make directories.

`more, page`   Browse or page through a text file.

`mv`   Move files.

`pathchk`   Check path names.

`pg`   File perusal filter.

`ps`   Report process status.

`pwd`   Return working directory name.

`rm, rmdir`   Remove directory entries.

`setfacl`   Modify the Access Control List (ACL) for a file or files.

New!   `setpgrp`   Set process group ID.

`tail`   Deliver the last part of a file.

`tee`   Replicate the standard output.

`touch`   Change file access and modification times.

`type`   Write a description of command type.

`umask`   Get or set the file-mode creation mask.

`which`   Locate a command; display its path name or alias.

Localization Commands

dumpcs	Show codeset table for the current locale.
geniconvtbl	Generate `iconv` code-conversion tables.
gettext	Retrieve text string from message database.
iconv	Code set conversion utility.
isalist	Display the native instruction sets for this platform.
localedef	Define locale environment.
xstr	Extract strings from C programs.

See also "System Localization (SUNWloc)" on page 20.

Miscellaneous

Intro, intro	Introduction to commands and application programs.
newgrp	Log in to a new group.
passwd	Change login password and password attributes.
pwck, grpck	Password and group file checkers.
rpcgen	RPC protocol compiler.
script	Make record of a terminal session.
tplot, t300, t300s, t4014, t450, tek, ver	
	Graphics filters for various plotters.

NIS+/Secure RPC Commands

chkey	Change user's secure RPC key pair.
keylogin	Decrypt and store secret key with `keyserv`.
keylogout	Delete stored secret key with `keyserv`.

Package Commands

pkginfo	Display software package information.
pkgmk	Produce an installable package.
pkgparam	Display package parameter values.
pkgproto	Generate prototype file entries for input to `pkgmk` command.
pkgtrans	Translate package format.

Platform Resource Commands

arch	Display the architecture of the current host.
hostid	Print the numeric identifier of the current host.
hostname	Set or print name of current host system.

isainfo	Describe instruction set architectures.
kbd	Keyboard command.
loadkeys, dumpkeys	
	Load and dump keyboard translation tables.
mach	Display the processor type of the current host.
machid, sun, pdp11, sparc, u3b, u3b2, u3b5, u3b15, vax, u370	
	Get processor type truth value.
optisa	Determine which variant instruction set is optimal.
pagesize	Display the size of a page of memory.
tput	Initialize a terminal or query terminfo database.
tty	Return user's terminal name.
uname	Print name of current system.

Programming Commands

New!

amt	Run abstract machine test.
asa	Convert FORTRAN carriage-control output to printable form.
install	Install commands.
ld.so.1	Runtime linker for dynamic objects.

Role-Based Access Control (RBAC) Commands

New! auths — Print authorizations granted to a user.

New! newtask — Create new task.

New! pfexec, pfsh, pfcsh, pfksh

Execute a command in a profile.

New! profiles — Print execution profiles for a user.

New! projects — Print project membership of user.

New! roles — Print roles granted to a user.

Search Commands

egrep	Search a file for a pattern, using full regular expressions.
fgrep	Search a file for a fixed-character string.
find	Find files.
grep	Search a file for a pattern.

Shell Programming Commands

alias, unalias	Create or remove a pseudonym.

`basename, dirname`

> Deliver portions of path names.

`break, continue` Shell built-in functions.

`command` Execute a simple command.

`csh` Shell command interpreter with a C-like syntax.

`echo` Write arguments to standard output.

`exec, eval, source`

> Shell built-in functions to execute other commands.

`exit, return, goto`

> Shell built-in functions to enable the shell to advance beyond its sequence of steps.

`expr` Evaluate argument as an expression.

`function` Shell built-in command to define a shell function.

`getopt` Parse command options.

`getoptcvt` Convert to `getopts` to parse command options.

`getopts` Parse utility options.

`glob` Shell built-in function to expand a word list.

`goto, exit, return`

> Shell built-in functions.

`hash, rehash, unhash, hashstat`

> Evaluate the internal hash table of the contents of directories.

`history, fc` Process command history list.

`jobs, fg, bg, stop, notify`

> Control process execution.

`ksh, rksh` Korn shell, a standard/restricted command and programming language.

`let` Shell built-in function to evaluate one or more arithmetic expressions.

`logout` Shell built-in function to exit from a login session.

`nohup` Run a command immune to hangups.

`print` Shell built-in function to output characters to the screen or window.

`read` Read a line from standard input.

`readonly` Shell built-in function to protect the value of the given variable from reassignment.

`set, unset, setenv, unsetenv, export`

> Shell environment variable built-in functions.

`sh, jsh`	Standard and job control shell and command interpreter.
`shell_builtins`	Shell command interpreter built-in functions.
`shift`	Shell built-in function to traverse either a shell's argument list or a list of field-separated words.
`sleep`	Suspend execution for an interval.
`stop`	Control process execution.
`suspend`	Shell built-in function to halt the current shell.
`test`	Evaluate conditions.
`times`	Shell built-in function to report time use of the current shell.
`trap, onintr`	Shell built-in functions to respond to hardware signals.
`true, false`	Provide truth values.
`typeset, whence`	Shell built-in command to get or set attributes and values for shell variables and functions.
`ulimit, unlimit`	Set or get shell limitations on system resources.
`wait`	Await process completion.

System Status Commands

`atq`	Display the jobs queued to run at specified times.
`atrm`	Remove jobs spooled by `at` or `batch`.
`crontab`	User chronological table file.
`date`	Write the date and time.
`dispgid`	Display a list of all valid group names.
`dispuid`	Display a list of all valid user names.
`du`	Report number of free disk blocks and files.
`env`	Set environment for command invocation.
`fmtmsg`	Display a message on standard error or system console.
`getconf`	Get configuration values.
`groups`	Print group membership of user.
`limit, ulimit, unlimit`	
	Set or get limitations on available system resources.
`listusers`	List user login information.
`logger`	Add entries to the system log.
`nice`	Invoke a command with an altered scheduling priority.
`pgrep, pkill`	Find or signal processes.
`priocntl`	Display or set scheduling parameters of specified process(es).
`renice`	Alter priority of running processes.

`time`	Time a simple command.
`uptime`	Show how long a system has been up.
`w`	Display information about currently logged-in users.
`who`	Report who is on the system.

Terminal Commands

`clear`	Clear the terminal screen.
`stty`	Set the options for a terminal.
`tabs`	Set tabs on a terminal.

Text Processing

`cut`	Cut out selected fields of each line of a file.
`ed, red`	Text editor.
`edit`	Text editor (variant of ex for casual users).
`ex`	Display-based text editor.
`fmt`	Simple text formatter.
`fold`	Filter for folding lines.
`join`	Relational database operator.
`line`	Read one line.
`m4`	Macro processor.
`nawk`	Pattern scanning and processing language.
`patch`	Apply changes to files.
`pr`	Print files.
`sed`	Stream editor.
`tr`	Translate characters.
`vi, view, vedit`	Screen-oriented visual display editor based on ex.
`wc`	Display a count of lines, words, and characters in a file.
`xargs`	Construct argument lists and invoke command.

Core Solaris (root) (SUNWcsr)

`dhcpinfo`	Display value of parameters received through DHCP.

Apptrace Utility (SUNWcstl, SUNWcstlx)

`apptrace`	Trace application function calls to Solaris shared libraries.

New!

Documentation Tools (SUNWdoc)

addbib	Create or extend a bibliographic database.
apropos	Locate commands by keyword lookup.
checkeq	Typeset mathematics test.
checknr	Check nroff and troff input files for errors.
deroff	Remove nroff/troff, tbl, and eqn constructs.
diffmk	Mark differences between versions of a troff input file.
eqn, neqn, checkeq	
	Typeset mathematics test.
indxbib	Create an inverted index to a bibliographic database.
lookbib	Find references in a bibliographic database.
man	Find and display reference manual pages.
nroff	Format documents for display or line printer.
refer	Expand and insert references from a bibliographic database.
roffbib	Format and print a bibliographic database.
soelim	Resolve and eliminate .so requests from nroff or troff input.
sortbib	Sort a bibliographic database.
tbl	Format tables for nroff or troff.
troff	Typeset or format documents.
ul	Underline text on terminal display.
vgrind	Format program listings.
whatis	Display a one-line summary about a command.

Extended System Utilities (SUNWesu, SUNWesxu)

at, batch	Execute commands at a later time.
awk	Pattern scanning and processing language.
banner	Make posters.
bc	Binary calculator.
bdiff	Big diff.
bfs	Big file scanner.
cal	Display a calendar.
calendar	Reminder service.
col	Reverse linefeeds filter.
comm	Select or reject lines common to two files.

`compress, uncompress, zcat`	
	Compress, uncompress files or display expanded files.
`csplit`	Split files, based on context.
`dc`	Desk calculator.
`diff`	Display line-by-line differences between pairs of text files.
`diff3`	Three-way differential file comparison.
`dircmp`	Directory comparison.
`dos2unix`	Convert text file from DOS format to ISO format.
`expand, unexpand`	Expand Tab characters to space characters, and vice versa.
`factor`	Obtain the prime factors of a number.
`graph`	Draw a graph.
`last`	Display login and logout information.
`lastcomm`	Display the last commands executed, in reverse order.
`logname`	Return user's login name.
`look`	Find words in the system dictionary or lines in sorted list.
`mpss.so.1`	Shared object for setting preferred page size. *New!*
`newform`	Change the format of a text file.
`news`	Print news items.
`nl`	Line numbering filter.
`pack, pcat, unpack`	
	Compress and expand files.
`paste`	Merge corresponding or subsequent lines of files.
`ppgsz`	Set preferred stack and/or heap page size. *New!*
`plimit`	Get or set the resource limits of running processes.
`prctl`	Get or set the resource controls of running processes, tasks, and projects. *New!*
`preap`	Force a defunct process to be reaped by its parent. *New!*
`proc, pargs, pcred, pfiles, pflags, pldd, pmap, prun, psig, pstack, pstop, ptime, ptree, pwait, pwdx`	
	`proc` tools.
`sdiff`	Print differences between two files side-by-side.
`sort`	Sort, merge, or sequence-check text files.
`spell, hashmake, spellin, hashcheck`	
	Report spelling errors.
`spline`	Interpolate smooth curve.

split	Split a file into pieces.
strchg, strconf	Change or query stream configuration.
sum	Print checksum and block count for a file.
tcopy	Copy a magnetic tape.
uniq	Report or filter out repeated lines in a file.
units	Convert quantities expressed in standard scales to other units.
unix2dos	Convert text file from ISO format to DOS format.
uuencode, uudecode	
	Encode or decode a binary file.
New! yes	Generate repetitive affirmative output.
zcat	Compress or uncompress files or display expanded files.

Federated Naming System (SUNWfns)

fnattr	Update and examine attributes associated with an FNS named object.
fnbind	Bind a reference to an FNS name.
fnlist	Display the names and references bound in an FNS context.
fnlookup	Display the reference bound to an FNS name.
fnrename	Rename the binding of an FNS name.
fnsearch	Search for FNS objects with specified attributes.
fnunbind	Unbind the reference from an FNS name.

FTP Server (Usr) (SUNWftpu)

New! ftpcount	Show current number of users in each FTP server class.
New! ftpwho	Show current process information for each FTP server user.

Layout Table Generation Command (SUNWglt)

New! genlayouttbl	Generate layout table for complex text layout.

New! The GNU Zip (gzip) Compression Utility (SUNWgzip)

gunzip	Uncompress files.
gzcat	Uncompress files.
gzcomp	Compare compressed files.
gzdiff	Compare compressed files.
gzexe	Compress executable files in place.

gzforce	Force a .gz extension on all gzip files.
gzip	Compress files.
gzmore	File filter for viewing of compressed text.
gznew	Recompress .Z files to .gz files.

Interprocess Communications (SUNWipc)

ipcrm	Remove a message queue, semaphore set, or shared memory ID.
ipcs	Report interprocess communication facilities status.

Kerberos Version 5 Support (SUNWkrbu)   *New!*

kdestroy	Destroy Kerberos tickets. Moved from SUNWcsu in the Solaris 9 release.
kinit	Kerberos login command. Moved from SUNWcsu in the Solaris 9 release.
klist	List currently held Kerberos tickets. Moved from SUNWcsu in the Solaris 9 release.
kpasswd	Change a user's Kerberos password. Moved from SUNWcsu in the Solaris 9 release. *New!*
ktutil	Kerberos keytab maintenance command. Moved from SUNWcsu in the Solaris 9 release. *New!*

LLC2 Driver and its Initialization Programs (SUNWllc)

llc2_autoconfig	
	Generate LLC2 configuration files. *New!*
llc2_config	Configure LLC2 interface parameters. *New!*
llc2_stats	LLC2 station, SAP, and connection statistics. *New!*

LDAP Libraries for Software Development of Dynamically Linked Executables (SUNWlldap)

ldap	LDAP as a naming repository. *New!*
ldapdelete	ldap delete entry tool.
ldapmodify, ldapadd	
	ldap entry addition and modification tools.
ldapmodrdn	ldap modify entry RDN tool.
ldapsearch	ldap search tool.

Modular Debugger (SUNWmdb, SUNWmdbx)

| | adb | General-purpose debugger (link to mdb). |
| New! | mdb | Modular debugger. |

MP Print Filter (SUNWmp)

New! mailp, newsp, digestp, filep, filofaxp, franklinp, timemanp, timesysp

| | | Front ends to the mp text to PDL pretty print filter. |
| New! | mp | Text to PDL pretty print filter. |

Solaris Network Cache and Accelerator (root) (SUNWncar, SUNWncarx)

| New! | nca, snca | The Solaris Network Cache and Accelerator (NCA). |
| New! | ncakmod | Start or stop the NCA kernel module. |

Solaris Network Cache and Accelerator (Usr) (SUNWncau)

| New! | ncab2clf | Convert binary log file to common log file format. |

New! Network File System (NFS) Client Support (Usr) (SUNWnfscu)

| | on | Execute a command on a remote system with the local environment. Moved from SUNWcsu in the Solaris 9 release. |

Network Information System (Usr) (SUNWnisu)

New!	ldaplist	Search and list naming information from an LDAP directory service.
	nis+, NIS+, nis	New version of the Network Information Name Service.
	niscat	Display NIS+ tables and objects.
	nischgrp	Change the group owner of an NIS+ object.
	nischmod	Change access rights on an NIS+ object.
	nischown	Change the owner of an NIS+ object.
	nischttl	Change the time-to-live value of an NIS+ object.
	nisdefaults	Display NIS+ default values.
	niserror	Display NIS+ error messages.
	nisgrep	Search NIS+ tables.
	nisgrpadm	NIS+ group administration command.
	nisln	Symbolically link NIS+ objects.
	nisls	List the contents of an NIS+ directory.

```
nismatch, nisgrep
```
        Search NIS+ tables.

`nismkdir`   Create NIS+ directories.

`nisopaccess`   NIS+ operation access control administration command.   *New!*

`nispasswd`   Change NIS+ password information.

`nisrm`   Remove NIS+ objects from the namespace.

`nisrmdir`   Remove NIS+ directories.

`nistbladm`   Administer NIS+ tables.

`nistest`   Return the state of the NIS+ namespace, using conditional expression.

`ypcat`   Print values in an NIS database.

`ypmatch`   Print the value of keys from an NIS map. Moved from `SUNWcsu` in the Solaris 9 release   *New!*

`yppasswd`   Change your network password in the NIS database. Moved from `SUNWcsu` in the Solaris 9 release.   *New!*

`ypwhich`   Return name of NIS server of map master.

Network File System (NFS) Server Support (Usr) (SUNWnfssu)   *New!*

`exportfs`   Translate `exportfs` options to share or unshare commands. Moved from `SUNWcsu` in the Solaris 9 release.

Perl 5.6.1 (Core) (SUNWpl5u)
Perl 5.6.1 (POD Documentation (SUNWpl5p)
Perl 5 Online Manual Pages (SUNWpl5m)

`perl`   Practical extraction and report language.   *New!*

PostScript Filters (Usr) (SUNWpsf)

`download`   Download host-resident PostScript font.

`dpost`   `troff` postprocessor for PostScript printers.

`postdaisy`   PostScript translator for Diablo 630 daisy-wheel files.

`postdmd`   PostScript translator for DMD bitmap files.

`postio`   Serial interface for PostScript printers.

`postmd`   Matrix display program for PostScript printers.

`postplot`   PostScript translator for `plot`(4) graphics files.

`postprint`   PostScript translator for text files.

`postreverse`   Reverse the page order in a PostScript file.

`posttek`   PostScript translator for Tektronix 4014 files.

New! *Remote Network Client Commands (SUNWrcmdc)*

`filesync`	Synchronize ordinary, directory, or special files. Moved from SUNWcsu in the Solaris 9 release.
`rcp`	Remote file copy. Moved from SUNWcsu in the Solaris 9 release.
`rdist`	Remote file distribution program. Moved from SUNWcsu in the Solaris 9 release.
`rlogin`	Remote login. Moved from SUNWcsu in the Solaris 9 release.
`rup`	Show host status of remote systems (RPC version). Moved from SUNWesu in the Solaris 9 release.
`ruptime`	Show host status of local systems. Moved from SUNWcsu in the Solaris 9 release.
`rusers`	Display who is logged in on remote systems. Moved from SUNWesu in the Solaris 9 release.
`rwho`	Display who is logged in on local systems. Moved from SUNWcsu in the Solaris 9 release.
`whois`	Internet user name directory service. Moved from SUNWcsu in the Solaris 9 release.

New! *Remote Network Server Commands (Usr) (SUNWrcmds)*

`finger`	Display information about local and remote users. Moved from SUNWcsu in the Solaris 9 release.
`talk`	Talk to another user. Moved from SUNWcsu in the Solaris 9 release.

Commands for Processing RPM Archives (SUNWrpm)

New! `rpm2cpio`	Convert Red Hat package (RPM) to `cpio` archive.

Sendmail User (SUNWsndmu)

New! `praliases`	Display system mail aliases.

SSH Client and Commands (SUNWsshu)

New! `scp`	Secure copy (remote file copy program).
New! `sftp`	Secure file transfer program.
New! `ssh`	Open SSH secure shell client (remote login program).
New! `ssh-add`	Add RSA or DSA identities for the authentication agent.
New! `ssh-agent`	Authentication agent.
New! `ssh-http-proxy-connect`	
	Secure shell proxy for HTTP.

`ssh-keygen`	Authentication key generation.	New!
`ssh-socks5-proxy-connect`		New!
	Secure shell proxy for SOCKS5.	

Trivial File Transfer Server (SUNWtftp)   New!

| `tftp` | Trivial file transfer program. Moved from `SUNWcsu` in the Solaris 9 release. |

Telnet Command (Client) (SUNWtnetc)   New!

| `telnet` | User interface to a remote system using the TELNET protocol. Moved from `SUNWcsu` in the Solaris 9 release. |

Programming Tools (SUNWtoo)

`crle`	Configure runtime linking environment.	New!
`ctags`	Create a `tags` file for use with `ex` and `vi`.	
`exstr`	Extract strings from source files.	
`gcore`	Get core images of running processes.	
`ld`	Link editor for object files.	
`ldd`	List dynamic dependencies of executable files or shared objects.	
`od`	Octal dump.	
`pvs`	Display the internal information of dynamic objects.	
`regcmp`	Compile regular expressions.	
`sotruss`	Trace shared library procedure calls.	
`strings`	Find printable strings in an object or binary file.	
`truss`	Trace system calls and signals.	
`whocalls`	Report on the calls to a specific procedure.	

sendmail User (SUNWsndmu)

`mailq`	Print the mail queue.	
`mailstats`	Print statistics collected by `sendmail`.	
`newaliases`	Rebuild the database for the mail aliases file. Moved from `SUNWnisu` in the Solaris 9 release.	New!

Solaris Bundled Tools (SUNWsprot)

| `as` | Assembler. |
| `cpp` | C language preprocessor. |

make	Maintain, update, and regenerate related programs and files.
sccs	Front end for the source code control system (SCCS).
sccs-admin, admin	
	Create and administer SCCS history files.
sccs-cdc, cdc	Change the commentary of an SCCS delta.
sccs-comb, comb	Combine SCCS deltas.
sccs-delta, delta	
	Make a delta to an SCCS file.
sccs-get, get	Retrieve a version of an SCCS file.
sccs-help, help	Ask for help regarding SCCS error or warning messages.
sccs-prs, prs	Display selected portions of an SCCS history.
sccs-prt, prt	Display delta table information from an SCCS file.
sccs-rmdel, rmdel	
	Remove a delta from an SCCS file.
sccs-sact, sact	Show editing activity status of an SCCS file.
sccs-sccsdiff, sccsdiff	
	Compare two versions of an SCCS file.
sccs-unget, unget	
	Undo a previous get of an SCCS file.
sccs-val, val	Validate an SCCS file.
sysV-make	Maintain, update, and regenerate groups of programs.
vc	Version control.
what	Extract SCCS version information from a file.

Solaris Documentation Server Lookup (SUNWab2m)

answerbook2	Online documentation system.

Solaris User Registration (SUNWsregu)

solregis	Solaris user registration.

Source Compatibility (Usr) (SUNWscpu)

biff	Give notice of incoming mail messages.
cc	C compiler.
df	Display status of disk space on file systems.
du	Summarize disk usage.

`fastboot, fasthalt`
              Reboot/halt the system without checking the disks.

`from`   Display the sender and date of newly arrived mail messages.

`lint`   C program verifier.

`mkstr`   Create an error message file by massaging C source files.

`plot, aedplot, atoplot, bgplot, crtplot, dumbplot, gigiplot, hpplot, implot, plottoa, t300, t300s, t4013, tek, vplot, hp7221plot`
              Graphics filters for various plotters.

`printenv`   Display current environment variable.

`rusage`   Print resource usage for a command.

`shutdown`   Close down the system at a given time.

`tset, reset`   Establish or restore terminal characteristics.

`ucblinks`   Add /dev entries for SunOS 4.x compatibility.

`users`   Display a compact list of logged-in users.

`vipw`   Edit the password file.

`whereis`   Locate the binary, source, and manual page files for a command.

`whoami`   Display the effective current user name.

SunSoft Print—Client (Usr) (SUNWpcu)

`cancel`   Cancel print request.

`enable, disable`
              Enable or disable LP printers.

`lp`   Submit print request.

`lpstat`   Display information about the status of the print service.

SunSoft Print—Source Compatibility (Usr) (SUNWscplp)

`lpc`   Line printer control program.

`lpq`   Display the contents of a print queue.

`lpr`   Submit print requests.

`lprm`   Remove print requests from the print queue.

`lptest`   Generate line printer ripple pattern.

System Accounting (Usr) (SUNWaccu)

`acctcom`   Search and print process accounting files.

`sag`   System activity graph.

sar	System activity reporter.
timex	Time a command; report process data and system activity.

System Localization (SUNWloc)

gencat	Generate a formatted message catalog.
genmsg	Generate a message source file by extracting messages from source files.
locale	Get locale-specific information.
mkmsgs	Create message files for use by gettxt.
msgfmt	Create a message object from a message file.
printf	Write formatted output.
srchtxt	Display contents of, or search for, a text string in message databases.
xgettext	Extract gettext call strings from C programs.

See also "Localization Commands" on page 5.

TNF Core Components (SUNWtnfc)

prex	Control tracing in a process or the kernel.
tnfdump	Convert binary trace normal form (TNF) file to ASCII.
tnfxtract	Extract kernel probes output into a trace file.

UUCP Utilities and Daemon (SUNWbnuu)

ct	Spawn login to a remote terminal.
cu	Call another UNIX system.
uucp, uulog, uuname	
	UNIX-to-UNIX system copy.
uuglist	Print the list of available service grades.
uupick	Public UNIX-to-UNIX system file copy.
uustat	uucp status inquiry and job control.
uuto, uupick	Public UNIX-to-UNIX system file copy.
uux	UNIX-to-UNIX system command execution.

Volume Management (Usr) (SUNWvolu)

volcancel	Cancel request for removable media not currently in drive.
volcheck	Check for media in a drive.
volmissing	Notify user that volume requested is not in the CD-ROM or diskette drive.

volrmmount   Call rmmount to mount or unmount media.

XCU4 Utilities (SUNWxcu4)

The XCU4 commands are an XPG4 superset of POSIX.1-1990, Solaris 2.4
POSIX.2-1992, and POSIX.2a-1992 containing extensions to POSIX standards from
XPG3.

ar   Maintain portable archive or library.

awk   Pattern scanning and processing language.

basename, dirname

                    Deliver portions of path names.

cp   Copy files.

ct   Spawn login to a remote terminal.

date   Write the date and time.

du   Display the number of disk blocks used per directory or file.   *New!*

ed, red   Text editor.

edit   Text editor (variant of ex for casual users).

egrep   Search a file for a pattern, using full regular expressions.

env   Set environment for command invocation.

ex   Display-based text editor.

fgrep   Search a file for a fixed-character string.

find   Find files.   *New!*

get   Retrieve a version of an SCCS file.   *New!*

getopts   Parse command options.   *New!*

grep   Search a file for a pattern.

ipcs   Report interprocess communication facilities status.   *New!*

jobs   Control process execution.   *New!*

kill   Terminate or signal processes.   *New!*

ksh, rksh   Korn shell, a standard and restricted command and
                    programming language.

ln   Make hard or symbolic links to files.

ls   List contents of directory.

m4   Macro processor.

make   Maintain, update, and regenerate related programs and files.

more, page   Browse or page through a text file.

mv   Move files.

nice   Invoke a command with an altered scheduling priority.

nl   Line-numbering filter.

nm	Print name list of an object file.
nohup	Run a command immune to hangups.
od	Octal dump.
pr	Print files.
rm, rmdir	Remove directory entries.
sccs	Front end for the Source Code Control System (SCCS).
sed	Stream editor.
sh, jsh	Standard and job control shell and command interpreter.
sort	Sort, merge, or sequence-check text files.
stty	Set the options for a terminal.
tail	Deliver the last part of a file.
tr	Translate characters.
vi, view, vedit	
	Screen-oriented visual display editor based on ex.
New! wait	Await process completion.
who	Report who is on the system.

New! Commands New in Solaris 8 Releases

apptrace	Trace application function calls to Solaris shared libraries.
auths	Print authorizations granted to a user.
cputrack	Monitor process and LWP behavior with CPU performance counters.
crle	Configure runtime linking environment.
geniconvtbl	Generate iconv code conversion tables.
genlayouttbl	Generate layout table for complex text layout.
gunzip	Uncompress files.
gzcat	Uncompress files.
gzcomp	Compare compressed files.
gzdiff	Compare compressed files.
gzexe	Compress executable files in place.
gzforce	Force a .gz extension on all gzip files.
gzip	Compress files.
gzmore	File filter for viewing of compressed text.
gznew	Recompress .Z files to .gz files.
kpasswd	Change a user's Kerberos password.
ktutil	Kerberos keytab maintenance command.

ldap	LDAP as a naming repository.
ldaplist	Search and list naming information from an LDAP directory service.
llc2_autoconfig	
	Generate LLC2 configuration files.
llc2_config	Configure LLC2 interface parameters.
llc2_stats	LLC2 station, SAP, and connection statistics.
mailp, digestp, filep, filofaxp, franklinp, newsp, timemanp, timesysp	
	Front ends to the mp text to PDL pretty print filter.
mdb	Modular debugger.
mixerctl	Audio mixer control command-line application.
mp	Text to PDL pretty print filter.
nca, snca	The Solaris network cache and accelerator (NCA).
ncab2clf	Convert binary log file to common log file format.
ncakmod	Start or stop the NCA kernel module.
netscape	Start Netscape Communicator for Solaris.
nisopaccess	NIS+ operation access control administration command.
perl	Practical extraction and report language.
pfexec, pfsh, pfcsh, pfksh	
	Execute a command in a profile.
praliases	Display system mail aliases.
profiles	Print execution profiles for a user.
roles	Print roles granted to a user.

Commands Removed from Solaris 8 Releases   *New!*

appletviewer	View Java applets.
makekey	Generate encryption key.
native2ascii	Native-to-ASCII converter.
pcmapkeys	Set keyboard extended map and scan code translation for the PC console in text mode.
rmic	Java RMI stub compiler.
rmiregistry	Register remote Java objects.
serialver	Show serial version.

New! *Commands New in the Solaris 9 Release*

allocate	Device allocation.
amt	Run abstract machine test.
appcert	Examine application-level products for unstable use of Solaris interfaces.
cdrw	CD read and write.
deallocate	Device deallocation.
ftpcount	Show current number of users in each FTP server class.
ftpwho	Show current process information for each FTP server user.
list_devices	List allocatable devices.
mpss.so.1	Shared object for setting preferred page size.
newtask	Create new task.
ppgsz	Set preferred stack and/or heap page size.
prctl	Get or set the resource controls of running processes, tasks, and projects.
preap	Force a defunct process to be reaped by its parent.
projects	Print project membership of user.
rmformat	Removable rewritable media format command.
rpm2cpio	Convert Red Hat Package (RPM) to cpio archive.
runat	Execute command in extended attribute name space.
scp	Secure copy (remote file copy program).
setpgrp	Set process group ID.
sftp	Secure file transfer program.
ssh	Open SSH secure shell client (remote login program).
ssh-add	Add RSA or DSA identities for the authentication agent.
ssh-agent	Authentication agent.
ssh-http-proxy-connect	
	Secure shell proxy for HTTP.
ssh-keygen	Authentication key generation.
ssh-socks5-proxy-connect	
	Secure shell proxy for SOCKS5.
yes	Generate repetitive affirmative output.

New! *Commands Removed from the Solaris 9 Release*

adb	General-purpose debugger. Now a link to mdb(1).

case, switch, select

      Shell built-in functions.

for, foreach, repeat

      Shell built-in repeat functions.

if	Evaluate conditions.
jar	Java archive tool.
javac	Java compiler.
javadoc	Java API documentation generator.
javah	C header and stub file generator.
javald	Create Java application wrappers.
javap	Java class file disassembler.
jre	Java runtime interpreter.
kerberos	Introduction to the Kerberos security system. Refer to SEAM(5) instead.
ksrvtgt	Fetch and store Kerberos ticket-granting ticket, using a service key.
loadfont	Display or change IA video card font information.
smart2cfg	Compaq Smart-2 EISA/PCI and Smart-2SL PCI array controller ioctl command.
while	Shell built-in function to execute conditional actions.

A

acctcom — Search and Print Process Accounting Files

Synopsis

```
/usr/bin/acctcom [-abfhikmqrtv] [-C sec] [-e time] [-E time] [-g group]
    [-H factor] [-I chars] [-l line] [-n pattern] [-o output-file]
    [-O sec] [-s time] [-S time] [-u user] [filename...]
```

Description

acctcom is one of the suite of commands that you use with the structured set of tools to build accounting systems. Use the acctcom command to search process accounting files created by acct(4) and to display selected records to standard output.

acctcom reads file names, the standard input, or /var/adm/pacct in the form described by acct(4) and writes selected records to standard output. Each record represents the execution of one process. The output shows the COMMAND, USER, TTY, START TIME, END TIME, REAL (SEC), CPU (SEC), MEAN SIZE (K), and optionally, F (the fork()/exec() flag: 1 for fork() without exec()), STAT (the system exit status), HOG FACTOR, KCORE MIN, CPU FACTOR, CHARS TRNSFD, and BLOCKS READ (total blocks read and written).

When you execute the command with superuser privileges, a pound sign (#) is prepended to the command name. When a process is not associated with a known terminal, a ? is displayed in the TTY field.

/var/adm/pacct is read when you do not specify a file name and when the standard input is associated with a terminal or /dev/null (as is the case when using & in the shell). Otherwise, the standard input is read.

Any file-name arguments are read in their respective order. Each file is normally read forward, that is, in chronological order by process completion time. The file

27

/var/adm/pacct is usually the current file to be examined; a busy system may need several such files, of which all but the current file are found in /var/adm/pacctincr. acctcom reports only on terminated processes. Use ps(1) for active processes.

Options

-a	Show some average statistics about the processes selected. Print the statistics after the output records.
-b	Read backward, showing latest commands first. This option has no effect when standard input is read.
-C *sec*	Show only processes with total CPU time (system-time + user-time) that exceed *sec* seconds.
-e *time*	Show processes existing at or before *time*.
-E *time*	Show processes ending at or before *time*. Using the same time for both -S and -E, show the processes that existed at *time*.
-f	Print the fork()/exec() flag and system exit status columns in the output. Display the numeric output in octal.
-g *group*	Show only processes belonging to *group*. You can designate the group by either the group ID or group name.
-h	Instead of mean memory size, show the fraction of total available CPU time consumed by the process during its execution. This hog factor is computed as (total CPU time)/(elapsed time).
-H *factor*	Show only processes that exceed *factor*, where *factor* is the hog factor, as explained in option -h, above.
-i	Print columns containing the I/O counts in the output.
-I *chars*	Show only processes transferring more characters than the cutoff number given by *chars*.
-k	Instead of memory size, show total kcore-minutes.
-l *line*	Show only processes belonging to terminal /dev/term/*line*.
-m	Show mean core size (the default).
-n *pattern*	Show only commands matching *pattern* that may be a regular expression, as in regcmp(3C), except + means one or more occurrences.
-o *output-file*	Copy selected process records in the input data format to *output-file*, suppress printing to standard output.
-O *sec*	Show only processes with CPU system time exceeding *sec* seconds.
-q	Do not print any output records, just print the average statistics, as with the -a option.
-r	Show CPU factor (user-time/(system-time + user-time)).
-s *time*	Show processes existing at or after *time*, given in the format *hr*[:*min*[:*sec*]].
-S *time*	Show processes starting at or after *time*.

-t	Show separate system and user CPU times.
-u *user*	Show only processes belonging to *user*. You can specify a user ID, a login name that is then converted to a user ID, # (which designates only those processes executed with superuser privileges), or ? (which designates only those processes associated with unknown user IDs).
-v	Exclude column headings from the output.

Examples

The following example turns on accounting, lists the contents of the /var/adm/pacct file by using the acctcom command without any arguments, and then turns off accounting. Notice that the accton command used to turn on accounting has a pound sign in front of it because it was run by superuser.

```
castle% su
castle#/usr/lib/acct/accton /var/adm/pacct
castle# exit
castle% acctcom
COMMAND                        START    END       REAL    CPU     MEAN
NAME        USER    TTYNAME    TIME     TIME     (SECS) (SECS) SIZE(K)
#accton     root    pts/3      12:09:16 12:09:16  0.12   0.05   543.20
csh         root    pts/3      12:09:21 12:09:21  0.01   0.01   748.00
ls          root    pts/3      12:09:29 12:09:29  0.03   0.03   548.00
more        root    pts/3      12:09:34 12:09:34  0.03   0.03   537.33
acctcom     root    pts/3      12:09:47 12:09:47  0.08   0.07   689.14
dtfile      winsor  ?          12:09:59 12:09:59  0.03   0.03  2510.67
dtfile      winsor  ?          12:10:02 12:10:02  0.02   0.02  3350.00
uusched     uucp    ?          12:11:00 12:11:00  0.05   0.05   409.60
uuxqt       uucp    ?          12:11:00 12:11:00  0.06   0.05   449.60
uudemon.    uucp    ?          12:11:00 12:11:00  0.15   0.04   489.00
#sh         uucp    ?          12:11:00 12:11:00  0.20   0.06   477.33
dtfile      winsor  ?          12:13:00 12:13:00  0.02   0.02  3298.00
dtfile      winsor  ?          12:13:03 12:13:03  0.02   0.02  3338.00
dtfile      winsor  ?          12:16:00 12:16:00  0.03   0.03  2514.67
dtfile      winsor  ?          12:16:03 12:16:03  0.02   0.02  3212.00
dtfile      winsor  ?          12:19:01 12:19:01  0.03   0.03  2472.00
dtfile      winsor  ?          12:19:04 12:19:04  0.02   0.02  3326.00
accton      winsor  pts/5      12:20:06 12:20:06  0.03   0.03   677.33
castle% su
castle# /usr/lib/acct/accton
castle# exit
castle%
```

Files

/etc/group	System group file.

/etc/passwd

System password file.

/var/adm/pacctincr

Active processes accounting file.

Attributes

See `attributes`(5) for descriptions of the following attributes:

Attribute Type	Attribute Value
Availability	SUNWcsu
CSI	Enabled

See Also

`ps(1)`, `acct(1M)`, `acctcms(1M)`, `acctcon(1M)`, `acctmerg(1M)`, `acctprc(1M)`,
`acctsh(1M)`, `fwtmp(1M)`, `runacct(1M)`, `su(1M)`, `acct(2)`, `regcmp(3C)`, `acct(4)`,
`utmp(4)`, `attributes(5)`
   System Administration Guide

---

adb — General-Purpose Debugger

Synopsis

```
/usr/bin/adb [-k] [-w] [-I dir] [-P prompt] [-V mode] [objectfile
   [corefile [swapfile]]]
```

Description

The `adb` command is an interactive, general-purpose debugger. You can use it to
examine files. It also provides a controlled environment for the execution of programs.

New!
   Starting with the Solaris 9 release, the `adb` command is a link to the `mdb`(1) command.
The `mdb` command is a low-level debugger that you can use to examine user processes,
the live operating system, and operating system crash dumps. The new `mdb` command
provides complete backwards compatibility with the existing syntax and features of `adb`,
including support for processing `adb` macro files. The *Solaris Modular Debugger Guide*
and `mdb`(1) manual page describe the features of `mdb`, including its `adb` compatibility
mode. This mode is activated by default if the `adb` link is present and is executed.

Attributes

See `attributes`(5) for descriptions of the following attributes:

Attribute Type	Attribute Value
Availability	SUNWmdb (32-bit)
	SUNWmdbx (64-bit)

See Also

New!
   `mdb(1)`, `attributes(5)`
   Solaris Modular Debugger Guide

addbib — Create or Extend a Bibliographic Database

Synopsis

/usr/bin/addbib [-a] [-p *promptfile*] *database*

Description

Use the addbib command to create or add entries to a bibliographic database. Once you create the database, you can search, index, sort, and format the database by using the related *bib commands. When you start addbib, you can display instructions by typing **y** at the Instructions? prompt. Typing **n** or Return skips them. addbib then prompts you for various bibliographic fields, reads responses from the terminal, and sends output records to *database*. A null response (just pressing Return) means to leave out that field. A minus sign (-) means to go back to the previous field. A trailing backslash (\) enables you to continue a field on the next line. You can, however, type a multiple-line abstract without using the trailing backslash. The repeating Continue? prompt enables you to resume either by typing **y** or by pressing Return. To quit the current session, type **n** or **u**. You can edit the database with any system editor such as vi(1), ex(1), or ed(1) by typing the name of the editor at the Continue? prompt.

Options

-a
: Suppress prompting for an abstract; asking for an abstract is the default. You end abstracts by pressing Control-D.

-p *promptfile*
: Use a new prompting skeleton, defined in *promptfile*. This file should contain prompt strings, a Tab, and the key letters to be written to the database.

Usage

The most common bibliography key letters and their meanings are listed below. When you use the addbib command to add entries, the prompts are displayed in English. However, if you later edit the bibliography file, the bibliography key letters are displayed as part of the file.

Key Letter	Description
%A	Author's name.
%B	Book containing article referenced.
%C	City (place of publication).
%D	Date of publication.
%E	Editor of book containing article referenced.
%F	Footnote number or label (supplied by refer).
%G	Government order number.
%H	Header commentary, printed before reference.
%I	Issuer (publisher).

Key Letter	Description
%J	Journal containing article.
%K	Keywords to use in locating reference.
%L	Label field used by -k option of refer.
%M	Bell Labs Memorandum (undefined).
%N	Number within volume.
%O	Other commentary, printed at end of reference.
%P	Page number(s).
%Q	Corporate or foreign author (unreversed).
%R	Report, paper, or thesis (unpublished).
%S	Series title.
%T	Title of article or book.
%V	Volume number.
%X	Abstract—used by roffbib, not by refer.
%Y,Z	Ignored by refer.

Examples

The following example creates a *database* named bibliography, displays the instructions, adds one entry, and then displays the contents of the database by means of the vi editor.

```
castle% addbib bibliography
Instructions? y

Addbib will prompt you for various bibliographic fields.
If you don't need a particular field, just hit Return,
        and that field will not appear in the output file.
If you want to return to previous fields in the skeleton,
        a single minus sign will go back a field at a time.
        (This is the best way to input multiple authors.)
If you have to continue a field or add an unusual field,
        a trailing backslash will allow a temporary escape.
Finally, (without -a) you will be prompted for an abstract
Type in as many lines as you need, and end with a ctrl-d.
To quit, type `q' or `n' when asked if you want to continue.
To edit the database, type `edit', `vi', or `ex' instead.

    Author:    Janice Winsor
     Title:    Opening the Dream Door
   Journal:
    Volume:
     Pages:    153
 Publisher:    Merrill-West Publishing
      City:    Carmel, California
      Date:    1998
     Other:
```

```
      Keywords:      dreams, psychic development
      Abstract: (ctrl-d to end)
Not just another dream interpretation book! Opening the Dream Door
is a practical guide to psychic development. Written in a
friendly, personal style, Opening the Dream Door does not
attempt to interpret dream symbology. It is the author's belief
that each person has their own personal myths and symbols that
cannot be deciphered in a collective fashion. By using her own
dreams as an example, Janice Winsor makes practical suggestions
for expanding the subconscious life and connecting to other realms.
Processes for remembering and accessing dreams are taught in an
easy to understand style.
^D
Continue? vi
%A Janice Winsor
%T Opening the Dream Door
%P 153
%I Merrill-West Publishing
%C Carmel, California
%D 1998
%K dreams, psychic development
%X Not just another dream interpretation book! Opening the Dream Door
is a practical guide to psychic development. Written in a
friendly, personal style, Opening the Dream Door does not
attempt to interpret dream symbology. It is the author's belief
that each person has their own personal myths and symbols that
cannot be deciphered in a collective fashion. By using her own
dreams as an example, Janice Winsor makes practical suggestions
for expanding the subconscious life and connecting to other realms.
Processes for remembering and accessing dreams are taught in an
easy to understand style.
~
~
~
"bibliography" 27 lines, 946 characters
```

Attributes

See attributes(5) for descriptions of the following attributes:

Attribute Type	Attribute Value
Availability	SUNWcsu

See Also

ed(1), ex(1), indxbib(1), lookbib(1), refer(1), roffbib(1), sortbib(1),
vi(1), attributes(5)

admin, sccs-admin — Create and Administer SCCS History Files

Synopsis

```
/usr/ccs/bin/admin [-bhnz] [-a username |groupid]... [-d flag]...
    [-e username |groupid]... [-f flag [value]]... [-i [filename]]
    [-m mr-list] [-rrelease] [-t [description-file]] [-y[comment]]
    s.filename...
```

Description

See sccs-admin(1).

aedplot — Graphics Filters for Various Plotters

Synopsis

```
/usr/ucb/plot [-Tterminal]
```

Description

See plot(1).

alias, unalias — Create or Remove a Pseudonym

Synopsis

```
/usr/bin/alias [alias-name[=string]...]
/usr/bin/unalias alias-name...
/usr/bin/unalias -a
```

csh

```
alias [name [def]]
unalias pattern
```

ksh

```
**
alias [-tx] [alias-name[=value]]...
unalias alias-name...
```

Description

New!

The alias command enables you to define simple aliases. An alias is a pseudonym or shorthand term for a command or series of commands. The functionality of aliases is different in the C and Korn shell environments.

You specify the name you want to use as the alias and define some text that is substituted by the shell whenever that word is used as a command. For example, because one engineer so consistently mistyped the more command as moer, he created an alias so that when he typed moer, the more command was executed. You can also create aliases to simplify complicated commands. You use the unalias command to remove an alias.

An alias can contain as many words as you want, provided you enclose them in quotation marks. You can also include several commands connected by a pipe.

The /usr/bin directory contains alias and unalias commands. The C and Korn shells also provide built-in alias and unalias commands. The Bourne shell does not provide aliasing capabilities. The syntax for defining aliases is slightly different, depending on the environment.

/usr/bin/alias

To display a list of defined aliases, type alias and press Return. An alias definition affects the current shell execution environment and the execution environments of the subshells of the current shell. When used as specified here, the alias definition does not affect the parent process of the current shell or any command environment invoked by the shell.

/usr/bin/unalias

The unalias command removes the definition for each alias name specified. The aliases are removed from the current shell execution environment.

C Shell

To display a list of currently defined aliases on standard output, type **alias** with no arguments and press Return.

To define an alias for the current shell, type **alias** *name def* and press Return. Because they are reserved words, you cannot use the names alias or unalias for *alias-name*. To include spaces in *def*, enclose the definition in quotes.

To display the definition for a specific alias, type **alias** *alias-name* and press Return.

When defining aliases for the current shell, you must have entered an alias definition on a previous command line before you can use it.

Use the unalias command to discard aliases that match *alias-name*. To remove all aliases, type **unalias** * and press Return.

To make your favorite aliases more readily available, include them in your .cshrc file.

Korn Shell

The Korn shell comes with a default set of predefined aliases. To display the list on standard output, type **alias** with no arguments and press Return.

To define an alias for the current shell, type **alias** *alias-name=value* and press Return. A trailing space in *value* checks the next word for alias substitution. Because they are reserved words, you cannot use the names alias or unalias for *alias-name*.

To display the definition for a specific alias, type **alias** *alias-name* and press Return.

Use the unalias command to discard aliases that match *alias-name*. To remove all aliases, type **unalias** * and press Return.

To make your favorite aliases more readily available, include them in your Korn shell ENV file.

> **Note** — If you set aliases in your .profile file, only the login shell has access to them unless you use the -x option to export the aliases. Any shell you invoke after you log in—such as those in xterms in an X Windows environment—will not have unexported aliases defined.

To create a Korn shell ENV file, create a file named *filename* and put your aliases in it. Then export the environment file with the following command.

ENV=*filename*;export ENV

Options

Korn Shell
The Korn shell provides the following options for the built-in alias command.

-t   Create a tracked alias. The Korn shell remembers the full path name of the command to enable it to be found more quickly and to be issued from any directory. If you supply no *alias-name* argument, list all currently tracked aliases.

-x   Export the alias so that it can be used in shell scripts and other subshells. If you supply no *alias-name* argument, list all current exported aliases.

The following option is supported by unalias.

-a   Remove all alias definitions from the current shell execution environment.

Operands
The following operand is supported for the alias command.

alias-name   Write the alias definition to standard output.

The following operands are supported for the unalias command:

alias-name   The name of an alias to be removed.

alias-name=string

Assign the value of string to the alias *alias-name*.

When you specify no operands, all alias definitions are written to standard output.

Output
The format for displaying aliases (when no operands or only name operands are specified) is:

`"%s=%s\n"` *name, value*

The *value* string is written with appropriate quoting so that it is suitable for reinput to the shell.

Examples

C Shell

The following example creates an alias for the `alias` command and uses the alias shortcut to create an alias for the `history` command and to create a `moer` alias for the `more` command.

```
castle% alias a alias
castle% a h history
castle% a moer more
```

The following example lists aliases that are set in the `.cshrc` file.

```
castle% alias
G3      172.16.8.21
a       alias
c       clear
h       history
mac     172.16.8.20
castle%
```

Korn Shell

The following alias changes `ls` to give a more annotated output in columnar format.

```
alias ls="ls -CF"
```

The following alias creates a simple redo command to repeat previous entries in the command history file.

```
alias r='fc -s'
```

The following alias uses 1-kilobyte units for `du`.

```
alias du="du -k"
```

Alternatively, you can create the alias in the following form, using a backslash to escape the space character and omitting the double quotes around the command.

```
alias du=du\ -k
```

The following alias sets up `nohup` so that it can deal with an argument that is itself an alias name.

```
alias nohup="nohup "
```

The following example lists the default aliases that are set for the Korn shell.

```
$ alias
autoload='typeset -fu'
command='command '
functions='typeset -f'
history='fc -l'
integer='typeset -i'
local=typeset
nohup='nohup '
r='fc -e -'
```

```
stop='kill -STOP'
suspend='kill -STOP $$'
$
```

Environment Variables

See environ(5) for descriptions of the following environment variables that affect the execution of alias and unalias: LC_CTYPE, LC_MESSAGES, and NLSPATH.

Exit Status

0	Successful completion.
>0	One of the *alias-name* operands specified did not have an alias definition, or an error occurred.

Attributes

See attributes(5) for descriptions of the following attributes:

Attribute Type	Attribute Value
Availability	SUNWcsu

See Also

csh(1), ksh(1), shell_builtins(1), attributes(5), environ(5)

New! allocate — Device Allocation

Synopsis

```
/usr/sbin/allocate [-s] [-U uname] device
/usr/sbin/allocate [-s] [-U uname] -g dev-type
/usr/sbin/allocate [-s] [-U uname] -F device
```

Description

Use the allocate command, new in the Solaris 9 Operating Environment, to manage the ownership of devices with its allocation mechanism. The allocate command ensures that each device is used by only one qualified user at a time.

> **Note —** The functionality described in this manual page is available only if the Basic Security Module (BSM) has been enabled. See bsmconv(1M) for more information.

The Solaris 9 Operating Environment provides a device-allocation method—with the allocate(1), deallocate(1), dminfo(1M), and list_devices(1) commands—that fulfills the Trusted Computer System Evaluation Criteria (TCSEC) object-reuse requirement for computing systems at C2 level and above. The device allocation mechanism prevents simultaneous access to a device, prevents one user from reading media being written to by another user, and prevents one user from accessing any information from the device or driver internal storage after another user is finished with the device.

For example, several users often share a single tape drive that may not be located at an individual user's location. If the tape drive is located remotely, some time can elapse between the time the user loads a tape in the drive and the time the user invokes a command to access the tape in the drive. Because other users could access the drive while the tape is unattended, another user could access or overwrite the data on the tape. With the device allocation mechanism, you can ensure that one user at a time has access to a specific tape device.

To preserve the integrity of the owner of the device, the allocate operation is executed on all the device special files associated with that device.

Only authorized users can allocate a device. The required authorizations are specified in device_allocate(4).

Options

-g *dev-type*

Allocate a nonallocated device with a device type matching *dev-type*.

Use the *dev-type* argument to specify the type of device. You can determine the type of device from the output of the list_devices -l command. See "Examples" for an example.

-s   Suppress any diagnostic output.

-F *device*   Reallocate a device allocated to another user. This option is often used with -U to reallocate a specific device to a specific user. Only a user with the solaris.devices.revoke authorization is permitted to use this option.

Use the *device* argument to specify the device to be manipulated, for example st0 for a streaming tape device. You can display a list of available devices with the -l option to the list_devices(1) command, also new in the Solaris 9 Operating Environment. See "Examples" on page 685 for an example of the output from list_devices -l. The default allocate operation allocates the device special files associated with *device* to the UID of the current process.

When you specify the -F option, the device-cleaning program is executed when allocation is performed. This cleaning program is found in /etc/security/lib. The name of this program is found in the device_allocate(4) entry for the device in the *dev-exec* field.

-U *uname*   Use the user ID *uname* instead of the user ID of the current process when performing the allocate operation. Only a user with the solaris.devices.revoke authorization is permitted to use this option.

Examples

The following example allocates a tape drive.

```
mopoke% allocate st0
mopoke%
```

The following example allocates audio files by type.

```
mopoke% allocate -g audio files
mopoke%
```

Diagnostics

allocate returns a non-zero exit status in the event of an error.

Files

/etc/security/device_allocate

Mandatory access control information about each device.

/etc/security/device_maps

Access control information about each physical device.

/etc/security/dev/*

Lock files that must exist for each allocatable device.

/etc/security/lib/*

Device allocate files.

Attributes

See attributes(5) for descriptions of the following attributes.

Attribute Type	Attribute Value
Availability	SUNWcsu

See Also

deallocate(1), list_devices(1), bsmconv(1M), dminfo(1M),
device_allocate(4), device_maps(4), attributes(5)

New! amt — Run Abstract Machine Test

Synopsis

/usr/bin/amt [-s]

Description

Use the amt command, new in the Solaris 9 Operating Environment, for a Common
Criteria security certified system. Use the command to verify that the low-level
functions necessary to enforce the object reuse requirements of the Controlled Access
Protection Profile are working correctly. /usr/bin/amt is a shell script that executes
tests specific to your system. For a 32-bit system, the tests run as a 32-bit application.
For a 64-bit system, the tests run twice; once as a 32-bit application and once as a 64-bit
application.

amt lists test results with a PASS or FAIL for each test it performs unless you suppress output with the -s option.

Options

-s   Suppress output.

Examples

The following example shows the output of the amt command on a 64-bit system.

```
mopoke% amt


AMT Test Program -- 64 bit application
=================


Test 1- stack Side Boundary Test
TEST 1 PASSED


Test 2- Data Side Boundary Test.
PASS: Successful read/write in data area.
TEST 2 PASSED


Test 3- Text Area Not Writeable
Verify that a write to the text space does not cause a write to the
    executable file from which it came, or to another process which
    shares that text.
PASS: Caught the segmentation fault, meaning we can't write to text
    area.
TEST 3 PASSED


Test 4- Memory Not Shared After Write
Verify that anonymous memory initially shared by two processes (e.g.
    after a fork) is not shared after either process writes to it.
TEST 4 PASSED


Test 5- Memory Allocation is Not Shared
Verify that newly allocated memory in one of two processes created by
    forking does not result in newly allocated memory in the other.
Parent address of hole before child change: 0010BD50
Child end of hole before change: 0010BD50
Child end of hole after change: 0010DD50
Parent address of hole after child change: 0010BD50
PASS: Hole is same size in parent.
TEST 5 PASSED

TESTS SUCCEEDED
```

```
AMT Test Program -- 32 bit application
=================

Test 1- stack Side Boundary Test
TEST 1 PASSED


Test 2- Data Side Boundary Test.
PASS: Successful read/write in data area.
TEST 2 PASSED


Test 3- Text Area Not Writeable
Verify that a write to the text space does not cause a write to the
   executable file from which it came, or to another process which
   shares that text.
PASS: Caught the segmentation fault, meaning we can't write to text
   area.
TEST 3 PASSED


Test 4- Memory Not Shared After Write
Verify that anonymous memory initially shared by two processes (e.g.
   after a fork) is not shared after either process writes to it.
TEST 4 PASSED


Test 5- Memory Allocation is Not Shared
Verify that newly allocated memory in one of two processes created by
   forking does not result in newly allocated memory in the other.
Parent address of hole before child change: 00024818
Child end of hole before change: 00024818
Child end of hole after change: 00026818
Parent address of hole after child change: 00024818
PASS: Hole is same size in parent.
TEST 5 PASSED

TESTS SUCCEEDED

mopoke%
```

Exit Status

0	All tests passed.
>0	Count of the number of tests that failed.
<0	Incorrect command-line argument.

Attributes

See attributes(5) for descriptions of the following attributes.

Attribute Type	Attribute Value
Availability	SUNWcsu (32 bit)
	SUNWcsxu (64 bit)
Interface Stability	Evolving

See Also

attributes(5)

answerbook2 — Online Documentation System

Synopsis

/usr/dt/bin/answerbook2 [-h]

Description

The answerbook2 command brings up the default Web browser and shows any online documentation installed in the default AnswerBook2 server. If an AnswerBook2 server has not been defined, answerbook2 checks whether one is running on the user's system. If so, it displays that server's information.

To define a default AnswerBook2 server, use the environment variable AB2_DEFAULTSERVER.

This functionality is also accessible through the AnswerBook2 option on the CDE front panel Help menu.

Note — Once the Web browser is opened and you can view the AnswerBook2 library, you can use the online Help system to find out more about the AnswerBook2 product.

Options

-h   Display a usage statement.

Usage

At startup time, answerbook2 starts up the default Web browser (for example, HotJava or Netscape) and displays the URL specified for the default AnswerBook2 server. If no default AnswerBook2 server is defined, answerbook2 looks for http://localhost:8888.

Environment Variables

AB2_DEFAULTSERVER

> Fully qualified URL that identifies the default AnswerBook2 server to use. For example: `http://imaserver.eng.sun.com:8888/`.

Attributes

See `attributes`(5) for descriptions of the following attributes:

Attribute Type	Attribute Value
Availability	SUNWab2m

See Also

`ab2cd`(1M), `ab2admin`(1M), `attributes`(5)

New! appcert — Examine Application-Level Products for Unstable Use of Solaris Interfaces

Synopsis

```
/bin/appcert [-h][-n][-f infile][-w working_dir] [-B] [-L]
   [-S] {obj | dir}...
```

Description

Use the `appcert` command, new in the Solaris 9 Operating Environment, to examine an application's conformance to the Solaris Application Binary Interface (ABI). The Solaris ABI defines the runtime library interfaces in Solaris that are safe and stable for application use. More specifically, `appcert` identifies any dependencies on unstable runtime interfaces. It also can identify other risks that might break the product in a subsequent release of Solaris.

`appcert` checks for the following elements.

- Private symbol usage in Solaris libraries. These private symbols, that is, functions or data, are not intended for developer consumption. Solaris libraries use these interfaces to call one another. These symbols might change their semantic behavior or even disappear altogether (so-called demoted symbols), so it is a good practice to make sure your application does not depend on any of them.

- Static linking refers, specifically, to static linking of archives `libc.a`, `libsocket.a`, and `libnsl.a` instead of dynamically linking the corresponding `.so` files of the shared object. Because the semantics of private symbol calls from one Solaris library to another can change from one release to another, it is not a good practice to "hardwire" library code into your binary objects.

- Unbound symbols are library symbols (that is, functions or data) that the dynamic linker could not resolve when appcert was run. The unbound symbols might be an environment problem (for example, LD_LIBRARY_PATH) or a build problem (for example, not specifying -llib and/or -z *defs* with compiling). Unbound symbols are flagged to point out these problems in case a more serious problem is indicated.

You can readily examine an entire product with appcert—for example, if the product is a collection of many programs and supporting shared objects—by referring appcert to the directories where the product is installed.

To perform its task, appcert constructs a profile of interface dependencies for each object file within the product (whether an executable object or shared object), to determine all the dependent Solaris system interfaces. (Notice that appcert uses the Solaris runtime linker to make this determination.) These dependency profiles are then compared to a definition of the Solaris ABI to identify any interfaces that are Private (unsafe and unstable for application-level use).

appcert generates a simple rollup report that indicates which of the product's components had liabilities and what those liabilities were. The report aids developers who are examining their product's release-to-release stability.

Notice that appcert produces complete interface dependency information, both the Public (safe and stable) Solaris interfaces and the Private (non-ABI) interfaces. This information can also be examined for each product component if you want.

You must run appcert in the same environment in which the application being checked runs. Otherwise, it might not be able to resolve references correctly to interfaces in the Solaris libraries. Take the following steps.

1. Make sure that LD_LIBRARY_PATH and any other aspects of the environment are set to whatever settings are used when the application is run. Also make sure that it contains the directories that contain any non-Solaris shared objects that are part of the product, so that they can be found when referenced.

2. Make sure that all the binaries to be checked:
   - Are dynamically linked ELF objects.
   - Have execute permission set on executables (not necessary for shared objects).
   - Are not suid root (otherwise you have to be root to check them; make non-suid copies and check those if necessary).

You might find it useful to write a shell script that sets up the environment correctly and then runs appcert.

Some potential problems that can be encountered are listed below.

- appcert reports unbound symbols that appear to be part of Solaris libraries.

  This problem occurs when the application uses dlopen(3DL) to access a shared object that does not have its Solaris dependencies recorded. appcert cannot resolve symbol use in such cases, because the dynamic linker is never invoked on the shared object and there is no other dependency information that could be used to resolve the Solaris symbol bindings. This problem can also occur with non-Solaris symbols.

  To avoid this problem, make sure that when a shared object is built, its dependencies on Solaris libraries are explicitly recorded by using the -llib option on the compile line (see cc(1) and ld(1)).

- appcert reports that the application uses a Solaris private symbol that is not referenced in the application's source code.

This problem is most likely because of static linking of a Solaris library that references that symbol. Because appcert uses the dynamic linker to resolve symbols, statically linked libraries appear to appcert to be part of the application code (which, in a sense, they are). This problem can also sometimes happen as a result of macro substitution in a Solaris header file.

To avoid this problem, whenever possible do not statically link Solaris library archives into your application.

- appcert does not recognize a library as part of Solaris.

Some obsolete Solaris libraries are so old that they were obsoleted before their symbols could be versioned. Consequently, appcert cannot recognize them as being part of Solaris.

Options

-B	Run in batch mode. When you use this option, the output report contains one line per binary, beginning with PASS if no problems were detected for the binary, FAIL if any problems were found, or INC if the binary could not be completely checked. Do not interpret these labels too literally. For example, PASS just means that none of the appcert warnings were triggered. These strings are flush left and so can be selected by grep ^FAIL..., and so forth.
-f *infile*	Specify the file *infile* that contains a list of files (one per line) to check. This list is appended to the list determined from the command-line operands.
-h	Print the usage information.
-L	Prevent appcert from automatically appending shared object directories to LD_LIBRARY_PATH. By default, appcert examines your product for the presence of shared objects. If some are found, it appends the directories they reside in to LD_LIBRARY_PATH.
-n	Do not follow symbolic links when searching directories for binaries to check. See find(1).
-S	Append Solaris library directories (that is, /usr/openwin/lib:/usr/dt/lib) to LD_LIBRARY_PATH.
-w *working_dir*	Identify the directory in which to run the library components and create temporary files (default is /tmp).

Operands

{*obj* | *dir*}...

A complete list of objects or directories that contain the objects constituting the product to be checked. appcert recursively searches directories looking for object files; it ignores nonobject files.

Exit Status

0	Ran successfully and found no potential binary stability problems.

1	Failed to run successfully.
2	Some of the objects checked have potential binary stability problems.
3	No binary objects were located that could be checked.

Limitations

If the object file to be examined depends on libraries, those dependencies must be recorded in it (with the compiler's -l option).

If the object file to be examined depends on other shared libraries, those libraries must be accessible via LD_LIBRARY_PATH or RPATH when you run appcert.

For checking 64-bit applications, the machine must be running the 64-bit Solaris kernel. See isalist(1). Also, the checks for static linking are currently not done on 64-bit applications.

appcert cannot examine the following elements.

- Object files that are completely or partially statically linked.

  Completely statically linked objects are reported as unstable.
- Executable files that do not have execute permission set.

  These files are skipped. Shared objects without execute permission are not skipped.
- Object files that are setuid root.

  Because of limitations in ldd(1), setuid root files are skipped. Copy and/or change the permissions to check them.
- Non-ELF file executables such as shell scripts.
- Non-C language interfaces to Solaris; for example, C++ and Java.

  The code itself need not be in C as long as the calls to Solaris libraries are in C.

Output Files

appcert records its findings in the following files in the working directory (/tmp/appcert. ????? by default).

Index	A mapping between checked binaries and the subdirectory in the working directory in which the output specific to that binary can be found.
Report	A copy of the rollup report that was displayed on standard output when you ran appcert.
Skipped	A list of binaries that appcert was asked to check but had to skip, along with a brief reason why each was skipped.

In addition, per-object information is stored in the subdirectories under appcert. ?????/objects/, in the following files:

check.demoted_symbols

A list of symbols suspected to be demoted Solaris symbols.

check.dynamic.private

A list of private Solaris symbols to which the object makes direct bindings.

`check.dynamic.public`

> A list of public Solaris symbols to which the object makes direct bindings.

`check.dynamic.unbound`

> A list of symbols not bound by the dynamic linker when `ldd -r` was run. For convenience, `ldd` output lines containing `file not found` are also included.

`summary.dynamic`

> A pretty-printed summary of dynamic bindings for the objects examined, including tables of public and private symbols used from each Solaris library.

Other files are temporary files used internally by `appcert`.

Output Messages

Private Symbol Use

Private symbols are functions or data variables in a Solaris library that are not intended for developer or external use. These symbols are interfaces that the Solaris libraries use to call and communicate with one another. They are marked in `pvs(1)` output with the symbol version name `SUNWprivate`.

Private symbols can change their semantic behavior or even disappear altogether ("demoted" or "deprecated" symbols), so your application should not depend on any of them.

Demoted Symbols

Demoted symbols are functions or data variables in a Solaris library that were once private to that library and have been removed (or possibly scoped local to the library) in a later Solaris release. If your application directly calls one of these demoted symbols, it will fail to run (relocation error), starting with the release in which the symbol was removed.

In some rare cases, a demoted symbol returns in a later release. Nevertheless, the application will still not run on some releases.

Sun Microsystems, Inc., performed most of the library scoping in the transition from Solaris 2.5.1 to 2.6. This action was done to increase binary stability. Because these completely internal interfaces were made invisible (that is, they cannot be dynamically linked against), a developer cannot accidentally or intentionally call these interfaces. For more information, see the *Linker and Libraries Guide*, in particular the chapter on versioning. You can find this document online at `http://docs.sun.com`.

Unbound Symbols

Unbound symbols are library symbols (that is, functions or data) referenced by the application that the dynamic linker could not resolve when `appcert` was run.

> **Note —** `appcert` does not actually run your application, so some aspect of the environment that affects dynamic linking might not be set properly.

Unbound symbols do not necessarily indicate a potential binary stability problem. They mean only that when `appcert` was run, the runtime dynamic linker could not resolve these symbols.

Unbound symbols might be the result of LD_LIBRARY_PATH not set correctly. Make sure LD_LIBRARY_PATH is set so that all of your binary objects can find all of the libraries they depend on (either your product's own libraries, Solaris libraries, or those of a third party). Then rerun appcert.

You might find it useful to write a shell script that sets up the environment correctly and then runs appcert on the binaries you want to check.

Another common reason for unbound symbols is that a shared object under test has not recorded its dynamic dependencies, that is, at build time the -l option was not supplied to the compiler and ld(1). The shared object requires that the executables that link against it have the correct dependencies recorded.

Notice that such a shared object can either be linked in the standard way (that is, specified at an executable's build time) or be dynamically opened (for example, an executable calls dlopen(3DL) on the shared object which may be running). Either case can give rise to unbound symbols when appcert is run. You can usually resolve the former by setting LD_LIBRARY_PATH appropriately before running appcert. The latter (dlopen) is usually difficult to resolve. Under some circumstances, you might be able to set LD_PRELOAD appropriately to preload the needed libraries, but this procedure does not always work.

How do you know whether the environment has been set up correctly so that there will be no unbound symbols? It must be set up so that running ldd -r on the binary yields no file not found or symbol not found errors. See ld.so.1(1) and ldd(1) for more information on dynamic linking.

In any event, appcert flags unbound symbols as a warning in case they might indicate a more serious problem. Unbound symbols can be an indicator of dependencies on demoted symbols (symbols that have been removed from a library or scoped local to it). Dependencies on demoted symbols lead to serious binary stability problems.

However, setting up the environment properly should remove most unbound symbols. In general, it is good practice to record library dependencies at build time whenever possible because it helps make the binary object better defined and self-contained. Also recommended is the use of the -z *defs* option when building shared objects, to force the resolution of all symbols during compilation. See ld(1) for more information.

No Bindings Found

appcert runs /bin/ldd -r on each binary object to be tested. It sets the environment variable LD_DEBUG="files,bindings". (See ldd(1) and ld.so.1(1) for more information.) If that command fails for some reason, appcert has no dynamic symbol-binding information and finds no bindings.

appcert can fail if any of the following conditions is true.

- The binary object does not have read permission.
- The binary object is suid or sgid and the user does not have sufficient privileges.
- The binary object is an executable without the execute permission bit set.
- The binary object is a 64-bit application, but the kernel running on the current machine supports only 32-bit applications.
- The binary object is completely statically linked.
- The binary object has no library dependency information recorded.

Other cases exist as well (for example, out of memory). In general, this flag means that appcert could not completely examine the object because of permissions or environment. Try to modify the permissions or environment so that the dynamic bindings can be recorded.

Obsolete Library

An obsolete library is one whose use is deprecated and that might, in some future release, be removed from Solaris altogether. appcert flags these because applications depending on them might not run in future releases of Solaris. All interfaces, including Private ones, in an obsolete library are frozen and will not change.

Use of sys_errlist/sys_nerr

Direct use of the symbols sys_errlist or sys_nerr presents a risk in which reference might be made past the end of the sys_errlist array. These symbols are deprecated in 32-bit versions of Solaris and are absent altogether in 64-bit versions. Use strerror(3C) instead.

Use of Strong vs. Weak Symbols

The "strong" symbols (for example, _socket) associated with "weak" symbols (for example, socket) are reserved as private (their behavior could change in the future). Your application should directly reference only the weak symbol (usually the strong symbols begin with _).

Note — Under certain build environments, the strong/private symbol dependency gets recorded into your binary instead of the weak/public one, even though the source code doesn't appear to reference the private symbol. Nevertheless, you should take steps to trace down why this problem is occurring and fix the dependency.

Bugs

The use of the terms "public" and "private" as equivalent to "stable" and "unstable" is unfortunately somewhat confusing. In particular, experimental or evolving interfaces are Public in the sense that they are documented and their use is encouraged. But, they are unstable because an application built with them might not run on subsequent releases. Thus, they are classified as Private for appcert's purposes until they are no longer evolving. Conversely, obsolete interfaces eventually disappear, and so are unstable, even though they have been Public and stable in the past and are still treated as Public by appcert. Fortunately, these two situations are rare.

Attributes

See attributes(5) for descriptions of the following attributes.

Attribute Type	Attribute Value
Availability	SUNWapct
Interface Stability	Stable

See Also

cc(1), find(1), isalist(1), ld(1), ldd(1), ld.so.1(1), pvs(1), dlopen(3DL), strerror(3C), intro(4), attributes(5)
Linker and Libraries Guide

apptrace — Trace Application Function Calls to Solaris   *New!*
Shared Libraries

Synopsis

```
/bin/apptrace [-f][-F [!] tracefromlist][-T [!] tracetolist]
    [-o outputfile]
[[-tv][!] call , ...] command [command arguments]
```

Description

Use the apptrace command, new in the Solaris 8 Operating Environment, to run the
executable program specified by *command* and trace all calls that the program *command*
makes to the Solaris shared libraries. Tracing means that for each call the program
makes, apptrace reports the name of the library interface called, the values of the
arguments passed, and the return value.

By default, apptrace traces calls directly from the executable object to any of the
shared objects it depends on. Indirect calls (that is, calls made between shared objects
that the executable depends on) are not reported by default.

You can trace calls from or to additional shared objects with the -F or -T options. See
"Options."

The default format reports a single line per call, with no formatted printing of
arguments that are passed by reference or of data structures.

You can specify additional options to format printing with the -v option.

By default, every interface provided by a shared object is traced if called. However,
you can restrict the set of interfaces to be traced with the -t or -v option.

Because you generally can trace calls between any of the dynamic objects linked at
runtime (the executable object and any of the shared objects depended on), the report of
each traced call gives the name of the object from which the call was made. apptrace
traces all of the procedure calls that occur between dynamic objects via the procedure
linkage table, so only those procedure calls that are bound via the table are traced. See
the *Linker and Libraries Guide*.

Options

-f   Follow all children created by fork(2), and print truss(1) output on
               each. This option outputs a *pid* on each truss(1) output line.

-F [!] *tracefromlist*

               Trace calls from a comma-separated list of shared objects. Trace calls
               only from these shared objects. The default is to trace calls from the
               main executable only. Specify only the basename of the shared object.
               For example, libc matches /usr/lib/libc.so.1. Additionally,
               shell-style wildcard characters are supported as

               described in fnmatch(5). A list preceded by a ! defines a list of objects
               from which calls are excluded from the trace. If you require the tracing
               of calls from *command*, then *command* must be a member of
               tracefromlist.

-o *outputfile*

> Direct apptrace output to *outputfile*. By default, output is placed on the standard error.

-t [!]*call*, . . .

> Trace or exclude function calls. Trace those calls specified in the comma-separated list. If the list begins with a !, exclude the specified function calls from the trace output. The default is -t all. The use of shell-style wildcards is allowed.

-T [!]*tracetolist*

> Trace calls to a comma-separated list of shared objects. The default is to trace calls to all shared objects. As above, specify only the basename. Wildcards are allowed. A list preceded by a ! denotes a list of objects from which calls are excluded from the trace.

-v [!]*call*, . . .

> Provide verbose, formatted output of the arguments and return values of the function calls specified (as above in the -t option). Unlike truss(1) calls, calls named by the -v option do not need to be named by the -t option. For example, apptrace -v open is equivalent to truss -t open -v open.

Examples

The following example traces the date command.

```
mopoke% apptrace date
date      -> libc.so.1:atexit(func = 0xff3bb0ec) = 0x0
date      -> libc.so.1:atexit(func = 0x115cc) = 0x0
date      -> libc.so.1:setlocale(category = 0x6, locale = "") = "C"
date      -> libc.so.1:textdomain(domainname = "SUNW_OST_OSCMD") =
   "SUNW_OST_OSCMD"
date      -> libc.so.1:getopt(argc = 0x1, argv = 0xffbef57c, optstring =
   "a:u") = 0xffffffff errno = 0 (Error 0)
date      -> libc.so.1:time(tloc = 0x21cbc) = 0x3bf9f39f
date      -> libc.so.1:nl_langinfo(item = 0x3a) = "%a %b %e %T %Z %Y"
date      -> libc.so.1:localtime(clock = 0x21cbc) = 0xff0bea20
date      -> libc_psr.so.1:memcpy(s1 = 0xffbef4ec, s2 = 0xff0bea20, n =
   0x24) = 0xffbef4ec
date      -> libc.so.1:strftime(s = "Tue Nov 20 14:09:35 ", maxsize =
   0x400, format = "%a %b %e %T %Z %Y", timeptr = 0xffbef4ec) = 0x1c
date      -> libc.so.1:puts(Tue Nov 20 14:09:35 WST 2001
s = "Tue Nov 20 14:09:35 ") = 0x1d
date      -> libc.so.1:exit(status = 0)
mopoke%
```

The following example traces a specific set of interfaces with verbosity set.

```
mopoke% apptrace -v '*gid*' id -a
id        -> libc.so.1:getgid() = 0xa
  return = (gid_t) 10     (0xa)
id        -> libc.so.1:getegid() = 0xa
```

```
   return = (gid_t) 10    (0xa)
id          -> libc.so.1:getgrgid(gid = 0xa) = 0x2325c
  gid = (gid_t) 10       (0xa)
  return = (struct group *) 0x2325c (struct group) {
    gr_name: (char *) 0x23270 "staff"
    gr_passwd: (char *) 0x23276 ""
    gr_gid: (gid_t) 10   (0xa)
    gr_mem: (char **) 0x2326c
}

id          -> libc.so.1:getgrgid(gid = 0xa) = 0x2325c
  gid = (gid_t) 10       (0xa)
  return = (struct group *) 0x2325c (struct group) {
    gr_name: (char *) 0x23270 "staff"
    gr_passwd: (char *) 0x23276 ""
    gr_gid: (gid_t) 10   (0xa)
    gr_mem: (char **) 0x2326c
}

uid=1001(winsor) gid=10(staff) groups=10(staff)
mopoke%
```

Files

The link auditing feature of the Solaris runtime linker (ld.so.1(1)) provides basic
runtime support for apptrace. The apptrace command's use of the runtime support
relies on an auditing object (apptrace.so.1) in the /usr/lib/abi directory.

To perform formatted printing of arguments when tracing calls (as selected by the -v
option), apptrace needs to know the number and data types of the arguments supplied
to the called interface. apptrace relies on special runtime support shared objects to
perform formatted printing. A runtime support object is provided for each Solaris shared
library, which contains an interceptor function for each interface within the shared
library. These supporting shared objects are in the /usr/lib/abi directory. apptrace
uses a simple algorithm to map from the name of a library interface to the name of an
interceptor function in the library's object that supports verbose-tracing. When
apptrace does not find an interceptor in the library's shared object that supports
tracing, apptrace cannot determine the number or data types of the arguments for that
interface. apptrace then uses a default output for the call-tracing report (hex-formatted
printing of the first three arguments).

Limitations

In general, apptrace cannot trace calls to functions accepting variable argument lists.
Some clever coding in several specific cases works around this limitation, most notably
in the printf family.

Functions that try to probe the stack or otherwise extract information about the
caller cannot be traced. Some examples are [gs]etcontext(), getsp(),
[sig]longjmp(), [sig]setjmp(), and vfork().

Functions such as exit(2) that do not return can also produce strange output. Also, *New!*
functions that call other traced functions before returning produce slightly garbled
output.

For security reasons, only root can run apptrace on setuid/setgid programs. *New!*

Tracing functions, such as vwprintw(3XCURSES) and vwscanw(3XCURSES), whose
usage requires the inclusion of varargs.h, do not provide formatted printing of *New!*
arguments.

Attributes

See attributes(5) for descriptions of the following attributes.

Attribute Type	Attribute Value
Availability	SUNWcstl (**32 bit**)
	SUNWcstlx (**64 bit**)

See Also

New!

ld.so.1(1), truss(1), vwprintw(3XCURSES), vwscanw(3XCURSES), attributes(5), fnmatch(5)
Linker and Libraries Guide

apropos — Locate Commands by Keyword Lookup

Synopsis

/usr/bin/apropos *keyword*...

Description

apropos displays the manual page name, section number, and a short description for each manual page whose line contains the *keyword.* This information is contained in the /usr/share/man/windex database created by catman(1M). If catman(1M) was not run or was run with the –n option, apropos fails. Each word is considered separately, and the case of letters is ignored. Words that are part of other words are considered; for example, when looking for compile, apropos also finds all instances of compiler.

Note — apropos is actually just the –k option to the man(1) command.

Examples

The following examples show manual page information for the password, editor, and format keywords.

```
castle% apropos password
d_passwd        d_passwd (4)      - dial-up password file
dialups         dialups (4)       - list of terminal devices requiring a dial-up
     password
endpwent        getpwnam (3c)     - get password entry
endspent        getspnam (3c)     - get password entry
fgetpwent       getpwnam (3c)     - get password entry
fgetpwent_r     getpwnam (3c)     - get password entry
fgetspent       getspnam (3c)     - get password entry
fgetspent_r     getspnam (3c)     - get password entry
getpwent        getpwnam (3c)     - get password entry
getpwent_r      getpwnam (3c)     - get password entry
getpwnam        getpwnam (3c)     - get password entry
getpwnam_r      getpwnam (3c)     - get password entry
getpwuid        getpwnam (3c)     - get password entry
getpwuid_r      getpwnam (3c)     - get password entry
```

```
getspent       getspnam (3c)    - get password entry
getspent_r     getspnam (3c)    - get password entry
getspnam       getspnam (3c)    - get password entry
getspnam_r     getspnam (3c)    - get password entry
grpck          pwck (1m)        - password/group file checkers
lckpwdf        lckpwdf (3c)     - manipulate shadow password database lock file
nispasswd      nispasswd (1)    - change NIS+ password information
nispasswdd     rpc.nispasswdd (1m) - NIS+ password update daemon
...
castle% apropos editor
ed             ed (1)           - text editor
edit           edit (1)         - text editor (variant of ex for casual users)
ex             ex (1)           - text editor
ld             ld (1)           - link-editor for object files
ld             ld (1b)          - link editor, dynamic link editor
red            ed (1)           - text editor
sed            sed (1)          - stream editor
sed            sed (1b)         - stream editor
vedit          vi (1)           - screen-oriented (visual) display editor
                                  based on ex
vi             vi (1)           - screen-oriented (visual) display editor
                                  based on ex
view           vi (1)           - screen-oriented (visual) display editor
                                  based on ex
...
castle% apropos format
COLOR_PAIR     can_change_color (3xc)  - manipulate color information
Intro          Intro (4)        - introduction to file formats
NIS+           nis+ (1)         - a new version of the network information
                                  name service
PAIR_NUMBER    can_change_color (3xc)  - manipulate color information
_lwp_info      _lwp_info (2)    - return the time-accounting information of
                                  a single LWP
a.out          a.out (4)        - Executable and Linking Format (ELF) files
acct           acct (4)         - per-process accounting file format
ar             ar (4)           -  archive file format
asysmem        sysmem (3)       - return physical memory information
audioconvert   audioconvert (1)   - convert audio file formats
audit_control  audit_control (4)   - control information for system audit
                                     daemon
audit_data     audit_data (4)   - current information on audit daemon
can_change_color                 can_change_color (3xc)  - manipulate color
                                  information
catman         catman (1m)      - create the formatted files for the reference
                                  manual
...
```

Files

/usr/share/man/windex

Table of contents and keyword database.

Attributes

See attributes(5) for descriptions of the following attributes:

Attribute Type	**Attribute Value**
Availability	SUNWdoc
CSI	Enabled

See Also

man(1), whatis(1), catman(1M), attributes(5)

Diagnostics

/usr/share/man/windex: No such file or directory

This database does not exist. You must run catman(1M) to create it.

ar — Maintain Portable Archive or Library

Synopsis

```
/usr/ccs/bin/ar -d [-Vv] archive file...
/usr/ccs/bin/ar -m [-abiVv] [posname] archive file...
/usr/ccs/bin/ar -p [-sVv] archive [file...]
/usr/ccs/bin/ar -q [-cVv] archive file...
/usr/ccs/bin/ar -r [-abciuVv] [posname] archive file...
/usr/ccs/bin/ar -t [-sVv] archive [file...]
/usr/ccs/bin/ar -x [-CsTVv] archive [file...]

/usr/xpg4/bin/ar -d [-Vv] archive file...
/usr/xpg4/bin/ar -m [-abiVv] [posname] archive file...
/usr/xpg4/bin/ar -p [-sVv] archive [file...]
/usr/xpg4/bin/ar -q [-cVv] archive file...
/usr/xpg4/bin/ar -r [-abciuVv] [posname] archive file...
/usr/xpg4/bin/ar -t [-sVv] archive [file...]
/usr/xpg4/bin/ar -x [-CsTVv] archive [file...]
```

Description

The ar command maintains groups of files combined into a single archive file. Its main use is to create and update library files; however, you can use it for any similar purpose. The magic string and the file headers used by ar consist of printable ASCII characters. If an archive is composed of printable files, the entire archive is printable.

When ar creates an archive, it creates headers in a format that is portable across all machines. The portable archive format and structure are described in detail in ar(4).

The archive symbol table (described in ar(4)) is used by the link-editor ld to effect multiple passes over libraries of object files in an efficient manner. An archive symbol table is created and maintained by ar only when there is at least one object file in the archive. The archive symbol table is in a specially named file that is always the first file in the archive. This file is never mentioned or accessible to the user. Whenever you use the ar command to create or update the contents of such an archive, the symbol table is rebuilt. You can force the symbol table to be rebuilt by using the -s option.

Note — If you mention the same file twice in an argument list, that file may be put in the archive twice.

By convention, archives are suffixed with the characters .a.

Options

-a	Position new files in *archive* after the file named by the *posname* operand.
-b	Position new files in *archive* before the file named by the *posname* operand.
-c	Suppress the diagnostic message that is written to standard error by default when *archive* is created.
-C	Prevent extracted files from replacing like-named files in the file system. This option is useful when you also use -T to prevent truncated file names from replacing files with the same prefix.
-d	Delete one or more files from *archive*.
-i	Position new files in *archive* before the file named by the *posname* operand (equivalent to -b).
-m	Move files. If you specify -a, -b, or -i with the *posname* operand, move files to the new position; otherwise, move files to the end of *archive*.
-p	Print the contents of files in *archive* to standard output. If you specify no files, write the contents of all files in *archive* in the order of the archive.
-q	Quickly append files to the end of *archive*. Positioning options -a, -b, and -i are invalid. The command does not check whether the added files are already in *archive*. This option is useful to avoid quadratic behavior when creating a large archive piece-by-piece.
-r	Replace or add files in *archive*. If *archive* does not exist, create a new archive file and write a diagnostic message to standard error (unless you specify the -c option). If no files are specified and the archive exists, the results are undefined. Files that replace existing files do not change the order of the archive. If you use the -u option with the -r option, then only those files with dates of modification later than the archive files are replaced. If you use the -a, -b, or -i option, then you must specify the *posname* and indicate that new files are to be placed after (-a) or before (-b or -i) *posname*; otherwise, the new files are placed at the end.

-s   Force the regeneration of the archive symbol table even if you do not invoke ar with an option that modifies the archive contents. This command is useful to restore the archive symbol table after the strip(1) command is used on the archive.

-t   Print a table of contents of *archive*. The files specified by the file operands are included in the written list. If no file operands are specified, include all files in *archive* in the order of the archive.

-T   Allow file-name truncation of extracted files whose archive names are longer than the file system can support. By default, extracting a file with a name that is too long is an error; a diagnostic message is written and the file is not extracted.

-u   Update older files. When used with the -r option, replace files within *archive* only if the corresponding file has a modification time that is at least as new as the modification time of the file within archive.

-V   Print version number on standard error.

/usr/bin/ar

-v   Give verbose output. When used with the -d, -r, or -x options, write a detailed file-by-file description of the archive creation, the constituent files, and maintenance activity.

          When used with -p, write the name of the file to the standard output before writing the file itself to the standard output.

          When used with -t, include a long listing of information about the files within the archive.

          When used with -x, print the file name preceding each extraction.

          When writing to an archive, write a message to the standard error.

/usr/xpg4/bin/ar

-v   Same as /usr/bin/ar version, except when writing to an archive, write no message to the standard error.

-x   Extract the files named by the *file* operands from *archive*. The contents of archive are not changed. If you specify no file operands, extract all files in *archive*. If the name of a file extracted from *archive* is longer than that supported in the directory to which it is being extracted, the results are undefined. Set the modification time of each file extracted to the time *file* is extracted from *archive*.

Operands

archive   A path name of the archive file.

file	A path name. Only the last component is used when comparing against the names of files in the archive. If two or more *file* operands have the same last path-name component (basename(1)), the results are unspecified. The implementation's archive format does not truncate valid names of files added to or replaced in the archive.
posname	The name of a file in the archive file, used for relative positioning; see options -m and -r.

Examples

The following example shows how to find which object modules make up the libexample.a archive.

```
castle% ar t libexample.a
```

The following example shows how to extract a module from a shared object. If module.o is part of the archive library libexample.a, you can extract the module with the following command.

```
castle% ar x libexample.a module.o
```

The ranlib command in SunOS 4.x was used to add a table of contents to archive libraries. The ranlib command is now incorporated into /usr/ccs/bin/ar. When ar is archiving object files, it automatically creates a symbol table, as shown in the following example.

```
castle% ar rcv libfoo.a foo.o bar.o
```

The following command forces a rebuild of the symbol table in an archive library.

```
castle% ar ts libfoo.a
```

Environment Variables

See environ(5) for descriptions of the following environment variables that affect the execution of ar: LC_CTYPE, LC_MESSAGES, and NLSPATH.

Exit Status

0	Successful completion.
>0	An error occurred.

Attributes

See attributes(5) for descriptions of the following attributes:

/usr/bin/ar

Attribute Type	Attribute Value
Availability	SUNWbtool

/usr/xpg4/bin/ar

Attribute Type	Attribute Value
Availability	SUNWxci4

See Also

```
basename(1), cpio(1), ld(1), lorder(1), strip(1), tar(1), cc(1B),
a.out(4), ar(4), attributes(5), environ(5), XPG4(5)
```

arch — Display the Architecture of the Current Host

Synopsis

```
/usr/bin/arch [-k | archname]
```

Description

Systems can be broadly classified by their architectures, which define what executables run on which machines. You can make a distinction between kernel architecture and application architecture (or, commonly, just architecture). Systems that run different kernels because of underlying hardware differences may be able to run the same application programs.

arch displays the application architecture of the current host system. Because of extensive historical use of this command without any options, all SunOS 5.x SPARC-based systems return sun4 as their application architecture.

This command is provided for compatibility with previous releases and its use is discouraged. Instead, use the uname command. See uname(1) for usage information.

Options

    -k   Display the kernel architecture, such as sun4m, sun4c, and so forth. This option defines which specific SunOS kernel runs on the system and has implications only for programs such as ps(1) that depend on a specific kernel architecture.

Operands

    archname   Use *archname* to determine whether the application binaries for this application architecture can run on the current host system. The *archname* must be a valid application architecture, such as sun4, i86pc, and so forth. If application binaries for *archname* can run on the current host system, return true (0); otherwise, return false (1).

Examples

The following example shows the value the arch command returns on a SPARCstation 10.

```
castle% arch
sun4
castle%
```

Exit Status

0	Successful completion.
>0	An error occurred.

Attributes

See attributes(5) for descriptions of the following attributes:

Attribute Type	Attribute Value
Availability	SUNWcsu

See Also

mach(1), ps(1), uname(1), attributes(5)

---

as — Assembler

Synopsis

SPARC

```
/usr/ccs/bin/as [-b] [-K PIC] [-L] [-m] [-n] [-o outfile] [-P] [-Dname]
    [-Dname=def] [-Ipath] [-Uname...] [-q] [-Q y|n] [-s] [-S[a | b | c |
    1 | A | B | C | L]][-T][-V] [-xarch=v7 | -xarch=v8 | -xarch=v8a |
    -xarch=v8plus | -xarch=v8plusa | -xarch=v9 | -xarch=v9a][-xF]
    filename...
```

IA

```
/usr/ccs/bin/as [-b] [-K PIC] [-L] [-m] [-n] [-o outfile] [-P] [-Dname]
    [-Dname=def] [-Ipath] [-Uname...] [-Qy | n] [-s] [-S [a | b | c | 1 |
    A | B | C | L]] [-T] [-V] filename...
```

Description

The as command creates object files from assembly language source files.

Note — If you use the -m (invoke the m4(1) macro processor) option, you cannot use keywords for m4(1) as symbols (variables, functions, labels) in the input file because m4(1) cannot determine which keywords are assembler symbols and which keywords are real m4(1) macros.

Whenever possible, access the assembler through a compilation system interface program such as cc(1B).

All undefined symbols are treated as global.

Options

The following options for the as command are common to both SPARC and IA. You can specify the options in any order.

-b	Generate extra symbol table information for the Sun Source Browser.
-D*name* -D*name=def*	When the -P option is in effect, pass these options to the cpp(1) preprocessor without interpretation by the as command; otherwise, ignore them.
-I*path*	When the -P option is in effect, pass this option to the cpp(1) C preprocessor without interpretation by the as command; otherwise, ignore it.
-K PIC	Generate position-independent code.
-L	Save all symbols in the ELF symbol table, including temporary labels that are normally discarded to save space.
-m	Run the m4(1) macro processor on the input to the assembler.
-n	Suppress all the warnings while assembling.
-o *outfile*	Put the output of the assembly in *outfile*. By default, form the output file name by removing the .s suffix, if there is one, from the input file name and appending an .o suffix.
-P	Run cpp(1), the C preprocessor, on the files being assembled. The preprocessor is run separately on each input file, not on their concatenation. Pass the preprocessor output to the assembler.
Q y | n	If you specify the n option, produce the assembler version information in the comment section of the output object file. If you specify the y option, suppress the information.
-s	Place all stabs in the .stabs section. By default, put stabs in stabs.excl sections, which are stripped out by the static linker, ld(1), during final execution. When you use the -s option, stabs remain in the final executable because .stab sections are not stripped by the static linker.

-S [a | b | c | l | A | B | C | L]

Produce a disassembly of the emitted code to the standard output. Adding each of the following characters to the -S option produces:

a	Disassemble with address.
b	Disassemble with .bof.
c	Disassemble with comments.
l	Disassemble with line numbers.

Capital letters turn the switch off for the corresponding option.

-T	Interpret symbol names in 4.x assembly files as 5.x symbol names. This option is for 4.x assembly files to be assembled on 5.x systems.
-U*name*	When the -P option is in effect, pass this option to the cpp(1) preprocessor without interpretation by the as command; otherwise, ignore it.

-V	Write the version number of the assembler being run on the standard error output.
-xF	Generate additional information for performance analysis of the executable, using Sun WorkShop analyzer. If the input file does not contain any stabs (debugging directives), then the assembler generates some default stabs that are needed by the Sun WorkShop analyzer. Also, see the dbx manual page available with Sun WorkShop.

The following options are for SPARC only.

-q	Perform a quick assembly. When you use the -q option, many error checks are not performed. Note: This option disables many error checks. It is recommended that you do not use this option to assemble handwritten assembly language.
-xarch=v7	Instruct the assembler to accept instructions defined in the SPARC version 7 (V7) architecture. The resulting object code is in ELF format.
-xarch=v8	Instruct the assembler to accept instructions defined in the SPARC V8 architecture, less the quad-precision floating-point instructions. The resulting object code is in ELF format.
-xarch=v8a	Instruct the assembler to accept instructions defined in the SPARC V8 architecture, less the quad-precision floating-point instructions and less the fsmuld instruction. The resulting object code is in ELF format. This choice is the default of the -xarch=*options*.

-xarch=v8plus

Instruct the assembler to accept instructions defined in the SPARC V9 architecture, less the quad-precision floating-point instructions. The resulting object code is in ELF format. It does not execute on a Solaris V8 system (a machine with a V8 processor). It does execute on a Solaris V8+ system.

-xarch=v8plusa

Instruct the assembler to accept instructions defined in the SPARC V9 architecture, less the quad-precision floating-point instructions, plus the instructions in the Visual Instruction Set (VIS). The resulting object code is in V8+ ELF format. It does not execute on a Solaris V8 system (a machine with a V8 processor). It does execute on a Solaris V8+ system

-xarch=v9	Limit the instruction set to the SPARC V9 architecture. The resulting .o object files are in 64-bit ELF format and can be linked only with other object files in the same format. The resulting executable can be run only on a 64-bit SPARC processor running 64-bit Solaris with the 64-bit kernel.

-xarch=v9a Limit the instruction set to the SPARC V9 architecture, adding the Visual Instruction Set (VIS) and extensions specific to UltraSPARC processors. The resulting .o object files are in 64-bit ELF format and can be linked only with other object files in the same format. The resulting executable can be run only on a 64-bit SPARC processor running 64-bit Solaris with the 64-bit kernel.

Operands

filename Assembly language source file.

Examples

The following example performs a quick assembly with no error checking.

```
castle% as -q inputfile
```

The -V option to the compiler is a very important flag. It prints the version number of the compiler so that you know exactly what compiler you are using. If the compiler is patched, the patch information is also displayed.

```
castle% as -V inputfile
```

Environment Variables

TMPDIR as normally creates temporary files in the directory /tmp. You can specify another directory by setting the environment variable TMPDIR to your chosen directory. (If TMPDIR isn't a valid directory, then as uses /tmp.)

Files

By default, as creates its temporary files in /tmp. When you set the TMPDIR environment variable, as creates its files in the directory you specify unless TMPDIR is not a valid directory.

Attributes

See attributes(5) for descriptions of the following attributes:

Attribute Type	Attribute Value
Availability	SUNWsprot

See Also

cc(1B), cpp(1), ld(1), m4(1), nm(1), strip(1), tmpnam(3C), a.out(4), attributes(5)

The dbx manual page available with Sun WorkShop.

asa — Convert FORTRAN Carriage-control Output to Printable Form

Synopsis

`/usr/bin/asa [-f] [`*file*`...]`

Description

The asa command writes its input files to standard output, mapping carriage-control characters from the text files to line-printer control sequences.

The first character of every line is removed from the input, and the following actions are performed.

When the Character is a:	Then:
space	Output the rest of the line without change.
0	Replace it by a newline control sequence followed by the rest of the input line.
1	Replace it by a newpage control sequence followed by the rest of the input line.
+	Replace it by a control sequence that returns to the first column of the previous line, where the rest of the input line is printed.

For any other character in the first column of an input line, asa skips the character and prints the rest of the line unchanged.

If you call asa without providing a file name, the standard input is used.

Options

-f	Start each file on a new page.

Operands

file	A path name of a text file used for input. If you specify no file operands or specify -, then use the standard input.

Examples

You can use asa as a filter to view the output of FORTRAN programs that use ASA carriage-control characters so that they are displayed in normal form. The following example properly formats and paginates the output and then directs it to a line printer.

```
castle% a.out | asa | lp
```

You can view FORTRAN output previously sent to the file on a terminal screen with the following command.

```
castle% asa output
```

The following program is used in the next two examples.

```
write(*,'(" Blank")')
write(*,'("0Zero ")')
write(*,'("+ Plus ")')
write(*,'("1One ")')
end
```

With actual files.

```
castle% a.out > MyOutputFile asa < MyOutputFile | lp
```

With only pipes.

```
castle% a.out | asa | lp
```

Both of the above examples produce two pages of output.

```
Page 1:
  Blank

  ZeroPlus
Page 2:
  One
```

Environment Variables

See environ(5) for descriptions of the following environment variables that affect the execution of asa: LC_CTYPE, LC_MESSAGES, and NLSPATH.

Exit Status

0	All input files were output successfully.
>0	An error occurred.

Attributes

See attributes(5) for descriptions of the following attributes:

Attribute Type	Attribute Value
Availability	SUNWcsu

See Also

lp(1), environ(5), attributes(5)

at, batch — Execute Commands at a Later Time

Synopsis

```
/usr/bin/at [-c|-k|-s] [-m] [-f file] [-p project] [-q queuename]
    -t time
/usr/bin/at [-c|-k|-s] [-m] [-f file] [-p project] [-q queuename]
    timespec...
/usr/bin/at -l [-p project] [-q queuename] [at-job-id...]
/usr/bin/at -r at-job-id...

/usr/bin/batch [-p project]
```

Description

at

Use the at command to schedule jobs for later execution. You can queue any command line or shell script. The at command reads commands from standard input and groups them together as an *at-job*, to be executed at a later time.

The *at-job* is executed in a separate invocation of the shell, running in a separate process group with no controlling terminal, except that the environment variables, current working directory, file creation mask (see umask(1)), and system resource limits (for sh and ksh only, see ulimit(1)) in effect when the at command is executed are retained and used when the *at-job* is executed.

When you submit the *at-job*, the system assigns a unique *at-job-id* and displays it when you schedule the *at-job*. The *at-job-id* is an identifier that is a string consisting of alphanumeric characters and the period character. You can also display a list of currently scheduled jobs by using the at -l command.

See the -m command for a description of user notification and processing of the job's standard output and standard error.

Users are permitted to use at and batch if their name appears in the file /usr/lib/cron/at.allow. If that file does not exist, the file /usr/lib/cron/at.deny is checked to determine if the user should be denied access to at. The at.allow and at.deny files consist of one user name per line. Starting in the Solaris 8 release, if neither file exists, only a user with the solaris.jobs.user authorization is permitted to submit a job. If only at.deny exists and is empty, global usage is permitted.

> **Note —** Regardless of the queue used, cron has a limit of 100 jobs in execution at any time.

There can be delays in cron at job execution. In some cases, these delays can compound to the point that cron job processing seems to be hung. All jobs are executed eventually. When the delays are excessive, the only workaround is to kill cron and restart it.

batch

The batch command reads commands to be executed at a later time. It is the equivalent of the command at -q b -m now, where queue b is a special at queue specifically for batch jobs. Batch jobs are submitted to the batch queue for immediate execution.

Options

If you do not use the -c, -k, or -s options, the SHELL environment variable determines which shell is used.

-c	Use C shell, csh(1), to execute the *at-job.*
-k	Use Korn shell, ksh(1), to execute the *at-job.*
-s	Use Bourne shell, sh(1), to execute the *at-job.*
-f *file*	Specify the path of a file to be used as the source of the *at-job,* instead of standard input.
-l	(ell) Report all jobs scheduled for the invoking user if you specify no *at-job-id* operands. If you specify *at-job-id*s, report information only for these jobs.
-m	Send mail to the invoking user after the *at-job* has run, announcing its completion. Mail standard output and standard error produced by the *at-job* to the user as well unless redirected elsewhere. Send mail even if the job produces no output. If you do not use -m, the job's standard output and standard error are mailed to the user unless they are redirected elsewhere; if there is no such output to provide, the user is not notified of the job's completion.
-p *project*	Starting with the Solaris 8 release, specify under which project the at or batch job is run. When used with the -l option, limit the search to that particular project. Values for project are interpreted first as a project name and then as a possible project ID if entirely numeric. By default, the user's current project is used.

New! (margin note beside -p *project*)

-q *queuename*

Specify the queue to schedule a job for submission. When used with the -l option, limit the search to that particular queue. Values for *queuename* are limited to the lowercase letters a through z. By default, *at-job*s are scheduled in queue a. In contrast, queue b is reserved for batch jobs. Because queue c is reserved for cron jobs, you cannot use it with the -q option.

-r *at-job-id*

Remove the jobs with the specified *at-job-id* operands that were previously scheduled by the at command.

-t *time*	Submit the job to be run at the time specified by the *time* option argument, which must have the decimal format [[*CC*]*YY*]*MMDDhhmm*[.*SS*], where each two-digit pair represent the following:

MM	The month of the year [01-12].
DD	The day of the month [01-31].
hh	The hour of the day [00-23].
mm	The minute of the hour [00-59].
CC	The first two digits of the year.

YY	The second two digits of the year.
SS	The second of the minute [00-61].

Refer to the touch(1) manual page for more details.

Operands

at_job_id The identification number for a scheduled *at-job.*

timespec Submit the job to be run at the date and time specified. All of the *timespec* operands are interpreted as if they were separated by space characters and concatenated. The date and time are interpreted as being in the time zone of the user (as determined by the TZ variable) unless a time zone name appears as part of *time.*

In the C locale, the following describe the three parts of the time specification string. All of the values from the LC_TIME categories in the C locale are case insensitive.

time You can specify the time as one, two, or four digits. One- and two-digit numbers are interpreted as hours. Four-digit numbers are interpreted as hours and minutes. Alternatively, you can specify the time as two numbers separated by a colon, meaning *hour:minute.* You can indicate an a.m./p.m. value (one of the values from the *am_pm* keywords in the LC_TIME locale category). This value can follow the time. Otherwise, a 24-hour clock time is understood. A time zone name of GMT, UCT, or ZULU (case insensitive) can follow to specify that the time is in Coordinated Universal Time. You can specify other time zones by using the TZ environment variable. The time field can also be one of the following tokens in the C locale:

midnight Indicates the time 12:00 a.m. (00:00).

noon Indicates the time 12:00 p.m.

now Indicate the current day and time. Invoking at now submits an *at-job* for potentially immediate execution (that is, subject only to unspecified scheduling delays).

date You can specify an optional date as either a month name (one of the values from the mon or abmon keywords in the LC_TIME locale category) followed by a day number (and possibly year number preceded by a comma) or a day of the week (one of the values from the day or abday keywords in the LC_TIME locale category). Two special days are recognized in the C locale:

today The current day.

| tomorrow | The day following the current day. If no date is given, today is assumed if the given time is greater than the current time, and tomorrow is assumed if it is less. If the given month is less than the current month (and no year is given), next year is assumed. |
| *increment* | The optional increment is a number preceded by a plus sign (+) and suffixed by one of the following: minutes, hours, days, weeks, months, or years. (The singular forms are also accepted.) The keyword next is equivalent to an increment number of +1. For example, the following are equivalent commands: |

```
at 2pm + 1 week
at 2pm next week
```

Usage

The format of the at command line shown here is guaranteed only for the C locale. Other locales are not supported for midnight, noon, now, mon, abmon, day, abday, today, tomorrow, minutes, hours, days, weeks, months, years, and next.

Because the commands run in a separate shell invocation, running in a separate process group with no controlling terminal results in the loss of open file descriptors, traps, and priority inherited from the invoking environment.

at Examples

The following two examples produce the same result. The first example uses the -t option to specify the time to run the script named tryit.

```
castle% at -f /export/home/winsor/bin/tryit -t 08281215
commands will be executed using /bin/csh
job 904277700.a at Fri Aug 28 12:15:00 1998
castle%
```

Note — It is a good idea to use the full path name for scripts scheduled with the at command. Otherwise, like cron, at may not find the script when the time comes to run it.

The next example uses the *timespec* operand to specify the time to run the script named tryit.

```
castle% at -f /export/home/winsor/bin/tryit 1230pm
commands will be executed using /bin/csh
job 904278600.a at Fri Aug 28 12:30:00 1998
castle%
```

The following example lists the *at-job-id* for the two scheduled jobs.

```
castle% at -l
904277700.a     Fri Aug 28 12:15:00 1998
904278600.a     Fri Aug 28 12:30:00 1998
castle%
```

You can also schedule multiple at jobs by typing a *timespec* and pressing Return. Put one command on each line and press Return. Then type Control-D when you have scheduled all of the jobs. The following example schedules only one job.

```
castle% at 1230pm
at> tryit
at> Control-D <EOT>
commands will be executed using /bin/csh
job 904278601.a at Fri Aug 28 12:30:00 1998
castle%
```

By default, results of *at-jobs* are e-mailed to the person who scheduled the job. The following screen shot shows the in-box with the results of the previous examples.

You can use the following sequence from a terminal.

```
$ at -m 0730 tomorrow
at> sort < file > outfile
at> Control-D <EOT>
commands will be executed using /bin/sh
job 904380100.a at Sat Aug 29 07:30:00 1998
$
```

The following sequence demonstrates redirecting standard error to a pipe. It is useful in a command procedure. Note that the sequence of output redirection is significant.

```
$ at now + 5 min
at> <<! diff file1 file2 2>&1 > outfile | mailx mygroup!
at> Control-D <EOT>
commands will be executed using /bin/sh
job 904280212.a at Fri Aug 28 12:56:52 1998
$ at -l
904347000.a     Sat Aug 29 07:30:00 1998
904280100.a     Fri Aug 28 12:55:00 1998
904280212.a     Fri Aug 28 12:56:52 1998
$
```

You can have a job reschedule itself by calling at from within the *at-job*. For example, this daily-processing script named my.daily runs every day (although crontab is a more appropriate vehicle for such work).

```
# my.daily runs every day at now tomorrow < my.daily daily-processing
```

You have quite a bit of flexibility in the spacing of the three portions of the C locale *timespec*, as long as there are no ambiguities. Examples of various times and operand presentations include:

```
at 0815am Jan 24
at 8 :15amjan24
at now "+ 1day"
at 5 pm FRIday
at '17
        utc+
        30minutes'
```

batch Examples

You can use the following sequence at a terminal. Notice that batch uses the at prompt and that batch job files end with a .b suffix.

```
$ batch
at> at> sort <file > outfile
at> Control-D <EOT>
commands will be executed using /bin/sh
job 904280755.b at Fri Aug 28 13:00:55 1998
$
```

The following sequence demonstrates redirecting standard error to a pipe. It is useful in a command procedure. Note that the sequence of output redirection is significant.

```
$ batch
at> <<!
at> diff file1 file2 2>&1 > outfile | mailx mygroup
at> !
at> Control-D <EOT>
commands will be executed using /bin/sh
job 904280756.b at Fri Aug 28 13:05:55 1998
$
```

Environment Variables

See environ(5) for descriptions of the following environment variables that affect the execution of at and batch: LC_CTYPE, LC_MESSAGES, NLSPATH, and LC_TIME.

SHELL   Determine a name of a command interpreter to be used to invoke the *at-job*. If the variable is unset or null, sh is used. If it is set to a value other than sh, the implementation uses that shell; a warning diagnostic is printed telling which shell is used.

TZ   Determine the time zone. The job is submitted for execution at the time specified by *timespec* or -t *time* relative to the time zone specified by the TZ variable. If timespec specifies a time zone, it overrides TZ. If *timespec* does not specify a time zone and TZ is unset or null, an unspecified default time zone is used.

DATEMSK   If the environment variable DATEMSK is set, at uses its value as the full path name of a template file containing format strings. The strings consist of format specifiers and text characters that are used to provide a richer set of allowable date formats in different languages by appropriate settings of the environment variable LANG or LC_TIME. The list of allowable format specifiers is located in the getdate(3C) manual page. The formats described in the Operands section for the *time* and *date* arguments, the special names noon, midnight, now, next, today, tomorrow, and the increment argument are not recognized when DATEMSK is set.

Exit Status

0   The at command successfully submitted, removed, or listed a job or jobs.

>0   An error occurred, and the job is not scheduled.

Files

/usr/lib/cron/at.allow

    Names of users, one per line, who are authorized access to the at and batch commands.

/usr/lib/cron/at.deny

    Names of users, one per line, who are denied access to the at and batch commands.

Attributes

See attributes(5) for descriptions of the following attributes:

at

Attribute Type	Attribute Value
Availability	SUNWcsu
CSI	Enabled

batch

Attribute Type	Attribute Value
Availability	SUNWesu
CSI	Enabled

See Also

auths(1), crontab(1), csh(1), date(1), ksh(1), sh(1), touch(1), ulimit(1), umask(1), cron(1M), getdate(3C), auth_attr(4), attributes(5), environ(5)

New!

atoplot — Graphics Filters for Various Plotters

Synopsis
/usr/ucb/plot [-T*terminal*]

Description
See plot(1).

atq — Display the Jobs Queued to Run at Specified Times

Synopsis
/usr/bin/atq [-c] [-n] [*username*...]

Description
The at command enables users to execute commands at a later date. Use the atq command to display for the current user *at-jobs* that were created by the at(1) command. Starting in the Solaris 8 release, if invoked by a user with the solaris.jobs.admin authorization, atq displays all jobs in the queue.

New!

If you use no options, jobs are displayed in chronological order of execution.

When superuser uses the atq command without specifying *username*, the entire queue is displayed; when you specify a user name, those jobs belonging only to the named user are displayed.

Options

-c   Display the queued jobs in the order they were created (that is, the time that the at command was given).

-n   Display only the total number of jobs currently in the queue.

Examples
The following example shows output from the atq command with no arguments. The list shows the jobs only for the current user, winsor.

```
castle% atq
 Rank      Execution Date      Owner    Job        Queue   Job Name
 1st   Aug 28, 1998 17:00    winsor   904294800.a    a      tryit
 2nd   Aug 29, 1998 01:00    winsor   904323600.a    a      tryit
 3rd   Aug 29, 1998 07:30    winsor   904347000.a    a      stdin
 4th   Aug 30, 1998 15:00    winsor   904460400.a    a      tryit
```

For comparison, the following example shows the output from the at -1 command, which also lists at and batch jobs in the queue.

```
castle% at -1
904347000.a      Sat Aug 29 07:30:00 1998
904294800.a      Fri Aug 28 17:00:00 1998
```

```
904323600.a     Sat Aug 29 01:00:00 1998
904460400.a     Sun Aug 30 15:00:00 1998
```

The following example shows the output from the atq command when executed as superuser.

```
castle% su
Password:
castle# atq
 Rank      Execution Date      Owner     Job          Queue   Job Name
  1st    Aug 28, 1998 16:00    root      904291200.a    a      tryit
  2nd    Aug 28, 1998 17:00    winsor    904294800.a    a      tryit
  3rd    Aug 28, 1998 18:00    root      904298400.a    a      tryit
  4th    Aug 28, 1998 19:00    ray       904302000.a    a      tryit
  5th    Aug 28, 1998 21:00    ray       904309200.a    a      tryit
  6th    Aug 29, 1998 01:00    winsor    904323600.a    a      tryit
  7th    Aug 29, 1998 07:30    winsor    904347000.a    a      stdin
  8th    Aug 30, 1998 15:00    winsor    904460400.a    a      tryit
```

The following example shows the same example sorted by creation time.

```
castle# atq -c
 Rank      Execution Date      Owner     Job          Queue   Job Name
  1st    Aug 29, 1998 07:30    winsor    904347000.a    a      stdin
  2nd    Aug 28, 1998 17:00    winsor    904294800.a    a      tryit
  3rd    Aug 29, 1998 01:00    winsor    904323600.a    a      tryit
  4th    Aug 30, 1998 15:00    winsor    904460400.a    a      tryit
  5th    Aug 28, 1998 16:00    root      904291200.a    a      tryit
  6th    Aug 28, 1998 18:00    root      904298400.a    a      tryit
  7th    Aug 28, 1998 19:00    ray       904302000.a    a      tryit
  8th    Aug 28, 1998 21:00    ray       904309200.a    a      tryit
```

The following example shows the value returned by the atq -n command. This option lists only the number of items in the queue.

```
castle# atq -n
8
castle#
```

The following example shows the jobs queued only by user ray.

```
castle# atq ray
 Rank      Execution Date      Owner     Job          Queue   Job Name
  1st    Aug 28, 1998 19:00    ray       904302000.a    a      tryit
  2nd    Aug 28, 1998 21:00    ray       904309200.a    a      tryit
castle#
```

Files

/var/spool/cron/atjobs

Spool area for at jobs.

Attributes

See attributes(5) for descriptions of the following attributes:

Attribute Type	Attribute Value
Availability	SUNWcsu

See Also

at(1), atrm(1), auths(1) cron(1M), auth_attr(4), attributes(5)

atrm — Remove Jobs Spooled by at or batch

Synopsis

/usr/bin/atrm [-afi] [[*job* #] [*user*]...]

Description

Use the atrm command to remove delayed-execution jobs created with the at(1) command that have not yet executed. You can display a list of these jobs and associated job numbers by using atq(1).

atrm removes each job number you specify and/or all jobs belonging to the *user* you specify, provided that you own the indicated jobs.

Starting in the Solaris 8 release, you can remove jobs belonging to other users only if you have solaris.jobs.admin privileges.

Options

-a	Remove all unexecuted jobs that were created by the current user. If invoked by superuser, flush the entire queue.
-f	Force suppression of all information regarding the removal of the specified jobs.
-i	Interactively ask if a job should be removed. If you respond with a y, remove the job.

Examples

The following example first lists the jobs in the at queue by using the atq command, and then, as superuser, removes jobs queued by user ray.

```
castle# atq
Rank     Execution Date        Owner    Job          Queue    Job Name
 1st     Aug 28, 1998 16:00    root     904291200.a    a       tryit
 2nd     Aug 28, 1998 17:00    winsor   904294800.a    a       tryit
 3rd     Aug 28, 1998 18:00    root     904298400.a    a       tryit
 4th     Aug 28, 1998 19:00    ray      904302000.a    a       tryit
 5th     Aug 28, 1998 21:00    ray      904309200.a    a       tryit
 6th     Aug 29, 1998 01:00    winsor   904323600.a    a       tryit
 7th     Aug 29, 1998 07:30    winsor   904347000.a    a       stdin
 8th     Aug 30, 1998 15:00    winsor   904460400.a    a       tryit
```

```
castle# atrm ray
904302000.a: removed
904309200.a: removed
```

If you want to suppress display of the list of removed jobs, use the atrm -f option. The following example removes a job by specifying the *at-job* number.

```
castle# atrm 904291200.a
904291200.a: removed
castle#
```

In the following example, superuser uses the atrm -i option to be prompted to interactively remove individual jobs queued by user winsor.

```
castle# atrm -i winsor
904347000.a:    (owned by winsor) remove it? y
904294800.a:    (owned by winsor) remove it? y
904323600.a:    (owned by winsor) remove it? y
904460400.a:    (owned by winsor) remove it? y
castle#
```

Files

/var/spool/cron/atjobs

Spool area for at jobs.

Attributes

See attributes(5) for descriptions of the following attributes:

Attribute Type	Attribute Value
Availability	SUNWcsu

See Also

at(1), atq(1), auths(1), cron(1M), auth_attr(4), attributes(5)

New!

audioconvert — Convert Audio File Formats

Synopsis

/usr/bin/audioconvert [-pF] [-f *outfmt*] [-o *outfile*] [[-i *nfmt*]
    [*file*...]]...

Description

audioconvert converts audio data between a set of supported audio encodings and file formats. You can use it to compress and decompress audio data, to add audio file headers to raw audio data files, and to convert between standard data encodings, such as ulaw and linear PCM.

If no file names are present, audioconvert reads the data from the standard input stream and writes an audio file to the standard output. Otherwise, input files are processed in order, concatenated, and written to the output file.

Input files are expected to contain audio file headers that identify the audio data format. If the audio data does not contain a recognizable header, you must specify the format with the -i option, using the rate, encoding, and channels keywords to identify the input data format.

The output file format is derived by updating the format of the first input file with the format options in the -f specification. If you do not specify -p, all subsequent input files are converted and concatenated. The output file contains an audio file header unless you specify format=raw in the output format options.

You can convert input files in place by using the -p option. When -p is in effect, the format of each input file is modified according to the -f option to determine the output format. The existing files are then overwritten with the converted data.

The file(1) command decodes and prints the audio data format of Sun audio files.

The algorithm used for converting multichannel data to single channel is implemented by simply summing the channels. If the input data is perfectly in phase (as would be the case if a mono file is converted to stereo and back to mono), the resulting data may contain some distortion.

Options

-?	Help: Print a command-line usage message.
-f *outfmt*	Specify the file format and data encoding of the output file. Derive defaults for unspecified fields from the input file format. Valid keywords and values are listed in the next section.
-F	Ignore any file header for input files whose format is specified by the -i option. If you do not specify -F, audioconvert ignores the -i option for input files that contain valid audio file headers.
-i *infmt*	Specify the data encoding of raw input files. Ordinarily, the input data format is derived from the audio file header. This option is required when converting audio data that is not preceded by a valid audio file header. If you specify -i for an input file that contains an audio file header, the input format string is ignored unless you also use the -F option. The format specification syntax is the same as the -f output file format. You can specify multiple input formats. An input format describes all input files following that specification until a new input format is specified.
-o *outfile*	Concatenate all input files, convert to the output format, and write to the named output file. If you do not specify either -o or -p, write the concatenated output to the standard output. You cannot combine the -p and -o options.
-p	In place, convert individual input files to the format specified by the -f option and rewrite them. If a target file is a symbolic link, rewrite the underlying file. You cannot combine the -o and -p options.

Operands

file   Concatenate and convert the named audio files to the output format, and write them out. If you specify no file name or if you specify the special file-name dash (-), read audio data from the standard input.

Format Specification

The syntax for the input and output format is a set of *keyword=value* pairs with no intervening white space.

keyword=value[,keyword=value...]

If values are unambiguous, you can omit the preceding *keyword=*.

rate   Specify the audio sampling rate in samples per second. If a number is followed by the letter k, it is multiplied by 1000 (for example, 44.1k = 44100). Standard, commonly used sample rates are 8k, 16k, 32k, 44.1k, and 48k.

channels   Specify the number of interleaved channels as an integer. You can also use the words mono or stereo to specify one- or two-channel data.

encoding   Specify the digital audio data representation. Encodings determine precision implicitly (ulaw implies 8-bit precision) or explicitly as part of the name (for example, linear16). Valid encoding values are:

ulaw   CCITT G.711 u-law encoding is an 8-bit format primarily used for telephone-quality speech.

alaw   CCITT G.711 a-law encoding is an 8-bit format primarily used for telephone-quality speech in Europe.

linear8,   Linear Pulse Code Modulation (PCM) encoding. The
linear16,   name identifies the number of bits of precision.
linear32   linear16 is typically used for high-quality audio data.

pcm   Same as linear16.

g721   CCITT G.721 compression format uses Adaptive Delta Pulse Code Modulation (ADPCM) with 4-bit precision. Its primary use is to compress u-law voice data with a 2:1 compression ratio.

g723   CCITT G.723 compression format uses Adaptive Delta Pulse Code Modulation (ADPCM) with 3-bit precision. Its primary use is to compress u-law voice data with an 8:3 compression ratio. The audio quality is similar to that of G.721 but may result in lower quality when used for nonspeech data.

The following encoding values are also accepted as shorthand to set the sample rate, channels, and encoding:

	voice	Equivalent to encoding=ulaw,rate=8k,channels=mono.
	cd	Equivalent to encoding=linear16,rate=44.1k,channels=stereo
	dat	Equivalent to encoding=linear16,rate=48k,channels=stereo.
format		Specify the audio file format. Valid formats are:
	sun	Sun-compatible file format (the default).
	raw	Read or write raw audio data with no audio header or in conjunction with an offset to import a foreign audio file format.
	offset	(-i only) Specify a byte offset to locate the start of the audio data. You can use this option to import audio data that contains an unrecognized file header.

Usage

See largefile(5) for the description of the behavior of audioconvert when encountering files greater than or equal to 2 Gbytes (2**31 bytes).

Examples

The following example records voice data and compresses it before storing it in a file.

```
castle% audiorecord | audioconvert -f g721 > mydata.au
```

The following example uses the file command to verify that the mydata.au file was converted.

```
castle% file mydata.au
mydata.au:  audio data: compressed (4-bit G.721 ADPCM), mono, 8000 Hz
castle%
```

The following example concatenates two Sun format audio files, regardless of their data format, and outputs an 8-bit u-law, 16 kHz, mono file.

```
% audioconvert -f ulaw,rate=16k,mono -o outfile.au infile1 infile2
```

The following example uses the file command to verify that the outfile.au file was converted.

```
castle% file outfile.au
outfile.au:      audio data: 8-bit u-law, mono, 16000 Hz
castle%
```

The following example converts a directory containing raw voice data files, in place, to Sun format and adds a file header to each file.

```
castle% audioconvert -p -i voice -f sun *.au
```

The following example uses the `file *` command to verify that both the files in the directory were converted.

```
castle% file *
mydata.au:        audio data: 8-bit u-law, mono, 16000 Hz
outfile.au:       audio data: 8-bit u-law, mono, 16000 Hz
castle%
```

Attributes

See `attributes(5)` for descriptions of the following attributes:

Attribute Type	Attribute Value
Architecture	SPARC, IA
Availability	SUNWauda
Interface Stability	Evolving

New!

See Also

`audioplay(1)`, `audiorecord(1)`, `file(1)`, `attributes(5)`, `largefile(5)`

audioplay — Play Audio Files

Synopsis

```
/usr/bin/audioplay [-iV] [-v vol] [-b bal] [-p speaker | headphone |
    line][-d dev] [file...]
```

Description

`audioplay` copies the named audio files (or the standard input if you specify no file names) to the audio device. If you do not specify an input file and standard input is a TTY, the port, volume, and balance settings specified on the command line are applied and the program exits.

The input files must contain a valid audio file header. The encoding information in this header is matched against the capabilities of the audio device and, if the data formats are incompatible, an error message is printed and the file is skipped. Compressed ADPCM (G.721) monaural audio data is automatically uncompressed before playing.

Minor deviations in sampling frequency (that is, less than 1 percent) are ordinarily ignored. For example, data sampled at 8012 Hz can be played on an audio device that only supports 8000 Hz. If you use the -V option, such deviations are flagged with warning messages.

Bugs

`audioplay` currently supports a limited set of audio format conversions. If the audio file is not in a format supported by the audio device, you must first convert it. For example, to convert to voice format on-the-fly, use the following command.

```
castle% audioconvert -f voice myfile | audioplay
```

The format conversion does not always keep up with the audio output. If this is the case, convert to a temporary file before playing the data.

Options

-\?   Print a command-line usage message.

-b *bal*   Set the output balance to the specified value before playing begins and reset it to its previous level when audioplay exits. The *bal* argument is an integer value between -100 and 100, inclusive. A value of -100 indicates left balance, 0 middle, and 100 right. If you do not specify this argument, leave the output balance at the level most recently set by any process.

-d *dev*   Direct output to an alternate audio device. If you do not specify the -d option, consult the AUDIODEV environment variable. Otherwise, use /dev/audio as the default audio device.

-i   Immediately exit if the audio device is unavailable (that is, another process currently has write access). audioplay ordinarily waits until it can obtain access to the device. When you use the -i option and the device is busy, print an error message and exit immediately.

-p speaker | headphone | line

Select the built-in speaker, (the default), headphone jack, or line out as the destination of the audio output signal. If you do not specify this argument, the output port remains unchanged. Not all audio adapters support all of the output ports. If the named port does not exist, use an appropriate substitute.

-v *vol*   Set the output volume to the specified value before playing begins and reset it to its previous level when audioplay exits. The *vol* argument is an integer value between 0 and 100, inclusive. If you do not specify this argument, leave the output volume at the level most recently set by any process.

-V   Give verbose output on the standard error when waiting for access to the audio device or when sample rate deviations are detected.

Operands

file   Audio files named on the command line are played sequentially. If you specify no file names, the standard input stream (if it is not a TTY) is played. The input stream must contain an audio file header. You can use the special file name - to read the standard input stream instead of a file. If you supply a relative path name, the AUDIOPATH environment variable is consulted.

Usage

See largefile(5) for the description of the behavior of audioplay when encountering files greater than or equal to 2 Gbytes (2**31 bytes).

Environment Variables

AUDIODEV   The full path name of the audio device to write to if you supply no
            -d argument. If the AUDIODEV variable is not set, use /dev/audio.

AUDIOPATH   Specify a colon-separated list of directories to search for audio files
            whose names are given by relative path names. You can explicitly
            specify the current directory (.) in the search path. If the
            AUDIOPATH variable is not set, search only the current directory.

Attributes

See attributes(5) for descriptions of the following attributes:

Attribute Type	Attribute Value
Architecture	SPARC, IA
Availability	SUNWauda
Interface Stability	Evolving

New!

See Also

audioconvert(1), audiorecord(1), mixerctl(1), attributes(5),
largefile(5), usb_ac(7D), audio(7I), mixer(7I)

New!

SPARC Only

audioamd(7D), dbri(7D)

IA Only

sbpro(7D)

audiorecord — Record an Audio File

Synopsis

/usr/bin/audiorecord [-af] [-v *vol*] [-b *bal*] [-m *monvol*]
    [-p mic | line | internal-cd] [-c *channels*] [-s *rate*] [-e *encoding*]
    [-t *time*] [-i *info*] [-d *dev*] [*file*]

Description

audiorecord copies audio data from the audio device to a named audio file (or the
standard output if you specify no file name). If you do not specify an output file and
standard output is a TTY, the volume, balance, monitor volume, port, and audio format
settings specified on the command line are applied and the program exits.

By default, monaural audio data is recorded at 8 kHz and encoded in ulaw format. If
the audio device supports additional configurations, you can use the -c, -s, and -e
options to specify the data format. The output file is prefixed by an audio file header that
identifies the format of the data encoded in the file.

Recording begins immediately and continues until a SIGINT signal (for example,
Control-C) is received. If you specify the -t option, audiorecord stops when the
specified time expires.

If the audio device is unavailable (that is, another process currently has read access), audiorecord prints an error message and exits immediately.

Options

-\?   Print a command-line usage message.

-a   Append the data onto the end of the named audio file. The audio device must support the audio data format of the existing file.

-b *bal*   Set the recording balance to the specified value before recording begins, and reset it to its previous level when audiorecord exits. The *bal* argument is an integer value between -100 and 100. A value of -100 indicates left balance, 0 middle, and 100 right. If you do not specify this argument, leave the input balance at the level most recently set by any process.

-c *channels*

Specify the number of audio channels (1 or 2). You can specify the value as an integer or as the string mono or stereo. The default value is mono.

-d *dev*   Specify an alternative audio device from which to take input. If you do not specify the -d option, consult the AUDIODEV environment variable. Otherwise, use /dev/audio as the default audio device.

-e *encoding*

Specify the audio data encoding. This value may be ulaw, alaw, or linear. The default encoding is ulaw.

-f   When you specify the -a flag, the sample rate of the audio device must match the sample rate at which the original file was recorded. If you also specify the -f flag, ignore sample rate differences and print a warning message on the standard error.

-i *info*   Set the information field of the output file header to the string specified by the *info* argument. You cannot specify this option in conjunction with the -a argument.

-m *monvol*   Set the input monitor volume to the specified value before recording begins, and reset it to its previous level when audiorecord exits. The *monvol* argument is an integer value between 0 and 100. A non-zero value allows a directly connected input source to be heard on the output speaker while recording is in progress. If you do not specify this argument, leave the monitor volume at the level most recently set by any process.

-p mic | line | internal-cd

Select the mic, line, or internal-cd input as the source of the audio output signal. If you do not specify this argument, the input port remains unchanged. Some systems do not support all possible input ports. If the named port does not exist, ignore this option.

-s *rate*   Specify the sample rate, in samples per second. If a number is followed by the letter k, it is multiplied by 1000 (for example, 44.1k = 44100). The default sample rate is 8 kHz.

-t *time*   Specify the maximum length of time to record. You can specify time as a floating-point value, indicating the number of seconds, or in the form *hh*:*mm*:*ss.dd*, where the hour and minute specifications are optional.

-v *vol*   Set the recording gain to the specified value before recording begins, and reset it to its previous level when audiorecord exits. The *vol* argument is an integer value between 0 and 100. If you do not specify this argument, leave the input volume at the level most recently set by any process.

Operand

file   Rewrite or append the named audio file. If you do not specify a file name (and standard output is not a TTY) or if you specify the special file-name dash (-), direct output to the standard output.

Usage

See largefile(5) for the description of the behavior of audiorecord when encountering files greater than or equal to 2 Gbytes (2**31 bytes).

Environment Variables

AUDIODEV   The full path name of the audio device to record from if you do not supply a -d argument. If the AUDIODEV variable is not set, use /dev/audio.

Attributes

See attributes(5) for descriptions of the following attributes:

Attribute Type	Attribute Value
Architecture	SPARC, IA
Availability	SUNWauda
Interface Stability	Evolving

See Also

audioconvert(1), audioplay(1), mixerctl(1), attributes(5), largefile(5), usb_ac(7D), audio(7I), mixer(7I)

auths — Print Authorizations Granted to a User

Synopsis

/bin/auths [*user...*]

Description

Use the auths command, new in the Solaris 8 Operating Environment, to print on standard output the role-based access control (RBAC) authorizations that you or the optionally specified user or role have been granted. Authorizations are rights that are checked by certain privileged programs to determine whether a user can execute restricted functionality.

Each user can have zero or more authorizations. Authorizations are represented by fully qualified names that identify the organization that created the authorization and the functionality that it controls. Following the convention of the Java programming language, the hierarchical components of an authorization are separated by dots (.), starting with the reverse order Internet domain name of the creating organization and ending with the specific function within a class of authorizations.

An asterisk (*) indicates all authorizations in a class.

Starting with the Solaris 9 release, a user's authorizations are looked up in user_attr(4) and in the /etc/security/policy.conf file (see policy.conf(4)). Authorizations can be specified directly in user_attr(4) or indirectly through prof_attr(4). Authorizations can also be assigned to every user in the system directly as default authorizations or indirectly as default profiles in the /etc/security/policy.conf file.

Examples

The auths output has the following form.

```
mopoke% auths tester01 tester02
tester01 : com.sun.system.date, com.sun.jobs.admin
tester02: com.sun.system.*
mopoke%
```

The following example shows the output from the auths command with no arguments, which shows the authorizations for the current user.

```
mopoke% auths
solaris.profmgr.read,solaris.jobs.users,solaris.admin.usermgr.read,sola
    ris.admin.logsvc.read,solaris.admin.fsmgr.read,solaris.admin.serialmg
    r.read,solaris.admin.diskmgr.read,solaris.admin.procmgr.user,solaris.
    compsys.read,solaris.admin.printer.read,solaris.admin.prodreg.read,so
    laris.admin.dcmgr.read
mopoke%
```

The following example shows the authorizations for root.

```
mopoke% auths root
solaris.*
mopoke%
```

Exit Status

0	Successful completion.
1	An error occurred.

Files

/etc/user_attr

        RBAC extended user attributes database.

/etc/security/auth_attr

        RBAC authorization descriptions database.

/etc/security/policy.conf   *New!*

        Configuration file for security policy.

/etc/security/prof_attr

        RBAC profile description database

Attributes

See attributes(5) for descriptions of the following attributes.

Attribute Type	Attribute Value
Availability	SUNWcsu

See Also

profiles(1), roles(1), getauthattr(3SECDB), auth_attr(4), policy.conf(4), *New!*
prof_attr(4), user_attr(4), attributes(5)

---

awk — Pattern Scanning and Processing Language

Synopsis

/usr/bin/awk [-f *progfile*] [-Fc] ['*prog*'] [*parameters*] [*filename*...]
/usr/xpg4/bin/awk [-F *ERE*] [-v *assignment*...] '*program*' | -f *progfile*...
   [*argument*...]

Description

The awk command is a complete programming language that is very useful for computation and pattern matching. The name awk is an acronym composed of the last initials of the three developers of the language: Aho, Weinberger, and Kernighan. The /usr/xpg4/bin/awk command is described on the nawk(1) manual page. The nawk (new awk) command is a greatly enhanced and optimized version of awk.

    The /usr/bin/awk command scans a list of input files for lines that match any of a set of patterns specified in *prog*. The *prog* string must be enclosed in single quotes (') to protect it from the shell. For each pattern in *prog* there may be an associated action performed when a line of a file name matches the pattern. The set of pattern-action statements may appear literally as *prog* or in a file specified with the -f *progfile* option. Input files are read in order; if there are no files, the standard input is read. The file-name dash (-) means the standard input.

Notes

Input white space is not preserved on output if fields are involved.

There are no explicit conversions between numbers and strings. To force an expression to be treated as a number, add 0 to it; to force it to be treated as a string, concatenate the null string ("") to it.

Options

-f *progfile*

Read the set of patterns from *progfile*.

-F*c*

Use the character *c* as the field separator (FS) character. See the discussion of FS below.

Usage

Input Lines

Each input line is matched against the pattern portion of every pattern-action statement; the associated action is performed for each matched pattern. Any file name of the form *var=value* is treated as an assignment, not a file name, and is executed at the time it would have been opened if it were a file name. Variables assigned in this manner are not available inside a BEGIN rule and are assigned after previously specified files have been read.

An input line is normally made up of fields separated by white spaces. (You can change this default by using the built-in field separator variable, FS, or the -F*c* option.) The default is to ignore leading blanks and to separate fields by blanks and/or Tab characters. However, if FS is assigned a value that does not include any of the white spaces, then leading blanks are not ignored. The fields are denoted $1, $2, . . .; $0 refers to the entire line.

Pattern-Action Statements

A pattern-action statement has the form:

pattern {action}

You can omit either *pattern* or *action*. If there is no *pattern*, the action is performed on every input line. If there is no *action*, the matching line is printed. Pattern-action statements are separated by newlines or semicolons.

Patterns are arbitrary Boolean combinations (!, | |, &&, and parentheses) of relational expressions and regular expressions. A relational expression is one of the following:

expression relop expression
expression matchop regular-expression

where a *relop* is any of the six relational operators in C, and a *matchop* is either ~ (contains) or !~ (does not contain). An expression is an arithmetic expression, a relational expression, the special expression var in array, or a Boolean combination of these.

Regular expressions are specified as in egrep(1). In patterns you must surround the regular expressions with slashes. Isolated regular expressions in a pattern apply to the entire line. You can also use regular expressions in relational expressions. A pattern can consist of two patterns separated by a comma; in this case, the action is performed for all lines between the occurrence of the first pattern to the occurrence of the second pattern.

You can use the special patterns BEGIN and END to capture control before the first input line has been read and after the last input line has been read. These keywords do not combine with any other patterns.

Built-in Variables
Built-in variables include:

FILENAME	Name of the current input file.
FS	Input field separator regular expression (default blank and Tab).
NF	Number of fields in the current record.
NR	Ordinal number of the current record.
OFMT	Output format for numbers (default, %.6g).
OFS	Output field separator (default, blank).
ORS	Output record separator (default, newline).
RS	Input record separator (default, newline).

An action is a sequence of statements. A statement can be one of the following:

```
if (expression) statement [else statement]
while (expression) statement
do statement while (expression)
for (expression; expression; expression) statement
for (var in array) statement
break
continue
{[statement]...}
expression # commonly variable = expression
print [expression-list] [>expression]
printf format [, expression-list] [>expression]
next # skip remaining patterns on this input line
exit [expr] # skip the rest of the input; exit status is expr
```

Terminate statements by semicolons, newlines, or right braces. An empty *expression-list* stands for the whole input line. Expressions take on string or numeric values as appropriate and are built using the operators +, -, *, /, %, ^, and concatenation (indicated by a blank). The operators ++, --, +=, -=, *=, /=, %=, ^=, >, >=, <, <=, ==, !=, and ?: are also available in expressions. Variables may be scalars, array elements (denoted x[i]), or fields. Variables are initialized to the null string or 0. Array subscripts can be any string, not necessarily numeric; this syntax allows for a form of associative memory. String constants are quoted (" "), with the usual C escapes recognized within.

The print statement prints its arguments on the standard output, on a file if >*expression* is present, or on a pipe if |cmd is present. The output resulting from the print statement is terminated by the output record separator with each argument separated by the current output field separator. The printf statement formats its expression list according to the format described for printf (see printf(3S)).

Built-in Functions

The arithmetic functions are as follows:

cos(x)	Return cosine of x, where x is in radians.
sin(x)	Return sine of x, where x is in radians.
exp(x)	Return the exponential function of x.
log(x)	Return the natural logarithm of x.
sqrt(x)	Return the square root of x.
int(x)	Truncate its argument to an integer. It is truncated toward 0 when $x > 0$.

The string functions are as follows:

index(s, t)

Return the position in string s where string t first occurs, or 0 if it does not occur at all.

int(s)   Truncate s to an integer value. If s is not specified, use $0.

length(s)   Return the length of its argument taken as a string, or of the whole line if there is no argument.

split(s, a, fs)

Split the string s into array elements a[1], a[2], a[n], and return n. The separation is done with the regular expression fs or with the field separator FS if fs is not given.

sprintf(fmt, $expr$, $expr$, ...)

Format the expressions according to the printf(3S) format given by fmt and return the resulting string.

substr(s, m, n)

Return the n-character substring of s that begins at position m.

The input/output function is as follows:

getline   Set $0 to the next input record from the current input file. getline returns 1 for successful input, 0 for end of file, and –1 for an error.

Large File Behavior

See largefile(5) for the description of the behavior of awk when encountering files greater than or equal to 2 Gbytes (2**31 bytes).

Examples

Make sure awk has a source of input. The following example doesn't do anything because there is no source of input.

```
castle% awk '{print "Hello, Everyone" }'
```

The following example uses a file named file1 that contains the following lines.

```
bill tom willy nikki
keith harry ed
```

```
mary linda
glenda willy neil
```

The following example prints out all lines from a file whose first record begins with the letter D or greater (in ASCII sorting sequence).

```
castle% awk '$1 > "D" {print $0}' /tmp/file1
keith karry ed
mary linda
glenda willy neil
castle%
```

You can use the pipe symbol (|) to match two patterns in awk, as shown in the following example.

```
castle% awk '$1 ~/(glenda|bill)/ {print $0}' file1
bill tom willy nikki
glenda willy neil
castle%
```

Here are some more examples of searching for patterns.

/Chicago/	Match any occurrence of Chicago in the record.
/^Detroit/	Match only when Detroit is at the beginning of the line.
/Chicago|Detroit/	
	Match any occurrence of Chicago or Detroit.
$2 ~ /Traverse/	
	The second field in the record matches Traverse.
$2 !~ /Bill/	
	The second field does not match Bill.
$4 > "k"	The fourth field follows k in alphabetical order.

The following example matches willy only when the name is not in the second field.

```
castle% awk '$2 !~/willy/ {print $0}' file1
bill tom willy nikki
keith karry ed
mary linda
castle%
```

It does not match the line glenda willy neil.

The following example matches lines that contain the names ed and mary.

```
castle% awk '/ed|mary/ {print $0}' file1
keith harry ed
mary linda
castle%
```

The following example prints the second field in the lines that contain the names ed and mary.

```
castle% awk '/ed|mary/ {print $2}' file1
harry
```

```
linda
castle%
```

Each of the examples above assumes that the fields are separated by a space or Tab. If the field is separated by a colon (:), use −F as shown in the following example.

```
castle% awk -F: ' /ed|mary/ {print $2}' file1
```

The following example prints lines longer than 72 characters.

```
length > 72
```

The following example prints the first two fields in opposite order.

```
{ print $2, $1 }
```

The following example prints the first two fields in opposite order, with input fields separated by comma and/or blanks and tabs.

```
BEGIN { FS = ",[\t]*|[\t]+" }
{ print $2, $1 }
```

The following example adds up first column, print sum, and average.

```
{ s += $1 }
END { print "sum is", s, " average is", s/NR }
```

The following example prints fields in reverse order.

```
{ for (i = NF; i > 0; --i) print $i }
```

The following example prints all lines between start/stop pairs.

```
/start/, /stop/
```

The following example prints all lines whose first field is different from the previous one.

```
$1 != prev { print; prev = $1 }
```

The following example prints a file, filling in page numbers starting at 5.

```
/Page/ { $2 = n++; } { print }
```

Assuming this program is in a file named prog, the following command line prints the file input numbering its pages starting at 5.

```
castle% awk -f prog n=5 input
```

Environment Variables

See environ(5) for descriptions of the following environment variables that affect the execution of awk: LC_CTYPE and LC_MESSAGES.

LC_NUMERIC   Determine the radix character used when interpreting numeric input, *New!*
performing conversions between numeric and string values, and
formatting numeric output. Regardless of locale, the period character
(the decimal-point character of the POSIX locale) is the decimal-point
character recognized in processing awk programs including
assignments in command-line arguments. New in the Solaris 8 release.

Attributes

See attributes(5) for descriptions of the following attributes:

/usr/bin/awk

Attribute Type	Attribute Value
Availability	SUNWesu
CSI	Enabled

/usr/xpg4/bin/awk

Attribute Type	Attribute Value
Availability	SUNWxcu4
CSI	Enabled

See Also

egrep(1), grep(1), nawk(1), sed(1), printf(3C), attributes(5),
environ(5), largefile(5), XPG4(5)

B

banner — Make Posters

Synopsis

/usr/bin/banner *strings*

Description

banner prints its arguments in large letters on the standard output, one argument per line, up to a maximum of 10 characters.

Examples

The following example prints happy birthday.

castle% **banner happy birthday**

```
castle%
```

In the following example, the word congratulations is 14 characters, so only the first 10 characters are displayed.

```
castle% banner congratulations
```

```
castle%
```

If you want to print the banner, you can pipe the output to a printer, as shown in the following example.

```
castle% banner happy birthday | lp
castle%
```

Attributes

See attributes(5) for descriptions of the following attributes:

Attribute Type	Attribute Value
Availability	SUNWesu

See Also

echo(1), attributes(5)

basename, dirname — Deliver Portions of Path Names

Synopsis

/usr/bin/basename *string* [*suffix*]
/usr/xpg4/bin/basename *string* [*suffix*] *dirname string*

Description

You can use the basename command to strip path names off a file name. For example, if you have an environment variable that contains a complete path name, you might want to extract just the name of the file without the complete path. This command is normally used inside substitution marks (``` `` ```) within shell procedures.

/usr/bin/basename

The suffix is a pattern defined on the expr(1) manual page.

/usr/xpg4/bin/basename

/usr/xpg4/bin/basename is a POSIX-compliant version of the /usr/bin/basename command. See standards(5).

The suffix is a string with no special significance attached to any of the characters it contains.

Conversely, you can use the dirname command to strip the file name and return the directory that includes all but the last level of the path name in string.

Examples

The following example first shows the complete path for the EDITOR environment variable. Then, it uses the basename command to display the name of the editor and the dirname file to display the path without the file name.

```
castle% env | grep EDITOR
EDITOR=/usr/dt/bin/dtpad
castle% basename $EDITOR
dtpad
castle% dirname $EDITOR
/usr/dt/bin
castle%
```

Environment Variables

See environ(5) for descriptions of the following environment variables that affect the execution of basename and dirname: LC_CTYPE, LC_MESSAGES, and NLSPATH.

Exit Status

0	Successful completion.
>0	An error occurred.

Attributes

See attributes(5) for descriptions of the following attributes:

/usr/bin/basename

Attribute Type	Attribute Value
Availability	SUNWcsu

/usr/xpg4/bin/basename

Attribute Type	Attribute Value
Availability	SUNWxcu4

See Also

expr(1), attributes(5), environ(5), xpg4(5)

batch — Execute Commands at a Later Time

Syntax

    /usr/bin/batch

Description

See at(1).

bc — Binary Calculator

Synopsis

    /usr/bin/bc [-c] [-l] [*file*...]

Description

bc is both a calculator and a C-like language that you can use to write numerical programs. bc is actually a preprocessor for the dc desktop calculator and uses the dc command to do its work. However, bc contains many more functions than does dc, including named functions, logical operators, and mathematical functions such as sqrt (square root). bc uses an infix notation, where you place operators between the numbers on which they operate. For example, 2 + 2 = 4.

You execute bc from a command line. It can take input from a command line or directly from a file and then from the command. When you use a file name as an argument, bc reads the file, processes its commands, and then switches to the command line for its input. In this way you can store complex commands and functions in a file and use them directly from a command line.

bc automatically displays the results of its calculations for every line. All of the information for a single calculation must be on one line.To exit from bc, type **quit** and press Return, or type **Control-D** to signal end-of-file.

The bc command language resembles the C language.

Notes

The bc command does not recognize the logical operators && and ||. The for statement must have all three expressions.

Options

-c   Compile only. Send the dc command output to the standard output.

-l   Define the math functions, and initialize scale to 20 instead of the default 0.

Operands

file   A path name of a text file containing bc program statements. After all cases of *file* have been read, bc reads the standard input.

Usage

The following list describes in more detail the syntax for bc programs:

Letter   A single letter between a and z.

Expression

An expression: a mathematical or logical value, an operand that takes a value, or a combination of operands and operators that evaluates to a value.

Statement   A statement.

Comments

Comments are enclosed between /* and */.

Names (Operands)

Letter   Simple one-letter variables.

Letter [*Expression*] (up to BC_DIM_MAX dimensions)

Array elements.

ibase   Input base.

obase (limited to BC_BASE_MAX)

Output base.

scale (limited to BC_SCALE_MAX)

The number of digits to the right of the decimal point that bc retains in its calculations.

Other Operands

- Arbitrarily long numbers with optional sign and decimal point.
- Strings of fewer than BC_STRING_MAX characters between double quotes (").
- (*Expression*).
- sqrt (*Expression*) (Square root).
- length (*Expression*) (Number of significant decimal digits).
- scale (*Expression*) (Number of digits right of decimal point).
- *Letter* (*Expression* , . . . , *Expression*).

Operators

- + - * / % ^ (% is remainder; ^ is power.)
- ++ -- (prefix and postfix; apply to names.)
- == <= >= != < >
- = =+ =- =* =/ =% =^

Statements

- *Expression*
- { *Statement* ; . . . ; *Statement* }
- if (*Expression*) *Statement*
- while (*Expression*) *Statement*
- for (*Expression* ; *Expression* ; *Expression*) *Statement*
- null statement.
- break
- quit
- *string*

Function Definitions

```
define Letter ( Letter ,..., Letter ) {
  auto Letter ,..., Letter
  Statement ;... Statement
  return ( Expression )
}
```

Functions in -l Math Library

s (*x*)	Sine.
c (*x*)	Cosine.
e (*x*)	Exponential.
l (*x*)	Log.
a (*x*)	Arctangent.
j (*n*, *x*)	Bessel function.

All function arguments are passed by value.

The value of a statement that is an expression is printed unless the main operator is an assignment. You can separate statements with either semicolons or newlines. Assignment to scale influences the number of digits retained on arithmetic operations in the manner of dc. Assignments to ibase or obase set the input and output number radix.

You can simultaneously use the same letter as an array, a function, and a simple variable. All variables are global to the program. auto variables are stacked during function calls. When arrays are used as function arguments or define them as automatic variables, empty square brackets must follow the array name.

Examples

You can use bc for normal arithmetic computations. Type **bc** and press Return. No prompt is displayed. To exit, type **quit** or **Control-D**. The entire calculation must be all on the same line. bc displays the results of each calculation as soon as you press Return.

```
castle% bc
2 + 2
4
Control-D
castle%
```

You can use a minus sign to indicate negative numbers. In the following examples, subtracting by a negative number adds it. Adding a negative number subtracts it.

```
castle% bc
1 + 2 + 3 - -3.12195
9.12195
1 + 2 + 3 + -2.14197
3.85803
Control-D
castle%
```

You can use the scale operator to specify how many digits to the right of the decimal point are retained in your calculations. The scale setting remains in effect for the current session.

```
castle% bc
scale = 3
1.2345/.9876
1.250
Control-D
castle%
```

You can define and use variables by assigning the value to a single letter. In the following example, x is set to 7 and used in the subsequent calculation.

```
castle% bc
x=7
5*7
35
Control-D
castle%
```

In the shell, the following assigns an approximation of the first 10 digits of -?n to the variable x.

```
x=$(printf "%s\n" 'scale = 10; 104348/33215' | bc)
```

The following example.dc file defines a function to compute an approximate value of the exponential function and prints approximate values of the exponential function of the first 10 integers.

```
scale = 20
define e(x){
auto a, b, c, i, s
a = 1
b = 1
s = 1
for(i=1; 1==1; i++){
 a = a*x
 b = b*i
 c = a/b
 if(c == 0) return(s)
 s = s+c
}
}
for(i=1; i<=10; i++) e(i)
```

Reading the file into bc produces the following results.

```
castle% bc example.bc
2.71828182845904523526
7.38905609893065022713
20.08553692318766774083
54.59815003314423907790
148.41315910257660342091
403.42879349273512260821
1096.63315842845859926350
2980.95798704172827474335
8103.08392757538400770974
22026.46579480671651695759
```

After the file is processed, you are still in bc and can perform additional computations, or you can press **Control-D**, or type **quit** and press Return to exit.

The following examples show bc's ability to perform base conversion on input and output separately. The ibase= (input base) command can change the way numbers you input are interpreted, and the obase= (output base) command can change the way numbers output by bc are interpreted. The comments in italic are not part of the screen output.

New!

```
$ bc
# Decimal to hexidecmal conversion.
obase=16
255        # I input 255, which is converted to hex FF.
FF
10         # I input 10.
A
# Decimal to octal conversion.
obase=8
10         # Decimal 10 is octal 12.
12
8          # Decimal 8 is octal 10.
10
7          # Decimal 7 is octal 7.
7
# Decimal to binary conversion.
obase=2
8          # Decimal 8 is binary 1000.
1000
255        # Decimal 255 is binary 11111111.
11111111
1          # Decimal 1 is binary 1.
1
2          # Decimal 2 is binary 10.
10
Control-D
$
```

The ibase command can be useful and can also trip you up because once you enter it, *all* subsequent numbers you enter are interpreted in that base, as shown in the following example.

```
# convert binary to decimal - obase is already set to 10
ibase=2
10  # binary 10 is decimal 2
2
# Now set input base back to decimal - NOT!
# Because bc is still interpreting your input as base 2, the next line is read as
# ibase=(binary) 10 = (decimal) 2, so all numbers you input are still interpreted
# as binary.
ibase=10
10
2    # What?
# To get back to decimal input mode, you have to enter the binary
# equivalent of decimal 10: 1010
ibase=1010
10
10   # decimal 10 = decimal 10
```

Environment Variables

See environ(5) for descriptions of the following environment variables that affect the execution of bc: LC_CTYPE, LC_MESSAGES, and NLSPATH.

Exit Status

0   All input files were processed successfully.

unspecified

An error occurred.

Files

/usr/lib/lib.b

Mathematical library.

/usr/include/limits.h

Use to define BC_ parameters.

Attributes

See attributes(5) for descriptions of the following attributes:

Attribute Type	Attribute Value
Availability	SUNWesu

See Also

awk(1), dc(1), attributes(5)

bdiff — Big diff

Synopsis

```
/usr/bin/bdiff filename1 filename2 [n] [-s]
```

Description

bdiff is similar to diff, except that you can use it to process files that are too large for diff. A large file is a regular file whose size is greater than or equal to 2 Gbytes (2**31 bytes). A small file is a regular file whose size is less than 2 Gbytes.

If *filename1* (*filename2*) is -, the standard input is read.

bdiff ignores lines common to the beginning of both files, splits the remainder of each file into *n*-line segments, and invokes diff on corresponding segments. If both optional arguments are specified, you must use them in the order indicated above.

The output of bdiff is exactly that of diff, with line numbers adjusted to make it look as if the files had been processed as one. The first part of the bdiff output lists the line numbers that differ in the two files, separated by c for changed. Lines from the first file are marked with <, and lines from the second file are marked with >.

Note — Because of the segmenting of the files, bdiff does not necessarily find a smallest sufficient set of file differences.

Options

n	Specify the number of line segments. By default, the value of *n* is 3500. This option is useful in those cases in which 3500-line segments are too large for diff, causing it to fail.
-s	Do not print bdiff diagnostics (silent option). This option does not suppress possible diagnostic messages from diff, which bdiff calls.

Usage

See largefile(5) for the description of the behavior of bdiff when encountering files greater than or equal to 2 Gbytes (2**31 bytes).

Examples

In the following example, two (small) files are first displayed by the cat command, and then bdiff compares the two files. You can use bdiff on small files; however, diff has more options available for comparing small files.

```
castle% cat kookaburra1
Kookaburra sits in the old gum tree
Merry merry king of the bush is he
Laugh, kookaburra, laugh
Gay your life must be.

Kookaburra sits in the old gum tree
Eating all the gumdrops he can see
Laugh, kookaburra, laugh
Leave some there for me.
castle% cat kookaburra2
Kookaburra sits in the old gum tree
```

```
Merry merry king of the bush is he
Laugh, kookaburra, laugh
Glad your life must be.

Kookaburra sits in the old gum tree
Eating all the gumdrops he can see
Laugh, kookaburra, laugh
Leave some there for me.
castle% bdiff kookaburra1 kookaburra2
4c4
< Gay your life must be.
---
> Glad your life must be.
castle%
```

Files

/tmp/bd*?????*

        Temporary file used for comparison.

While bdiff is comparing files, it creates temporary files in the /tmp directory. When the comparison is done, the files are automatically removed. The following example shows two bdiff temporary files.

```
castle% ls /tmp/bd*
bdCg4GX   bdowlVW
castle%
```

Attributes

See attributes(5) for descriptions of the following attributes:

Attribute Type	Attribute Value
Availability	SUNWesu
CSI	Enabled

See Also

diff(1), attributes(5), largefile(5)

Diagnostics

Use help for explanations.

---

bfs — Big File Scanner

Synopsis

/usr/bin/bfs [-] *filename*

Description

The bfs command is similar to ed(1) except that it is read-only and processes much larger files. Files can be up to 1024 Kbytes and 32-Kbyte lines, with up to 512 characters, including newline, per line (255 for 16-bit machines). bfs is usually more efficient than ed(1) for scanning a file because the file is not copied to a buffer. It is most useful for identifying sections of a large file where you can use csplit(1) to divide the file into more manageable pieces for editing.

Normally, the size of the file being scanned is printed, as is the size of any file written with the w (write) command. The optional – suppresses printing of sizes. You can turn on prompting for input with * if you type **P** and press Return, as in ed(1). You can turn prompting off again by typing another **P** and pressing Return. Note that when prompting is turned on, messages are displayed in response to errors.

All address expressions described under ed(1) are supported. In addition, you can surround regular expressions with two symbols besides / and ?: > indicates downward search without wrap-around, and < indicates upward search without wrap-around.

You can use only the letters a through z for mark names, and all 26 marks are remembered.

bfs Commands

The e, g, v, k, p, q, w, =, !, and null commands operate as described under ed(1). Commands such as ---, +++-, +++=, -12, and +4p are accepted. Note that 1,10p and 1,10 both print the first 10 lines. The f command prints only the name of the file being scanned; there is no remembered file name. The w command is independent of output diversion, truncation, or crunching (see the xo, xt, and xc commands, below). Additional commands that are available are listed below.

: *label*   Position a *label* in a command file. Terminate the *label* by newline, and ignore blanks between the : (colon) and the start of the *label*. You can also use this command to insert comments into a command file, because labels need not be referenced.

(. , .)xb/*regular expression*/*label*

Jump (either upward or downward) to *label* if the command succeeds. It fails under any of the following conditions:

- Either address is not between 1 and $.

- The second address is less than the first.

- The regular expression does not match at least one line in the specified range, including the first and last lines.

On success, set dot (.) to the line matched and jump to label. This command is the only one that does not issue an error message on bad addresses, so it can be used to test whether addresses are bad before other commands are executed. Note that the command xb/^/ *label* is an unconditional jump.

The xb command is allowed only if it is read from someplace other than a terminal. If it is read from a pipe, you can only jump downward.

xbz *label*   Test the last saved return code from the execution of a UNIX system
xbn *label*   command (! *command*) or non-zero value to the specified *label*. The two examples below both search for the next five lines containing the string size.

Example 1:
```
xv55
: 1
/size/
xv5!expr %5 - 1
!if 0%5 != 0 exit 2
xbn 1
```

Example 2:
```
xv45
: 1
/size/
xv4!expr %4 - 1
!if 0%4 = 0 exit 2
xbz 1
```

xc [*switch*] If *switch* is 1, crunch output from the p and null commands; if *switch* is 0, don't crunch output. Without an argument, xc reverses *switch*. Initially, *switch* is set for no crunching. Crunched output reduces strings of tabs and blanks to one blank and suppresses blank lines.

xf *file* Take further commands from the named file. When an end-of-file is reached, an interrupt signal is received, or an error occurs, resume reading with the file containing the xf. You can nest the xf commands to a depth of 10.

xn List the marks currently in use (you set marks with the k command).

xo [*file*] Divert further output from the p and null commands to the named file, which, if necessary, is created mode 666 (readable and writable by everyone) unless your umask setting (see umask(1)) dictates otherwise. If *file* is missing, divert output to the standard output. Note that each diversion causes truncation or creation of the file.

xt *number* Truncate output from the p and null commands to, at most, *number* characters. The initial number is 255.

xv [*digit*] [*spaces*] [*value*]

Set the variable name to the specified digit following xv. The commands xv5100 or xv5 100 both assign the value 100 to the variable 5. The command xv61,100p assigns the value 1,100p to the variable 6. To reference a variable, put a % in front of the variable name. For example, using the above assignments for variables 5 and 6, the following commands all print the first 100 lines.
```
1,%5p
1,%5
%6
```

g/%5/p globally searches for the characters 100 and prints each line containing a match.

To escape the special meaning of %, precede it with a backslash (\). For example, you can use g/".*\%[cds]/p to match and list %c, %d, or %s formats (for example, printf-like statements) of characters, decimal integers, or strings.

Another feature of the xv command is that you can store the first line of output from a UNIX system command in a variable. The only requirement is that the first character of value be an !. For example, the following lines put the current line into variable 35, print it, and increment the variable 36 by 1.

```
.w junk
xv5!cat junk
!rm junk
!echo "%5"
xv6!expr %6 + 1
```

To escape the special meaning of ! as the first character of value, precede it with a \. The following statement stores the value !date in variable 7.

```
xv7\!date
```

Operands

filename   Any file up to 1,024 Kbytes and 32-Kbyte lines, with up to 512 characters, including newline, per line (255 for 16-bit machines). *filename* can be a section of a larger file that has been divided into more manageable sections for editing by the use of csplit(1).

Examples

The following example returns the total number of characters in the core file and exits with Control-D.

```
castle% bfs core
11890
^D
castle%
```

The following example returns the total number of characters in the bibliography file, assigns the value 100 to a variable named 5, prints lines 1–100 of the file, and exits with Control-D. The example shows only the first few of the 100 lines.

```
castle% bfs bibliography
4471
xv5100
1,%5p
%A Janice Winsor
%T Opening the Dream Door
%P 153
%I Merrill-West Publishing
^D
castle%
```

The following example uses the – option to suppress printing of the total number of characters in the bibliography file. It then assigns the value dreams to the variable 1, displays the value of the variable, searches for all lines in the file that contain the word dreams, and exits with Control-D.

```
castle% bfs - bibliography

xv1dreams
!echo "%1"
dreams
g/%1/p
%K dreams, psychic development
dreams as an example, Janice Winsor makes practical suggestions
Processes for remembering and accessing dreams are taught in an
^D
castle%
```

The following example returns the total number of characters in the bibliography file, assigns the value date to a variable named 7, displays the value of the variable, and exits with Control-D.

```
castle% bfs bibliography
4471
xv7!date
!echo "%7"
Thursday March 18 08:36:52 WST 1999
^D
castle%
```

Exit Status

0	Successful completion without any file or command errors.
>0	An error occurred.

Attributes

See attributes(5) for descriptions of the following attributes:

Attribute Type	Attribute Value
Availability	SUNWesu

See Also

csplit(1), ed(1), umask(1), attributes(5)

Diagnostics

Message is ? for errors in commands if prompting is turned off. Self-explanatory error messages are displayed when prompting is on.

bg — Control Process Execution

Synopsis
/usr/bin/bg [%*job-id*...]

Description
See jobs(1).

bgplot — Graphics Filters for Various Plotters

Synopsis
/usr/ucb/plot [-T*terminal*]

Description
See plot(1).

biff — Give Notice of Incoming Mail Messages

Synopsis
/usr/ucb/biff [y | n]

Description
Use biff to turn mail notification on or off for the terminal session. With no arguments, biff displays the current notification status for the terminal.

If notification is enabled, the terminal rings the bell and displays the header and the first few lines of each arriving mail message. biff operates asynchronously. For synchronized notices, use the MAIL variable of sh(1) or the mail variable of csh(1).

You can include a biff y command in your ~/.login or ~/.profile file for execution when you log in.

Options

y	Enable mail notification for the terminal.
n	Disable notification for the terminal.

Examples
The following example turns biff on, displays the current notification status, turns biff off, and displays the current notification status again.

```
castle% biff y
castle% biff
```

```
is y
castle% biff n
castle% biff
is n
castle%
```

Files

~/.login   User's login file.

~/.profile   User's profile file.

Attributes

See attributes(5) for descriptions of the following attributes:

Attribute Type	Attribute Value
Availability	SUNWscpu

See Also

csh(1), mail(1), sh(1), attributes(5)

break, continue — Shell Built-in Functions to Break Out of Loops

Synopsis

sh
```
break [n]
continue [n]
```

csh
```
break
continue
```

ksh
```
*
break [n]
*
continue [n]
```

Description

Bourne Shell

break exits from the enclosing for or while loop if any. If you specify *n*, break *n* levels.
continue resumes the next iteration of the enclosing for or while loop. If you specify
n, resume at the *n*-th enclosing loop.

C Shell

break resumes execution after the end of the nearest enclosing foreach or while loop. The remaining commands on the current line are executed. You can write multilevel breaks as a list of break commands, all on one line.

continue continues execution of the next iteration of the nearest enclosing while or foreach loop.

Korn Shell

break exits from the enclosed for, while, until, or select loop, if any. If you specify n, then break n levels.

continue resumes the next iteration of the enclosed for, while, until, or select loop. If you specify n, resume at the n-th enclosed loop.

ksh(1) commands that are preceded by one or two asterisks (*) are treated specially in the following ways:

- Variable assignment lists preceding the command remain in effect when the command completes.
- I/O redirections are processed after variable assignments.
- Errors abort a script that contains them.
- Words following a command preceded by ** and that are in the format of a variable assignment are expanded with the same rules as a variable assignment. Thus, tilde substitution is performed after the = sign, and word-splitting and file-name generation are not performed.

Examples

In the following C shell example, the script continues running the while loop until the user answers Yes (or yes, y, or Y). When the user does answer **yes**, the break terminates the while loop and, in this case, exits because there are no additional commands to execute.

```
#!/bin/csh -f
#
while (1)
        echo "Finished yet? \
        set answer = $<
        if ($answer =- [Yy]*) break
endp
```

Attributes

See attributes(5) for descriptions of the following attributes:

Attribute Type	Attribute Value
Availability	SUNWcsu

See Also

csh(1), exit(1), ksh(1), select(1), sh(1), until(1), attributes(5)

C

cal — Display a Calendar

Synopsis

```
/usr/bin/cal [[month] year]
```

Description

The cal command writes a Gregorian calendar to standard output. If you specify a four-digit year operand, a calendar for that year is written. If you specify no operands, a calendar for the current month is written. You can display a calendar for any month of any year by specifying the month, as a digit from 1 to 12, followed by any four-digit year up to 9999.

An unusual calendar is printed for September 1752. That is the month 11 days were skipped to make up for lack of leap year adjustments. To see this calendar, type:

```
castle% cal 9 1752
```

The command cal 83 refers to the year 83, not 1983. The year is always considered to start in January.

Operands

month	Specify the month to be displayed, represented as a decimal integer from 1 (January) to 12 (December). The default is the current month.
year	Specify the year for which the calendar is displayed, represented as a decimal integer from 1 to 9999. The default is the current year.

113

Examples

The following example uses the `cal` command with no arguments to display the current month.

```
castle% cal
      January 1999
   S  M Tu  W Th  F  S
               1  2
   3  4  5  6  7  8  9
  10 11 12 13 14 15 16
  17 18 19 20 21 22 23
  24 25 26 27 28 29 30
  31
castle%
```

The following example displays a calendar for the year 2000.

```
castle% cal 2000


                              2000
         Jan                  Feb                  Mar
 S  M Tu  W Th  F  S    S  M Tu  W Th  F  S    S  M Tu  W Th  F  S
                  1           1  2  3  4  5              1  2  3  4
 2  3  4  5  6  7  8    6  7  8  9 10 11 12    5  6  7  8  9 10 11
 9 10 11 12 13 14 15   13 14 15 16 17 18 19   12 13 14 15 16 17 18
16 17 18 19 20 21 22   20 21 22 23 24 25 26   19 20 21 22 23 24 25
23 24 25 26 27 28 29   27 28 29               26 27 28 29 30 31
30 31
         Apr                  May                  Jun
 S  M Tu  W Th  F  S    S  M Tu  W Th  F  S    S  M Tu  W Th  F  S
                  1        1  2  3  4  5  6              1  2  3
 2  3  4  5  6  7  8    7  8  9 10 11 12 13    4  5  6  7  8  9 10
 9 10 11 12 13 14 15   14 15 16 17 18 19 20   11 12 13 14 15 16 17
16 17 18 19 20 21 22   21 22 23 24 25 26 27   18 19 20 21 22 23 24
30                     28 29 30 31            25 26 27 28 29 30
         Jul                  Aug                  Sep
 S  M Tu  W Th  F  S    S  M Tu  W Th  F  S    S  M Tu  W Th  F  S
                  1        1  2  3  4  5                    1  2
 2  3  4  5  6  7  8    6  7  8  9 10 11 12    3  4  5  6  7  8  9
 9 10 11 12 13 14 15   13 14 15 16 17 18 19   10 11 12 13 14 15 16
16 17 18 19 20 21 22   20 21 22 23 24 25 26   17 18 19 20 21 22 23
23 24 25 26 27 28 29   27 28 29 30 31         24 25 26 27 28 29 30
30 31
         Oct                  Nov                  Dec
 S  M Tu  W Th  F  S    S  M Tu  W Th  F  S    S  M Tu  W Th  F  S
 1  2  3  4  5  6  7           1  2  3  4                    1  2
 8  9 10 11 12 13 14    5  6  7  8  9 10 11    3  4  5  6  7  8  9
15 16 17 18 19 20 21   12 13 14 15 16 17 18   10 11 12 13 14 15 16
22 23 24 25 26 27 28   19 20 21 22 23 24 25   17 18 19 20 21 22 23
29 30 31              26 27 28 29 30          24 25 26 27 28 29 30
                                              31
castle%
```

The following example displays a calendar for March 1946.

```
castle% cal 3 1946
    March 1946
 S  M Tu  W Th  F  S
                1  2
 3  4  5  6  7  8  9
10 11 12 13 14 15 16
17 18 19 20 21 22 23
24 25 26 27 28 29 30
31

castle%
```

Environment Variables

See environ(5) for descriptions of the following environment variables that affect the execution of cal: LC_TIME, LC_CTYPE, and NLSPATH.

Exit Status

0   Successful completion.

>0   An error occurred.

Attributes

See attributes(5) for descriptions of the following attributes:

Attribute Type	Attribute Value
Availability	SUNWesu

See Also

calendar(1), attributes(5), environ(5)

calendar — Reminder Service

Synopsis

/usr/bin/calendar [-]

Description

You can use the calendar command as a simple reminder service to record your appointments. The calendar command consults a file named calendar in the current directory and writes to the standard output any lines that contain today's or tomorrow's date anywhere in the line. calendar recognizes most reasonable month-day dates such as Aug. 24, august 24, 8/24. It does not recognize date formats such as 24 August or 24/8. On Fridays and weekends, "tomorrow" extends through Monday. You can run calendar regularly by using the crontab(1) or at(1) commands.

When the optional argument - is present, calendar does its job for all users who have a calendar file in their login directory and sends any positive results by mail(1).

Normally, this action is done daily by facilities in the UNIX operating system (see cron(1M)).

If the environment variable DATEMSK is set, calendar uses its value as the full path name of a template file containing format strings. The strings consist of conversion specifications and text characters and can provide a richer set of allowable date formats in different languages by appropriate settings of the environment variable LANG or LC_TIME; see environ(5). See strftime(3C) for the list of allowable conversion specifications.

Notes

Appropriate lines beginning with white space are not printed.

Your calendar must be public information for you to get reminder service.

calendar's extended idea of tomorrow does not account for holidays.

The - argument works only on calendar files that are local; calendar is intended not to work on calendar files that are mounted remotely with NFS. Thus, you should run **calendar** - only on diskful machines where home directories exist; running it on a diskless client has no effect.

calendar is no longer in the default root crontab. Because of the network burden, it is inadvisable to run calendar - in an environment running ypbind (1M) with a large passwd name map. If, however, the usefulness of calendar outweighs the network impact, the superuser can run crontab -e to edit the root crontab. Otherwise, individual users can use crontab -e to edit their own crontab to have cron invoke calendar without the - argument, piping output to mail addressed to themselves.

Examples

If there is no calendar file in the current directory, an error message is displayed.

```
castle% calendar
/bin/calendar: /export/home/winsor/calendar not found
castle%
```

In the following example, the calendar file in the user's home directory has three entries in it: one for today, one for tomorrow, and one for a few weeks from now. As you can see from the example, only the current calendar items are displayed.

```
castle% cat calendar
Sep 15 - Dentist, 4:30
Chiropractic appointment, Sept 16 at 10:00 AM
Monday, September 28. Start new contract
castle%
castle% calendar
Sep 15 - Dentist, 4:30
Chiropractic appointment, Sept 16 at 10:00 AM
castle%
```

You can extend date formats that are recognized by the calendar command by using the DATEMSK environment variable. First, create a template file named datemask. In that file, put the following template format:

```
%B %eth of the year %Y
```

%B represents the full month name,%e the day of the month, and %Y a four-digit year. This template recognizes dates of the following format:

```
March 7th of the year 1999 <Reminder>
```

When you set the DATEMSK environment variable to reference the datemask file, calendar recognizes traditional dates as well as dates with the extended format.

```
castle% setenv DATEMSK datemask
castle% calendar
Chiropractic appointment September 16th of the year 1998.
castle%
```

Environment Variables

See environ(5) for descriptions of the following environment variables that affect the execution of calendar: LC_CTYPE, LC_TIME, LC_CTYPE, LC_MESSAGES, LC_MESSAGES, and TZ.

Exit Status

0   Successful completion.

>0   An error occurred.

Files

/etc/passwd

System password file.

/tmp/cal*   Temporary files used by calendar.

/usr/lib/calprog

Program used to determine dates for today and tomorrow.

Attributes

See attributes(5) for descriptions of the following attributes:

Attribute Type	Attribute Value
Availability	SUNWesu

See Also

at(1), crontab(1), mail(1), cron(1M), ypbind(1M), trftime(3C), attributes(5), environ(5)

cancel — Cancel Print Request

Synopsis

/usr/bin/cancel [*request-ID*...] [*destination*...]
/usr/bin/cancel -u *username*... [*destination*...]

Description

Use the cancel command to cancel print requests while they are in the queue or while they are printing. To cancel a specific print request, you need to know the request ID for the print job. The request ID always includes the name of the printer, a dash, and the number of the print request. When a request is submitted from standard input, the request ID is displayed. To find the request ID, type **lpstat** and press Return. Only the user who submitted the request or someone logged in as root or lp can cancel a print request.

You can also use the cancel command in the following ways:

- Cancel a specific print job on a specific printer by specifying the *request-ID* and *destination* arguments.
- Cancel all jobs on a specific destination by specifying a *destination* argument.
- Cancel all requests for a specific user by specifying the -u *username* option.
- Cancel all requests for a specific user on a specific printer by specifying the -u *username* and *destination* arguments.

Users can cancel only their own print requests. By default, users can only cancel print requests on the host from which the print request was submitted. If a superuser has set user-equivalence=true in /etc/printers.conf on the print server, users can cancel print requests associated with their user name on any host. Superusers can cancel print requests on the host from which the print request was submitted. Superusers can also cancel print requests from the print server.

The print client commands locate destination information in the printers database in the name service switch file. See nsswitch.conf(4), printers(4), and printers.conf(4) for details.

Options

-u *username*

Specify the name of the user for whom print requests are to be canceled.

Operands

destination

Specify the destination on which the print requests are to be canceled. *destination* is the name of a printer or class of printers (see lpadmin(1M)). If you do not specify *destination*, cancel cancels the requested print request on all destinations.

Specify destination using atomic, POSIX-style (*server:destination*), or Federated Naming Service (FNS) (*.../service/printer/...*) names.

The print client commands locate destination information in a very specific order. See printers.conf(4) and printers(4) for details.

POSIX-style destination names (*server:destination*) are treated as print requests if *destination* has the same format as an LP-style *request-ID*. See standards(5).

request-ID   Specify the ID for the print request to be canceled, using LP-style request IDs (destination-number).

Examples

The following example lists the jobs in the print queue and then cancels them, using the different options and operands.

In the first example, user `winsor` tries to cancel print jobs owned by user `ray`. The prompt is returned but the jobs are not removed from the print queue. Notice that when you do not have permission to cancel a job, the `cancel` command does not display an error message.

```
castle% lpstat
seachild-077        castle!winsor        615      Sep 29 08:30
seachild-078        castle!winsor        615      Sep 29 08:32
seachild-079        castle!winsor        615      Sep 29 08:33
seachild-080        castle!ray           615      Sep 29 08:36
seachild-081        castle!ray           615      Sep 29 08:37
seachild-082        castle!root          615      Sep 29 08:40
castle% whoami
winsor
castle% cancel -u ray
castle%
```

Still as user `winsor`, the next example removes all `winsor`'s print jobs from the printer destination `seachild`. Then, user `winsor` tries to remove a print job owned by root by using the request ID.

```
castle% cancel -u winsor seachild
        seachild-77: canceled
        seachild-78: canceled
        seachild-79: canceled
castle% cancel seachild-82
castle% lpstat
seachild-080        castle!ray           615      Sep 29 08:36
seachild-081        castle!ray           615      Sep 29 08:37
seachild-082        castle!root          615      Sep 29 08:40
castle%
```

In the following example, root removes a print job owned by `root` and then removes all print jobs from the printer destination `seachild`. Notice that when you cancel all of the print jobs for a destination printer, no list of the jobs canceled is displayed, even when there are print jobs listed in the queue.

```
castle% su
Password:
castle# cancel seachild-82
        seachild-82: canceled
castle# cancel seachild
castle# lpstat
castle#
```

Exit Status

0   Successful completion.

non-zero   An error occurred.

Files

/var/spool/print/*

                LP print queue.

```
$HOME/.printers
```
> User-configurable printer database.

```
/etc/printers.conf
```
> System printer configuration database.

```
printers.conf.byname
```
> NIS version of `/etc/printers.conf`.

New!
```
printers.org_dir
```
> NIS+ version of `/etc/printers.conf`.

```
fns.ctx_dir.domain
```
> FNS version of `/etc/printers.conf`.

Attributes

See attributes(5) for descriptions of the following attributes:

Attribute Type	Attribute Value
Availability	SUNWpcu

See Also

New!
lp(1), lpstat(1), lpq(1B), lpr(1B), lprm(1B), lpadmin(1M),
nsswitch.conf(4), printers(4), printers.conf(4), attributes(5),
standards(5)

cat — Concatenate and Display Files

Synopsis

```
/usr/bin/cat [-nbsuvet] [file...]
```

Description

Use the cat command to create short files, to concatenate two files into a third one, to append one file to the end of another, or to display the contents of files in sequence on the standard output.

The following syntax creates a new file named *file*. Everything that you type is written to *file*. cat sends one line at a time to the file after you press Return. You can use the backspace key to correct typos on the current line, but you cannot back up across lines. When you are finished, type **Control-D** on a line by itself to terminate the session and close the file. If the file does not exist, it is created. If it already exists, the contents are overwritten with no warning.

```
cat > file
```

The following syntax displays the contents of *file* on your terminal.

```
cat file
```

The following syntax concatenates *file1* and *file2* and writes the results into *file3*. If you give no input file, cat reads from the standard input file.

cat *file1 file2* >*file3*

The following syntax appends the contents of *file1* to the end of *file2*.

cat *file1* >> *file2*

The following syntax displays the contents of *file1, file2,* and *file3* in sequence on your terminal.

cat *file1 file2 file3*

Note — Redirecting the output of cat onto one of the files being read overwrites the data originally in the file without any warning message.

Options

-n	Precede each line output with its line number.
-b	Number the lines, as with –n, but omit the line numbers from blank lines.
-s	Be silent about nonexistent files.
-u	Do not buffer the output. (The default is buffered output.)
-v	Display nonprinting characters (with the exception of Tabs, newlines, and formfeeds). ASCII control characters (octal 000–037) are printed as ^*n*, where *n* is the corresponding ASCII character in the range octal 100–137 (@) A, B, C, . . . , X, Y, Z, [, \,], ^, and _); the DEL character (octal 0177) is printed ^?. Other nonprintable characters are printed as M-*x*, where *x* is the ASCII character specified by the low-order seven bits.

You can combine the following options with the –v option.

-e	Print a $ character at the end of each line (before the newline).
-t	Print Tabs as ^I's and formfeeds as ^L's.

The –e and –t options are ignored if you do not specify the –v option.

Operands

file	A path name of an input file. If no file is specified, use the standard input. If *file* is -, read from the standard input at that point in the sequence. cat does not close and reopen standard input when it is referenced in this way but accepts multiple occurrences of dash (–) as *file*.

Usage

See largefile(5) for the description of the behavior of cat when encountering files greater than or equal to 2 Gbytes (2**31 bytes).

Examples

The following command writes the contents of the file kookaburra to standard output:

```
castle% cat kookaburra
Kookaburra sits in the old gum tree
Merry merry king of the bush is he
Laugh, kookaburra, laugh, kookaburra
Gay your life must be.

Kookaburra sits in the old gum tree
Eating all the gumdrops he can see
Stop, kookaburra, stop, kookaburra
Leave some there for me.
castle%
```

The following example concatenates kookaburra1 and kookaburra2 and writes the result to kookaburra3. It then uses the cat command to display the combined result.

```
castle% cat kookaburra1 kookaburra2 > kookaburra3
castle% cat kookaburra3
Kookaburra sits in the old gum tree
Merry merry king of the bush is he
Laugh, kookaburra, laugh, kookaburra
Gay your life must be.

Kookaburra sits in the old gum tree
Eating all the gumdrops he can see
Stop, kookaburra, stop, kookaburra
Leave some there for me.
Kookaburra sits in the old gum tree
Merry merry king of the bush is he
Laugh, kookaburra, laugh, kookaburra
Glad your life must be.

Kookaburra sits in the old gum tree
Eating all the gumdrops he can see
Stop, kookaburra, stop, kookaburra
Leave some there for me.
castle%
```

The following example uses the -n option to display line numbers for the file kookaburra.

```
castle% cat -n kookaburra
     1  Kookaburra sits in the old gum tree
     2  Merry merry king of the bush is he
     3  Laugh, kookaburra, laugh, kookaburra
     4  Gay your life must be.
     5
     6  Kookaburra sits in the old gum tree
     7  Eating all the gumdrops he can see
     8  Stop, kookaburra, stop, kookaburra
     9  Leave some there for me.
```

The following example uses the -b option to display line numbers, omitting any numbers for blank lines. Compare the results with those for the -n command above.

```
castle% cat -b kookaburra
     1  Kookaburra sits in the old gum tree
     2  Merry merry king of the bush is he
     3  Laugh, kookaburra, laugh, kookaburra
     4  Gay your life must be.

     5  Kookaburra sits in the old gum tree
     6  Eating all the gumdrops he can see
     7  Stop, kookaburra, stop, kookaburra
     8  Leave some there for me.
```

The following example displays the contents of three files, the first two of which do not exist. It then uses the -s option to suppress error messages about nonexistent files.

```
castle% cat file1 file2 kookaburra
cat: cannot open file1
cat: cannot open file2
Kookaburra sits in the old gum tree
Merry merry king of the bush is he
Laugh, kookaburra, laugh, kookaburra
Gay your life must be.

Kookaburra sits in the old gum tree
Eating all the gumdrops he can see
Stop, kookaburra, stop, kookaburra
Leave some there for me.
castle% cat -s file1 file2 kookaburra
Kookaburra sits in the old gum tree
Merry merry king of the bush is he
Laugh, kookaburra, laugh, kookaburra
Gay your life must be.

Kookaburra sits in the old gum tree
Eating all the gumdrops he can see
Stop, kookaburra, stop, kookaburra
Leave some there for me.
```

The following example uses the -vet options to display all nonprinting characters in the file kookaburra. The only nonprinting characters in this file are the newlines at the end of each line, which are displayed as a dollar sign ($).

```
castle% cat -vet kookaburra
Kookaburra sits in the old gum tree$
Merry merry king of the bush is he$
Laugh, kookaburra, laugh, kookaburra$
Gay your life must be.$
$
Kookaburra sits in the old gum tree$
Eating all the gumdrops he can see$
Stop, kookaburra, stop, kookaburra$
Leave some there for me.$
castle%
```

Environment Variables

See environ(5) for descriptions of the following environment variables that affect the execution of cat: LC_CTYPE, LC_MESSAGES, and NLSPATH.

Exit Status

0	All input files were output successfully.
>0	An error occurred.

Attributes

See attributes(5) for descriptions of the following attributes:

Attribute Type	Attribute Value
Availability	SUNWcsu
CSI	Enabled

See Also

touch(1), environ(5), attributes(5), largefile(5)

---

cc — C Compiler

Synopsis

/usr/ucb/cc [*options*]

Description

/usr/ucb/cc is the interface to the BSD Compatibility package C compiler. It is a script that looks for the link /usr/ccs/bin/ucbcc to the C compiler. /usr/ccs/bin/ucbcc is available only with the SPROcc package, whose default location is /opt/SUNWspro. /usr/ucb/cc is identical to /usr/ccs/bin/ucbcc, except that it uses BSD headers and links BSD libraries before base libraries. The /opt/SUNWspro/man/man1/acc.1 manual page is available only with the SPROcc package.

Options

/usr/ucb/cc accepts the same options as /usr/ccs/bin/ucbcc, with the exceptions noted below.

-I*dir*	Search *dir* for included files whose names do not begin with a slash (/) before searching the usual directories. cc searches the directories for multiple -I options in the order specified. The preprocessor first searches for #include files in the directory containing *sourcefile*, and then in directories named with -I options (if any), then /usr/ucbinclude, and finally, in /usr/include.

`-L`*dir*	Add *dir* to the list of directories searched for libraries by `/usr/ccs/bin/ucbcc`. Pass this option to `/usr/ccs/bin/ld` and `/usr/ccs/lib`. Search directories specified with this option before `/usr/ucblib` and `/usr/lib`.
`-Y P,` *dir*	Change the default directory used for finding libraries. Note that this option may have unexpected results and should not be used.

Exit Status

`0`	Successful compilation or link-edit.
`>0`	An error occurred.

Files

`/usr/ccs/bin/ld link`

Editor.

`/usr/lib/libcC`

Library.

`/usr/ucbinclude`

BSD Compatibility directory for header files.

`/usr/ucblib`

BSD Compatibility directory for libraries.

`/usr/ucblib/libuc`

BSD Compatibility C library.

`/usr/lib/libsocket`

Library containing socket routines.

`/usr/lib/libnsl`

Library containing network functions.

`/usr/lib/libelf`

Library containing routines to process ELF object files.

`/usr/lib/libaio`

Library containing asynchronous I/O routines.

Attributes

See `attributes`(5) for descriptions of the following attributes:

Attribute Type	Attribute Value
Availability	`SUNWscpu`

See Also

`ld(1)`, `a.out(4)`, `attributes(5)`

cd, chdir, pushd, popd, dirs — Change Working Directory

Synopsis
/usr/bin/cd [*directory*]

sh
cd [*argument*]
chdir [*argument*]

csh
cd [*dir*]
chdir [*dir*]
pushd [+*n* | *dir*]
popd [+*n*]
dirs [-l]

ksh
cd [*arg*]
cd *old new*

Description
You can move between directories with the cd (change directory) command. Depending on the shell you are using, you may have alternative ways to change directories.

New!

The /usr/bin/cd command changes the working directory in the context of the cd command only, in contrast to the version built into the shell, as described below. /usr/bin/cd has no effect on the invoking process but can be used to determine whether a given directory can be set as the current directory.

Bourne Shell
The Bourne shell built-in cd command changes the current directory to *argument*. The shell parameter HOME is the default argument. The shell parameter CDPATH defines the search path for the directory containing *argument*. Separate alternative directory names by a colon (:). The default path is null (specifying the current directory).

Note — The current directory is specified by a null path name, which can appear immediately after the equal sign or between the colon delimiters anywhere else in the path list. If *argument* begins with /, ., or .., the search path is not used. Otherwise, each directory in the path is searched for *argument*. cd must have execute (search) permission in *argument*. Because a new process is created to execute each command, cd is ineffective if it is written as a normal command; therefore, it is recognized by and is internal to the shell. (See pwd(1), sh(1), and chdir(2).)

---

chdir is just another way to call cd.

C Shell
If you do not specify *dir*, the C shell built-in cd uses the value of the shell parameter HOME as the new working directory.

If *dir* specifies a complete path starting with /, ., or .., *dir* becomes the new working directory. If *dir* does not start with /, ., or .., cd tries to find the designated directory relative to one of the paths specified by the CDPATH shell variable. CDPATH has the same syntax as, and similar semantics to, the PATH shell variable. cd must have execute (search) permission in *dir*. Because a new process is created to execute each command, cd is ineffective if it is written as a normal command; therefore, it is recognized by and is internal to the C shell. (See pwd(1), csh(1), and chdir(2).)

chdir changes the shell's working directory to directory *dir*. If no argument is given, change to the home directory of the user. If *dir* is a relative path name not found in the current directory, check for it in those directories listed in the cdpath variable. If *dir* is the name of a shell variable whose value starts with a /, change to the directory named by that value.

pushd pushes a directory onto the directory stack. With no arguments, it exchanges the top two elements. You can also use the following arguments for pushd.

+n	Rotate the *n*-th entry to the top of the stack and use cd to change to it.
dir	Push the current working directory onto the stack and change to *dir*.

popd pops the directory stack and changes to the new top directory. The elements of the directory stack are numbered from 0, starting at the top. You can use the following arguments for popd.

+n	Discard the *n*-th entry in the stack.
dirs	Print the directory stack, most recent to the left; the first directory shown is the current directory. With the -l argument, produce an unabbreviated printout; suppress use of the ~ notation.

Korn Shell

The Korn shell built-in cd command can be in either of two forms. In the first form, cd changes the current directory to *arg*. If *arg* is -, the directory is changed to the previous directory. The shell variable HOME is the default *arg*. The variable PWD is set to the current directory. The shell variable CDPATH defines the search path for the directory containing *arg*. Separate alternative directory names by a colon (:). The default path is <null> (specifying the current directory). Note that the current directory is specified by a null path name, which can appear immediately after the equal sign or between the colon delimiters anywhere else in the path list. If *arg* begins with a /, ., or .., then the search path is not used. Otherwise, each directory in the path is searched for *arg*.

The second form of cd substitutes the string *new* for the string *old* in the current directory name, PWD, and tries to change to this new directory.

The cd command may not be executed by rksh. Because a new process is created to execute each command, cd is ineffective if it is written as a normal command; therefore, it is recognized by and is internal to the Korn shell. (See pwd(1), ksh(1), and chdir(2).)

Operands

directory	An absolute or relative path name of the directory that becomes the new working directory. The interpretation of a relative path name by cd depends on the CDPATH environment variable.

Environment Variables

See environ(5) for descriptions of the following environment variables that affect the execution of cd: LC_CTYPE, LC_MESSAGES, and NLSPATH.

CDPATH	A colon-separated list of path names that refer to directories. If the directory operand does not begin with a slash (/) character and the first component is not dot or dot-dot, cd searches for a directory relative to each directory named in the CDPATH variable, in the order listed. The new working directory is set to the first matching directory found. An empty string in place of a directory path name represents the current directory. If CDPATH is not set, it is treated as if it were an empty string.
	When CDPATH is defined, the cd command for the Korn and Bourne shells displays the absolute path name of the new directory to the standard output. If CDPATH is not set, there is no output.
HOME	The name of the home directory, used when no directory operand is specified.
PWD	A path name of the current working directory, set by cd after it has changed to that directory.

Exit Status

0	The directory was successfully changed.
>0	An error occurred.

Attributes

See attributes(5) for descriptions of the following attributes:

Attribute Type	Attribute Value
Availability	SUNWcsu

See Also

csh(1), ksh(1), pwd(1), sh(1), chdir(2), attributes(5), environ(5)

cdc, sccs-cdc — Change the Delta Commentary of an SCCS Delta

Synopsis

/usr/ccs/bin/cdc -rsid [-mmr-list] [-y [comment]] s.filename...

Description

See sccs-cdc(1).

cdrw — CD Read and Write   *New!*

Synopsis

```
/bin/cdrw -i [-vSCO] [-d device] [-p speed] [imagefile]
/bin/cdrw -a [-vSCO] [-d device] [-p speed] [-T audio-type] audio-file1
   [audio-file2...]
/bin/cdrw -x [-v] [-d device] [-T audio-type] track-number out-file
/bin/cdrw -c [-vSC] [-d device] [-p speed] [-m tmp-dir] [-s src-device]
/bin/cdrw -b [-v] [-d device] all| session
/bin/cdrw -M [-v] [-d device]
/bin/cdrw -l [-v]
/bin/cdrw -h
```

Description

Use the cdrw command to create data and audio CDs. cdrw also enables you to extract audio tracks from an audio CD. You can use any MMC-compliant CD-R or CD-RW drive with cdrw.

The cdrw command was initially provided starting with the Solaris 8 update 2 (10/00) release on the separate Software Supplement CD for the Solaris 8 Operating Environment. Starting with the Solaris 9 release, the cdrw command is included with the Solaris 9 release and is available when you install the SUNWcdrw package.

cdrw searches for a CD writer device connected to the system unless you specify a device with the -d option. If cdrw finds a single such writer device, it uses that as the default CD writer device for the command.

When more than one CD writer is connected to the system, use the -d option to indicate which device to use. You can specify the device name in one of the following ways.

- /dev/rdsk/c*Nt*N*d*N*s*N, c*Nt*N*d*N*s*N, c*Nt*N*d*N.
- A symbolic name used by volume manager, such as cdrom or cdrom1.

You can use the -l option to display a list of CD writers.

For instructions on adding to your system a CD-RW that complies with the USB mass-storage class, see scsa2usb(7D).

Creating Data CDs

Typically, you first prepare the data with the mkisofs(1M) command to convert the file and file information into the High Sierra format used on CDs. See the examples that include use of this command in "Examples" on page 132.

When creating data CDs, cdrw uses the track-at-once mode of writing. Use the -i option to specify a file that contains the data to write on CD media. In the absence of such a file, cdrw reads data from standard input.

Creating Audio CDs

To create an audio CD with the -a option, you can specify single or multiple audio files. All of the audio files should be in the supported audio formats. Currently approved formats are listed below.

sun	Sun .au files with data in Red Book CDDA form.
wav	RIFF (.wav) files with data in Red Book CDDA form.

cda   .cda files with raw CD audio data (that is, 16-bit PCM stereo at 44.1
               kHz sample rate in little-endian byte order).

aur   .aur files with raw CD data in big-endian byte order.

   If you specify no audio format, cdrw tries to understand the audio file format based on
the file extension. The case of the characters in the extension is ignored. If you specify a
format with the -T option, it is assumed as the audio file type for all the files specified.
Also, -cdrw closes the session after writing the audio tracks. Therefore, you should
specify the tracks to be written in a single command line.

Extracting Audio
You can also use cdrw to extract audio data from an audio CD with the -x option. The CD
should have tracks in Red Book CDDA form. By default, the output format is based on
the file extension. You can specify a sun, wav, cda, or aur output format with the -T
option.

Copying CDs
You can use cdrw to copy single session data CD-ROMs and Red Book audio CDs. For
copying a CD, cdrw looks for a specified source device. If you specify no source device
with the -c option, the current CD writing device is assumed to be the source. cdrw
extracts the track or tracks into a temporary file and looks for a blank writable
CD-R/RW in the current CD writing device. If no such medium is found, you are asked
to insert a blank writable CD in the current CD writing device. If enough space is not
available in the default temporary directory, you can specify an alternative directory
with the -m option.

Erasing CD-RWDiscs
You have to erase the CD-RWdisc before it can be rewritten. With the -b option, the
following flavors of erasing are currently supported.

session   Erase the last session.

all   Erase the entire CD.

   If you use the session erasing type, cdrw erases the last session. If only one session
is recorded on the CD-RW (for example, a data/audio CD-RW created by this tool), then
session erasing is useful because it erases only the portion that is recorded, leaving
behind a blank disc, which is faster than erasing the entire disc.
   Use the all erasing type for a multisession disc, if the last session is not closed or if
the disc status is unknown and you want to erase the disc. With this type of erase, cdrw
erases the entire CD.

Checking device-list or media-status
You can display a list of CD writing devices currently present in the system with the -l
option. Also, for a particular disc, you can display the blanking status and table of
contents with the -M option. The -M option also prints information about the last session
start address and the next writable address. You can use this information, along with
the -O option, to create multisession CDs. Please refer to mkisofs(1M) for more
information.

Notes

The CD writing process requires data to be supplied at a constant rate to the drive. It is advised to keep I/O activity to a minimum and shut down the related applications while writing CDs.

When making copies or extracting audio tracks, it is better to use an MMC compliant source CD-ROM drive. The CD writing device can be used for this purpose.

Before writing a CD, ensure it is blank by using the -M option and then use the -s simulation mode to test the system to make sure it can provide data at the required rate. In case the system is not able to provide data at the required rate, try simulation with a slower write speed set with the -p option. You can also try to run cdrw at a higher priority with the priocntl(1) command.

The -p option is provided for users who are aware of the CD-R/RW drive and its capabilities to operate at different write speeds. Some commercially available drives handle the drive speed setting command differently, so use this option judiciously.

Most commercially available drives allow writing beyond 74 minutes as long as the media has the capacity (such as 80-minute disc). However, such capability of writing beyond 74 minutes might not be supported by the drive. If the drive supports such capability, then use the -C option to indicate that the tool should rely on the capacity indicated by the CD.

The cdrw command uses rbac(5) to control user access to the devices. By default, cdrw is accessible to all users but can be restricted to individual users. Please refer to "Administering CD-R/CD-RW Devices" in the *System Administration Guide: Basic Administration* for more information.

Options

-a
Create an audio disc. You must specify at least one audio-file name. Because a CD cannot have more than 99 audio tracks, you can specify no more than 99 audio files. The maximum audio data that can be written to the CD by default is 74 minutes unless you specify the -C option.

-b all | session
Blank a CD-RW disc. You must specify the type of erasing by specifying the all or session argument.

-c
Copy a CD. If you specify no other argument, the default CD writing device is assumed to be the source device as well. In this case, the copying operation reads the source CD into a temporary directory and prompts you to put a blank CD into the drive for copying to proceed.

-C
Use the CD stated capacity. Without this option, cdrw uses a default value for writable discs, which is 74 minutes for an audio CD or 681984000 bytes for a data CD.

-d
Specify CD writing device.

-h
Help. Print usage message.

<table>
<tr><td>-i</td><td>Specify an image file for creating data CDs. The file size should be less than what can be written on a CD-R or CD-RW disc, which is 681984000 bytes by default or the CD stated capacity when you use the -C option. Also, it is better to have the file locally available instead of having it on an NFS-mounted filesystem, because the CD writing process expects data to be available continuously without interruptions.</td></tr>
<tr><td>-l</td><td>List all the CD writers found in the system.</td></tr>
<tr><td>-m</td><td>Use an alternate temporary directory instead of system default temporary directory for storing track data while copying a CD. You might use an alternate temporary directory because the amount of data on a CD can be huge (as much as 800 Mbytes for an 80-minute audio CD) and the system default temporary directory might not have that much space.</td></tr>
<tr><td>-M</td><td>Report CD status. cdrw reports whether the disc is blank, its table of contents, the last session's start address, and the next writable address if the disc is open.</td></tr>
<tr><td>-O</td><td>Keep the disc open. cdrw closes the session, but it keeps the disc open so that another session can be added later to create a multisession disc.</td></tr>
<tr><td>-p</td><td>Set the CD writing speed. For example, -p 4 sets the speed to 4X. If you do not specify this option, cdrw uses the default speed of the CD writer. If you specify this option, cdrw tries to set the drive write speed to this value, but there is no guarantee of the speed actually used by the drive.</td></tr>
<tr><td>-s</td><td>Specify the source device for copying to the CD.</td></tr>
<tr><td>-S</td><td>Simulation mode. In this mode, cdrw does everything with the drive laser turned off, so nothing is written to the CD. You can use this option to verify if the system can provide data at a rate good enough for CD writing.</td></tr>
<tr><td>-T</td><td>Specify the audio format to use extracting audio files or reading audio files for audio CD creation. The audio-type can be sun, wav, cda, or aur.</td></tr>
<tr><td>-v</td><td>Verbose mode.</td></tr>
<tr><td>-x</td><td>Extract audio data from an audio track.</td></tr>
</table>

Examples

The following example creates a data CD.

```
example% cdrw -i /local/iso_image
```

The following example creates a CD from the directory tree /home/foo.

```
example% mkisofs -r /home/foo 2>/dev/null | cdrw -i -p 1
```

The following example extracts an audio track number 1 to /home/foo/song1.wav.

```
example% cdrw -x -T wav 1 /home/foo/song1.wav
```

The following example creates an audio CD from wav files on disc.

```
example% cdrw -a song1.wav song2.wav song3.wav song4.wav
```

The following example erases all data from a CD-RW disc in a CD-RW drive.

```
example% cdrw -b all
```

The following example creates a data CD on a system with multiple CD-R/RW drives.

```
example% cdrw -d c1t6d0s2 -i /home/foo/iso-image
```

The following example checks whether the system can provide data to a CD-RW drive at a rate sufficient for the write operation.

```
example% cdrw -S -i /home/foo/iso-image
```

The following example runs cdrw at a higher priority (for root user only).

```
example# priocntl -e -p 60 cdrw -i /home/foo/iso-image
```

The following example creates the first session image in a multisession disc and records it onto the disc without closing it.

```
example% cdrw -O -i /home/foo/iso-image
```

You can then add more sessions to an open disc by creating an image with mkisofs(1M), using the session start and next writable address reported by cdrw.

```
example% cdrw -M
Track No. |Type     |Start address
----------+--------+------------ 1      |Data     | 0
Leadout   |Data    | 166564
Last session start address: 162140
Next writable address: 173464

example% mkisofs -o /tmp/image2 -r -C 0,173464 -M /dev/rdsk/c0t2d0s2 /home/foo
```

Attributes

See attributes(5) for descriptions of the following attributes.

Attribute Type	Attribute Value
Availability	SUNWcdrw

See Also

audioconvert(1), mkisofs(1M), priocntl(1), attributes(5), rbac(5), scsa2usb(7D), sd(7D)

chdir — Change Working Directory

Synopsis

sh

chdir [*argument*]

csh

chdir [*dir*]

Description

See cd(1).

checkeq — Typeset Mathematics Test

Synopsis

/usr/bin/checkeq [*file*] ...

Description

See eqn(1).

checknr — Check nroff and troff Input Files for Errors

Synopsis

/usr/bin/checknr [-fs] [-a *.x1 .y1 .x2 .y2... .xn .yn*]
[-c *.x1 .x2 .x3... .xn*] [*filename...*]

Description

checknr checks a list of nroff(1) or troff(1) input files for certain kinds of errors
involving mismatched opening and closing delimiters and unknown commands. If you
specify no files, checknr checks the standard input. Delimiters checked are:

- Font changes using \f$x$ ... \fP.
- Size changes using \s$x$ ... \s0.
- Macros that come in open... close forms, for example, the .TS and .TE macros,
  which must always come in pairs.

checknr knows about the ms(5) and me(5) macro packages.

Use checknr on documents that are prepared with checknr in mind. It expects a
certain document writing style for \f and \s commands, in that each \f$x$ must be
terminated with \fP and each \s$x$ must be terminated with \s0. Although it works to go
directly into the next font or to explicitly specify the original font or point size (and many

existing documents actually do this), such a practice produces complaints from checknr. Because it is probably better to use the \fP and \s0 forms anyway, think of this restriction as a contribution to your document preparation style.

Bugs

You cannot define a one-character macro name by using the -a option.

Options

-f   Ignore \f font changes.

-s   Ignore \s size changes.

-a.*x1* .*y1*...

Add pairs of macros to the list. The pairs of macros are assumed to be those (such as .DS and .DE) that should be checked for balance. Follow the -a option by groups of six characters, each group defining a pair of macros. The six characters are a period, the first macro name, another period, and the second macro name. For example, to define a pair .BS and .ES, use -a.BS.ES

-c .*x1*...   Define commands that checknr would otherwise complain about as undefined.

Examples

The following example runs the checknr command on the checknr.1 manual page from the /usr/share/man directory.

```
castle% checknr checknr.1
13: Unknown command: .BI
14: Unknown command: .BI
15: Unknown command: .BI
16: Unknown command: .BI
18: Unknown command: .BI
19: Unknown command: .BI
24: Unknown command: .BI
25: Unknown command: .BI
26: Unknown command: .BI
28: Unknown command: .BI
42: Unknown command: .BR
44: Unknown command: .BR
62: Unknown command: .SB
64: Unknown command: .SB
54: Unmatched \f3
54: Unmatched \f2
54: Unmatched \f1
54: Unmatched \f3
54: Unmatched \f1
57: Unmatched \f3
57: Unmatched \f2
57: Unmatched \f1
57: Unmatched \f3
57: Unmatched \f1
70: Unknown command: .BR
```

```
72: Unknown command: .BR
84: Unknown command: .BI
88: Unknown command: .BI
90: Unknown command: .BR
96: Unknown command: .BR
116: Unknown command: .BI
120: Unknown command: .SB
122: Unknown command: .BR
131: Unknown command: .SB
133: Unknown command: .BR
135: Unknown command: .RB
137: Unknown command: .BI
144: Unknown command: .BR
156: Unknown command: .BR
157: Unknown command: .BR
158: Unknown command: .BR
159: Unknown command: .BR
160: Unknown command: .BR
161: Unknown command: .BR
137: Unmatched \f1
116: Unmatched \f1
castle%
```

The following example uses the -a option to suppress the Unknown command messages for .BI and .BR.

```
castle% checknr -a.BI.BR checknr.1
62: Unknown command: .SB
64: Unknown command: .SB
54: Unmatched \f3
54: Unmatched \f2
54: Unmatched \f1
54: Unmatched \f3
54: Unmatched \f1
57: Unmatched \f3
57: Unmatched \f2
57: Unmatched \f1
57: Unmatched \f3
57: Unmatched \f1
120: Unknown command: .SB
131: Unknown command: .SB
135: Unknown command: .RB
137: Unmatched \f1
116: Unmatched \f1
castle%
```

Attributes

See attributes(5) for descriptions of the following attributes:

Attribute Type	Attribute Value
Availability	SUNWdoc

See Also

eqn(1), nroff(1), troff(1), attributes(5), me(5), ms(5)

chgrp — Change File Group Ownership

Synopsis

/usr/bin/chgrp [-fhR] *group file*

Description

You can use the chgrp command to change the group that owns a file, provided that you own the file and are a member of the group that owns it. The chgrp command sets the group ID of the file named by each *file* operand to the group ID specified by the *group* operand.

For each file operand, chgrp performs actions equivalent to the chown(2) function, called with the following arguments:

- The *file* operand is used as the path argument.
- The user ID of the file is used as the *owner* argument.
- The specified group ID is used as the *group* argument.

Unless chgrp is invoked by a process with appropriate privileges, the set-user-ID and set-group-ID bits of a regular file are cleared on successful completion; the set-user-ID and set-group-ID bits of other file types may be cleared.

The operating system has a {_POSIX_CHOWN_RESTRICTED} configuration option to restrict ownership changes. When this option is in effect, the owner of the file can change the group of the file only to a group to which the owner belongs. Only superuser can arbitrarily change owner IDs, regardless of whether this option is in effect. To set this configuration option, include the following line in /etc/system:

set rstchown = 1

To disable this option, include the following line in /etc/system:

set rstchown = 0

{_POSIX_CHOWN_RESTRICTED} is enabled by default. See system(4) and fpathconf(2).

Options

-f	Do not report errors.
-h	If the file is a symbolic link, change the group of the symbolic link. Without this option, change the group of the file referenced by the symbolic link.
-R	Recursively descend through the directory and any subdirectories, setting the specified group ID as chgrp proceeds. When chgrp encounters a symbolic link, change the group of the target file (unless you specify the -h option), but do no recursion.

Operands

   group   A group name from the group database or a numeric group ID. Either specifies a group ID to be given to each file named by one of the file operands. If a numeric group operand exists in the group database as a group name, the group ID number associated with that group name is used as the group ID.

   file   A path name of a file whose group ID is to be modified.

Usage

See largefile(5) for the description of the behavior of chgrp when encountering files greater than or equal to 2 Gbytes (2**31 bytes).

Examples

In the following example, winsor, the owner of the file, changes the group for the file named tryit to other.

```
castle% chgrp other tryit
castle% ls -l tryit
-rw-rw-rw-   1 winsor     other        18 Aug 27 17:45 tryit
castle%
```

In the following example, user ray tries to change the group for the file named tryit back to staff but does not own the file. An error message is displayed.

```
castle% whoami
ray
castle% chgrp staff tryit
chgrp: tryit: Not owner
castle%
```

In the following example, superuser changes the group for the file named tryit back to staff.

```
castle% su
Password:
castle# chgrp staff tryit
castle# ls -l tryit
-rw-rw-rw-   1 winsor     staff        18 Aug 27 17:45 tryit
castle#
```

Environment Variables

See environ(5) for descriptions of the following environment variables that affect the execution of chgrp: LC_CTYPE, LC_MESSAGES, and NLSPATH.

Exit Status

   0   The command executed successfully, and all requested changes were made.

   >0   An error occurred.

Files

`/etc/group`   Group file.

Attributes

See `attributes`(5) for descriptions of the following attributes:

Attribute Type	Attribute Value
Availability	SUNWcsu
CSI	Enabled

Note — `chgrp` is CSI-enabled except for the group name.

See Also

`chmod(1)`, `chown(1)`, `id(1M)`, `chown(2)`, `fpathconf(2)`, `group(4)`, `passwd(4)`, `system(4)`, `attributes(5)`, `environ(5)`, `largefile(5)`

chkey — Change User's Secure RPC Key Pair

Synopsis

`/usr/bin/chkey [-p] [-s nisplus | nis | files] [-m mechanism]`

Description

Use `chkey` to change a user's secure RPC public key and secret key pair. `chkey` prompts for the old secure RPC password and verifies that it is correct by decrypting the secret key. If the user has not already keylogged in, `chkey` registers the secret key with the local `keyserv`(1M) daemon. If the secure RPC password does not match the login password, `chkey` prompts for the login password. `chkey` uses the login password to encrypt the user's secret Diffie-Hellman (192-bit) cryptographic key.

`chkey` ensures that the login password and the secure RPC password are kept the same, thus enabling password shadowing (see `shadow`(4)).

The key pair can be stored in the `/etc/publickey` file, (see `publickey`(4)), NIS public key map, or the NIS+ `cred.org_dir` table. If a new secret key is generated, it is registered with the local `keyserv`(1M) daemon.

You can change or reencrypt specific mechanisms with the `-m` option followed by the authentication mechanism name. You can use multiple `-m` options to change one or more keys. However, only mechanisms configured with `nisauthconf`(1M) can be changed with `chkey`.

If you do not specify the source of the public key with the `-s` option, `chkey` consults the public key entry in the name service switch configuration file (see `nsswitch.conf`(4)). If the public key entry specifies one and only one source, then `chkey` changes the key in the specified name service. However, if multiple name services are listed, `chkey` cannot decide which source to update and displays an error message. Specify the source explicitly with the `-s` option.

Non-root users are not allowed to change their key pair in the `files` database.

Options

`-p`	Reencrypt the existing secret key with the user's login password.
`-s nisplus`	Update the NIS+ database.
`-s nis`	Update the NIS database.
`-s files`	Update the `files` database.
`-m mechanism`	

        Change or reencrypt the secret key for the specified mechanism.

Examples

The following example changes the NIS secure RPC key pair for user `ray`.

```
seachild% chkey -p
Updating nis publickey database.
Reencrypting key for unix.1002@Castle.Abc.COM
Please enter the Secure-RPC password for ray:
Please enter the login password for ray:
Sending key change request to castle...
Seachild%
```

Files

/etc/nsswitch.conf

/etc/publickey

Attributes

See `attributes`(5) for descriptions of the following attributes:

Attribute Type	Attribute Value
Availability	SUNWcsu

See Also

keylogin(1), keylogout(1), keyserv(1M), newkey(1M), nisaddcred(1M), nsswitch.conf(4), publickey(4), shadow(4), attributes(5)

chmod — Change the Permissions Mode of a File

Synopsis

/usr/bin/chmod [-fR] *absolute-mode file...*
/usr/bin/chmod [-fR] *symbolic-mode-list file...*

Description

Use the chmod (change mode) command to change the mode of a file. The mode of a file specifies its permissions and other attributes. You can specify the mode in one of two ways: absolute or symbolic.

Absolute Mode

You specify an absolute mode in octal numbers by using the following syntax:

chmod [*options*] *absolute-mode file...*

where you specify absolute mode with octal numbers *nnnn*, where *n* is a number from 0 to 7. You construct an absolute mode from the OR of any of the following modes.

4000	Set user ID on execution.
20#0	Set group ID on execution if # is 7, 5, 3, or 1. Enable mandatory locking if # is 6, 4, 2, or 0. For directories, create files with BSD semantics for propagation of the group ID. With this option, files and subdirectories created in the directory inherit the group ID of the directory instead of the current process. You can clear the group ID bit only by using symbolic mode.
1000	Turn on sticky bit. See chmod(2).
0400	Allow read by owner.
0200	Allow write by owner.
0100	Allow execute (search in directory) by owner.
0700	Allow read, write, and execute (search) by owner.
0040	Allow read by group.
0020	Allow write by group.
0010	Allow execute (search in directory) by group.
0070	Allow read, write, and execute (search) by group.
0004	Allow read by others.
0002	Allow write by others.
0001	Allow execute (search in directory) by others.
0007	Allow read, write, and execute (search) by others.

Note — You cannot set or clear the setgid bit in absolute mode; you must set (or clear) it in symbolic mode, using g+s (or g-s).

Symbolic Mode

You specify a symbolic mode by using the following syntax:

chmod [*options*] *symbolic-mode-list file...*

where *symbolic-mode-list* is a comma-separated list (with no intervening white space) of symbolic mode expressions of the form:

[*who*] *operator* [*permissions*]

Operations are performed in the order given. Multiple permissions letters following a single operator perform the corresponding operations simultaneously.

The modes for the chmod command are shown below.

who　　　　Zero or more of the characters u, g, o, and a, specifying whose permissions are to be changed or assigned.

　　　　u　　　User's permissions.

　　　　g　　　Group's permissions.

　　　　o　　　Others' permissions.

　　　　a　　　All permissions (user, group, and other).

If you omit *who*, it defaults to a, but the setting of the file mode creation mask (see umask in sh(1) or csh(1) for more information) is taken into account. When you omit *who*, chmod does not override the restrictions of your user mask.

operator　　Either +, -, or =, signifying how permissions are to be changed.

　　　　+　　　Add permissions.

　　　　　　　If you omit *permissions*, nothing is added.

　　　　　　　If you omit *who*, add the file-mode bits represented by *permissions*, except for those with corresponding bits in the file-mode creation mask.

　　　　　　　If you specify *who*, add the file-mode bits represented by the *permissions*.

　　　　-　　　Take away *permissions*.

　　　　　　　If you omit *permissions*, do nothing.

　　　　　　　If you omit *who*, clear the file-mode bits represented by permissions, except for those with corresponding bits in the file-mode creation mask.

　　　　　　　If you specify *who*, clear the file-mode bits represented by permissions.

　　　　=　　　Assign permissions absolutely.

　　　　　　　If you omit *who*, clear all file-mode bits; if you specify *who*, clear the file-mode bits represented by *who*.

　　　　　　　If you omit *permissions*, do nothing else.

　　　　　　　If you omit *who*, add the file-mode bits represented by *permissions*, except for those with corresponding bits in the file-mode creation mask.

　　　　　　　If you specify *who*, add the file-mode bits represented by *permissions*.

Unlike other symbolic operations, = has an absolute effect in that it resets all other bits represented by *who*. Omitting permissions is useful only with = to take away all permissions.

permissions

Any compatible combination of the following letters:

l   Mandatory locking.

r   Read permission.

s   User or group set-ID.

t   Sticky bit.

u,g,o   Take permission from the current user, group, or other mode.

w   Write permission.

x   Execute permission.

X   Execute permission if the file is a directory or if one of the *New!* other classes has execute permission. New in the Solaris 9 release.

Permissions to a file can vary depending on your user identification number (UID) or group identification number (GID). Permissions are described in three sequences, each having three characters. The following example shows the access class for each group of permissions and the permissions themselves. It gives user, group, and others permission to read, write, and execute a given file.

```
User Group Other
rwx   rwx   rwx
```

The letter s is meaningful only with u or g, and t works only with u.

Mandatory file and record locking refers to a file's ability to have its reading or writing permissions locked while a program is accessing that file.

In a directory that has the set-group-ID bit set (reflected as either -----s--- or ----- l--- in the output of ls -ld), files and subdirectories are created with the group ID of the parent directory, not that of current process.

You cannot permit group execution and enable a file to be locked on execution at the same time. In addition, you cannot turn on the set-group-ID bit and enable a file to be locked on execution at the same time. The following examples, therefore, are invalid and result in error messages.

```
chmod g+x,+l file
chmod g+s,+l file
```

Only the owner of a file or directory (or the superuser) can change its mode. Only the superuser can set the sticky bit on a nondirectory file. If you are not superuser, chmod masks the sticky bit but does not return an error. To turn on a file's set-group-ID bit, your own group ID must correspond to that of the file and group execution must be set.

Notes

Absolute changes don't work for the set-group-ID bit of a directory. You must use g+s or g-s. chmod permits you to produce useless modes as long as they are not illegal (for instance, making a text file executable). chmod does not check the file type to see if mandatory locking is meaningful.

If the file system is mounted with the nosuid option, setuid(2) execution is not allowed.

Options

-f	Do not complain if chmod fails to change the mode of a file.
-R	Recursively descend through directory arguments, setting the mode for each file as described above. When symbolic links are encountered, change the mode of the target file, but do no recursion.

Operands

absolute-mode
symbolic-mode-list

The change to be made to the file-mode bits of each file named by one of the file operands.

file   A path name of a file whose file-mode bits are to be modified.

Usage

See largefile(5) for the description of the behavior of chmod when encountering files greater than or equal to 2 Gbytes (2**31 bytes).

Examples

The following example denies execute permissions to everyone.

castle% **chmod a-x** *file*

The following example gives everyone only read permission.

castle% **chmod 444** *file*

The following examples makes a file readable and writable by the group and others.

castle% **chmod go+rw** *file*
castle% **chmod 066** *file*

The following example locks a file during access.

castle% **chmod +l** *file*

The following example enables everyone to read, write, and execute the file and turns on the set group-ID.

castle% **chmod a=rwx,g+s** *file*
castle% **chmod 2777** *file*

Environment Variables

See environ(5) for descriptions of the following environment variables that affect the execution of chmod: LC_CTYPE, LC_MESSAGES, and NLSPATH.

Exit Status

0	Successful completion.
>0	An error occurred.

Attributes

See attributes(5) for descriptions of the following attributes:

Attribute Type	Attribute Value
Availability	SUNWcsu
CSI	Enabled

See Also

getfacl(1), ls(1), setfacl(1), chmod(2), attributes(5), environ(5), largefile(5)

New!

chown — Change File Ownership

Synopsis

/usr/bin/chown [-fhR] *owner*[:group] *file*...

Description

Use the chown (change owner) command to change the user ID of files that you own. You can also optionally change the group ID with this command. If chown is used by somebody other than the superuser, the setuser-ID bit is cleared.

Only the owner of a file (or the superuser) can change the owner of that file.

The operating system has a configuration option, {_POSIX_CHOWN_RESTRICTED}, to restrict ownership changes. When this option is in effect, even the owner of the file cannot change the owner ID of the file. Only the superuser can arbitrarily change owner IDs regardless of whether this option is in effect.

To set the {_POSIX_CHOWN_RESTRICTED} configuration option, include the following line in /etc/system:

set rstchown = 1

To disable the {_POSIX_CHOWN_RESTRICTED} option, include the following line in /etc/system:

set rstchown = 0

{_POSIX_CHOWN_RESTRICTED} is enabled by default. See system(4) and fpathconf(2).

Options

-f   Do not report errors.

-h   If the file is a symbolic link, change the owner of the symbolic link. Without this option, the owner of the file referenced by the symbolic link is changed.

-R   Recursively descend through the directory and any subdirectories, setting the ownership ID. When a symbolic link is encountered, change the owner of the target file (unless you specify the -h option), but do no recursion.

Operands

owner[:*group*]

A user ID and optional group ID to be assigned to file. The owner portion of this operand must be a user name from the user database or a numeric user ID. Either specifies a user ID to be given to each file named by *file*. If a numeric owner exists in the user database as a user name, chown uses the user ID number associated with that user name. Similarly, if you use the *group* portion of this operand, it must be a group name from the group database or a numeric group ID. Either specifies a group ID to be given to each file. If a numeric group operand exists in the group database as a group name, chown uses the group ID number associated with that group name as the group ID.

file   A path name of a file whose user ID is to be modified.

Usage

See largefile(5) for the description of the behavior of chown when encountering files greater than or equal to 2 Gbytes (2**31 bytes).

Examples

In the following example, although user winsor owns the file named kookaburra, {_POSIX_CHOWN_RESTRICTED} is enabled (by default) and so the Not owner error message is displayed.

```
castle% ls -l kookaburra
-rw-rw-rw-  1 winsor    staff        242 Oct  1 16:12 kookaburra
castle% chown ray kookaburra
chown: kookaburra: Not owner
castle%
```

In the following example, superuser changes the ownership of the file named kookaburra to ray and the group to other.

```
castle% su
Password:
castle# chown ray kookaburra
castle# ls -l kookaburra
-rw-rw-rw-  1 ray       staff        242 Oct  1 16:12 kookaburra
castle# chown ray:other kookaburra
castle# ls -l kookaburra
-rw-rw-rw-  1 ray       other        242 Oct  1 16:12 kookaburra
castle#
```

Environment Variables

See environ(5) for descriptions of the following environment variables that affect the execution of chown: LC_CTYPE, LC_MESSAGES, and NLSPATH.

Exit Status

0	The command executed successfully and all requested changes were made.
>0	An error occurred.

Files

/etc/passwd

System password file.

Attributes

See attributes(5) for descriptions of the following attributes:

Attribute Type	Attribute Value
Availability	SUNWcsu
CSI	Enabled

Note — chown is CSI-enabled except for the owner and group names.

See Also

chgrp(1), chmod(1), chown(2), fpathconf(2), passwd(4), system(4),
attributes(5), environ(5), largefile(5)

cksum — Write File Checksums and Sizes

Synopsis

/usr/bin/cksum [*file*...]

Description

The cksum command calculates and writes to standard output a cyclic redundancy check (CRC) for each input file and also writes to standard output the number of octets in each file.

For each file processed successfully, cksum writes in the following format.

"%u %d %s\n" *checksum*, # of octets, *pathname*

If you do not specify a file operand, the path name and its leading space are omitted.
The CRC is based on the polynomial used for CRC error checking in the referenced Ethernet standard.

The encoding for the CRC checksum is defined by the generating polynomial

$G(x) = x^{32} + x^{26} + x^{23} + x^{22} + x^{16} + x^{12} + x^{11} + x^{10} + x^8 + x^7 + x^5 + x^4 + x^2 + x + 1$

Mathematically, the CRC value corresponding to a given file is defined by the following procedure.

1. The n bits to be evaluated are considered to be the coefficients of a mod 2 polynomial M(x) of degree n-1. These n bits are the bits from the file; the most significant bit is the most significant bit of the first octet of the file, and the last bit is the least significant bit of the last octet, padded with zero bits (if necessary) to achieve an integral number of octets. The last bit is followed by one or more octets representing the length of the file as a binary value, with least significant octet first. The smallest number of octets capable of representing this integer is used.

2. M(x) is multiplied by x 32 (that is, shifted left 32 bits) and divided by G(x) with mod 2 division, producing a remainder R(x) of degree < 31.

3. The coefficients of R(x) are considered to be a 32-bit sequence.

4. The bit sequence is complemented, and the result is the CRC.

Examples

You can display a checksum for an individual file or directory, for a list of files, or for all of the files in a directory. The following example displays checksums for all the directories and files in the current working directory.

```
castle% cksum *
1583778740      1024    Art
2849654401      512     DeadLetters
4294967295      0       Design.book
3648788112      512     Mail
1811574335      737     bibliography
2131326963      526     commands
3414952850      934     examples
4294967295      0       file
2520900578      12      file1
3048412797      241     file3
599464025       242     kookaburra
3048412797      241     kookaburra1
2464961294      242     kookaburra2
40181032        483     kookaburra3
1589184179      2007    listfile
766785258       124     local.cshrc
1383060028      560     local.profile
50931726        85      mycode
2025597153      3673    permissions
3135107960      4182    printing
1365772283      18      script
1580610504      20      sortfile
1681251586      20      sortoutput
2655897922      23      template
2618551756      84      typescript
2176151109      40020   whtpaper.html
castle%
```

clear — Clear the Terminal Screen

Synopsis

```
/usr/bin/clear
```

Description

The clear command clears your screen or the current shell window if it can. It looks in the environment for the terminal type and then in the terminfo database to figure out how to clear the screen.

Attributes

See attributes(5) for descriptions of the following attributes:

Attribute Type	Attribute Value
Availability	SUNWcsu

See Also

```
attributes(5)
```

cmp — Compare Two Files

Synopsis

```
/usr/bin/cmp [-l] [-s] file1 file2 [skip1] [skip2]
```

Description

Use the cmp command to compare two files. If the files are the same, cmp writes no output. Under default options, if the files differ, cmp writes to standard output the byte and line numbers at which the first difference occurred. Bytes and lines are numbered beginning with 1. If one file is an initial subsequence of the other, that fact is noted. *skip1* and *skip2* are initial byte offsets into *file1* and *file2* and can be either octal or decimal; a leading 0 denotes octal.

Options

-l   Write the byte number (decimal) and the differing bytes (octal) for each difference.

-s   Write nothing for differing files; return exit statuses only.

Operands

file1   A path name of the first file to be compared. If *file1* is -, use the standard input.

file2   A path name of the second file to be compared. If *file2* is -, use the
                 standard input.

If both *file1* and *file2* refer to standard input or refer to the same FIFO special,
block special, or character special file, an error results.

Usage

See largefile(5) for the description of the behavior of cmp when encountering files
greater than or equal to 2 Gbytes (2**31 bytes).

Examples

The following example does a byte-for-byte comparison of kookaburra1 and
kookaburra2.

```
castle% cmp kookaburra1 kookaburra2
kookaburra1 kookaburra2 differ: char 110, line 4
castle%
```

The following example does a byte-for-byte comparison of kookaburra1 and
kookaburra2 and skips the first 64 bytes in kookaburra2 before starting the
comparison. Notice that the line and character numbers differ because of the skip offset.

```
castle% cmp kookaburra1 kookaburra2 0 64
kookaburra1 kookaburra2 differ: char 1, line 1
castle%
```

Environment Variables

See environ(5) for descriptions of the following environment variables that affect the
execution of cmp: LC_CTYPE, LC_MESSAGES, and NLSPATH.

Exit Status

0   The files are identical.

1   The files are different; this includes the case where one file is identical
             to the first part of the other.

>1   An error occurred.

Attributes

See attributes(5) for descriptions of the following attributes:

Attribute Type	Attribute Value
Availability	SUNWcsu
CSI	Enabled

See Also

comm(1), diff(1), attributes(5), environ(5), largefile(5)

col — Reverse Linefeeds Filter

Synopsis

    /usr/bin/col [-bfpx]

Description

The col command is a postprocessing filter that handles escape characters and removes reverse linefeeds that are used to handle underlining, superscripts, and subscripts. Use col to convert reverse line motions into single-line combinations of backspaces and characters. col removes superscripts and subscripts from nroff output. It is particularly useful for filtering multicolumn output made with the .rt command of nroff(1) and output resulting from use of the tbl(1) preprocessor.

col reads from the standard input and writes to the standard output. It performs the line overlays implied by reverse linefeeds and by forward and reverse half-linefeeds. Unless you use the -x option, all blank characters in the input are converted to Tab characters wherever possible.

The ASCII control characters SO and SI are assumed to start and end text in an alternative character set. The character set to which each input character belongs is remembered, and on output SI and SO characters are generated as appropriate to ensure that each character is written in the correct character set.

On input, the only control characters accepted are space, backspace, Tab, Return, and newline characters, SI, SO, VT, reverse linefeed, forward half-linefeed, and reverse half-linefeed. The VT character is an alternative form of full reverse linefeed, included for compatibility with some earlier programs of this type. The only other characters to be copied to the output are those that are printable.

The ASCII codes for the control functions and line-motion sequences mentioned above are shown below. Esc stands for the ASCII escape character, with the octal code 033; Esc- means a sequence of two characters, Esc followed by the character *x*.

Code	Description
Esc-7	Reverse linefeed
Esc-8	Reverse half-linefeed
Esc-9	Forward half-linefeed
013	Vertical-Tab (VT)
016	Start-of-text (SO)
017	End-of-text (SI)

Notes

The input format accepted by col matches the output produced by nroff with either the -T37 or -Tlp options. Use -T37 (and the -f option of col) if the ultimate disposition of the output of col is a device that can interpret half-line motions. Otherwise, use -Tlp.

col cannot back up more than 128 lines or handle more than 800 characters per line.

Local vertical motions that would result in backing up over the first line of the document are ignored. As a result, the first line must not have any superscripts.

Options

-b   Assume that the output device in use is not capable of backspacing. In this case, if two or more characters are to appear in the same place, only the last one read is output.

-f   Include forward half-linefeeds (Esc-9) but do not include reverse line motion. Usually half-line input motion is displayed on the next full line.

-p   Esc-7.

-x   Esc-8.

Examples

The following example runs a file through `tbl` and `nroff` and then displays output on the screen by filtering through `col` and `more`.

```
castle% tbl file | nroff | col | more
```

The following example runs `nroff` output from a VDT through `col`.

```
castle% nroff -cm -rO8 -rW79 document | col
```

The following example removes the ^M's from a DOS text document.

```
castle% cat filename | col output-file
```

Before the `col` command, the file looks like this:

```
The od command copies sequentially each input file to  stan-^M
dard output and transforms the input data according to the^M
output types specified by the -t or -bcCDdFfOoSsvXx options.^M
If  no output type is specified, the default output is as if^M
-t o2 had been specified. Multiple types can be specified^M
by using multiple -bcCDdFfOoSstvXx options. Output lines^M
are written for each type specified in the order in which^M
the types are specified. If no file is specified, the stan-^M
dard input is used. The [offset_string] operand is mutually^M
exclusive from the -A, -j, -N, and -t options. For the pur-^M
poses of this description, the following terms are used:^M
^M

^M
^M
^M
^M
```

After the `col` command, the file looks like this:

```
The od command copies sequentially each input file to  stan-
dard output  and transforms  the input data according to the
output types specified by the -t or -bcCDdFfOoSsvXx options.
If  no output type is specified, the default output is as if
-t o2 had been specified.  Multiple types can  be  specified
by  using  multiple  -bcCDdFfOoSstvXx options.  Output lines
are written for each type specified in the  order  in  which
```

the types are specified. If no file is specified, the standard input is used. The [offset_string] operand is mutually
exclusive from the -A, -j, -N, and -t options. For the purposes of this description, the following terms are used:

Alternatively, you can use the dos2unix command for DOS formatted files, as shown
below.

castle% **dos2unix** *input-file output-file*

The following example filters reverse linefeeds from input to print a manual page
without the formatting.

castle% **man od | col -b lpr**

Without the use of the col command, the output looks like this:

NAME

     od - octal dump

SYNOPSIS

     /usr/bin/od [-bcCDdFfOoSsvXx] [-] [_ f_ i_ l_ e]

          [_ o_ f_ f_ s_ e_ t__ s_ t_ r_ i_ n_ g]

     /usr/bin/od [-bcCDdFfOoSsvXx] [-A _ a_ d_ d_ r_ e_ s_ s__ b_ a_
     s_ e]
          [-j _ s_ k_ i_ p] [-N _ c_ o_ u_ n_ t] [-t _ t_ y_ p_ e__
     s_ t_ r_ i_ n_ g] ...
               [-] [_ f_ i_ l_ e

     /usr/xpg4/bin/od [-bcCDdFfOoSsvXx] [-] [_ f_ i_ l_ e]
          [_ o_ f_ f_ s_ e_ t__ s_ t_ r_ i_ n_ g]
     /usr/xpg4/bin/od [-bcCDdFfOoSsvXx] [-A _ a_ d_ d_ r_ e_ s_ s__
     b_ a_ s_ e]
          [-j _ s_ k_ i_ p] [-N _ c_ o_ u_ n_ t] [-t _ t_ y_ p_ e__
     s_ t_ r_ i_ n_ g
               [-] [_ f_ i_ l_ e

The col command strips out the formatting so that the output is a normal text file
like this:

NAME

     od - octal dump

SYNOPSIS

     /usr/bin/od [-bcCDdFfOoSsvXx] [-] [file]

```
        [ offset_string ]

    /usr/bin/od [ -bcCDdFfOoSsvXx ] [ -A address_base ]

        [ -j skip ] [-N count ] [ -t type_string ] ...
        [ - ]      [ file

    /usr/xpg4/bin/od [-bcCDdFfOoSsvXx [ -] [ file ]
        [ offset_string ]
    /usr/xpg4/bin/od [-bcCDdFfOoSsvXx [ -A address_base ]
        [ -j skip ] [-N count ] [ -t type_string
        [ - ]      [ file
```

The nroff formatter produces outputs for line printers and CRT displays. To bold characters, it prints the character followed by a backspace and then prints the same character again. Underlining is done by printing an underscore, a backspace, and then the character to be underlined. At times you need to strip these special effects, such as when you want to use the grep command to search formatted manual pages for a particular string. The following example uses col to get rid of these special effects.

```
castle% col -b nroff-output stripped-output
```

Environment Variables

See environ(5) for descriptions of the following environment variables that affect the execution of col: LC_CTYPE, LC_MESSAGES, and NLSPATH.

Exit Status

0	Successful completion.
>0	An error occurred.

Attributes

See attributes(5) for descriptions of the following attributes:

Attribute Type	**Attribute Value**
Availability	SUNWesu
CSI	Enabled

See Also

nroff(1), tbl(1), ascii(5), attributes(5), environ(5)

comb, sccs-comb — Combine SCCS Deltas

Synopsis

```
/usr/ccs/bin/comb [-os] [-csid-list] [-psid] s.filename...
```

Description

See sccs-comb(1).

---

comm — Select or Reject Lines Common to Two Files

Synopsis

/usr/bin/comm [-123] *file1* *file2*

Description

Use the comm command to compare lines common to the sorted files or to display lines unique to each file. comm reads *file1* and *file2*, which should be ordered in the current collating sequence, and produces three text columns as output:

1. Lines only in *file1*.
2. Lines only in *file2*.
3. Lines in both files.

If the input files were ordered according to the collating sequence of the current locale, the lines written are in the collating sequence of the original lines. If not, the results are unspecified.

Options

-1	Suppress the output column of lines unique to *file1*.
-2	Suppress the output column of lines unique to *file2*.
-3	Suppress the output column of lines duplicated in *file1* and *file2*.

By combining these options, you can display specific information. For example:

comm -12 Print only lines that are common to the two files.
comm -13 Print only lines that are unique in *file2*.
comm -23 Print only lines that are unique to *file1*.

Operands

file1	A path name of the first file to be compared. If *file1* is -, use the standard input.
file2	A path name of the second file to be compared. If *file2* is -, use the standard input.

Usage

See largefile(5) for the description of the behavior of comm when encountering files greater than or equal to 2 Gbytes (2**31 bytes).

Examples

The following example compares kookaburra1 with kookaburra2, using none of the options.

castle% **comm kookaburra1 kookaburra2**
                Kookaburra sits in the old gum tree

```
                    Merry merry king of the bush is he
                    Laugh, kookaburra, laugh, kookaburra
        Gay your life must be.

            Glad your life must be.

                    Kookaburra sits in the old gum tree
                    Eating all the gumdrops he can see
                    Stop, kookaburra, stop, kookaburra
                    Leave some there for me.
        castle%
```

The following example uses the -12 option to display files that are common to the two files.

```
castle% comm -12 kookaburra1 kookaburra2
Kookaburra sits in the old gum tree
Merry merry king of the bush is he
Laugh, kookaburra, laugh, kookaburra
Kookaburra sits in the old gum tree
Eating all the gumdrops he can see
Stop, kookaburra, stop, kookaburra
Leave some there for me.
castle%
```

The following example uses the -13 option to display lines that are unique to kookaburra2.

```
castle% comm -13 kookaburra1 kookaburra2
Glad your life must be.

castle%
```

The following example uses the -23 option to display lines that are unique to kookaburra1.

```
castle% comm -23 kookaburra1 kookaburra2
Gay your life must be.

castle%
```

Environment Variables

See environ(5) for descriptions of the following environment variables that affect the execution of comm: LC_COLLATE, LC_CTYPE, LC_MESSAGES, and NLSPATH.

Exit Status

0	All input files were successfully output as specified.
>0	An error occurred.

Attributes

See attributes(5) for descriptions of the following attributes:

Attribute Type	Attribute Value
Availability	SUNWesu
CSI	Enabled

See Also

cmp(1), diff(1), sort(1), uniq(1), attributes(5), environ(5), largefile(5)

command — Execute a Simple Command

Synopsis

```
/usr/bin/command [-p] command-name [argument...]
/usr/bin/command [-v | -V] command-name
```

Description

You can use the command command to escape commands that a shell would otherwise treat as built-in functions. With command, the shell treats the arguments as a simple command,

If the *command-name* is the same as the name of one of the special built-in commands, the special properties are not used. In every other respect, if *command-name* is not the name of a function, the effect of command is the same as omitting command.

The command command also provides information concerning how a command name is interpreted by the shell; see -v and -V.

Options

-p   Perform the command search using a default value for PATH that is guaranteed to find all of the standard commands.

-v   Write a string to standard output that indicates the path or command that is used by the shell in the current shell execution environment to invoke *command-name*.

Write commands, regular built-in commands, *command-name* including a slash character, and any implementation-provided functions that are found, using the PATH variable as absolute path names.

Write shell functions, special built-in commands, regular built-in commands not associated with a PATH search, and shell reserved words as just their names.

Write an alias as a command line that represents its alias definition.

Otherwise, write no output and return an exit status that reflects that the name was not found.

-v
Write a string to standard output that indicates how the name given in the *command-name* operand is interpreted by the shell in the current shell execution environment. Although the format of this string is unspecified, it indicates in which of the following categories *command-name* falls and includes the information stated below.

Identify commands, regular built-in commands, and any implementation-provided functions that are found, using the PATH variable, and include the absolute path name in the string.

Identify other shell functions.

Identify aliases and include their definitions in the string.

Identify special built-in commands.

Identify regular built-in commands not associated with a PATH search.

Identify shell reserved words.

Operands

argument   One of the strings treated as an argument to *command-name*.

command-name

The name of a command or a special built-in command.

Examples

The following example makes a version of cd that always prints out the new working directory exactly once.

```
cd() {
command cd "$@" >/dev/null
pwd
}
```

The following example starts up a secure shell script in which the script avoids being fooled by its parent.

```
IFS='
'
# The preceding value should be <space><tab><newline>.
# Set IFS to its default value.
\unalias -a
# Unset all possible aliases.
# Note that unalias is escaped to prevent an alias
# being used for unalias.
unset -f command
# Ensure command is not a user function.
PATH="$(command -p getconf _CS_PATH):$PATH"
# Put on a reliable PATH prefix.
# ...
```

At this point, given correct permissions on the directories called by PATH, the script can ensure that any command it calls is the intended one. The script is being very cautious because it assumes that implementation extensions may be present that would allow user functions to exist when it is invoked; this capability is not specified by this document, but it is not prohibited as an extension. For example, the ENV variable precedes the invocation of the script with a user startup script. Such a script could define functions to spoof the application.

Environment Variables

See environ(5) for descriptions of the following environment variables that affect the execution of command: LC_CTYPE, LC_MESSAGES, and NLSPATH.

PATH   Determine the search path used during the command search, except as described under the -p option.

Exit Status

When you use the -v or -V options, the following exit values are returned:

0   Successful completion.

\>0   The *command-name* could not be found, or an error occurred.

    Otherwise, the following exit values are returned:

126   The command specified by *command-name* was found but could not be invoked.

127   An error occurred in the command command, or the command specified by *command-name* could not be found.

    Otherwise, the exit status of command is that of the simple command specified by the arguments to command.

Attributes

See attributes(5) for descriptions of the following attributes:

Attribute Type	Attribute Value
Availability	SUNWcsu

See Also

sh(1), type(1), attributes(5)

---

compress, uncompress, zcat — Compress, Uncompress Files or Display Expanded Files

Synopsis

```
/usr/bin/compress [-fv] [-b bits] [file...]
/usr/bin/compress [-cfv] [-b bits] [file]
/usr/bin/uncompress [-cfv] [file...]
/usr/bin/zcat [file...]
```

Description

compress

The compress command tries to reduce the size of the named files by using adaptive Lempel-Ziv coding. Except when the output is to the standard output, each file is replaced by one with the extension .z, while keeping the same ownership modes, change times, and modification times.

If appending the .z to the file name would make the name exceed 14 bytes, the command fails. If no files are specified, the standard input is compressed to the standard output.

The amount of compression obtained depends on the size of the input, the number of bits per code, and the distribution of common substrings. Typically, text such as source code or English is reduced by 50-60 percent. Compression is generally much better than that achieved by Huffman coding (as used in pack(1)) and takes less time to compute. The bits parameter specified during compression is encoded within the compressed file, along with a magic number to ensure that neither decompression of random data nor recompression of compressed data is subsequently allowed.

Note — Although compressed files are compatible between machines with large memory, use -b 12 for file transfer to architectures with a small process data space (64 kilobytes or less).

New! compress should be more flexible about the existence of the .z suffix.

uncompress

The uncompress command restores files to their original state after they have been compressed by the compress command. If you specify no files, the standard input is uncompressed to the standard output.

This command supports the uncompressing of any files produced by compress. For files produced by compress on other systems, uncompress supports 9- to 16-bit compression (see -b).

zcat

The zcat command writes to standard output the uncompressed form of files that have been compressed with compress. It is the equivalent of uncompress -c. Input files are not affected.

Options

-b *bits*   Set the upper limit (in bits) for common substring codes. Bits must be between 9 and 16 (16 is the default). Lowering the number of bits results in larger, less compressed files.

-c   Write to the standard output; change no files and create no .z files. The behavior of zcat is identical to that of uncompress -c.

-f	When compressing, force compression of file, even if it does not actually reduce the size of the file or if the corresponding *file*.Z file already exists. If you do not use the -f option and the process is not running in the background, prompt to verify whether to overwrite an existing *file*.Z file. When uncompressing, do not prompt for overwriting files. If the standard input is not a terminal and you do not use the -f option, write a diagnostic message to standard error and exit with a status greater than 0.
-v	Write to standard error messages concerning the percentage reduction or expansion of each file.

Operands

file	A path name of a file to be compressed. If *file* is - or if no file is specified, use the standard input.

Examples

The following example compresses and uncompresses a file named testcompress and uses the ls -l command to display the uncompressed and compressed file size. As you can see, the compressed file is about 50 percent smaller than the uncompressed file.

```
castle% ls -l testcompress
-r--r--r--   1 winsor    staff      13054 Dec 30 15:21 testcompress
castle% compress testcompress
castle% ls -l testcompress.Z
-r--r--r--   1 winsor    staff       6486 Dec 30 15:21 testcompress.Z
castle% uncompress testcompress.Z
castle% ls -l testcompress
-r--r--r--   1 winsor    staff      13054 Dec 30 15:21 testcompress
castle%
```

Usage

See largefile(5) for the description of the behavior of compress, uncompress, and zcat when encountering files greater than or equal to 2 Gbytes (2**31 bytes).

Environment Variables

See environ(5) for descriptions of the following environment variables that affect the execution of compress, uncompress, and zcat: LC_CTYPE, LC_MESSAGES, and NLSPATH.

Exit Status

0	Successful completion.
1	An error occurred.
2	One or more files were not compressed because they would have increased in size (and you did not specify the -f option).
>2	An error occurred.

Attributes

See attributes(5) for descriptions of the following attributes:

Attribute Type	Attribute Value
Availability	SUNWesu
CSI	Enabled

See Also

ln(1), pack(1), attributes(5), environ(5), largefile(5)

Diagnostics

Usage: compress [-fvc] [-b maxbits] [file...]

         Invalid options were specified on the command line.

Missing maxbits

         maxbits must follow -b, invalid maxbits, or not a numeric value.

file: not in compressed format

         The file specified to uncompress has not been compressed.

file: compressed with xxbits, can only handle yybits

         The file was compressed by a program that could deal with more bits than the compress code on this machine. Recompress the file with smaller bits.

file: already has .Z suffix -- no change

         The file is assumed to be already compressed. Rename the file and try again.

file: already exists; do you wish to overwrite (y or n)?

         Respond y if you want the output file to be replaced; n if not.

uncompress: corrupt input

         A SIGSEGV violation was detected, which usually means that the input file is corrupted.

Compression: *xx.xx*%

         Percentage of the input saved by compression. (Relevant only for -v.)

-- not a regular file: unchanged

         When the input file is not a regular file (such as a directory), it is left unaltered.

-- has *xx* other links: unchanged

         The input file has links; it is left unchanged. See ln(1) for more information.

```
-- file unchanged
```
> No savings are achieved by compression. The input remains uncompressed.

```
filename too long to tack on .Z
```
> The path name is too long and the .Z suffix cannot be appended.

continue, break — Shell Built-in Functions

Synopsis

sh
```
continue [n]
```

csh
```
continue
```

ksh
```
*
continue [n]
```

Description
See break(1).

cp — Copy Files

Synopsis
```
/usr/bin/cp [-fip@] source_file target_file
/usr/bin/cp [-fip@] source_file... target
/usr/bin/cp -r | -R [-fip@] source_dir... target
/usr/xpg4/bin/cp [-fip@] source_file target_file
/usr/xpg4/bin/cp [-fip@] source_file... target
/usr/xpg4/bin/cp -r | -R [-fip@] source_dir... target
```

New!

Description
With the cp command, you can do the following actions:

- Make copies of individual files and assign new names to them.
- Copy one or more files into a different existing directory, keeping the existing file names.
- Recursively copy an entire directory structure to another directory.
- Copy extended file attributes.

New!

In the Solaris 9 Operating Environment, the UFS, NFS, and TMPFS file systems are enhanced to include extended file attributes. These file attributes enable application developers to associate specific attributes with a file. For example, a developer of a file management application for a windowing system might choose to associate a display icon with a file.

In the first synopsis form, neither *source_file* nor *target_file* are directory files, nor can they have the same name. The cp command copies the contents of *source_file* to the destination path named by *target_file*.

If *target_file* exists, it is overwritten, but the mode (and access control list (ACL) if applicable), owner, and group associated with it are not changed. The last modification time of *target_file* and the last access time of *source_file* are set to the time the copy was made.

When you make a copy of a *source_file*, *target_file* is created if it does not already exist. The *target_file* has the same owner, group, and modes as *source_file*, except that the sticky bit is not set unless the user is superuser. In this case, the owner and group of *target_file* are those of the user unless the setgid bit is set on the directory containing the newly created file. If the directory's setgid bit is set, the newly created file has the group of the containing directory instead of the creating user.

If *target_file* is a link to another file with links, the other links remain and *target_file* becomes a new file.

In the second synopsis form, one or more *source_files* are copied to the directory specified by *target*. For each *source_file* specified, a new file with the same mode (and ACL if applicable) is created in *target*; the owner and group are those of the user making the copy. It is an error if any *source_file* is a file of type directory and if *target* either does not exist or is not a directory.

In the third synopsis form, one or more directories specified by *source_dir* are copied to the directory specified by *target*. You must specify either -r or -R. For each *source_dir*, cp -r | -R recursively copies all files and subdirectories.

You can use a double-dash (--) to explicitly mark the end of any command-line options to enable cp to recognize file-name arguments that begin with a dash (-).

Options

The following options are supported for both /usr/bin/cp and /usr/xpg4/bin/cp.

@	Preserve extended attributes. cp tries to copy all of the extended attributes of the source file along with the file data to the destination file. Extended attributes are new in the Solaris 9 release.
-f	If a file descriptor for a destination file cannot be obtained, try to unlink the destination file and proceed.
-i	Interactively prompt for confirmation whenever the copy would overwrite an existing *target*. A y answer means proceed with the copy. Any other answer prevents cp from overwriting *target*.
-r	Recursively copy the directory and all its files, including any subdirectories and their files, to *target*.
-R	Same as -r, except replicate pipes.

The following options are supported for `/usr/bin/cp` only.

-p   Duplicate not only the contents of *source-file*, but also preserve ID, permission modes, modification and access time, and ACLs if applicable. Note that the command may fail if you copy ACLs to a file system that does not support them. The command does not fail if unable to preserve modification and access time or permission modes. If unable to preserve owner and group ID, cp does not fail and it clears S_ISUID and S_ISGID bits in the *target*. Print a diagnostic message to standard error and return a non-zero exit status if unable to clear these bits.

To preserve the owner and group ID, permission modes, and modification and access times, users must have the appropriate file access permissions; this includes being superuser or the same owner ID as the destination file.

The following option is supported for `/usr/xpg4/bin/cp` only.

-p   Same as -p, above, except the command fails if unable to duplicate the modification and access time or the permission modes. Print a diagnostic message to standard error and return a non-zero exit status.

Operands

source-file

A path name of a regular file to be copied.

source-dir

A path name of a directory to be copied.

target-file

A path name of an existing or nonexisting file, used for the output when a single file is copied.

target   A path name of a directory to contain the copied files.

Usage

See `largefile(5)` for the description of the behavior of cp when encountering files greater than or equal to 2 Gbytes (2**31 bytes).

Examples

The following example copies a file.

```
castle% cp goodies goodies.old
castle% ls goodies*
goodies goodies.old
castle%
```

The following example copies all of the files in one directory to a destination directory.

```
castle% cp ~/src/* /tmp
```

The following example copies a directory, first to a new, and then to an existing
destination directory.

```
castle% ls ~/bkup
/usr/example/fred/bkup not found
castle% cp -r ~/src ~/bkup
castle% ls -R ~/bkup
x.c y.c z.sh
castle% cp -r ~/src ~/bkup
castle% ls -R ~/bkup
src x.c y.c z.sh
src:
x.c y.c z.sh
castle%
```

Environment Variables

See environ(5) for descriptions of the following environment variables that affect the
execution of cp: LC_COLLATE, LC_CTYPE, LC_MESSAGES, and NLSPATH.

Exit Status

0	All files were copied successfully.
>0	An error occurred.

Attributes

See attributes(5) for descriptions of the following attributes:

/usr/bin/cp

Attribute Type	Attribute Value
Availability	SUNWcsu
CSI	Enabled
Interface Stability	Stable

/usr/xpg4/bin/cp

Attribute Type	Attribute Value
Availability	SUNWxcu4
CSI	Enabled
Interface Stability	Standard

See Also

chmod(1), chown(1), setfacl(1), utime(2), attributes(5), environ(5),
fsattr(5), largefile(5), xpg4(5)

cpio — Copy File Archives In and Out

Synopsis

```
/usr/bin/cpio -i [bBcdfkmPrsStuvV6@] [-C bufsize] [-E file]
    [-H header] [-I file [-M message]] [-R id] [pattern...]
/usr/bin/cpio -o [aABcLPvV@] [-C bufsize] [-H header] [-O file
    [-M message]]
/usr/bin/cpio -p [adlLmPuvV@] [-R id] directory
```

New!

Description

Use the cpio command to copy files, special files (files used to represent peripheral devices attached to a system), and file systems that require multiple tape volumes. cpio provides compatibility for copying files from SunOS 5.x systems to SunOS 4.x systems. Advantages of using the cpio command are that it packs data onto tape more efficiently than does the tar command, skips over any bad spots in a tape when restoring files, provides options for writing files with different header formats (tar, ustar, crc, odc, bar) for portability between different system types, and creates multiple tape volumes.

The cpio command, when used to create an archive, takes a list of files or path names from standard input and writes to standard output. The output is almost always redirected to a file or to a device.

You use the -i (copy in), -o (copy out), or -p (pass) option to choose the actions to perform.

Note — cpio assumes 4-byte words. If, when writing to a character device (-o) or reading from a character device (-i), cpio reaches the end of a medium (such as the end of a diskette) and you do not use the -O and -I options, cpio prints the following message: To continue, type device/file name when ready. To continue, you must replace the medium and type the character special device name (/dev/rdiskette, for example) and press Return. You may want to continue by directing cpio to use a different device. For example, if you have two diskette drives, you may want to switch between them so cpio can proceed while you are changing the diskettes. (Simply pressing Return exits cpio.)

In the Solaris 9 Operating Environment, the UFS, NFS, and TMPFS file systems are enhanced to include extended file attributes. These file attributes enable application developers to associate specific attributes with a file. For example, a developer of a file management application for a windowing system might choose to associate a display icon with a file. You can use the new -@ option to copy extended file attributes.

New!

Copy-In Mode

cpio -i (copy in) extracts files from the standard input, which is assumed to be the product of a previous cpio -o. Only files with names that match patterns are selected.

Extracted files are conditionally created and copied into the current directory tree, based on the options described below. The permissions of the files are those of the previous cpio -o. Owner and group are the same as the current user unless the current user is superuser. If the user is superuser, owner and group are the same as those resulting from the previous cpio -o. Note that if cpio -i tries to create a file that already exists and the existing file is the same age or younger (newer), cpio outputs a warning message and does not replace the file. (You can use the -u option to unconditionally overwrite the existing file.)

Copy-Out Mode

cpio -o (copy out) reads the standard input to obtain a list of path names and copies those files onto the standard output together with path name and status information. Output is padded to a 512-byte boundary by default, to the block size specified by the -B or -C options, or to some device-dependent block size where necessary (as with the CTC tape).

Pass Mode

cpio -p (pass) reads the standard input to obtain a list of path names of files that are conditionally created and copied into the destination directory tree, based on the options described below.

Notes

The maximum path-name length allowed in a cpio archive is determined by the header type. The following table shows the proper value for each supported archive header type.

Header Type	Command-Line Options	Maximum Path Name Length
BINARY	-o	256
POSIX	-oH odc	256
ASCII	-oc	1023
CRC	-oH crc	1023
USTAR	-oH ustar	255

When you specify the command-line options -o -H tar, the archive created is of type USTAR, which means that it is an error to read the same archive with the command-line options -i -H tar. Instead, read the archive with the command line options -i -H ustar. The options -i -H tar refer to an older tar archive format. The above changes are new in the Solaris 9 release.

Only superuser can copy special files.

Blocks are reported in 512-byte quantities.

If a file has 000 permissions, contains more than 0 characters of data, and the user is not root, the file is not saved or restored.

The inode number stored in the header (/usr/include/archives.h) is an unsigned short, which is 2 bytes. This restriction limits the range of inode numbers from 0 to 65535. Files that are hard-linked must fall in this inode range, which can be a problem when moving cpio archives between different vendors' machines.

When the Volume Management daemon is running, access to diskette devices through the conventional device names (for example, /dev/rdiskette) may not succeed. See vold(1M) for further details.

You must use the same blocking factor when you retrieve or copy files from the tape to the hard disk as you did when you copied files from the hard disk to the tape. Therefore, you must specify the -B option.

Options

-i	Copy in. Extract files from the standard input.
-o	Copy out. Read the standard input to obtain a list of path names and copy those files onto the standard output.
-p	Pass. Read the standard input to obtain a list of path names of files.

You can append the following options in any sequence to the -o, -i, or -p option.

@	Include extended attributes in archive. By default, cpio does not put extended attributes in the archive. With this option, cpio looks for extended attributes on the files to be placed in the archive and adds them, as regular files, to the archive. The extended attribute files go in the archive as special files with special file types. Using the -@ option with -i or -p instructs cpio to restore extended attribute data along with the normal file data. You can extract extended attribute files from an archive only as part of a normal file extract. Attempts to explicitly extract attribute records are ignored. Extended file attributes are new in the Solaris 9 release.

New!

-a	Reset access times of input files after they have been copied. Access times are not reset for linked files when you specify cpio -pla (mutually exclusive with -m).
-A	Append files to an archive. The -A option requires the -O option. Valid only with archives that are files or that are on diskettes or hard disk partitions.
-b	Reverse the order of the bytes within each word. (Use only with the -i option.)
-B	Block input/output 5120 bytes to the record. The default buffer size is 512 bytes when you do not use this and the -C option. -B does not apply to the pass option; -B is meaningful only with data directed to or from a character special device, for example, /dev/rmt/0m.
-c	Read or write header information in ASCII character form for portability. There are no UID or GID restrictions associated with this header format. Use this option between SVR4-based machines, or the -H odc option between unknown machines. The -c option implies the use of expanded device numbers, which are only supported on SVR4-based systems. When transferring files between Solaris 1.x or INTERACTIVE UNIX and Solaris 2.x, use -H odc.
-C *bufsize*	Block input/output *bufsize* bytes to the record, where *bufsize* is replaced by a positive integer. The default buffer size is 512 bytes when you do not use this and the -B option. (-C does not apply to the pass option; -C is meaningful only with data directed to or from a character special device, for example, /dev/rmt/0m.)
-d	Create directories as needed.
-E *file*	Specify an input file (*file*) that contains a list of file names to be extracted from the archive (one file name per line).

-f   Copy in all files except those in *patterns*.

-H *header*   Read or write header information in *header* format. Always use this option or the -c option when the origin and the destination machines are different types (mutually exclusive with -c and -6). Available *header* formats are listed below.

bar   Bar head and format. Use only with the -i option (read-only)

crc|CRC   ASCII header with expanded device numbers and an additional per file checksum. No UID or GID restrictions are associated with this header format.

odc   ASCII header with small device numbers. This is the IEEE/P1003 Data Interchange Standard cpio header and format. It has the widest range of portability of any of the header formats. It is the official format for transferring files between POSIX-conforming systems (see standards(5)). Use this format to communicate with Solaris 1.x and INTERACTIVE UNIX. This header format enables UIDs and GIDs up to 262143 to be stored in the header.

tar|TAR   tar header and format. This header format enables UIDs and GIDs up to 2097151 to be stored in the header.

ustar|USTAR   IEEE/P1003 Data Interchange Standard tar header and format. This header format enables UIDs and GIDs up to 2097151 to be stored in the header.

Files with UIDs and GIDs greater than the limit stated above are archived with the UID and GID of 60001.

New!   To transfer a large file (8 GB–1 byte), the header format can be tar | TAR, ustar | USTAR, or odc only.

-I *file*   Read the contents of *file* as an input archive. If *file* is a character special device and the current medium has been completely read, you should replace the medium and press Return to continue to the next medium. Use this option only with the -i option.

-k   Try to skip corrupted file headers and I/O errors that may be encountered. If you want to copy files from a medium that is corrupted or out of sequence, this option lets you read only those files with good headers. (For cpio archives that contain other cpio archives, if an error is encountered, cpio may terminate prematurely. cpio finds the next good header, which may be one for a smaller archive, and terminates when the smaller archive's trailer is encountered.) Use only with the -i option.

-l	Whenever possible, link files instead of copying them. (Use only with the -p option.)
-L	Follow symbolic links. The default is not to follow symbolic links.
-m	Retain previous file modification time. This option is ineffective on directories that are being copied (mutually exclusive with -a).
-M *message*	Define a *message* to use when switching media. When you use the -O or -I options and specify a character special device, you can use this option to define the message that is printed when you reach the end of the medium. You can put one %d in *message* to print the sequence number of the next medium needed to continue.
-O *file*	Direct the output of cpio to *file*. If *file* is a character special device and the current medium is full, you should replace the medium and press Return to continue to the next medium. Use only with the -o option.
-P	Preserve access control lists (ACLs). If the option is used for output, write existing ACLs along with other attributes to the standard output. ACLs are created as special files with a special file type. If the option is used for input, extract existing ACLs along with other attributes from standard input. The option recognizes the special file type. Note that errors occur if a cpio archive with ACLs is extracted by previous versions of cpio. Do not use this option with the -c option because ACL support may not be present on all systems, and hence is not portable. Use ASCII headers for portability.
-r	Interactively rename files. Use a Return alone to skip the file and a dot (.) to retain the original path name. (Not available with cpio -p.)
-R *id*	Reassign ownership and group information for each file to user ID (ID must be a valid login ID from /etc/passwd). This option is valid only for the superuser.
-s	Swap bytes within each half-word.
-S	Swap half-words within each word.
-t	Print a table of contents of the input. No files are created (mutually exclusive with -V).
-u	Copy unconditionally (normally, an older file does not replace a newer file with the same name).
-v	Print a list of file names. When you use the verbose option with the -t option, the table of contents looks like the output of an ls -l command.
-V	Print a dot for each file read or written. This special verbose option is useful to assure you that cpio is working without printing out all file names.
-6	Process a UNIX System Sixth Edition archive format file. Use only with the -i option (mutually exclusive with -c and -H).

Operands

directory   A path name of an existing directory to be used as the target of cpio -p.

pattern   Expressions making use of a pattern-matching notation similar to that used by the shell (see sh(1)) for file-name pattern matching and similar to regular expressions. The following metacharacters are defined:

*   Match any string, including the empty string.

?   Match any single character.

[...]   Match any one of the enclosed characters. A pair of characters separated by a dash (-) matches any symbol between the pair (inclusive), as defined by the system default collating sequence. If the first character following the opening [is a !, the results are unspecified.

!   Don't match. (For example, the !abc* pattern excludes all files that begin with abc.)

In patterns, metacharacters ?, *, and [...] match the slash (/) character, and backslash (\) is an escape character. You can specify multiple cases of *pattern* and, if no pattern is specified, the default for *pattern* is * (that is, select all files).

Enclose each pattern in double quotes; otherwise, the name of a file in the current directory might be used.

Usage

See largefile(5) for the description of the behavior of cpio when encountering files greater than or equal to 2 Gbytes (2**31 bytes).

Examples

The following example lists files and pipes the output to cpio -o so it can be directed (>) to a single file (../newfile). The -c option ensures that the file is portable to other machines (as would the -H option).

```
castle% ls | cpio -oc > ../newfile
```

Instead of ls(1), you could use find(1), echo(1), cat(1), and so on, to pipe a list of names to cpio. You could also direct the output to a device instead of to a file.

The following example of cpio -i uses the output file of cpio -o (directed through a pipe with cat in the example below), extracts those files that match the patterns (memo/a1, memo/b*), creates directories below the current directory as needed (-d option), and puts the files in the appropriate directories. Use the -c option if the input file was created with a portable header. If no patterns are given, all files from newfile are put in the directory.

```
castle% cat newfile | cpio -icd "memo/a1" "memo/b*"
```

The following example of cpio -p takes the file names piped to it and copies or links (-l option) those files to another directory (newdir). The -d option creates directories as needed. The -m option retains the modification time.

```
castle% find . -depth -print | cpio -pdlmv newdir
```

> **Note** — It is important to use the -depth option of find(1) to generate path names for cpio. This option eliminates problems cpio could have trying to create files under read-only directories. The destination directory, newdir, must exist.
>
> When you use cpio in conjunction with find, if you use the -L option with cpio, then you must use the -follow option with find, and vice versa. Otherwise, you will get undesirable results.

For multiple-reel archives, dismount the old volume, mount the new one, and continue to the next tape by typing the name of the next device (probably the same as the first reel). To stop, press Return and cpio exits.

Environment Variables

See environ(5) for descriptions of the following environment variables that affect the execution of cpio: LC_COLLATE, LC_CTYPE, LC_MESSAGES, LC_TIME, TZ, and NLSPATH.

TMPDIR   By default, cpio creates its temporary file in /var/tmp. When   *New!*
          TMPDIR is specified, cpio uses the TMPDIR directory to create its
          temporary file. New in the Solaris 9 release.

Exit Status

0   Successful completion.

>0   An error occurred.

Attributes

See attributes(5) for descriptions of the following attributes:

Attribute Type	Attribute Value
Availability	SUNWcsu
CSI	Enabled
Interface Stability	Stable

New!

See Also

ar(1), cat(1), echo(1), find(1), ls(1), setfacl(1), sh(1), tar(1), vold(1M), archives(4), attributes(5), environ(5), fsattr(5), largefile(5), standards(5)

New!

cpp — C Language Preprocessor

Synopsis

/usr/ccs/lib/cpp [-BCHMpPRT] [-undef] [-Dname] [-Dname=def]
    [-Idirectory] [-Uname] [-Ydirectory] [input-file [output-file]]

Description

cpp is the C language preprocessor. It is invoked as the first pass of any C compilation started with the cc(1B) command; however, you can also use cpp as a first-pass preprocessor for other Sun compilers.

> **Note** — Although you can use cpp as a macro processor, it is not normally recommended because its output is designed to be acceptable as input to a compiler's second pass. The preferred way to invoke cpp is through the cc(1B) command or some other compilation command. For general-purpose macro processing, see m4(1), and the chapter on m4 in *Programming Utilities Guide*.

cpp optionally accepts two file names as arguments: *input-file* and *output-file* are the input and output files for the preprocessor. They default to the standard input and the standard output.

Options

-B	Support the C++ comment indicator //. With this indicator, treat everything on the line after the // as a comment.
-C	Pass all comments (except those that appear on cpp directive lines) through the preprocessor. By default, cpp strips out C-style comments.
-D*name*	Define *name* as 1 (one). This option is the same as if you included the -D*name*=1 option on the cpp command line, or as if a #define *name* 1 line is included in the source file that cpp is processing.
-D*name*=*def*	Define *name* as if by a #define directive. This option is the same as if a #define *name* *def* line is included in the source file that cpp is processing. The -D option has lower precedence than the -U option. That is, if the same name is used in both a -U option and a -D option, the name is undefined regardless of the order of the options.
-I*directory*	Insert *directory* into the search path for #include files with names not beginning with /. *directory* is inserted ahead of the standard list of include directories. Thus, #include files with names enclosed in double quotes (") are searched for first in the directory of the file with the #include line, then in directories named with -I options, and lastly, in directories from the standard list. For #include files with names enclosed in angle brackets (<>), do not search the directory of the file with the #include line.
-H	Print the path names of included files, one per line on the standard error.
-M	Generate a list of makefile dependencies, and write them to the standard output. This list indicates that the object file that is generated from the input file depends on the input file as well as the include files referenced.
-p	Use only the first eight characters to distinguish preprocessor symbols, and issue a warning if extra tokens appear at the end of a line containing a directive.

-P	Preprocess the input without producing the line control information used by the next pass of the C compiler.
-R	Allow recursive macros.
-T	Use only the first eight characters for distinguishing different preprocessor names. This option is included for backward compatibility with systems that always use only the first eight characters.
-undef	Remove initial definitions for all predefined symbols.
-U*name*	Remove any initial definition of *name*, where *name* is a symbol that is predefined by a particular preprocessor. The following partial list shows symbols you can predefine, depending on the architecture of the system:

ibm, gcos, os, tss, unix	Operating system.
interdata, pdp11, u370, u3b, u3b2, u3b5, u3b15, u3b20d, vax, ns32000, iAPX286, i386, sparc, sun	Hardware.
RES, RT	UNIX system variant.
lint	The lint command.

The symbols sun, sparc, and unix are defined for all Sun systems.

-Y*directory*

Use *directory* in place of the standard list of directories when searching for #include files.

Usage

Directives

Start all cpp directives with a hash symbol (#) as the first character on a line. You can include white space (space or Tab characters) after the initial # for proper indentation.

#define *name token-string*

Replace subsequent instances of *name* with *token-string*.

#define *name*(*argument* [, *argument*] ...) *token-string*

Leave no space between *name* and the (. Replace subsequent instances of *name*, followed by a parenthesized list of arguments, with *token-string*, where each occurrence of an argument in the token string is replaced by the corresponding token in the comma-separated list. When a macro with arguments is expanded, the arguments are placed into the expanded *token-string* unchanged. After the entire *token-string* has been expanded, cpp restarts its scan for names to expand at the beginning of the newly created token string.

#undef *name*

Remove any definition for the symbol *name*. No additional tokens are permitted on the directive line after *name*.

```
#include
#include <filename>
```

> Read in the contents of *filename* at this location. This data is processed by cpp as if it were part of the current file. When the <*filename*> notation is used, *filename* is searched for only in the standard include directories. See the -I and -Y options above for more detail. No additional tokens are permitted on the directive line after the final " or >.

`#line` *integer-constant* `"filename"`

> Generate line control information for the next pass of the C compiler. *integer-constant* is interpreted as the line number of the next line, and *filename* is interpreted as the file that contains it. If "*filename*" is not given, the current *filename* is unchanged. No additional tokens are permitted on the directive line after the optional *filename*.

`#if` *constant-expression*

> Include subsequent lines up to the matching #else, #elif, or #endif directive in the output only if *constant-expression* yields a non-zero value. All binary nonassignment C operators, including &&, ||, and ,, are legal in *constant-expression*. The ?: operator, and the unary -, !, and ~ operators are also legal in *constant-expression*.

> The precedence of these operators is the same as that for C. In addition, the defined unary operator can be used in *constant-expression* in these two forms: defined (name) or defined name. This allows the effect of #ifdef and #ifndef directives in the #if directive. Only use these operators, integer constants, and names known by cpp within *constant-expression*. In particular, the size of operator is not available.

`#ifdef` *name*

> Include subsequent lines up to the matching #else, #elif, or #endif in the output only if *name* has been defined either with a #define directive or a -D option, and in the absence of an intervening #undef directive. Additional tokens after *name* on the directive line are silently ignored.

`#ifndef` *name*

> Include subsequent lines up to the matching #else, #elif, or #endif in the output only if *name* has not been defined or if its definition has been removed with an #undef directive. No additional tokens are permitted on the directive line after *name*.

`#elif` *constant-expression*

> Any number of #elif directives can appear between an #if, #ifdef, or #ifndef directive and a matching #else or #endif directive. Include the lines following the #elif directive in the output only if *all* of the following conditions hold.

- The constant-expression in the preceding #if directive evaluates to zero, the *name* in the preceding #ifdef is not defined, or the *name* in the preceding #ifndef directive was defined.
- The *constant-expression* in all intervening #elif directives evaluates to zero.
- The current *constant-expression* evaluates to non-zero. If the *constant-expression* evaluates to non-zero, ignore subsequent #elif and #else directives up to the matching #endif. Any *constant-expression* allowed in an #if directive is allowed in an #elif directive.

#else   Invert the sense of the conditional directive otherwise in effect. If the preceding conditional would indicate that lines are to be included, then ignore lines between the #else and the matching #endif. If the preceding conditional indicates that lines are ignored, include subsequent lines in the output. You can nest conditional directives and corresponding #else directives.

#endif   End a section of lines begun by one of the conditional directives #if, #ifdef, or #ifndef. Each such directive must have a matching #endif.

Because the standard directory for included files may be different in different environments, use the following form of #include directive:

```
#include <file.h>
```

instead of one with an absolute path, like:

```
#include "/usr/include/file.h"
```

cpp warns about the use of the absolute path name.

Note — While the compiler allows 8-bit strings and comments, 8 bits are not allowed anywhere else.

Macros

Formal parameters for macros are recognized in #define directive bodies, even when they occur inside character constants and quoted strings. For instance, the output from:

```
#define abc(a)  |`|a|
abc(xyz)
```

is:

```
# 1 ""

|`|xyz|
```

The second line is a newline. The last seven characters are |`|xyz| (vertical-bar, backquote, vertical-bar, x, y, z, vertical-bar). Macro names are not recognized within character constants or quoted strings during the regular scan.

Thus:

```
#define abc xyz
printf("abc");
```

does not expand abc in the second line, because it is inside a quoted string that is not part of a #define macro definition.

Macros are not expanded while processing a #define or #undef. Thus:

```
#define abc zingo
#define xyz abc
#undef abc
xyz
```

produces abc. The token appearing immediately after an #ifdef or #ifndef is not expanded.

Macros are not expanded during the scan that determines the actual parameters to another macro call. Thus:

```
#define reverse(first,second)second first
#define greeting hello
reverse(greeting,
#define greeting goodbye
)
```

produces

```
#define hello goodbye hello
```

In some previous versions of cpp, when newline characters were found in argument lists for macros to be expanded, the newline characters were put out as they were found and expanded. The current version of cpp replaces them with space characters.

Output

Output consists of a copy of the input file, with modifications, plus lines of the form:

```
#lineno "filename" "level"
```

indicating the original source line number and *filename* of the following output line and whether this is the first such line after an include file has been entered (level=1), the first such line after an include file has been exited (level=2), or any other such line (level is empty).

Directory Search Order

#include files are searched for in the following order:

1. The directory of the file that contains the #include request (that is, #include is relative to the file being scanned when the request is made).
2. The directories specified by -I options, in left-to-right order.
3. The standard directory(s) (/usr/include on UNIX systems).

Special Names

cpp understands two special names:

- __LINE__ is defined as the current line number (a decimal integer) as known by cpp.

- __FILE__ is defined as the current *filename* (a C string) as known by cpp.

You can use these special names anywhere, including in macros, just as any other defined name.

Newline Characters
A newline character terminates a character constant or quoted string. You can use an escaped newline (that is, a backslash immediately followed by a newline) in the body of a #define statement to continue the definition onto the next line. The escaped newline is not included in the macro value.

Comments
Comments are removed (unless you use the -C option on the command line). Comments are also ignored, except that a comment terminates a token.

Exit Status

0	Successful completion.
non-zero	An error occurred.

Attributes
See attributes(5) for descriptions of the following attributes:

Attribute Type	Attribute Value
Availability	SUNWsprot

See Also
cc(1B), m4(1), attributes(5)

Diagnostics
The error messages produced by cpp are intended to be self-explanatory. The line number and *filename* where the error occurred are printed along with the diagnostic.

cputrack — Monitor Process and LWP Behavior with CPU Performance Counters

New!

Synopsis
```
/bin/cputrack -c eventspec [-c eventspec]... [-efntvD] [-N count]
    [-o pathname] [-T interval] command [args]
/bin/cputrack -c eventspec [-c eventspec]... -p pid [-efntvD] [-N count]
    [-o pathname] [-T interval]
/bin/cputrack -h
```

Description

With the cputrack command, new in the Solaris 8 Operating Environment, you can use CPU performance counters to monitor the behavior of a process or family of processes running on the system. When you specify *interval* with the -T option, cputrack samples activity every *interval* seconds, repeating forever. When you specify a *count* with the -N option, the statistics are repeated *count* times for each process tracked. When you specify neither *interval* nor *count*, an interval of one second is used. When you specify *command* and optional *args*, cputrack runs the command with the specified arguments while monitoring the specified CPU performance events. Alternatively, you can specify the process ID of an existing process with the -p option.

Because cputrack is an unprivileged program, it is subject to the same restrictions that apply to truss(1). For example, you cannot track setuid(2) executables.

Options

-c *eventspec*

> Specify a set of events for the CPU performance counters to monitor. You can determine the list of available events and the syntax of the event specifications for the system with the -h option. Read the CPU manufacturers' documentation to determine the semantics of these event specifications. See cpc_strtoevent(3CPC) for a description of the syntax. You can specify multiple -c options to cycle cputrack between the different event settings on each sample.

-D
> Enable debug mode.

-e
> Follow all exec(2), or execve(2) system calls. Without this option, cputrack terminates when the process image is overlaid with a new executable.

-f
> Follow all children created by fork(2), fork1(2), or vfork(2) system calls.

-h
> Print an extended help message on how to use the command and how to program the processor-dependent counters.

-n
> Omit all header output (useful if cputrack is the beginning of a pipeline).

-N *count*
> Specify the maximum number of CPU performance counter samples to take before exiting.

-o *outfile*
> Specify the file to be used for cputrack output.

-p *pid*
> Interpret the argument as the process ID of an existing process to attach and monitor process counter context.

-t
> Print an additional column of processor cycle counts if available on the current architecture.

-T *interval*

> Specify the interval between CPU performance counter samples in seconds.

-v
> Enable more verbose output.

Usage

The operating system enforces certain restrictions on the tracing of processes. In particular, a user cannot track a command when the object file cannot be read by that user; setuid and setgid commands can be tracked only by a privileged user. Unless run by a privileged user, cputrack loses control of any process that performs an exec() of a setuid, setgid, or unreadable object file; such processes continue normally, independently of cputrack, from the point of the exec().

Because cputrack runs one controlling process for each process it tracks, the system can run out of per user process slots when you use the -f option.

The times cputrack prints correspond to the wall clock time when the hardware counters were actually sampled, instead of when the program told the kernel to sample them.

The time is derived from the same timebase as gethrtime(3C).

The cputrack command attaches performance counter context to each process it examines. This context enables the performance counters to be multiplexed between different processes on the system, but you cannot use it at the same time as the cpustat(1M) command. Once an instance of the cpustat command is running, further attempts to run cputrack fail until all instances of cpustat terminate.

Sometimes cputrack provides enough flexibility and prints sufficient statistics that you don't need to add the event selection code to an application. However, you occasionally want more control. Because the same performance counter context is used by both the application itself and by the agent LWP injected into the application by cputrack, an application can interact with the counter context to achieve some interesting capabilities. See cpc_count_usr_events(3CPC) for more information.

The processor cycle counts enabled by the -t option always apply to both user and system modes, regardless of the settings applied to the performance counter registers.

The output of cputrack is designed to be readily parsable by nawk(1) and perl(1). Therefore, you can compose performance tools by embedding cputrack in scripts. Alternatively, you can construct tools directly by using libcpc(3LIB) and libpctx(3LIB), which use the same APIs as cputrack. See cpc(3CPC) for more information.

Although cputrack uses performance counter context to maintain separate performance counter values for each LWP, some of the events that can be counted are inevitably impacted by other activities on the system, particularly for limited resources that are shared between processes (for example, cache miss rates.) For such events, you may find it interesting to use cpustat(1M) to observe overall system behavior.

Warning — By running any instance of the cpustat(1M) command, you forcibly invalidate all existing performance counter context across the machine. In turn, all invocations of the cputrack command may exit prematurely with unspecified errors.

Examples

SPARC

In the following example, the cputrack command is used on a system with an UltraSPARC I processor. The counters are set to count processor clock cycles and instructions dispatched in user mode while the sleep(1) command is running.

```
mopoke% cputrack -c pic0=Cycle_cnt,pic1=Instr_cnt sleep 10
   time lwp      event      pic0       pic1
  1.019   1       tick    720627     248732
  2.019   1       tick         0          0
```

```
 3.019    1      tick        0         0
 4.019    1      tick        0         0
 5.019    1      tick        0         0
 6.019    1      tick        0         0
 7.019    1      tick        0         0
 8.019    1      tick        0         0
 9.019    1      tick        0         0
10.009    1      exit     797318    262678
mopoke%
```

The following example shows more verbose output while following the fork() and exec() of a simple shell script on an UltraSPARC machine. The counters are measuring the number of external cache references and external cache hits. Note that explicit pic0 and pic1 names may be omitted when there are no ambiguities.

```
mopoke% cputrack -fev -c EC_ref,EC_hit /bin/ulimit -c
   time    pid lwp      event      pic0      pic1
   0.014   470   1   init_lwp        0         0
   0.037   470   1       fork                      # 471
   0.039   471   1   init_lwp        0         0
   0.043   471   1   fini_lwp     10014      3304
   0.043   471   1       exec     10014      3304
   0.000   471   1       exec                      # '/usr/bin/sh
   /bin/basename /bin/ulimit'
   0.058   471   1   init_lwp        0         0
   0.070   471   1   fini_lwp     92203     45185
   0.070   471   1       exec     92203     45185
   0.000   471   1       exec                      # '/usr/bin/expr
   //bin/ulimit : \(.*[^/]\)/*$ : .*/\(..*\) : \(.*\)$ | //bin/ulimi'
   0.079   471   1   init_lwp        0         0
   0.089   471   1   fini_lwp     93054     48354
   0.089   471   1       exit     93054     48354
unlimited
   0.094   470   1   fini_lwp    151387     69280
   0.094   470   1       exit    151387     69280
mopoke%
```

IA

The following example shows how many instructions were executed in the application and in the kernel to print the date on a Pentium machine.

```
% cputrack -c inst_retired,inst_retired,nouser1,sys1 date
   time     lwp      event      pic0      pic1
Sun Nov 25 20:03:08 PDT 2001
   0.072      1       exit     246725    339666
%
```

Attributes

See attributes(5) for descriptions of the following attributes.

Attribute Type	Attribute Value
Availability	SUNWcpcu (32 bit)
	SUNWcpcux (64 bit)
Interface stability	Evolving

See Also

nawk(1), perl(1), proc(1), prstat(1), truss(1), cpustat(1M),
gethrtime(3C), cpc(3CPC), cpc_strtoevent(3CPC),
cpc_count_usr_events(3CPC), libcpc(3LIB), libpctx(3LIB), proc(4),
attributes(5).

> *Sun Microelectronics UltraSPARC I&II User's Manual,* January
> 1997, STP1031, http://www.sun.com/sparc
> *Intel Architecture Software Developer's Manual,* Volume 3.
> *System Programmers Guide,* 243192, http://developer.intel.com

crle — Configure Runtime Linking Environment   *New!*

Synopsis

```
/bin/crle [-64] [-a name] [-c conf] [-f flags] [-i name] [-I name]
    [-g name] [-G name] [-l dir] [-o dir] [-s dir] [-t [ELF | AOUT]]
    [-u] [-v]
```

Description

The crle command, new in the Solaris 8 Operating Environment, enables you to create
and display a runtime linking configuration file. Without any arguments or with just the
-c option, crle displays the contents of a configuration file, any system defaults, and the
command-line options required to regenerate the configuration file. When used with any
other options, a new configuration file is created or updated. The configuration file is
read and interpreted by the runtime linker ld.so.1(1) during process startup.

The default configuration file is /var/ld/ld.config for 32-bit objects and
/var/ld/64/ld.config for 64-bit objects.

> **Note** — It is recommended you first create any new configuration file in a
> temporary location. You can set the environment variable LD_CONFIG to this
> new configuration file so it is used by the runtime linker instead of any
> default. After verification, you can move the new configuration file to the
> default location if desired. When the environment variable LD_NOCONFIG is
> set to any value, the runtime linker ignores any configuration files. This
> capability can be useful during experimentation.

The configuration file may contain the following information.

Default Search Paths

The runtime linker uses a prescribed search path to locate the dynamic dependencies of an object. This search path starts with the components of any LD_LIBRARY_PATH definition, followed by the components of an object's runpath and finally any defaults specific to the object's type. You can express this last component of the search path within the configuration file.

Note — Typical use of default search paths should augment any system defaults; see the -l option.

Trusted Directories

When processing a secure application the runtime linker restricts to known trusted directories the use of LD_LIBRARY_PATH and the directories from which preload and audit libraries can be used. You can express these trusted directories within the configuration file.

Note — Typical use of trusted directories should augment any system defaults; see the -s option.

Directory Cache

You can maintain the location of shared objects within defined directories as a cache within the configuration file. This directory cache can reduce the overhead of searching for application dependencies.

Alternative Objects

In conjunction with the directory cache, shared objects can have alternative objects specified for use at runtime. These alternative objects can be supplied by the user or can be created by crle as copies of shared objects are fixed to known memory locations. These fixed alternative objects can require less processing at runtime than their original shared object counterpart.

Defining alternative default search paths or additional trusted directories can be useful for administrators who want to install third-party software in a central location or otherwise alter the search path of applications that may not have been coded with suitable runpaths.

Defining user-supplied alternative objects provides a way to replace dependencies other than by symbolic links or by requiring LD_LIBRARY_PATH settings.

The directory cache and crle-generated alternate objects can provide a way to reduce the runtime startup overhead of applications that require many dependencies, or whose dependencies are expensive to relocate (this may be the case when shared objects contain position-dependent code).

When crle-generated alternative objects are specified within a configuration file, ld.so.1(1) performs some minimal consistency verification of the alternative objects against their originating objects. This verification is intended to avert application failure should an application's configuration information become out of sync with the underlying system components. When this situation arises, the flexibility offered by dynamic linking system components can be compromised. Diagnosing the application failure can be difficult.

Note — No verification of directory cache information is performed. Any changes to the directory structure are not seen by a process until the cache is rebuilt.

System shared objects are often well tuned and may not benefit by being cached. The directory cache and alternative object features are typically applicable to user applications and shared objects.

crle creates alternative objects for the shared objects discovered by calls to dldump(3DL) when the -I and -G options are used. The alternative object is created in the directory specified by the preceding -o option or defaults to the directory in which the configuration file is created. The flags used for the dldump() are specified with the -f option, or they default to RTLD_REL_RELATIVE.

Options

-64	Process 64-bit objects, the default is 32.
-a *name*	Add an alternative to *name* to the configuration file. You must supply the actual alternative file. You can use this option multiple times. If *name* is a directory, each shared object within the directory is added to the cache. If *name* does not exist, it is marked in the cache as a nonexistent file.
-c *conf*	Use the configuration file name *conf*. If you do not specify this option, the default configuration file is used.
-f *flags*	Provide the symbolic flags argument to the dldump(3DL) calls used to generate alternative objects. You can use any of the RTLD_REL flags defined in /usr/include/dlfcn.h. You can OR multiple flags with the | character and, in this case, you should quote the string to avoid expansion by the shell. If you specify no *flags* values, the default flag is RTLD_REL_RELATIVE.
-i *name*	Add an individual name to the configuration cache. You can specify this option multiple times. *name* can be a shared object or a directory. If *name* is a directory, crle adds each shared object within the directory to the cache. Note: If *name* does not exist, it is marked in the cache as a nonexistent directory.
-I *name*	The same as -i and, in addition, any shared objects have alternatives created by dldump(3DL). If -f *flag* contains RTLD_REL_EXEC, then *name* can be a dynamic executable for which an alternative is created. You can specify only one dynamic executable in this way because the cache created is specific to this application.
-g *name*	Add the group name to the configuration cache. Each object is expanded to determine its dependencies. You can specify this option multiple times. *name* can be a dynamic executable, shared object, or a directory. If *name* itself is a shared object, its dependencies are added to the cache. If *name* is a directory each shared object and its dependencies are added to the cache.
-G name	The same as -g and, in addition, any shared objects have alternatives created by dldump(3DL). If *name* is a dynamic executable and the -f *flag* contains RTLD_REL_EXEC, then crle also creates an alternative for the dynamic executable. You can specify only one dynamic executable in this way because the cache created is specific to this application.

-l *dir*	Specify a new default search directory *dir* for ELF or AOUT objects. You can specify this option multiple times. The type of object applicable to the search is either specified by the preceding -t option or defaults to ELF.

The system default search path for ELF objects is /usr/lib for 32-bit objects, and /usr/lib/64 for 64-bit objects. The system default search paths for AOUT objects is /usr/4lib, /usr/lib, and /usr/local/lib.

This option replaces the system default search path, and thus you must normally use an -l option to specify the original system default in relation to any new paths being applied. However, if you specify the -u option and a configuration file does not exist, the system defaults are added to the new configuration file before the new paths specified with the -l option.

-o *dir*   Specify the directory *dir* in which any alternate objects are created. Without this option alternate objects are created in the directory in which the configuration file is created. You can specify this option multiple times; the directory *dir* is used to locate alternatives for any following command-line options. Alternative objects are not permitted to override their associated originals.

-s *dir*   Specify a new trusted directory *dir* for secure ELF or AOUT objects. See "Security" on page 665 in ld.so.1(1) for a definition of secure objects.

You can specify this option multiple times. The type of object applicable to the search is either specified by the preceding -t option or defaults to ELF.

The system default trusted directory for secure ELF objects is /usr/lib/secure for 32-bit objects and /usr/lib/secure/64 for 64-bit objects. The system default trusted directories for secure AOUT objects are /usr/4lib, /usr/lib, /usr/ucblib, and /usr/local/lib.

Because this option replaces the system default trusted directories, you are normally required to use the -s option to specify the original system default in relation to any new directories being applied. However, if you specify the -u option and a configuration file does not exist, the system defaults are added to the new configuration file before the new directories specified with the -s option.

-t ELF | AOUT

Toggle the object type applicable to any -l or -s options that follow. The default object type is ELF.

-u   Update a configuration file, possibly with the addition of new information. Without other options, any existing configuration file is inspected and its contents recomputed. Additional arguments allow information to be appended to the recomputed contents.

The -u option requires version 2 of crle. The configuration file contains the version level. You can display it with the crle command.

```
example% crle
Configuration file [2]: /var/ld/ld.config
......
example%
```

With a version 2 configuration file, crle can construct the command-line arguments required to regenerate the configuration file and to provide full update capabilities. Although the update of a version 1 configuration file is possible, the contents of the configuration file may be insufficient for crle to compute the entire update requirements.

If a configuration file does not exist, it is created as directed by the other arguments. In the case of the -l and -s options, any system defaults are first applied to the configuration file before the directories specified with these options.

-v   Verbose mode. When creating a configuration file, write a trace of the files being processed to the standard out. When printing the contents of a configuration file, crle provides more extensive directory and file information.

By default, the runtime linker tries to read the configuration file /var/ld/ld.config for each 32-bit application it processes, or /var/ld/64/ld.config for each 64-bit application. When processing an alternative application, the runtime linker uses a $ORIGIN/ld.config.*app-name* configuration file if present. Applications may reference an alternative configuration file either by setting the LD_CONFIG environment variable (see ld.so.1(1)), or by recording a configuration file name in the application at the time it is built with the link-editor -c option (see ld(1)).

Tagging an alternative application to use an application-specific configuration file can be achieved only if the original application contains one of the .dynamic tags DT_FLAGS_1 or DT_FEATURE_1. Without these entries, you must specify any application-specific configuration file with the LD_CONFIG environment variable. Exercise care with this latter method because this environment variable is visible to any forked applications.

Examples

The following example updates and displays a new default search path for ELF objects.

```
example% crle -u -l /local/lib
example% crle
Configuration file [2]: /var/ld/ld.config
  Default Library Path (ELF):  /usr/lib:/local/lib
  Trusted Directories (ELF):   /usr/lib/secure  (system default)

Command line:
  crle -l /usr/lib:/local/lib

example% crle -u -l /usr/local/lib
example% crle

Configuration file [2]: /var/ld/ld.config
  Default Library Path (ELF):  /usr/lib:/local/lib:/usr/local/lib
  Trusted Directories (ELF):   /usr/lib/secure  (system default)
```

```
Command line:
  crle -l /usr/lib:/local/lib:/usr/local/lib
example%
```

In the above example, the default configuration file initially did not exist, and thus the new search path /local/lib is appended to the system default. The next update appends the search path /usr/local/lib to those already established in the configuration file.

The following example creates and displays a new default search path and new trusted directory for ELF objects.

```
example% crle -l /local/lib -l /usr/lib -s /local/lib
example% crle

Configuration file [2]: /var/ld/ld.config
  Default Library Path (ELF):  /local/lib:/usr/lib
  Trusted Directories (ELF):   /local/lib

Command line:
  crle -l /local/lib:/usr/lib -s /local/lib
example%
```

With this configuration, you can install third-party applications in /local/bin and their associated dependencies in /local/lib. The default search path enables the applications to locate their dependencies without the need to set LD_LIBRARY_PATH.

Note — This example replaces the system default trusted directory.

The following example creates a directory cache for ELF objects.

```
example% crle -i  /usr/dt/lib -i /usr/openwin/lib -i /usr/lib -c config
example% ldd -s ./main
    ....
      find object=libc.so.1; required by ./main
       search path=/usr/dt/lib:/usr/openwin/lib  (RPATH ./main)
       trying path=/usr/dt/lib/libc.so.1
       trying path=/usr/openwin/lib/libc.so.1
       search path=/usr/lib  (default)
       trying path=/usr/lib/libc.so.1
          libc.so.1 =>     /usr/lib/libc.so.1

example% LD_CONFIG=config  ldd  -s  ./main
    ....
      find object=libc.so.1; required by ./main
       search path=/usr/dt/lib:/usr/openwin/lib  (RPATH ./main)
       search path=/usr/lib  (default)
       trying path=/usr/lib/libc.so.1
          libc.so.1 =>     /usr/lib/libc.so.1
example%
```

With this configuration, the cache reflects that the system library libc.so.1 does not exist in the directories /usr/dt/lib or /usr/openwin/lib. Therefore, the search for this system file ignores these directories even though the application's runpath indicates they should be searched.

The following example creates an alternative object cache for an ELF executable.

```
example% crle -c /local/$HOST/.xterm/ld.config -f RTLD_REL_ALL
  -G /usr/openwin/bin/xterm
example% ln  -s /local/$HOST/.xterm/xterm  /local/$HOST/xterm
example% ldd /usr/local/$HOST/xterm
        libXaw.so.5 =>  /local/$HOST/.xterm/libWaw.so.5  (alternate)
        libXmu.so.4 =>  /local/$HOST/.xterm/libXmu.so.4  (alternate)
        ....
        libc.so.1 =>    /local/$HOST/.xterm/libc.so.1  (alternate)
        ....
example%
```

With this configuration, a new xterm and its dependencies are created. These new objects are fully relocated to themselves and result in faster startup than the originating objects.

> **Note —** The execution of this application uses its own specific configuration file. Using this model is generally more flexible than using the environment variable LD_CONFIG, because the configuration file is not erroneously used by other applications such as ldd(1) or truss(1).

The following example creates an alternative object cache to replace an ELF shared object.

```
example% ldd /usr/sbin/vold
        libthread.so.1 =>  /usr/lib/libthread.so.1
        ....

example% crle -a /usr/lib/libthread.so.1 -o /usr/lib/lwp
example% crle

Configuration file [2]: /var/ld/ld.config
  Default Library Path (ELF):   /usr/lib  (system default)
  Trusted Directories (ELF):    /usr/lib/secure  (system default)

Directory: /usr/lib
  libthread.so.1  (alternate: /usr/lib/lwp/libthread.so.1)

example% ldd /usr/sbin/vold
        libthread.so.1 =>  /usr/lib/lwp/libthread.so.1  (alternate)
        ....
example%
```

With this configuration, any dependency that would normally resolve to /usr/lib/libthread.so.1 instead resolves to /usr/lib/lwp/libthread.so.1. See threads(3THR).

Exit Status

The creation or display of a configuration file returns 0; otherwise, any error condition is accompanied by a diagnostic message and a non-zero value is returned.

Files

/var/ld/ld.config

>   Default configuration file for 32-bit applications.

/var/ld/64/ld.config

>   Default configuration file for 64-bit applications.

/var/tmp   Default location for temporary configuration file (see tempnam(3C)).

/usr/lib/lddstub

>   Stub application employed to dldump(3DL) 32-bit objects.

/usr/lib/64/lddstub

>   Stub application employed to dldump(3DL) 64-bit objects.

/usr/lib/libcrle.so.1

>   Audit library employed to dldump(3DL) 32-bit objects.

/usr/lib/64/libcrle.so.1

>   Audit library employed to dldump(3DL) 64-bit objects.

Attributes

See attributes(5) for descriptions of the following attributes.

Attribute Type	Attribute Value
Availability	SUNWtoo

See Also

ld(1), ld.so.1(1), dldump(3DL), tempnam(3C), threads(3THR), attributes(5)

crontab — User Chronological Table File

Synopsis

/usr/bin/crontab [*filename*]
/usr/bin/crontab [-elr] *username*

Description

Use the crontab command to manage a user's access with cron by copying, creating, listing, and removing crontab files. If invoked without options, crontab copies the specified file, or the standard input if no file is specified, into a directory that holds all users' crontabs.

crontab Access Control

User access to crontab is allowed:

- If the user's name appears in /etc/cron.d/cron.allow.

- If `/etc/cron.d/cron.allow` does not exist and the user's name is not in `/etc/cron.d/cron.deny`.

User access to `crontab` is denied:

- If `/etc/cron.d/cron.allow` exists and the user's name is not in it.
- If `/etc/cron.d/cron.allow` does not exist and user's name is in `/etc/cron.d/cron.deny`.
- If neither file exists, starting with the Solaris 8 release, only a user with the `solaris.jobs.user` authorization is allowed to submit a job.

New!

Note that the rules for `allow` and `deny` apply to root only if the allow/deny files exist. The allow/deny files consist of one user name per line.

crontab Entry Format

A `crontab` file consists of lines of six fields each. The fields are separated by spaces or tabs. The first five fields are integer patterns that specify the following:

- Minute (`0-59`).
- Hour (`0-23`).
- Day of the month (`1-31`).
- Month of the year (`1-12`).
- Day of the week (`0-6` with `0`=Sunday).

Each of these patterns can be either an asterisk (meaning all legal values) or a list of elements separated by commas.

An element is either a number or two numbers separated by a dash (meaning an inclusive range). Note that the specification of days can be made by two fields (day of the month and day of the week). Both are adhered to if specified as a list of elements.

The sixth field of a line in a `crontab` file is a string that is executed by the shell at the specified times. A `%` character in this field (unless escaped by `\`) is translated to a newline character.

Only the first line (up to a percent sign (`%`) or end of line) of the command field is executed by the shell. Other lines are made available to the command as standard input. Any line beginning with a hash mark (`#`) is a comment and is ignored. The file should not contain blank lines.

The shell is invoked from a `$HOME` directory with an `arg0` of `sh`. Users who want to have their `.profile` executed must explicitly do so in the `crontab` file. `cron` supplies a default environment for every shell, defining `HOME`, `LOGNAME`, `SHELL`(`=/bin/sh`), `TZ`, and `PATH`. The default `PATH` for user `cron` jobs is `/usr/bin`; root `cron` jobs default to `/usr/sbin:/usr/bin`. You can set the default `PATH` in `/etc/default/cron`; see `cron`(1M).

If you do not redirect the standard output and standard error of your commands, any generated output or errors are e-mailed to you.

Warning — If you inadvertently enter the `crontab` command with no argument(s), do not use Control-D to get out. This key sequence removes all entries in your `crontab` file. Instead, exit with Control-C.

If a different user modifies another user's `crontab` file, resulting behavior may be unpredictable. Instead, the privileged user should first invoke `su`(1M) with the other user's login before making any changes to the `crontab` file.

When updating a user's `crontab` file with the `crontab` command, first check for existing `crontab` entries that may be scheduled close to the time of the update. Such entries can be lost if the update process completes after the scheduled event. This

New!

situation can occur because when cron is notified by crontab to update the internal view of a user's crontab file, it first removes the user's existing internal crontab and any internal scheduled events. Then, it reads the new crontab file and rebuilds the internal crontab and events. This last step takes time, especially with a large crontab file, and can complete after an existing crontab entry is scheduled to run if it is scheduled too close to the update. To be safe, start a new job at least 60 seconds after the current date and time.

Options

-e   Edit a copy of the current user's crontab file, or create an empty file to edit if crontab does not exist. When editing is complete, install the file as the user's crontab file. If a *username* is given, edit the specified user's crontab file instead of the current user's crontab file; this action can be done only by a superuser. The environment variable EDITOR determines which editor is invoked with the -e option. The default editor is ed(1). Note that all crontab jobs should be submitted via crontab; you should not add jobs by just editing the crontab file because cron is not aware of changes made in this way.

New!

If you delete all lines in the crontab file, the old crontab file is restored. The correct way to delete all lines is to remove the crontab file with the -r option.

-l   List the crontab file for the invoking user. Only a superuser can specify a *username* following the -r or -l options to remove or list the crontab file of the specified user.

-r   Remove a user's crontab from the crontab directory.

Examples

The following example cleans up core files every weekday morning at 3:15 a.m.

```
15 3 * * 1-5 find $HOME -name core 2>/dev/null | xargs
rm -f
```

The following example e-mails a birthday greeting.

```
0 12 14 2 * mailx john%Happy Birthday!%Time for lunch.
```

The following example runs a command on the first and fifteenth of each month, as well as on every Monday.

```
0 0 1,15 * 1
```

To specify days by only one field, set the other field to *. The following example runs a command only on Mondays.

```
0 0 * * 1
```

Environment Variables

See environ(5) for descriptions of the following environment variables that affect the execution of crontab: LC_TYPE, LC_CTYPE, and NLSPATH.

EDITOR   Determine the editor to be invoked when the -e option is specified. The default editor is ed(1). If both the EDITOR and VISUAL environment variables are set, the value of the VISUAL variable is used as the editor.

Exit Status

0   Successful completion.

>0   An error occurred.

Files

/etc/cron.d

          Main cron directory.

/etc/cron.d/cron.allow

          List of allowed users.

/etc/default/cron

          Contains cron default settings.

/etc/cron.d/cron.deny

          List of denied users.

/var/cron/log

          Accounting information.

/var/spool/cron/crontabs

          Spool area for crontab.

Attributes

See attributes(5) for descriptions of the following attributes:

Attribute Type	Attribute Value
Availability	SUNWcsu

See Also

atq(1), atrm(1), auths(1), ed(1), sh(1), cron(1M), su(1M), auth_attr(4), **New!**
attributes(5), environ(5)

crtplot — Graphics Filters for Various Plotters

Synopsis

/usr/ucb/plot [-T*terminal*]

Description

See plot(1).

crypt — Encrypt or Decrypt a File

Synopsis

/usr/bin/crypt [*password*]

Description

crypt encrypts and decrypts the contents of a file. crypt reads from the standard input and writes on the standard output. The password is a key that selects a particular transformation. If no password is given, crypt demands a key from the terminal and turns off printing while the key is being typed in. crypt encrypts and decrypts with the same key, as shown in the following example.

```
castle% crypt key < clear.file > encrypted.file
castle% crypt key < encrypted.file | pr
```

Files encrypted by crypt are compatible with those treated by the editors ed(1), ex(1), and vi(1) in encryption mode.

The security of encrypted files depends on three factors:

- The fundamental method must be hard to solve.
- Direct search of the key space must be infeasible.
- "Sneak paths" by which keys or cleartext can become visible must be minimized.

crypt implements a one-rotor machine designed along the lines of the German Enigma, but with a 256-element rotor. Methods of attack on such machines are widely known; thus, crypt provides minimal security.

The transformation of a key into the internal settings of the machine is deliberately designed to be expensive, that is, to take a substantial fraction of a second to compute. However, if keys are restricted to (say) three lowercase letters, then encrypted files can be read by expending only a substantial fraction of five minutes of machine time.

Because the key is an argument to the crypt command, it is potentially visible to users executing ps(1) or a derivative command. To minimize this possibility, crypt destroys any record of the key immediately on entry. No doubt the choice of keys and key security are the most vulnerable aspect of crypt.

Files

/dev/tty   For typed key.

Attributes

See attributes(5) for descriptions of the following attributes:

Attribute Type	Attribute Value
Availability	SUNWcsu

See Also

ed(1), ex(1), ps(1), vi(1), attributes(5)

csh — Shell Command Interpreter with a C-like Syntax

Synopsis

/usr/bin/csh [-bcefinstvVxX] [*argument*...]

Description

csh, the C shell, is a command interpreter with a syntax reminiscent of the C language. It provides a number of convenient features for interactive use that are not available with the Bourne shell, including file-name completion, command aliasing, history substitution, job control, and a number of built-in commands. As with the Bourne shell, the C shell provides variable, command and file-name substitution.

> **Note** — Although the C shell is robust enough for general use, adventures into its esoteric periphery may reveal unexpected quirks.

Initialization and Termination

When first started, the C shell normally performs commands from the .cshrc file in your home directory, provided that it is readable and you either own it or your real group ID matches its group ID. If the shell is invoked with a name that starts with a dash (-), as when started by login(1), the shell runs as a login shell.

If the shell is a login shell, it is invoked in the following sequence:

1. Execute commands in /etc/.login.
2. Execute commands from the .cshrc file in your home directory.
3. Execute commands from the .login file in your home directory; the same permission checks as those for .cshrc are applied to this file. Typically, the .login file contains commands to specify the terminal type and environment.

As a login shell terminates, it performs commands from the .logout file in your home directory; the same permission checks as those for .cshrc are applied to this file.

Interactive Operation

After startup processing is complete, an interactive C shell begins reading commands from the terminal, prompting with *hostname%* (or *hostname#* for superuser). The shell then repeatedly performs the following actions:

1. Reads a line of command input and breaks it into words.
2. Puts the sequence of words in the history list and then parses them.
3. Executes each command in the current line.

Noninteractive Operation

When running noninteractively, the shell does not prompt for input from the terminal. A noninteractive C shell can execute a command supplied as an argument on its command line or can interpret commands from a file, also known as a script.

Note — When the shell executes a shell script that attempts to execute a nonexistent command interpreter, the shell returns an erroneous diagnostic message that the shell script file does not exist.

Options

-b	Force a "break" from option processing. Do not interpret subsequent command-line arguments as C shell options. This option enables the passing of options to a script without confusion. You must use this option or the shell will not run setuid or setgid scripts.
-c	Execute the first argument (which must be present). Remaining arguments are placed in argv, the argument-list variable, and passed directly to csh.
-e	Exit if a command terminates abnormally or yields a non-zero exit status.
-f	For a fast start, read neither the .cshrc file nor the .login file (if a login shell) on startup.
-i	Force interactive mode. Prompt for command-line input, even if the standard input does not appear to be a terminal (character special device).
-n	Parse (interpret), but do not execute commands. You can use this option to check C shell scripts for syntax errors.
-s	Take commands from the standard input.
-t	Read and execute a single command line. You can use a backslash (\) to escape each newline for continuation of the command line onto subsequent input lines.
-v	Set the verbose predefined variable; echo command input after history substitution (but before other substitutions) and before execution.
-V	Set verbose before reading .cshrc.
-x	Set the echo variable. Echo commands after all substitutions and just before execution.
-X	Set echo before reading .cshrc.

Except with the options -c, -i, -s, or -t, take the first non-option argument to be the name of a command or script. Pass it as argument zero, and add subsequent arguments to the argument list for that command or script.

Usage

File-name Completion

When you enable the file-completion variable, filec, an interactive C shell can complete a partially typed file name or user name. When you type an unambiguous beginning of a file name and press the Escape key, the shell fills in the remaining characters of a matching file name from the working directory.

If you follow a partial file name with the EOF character (usually typed as Control-D), the shell lists all file names that match. It then prompts once again, supplying the incomplete command line typed in so far.

When the last (partial) word begins with a tilde (~), the shell tries to complete with a user name, instead of a file in the working directory.

If there is no match or multiple matches, the terminal bell beeps. You can turn the beep off by setting the nobeep variable. You can exclude files with certain suffixes by listing those suffixes in the fignore variable. If, however, the only possible completion includes a suffix in the list, it is not ignored. fignore does not affect the listing of file names by the EOF character.

Lexical Structure

The shell splits input lines into words at space and Tab characters, except as noted below. The characters &, |, ;, <, >, (, and) form separate words; if paired, the pairs form single words. These shell metacharacters can be made part of other words, and their special meaning can be suppressed by a backslash (\) preceding them. A newline preceded by a \ is equivalent to a space character.

In addition, a string enclosed in matched pairs of single quotes ('), double quotes ("), or backquotes (`) forms a partial word; metacharacters in such a string, including any space or Tab characters, do not form separate words. Within pairs of backquote (`) or double quote (") characters, a newline preceded by a backslash (\) gives a true newline character. Additional functions of each type of quote are described, below, under Variable Substitution, Command Substitution, and File-name Substitution.

When the shell's input is not a terminal, the character # introduces a comment that continues to the end of the input line. Its special meaning is suppressed when preceded by a \ or enclosed in matching quotes.

Note — Words can be no longer than 1,024 bytes. The system limits argument lists to 1,048,576 bytes. However, the maximum number of arguments to a command for which file-name expansion applies is 1,706. Command substitutions may expand to no more characters than are allowed in the argument list. To detect looping, the shell restricts the number of alias substitutions on a single line to 20.

Command-Line Parsing

A simple command is composed of a sequence of words. The first word (that is not part of an I/O redirection) specifies the command to be executed. A simple command, or a set of simple commands separated by | or |& characters, forms a pipeline. With |, the standard output of the preceding command is redirected to the standard input of the command that follows. With |&, both the standard error and the standard output are redirected through the pipeline.

Pipelines can be separated by semicolons (;), in which case they are executed sequentially. Pipelines that are separated by && or || form conditional sequences in which the execution of pipelines on the right depends on the success or failure of the pipeline on the left.

A pipeline or sequence can be enclosed within parentheses ( ) to form a simple command that can be a component in a pipeline or sequence.

A sequence of pipelines can be executed asynchronously or "in the background" by appending an ampersand (&); instead of waiting for the sequence to finish before issuing a prompt, the shell displays the job number (see "Job Control" on page 206) and associated process IDs and prompts immediately.

> **Note** — Quote conventions are confusing. Overriding the escape character to force variable substitutions within double quotes is counterintuitive and inconsistent with the Bourne shell.

History Substitution

History substitution enables you to use words from previous command lines in the command line you are typing. This process simplifies spelling corrections and the repetition of complicated commands or arguments. Command lines are saved in the history list, the size of which is controlled by the history variable. The most recent command is retained in any case. A history substitution begins with a ! (although you can change this with the histchars variable) and can occur anywhere on the command line; history substitutions do not nest. You can escape the ! with \ to suppress its special meaning.

Input lines containing history substitutions are echoed on the terminal after being expanded but before any other substitutions take place or the command gets executed.

> **Note** — The g (global) flag in history substitutions applies only to the first match in each word, instead of to all matches in all words. The common text editors consistently do the latter when given the g flag in a substitution command.

Refer to history(1) for more details.

Event Designators

An event designator is a reference to a command-line entry in the history list.

!	Start a history substitution, except when followed by a space character, Tab, newline, =, or (.
!!	Refer to the previous command. By itself, this substitution repeats the previous command.
!n	Refer to command line *n*.
!-*n*	Refer to the current command line minus *n*.
!*str*	Refer to the most recent command starting with *str*.
!?*str*?	Refer to the most recent command containing *str*.

!?*str*? *additional*

Refer to the most recent command containing *str*, and append *additional* to that referenced command.

!{*command*} *additional*

Refer to the most recent command beginning with *command* and append *additional* to that referenced command.

*^previous-word^replacement^*

> Repeat the previous command line, replacing the string *previous-word* with the string replacement. This is equivalent to the history substitution: `!:s`*/previous-word/replacement/*.

> To reexecute a specific previous command *and* make such a substitution, say, reexecuting command #6, `!:6s`*/previous-word/replacement/*.

Word Designators

A colon (`:`) separates the event specification from the word designator. You can omit it if the word designator begins with a `^`, `$`, `*`, or `%`. If the word is to be selected from the previous command, you can omit the second `!` character from the event specification. For instance, `!!:1` and `!:1` both refer to the first word of the previous command, whereas `!!$` and `!$` both refer to the last word in the previous command. Word designators include:

`#`	The entire command line typed so far.
`0`	The first input word (command).
n	The *n*-th argument.
`^`	The first argument, that is, 1.
`$`	The last argument.
`%`	The word matched by (the most recent) `?s` search.
x-y	A range of words; *-y* abbreviates `0-`*y*.
`*`	All the arguments, or a null value if there is just one word in the event.
x*	Abbreviates *x-*`$`.
x-	Like *x** but omitting word `$`.

Modifiers

After the optional word designator, you can add one of the following modifiers, preceded by a colon (`:`).

`h`	Remove a trailing path name component, leaving the head.
`r`	Remove a trailing suffix of the form `.`*xxx*, leaving the basename.
`e`	Remove all but the suffix, leaving the extension.
`s/`*l*`/`*r*`/`	Substitute *r* for *l*.
`t`	Remove all leading path-name components, leaving the tail.
`&`	Repeat the previous substitution.
`g`	Apply the change to the first occurrence of a match in each word by prefixing the above (for example, `g&`).
`p`	Print the new command but do not execute it.
`q`	Quote the substituted words, escaping further substitutions.
`x`	Like `q`, but break into words at each space character, Tab, or newline.

> **Note** — Although it should be possible to use the : modifiers on the output of command substitution, there are two problems with : modifier usage on variable substitutions: not all of the modifiers are available, and only one modifier per substitution is allowed.

Unless preceded by a g, the modification is applied only to the first string that matches l; an error results if no string matches.

The left-hand side of substitutions are not regular expressions, but character strings. You can use any character as the delimiter in place of /. A backslash quotes the delimiter character. The character &, in the right-hand side, is replaced by the text from the left-hand side. You can escape the & with a backslash. A null l uses the previous string either from a l or from a contextual scan string s from !?s. You can omit the rightmost delimiter if a newline immediately follows r; similarly, you can omit the rightmost ? in a context scan.

Without an event specification, a history reference refers either to the previous command or to a previous history reference on the command line (if any).

Quick Substitution

^l^r^ is equivalent to the history substitution !:s/l/r/.

Aliases

The C shell maintains a list of aliases that you can create, display, and modify by using the alias and unalias commands. The shell checks the first word in each command to see if it matches the name of an existing alias. If it does, the command is reprocessed with the alias definition replacing its name; the history substitution mechanism is made available as though that command were the previous input line. History substitutions, escaped with a backslash in the definition, can be replaced with actual command-line arguments when you use the alias. If no history substitution is called for, the arguments remain unchanged.

You can nest aliases. That is, an alias definition can contain the name of another alias. Nested aliases are expanded before any history substitution is applied. This expansion is useful in pipelines such as

```
alias lm 'ls -l \!* | more'
```

which when called, pipes the output of ls(1) through more(1).

Except for the first word, the name of the alias may not appear in its definition nor in any alias referred to by its definition. Such loops are detected and display an error message.

I/O Redirection

The following metacharacters indicate that the subsequent word is the name of a file to which to redirect the command's standard input, standard output, or standard error; this word is variable, command, and file-name expanded separately from the rest of the command.

    <   Redirect the standard input.

<<*word*   Read the standard input, up to a line that is identical with *word*, and
              place the resulting lines in a temporary file. Unless *word* is escaped or
              quoted, perform variable and command substitutions on these lines.
              Then, invoke the pipeline with the temporary file as its standard
              input. *word* is not subjected to variable, file-name, or command
              substitution, and each line is compared to it before any substitutions
              are performed by the shell.

> >! >& >&! Redirect the standard output to a file. If the file does not exist, create
              it. If it does exist, overwrite it; its previous contents are lost.

              When set, the variable `noclobber` prevents destruction of existing
              files. It also prevents redirection to terminals and `/dev/null` unless
              you use one of the ! forms. The & forms redirect both standard output
              and the standard error (diagnostic output) to the file.

>> >>& >>! >>&!

              Append the standard output. Like >, but place output at the end of the
              file instead of overwriting it. If `noclobber` is set, it is an error for the
              file not to exist unless you use one of the ! forms. The & forms append
              both the standard error and standard output to the file.

Note — Control over terminal output after processes are started is
primitive; use the Sun window system if you need better output control.

The only way to direct the standard output and standard error separately is
by invoking a subshell, as follows:

`castle% `**`(command > outfile) >& errorfile`**

Variable Substitution

The C shell maintains a set of variables, each of which is composed of a *name* and a
value. A variable name consists of up to 20 letters and digits, and starts with a letter
(the underscore is considered a letter). A variable's value is a space-separated list of zero
or more words.

To refer to a variable's value, precede its name with a dollar sign ($). You can use
certain references (described below) to select specific words from the value or to display
other information about the variable. You can use braces to insulate the reference from
other characters in an input-line word.

Variable substitution takes place after the input line is analyzed, aliases are
resolved, and I/O redirections are applied. Variable references in I/O redirections and
backquoted strings, however, are substituted at the time the redirection is made.

You can suppress variable substitution by preceding the $ with a \, except within
double quotes where it always occurs. Variable substitution is suppressed inside of
single quotes. A $ is escaped if followed by a space character, Tab, or newline.

You can use the `set` and `unset` commands to create, display, or destroy variables.
Some variables are maintained or used by the shell. For instance, the `argv` variable
contains an image of the shell's argument list. Of the variables used by the shell, a
number are toggles; the shell does not care what their value is, only whether they are set
or not.

You can operate on numerical values as numbers (as with the @ built-in command).
With numeric operations, an empty value is considered to be 0; the second and

subsequent words of multiword values are ignored. For instance, when the verbose variable is set to any value (including an empty value), command input is echoed on the terminal.

Command- and file-name substitution is subsequently applied to the words that result from the variable substitution, except when suppressed by double quotes, when noglob is set (suppressing file-name substitution), or when you quote the reference with the :q modifier. Within double quotes, a reference is expanded to form (a portion of) a quoted string; multiword values are expanded to a string with embedded space characters. When the :q modifier is applied to the reference, it is expanded to a list of space-separated words, each of which is quoted to prevent subsequent command or file-name substitutions.

Except as noted below, it is an error to refer to a variable that is not set.

$*var*   Replace by words from the value of *var*, each separated by a space
${*var*}   character. If *var* is an environment variable, return its value (but :
                  modifiers and the other forms given below are not available).

$*var*[*index*]
${*var*[*index*]}

                  Select only the indicated words from the value of *var*. Variable
                  substitution is applied to *index*, which may consist of (or result in)
                  either a single number, two numbers separated by a dash (–), or an
                  asterisk (*). Words are indexed starting from 1; an asterisk selects all
                  words. If you omit the first number of a range (as with $argv[-2]), it
                  defaults to 1. If you omit the last number of a range (as with
                  $argv[1-]), it defaults to $#*var* (the word count). It is not an error for
                  a range to be empty if you omit the second argument (or it is within
                  range).

$#*name*   Give the number of words in the variable.
${#*name*}

$0   Substitute the name of the file from which command input is being
                  read except for setuid shell scripts. An error occurs if the name is not
                  known.

$*n*   Equivalent to $argv[*n*].
${*n*}

$*   Equivalent to $argv[*].

You can apply the modifiers :e, :h, :q, :r, :t, and :x (see "History Substitution" on page 198), :gh, :gt, and :gr. If you use braces ({}), then the modifiers must appear within the braces. The current implementation allows only one such modifier per expansion.

You cannot use : modifiers with the following references.

$?*var*   Substitute the string 1 if *var* is set, or 0 if it is not set.
${?*var*}

$?0   Substitute 1 if the current input file name is known, or 0 if it is not.

$$ Substitute the process number of the (parent) shell.

$<   Substitute a line from the standard input, with no further
            interpretation thereafter. You can use this modifier to read from the
            keyboard in a C shell script.

Command- and File-name Substitutions

Command- and file-name substitutions are applied selectively to the arguments of
built-in commands. Portions of expressions that are not evaluated are not expanded. For
non-built-in commands, file-name expansion of the command name is done separately
from that of the argument list; expansion occurs in a subshell after I/O redirection is
performed.

Command Substitution

A command enclosed by backquotes (`` ` ... ` ``) is performed by a subshell. Its standard
output is broken into separate words at each space character, Tab, and newline; null
words are discarded. This text replaces the backquoted string on the current command
line. Within double quotes, only newline characters force new words; space and Tab
characters are preserved. However, a final newline is ignored. It is, therefore, possible
for a command substitution to yield a partial word.

File-name Substitution

Unquoted words containing any of the characters *, ?, [, or { or that begin with ~ are
expanded (also known as globbing) to an alphabetically sorted list of file names, as
follows:

*   Match any (0 or more) characters.

?   Match any single character.

[...]   Match any single character in the enclosed list(s) or range(s). A list is a
            string of characters. A range is two characters separated by a dash (-)
            and includes all the characters in between in the ASCII collating
            sequence (see ascii(5)).

{ str, str, ... }
            Expand to each string (or file-name-matching pattern) in the
            comma-separated list. Unlike the pattern-matching expressions above,
            the expansion of this construct is not sorted. For instance, {b,a}
            expands to b a, (not a b). As special cases, the characters { and }, along
            with the string {}, are passed undisturbed.

~[user]   Your home directory, as indicated by the value of the variable *home*, or
            that of *user*, as indicated by the password entry for user.

Only the patterns *, ? and [...] imply pattern matching; an error results if no file
name matches a pattern that contains them. The dot character (.) must be matched
explicitly when it is the first character in a file-name or path-name component. The
slash (/) must also be matched explicitly.

Expressions and Operators

A number of C shell built-in commands accept expressions in which the operators are
similar to those of C and have the same precedence. These expressions typically appear
in the @, exit, if, set, and while commands and are often used to regulate the flow of

control for executing commands. Components of an expression are separated by white space.

Null or missing values are considered 0. The result of all expressions is a string, which may represent decimal numbers.

The following C shell operators are grouped in order of precedence:

(...)   Grouping.

~   One's complement.

!   Logical negation.

* / %   Multiplication, division, remainder. (These operators are right-associative, which can lead to unexpected results. Group combinations explicitly with parentheses.)

+ −   Addition, subtraction (also right-associative).

<< >>   Bitwise shift left, bitwise shift right.

< > <= >=   Less than, greater than, less than or equal to, greater than or equal to.

== != =~ !~   Equal to, not equal to, file-name-substitution pattern match (described below), file-name-substitution pattern mismatch.

&   Bitwise AND.

^   Bitwise XOR (exclusive OR).

| Bitwise inclusive OR.

&&   Logical AND.

|| Logical OR.

The operators ==, !=, =~, and !~ compare their arguments as strings; other operators use numbers. The operators =~ and !~ each check whether a string to the left matches a file-name substitution pattern on the right. This checking reduces the need for switch statements when pattern matching between strings is all that is required.

Also available are file inquiries:

-r *filename*

         Return true, or 1 if the user has read access. Otherwise, return false, or 0.

-w *filename*

         true if the user has write access.

-x *filename*

         true if the user has execute permission (or search permission on a directory).

-e *filename*

         true if *filename* exists.

-o *filename*

         true if the user owns *filename*.

-z *filename*

>true if *filename* is of 0 length (empty).

-f *filename*

>true if *filename* is a plain file.

-d *filename*

>true if *filename* is a directory.

If *filename* does not exist or is inaccessible, then all inquiries return false. An inquiry as to the success of a command is also available:

{ *command* } If *command* runs successfully, the expression evaluates to true, 1. Otherwise, it evaluates to false, 0. (Note: Conversely, *command* itself typically returns 0 when it runs successfully, or some other value if it encounters a problem. If you want to get at the status directly, use the value of the status variable instead of this expression.)

Control Flow
The shell contains a number of commands to regulate the flow of control in scripts and, within limits, from the terminal. These commands operate by forcing the shell either to reread input (to loop) or to skip input under certain conditions (to branch).

Each occurrence of a foreach, switch, while, if...then, or else built-in command must appear as the first word on its own input line.

If the shell's input is not seekable and a loop is being read, that input is buffered. The shell performs seeks within the internal buffer to accomplish the rereading implied by the loop. (To the extent that this action allows, backward goto commands succeed on nonseekable inputs.)

Note — Commands within loops, prompted for by ?, are not placed in the history list.

Command Execution
If the command is a C shell built-in command, the shell executes it directly. Otherwise, the shell searches for a file by that name with execute access. If the command name contains a /, the shell takes it as a path name and searches for it. If the command name does not contain a /, the shell attempts to resolve it to a path name, searching each directory in the path variable for the command. To speed the search, the shell uses its hash table (see the rehash built-in command) to eliminate directories that have no applicable files. You can disable this hashing with the -c or -t options or by using the unhash built-in command.

As a special case, if there is no / in the name of the script and there is an alias for the word shell, the expansion of the shell alias is prepended (without modification) to the command line. The system tries to execute the first word of this special (late-occurring) alias, which should be a full path name. Remaining words of the alias's definition, along with the text of the input line, are treated as arguments.

When a path name is found that has proper execute permissions, the shell forks a new process and passes it, along with its arguments, to the kernel, using the execve() system call (see exec(2)). The kernel then tries to overlay the new process with the desired program. If the file is an executable binary (in a.out(4) format), the kernel succeeds and begins executing the new process. If the file is a text file and the first line begins with #!, the next word is taken to be the path name of a shell (or command) to interpret that script. Subsequent words on the first line are taken as options for that shell. The kernel invokes (overlays) the indicated shell, using the name of the script as an argument.

If neither of the above conditions holds, the kernel cannot overlay the file and the execve() call fails (see exec(2)); the C shell then tries to execute the file by spawning a new shell, as follows:

- If the first character of the file is a #, the file invokes a C shell.
- Otherwise, the file invokes a Bourne shell.

Signal Handling

The shell normally ignores QUIT signals. Background jobs are immune to signals generated from the keyboard, including hangups (HUP). Other signals have the values that the C shell inherited from its environment. You can control the shell's handling of interrupt and terminate signals within scripts by using the onintr built-in command. Login shells catch the TERM signal; otherwise, this signal is passed on to child processes. In no case are interrupts allowed when a login shell is reading the .logout file.

Job Control

The shell associates a numbered job with each command sequence to keep track of those commands that are running in the background or have been stopped with TSTP signals (typically Control-Z). When a command or command sequence in a semicolon-separated list is started in the background by use of the & metacharacter, the shell displays a line with the job number in brackets and a list of associated process numbers, for example:

```
[1] 1234
```

To see the current list of jobs, use the jobs built-in command. The job most recently stopped (or put into the background if none are stopped) is referred to as the current job and is indicated with a +. The previous job is indicated with a –; when the current job is terminated or moved to the foreground, this job takes its place (becomes the new current job).

To manipulate jobs, refer to the bg, fg, kill, stop, and % built-in commands.

A reference to a job begins with a %. By itself, the percent sign refers to the current job.

% %+ %%	The current job.
%-	The previous job.
%j	Refer to job *j*, as in kill -9 %*j*. *j* can be a job number or a string that uniquely specifies the command line that started it; for example, fg %vi might bring a stopped vi job to the foreground.
%?*string*	Specify the job for which the command line uniquely contains *string*.

A job running in the background stops when it tries to read from the terminal. Background jobs can normally produce output, but you can suppress this output by using the stty tostop command.

Status Reporting

While running interactively, the shell tracks the status of each job and reports whenever the job finishes or becomes blocked. To avoid disturbing the appearance of your input, the shell normally displays a message to this effect as it issues a prompt. When set, the notify variable indicates that the shell is to report status changes immediately. By default, the notify command marks the current process; after starting a background job, type **notify** to mark it.

Built-in Commands

Built-in commands are executed within the C shell. If a built-in command occurs as any component of a pipeline except the last, it is executed in a subshell.

Note — Shell built-in functions are not stoppable/restartable. Command sequences of the form a ; b ; c are also not handled gracefully when stopping is attempted. If you suspend b, the shell never executes c. This problem is especially noticeable if the expansion results from an alias. It can be avoided by placing the sequence in parentheses to force it into a subshell.

It is up to the user to manually remove all duplicate path names accrued from using built-in commands as set path = *pathnames* or setenv PATH *pathnames* more than once. For example, these duplicates often occur because a shell script or a .cshrc file does something like set path=(/usr/local /usr/hosts $path) to ensure that the named directories are in the path-name list.

The C shell built-in commands are shown below. For more details, refer to the individual manual page for each built-in command.

: Null command

Interpret the command but perform no action.

alias [*name* [*def*]]

Assign *def* to the alias *name*. *def* is a list of words that may contain escaped history-substitution metasyntax. *name* is not allowed to be alias or unalias. If you omit *def*, display the current definition for the alias name. If you omit both *name* and *def*, display all aliases with their definitions.

bg [%*job*...]

Run the current or specified jobs in the background.

break   Resume execution after the end of the nearest enclosing foreach or while loop. Execute the remaining commands on the current line. You can write multilevel breaks as a list of break commands, all on one line.

breaksw   Break from a switch, resuming after the endsw.

case *label*: A label in a switch statement.

cd [*dir*]
chdir [*dir*]

> Change the shell's working directory to directory *dir*. If no argument is given, change to the home directory of the user. If *dir* is a relative pathname not found in the current directory, check for it in those directories listed in the cdpath variable. If *dir* is the name of a shell variable whose value starts with a /, change to the directory named by that value.

continue Continue execution of the next iteration of the nearest enclosing while or foreach loop.

default: Label the default case in a switch statement. The default should come after all case labels. First, execute any remaining commands on the command line.

dirs [-1] Print the directory stack, most recent to the left; the first directory shown is the current directory. With the -l argument, produce an unabbreviated printout; suppress use of the ~ notation.

echo [-n] *list*

> Write the words in *list* to the shell's standard output, separated by space characters. Terminate the output with a newline unless you use the -n option. csh, by default, invokes its built-in echo if echo is called without the full path name of a UNIX command, regardless of the configuration of your PATH (see echo(1)).

eval *argument*...

> Read the arguments as input to the shell and execute the resulting command(s). This command is usually used to execute commands generated as the result of command or variable substitution. See tset(1B) for an example of how to use eval.

exec *command*

> Execute *command* in place of the current shell, which terminates.

exit [(*expr*)]

> Exit the calling shell or shell script, either with the value of the status variable or with the value specified by the expression *expr*.

fg [%*job*] Bring the current or specified job into the foreground.

foreach *var* (*wordlist*)
...
end

> Successively set the variable *var* to each member of *wordlist*. Execute the sequence of commands between this command and the matching end for each new value of *var*. Both foreach and end must appear alone on separate lines.

You can use the built-in `continue` command to terminate the execution of the current iteration of the loop, and the built-in command `break` to terminate execution of the `foreach` command. When this command is read from the terminal, the loop is read once, prompting with ? before any statements in the loop are executed.

`glob` *wordlist*

Perform file-name expansion on *wordlist*. Like `echo`, but no \ escapes are recognized. Words are delimited by NULL characters in the output.

`goto` *label*   The specified *label* is a file name and a command expanded to yield a label. The shell rewinds its input as much as possible and searches for a line of the form *label*: possibly preceded by space or Tab characters. Execution continues after the indicated line. It is an error to jump to a label that occurs between a `while` or `for` built-in command and its corresponding `end`.

`hashstat`   Print a statistics line indicating how effective the internal hash table for the path variable has been at locating commands (and avoiding `execs`). Try an `exec` for each component of the path where the `hash` function indicates a possible hit and in each component that does not begin with a /. These statistics reflect only the effectiveness of the path variable, not the `cdpath` variable.

`history` [-hr] [*n*]

Display the history list; if *n* is given, display only the *n* most recent events.

-h   Display the history list without leading numbers. Use this option to produce files suitable for sourcing, using the -h option to source.

-r   Reverse the order of printout to be most recent first instead of oldest first.

`if` (*expr*) *command*

If the specified expression evaluates to `true`, execute the single command with arguments. Variable substitution on *command* happens early, at the same time it does for the rest of the `if` command. *command* must be a simple command, not a pipeline, a command list, or a parenthesized command list. Note: I/O redirection occurs even if *expr* is `false` when *command* is not executed (this is a bug).

`if (expr)`
`then`
`...`
`else if`
`(expr2)`
`then`
`...`
`else`
`...`
`endif`
	If *expr* is true, execute commands up to the first `else`. Otherwise, if *expr2* is true, execute the commands between the `else if` and the second `else`. Otherwise, execute commands between the `else` and the `endif`. Any number of `else if` pairs are allowed, but only one `else`. You need only one `endif`, but it is required. The words `else` and `endif` must be the first nonwhite characters on a line. The `if` must appear alone on its input line or after an `else`.

`jobs[-l]` List the active jobs under job control.

`-l` List process IDs, in addition to the normal information.

`kill [-sig] [pid] [%job] ...`

`kill -l` Send either the TERM (terminate) signal, by default, or the signal specified, to the specified process ID, the job indicated, or the current job. Give signals either by number or by name. There is no default. Typing `kill` does not send a signal to the current job. If the signal being sent is TERM (terminate) or HUP (hang up), then the job or process is sent a CONT (continue) signal as well.

`-l` List the signal names that can be sent.

`limit [-h] [resource [max-use]]`

Limit the consumption by the current process or any process it spawns, each not to exceed *max-use* on the specified resource. If you omit *max-use*, print the current limit; if you omit *resource*, display all limits. (Run the sysdef(1M) command to obtain the maximum possible limits for your system. The values reported are in hexadecimal, but you can translate them into decimal numbers by using the bc(1) command.)

`-h`	Use hard limits instead of the current limits. Hard limits impose a ceiling on the values of the current limits. Only superuser can raise the hard limits.

resource can be one of the following values:

`cputime`	Maximum CPU seconds per process.
`filesize`	Largest single file allowed; limited to the size of the file system. See df(1M).
`datasize` `(heapsize)`	Maximum data size (including stack) for the process; the size of your virtual memory. See swap(1M).
`stacksize`	Maximum stack size for the process. See swap(1M).
`coredumpsize`	Maximum size of a core dump (file); limited to the size of the file system.
`descriptors`	Maximum number of file descriptors. Run sysdef().
`memorysize`	Maximum size of virtual memory.

max-use is a number, with an optional scaling factor, as follows:

*n*h	Hours (for cputime).
*n*k v	Kilobytes; the default for all but cputime.
*n*m v	Megabytes or minutes (for cputime).
mm:v	Minutes and seconds (for cputime).

Example of limit: to limit the size of a corefile dump to 0 megabytes, type the following:

```
limit coredumpsize 0M
```

login [*username*| -p]

Terminate a login shell and invoke login(1). Do not process the .logout file. If you omit *username*, prompt for the name of a user.

-p   Preserve the current environment (variables).

logout   Terminate a login shell.

nice [+*n* | -*n*] [*command*]

Increment the process priority value for the shell or for command by *n*. The higher the priority value, the lower the priority of a process and the slower it runs. When given, *command* is always run in a subshell. If command is omitted, nice increments the value for the current shell. If you specify no increment, set the process priority value to 4. The range of process priority values is from -20 to 20. Values of *n* outside this range set the value to the lower or to the higher boundary, respectively.

+*n*   Increment the process priority value by *n*.

-*n*   Decrement by *n*. This argument can be used only by superuser.

nohup [*command*]

Run command with HUPs ignored. With no arguments, ignore HUPs throughout the remainder of a script. When given, always run *command* in a subshell; the restrictions placed on commands in simple if statements apply. All processes detached with & are effectively nohup'd.

notify [%*job*]...

Notify the user asynchronously when the status of the current job or specified jobs changes.

onintr [-| *label*]

Control the action of the shell on interrupts. With no arguments, restore the default action of the shell on interrupts. (The shell terminates shell scripts and returns to the terminal command input level.) With the - argument, the shell ignores all interrupts. With a *label* argument, the shell executes a goto *label* when it receives an interrupt or a child process terminates because it was interrupted.

popd [+*n*]   Pop the directory stack and change to the new top directory. Number the elements of the directory stack from 0, starting at the top. When you specify +*n*, discard the *n*-th entry in the stack.

pushd [+*n* | *dir*]

Push a directory onto the directory stack. With no arguments, exchange the top two elements. When you specify +*n*, rotate the *n*-th entry to the top of the stack and change to it. With the *dir* argument, push the current working directory onto the stack and change to *dir*.

rehash   Recompute the internal hash table of the contents of directories listed in the path variable to account for new commands added. Recompute the internal hash table of the contents of directories listed in the cdpath variable to account for new directories added.

repeat *count command*

Repeat *command count* times. *command* is subject to the same restrictions as with the one-line if statement.

set [*var* [= *value*]]

set *var*[*n*]
= *word*   With no arguments, display the values of all shell variables. Display multiword values as a parenthesized list. With the *var* argument alone, assign an empty (null) value to the variable *var*. With arguments of the form *var* = *value*, assign *value* to *var*, where *value* is one of:

    word   A single word (or quoted string).

    (*wordlist*)   A space-separated list of words enclosed in parentheses.

Values are command and file-name expanded before being assigned. The form set *var*[*n*] = *word* replaces the *n*-th word in a multiword value with *word*.

setenv [*VAR* [*word*]]

With no arguments, display all environment variables. With the *VAR* argument, set the environment variable *VAR* to have an empty (null) value. (By convention, environment variables are normally given uppercase names.) With both *VAR* and *VAR arguments*, set the environment variable NAME to the value *word*, which must be either a single word or a quoted string. The most commonly used environment variables, USER, TERM, and PATH, are automatically imported to and exported from the csh variables user, term, and path; you do not need to use setenv for these. In addition, the shell sets the PWD environment variable from the csh variable cwd whenever the latter changes.

The environment variables LC_CTYPE, LC_MESSAGES, LC_TIME, LC_COLLATE, LC_NUMERIC, and LC_MONETARY take immediate effect when changed within the C shell.

If any of the LC_* variables (LC_CTYPE, LC_MESSAGES, LC_TIME, LC_COLLATE, LC_NUMERIC, and LC_MONETARY) (see environ(5)) are not set in the environment, the operational behavior of csh for each corresponding locale category is determined by the value of the LANG environment variable. If LC_ALL is set, its contents are used to override both the LANG and the other LC_* variables. If none of the above variables are set in the environment, the C (U.S. style) locale determines how csh behaves.

LC_CTYPE	Determine how csh handles characters. When LC_CTYPE is set to a valid value, csh can display and handle text and file names containing valid characters for that locale.
LC_CTYPE	Determine how diagnostic and informative messages are presented. This presentation includes the language and style of the messages and the correct form of affirmative and negative responses. In the C locale, the messages are presented in the default form found in the program itself (in most cases, U.S. English).
LC_NUMERIC	Determine the value of the radix character (decimal point (.) in the C locale) and thousand separator (empty string (" ") in the C locale).

shift [*variable*]

Shift the components of argv or *variable*, if supplied, to the left, discarding the first component. It is an error for the variable not to be set or to have a null value.

source [-h] *name*

Read commands from *name*. You can nest source commands, but if they are nested too deeply, the shell may run out of file descriptors. An error in a sourced file at any level terminates all nested source commands.

-h   Place commands from the file *name* on the history list without executing them.

stop %*jobid*...

Stop the current or specified background job.

stop *pid*...

Stop the specified process, *pid* (see ps(1)). Note that when you restart a command from a stop, the shell prints the directory it started in if this is different from the current directory; this result can be misleading (that is, wrong) as the job may have changed directories internally.

suspend   Stop the shell in its tracks, much as if it had been sent a stop signal with ^Z. This command is most often used to stop shells started by su.

switch	Successively match each *label* against the specified *string*, which is
(*string*)	first command- and file-name expanded. You can use the file
case *label*:	metacharacters *, ?, and [...] in the case labels, which are variable
...	expanded. If none of the labels match before a default *label* is found,
breaksw	begin execution after the default *label*. Each case statement and the
....	default statement must appear at the beginning of a line. The
default:	command breaksw continues execution after the endsw. Otherwise,
...	control falls through subsequent case and default statements as with
breaksw	C. If no *label* matches and there is no default, execution continues
endsw	after the endsw.

time [*command*]

> With no argument, print a summary of time used by this C shell and its children. With an optional *command*, execute *command* and print a summary of the time it uses.
>
> As of this writing, the time built-in command does *not* compute the last six fields of output, erroneously reporting the value 0 for these fields.
>
> example% **time**
> 9.0u 11.0s 3:32 10% 0+0k 0+0io 0pf+0w

umask [*value*]

> Display the file creation mask. With an optional *value*, set the file creation mask. With *value* given in octal, you can turn off any bits, but you cannot turn on bits to allow new permissions. Common values include 077, restricting all permissions from everyone else; 022, giving complete access to the group and read (and directory search) access to others; or 022, giving read (and directory search) but not write permission to the group and others.

unalias *pattern*

> Discard aliases that match (file-name substitution) *pattern*. unalias * removes all aliases.

unhash

Disable the internal hash tables for the path and cdpath variables.

unlimit [-h] [*resource*]

> Remove a limitation on *resource*. If you specify no resource, then remove all resource limitations. See the description of the limit command for the list of resource names. Only superuser can use the –h option to remove corresponding hard limits.

unset *pattern*

> Remove variables whose names match (file-name substitution) *pattern*. unset * removes all variables, which has noticeably distasteful side effects.

unsetenv *variable*

> Remove *variable* from the environment. As with unset, pattern matching is not performed.

wait   Wait for background jobs to finish (or for an interrupt) before prompting.

while (*expr*)
...
end

          While *expr* is true (evaluates to non-zero), repeat commands between the `while` and the matching `end` statement. You can use `break` and `continue` to terminate or continue the loop prematurely. The `while` and `end` must appear alone on their input lines. If the shell's input is a terminal, it prompts for commands with a question mark until the `end` command is entered and then performs the commands in the loop.

%[*job*] [&]   Bring the current or indicated job to the foreground. With the optional ampersand, continue running job in the background.

@ [*var* =*expr*]
@ [*var*[*n*] =*expr*]

          With no arguments, display the values for all shell variables. With arguments, set the variable *var*, or the *n*-th word in the value of *var*, to the value that *expr* evaluates to. (If you supply [*n*], both *var* and its *n*-th component must already exist.)

          If the expression contains the characters >, <, &, or |, then at least this part of *expr* must be placed within parentheses.

          The operators *=, +=, and so forth, are available as in C. The space separating the name from the assignment operator is optional. Spaces are, however, mandatory in separating components of *expr* that would otherwise be single words.

          Special postfix operators, ++ and --, increment or decrement *expr*.

Environment Variables and Predefined Shell Variables

Unlike the Bourne shell, the C shell maintains a distinction between environment variables and shell variables. Environment variables are automatically exported to processes the shell invokes. Shell variables are not. Both types of variables are treated similarly under variable substitution. The shell sets the variables argv, cwd, home, path, prompt, shell, and status on initialization. The shell copies the environment variable USER into the shell variable user, TERM into term, and HOME into home, and copies each back into the respective environment variable whenever the shell variables are reset. PATH and path are handled similarly. You need set path only once in the .cshrc or .login file. The environment variable PWD is set from cwd whenever the latter changes. The shell variables shown below have predefined meanings.

argv   The list of command-line arguments supplied to the current invocation of the shell. This variable determines the value of the positional parameters $1, $2, and so on.

cdpath   A list of directories to be searched by the cd, chdir, and popd commands if the directory argument each accepts is not a subdirectory of the current directory.

cwd   The full path name of the current directory.

echo   Echo commands (after substitutions) just before execution.

fignore   A list of file-name suffixes to ignore when attempting file-name completion. Typically, the single word .o.

filec   Enable file-name completion, in which case the Control-D character EOT and the ESC character have special significance when typed in at the end of a terminal input line.

            EOT   Print a list of all file names that start with the preceding string.

            ESC   Replace the preceding string with the longest unambiguous extension.

hardpaths   Resolve path names in the directory stack to contain no symbolic-link components. Note that symbolic links can fool the shell. Setting the hardpaths variable alleviates this.

histchars   A two-character string. The first character replaces ! as the history-substitution character. The second replaces the carat (^) for quick substitutions.

history   The number of lines saved in the history list. A very large number can use up all of the C shell's memory. If not set, the C shell saves only the most recent command.

home   The user's home directory. The file-name expansion of ~ refers to the value of this variable.

ignoreeof   Ignore EOF from terminals. This variable protects against accidentally killing a C shell by typing a Control-D.

mail   A list of files that the C shell checks for mail. If the first word of the value is a number, it specifies a mail-checking interval in seconds (default, 5 minutes).

nobeep   Suppress the bell during command completion when asking the C shell to extend an ambiguous file name.

noclobber   Restrict output redirection so that existing files are not destroyed by accident. > redirections can be made only to new files. >> redirections can be made only to existing files.

noglob   Inhibit file-name substitution. This variable is most useful in shell scripts once file names (if any) are obtained and no further expansion is desired.

nonomatch   Returns the file-name substitution pattern, instead of an error, if the pattern is not matched. Malformed patterns still result in errors.

notify   Notify you immediately as jobs are completed, instead of waiting until just before issuing a prompt.

path   The list of directories to search for commands. path is initialized from the environment variable PATH, which the C shell updates whenever path changes. A null word specifies the current directory. The default is typically (/usr/bin .). If path becomes unset, execute only full path names. An interactive C shell normally hashes the contents of the directories listed after reading .cshrc and whenever path is reset. If new commands are added, use the rehash command to update the table.

prompt   The string an interactive C shell prompts with. Noninteractive shells leave the prompt variable unset. Aliases and other commands in the .cshrc file that are useful only interactively can be placed after the following test: 'if ($?prompt == 0) exit', to reduce startup time for noninteractive shells. A ! in the prompt string is replaced by the current event number. The default prompt is *hostname*% for mere mortals, or *hostname*# for superuser.

The setting of $prompt has three values:

$prompt not set

> Noninteractive shell, test $? prompt.

$prompt set but == ""

> .cshrc called by the which(1) command.

$prompt set and != ""

> Normal interactive shell.

savehist   The number of lines from the history list that are saved in ~/.history when the user logs out. Large values for savehist slow down the C shell during startup.

shell   The file in which the C shell resides. This variable is used in forking shells to interpret files that have execute bits set but that are not executable by the system.

status   The status returned by the most recent command. If that command terminated abnormally, 0200 is added to the status. Built-in commands that fail return exit status 1; all other built-in commands set status to 0.

time   Control automatic timing of commands. Can be supplied with one or two values. The first is the reporting threshold in CPU seconds. The second is a string of tags and text indicating which resources to report on. A tag is a percent sign (%) followed by a single, uppercase letter (unrecognized tags print as text):

%D   Average amount, in kilobytes, of unshared data space used.

%E   Elapsed (wall clock) time for the command.

%F   Page faults.

%I   Number of block input operations.

%K	Average amount of unshared stack space used, in kilobytes.
%M	Maximum real memory used during execution of the process.
%O	Number of block output operations.
%P	Total CPU time—U (user) plus S (system)—as a percentage of E (elapsed) time.
%S	Number of seconds of CPU time consumed by the kernel on behalf of the user's process.
%U	Number of seconds of CPU time devoted to the user's process.
%W	Number of swaps.
%X	Average amount of shared memory used, in kilobytes.

The default summary display outputs from the %U, %S, %E, %P, %X, %D, %I, %O, %F, and %W tags, in that order.

verbose Display each command after history substitution takes place.

Large File Behavior

See largefile(5) for the description of the behavior of csh when encountering files greater than or equal to 2 Gbytes (2**31 bytes).

Files

~/.cshrc	Read at beginning of execution by each shell.
~/.login	Read by login shells after .cshrc at login.
~/.logout	Read by login shells at logout.
~/.history	Saved history for use at next login.
/usr/bin/sh	
	The Bourne shell, for shell scripts not starting with a #.
/tmp/sh*	Temporary file for <<.
/etc/passwd	
	Source of home directories for ~name.

Attributes

See attributes(5) for descriptions of the following attributes:

Attribute Type	Attribute Value
Availability	SUNWcsu
CSI	Enabled

See Also

bc(1), echo(1), login(1), ls(1), more(1), ps(1), sh(1),
shell_builtins(1), which(1), tset(1B), df(1M), swap(1M), sysdef(1M),
access(2), exec(2), fork(2), pipe(2), a.out(4), environ(4), ascii(5),
attributes(5), environ(5), largefile(5), termio(7I)

Diagnostics

You have stopped jobs.

> You exited the C shell with stopped jobs under job control. An
> immediate second attempt to exit succeeds, terminating the stopped
> jobs.

Warnings

The use of setuid shell scripts is strongly discouraged.

csplit — Split Files, Based on Context

Synopsis

/usr/bin/csplit [-ks] [-f *prefix*] [-n *number*] *file arg1 argn*

Description

Use the csplit command to split a file into sections. The csplit command reads the file
named by the *file* operand, writes all or part of that file into other files as directed by
the *arg* operands, and writes the sizes of the files.

Options

-f *prefix*	Name the created files *prefix*00, *prefix*01, *prefixn*. The default is xx00 ... xxn. If the *prefix* argument would create a file name exceeding 14 bytes, an error results; csplit exits with a diagnostic message and no files are created.
-k	Leave previously created files intact. By default, csplit removes created files if an error occurs.
-n *number*	Specify the *number* of decimal digits used to form file names for the file pieces. The default is 2, starting with 00. For example, if you specify -n 4, output files are numbered starting with xx0000.
-s	Suppress the output of file size messages.

Operands

file	The path name of a text file to be split. If *file* is -, use the standard input.
arg1...argn	The operands *arg1...argn* can be a combination of the following:

/*rexp*/[*offset*]

Create a file using the content of the lines from the current line up to, but not including, the line that results from the evaluation of the regular expression with *offset*, if any, applied. The regular expression *rexp* must follow the rules for basic regular expressions. The optional offset must be a positive or negative integer value representing a number of lines. The integer value must be preceded by + or -. If the selection of lines from an offset expression of this type would create a file with zero lines or one with greater than the number of lines left in the input file, the results are unspecified. After the section is created, the current line is set to the line that results from the evaluation of the regular expression with any offset applied. The pattern match of *rexp* is always applied from the current line to the end of the file.

%*rexp*%[*offset*]

This operand is the same as /*rexp*/[*offset*], except create no file for the selected section of the input file.

line-no

Create a file from the current line up to, but not including, the line number *line-no*. Lines in the file are numbered starting at 1. The current line becomes *line-no*. For example, an *in-line* argument of 100 puts 99 lines in each file.

"{*num*}"

Repeat operand. This operand can follow any of the operands described previously. If it follows a *rexp* type operand, that operand is applied *num* more times. If it follows a *line-no* operand, the files are split every *line-no* lines, *num* times, from that point. You must enclose the {*num*} operand in double quotes (" ") or it does not work properly.

csplit reports an error if an operand does not reference a line between the current position and the end of the file.

Usage

See largefile(5) for the description of the behavior of csplit when encountering files greater than or equal to 2 Gbytes (2**31 bytes).

Examples

The following example splits the file named whtpaper.html in two.

```
castle% csplit whtpaper.html 100
4884
35136
castle%
```

The output displays the number of blocks in each file.
The following example creates four files, cobol00...cobol03.

```
castle% csplit -f cobol filename '/procedure division/' /par5./ /par16./
```

After editing the split files, you can recombine them as follows.

```
castle% cat cobol0[0-3] > filename
```

> **Note —** This example overwrites the original file.

The following example splits the file at every 100 lines, up to 10,000 lines. The -k
option retains the created files if there are fewer than 10,000 lines; however, an error
message is still printed.

```
castle% csplit -k testfile 100 "{99}"
2821
3670
3617
3195
3896
3754
2787
3691
3609
3207
3760
3849
csplit: {99} - out of range
1780
castle% ls -l xx*
-rw-rw-rw-   1 winsor    staff      2821 Jan  6 12:23 xx00
-rw-rw-rw-   1 winsor    staff      3670 Jan  6 12:23 xx01
-rw-rw-rw-   1 winsor    staff      3617 Jan  6 12:23 xx02
-rw-rw-rw-   1 winsor    staff      3195 Jan  6 12:23 xx03
-rw-rw-rw-   1 winsor    staff      3896 Jan  6 12:23 xx04
-rw-rw-rw-   1 winsor    staff      3754 Jan  6 12:23 xx05
-rw-rw-rw-   1 winsor    staff      2787 Jan  6 12:23 xx06
-rw-rw-rw-   1 winsor    staff      3691 Jan  6 12:23 xx07
-rw-rw-rw-   1 winsor    staff      3609 Jan  6 12:23 xx08
-rw-rw-rw-   1 winsor    staff      3207 Jan  6 12:23 xx09
-rw-rw-rw-   1 winsor    staff      3760 Jan  6 12:23 xx10
-rw-rw-rw-   1 winsor    staff      3849 Jan  6 12:23 xx11
-rw-rw-rw-   1 winsor    staff      1780 Jan  6 12:23 xx12
castle%
```

> **Note —** The online csplit manual page does not show double quotes
> around the number in curly braces. Without the double quotes, the first
> output file contains the specified number of lines but subsequent files are
> not split properly.

If prog.c follows the normal C coding convention (the last line of a routine consists
only of a } in the first character position), the following example creates a file for each
separate C routine (up to 21) in prog.c.

```
castle% csplit -k prog.c '%main(%' '/^}/+1' "{20}"
```

Environment Variables

See environ(5) for descriptions of the following environment variables that affect the execution of csplit: LC_COLLATE, LC_CTYPE, LC_MESSAGES, and NLSPATH.

Exit Status

0	Successful completion.
>0	An error occurred.

Attributes

See attributes(5) for descriptions of the following attributes:

Attribute Type	Attribute Value
Availability	SUNWcsu
CSI	Enabled

See Also

sed(1), split(1), attributes(5), environ(5), largefile(5)

Diagnostics

The diagnostic messages are self-explanatory, except for the following:

arg out of range

> The given argument did not reference a line between the current position and the end of the file.

ct — Spawn Login to a Remote Terminal

Synopsis

/usr/bin/ct [-h] [-s*speed*] [-v] [-w*n*] *telno*...

Description

ct dials the telephone number of a modem that is attached to a terminal and spawns a login process to that terminal. *telno* is a telephone number, with equal signs for secondary dial tones and minus signs for delays at appropriate places. (The set of legal characters for *telno* is 0 through 9, -, =, *, and #. The maximum length of *telno* is 31 characters.) If you specify more than one telephone number, ct tries each in succession until one answers; this feature is useful for specifying alternate dialing paths.

ct tries each line listed in the file /etc/uucp/Devices until it finds an available line with appropriate attributes or until it runs out of entries.

After the user on the destination terminal logs out, two things could occur, depending on what type of port monitor is monitoring the port. When there is no port monitor, ct prompts: Reconnect? If the response begins with the letter n, the line is dropped;

otherwise, `ttymon` is started again and the `login:` prompt is printed. When a port monitor is monitoring the port, the port monitor reissues the `login:` prompt. The user should log out properly before disconnecting.

Note — The `ct` program does not work with a DATAKIT Multiplex interface.

For a port that is shared for both dial-in and dial-out, the `ttymon` program running on the line must have the `-r` and `-b` options specified (see `ttymon`(1M)).

Options

`-h`	Prevent `ct` from hanging up the current line so that it can be used to answer the incoming call. Also, wait for the termination of the specified `ct` process before returning control to the user's terminal.
`-s speed`	Set the data rate. *speed* is expressed in baud rates. The default baud rate is 1200.
`-v`	Send a running narrative to the standard error output stream.
`-wn`	Override the default action of asking if `ct` should wait if there are no free lines, and if so, specifying how many minutes to wait. *n* specifies the maximum number of minutes that `ct` should wait for a free line.
`-xn`	Produce a detailed output of the program execution on `stderr`. *n* specifies the level of detail of debugging information as a single number between 0 and 9. As *n* increases to 9, give more detailed debugging information.

Files

`/etc/uucp/Devices`

`/var/adm/ctlog`

Attributes

See `attributes`(5) for descriptions of the following attributes:

Attribute Type	Attribute Value
Availability	SUNWbnuu

See Also

`cu`(1C), `login`(1), `uucp`(1C), `ttymon`(1M), `attributes`(5)

ctags — Create a Tags File for Use with ex and vi

Synopsis

```
/usr/bin/ctags [-aBFtuvwx] [-f tagsfile] file...
/usr/xpg4/bin/ctags [-aBFuvwx] [-f tagsfile] file...
```

Description

The ctags command makes a tags file for ex(1) from the specified C, C++, Pascal, FORTRAN, yacc(1), and lex(1) sources. A tags file gives the locations of specified objects (in this case, functions and typedefs) in a group of files. Each line of the tags file contains the object name, the file in which it is defined, and an address specification for the object definition. Functions are searched with a pattern, typedefs with a line number. Specifiers are given in separate fields on the line, separated by space or Tab characters. Using the tags file, ex can quickly find these object definitions.

Normally, ctags places the tag descriptions in a file called tags; you can override this default by using the -f option.

Files with names ending in .c or .h are assumed to be either C or C++ source files and are searched for C/C++ routine and macro definitions. Files with names ending in .cc, .C, or .cxx are assumed to be C++ source files. Files with names ending in .y are assumed to be yacc source files. Files with names ending in .l are assumed to be lex files. Others are first examined to see if they contain any Pascal or FORTRAN routine definitions; if not, they are processed again, looking for C definitions.

The tag main is treated specially in C or C++ programs. The tag formed is created by prepending M to *file*, with a trailing .c, .cc, .C, or .cxx removed, if any, and leading path-name components also removed. This behavior makes use of ctags practical in directories with more than one program.

Options

When printing, specify first the -x and -v options, then the remaining options.

-a	Append output to an existing tags file.
-B	Use backward searching patterns (?...?).
-f *tagsfile*	
	Place the tag descriptions in a file called *tagsfile* instead of tags.
-F	Use forward searching patterns (/.../) (default).
-t	Create tags for typedefs. /usr/xpg4/bin/ctags creates tags for typedefs by default.
-u	Update the specified files in tags, that is, delete all references to them, and append the new values to the file. Beware: This option is implemented in a way that is rather slow; it is usually faster to simply rebuild the tags file.
-v	Produce on the standard output an index listing the function name, file name, and page number (assuming 64-line pages). Because the output is sorted into lexicographic order, you may want to run the output through sort -f.
-w	Suppress warning diagnostics.

-x   Produce a list of object names, the line number, and file name on which
            each is defined, as well as the text of that line and print it on the
            standard output. This list provides a simple index that can be printed
            as an off-line readable function index.

Operands

file.c   Treat files with basenames ending with the .c suffix as C-language
            source code.

file.h   Treat files with basenames ending with the .h suffix as C-language
            source code header files.

file.f   Treat files with basenames ending with the .f suffix as
            FORTRAN-language source code.

Usage

The -v option is used mainly with vgrind, which is part of the optional BSD
Compatibility package.

Notes

Recognition of functions, subroutines, and procedures for FORTRAN and Pascal is done
in a simple-minded way. No attempt is made to deal with block structure; if you have two
Pascal procedures in different blocks with the same name, you lose.

The ctags command does not know about #ifdefs.

The ctags command should know about Pascal types. It relies on the input being well
formed to detect typedefs. Use of -tx shows only the last line of typedefs.

Examples

Using ctags with the -v option produces entries in an order that may not always be
appropriate for vgrind. To produce results in alphabetical order, you may want to pipe
the output through sort -f, as shown in the following example.

```
castle% ctags -v filename.c filename.h | sort -f > index
castle% vgrind -x index
```

To build a tags file for C sources in a directory hierarchy rooted at sourcedir, first
create an empty tags file, and then run find(1), as shown in the following example

```
castle% cd sourcedir ; rm -f tags ; touch tags
castle% find . \( -name SCCS -prune -name '*.c' -o -name '*.h' \) -exec
    ctags -u {} \;
```

Note — Spaces must be entered exactly as shown.

Environment Variables

See environ(5) for descriptions of the following environment variables that affect the
execution of ctags: LC_COLLATE, LC_CTYPE, LC_MESSAGES, and NLSPATH.

Exit Status

0	Successful completion.
>0	An error occurred.

Files

tags Output tags file.

Attributes

See attributes(5) for descriptions of the following attributes:

/usr/bin/ctags

Attribute Type	Attribute Value
Availability	SUNWtoo

/usr/xpg4/bin/ctags

Attribute Type	Attribute Value
Availability	SUNWxcu4

See Also

ex(1), lex(1), vgrind(1), vi(1), yacc(1), attributes(5), environ(5), XPG4(5)

cu — Call Another UNIX System

Synopsis

/usr/bin/cu [-c *device* | -l *line*] [-s *speed*] [-b *bits*] [-h] [-n] [-t]
   [-d] [-o | -e] [-L] [-C] [-H] *telno*|*systemname* [*local-cmd*]

Description

cu calls up another UNIX system, a terminal, or possibly a non-UNIX system. It manages an interactive conversation with possible transfers of files. It is convenient to think of cu as operating in two phases. The first phase is the connection phase in which the connection is established. cu then enters the conversation phase. The -d option is the only one that applies to both phases.

Options

The -c, -l, and -s options play a part in selecting the medium; the remaining options are used in configuring the line.

-b *bits* Force *bits* to be the number of bits processed on the line. *bits* is either 7 or 8. This option enables connection between systems with different character sizes. By default, the character size of the line is set to that of the current local terminal.

-c *device* Use entries only in the Type field (the first field in the /etc/uucp/Devices file) that match the user-specified device, usually the name of a local area network.

-C   Run the local-cmd specified at the end of the command line instead of entering interactive mode. The standard in and standard out of the command that is run refer to the remote connection.

-d   Print diagnostic traces.

-e   Set an EVEN data parity for data sent to the remote system.

-h   Set communication mode to half-duplex. This option emulates local echo to support calls to other computer systems that expect terminals to be set to half-duplex mode.

-H   Ignore one hangup. This option enables the user's system to remain in cu while the remote machine disconnects and places a call back to the local machine. Use this option when connecting to systems with callback or dialback modems. Once the callback occurs, subsequent hangups terminate cu. You can specify this option more than once. For more information about dialback configuration, see remote(4) and *TCP/IP and Data Communications Administration Guide.*

-l *line* Specify a device name to use as the communication line. You can use this option to override the search that would otherwise take place for the first available line with the right speed. When you use the -l option without the -s option, the speed of a line is taken from the /etc/uucp/Devices file record in which *line* matches the second field (the Line field). When you use the -l and -s options together, cu searches the /etc/uucp/Devices file to check whether the requested speed for the requested line is available. If so, the connection is made at the requested speed; otherwise, an error message is printed and the call is not made. In the general case in which a specified device is a directly connected asynchronous line (for instance, /dev/term/a), a telephone number (*telno*) is not required. The specified device need not be in the /dev directory. If the specified device is associated with an autodialer, you must provide a telephone number.

-L   Go through the login chat sequence specified in the /etc/uucp/Systems file. For more information about the chat sequence, see *TCP/IP and Data Communications Administration Guide.*

-n	Request user prompt for telephone number. For added security, this option prompts the user to provide the telephone number to be dialed, instead of taking it from the command line.
-o	Set an ODD data parity for data sent to the remote system.
-s *speed*	Specify the transmission speed (300, 1200, 2400, 4800, 9600, 19200, 38400). The default value is Any speed that depends on the order of the lines in the /etc/uucp/Devices file.
-t	Dial a terminal that has been set to autoanswer. Appropriate mapping of Return to Return-linefeed pairs is set.

Operands

telno	When using an automatic dialer, specify the telephone number with equal signs for secondary dial tone or minus signs placed appropriately for delays of 4 seconds.
systemname	Specify a uucp system name that can be used instead of a telephone number; in this case, cu obtains an appropriate direct line or telephone number from a system file.

Usage

Connection Phase

cu uses the same mechanism that uucp(1C) does to establish a connection. It uses the uucp control files /etc/uucp/Devices and /etc/uucp/Systems, enabling cu to choose from several different media to establish the connection. The possible media include telephone lines, direct connections, and local area networks (LANs). The /etc/uucp/Devices file contains a list of media available on your system. The /etc/uucp/Systems file contains information for connecting to remote systems, but it is not generally readable.

Note — cu determines which /etc/uucp/Systems and /etc/uucp/Devices files to use, based on the name used to invoke cu. In the simple case, this name is cu, but you could also have created a link to cu with another name, such as pppcu, in which case, cu then looks for a service=pppcu entry in the /etc/uucp/Sysfiles file to determine which /etc/uucp/Systems file to use.

The *telno* or *systemname* parameter from the command line tells cu what system you want to connect to. This parameter can be blank, a telephone number, a system name, or a LAN-specific address, as described below.

telephone number

A string consisting of the dial tone characters (the digits 0 through 9, *, and #) plus the special characters = and -. The equal sign designates a secondary dial tone, and the minus sign creates a 4-second delay.

system name

> The name of any computer that uucp can call; you can print a list of these names by using the uuname(1C) command.

LAN address

> The documentation for your LAN shows the form of the LAN-specific address.

If cu's default behavior is invoked (not using the -c or -l options), cu uses the *telno* or *systemname* parameter to determine what medium to use. If you specify a telephone number, cu assumes that you want to use a telephone line and selects an automatic call unit (ACU). Otherwise, cu assumes that the parameter is a system name. cu follows the uucp calling mechanism and uses the /etc/uucp/Systems and /etc/uucp/Devices files to obtain the best available connection. Because cu chooses a speed that is appropriate for the medium, you may not use the -s option when this parameter is a system name.

You can use the -c and -l options to modify the default behavior. -c is most often used to choose a LAN by specifying a Type field from the /etc/uucp/Devices file. You must include either a *telno* or *systemname* value when using the -c option. If the connection to *systemname* fails, a connection is attempted, using *systemname* as a LAN-specific address. Use the -l option to specify a device associated with a direct connection. If the connection is truly a direct connection to the remote system, then there is no need to specify a *systemname*. This case is the only one where a *telno* or *systemname* parameter is unnecessary. On the other hand, there may be cases in which the specified device connects to a dialer, so it is valid to specify a telephone number. Do not specify both the -c and -l options on the same command line.

Conversation Phase

After making the connection, cu runs as two processes:

- The transmit process reads data from the standard input and, except for lines beginning with ~, passes it to the remote system.
- The receive process accepts data from the remote system and, except for lines beginning with ~, passes it to the standard output. Normally, an automatic DC3/DC1 protocol controls input from the remote so the buffer is not overrun. Lines beginning with ~ have special meanings.

Commands

The transmit process interprets the following user-initiated commands:

~.	Terminate the conversation.
~!	Escape to an interactive shell on the local system.
~%break	Transmit a BREAK to the remote system (can also be specified as ~%b).
~%cd	Change the directory on the local system. Note: ~!cd runs the command in a subshell, probably not what was intended.
~!*cmd*...	Run *cmd* on the local system (by using sh -c).
~$*cmd*...	Run *cmd* locally and send its output to the remote system.
~%debug	Toggle the -d debugging option on or off (can also be specified as ~%d).

~%divert	Allow/disallow unsolicited diversions not specified by ~%take.
~%ifc	Toggle between DC3/DC1 input control protocol and no input control. This command is useful when the remote system does not respond properly to the DC3 and DC1 characters (can also be specified as ~%nostop).
~l	Print the values of the termio structure variables for the remote communication line (useful for debugging).
~~*line*	Send the line ~ *line* to the remote system.
~%nostop	Same as ~%ifc.
~%ofc	Toggle the output flow control setting. When enabled, outgoing data may be flow-controlled by the remote host (can also be specified as ~%nostop).
~%old	Allow/disallow old-style syntax for received diversions.
~%put *from* [*to*]	
	Copy file *from* (on local system) to file *to* on remote system. If you omit *to*, use the *from* argument in both places.
~t	Print the values of the termio structure variables for the user's terminal (useful for debugging).
~%take *from* [*to*]	
	Copy file *from* (on the remote system) to file *to* on the local system. If you omit *to*, use the *from* argument in both places.

The receive process normally copies data from the remote system to the standard output of the local system. It may also direct the output to local files.

The use of ~%put requires stty(1) and cat(1) on the remote side. It also requires that the current erase and kill characters on the remote system be identical to these current control characters on the local system. Backslashes are inserted at appropriate places.

The use of ~%take requires the existence of echo(1) and cat(1) on the remote system and also requires that the remote system must be using the Bourne shell, sh. Also, Tabs mode (see stty(1)) should be set on the remote system if Tabs are to be copied without expansion to spaces.

When cu is used on system X to connect to system Y and subsequently used on system Y to connect to system Z, commands on system Y can be executed by use of ~~. Executing a tilde command reminds the user of the local system uname. For example, uname can be executed on Z, X, and Y as follows.

```
uname
Z
~[X]!uname
X
~~[Y]!uname
Y
```

In general, ~ executes the command on the original machine. ~~ executes the command on the next machine in the chain.

Notes

The cu command takes the default action on receipt of signals, with the exception of the following signals.

SIGHUP   Close the connection and terminate.

SIGINT   Forward to the remote system.

SIGQUIT   Forward to the remote system.

SIGUSR1   Terminate the cu process without the normal connection closing sequence.

The cu command does not do any integrity checking on data it transfers. Data fields with special cu characters may not be transmitted properly. Depending on the interconnection hardware, it may be necessary to use a ~. to terminate the conversion, even if you use stty 0. Nonprinting characters are not dependably transmitted with either the ~%put or ~%take commands. You cannot use ~%put and ~%take over multiple links. You must move files one link at a time.

cu artificially slows transmission during the ~%put operation so that loss of data is unlikely. Files transferred with ~%take or ~%put must contain a trailing newline; otherwise, the operation hangs. Entering a Control-D command usually clears the hang condition.

Examples

The following example dials a system whose telephone number is 9 1 201 555 1234, using 1200 baud (where dial tone is expected after the 9). If you do not specify a speed, Any is the default value.

```
castle% cu -s 1200 9=12015551234
```

The following example logs in to a system connected by a direct line.

```
castle% cu -l /dev/term/b
```

or

```
castle% cu -l term/b
```

The following example dials a system with a specific line and speed.

```
castle% cu -s 1200 -l term/b
```

To connect to a specific system by name, use

```
castle% cu systemname
```

Environment Variables

See environ(5) for descriptions of the following environment variables that affect the execution of cu: LC_CTYPE, LC_MESSAGES, and NLSPATH.

Exit Status

0   Successful completion.

>0   An error occurred.

Files

/etc/uucp/Devices

Device file.

/etc/uucp/Sysfiles

System file.

/etc/uucp/Systems

System file.

/var/spool/locks/*

Lock file.

Attributes

See attributes(5) for descriptions of the following attributes:

Attribute Type	Attribute Value
Availability	SUNWbnuu

See Also

New!

cat(1), echo(1), stty(1), tip(1), uname(1), ct(1C), uuname(1C), uucp(1C), remote(4), attributes(5), environ(5)
System Administration Guide: IP Services

cut — Cut Out Selected Fields of Each Line of a File

Synopsis

```
/usr/bin/cut -b list [-n] [file...]
/usr/bin/cut -c list [file...]
/usr/bin/cut -f list [-d delim] [-s] [file...]
```

Description

Use cut to cut out columns from a table or fields from each line of a file; in database parlance, cut implements the projection of a relation. The fields as specified by *list* can be fixed length, that is, character positions as on a punched card (-c option), or the length can vary from line to line and be marked with a field delimiter character like Tab (-f option). You can use cut as a filter.

Note — You must specify the -b, -c, or -f option.

Use grep(1) to make horizontal cuts (by context) through a file, or paste(1) to put files together column-wise (that is, horizontally). To reorder columns in a table, use cut and paste.

Options

-b *list*	Specify byte positions (for instance, -b1-72 would pass the first 72 bytes of each line). When you use -b and -n together, *list* is adjusted so that no multibyte character is split. If you use -b, the input line should contain 1023 bytes or less.
-c *list*	Specify character positions (for instance, -c1-72 would pass the first 72 characters of each line).
-d *delim*	Specify the field delimiter character (-f option only). Default is t for Tab. You must quote space or other characters with special meaning to the shell. *delim* can be a multibyte character.
-f *list*	Specify list of fields assumed to be separated in the file by a delimiter character (see -d); for instance, -f1,7 copies the first and seventh field only. Lines with no field delimiters are passed through intact (useful for table subheadings) unless you specify -s. If you use -f, the input line should contain 1023 characters or less.
-n	Do not split characters. When you use -b*list* and -n together, *list* is adjusted so that no multibyte character is split.
-s	Suppress lines with no delimiter characters for the -f option. Unless specified, lines with no delimiters are passed through untouched.

Operands

file	A path name of an input file. If you specify no *file* operands or if a *file* operand is -, use the standard input.
list	A comma-separated or blank-character-separated list of integer field numbers (in increasing order), with optional - to indicate ranges (for instance, 1,4,7; 1-3,8; -5,10 (short for 1-5,10); or 3 (short for third through last field)).

Usage

See largefile(5) for the description of the behavior of cut when encountering files greater than or equal to 2 Gbytes (2**31 bytes).

Examples

The following example maps user IDs to names.

```
castle% cut -d: -f1,5 /etc/passwd
root:Super-User
daemon:
bin:
sys:
adm:Admin
lp:Line Printer Admin
smtp:Mail Daemon User
uucp:uucp Admin
nuucp:uucp Admin
listen:Network Admin
nobody:Nobody
```

```
noaccess:No Access User
nobody4:SunOS 4.x Nobody
winsor:
ray:
des:
rob:
castle%
```

The following Bourne shell example sets name to the current login name.

```
$ name=`who am i | cut -f1 -d' '`
$ echo $name
winsor
$
```

Environment Variables

See environ(5) for descriptions of the following environment variables that affect the execution of cut: LC_CTYPE, LC_MESSAGES, and NLSPATH.

Exit Status

0   All input files were output successfully.

>0   An error occurred.

Attributes

See attributes(5) for descriptions of the following attributes:

Attribute Type	Attribute Value
Availability	SUNWcsu
CSI	Enabled

See Also

grep(1), paste(1), attributes(5), environ(5), largefile(5)

Diagnostics

cut: -n may only be used with -b

cut: -d may only be used with -f

cut: -s may only be used with -f

cut: cannot open <file>

> Either *file* cannot be read or does not exist. If multiple files are present, processing continues.

cut: no delimiter specified

> Missing *delim* on -d option.

cut: invalid delimiter

cut: no list specified

> Missing *list* on -b, -c, or -f option.

```
cut: invalid range specifier
cut: too many ranges specified
cut: range must be increasing
cut: invalid character in range
cut: internal error processing input
cut: invalid multibyte character
cut: unable to allocate enough memory
```

D

---

date — Write the Date and Time

Synopsis

```
/usr/bin/date [-u] [+format]
/usr/bin/date [-a [-]sss.fff]
/usr/bin/date [-u] [[mmdd]HHMM | mmddHHMM[cc]yy] [.SS]

/usr/xpg4/bin/date [-u] [+format]
/usr/xpg4/bin/date [-a [-]sss.fff]
/usr/xpg4/bin/date [-u] [[mmdd]HHMM | mmddHHMM[cc]yy] [.SS]
```

New!

Description

The date command writes the date and time to standard output or tries to set the system date and time. By default, the current date and time are written.

Specifications of native language translations of month and weekday names are supported. The month and weekday names used for a language are based on the locale specified by the environment variable LC_TIME; see environ(5).

The following is the default form for the C locale:

```
%a %b %e %T %Z %Y
```

where

%a	Day of the week.
%b	Month.
%e	Date.

%T	Time.
%Z	Time zone.
%Y	Year.

For example:

```
Fri Jan  8 13:15:42 WST 1999
```

Note — If you try to set the current date to one of the dates that the
standard and alternate time zones change (for example, the date that
daylight saving time is starting or ending), and you try to set the time to a
time in the interval between the end of standard time and the beginning of
the alternate time (or the end of the alternate time and the beginning of
standard time), the results are unpredictable.

New!

Changing the date with the date command within windowing environments
is unsafe and can lead to unpredictable results. If you change the date
rapidly back and forth, it can also be unsafe to change the date in multiuser
mode, that is, outside of a windowing system. The recommended way to
change the date is date -a.

Options

-a [-]*sss.fff*

Slowly adjust the time by *sss.fff* seconds (*fff* represents fractions of
a second). This adjustment can be positive or negative. The system's
clock is speeded up or slowed down until it has drifted by the number
of seconds specified.

-u

Display (or set) the date in Greenwich Mean Time (GMT-universal
time), bypassing the normal conversion to (or from) local time.

Operands

+*format*

If the argument begins with +, the output of date is the result of passing
format and the current time to strftime(). date uses the conversion
specifications listed on the strftime(3C) manual page, with the
conversion specification for %C determined by whether you use
/usr/bin/date or /usr/xpg4/bin/date:

| /usr/bin/date | Locale's date and time representation. This is the default output for date. |
| /usr/xpg4/bin/date | Century (a year divided by 100 and truncated to an integer) as a decimal number [00-99]. |

The string is always terminated with a newline. You must quote an
argument containing blanks.

mm

Month number.

dd

Day number in the month.

HH	Hour number (24-hour system).
MM	Minute number.
SS	Second number
cc	Century (a year divided by 100 and truncated to an integer) as a decimal number [00-99]. For example, *cc* is 19 for the year 1988 and 20 for the year 2007.
yy	Last two digits of the year number. If you do not specify century (*cc*), then values in the range 66-99 refer to years 1969-1999, and values in the range 00-68 refer to the years 2000 to 2068.

You can omit the month, day, year, and century. The current values are applied as defaults. The following example sets the date to Oct 8, 12:45 a.m.

```
date 10080045
```

Because no year is supplied, the current year is the default. The system operates in GMT. date takes care of the conversion to and from local standard and daylight time. Only superuser can change the date. After successfully setting the date and time, date displays the new date according to the default format. The date command uses TZ to determine the correct time zone information. See environ(5).

Examples

The following command displays the current date and time in a format different from that of the default.

```
castle% date '+DATE: %m/%d/%y%nTIME: %H:%M:%S'
DATE: 01/08/99
TIME: 13:59:38
castle%
```

The following command sets the current time to 12:34:56.

```
castle% su
Password:
castle# date 1234.56
Fri Jan  8 12:34:56 WST 1999
castle#
```

The following command sets the date to January 1, 12:30 a.m., 2002.

```
# date -u 010100302002
#
```

This date is displayed as follows.

```
Thu Jan 01 00:30:00 GMT 2002
```

Environment Variables

See environ(5) for descriptions of the following environment variables that affect the execution of date: LC_CTYPE, LC_TIME, LC_MESSAGES, and NLSPATH.

TZ   Determine the time zone in which the time and date are written, unless you specify the -u option. If the TZ variable is not set and you do not specify the -u option, the system default time zone is used.

Exit Status

0   Successful completion.

>0   An error occurred.

Attributes

See attributes(5) for descriptions of the following attributes:

/usr/bin/date

Attribute Type	Attribute Value
Availability	SUNWcsu
CSI	Enabled

/usr/xpg4/bin/date

Attribute Type	Attribute Value
Availability	SUNWxcu4
CSI	Enabled

See Also

strftime(3C), attributes(5), environ(5), xpg4(5)

Diagnostics

no permission

        You are not superuser and you tried to change the date.

bad conversion

        The date set is syntactically incorrect.

dc — Desk Calculator

Synopsis

/usr/bin/dc [*filename*]

Description

The dc desktop calculator is an arbitrary-precision arithmetic package. Ordinarily, it operates on decimal integers, but you can specify an input base, output base, and a number of fractional digits to be maintained. The dc command uses postfix notation (so-called reverse Polish). With postfix notation, first you type two numbers, one on each line, and then the operator. To print the results on the screen, you type the **p** command as shown in the following example.

```
castle% dc
2
2
+
p
4
q
castle%
```

Type **q** to exit dc.

The dc command also can accept several commands on a single line. You must delimit numbers by white space, but you can run other commands together. For example, you could write the previous example in the following way:

```
castle% dc
2 2+p
4
q
castle%
```

The dc command is stack oriented, which means that all operations take place on a single variable stack. The dc command recognizes the arithmetic operators + (addition), – (subtraction), / (division), * (multiplication), % (remainder), and ^ (exponentiation). Each of these operators pops the top two numbers off the stack, performs the operation, and pushes the result of the operation back onto the stack in place of the two numbers. You use the p (print) command to display the results. Additional special commands enable you to further control operations.

If you give a *filename* argument, dc takes input from that file until its end, then accepts further input from the standard input.

Note — bc is a preprocessor for dc. bc provides infix notation and a C-like syntax that implements functions. bc also provides reasonable control structures for programs. See bc(1).

Usage

The constructions that the dc command recognizes are listed below.

number	Push the value of *number* onto the stack. A number is an unbroken string of the digits 0-9. You can precede *number* by an underscore (_) to input a negative number. Numbers can contain decimal points.
+ - / * % ^	Add (+), subtract (-), multiply (*), divide (/), remainder (%), or exponentiate (^) the top two values onto the stack. Pop the two entries off the stack; push the result onto the stack in their place. Ignore any fractional part of an exponent.
s*x*, S*x*	Pop the top of the stack, and store into a register named *x*, where *x* can be any character. If you capitalize the S, treat *x* as a stack and push the value onto it.
l*x*, L*x*	Push the value in register *x* onto the stack. The register *x* is not altered. All registers start with zero value. If you capitalize the L, treat register *x* as a stack and pop its top value onto the main stack.
d	Duplicate the top value onto the stack.
p	Print the top value onto the stack. The top value remains unchanged.
P	Interpret the top of the stack as an ASCII string, remove it, and print it.
f	Print all values onto the stack.
q	Exit the program. If executing a string, pop the recursion level by 2.
Q	Exit the program. Pop the top value onto the stack, and pop the string execution level by that value.
x	Treat the top element of the stack as a character string and execute it as a string of dc commands.
X	Replace the number on the top of the stack with its scale factor.
[...]	Put the bracketed ASCII string onto the top of the stack.
<*x* >*x* =*x*	Pop the top two elements of the stack and compare. Evaluate register *x* if they obey the stated relation.
v	Replace the top element on the stack by its square root. Take into account any existing fractional part of the argument, but otherwise ignore the scale factor.
!	Interpret the rest of the line as a shell command.
c	Pop all values onto the stack.
i	Pop the top value onto the stack, and use as the number radix for further input.
I	Push the input base on the top of the stack.
o	Pop the top value onto the stack, and use as the number radix for further output.
O	Push the output base on the top of the stack.

k   Pop the top of the stack. and use that value as a nonnegative scale factor: print the appropriate number of places on output, and maintain during multiplication, division, and exponentiation. The interaction of scale factor, input base, and output base are reasonable if all are changed together.

K   Push the current scale factor on the top of the stack.

z   The stack level is pushed on the stack.

Z   Replace the number on the top of the stack with its length.

?   Take a line of input from the input source (usually the terminal) and execute it.

Y   Display dc debugging information.

; :   Used by bc(1) for array operations.

Examples

The following example prints the first ten values of n!. First we create a file named examples that contains the following three lines.

```
[la1+dsa*pla10>y]sy
0sa1
1yx
```

When you run the command, the first ten values of n! are displayed.

```
castle% dc examples
1
2
6
24
120
720
5040
40320
362880
3628800
```

Attributes

See attributes(5) for descriptions of the following attributes:

Attribute Type	Attribute Value
Availability	SUNWesu

See Also

bc(1), attributes(5)

Diagnostics

```
x is unimplemented
```

x is an octal number.

out of space The free list is exhausted (too many digits).

out of stack space

Too many pushes onto the stack (stack overflow).

empty stack Too many pops from the stack (stack underflow).

nesting depth

Too many levels of nested execution.

divide by 0 Division by zero.

sqrt of neg number

Square root of a negative number is not defined (no imaginary numbers).

exp not an integer

dc processes only integer exponentiation.

exp too big The largest exponent allowed is 999.

input base is too large

The input base x: 2<= x <= 16.

input base is too small

The input base x: 2<= x <= 16.

output base is too large

The output base must be no larger than BC_BASE_MAX.

invalid scale factor

Scale factor cannot be less than 1.

scale factor is too large

A scale factor cannot be larger than BC_SCALE_MAX.

symbol table overflow

You have specified too many variables.

invalid index

Index cannot be less than 1.

index is too large

An index cannot be larger than BC_DIM_MAX.

deallocate — Device Deallocation

New!

Synopsis

```
/usr/sbin/deallocate [-s] device
/usr/sbin/deallocate [-s] [-F] device
/usr/sbin/deallocate [-s] -I
```

Description

Use the deallocate command, new in the Solaris 9 Operating Environment, to deallocate a device allocated to the evoking user.

The Solaris 9 Operating Environment provides a device-allocation method—with the allocate(1), deallocate(1), dminfo(1M), and list_devices(1) commands—that fulfills the Trusted Computer System Evaluation Criteria (TCSEC) object-reuse requirement for computing systems at C2 level and above. The device allocation mechanism prevents simultaneous access to a device, prevents one user from reading media written to by another user, and prevents one user from accessing any information from the device or driver internal storage after another user is finished with the device.

When you perform deallocation or forced deallocation, the appropriate device cleaning program is executed, based on the contents of device_allocate(4). These cleaning programs are normally stored in /etc/security/lib.

Options

device	Deallocate the device associated with the device special file specified by *device*.
	device can be a device defined in device_allocate(4) or one of the device special files associated with the device. The command resets the ownership and the permission on all device special files associated with *device*, disabling the user's access to that device. An authorized user can use this option to remove access to the device by another user. The required authorization is solaris.device.allocate.
-F device	Force deallocation of the device associated with the file specified by device. Only a user with the solaris.devices.revoke authorization is permitted to use this option.
-I	Force deallocation of all allocatable devices. Only a user with the solaris.devices.revoke authorization is permitted to use this option. Use this option only at system initialization.
-s	Silent. Suppress any diagnostic output.

Diagnostics

deallocate returns a non-zero exit status in the event of an error.

Files

/etc/security/device_allocate

>   Mandatory access control information about each device.

/etc/security/device_maps

>   Access control information about each physical device.

/etc/security/dev/*

>   Lock files that must exist for each allocatable device.

/etc/security/lib/*

>   Device allocate files.

Attributes

See attributes(5) for descriptions of the following attributes.

Attribute Type	Attribute Value
Availability	SUNWcsu

See Also

allocate(1), list_devices(1), bsmconv(1M), dminfo(1M), device_allocate(4), device_maps(4), attributes(5)

delta, sccs-delta — Make a Delta to an SCCS File

Synopsis

/usr/ccs/bin/delta [-dnps] [-g *sid-list* | -g*sid-list*] [-m *mr-list* | -m*mr-list*] [-r *sid* | -r*sid*] [-y[*comment*]] s.*filename*...
/usr/xpg4/bin/delta [-dnps] [-g *sid-list* | -g*sid-list*] [-m *mr-list* | -m*mr-list*] [-r *sid* | -r*sid*] [-y[*comment*]] s.*filename*...

Description

See sccs-delta(1).

deroff — Remove nroff/troff, tbl, and eqn Constructs

Synopsis

/usr/bin/deroff [-m [m | s | l] [-w] [-i] [*filename*...]

Description

deroff reads each of the file names in sequence; it removes all troff(1) requests, macro calls, backslash constructs, eqn(1) constructs (between .EQ and .EN lines and between delimiters), and tbl(1) descriptions, perhaps replacing them with white space (blanks and blank lines). Then, deroff writes the remainder of the file on the standard output. deroff follows chains of included files (.so and .nx troff commands); if a file has already been included, a .so naming that file is ignored and a .nx naming that file terminates execution.

If you specify no input file, deroff reads the standard input.

Note — deroff is not a complete troff interpreter, so it can be confused by subtle constructs. Most such errors result in too much instead of too little output.

Options

-mm | s | l   You can follow the –m option with an m, s, or l. The –mm option interprets the macros so that only running text is output (that is, no text from macro lines). The –ml option forces the –mm option and also deletes lists associated with the mm macros. Note that the –ml option does not handle nested lists correctly.

-w   Output a word list, one word per line, and delete all other characters. In text, a word is any string that contains at least two letters and is composed of letters, digits, ampersands (&), and apostrophes (ꞌ); in a macro call, however, a word is a string that begins with at least two letters and contains a total of at least three letters. Delimiters are any characters other than letters, digits, apostrophes, and ampersands. Trailing apostrophes and ampersands are removed from words.

-i   Ignore troff .so and .nx commands.

Examples

The following example uses the more command to display the beginning lines of the deroff.1 manual page, then uses the deroff command to remove formatting constructs.

```
castle% more deroff.1
'\" t
.\" @(#)deroff.1 1.26 97/01/03 SMI;
.\" Copyright 1989 AT&T
.nr X
.TH deroff 1 "14 Sep 1992"
.SH NAME
deroff \- remove nroff/troff, tbl, and eqn constructs
.SH SYNOPSIS
.B deroff
[
.B \-m
[
.B m
\|]\|
.B s
\|]\|
```

```
.B l
] [
.B \-w
] [
.B \-i
] [
.IR filename \|.\|.\|.\|
]
.SH DESCRIPTION
.IX "deroff command" "" "\fLderoff\fP \(em remove \fLnroff\fP,
  \fLtroff\fP, \fLtbl\fP and \fL
eqn\fP constructs"
.IX "nroff utilities" "remove nroff/troff, tbl, and eqn constructs" ""
  "remove \fLnroff\fP, \
fLtroff\fP, \fLtbl\fP and \fLeqn\fP constructs \(em \fLderoff\fP"
.IX "troff utilities" "remove nroff/troff, tbl, and eqn constructs" ""
  "remove \fLnroff\fP, \
fLtroff\fP, \fLtbl\fP and \fLeqn\fP constructs \(em \fLderoff\fP"
.IX "tbl" "remove nroff/troff, tbl, and eqn constructs" "" "remove
  \fLnroff\fP, \fLtroff\fP,
\fLtbl\fP and \fLeqn\fP constructs \(em \fLderoff\fP"
.IX "eqn" "remove nroff/troff, tbl, and eqn constructs" "" "remove
  \fLnroff\fP, \fLtroff\fP,
\fLtbl\fP and \fLeqn\fP constructs \(em \fLderoff\fP"
.IX "document production" "remove nroff/troff, tbl, and eqn constructs"
  "" "remove \fLnroff\f
P, \fLtroff\fP, \fLtbl\fP and \fLeqn\fP constructs \(em \fLderoff\fP"
.B deroff
reads each
of the
.I filenames
in sequence
and removes all
.BR troff (1)
requests, macro calls, backslash constructs,
.BR eqn (1)
constructs
(between
.B \&.EQ
and
.SM
...
castle% deroff deroff.1

    SMI;
 Copyright  AT&T

 deroff    Sep
 NAME
deroff    remove nroff/troff, tbl, and eqn constructs
 SYNOPSIS
 deroff
 [
```

```
[

  |

  |

] [

] [

] [
 filename
]
DESCRIPTION
deroff command    deroff    remove   nroff    troff    tbl   and   eqn
  constructs
 nroff utilities remove nroff/troff, tbl, and eqn constructs   remove
  nroff    troff    tbl   and   eqn   constructs     deroff
 troff utilities remove nroff/troff, tbl, and eqn constructs   remove
  nroff    troff    tbl   and   eqn   constructs     deroff
 tbl remove nroff/troff, tbl, and eqn constructs   remove  nroff   troff
  tbl   and   eqn   constructs     deroff
 eqn remove nroff/troff, tbl, and eqn constructs   remove  nroff   troff
  tbl   and   eqn   constructs     deroff
 document production remove nroff/troff, tbl, and eqn constructs   remove
  nroff    troff    tbl   and   eqn   constructs     deroff
 deroff
reads each
of the
 filenames
in sequence
and removes all
 troff
requests, macro calls, backslash constructs,
 eqn
constructs
(between

and
...
```

Attributes

See attributes(5) for descriptions of the following attributes:

Attribute Type	Attribute Value
Availability	SUNWdoc

See Also

eqn(1), nroff(1), tbl(1), troff(1), attributes(5)

df — Display Status of Disk Space on File Systems

Synopsis

    /usr/ucb/df [-a] [-i] [-t *type*] [*filesystem*...] [*filename*...]

Description

> **Note —** The /usr/bin/df command is in Section 1M.

The /usr/ucb/df command, provided for BSD compatibility, displays the amount of disk space occupied by currently mounted file systems, the amount of used and available space, and the amount of the file system's total capacity that has been used.

If arguments to df are path names, df produces a report on the file system containing the named file. Thus df . shows the amount of space on the file system containing the current directory.

Options

-a	Report on all file systems including the uninteresting ones that have zero total blocks (that is, automounter).
-i	Report the number of used and free inodes. Print * if no information is available.
-t *type*	Report on file systems of a given type (for example, nfs or ufs),

Examples

The following example shows the output of the df command.

```
example% df
Filesystem     kbytes   used   avail   capacity   Mounted on
sparky:/         7445   4714   1986       70%      /
sparky:/usr    42277  35291   2758       93%      /usr
example%
```

Note that used + avail is less than the amount of space in the file system (kbytes) because the system reserves a fraction of the space in the file system to allow its file system allocation routines to work well. The amount reserved is typically about 10 percent; you can adjust this amount with tunefs (see tunefs(1M)). When all the space on a file system except for this reserve is in use, only superuser can allocate new files and data blocks to existing files. When a file system is overallocated in this way, df may report that the file system is more than 100 percent used.

Files

    /etc/mnttab

> List of file systems currently mounted.

    /etc/vfstab

> List of default parameters for each file system.

Attributes

See attributes(5) for descriptions of the following attributes:

Attribute Type	Attribute Value
Availability	SUNWscpu

See Also

du(1M), quot(1M), tunefs(1M), mnttab(4), attributes(5)

dhcpinfo — Display Value of Parameters Received through DHCP

Synopsis

```
/sbin/dhcpinfo [-c] [-i interface] [-n limit] code
/sbin/dhcpinfo [-c] [-i interface] [-n limit] identifier
```

New!

Description

DHCP (Dynamic Host Configuration Protocol) permits a client to establish an endpoint for communication with a network by delivering an IP address of one or more of the client's network interfaces and a "lease" on that address. Use the dhcpinfo command to print the value(s) of the parameter requested on the command line as supplied by the DHCP protocol. If the DHCP parameter implies more than one value (that is, a list of gateways), the values are printed, separated by newline characters. The parameter can be identified either by its numeric value in the DHCP protocol, by its mnemonic identifier, or by its long name. This value is intended to be used in command substitutions in the shell scripts invoked by init(1M) at system boot. init first contacts the DHCP agent daemon dhcpagent(1M) to verify that DHCP has successfully completed. When a particular interface is given with the -i option, the daemon verifies successful DHCP configuration of that specific interface; otherwise, the client verifies that the interface marked as the "primary" has successfully configured and supplies the name of that interface back to dhcpinfo. You should not use parameter values echoed by dhcpinfo without checking the exit status.

See dhcptags(4) for the list of mnemonic identifier codes and names of all DHCP parameters. See *DHCP Options and BOOTP Vendor Extensions* (RFC 2132) for more detail.

Output Format

New!

New in the Solaris 8 release, the output from dhcpinfo consists of one or more lines of ASCII text. The format of the output depends on the requested parameter. The number of values returned per line is determined by the parameter's granularity. The total number of lines output for a given parameter is determined by the parameter's maximum values as defined by dhcp_inittab(4).

The format of each individual value is determined by the data type of the option, as determined by dhcp_inittab(4).

The possible data types and their formats are listed below.

Data Type	Format	dhcp_inittab(4) Type
Unsigned Number	One or more decimal digits	UNUMBER8, UNUMBER16, UNUMBER32, UNUMBER64
Signed Number	One or more decimal digits optional, preceded with a minus sign	SNUMBER8, SNUMBER16, SNUMBER64
IP Address	Dotted-decimal notation	IP
Octet	The string 0xR followed by a two-digit hexadecimal value	OCTET
String	Zero or more ASCII characters	ASCII

Options

New!   -c   Display the output in a canonical format. This format is identical to the OCTET format with a granularity of 1. New in the Solaris 8 release.

-i *interface*

In general, you should need to use this option only on hardware with two or more interfaces configurable by DHCP, and for a parameter that is interface specific.

-n *limit*   When the *tag* is one with a list of values, limit the number printed.

Operands

New!   *code*   Numeric code for the requested DHCP parameter as defined by the DHCP specification. Vendor options are specified by adding 256 to the actual vendor code. New in the Solaris 8 release.

New!   *identifier*   Mnemonic symbol for the requested DHCP parameter as listed in dhcp_inittab(4).

Exit Status

0   Successful operation.

2   DHCP was not successful. The DHCP agent may not be running, the interface might have failed to configure, or no satisfactory DHCP responses were received.

3   Bad arguments.

4   A timer was set with wait (see ifconfig(1M)), and the interface had not configured before it expired.

6   Some system error (should never occur).

Attributes

See `attributes`(5) for descriptions of the following attributes:

Attribute Type	Attribute Value
Availability	SUNWcsr

See Also

`dhcpagent(1M)`, `ifconfig(1M)`, `init(1M)`, `dhcp_inittab(4)`, `attributes(5)`   *New!*
Alexander, S., and R. Droms, *DHCP Options and BOOTP Vendor Extensions*, RFC 2132,
Silicon Graphics, Inc., Bucknell University, March 1997.

diff — Display Line-by-Line Differences between Pairs of Text Files

Synopsis

```
/usr/bin/diff [-bitw] [-c | -e | -f | -h | -n | -u] file1 file2
/usr/bin/diff [-bitw] [-C number | -U number] file1 file2
/usr/bin/diff [-bitw] [-D string] file1 file2
/usr/bin/diff [-bitw] [-c | -e | -f | -h | -n] [-l] [-r] [-s] [-S name]
    file1 file2
```

New!
New!

Description

The `diff` command compares the contents of *file1* and *file2* line by line and produces
a complete index of all of the lines that differ between the two files, along with their line
numbers. It also reports what must be changed to make the files match. No output is
produced if the files are identical.

The following example illustrates the `diff` output for two simple files.

```
castle% diff kookaburra1 kookaburra2
4c4
< Gay your life must be.
---
> Glad your life must be.
castle%
```

Each section of the `diff` output begins with a code that indicates what kinds of
differences the following lines refer to. In the previous example, the differences are
marked with the code 4c4. This code tells you that there is a change (c) between line 4
in the first file and line 4 in the second file. Lines containing text found only in the first
file begin with <. Lines containing text found only in the second file begin with >. The
dashed line separates parts of the output that refer to different sections of the files.

The normal output contains lines of these forms:

```
n1 a n3,n4
n1,n2 d n3
n1,n2 c n3,n4
```

where $n1$ and $n2$ represent lines in *file1* and $n3$ and $n4$ represent lines in *file2*. The a (append) code indicates that a line is added following the line in the first file. The d (delete) code indicates that lines are found in one file but not in the other. The c (change) code indicates that there is a change between the lines in the two files.

These lines resemble ed(1) or vi(1) commands to convert *file1* to *file2*. By exchanging a for d and reading backward, you can convert *file2* to *file1*. As in ed, identical pairs, where $n1=n2$ or $n3=n4$, are abbreviated as a single number.

Following each of these lines come all the lines that are affected in the first file flagged by <, then all the lines that are affected in the second file flagged by >.

Note — Editing scripts produced under the -e or -f options are naive about creating lines consisting of a single period (.).

A missing newline at end-of-file indicates that the last line of the file in question did not have a newline. If the lines are different, they are flagged and output, although the output seems to indicate they are the same.

Options

-b   Ignore trailing blanks (spaces and tabs) and treat other strings of blanks as equivalent.

-i   Ignore the case of letters; for example, compare A equal to a.

-t   Expand Tab characters in output lines. Normal or -c output adds character(s) to the front of each line that may adversely affect the indentation of the original source lines and make the output lines difficult to interpret. This option preserves the original source's indentation.

-w   Ignore all blanks (space and Tab characters) and treat all other strings of blanks as equivalent; for example, if (a == b) compares equal to if(a==b).

Options for the diff command that are mutually exclusive are listed below.

-c   Produce a listing of differences with three lines of context. With this option, output format is modified slightly: Output begins with identification of the files involved and their creation dates, then each change is separated by a line with a dozen asterisks. The lines removed from *file1* are marked with –; those added to *file2* are marked +. Lines that are changed from one file to the other are marked in both files with !.

-C *number*   Produce a listing of differences identical to that produced by -c with *number* lines of context.

-D *string*   Create a merged version of *file1* and *file2* with C preprocessor controls included so that a compilation of the result without defining *string* is equivalent to compiling *file1*, while defining *string* yields *file2*.

-e	Produce a script of only a, c, and d commands for the editor ed, which recreates *file2* from *file1*. In connection with -e, the following shell program may help maintain multiple versions of a file. Only an ancestral file ($1) and a chain of version-to version ed scripts ($2,$3,...) made by diff need be on hand. A latest version appears on the standard output.

```
(shift; cat $*; echo '1,$p') | ed - $1
```

Except in rare circumstances, diff finds a smallest sufficient set of file differences.

-f	Produce a script similar to -e in the opposite order. Not useful with ed.
-h	Do a fast, half-hearted job. This option works only when changed stretches are short and well separated but does work on files of unlimited length. Options -c, -e, -f, and -n are unavailable with -h. diff does not descend into directories with this option.
-n	Produce a script similar to -e, but in the opposite order and with a count of changed lines on each insert or delete command.
-u	List differences with three lines of context. The output is similar to the -c option except that the context is unified. Removed and changed lines in *file1* are marked with a -; lines added or changed in *file2* are marked with a +. Both versions of changed lines are shown in the output. Added, removed, and context lines are shown only once. The identification of *file1* and *file2* is different, with --- used instead of the -c option *** and +++ instead of the -c option ---. Each option is separated by a line of the following form.

New!

```
@@ -n1,n2+n3,n4 @@
```

This option is new in the Solaris 9 release.

-U	List differences in the same way as the -u option with numbered lines of context. This option is new in the Solaris 9 release.

New!

The following options for the diff command are used to compare directories.

-l	Produce output in long format. Before the diff, pipe each text file through pr(1) to paginate it. Remember other differences and summarize them after all text file differences are reported.
-r	Apply diff recursively to common subdirectories encountered.
-s	Report files that are the identical; these would not otherwise be mentioned.
-S *name*	Start a directory diff in the middle, beginning with the file *name*.

Operands

file1 *file2*	A path name of a file or directory to be compared. If either *file1* or *file2* is -, use the standard input in its place.
directory1 *directory2*	A path name of a directory to be compared.

If only one of *file1* and *file2* is a directory, diff is applied to the nondirectory file and the file contained in the directory file with a file name that is the same as the last component of the nondirectory file.

Usage

See largefile(5) for the description of the behavior of diff when encountering files greater than or equal to 2 Gbytes (2**31 bytes).

Examples

If dir1 is a directory containing a directory named x, dir2 is a directory containing a directory named x, dir1/x and dir2/x both contain files named date.out, and dir2/x contains a file named y, then the command:

castle% **diff -r dir1 dir2**

could produce output similar to:

```
Common subdirectories: dir1/x and dir2/x
Only in dir2/x: y
diff -r dir1/x/date.out dir2/x/date.out
1c1
< Mon Jul 2 13:12:16 PDT 1990
---
> Tue Jun 19 21:41:39 PDT 1990
```

The following example shows a comparison between two files. The test1 file was generated by the command deroff deroff.1. The test2 file was generated by the command deroff -mm deroff.1. As you can see from the diff output, the deroff -mm command dropped data from the file.

```
castle% diff test1 test2
6,10d5
<  NAME
< deroff    remove nroff/troff, tbl, and eqn constructs
<  SYNOPSIS
<  deroff
<  [
25,26d19
<  DESCRIPTION
<  deroff command    deroff    remove   nroff    troff    tbl   and   eqn
   constructs
72,73d64
<  OPTIONS
<
140,141d130
<  ATTRIBUTES
< See
145,149d133
< ATTRIBUTE TYPE          ATTRIBUTE VALUE
< =
< Availability  SUNWdoc
<  SEE ALSO
<  eqn
154,160d137
<  NOTES
```

```
< deroff
< is not a complete
<  troff
< interpreter,
< so it can be confused by subtle constructs.
< Most such errors result in too much rather than too little output.
castle%
```

Environment Variables

See environ(5) for descriptions of the following environment variables that affect the execution of diff: LC_CTYPE, LC_MESSAGES, LC_TIME, and NLSPATH.

TZ   Determine the locale for affecting the time zone used for calculating file timestamps written with the -C and -c options.

Exit Status

0   No differences were found.

1   Differences were found.

>1   An error occurred.

Files

/tmp/d?????

               Temporary file used for comparison.

/usr/lib/diffh

               Executable file for -h option.

Attributes

See attributes(5) for descriptions of the following attributes:

Attribute Type	Attribute Value
Availability	SUNWesu
CSI	Enabled

See Also

bdiff(1), cmp(1), comm(1), dircmp(1), ed(1), pr(1), sdiff(1), attributes(5), environ(5), largefile(5)

diff3 — Three-Way Differential File Comparison

Synopsis

/usr/bin/diff3 [-exEX3] *filename1 filename2 filename3*

Description

diff3 compares three versions of a file and publishes disagreeing ranges of text flagged with these codes:

====	All three files differ.
====1	*filename1* is different.
====2	*filename2* is different.
====3	*filename3* is different.

The type of change in converting a given range of a given file to some other is indicated in one of these ways:

f : n1 a — Text is to be appended after line number n1 in file *f*, where *f* = 1, 2, or 3.

f : n1 , n2 c

Text is to be changed in the range line n1 to line n2. If n1 = n2, the range may be abbreviated to n1.

The original contents of the range follow immediately after a c (change) indication. When the contents of two files are identical, the contents of the lower-numbered file are suppressed.

The following command applies the resulting script to *filename1*.

```
(cat script; echo '1,$p') | ed - filename1
```

Note — Text lines that consist of a single dot (.) defeat -e. Files longer than 64 Kbytes do not work.

Options

-3	Produce a script to incorporate only changes flagged ====3.
-e	Produce a script for the editor ed(1) that incorporates into *filename1* all changes between *filename2* and *filename3*, that is, the changes that normally would be flagged ==== and ====3.
-E	Produce a script that incorporates all changes between *filename2* and *filename3*, but treat overlapping changes (that is, changes that would be flagged with ==== in the normal listing) differently. The overlapping lines from both files are inserted by the edit script, bracketed by <<<<<< and >>>>>> lines.
-x	Produce a script to incorporate only changes flagged ====.
-X	Produce a script that incorporates only changes flagged ====, but treat these changes in the manner of the -E option.

Examples

The following example compares three files. The test1 file was generated by the command deroff deroff.1. The test2 file was generated by the command deroff -mm deroff.1. The test3 file was generated by the command deroff -ml deroff.1.

```
castle% diff3 test1 test2 test3
====1
1:6,10c
   NAME
    deroff    remove nroff/troff, tbl, and eqn constructs
    SYNOPSIS
    deroff
    [
2:5a
3:5a
====1
1:25,26c
    DESCRIPTION
    deroff command   deroff    remove  nroff   troff   tbl   and  eqn
    constructs
2:19a
3:19a
====1
1:72,73c
    OPTIONS

2:64a
3:64a
====1
1:140,141c
   ATTRIBUTES
   See
2:130a
3:130a
====1
1:145,149c
   ATTRIBUTE TYPE          ATTRIBUTE VALUE
   =
   Availability  SUNWdoc
    SEE ALSO
    eqn
2:133a
3:133a
====1
1:154,160c
    NOTES
    deroff
   is not a complete
    troff
   interpreter,
   so it can be confused by subtle constructs.
   Most such errors result in too much rather than too little output.
2:137a
3:137a
castle%
```

Usage

See largefile(5) for the description of the behavior of diff3 when encountering files greater than or equal to 2 Gbytes (2**31 bytes).

Files

/tmp/d3*

/usr/lib/diff3prog

Attributes

See attributes(5) for descriptions of the following attributes:

Attribute Type	Attribute Value
Availability	SUNWesu
CSI	Enabled

See Also

diff(1), attributes(5), largefile(5)

---

diffmk — Mark Differences between Versions of a troff Input File

Synopsis

/usr/bin/diffmk *oldfile newfile markedfile*

Description

diffmk compares two versions of a file and creates a third version that includes "change mark" (.mc) commands for nroff(1) and troff(1). *oldfile* and *newfile* are the old and new versions of the file. diffmk generates *markedfile*, which contains the text from *newfile* with troff(1) change-mark requests (.mc) inserted where *newfile* differs from *oldfile*. Formatted, changed, or inserted text in *markedfile* shows a | at the right margin of each line. The position of deleted text is shown by a single *.

Usage

See largefile(5) for the description of the behavior of diffmk when encountering files greater than or equal to 2 Gbytes (2**31 bytes).

Examples

You can also use diffmk in conjunction with the proper troff requests to produce program listings with marked changes. In the command line

castle% **diffmk old.c new.c marked.c ; nroff reqs marked.c | pr**

the file reqs contains the following troff requests that eliminate page breaks, adjust the line length, set no-fill mode, ignore escape characters, and turn off hyphenation.

```
.pl 1
.ll 77
.nf
.eo
.nh
```

   If the characters | and * are inappropriate, you might run `markedfile` through
sed(1) to globally change them.

Attributes

   See `attributes`(5) for descriptions of the following attributes:

Attribute Type	**Attribute Value**
Availability	SUNWdoc

See Also

   diff(1), nroff(1), sed(1), troff(1), attributes(5), largefile(5)

Bugs

   Aesthetic considerations may dictate manual adjustment of some output. File
   differences involving only formatting requests may produce undesirable output, that is,
   replacing `.sp` by `.sp 2` produces a change mark on the preceding or following line of
   output.

digestp — Front Ends to the mp Text to PDL Pretty Print Filter   *New!*

Synopsis

   /bin/digestp [*options*] *filename*...

Description

   See `mailp`(1).

dircmp — Directory Comparison

Synopsis

   /usr/bin/dircmp [-ds] [-w n] *dir1 dir2*

Description

   The `dircmp` command compares the contents of two directory structures. It reports on
   the files from only one directory and uses the `cmp` command to compare the files that
   appear in both directories. If you want the output to be generated in `diff` format, specify

the -d option. If you specify no options, dircmp generates a list indicating whether the file names common to both directories have the same contents.

Options

-d	Compare the contents of files with the same name in both directories and output a list telling what must be changed in the two files to bring them into agreement. The list format is described in diff(1).
-s	Suppress messages about identical files.
-w *n*	Change the width of the output line to *n* characters. The default width is 72.

Operands

dir1 *dir2*	A path name of directories to be compared.

Examples

The following example compares the contents of the two directories
/export/home/winsor/Audiofiles and /usr/demo/SOUND/sounds.

```
castle% dircmp /export/home/winsor/Audiofiles/ /usr/demo/SOUND/sounds

Jan  8 17:13 1999  /export/home/winsor/Audiofiles/ only and
   /usr/demo/SOUND/sounds only Page 1

./Audiotest
./Audiotest/mydata.au
./Audiotest/outfile.au
./file1

Jan  8 17:13 1999  Comparison of /export/home/winsor/Audiofiles/
   /usr/demo/SOUND/sounds Page 1

directory          .
same               ./bark.au
same               ./bong.au
same               ./bubbles.au
same               ./busy.au
...
castle%
```

Note — The dircmp file generated quite a few extra linefeeds, which have been removed from this example along with a number of the files that were marked same.

Usage

See largefile(5) for the description of the behavior of dircmp when encountering files greater than or equal to 2 Gbytes (2**31 bytes).

Environment Variables

See environ(5) for descriptions of the following environment variables that affect the execution of dircmp: LC_COLLATE, LC_CTYPE, LC_MESSAGES, and NLSPATH.

Exit Status

0	Successful completion.
>0	An error occurred. (Differences in directory contents are not considered errors.)

Attributes

See attributes(5) for descriptions of the following attributes:

Attribute Type	**Attribute Value**
Availability	SUNWesu

See Also

cmp(1), diff(1), attributes(5), environ(5), largefile(5)

dirname — Deliver Portions of Path Names

Synopsis

/usr/bin/dirname *string*

Description

See basename(1).

dirs — Change Working Directory

Synopsis

csh

dirs [-l]

Description

See cd(1).

dis — Object Code Disassembler

Synopsis

```
/usr/ccs/bin/dis [-C] [-o] [-V] [-L] [-d sec] [-D sec] [-F function]
    [-l string] [-t sec] file...
```

Description

New!

The dis command produces an assembly language listing of *file*, which may be an object file or an archive of object files. The listing includes assembly statements and an octal or hexadecimal representation of the binary that produced those statements. However, the IA64 listing is limited to assembly statements only.

Options

The options are interpreted by the disassembler. You can specify them in any order.

-C   Display demangled C++ symbol names in the disassembly.

-d *sec*   Disassemble the named section as data, printing the offset of the data from the beginning of the section.

-D *sec*   Disassemble the named section as data, printing the actual address of the data.

-F *function*

Disassemble only the named function in each object file specified on the command line. You can specify the -F option multiple times on the command line.

-l *string* Disassemble the archive file specified by *string*. For example, you would issue the command dis -l x -l z to disassemble libx.a and libz.a, which are assumed to be in LIB-DIR.

-L   Invoke a lookup of C-language source labels in the symbol table for subsequent writing to standard output.

-o   Print numbers in octal. The default is hexadecimal.

-t *sec*   Disassemble the named section as text.

-V   Print, on standard error, the version number of the disassembler being executed.

If you specify the -d, -D, or -t options, only those named sections from each user-supplied file are disassembled. Otherwise, all sections containing text are disassembled.

On output, a number enclosed in brackets, such as [5], at the beginning of a line indicates that the break-pointable line number starts with the following instruction. These line numbers are printed only if the file was compiled with additional debugging information, for example, the -g option of cc(1B). An expression such as <40> in the operand field or in the symbolic disassembly, following a relative displacement for control transfer instructions, is the computed address within the section to which control is transferred. A function name is displayed in the first column, followed by () if the object file contains a symbol table.

Operands

  file   A path name of an object file or an archive (see ar(1)) of object files.

Environment Variables

  See environ(5) for descriptions of the following environment variables that affect the execution of dis: LC_CTYPE, LC_MESSAGES, and NLSPATH.

  LIBDIR   Use this as the path to search for the library. If the variable contains a null value or is not set, search for the library under /usr/lib.

Exit Status

  0   Successful completion.

  >0   An error occurred.

Files

  /usr/lib Default LIBDIR.

Attributes

  See attributes(5) for descriptions of the following attributes:

Attribute Type	Attribute Value
Availability	SUNWbtool

See Also

  ar(1), as(1), ld(1), cc(1B), a.out(4), attributes(5), environ(5)

Diagnostics

  The self-explanatory diagnostics indicate errors in the command line or problems encountered with the specified files.

disable — Disable LP Printers

Synopsis

  /usr/bin/disable [-c | -W] [-r [*reason*]] *printer*...

Description

  See enable(1).

dispgid — Display a List of All Valid Group Names

Synopsis

/usr/bin/dispgid

Description

dispgid displays a list of all group names on the system (one group per line).

Examples

The following example displays the group names for the system castle.

```
castle% dispgid
root
other
bin
sys
adm
uucp
mail
tty
lp
nuucp
staff
daemon
sysadmin
nobody
noaccess
nogroup
castle%
```

Exit Status

0	Successful execution.
1	Cannot read the group file.

Attributes

See attributes(5) for descriptions of the following attributes:

Attribute Type	Attribute Value
Availability	SUNWcsu

See Also

attributes(5)

dispuid — Display a List of All Valid User Names

Synopsis
```
/usr/bin/dispuid
```

Description
dispuid displays a list of all user names on the system (one line per name).

Examples
The following example displays the user names for the system castle.

```
castle% dispuid
root
daemon
bin
sys
adm
lp
smtp
uucp
nuucp
listen
nobody
noaccess
nobody4
winsor
ray
des
rob
castle%
```

Exit Status

0	Successful execution.
1	Cannot read the password file.

Attributes
See attributes(5) for descriptions of the following attributes:

Attribute Type	Attribute Value
Availability	SUNWcsu

See Also
attributes(5)

dos2unix — Convert Text File from DOS Format to ISO Format

Synopsis

```
/usr/bin/dos2unix [-ascii] [-iso] [-7] [0437 | -850 | -860 | -863 |
    -865] originalfile convertedfile
```

Description

dos2unix converts characters in the DOS extended character set to the corresponding ISO standard characters.

You can invoke this command from either DOS or SunOS. However, the file names must conform to the conventions of the environment in which you invoke the command.

If *originalfile* and *convertedfile* are the same, dos2unix rewrites the original file after converting it.

Options

-ascii	Remove extra Returns, and convert end-of-file characters in DOS format text files to conform to SunOS requirements.
-iso	Convert characters in the DOS extended character set to the corresponding ISO standard characters (the default).
-7	Convert 8-bit DOS graphics characters to 7-bit space characters so that SunOS can read the file.

New!

On non-i386 systems, dos2unix tries to obtain the keyboard type to determine which code page to use. Otherwise, the default is US. You can override the code page with one of the following options, new in the Solaris 9 release.

-437	Use US code page.
-850	Use multilingual code page.
-860	Use Portuguese code page.
-863	Use French Canadian code page.
-865	Use Danish code page.

New! Operands

The following operands are required.

originalfile

The original file in DOS format that is being converted to ISO format.

convertedfile

The new file in ISO format that has been converted from the original DOS file format.

Attributes

See attributes(5) for descriptions of the following attributes:

Attribute Type	Attribute Value
Availability	SUNWesu

See Also

unix2dos(1), ls(1), attributes(5)

New!

Diagnostics

File *filename* not found, or no read permission

> The input file you specified does not exist, or you do not have read permission (check with the SunOS ls -l command).

Bad output filename *filename*, or no write permission

> The output file you specified is invalid or you do not have write permission for that file or the directory that contains it.

> Check also that the drive or diskette is not write protected.

Error while writing to temporary file

> An error occurred while converting your file, possibly because there is not enough space on the current drive. Check the amount of space on the current drive, using the DIR command. Also be certain that the default diskette or drive is write enabled (not write protected). Note that when this error occurs, the original file remains intact.

Could not rename temporary file to *filename*

Translated temporary file name = *filename*

> The command could not perform the final step in converting your file. Your converted file is stored under the name indicated on the second line of this message.

download — Download Host-Resident PostScript Font

Synopsis

```
/usr/lib/lp/postscript/download [-f] [-p printer] [-m name]
   [-H directory] [file...]
/usr/lib/lp/postscript/download
```

Description

download prepends host-resident fonts to files and writes the results on the standard output. If you specify no files or if - is one of the input files, download reads the standard input. download assumes the input files make up a single PostScript job and that requested fonts can be included at the start of each input file.

Requested fonts are named in a comment (marked with %%DocumentFonts:) in the input files. Available fonts are the ones listed in the map table selected with the -m option.

The map table consists of fontname-file pairs. The fontname is the full name of the PostScript font, exactly as it would appear in a %%DocumentFonts: comment. The file is the path name of the host-resident font. A file that begins with a / is used as is. Otherwise, the path name is relative to the host font directory. Comments are introduced by % (as in PostScript) and extend to the end of the line.

The only candidates for downloading are fonts listed in the map table that points download to readable files. A font is downloaded once, at most. Requests for unlisted fonts or inaccessible files are ignored. All requests are ignored if the map table cannot be read.

Note — download does not look for %%PageFonts: comments and there is no way to force multiple downloads of a particular font.

Using full path names in either map tables or the names of map tables is not recommended.

Options

-f   Force a complete scan of each input file. In the absence of an explicit comment pointing download to the end of the file, stop the default scan immediately after the PostScript header comments.

-H *directory*

Use *directory* as the host font directory. The default is /usr/lib/lp/postscript.

-m *name*   Use *name* as the font map table. A name that begins with / is the full path name of the map table and is used as is. Otherwise, *name* is appended to the path name of the host font directory.

-p *printer*

Check the list of printer-resident fonts in /etc/lp/printers/printer/residentfonts before downloading.

Examples

You could use the following map table to control the downloading of the Bookman font family:

```
%
% The first string is the full PostScript font name. The second string
% is the file name - relative to the host font directory unless it begins
% with a /.
%

Bookman-Light          bookman/light
Bookman-LightItalic    bookman/lightitalic
Bookman-Demi           bookman/demi
Bookman-DemiItalic     bookman/demiitalic
```

Using the file myprinter/map (in the default host font directory) as the map table, you could download fonts by issuing the following command.

castle% **download -m myprinter/map file**

Exit Status

0	Successful completion.
non-zero	An error occurred.

Attributes

See attributes(5) for descriptions of the following attributes:

Attribute Type	Attribute Value
Availability	SUNWpsf

See Also

dpost(1), postdaisy(1), postdmd(1), postio(1), postmd(1), postprint(1), posttek(1), attributes(5)

dpost — troff Postprocessor for PostScript Printers

Synopsis

/usr/lib/lp/postscript/dpost [-c *num*] [-e *num*] [-m *num*] [-n *num*]
    [-o *list*] [-p *mode*] [-w *num*] -x *num*] [-y *num*] [-F *dir*] [-H *dir*]
    [-L *file*] [-O] [-T *name*] [*file*...]
/usr/lib/lp/postscript/dpost

Description

dpost translates files created by troff(1) into PostScript and writes the results on the standard output. If you specify no files or if – is one of the input files, the standard input is read.

The files should be prepared by troff. The default font files in /usr/lib/font/devpost produce the best and most efficient output. They assume a resolution of 720 dpi, and you can use them to format files by adding the –Tpost option to the troff call. Older versions of the eqn and pic preprocessors need to know the resolution that troff is using to format the files. If those are the versions installed on your system, use the –r720 option with eqn and –T720 with pic.

dpost makes no assumptions about resolutions. The first x res command sets the resolution used to translate the input files, the DESC.out file, usually /usr/lib/font/devpost/DESC.out, defines the resolution used in the binary font files, and the PostScript prologue is responsible for setting up an appropriate user coordinate system.

Output files often do not conform to the file structuring conventions of Adobe. Piping the output of dpost through postreverse(1) should produce a minimally conforming PostScript file.

Although dpost can handle files formatted for any device, emulation is expensive and can easily double the print time and the size of the output file. No attempt has been made to implement the character sets or fonts available on all devices supported by troff. Missing characters are replaced by white space, and unrecognized fonts usually default to one of the Times fonts (that is, R, I, B, or BI).

An x res command must precede the first x init command, and all the input files should have been prepared for the same output device.

Note — Use of the -T option is not encouraged. Its only purpose is to enable the use of other PostScript font and device description files that, perhaps, use different resolutions, character sets, or fonts.

Although level 0 encoding is the only scheme that has been thoroughly tested, level 2 is fast and may be worth a try.

Options

-c *num*   Print *num* copies of each page. By default, only one copy is printed.

-e *num*   Set the text encoding level to *num*. The recognized values are 0, 1, and 2. The size of the output file and print time should decrease as *num* increases. Level 2 encoding typically is about 20 percent faster than level 0 (the default) and produces output essentially identical to previous versions of dpost.

-F *dir*   Use *dir* as the font directory. The default *dir* is /usr/lib/font, and dpost reads binary font files from directory /usr/lib/font/devpost.

-H *dir*   Use *dir* as the host-resident font directory. Files in this directory should be complete PostScript font descriptions. They must be assigned a name that corresponds to the appropriate two-character troff font name. Each font file is copied to the output file only when needed and at most once during each job. There is no default directory.

-L *file*   Use *file* as the PostScript prologue. The default is /usr/lib/lp/postscript/dpost.ps.

-m *num*   Magnify each logical page by the factor *num*. Scale pages uniformly about the origin, which is located near the upper-left corner of each page. The default magnification is 1.0.

-n *num*   Print *num* logical pages on each piece of paper, where *num* can be any positive integer. By default, *num* is set to 1.

-O   Disable PostScript picture inclusion. A recommended option when running dpost by a spooler in a networked environment.

-o *list*　　　Print those pages for which numbers are given in the comma-separated list. The list contains single numbers *N* and ranges *N1*–*N2*. A missing *N1* means the lowest numbered page, a missing *N2* means the highest. The page range is an expression of logical pages instead of physical sheets of paper. For example, if you are printing two logical pages to a sheet and you specify a range of 4, then two sheets of paper print, containing four page layouts. If you specified a page range of 3–4 when requesting two logical pages to a sheet, then only page 3 and page 4 layouts print on one physical sheet of paper.

-p *mode*　　　Print files in either p (portrait) or l (landscape) mode. Only the first character of *mode* is significant. The default mode is portrait.

-T *name*　　　Use font files for device *name* as the best description of available PostScript fonts. By default, *name* is set to post, and dpost reads binary files from /usr/lib/font/devpost.

-w *num*　　　Set the line width used to implement troff graphics commands to *num* points, where a point is approximately 1/72 of an inch. By default, *num* is set to 0.3 points.

-x *num*　　　Translate the origin *num* inches along the positive x axis. The default coordinate system has the origin fixed near the upper-left corner of the page, with positive x to the right and positive y down the page. Positive *num* moves everything right. The default offset is 0 inches.

-y *num*　　　Translate the origin *num* inches along the positive y axis. Positive *num* moves text up the page. The default offset is 0.

Examples

If the old versions of eqn and pic are installed on your system, you can obtain the best-looking output possible by issuing a command such as the following.

```
castle% pic -T720 file | tbl | eqn -r720 | troff -mm -Tpost | dpost
```

Otherwise, the following command should give the best results.

```
castle% pic file | tbl | eqn | troff -mm -Tpost | dpost
```

Exit Status

0　　　　　Successful completion.

non-zero　An error occurred.

Files

/usr/lib/font/devpost/*.out

/usr/lib/font/devpost/charlib/*

/usr/lib/lp/postscript/color.ps

/usr/lib/lp/postscript/draw.ps

/usr/lib/lp/postscript/forms.ps

/usr/lib/lp/postscript/ps.requests

/usr/lib/macros/pictures

/usr/lib/macros/color

Attributes

See attributes(5) for descriptions of the following attributes:

Attribute Type	Attribute Value
Availability	SUNWpsf

See Also

download(1), postdaisy(1), postdmd(1), postio(1), postmd(1),postprint(1), postreverse(1), posttek(1), troff(1), attributes(5)

du — Summarize Disk Usage

Synopsis

/usr/bin/du [-adkLr][-k | -h | -H] [-s | -o] [*file*...]
/usr/xpg4/bin/du [-a | -s][-k | -h | -H] [-rx] [*file*...]

Description

Use the du command to write to standard output the size of the file space allocated to, and the size of the file space allocated to each subdirectory of the file hierarchy rooted in each of the specified files. The size of the file space allocated to a file of type directory is defined as the sum total of space allocated to all files in the file hierarchy rooted in the directory plus the space allocated to the directory itself.

Files with multiple links are counted and written for only one entry. The directory entry that is selected in the report is unspecified. By default, file sizes are written in 512-byte units, rounded up to the next 512-byte unit.

Note — The du command was moved from section (1M) to section (1) in the Solaris 9 release.

/usr/xpg4/bin/du

When du cannot obtain file attributes or read directories (see stat(2)), it reports an error condition and the final exit status is affected.

Note — A file with two or more links is counted only once. If, however, there are links between files in different directories where the directories are on separate branches of the file system hierarchy, du counts the excess files more than once.

Files containing holes result in an incorrect block count.

Options

The following options are supported for /usr/bin/du and /usr/xpg4/bin/du.

-a   In addition to the default output, report the size of each file not of type *directory* in the file hierarchy rooted in the specified file. Regardless of the presence of the -a option, nondirectories given as file operands are always listed.

-h   Scale all sizes to a human-readable format, for example 14K, 234M, 2.7G, or 3.0T. Scaling is done by repetitively dividing by 1024. New in the Solaris 9 release.   *New!*

-H   Same as the -h option, but scaling is done by dividing by 1000 instead of 1024. New in the Solaris 9 release.   *New!*

-k   Write the files sizes in units of 1024 bytes instead of the default 512-byte units.

-s   Instead of the default output, report only the total sum for each of the specified files.

The following options are supported for /usr/bin/du only.

-d   Do not cross file-system boundaries. For example, du -d / reports usage only on the root partition.

-L   Process symbolic links by using the file or directory that the symbolic link references instead of the link itself. This option is new in the Solaris 8 release.

-o   Do not add child directories' usage to a parent's total. Without this option, the usage listed for a particular directory is the space taken by the files in that directory, as well as the files in all directories beneath it. This option does nothing if you specify -s.

-r   Generate messages about directories that cannot be read, files that cannot be opened, and so forth, instead of being silent (the default).

The following options are supported for /usr/xpg4/bin/du only.

-r   By default, generate messages about directories that cannot be read, files that cannot be opened, and so forth.

-x   When evaluating file sizes, evaluate only those files that have the same device as the file specified by the *file* operand.

Operands

file   The path name of a file whose size is to be written. If you specify no file, use the current directory.

Output

The output from du consists of the amount of the space allocated to a file and the name of the file. The following example displays the output in 512-byte blocks.

```
paperbark% du /export/home/winsor/Docs
7452    /export/home/winsor/Docs
paperbark%
```

The following example uses the -k option to display the output for the same directory in 1024-byte blocks.

```
paperbark% du -k /export/home/winsor/Docs
3726   /export/home/winsor/Docs
paperbark%
```

The following example uses the -h option to display the output for the /export/home/winsor/Man-9 directory.

```
mopoke% du -h /export/home/winsor/Man-9
 1.5M   /export/home/winsor/Man-9
mopoke%
```

Usage

See largefile(5) for the description of the behavior of du when encountering files greater than or equal to 2 Gbytes (2**31 bytes).

Environment Variables

See environ(5) for descriptions of the following environment variables that affect the execution of du: LC_CTYPE, LC_MESSAGES, and NLSPATH.

Exit Status

0	Successful completion.
>0	An error occurred.

Attributes

See attributes(5) for descriptions of the following attributes.

/usr/bin/du

Attribute Type	Attribute Value
Availability	SUNWcsu
CSI	Enabled
Interface Stability	Stable

/usr/xpg4/bin/du

Attribute Type	Attribute Value
Availability	SUNWxcu4
CSI	Enabled
Interface Stability	Standard

See Also

ls(1), stat(2), attributes(5), environ(5), fsattr(5), largefile(5), XPG4(5)

System Administration Guide: Basic Administration

du (ucb) — Summarize Disk Usage

Synopsis

```
/usr/ucb/du
/usr/ucb/du [-a] [-s] [filename]
```

Description

The `/usr/ucb/du` command, provided for BSD compatibility, displays the number of kilobytes contained in all files and, recursively, directories within each specified directory or file name. If you do not specify *filename*, then the current directory (.) is used.

A file that has multiple links is counted only once.

Entries are generated only for each directory in the absence of options. Unless you use the -a option, *filename* arguments that are not directory names are ignored.

Note — If there are too many distinct linked files, du counts the excess files more than once.

Options

-a	Generate an entry for each file.
-s	Display only the grand total for each of the specified file names.

Examples

The following example uses the pwd command to identify the directory, then uses the du command to show the usage of all the subdirectories in that directory. The grand total for the directory, in kilobytes, is the last entry.

```
castle% pwd
/export/home/winsor/Misc
castle% du
5     ./Jokes
33    ./Squash
44    ./Tech.papers/lpr.document
217   ./Tech.papers/new.manager
401   ./Tech.papers
144   ./Memos
80    ./Letters
388   ./Window
93    ./Messages
15    ./Useful.news
1211  .
castle%
```

Environment Variables

If any of the LC_* variables (LC_CTYPE, LC_MESSAGES, LC_TIME, LC_COLLATE, LC_NUMERIC, and LC_MONETARY) (see environ(5)) are not set in the environment, the operational behavior of du for each corresponding locale category is determined by the value of the LANG environment variable. If LC_ALL is set, its contents are used to override both the LANG and the other LC_* variables. If none of the above variables are set in the environment, the C (U.S. style) locale determines how du behaves.

LC_CTYPE   Determine how du handles characters. When LC_CTYPE is set to a valid value, du can display and handle text and file names containing valid characters for that locale. du can display and handle Extended UNIX Code (EUC) characters, where any individual character can be 1, 2, or 3 bytes wide. du can also handle EUC characters of 1, 2, or more column widths. In the C locale, only characters from ISO 8859-1 are valid.

LC_MESSAGES

Determine how diagnostic and informative messages are presented, including the language and style of the messages, and the correct form of affirmative and negative responses. In the C locale, the messages are presented in the default form found in the program itself (in most cases, U.S. English).

Attributes

See attributes(5) for descriptions of the following attributes:

Attribute Type	Attribute Value
Availability	SUNWscpu

See Also

pwd(1), df(1M), quot(1M), attributes(5), environ(5)

dumbplot — Graphics Filters for Various Plotters

Synopsis

/usr/ucb/plot [-T*terminal*]

Description

See plot(1).

dump — Dump Selected Parts of an Object File for Shell Scripts

Synopsis

```
/usr/ccs/bin/dump [-aCcfghLlorstV] [-T index [, indexn]] filename...
/usr/ccs/bin/dump [-afhorstL [v]] filename...
/usr/ccs/bin/dump [-hsr [-d number [, numbern]]] filename...
/usr/ccs/bin/dump [-hsrt [-n name]] filename...
```

New!

Description

The dump command dumps selected parts of each of its object file arguments to the standard output.

The dump command is best suited for use in shell scripts. The elfdump(1) command is recommended for more human-readable output.

Options

The dump command accepts both object files and archives of object files. It processes each file argument according to one or more of the options listed below.

Note — The -D and -l options were removed starting with the Solaris 8 release.   *New!*

-a	Dump the archive header of each member of an archive.
-c	Dump the string table(s).
-C	Dump decoded C++ symbol table names.
-f	Dump each file header.
-g	Dump the global symbols in the symbol table of an archive.
-h	Dump the section headers.
-L	Dump dynamic linking information and static shared library information if available.
-o	Dump each program execution header.
-r	Dump relocation information.
-s	Dump section contents in hexadecimal.
-t	Dump symbol table entries.

-T *index*
-T *index1, index2*

> Dump only the indexed symbol table entry defined by *index* or a range of entries defined by *index1, index2*.

-V	Print version information.

You can use the following modifiers to modify the capabilities of the options listed above.

Modifier   **Description**

-d *number*
-d *number1, number2*

> Dump the section number indicated by *number* or the range of sections starting at *number1* and ending at *number2*. You can use this modifier with -h, -s, and -r. When you use -d with -h or -s, treat the argument as the number of a section or range of sections. When you use -d with -r, treat the argument as the number of the section or range of sections to which the relocation applies. For example, to print out all relocation entries associated with the .text section, specify the number of the section as the argument to -d. If .text is section number 2 in the file, dump -r -d 2 prints all associated entries. To print out a specific relocation section, use dump -s -n *name* for raw data output or dump -sv -n *name* for interpreted output.

-n *name*

> Dump information pertaining only to the named entity. You can use this modifier with -h, -s, -r, and -t. When you use -n with -h or -s, treat the argument as the name of a section. When you use -n with -t or -r, treat the argument as the name of a symbol. For example, dump -t -n .text dumps the symbol table entry associated with the symbol whose name is .text, where dump -h -n .text dumps the section header information for the .text section.

-p

> Suppress printing of the headings.

-v

> Dump information in symbolic representation instead of numeric. You can use this modifier with the following options.
> -a   (date, user ID, group ID).
> -f   (class, data, type, machine, version, flags).
> -h   (type, flags).
> -o   (type, flags).
> -r   (name, type).
> -s   (interpret section contents wherever possible).
> -t   (type, bind).
> -L   (value).
> When you use -v with -s, all sections that can be interpreted, such as the string table or symbol table, are interpreted. For example, dump -sv -n .symtab *filename*... produces the same formatted output as dump -tv *filename*..., but dump -s -n .symtab *filename*... prints raw data in hexadecimal. Without additional modifiers, dump -sv *filename*... dumps all sections in the files, interpreting all those that it can and dumping the rest (such as .text or .data) as raw data.

The dump command tries to format the information it dumps in a meaningful way, printing certain information in character, hexadecimal, octal, or decimal representation as appropriate.

Examples

The following example shows the first few lines of the section header information for the
zipinfo command.

```
castle% /usr/ccs/bin/dump -h /bin/zipinfo

/bin/zipinfo:

          **** SECTION HEADER TABLE ****
[No]    Type    Flags   Addr          Offset          Size          Name
        Link    Info    Adralgn       Entsize

[1]     1       2       0x100d4       0xd4            0x11          .interp
        0       0       0x1           0

[2]     5       2       0x100e8       0xe8            0x64c         .hash
        3       0       0x4           0x4

[3]     11      2       0x10734       0x734           0xbe0         .dynsym
        4       28      0x4           0x10

[4]     3       2       0x11314       0x1314          0xc25         .dynstr
        0       0       0x1           0

[5]     1879048190      2       0x11f3c       0x1f3c        0x20
    .SUNW_version
                4       1       0x4           0
...
```

For contrast, the following example shows the first few lines of the output from the
elfdump command for the zipinfo command.

```
castle% /usr/ccs/bin/elfdump -c /bin/zipinfo

Section Header[1]:  sh_name: .interp
    sh_addr:       0x100d4          sh_flags:    [ SHF_ALLOC ]
    sh_size:       0x11             sh_type:     [ SHT_PROGBITS ]
    sh_offset:     0xd4             sh_entsize: 0
    sh_link:       0                sh_info:     0
    sh_addralign: 0x1

Section Header[2]:  sh_name: .hash
    sh_addr:       0x100e8          sh_flags:    [ SHF_ALLOC ]
    sh_size:       0x64c            sh_type:     [ SHT_HASH ]
    sh_offset:     0xe8             sh_entsize: 0x4
    sh_link:       3                sh_info:     0
    sh_addralign: 0x4

Section Header[3]:  sh_name: .dynsym
    sh_addr:       0x10734          sh_flags:    [ SHF_ALLOC ]
    sh_size:       0xbe0            sh_type:     [ SHT_DYNSYM ]
    sh_offset:     0x734            sh_entsize: 0x10
    sh_link:       4                sh_info:     28
    sh_addralign: 0x4
...
```

The following example displays the program execution headers for the `zipinfo` command.

```
castle% /usr/ccs/bin/dump -o /bin/zipinfo

/bin/zipinfo:
  ***** PROGRAM EXECUTION HEADER *****
  Type        Offset        Vaddr         Paddr
  Filesz      Memsz         Flags         Align

  6           0x34          0x10034       0
  0xa0        0xa0          5             0

  3           0xd4          0             0
  0x11        0             4             0

  1           0             0x10000       0
  0x14a5a     0x14a5a       5             0x10000

  1           0x14a5c       0x34a5c       0
  0x4460      0x11858       7             0x10000

  2           0x14d34       0x34d34       0
  0xa8        0             7             0

castle%
```

Attributes

See `attributes`(5) for descriptions of the following attributes:

Attribute Type	Attribute Value
Availability	SUNWbtool

See Also

`elfdump(1)`, `nm(1)`, `a.out(4)`, `ar(4)`, `attributes(5)`

dumpcs — Show Codeset Table for the Current Locale

Synopsis

```
/usr/bin/dumpcs [-0123vw]
```

Description

`dumpcs` displays a list of printable characters for the user's current locale, along with their hexadecimal code values. The display device is assumed to be capable of displaying characters for a given locale. With no option, `dumpcs` displays the entire list of printable characters for the current locale.

With one or more numeric options specified, dumpcs shows EUC codeset(s) for the current locale according to the numbers specified and in order of codeset number. Each nonprintable character is represented by an asterisk (*) and enough ASCII space character(s) to fill that codeset's column width.

Note — dumpcs can handle only EUC locales.

Options

-0	Show ASCII (or EUC primary) codeset.
-1	Show EUC codeset 1 if used for the current locale.
-2	Show EUC codeset 2 if used for the current locale.
-3	Show EUC codeset 3 if used for the current locale.
-v	Verbose. Normally, ranges of nonprintable characters are collapsed into a single line. This option produces one line for each nonprintable character.
-w	Replace code values with corresponding wide character values (process codes).

Examples

The following example first uses the dumpcs command with no arguments, then uses the -0 option. Notice that the output from these two commands is identical.

```
castle% dumpcs
::::::::::::::::
LC_CTYPE:C CS:0
::::::::::::::::
20    ! " # $ % & ' ( ) * + , - . / 0 1 2 3 4 5 6 7 8 9 : ; < = > ?
40  @ A B C D E F G H I J K L M N O P Q R S T U V W X Y Z [ \ ] ^ _
60  ` a b c d e f g h i j k l m n o p q r s t u v w x y z { | } ~*
::::::::::::::::
LC_CTYPE:C CS:1
::::::::::::::::
*
castle% dumpcs -0
::::::::::::::::
LC_CTYPE:C CS:0
::::::::::::::::
20    ! " # $ % & ' ( ) * + , - . / 0 1 2 3 4 5 6 7 8 9 : ; < = > ?
40  @ A B C D E F G H I J K L M N O P Q R S T U V W X Y Z [ \ ] ^ _
60  ` a b c d e f g h i j k l m n o p q r s t u v w x y z { | } ~*
castle% dumpcs -1
::::::::::::::::
LC_CTYPE:C CS:1
::::::::::::::::
*
castle%
```

Environment Variables

The environment variables LC_CTYPE and LANG control the character classification throughout dumpcs. On entry to dumpcs, these environment variables are checked in that order, which means that a new setting for LANG does not override the setting of LC_CTYPE. When none of the values are valid, the character classification defaults to the POSIX.1 C locale.

Attributes

See attributes(5) for descriptions of the following attributes:

Attribute Type	Attribute Value
Availability	SUNWcsu

See Also

localedef(1), attributes(5)

dumpkeys — Dump Keyboard Translation Tables

Synopsis

/usr/bin/dumpkeys

Description

See loadkeys(1).

E

echo — Write Arguments to Standard Output

Synopsis

```
/usr/bin/echo [string...]
/usr/ucb/echo [-n] [string...]
```

Description

The echo command writes its arguments, separated by blanks and terminated by a newline, to the standard output. If you provide no arguments, only the newline character is written.

echo is useful for producing diagnostics in command files, sending known data into a pipe, and displaying the contents of environment variables.

The C shell, the Korn shell, and the Bourne shell all have echo built-in commands, which, by default, are invoked if you call echo without a full path name. See shell_builtins(1).

The sh echo, ksh echo, and /usr/bin/echo commands understand the backslashed *New!* escape characters, except that the sh echo command does not understand \a as the alert character. In addition, the ksh echo command does not have an -n option. The sh echo and /usr/bin/echo command have an -n option only if the SYSV3 environment variable is set. If it is, none of the backslashed characters mentioned above are available. The csh echo and /usr/ucb/echo commands, on the other hand, have an -n option but do not understand the backslashed escape characters.

Options

/usr/ucb/echo

-n   Do not add the newline to the output.

Note — The -n option is provided for transition for BSD applications and may not be supported in future releases.

Operands

string   A string to be written to standard output. If any operand is -n, it is treated as a string, not an option.

/usr/bin/echo

The following character sequences are recognized within any of the arguments:

\a   Alert character.

\b   Backspace.

\c   Print line without newline.

\f   Formfeed.

\n   Newline.

\r   Return.

\t   Tab.

\v   Vertical tab.

\\   Backslash.

\0*n*   Where *n* is the 8-bit character whose ASCII code is the 1-, 2-, or 3-digit octal number representing that character.

When an 8-bit character is represented by the escape convention \0*n*, the *n* must always be preceded by the digit zero (0).

For example, the following command prints the phrase WARNING: and sounds the bell on your terminal.

```
$ echo 'WARNING:\07'
WARNING:
$
```

The single (or double) quotes (or two backslashes) are required to protect the backslash that precedes the 07.

Following the \0, you can use up to three digits in constructing the octal output character. If, following the \0*n*, you want to echo additional digits that are not part of the octal representation, you must use the full 3-digit *n*. For example, if you want to echo ESC 7, you must use the three digits 033 instead of just the two digits 33 after the \0.

The following example shows that using only two digits is incorrect.

```
$ echo "\0337" | od -xc
0000000    df0a
            337  \n
0000002
$
```

The following example shows that the 3-digit syntax produces the correct results.

```
$ echo "\00337" | od -xc
0000000     1b37    0a00
          033    7   \n
0000003
$
```

For the octal equivalents of each character, see ascii(5).

Usage

Portable applications should not use −n (as the first argument) or escape sequences. The printf(1) command can be used portably to emulate any of the traditional behaviors of the echo command as follows.

The Solaris 2.x /usr/bin/echo is equivalent to:

```
printf "%b\n" "$*"
```

The /usr/ucb/echo is equivalent to:

```
if ["X$1" = "X-n"]
then
 shift
 printf "%s" "$*"
else
 printf "%s\n" "$*"
fi
```

New applications are encouraged to use printf instead of echo.

Examples

You can use the echo command to display the value for a variable by preceding the variable name with a dollar sign ($). The following example displays the values for the PATH environment variable.

```
castle% echo $PATH
/usr/openwin/bin:/usr/dt/bin:/bin:/usr/bin:/usr/sbin:/usr/ucb:/etc:/usr
   /proc/bin:/opt/hpnp/bin:/usr/local/games:.
castle%
```

The following example shows how you can use the echo command in combination with the tr and wc commands to determine how many subdirectories are between the root directory (/) and your current directory. The example has the following parts:

- Echo the full path name of your current working directory.

- Pipe the output through tr to translate the path's embedded slash characters into space characters.

- Pipe that output through wc −w for a count of the names in your path.

```
castle% /usr/bin/echo $PWD | tr '/' ' ' | wc -w
        3
castle%
```

See tr(1) and wc(1) for their functionality.

The following examples show the different ways you can echo a string without a newline.

/usr/bin/echo

```
castle% /usr/bin/echo "$USER's current directory is $PWD\c"
winsor's current directory is /export/home/winsorcastle%
```

Bourne and Korn Shells

```
$ /usr/bin/echo "$USER's current directory is $PWD\c"
winsor's current directory is /export/home/winsor$
```

C Shell

```
castle% echo -n /usr/bin/echo "$USER's current directory is $PWD"
/usr/bin/echo winsor's current directory is /export/home/winsorcastle%
```

/usr/ucb/echo

```
castle% /usr/ucb/echo -n "$USER's current directory is $PWD"
winsor's current directory is /export/home/winsorcastle%
```

Environment Variables

SYSV3   Provide compatibility with INTERACTIVE UNIX System and SCO UNIX installation scripts. SYSV3 is intended for compatibility only and should not be used in new scripts.

See environ(5) for descriptions of the following environment variables that affect the execution of echo: LC_CTYPE, LC_MESSAGES, and NLSPATH.

Exit Status

0   Successful completion.

>0   An error occurred.

Attributes

See attributes(5) for descriptions of the following attributes:

/usr/bin/echo

Attribute Type	Attribute Value
Availability	SUNWcsu
CSI	Enabled

/usr/ucb/echo

Attribute Type	Attribute Value
Availability	SUNWscpu

See Also

```
printf(1), shell_builtins(1), tr(1), wc(1), echo(1B), ascii(5),
attributes(5), environ(5)
```

ed, red — Text Editor

Synopsis

```
/usr/bin/ed [-s|-] [-p string] [-x] [-C] [file]
/usr/xpg4/bin/ed [-s|-] [-p string] [-x] [-C] [file]
/usr/bin/red [-s|-] [-p string] [-x] [-C] [file]
```

Description

The ed command is the standard text editor. If you specify a file, ed reads the file into ed's buffer so that it can be edited.

> **Note** — Although vi and ex have superseded ed as a line editor, some commands such as diff continue to use ed.

The ed command operates on a copy of the file it is editing; the original file remains unchanged until you issue a w (write) command. The copy of the text being edited resides in a temporary file called the buffer. There is only one buffer.

Unlike the vi and ex commands, ed does not display any of the text in its buffer unless you ask for it. As a result, it can be difficult to keep track of the current contents of the buffer.

The red command is a restricted version of ed. It enables editing of files in the current directory only. It prohibits executing shell commands by using the !shell command. Attempts to bypass these restrictions result in an error message (restricted shell).

Both ed and red support the fspec(4) formatting capability. The default terminal mode is either stty -tabs or stty tab3, where Tab stops are set at eight columns (see stty(1)). If, however, the first line of file contains a format specification, that specification overrides the default mode. The following example of the first line of a file sets Tab stops at 5, 10, and 15, and a maximum line length of 72.

```
<:t5,10,15 s72:>
```

Commands to ed have a simple and regular structure: zero, one, or two addresses followed by a single-character command, possibly followed by parameters to that command. The addresses specify one or more lines in the buffer. Every command that requires addresses has default addresses, so that you can often omit the addresses. In general, you can specify only one command per line.

ed has separate input and command modes. If you enter an invalid command, ed writes the string ?\n (followed by an explanatory message if you have enabled help mode with the H command) to standard output and continues in command mode with the current line number unchanged.

Certain commands allow the input of text. This text is put in the appropriate place in the buffer. While ed is accepting text, it is said to be in input mode. In this mode, ed recognizes no commands; it merely collects all input. You leave input mode by typing a period (.) at the beginning of a line, followed immediately by a Return.

> **Note** — If the editor input is coming from a command file (for example, ed file < ed-cmd-file), the editor exits at the first failure.

ed has the following size limitations:

- 512 characters in a line.
- 256 characters in a global command list.
- 255 characters in the path name of a file (counting slashes).

The limit on the number of lines depends on the amount of user memory; each line takes one word. When reading a file, ed discards ASCII and null characters.

If a file is not terminated by a newline character, ed adds one and puts out a message explaining what it did.

/usr/bin/ed

If ed executes commands with arguments, it uses the default shell /usr/bin/sh (see sh(1)).

/usr/xpg4/bin/ed

/usr/xpg4/bin/ed is a POSIX-compliant version of the /usr/bin/ed command. See standards(5).

If ed executes commands with arguments, it uses /usr/xpg4/bin/sh, which is equivalent to /usr/bin/ksh (see ksh(1)).

Regular Expressions

The ed command supports a limited form of regular expression notation. You can use regular expressions in addresses to specify lines and in some commands (for example, s) to specify portions of a line that are to be substituted. With ed addressing, at any time there is a current line. Generally, the current line is the last line affected by a command; the exact effect on the current line is discussed under the description of each command.

Internationalized Basic Regular Expressions are used for all system-supplied locales. See regex(5).

If the closing delimiter of an *RE* or of a replacement string (for example, /) would be the last character before a newline, you can omit that delimiter, in which case the addressed line is written. The following pairs of commands are equivalent:

```
s/s1/s2      s/s1/s2/p

g/s1         g/s1/p

?s1          ?s1?
```

ed Commands

Commands may require zero, one, or two addresses. Commands that require no addresses regard the presence of an address as an error. Commands that accept one or two addresses assume default addresses when you specify an insufficient number of addresses; if you specify more addresses than such a command requires, ed uses the last one(s).

Typically, you separate addresses from each other by a comma (,) or a semicolon (;). If you use a semicolon separator, the first address is calculated, the current line (.) is set to that value, and then the second address is calculated. You can use this feature to determine the starting line for forward and backward searches. The second address of any two-address sequence must correspond to a line in the buffer that follows the line corresponding to the first address.

In the following list of ed commands, the parentheses shown before the command are not part of the address; instead, they show the default address(es) for the command.

You can precede each address component by zero or more blank characters. You can precede the command letter by zero or more blank characters. If you use a suffix letter (l, n, or p), it must immediately follow the command.

The e, E, f, v, and w commands take an optional file parameter, separated from the command letter by one or more blank characters.

If changes have been made in the buffer since the last w command that wrote the entire buffer, ed warns you if you use either the e or q commands because such use would destroy the buffer. The ed command writes the string: ?\n (followed by an explanatory message if you have used the H command to enable help mode) to standard output and continues in command mode with the current line number unchanged. If you repeat the e or q command with no other intervening command, the buffer is cleared and ed exits.

If an end-of-file is detected on standard input when a command is expected, the ed command acts as if a q command had been entered.

It is generally illegal for more than one command to appear on a line. However, you can suffix any command (except e, f, r, or w) by l, n, or p, in which case the current line is either listed, numbered, or written.

The ed commands are listed below.

(.)a *text* .	Append zero or more lines of text after the addressed line in the buffer. Leave the current line (.) at the last inserted line, or, if there was none, at the addressed line. Address 0 is legal for this command, placing the appended text at the beginning of the buffer. The maximum number of characters per line is 256, including the newline character.
(.)c *text* .	Change the addressed lines from the buffer with zero or more lines of text. Leave the current line (.) at the last line input, or, if there was none, at the first line that was not deleted; if the lines deleted were originally at the end of the buffer, set the current line number to the address of the new last line; if no lines remain in the buffer, set the current line number to 0.
C	Assume that all text read in for the e and r commands is encrypted unless a null key is typed in.
(.,.)d	Delete the addressed lines from the buffer. The line after the last line deleted becomes the current line; if the lines deleted were originally at the end of the buffer, the new last line becomes the current line. If no lines remain in the buffer, set the current line number to 0.
e *file*	Edit by deleting the entire contents of the buffer and then reading the contents of *file* into the buffer. Set the current line (.) to the last line of the buffer. If you do not specify *file*, use the currently remembered file name if any (see the f command). Write the number of bytes read to standard output in the following format, unless you specify the -s option: %d\n *number of bytes read* Remember *file* for possible use as a default file name in subsequent e, E, r, and w commands. If you replace *file* with !, take the rest of the line to be a shell command (see sh(1)) whose output is to be read. Such a shell command is not remembered as the current file name. Discard all marks on completion of a successful e command. If the buffer has changed since the last time the entire buffer was written, you are warned, as described previously.
E *file*	Edit as with the e command but do not check to see if any changes have been made to the buffer since the last w command.

f [*file*]   Change the currently remembered path name to *file* if given. Then, write the (possibly new) currently remembered path name to the standard output in the following format:
"%s\n" *pathname*
The current line number is unchanged.

(1,$)g/*RE*/*command list*

Make global changes by first marking every line that matches the given *RE*. Then, for every marked line, execute the given command with the current line (.) initially set to that line. When the g command completes, the current line number has the value assigned by the last command in the command list. Leave the line number unchanged if no lines were matched. A single command or the first of a list of commands appears on the same line as the global command. You must end all lines of a multiline list except the last line with a backslash (\); a, i, and c commands and associated input are permitted. If the . terminating input mode would be the last line of the command, you can omit it. An empty command list is equivalent to the p command. The g, G, v, V, and ! commands are not permitted in the command list. You can use any character other than space or newline instead of a slash to delimit *RE*. Within *RE*, you can use the *RE* delimiter itself as a literal character by preceding it with a backslash.

(1,$)G/*RE*/   Make interactive global changes by first marking every line that matches the given *RE*. Then, write each such line to standard output. Change the current line (.) to that line, and you can input any single command except a, c, i, g, G, v, and V. After the execution of that command, write the next marked line, and so on; a newline acts as a null command; an & reexecutes the most recent non-null command within the current invocation of G. The commands input as part of the execution of the G command can address and affect any lines in the buffer. The final value of the current line number is the value set by the last command successfully executed. (Note that the last command successfully executed is the G command itself if a command fails or you specify the null command.) The current line number is not changed if no lines matched. You can terminate the G command by a SIGINT signal, an ASCII DEL, or BREAK. You can use any character other than space or newline instead of a slash to delimit *RE*. Within *RE*, you can use the *RE* delimiter itself as a literal character by preceding it with a backslash. Note that the sequence \n in an *RE* does not match a newline character.

h   Display a short help message that explains the reason for the most recent ? diagnostic. The current line number is unchanged.

H   Enter a mode that displays help messages for all subsequent ? diagnostics. Explain the previous ? diagnostic if there was one. Enter the H command again to exit this mode. The current line number is unchanged.

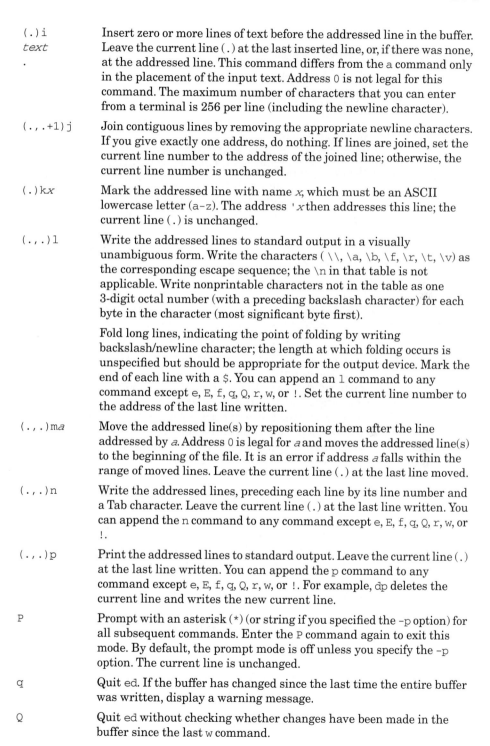

(.)i
text
.

Insert zero or more lines of text before the addressed line in the buffer. Leave the current line (.) at the last inserted line, or, if there was none, at the addressed line. This command differs from the a command only in the placement of the input text. Address 0 is not legal for this command. The maximum number of characters that you can enter from a terminal is 256 per line (including the newline character).

(.,.+1)j

Join contiguous lines by removing the appropriate newline characters. If you give exactly one address, do nothing. If lines are joined, set the current line number to the address of the joined line; otherwise, the current line number is unchanged.

(.)k*x*

Mark the addressed line with name *x*, which must be an ASCII lowercase letter (a-z). The address '*x* then addresses this line; the current line (.) is unchanged.

(.,.)l

Write the addressed lines to standard output in a visually unambiguous form. Write the characters (\\, \a, \b, \f, \r, \t, \v) as the corresponding escape sequence; the \n in that table is not applicable. Write nonprintable characters not in the table as one 3-digit octal number (with a preceding backslash character) for each byte in the character (most significant byte first).

Fold long lines, indicating the point of folding by writing backslash/newline character; the length at which folding occurs is unspecified but should be appropriate for the output device. Mark the end of each line with a $. You can append an l command to any command except e, E, f, q, Q, r, w, or !. Set the current line number to the address of the last line written.

(.,.)m*a*

Move the addressed line(s) by repositioning them after the line addressed by *a*. Address 0 is legal for *a* and moves the addressed line(s) to the beginning of the file. It is an error if address *a* falls within the range of moved lines. Leave the current line (.) at the last line moved.

(.,.)n

Write the addressed lines, preceding each line by its line number and a Tab character. Leave the current line (.) at the last line written. You can append the n command to any command except e, E, f, q, Q, r, w, or !.

(.,.)p

Print the addressed lines to standard output. Leave the current line (.) at the last line written. You can append the p command to any command except e, E, f, q, Q, r, w, or !. For example, dp deletes the current line and writes the new current line.

P

Prompt with an asterisk (*) (or string if you specified the -p option) for all subsequent commands. Enter the P command again to exit this mode. By default, the prompt mode is off unless you specify the -p option. The current line is unchanged.

q

Quit ed. If the buffer has changed since the last time the entire buffer was written, display a warning message.

Q

Quit ed without checking whether changes have been made in the buffer since the last w command.

($)r *file*   Read the contents of *file* into the buffer. If you do not specify *file*, use the currently remembered file name if any (see the e and f commands). Leave the currently remembered file name unchanged unless *file* is the very first file name mentioned since ed was invoked. Address 0 is legal for r and reads the file in at the beginning of the buffer. If the read is successful and you did not specify the -s option, write to standard output the number of characters read in the following format.

%d\n, <number of bytes read>

Set the current line (.) to the last line read. If you replace *file* with !, take the rest of the line to be a shell command (see sh(1)) whose output is to be read. For example, $r !ls appends the current directory to the end of the file being edited. Such a shell command is not remembered as the current file name.

(.,.)s/*RE*/*replacement*/
(.,.)s/*RE*/*replacement*/ *count*, *count*=[1-512]
(.,.)s/*RE*/*replacement*/g
(.,.)s/*RE*/*replacement*/l
(.,.)s/*RE*/*replacement*/n
(.,.)s/*RE*/*replacement*/p

Substitute by searching each addressed line for an occurrence of the specified *RE*. You can specify zero or more substitution commands. In each line in which a match is found, replace all (nonoverlapped) matched strings by the replacement if you use the global replacement indicator g after the command. If you do not use the global indicator, replace only the first occurrence of the matched string. If you specify a number *count* after the command, replace only the *count*-th occurrence of the matched string on each addressed line. It is an error if the substitution fails on all addressed lines. You can use any character other than space or newline instead of the slash (/) to delimit the *RE* and the replacement. Leave the current line (.) at the last line on which a substitution occurred. Within the *RE*, you can use the *RE* delimiter itself as a literal character by preceding it with a backslash.

Replace an ampersand (&) in the *replacement* with the string matching the *RE* on the current line. You can escape the special meaning of & in this context by preceding it with a backslash. As a more general feature, replace the characters *n*, where *n* is a digit, with the text matched by the *n*-th regular subexpression of the specified *RE* enclosed between \\(and \\). When you use nested parenthesized subexpressions, *n* is determined by counting occurrences of \\(starting from the left. When the character % is the only character in the replacement, use the replacement used in the most recent substitute command as the replacement in the current substitute command; if there was no previous substitute command, the use of % in this manner is an error. The % loses its special meaning when it is in a replacement string of more than one character or is preceded by a backslash. For each backslash encountered in scanning *replacement* from beginning to end, the character following loses its special meaning (if any). It is unspecified what special meaning is given to any character other than &, \, %, or digits.

You can split a line by substituting a newline character into it. You must escape the newline in the replacement by preceding it with a backslash. You cannot do such substitution as part of a g or v command list. Set the current line number to the address of the last line on which a substitution is performed. If no substitution is performed, the current line number is unchanged. If a line is split, a substitution is considered to have been performed on each of the new lines for the purpose of determining the new current line number. A substitution is considered to have been performed even if the replacement string is identical to the string that it replaces.

The substitute command supports the following indicators:

count	Substitute for the *count*-th occurrence only of the *RE* found on each addressed line. *count* must be between 1 and 512, inclusive.
g	Globally substitute for all nonoverlapping instances of the *RE* instead of just the first one. If you specify both g and *count*, the results are unspecified.
l	Write to standard output the final line in which a substitution was made. The line is written in the format specified for the l command.
n	Write to standard output the final line in which a substitution was made. The line is written in the format specified for the n command.
p	Write to standard output the final line in which a substitution was made. The line is written in the format specified for the p command.

(.,.)t*a*   Copy the addressed lines after address *a* (which may be 0). Leave the current line (.) at the last line copied. This command is similar to the m command.

u   Undo the most recent command that modified anything in the buffer, namely, the most recent a, c, d, g, i, j, m, r, s, t, u, v, G, or V command. Undo all changes made to the buffer by a g, G, v, or V global command as a single change; if the global command made no changes (such as with g/ *RE* /p), the u command has no effect. Set the current line number to the value it had immediately before the command being undone started.

(1,$)v/*RE*/*command list*

Make global changes as with the g command except, during the first step, mark the lines that do not match the *RE*.

(1,$)V/*RE*/   Make interactive global changes as with the G command except, during the first step, mark the lines marked that do not match the *RE*.

(1,$)w *file*   Write the addressed lines into *file*. If *file* does not exist, create it with mode 666 (readable and writable by everyone), unless your file creation mask dictates otherwise; see the description of the umask special command on sh(1). Leave the currently remembered file name unchanged unless *file* is the very first file name mentioned since ed was invoked. If you specify no *file*, use the currently remembered file name if any (see the e and f commands). Leave the current line (.) unchanged. If the command is successful, print the number of characters written, unless you specify the -s option in the following format: "%d\n", *number-of-bytes-written*

If you replace *file* with !, take the rest of the line to be a shell command (see sh(1)) whose standard input is the addressed lines. Such a shell command is not remembered as the current path name. This usage of the write command with ! is considered as a last w command that wrote the entire buffer.

(1,$)W *file*   Write the addressed lines into *file* as the write command above but append the addressed lines to the end of *file* if it exists. If *file* does not exist, create it as described above for the w command.

X   Determine whether text read for the e and r commands is encrypted. A null key turns off encryption. Subsequent e, r, and w commands use this key to encrypt or decrypt the text. An explicitly empty key turns off encryption. Also, see the -x option of ed.

($)=   Write the number of the addressed line to standard output in the following format: "%d\n" *line-number*

The current line number is unchanged.

!shell *command*

Send the remainder of the line after the ! to the UNIX system shell (see sh(1)) to be interpreted as a command. Within the text of that command, replace the unescaped character % with the remembered file name; if you use a ! as the first character of the shell command, replace it with the text of the previous shell command. Thus, !! repeats the last shell command. If any replacements of % or ! are performed, write the modified line to the standard output before *command* is executed. The ! command writes !\n to standard output on completion, unless you specify the -s option. The current line number is unchanged. Note that a ! command cannot be subject to a g or v command. You cannot use the ! command and the ! escape from the e, r, and w commands if you invoke ed from a restricted shell (see sh(1)).

(.+1)newline

Write the addressed line. A newline alone, equivalent to .+1p, is useful for stepping forward through the buffer. Set the current line number to the address of the written line.

If you send an interrupt signal (ASCII DEL or BREAK), ed writes a ?\n and returns to its command level. The ed command takes the standard action for all signals with the following exceptions:

SIGINT   Interrupt current activity, write the string ?\n to standard output, and return to command mode.

SIGHUP   If the buffer is not empty and has changed since the last write, write a copy of the buffer in a file. First, use the file named ed.hup in the current directory; if that fails, use the file named ed.hup in the directory named by the HOME environment variable. In any case, the ed command exits without returning to command mode.

Options

-C   Simulate a C encryption command. The C command is like the X command, except that all text read in is assumed to have been encrypted.

-p *string* Specify a prompt string. By default, there is no prompt string.

-s | -   Suppress the writing of character counts by e, r, and w commands, of diagnostics from e and q commands, and of the ! prompt after a !shell command. Although the - option is still supported, it has been replaced in the documentation by the -s option that follows the Command Syntax Standard (see intro(1)).

-x   Simulate an X encryption command and prompt for a key. The X command makes an educated guess to determine whether text read in is encrypted or not. The temporary buffer file is encrypted also, using a transformed version of the key typed in for the -x option.

Operands

file   Simulate an e command on the named *file* before accepting commands from the standard input.

Examples

The following examples show some of the basic ed editing commands. First we create a new file named edfile and use the a (append) command to append text to it. If the file already contained text, the new input would be appended to the end of the file. The dot (.) on a separate line at the end exits input mode.

```
castle% ed edfile
?edfile
a
Kookaburra sits in the old gum tree
Merry merry king of the bush is he
Laugh, kookaburra, laugh
Gay your life must be.

Kookaburra sits in the old gum tree
Eating all the gumdrops he can see
Laugh, kookaburra, laugh
```

Leave some there for me.

.

To save the file, we use the w (write) command. The text is written to the buffer, and the number of characters is displayed. Then we use the q (quit) command to quit ed.

```
w
240
q
castle%
```

Now let's open the file again by typing **ed** and the file name. The contents of the file are written into the ed buffer, and the number of characters in the file is displayed.

```
castle% ed edfile
240
```

To display the last line of the file, we use the p (print) command.

```
p
Leave some there for me.
```

To display the first line of the file, we use 1p.

```
1p
Kookaburra sits in the old gum tree
```

To display the first five lines of the file, we use 1,5p.

```
1,5p
Kookaburra sits in the old gum tree
Merry merry king of the bush is he
Laugh, kookaburra, laugh
Gay your life must be.
```

To display everything in the buffer, we use 1,$p.

```
1,$p
Kookaburra sits in the old gum tree
Merry merry king of the bush is he
Laugh, kookaburra, laugh
Gay your life must be.

Kookaburra sits in the old gum tree
Eating all the gumdrops he can see
Laugh, kookaburra, laugh
Leave some there for me.
```

Because ed is a line-oriented text editor, it helps a great deal to know what line you want to edit. The n (number) command is like the p (print) command except that it displays a line number at the beginning of each line. The n command uses the same syntax as the p command. In the following example, we print the contents of the buffer with line numbers.

```
1,$n
1       Kookaburra sits in the old gum tree
```

```
2          Merry merry king of the bush is he
3          Laugh, kookaburra, laugh
4          Gay your life must be.
5
6          Kookaburra sits in the old gum tree
7          Eating all the gumdrops he can see
8          Laugh, kookaburra, laugh
9          Leave some there for me.
```

To delete a line of text, use the d (delete) command. In the following example, we delete the fifth line that contains just a newline character and then use the n command again to display the contents of the buffer. As you can see, the blank line has been deleted.

5d
1,$n
```
1          Kookaburra sits in the old gum tree
2          Merry merry king of the bush is he
3          Laugh, kookaburra, laugh
4          Gay your life must be.
5          Kookaburra sits in the old gum tree
6          Eating all the gumdrops he can see
7          Laugh, kookaburra, laugh
8          Leave some there for me.
```

Now we decide to quit the file, but we've forgotten to write the changes in the buffer. ed displays a ? prompt to remind us that we haven't saved the changes. We then write the changes and quit again.

q
```
?
```
w
```
239
```
q
```
castle%
```

Usage
See largefile(5) for the description of the behavior of ed and red when encountering files greater than or equal to 2 Gbytes (2**31 bytes).

Environment Variables
See environ(5) for descriptions of the following environment variables that affect the execution of ed: HOME, LC_CTYPE, LC_COLLATE, LC_MESSAGES, and NLSPATH.

Exit Status

0	Successful completion without any file or command errors.
>0	An error occurred.

Files

$TMPDIR	If this environment variable is not null, use its value in place of /var/tmp as the directory name for the temporary work file.

/var/tmp   If /var/tmp exists, use it as the directory name for the temporary work
            file.

/tmp   If the environment variable TMPDIR does not exist or is null and if
            /var/tmp does not exist, then use /tmp as the directory name for the
            temporary work file.

ed.hup   Save work here if the terminal is hung up.

Attributes

See attributes(5) for descriptions of the following attributes:

/usr/bin/ed, /usr/bin/red

Attribute Type	Attribute Value
Availability	SUNWcsu
CSI	Enabled

/usr/xpg4/bin/ed

Attribute Type	Attribute Value
Availability	SUNWxcu4
CSI	Enabled

See Also

bfs(1), edit(1), grep(1), ksh(1), lex(1), sh(1), stty(1), umask(1), vi(1),
fspec(4), attributes(5), environ(5), largefile(5), regex(5), xpg4(5)

Diagnostics

?   Command errors.

?*file*   An inaccessible file. (Use the h and H commands for detailed
            explanations.)

If changes have been made in the buffer since the last w command that wrote the
entire buffer, ed warns you if you use the e or q commands, which would destroy the
buffer. It writes ? and enables you to continue editing. Issuing a second e or q command
at this point executes the command. You can inhibit this feature by using the -s
command-line option.

edit — Text Editor (Variant of ex for Casual Users)

Synopsis

/usr/bin/edit [- | -s] [-l] [-L] [-R] [-r [*filename*]] [-t *tag*] [-v] [-V]
    [-x] [-w*n*] [-C] [+*command* | -c *command*] *filename*...
/usr/xpg4/bin/edit [- | -s] [-l] [-L] [-R] { -r [*filename*]} [-t *tag*]
    [-v] [-V] [-x] [-w*n*] [-C] [+*command* | -c *command*] *filename*...

Description

The edit command is a variant of the text editor ex and is recommended for new or casual users who want to use a command-oriented editor. It operates precisely as ex with the following options automatically set:

novice	On.
report	On.
showmode	On.
magic	Off.

The following brief introduction should help you get started with edit. If you are using a CRT terminal, you may want to learn about the display editor vi.

The edit command operates on a copy of the file it is editing; the original file remains unchanged until you issue a w (write) command. The copy of the text being edited resides in a temporary file called a buffer. The edit command also has 26 additional buffers, named a through z, that you can use as temporary storage areas for copying and moving text between files.

The edit command numbers the lines in the buffer, with the first line as number 1. If you execute the command 1, then edit types the first line of the buffer. If you then execute the command d, edit deletes the first line, line 2 becomes line 1, and edit prints the current line (the new line 1) so you can see where you are. In general, the current line is always the last line affected by a command. The current line has the symbolic name dot (.).

See ex(1) for a complete list of edit commands and syntax.

Starting the Editor

To create a new file, you begin at a shell prompt by typing:

```
castle% edit filename
```

The editor displays the file name, tells you it is a new file, and displays the colon (:) prompt, as shown in the following example.

```
castle% edit editfile
"editfile" [New File]
:
```

To edit an existing file, you also type edit *filename* and press Return. The editor makes a copy of the file, stores it in the buffer, and tells you how many lines and characters are in the file, as shown in the following example.

```
castle% edit editfile2
"editfile2" 9 lines, 263 characters
:
```

To edit the file, you type an edit command and press Return. The edit command prompt is the colon (:), which you should see after starting the editor. If you are editing an existing file, then you have some lines in edit's buffer. When you start editing, edit makes the last line of the file the current line. Most commands to edit use the current line if you do not tell them which line to use. Thus, if you type print (which can be abbreviated p) and press Return (as you should after all edit commands), edit prints the current line. If you delete (d) the current line, edit prints the new current line, which is usually the next line in the file. If you delete the last line, then the new last line becomes the current one.

Appending Text

If you start with an empty file or want to add some new lines, use the append (a) command. After you execute this command (pressing a Return after the word append), edit reads lines from your terminal until you type a line consisting of just a dot (.); edit places these lines after the current line. The last line you type then becomes the current line. The insert (i) command is like append but places the lines you type before, instead of after, the current line.

Changing Text

You can make a change to some text within the current line by using the substitute (s) command: s/*old*/*new*/, where *old* is the string of characters you want to replace and *new* is the string of characters you want to replace *old* with.

The filename (f) command tells you how many lines are in the buffer you are editing and displays [Modified] if you have changed the buffer.

By using the d and a commands and giving line numbers to see lines in the file, you can make any changes you want. You should learn at least a few more things, however, if you use edit more than a few times.

The change (c) command changes the current line to a sequence of lines you supply (as in append, you type lines up to a line consisting of only a dot (.). You can tell change to change more than one line by giving the line numbers of the lines you want to change, for example, 3,5c.

Saving Edits and Quitting the Editor

After modifying a file, you can save the contents of the file by executing a write (w) command. You can leave the editor by issuing a quit (q) command. If you run edit on a file but do not change the file, you need not (but it does no harm) write the file back. If you try to quit from edit after modifying the buffer without writing it out, you receive the message No write since last change (:quit! overrides), and edit waits for another command. If you do not want to write the buffer out, issue the quit command followed by an exclamation point (q!). The buffer is then irretrievably discarded, and the shell returns.

The undo (u) command reverses the effect of the last command you executed that changed the buffer. Thus, if you execute a substitute command that does not do what you want, type u and the old contents of the line are restored. You can also undo an undo command. edit warns you when a command affects more than one line of the buffer. Note that you cannot undo commands such as write and quit.

Displaying Lines in the Buffer

edit provides a number of different commands that enable you to display what's in the buffer.

- Find the current line number by typing .=
- Use the print command to display a set of line numbers: 1,23p prints the first 23 lines of the file, 1,$p prints the complete file, and .,$p prints the current line plus the rest of the lines in the file.
- Use the number (nu) command to display the contents of the buffer with line numbers. You can find the number of the current line (nu), a range of lines (for example, 5,10nu displays numbered lines 5 through 10), or all of the lines in the file (1,$pnu).
- To look at the next line in the buffer, press Return.

- To look at a number of lines, enter Control-D (while holding down the Control key, press the d key) instead of Return. This key sequence shows you a half-screen of lines on a CRT or 12 lines on a hardcopy terminal. You can look at nearby text by executing the z command. The current line is displayed in the middle of the text displayed, and the last line displayed becomes the current line; you can get back to the line where you were before you executed the z command by typing ' '. The z command has other options: z- prints a screen of text (or 24 lines) ending where you are; z+ prints the next screenful. If you want less than a screenful of lines, type z.11 to display five lines before and five lines after the current line. (Typing z.n, when n is an odd number, displays a total of n lines, centered about the current line; when n is an even number, it displays $n-1$ lines, so that the lines displayed are centered around the current line.) You can give counts after other commands; for example, with the command d5 you can delete 5 lines starting with the current line.

You can also do arithmetic with line references. Thus, the line $-5 is the fifth before the last and .+20 is 20 lines after the current line.

> **Note** — edit also has a vi mode that enables you to view the contents of the file as you edit it. For more information on using the vi mode, see ex(1).

Finding Text

To find things in the file, you can use line numbers. You can also search backward and forward in the file for strings by giving commands of the form /*text*/ to search forward for text or ?*text*? to search backward for text. If a search reaches the end of the file without finding text, it wraps around and continues to search back to the line where you are. A useful feature here is a search of the form /^*text*/ which searches for text at the beginning of a line. Similarly, /*text*$/ searches for text at the end of a line. You can omit the trailing / or ? in these commands.

Copying or Moving Text

You can copy or move text within the same file by using the copy (c) or move (m) commands. You specify the line or range of lines you want to move, followed by the command and then the number of the line after which you want the text to be placed. For example, the command 5,10c 20 makes a copy of lines 5 through 10 and inserts it after line 20 in the buffer. The symbolic name dot (.) syntax, which represents the current line, is most useful in a range of lines. To move to the last line in the file, you can refer to it by its symbolic name $. Thus, the command $d deletes the last line in the file, no matter what the current line is, and the command 10,20m $ moves lines 10 through 20 to the end of the file.

Using the Internal Buffers

The edit command has 26 internal buffers, named a through z, that you can use as temporary clipboards for copying or moving text from one file to another. Before you begin the copy or move, find the first and last line numbers you want to copy or move. For example, to move lines 10 through 20, type 10,20d a and press Return. The lines are deleted from the file and put into a buffer named a. To put the contents of buffer a after the current line, type put a and press Return. If you want to move or copy these lines to another file, first copy the lines by using the yank (y) command, then type e *filename* and press Return, where *filename* is the name of the other file you want to edit, for example, e chapter2.

> **Note —** The contents of the a through z buffers are not preserved if you exit edit. When you use the e or q commands, edit does not warn you when these buffers contain text.

The /usr/xpg4/bin/edit command is identical to /usr/bin/edit.

Options

You can turn the following options on or off by using the set command in ex(1).

-	-s	Suppress all interactive user feedback. This option is useful when processing editor scripts.
-C	Simulate the C command of ex, which assumes that all text read in has been encrypted.
+command	-c command	
	Begin editing by executing the specified editor command (usually a search or positioning command).
-l	Set up for editing LISP programs.
-L	List the names of all files saved as the result of an editor or system crash.
-R	Set the read-only flag to prevent accidental overwriting of the file.
-r filename	Recover the version of filename that was in the buffer when a system crash occurred.
-t tag	Edit the file containing tag, and position the editor at its definition.
-v	Start up in display-editing state using vi. You can achieve the same effect by simply typing the vi command.
-V	Verbose. When ex commands are read by means of standard input, the input is echoed to standard error. This option is useful for processing ex commands within shell scripts.
-wn	Set the default window size to n. This option is useful when you are using the editor over a slow-speed line.
-x	Simulate the X encryption command of ex, and prompt for a key. This key encrypts and decrypts text, using the algorithm of the crypt command. The X command makes an educated guess to determine whether text read in is encrypted or not. The temporary buffer file is encrypted also, using a transformed version of the key typed in for the -x option. Note that the encryption options are provided with the Security Administration Utilities package, which is available only in the United States.

The filename argument indicates one or more files to be edited.

Attributes

See attributes(5) for descriptions of the following attributes:

/usr/bin/edit

Attribute Type	Attribute Value
Availability	SUNWcsu
CSI	Enabled

/usr/xpg4/bin/edit

Attribute Type	Attribute Value
Availability	SUNWxcu4
CSI	Enabled

See Also

ed(1), ex(1), vi(1), attributes(5), XPG4(5)

---

egrep — Search a File for a Pattern, Using Full Regular Expressions

Synopsis

```
/usr/bin/egrep [-bchilnsv] [-e pattern-list] [-f file] [strings]
    [file...]
/usr/xpg4/bin/cgrep [-bchilnsvx] [-e pattern-list] [-f file] [strings]
    [file...]
```

Description

The egrep (expression grep) command searches files for a pattern of characters and prints all lines that contain that pattern. egrep uses full regular expressions (expressions that have string values that use the full set of alphanumeric and special characters) to match the patterns. It uses a fast deterministic algorithm that sometimes needs exponential space.

If you specify no files, egrep assumes standard input. Normally, each line found is copied to the standard output. The file name is printed before each line found if there is more than one input file.

/usr/bin/egrep

The /usr/bin/egrep command accepts full regular expressions as described on the regexp(5) manual page, except for \(and \), and with the addition of the following expressions:

- A full regular expression followed by + that matches one or more occurrences of the full regular expression.
- A full regular expression followed by ? that matches 0 or 1 occurrence of the full regular expression.
- Full regular expressions separated by | or by a newline that match strings that are matched by any of the expressions.

- A full regular expression that may be enclosed in parentheses () for grouping.

Be careful when using the characters $, *, [, ^, |, (,), and \ in full regular expression because they are also meaningful to the shell. It is safest to enclose the entire full regular expression in single quotes ' . . . '.

The order of precedence of operators is [], then *?+, then concatenation, then | and newline.

/usr/xpg4/bin/egrep

/usr/xpg4/bin/egrep is a POSIX-compliant version of the /usr/bin/egrep command. See standards(5).

The /usr/xpg4/bin/egrep command uses the regular expressions described in the Extended Regular Expressions section of the regex(5) manual page.

Notes

Ideally, there should be only one grep command, but there is not a single algorithm that spans a wide enough range of space-time trade-offs.

Lines are limited only by the size of the available virtual memory.

The /usr/xpg4/bin/egrep command is identical to /usr/xpg4/bin/grep -E (see grep(1)). Portable applications should use /usr/xpg4/bin/grep -E.

Options

The options listed below are supported for both /usr/bin/egrep and /usr/xpg4/bin/egrep except for the -x option, which is available only for the /usr/xpg4/bin/egrep command.

-b	Precede each line by the block number on which it was found. This option can be useful in locating block numbers by context (first block is 0).
-c	Print only a count of the lines that contain the pattern.
-e *pattern-list*	Search for a *pattern-list* (full regular expression that begins with a -).
-f *file*	Take the list of full regular expressions from *file*.
-h	Suppress printing of file names when searching multiple files.
-i	Ignore upper-/lowercase distinction during comparisons.
-l	Print the names of files with matching lines once, separated by newlines. Do not repeat the names of files when the pattern is found more than once.
-n	Precede each line by its line number in the file (first line is 1).
-s	Work silently, that is, display nothing except error messages. This option is useful for checking the error status.
-v	Print all lines except those that contain the pattern.
-x	Consider only input lines that use all characters in the line to match an entire fixed string or regular expression to be matching lines. This option is supported for /usr/xpg4/bin/egrep only.

Operands

`file`	A path name of a file to be searched for the patterns. If you specify no file operands, use the standard input.
`pattern`	For `/usr/bin/egrep`, specify a pattern to be used during the search for input. For `usr/xpg4/bin/egrep`, specify one or more patterns to be used during the search for input. This operand is treated as if it were specified as `-e` `pattern-list`.

Examples

Suppose you want to find lines in one of your files that contain the words Michigan, Ohio, or Indiana. A single grep command cannot perform searches for more than one pattern. You can use egrep to search for more than one pattern in a file or group of files with a similar extension.

egrep provides the following capabilities:

- The capability to search for several patterns at a time in an "either or" condition.
- The capability to use a file containing patterns as the basis for its search.
- An extended set of regular expression metacharacters.

egrep is slower than grep but it can do more complex searches.

> **Note —** When using the egrep command, \ (—backslash followed by open parenthesis—or \)—backslash followed by close parenthesis—match parentheses as literal text. Open parenthesis and closed parenthesis are special characters that group parts of the pattern. The reverse is true with the grep command.

The following example searches all the files in the current directory with a .doc extension, for lines containing either Michigan or Ohio.

```
castle% egrep "Michigan|Ohio" *.doc
```

The following example forces egrep to look for lines that begin with Michigan or Ohio. The –i option looks for both upper- and lowercase.

```
castle% egrep -i "^Michigan|^Ohio" *.doc
```

You can include search patterns in a file and specify the file name as an argument to the egrep command. Using a file is convenient when developing complex patterns that you do not want to type at the command line.

In the following example, a file named pattern.file contains the line

```
(Michigan|Ohio)
```

The patterns do not require quotes but do require parentheses. The following example uses -f pattern.file as an egrep argument.

```
castle% egrep -f pattern.file *.doc
```

The following example searches all files with a .doc extension for lines that contain a string of one or more digits or the string ABC.

```
castle% egrep  "( [0-9]+  )|ABC)" *.doc
file1.doc: ABCDEFGHI
```

```
file5.doc: The following are numbers 1234567
file7.doc: 1 2 3 4 5 6
castle%
```

The following example searches `file1.doc` for lines that contain either the strings `bill`, `tom`, or any number that is enclosed in `()`:

```
castle% egrep "\((bill)|(tom)|(0-9)\)" file1.doc
(1)
(5)
(bill)
(tom)
castle%
```

The search does not match the following strings.

```
(123)
(bill123)
```

Usage

See `largefile`(5) for the description of the behavior of `egrep` when encountering files greater than or equal to 2 Gbytes (2**31 bytes).

Environment Variables

See `environ`(5) for descriptions of the following environment variables that affect the execution of `egrep`: LC_COLLATE, LC_CTYPE, LC_MESSAGES, and NLSPATH.

Exit Status

0	If any matches are found.
1	If no matches are found.
2	For syntax errors or inaccessible files (even if matches were found).

Attributes

See `attributes`(5) for descriptions of the following attributes:

/usr/bin/egrep

Attribute Type	Attribute Value
Availability	SUNWcsu
CSI	Enabled

/usr/xpg4/bin/egrep

Attribute Type	Attribute Value
Availability	SUNWxcu4
CSI	Enabled

See Also

fgrep(1), grep(1), sed(1), sh(1), attributes(5), environ(5),
largefile(5), regex(5), regexp(5), XPG4(5)

eject — Eject Media such as CD-ROM and Diskette from Drive

Synopsis

/usr/bin/eject [-dfnpq] [*device* | *nickname*]

Description

Use the eject command for those removable media devices that do not have a manual eject button or for those that do but are managed by Volume Management (see vold(1M)). You can specify the device by its name or by a nickname; if Volume Management is running and no device is specified, eject uses the default device.

Note — Only devices that support eject under program control respond to this command. eject responds differently, depending on whether or not Volume Management is running.

---

eject can also display its default device and a list of nicknames.

With Volume Management

When you use eject on media that can be ejected only manually, it does everything except remove the media, including unmounting the file system if it is mounted. In this case, eject displays a message that the media can now be manually ejected. If a window system is running, the message is displayed as a pop-up window, unless you use the -p option. If no window system is running or you use the -p option, a message is displayed both to standard error and to the system console that the media can now be physically removed.

Volume Management has the concept of a default device, which eject uses if you specify no path name or nickname. Use the -d option to check what default device is used.

Without Volume Management

When Volume Management is not running and you specify a path name, eject sends the eject command to that path name. If you supply a nickname instead of a path name, eject recognizes the nicknames shown below. To display this list, you can type **eject -n** and press Return.

Nickname	Path
fd	/dev/rdiskette
fd0	/dev/rdiskette
fd1	/dev/rdiskette1
diskette	/dev/rdiskette

Nickname	Path
diskette0	/dev/rdiskette0
diskette1	/dev/rdiskette1
rdiskette	/dev/rdiskette
rdiskette0	/dev/rdiskette0
rdiskette1	/dev/rdiskette1
floppy	/dev/rdiskette
floppy0	/dev/rdiskette0
floppy1	/dev/rdiskette1

Do not physically eject media from a device that contains mounted file systems. eject automatically searches for any mounted file systems that reside on the device and tries to unmount them before ejecting the media (see mount(1M)). If the umount operation fails, eject prints a warning message and exits. You can use the -f option to specify an eject even if the device contains mounted partitions; this option works only if Volume Management is not running.

If you have inserted a diskette, you must use volcheck(1) before ejecting the medium, to inform Volume Management of the diskette's presence.

Bugs

There should be a way to change the default on a per-user basis.

If Volume Management is not running, it is possible to eject a volume that is currently mounted (see mount(1M)). For example, if you have a CD-ROM drive at /dev/dsk/c0t3d0s2 mounted on /mnt, the following command (without Volume Management running) ejects the CD-ROM because both slices s0 and s2 reference the whole CD-ROM drive.

```
castle% eject /dev/dsk/c0t3d0s0
```

Options

-d	Display the name of the default device to be ejected.
-f	Force the device to eject even if it is busy, if Volume Management is not running.
-n	Display the nickname to the device name translation table.
-p	Do not try to call the eject_popup program.
-q	Query to see if the media are present.

Operands

device	Specify which device to eject, by the name in the /dev directory.
nickname	Specify which device to eject, by its nickname as known to this command.

Example

The following example uses the -d option to find out the default eject device. In the first example, no medium is in either the diskette or CD-ROM drive. In the second example, a diskette is in the diskette drive, and the volcheck command is used to let the system know that it is there. In the third example, a CD is in the CD-ROM drive and nothing is in the diskette drive.

```
castle% eject -d
Default device is: nothing inserted
castle% volcheck
castle% eject -d
Default device is: /vol/dev/rdiskette0/unnamed_floppy
castle% eject
castle% eject -d
Default device is: /vol/dev/rdsk/c0t6d0/jumpingjavascript
castle% eject
```

The following example ejects a CD from its drive while Volume Management is running (assuming only one CD-ROM drive).

```
castle% eject cdrom0
castle%
```

The following example ejects a diskette whether or not Volume Management is running.

```
castle% eject floppy0
castle%
```

The following example ejects a CD-ROM drive with path name /dev/dsk/c0t3d0s2 without Volume Management running.

```
# eject /dev/dsk/c0t3d0s2
#
```

Note — You must be superuser to mount, unmount, and eject a CD-ROM without Volume Management running.

Exit Status

0	The operation was successful or, with the -q option, the medium is in the drive.
1	The operation was unsuccessful or, with the -q option, the medium is not in the drive.
2	You specified invalid options.
3	An ioctl() request failed.
4	Manually ejectable medium is now okay to remove.

Files

/dev/diskette0

> Default diskette file.

/dev/sr0   Default CD-ROM file (deprecated).

/dev/dsk/c0t6d0s2

> Default CD-ROM file.

/usr/lib/vold/eject_popup

> Pop-up used for manually ejected media.

Attributes

See attributes(5) for descriptions of the following attributes:

Attribute Type	Attribute Value
Availability	SUNWcsu

See Also

volcancel(1), volcheck(1), volmissing(1), mount(1M), rmmount(1M), vold(1M), ioctl(2), rmmount.conf(4), vold.conf(4), attributes(5), volfs(7FS)

Diagnostics

A short help message is printed if you specify an unknown option. A diagnostic is printed if the device name cannot be opened or does not support eject.

Device Busy   An attempt was made to eject a device that has a mounted file system. A warning message is printed when doing a forced eject of a mounted device.

---

elfdump — Dump Selected Parts of an Object File

Synopsis

New!

/usr/ccs/bin/elfdump [-cCdehikmnprsvGy] [-w *file*] [-N *name*] *filename*...

Description

Use the elfdump command to symbolically dump selected parts of the specified object file(s). The options enable you to display specific portions of the file.

The elfdump command is similar in function to the dump(1) command, which offers an older and less user-friendly interface than elfdump, although dump(1) may be more appropriate for certain uses, such as in shell scripts.

For a complete description of the displayed information, refer to the *Linker and Libraries Guide*.

Options

-c	Dump section header information.
-C	Demangle C++ symbol names. New in the Solaris 8 release. *New!*
-d	Dump the contents of the .dynamic section.
-e	Dump the ELF header.
-G	Dump the contents of the .got section.
-h	Dump the contents of the .hash section.
-i	Dump the contents of the .interp section.
-k	Calculate the elf checksum. See gelf_checksum(3ELF). New in the Solaris 8 release. *New!*
-m	Dump the contents of the .note section. New in the Solaris 8 release. *New!*
-n	Dump the contents of the .note section.
-N *name*	Qualify an option with a specific name. For example, in a file that contains more than one symbol table, you can display the .dynsym table with the following command.

```
% elfdump -s -N .dynsym filename
```

-p	Dump the program headers.
-r	Dump the contents of the relocation sections (that is, .rel[a]).
-s	Dump the contents of the symbol table sections (that is, .dynsym and/or .symtab).

In the case of archives, dump the archive symbol table. You can specify individual sections with the -N option or you can specify an archive symbol table with the special section name -N ARSYM. In addition to the standard symbol table information, the version definition index of the symbol is also provided under the ver heading. New in the Solaris 8 release. *New!*

-v	Dump the contents of the version sections (that is, .SUNW_version). If you also use the -s option, then the st_other entry reported for symbols from the .dynsym section are their version index.
-w *file*	Write the contents of a specified section to the named file. This option is useful for extracting an individual section's data for additional processing.

For example, you can extract the .text section of a file with the following syntax. *New!*

```
% elfdump -w text.out -N .text filename
```

-y	Dump the contents of the .SUNW_syminfo section. New in the Solaris 9 release. *New!*

Operands

filename   The name of the specified object file.

Examples

The following example shows the first few lines of the output from the elfdump command for the zipinfo command.

castle% **/usr/ccs/bin/elfdump -c /bin/zipinfo**

```
Section Header[1]:  sh_name: .interp
    sh_addr:       0x100d4        sh_flags:    [ SHF_ALLOC ]
    sh_size:       0x11           sh_type:     [ SHT_PROGBITS ]
    sh_offset:     0xd4           sh_entsize: 0
    sh_link:       0              sh_info:     0
    sh_addralign: 0x1

Section Header[2]:  sh_name: .hash
    sh_addr:       0x100e8        sh_flags:    [ SHF_ALLOC ]
    sh_size:       0x64c          sh_type:     [ SHT_HASH ]
    sh_offset:     0xe8           sh_entsize: 0x4
    sh_link:       3              sh_info:     0
    sh_addralign: 0x4

Section Header[3]:  sh_name: .dynsym
    sh_addr:       0x10734        sh_flags:    [ SHF_ALLOC ]
    sh_size:       0xbe0          sh_type:     [ SHT_DYNSYM ]
    sh_offset:     0x734          sh_entsize: 0x10
    sh_link:       4              sh_info:     28
    sh_addralign: 0x4
...
```

Files

liblddbg.so

Linker debugging library.

Attributes

See attributes(5) for descriptions of the following attributes:

Attribute Type	Attribute Value
Availability	SUNWbtool

See Also

ar(1), dump(1), nm(1), pvs(1), elf(3ELF), attributes(5)
Linker and Libraries Guide

enable, disable — Enable/Disable LP Printers

Synopsis

```
/usr/bin/enable printer...
/usr/bin/disable [-c | -W] [-r [reason]] printer...
```

Description

The enable command activates printers, enabling them to print requests submitted by the lp command. You must run the enable command on the printer server.

The disable command deactivates printers, disabling them from printing requests submitted by the lp command. By default, any requests that are currently printing on *printer* are reprinted in their entirety either on *printer* or another member of the same class of printers. You must run the disable command on the print server.

Use lpstat -p to check the status of printers.

enable and disable affect queueing only on the print server's spooling system. Executing these commands from a client system has no effect on the server.

Options

-c
Cancel any requests that are currently printing on *printer*. You cannot use this option with the -W option. If the printer is remote, the -c option is silently ignored.

-r [*reason*]

Assign a reason for the disabling of the printer(s). This reason applies to all printers specified. This reason is reported by lpstat -p. Enclose *reason* in quotes if it contains blanks. The default reasons are unknown reason for the existing printer and new printer for a printer that has been added to the system but not yet enabled.

-W
Wait until the request currently being printed is finished before disabling *printer*. You cannot use this option with the -c option. If the printer is remote, the -W option is silently ignored.

Operands

printer
The name of the printer to be enabled or disabled. Specify *printer* using atomic name. See printers.conf(4) for information regarding the naming conventions for atomic names.

Exit Status

0   Successful completion.

non-zero   An error occurred.

Files

/var/spool/lp/*

LP print queue.

Attributes

See attributes(5) for descriptions of the following attributes:

Attribute Type	Attribute Value
Availability	SUNWpcu
CSI	Enabled

See Also

lp(1), lpstat(1), printers.conf(4), attributes(5)

env — Set Environment for Command Invocation

Synopsis

/usr/bin/env [-i | -] [*name=value*]... [*command* [*arg*...]]
/usr/xpg4/bin/env [-i | -] [*name=value*]...[*command* [*arg*...]]

Description

Using the env command with no arguments displays the current environment variable settings. The env command with options obtains the current environment, modifies it according to its arguments, then invokes the command named by the *command* operand with the modified environment.

Optional arguments are passed to *command*. If you specify no *command* operand, the resulting environment is written to the standard output, with one *name=value* pair per line.

/usr/bin/env

If env executes commands with arguments, it uses the default shell /usr/bin/sh (see sh(1)).

/usr/xpg4/bin/env

/usr/xpg4/bin/env is a POSIX-compliant version of the /usr/bin/env command. See standards(5).

If env executes commands with arguments, it uses /usr/xpg4/bin/sh, which is equivalent to /usr/bin/ksh (see ksh(1)).

Options

-i | - Ignore the environment that would otherwise be inherited from the current shell. Restrict the environment for *command* to that specified by the arguments.

Operands

name=value Arguments of the form *name=value* modify the execution environment and are placed into the inherited environment before command is invoked.

command The name of the command to be invoked. If *command* names any of the special shell built-in commands, the results are undefined.

arg A string to pass as an argument for the invoked command.

Examples

The following example uses the env command without any arguments to display the current values for the environment variables. The list has been truncated to save space.

```
castle% env
MANPATH=/usr/openwin/share/man:/usr/openwin/man:/usr/share/man:/usr/dt/
    share/man:/usr/dt/man:/usr/man:/opt/SUNWrtvc/man:/opt/hpnp/man
DTDATABASESEARCHPATH=/export/home/winsor/.dt/types,/etc/dt/appconfig/ty
    pes/%L,/etc/dt/appconfig/types/C,/usr/dt/appconfig/types/%L,/usr/dt/a
    ppconfig/types/C
DTXSERVERLOCATION=local
LANG=C
HELPPATH=/usr/openwin/lib/locale:/usr/openwin/lib/help
DTSOURCEPROFILE=true
PATH=/usr/openwin/bin:/usr/dt/bin:/bin:/usr/bin:/usr/sbin:/usr/ucb:/etc
    :/usr/proc/bin:/opt/hpnp/bin:/usr/local/games:.
...
castle%
```

The following example pipes the output of the env command through grep and searches for the value for the MANPATH environment variable.

```
castle% env | grep MANPATH
MANPATH=/usr/openwin/share/man:/usr/openwin/man:/usr/share/man:/usr/dt/
    share/man:/usr/dt/man:/usr/man:/opt/SUNWrtvc/man:/opt/hpnp/man
castle%
```

The following command invokes the command named mygrep with a new PATH value as the only entry in its environment. In this case, PATH is used to locate mygrep, which then must reside in /mybin.

```
castle% env -i PATH=/mybin mygrep xyz myfile
```

Environment Variables

See environ(5) for descriptions of the following environment variables that affect the execution of env: LC_CTYPE, LC_MESSAGES, and NLSPATH.

Exit Status

If *command* is invoked, the exit status of env is the exit status of *command*, otherwise, the env command exits with one of the following values:

0	Successful completion.
1-125	An error occurred.
126	*command* was found but could not be invoked.
127	*command* could not be found.

Attributes

See attributes(5) for descriptions of the following attributes:

/usr/bin/env

Attribute Type	Attribute Value
Availability	SUNWcsu
CSI	Enabled

/usr/xpg4/bin/env

Attribute Type	Attribute Value
Availability	SUNWxcu4
CSI	Enabled

See Also

ksh(1), sh(1), exec(2), profile(4), attributes(5), environ(5), XPG4(5)

eqn, neqn, checkeq — Typeset Mathematics Test

Synopsis

```
/usr/bin/eqn [-dxy] [-fn] [-pn] [-sn] [file]...
/usr/bin/neqn [file]...
/usr/bin/checkeq [file]...
```

Description

eqn and neqn are language processors to assist in describing equations. eqn is a preprocessor for troff(1) and is intended for devices that can print troff's output. neqn is a preprocessor for nroff(1) and is intended for use with terminals. Usage is almost always:

```
castle% eqn file... | troff
castle% neqn file... | nroff
```

If you specify no files, eqn and neqn read from the standard input. A line beginning with .EQ marks the start of an equation; the end of an equation is marked by a line beginning with `.EN`. Neither of these lines is altered, so they may be defined in macro packages to get centering, numbering, and so on. It is also possible to set two characters as delimiters; subsequent text between delimiters is also treated as eqn input.

checkeq reports missing or unbalanced delimiters and `.EQ`/`.EN` pairs.

Options

-dxy Set equation delimiters to characters x and y with the command-line argument. The more common way to do this is with delim xy between `.EQ` and `.EN`. The left and right delimiters can be identical. Delimiters are turned off by delim off in the text. All text that is neither between delimiters nor between `.EQ` and `.EN` is passed through untouched.

-fn Change font to n globally in the document. The font can also be changed globally in the body of the document by the gfont n directive, where n is the font specification.

-pn Reduce subscripts and superscripts by n point sizes from the previous size. In the absence of the -p option, subscripts and superscripts are reduced by three point sizes from the previous size.

-sn Change point size to n globally in the document. The point size can also be changed globally in the body of the document by the gsize n directive, where n is the point size.

Operands

file   The nroff or troff file processed by eqn or neqn.

Eqn Language

The nroff version of this description depicts the output of neqn to the terminal screen exactly as neqn is able to display it. Use neqn to view an accurate depiction of the printed output on the screen.

Tokens within eqn are separated by braces, double quotes, tildes, circumflexes, space, Tab, or newline characters. Braces {} are used for grouping; generally, anywhere a single character like x could appear, you can use a complicated construction enclosed in braces instead. Tilde (~) represents a full space in the output, circumflex (^), half as much.

Make subscripts and superscripts with the keywords sub and sup.

```
 x sub i makes xi
 2
a sub i sup 2 produces ai
 e sup {x sup 2 + y sup 2} gives ex2+y2
```

Make fractions with over.

```
a?_
a over b yields b
```

Make square roots with sqrt.

```
1
1 over sqrt {ax sup 2 +bx+c} results in _____
\|ax2+bx+c
```

Use the keywords `from` and `to` to introduce lower and upper limits on arbitrary things.

```
lim from {n-> inf } sum from 0 to n x sub i
```

makes

```
n
lim ~?>?_xi
n->oo0
```

Note — The SIGMA symbol cannot be displayed in `nroff`.

Make left and right brackets and braces of the right height with `left` and `right`.

```
left [x sup 2 + y sup 2 over alpha right] ~=~1
```

produces

```
|
|  y?_2?_|  = 1.
|x2+<?a  |
|
```

The `right` clause is optional. Legal characters after `left` and `right` are braces, brackets, bars, `c` and `f` for ceiling and floor, and `""` for nothing at all (useful for a right-side-only bracket).

Make vertical piles of things with `pile`, `lpile`, `cpile`, and `rpile`.

```
pile {a above b above c}
```

produces

```
a
b
c
```

There can be an arbitrary number of elements in a pile. `lpile` left-justifies, `pile` and `cpile` center, with different vertical spacing, and `rpile` right-justifies.

Make matrices with `matrix`.

```
matrix { lcol { x sub i above y sub 2 } ccol { 1 above 2 } }
```

produces

```
xi
y2
1
2
```

In addition, you can use `rcol` for a right-justified column.

Make diacritical marks with `dot`, `dotdot`, `hat`, `tilde`, `bar`, `vec`, `dyad`, and `under`.

```
x dot = f(t) bar
```

is

```
.   ___
x=f(t)
```

```
y dotdot bar ~=~ n under
```

is

```
 .?_.?_
 y = n?_
```

```
x vec ~=~ y dyad
```

is

```
_ _
x = y
```

Sizes and Fonts

Change sizes and fonts with `size` *n* or `size +-n`, `roman`, `italic`, `bold`, and `font` *n*.
Change sizes and fonts globally in a document by `gsize` *n* and `gfont` *n* or by the
command-line arguments `-sn` and `-fn`.

Successive Display Arguments

You can line up successive display arguments by placing `mark` before the desired lineup
point in the first equation; place `lineup` at the place that is to line up vertically in
subsequent equations.

Shorthands

Define shorthands or redefine existing keywords with `define`. The following statement
defines a new token called *thing* that is replaced by *replacement* whenever it appears
thereafter. The `%` can be any character that does not occur in *replacement*.

```
define thing % replacement %
```

Keywords and Shorthands

Recognized keywords are `sum` (SIGMA is not reproducible in `nroff`), `int` (integral sign
is not reproducible in `nroff`), `inf` (infinity sign is not reproducible in `nroff`), and
shorthands like `>=` (greater than or equal to is not reproducible in `nroff`) `->` (`->`), and
`!=` (not equal to is not reproducible in `nroff`).

Greek Letters

Greek letters are spelled out in the desired case, as in alpha or GAMMA.

Mathematical Words

Mathematical words like `sin`, `cos`, and `log` are made Roman automatically.

You can use `troff(1)` four-character escapes like `\ (bu (o)` anywhere. Strings enclosed
in double quotes `" . . . "` are passed through untouched to permit keywords to be entered
as text. You can use them to communicate with `troff` when all else fails.

Attributes

See `attributes(5)` for descriptions of the following attributes:

Attribute Type	Attribute Value
Availability	SUNWdoc

See Also
nroff(1), tbl(1), troff(1), attributes(5), ms(5)

Bugs
To bold characters such as digits and parentheses, you must quote them, as in 'bold "12.3"'.

---

eval — Shell Built-in Functions to Execute Other Commands

Synopsis

sh and ksh

eval [*argument*...]

ksh

* eval [*arg*...]

Description
See exec(1).

---

ex — Display-Based Text Editor

Synopsis
/usr/bin/ex [- | -s] [-l] [-L] [-R] [-r [*file*]] [-t *tag*] [-v] [-V] [-x] [-wn] [-C] [+*command* | -c *command*] *file*...
/usr/xpg4/bin/ex [- | -s] [-l] [-L] [-R] [-r [*file*]] [-t *tag*] [-v] [-V] [-x] [-wn] [-C] [+*command* | -c *command*] *file*...

Description
The ex command is the root of a family of editors: ex, edit, and vi. ex is a superset of ed(1), with the most notable extension being a display-editing facility. Display-based editing is the focus of vi.

If you have a CRT terminal, you may want to use a display-based editor; in this case, see vi(1), which is a command that focuses on the display-editing portion of ex.

If you have used ed, you will find that, in addition to having all of the ed commands available, ex has a number of additional features useful on CRT terminals. Intelligent terminals and high-speed terminals are very pleasant to use with vi. Generally, the ex editor uses far more of the capabilities of terminals than does ed. The ex editor uses the terminal capability database (see terminfo(4)) and the type of the terminal you are using from the environment variable TERM to determine how to drive your terminal efficiently. The editor makes use of features such as "insert and delete character and line" in its visual command (the vi command).

The ex command contains a number of features to allow easy viewing the text of a file. The z command gives easy access to windows of text. Entering Control-D scrolls a half-window of text and is more useful for quickly stepping through a file than just pressing Return. Of course, the screen-oriented visual mode gives constant access to editing context.

The ex command provides help when you make mistakes. The undo (u) command enables you to reverse any single change that goes astray. ex gives you a lot of feedback, normally printing changed lines, and indicates when more than a few lines are affected by a command so that it is easy to detect when a command has affected more lines than it should have.

The editor also normally prevents overwriting existing files, unless you edited them, so that you do not accidentally overwrite a file other than the one you are editing. If the system (or editor) crashes or you accidentally hang up the telephone, you can use the editor recover command (or -r *file* option) to retrieve your work. This facility gets you back to within a few lines of where you left off.

The ex command has several features for dealing with more than one file at a time. You can give it a list of files on the command line and use the next (n) command to deal with each in turn. You can also give the next command a list of file names, or a pattern as used by the shell, to specify a new set of files to be dealt with. In general, you can form file names in the editor with full shell metasyntax. The metacharacter % is also available in forming file names and is replaced by the name of the current file.

The editor has a group of buffers whose names are the ASCII lowercase letters (a-z). You can place text in these named buffers, where it is available to be inserted elsewhere in the file. The contents of these buffers remain available when you begin editing a new file using the edit (e) command.

Note — The editor does not warn you when you exit if you put text in named buffers and have not used them.

The & command repeats the last substitute command. In addition, ex provides a confirmed substitute command. You give a range of substitutions to be done, and the editor interactively asks whether each substitution is desired.

You can specify whether searches and substitutions are case insensitive. ex also allows regular expressions that match words to be constructed. This pattern matching is convenient, for example, in searching for the word edit if your document also contains the word editor.

ex has a set of options that you can tailor to your liking. One option that is very useful is the autoindent option, which enables the editor to supply leading white space to align text automatically. You can then use ^D as a backtab and space or Tab to move forward to align new code easily.

Miscellaneous useful features include an intelligent join (j) command that automatically supplies white space between joined lines, commands < and > that shift groups of lines, and the ability to filter portions of the buffer through commands such as sort.

Note — Null characters are discarded in input files and cannot appear in resultant files.

Options

- | -s   Suppress all interactive user feedback. This option is useful when processing editor scripts. Note that file input/output errors do not print a name if you use the command-line -s option.

+command | *-c command*

Begin editing by executing the specified editor command (usually a search or positioning command).

-C   Simulate the C command. The C command is like the X command, except that all text read in is assumed to have been encrypted.

-l   Set up for editing LISP programs.

-L   List the name of all files saved as the result of an editor or system crash.

-R   Set the read-only flag to prevent accidental overwriting of the file.

-r *file*   Edit *file* after an editor or system crash. (Recover the version of *file* that was in the buffer when the crash occurred.) Note that the message file too large to recover with -r option that you see when you load a file indicates that you can successfully edit and save the file. However, if the editing session is lost, you cannot recover the file with the -r option.

-t *tag*   Edit the file containing the *tag*, and position the editor at its definition.

-v   Start up in display-editing state using vi. You can achieve the same effect by simply typing the vi command.

-V   When ex commands are read by means of standard input, echo the input to standard error. This verbose option can be useful for processing ex commands within shell scripts.

-wn   Set the default window size to *n*. This option is useful when you are using the editor over a slow-speed line.

-x   Simulate the X command, and prompt for an encryption key. This key encrypts and decrypts text using the algorithm of the crypt command. The X command makes an educated guess to determine whether text read in is encrypted or not. The temporary buffer file is encrypted also, using a transformed version of the key typed in for the -x option.

> **Note** — Although the following options continue to be supported, they have been replaced in the documentation by options that follow the Command Syntax Standard (see intro(1)). The - option has been replaced by -s; a -r option that is not followed with an option-argument has been replaced by -L, and +*command* has been replaced by -c *command*.

/usr/xpg4/bin/ex

If you specify both the -t *tag* and the -c *command* options, the -t *tag* is processed first. That is, the file containing *tag* is selected by -t and then the command is executed.

> **Note** — The standard Solaris version of ex will be replaced by the POSIX.2-conforming version (see standards(5)) in the future. Scripts that use the ex family of addressing and features should use the /usr/xpg4/bin version of these commands.

Operands

file   A path name of a file to be edited.

Usage

The states for the ex command are listed below.

State	Description
Command	Normal and initial state. Input prompted for by a colon (:). Your line-kill character cancels a partial command.
Insert	Entered by a, i, or c. You can enter arbitrary text. Insert state normally is terminated by a line having only . on it, or, abnormally, with an interrupt.
Visual	Entered by typing vi; terminated by typing Q or ^\ (Control-\).

The commands, abbreviations, and command arguments for the ex command are listed below. For /usr/xpg4/bin/ex, if you specify both a *count* and a *range* for a command that uses them, the number of lines affected is taken from the *count* value instead of the *range*. The starting line for the command is taken to be the first line addressed by the *range*.

Command	Abbreviation	Arguments
Abbreviate	ab	ab[brev] *word* rhs
Adjust Window		[*line*] z [type] [*count*] [*flags*]
Append	a	[*line*] a[ppend] [!]
Arguments	ar	ar[gs]
Change	c	[*range*] c[hange] [!] [*count*]
Change Directory	chd	chd[ir] [!] [*directory*]; cd[!] [*directory*]
Copy	co	[*range*] co[py] *line* [*flags*]; [*range*] t *line* [*flags*]
Delete	d	[*range*] d[elete] [*buffer*] [*count*] [*flags*]
Edit	e	e[dit] [!] [+*line*] [*file*]; ex[!] [+*line*] [*file*]
Escape		! *command* [*range*]! *command*
Execute		@ *buffer*; * *buffer*
File	f	f[ile] [*file*]
Global	g	[*range*] g[lobal] /*pattern*/ [*commands*]; [*range*] v /*pattern*/ [commands]
Insert	i	[*line*] i[nsert] [!]
Join	j	[*range*] j[oin] [!] [*count*] [*flags*]

Command	Abbreviation	Arguments
List	l	[*range*] l[ist] [*count*] [*flags*]
Map	map	map[!] [x rhs]
Mark	ma	[*line*] ma[rk] x; [*line*] k x
Move	m	[*range*] m[ove] *line*
Next	n	n[ext] [!] [*file* ...]
Number	nu	[*range*] nu[mber] [*count*] [*flags*]; [*range*] # [*count*] [*flags*]
Open	o	[*line*] o[pen] /*pattern*/ [*flags*]
Preserve	pre	pre[serve]
Print	p	[*range*] p[rint] [*count*] [*flags*]
Put	pu	[*line*] pu[t] [*buffer*]
Quit	q	q[uit] [!]
Read	r	[*line*] r[ead] [!] [*file*]
Recover	rec	rec[over] *file*
Resubstitute		[*range*] & [*options*] [*count*] [*flags*]; [*range*] s[ubstitute] [*options*] [*count*] [*flags*]; [*range*] ~ [*options*] [*count*] [*flags*]
Rewind	rew	rew[ind] [!] Set se[t] [*option*[=[*value*]]...] [nooption...] [*option*?...] [all]
Scroll		EOF
Shell	sh	sh[ell]
Shift Left		[*range*] < [*count*] [*flags*]
Shift Right		[*range*] > [*count*] [*flags*]
Source	so	so[urce] *file*
Substitute	s	[*range*] s[ubstitute] [/*pattern*/*repl*/[*options*] [*count*] [*flags*]]
Suspend	su	su[spend] [!]; st[op] [!]
Tag	ta	ta[g] [!] *tagstring*
Unabbreviate	una	una[bbrev] *word*
Undo	u	u[ndo]
Unmap	unm	unm[ap] [!] x
Visual	vi	[*line*] vi[sual] [*type*] [*count*] [*flags*]

Command	Abbreviation	Arguments
Write	w	[*range*} w[rite] [!] [>>] [*file*]; [*range*} w[rite] [!] [*file*]; [*range*} wq[!] [>>] [*file*]
Write and Exit	x	[*range*] x[it] [!] [*file*]
Write Line Number		[*line*] = [*flags*]
Yank	ya	[*range*] ya[nk] [*buffer*] [*count*]

The ex commands are listed below.

Command	Description
C	Forced encryption.
X	Heuristic encryption.
&	Resubstitute.
CR	Print next.
>	Right shift.
<	Left shift.
^D	Scroll.
z	Window.
!	Shell escape.

Note — The z command prints the number of logical instead of physical lines. More than one screen of output may result if long lines are present.

The ex command addresses are listed below.

Address	Description
n	Line *n*.
.	Current.
$	Last.
+	Next.
–	Previous.
+*n*	*n* forward.
/*pat*	Next with *pat*.
?*pat*	Previous with *pat*.
x-*n*	*n* before *x*.
x,y	*x* through *y*.
'*x*	Marked with *x*.
' '	Previous context.

Address	Description
`%`	`1,$.`

The ex initialization options are listed below.

Option	Description
`$HOME/.exrc`	
	Editor initialization file.
`./.exrc`	Editor initialization file.
`EXINIT`	Place `set` commands in the `EXINIT` environment variable.
`set`	Show changed options.
`set al`	Show all options.
`set no`*x*	Disable option *x*.
`set` *x*	Enable option *x*.
`set` *x*=*val*	Give value *val* to option *x*.
`set` *x*?	Show value of option *x*.

The most useful ex options and their abbreviations are listed below.

Option	Abbrev.	Description
`autoindent`	`ai`	Supply indent.
`autowrite`	`aw`	Write before changing files.
`directory`		Path name of directory for temporary work files.
`exrc`	`ex`	Enable vi/ex to read the `.exrc` in the current directory. This option is set in the `EXINIT` shell variable or in the `.exrc` file in the `$HOME` directory.
`ignorecase`	`ic`	Ignore case of letters in scanning. Note that there is no easy way to do a single scan ignoring case.
`list`		Print ^I for Tab, $ at end.
`magic`		Treat `.` `[* as special in patterns.
`modelines`		Execute first five lines and last five lines as vi/ex commands if they are of the form ex: *command*: or vi: *command*:.
`number`	`nu`	Number lines.
`paragraphs`	`para`	Macro names that start paragraphs.
`redraw`		Simulate smart terminal.
`report`		Inform you if the number of lines modified by the last command is greater than the value of the report variable.
`scroll`		Command-mode lines.

Option	Abbrev.	Description
sections	sect	Macro names that start sections.
shiftwidth	sw	For < >, and input ^D.
showmatch	sm	To) and } as typed.
showmode	smd	Show insert mode in vi.
slowopen	slow	Stop updates during insert.
term		Specifies to vi the type of terminal being used (the default is the value of the environment variable TERM).
window		Visual mode lines.
wrapmargin	wm	Automatic line splitting.
wrapscan	ws	Search around end (or beginning) of buffer.

The ex scanning pattern formations are listed below.

Pattern	Description
^	Beginning of line.
$	End of line.
.	Any character.
\<	Beginning of word.
\>	End of word.
[*str*]	Any character in *str*.
[^*str*]	Any character not in *str*.
[*x*-v]	Any character between *x* and *y*.
*	Any number of preceding characters.

Environment Variables

See environ(5) for descriptions of the following environment variables that affect the execution of ex: HOME, PATH, SHELL, TERM, LC_COLLATE, LC_CTYPE, LC_MESSAGES, and NLSPATH.

COLUMNS	Override the system-selected horizontal screen size.
EXINIT	Determine a list of ex commands that are executed on editor startup, before reading the first file. The list can contain multiple commands separated by the pipe (|) character.
LINES	Override the system-selected vertical screen size, used as the number of lines in a screenful and the vertical screen size in visual mode.

The editing environment defaults to certain configuration options. When you initiate an editing session, ex tries to read the EXINIT environment variable. If it exists, the editor uses the values defined in EXINIT; otherwise, the values set in $HOME/.exrc are used. If $HOME/.exrc does not exist, the default values are used.

To use a copy of `.exrc` located in the current directory other than $HOME, set the `exrc` option in EXINIT or $HOME/`.exrc`. Options set in EXINIT can be turned off in a local `.exrc` only if `exrc` is set in EXINIT or $HOME/`.exrc`.

Exit Status

0	Successful completion.
>0	An error occurred.

Files

/var/tmp/Ex*nnnnn*

Editor temporary file.

/var/tmp/Rx*nnnnn*

Named buffer temporary file.

/usr/lib/expreserve

Preserve command.

/usr/lib/exrecover

Recover command.

/usr/lib/exstrings

Error messages.

/usr/share/lib/terminfo/*

Describes capabilities of terminals.

/var/preserve/login

Preservation directory (where login is the user's login).

$HOME/.exrc

Editor startup file.

./.exrc   Editor startup file.

Attributes

See `attributes`(5) for descriptions of the following attributes:

/usr/bin/ex

Attribute Type	Attribute Value
Availability	SUNWcsu
CSI	Enabled

/usr/xpg4/bin/ex

Attribute Type	Attribute Value
Availability	SUNWxcu4
CSI	Enabled

See Also

ed(1), edit(1), grep(1), sed(1), sort(1), vi(1), curses(3X), term(4),
terminfo(4), attributes(5), environ(5), standards(5)
  Solaris Advanced User's Guide

Author

The vi and ex commands are based on software developed by The University of
California, Berkeley, California, Computer Science Division, Department of Electrical
Engineering and Computer Science.

---

exec, eval, source — Shell Built-in Functions to Execute Other Commands

Synopsis

sh

exec [*argument...*]
cval [*argument...*]

csh

exec *command*
eval *argument...*
source [-h] *name*

ksh

* exec [*arg...*]
* eval [*arg...*]

Description

Bourne Shell

The exec *command* specified by the arguments is executed in place of this shell without
creating a new process. Input/output arguments may appear, and if you give no other
arguments, they modify the shell input/output.

   The arguments to the eval built-in are read as input to the shell and the resulting
command(s) executed.

C Shell

exec executes *command* in place of the current shell, which terminates.

   eval reads its arguments as input to the shell and executes the resulting
command(s). This command is usually used to execute commands generated as the
result of command or variable substitution.

   source reads commands from *name*. You can nest source commands, but if they are
nested too deeply, the shell may run out of file descriptors. An error in a sourced file at
any level terminates all nested source commands.

-h   Put commands from the file name on the history list without executing
                      them.

Korn Shell

With the exec built-in function, if you specify *arg*, the command specified by the arguments is executed in place of this shell without creating a new process. You can specify input/output arguments that affect the current process. If you specify no arguments, the effect of this command is to modify file descriptors as prescribed by the input/output redirection list. In this case, any file descriptor numbers greater than 2 that are opened with this mechanism are closed when another program is invoked.

The arguments to eval are read as input to the shell, and the resulting command(s) executed.

ksh(1) commands that are preceded by one or two asterisks (*) are treated specially in the following ways:

- Variable assignment lists preceding the command remain in effect when the command completes.
- I/O redirections are processed after variable assignments.
- Errors cause a script that contains them to abort.
- Words following a command preceded by ** and that are in the format of a variable assignment are expanded with the same rules as a variable assignment. Tilde substitution is performed after the equal sign, and word-splitting and file-name generation are not performed.

Attributes

See attributes(5) for descriptions of the following attributes:

Attribute Type	Attribute Value
Availability	SUNWcsu

See Also

csh(1), ksh(1), sh(1), attributes(5)

exit, return, goto — Shell Built-in Functions to Enable the Shell to Advance Beyond Its Sequence of Steps

Synopsis

sh
```
exit [n]
return [n]
```

csh
```
exit [(expr)]
goto label
```

ksh
```
* exit [n]
* return [n]
```

Description

Bourne Shell

exit exits the calling shell or shell script with the exit status specified by *n*. If you omit *n*, the exit status is that of the last command executed (an end-of-file exits the shell).

return exits a function with the return value specified by *n*. If you omit *n*, the return status is that of the last command executed.

C Shell

exit exits the calling shell or shell script, either with the value of the status variable or with the value specified by the expression *expr*.

The goto built-in uses a specified label as a search string among commands. The shell rewinds its input as much as possible and searches for a line of the form *label*: possibly preceded by space or Tab characters. Execution continues after the indicated line. It is an error to jump to a label that occurs between a while or for built-in command and its corresponding end.

Korn Shell

exit exits the calling shell or shell script with the exit status specified by *n*. The value is the least significant 8 bits of the specified status. If you omit *n*, the exit status is that of the last command executed. When exit occurs when a trap is being executed, the last command refers to the command that executed before the trap was invoked. An end-of-file also exits the shell except for a shell that has the ignoreeof option turned on.

return returns a shell function or . script to the invoking script with the return status specified by *n*. The value is the least significant 8 bits of the specified status. If you omit *n*, the return status is that of the last command executed. If you invoke return while not in a function or a . script, then it is the same as an exit.

For the exit and return commands, ksh(1) commands that are preceded by one or two asterisks (*) are treated specially in the following ways:

1. Variable assignment lists preceding the command remain in effect when the command completes.

2. I/O redirections are processed after variable assignments.

3. Errors cause a script that contains them to abort.

4. Words, following a command preceded by ** and that are in the format of a variable assignment, are expanded with the same rules as a variable assignment. Tilde substitution is performed after the equal sign (=), and word-splitting and file-name generation are not performed.

Attributes

See attributes(5) for descriptions of the following attributes:

Attribute Type	Attribute Value
Availability	SUNWcsu

See Also

break(1), csh(1), ksh(1), sh(1), attributes(5)

expand, unexpand — Expand Tab Characters to Space Characters, and Vice Versa

Synopsis
```
/usr/bin/expand [-t tablist] [file...]
/usr/bin/expand [-tabstop] [-tab1,tab2,...,tabn] [file...]
/usr/bin/unexpand [-a] [-t tablist] [file...]
```

Description
expand copies files (or the standard input) to the standard output, with Tab characters expanded to space characters. Backspace characters are preserved in the output and decrement the column count for Tab calculations. expand is useful for preprocessing character files (before sorting, looking at specific columns, and so forth) that contain Tab characters.

unexpand copies files (or the standard input) to the standard output, putting Tab characters back into the data. By default, only leading space and Tab characters are converted to strings of tabs. You can override the default behavior with the -a option.

Options
The options for the expand command are listed below.

-t *tablist*   Specify the Tab stops. The argument *tablist* must consist of a single, positive decimal integer or multiple, positive, decimal integers separated by blank characters or commas, in ascending order. If you specify a single number, Tabs are set *tablist* column positions apart instead of the default 8. If you specify multiple numbers, the Tabs are set at those specific column positions.

Each Tab-stop position N must be an integer value greater than 0, and the list must be in strictly ascending order. From the start of a line of output, tabbing to position N outputs the next character in the (N+1)-th column position on that line.

If expand processes a Tab character at a position beyond the last of those specified in a multiple Tab-stop list, the Tab character is replaced by a single space character in the output.

-*tabstop*   Set Tab characters *tabstop* space characters apart, where *tabstop* is a single integer, instead of the default 8.

-*tab1*,*tab2*,...,*tabn*

Set Tab characters at the columns specified by -*tab1*, *tab2*,..., *tabn*.

The options for the unexpand command are listed below.

-a   Insert Tab characters when replacing a run of two or more space characters would produce a smaller output file.

-t *tablist*　　Specify the Tab stops. The *tablist* must be a single argument consisting of a single, positive, decimal integer or multiple, positive, decimal integers separated by blank characters or commas, in ascending order. If you specify a single number, set Tabs *tablist* column positions apart instead of the default 8. If you specify multiple numbers, the tabs are set at those specific column positions.

Each Tab-stop position N must be an integer value greater than 0, and the list must be in strictly ascending order. From the start of a line of output, tabbing to position N outputs the next character in the $(N+1)$-th column position on that line. When you do not specify the -t option, the default is the equivalent of specifying -t 8 (except for the interaction with -a).

No space-to-Tab character conversions occur for characters at positions beyond the last of those specified in a multiple Tab-stop list.

When you specify -t, the presence or absence of the -a option is ignored; conversion is not limited to the processing of leading blank characters.

Operands

file　　The path name of a text file to be used as input.

Environment Variables

See environ(5) for descriptions of the following environment variables that affect the execution of expand and unexpand: LC_CTYPE, LC_MESSAGES, and NLSPATH.

Exit Status

0　　Successful completion.

>0　　An error occurred.

Attributes

See attributes(5) for descriptions of the following attributes:

Attribute Type	Attribute Value
Availability	SUNWesu
CSI	Enabled

See Also

tabs(1), attributes(5), environ(5)

export — Shell Built-in Environment Variable Function

Synopsis

sh
export [*name*...]

ksh
export [*name*[=*value*]]...

Description

See set(1).

exportfs — Translate exportfs Options to share/unshare Commands

Synopsis

/usr/sbin/exportfs [-aiuv] [-o *options*] [*pathname*]

Description

exportfs translates SunOS 4.x exportfs options to the corresponding share/unshare options and invokes share/unshare with the translated options.

With no options or arguments, exportfs invokes share to print out the list of all currently shared NFS file systems.

Note — exportfs is the BSD/Compatibility Package command of share(1M) and unshare(1M). Use share(1M)/unshare(1M) whenever possible.

Options

-a   Invoke shareall(1M), or if –u is specified, invoke unshareall(1M).

-i   Ignore options in /etc/dfs/dfstab.

-o *options*   Specify a comma-separated list of optional characteristics for the file systems being exported. exportfs translates options to share-equivalent options. (See share(1M) for information about individual options.)

-u   Invoke unshare(1M) on path name.

-v   Verbose.

Attributes

See attributes(5) for descriptions of the following attributes:

Attribute Type	Attribute Value
Availability	SUNWnfssu

New!

See Also

share(1M), shareall(1M), unshare(1M), unshareall(1M), attributes(5)

expr — Evaluate Arguments as an Expression

Synopsis

```
/usr/bin/expr argument...
/usr/xpg4/bin/expr argument...
/usr/ucb/expr argument...
```

Description

The expr command evaluates the expression and writes the result to standard output. Each token of the expression is a separate argument, so you must separate terms of the expression by blanks. Quote strings containing blanks or other special characters. You can precede integer-valued arguments by a unary minus sign. Escape characters special to the shell. The length of the expression is limited to LINE_MAX (2048 characters).

> **Note —** The character 0 is written to indicate a zero value and nothing is written to indicate a null string.

Operands

argument   Evaluated as an expression. Separate terms of the expression with blanks. You must escape characters special to the shell (see sh(1)). Quote strings containing blanks or other special characters. The length of the expression is limited to LINE_MAX (2048 characters).

New!

The operators and keywords are listed below. The list is in order of increasing precedence, with equal precedence operators grouped within { } symbols. All of the operators are left-associative.

expr \| *expr*

Return the first *expr* if it is neither null nor 0; otherwise, return the second *expr*.

expr \& *expr*

Return the first *expr* if neither *expr* is null or 0; otherwise, return 0.

expr { =, \>, \>=, \<, \<=, != } *expr*

> Return the result of an integer comparison if both arguments are integers; otherwise, return the result of a string comparison, using the locale-specific coalition sequence. The result of each comparison is 1 if the specified relationship is true, 0 if the relationship is false.

expr { +, - } *expr*

> Add or subtract integer-valued arguments.

expr { *, /, % } *expr*

> Multiply, divide, or remainder the integer-valued arguments.

expr : *expr* Compare the first argument with the second argument, which must be an internationalized basic regular expression (BRE); see regex(5). Normally, the /usr/bin/expr colon (:) matching operator returns the number of bytes matched, and the /usr/xpg4/bin/expr matching operator returns the number of characters matched (0 on failure). If the second argument contains at least one BRE subexpression [\(...\)], the matching operator returns the string corresponding to \1.

integer   An argument consisting only of an (optional) unary minus followed by digits.

string   A string argument that cannot be identified as an integer argument or as one of the expression operator symbols.

Compatibility Operators (IA only)

The following operators are included for compatibility with INTERACTIVE UNIX System only and are not intended to be used by non-INTERACTIVE UNIX System scripts.

index string character-list

> Report the first position in which any one of the bytes in *character-list* matches a byte in string.

length string

> Return the length (that is, the number of bytes) of *string*.

substr string integer-1 integer-2

> Extract the substring of *string* starting at position *integer-1* and of length *integer-2* bytes. If *integer-1* has a value greater than the number of bytes in *string*, *expr* returns a null string. If you try to extract more bytes than there are in *string*, *expr* returns all the remaining bytes from *string*. Results are unspecified if either *integer-1* or *integer-2* is a negative value.

Notes

After argument processing by the shell, expr cannot tell the difference between an operator and an operand except by the value. If $a is an =, the command:

```
$ expr $a = '='
```

looks like:

```
$ expr = = =
```

because the arguments are passed to expr (and they are all taken as the = operator). The following works:

```
$ expr X$a = X=
```

Regular Expressions

Unlike some previous versions, expr uses Internationalized Basic Regular Expressions for all system-provided locales. Internationalized Regular Expressions are explained on the regex(5) manual page.

Examples

You can use expr to perform basic integer math, which is useful for simple mathematical processing and for controlling loops.

The following example performs a simple calculation.

```
castle% expr 1 + 9
10
castle%
```

You can use expr to evaluate various string comparisons, as shown in the following example.

```
a=bill
b=tom

 if expr $a = $b
then
   echo "They are the same."
else
   echo "They are different."
fi
```

The script returns:

```
They are different.
```

You can use expr to evaluate alphabetic or arithmetic variables, as shown in the following example.

```
a=bill
expr $a : '[a-zA-Z]*'
or
n=100
expr $n : '[-+]*[0-9.]*'


if [ 'expr $n : '[-+]*[0-9.]*'' -eq 'expr $n : '.*'' ]
 then
    echo "It's numeric."
 else
```

```
      echo "It's not numeric."
fi
```

The system returns:

```
It's numeric.
```

The following example adds 1 to the shell variable a.

```
a=0
a=`expr $a + 1`
```

The following example emulates basename(1). It returns the last segment of the path name $a. For $a equal to either /usr/abc/file or just file, the example returns file. (Watch out for / alone as an argument: expr takes it as the division operator.)

```
a='/etc/dfs/dfstab'
expr $a : '.*/\(.*\)' \| $a
```

The expression returns dfstab.
The following example is a better version of the previous example. The addition of the // characters eliminates any ambiguity about the division operator and simplifies the whole expression.

```
a='/etc/dfs/dfstab'
expr //$a : '.*/\(.*\)'
```

/usr/bin/expr
The following example returns the number of bytes in $VAR.

```
VAR=bill
expr "$VAR" : '.*'
```

The expression returns 4.

/usr/xpg4/bin/expr
The following example returns the number of characters in $VAR.

```
VAR=bill
expr "$VAR" : '.*'
```

Environment Variables
See environ(5) for descriptions of the following environment variables that affect the execution of expr: LC_COLLATE, LC_CTYPE, LC_MESSAGES, and NLSPATH.

Exit Status
As a side effect of expression evaluation, expr returns the following exit values:

0	The expression is neither null nor 0.
1	The expression is either null or 0.
2	Invalid expression.
>2	An error occurred.

Attributes

See attributes(5) for descriptions of the following attributes:

Attribute Type	Attribute Value
Availability	SUNWcsu
CSI	Enabled

See Also

basename(1), ed(1), sh(1), Intro(3), attributes(5), environ(5), regex(5), XPG4(5)

Diagnostics

syntax error   Operator and operand errors.

non-numeric argument

        Arithmetic is attempted on such a string.

exstr — Extract Strings from Source Files

Synopsis

```
/usr/bin/exstr filename...
/usr/bin/exstr -e filename...
/usr/bin/exstr -r [-d] filename...
```

Description

Use the exstr command to extract strings from C-language source files and replace them by calls to the message retrieval function (see gettxt(3C)). This command extracts all character strings surrounded by double quotes, not just strings used as arguments to the printf command or the printf routine. In the first form, exstr finds all strings in the source files and writes them on the standard output. Each string is preceded by the source file name and a colon.

Use the following steps to extract strings from a source file:

1. Use exstr -e to extract a list of strings and save it in a file.

2. Examine the list and determine which strings can be translated and subsequently retrieved by the message retrieval function.

3. Modify the file by deleting lines that can't be translated and, for lines that can be translated, by adding the message file names and the message numbers as the fourth (msgfile) and fifth (msgnum) entries on a line. The message files named must have been created by mkmsgs(1) and exist in /usr/lib/locale/locale/LC_MESSAGES. (The directory locale corresponds to the language in which the text strings are written; see setlocale(3C)). Use message numbers that correspond to the sequence numbers of strings in the message files.

4. Use this modified file as input to exstr -r to produce a new version of the original C-language source file in which the strings have been replaced by calls to the

message retrieval function `gettxt()`. The `msgfile` and `msgnum` fields are used to construct the first argument to `gettxt()`. The second argument to `gettxt()` is printed if the message retrieval fails at runtime. This argument is the null string, unless you use the `-d` option.

The `exstr` command cannot replace strings in all instances. For example, a static initialized character string cannot be replaced by a function call. A second example is that a string could be in a form of an escape sequence that could not be translated. To not break existing code, you must examine the files created by invoking `exstr -e` and delete lines containing strings not replaceable by function calls. In some cases, the code may require modifications so that strings can be extracted and replaced by calls to the message retrieval function.

Options

-e   Extract a list of strings from the named C-language source files, with positional information. This list is produced on standard output in the following format:

file: *line*: *position*: *msgfile*: *msgnum*: *string*

file	The name of a C-language source file.
line	Line number in the file.
position	Character position in the line.
msgfile	Null.
msgnum	Null.
string	The extracted text string.

Normally, you redirect this output into a file. Then, you edit this file to add the values you want to use for *msgfile* and *msgnum*.

msgfile	The file that contains the text strings that replace *string*. A file with this name must be created and installed in the appropriate place by the mkmsgs(1) command.
msgnum	The sequence number of the string in *msgfile*.

The next step is to use `exstr -r` to replace strings in *file*.

-r   Replace strings in a C-language source file with function calls to the message retrieval function `gettxt()`.

-d   Use together with the `-r` option. If the message retrieval fails when `gettxt()` is invoked at runtime, then the extracted string is printed. You use the capability provided by `exstr` on an application program that needs to run in an international environment and have messages print in more than one language. `exstr` replaces text strings with function calls that point at strings in a message database. The database used depends on the runtime value of the LC_MESSAGES environment variable (see `environ(5)`).

Examples

The following examples show uses of `exstr`.

Assume that the file example.c contains two strings.

```
main()
{
 printf("This is an example\n");
 printf("Hello world!\n");
}
```

The following example invokes the exstr command with the argument example.c to extract strings from the named file and print them on the standard output.

```
castle% exstr example.c
example.c:This is an example\n
example.c:Hello world!\n
castle%
```

Next, use the -e option to extract the strings and redirect the output to a file named example.stringout.

```
castle% exstr -e example.c > example.stringout
castle% more example.stringout
example.c:3:22:::This is an example\n
example.c:4:22:::Hello world!\n
castle%
```

You must edit example.stringout to add the values you want to use for the msgfile and msgnum fields before these strings can be replaced by calls to the retrieval function. The following example uses UX as the name of the message file and the numbers 1 and 2 as the sequence number of the strings in the file to produce a file that looks like the following.

```
castle% more example.stringout
example.c:3:22:UX:1:This is an example\n
example.c:4:22:UX:2:Hello world!\n
castle%
```

Now, invoke the exstr command with the -r option to replace the strings in the source file by the calls to the message retrieval function gettxt().

```
castle% exstr -r example.c < example.stringout > intlexample.c
castle% more intlexample.c
extern char *gettxt();
        main()
        {
            printf(gettxt("UX:1", ""));
            printf(gettxt("UX:2", ""));
        }
castle%
```

Using exstr with the -rd option displays the extracted strings as a second argument to gettxt().

```
castle% exstr -rd example.c < example.stringout > intlexample.c
castle% more intlexample.c
extern char *gettxt();
        main()
          {
```

```
            printf(gettxt("UX:1", "This is an example\n"));
            printf(gettxt("UX:2", "Hello world!\n"));
      }
castle%
```

Files

/usr/lib/locale/locale/LC_MESSAGES/*

Files created by mkmsgs(1).

Attributes

See attributes(5) for descriptions of the following attributes:

Attribute Type	Attribute Value
Availability	SUNWtoo

See Also

gettxt(1), mkmsgs(1), printf(1), srchtxt(1), gettxt(3C), setlocale(3C), printf(3S), attributes(5), environ(5)

Diagnostics

The error messages produced by exstr are self-explanatory. They indicate errors in the command line or format errors encountered within the input file.

F

factor — Obtain the Prime Factors of a Number

Synopsis

`/usr/bin/factor [`*`integer`*`]`

Description

`factor` writes to standard input all prime factors for any positive integer of fewer than 15 digits. The prime factors are written the proper number of times.

If you type `factor` without an argument, it waits for you to type an integer and press Return. After you enter the integer, `factor` factors it, writes its prime factors the proper number of times, and then waits for another integer. `factor` exits if you enter a 0 or any nonnumeric character.

If you invoke `factor` with an argument (*`integer`*), it writes the integer, factors it, writes all the prime factors as described above, and then exits. If the argument is 0 or nonnumeric, `factor` writes a 0 and then exits.

The maximum time to factor an integer is proportional to sqrt (n), where n is the integer that you enter. `factor` takes this time when n is prime or the square of a prime.

Operands

`integer`   Any positive integer less than 15 digits.

Examples

The following example enters a number of 15 digits, and `factor` displays the Ouch! error message. It then factors a number of 14 digits. Type **q** and press Return to quit `factor`.

```
castle% factor
123456789012345
Ouch!
12345678901234
        2
        7
        73
        12079920647

q
castle%
```

Exit Status

0	Successful completion.
1	An error occurred.

Diagnostics

factor prints the error message Ouch! for input out of range or for garbage input.

Attributes

See attributes(5) for descriptions of the following attributes:

Attribute Type	Attribute Value
Availability	SUNWesu

See Also

attributes(5)

false — Provide Truth Values

Synopsis

/usr/bin/false

Description

See true(1).

fastboot, fasthalt — Reboot/Halt the System Without Checking the Disks

Synopsis

/usr/ucb/fastboot [*boot-options*]
/usr/ucb/fasthalt [*halt-options*]

Description

fastboot and fasthalt are shell scripts that invoke reboot and halt with the proper arguments.

Note — These commands are provided for BSD compatibility only.

Attributes

See attributes(5) for descriptions of the following attributes:

Attribute Type	Attribute Value
Availability	SUNWscpu

See Also

fsck(1M), halt(1M), init(1M), reboot(1M), init.d(4), attributes(5)

fc — Process Command History List

Synopsis

/usr/bin/fc [*first*[*last*]]
/usr/bin/fc -l [-nr] [*first*[*last*]]
/usr/bin/fc -s [*old=new*] [*first*]

ksh

fc -e - [*old=new*] [*command*]
fc [-e *ename*] [-nlr] [*first* [*last*]]

Description

See history(1).

fdformat — Format Diskette or PCMCIA Memory Card

Synopsis

```
/usr/bin/fdformat [-dDeEfHlLmMUqvx] [-b label] [-B filename] [-t dos]
[-t nec] [devname]
```

Description

Note — Starting with the Solaris 8 release, fdformat has been superseded by rmformat(1), which provides most but not all fdformat functionality.

Use the fdformat command to format both diskettes and PCMCIA memory cards. You must format all new, blank diskettes or PCMCIA memory cards before you can use them. fdformat formats and verifies the media and indicates whether it encountered any bad sectors. All existing data on the diskette or PCMCIA memory card, if any, is destroyed by formatting. If you specify no device name, fdformat uses the diskette as a default.

By default, fdformat uses the configured capacity of the drive to format the diskette. A 3.5-inch, high-density drive uses diskettes with a formatted capacity of 1.44 megabytes. A 5.25-inch, high-density drive uses diskettes with a formatted capacity of 1.2 megabytes. In either case, you need not specify a density option to fdformat. You must, however, specify a density option when using a diskette with a lower capacity than that of the drive's default. Use the -H option to format high-density diskettes (1.44-megabyte capacity) in an extra-high-density (ED) drive. Use the -D option, the -l option, or the -L option to format double-density (or low-density) diskettes (720-kilobyte capacity) in an HD or ED drive. To format medium-density diskettes (1.2-megabyte capacity), use the -M option with -t nec (this is the same as using the -m option with -t nec).

Extended density uses double-sided, extended-density (or extra-high-density) (DS/ED) diskettes. Medium and high densities use the same media: double-sided, high-density (DS/HD) diskettes. Double (low) density uses double-sided, double-density (DS/DD) diskettes.

Note — Substituting diskettes of one density for diskettes of either a higher or lower density generally does not work. Data integrity cannot be assured whenever a diskette is formatted to a capacity not matching its density.

You can use the fdformat command to format a PCMCIA memory card with densities from 512-kilobytes to 64-megabytes.

fdformat writes new identification and data fields for each sector on all tracks unless you specify the -x option. For diskettes, if you specify the -v option, each sector is verified.

After formatting and verifying, fdformat writes an operating-system label on block 0. Use the -t dos option (same as the -d option) to put an MS-DOS file system on the diskette or PCMCIA memory card after the format is done. Use the -t nec option with the -M option (same as the -m option) to put an NEC-DOS file system on a diskette. Otherwise, fdformat writes a SunOS label in block 0.

> **Note** — A diskette or PCMCIA memory card containing a ufs file system created on a SPARC-based system (by using fdformat and newfs(1M)) is not identical to a diskette or PCMCIA memory card containing a ufs file system created on an IA-based system. Do not interchange ufs diskettes or memory cards between these platforms; use cpio(1) or tar(1) to transfer files on diskettes or memory cards between them.
>
> A diskette or PCMCIA memory card formatted with the -t dos option (or -d) for MS-DOS does not have the necessary system files and is therefore not bootable. Trying to boot from it on a PC displays the following message:
>
> ```
> Non-System disk or disk error
> Replace and strike any key when ready
> ```

Bugs

Currently, bad sector mapping is not supported on diskettes or PCMCIA memory cards. Therefore, a diskette or memory card is unusable if fdformat finds an error (bad sector).

Options

-b *label*   Label the media with volume label. A SunOS volume label is restricted to 8 characters. A DOS volume label is restricted to 11 uppercase characters.

-B *filename*

    Install special boot loader in *filename* on an MS-DOS diskette. This option is meaningful only when you also specify the -d option (or -t dos).

-D   Format a 720-kilobyte (3.5-inch) or 360-kilobyte (5.25-inch) double-density diskette (same as the -l or -L options). This option is the default for double-density type drives. Use it only if the drive is a high- or extended-density type.

-e   Eject the diskette when done. (This feature is not available on all systems.)

-E   Format a 2.88-megabyte (3.5-inch) extended-density diskette. This option is the default for extended-density type drives.

-f   Do not ask for confirmation before starting format.

-H   Format a 1.44-megabyte (3.5-inch) or 1.2-megabyte (5.25-inch) high-density diskette. This option is the default for high-density type drives; use it only if the drive is the extended-density type.

-M   Write a 1.2-megabyte (3.5-inch) medium-density format on a high-density diskette (use only with the -t nec option). This option is the same as using -m. (This feature is not available on all systems.)

-q   Do not print status messages.

-t dos   Install an MS-DOS file system and boot sector formatting. This is equivalent to the DOS format command or the -d option.

-t nec	Install an NEC-DOS file system and boot sector on the disk after formatting. Use this option only with the -M option. (This feature is not available on all systems.)
-U	Unmount any file systems and then format.
-v	Verify each block of the diskette after the format.
-x	Skip the format, and write only a SunOS label or an MS-DOS file system.

The following options are provided for compatibility with previous versions of fdformat; their use is discouraged.

-d	Format an MS-DOS diskette or PCMCIA memory card (same as -t). This option is equivalent to the MS-DOS FORMAT command.
-l	Format a 720-kilobyte (3.5-inch) or 360-kilobyte (5.25-inch) double-density diskette (same as -D or -L). This option is the default for double-density type drives; use it only if the drive is the high- or extended-density type.
-L	Format a 720-kilobyte (3.5-inch) or 360-kilobyte (5.25-inch) double-density diskette (same as -l or -D). This option is the default for double-density type drives; use it only if the drive is the high- or extended-density type.
-m	Write a 1.2-megabyte (3.5-inch) medium-density format on a high-density diskette (use only with the -t nec option). This option is the same as using -M. (This feature is not available on all systems.)

Operands

devname	Replace *devname* with rdiskette0 (systems without Volume Management) or floppy0 (systems with Volume Management) to use the first drive or rdiskette1 (systems without Volume Management) or floppy1 (systems with Volume Management) to use the second drive. If you omit *devname*, use the first drive, if one exists.

For PCMCIA memory cards, replace *devname* with the device name for the PCMCIA memory card that resides in /dev/rdsk/cNtNdNsN or /dev/dsk/cNtNdNsN.

If you omit *devname*, use the default diskette drive, if one exists. N represents a decimal number and can be specified as follows:

cN	Controller N.
tN	Technology type N.

0x1	ROM.
0x2	OTPROM.
0x3	EPROM.
0x4	EEPROM.
0x5	FLASH.

0x6	SRAM.
0x7	DRAM.

d*N*   Technology region in type *N*.

s*N*   Slice *N*.

Files

/vol/dev/diskette0

> Directory providing block device access for the media in diskette drive 0.

/vol/dev/rdiskette0

> Directory providing character device access for the media in diskette drive 0.

/vol/dev/aliases/floppy0

> Symbolic link to the character device for the media in diskette drive 0.

/dev/rdiskette

> Directory providing character device access for the media in the primary diskette drive, usually drive 0.

/vol/dev/dsk/c*N*t*N*d*N*s*N*

> Directory providing block device access for the PCMCIA memory card.

/vol/dev/rdsk/c*N*t*N*d*N*s*N*

> Directory providing character device access for the PCMCIA memory card.

/vol/dev/aliases/pcmemS

> Symbolic link to the character device for the PCMCIA memory card in socket S, where S represents a PCMCIA socket number.

/dev/rdsk/c*N*t*N*d*N*s*N*

> Directory providing character device access for the PCMCIA memory card.

/dev/dsk/c*N*t*N*d*N*s*N*

> Directory providing block device access for the PCMCIA memory card.

Note — See the *devname* section above for a description of the values for *N*.

Examples

In the following example, the diskette has been mounted with the volcheck command. fdformat displays an error message telling you to use the -U option to unmount the diskette before formatting it.

```
castle% volcheck
castle% fdformat
fdformat: /vol/dev/rdiskette0/unnamed_floppy is mounted (use -U flag)
castle%
```

In the following example, using the `fdformat -U` command, `fdformat` detects a formatting error, as indicated by the `e`, and exits.

```
castle% fdformat -U
Formatting 1.44 MB in /vol/dev/rdiskette0/unnamed_floppy
Press return to start formatting floppy.
.......................................................e
fdformat: can't read format data, I/O error
castle% eject
```

The following example uses `fdformat` with no arguments (on a new diskette) to successfully create a SunOS file system on the diskette.

```
castle% fdformat
Formatting 1.44 MB in /vol/dev/rdiskette0/untitled
Press return to start formatting floppy.
...............................................................
castle%
```

The following example uses the `-d` option to successfully create a DOS file system on a diskette.

```
castle% fdformat -d
Formatting 1.44 MB in /vol/dev/rdiskette0/untitled
Press return to start formatting floppy.
...............................................................
castle%
```

Attributes

See `attributes`(5) for descriptions of the following attributes:

Attribute Type	Attribute Value
Availability	SUNWcsu

See Also

cpio(1), eject(1), tar(1), volcancel(1), volcheck(1), volmissing(1), volrmmount(1), mount(1M), newfs(1M), rmmount(1M), vold(1M), rmmount.conf(4), vold.conf(4), attributes(5), pcfs(7FS), volfs(7FS)

IA Only
fd(7D)

fg — Control Process Execution

Synopsis

sh, ksh
fg [%*job-id*...]

csh
fg [%*job-id*]

Description

See jobs(1).

---

fgrep — Search a File for a Fixed-Character String

Synopsis

    /usr/bin/fgrep [-bchilnsvx] [-e *pattern-list*] [-f *pattern-file*]
       [*pattern*] [*file*...]
    /usr/xpg4/bin/fgrep [-bchilnsvx] [-e p*attern-list*] [-f *pattern-file*]
       [*pattern*] [*file*...]

Description

The fgrep (fast grep) command searches files for a character string and prints all lines that contain that string. fgrep is different from grep(1) and egrep(1) because it searches for a string instead of searching for a pattern that matches an expression. fgrep uses a fast and compact algorithm.

fgrep interprets the characters $, *, [, ^, |, (,), and \ literally; that is, fgrep does not recognize full regular expressions as does egrep. Because these characters have special meaning to the shell, it is safest to enclose the entire string in single quotes ' ... '.

If you specify no files, fgrep uses the standard input. Normally, each line found is copied to the standard output.The file name is printed before each line found if there is more than one input file.

> **Note** — Ideally there should be only one grep command; however, no single algorithm spans a wide enough range of space-time trade-offs.
>
> Lines are limited only by the size of the available virtual memory.
>
> The /usr/xpg4/bin/fgrep command is identical to/usr/xpg4/bin/grep -F (see grep(1)). Portable applications should use /usr/xpg4/bin/grep -F.

Options

-b	Precede each line by the block number on which it was found. This option can be useful in locating block numbers by context (first block is 0).
-c	Print a count only of the lines that contain the pattern.
-e *pattern-list*	
	Search for a string in *pattern-list* (useful when the string begins with a -).
-f *pattern-file*	
	Take the list of patterns from *pattern-file*.

-h	Suppress printing of files when searching multiple files.
-i	Ignore upper-/lowercase distinction during comparisons.
-l	Print the names of files with matching lines once, separated by newlines. Do not repeat the names of files when the pattern is found more than once.
-n	Precede each line by its line number in the file (first line is 1).
-s	Work silently, that is, display nothing except error messages. This option is useful for checking the error status.
-v	Print all lines except those that contain the pattern.
-x	Print only lines matched entirely.

Operands

file	A path name of a file to be searched for the patterns. If you specify no file operands, use the standard input.
pattern	For /usr/bin/fgrep, specify a pattern to be used during the search for input. For /usr/xpg4/bin/fgrep, specify one or more patterns to be used during the search for input. This operand is treated as if it were specified as -e *pattern-list*.

Examples

Because you do not need to quote special characters, the fgrep command is useful for searching for patterns that have literal backslashes, asterisks, and the like. You can also search for more than one target string. With the fgrep command, you put each target on a separate line.

Suppose you have a file named foo that has lots of special characters.

```
$ cat foo
@ # $ &
^
\
* ( )
$
```

The following example uses the fgrep command to search the file foo.

```
$ fgrep "$
> *" foo
@ # $
* ( )
$
```

Usage

See largefile(5) for the description of the behavior of fgrep when encountering files greater than or equal to 2 Gbytes (2**31 bytes).

Environment Variables

See environ(5) for descriptions of the following environment variables that affect the execution of fgrep: LC_COLLATE, LC_CTYPE, LC_MESSAGES, and NLSPATH.

Exit Status

0	Matches are found.
1	No matches are found.
2	Syntax errors or inaccessible files (even if matches are found).

Attributes

See attributes(5) for descriptions of the following attributes:

/usr/bin/fgrep

Attribute Type	Attribute Value
Availability	SUNWcsu

/usr/xpg4/bin/fgrep

Attribute Type	Attribute Value
Availability	SUNWxcu4
CSI	Enabled

See Also

ed(1), egrep(1), grep(1), sed(1), sh(1), attributes(5), environ(5), largefile(5), XPG4(5)

file — Determine File Type

Synopsis

```
/usr/bin/file [-h] [-m mfile] [-f ffile] file
/usr/bin/file [-h] [-m mfile] -f ffile
/usr/bin/file -c [-m mfile]
```

Description

The file command performs a series of tests on each file supplied by *file* and, optionally, on each file listed in *ffile* in an attempt to classify it. If the file is not a regular file, its file type is identified. The file types directory, FIFO, block special, and character special are identified as such. If the file is a regular file and the file is 0-length, it is identified as an empty file.

If *file* is a text file, file examines the first 512 bytes and tries to determine its programming language. If *file* is an executable a.out, file prints the version stamp, provided it is greater than 0. If *file* is a symbolic link, by default the link is followed and file tests the file to which the symbolic link refers.

A magic number is a numeric or string constant that indicates the file type. By default, file tries to use the localized magic file /usr/lib/locale/locale/LC_MESSAGES/magic, if it exists, to identify files that have a magic number. If a localized magic file does not exist, file uses /etc/magic. See magic(4) for an explanation of the format of /etc/magic.

If *file* does not exist, cannot be read, or its file status could not be determined, it is not considered an error that affects the exit status. The output indicates that the file was processed, but that its type could not be determined.

Options

-c	Check the magic file for format errors. For reasons of efficiency, this validation is normally not carried out.
-f *ffile*	Examine the files listed in *ffile*.
-h	Do not follow symbolic links.
-m *mfile*	Use *mfile* as an alternative magic file, instead of /etc/magic.

Operands

ffile	A file containing a list of the names of files to be examined.
file	A path name of a file to be tested.
mfile	An alternative magic file.

Usage

See largefile(5) for the description of the behavior of file when encountering files greater than or equal to 2 Gbytes (2**31 bytes).

Examples

The following example displays the file types for all of the files in a directory.

```
castle% file *
Art:            directory
Design.book:    empty file
Mail:           directory
Menu.start:     empty file
bibliography:   ascii text
checknr.1:      [nt]roff, tbl, or eqn input text
dosfile:        ascii text
example.c:      c program text
example.stringout:      ascii text
kerberos:       English text
local.cshrc:    assembler program text
local.profile:  ascii text
castle%
```

The following example determines whether a file is a binary executable file.

```
castle% file "$1" | grep -Fq executable && printf "%s is executable.\n"
"$1"
```

Environment Variables

See environ(5) for descriptions of the following environment variables that affect the execution of file: LC_CTYPE, LC_MESSAGES, and NLSPATH.

Exit Status

0	Successful completion.
>0	An error occurred.

Files

/etc/magic   Magic number file.

Attributes

See attributes(5) for descriptions of the following attributes:

Attribute Type	Attribute Value
Availability	SUNWcsu
CSI	Enabled

See Also

ls(1), filehdr(4), magic(4), attributes(5), environ(5), largefile(5)

Diagnostics

When you specify the -h option and *file* is a symbolic link, file prints the error message:

symbolic link to file

---

filep — Front Ends to the mp Text to PDL Pretty Print Filter   New!

Synopsis

/bin/filep [*options*] *filename*...

Description

See mailp(1).

filesync — Synchronize Ordinary, Directory, or Special Files

Synopsis
```
/usr/bin/filesync [-aehmnqvy] [-o src | dst] [-f src | dst] |old | new]
    [-r directory...]
/usr/bin/filesync [-aehmnqvy] -s source-dir -d dest-dir filename...
```

Description
filesync synchronizes files between multiple computer systems, typically a server and a portable computer. filesync synchronizes ordinary, directory, or special files. Although intended for use on nomadic systems, filesync is useful for backup and file replication on more permanently connected systems.

If files are synchronized between systems, the corresponding files on each of the systems are identical. Changing a file on one or both of the systems can unsynchronize the files. To make the files identical again, the differences between the files must be reconciled.

There are two forms of the filesync command. You invoke the first form of filesync without file arguments. This form of filesync reconciles differences between the files and systems specified in the $HOME/.packingrules file. $HOME/.packingrules is a packing rules list for filesync and cachefspack and contains a list of files to be kept synchronized. See packingrules(4) and cachefspack(1M).

The second form of filesync copies specific files from a directory on the source system to a directory on the destination system. In addition, this form of filesync adds the file or files specified as arguments (*filename*) to $HOME/.packingrules. See -s and -d for information about specifying directories on source and destination systems.

Multiple filesync commands are cumulative (that is, the specified files are added to the already existing packing rules file list).

Reconciling and Synchronizing Files
filesync synchronizes files between computer systems by performing the following tasks:

1. filesync examines the directories and files specified in the packing rules file on both systems and determines whether or not they are identical. Any file that differs requires reconciliation.

2. filesync also maintains a baseline summary in the $HOME/.filesync-base file for all of the files that are being monitored. This file lists the names, types, and sizes of all files as of the last reconciliation.

3. Based on the information contained in the baseline file and the specified options, filesync determines which of the various copies is the correct one and makes the corresponding changes to the other system. Once this has been done, the two copies are again identical (synchronized).

4. If a source file has changed and the destination file has not, the changes on the source system are propagated to the destination system. If a destination file has changed and the corresponding source file has not, the changes on the destination file are propagated to the source system. If both systems have changed (and the files are not still identical) a warning message is printed, asking you to resolve the conflict manually.

Resolving Conflicts

When files on both sides have changed, `filesync` tries to determine which version should be chosen. If `filesync` cannot automatically determine which version should be selected, it prints out a warning message and leaves the two incompatible versions of the file unreconciled.

In these cases, you must either resolve the differences manually or tell `filesync` how to choose which file should win. Use the `-o` and `-f` options to tell `filesync` how to resolve conflicts.

Alternatively, for each conflicting file, you can examine the two versions, determine which one should be kept, and manually bring the two versions into agreement (by copying, deleting, or changing the ownership or protection to be correct). You can then rerun `filesync` to see whether any other conflicts remain.

Packing Rules File

The packing rules file `$HOME/.packingrules` contains a list of files to be kept synchronized. The syntax of this file is described in `packingrules`(4).

If you invoke `filesync` with *filename* arguments, the `$HOME/.packingrules` file is automatically created. By using `filesync` options, you can augment the packing rules in `$HOME/.packingrules`.

Many users choose to create the packing rules file manually and edit it by hand. You can edit `$HOME/.packingrules` (using any editor) to permanently change the `$HOME/.packingrules` file or to gain access to more powerful options that are not available from the command line (such as `IGNORE` commands). By editing the `$HOME/.packingrules` file, you can easily enter complex wild-card expressions.

Baseline Files

`$HOME/.filesync-base` is the `filesync` baseline summary file. `filesync` uses the information in `$HOME/.filesync-base` to identify the differences between files during reconciliation and synchronization. You do not create or edit the baseline file. It is created automatically by `filesync` and records the last-known state of agreement between all of the files being maintained.

Multiple filesync Commands

Over time, the set of files you want to keep synchronized can change. It is common, for instance, to want to keep files pertaining to only a few active projects on your notebook. If you continue to synchronize files associated with every project you have ever worked on, your notebook's disk would fill up with old files. In addition, each `filesync` command would waste a lot of time updating files you no longer care about.

If you simply delete the files from your notebook, `filesync` wants to perform the corresponding deletes on the server, which is not what you want. Instead, you can tell `filesync` to stop synchronizing some of the files in one of the following two ways:

- Edit `$HOME/.packingrules` and delete the rules for the files that you want to delete from your notebook.

- Delete `$HOME/.packingrules`. Then, use the `filesync` command to specify the files that you want synchronized.

Either way works, and you can choose the one that seems easier to you. For minor changes, it is probably easier to edit `$HOME/.packingrules`. For major changes, it is probably easier to start from scratch.

Once `filesync` is no longer synchronizing a set of files, you can delete them from your notebook without affecting the files on the server.

Nomadic Machines

When using `filesync` to keep files synchronized between nomadic machines and a server, store the packing rules and baseline files on the nomadic machines, not the server. If, when you are logged into your notebook, the HOME environment variable does not normally point to a directory on your notebook, you can use the FILESYNC environment variable to specify an alternate location for the packing rules and baseline files.

Each nomadic machine should carry its own packing rules and baseline file. Incorrect file synchronization can result if a server carries a baseline file and multiple nomadic machines attempt to reconcile against the server's baseline file. In this case, a nomadic machine could be using a baseline file that does not accurately describe the state of its files, which might result in incorrect reconciliations.

To safeguard against the dangers associated with a single baseline file being shared by more than two machines, `filesync` adds a default rule to each new packing rules file. This default rule prevents the packing rules and baseline files from being copied.

Options

`-a`	Force the checking of Access Control Lists (ACLs), and try to make them agree for all new and changed files. If it is not possible to set the ACL for a particular file, `filesync` stops ACL synchronization for that file.
	Some file systems do not support ACLs. It is not possible to synchronize ACLs between file systems that support ACLs and those that do not; trying to do so results in numerous error messages.
`-d` *dest-dir*	
	Specify the directory on the destination system into which *filename* is to be copied. Use with the `-s` *source-dir* option and the *filename* operand. See `-s`.
`-e`	Flag all differences. It may not be possible to resolve all conflicts involving modes and ownership (unless `filesync` is being run with root privileges). If you cannot change the ownership or protections on a file, `filesync` normally ignores conflicts in ownership and protection. If you specify the `-e` (everything must agree) flag, `filesync` flags these differences.
`-f src	dst	old	new`	
	Specify how to resolve conflicting changes. If a file has been changed on both systems and you specify the `-f` option, retain the changes made on the favored system and discard the changes made on the unfavored system.
	Specify `-f src` to favor the source system file. Specify `-f dst` to favor the destination system file. Specify `-f old` to favor the older version of the file. Specify `-f new` to favor the newer version of the file.
	You can combine the `-f` and `-o` options if they both specify the same preference (src or dst). If `-f` and `-o` conflict, ignore the `-f` option.

-h   Halt on error. Normally, if filesync encounters a read or write error
            while copying files, it notes the error and the program continues trying
            to reconcile other files. If you specify the -h option, filesync
            immediately halts when one of these errors occurs and does not process
            any more files.

-m   Ensure that both copies of the file have the same modification time. Set
            the modification time for newly copied files to the time of reconciliation
            by default. Order file changes by increasing modification times so that
            the propagated files have the same relative modification time ordering
            as the original changes. There is usually some time skew between any
            two systems, and transferring modification times from one system to
            another can occasionally produce strange results.

            At times, using filesync to update some (but not all) files in a
            directory confuses the make program. If, for example, filesync is
            keeping .c files synchronized but ignoring .o files, a changed .c file
            may show up with a modification time before a .o file that was built
            from a previous version of the .c file.

-n   Display the change and reconciliation information on standard output,
            but do not make the changes.

            Specifying both the -n and -o options analyzes the prevailing system
            and reports the changes that have been made on that system. Using -n
            and -o in combination is useful if your machine is disconnected (and
            you cannot access the server) but you want to know what changes have
            been made on the local machine.

-o src | dst

            Force a one-way reconciliation, favoring either the source system (src)
            or destination system (dst). filesync aborts if it cannot access a
            source or destination directory.

            Specify -o src to propagate changes from the source system to the
            destination system only. Ignore changes made on the destination
            system. filesync aborts if it cannot access a source or destination
            directory.

            Specify -o dst to propagate changes only from the destination system
            to the source system. Ignore changes made on the source system.

            Specifying both the -n and -o options analyzes the prevailing system
            and reports the changes that have been made on that system. Using -n
            and -o in combination is useful if your machine is disconnected (and
            you cannot access the server) but you want to know what changes have
            been made on the local machine.

            You can combine the -f and -o options if they both specify the same
            preference (src or dst). If -f and -o conflict, ignore the -f option.

-q   Suppress the standard filesync messages that describe each
            reconciliation action as it is performed.

The standard `filesync` message describes each reconciliation action in the form of a UNIX shell command (for example, `mv`, `ln`, `cp`, `rm`, `chmod`, `chown`, `chgrp`, `setfacl`, and so forth).

-r directory

Limit the reconciliation to *directory*. Specify multiple directories with multiple `-r` specifications.

-s source-dir

Specify the directory on the source system from which the *filename* to be copied is located. Use with the *-d dest-dir* option and the *filename* operand.

-v

Display additional information about each file comparison as it is made on the standard output.

-y

Bypass safety check prompts. Nomadic machines occasionally move between domains, and many of the files on which `filesync` operates are expected to be accessed by NFS. It is possible that you could ask `filesync` to reconcile local changes against the wrong file system or server, resulting in a large number of inappropriate copies and deletions. To prevent such a mishap, `filesync` performs a few safety checks before reconciliation. If large numbers of files are likely to be deleted or if high-level directories have changed their I-node numbers, `filesync` prompts for a confirmation before reconciliation. If you know that this is likely and do not want to be prompted, use the `-y` (yes) option.

Operands

filename

The name of the ordinary file, directory, symbolic link, or special file in the specified source directory (*source-dir*) to be synchronized. Specify multiple files by separating each *filename* by spaces. Use the *filename* operand with the `-s` and *-d* options.

If *filename* is an ordinary file, replicate that ordinary file (with the same *filename*) in the specified destination directory (*dest-dir*).

If *filename* is a directory, replicate that directory and all of the files and subdirectories under it (recursively) in the specified destination directory (*dest-dir*).

If *filename* is a symbolic link, replicate a copy of that symbolic link in the specified destination directory (*dest-dir*).

If *filename* is a special file, replicate a special file with the same major or minor device numbers in the specified destination directory (*dest-dir*). Only superusers can use `filesync` to create special files.

Files created in the destination directory (*dest-dir*) have the same owner, group, and other permissions as the files in the source directory.

If *filename* contains escaped shell wild-card characters, filesync stores the wild-card characters in $HOME/packingrules and evaluates them each time you run the command.

For example, the following command makes sure that the two specified files, currently in $RHOME, are replicated in $HOME.

```
castle% filesync -s $RHOME -d $HOME a.c b.c
```

The following example ensures that all of the *.c files in $RHOME are replicated in $HOME, even if those files are not created until later.

```
castle% filesync -s $RHOME -d $HOME '*.c'
```

If any of the destination files already exist, filesync ensures that they are identical and issues warnings if they are not.

Once files have been copied, the distinction between the source and destination is a relatively arbitrary one (except for its use in the -o and -f switches).

Environment Variables

FILESYNC   Specify the default location of the filesync packing rules and baseline files. The default value for this variable is $HOME. The suffixes .packingrules and .filesync-base are appended to form the names of the packing rules and baseline files.

LC_MESSAGES

Determine how diagnostic and informative messages are presented. In the C locale, the messages are presented in the default form found in the program itself (in most cases, U.S. English).

Exit Status

Normally, if all files are already up-to-date or if all files are successfully reconciled, filesync exits with a status of 0. However, if you specify the -n option or any errors occurred, the exit status is the logical OR of the following:

0	No conflicts, all files up to date.
1	Some resolvable conflicts.
2	Some conflicts requiring manual resolution.
4	Some specified files did not exist.
8	Insufficient permission for some files.
16	Errors accessing packing rules or baseline file.
32	Invalid arguments.
64	Unable to access either or both of the specified source or destination directories.
128	Miscellaneous other failures.

Files

$HOME/.packingrules

>   List of files to be kept synchronized.

$HOME/.filesync-base

>   Baseline summary file.

Attributes

See attributes(5) for descriptions of the following attributes:

Attribute Type	Attribute Value
Availability	SUNWrcmdc

New!

See Also

cachefspack(1M), packingrules(4), attributes(5)

New! **filofaxp** — Front Ends to the mp Text to PDL Pretty Print Filter

Synopsis

/bin/filofaxp [*options*] *filename*...

Description

See mailp(1).

find — Find Files

Synopsis

/usr/bin/find *path*... *expression*
/usr/xpg/find *path*... *expression*

New!

Description

You can use the find command to search through any part of the file system, looking for files with a particular name. find recursively descends the directory hierarchy for each path, seeking files that match *expression*.

find descends to arbitrary depths in a file hierarchy and does not fail because of path-length limitations (unless a path operand specified by the application exceeds PATH_MAX requirements).

Operands

path	A path name of a starting point in the directory hierarchy.
expression	Interpret the first argument that starts with a -, or is a ! or a (, and all subsequent arguments as an expression made up of the following primaries and operators. In the descriptions, wherever you use *n* as a primary argument, interpret it as a decimal integer optionally preceded by a plus (+) or minus (-) sign, as follows:

+*n*	More than *n*.
n	Exactly *n*.
−*n*	Less than *n*.

Expressions

-atime *n*
: true if the file was accessed *n* days ago. The access time of directories in path is changed by find itself.

-cpio *device*

Always true; write the current file on device in cpio format (5120-byte records).

-ctime *n*
: true if any aspect of the file's inode was changed *n* days ago.

-depth
: Always true; descend the directory hierarchy so that all entries in a directory are acted on before the directory itself. This option can be useful when find is used with cpio(1) to transfer files that are contained in directories without write permission.

-exec *command*

true if the executed command returns a 0 value as exit status. You must punctuate the end of *command* with an escaped semicolon. A command argument {} is replaced by the current path name.

If the last argument to -exec is {} and you specify + instead of the semicolon (;), the command is invoked fewer times, with {} replaced by groups of path names. New in the Solaris 9 release. *New!*

-follow
: Always true; follow symbolic links. When following symbolic links, find keeps track of the directories visited so that it can detect infinite loops. For example, such a loop would occur if a symbolic link pointed to an ancestor. Do not use this expression with the -type l expression.

-fstype *type*

true if the file system to which the file belongs is of type *type*.

-group *gname*

true if the file belongs to the group *gname*. If *gname* is numeric and does not appear in the /etc/group file or in the NIS or NIS+ tables, it is taken as a group ID. *New!*

-inum *n*
: true if the file has inode number *n*.

-links *n*
: true if the file has *n* links.

-local   true if the file-system type is not a remote file-system type as defined in the /etc/dfs/fstypes file. find uses nfs as the default remote file-system type if the /etc/dfs/fstypes file is not present.

Note that -local descends the hierarchy of nonlocal directories. See "Examples" on page 369 for an example of how to search for local files without descending.

-ls   Always true; print current path name together with its associated statistics:

   • Inode number.

   • Size in kilobytes (1024 bytes).

   • Protection mode.

   • Number of hard links.

   • User.

   • Group.

   • Size in bytes.

   • Modification time.

If the file is a special file, the size field contains the major and minor device numbers.

If the file is a symbolic link, the path name of the linked-to file is printed preceded by ->. The format is identical to that of ls -gilds (see ls(1)). Formatting is done internally, without executing the ls command.

-mount   Always true; restrict the search to the file system containing the directory specified. Do not list mount points to other file systems.

-mtime *n*   true if the contents of the file was modified *n* days ago.

-name *pattern*

true if *pattern* matches the current file name. You can use normal shell file-name generation characters (see sh(1)). Use a backslash (\) as an escape character within the pattern. Escape or quote the pattern when you invoke find from the shell.

Unless you explicitly specify the . character at the beginning of a pattern, a current file name beginning with . does not match *pattern* with the /usr/bin/find command. The /usr/xpg4/bin/find command does not make this distinction. Wild-card file-name generation characters can match file names beginning with a dot (.). New in the Solaris 9 release.

-ncpio *device*

Always true; write the current file on device in cpio -c format (5120-byte records).

-newer *file*

> true if the current file has been modified more recently than the argument *file*.

-nogroup

> true if the file belongs to a group not in the /etc/group file or not in the NIS or NIS+ tables.

New!

-nouser

> true if the file belongs to a user not in the /etc/passwd file or not in the NIS or NIS+ tables.

New!

-ok *command*

> Like -exec except print the generated command line with a question mark first, and execute it only if the user responds by typing **y**.

-perm [-]*mode*

> The *mode* argument represents file-mode bits. It is identical in format to the *symbolic-mode* operand described in chmod(1) and is interpreted in the following way. To start, assume a template with all file mode bits cleared. For an operator symbol of:
>
> +   Set the appropriate mode bits in the template.
>
> -   Clear the appropriate bits.
>
> =   Set the appropriate mode bits without regard to the contents of the process file-mode creation mask.
>
> You cannot use the - symbol as the first character of *mode*; this restriction avoids ambiguity with the optional leading dash. Because the initial mode is all bits off, no symbolic modes need to use - as the first character.
>
> If you omit the dash, the primary evaluates as true when the file permission bits exactly match the value of the resulting template.
>
> Otherwise, if *mode* is prefixed by a dash, the primary evaluates as true if at least all the bits in the resulting template are set in the file permission bits.

-perm [-]*onum*

> true if the file permission flags exactly match the octal number *onum* (see chmod(1)). If *onum* is prefixed by a dash (-), compare only the bits that are set in *onum* with the file permission flags and evaluate the expression true if they match.

-print

> Always true; print the current path name.

-prune

> Always true. Do not examine any directories or files in the directory structure below the pattern just matched.

-size *onum*[c]

> true if the file is *onum* blocks long (512 bytes per block). If you follow *onum* with a c, the size is in bytes.

-type *c*	true if the type of the file is *c*, where c is b (block special file), c (character special file), d (directory), l (symbolic link), p (fifo: named pipe), s (socket), or f (plain file).
-user *uname*	

New! true if the file belongs to the user *uname*. If *uname* is numeric and does not appear as a login name in the /etc/passwd file or in the NIS or NIS+ tables, take it as a user ID.

New! -xattr   true if the file has extended attributes. New in the Solaris 9 release.

-xdev   Same as the -mount primary.

Note — When using find to determine files modified within a range of time, specify the -atime, -ctime, or -mtime option before the -print option; otherwise, find gives all files.

New! Some files that may be under the Solaris root file system are actually mount points for virtual file systems such as mntfs or namefs. When comparing against a UFS file system, they are not selected if you specify -mount or -xdev in the find expression.

The following options are obsolete and will not be supported in future releases.

-cpio *device*

Always true; write the current file on *device* in cpio format (5120-byte records).

-ncpio *device*

Always true; write the current file on *device* in cpio -c format (5120-byte records).

Complex Expressions

You can combine the primaries by using the operators listed below, in order of decreasing precedence.

(*expression*)

true if the parenthesized expression is true (parentheses are special to the shell and must be escaped).

! *expression*

The negation of a primary (! is the unary not operator).

expression [-a] *expression*

Concatenation of primaries (the and operation is implied by the juxtaposition of two primaries).

expression -o expression

Alternation of primaries (-o is the or operator).

Note — When you use find in conjunction with cpio, if you use the -L
option with cpio, then you must use the -follow expression with find, and
vice versa. Otherwise, you get undesirable results.

If no expression is present, -print is used as the expression. Otherwise, if the given
expression does not contain any of the primaries -exec, -ok, or -print, the given
expression is effectively replaced by:

(*given-expression*) -print

The -user, -group, and -newer primaries each evaluate their respective arguments
only once. Invoking the command specified by -exec or -ok does not affect subsequent   *New!*
primaries on the same file.

Usage

See largefile(5) for the description of the behavior of find when encountering files
greater than or equal to 2 Gbytes (2**31 bytes).

Examples

The following commands are equivalent. Both write out the entire directory hierarchy
from the current directory.

```
castle% find .
castle% find . -print
```

The following example searches from the root directory (/) and lists all core files on
the system.

```
castle# find / -name core -print
/export/home/winsor/core
/files/winsor/bookgames/src/xblackjack/core
/core
castle#
```

The following example searches the current directory and silently removes all core
files.

```
castle% pwd
/export/home/winsor
castle% ls core
core
castle% find . -name core -exec rm {} \;
castle% ls core
core: No such file or directory
castle%
```

If you want to see a list of the files that are removed, add the -print option to the
command line as shown in the following example.

```
castle% find . -name core -exec rm {} \; -print
```

The following example recursively prints all file names whose permission mode
exactly matches read, write, and execute access for user, and read and execute access for
group and other.

```
castle% find . -perm u+rwx,g=rx,o=rx
./.dt
./.dt/sessions
./.dt/sessions/current
./.dt/sessions/current.old
./.dt/types
./.dt/types/fp_dynamic
./.dt/tmp
./.dt/sessionlogs
./.dt/icons
./.dt/appmanager
./.dt/help
./.dt/help/winsor-castle-0
./.dt/Trash
./.dt/palettes
./.dt/.Printers/seachild1_Print
./.dtprofile
castle% find . -perm -o+w
.
./local.cshrc
./.dt/sessions/current/dt.session
./.dt/sessions/current/dt.settings
./.dt/sessions/current/dt.resources
./.dt/sessions/current.old/dt.session
...
castle%
```

The following example removes all files in your home directory named a.out or *.o* that have not been accessed for a week.

```
castle% find $HOME \( -name a.out -o -name '*.o*' \) -atime +7 -exec rm {} \;
```

The following example recursively prints all file names in the current directory and below but skips SCCS directories.

```
castle% find . -name SCCS -prune -o -print
```

The following example recursively prints all file names in the current directory and below, skipping the contents of SCCS directories but printing out the SCCS directory name.

```
castle% find . -print -name SCCS -prune
```

The following command is basically equivalent to the -nt extension to test(1).

```
castle$ if [-n "$(find file1 -prune -newer file2)"]; then printf %s
    "file1 is newer than file2"
```

The following command recursively prints all file names whose permission mode exactly matches read, write, and execute access for user, and read and execute access for group and other.

```
castle% find . -perm u=rwx,g=rx,o=rx
```

You could also specify the above command in the following way.

```
castle% find . -perm a=rwx,g-w,o-w
```

The following command recursively prints all file names whose permissions include, but are not limited to, write access for other.

```
castle% find . -perm -o+w
```

The descriptions of -atime, -ctime, and -mtime use the terminology *n 24-hour periods*. The midnight boundary between days does not affect the 24-hour calculation. -atime looks for files that have been accessed, which means files that have been read or changed or directories that have been listed or changed into. -mtime looks for files that have been modified, which means files that have been altered in some way, such as being edited, moved, renamed, or revised. -ctime looks for files that have had a change in file status such as a change of owner or a change of group.

The following example looks for a file that has been accessed no more than one day ago.

```
castle% find . -atime -1 -print
```

Suppose your disk has filled up recently and you want to find large files that are less than three days old. With the following example, you search your home directory for files that are 200c or larger. The c specifies the size in bytes. Without the c, you would be specifying blocks of 512 kilobytes.

```
castle% find $HOME -size 200c -mtime -3 -user winsor -print
```

The -mtime -3 option looks for files modified less than three days ago. To look for files modified more than three days ago, use -mtime +3. To look for files modified exactly three days ago, use -mtime 3.

The following example looks for files older than three days but less than six days.

```
castle% find $HOME -size 200c -mtime +3 -mtime -6 -user winsor -print
```

The following example looks for files owned by winsor not accessed for three or more days and not modified within 14 days.

```
castle% find $HOME \( -atime +3 -o -mtime +14 \) -user winsor -print
```

The following example looks for core files older than seven days and then prompts you to verify that it is OK to remove them.

```
castle% find / -name core -mtime +7 -ok -exec {} \;
```

The following example prints local files without descending nonlocal directories.   *New!*

```
castle% find . ! -local -prune -o -print
```

The following example prints files in the namespace that possess extended   *New!*
attributes.

```
mopoke% find . -xattr
```

In the following example, suppose you have just compiled a package from source code *New!* and want to install it under /usr/local. And, you'd like a list of all the files that are part of the installation so you can create a Solaris package later.

```
talos# touch /tmp/timestamp      # Create a file that has a time on it.
talos# make install              # Install the package.
talos# find /usr/local -newer /tmp/timestamp -print
```

This example lists all files under `/usr/local` that are newer than the `/tmp/timestamp` file. You now have a list of all files that have been installed by your `make install` command.

Environment Variables

See `environ`(5) for descriptions of the following environment variables that affect the execution of `find`: LC_COLLATE, LC_CTYPE, LC_MESSAGES, and NLSPATH.

Exit Status

0	All path operands were traversed successfully.
>0	An error occurred.

Files

`/etc/passwd` Password file.

`/etc/group` Group file.

`/etc/dfs/fstypes`

File that registers distributed file system packages.

Attributes

See `attributes`(5) for descriptions of the following attributes:

Attribute Type	Attribute Value
Availability	SUNWcsu
CSI	Enabled
Interface Stability	Stable

New!

See Also

New!

`chmod`(1), `cpio`(1), `ls`(1), `sh`(1), `test`(1), `stat`(2), `umask`(2), `attributes`(5), `environ`(5), `fsattr`(5), `largefile`(5)

finger — Display Information About Local and Remote Users

Synopsis

```
/usr/bin/finger [-bfhilmpqsw] [username...]
/usr/bin/finger [-l] [username@hostname1[@hostname2...@hostnamen]...
/usr/bin/finger [-l] [@hostname1[@hostname2...@hostnamen]...]
```

Description

By default, the `finger` command displays, in a multicolumn format, the following information about each logged-in user:

- User name.
- User's full name.

- Terminal name (prepended with an asterisk (*) if write permission is denied).
- Idle time.
- Login time.
- Host name if logged in remotely.

The following example shows the output from the `finger` command with no arguments.

```
castle% finger
Login      Name              TTY           Idle    When     Where
winsor     ???               console               Thu 15:38  :0
castle%
```

Idle time is displayed in minutes if it is a single integer, in hours and minutes if a colon (`:`) is present, or in days and hours if a `d` is present.

When you specify one or more *username* arguments, more detailed information is shown for each user name specified, whether the user is logged in or not. *username* must be that of a local user and can be a first or last name or an account name. Information is presented in multiline format as follows:

- The user name and the user's full name.
- The user's home directory and login shell.
- Time the user logged in if currently logged in or the time the user last logged in, and the terminal or host from which the user logged in.
- Last time the user received mail and the last time the user read mail.
- The first line of the `$HOME/.project` file if it exists.
- The contents of the `$HOME/.plan` file if it exists.

Note — When the comment (GECOS) field in `/etc/passwd` includes a comma, `finger` does not display the information following the comma.

The following example shows the output from the `finger` command with three user names specified. None of these users were logged in at the time the command was invoked.

```
castle% finger ray des rob
Login name: ray
Directory: /export/home/ray          Shell: /bin/csh
Last login Tue Nov 25, 1997 on pts/6 from castle
Unread mail since Thu Nov 13 08:37:58 1997
No Plan.

Login name: des
Directory: /export/home/des          Shell: /bin/csh
Last login Thu Oct  9, 1997 on console from :0
No unread mail
No Plan.

Login name: rob
Directory: /export/home/rob          Shell: /bin/csh
Never logged in.
No unread mail
No Plan.
castle%
```

If you specify the arguments *username@hostname1*[*@hostname2...* *@hostnamen*] or *@hostname1*[*@hostname2...@hostnamen*], the request is sent first to *hostnamen* and forwarded through each *hostnamen-1* to *hostname1*. The program uses the finger user information protocol (see RFC 1288) to query that remote host for information about the named user (if you specify a *username*) or about each logged-in user. The information displayed is server dependent.

As required by RFC 1288, finger passes only printable, 7-bit ASCII data. A system administrator can modify this behavior by using the PASS option in /etc/default/finger. Specifying PASS=low enables all characters less than decimal 32 ASCII. Specifying PASS=high enables all characters greater than decimal 126 ASCII. PASS=low,high or PASS=high,low enables both characters less than 32 and greater than 126 to pass through.

Note — The finger user information protocol limits the options that can be used with the remote form of this command.

```
castle% finger winsor@castle
[castle]
Login       Name            TTY        Idle    When      Where
winsor      ???             console         Thu 15:38  :0
winsor      ???             pts/3       2 Thu 15:39  :0.0
winsor      ???             pts/4       9 Thu 15:39  :0.0
winsor      ???             pts/5      25 Thu 15:42  :0.0
castle%
```

Options

-b	Suppress printing of the user's home directory and shell in a long format printout.
-f	Suppress printing of the header that is normally printed in a short format printout.
-h	Suppress printing of the .project file in a long format printout.
-i	Force idle output format, which is similar to short format except print only the login name, terminal, login time, and idle time.
-l	Force long output format.
-m	Match arguments only on user name (not first or last name).
-p	Suppress printing of the .plan file in a long format printout.
-q	Force quick output format, which is similar to short format except print only the login name, terminal, and login time.
-s	Force short output format.
-w	Suppress printing of the full name in a short format printout.

Files

$HOME/.plan   User's plan.

$HOME/.project

User's projects.

/etc/default/finger

> `finger` options file.

/etc/passwd Password file.

var/adm/lastlog

> Time of last login.

/var/adm/utmpx

> Accounting.

Attributes

See `attributes`(5) for descriptions of the following attributes:

Attribute Type	Attribute Value
Availability	SUNWrcmds

See Also

`passwd(1)`, `who(1)`, `whois(1)`, `passwd(4)`, `attributes(5)`

> Zimmerman, D., *The Finger User Information Protocol*, RFC 1288, Center for Discrete Mathematics and Theoretical Computer Science (DIMACS), Rutgers University, December 1991.

fmt — Simple Text Formatter

Synopsis

/usr/bin/fmt [-cs] [-w *width* | -*width*] [*inputfile*...]

Description

`fmt` is a simple text formatter that fills and joins lines to produce output lines of (up to) the number of characters specified in the -w *width* option. The default width is 72. `fmt` concatenates the *inputfiles* listed as arguments. If you specify no input files, `fmt` formats text from the standard input.

Blank lines are preserved in the output, as is the spacing between words. For compatibility with `nroff` (1), `fmt` does not fill or split lines beginning with a dot (.). It does not fill or split a set of contiguous nonblank lines that is recognized as a mail header, the first line of which must begin with From.

Indentation is preserved in the output, and input lines with differing indentation are not joined unless you use the -c option.

You can also use `fmt` as an inline text filter for `vi`(1). The following `vi` command reformats the text between the cursor location and the end of the paragraph.

!}fmt

Options

-c   Preserve the indentation of the first two lines within a paragraph and align the left margin of each subsequent line with that of the second line. This crown width mode is useful for tagged paragraphs.

-s   Do not join short lines to form longer ones. This split-lines-only option prevents sample lines of code, and other such formatted text, from being unduly combined.

-w *width* | *-width*

Fill output lines to up to *width* columns. Note that the -width option is acceptable for BSD compatibility, but it may go away in future releases.

Operands

inputfile   Input file.

Examples

The following example combines three files and displays the output on standard output. The original files are unaffected.

```
castle% fmt -72 kookaburra-1 kookaburra-2 kookaburra-3
Kookaburra sits in the old gum tree Merry merry king of the bush is he
Laugh, kookaburra, laugh Gay your life must be.

Kookaburra sits in the old gum tree Eating all the gumdrops he can see
Laugh, kookaburra, laugh Leave some there for me. Kookaburra sits in
the old gum tree Merry merry king of the bush is he Laugh, kookaburra,
laugh Glad your life must be.

Kookaburra sits in the old gum tree Eating all the gumdrops he can see
Laugh, kookaburra, laugh Leave some there for me. Kookaburra sits in
the old gum tree Merry merry king of the bush is he Laugh, kookaburra,
laugh Gay your life must be.

Kookaburra sits in the old gum tree Eating all the gumdrops he can see
Laugh, kookaburra, laugh Leave some there for me. Kookaburra sits in
the old gum tree Merry merry king of the bush is he Laugh, kookaburra,
laugh Glad your life must be.

Kookaburra sits in the old gum tree Eating all the gumdrops he can see
Laugh, kookaburra, laugh Leave some there for me.
castle%
```

Environment Variables

See environ(5) for a description of the LC_CTYPE environment variable that affects the execution of fmt.

Attributes

See attributes(5) for descriptions of the following attributes:

Attribute Type	Attribute Value
Availability	SUNWcsu

See Also

nroff(1), vi(1), attributes(5), environ(5)

---

fmtmsg — Display a Message on Standard Error or System Console

Synopsis

```
/usr/bin/fmtmsg [-c hard | soft | firm] [-u subclass] [-l label]
    [-s severity] [-t tag] [-a action] text
```

Description

Based on the message classification component, fmtmsg either writes a formatted message to standard error or writes a formatted message to the console.

A formatted message consists of up to five standard components (see environment variable MSGVERB.) The classification and subclass components are not displayed as part of the standard message, but they define the source of the message and direct the display of the formatted message.

Options

-c hard | soft | firm

   Describe the source of the message as hardware, software, or firmware.

-u subclass

   A list of keywords (separated by commas) that further defines the message and direct the display of the message. Valid keywords are:

   appl   The condition originated in an application. Do not use this keyword in combination with either util or opsys.

   util   The condition originated in a command. Do not use this keyword in combination with either appl or opsys.

   opsys   The message originated in the kernel. Do not use this keyword in combination with either appl or util.

   recov   The application recovers from the condition. Do not use this keyword in combination with nrecov.

   nrecov   The application does not recover from the condition. Do not use this keyword in combination with recov.

print	Print the message to the standard error stream stderr. You can use print, console, or both.
console	Write the message to the system console. You can use print, console, or both.

-l *label*   Identify the source of the message.

-s *severity*

Indicate the seriousness of the error. The keywords and definitions of the standard levels of severity are:

halt	The application has encountered a severe fault and is halting.
error	The application has detected a fault.
warn	The application has detected a condition that is unusual and might be a problem.
info	The application is providing information about a condition that is not in error.

-t *tag*   Specify the string containing an identifier for the message.

-a *action*   Specify a text string describing the first step in the error recovery process. You must write this string so that the entire *action* argument is interpreted as a single argument. fmtmsg precedes each action string with the TO FIX: prefix.

text   Specify a quoted text string describing the condition. You must write this string so that the entire *text* argument is interpreted as a single argument.

Examples

The following example of fmtmsg produces a complete message in the standard message format and displays it to standard error.

```
castle% fmtmsg -c soft -u recov,print,appl -l UX:cat  -s error
   -t UX:cat:001 -a "Refer to manual" "Invalid syntax"
UX:cat: ERROR: Invalid syntax
       TO FIX: Refer to manual  UX:cat:001
castle%
```

If you set the MSGVERB environment variable, in the C shell, as follows,

```
castle% setenv MSGVERB severity:text:action
```

then the previous example produces

```
ERROR: invalid syntax
TO FIX: refer to manual
```

If you set the environment variable SEV_LEVEL, in the C shell, as follows,

```
castle% setenv SEV_LEVEL=note,5,NOTE
```

then the following command displays the NOTE: tag on standard error.

```
castle% fmtmsg -c soft -u print -l UX:cat -s note -a "refer to manual"
  "Invalid syntax"
UX:cat: INFO: Invalid syntax
      TO FIX: refer to manual
castle%
```

> **Note —** If you do not set the SEV_LEVEL environment variable, fmtmsg
> displays a syntax error message because note is not one of the default
> arguments for the -s option.

Environment Variables

The environment variables MSGVERB and SEV_LEVEL control the behavior of fmtmsg.
MSGVERB is set by the administrator in /etc/profile for the system. You can override
the value of MSGVERB set by the system by resetting MSGVERB in your own .profile files
or by changing the value in the current shell session. You can use the SEV_LEVEL
environment variable in shell scripts.

MSGVERB tells fmtmsg what message components to select when writing messages to
standard error. The value of MSGVERB is a colon-separated list of optional keywords. You
can set MSGVERB as follows for the Bourne and Korn shell.

```
$ MSGVERB=[keyword[:keyword[:...]]]
$ export MSGVERB
```

You can set MSGVERB as follows for the C shell.

```
castle% setenv MSGVERB [keyword[:keyword[:...]]]
```

Valid keywords are label, severity, text, action, and tag. If MSGVERB contains a
keyword for a component and the component's value is not the component's null value,
fmtmsg includes that component in the message when writing the message to stderr. If
MSGVERB does not include a keyword for a message component, that component is not
included in the display of the message. You can specify the keywords in any order. If
MSGVERB is not defined, if its value is the null string, if its value is not of the correct
format, or if it contains keywords other than the valid ones listed above, fmtmsg selects
all components.

MSGVERB affects only the selection of message components for display on stderr. All
message components are included in console messages.

SEV_LEVEL defines severity levels and associates print strings with them for use by
fmtmsg. You cannot modify the standard severity levels shown below. You can define,
redefine, and remove additional severity levels.

0	(No severity is used).
1	HALT.
2	ERROR.
3	WARNING.
4	INFO.

You set SEV_LEVEL as follows for the Bourne and Korn shell.

```
$ SEV_LEVEL=[description[:description[:...]]]; export SEV_LEVEL
```

For the C shell, you set it as follows,

```
castle% setenv SEV_LEVEL [description[:description[:...]]]
```

description is a comma-separated list containing three fields.
description=severity-keyword,level,printstring

severity-keyword

>A character string used as the keyword with the -s severity option to fmtmsg.

level   A character string that evaluates to a positive integer (other than 0, 1, 2, 3, or 4, which are reserved for the standard severity levels). If you use the keyword *severity-keyword*, *level* is the severity value passed on to fmtmsg(3C).

printstring

>The character string used by fmtmsg in the standard message format whenever the severity value level is used.

If SEV_LEVEL is not defined or if its value is null, no severity levels other than the defaults are available. If a description in the colon-separated list is not a comma-separated list containing three fields or if the second field of a comma-separated list does not evaluate to a positive integer, that description in the colon-separated list is ignored.

Exit Status

0	All the requested functions were executed successfully.
1	The command contains a syntax error, an invalid option, or an invalid argument to an option.
2	The function executed with partial success; however, the message was not displayed on standard error.
4	The function executed with partial success; however, the message was not displayed on the system console.
32	No requested functions were executed successfully.

Attributes

See attributes(5) for descriptions of the following attributes:

Attribute Type	Attribute Value
Availability	SUNWcsu

See Also

addseverity(3C), fmtmsg(3C), attributes(5)

fnattr — Update and Examine Attributes Associated with an FNS Named Object

Synopsis

```
/usr/bin/fnattr [-AL] composite-name [[-O | -U] identifier]...
/usr/bin/fnattr [-L] composite-name [{ -a [-s] [-O | -U] identifier
    [value...] } | { -d [[-O | -U] identifier [value...]] } |{ -m [-O |
    -U] identifier old-value new-value }]...
```

Description

Use the fnattr command to update and examine attributes associated with a Federated Naming Service (FNS) named object. This command has four uses:

- Add an attribute or value.
- Delete an attribute or value.
- Modify an attribute's value.
- List the contents of an attribute.

Note — You cannot update built-in attributes, such as onc_unix_passwd for users, by using the fnattr command. Their contents are affected by updates to the underlying naming service, such as NIS+ or NIS.

Options

You can combine the options for adding, modifying, and deleting attributes and their values in the same command line. The modifications are executed in the order in which you specify them.

Any unsuccessful modification aborts all subsequent modifications specified in the command line; any modifications already carried out remain. The unsuccessful modifications are displayed as output of fnattr.

-a	Add an attribute, or add a value to an attribute associated with object named by *composite-name*. *identifier* is the identifier of the attribute to manipulate; its format is FN_ID_STRING unless you use the -O or -U option. *value*... represents the attribute values to add. The attribute syntax used for storing value is fn_attr_syntax_ascii.
-A	Consult the authoritative source to get attribute information.
-d	Delete attributes associated with object named by *composite-name*. If you do not specify *identifier*, delete all attributes associated with the named object. If you specify *identifier* without accompanying values (*value*...), remove the entire attribute identified by *identifier*. If you specify individual attribute values (*value*...), then remove only these from the attribute. Removal of the last value of an attribute entails removal of the attribute as well. The format of identifier is FN_ID_STRING unless you use the -O or -U option.

-L	If the composite name is bound to an X/Open Federated Naming (XFN) link, manipulate the attributes associated with the object pointed to by the link. If you do not specify -L, manipulate the attributes associated with the XFN link.
-m	Modify the values of the attribute identified by *identifier* associated with the object named by *composite-name*. *old-value* is replaced by *new-value* in the specified attribute. Leave other attributes and values associated with *composite-name* unaffected. The format of identifier is FN_ID_STRING unless you use the -O or -U option.
-O	The format of *identifier* is FN_ID_ISO_OID_STRING, an ASN.1, dot-separated, integer list string.
-s	Add in supersede mode. If an attribute with the same identifier as *identifier* already exists, remove all its values and replace with *value*. If you omit this option, the resulting values for the specified attribute is a union of the existing values and *value*.
-U	The format of identifier is FN_ID_DCE_UUID, a DCE UUID in string form.

Operands

composite-name

> An FNS named object.

identifier   The identifier of the attribute to manipulate.

Examples

Adding
Use the -a option for adding attributes and values. The following command replaces the value of the shoesize attribute of user/jane with the value 7.5.

```
castle% fnattr user/jane -as shoesize 7.5
```

The following command adds the value Chameleon to the projects attribute of user/jane.

```
castle% fnattr user/jsmith -a projects Chameleon
```

Deleting
Use the -d option for deleting attributes and values. The following command deletes the attribute shoesize associated with user/jane.

```
castle% fnattr user/jane -d shoesize
```

The following command deletes the attribute value old_project from the projects attribute associated with user/jane.

```
castle% fnattr user/jane -d projects old_project
```

The following command deletes all the attributes associated with user/jane.

```
castle% fnattr user/jane -d
```

Modifying

Use the –m option to modify an attribute value. The following command replaces the value Chameleon with Dungeon in the projects attribute associated with user/jsmith.

castle% **fnattr user/jsmith -m projects Chameleon Dungeon**

The following command is an example of unsuccessful modification attempts. The user executing this command does not have permission to update user/jane's attributes but is allowed to add new attributes. Executing the command adds the attribute hatsize but does not delete shoesize or modify dresssize because -d shoesize fails and the command stops.

castle% **fnattr user/jane -a hatsize medium -d shoesize -m dresssize 5 6**

Listing

Use the fnattr command with no options to list attributes and their values. The following command lists all the attributes associated with user/jane.

castle% **fnattr user/jane**

The following command lists the values of the projects attribute of user/jane.

castle% **fnattr user/jane projects**

The following command lists the values of the project and shoesize attributes of user/jane.

castle% **fnattr user/jane project shoesize**

Exit Status

0	Operation was successful.
1	Operation failed.

Attributes

See attributes(5) for descriptions of the following attributes:

Attribute Type	Attribute Value
Availability	SUNWfns

See Also

fnlookup(1), attributes(5), fns(5)

fnbind — Bind a Reference to an FNS Name

Synopsis

```
/usr/bin/fnbind [-s] [-v] [-L] name new-name
/usr/bin/fnbind -r [-s] [-v] new-name [-O | -U] ref-type { [-O | -U]
    addr-type [-c | -x] addr-contents }...
```

Description

fnbind binds the Federated Naming Service (FNS) reference named by *name* to the name *new-name*. The second synopsis of fnbind (using the -r option) enables the binding of *new-name* to the reference constructed, using arguments supplied in the command line.

Options

-c	Store *addr-contents* in the given form; do not use XDR encoding.
-L	Create an X/Open Federated Naming (XFN) link by using *name* and bind it to *new-name*.
-O	Specify the identifier format as FN_ID_ISO_OID_STRING, an ASN.1 dot-separated integer list string.
-r	Create a reference using *ref-type* as the reference's type and one or more pairs of *addr-type* and *addr-contents* as the reference's list of addresses, and bind this reference to *new-name*. Unless you use the -O or -U options, use FN_ID_STRING as the identifier format for *ref-type* and *addr-type*. Unless you use the -c or -x options, store *addr-contents* as an XDR-encoded string.
-s	Bind to *new-name* even if it is already bound. If you omit this option, fnbind fails if *new-name* is already bound.
-U	Specify the identifier format as FN_ID_DCE_UUID, a DCE UUID in string form.
-v	Display the reference being bound to *new-name*.
-x	Specify *addr-contents* as a hexidecimal string. Convert it to its hexidecimal representation and store it; do not use XDR encoding.

Examples

The following command binds the name thisorgunit/service/pr to the reference named by thisorgunit/service/printer. Any reference bound to thisorgunit/service/pr is overwritten.

```
castle% fnbind -s thisorgunit/service/printer thisorgunit/service/pr
```

The following example binds the name thisorgunit/service/pr to the XFN link constructed using the name thisorgunit/service/printer.

```
castle% fnbind -L thisorgunit/service/printer thisorgunit/service/pr
```

The following command binds the name thisorgunit/service/calendar to the reference with reference type SUNW_cal, address type SUNW_cal_deskset_onc, and address contents of staff@exodus.

```
castle% fnbind -r thisorgunit/service/calendar SUNW_cal
     SUNW_cal_deskset_onc staff@exodus
```

Attributes

See attributes(5) for descriptions of the following attributes:

Attribute Type	Attribute Value
Availability	SUNWfns

See Also

fnlookup(1), fnrename(1), fnunbind(1), FN_identifier_t(3N), xdr(3N), xfn_links(3N), attributes(5), fns(5)

fnlist — Display the Names and References Bound in an FNS Context

Synopsis

/usr/bin/fnlist [-Alv] [*composite-name*]

Description

fnlist displays the Federated Naming Service (FNS) names and references bound in the context of *composite-name*.

If you do not specify *composite-name*, the default initial context is displayed, as shown in the following example.

```
castle% fnlist
_myorgunit
...
_orgunit
_x500
_thisens
myens
thisens
org
orgunit
_dns
myorgunit
thisorgunit
_thisorgunit
_myens
castle%
```

Options

-A   Consult the authoritative source for information.

-l   Display the references as well as the names bound in the context of *composite-name*. Without this option, display only the names.

-v   Display the reference in detail. For onc_fn* references, this option is useful for deriving the name of the NIS+ table that stores the reference for every name that is bound in the context of *composite-name*.

Operands

composite-name

A Federated Naming Service named object. Composite names, like UNIX file names, depend on the subcontexts created.

Examples of commands with valid *composite-name* operands are:

```
castle% fnlist thisorgunit
castle% fnlist thisorgunit/service
castle% fnlist thisorgunit/service/printer
```

When FNS is deployed, the composite name is specific to the deployed site.

Examples

In the following example, the command with no operand provides the listing with reference and address types for the initial context.

```
castle% fnlist -l
name: _myorgunit
Reference type: onc_fn_nsid
Address type: onc_fn_files
  context type: namespace id

name: ...
Reference type: fn_global
Address type: initial

name: _orgunit
Reference type: onc_fn_organization
Address type: onc_fn_files
  context type: organization

name: _x500
Reference type: fn_global
Address type: x500
  Warning: empty X.500 reference address
  length: 0
  data:

name: _thisens
Reference type: onc_fn_enterprise
Address type: onc_fn_files
  context type: enterprise root
```

```
...
castle%
```

In the following examples, where you specify a user context (that is, *composite-name* = user/), FNS must first be deployed with fncreate(1M), using one of the naming services NIS, NIS+, or files. If FNS is not deployed, there are no user contexts and the command fails with the Name not found error message.

The following command shows the names bound in the context of user/.

```
castle% fnlist user/
```

The following command displays the names and references bound in the context of user/.

```
castle% fnlist -l user/
```

Exit Status

0	Operation was successful.
1	Operation failed.

Attributes

See attributes(5) for descriptions of the following attributes:

Attribute Type	Attribute Value
Availability	SUNWfns

See Also

fnbind(1), fnlookup(1), fnunbind(1), fncreate(1M), fndestroy(1M), attributes(5), fns(5), fns_references(5)

fnlookup — Display the Reference Bound to an FNS Name

Synopsis

/usr/bin/fnlookup [-ALv] *composite-name*

Description

fnlookup displays the Federated Naming Service (FNS) binding of *composite-name*.

Options

-A   Consult the authoritative source for information.

-L   If the composite name is bound to an X/Open Federated Naming (XFN) link, display the reference that the link is bound to. Without the -L option, display the XFN link.

-v   Display the binding in detail. For onc_fn_* references, this option is useful for deriving the name of the NIS+ table that stores the reference for *composite-name* and a string representation of the reference, if applicable.

Operands

composite-name

An FNS named object.

Examples

The following example shows the calendar reference to which the name /usr/jsmith/service/calendar is bound.

castle% **fnlookup user/jsmith/service/calendar**

The following example shows the service context reference to which /usr/jsmith is bound.

castle% **fnlookup user/jsmith/service**

If the service reference is bound to an XFN link, then the following command displays the reference to which this link is bound.

castle% **fnlookup -L user/jsmith/service**

Exit Status

0   Operation was successful.

1   Operation failed.

Attributes

See attributes(5) for descriptions of the following attributes:

Attribute Type	Attribute Value
Availability	SUNWfns

See Also

fnbind(1), fnlist(1), fnunbind(1), fncreate(1M), fndestroy(1M), xfn_links(3N), attributes(5), fns(5), fns_references(5)

fnrename — Rename the Binding of an FNS Name

Synopsis

/usr/bin/fnrename [-s] [-v] *context-name old-atomic-name new-atomic-name*

Description

fnrename renames the Federated Naming Service (FNS) binding of *old-atomic-name*
to *new-atomic-name* in the context of *context-name*. Both *old-atomic-name* and
new-atomic-name must be atomic names, to be resolved in the context named by
context-name.

Options

-s   Overwrite any reference already bound to *new-atomic-name*. If you
            omit this option, fnrename fails if *new-atomic-name* is already bound.

-v   Display the binding being renamed.

Examples

The following example binds calcndar to the reference bound to clendar in the context
named by /usr/jsmith/service and unbinds clendar.

castle% **fnrename user/jsmith/service/ clendar calendar**

Attributes

See attributes(5) for descriptions of the following attributes:

Attribute Type	Attribute Value
Availability	SUNWfns

See Also

fnbind(1), fnlist(1), fnunbind(1), fncreate(1M), fndestroy(1M),
xfn_links(3N), attributes(5), fns(5), fns_references(5)

fnsearch — Search for FNS Objects with Specified Attributes

Synopsis

/usr/bin/fnsearch [-AlLv] [-n *max*] [-s *scope*] *composite-name*
    [-a *ident*]... [-O | -U] *filter-expr* [*filter-arg*]...

Description

The fnsearch command displays the names and, optionally, the attributes and
references of Federated Naming Service (FNS) objects bound at or below
composite-name whose attributes satisfy a given filter expression. Specify the filter

expression in terms of logical expressions involving the identifiers and values of the attributes and references of objects examined during the search.

For general information about FNS, see fns(5).

Options

-a *ident*	Display the given attribute of each object that satisfies the filter expression. If you do not use the -a option, display all attributes. An empty *ident* (" " from the shell) indicates that no attributes are to be displayed. You can give multiple -a options. The syntax of *ident* is described fully under "Displaying Selected Attributes" on page 392.
-A	Consult the authoritative source(s) for information.
-1	Display the reference of each object that satisfies the filter expression.
-L	Follow X/Open Federated Naming (XFN) links during the search.
-n *max*	Restrict the maximum number of objects displayed to the given number (a positive integer). There is no limit by default.
-s *scope*	Set the scope of the search. *scope* is one of:

* object   Search only the object *composite-name*.

* context   Search objects bound directly to *composite-name*.

* subtree   Search objects bound to *composite-name* or any of its subcontexts.

* constrained_subtree

> Like subtree, but restrict the search to a set of subcontexts in a manner defined by the implementation context.

You can abbreviate *scope* to any unambiguous prefix, such as o or cont.

If you do not specify the -s *scope* option, the default behavior is -s *context*.

-v	Display in detail the reference of each object that satisfies the filter expression. This option takes precedence over -1.

Operands

composite-name

> An FNS named object.

Usage

Simple Filter Expressions

The simplest form of filter expression is one that tests for the existence of an attribute. You form this expression simply by giving the attribute's name. For example, the following command searches for objects having an attribute named for_sale.

```
% fnsearch composite-name for_sale
```

Another simple filter expression is one that tests the value of a particular attribute. The following command finds objects with ages less than 17.

```
% fnsearch composite-name "age < 17"
```

String values are indicated by enclosing the string in single quotes. For example, the following command finds all red objects.

```
% fnsearch composite-name "color == 'red'"
```

Note that the double quotes (") in this example are not part of the filter expression. Instead, they prevent the shell from interpreting the white space and single quotes that are part of the expression.

Logical Operators

You can compose simple filter expressions by using the logical operators and, or, and not, as shown in the following example.

```
% fnsearch composite-name "age >= 35 and us_citizen"
```

You can use parentheses to group expressions, as shown in the following example.

```
% fnsearch composite-name "not (make == 'olds' and \ year == 1973)"
```

The precedence of operators is as follows, in order of increasing precedence:

- or.
- and.
- not.
- Relational operators.

The logical operators and and or are left-associative.

Relational Operators

You can use the following relational operators to compare an attribute to a supplied value:

==	true if at least one value of the attribute is equal to the supplied value.
!=	true if none of the attribute's values are equal to the supplied value.
<	true if at least one value of the attribute is less than the supplied value.
<=	true if at least one value of the attribute is less than or equal to the supplied value.
>	true if at least one value of the attribute is greater than the supplied value.
>=	true if at least one value of the attribute is greater than or equal to the supplied value.
~=	true if at least one value of the attribute matches the supplied value according to some context-specific approximate matching criterion. This criterion must subsume strict equality.

Comparisons and ordering are specific to the syntax or rules of the attribute being tested.

Displaying Selected Attributes

By default, the `fnsearch` command displays the names and all of the attributes of each object matching the search criteria. You can restrict the list of attributes by using the `-a` command-line option. In the following example, only the color and shape attributes of small objects are displayed.

```
% fnsearch composite-name -a color -a shape "size == 'small'"
```

The format of an attribute identifier is taken to be *FN_ID_STRING* (an ASCII string) by default. To name an attribute identifier that is an OSI OID or a DCE UUID, prefix the attribute name by `-O` or `-U`.

`-O`   The identifier format is *FN_ID_ISO_OID_STRING*, an ASN.1, dot-separated, integer list string.

`-U`   The identifier format is *FN_ID_DCE_UUID*, a DCE UUID in string form.

The following examples show the `-O` and `-U` attributes.

```
% fnsearch composite-name -a -O 2.5.4.0 "shoe_size < 9"
% fnsearch composite-name -a -U 0006a446-5e97-105f-9828-8190285baa77
   "bowling_avg > 200"
```

Filter Arguments

You can replace some parts of a filter expression with a substitution token which is a percent sign (%) followed by a single character. The value of this portion of the expression is then given in a filter argument that follows the filter expression, in much the same way as is done in `printf(1)`. The available substitution tokens are:

`%a`   Attribute.

`%s`   String.

`%i`   Identifier.

`%v`   Attribute value.

> **Note** — The only syntax currently supported for `%v` is `fn_attr_syntax_ascii`.

For example, you could write the following command

```
% fnsearch composite-name "color == 'red'"
```

as

```
% fnsearch composite-name "%a == 'red'" color
```

or as

```
% fnsearch composite-name "%a == %s" color red
```

Substitution tokens are helpful for writing shell scripts when the values of the filter arguments will be generated at runtime.

By default, the format of the identifier of an attribute, such as the `color` attribute above, is taken to be *FN_ID_STRING* (an ASCII string). Substitution tokens enable the use of OSI OIDs and DCE UUIDs instead. Prefix the filter argument by -O or -U, with the same meaning as in the -a command-line option:

-O   The identifier format is *FN_ID_ISO_OID_STRING*, an ASN.1, dot-separated, integer list string.

-U   The identifier format is *FN_ID_DCE_UUID*, a DCE UUID in string form.

For example:

```
% fnsearch composite-name "%a -O 2.5.4.0
```

and

```
% fnsearch composite-name "%a" =='red'" -U
    0006a446-5e97-105f-9828-8190285baa77
```

Wild-carded Strings

A wild-carded string consists of a sequence of alternating wild-card specifiers and strings. The wild-card specifier is denoted by the asterisk (*) and means 0 or more occurrences of any character.

Use wild-carded strings to specify substring matches. The following are some examples of wild-carded strings and their meanings.

*   Any string.

'tom'   The string tom.

'harv'*   Any string starting with harv.

*'ing'   Any string ending with ing.

'a'*'b'   Any string starting with a and ending with b.

'jo'*'ph'*'ne'*'er'

                Any string starting with jo and containing the substring ph, and containing the substring ne in the portion of the string following ph, and ending with er.

%s*   Any string starting with the string supplied as a filter argument.

'bix'*%s   Any string starting with bix and ending with the string supplied as a filter argument.

Extended Operations

Extended operators are predicates (functions that return true or false) that you can freely mix with other operators in a filter expression. You specify an extended operation by giving the operation name as a quoted string, followed by an argument in parentheses. The following three extended operations are currently defined:

'name'(WildcardedString)

                true if the name of the object matches the supplied wild-carded string.

'reftype'(Identifier)

                true if the reference type of the object is equal to the supplied identifier.

`'addrtype'(Identifier)`

> true if any of the address types in the reference of the object are equal to the supplied identifier.

The following example shows a search for objects whose names start with `bill` and who have IQ attributes over 80.

```
% fnsearch composite-name "'name'('bill'*) and IQ > 80"
```

Grammar of Filter Expressions

The complete grammar of filter expressions is given below. It is based on the grammar defined by the X/Open Federated Naming (XFN) specification (see `FN_search_filter_t(3N)`).

String literals in this grammar are enclosed in double quotes; the quotes are not themselves part of the expression. Use braces for grouping; brackets for optional elements. An unquoted asterisk (*) signifies 0 or more occurrences of the preceding element; a plus sign (+) signifies 1 or more occurrences.

```
FilterExpr ::= [Expr]

Expr ::= Expr "or" Expr
       | Expr "and" Expr
       | "not" Expr
       | "(" Expr ")"
       | Attribute [RelOp Value]
       | Ext

RelOp ::= "==" | "!=" | "<" | "<=" | ">" | ">=" | "~="

Attribute ::= Char*
            | "%a"

Value ::= Integer
        | WildcardedString
        | "%v"

WildcardedString ::=
        "*"
      | String
      | {String "*"}+ [String]
      | {"*" String}+ ["*"]
```

(that is, an alternating sequence of *String* and `"*"`)

```
String ::= "'" Char* "'"
         | "%s"

Ext ::= "'name'(" WildcardedString ")"
      | "'reftype'(" Identifier ")"
      | "'addrtype'(" Identifier ")"

Identifier ::= "'" Char* "'"
             | "%i"
```

Char ::=an element of the Portable Character Set (ASCII)
    | a character in the repertoire of a string representation

---

Note — If the filter expression is empty, it evaluates to true (all objects satisfy it).

If the identifier in any subexpression of the filter expression does not exist as an attribute of an object, then the innermost logical expression containing that identifier evaluates to false.

Exit Status

0   Operation was successful.

1   Operation failed.

Attributes

See attributes(5) for descriptions of the following attributes:

Attribute Type	Attribute Value
Availability	SUNWfns

See Also

printf(1), FN_search_control_t(3N), FN_search_filter_t(3N), fn_attr_ext_search(3N), fn_attr_search(3N), attributes(5), fns(5)

---

fnunbind — Unbind the Reference from an FNS Name

Synopsis

/usr/bin/fnunbind *composite-name*

Description

fnunbind unbinds the Federated Naming Service (FNS) reference of *composite-name*. For example, the following command unbinds the reference to which the name user/jsmith/fs/ was bound.

castle% **fnunbind user/jsmith/fs/**

Note — An fnunbind on a name of a context fails because such a context cannot be unbound unless it is first destroyed with the fndestroy command.

Attributes

See attributes(5) for descriptions of the following attributes:

Attribute Type	Attribute Value
Availability	SUNWfns

See Also

fnbind(1), fnlist(1), fnlookup(1), fnrename(1), fncreate(1M), fndestroy(1M), attributes(5), fns(5)

fold — Filter for Folding Lines

Synopsis

/usr/bin/fold [-bs] [-w *width* | -*width*] [*file...*]

Description

The fold command is a filter that folds lines from its input files, breaking the lines to have a maximum of *width* column positions (or bytes, if you specify the -b option). Lines are broken by insertion of a newline character so that each output line (referred to later in this section as a segment) is the maximum width possible that does not exceed the specified number of column positions (or bytes). A line is not broken in the middle of a character. The behavior is undefined if *width* is less than the number of columns any single character in the input would occupy.

If the Return, backspace, or Tab characters are encountered in the input and you do not specify the -b option, the characters are treated specially, as described below.

Backspace	Decrement the current count of line width by 1, although the count never becomes negative. Do not insert a newline character immediately before or after any backspace character.
Return	Set the current count of line width to 0. Do not insert a newline character immediately before or after any Return character.
Tab	Advance the column position pointer to the next Tab stop for each Tab character encountered. Tab stops are at each column position n so that n modulo 8 equals 1.

Note — You can use fold and cut(1) to create text files out of files with arbitrary line lengths. Use fold when you need to keep the contents of long lines contiguous. Use cut when you need the number of lines (or records) to remain constant.

fold is frequently used to send text files to line printers that truncate, instead of fold, lines wider than the printer is able to print (usually 80 or 132 column positions).

fold may not work correctly if underlining is present.

Options

-b   Count width in bytes instead of column positions.

-s   If a segment of a line contains a blank character within the first width column positions (or bytes), break the line after the last such blank character meeting the width constraints. If no blank character meets the requirements, the -s option has no effect for that output segment of the input line.

-w *width*|-*width*

Specify the maximum line length, in column positions (or bytes if you specify -b). If *width* is not a positive decimal number, return an error. The default value is 80.

Operands

file   A path name of a text file to be folded. If you specify no *file* operands, use the standard input.

Examples

The following example folds lines for the file kookaburra at 10 characters.

```
castle% fold -w 10 kookaburra
Kookaburra
 sits in t
he old gum
 tree
Merry merr
y king of
the bush i
s he
Laugh, koo
kaburra, l
augh
Gay your l
ife must b
e.

Kookaburra
 sits in t
he old gum
 tree
Eating all
 the gumdr
ops he can
 see
Laugh, koo
kaburra, l
augh
Leave some
 there for
 me.
castle%
```

The following example folds lines for the file kookaburra at 72 characters. Because the file contains no lines longer than 72 characters, the output looks exactly like the original file.

```
castle% fold -w 72 kookaburra
Kookaburra sits in the old gum tree
Merry merry king of the bush is he
Laugh, kookaburra, laugh
Gay your life must be.

Kookaburra sits in the old gum tree
Eating all the gumdrops he can see
Laugh, kookaburra, laugh
Leave some there for me.

castle%
```

The following example submits a file of possibly long lines to the line printer (under the assumption that you know the line width of the printer to be assigned by lp(1)).

```
castle% fold -w 132 bigfile | lp
```

Environment Variables

See environ(5) for descriptions of the following environment variables that affect the execution of fold: LC_CTYPE, LC_MESSAGES, and NLSPATH.

Exit Status

0   All input files were processed successfully.

>0   An error occurred.

Attributes

See attributes(5) for descriptions of the following attributes:

Attribute Type	Attribute Value
Availability	SUNWcsu
CSI	Enabled

See Also

cut(1), pr(1), attributes(5), environ(5)

New! **franklinp** — Front Ends to the mp Text to PDL Pretty Print Filter

Synopsis

/bin/franklinp [*options*] *filename*...

Description

See mailp(1).

from — Display the Sender and Date of Newly Arrived Mail Messages

Synopsis

/usr/ucb/from [-s *sender*] [*username*]

Description

from prints out the mail header lines in your mailbox file to show who your mail is from. If you specify *username*, then *username's* mailbox is examined instead of your own.

Options

-s *sender*   Display headers only for mail sent by *sender*.

Examples

The following example displays the header lines for the current user.

```
castle% from
From <IMAP4.psuedo.sims> Fri Aug 28 12:30:14 1998
From winsor Fri Aug 28 12:15:01 1998
From winsor Fri Aug 28 12:30:01 1998
From winsor Fri Aug 28 12:30:02 1998
From winsor Fri Aug 28 12:55:01 1998
From winsor Fri Aug 28 12:56:53 1998
From winsor Fri Aug 28 13:04:41 1998
From winsor Fri Aug 28 13:04:53 1998
From winsor Fri Aug 28 13:05:37 1998
From winsor Fri Aug 28 13:06:24 1998
From lp Tue Sep 29 13:11:29 1998
From lp Thu Oct  1 10:38:46 1998
castle%
```

In the following example, someone tries to use the from command to display the header lines for a different user.

```
castle% from ray
Can't open /var/mail/ray
castle%
```

In the following example, superuser examines the header lines for user ray.

```
castle% su
Password:
# /usr/ucb/from ray
From winsor@castle Wed Nov 12 16:37:58 1997
#
```

Usage

See largefile(5) for the description of the behavior of from when encountering files greater than or equal to 2 Gbytes (2**31 bytes).

Files

```
/var/spool/mail/*
```

Attributes

See attributes(5) for descriptions of the following attributes:

Attribute Type	Attribute Value
Availability	SUNWfac

See Also

```
biff(1B), mail(1B), attributes(5), largefile(5)
```

---

ftp — File Transfer Program

Synopsis

New!

```
/usr/bin/ftp [-T timeout] [-dgintv] [hostname]
```

Description

The ftp command is the user interface to the Internet standard File Transfer Protocol (FTP). Use ftp to transfer files to and from a remote network site.

You can specify the client host with which ftp is to communicate on the command line. If you do so, ftp immediately tries to establish a connection to an FTP server on that host; otherwise, ftp enters its command interpreter and awaits instructions. When ftp is awaiting commands, it displays the prompt ftp>.

Use the following steps to transfer files from your local system to a remote system with the ftp command.

Note — You may need to have an account on each system and an entry in the /.rhosts file to use the file transfer program. Some systems allow read-only ftp access to anybody who logs in as anonymous and types a login name at the password prompt.

If you have an NIS or an NIS+ account, you can use your login name and network password to access a remote system, using ftp.

1. Type **ftp** and press Return. The ftp> prompt is displayed.

2. Type **open *remote-system-name*** and press Return. System connection messages are displayed, and you are asked for a user name.

3. Type the user name for your account on the remote system and press Return. If a password is required, you are asked to enter it.

4. Type the password (if required) for your account on the remote system and press Return. A system login message and the ftp> prompt are displayed.

5. Type **bin** to set binary format or type **asc** to set ASCII format and press Return. The file type is set. (The default is ASCII.)

6. Type **put *local-filename destination-filename*** and press Return. File transfer messages and the ftp> prompt are displayed.

7. Type **quit** and press Return. A goodbye message and the command prompt are displayed.

The following example establishes an ftp connection from the system oak to the system elm, specifies ASCII format, puts the file quest from oak into the /tmp/quest directory on elm, and quits the session.

```
oak% ftp
ftp> open elm
Connected to elm
220 elm FTP server (UNIX(r) System V Release 4.0) ready.

Name (elm:ignatz): ignatz
331 Password required for ignatz.
Password:
230 User ignatz logged in.
ftp> asc
ftp> put quest /tmp/quest
200 PORT command successful.

150 ASCII data connection for /tmp/quest (129.144.52.119,1333).

226 Transfer complete.
ftp> quit
221 Goodbye.
oak%
```

You can use the send command as an alternative to the put command. You can copy multiple files by using the mput command. There is no msend command.

Follow these steps to transfer files from a remote system to your local system, using ftp.

1. Type **ftp** and press Return. The ftp> prompt is displayed.

2. Type **open *remote-system-name*** and press Return. System connection messages are displayed, and you are asked for a user name.

3. Type the user name for your account on the remote system and press Return. If a password is required, you are asked to enter it.

4. Type the password (if required) for your account on the remote system and press Return. A system login message and the ftp> prompt are displayed.

5. Type **bin** to set binary format or type **asc** to set ASCII format and press Return. The file type is set.

6. Type **get *remote-filename destination-filename*** and press Return. File transfer messages and the ftp> prompt are displayed.

7. Type **quit** and press Return. A goodbye message and the command prompt are displayed.

The following example establishes an `ftp` connection from the system `oak` to the system `elm`, specifies ASCII format, gets the file `quest` from `elm`, puts it into the `/tmp/quest` directory on `oak`, and quits the session.

```
oak% ftp
ftp> open elm
Connected to elm
220 elm FTP server (UNIX(r)System V Release 4.0) ready.

Name (elm:ignatz): ignatz
331 Password required for ignatz.
Password:
230 User ignatz logged in.

ftp> asc
ftp> get quest /tmp/quest
200 PORT command successful.
150 ASCII data connection for /tmp/quest (129.144.52.119,1333).
226 Transfer complete.

ftp> quit
221 Goodbye.
oak%
```

Note — Correct execution of many commands depends on proper behavior by the remote server.

An error in the treatment of Returns in the 4.2 BSD code that handles transfers with a representation type of network ASCII has been corrected. This correction may result in incorrect transfers of binary files to and from 4.2 BSD servers using a representation type of network ASCII. Avoid this problem by using the `image` type.

New! Failure to log in can result from an explicit denial by the remote FTP server because the account is listed in `/etc/ftpusers`. See `in.ftpd`(1M) and `ftpusers`(4). New in the Solaris 8 release.

Options

You can specify the following options for the `ftp` command either at the command line or to the `ftp` command interpreter.

-d   Enable debugging.

-g   Disable *filename* globbing.

-i   Turn off interactive prompting during multiple file transfers.

-n   Do not attempt auto-login on initial connection. If auto-login is not disabled, `ftp` checks the `.netrc` file in the user's home directory for an entry describing an account on the remote machine. If no entry exists, `ftp` prompts for the login name of the account on the remote machine (the default is the login name on the local machine) and, if necessary, prompts for a password and an account with which to log in.

-t   Enable packet tracing (unimplemented).

-T *timeout*   Enable global connection timer, specified in seconds (decimal). The
             timer is reset when anything is sent to the server on the control
             connection and is disabled while the client is prompting for user input.
             On the data connection, timeouts rely on TCP and can time out only on
             network outages between the client and server. It may not time out, for
             example, if the server is waiting for an NFS server. New in the Solaris
             8 release.

-v   Show all responses from the remote server, as well as report on data
             transfer statistics. This option is turned on by default if ftp is running
             interactively with its input coming from the user's terminal.

You can specify the following ftp commands to the ftp command interpreter.

! [*command*]   Run *command* as a shell command on the local machine. If no command
             is given, invoke an interactive shell.

$ *macro-name* [*args*]

             Execute the macro *macro-name* that was defined with the macdef
             command. Arguments are passed unglobbed to the macro.

account [*passwd*]

             Supply a supplemental password required by a remote system for
             access to resources once a login has been successfully completed. If no
             argument is included, the user is prompted for an account password in
             a nonechoing input mode.

append *local-file* [*remote-file*]

             Append a local file to a file on the remote machine. If you do not specify
             remote-file, use the local file name, subject to alteration by any
             ntrans or nmap settings. File transfer uses the current settings for
             representation type, file structure, and transfer mode.

ascii   Set the representation type to network ASCII (the default).

bell   Sound a bell after each file transfer command is completed.

binary   Set the representation type to image.

bye   Terminate the FTP session with the remote server, and exit ftp. An
             end-of-file also terminates the session and exits.

case   Toggle remote computer file-name case mapping during mget
             commands. When case is on (default is off), write remote computer file
             names with all letters in uppercase in the local directory with the
             letters mapped to lowercase.

cd *remote-directory*

             Change the working directory on the remote machine to
             remote-directory.

cdup   Change the remote-machine working directory to the parent of the
             current, remote-machine working directory.

close   Terminate the FTP session with the remote server, and return to the
             command interpreter. Erase any defined macros.

New!

cr   Toggle Return-stripping during network ASCII type file retrieval.
               Records are denoted by a Return/linefeed sequence during network
               ASCII type file transfer. When cr is on (the default), Return characters
               are stripped from this sequence to conform with the UNIX system
               single-linefeed record delimiter. Records on non-UNIX-system remote
               hosts can contain single linefeed characters; when a network ASCII
               type transfer is made, these linefeed characters can be distinguished
               from a record delimiter only when cr is off.

delete *remote-file*

               Delete the file *remote-file* on the remote machine.

debug   Toggle debugging mode. When debugging is on, ftp prints each
               command sent to the remote machine, preceded by the string -->.

dir [*remote-directory*] [*local-file*]

               Print a listing of the directory contents in the directory,
               remote-directory, and, optionally, place the output in *local-file*. If
               you specify no directory, use the current working directory on the
               remote machine. If you specify no local file or local-file is -, send
               output to the terminal.

disconnect   A synonym for close.

form [*format-name*]

               Set the carriage control format subtype of the representation type to
               format-name. The only valid *format-name* is nonprint, which
               corresponds to the default "nonprint" subtype.

get *remote-file* [*local-file*]

               Retrieve the *remote-file* and store it on the local machine. If you do
               not specify the local file name, give it the same name it has on the
               remote machine, subject to alteration by the current case, ntrans, and
               nmap settings. Use the current settings for representation type, file
               structure, and transfer mode while transferring the file.

glob   Toggle *filename expansion*, or globbing, for mdelete, mget, and mput.
               If globbing is turned off, take file names literally.

               Do globbing for mput as in sh(1). For mdelete and mget, expand each
               remote file name separately on the remote machine, and do not merge
               the lists.

               Expansion of a directory name is likely to be radically different from
               expansion of the name of an ordinary file: the exact result depends on
               the remote operating system and FTP server and can be previewed with
               mls *remote-files* -.

               mget and mput are not meant to transfer entire directory subtrees of
               files. You can transfer entire directory subtrees by transferring a tar(1)
               archive of the subtree (using a representation type of image as set by
               the binary command).

hash   Toggle hash sign (#) printing for each data block transferred. The size of
                a data block is 8,192 bytes.

help [*command*]

                Print an informative message about the meaning of *command*. If you
                specify no argument, ftp prints a list of the known commands.

lcd [*directory*]

                Change the working directory on the local machine. If you specify no
                directory, use the user's home directory.

ls [*remote-directory* | -al] [*local-file*]

                Print an abbreviated listing of the contents of a directory on the remote
                machine. If you specify no *remote-directory*, use the current working
                directory.

                The -a option lists all entries, including those that begin with a dot (.),
                that are normally not listed. The -l option lists files in long format,
                giving mode, number of links, owner, group, size in bytes, and time of
                last modification for each file. If the file is a special file, the size field
                contains the major and minor device numbers instead of a size. If the
                file is a symbolic link, the file name is printed, followed by -> and the
                path name of the referenced file.

                If you specify no local file or if local-file is -, send the output to the
                terminal.

macdef *macro-name*

                Define a macro. Store subsequent lines as the macro *macro-name*; a null
                line (consecutive newline characters in a file or Return characters from
                the terminal) terminates macro input mode. There is a limit of 16
                macros and 4,096 total characters in all defined macros. Macros remain
                defined until you execute a close command.

                The macro processor interprets $ and \ as special characters. A $
                followed by a number (or numbers) is replaced by the corresponding
                argument on the macro invocation command line. A $ followed by an i
                signals the macro processor to loop the executing macro. On the first
                pass, $i is replaced by the first argument on the macro invocation
                command line; on the second pass, it is replaced by the second
                argument, and so on. A \ followed by any character is replaced by that
                character. Use the \ to prevent special treatment of the $.

mdelete *remote-files*

                Delete the *remote-files* on the remote machine.

mdir *remote-files local-file*

                Like dir, except you can specify multiple remote files. If interactive
                prompting is on, prompt to verify that the last argument is indeed the
                target local file for receiving mdir output.

mget *remote-files*

> Expand the remote-files on the remote machine and do a get for each
> file name thus produced. See glob for details on the file-name
> expansion. Process resulting file names according to case, ntrans, and
> nmap settings. Transfer files into the local working directory, which you
> can change with lcd *directory*; you can create new local directories
> with ! mkdir *directory*.

mkdir *directory-name*

> Make a directory on the remote machine.

mls *remote-files local-file*

> Like ls(1), except you can specify multiple remote files. If interactive
> prompting is on, ftp prompts you to verify that the last argument is
> indeed the target local file for receiving mls output.

mode [*mode-name*]

> Set the transfer mode to *mode-name*. The only valid *mode-name* is
> stream, which corresponds to the default stream mode. This
> implementation supports only stream and requires that it be specified.

mput *local-files*

> Expand wild-cards in the list of local files given as arguments and do a
> put for each file in the resulting list. See glob for details of file-name
> expansion. Process resulting file names according to ntrans and nmap
> settings.

nmap [*inpattern outpattern*]

> Set or unset the file-name mapping mechanism. If you specify no
> arguments, unset the file-name mapping mechanism. If you specify
> arguments, map remote file names during mput and put commands
> issued without a specified remote target file name.
>
> The nmap command is useful when connecting to a non-UNIX system
> remote host with different file-naming conventions or practices. The
> mapping follows the pattern set by *inpattern* and *outpattern*.
> *inpattern* is a template for incoming file names (that may have
> already been processed according to the ntrans and case settings).
> Variable templating is accomplished by inclusion of the sequences $1,
> $2, ..., $9 in *inpattern*. Use \ to prevent this special treatment of
> the $ character. All other characters are treated literally and are used to
> determine the nmap *inpattern* variable values.
>
> For example, given *inpattern* $1.$2 and the remote file name,
> mydata.data, $1 would have the value mydata and $2 would have the
> value data.

The *outpattern* determines the resulting mapped file name. The sequences $1, $2, ..., $9 are replaced by any value resulting from the *inpattern* template. The sequence $0 is replaced by the original file name. Additionally, the sequence [*seq1,seq2*] is replaced by *seq1* if *seq1* is not a null string; otherwise, it is replaced by *seq2*.

For example, the command nmap $1.$2.$3 [$1,$2].[$2,file] yields the output file name myfile.data for input file names myfile.data and myfile.data.old; myfile.file for the input file name myfile; and myfile.myfile for the input file name .myfile. You can include space characters in *outpattern*, as in the example nmap $1 | sed "s/ *$//" > $1. Use the \ character to prevent special treatment of the $, [,], and , characters.

ntrans [*inchars* [*outchars*]]

Set or unset the file-name character translation mechanism. If you specify no arguments, unset the file-name character translation mechanism. If you specify arguments, translate characters in remote file names during mput and put commands issued without a specified remote target file name, and translate characters in local file names during mget and get commands issued without a specified local target file name.

The ntrans command is useful when connecting to a non-UNIX system remote host with different file-naming conventions or practices. Characters in a file name matching a character in *inchars* are replaced with the corresponding character in *outchars*. If the character's position in *inchars* is longer than the length of *outchars*, delete the character from the file name.

You can translate only 16 characters when using the ntrans command under ftp. Use case if you need to convert the entire alphabet.

open host [*port*]

Establish a connection to the specified host FTP server. You can supply an optional port number, in which case, ftp contacts an FTP server at that port. If the auto-login option is on (default setting), ftp also tries to automatically log the user in to the FTP server.

prompt Toggle interactive prompting. Interactive prompting occurs during multiple file transfers to enable you to selectively retrieve or store files. By default, prompting is turned on. If you turn prompting off, any mget command transfers all files, and any mdelete command deletes all files.

proxy *ftp-command*

Execute an FTP command on a secondary control connection. The proxy command enables simultaneous connection to two remote FTP servers for transferring files between the two servers. The first proxy command should be an open, to establish the secondary control connection. Enter the command proxy ? to see other FTP commands executable on the secondary connection.

The following commands behave differently when prefaced by proxy: open does not define new macros during the auto-login process; close does not erase existing macro definitions; get and mget transfer files from the host on the primary control connection to the host on the secondary control connection; and put, mputd, and append transfer files from the host on the secondary control connection to the host on the primary control connection.

Third-party file transfers depend on support of the PASV command by the server on the secondary control connection.

put *local-file* [*remote-file*]

Store a local file on the remote machine. If you do not specify *remote-file*, use the local file name after processing according to any ntrans or nmap settings in naming the remote file. File transfer uses the current settings for representation type, file structure, and transfer mode.

pwd   Print the name of the current working directory on the remote machine.

quit   A synonym for bye.

quote *arg1 arg2*...

Send the arguments specified, verbatim, to the remote FTP server. A single FTP reply code is expected in return. (The remotehelp command displays a list of valid arguments.) Use quote only if you are an experienced user familiar with the FTP protocol.

recv *remote-file* [*local-file*]

A synonym for get.

remotehelp [*command-name*]

Request help from the remote FTP server. If *command-name* is specified, it is supplied to the server as well.

rename *from to*

Rename the file named *from* on the remote machine to have the name *to*.

reset   Clear reply queue. This command resynchronizes command/reply sequencing with the remote FTP server. You may need to resynchronize following a violation of the FTP protocol by the remote server.

rmdir *directory-name*

Delete a directory on the remote machine.

runique   Toggle storing of files on the local system with unique file names. If a
             file already exists with a name equal to the target local file name for a
             get or mget command, append a .1 to the name. If the resulting name
             matches another existing file, append a .2 to the original name. If this
             process continues up to .99, print an error message, and abort the
             transfer. The generated unique file name is reported. runique does not
             affect local files generated from a shell command. The default value is
             off.

send *local-file* [*remote-file*]

             A synonym for put.

sendport   Toggle the use of PORT commands. By default, ftp tries to use a PORT
             command when establishing a connection for each data transfer. The
             use of PORT commands can prevent delays when performing multiple
             file transfers. If the PORT command fails, ftp uses the default data port.
             When you disable the use of PORT commands, no attempt is made to use
             PORT commands for each data transfer. This option is useful when
             connected to certain FTP implementations that ignore PORT commands
             but incorrectly indicate they have been accepted.

status   Show the current status of ftp.

struct [*struct-name*]

             Set the file structure to *struct-name*. The only valid *struct-name* is
             file, which corresponds to the default file structure. The
             implementation supports only file and requires that it be specified.

sunique   Toggle storing of files on a remote machine under unique file names.
             The remote FTP server must support the STOU command for successful
             completion. The remote server reports the unique name. Default value
             is off.

tenex   Set the representation type to that needed to talk to TENEX machines.

trace   Toggle packet tracing (unimplemented).

type [*type-name*]

             Set the representation type to *type-name*. The valid *type-name*s are
             ascii for network ASCII, binary or image for image, and tenex for
             local byte size with a byte size of 8 (used to talk to TENEX machines). If
             you do not specify a type, ftp prints the current type. The default type
             is network ASCII.

user *user-name* [*password*] [*account*]

             Identify yourself to the remote FTP server. If you do not specify the
             password and the server requires it, ftp prompts you for it (after
             disabling local echo). If you do not specify an account field and the FTP
             server requires it, you are prompted for it. If you specify an account
             field, relay an account command to the remote server after the login
             sequence is completed if the remote server did not require it for logging
             in. Unless ftp is invoked with auto-login disabled, this process is done
             automatically on initial connection to the FTP server.

verbose   Toggle verbose mode. In verbose mode, all responses from the FTP
           server are displayed. In addition, if verbose mode is on, then when a file
           transfer completes, statistics regarding the efficiency of the transfer are
           reported. By default, verbose mode is on if ftp's commands are coming
           from a terminal, and off otherwise.

? [*command*]

           A synonym for help.

You can quote command arguments that have embedded spaces with quote (") marks.
If you do not specify any command argument that is not indicated as being optional,
ftp prompts for that argument.

Aborting File Transfer

To abort a file transfer, use the terminal interrupt key. Sending transfers are
immediately halted. Receiving transfers are halted by sending an FTP protocol ABOR
command to the remote server and discarding any further data received. The speed at
which this is accomplished depends on the remote server's support for ABOR processing.
If the remote server does not support the ABOR command, an ftp> prompt is not
displayed until the remote server has completed sending the requested file.

The terminal interrupt key sequence is ignored when ftp has completed any local
processing and is awaiting a reply from the remote server. A long delay in this mode may
result from the ABOR processing described above, or from unexpected behavior by the
remote server, including violations of the ftp protocol. If the delay results from
unexpected remote server behavior, you must kill the local ftp program by hand.

File-Naming Conventions

Local files specified as arguments to ftp commands are processed according to the
following rules.

1. If you specify the file name -, use the standard input (for reading) or the standard
   output (for writing).
2. If the first character of the file name is |, interpret the remainder of the argument
   as a shell command. ftp then forks a shell, using popen(3S) with the argument
   supplied, and reads (writes) from the standard output (standard input) of that
   shell. If the shell command includes space characters, you must quote the
   argument; for example "| ls -lt". A particularly useful example of this
   mechanism is: "dir | more".
3. Failing the above checks, if you enable globbing, then expand local file names
   according to the rules used in the sh(1); see the glob command. If the ftp
   command expects a single local file (for example, put), use only the first *filename*
   generated by the globbing operation.
4. For mget and get commands with unspecified local file names, the local *filename*
   is the remote *filename*, which you can alter by using a case, ntrans, or nmap
   setting. You can then alter the resulting *filename* if runique is on.
5. For mput and put commands with unspecified remote file names, the remote
   filename is the local *filename*, which you can alter by using an ntrans or nmap
   setting. The resulting *filename* can then be altered by the remote server if
   sunique is on.

File Transfer Parameters

The following parameters from the FTP specification can affect file transfers.

Representation type

> ASCII, EBCDIC, image, or local byte size with a specified byte size (for PDP-10s and PDP-20s mostly). The network ASCII and EBCDIC types have a further subtype that specifies whether vertical format control such as newline characters and formfeeds is to be passed through (nonprint), provided in TELNET format (TELNET format controls), or provided in ASA (FORTRAN) (carriage control (ASA)) format. ftp supports the network ASCII (subtype nonprint only) and image types, plus local byte size with a byte size of 8 for communicating with TENEX machines.

File structure

> file (no record structure), record, or page. ftp supports only the default value, which is file.

Transfer mode

> stream, block, or compressed. ftp supports only the default value, which is stream.

Usage

See largefile(5) for the description of the behavior of ftp when encountering files greater than or equal to 2 Gbytes (2**31 bytes).

The ftp command is IPv6 enabled. See ip6 (7P).   *New!*

Files

~/.netrc

Attributes

See attributes(5) for descriptions of the following attributes:

Attribute Type	Attribute Value
Availability	SUNWbip
CSI	Enabled

New!

See Also

ls(1), rcp(1), sh(1), tar(1), in.ftpd(1M), popen(3C), ftpusers(4), netrc(4), attributes(5), largefile(5), ip6(7P)   *New!*

New! **ftpcount** — Show Current Number of Users in Each FTP Server Class

Synopsis

    /usr/sbin/ftpcount [-V]

Description

Use the ftpcount command, new in the Solaris 9 Operating Environment, to show the current number of users logged in and the login limit for each FTP Server class defined in the ftpaccess(4) file.

Options

-V	Display program copyright and version information, then terminate.

Examples

The following example shows that no FTP users are currently configured for the system mopoke.

```
mopoke% ftpcount
Service class realusers         -    1 users (no maximum)
Service class guestusers        -    0 users (no maximum)
Service class anonusers         -    0 users (no maximum)
mopoke%
```

Exit Status

0	Successful completion.
>0	An error occurred.

Files

/etc/ftpd/ftpaccess

    File used to configure the operation of the FTP server.

/var/run/ftp.pids-classnames

    FTP Server run file.

Attributes

See attributes(5) for descriptions of the following attributes.

Attribute Type	Attribute Value
Availability	SUNWftpu

See Also

ftpwho(1), in.ftpd(1M), ftpaccess(4), attributes(5)

ftpwho — Show Current Process Information for Each FTP Server User

New!

Synopsis

/usr/sbin/ftpwho [-V]

Description

Use the ftpwho command, new in the Solaris 9 Operating Environment, to show the current process information for each user logged in to the FTP Server. This information is in addition to information displayed by the ftpcount(1) command.

Options

-V   Display the program copyright and version information, then terminate.

Examples

The following example shows the output from the ftpwho command.

```
mopoke% ftpwho
Service class realusers:
winsor    596  0.0  1.9 2648 2176 ?          S 19:54:45  0:00 ftpd:
   castle: winsor: IDLE
   -    1 users (no maximum)
Service class guestusers:
   -    0 users (no maximum)
Service class anonusers:
   -    0 users (no maximum)
mopoke%
```

Exit Status

0   Successful completion.

>0   An error occurred.

Files

/etc/ftpd/ftpaccess

                   File used to configure the operation of the FTP server.

/var/run/ftp.pids-classnames

                   FTP Server run file.

Attributes

See `attributes`(5) for descriptions of the following attributes.

Attribute Type	Attribute Value
Availability	SUNWftpu

See Also

`ftpcount(1)`, `ps(1)`, `in.ftpd(1M)`, `ftpaccess(4)`, `attributes(5)`

function — Shell Built-in Command to Define a Shell Function

Synopsis

ksh
```
function identifier { list ;}
identifier() { list ;}
```

Description

Korn Shell

`function` defines a function that is referenced by *identifier*. The body of the function is the list of commands between the curly braces (`{}`).

Alternatively, you can define a function by omitting the `function` keyword and appending the identifier with a set of enclosed parentheses.

Examples

The following example creates a function called `status()` that returns the name of your current working directory and then lists it.

```
$ status() { cd $*; pwd;ls; }
$
$ functions
function status
{
cd $*; pwd;ls; }
$
$ status /home
/home
TT_DB        bill         lost+found
$
```

The following example creates a function called `scp()` for safe copy. It prevents you from overwriting an existing file. When you issue the same command twice, the second command is not executed and the `scp()` function displays an error message.

```
$ scp()
> {
> if test ! -s "$2"
```

```
> then cp "$1" "$2"
> else echo "scp: cannot copy $1: $2 exists"
> fi
> }
$ scp junk junk1
$ scp junk junk1
scp: cannot copy junk: junk1 exists
$
```

Attributes

See attributes(5) for descriptions of the following attributes:

Attribute Type	Attribute Value
Availability	SUNWcsu

See Also

ksh(1), attributes(5)

G

gcore — Get Core Images of Running Processes

Synopsis

/usr/bin/gcore [-o *filename*] *process-id*...

Description

gcore creates a core image of each specified process in the current working directory. By default, the name of the core image file for the process is core.*process-id*.

Options

-o *filename*

Substitute *filename* in place of core as the first part of the name of the core image files.

Operands

process-id   Process ID.

Examples

The following example creates a core image of process ID 450.

```
castle% gcore 450
gcore: core.450 dumped
castle% ls -l core*
-rw-rw-rw-   1 winsor    staff       66216 Jan 16 14:16 core.450
castle% file core.450
```

```
core.450:      ELF 32-bit MSB core file SPARC Version 1, from 'cat'
castle%
```

The following example tries to create a core image for process ID 461, which doesn't exist. Notice that gcore creates an output file named core.o, but it is an empty file.

```
castle% gcore 461
castle% ls -l core*
-rw-rw-rw-   1 winsor    staff           0 Jan 14 15:50 core.o
castle%
```

Exit Status

0   On success.

non-zero   On failure, such as nonexistent process ID.

Files

core.*process-id*

Core images.

Attributes

See attributes(5) for descriptions of the following attributes:

Attribute Type	Attribute Value
Availability	SUNWtoo (32-bit)
	SUNWtoox (64-bit)

See Also

kill(1), core(4), proc(4), attributes(5)

gencat — Generate a Formatted Message Catalog

Synopsis

/usr/bin/gencat *catfile msgfile*...

Description

Use the gencat command to merge the message text source file(s) *msgfile* into a formatted message database *catfile*. If the database *catfile* does not already exist, it is created. If *catfile* does exist, its messages are included in the new *catfile*. If set and message numbers collide, the new message text defined in *msgfile* replaces the old message text currently contained in *catfile*. The message text source file (or set of files) you input to gencat can contain either set and message numbers or simply message numbers, in which case the set NL_SETD (see nl_types(5)) is assumed.

Message Text Source File Format

The format of a message text source file is described below.

Note — The fields of a message text source line are separated by a single ASCII space or Tab character. Any other ASCII spaces or Tabs are considered as part of the subsequent field.

$set *n comment*

>Specify a set identifier, where *n* specifies the set identifier of the following messages until the next $set, $delset, or end-of-file. *n* must be a number in the range (1-{NL_SETMAX}). Set identifiers within a single source file need not be contiguous. Treat any string following the set identifier as a comment. If you specify no $set directive in a message text source file, locate all messages in the default message set NL_SETD.

$delset *n comment*

>Delete message set *n* from an existing message catalog. Treat any string following the set number as a comment. (Note: if *n* is not a valid set, it is ignored.)

$ *comment*

>Treat a line beginning with a dollar symbol $ followed by an ASCII space or Tab character as a comment.

m message-text

>The *m* denotes the message identifier, a number in the range (1-{NL_MSGMAX}). Store *message-text* in the message catalog with the set identifier specified by the last $set directive and with message identifier *m*. If *message-text* is empty and an ASCII space or Tab field separator is present, store an empty string in the message catalog. If a message source line has a message number but neither a field separator nor message text, delete the existing message with that number (if any) from the catalog. Message identifiers need not be contiguous. The length of *message-text* must be in the range (0-{NL_TEXTMAX}).

$quote *c*

>Specify an optional quote character *c* that can be used to surround *message-text* so that trailing spaces or null (empty) messages are visible in a message source line. By default or if you specify an empty $quote directive, no quoting of *message-text* is recognized.

Empty lines in a message text source file are ignored.

Text strings can contain the special characters and escape sequences defined below.

Description	Symbol	Sequence
Newline	NL(LF)	\n
Horizontal tab	HT	\t
Vertical tab	VT	\v
Backspace	BS	\b

Description	Symbol	Sequence
Return	CR	\r
Formfeed	FF	\f
Backslash	\	\\
Bit pattern	*ddd*	*ddd*

The escape sequence *ddd* consists of backslash followed by 1, 2, or 3 octal digits, which are taken to specify the value of the desired character. If the character following a backslash is not one of those specified, the backslash is ignored.

You can also use a backslash followed by an ASCII newline character to continue a string on the following line. Thus, the following two lines describe a single message string:

```
1 This line continues \
to the next line
```

is equivalent to:

```
1 This line continues to the next line
```

Operands

catfile   A path name of the formatted message catalogue. If you specify -, use the standard output.

msgfile   A path name of a message text source file. If you specify - for an instance of *msgfile*, use the standard input.

Environment Variables

See environ(5) for descriptions of the following environment variables that affect the execution of gencat: LC_CTYPE, LC_MESSAGES, and NLSPATH.

Exit Status

0   Successful completion.

>0   An error occurred.

Attributes

See attributes(5) for descriptions of the following attributes:

Attribute Type	Attribute Value
Availability	SUNWloc
CSI	Enabled

See Also

mkmsgs(1), catgets(3C), catopen(3C), gettxt(3C), attributes(5), environ(5), nl_types(5)

geniconvtbl — Generate iconv Code Conversion Tables   New!

Synopsis

```
/bin/geniconvtbl [-fnq] [-o outputfile] [-p preprocessor] [-W arg]
    [-Dname] [-Dname=def] [-Idirectory] [-Uname] [infile...]
```

Description

The geniconvtbl command, new in the Solaris 8 Operating Environment, accepts code conversion rules defined in flat text file(s) and writes code conversion binary table file(s) that can be used to support user-defined iconv code conversions (see iconv(1) and iconv(3C) for more detail on the iconv code conversion).

Options

-f	Overwrite output file if the output file exists.
-n	Do not generate an output file. This option is useful to check the contents of the input file.
-o outputfile	
	Specify the name of the output file.
-p preprocessor	
	Use specified preprocessor instead of the default preprocessor, /usr/lib/cpp.
-q	Quiet option. Suppress warning and error messages.
-W arg	Pass the argument arg to the preprocessor. If you specify this option more than once, pass all arguments to the preprocessor.
-Dname -Dname=def -Idirectory -Uname	
	Pass these options and their arguments to the preprocessor.

Operands

infile	A path name of an input file. If you specify no input file, geniconvtbl reads from the standard input stream. You can specify more than one input file.

Output

If input is from the standard input stream, geniconvtbl writes output to the standard output stream. If you specify one or more input files, geniconvtbl reads from each input file and writes to a corresponding output file. Each of the output file names is the same as the corresponding input file with .bt appended.

You must move the generated output files to the following directory before using the iconv(1) and iconv(3C) code conversions.

/usr/lib/iconv/geniconvtbl/binarytables/

Start the output file name with one or more printable ASCII characters as the fromcode name followed by a percent sign (%), followed by one or more printable ASCII characters as the tocode name, followed by the suffix .bt. The fromcode and tocode names are used to identify the iconv code conversion at iconv(1) and iconv_open(3C). Place the properly named output file in the /usr/lib/iconv/geniconvtbl/binarytables/ directory.

> **Note —** The generated and correctly placed output files /usr/lib/iconv/geniconvtbl/binarytables/*.bt are used in both 32-bit and 64-bit environments.

Examples

The following example uses the UTF-8_to_ISO8859-1.src example file in /usr/lib/iconv/geniconvtbl/srcs/ to generate the properly named binary version of the conversion table.

```
$ cd /tmp
$ geniconvtbl -o UTF-8%ISO8859-1.bt
  /usr/lib/iconv/geniconvtbl/srcs/UTF-8_to_ISO8859-1.src
$
```

The UTF-8%ISO8859-1.bt file is created in /tmp, which is the current directory. To use this conversion binary table, copy it to /usr/lib/iconv/geniconvtbl/binarytables/.

The following example generates two code-conversion binary tables with output files test1.bt and test2.bt.

```
example% geniconvtbl test1 test2
```

The following example generates a code conversion binary table once the specified preprocessor has processed the input file.

```
example% geniconvtbl -p /opt/SUNWspro/bin/cc -W -E convertB2A
```

To use the binary table created in the first example above as the engine of the conversion from code ABC to code DEF, become superuser and then rename the output file and put it in the following directory.

```
example# mv convertA2B.bt
  /usr/lib/icnv/geniconvtbl/binarytables/ABC%DEF.bt
```

Environment Variables

See environ(5) for descriptions of the LANG and LC_CTYPE environment variables that affect the execution of geniconvtbl.

Exit Status

0	No errors occurred, and the output files were successfully created.
1	Command-line options are not correctly used or an unknown command-line option was specified.

2	Invalid input or output file was specified.
3	Conversion rules in input files are not correctly defined.
4	Conversion rule limit of input files has been reached.
5	No more system resource error.
6	Internal error.

Files

/usr/lib/iconv/geniconvtbl/binarytables/*.bt

Conversion binary tables.

/usr/lib/iconv/geniconvtbl/srcs/*

Conversion source files for user reference.

Attributes

See attributes(5) for descriptions of the following attributes.

Attribute Type	**Attribute Value**
Availability	SUNWcsu

See Also

cpp(1), iconv(1), iconv(3C), iconv_close(3C), iconv_open(3C), geniconvtbl(4), attributes(5), environ(5), iconv(5)
Solaris Internationalization Guide for Developers

genlayouttbl — Generate Layout Table for Complex Text Layout   New!

Synopsis

/bin/genlayouttbl [-o *outfile*] [*infile*]

Description

The genlayouttbl command is new in the Solaris 8 Operating Environment. You can specify a locale's layout definition in a flat text file; the genlayouttbl command then writes a binary layout table file that can be used in the complex text layout of the locale.

Options

-o *outfile*   Write output of a binary layout table to the specified *outfile*.

Operands

infile   A path name of an input file. If you specify no input file, genlayouttbl reads from the standard input stream.

Output and Symbolic Links

If you specify no *outfile*, genlayouttbl writes output to the standard output stream.
Before you use the system, you must move the generated dat output file to
/usr/lib/locale/locale/LO_LTYPE/layout.dat.

The locale should also have a symbolic link,
/usr/lib/locale/locale/LO_LTYPE/locale.layout.so.1, to the 32-bit Universal
Multiscript Layout Engine (UMLE),
/usr/lib/locale/common/LO_LTYPE/umle.layout.so.1.

For proper 64-bit platform operations, the locale should also have a symbolic link, as
for instance, in the 64-bit SPARC platform,
/usr/lib/locale/locale/LO_LTYPE/sparcv9/locale.layout.so.1, to the 64-bit
UMLE, /usr/lib/locale/common/LO_LTYPE/sparcv9/umle.layout.so.1.

The locale is the locale that you want to provide and to use the layout functionality
you defined.

Input File Format

A layout definition file to genlayouttbl contains three different sections of definitions.

- Layout attribute definition.
- Bidirectional data and character type data definition.
- Shaping data definition.

For appropriate complex text layout support, all three sections must be defined in the
layout definition file.

Lexical Conventions

The following lexical conventions are used in the layout definition.

NAME   A string of characters that consists of printable ASCII characters.
It includes DECIMAL and HEXADECIMAL also. For example, test,
a1_src, b32, 123.

HEXADECIMAL_BYTE

Two-digit hexadecimal number. The number starts with a
hexadecimal digit followed by another hexadecimal digit. For
example, e0, E1, a7, fe.

HEXADECIMAL

A hexadecimal number. The hexadecimal representation consists
of an escape character, 0 followed by the constant x or X, and one or
more hexadecimal digits. For example, 0x0, 0x1, 0x1a, 0xA, 0x1b3.

DECIMAL   A decimal number, represented by one or more decimal digits. For
example, 0, 123, 2165.

Each comment must start with #. The comment ends at the end of the line.
The following keywords are reserved.

- active_directional
- active_shape_editing
- AL, ALGORITHM_BASIC
- ALGORITHM_IMPLICIT
- AN
- BN
- check_mode
- context
- CONTEXT_LTR
- CONTEXT_RTL
- CS
- EN
- END
- ES
- ET
- FALSE
- FILE_CODE_REPRESENTATION
- implicit_algorithm
- keep
- L
- LAYOUT_ATTRIBUTES
- LAYOUT_BIDI_CHAR_TYPE_DATA
- LAYOUT_SHAPE_DATA
- LRE
- LRO
- MODE_EDIT
- MODE_STREAM
- NSM
- national_numerals
- numerals
- NUMERALS_CONTEXTUAL
- NUMERALS_NATIONAL
- NUMERALS_NOMINAL
- ON
- orientation
- ORIENTATION_CONTEXTUAL
- ORIENTATION_LTR
- ORIENTATION_RTL
- ORIENTATION_TTBLR
- ORIENTATION_TTBRL
- PDF

- PROCESS_CODE_REPRESENTATION
- PS
- R
- repeat*
- repeat+
- RLE
- RLO
- S
- shape_charset
- shape_charset_size
- shape_context_size
- swapping
- SWAPPING_NO
- swapping_pairs
- SWAPPING_YES
- TEXT_EXPLICIT
- TEXT_IMPLICIT
- TEXT_NOMINAL
- TEXT_SHAPED
- text_shaping
- TEXT_VISUAL
- TRUE
- type_of_text
- WS.

The following symbols are also reserved as tokens.

```
( ) [ ] , : ; ... = -> +
```

Layout Attribute Definition

The layout attribute definition section defines the layout attributes and their associated values.

The definition starts with a keyword, LAYOUT_ATTRIBUTES, and ends with END LAYOUT_ATTRIBUTES, as shown in the following example.

```
LAYOUT_ATTRIBUTES
# Layout attributes here.
.
:END LAYOUT_ATTRIBUTES
```

In the layout attributes section, you can define a total of eight layout attribute value trios, as shown below.

- orientation
- context
- type_of_text
- implicit_algorithm

- swapping
- numerals
- text_shaping
- shape_context_size

Additionally, you can define five layout attribute value pairs in this section.

- active_directional
- active_shape_editing
- shape_charset
- shape_charset_size
- check_mode

Each attribute value trio has an attribute name, an attribute value for the input buffer, and an attribute value for the output buffer, as shown in the following example.

```
# Orientation layout attribute value trio. The input and output
# attribute values are separated by a colon and the left one
# is the input attribute value.
orientation    ORIENTATION_LTR:ORIENTATION_LTR
```

Each attribute value pair has an attribute name and an associated attribute value, as shown in the following example.

```
# Shape charset attribute value pair.
shape_charset    ISO8859-6
```

The orientation value trio defines the global directional text orientation. The possible values are described below.

ORIENTATION_LTR

> Left-to-right horizontal rows that progress from top to bottom.

ORIENTATION_RTL

> Right-to-left horizontal rows that progress from top to bottom.

ORIENTATION_TTBRL

> Top-to-bottom vertical columns that progress from right to left.

ORIENTATION_TTBLR

> Top-to-bottom vertical columns that progress from left to right.

ORIENTATION_CONTEXTUAL

> The global orientation is set according to the direction of the first significant (strong) character. If the text contains no strong characters and the attribute is set to this value, the global orientation of the text is set according to the value of the attribute context. This value is meaningful only for bidirectional text. If you define no value or value trio, the default is ORIENTATION_LTR.

The context value trio is meaningful only if the attribute orientation is set to ORIENTATION_CONTEXTUAL. It defines what orientation is assumed when no strong character appears in the text. The possible values are described below.

CONTEXT_LTR

> In the absence of characters with strong directionality in the text, orientation is assumed to be left-to-right rows progressing from top to bottom.

CONTEXT_RTL

> In the absence of characters with strong directionality in the text, orientation is assumed to be right-to-left rows progressing from top to bottom.

If you specify no value or value trio, the default is CONTEXT_LTR.

The type_of_text value trio specifies the ordering of the directional text. The possible values are described below.

TEXT_VISUAL

> Provide code elements in visually ordered segments that can be rendered without any segment inversion.

TEXT_IMPLICIT

> Provide code elements in logically ordered segments. Logically ordered means that the order in which the characters are provided is the same as the order in which the characters would be pronounced when the presented text is read or the order in which characters would be entered from a keyboard.

TEXT_EXPLICIT

> Provide code elements in logically ordered segments with a set of embedded controls.

Some examples of such embedded controls from ISO/IEC 10646-1 are shown below.

```
LEFT-TO-RIGHT EMBEDDING (LRE)
RIGHT-TO-LEFT EMBEDDING (RLE)
RIGHT-TO-LEFT OVERRIDE (RLO)
LEFT-TO-RIGHT OVERRIDE (LRO)
POP DIRECTIONAL FORMAT (PDF)
```

If you specify no value or value trio, the default is TEXT_IMPLICIT.

The implicit_algorithm value trio specifies the type of bidirectional implicit algorithm used in reordering and shaping of directional or context-dependent text. The possible values are described below.

ALGORITHM_IMPLICIT

> Reorder directional code elements with an implementation-defined implicit algorithm. The default value is ALGORITHM_IMPLICIT.

ALGORITHM_BASIC

> Reorder directional code elements with a basic implicit algorithm defined in the Unicode standard.

Note — Even though you can specify two different values for the implicit_algorithm, because the Solaris implementation-defined implicit algorithm is based on the Unicode standard, the behavior is the same whether you choose ALGORITHM_IMPLICIT or ALGORITHM_BASIC for this attribute.

The swapping value trio specifies whether symmetric swapping is applied to the text. The possible values are shown below.

SWAPPING_YES

> The text conforms to symmetric swapping.

SWAPPING_NO

> The text does not conform to symmetric swapping. If no value or value trio is specified, the default is SWAPPING_NO.

The numerals value trio specifies the shaping of numerals. The possible values are shown below. If no value or value trio is specified, the default is NUMERALS_NOMINAL.

NUMERALS_NOMINAL

> Nominal shaping of numerals using the Arabic numbers of the portable character set (in Solaris, ASCII digits).

NUMERALS_NATIONAL

> National shaping of numerals based on the script of the locale. For instance, Thai digits in the Thai locale.

NUMERALS_CONTEXTUAL

> Contextual shaping of numerals depending on the context script of surrounding text, such as Hindi numbers in Arabic text and Arabic numbers otherwise.

The text_shaping values specify the shaping; that is, choosing (or composing) the correct shape of the input or output text. The possible values are shown below.

TEXT_SHAPED

> The text has presentation form shapes.

TEXT_NOMINAL

> The text is in basic form. If no value or value trio is specified, the default is TEXT_NOMINAL for input and TEXT_SHAPED for output.

The shape_context_size values specify the size of the context (surrounding code elements) that must be accounted for when performing active shape editing. If not defined, the default value 0 is used for the number of surrounding code elements at both front and rear.

```
# The shape_context_size for both front and rear surrounding code
# elements are all zero.
shape_context_size 0:0
```

The front and rear attribute values are separated by a colon, with the front value to the left of the colon.

The `active_directional` value pair specifies whether the current locale requires (bi-)directional processing. The possible values are shown below.

TRUE   Requires (bi-)directional processing.

FALSE   Does not require (bi-)directional processing.

The `active_shape_editing` value pair specifies whether the current locale requires context-dependent shaping for presentation. The possible values are shown below.

TRUE   Requires context-dependent shaping.

FALSE   Does not require context-dependent shaping.

The `shape_charset` value pair specifies the current locale's shape charset on which the complex text layout is based. You can specify two different kinds of shape charset values.

- A single-shape charset.
- Multiple-shape charsets.

You can define a single-shape charset with NAME as defined in the Lexical Convention section above. Multiple shape charsets, however, should follow the syntax shown below in extended BNF form.

```
multiple_shape_charset
    : charset_list
    ;

charset_list  : charset
    | charset_list ; charset
    ;

charset       : charset_name '=' charset_id
    ;

charset_name  : NAME
    ;

charset_id    : HEXADECIMAL_BYTE
    ;
```

The following example is a valid multiple-shape charsets value for the `shape_charset` attribute.

```
# Multiple-shape charsets.
shape_charset    tis620.2533=e4;iso8859-8=e5;iso8859-6=e6
```

You must specify the `shape_charset`.

The `shape_charset_size` value pair specifies the encoding size of the current shape_charset. The valid value is a positive integer from 1 to 4. If you define the multiple-shape charsets value for the `shape_charset` attribute, the `shape_charset_size` must be 4.

The `shape_charset_size` must be specified.

The `check_mode` value pair specifies the level of checking of the elements in the input buffer for shaping and reordering purposes. The possible values are shown below.

MODE_STREAM

> The string in the input buffer is expected to have valid combinations of characters or character elements.

MODE_EDIT   The shaping of input text may vary depending on locale-specific validation or assumption. When you specify no value or value pair, the default value is MODE_STREAM.

Bidirectional Data and Character Type Data Definition

This section defines the bidirectional and other character types that are used in the Unicode Bidirectional Algorithm and the shaping algorithm part of the UMLE.

The definition starts with a keyword LAYOUT_BIDI_CHAR_TYPE_DATA and ends with END LAYOUT_BIDI_CHAR_TYPE_DATA, as shown in the following example.

```
LAYOUT_BIDI_CHAR_TYPE_DATA
    # Layout bidi definitions here.
    .
    .
    .
END LAYOUT_BIDI_CHAR_TYPE_DATA
```

You should define the bidirectional data and character type data definition for the two different kinds of text shape forms—TEXT_SHAPED and TEXT_NOMINAL—depending on the `text_shaping` attribute value. You should also define the two different kinds of text representations—file-code representation and process-code representation (that is, wide-character representation)—as shown in the following example.

```
LAYOUT_BIDI_CHAR_TYPE_DATA

    FILE_CODE_REPRESENTATION

        TEXT_SHAPED

            # TEXT_SHAPED bidi and character type data

            # definition in file code representation here.

            .
            .

        END TEXT_SHAPED
        TEXT_NOMINAL
            # TEXT_NOMINAL bidi and character type data
            # definition in file code representation here.
            .
            .
        END TEXT_NOMINAL
END FILE_CODE_REPRESENTATION
PROCESS_CODE_REPRESENTATION
        TEXT_SHAPED
            # TEXT_SHAPED bidi and character type data
            # definition in process code representation here.
```

```
            .
            .
            .
        END TEXT_SHAPED
        TEXT_NOMINAL
            # TEXT_NOMINAL bidi and character type data
            # definition in process code representation here.
                .
                .
                .
        END TEXT_NOMINAL
    END PROCESS_CODE_REPRESENTATION
END LAYOUT_BIDI_CHAR_TYPE_DATA
```

Each bidi- and character-type data definition can have the following definitions.

- Bidirectional data type definition.
- `swapping_pairs` character type definition.
- `national_numerals` character type definition.
- You can define 19 different bidirectional data types, as described below.

Keyword	Category	Description
L	Strong	Left-to-right.
LRE	Strong	Left-to-right embedding.
LRO	Strong	Left-to-right override.
R	Strong	Right-to-left.
AL	Strong	Right-to-left.
RLE	Strong	Right-to-left embedding.
RLO	Strong	Right-to-left override.
PDF	Weak	Pop directional format.
EN	Weak	European number.
ES	Weak	European number separator.
ET	Weak	European number terminator.
AN	Weak	Arabic number.
CS	Weak	Common number separator.
PS	Separator	Paragraph separator.
S	Separator	Segment separator.
WS	Neutral	White space.
ON	Neutral	Other neutrals.
NSM	Weak	Nonspacing mark.
BN	Weak	Boundary neutral.

If not defined in this section, the characters belong to the other neutrals type, ON. Each keyword list is accompanied by one or more HEXADECIMAL ranges of characters that belong to the bidirectional character type. The syntax is shown below.

```
bidi_char_type  : bidi_keyword : range_list\
    ;
bidi_keyword    : L
    | LRE
    | LRO
    | R
    | AL
    | RLE
    | RLO
    | PDF
    | EN
    | ES
    | ET
    | AN
    | CS
    | PS
    | S
    | WS
    | ON
    | NSM
    | BN
    ;

range_list    : range
    | range_list , range
    ;

range    : HEXADECIMAL
    | HEXADECIMAL '...' HEXADECIMAL
    ;
```

For example,

```
# Bidi character type definitions.
L:  0x26, 0x41...0x5a, 0xc380...0xc396, 0xe285a0...0xe28682
WS: 0x20, 0xc2a0, 0xe28080...0xe28086
```

swapping_pairs specifies the list of swappable characters if you specify SWAPPING_YES as a value at the swapping value trio. The syntax of swapping_pairs is shown below.

```
swapping_pair_list  : swapping_keyword : swap_pair_list
    ;
swapping_keyword  : swapping_pairs
    ;
swap_pair_list  : swap_pair
    | swap_pair_list , swap_pair
    ;
```

```
swap_pair      : ( HEXADECIMAL , HEXADECIMAL )
```

For example,

```
# Swapping pair definitions.
swapping_pairs:   (0x28, 0x29), (0x7b, 0x7d)
```

national_numerals specifies the list of national digits that can be converted as the numerals value trio specifies. The syntax of national_numerals is shown below.

```
numerals_list    : numerals_keyword :
      numerals_list ; contextual_range_list
      ;

numerals_keyword  : national_numerals
      ;

numerals_list    : [ zero , one , two , three , four , five , six , seven
   , eight , nine )

zero       : HEXADECIMAL
      ;

one        : HEXADECIMAL
      ;
two        : HEXADECIMAL
      ;

three      : HEXADECIMAL
      ;

four       : HEXADECIMAL
      ;

five       : HEXADECIMAL
      ;

six        : HEXADECIMAL
      ;

seven      : HEXADECIMAL
      ;

eight      : HEXADECIMAL
      ;

nine       : HEXADECIMAL
      ;
contextual_range_list
      : contextual_range
      | contextual_range_list ,
      contextual_range
      ;
```

```
contextual_range  : HEXADECIMAL
        | HEXADECIMAL '...' HEXADECIMAL
        .
```

For example,

```
# National numerals definition. The national number that
# replaces Arabic number 0 to 9 is 0, 0x41, 0x42, and so on.
# The contextual surrounding characters are 0x20 to 0x40 and
# 0x50 to 0x7f.
national_numerals.
(0x0, 0x41, 0x42, 0x43, 0x44, 0x45, 0x46, 0x47, 0x48, 0x49)
; 0x20...0x40, 0x50...0x7f
```

Unless NUMERALS_CONTEXTUAL is the value of the numerals attribute, the contextual range list definition is meaningless.

Shaping Data Definition

The shaping data definition section defines the context-dependent shaping rules that are used in the shaping algorithm of the UMLE.

The definition starts with a keyword, LAYOUT_SHAPE_DATA, and ends with END LAYOUT_SHAPE_DATA, as shown in the following example.

```
LAYOUT_SHAPE_DATA
# Layout shaping data definitions here.
    .
    .
END LAYOUT_SHAPE_DATA
```

The shaping data definition should be defined for the two different kinds of text shape forms, TEXT_SHAPED and TEXT_NOMINAL, depending on the text-shaping attribute value and also for the two different kinds of text representations, file-code representation and process-code representation (that is, wide-character representation).

```
LAYOUT_SHAPE_DATA
    FILE_CODE_REPRESENTATION
        TEXT_SHAPED

                # TEXT_SHAPED shaping data definition in file code
                # representation here.
                .
                .

        END TEXT_SHAPED

        TEXT_NOMINAL

                # TEXT_NOMINAL shaping data definition in file code
                # representation here.
                .
                .

END TEXT_NOMINAL
```

```
END FILE_CODE_REPRESENTATION
    PROCESS_CODE_REPRESENTATION
            TEXT_SHAPED

                # TEXT_SHAPED shaping data definition in process code
                # representation here.
                .
                .

            END TEXT_SHAPED
            TEXT_NOMINAL

                # TEXT_NOMINAL shaping data definition in process
                # code representation here.
                .
                .

            END TEXT_NOMINAL
END PROCESS_CODE_REPRESENTATION
END LAYOUT_SHAPE_DATA
```

Each shaping data definition consists of one or more of the shaping sequence definitions. Each shaping sequence definition is a representation of a series of state transitions triggered by an input character and the current state at each transition.

The syntax of the shaping sequence definition is shown below.

```
shaping_sequence  : initial_state + input ->
next_state_list
     ;

initial_state   : ()
     ;

input     : HEXADECIMAL
     ;

next_state_list   : next_state
     | next_state_list + input ->
     next_state
     | ( next_state_list + input )
     repeat+
     | ( next_state_list + input )
     repeat*
     ;

next_state    : ( out_buffer , in2out , out2in , property )
     ;

out_buffer    : [ out_char_list ]
     ;

out_char_list   : HEXADECIMAL
     | ( HEXADECIMAL ) repeat+
     | out_char_list ; HEXADECIMAL
```

```
           ;

in2out      : '[' i2o_list ]
           ;

i2o_list    : DECIMAL
           | ( DECIMAL ) repeat+
           | i2o_list ; DECIMAL
           ;

out2in      : [ o2i_list ]
           ;

o2i_list    : DECIMAL
           | ( DECIMAL ) repeat+
           | o2i_list ; DECIMAL
           ;

property    : [ prop_list ]
           ;

prop_list    : HEXADECIMAL
           | ( HEXADECIMAL ) repeat+
           | prop_list ; HEXADECIMAL
           ;
```

For example, you can define the following shaping sequences.

```
# A simple shaping sequence.
() + 0x21 ->
  ( [0x0021], [0], [0;0], [0x80] ) + 0x22 ->
  ( [0x0021;0x0022], [0;1], [0;0;1;1], [0x80;0x80] ) +
  0xc2a0 ->
  ( [0x0021;0x0022;0xe030], [0;1;2], [0;0;1;1;2;2],
  [0x80;0x80;0x80] )

# A repeating shaping sequence.
  () + 0x21 ->
    (
      ( [0x0021], [0], [0;0], [0x80] ) + 0x22 ->
      ( [0x0021;0x0022], [0;1], [0;0;1;1], [0x80;0x80] ) +
      0xc2a2
) repeat+
```

The first example shows a shaping sequence where, when 0x21, 0x22, and 0xc2a0 are the input buffer contents, the sequence is converted into an output buffer containing 0x0021, 0x0022, and 0xe030; an input to the output buffer containing 0, 1, and 2; an output to the input buffer containing 0, 0, 1, 1, 2, and 2; and a property buffer containing 0x80, 0x80, and 0x80.

The second example shows a repeating shaping sequence where, if the first input code element is 0x21, the second and third input code elements are 0x22 and 0xc2a2.

Exit Status

0	No errors occurred, and the output file was successfully created.
1	Command-line options are not correctly used, or unknown command-line option specified.
2	Invalid input or output file specified.
3	The layout definitions not correctly defined.
4	No more system resource error.
6	Internal error.

Files

`/usr/lib/locale/common/LO_LTYPE/umle.layout.so.1`

The Universal Multiscript Layout Engine for 32-bit platforms.

`/usr/lib/locale/common/LO_LTYPE/sparcv9/umle.layout.so.1`

The Universal Multiscript Layout Engine for the 64-bit SPARC platform.

`/usr/lib/locale/common/LO_LTYPE/ia64/umle.layout.so.1`

The Universal Multiscript Layout Engine for the 64-bit Intel platform.

`/usr/lib/locale/locale/LO_LTYPE/layout.dat`

The binary layout table file for the locale.

Attributes

See `attributes`(5) for descriptions of the following attributes.

Attribute Type	Attribute Value
Availability	SUNWglt

See Also

`m_create_layout`(3LAYOUT), `m_destroy_layout`(3LAYOUT),
`m_getvalues_layout`(3LAYOUT), `m_setvalues_layout`(3LAYOUT),
`m_transform_layout`(3LAYOUT), `m_wtransform_layout`(3LAYOUT),
`attributes`(5), `environ`(5)

  International Language Environments Guide
  Unicode Technical Report #9: The Bidirectional Algorithm from
`http://www.unicode.org/unicode/reports/`

genmsg — Generate a Message Source File by Extracting Messages from Source Files

Synopsis

```
/usr/bin/genmsg [-abdfnrtx] [-c message-tag] [-g project-file]
    [-l project-file] [-m prefix] [-M suffix] [-o message-file]
    [-p preprocessor] [-s set-tags] file...
```

Description

genmsg extracts message strings with calls to catgets(3C) from source files and writes them in a format suitable for input to gencat(1).

Invocation

genmsg reads one or more input files and, by default, generates a message source file whose name is composed of the first input file name with a .msg suffix. If you specify the -o option, genmsg uses the option argument for its output file.

Command	Output File
genmsg prog.c	prog.c.msg
gensmg main.c util.c tool.c	main.c.msg
genmsg -o prog.msg mail.c util.c	prog.msg

genmsg also enables you to invoke a preprocessor to solve the dependencies of macros and to define statements for the catgets(3C) calls.

Message Autonumbering

genmsg replaces message numbers with the calculated numbers based on the project file if the message numbers are -1. It generates copies of the input files with the new message numbers and a copy of the project file with the new maximum message numbers.

A project file is a database that stores a list of set numbers with their maximum message numbers. Each line in a project file is composed of a set number and its maximum message number:

Set_number   Maximum_message_number

In a project file, a line beginning with a number sign (#) or an ASCII space is considered as a comment and ignored.

genmsg also has the reverse operation to replace all message numbers with -1.

Comment Extraction

genmsg enables you to comment about messages and set numbers to inform the translator how to translate the messages. It extracts the comment, which is surrounded with the comment indicators and has the specified tag inside the comment, from the input file, and writes it with a dollar ($) prefix in the output file. genmsg supports the C and C++ comment indicators, /*, */, and //.

Testing

genmsg generates two kinds of messages for testing:

- Prefixed messages enable you to check that your program is retrieving the messages from the message catalog.
- Long messages enable you to check the appearance of your window program's initial size and position.

Notes

genmsg does not handle pointers or variables in the catgets(3C) call. For example:

```
const int set_num = 1;
extern int msg_num(const char *);
const char *msg = "Hello";

catgets(catd, set_num, msg_num(msg), msg);
```

When the message autonumbering is turned on with a preprocessor, if there are multiple –1's in the catgets(3C) line, genmsg replaces all of the –1's in the line with a calculated number. For example, given the input:

```
#define MSG(id, msg) catgets(catd, 1, (id), (msg))

if (ret == -1) printf("%s0, MSG(-1, "Failed"));
```

the command

```
genmsg -l proj -p "cc -E"
```

produces

```
#define MSG(id, msg) catgets(catd, 1, (id), (msg))

if (ret == 1) printf("%s0, MSG(1, "Failed"));
```

The workaround is to split the output into two lines as follows:

```
if (ret == -1)
  printf("%s0, MSG(-1, "Failed"));
```

Options

-a   Append the output into the message file *message-file* that is specified by the -o option. If two different messages that have the same set and message number are found, keep the message in the specified message file and discard the other message in the input file.

-b   Place the extracted comment after the corresponding message in the output file. This option changes the placement behavior of the -s or -c option.

-c *message-tag*

         Extract message comments having *message-tag* inside them from the input files, and write them with a $ prefix as a comment in the output file.

-d   Include an original text of a message as a comment to be preserved
           along with its translations. With this option, the translator can see the
           original messages even after they are replaced with their translations.

-f   Overwrite the input files and the project file when used with the -l or -r
           option. With the -r option, overwrite only the input files.

-g *project-file*

           Generate *project-file* that has a list of set numbers and their
           maximum message numbers in the input files.

-l *project-file*

           Replace message numbers with the calculated numbers based on
           project-file if the message numbers are -1 in the input files, then
           generate copies of the input files with the new message numbers and a
           copy of *project-file* with the new maximum message numbers. If
           project-file is not found, use the maximum message number in the
           input file as a base number and generate *project-file*.

-m *prefix*   Fill in the message with *prefix*. This option is useful for testing.

-M *suffix*   Fill in the message with *suffix*. This option is useful for testing.

-n   Add comment lines to the output file indicating the file name and line
           number in the input files where each extracted string is encountered.

-o *message-file*

           Write the output to *message-file*.

-p *processor*

           Invoke the preprocessor to preprocess macros and define statements for
           the catgets(3C) calls. genmsg first invokes the option argument as a
           preprocesser and then starts the normal process against the output
           from the preprocessor. genmsg initiates this process for all the input
           files.

-r   Replace message numbers with -1. This operation is the reverse of the
           -l option.

-s *set-tag*   Extract set number comments having *set-tag* inside them from the
           input files and write them with a $ prefix as a comment in the output
           file. If you specify multiple comments for one set number, extract the
           first one and discard the rest of them.

-t   Generate a message that is three times as long as the original message.
           This option is useful for testing.

-x   Suppress warning messages about message, set number range checks,
           and conflicts.

Operands

file   An input source file.

Examples

Suppose that you have the following source and project files.

```
castle% cat test.c
printf(catgets(catfd, 1, -1, "line too long0));
printf(catgets(catfd, 2, -1, "invalid code0));
castle% cat proj
1   10
2   20
```

The command

```
castle% genmsg -l proj test.c
```

assigns the calculated message numbers based on `proj` and generates the following files.

```
test.c.msg     message file
proj.new       updated project file
test.c.new     new source file
castle% cat test.c.msg
$quote "

$set    1
11       "line too long0

$set    2
21       "invalid code0
castle% cat proj.new
1   11
2   21
castle% cat test.c.new
printf(catgets(catfd, 1, 11, "line too long0));
printf(catgets(catfd, 2, 21, "invalid code0));
```

For a `test.c` file containing the following information

```
castle% cat test.c
/* SET: tar messages */
/* MSG: don't translate "tar". */
catgets(catfd, 1, 1, "tar: tape write error");
// MSG: don't translate "tar" and "-I".
catgets(catfd, 1, 2, "tar: missing argument for -I flag");
```

the following command extracts the comments and writes them in the `test.c.msg` output file.

```
castle% genmsg -s SET -c MSG test.c
castle% cat test.c.msg
$ /* SET: tar messages */
$set    1
$ /* MSG: don't translate "tar". */
1        "tar: tape write error"
$ // MSG: don't translate "tar" and "-I".
2        "tar: missing argument for -I flag"
```

The following command generates messages for testing.

```
castle% genmsg -m PRE: -M :FIX test.c
castle% cat test.c.msg
1        "PRE:OK:FIX"
2        "PRE:Cancel:FIX"
```

With the following input,

```
castle% cat example.c
#include <nl_types.h>

#define MSG1     "message1"
#define MSG2     "message2"
#define MSG3     "message3"

#define MSG(n)   catgets(catd, 1, n, MSG ## n)

void
main(int argc, char **argv)
{
         nl_catd catd = catopen(argv[0], NL_CAT_LOCALE);

         (void) printf("%s0, MSG(1));
         (void) printf("%s0, MSG(2));
         (void) printf("%s0, MSG(3));

         (void) catclose(catd);
}
```

the following command parses the MSG macros and writes the extracted messages in example.msg.

```
castle% genmsg -p "cc -E" -o example.msg example.c
```

Suppose that you have the following header, source, and project files:

```
castle% ../inc/msg.h
#define WARN_SET                  1
#define ERR_SET                   2

#define WARN_MSG(id, msg) catgets(catd, WARN_SET, (id), (msg))

#define ERR_MSG(id, msg) catgets(catd, ERR_SET, (id), (msg))
castle% example.c
#include "msg.h"
printf("%s0, WARN_MSG(-1, "Warning error"));
printf("%s0, ERR_MSG(-1, "Fatal error"));
example % proj
1        10
2        10
```

Then, the following command assigns each of the -1 message numbers a calculated number based on proj and overwrites the results to example.c and proj. This command also writes the extracted messages in example.msg.

```
castle% genmsg -f -p "cc -E -I../inc" -l proj -o example.msg example.c
```

Environment Variables

See environ(5) for descriptions of the following environment variables that affect the execution of genmsg: LC_MESSAGES and NLSPATH.

Exit Status

0	Successful completion.
>0	An error occurred.

Attributes

See attributes(5) for descriptions of the following attributes:

Attribute Type	Attribute Value
Availability	SUNWloc

See Also

gencat(1), catgets(3C), catopen(3C), attributes(5), environ(5)

get, sccs-get — Retrieve a Version of an SCCS File

Synopsis

```
/usr/ccs/bin/get [-begkmnpst] [-l[p]] [-asequence] [-c date-time |
    -cdate-time] [-Gg-file] [-i sid-list | -isid-list] [-r[sid]]
    [-x sid-list| -xsid-list] s.filename...
/usr/xpg4/bin/get [-begkmnpst] [-l[p]] [-asequence] [-c date-time |
    -cdate-time] [-Gg-file] [-i sid-list | -isid-list] [-r sid | -rsid]
    [-x sid-list | -xsid-list] s.filename...
```

Description

See sccs-get(1).

getconf — Get Configuration Values

Synopsis

```
/usr/bin/getconf [-v specification] system-var
/usr/bin/getconf [-v specification] path-var pathname
/usr/bin/getconf -a
```

Description

In the first synopsis form, the getconf command writes the value of the variable specified by *system-var* to the standard output. If you specify the -v option, getconf writes the value in accordance with *specification*.

In the second synopsis form, getconf writes the value of the variable specified by *path-var* for the path specified by *pathname* to the standard output. If you specify the -v option, getconf writes the value in accordance with *specification*.

In the third synopsis form, the getconf command writes the names of the current system configuration variables to the standard output.

The value of each configuration variable is determined as if it were obtained by calling the function from which it is defined. The value reflects conditions in the current operating environment.

Options

-a   Write the names of the current system configuration variables to the standard output.

-v *specification*

          Give the specification that governs the selection of values for configuration variables.

Operands

path-var   A name of a configuration variable whose value is available from the pathconf(2) function. All of the following values are supported:
LINK_MAX
NAME_MAX
POSIX_CHOWN_RESTRICTED
MAX_CANON
PATH_MAX
POSIX_NO_TRUNC
MAX_INPUT
PIPE_BUF POSIX_VDISABLE

pathname   A path name for which the variable specified by *path-var* is to be determined.

system-var   A name of a configuration variable whose value is available from confstr(3C) or sysconf(3C). All of the values in the following table are supported.

ARG_MAX	POSIX2_C_BIND
BC_BASE_MAX	POSIX2_C_DEV
BC_DIM_MAX	POSIX2_C_VERSION
BC_SCALE_MAX	POSIX2_CHAR_TERM
BC_STRING_MAX	POSIX2_COLL_WEIGHTS_MAX
CHAR_BIT	POSIX2_EXPR_NEST_MAX
CHAR_MAX	POSIX2_FORT_DEV
CHAR_MIN	POSIX2_FORT_RUN
CHARCLASS_NAME_MAX	POSIX2_LINE_MAX
CHILD_MAX	POSIX2_LOCALEDEF
CLK_TCK	POSIX2_RE_DUP_MAX
COLL_WEIGHTS_MAX	POSIX2_SW_DEV
CS_PATH	POSIX2_UPE
EXPR_NEST_MAX	POSIX2_VERSION
INT_MAX	RE_DUP_MAX
INT_MIN	SCHAR_MAX
LFS64_CFLAGS	SCHAR_MIN
LFS64_LDFLAGS	SHRT_MAX
LFS64_LIBS	SHRT_MIN
LFS64_LINTFLAGS	SSIZE_MAX
LFS_CFLAGS	STREAM_MAX
LFS_LDFLAGS	TMP_MAX
LFS_LIBS	TZNAME_MAX
LFS_LINTFLAGS	UCHAR_MAX
LINE_MAX	UINT_MAX
LONG_BIT	ULONG_MAX
LONG_MAX	USHRT_MAX
LONG_MIN	WORD_BIT
MB_LEN_MAX	XBS5_ILP32_OFF32
NGROUPS_MAX	XBS5_ILP32_OFF32_CFLAGS
NL_ARGMAX	XBS5_ILP32_OFF32_LDFLAGS
NL_LANGMAX	XBS5_ILP32_OFF32_LIBS
NL_MSGMAX	XBS5_ILP32_OFF32_LINTFLAGS
NL_NMAX	XBS5_ILP32_OFFBIG
NL_SETMAX	XBS5_ILP32_OFFBIG_CFLAGS

NL_TEXTMAX	XBS5_ILP32_OFFBIG_LDFLAGS
NZERO	XBS5_ILP32_OFFBIG_LIBS
OPEN_MAX	XBS5_ILP32_OFFBIG_LINTFLAGS
_POSIX_ARG_MAX	XBS5_LP64_OFF64
_POSIX_CHILD_MAX	XBS5_LP64_OFF64_CFLAGS
_POSIX_JOB_CONTROL	XBS5_LP64_OFF64_LDFLAGS
_POSIX_LINK_MAX	XBS5_LP64_OFF64_LIBS
_POSIX_MAX_CANON	XBS5_LP64_OFF64_LINTFLAGS
_POSIX_MAX_INPUT	XBS5_LPBIG_OFFBIG
_POSIX_NAME_MAX	XBS5_LPBIG_OFFBIG_CFLAGS
_POSIX_NGROUPS_MAX	XBS5_LPBIG_OFFBIG_LDFLAGS
_POSIX_OPEN_MAX	XBS5_LPBIG_OFFBIG_LIBS
_POSIX_PATH_MAX	XBS5_LPBIG_OFFBIG_LINTFLAGS
_POSIX_PIPE_BUF	_XOPEN_CRYPT
_POSIX_SAVED_IDS	_XOPEN_ENH_I18N
_POSIX_SSIZE_MAX	_XOPEN_LEGACY
_POSIX_STREAM_MAX	_XOPEN_SHM
_POSIX_TZNAME_MAX	_XOPEN_VERSION
_POSIX_VERSION	_XOPEN_XCU_VERSION
POSIX2_BC_BASE_MAX	_XOPEN_XPG2
POSIX2_BC_DIM_MAX	_XOPEN_XPG3
POSIX2_BC_SCALE_MAX	_XOPEN_XPG4
POSIX2_BC_STRING_MAX	

The symbol PATH also is recognized, yielding the same value as the confstr() name value CS_PATH.

Usage

See largefile(5) for the description of the behavior of getconf when encountering files greater than or equal to 2 Gbytes (2**31 bytes).

Examples

The following example shows the first few lines of the output generated by the getconf -a command.

```
castle% getconf -a
AIO_LISTIO_MAX:             256
AIO_MAX:                    undefined
AIO_PRIO_DELTA_MAX:         0
ARG_MAX:                    1048320
ATEXIT_MAX:                 32
BC_BASE_MAX:                99
BC_DIM_MAX:                 2048
```

```
BC_SCALE_MAX:                   99
BC_STRING_MAX:                  1000
CHARCLASS_NAME_MAX:             14
CHAR_BIT:                       8
CHAR_MAX:                       127
CHAR_MIN:                       -128
...
castle%
```

The following example returns the value of NGROUPS_MAX.

```
castle% getconf NGROUPS_MAX
16
castle%
```

The following example returns the value of NAME_MAX for a specific directory.

```
castle% getconf NAME_MAX /usr
255
castle%
```

The following example shows how to deal more carefully with results that might be unspecified.

```
if value=$(getconf PATH_MAX /usr); then
  if ["$value" = "undefined"]; then
    echo PATH_MAX in /usr is infinite.
  else
    echo PATH_MAX in /usr is $value.
  fi
else
  echo Error in getconf.
fi
```

Note — sysconf(_SC_POSIX_C_BIND); and system("getconf POSIX2_C_BIND"); in a C program could give different answers. The sysconf call supplies a value that corresponds to the conditions when the program was either compiled or executed, depending on the implementation; the system call to getconf always supplies a value corresponding to conditions when the program is executed.

Environment Variables

See environ(5) for descriptions of the following environment variables that affect the execution of getconf: LC_CTYPE, LC_MESSAGES, and NLSPATH.

Exit Status

0	The specified variable is valid and information about its current state was written successfully.
>0	An error occurred.

Attributes

See attributes(5) for descriptions of the following attributes:

Attribute Type	Attribute Value
Availability	SUNWcsu

See Also

pathconf(2), confstr(3C), sysconf(3C), attributes(5), environ(5), largefile(5)

getfacl — Display Discretionary File Information

Synopsis

/usr/bin/getfacl [-ad] *file*...

Description

Access Control Lists (ACLs) are extensions to standard UNIX file permissions. The ACL information is stored and associated with each file individually. You can determine if a file has an ACL with the getfacl command. For each argument that is a regular file, special file, or named pipe, getfacl displays the owner, the group, and the ACL. For each directory argument, getfacl displays the owner, the group, and the ACL and/or the default ACL. Only directories contain default ACLs.

You can execute getfacl on a file system that does not support ACLs. It reports the ACL based on the base permission bits.

If you specify no options, getfacl displays the file name, the owner, the group, and both the ACL and the default ACL if it exists.

Options

-a	Display the file name, the owner, the group, and the ACL of the file.
-d	Display the file name, the owner, the group, and the default ACL of the file if it exists.

Operands

file	The path name of a regular file, special file, or named pipe.

Output

The format for ACL output is as follows.

```
# file: filename
# owner: uid
# group: gid
user::perm
user:uid:perm
group::perm
group:gid:perm
```

```
mask:perm
other:perm
default:user::perm
default:user:uid:perm
default:group::perm
default:group:gid:perm
default:mask:perm
default:other:perm
```

When you specify multiple files on the command line, a blank line separates the ACLs for each file.

The ACL entries are displayed in the order in which they are evaluated when an access check is performed. The default ACL entries that may exist on a directory have no effect on access checks.

The first three lines display the file name, the file owner, and the file-owning group. Note that when you specify only the –d option and the file has no default ACL, only these three lines are displayed.

The user entry without a user ID indicates the permissions that are granted to the owner of the file. One or more additional user entries indicate the permissions that are granted to the specified users.

The group entry without a group ID indicates the permissions that are granted to the owning group of the file. One or more additional group entries indicate the permissions that are granted to the specified groups.

The mask entry indicates the file group mask permissions. These are the maximum permissions allowed to any user entries, except the file owner, and to any group entries, including the owning group. These permissions restrict the permissions specified in other entries.

The other entry indicates the permissions that are granted to others.

The default entries may exist only for directories and indicate the default entries that are added to a file created within the directory.

The uid is a login name or a user ID if there is no entry for the uid in the system password file, /etc/passwd. The gid is a group name or a group ID if there is no entry for the gid in the system group file, /etc/group. The perm is a three-character string composed of the letters representing the separate discretionary access rights: r (read), w (write), x (execute/search), or the placeholder character –. The perm is displayed in the following order: rwx. If permission is not granted by an ACL entry, the placeholder character is used.

The file-owner permission bits represent the access of the owning user ACL entry. The file-group class permission bits represent the most access that any additional user entries, additional group entries, or the owning group entry may grant. The file other-class permission bits represent the access that the other ACL entry has. If a user invokes the chmod(1) command and changes the file group class permission bits, the access granted by additional ACL entries may be restricted.

To indicate that the file group-class permission bits restrict an ACL entry, getfacl displays an additional Tab character, a pound sign (#), and the actual permissions granted, following the entry.

Note — The output from getfacl is in the correct format for input to the setfacl command. If the output from getfacl is redirected to a file, the file can be used as input to setfacl. In this way, you can easily assign one file's ACL to another file.

Examples

Given file foo, with an ACL six entries long, the command

```
castle% getfacl foo
```

prints

```
# file: foo
# owner: shea
# group: staff
user::rwx
user:spy:---
user:mookie:r--
group::r--
mask::rw-
other::---
```

Continuing with the above example, after issuing the **chmod 700 foo** command:

```
castle% getfacl foo
```

prints

```
# file: foo
# owner: shea
# group: staff
user::rwx
user:spy:---
user:mookie:r--      #effective:---
group::r--           #effective:---
mask::---
other::---
```

Given directory doo, with an ACL containing default entries, the command

```
castle% getfacl -d doo
```

prints

```
# file: doo
# owner: shea
# group: staff
default:user::rwx
default:user:spy:---
default:user:mookie:r--
default:group::r--
default:mask::---
default:other::---
```

Files

/etc/passwd   System password file.

/etc/group   Group file.

Attributes

See `attributes`(5) for descriptions of the following attributes:

Attribute Type	Attribute Value
Availability	SUNWcsu

See Also

`chmod(1)`, `ls(1)`, `setfacl(1)`, `acl(2)`, `aclsort(3)`, `group(4)`, `passwd(4)`, `attributes(5)`

getopt — Parse Command Options

Synopsis

`set -- `getopt optstring $*``

Description

The `/usr/bin/getopt` command is superseded by the `getopts` command.

> **Note —** `getopt` is not supported in the next major release. This release provides a `getoptcvt` conversion tool. For more information about `getopts` and `getoptcvt`, see `getopts`(1).

New!

> Reset *optind* to 1 when rescanning the options.
>
> `getopt` does not support the part of Rule 8 of the command syntax standard (see `intro(1)`) that permits groups of option-arguments following an option to be separated by white space and quoted. For example,
>
> `cmd` -a -b -o "xx z yy" *filename*
>
> is not handled correctly. To correct this deficiency, use the `getopts` command in place of `getopt`.
>
> If an option that takes an option-argument is followed by a value that is the same as one of the options listed in *optstring*, as shown in "Examples" on page 453, but with the following command line:
>
> `cmd` -l -a *filename*
>
> `getopt` always treats it as an option-argument to -o; it never recognizes -a as an option. For this case, the `for` loop in the example shifts past the *filename* argument.

Use `getopt` to break up options in command lines for easy parsing by shell procedures and to check for legal options; you use `getopts` in shell script loops to ensure standard syntax for command-line options. *optstring* is a string of recognized option letters; see `getopt(3C)`. If you follow a letter with a colon, the option is expected to have an argument that may or may not be separated from it by white space. Use the special option -- to delimit the end of the options. If you use it explicitly, getopt recognizes it; otherwise, getopt generates it; in either case, getopt puts it at the end of the options. The positional parameters ($1 $2...) of the shell are reset so that each option is preceded by a - and is in its own positional parameter; each option argument is also parsed into its own positional parameter.

Reset optind to 1 when rescanning the options.

getopt does not support the part of Rule 8 of the command syntax standard (see intro(1)) that permits groups of option-arguments following an option to be separated by white space and quoted. For example,

cmd - a - b - o "xxx z yy" *filename*

is not handled correctly. To correct this deficiency, use the getopts command in place of getopt.

Examples

The following code fragment shows how you might process the arguments for a command that can take the options a or b, as well as the option o, which requires an argument.

```
set -- `getopt abo: $*`
if [$? != 0]
then
   echo $USAGE
   exit 2
fi
for i in $*
do
   case $i in
   -a | -b)   FLAG=$i; shift;;
   -o)        OARG=$2; shift 2;;
   --)        shift; break;;
   esac
done
```

This code accepts any of the following as equivalent.

cmd - ao*arg filename1 filename2*
cmd - a - o *arg filename1 filename2*
cmd - o*arg* - a *filename1 filename2*
cmd - a - o*arg* - - *filename1 filename2*

Note — If an option that takes an option-argument is followed by a value that is the same as one of the options listed in *optstring*,

cmd - o - a *filename*

getopt always treats - a as an option-argument to - o; it never recognizes - a as an option. For this case, the for loop in the example shifts past the *filename* argument.

Attributes

See attributes(5) for descriptions of the following attributes:

Attribute Type	Attribute Value
Availability	SUNWcsu
CSI	Enabled

See Also

intro(1), getopts(1), getoptcv(1), sh(1), shell_builtins(1), getopt(3C), attributes(5)

Diagnostics

getopt prints an error message on the standard error when it encounters an option letter not included in *optstring*.

---

getoptcvt — Convert to getopts to Parse Command Options

Synopsis

```
/usr/lib/getoptcvt [-b] filename
/usr/lib/getoptcvt
```

Description

Use /usr/lib/getoptcvt to convert getopt output to use getopts instead. getoptcvt reads the shell script in *filename*, converts it to use getopts instead of getopt, and writes the results on the standard output.

getopts is a built-in Bourne shell command that parses positional parameters and checks for valid options. See sh(1). getopts supports all applicable rules of the command syntax standard (see Rules 3–10, intro(1)). You should use getopts instead of the getopt command. The syntax for the shell's built-in getopts command is

getopts *optstring name* [*argument...*]

optstring must contain the option letters recognized by the command using getopts; if a letter is followed by a colon, the option is expected to have an argument or group of arguments that must be separated from it by white space.

Each time you invoke it, getopts puts the next option in the shell variable name and the index of the next argument to be processed in the shell variable OPTIND. Whenever you invoke the shell or a shell script, OPTIND is initialized to 1.

When an option requires an option-argument, getopts puts it in the shell variable OPTARG.

If getops encounters an illegal option, ? is placed in *name.*

When the end-of-options is encountered, getopts exits with a non-zero exit status. You can use the special option -- to delimit the end of the options.

By default, getopts parses the positional parameters. If you specify extra arguments (*argument...*) on the getopts command line, getopts parses them instead.

So that all new commands adhere to the command syntax standard described in intro(1), they should use getopts or getopt to parse positional parameters and should check for options that are valid for that command.

Although relaxations of the following command syntax rule (see intro(1)) are permitted under the current implementation, you should not use them because they may not be supported in future releases of the system.

Options

-b   Make the converted script portable to earlier releases of the Solaris Operating Environment. /usr/lib/getoptcvt modifies the shell script in *filename* so that when the resulting shell script is executed, it determines at runtime whether to invoke getopts or getopt.

Examples

The following fragment of a shell program shows how you might process the arguments for a command that can take the options a or b, as well as the option o, which requires an option-argument.

```
while getopts abo: c
  do
    case $c in
    a | b)      FLAG=$c;;
    o)          OARG=$OPTARG;;
    \?)         echo $USAGE
                exit 2;;
    esac
  done
  shift `expr $OPTIND - 1`
```

This code accepts any of the following as equivalent.

```
cmd - a - b - o "xxx z yy" filename
cmd - a - b - o "xxx z yy" -- filename
cmd - ab - o xxx,z,yy filename
cmd - ab - o "xxx z yy" filename
cmd - o xxx,z,yy - b - a filename
```

Note that a and b are options, and the option o requires an option-argument. The following example violates Rule 5: options with option-arguments must not be grouped with other options.

```
castle% cmd - aboxxx filename
```

The following example violates Rule 6: there must be white space after an option that takes an option-argument.

```
castle% cmd - ab oxxx filename
```

Changing the value of the shell variable OPTIND or parsing different sets of arguments can lead to unexpected results.

Attributes

See attributes(5) for descriptions of the following attributes:

Attribute Type	Attribute Value
Availability	SUNWcsu
CSI	Enabled

See Also

intro(1), getopts(1), sh(1), shell_builtins(1), getopt(3C), attributes(5)

Diagnostics

getopts prints an error message on the standard error when it encounters an option letter not included in *optstring*.

---

getopts — Parse Utility Options

Synopsis

/usr/bin/getopts *optstring name* [*arg*...]

sh

getopts *optstring name* [*argument*...]

ksh

getopts *optstring name* [*arg*...]

Description

/usr/bin/getopts

You can use the getopts command to process command-line arguments and check for legal options. You use the getops command in shell script loops to ensure standard syntax for command-line options.

Each time it is invoked, the getopts command puts the value of the next option in the shell variable specified by the *name* operand and the index of the next argument to be processed in the shell variable OPTIND. Whenever the shell is invoked, OPTIND is initialized to 1.

When the option requires an option-argument, the getopts command puts it in the shell variable OPTARG. If no option is found or if the option that was found does not have an option-argument, OPTARG is unset.

If an option character not contained in the *optstring* operand is found where an option character is expected, the shell variable specified by *name* is set to the question-mark (?) character. In this case, if the first character in *optstring* is a colon (:), the shell variable OPTARG is set to the option character found but no output is written to standard error; otherwise, the shell variable OPTARG is unset and a diagnostic message is written to standard error. This condition is considered to be an error detected in the way arguments were presented to the invoking application but is not an error in getopts processing.

If an option-argument is missing, getopts handles it in the following ways:

- If the first character of *optstring* is a colon, the shell variable specified by *name* is set to the colon character and the shell variable OPTARG is set to the option character found.
- Otherwise, the shell variable specified by *name* is set to the question-mark character, the shell variable OPTARG is unset, and a diagnostic message is written to standard error. This condition is considered to be an error detected in the way arguments were presented to the invoking application but is not an error in getopts processing; a diagnostic message is written as stated, but the exit status is 0.

When the end-of-options is encountered, the getopts command exits with a return value greater than zero; the shell variable OPTIND is set to the index of the first non-option argument, where the first -- argument is considered to be an option-argument if no other nonoption arguments appear before it, or the value $# + 1 if there are no non-option arguments; the *name* variable is set to the question-mark character. Any of the following identify the end-of-options:

- The special option --.
- Finding an argument that does not begin with a -.
- Encountering an error.

The shell variables OPTIND and OPTARG are local to the caller of getopts and are not exported by default.

The shell variable specified by the *name* operand, OPTIND, or OPTARG affects the current shell execution environment.

If the application sets OPTIND to the value 1, a new set of parameters can be used: either the current positional parameters or new *arg* values. Any other attempt to invoke getopts multiple times in a single-shell execution environment with parameters (positional parameters or *arg* operands) that are not the same in all invocations, or with an OPTIND value modified to be a value other than 1, produces unspecified results.

Bourne Shell

getopts is a built-in Bourne shell command that parses positional parameters and checks for valid options. See sh(1). It supports all applicable rules of the command syntax standard (see Rules 3–10, intro(1)). You should use it instead of the getopt command.

optstring must contain the option letters recognized by the command using getopts; if a letter is followed by a colon, the option is expected to have an argument or group of arguments that must be separated from it by white space.

Each time getopts is invoked, it puts the next option in the shell variable *name* and the index of the next argument to be processed in the shell variable OPTIND. Whenever the shell or a shell script is invoked, OPTIND is initialized to 1. When an option requires an option-argument, getopts puts it in the shell variable OPTARG.

If an illegal option is encountered, ? is placed in *name*.

When the end-of-options is encountered, getopts exits with a non-zero exit status. You can use the special option -- to delimit the end of the options.

By default, getopts parses the positional parameters. If extra arguments (*argument...*) are given on the getopts command line, getopts parses them instead.

/usr/lib/getoptcvt reads the shell script in *filename*, converts it to use getopts instead of getopt, and writes the results on the standard output.

So that all new commands adhere to the command syntax standard described in intro(1), they should use getopts or getopt to parse positional parameters and to check for options that are valid for that command.

getopts prints an error message on the standard error when it encounters an option letter not included in *opstring*.

Although relaxations of the following command syntax rule (see intro(1)) are permitted under the current implementation, you should not use them because they may not be supported in future releases of the system.

Note that a and b are options, and the option o requires an option-argument. The following example violates Rule 5: options with option-arguments must not be grouped with other options.

```
castle% cmd - aboxxx filename
```

The following example violates Rule 6: there must be white space after an option that takes an option-argument.

```
castle% cmd - ab oxxx filename
```

Changing the value of the shell variable OPTIND or parsing different sets of arguments can lead to unexpected results.

Korn Shell

The Korn shell built-in getopts command checks *arg* for legal options. If you omit *arg*, the positional parameters are used. An option argument begins with a + or a -. An option not beginning with + or - or the argument -- ends the options. *optstring* contains the letters that getopts recognizes. If a letter is followed by a colon, that option is expected to have an argument. You can separate the options from the argument by blanks.

getopts puts the next option letter it finds inside variable *name* each time it is invoked with a + prepended when *arg* begins with a +. The index of the next *arg* is stored in OPTIND. The option argument, if any, is stored in OPTARG.

A leading : in *optstring* stores the letter of an invalid option in OPTARG, and sets *name* to ? for an unknown option and to : when a required option is missing. Otherwise, getopts prints an error message. The exit status is non-zero when there are no more options.

See the Bourne shell section, above, for a further discussion of the Korn shell's getopts built-in command.

Operands

    optstring   A string containing the option characters recognized by the command invoking getopts. If a character is followed by a colon, the option is expected to have an argument, which should be supplied as a separate argument. Applications should specify an option character and its option-argument as separate arguments, but getopts interprets the characters following an option character requiring arguments as an argument whether or not this specification is done. An explicit null option-argument need not be recognized if it is not supplied as a separate argument when getopts is invoked; see getopt(3C). An application must not use the characters ? and : as option characters. The use of other option characters that are not alphanumeric produces unspecified results. If the option-argument is not supplied as a separate argument from the option character, the value in OPTARG is stripped of the option character and the -. The first character in *optstring* determines how getopts behaves if an option character is not known or if an option-argument is missing.

     name   The name of a shell variable that is set by the getopts command to the option character that was found.

The getopts command by default parses positional parameters passed to the invoking shell procedure. If you specify *args*, they are parsed instead of the positional parameters.

Usage

Because getopts affects the current shell execution environment, it is generally provided as a shell regular built-in. If it is called in a subshell or separate command-execution environment, such as one of the following,

```
(getopts abc value "$@")
nohup getopts...
find . -exec getopts... \;
```

it does not affect the shell variables in the caller's environment.

Note — Shell functions share OPTIND with the calling shell even though the positional parameters are changed. Functions that use getopts to parse their arguments usually want to save the value of OPTIND on entry and restore it before returning. However, there are cases when a function wants to change OPTIND for the calling shell.

Examples

The following example script parses and displays its arguments.

```
aflag=
bflag=
while getopts ab: name
do
  case $name in
  a)      aflag=1;;
  b)      bflag=1
          bval="$OPTARG";;
  ?)      printf "Usage: %s: [-a] [-b value]  args\n"
$0
     exit 2;;
     esac
done
if [! -z "$aflag"]; then
  printf "Option -a specified\n"
fi
if [! -z "$bflag"]; then
  printf 'Option -b "%s" specified\n' "$bval"
fi
shift $(($OPTIND - 1))
printf "Remaining arguments are: %s\n" "$*"
```

The following fragment of a shell program shows how you could process the arguments for a command that can take the options –a or –b, as well as the option –o, which requires an option-argument.

```
while getopts abo: c
do
  case $c in
  a | b)    FLAG=$c;;
  o)        OARG=$OPTARG;;
  \?)       echo $USAGE
     exit 2;;
  esac
done
  shift `expr $OPTIND - 1`
```

This code accepts any of the following as equivalent.

```
cmd -a -b -o "xxx z yy" filename
cmd -a -b -o "xxx z yy" -- filename
cmd -ab -o xxx,z,yy filename
cmd -ab -o "xxx z yy" filename
cmd -o xxx,z,yy -b -a filename
```

Environment Variables

See environ(5) for descriptions of the following environment variables that affect the execution of getopts: LC_CTYPE, LC_MESSAGES, and NLSPATH.

OPTIND	This variable is used by getopts as the index of the next argument to be processed.
OPTART	This variable is used by getopts as the index of the next argument to be processed.

Exit Status

0	An option, specified or unspecified by *optstring*, was found.
>0	The end-of-options was encountered or an error occurred.

Attributes

See attributes(5) for descriptions of the following attributes:

Attribute Type	Attribute Value
Availability	SUNWcsu

See Also

getopt(1), getoptcvt(1), intro(1), ksh(1), sh(1), getopt(3C), attributes(5), environ(5)

Diagnostics

Whenever an error is detected and the first character in the *optstring* operand is not a colon (:), a diagnostic message is written to standard error with the following information in an unspecified format:

- The invoking program name is identified in the message. The invoking program name is the value of the shell special parameter 0 at the time the getopts command is invoked. A name equivalent to basename "$0" can be used.
- If an option is found that was not specified in *optstring*, this error is identified and the invalid option character is identified in the message.
- If an option requiring an option-argument is found but an option-argument is not found, this error is identified and the invalid option character is identified in the message.

gettext — Retrieve Text String from Message Database

Synopsis

```
/usr/bin/gettext [-d textdomain | --domain=textdomain] [textdomain]
    msgid
/usr/bin/gettext [-s [-e] [-n] [-d textdomain | --domain=textdomain]
    msgid
```

New!

New!

Description

gettext retrieves a translated text string corresponding to string *msgid* from a message object generated with msgfmt(1). The message object name is derived from the optional argument *textdomain* if present; otherwise, from the TEXTDOMAIN environment. If you specify no domain or if a corresponding string cannot be found, gettext prints *msgid*.

Ordinarily gettext looks for its message object in /usr/lib/locale/*lang*/LC_MESSAGES, where *lang* is the locale name. If present, the TEXTDOMAINDIR environment variable replaces the path-name component up to *lang*.

This command interprets C escape sequences such as \t for Tab. Use \\ to print a backslash. To produce a message on a line of its own, either put a \n at the end of *msgid* or use this command in conjunction with printf(1).

When used with the -s option, gettext behaves like echo(1). However, it does not simply copy its arguments to standard output. Instead, those messages found in the selected catalog are translated. The -s option is new in the Solaris 9 release.

New!

Note — This command is the shell equivalent of the library routine gettext(3C).

Options

New!

-d *textdomain*
--domain=*textdomain*

        Retrieve translated messages from the domain *textdomain*, if *textdomain* is not specified as an operand. New in the Solaris 9 release.

-e   Enable expansion of some escape sequences if used with the -s option. New in the Solaris 9 release.

-n   Suppress trailing newline if used with the -s option. New in the Solaris 9 release.

-s   Behave like echo(1). However, instead of simply copying its arguments
                to standard output, translate those messages found in the selected
                catalog. If you specify the -s option, gettext performs no expansion of
                C escape sequences and appends a newline character to the output by
                default. New in the Solaris 9 release.

New! ## Operands

textdomain   A domain name used to retrieve the messages. This operand overrides
             the specification by the -d or --domain option if present.

msgid   A key to retrieve the localized message.

Environment Variables

LANG   Specify locale name.

LC_MESSAGES   Specify messaging locale and, if present, override LANG for messages.

TEXTDOMAIN   Specify the text domain name, which is identical to the message object
                file name without the .mo suffix.

TEXTDOMAINDIR

                Specify the path name to the message database, and if present, use
                instead of /usr/lib/locale.

Attributes

See attributes(5) for descriptions of the following attributes:

Attribute Type	Attribute Value
Availability	SUNWcsu

See Also

New!   echo(1), msgfmt(1), printf(1), gettext(3C), setlocale(3C), attributes(5)

gigiplot — Graphics Filters for Various Plotters

Synopsis

/usr/ucb/plot [-T*terminal*]

Description

See plot(1).

glob — Shell Built-in Function to Expand a Word List

Synopsis

glob *wordlist*

Description

For csh, glob performs file-name expansion and history substitutions on *wordlist*. This command is much the same as the echo(1) command, but glob does not recognize \ escapes. Words are delimited by null characters in the output.

Attributes

See attributes(5) for descriptions of the following attributes:

Attribute Type	Attribute Value
Availability	SUNWcsu

See Also

csh(1), echo(1), attributes(5)

goto — Shell Built-in Functions

Synopsis

csh
goto *label*

Description

See exit(1).

gprof — Display Call-Graph Profile Data

Synopsis

/usr/ccs/bin/gprof [-abcCDlsz] [-e *function-name]* [-E *function-name*]
    [-f *function-name*] [-F *function-name*] [*image-file* [*profile-file*...]]
    [-n *number-of-functions*]

Description

gprof produces an execution profile of a program. The effect of called routines is incorporated in the profile of each caller. The profile data is taken from the call-graph profile file that is created by programs compiled with the –xpg option of cc(1), by the –pg option with other compilers, or by setting the LD_PROFILE environment variable for shared objects. See ld.so.1(1). These compiler options also link in versions of the library routines that are compiled for profiling. The symbol table in the executable image file *image-file*(a.out by default) is read and correlated with the call-graph profile file *profile-file*(gmon.out by default).

The gprof command works in the following way.

1. Execution times for each routine are propagated along the edges of the call graph.
2. Cycles are discovered, and calls into a cycle are made to share the time of the cycle. The first listing shows the functions sorted according to the time they represent, including the time of their call-graph descendants. Below each function entry is shown its (direct) call-graph children and how their times are propagated to this function. A similar display above the function shows how this function's time and the time of its descendants are propagated to its (direct) call-graph parents.
3. Cycles are also shown, with an entry for the cycle as a whole and a listing of the members of the cycle and their contributions to the time and call counts of the cycle.
4. A flat profile is given, similar to that provided by prof(1). This listing gives the total execution times and call counts for each of the functions in the program, sorted by decreasing time.
5. Finally, an index is given that shows the correspondence between function names and call-graph profile index numbers.

You can split a single function into subfunctions for profiling by means of the MARK macro. See prof(5).

Note — Beware of quantization errors. The granularity of the sampling is shown but remains statistical at best. It is assumed that the time for each execution of a function can be expressed by the total time for the function divided by the number of times the function is called. Thus, the time propagated along the call-graph arcs to parents of that function is directly proportional to the number of times that arc is traversed.

The profiled program must call exit(2) or return normally for the profiling information to be saved in the gmon.out file.

64-bit Profiling

You can use 64-bit profiling freely with dynamically linked executables, and profiling information is collected for the shared objects if the objects are compiled for profiling. Apply care to interpret the profile output because it is possible for symbols from different shared objects to have the same name. If name duplication occurs in the profile output, you can use the module ID prefix before the symbol name in the symbol index listing to identify the appropriate module for the symbol.

Note — Take care not to mix 32-bit profile files with 64-bit profile files when using the –s or –D option to sum multiple profile files.

32-bit Profiling

You can use 32-bit profiling with dynamically linked executables; however, you must be careful. In 32-bit profiling, you cannot use gprof to profile shared objects. Only the main portion of the image is sampled when you execute a profiled, dynamically linked program. This means that all time spent outside the main object (time spent in a shared object) is not included in the profile summary. Thus, the total time reported for the program may be less than the total time used by the program.

Because the time spent in a shared object cannot be accounted for, you should minimize the use of shared objects whenever a program is profiled with gprof. You can link the program to the profiled version of a library (or to the standard archive version if no profiling version is available), instead of to the shared object, to get profile information on the functions of a library. Versions of profiled libraries may be supplied with the system in the /usr/lib/libp directory. Refer to compiler driver documentation on profiling.

Consider an extreme case. A profiled program dynamically linked with the shared C library spends 100 units of time in some libc routine, say, malloc(). Suppose malloc() is called only from routine B and B consumes only 1 unit of time. Suppose further that routine A consumes 10 units of time, more than any other routine in the main (profiled) portion of the image. In this case, gprof concludes that most of the time is being spent in A and almost no time is being spent in B. From this result, it is almost impossible to tell that the greatest improvement can be made by looking at routine B and not routine A. The value of the profiler in this case is severely degraded; the solution is to use archives as much as possible for profiling.

Notes

If the executable image has been stripped and has no symbol table (.symtab), then gprof reads the dynamic symbol table (.dyntab) if present. If the dynamic symbol table is used, then only the information for the global symbols is available and the behavior is identical to that with the -a option.

LD_LIBRARY_PATH must not contain /usr/lib as a component when compiling a program for profiling. If LD_LIBRARY_PATH contains /usr/lib, the program links incorrectly with the profiling versions of the system libraries in /usr/lib/libp.

The times reported in successive, identical runs may show variances because of varying cache-hit ratios that result from sharing the cache with other processes. Even if a program seems to be the only one using the machine, hidden background or asynchronous processes may blur the data. In rare cases, the clock ticks initiating recording of the program counter may change because of loops in a program, grossly distorting measurements. Call counts are always recorded precisely, however.

Only programs that call exit or return from main are guaranteed to produce a profile file, unless a final call to monitor is explicitly coded.

Profiling can be used with dynamically linked executables, but care must be applied. Currently, shared objects cannot be profiled with gprof. Thus, when a profiled, dynamically linked program is executed, only the main portion of the image is sampled. This means that all time spent outside the main object, that is, time spent in a shared object, is not included in the profile summary; the total time reported for the program may be less than the total time used by the program.

Functions such as mcount(), _mcount(), moncontrol(), _moncontrol(), monitor(), and _monitor() may appear in the gprof report. These functions are part of the profiling implementation and thus account for some amount of the runtime overhead. Because these functions are not present in an unprofiled application, you can ignore time accumulated and call counts for these functions when evaluating the performance of an application.

Bugs

Parents that are not themselves profiled have the time of their profiled children propagated to them, but they appear to be spontaneously invoked in the call-graph listing and do not have their time propagated further. Similarly, signal catchers, even though profiled, appear to be spontaneous (although for more obscure reasons). Any profiled children of signal catchers should have their times propagated properly unless the signal catcher was invoked during the execution of the profiling routine, in which case all is lost.

Options

-a   Suppress printing statically declared functions. If you specify this option, all relevant information about the static function (for instance, time samples, calls to other functions, calls from other functions) belongs to the function loaded just before the static function in the a.out file.

-b   Suppress descriptions of each field in the profile.

-c   Discover the static call graph of the program by a heuristic that examines the text space of the object file. Indicate static-only parents or children with call counts of 0.

-C   Demangle C++ symbol names before printing them.

-D   Produce a profile file gmon.sum that represents the difference of the profile information in all specified profile files. You can give this summary profile file to subsequent executions of gprof (also with -D) to summarize profile data across several runs of an a.out file. See also the -s option.

              As an example, suppose function A calls function B n times in profile file gmon.sum, and m times in profile file gmon.out. With -D, create a new gmon.sum file showing the number of calls from A to B as $n-m$.

-e *function-name*

              Suppress printing the graph profile entry for routine *function-name* and all its descendants (unless they have other ancestors that are not suppressed). You can specify more than one -e option. You can specify only one *function-name* with each -e option.

-E *function-name*

              Suppress printing the graph profile entry for routine *function-name* and its descendants (as -e), and also exclude the time spent in *function-name* and its descendants from the total and percentage time computations. You can specify more than one -E option. For example, the default is

              `-E mcount -E mcleanup'

-f *function-name*

              Print the graph profile entry only for routine *function-name* and its descendants. You can give more than one -f option. You can specify only one *function-name* for each -f option.

-F *function-name*

> Print the graph profile entry only for routine *function-name* and its descendants (as -f), and also use only the times of the printed routines in total time and percentage computations. You can specify more than one -F option. You can specify only one *function-name* with each -F option. The -F option overrides the -E option.

-l

> Suppress the reporting of graph profile entries for all local symbols. This option is the equivalent of placing all of the local symbols for the specified executable image on the -E exclusion list.

-n *number-of-functions*

> Limit the size of flat and graph profile listings to the top *number-of-functions* offending functions.

-s

> Produce a profile file *gmon.sum* that represents the sum of the profile information in all of the specified profile files. You can give this summary profile file to subsequent executions of gprof (also with -s) to accumulate profile data across several runs of an a.out file. See also the -D option.

-z

> Display routines that have 0 usage (as indicated by call counts and accumulated time). This option is useful in conjunction with the -c option for discovering which routines are never called.

Environment Variables

PROFDIR

> Put profiling output within the specified directory, in a file named *pid.programname*. *pid* is the process ID, and *programname* is the name of the program being profiled, as determined by removing any path prefix from the argv[0] with which the program was called. If the variable contains a null value, no profiling output is produced. Otherwise, profiling output is placed in the file gmon.out.

LD_LIBRARY_PATH must not contain /usr/lib as a component when a program is compiled for profiling. If LD_LIBRARY_PATH contains /usr/lib, the program is not linked correctly with the profiling versions of the system libraries in /usr/lib/libp.

Files

a.out   Executable file containing *namelist*.

gmon.out   Dynamic call graph and profile.

gmon.sum   Summarized dynamic call graph and profile.

$PROFDIR/pid.programname

Attributes

See attributes(5) for descriptions of the following attributes:

Attribute Type	Attribute Value
Availability	SUNWbtool

See Also

cc(1), ld.so.1(1), prof(1), exit(2), pcsample(2), profil(2), malloc(3C), monitor(3C), malloc(3X), attributes(5), prof(5)

Graham, S. L., Kessler, P. B., McKusick, M. K., "gprof: A Call Graph Execution Profiler," *Proceedings of the SIGPLAN '82 Symposium on Compiler Construction*, SIGPLAN Notices, Vol.17, No. 6, pp. 120–126, June 1982.

Linker and Libraries Guide

graph — Draw a Graph

Synopsis

```
/usr/bin/graph [-a spacing [start]]  [-b]  [-c string]  [-g gridstyle]
   [-l label]  [-m connectmode]  [-s]  [-x [l] lower [upper [spacing]]]
   [-y [l]  lower [upper [spacing]]]  [-h fraction] [-w fraction]
   [-r fraction]  [-u fraction]  [-t]...
```

Description

If you type graph with no options, an se prompt is displayed. You can type a pair of numbers, separated by a comma or by white space, that are used as abscissas and ordinates of a graph. Successive points are connected by straight lines. The standard output from graph contains plotting instructions suitable for input to plot(1B) or to the command lpr -g (see lpr(1B)).

If the coordinates of a point are followed by a nonnumeric string, that string is printed as a label beginning on the point. You can surround labels with quotes "...", in which case they may be empty or contain blanks and numbers; labels never contain newline characters.

A legend indicating grid range is produced with a grid unless you specify the -s option.

Bugs

graph stores all points internally and drops those for which there is no room. Segments that run out of bounds are dropped, not windowed.

Logarithmic axes cannot be reversed.

Options

Represent each option as a separate argument. If a specified lower limit exceeds the upper limit, the axis is reversed.

-a *spacing*[*start*]

Supply abscissas automatically (they are missing from the input); *spacing* is the spacing (default 1). *start* is the starting point for automatic abscissas (default 0 or lower limit given by -x).

-b   Break (disconnect) the graph after each label in the input.

-c *string*   Use *string* as the default label for each point.

graph   **469**

-g *gridstyle*

> Use *gridstyle* as the grid style. Possible values are 0, no grid, 1, frame with ticks, 2, full grid (default).

-l *label*   Use *label* as the label.

-m *connectmode*

> Use *connectmode* as the style or mode of connecting lines. Possible values are 0, disconnected, 1, connected (default). Some devices give distinguishable line styles for other small integers.

-s   Save screen. Do not erase before plotting.

-x [1] *lower* [*upper* [*spacing*]]

> If you use 1, make the x axis logarithmic. *lower* and *upper* specify lower and upper x limits. If you use *spacing*, space the grid on the x axis. Normally, these quantities are determined automatically.

-y [1] *lower* [*upper* [*spacing*]]

> If you use 1, make the y axis logarithmic. *lower* and *upper* specify lower and upper x limits. If you use *spacing*, space the grid on the x axis. Normally, these quantities are determined automatically.

-h *fraction*

> Use *fraction* of space for height.

-w *fraction*

> Use *fraction* of space for width.

-r *fraction*

> Use *fraction* of space to move right before plotting.

-u *fraction*

> Use *fraction* of space to move up before plotting.

-t   Transpose horizontal and vertical axes. Option -x now applies to the vertical axis.

Examples

The following example uses the plot and graph capabilities. The file named data contains the following data points.

```
castle% cat data
1       1.0
2       4.0
3       5.0
4       6.5         "Optional Label"
7       10.3
8       11.4
9       9.5
10      8.9
11      7.0
12      10.5
13      5.0
```

```
14      2.8
castle%
```

The following example displays the data in a shell tool using the graph command.

```
castle% graph < data + plot -Tcrt
castle% ***********************************************************************
   *                        *                    *                          *
   *                        *                    *                          *
   *                        *                    *                          *
   *                        *              *      *                          *
   *                        *            *  *     *                          *
   *                        *          **   **    *              *           *
   ***************************************************************************
   *                    *         **        ** *          * *                *
   *                    *       **           ** *        *    *              *
   *                    *     **             **        *     *               *
   *                    *  **               * **   *        *                *
   *                  ***                   *  * *        *                  *
   *                **  *                   *     *       *                  *
   *              *Optional Label           *             *                  *
   *          *       *                     *                 *             *
   *        **        *                     *                   *           *
   *      *           *                     *                     *         *
   ***************************************************************************
   *          **         *                  *                     *          *
   *        **           *                  *                   *            *
   *      *              *                  *                  *             *
   *    *                *                  *                *               *
   *   *                 *                  *               *                *
   *  *                  *                  *                                *
   * *                   *                  *                                *
   *                     *                  *                                *
   ***************************************************************************
    0 -x- 15   0 -y- 15
```

graph clears the screen and displays the graph positioning the prompt at the top of the screen. Any subsequent commands you type are displayed on top of the graph. Use the clear command to clear the screen after you display the plot.

Attributes

See attributes(5) for descriptions of the following attributes:

Attribute Type	Attribute Value
Availability	SUNWesu

See Also

spline(1), lpr(1B), plot(1B), plot(3), attributes(5)

grep — Search a File for a Pattern

Synopsis

```
/usr/bin/grep [-bchilnsvw] limited-regular-expression [filename...]
/usr/xpg4/bin/grep [-E | -F] [-c | -l | -q] [-bhinsvwx] -e pattern-list
    [-f pattern-file]... [file...]
/usr/xpg4/bin/grep [-E | -F] [-c | -l | -q] [-bhinsvwx]
    [-e pattern-list -f pattern-file [file...]
/usr/xpg4/bin/grep [-E | -F] [-c | -l | -q] [-bhinsvwx] pattern
    [file...]
```

Description

The grep command searches files for a pattern in one or more files and prints all lines that contain that pattern. grep (which stands for global regular expression and print) uses a compact, nondeterministic algorithm.

> **Note** — Be careful using the characters $, *, [, ^, |, (,), and \ in the *pattern-list* because they are also meaningful to the shell. It is safest to enclose the entire *pattern-list* in single quotes '...'.

If you specify no files, grep assumes standard input. Normally, each line found is copied to standard output. The file name is printed before each line found if there is more than one input file.

/usr/bin/grep

The /usr/bin/grep command uses limited regular expressions like those described on the regexp(5) manual page to match the patterns.

Lines are limited only by the size of the available virtual memory. For a line with embedded nulls, grep matches only up to the first null; if it matches, grep prints the entire line.

/usr/xpg4/bin/grep

/usr/xpg4/bin/grep is a POSIX-compliant version of the /usr/bin/grep command. See standards(5).

The options -E and -F affect the way /usr/xpg4/bin/grep interprets *pattern-list*. If you specify -E, /usr/xpg4/bin/grep interprets *pattern-list* as a full regular expression. If you specify -F, grep interprets *pattern-list* as a fixed string. If you specify neither, grep interprets *pattern-list* as a basic regular expression, as described on the regex(5) manual page.

The results are unspecified if input files contain lines longer than LINE_MAX bytes or contain binary data. LINE_MAX is defined in /usr/include/limits.a.

Options

The following options are supported for both /usr/bin/grep and /usr/xpg4/bin/grep.

-b   Precede each line by the block number on which it was found. This option can be useful in locating block numbers by context (first block is 0).

-c   Print a count only of the lines that contain the pattern.

-h	Prevent the name of the file containing the matching line from being appended to that line. Used when searching multiple files.
-i	Ignore upper-/lowercase distinction during comparisons.
-l	Print the names of files only with matching lines, separated by newline characters. Do not repeat the names of files when the pattern is found more than once.
-n	Precede each line by its line number in the file (first line is 1).
-s	Suppress error messages about nonexistent or unreadable files.
-v	Print all lines except those that contain the pattern.
-w	Search for the expression as a word as if surrounded by \< and \>.

The following options are supported only for /usr/xpg4/bin/grep.

-e *pattern-list*

Specify one or more patterns to be used during the search for input. Separate patterns in *pattern-list* by a newline character. You can specify a null pattern with two adjacent newline characters in *pattern-list*. Unless you specify the -E or -F option, treat each pattern as a basic regular expression. grep accepts multiple -e and -f options. All of the specified patterns are used when matching lines, but the order of evaluation is not specified.

-E

Match, using full regular expressions. Treat each pattern specified as a full regular expression. If any entire full regular expression pattern matches an input line, the line is matched. A null full regular expression matches every line.

Interpret each pattern as a full regular expression as described on the regex(5) manual page, except for \(and \), and including:

- A full regular expression followed by + that matches one or more occurrences of the full regular expression.

- A full regular expression followed by ? that matches 0 or 1 occurrence of the full regular expression.

- Full regular expressions, separated by | or by a newline, that match strings that are matched by any of the expressions.

- A full regular expression that can be enclosed in parentheses () for grouping.

The order of precedence of operators is [], then *?+, then concatenation, then | and newline.

-f *pattern-file*

Read one or more patterns from the file named by the path-name *pattern-file*. Terminate patterns in *pattern-file* with a newline character. You can specify a null pattern by an empty line in *pattern-file*. Unless you also specify the -E or -F option, treat each pattern as a basic regular expression.

-F	Match, using fixed strings. Treat each pattern specified as a string instead of a regular expression. If an input line contains any of the patterns as a contiguous sequence of bytes, match the line. A null string matches every line. See fgrep(1) for more information.
-q	Do not write anything to the standard output, regardless of matching lines. Exit with 0 status if an input line is selected.
-x	Consider only input lines that use all characters in the line to match an entire fixed string or regular expression to be matching lines.

Operands

file	A path name of a file to be searched for the patterns. If no file operands are specified, use the standard input.

/usr/bin/grep *pattern*

Specify a pattern to be used during the search for input.

/usr/xpg4/bin/grep *pattern*

Specify one or more patterns to be used during the search for input. This operand is treated as if it were specified as -e *pattern-list*.

Usage

The -e *pattern-list* option has the same effect as the *pattern-list* operand but is useful when *pattern-list* begins with the hyphen delimiter. It is also useful when it is more convenient to provide multiple patterns as separate arguments.

grep accepts multiple -e and -f options and uses all of the patterns it is given to match input text lines.

Note — The order of evaluation is not specified. If an implementation finds a null string as a pattern, it is allowed to use that pattern first, matching every line, and effectively ignore any other patterns.

The -q option provides a means of easily determining whether or not a pattern (or string) exists in a group of files. When searching several files, it provides a performance improvement (because grep can quit as soon as it finds the first match) and requires less care by the user in choosing the set of files to supply as arguments (because grep exits with 0 if it finds a match even if grep detected an access or read error on earlier file operands).

Large File Behavior

See largefile(5) for the description of the behavior of grep when encountering files greater than or equal to 2 Gbytes (2**31 bytes).

Examples

The following example finds all uses of the word Posix (in any case) in the standards.5 manual page and displays the line with a line number preceding it. To save space, not all of the lines are shown in this example.

```
castle% /usr/bin/grep -i -n posix standards.5
7:standards, posix, POSIX, posix.1, POSIX.1, posix.2, POSIX.2, xnet,
    XNET, xnet4, XNET4, xpg, XPG, xpg3, XPG3, xpg4, XPG4, xpg4v2, XPG4v2
    \- standards and specifications supported by Solaris
```

```
33:.IX "standards and specifications supported by Solaris" "POSIX.2" ""
   "\(em \fLPOSIX.2\fP"
34:.IX "POSIX.2" "" "\fLPOSIX.2\fP \(em standards and specifications
   supported by Solaris"
35:.IX "standards and specifications supported by Solaris" "posix.2" ""
   "\(em \fLposix.2\fP"
...
castle%
```

You can combine the grep command with other commands to find specific information. In the following example, the output of the env command is piped to grep to search for environment variables that contain the word HOME. As you can see, the search results also include longer words that contain the HOME string.

```
castle% env | grep HOME
OPENWINHOME=/usr/openwin
HOME=/export/home/winsor
castle%
```

You can use either of the following commands to find all empty lines in the standard input.

```
castle% /usr/bin/grep ^$
castle% /usr/bin/grep -v .
```

Both of the following commands print all lines containing strings abc or def or both.

```
castle% /usr/xpg4/bin/grep -E 'abc def'
castle% /usr/xpg4/bin/grep -F 'abc def'
```

Both of the following commands print all lines matching exactly abc or def.

```
castle% /usr/xpg4/bin/grep -E '^abc$ ^def$'
castle% /usr/xpg4/bin/grep -F -x 'abc def'
```

You can use the grep command to search through several files to find a particular string. The following example uses the grep command to search all of the files in a directory for the string kookaburra.

```
castle% grep kookaburra *
kookaburra:Laugh, kookaburra, laugh
kookaburra:Laugh, kookaburra, laugh
kookaburra-1:Laugh, kookaburra, laugh
kookaburra-1:Laugh, kookaburra, laugh
kookaburra-2:Laugh, kookaburra, laugh
kookaburra-2:Laugh, kookaburra, laugh
kookaburra-3:Laugh, kookaburra, laugh
kookaburra-3:Laugh, kookaburra, laugh
kookaburra-3:Laugh, kookaburra, laugh
kookaburra-3:Laugh, kookaburra, laugh
castle%
```

As you can see from the output, grep displays the name of the file at the beginning of each line that it prints. Four files in this directory contain the word kookaburra. Also note that because we did not specify the -i option to ignore case, lines containing the word Kookaburra are not displayed.

Environment Variables

See environ(5) for descriptions of the following environment variables that affect the execution of grep: LC_COLLATE, LC_CTYPE, LC_MESSAGES, and NLSPATH.

Exit Status

0	One or more matches were found.
1	No matches were found.
2	Syntax errors or inaccessible files (even if matches were found).

Attributes

See attributes(5) for descriptions of the following attributes:

/usr/bin/grep

Attribute Type	Attribute Value
Availability	SUNWfac

/usr/xpg4/bin/grep

Attribute Type	Attribute Value
Availability	SUNWfac

See Also

egrep(1), fgrep(1), sed(1), sh(1), attributes(5), environ(5), largefile(5), regex(5), regexp(5), XPG4(5)

groups — Print Group Membership of User

Synopsis

/usr/bin/groups [*user*...]

Description

The groups command prints on standard output the groups to which you or the optionally specified *user* belong. Each user belongs to a group specified in /etc/passwd and possibly to other groups as specified in /etc/group. Note that /etc/passwd specifies the numerical ID (gid) of the group. The groups command converts gid to the group name in the output.

Examples

The following example shows the groups for users winsor, ray, and des.

```
castle% groups winsor ray des
winsor : staff other sysadmin
ray : staff other sysadmin
des : staff sysadmin
castle%
```

Files

/etc/passwd Password file.

/etc/group Group file.

Attributes

See attributes(5) for descriptions of the following attributes:

Attribute Type	Attribute Value
Availability	SUNWcsu

See Also

group(4), passwd(4), attributes(5)

grpck — Password/Group File Checkers

Synopsis

/usr/sbin/grpck [*filename*]

Description

See pwck(1).

New! gunzip — Compress or Expand Files

Synopsis

/bin/gunzip [-acfhlLnNrtvV] [-S *suffix*] [*name...*]

Description

See gzip(1).

gzcat — Compress or Expand Files

Synopsis

```
/bin/gzcat [-fhLV] [name...]
```

Description

See gzip(1).

gzcmp, gzdiff — Compare Compressed Files   *New!*

Synopsis

```
/bin/gzcmp [cmp_options] file1 [file2]
/bin/gzdiff [diff_options] file1 [file2]
```

Description

Use gzcmp and gzdiff, new in the Solaris 8 Operating Environment, to invoke the cmp or the diff program on compressed files. All specified options are passed directly to cmp or diff. When you specify only one file, then the files compared are file1 and an uncompressed file1.gz. When you specify two files, they are uncompressed if necessary and fed to cmp or diff. The exit status from cmp or diff is preserved.

Attributes

See attributes(5) for descriptions of the following attributes.

Attribute Type	Attribute Value
Availability	SUNWgzip

See Also

cmp(1), diff(1), gzforce(1), gzgrep(1), gzip(1), gzmore(1), gznew(1), gzexe(1)

Bugs

Messages from the cmp or diff programs refer to temporary file names instead of those specified.

gzdiff — Compare Compressed Files   *New!*

Synopsis

```
/bin/gzdiff [diff_options] file1 [file2]
```

Description

See gzcmp(1).

New! gzexe — Compress Executable Files in Place

Synopsis

/bin/gzexe [*name*...]

Description

Use the gzexe command, new in the Solaris 8 Operating Environment, to compress executables in place and have them automatically uncompress and execute when you run them (at a penalty in performance). For example, executing gzexe /bin/cat creates the following two files.

```
-r-xr-xr-x 1 root bin 9644 Feb 11 11:16 /bin/cat
-r-xr-xr-x 1 bin bin 24576 Nov 23 13:21 /bin/cat~
```

/bin/cat~ is the original file, and /bin/cat is the self-uncompressing executable file. You can remove /bin/cat~ once you are sure that /bin/cat works properly.

This command is most useful on systems with very small disks.

Options

-d   Decompress the given executables instead of compressing them.

Attributes

See attributes(5) for descriptions of the following attributes.

Attribute Type	Attribute Value
Availability	SUNWgzip

See Also

gzcmp(1), gzforce(1), gzip(1), gzmore(1), gznew(1)

Caveats

The compressed executable is a shell script. This script may create some security holes. In particular, the compressed executable relies on the PATH environment variable to find gzip and other commands such as tail, chmod, ln, and sleep.

Bugs

gzexe tries to retain the original file attributes on the compressed executable, but in some cases you may have to fix them manually with chmod or chown.

gzforce — Force a .gz Extension on all gzip Files

New!

Synopsis

```
/bin/gzforce [name...]
```

Description

Use the gzforce command, new in the Solaris 8 Operating Environment, to force a .gz extension on all gzip files so that gzip does not compress them twice. This command can be useful for files with names truncated after a file transfer. On systems with a 14-character limitation on file names, the original name is truncated to make room for the .gz suffix. For example, 12345678901234 is renamed to 12345678901.gz. A file name such as foo.tgz is left intact.

Attributes

See attributes(5) for descriptions of the following attributes.

Attribute Type	Attribute Value
Availability	SUNWgzip

See Also

gzdiff(1), gzexe(1), gzgrep(1), gzip(1), gzmore(1), gznew(1)

gzip, gunzip, gzcat — Compress or Expand Files

New!

Synopsis

```
/bin/gzip [-acdfhlLnNqrtvV#] [-S suffix] [name...]
/bin/gunzip [-acfhlLnNqrtvV] [-S suffix] [name...]
/bin/gzcat [-fhLV] [name...]
```

Description

Use the gzip command, new in the Solaris 8 Operating Environment, to reduce the size of the named files with Lempel-Ziv coding (LZ77).

> **Note** — Source for gzip is available in the SUNWgzipS package.

When possible, each file is replaced by one with the extension .gz, keeping the same ownership modes, access, and modification times. For VMS, the default extension is -gz. For MS-DOS, OS/2 FAT, Windows NT FAT, and Atari, the default extension is z. When you specify no files or if a file name is -, the standard input is compressed to the standard output. gzip tries to compress only regular files. It ignores symbolic links.

If the compressed file name is too long for the file system, gzip tries to truncate it. gzip truncates only the parts of the file name longer than 3 characters. A part is delimited by dots. If the name consists of small parts only, the longest parts are truncated. For example, if file names are limited to 14 characters, gzip.msdos.exe is compressed to `gzi.msd.exe.gz`. Names are not truncated on systems that have no limit on file-name length.

By default, `gzip` keeps the original file name and timestamp in the compressed file. They are used when the file is decompressed with the `-N` option. This feature is useful when the compressed file name was truncated or when the timestamp was not preserved after a file transfer.

You can restore compressed files to their original form with `gzip -d`, `gunzip`, or `gzcat`. If the original name saved in the compressed file is not suitable for its file system, a new, legal name is constructed from the original one.

`gunzip` replaces each file on the command line with names ending with `.gz`, `-gz`, `.z`, `-z`, `_z`, or `.Z` and beginning with the correct magic number with an uncompressed file without the original extension. `gunzip` also recognizes the special extensions `.tgz` and `.taz` as shorthands for `.tar.gz` and `.tar.Z`. When compressing, `gzip` uses the `.tgz` extension if necessary instead of truncating a file with a `.tar` extension.

`gunzip` can currently decompress files created by `gzip`, `zip`, `compress`, `compress -H`, or `pack`. Input format detection is automatic. With the first two formats, `gunzip` checks a 32-bit CRC. For `pack`, `gunzip` checks the uncompressed length. The standard compress format was not designed to allow consistency checks; however, `gunzip` is sometimes able to detect a bad `.Z` file. If you get an error when uncompressing a `.Z` file, do not assume that the `.Z` file is correct simply because the standard uncompress does not complain. This lack of complaint generally means that the standard uncompress does not check its input and happily generates garbage output. The SCO `compress -H` format (`lzh` compression method) does not include a CRC but does allow some consistency checks.

Files created by `zip` can be uncompressed by `gzip` only if they have a single member compressed with the deflation method. This feature is intended to help conversion of `tar.zip` files to the `tar.gz` format. To extract `zip` files with several members, use `unzip` instead of `gunzip`.

`gzcat` is identical to `gunzip -c`. (On some systems, `zcat` may be installed as `gzcat` to preserve the original link to `compress`.) `gzcat` uncompresses either a list of files on the command line or its standard input and writes the uncompressed data to standard output. `gzcat` uncompresses files that have the correct magic number regardless of whether they have a `.gz` suffix.

`gzip` uses the Lempel-Ziv algorithm used in `zip` and `PKZIP`. The amount of compression obtained depends on the size of the input and the distribution of common substrings. Typically, text such as source code or English is reduced by 60 to 70 percent. Compression is generally much better than that achieved by LZW (as used by `compress`), Huffman coding (as used by `pack`), or adaptive Huffman coding (`compact`).

Compression is always performed, even if the compressed file is slightly larger than the original. The worst-case expansion is a few bytes for the `gzip` file header plus 5 bytes every 32K blocks or an expansion ratio of 0.015 percent for large files. Note that the actual number of used disk blocks almost never increases. `gzip` preserves the mode, ownership, and timestamps of files when compressing or decompressing.

Options

`-a --ascii`   ASCII text mode. Convert end-of-lines with local conventions. This option is supported only on some non-UNIX systems. For MS-DOS, CR LF is converted to LF when compressing, and LF is converted to CR LF when decompressing.

-c --stdout --to-stdout

       Write output on standard output; keep original files unchanged. With several input files, the output consists of a sequence of independently compressed members. To obtain better compression, concatenate all input files before compressing them.

-d --decompress --uncompress

       Decompress.

-f --force   Force compression or decompression even if the file has multiple links or the corresponding file already exists or if the compressed data is read from or written to a terminal. If the input data is not in a format recognized by gzip and if you specify the --stdout option, copy the input data without change to the standard output. In this case, gzcat behaves as cat. If you do not specify the -f and gzip is not running in the background, prompt to verify whether to overwrite an existing file.

-h --help   Display a help screen, and quit.

-l --list   For each compressed file, list the following fields.

compressed size

       Size of the compressed file.

uncompressed size

       Size of the uncompressed file.

ratio   Compression ratio (0.0% if unknown).

uncompressed_name

       Name of the uncompressed file.

The uncompressed size is -1 for files not in gzip format, such as compressed .Z files. To get the uncompressed size for such a file, you can use the following command.

gzcat file.Z | wc -c

In combination with the --verbose option, the following fields are also displayed.

method   Compression method.

crc   The 32-bit CRC of the uncompressed data.

date & time   Time stamp for the uncompressed file.

The compression methods currently supported are deflate, compress, lzh (SCO compress -H), and pack. The crc is shown as ffffffff for a file not in gzip format.

With --name, the uncompressed name, date, and time are those stored within the compress file if present. With --verbose, the size totals and compression ratio for all files are also displayed unless some sizes are unknown. With --quiet, the title and totals lines are not displayed.

-L --license

> Display the gzip license, and quit.

-n --no-name

> When compressing, do not save the original file name and timestamp by default. (The original name is always saved if the name was truncated.) When decompressing, do not restore the original file name if present (remove only the gzip suffix from the compressed file name) and do not restore the original timestamp if present (copy it from the compressed file). This option is the default when decompressing.

-N --name

> When compressing, always save the original file name and timestamp (the default). When decompressing, restore the original file name and timestamp if present. This option is useful on systems that have a limit on file-name length or when the timestamp has been lost after a file transfer.

-q --quiet   Suppress all warnings.

-r --recursive

> Travel the directory structure recursively. If any of the file names specified on the command line are directories, gzip descends into the directory and compresses all the files it finds there (or decompresses them in the case of gunzip).

-S .suf --suffix .suf

> Use suffix .suf instead of .gz. You can specify any suffix, but you should avoid suffixes other than .z and .gz to prevent confusion when files are transferred to other systems. A null suffix forces gunzip to try decompression on all given files regardless of suffix, as shown in the following example.
>
> **gunzip -S "" * (*.*** for MS-DOS)
>
> Previous versions of gzip used the .z suffix. This suffix was changed to avoid a conflict with pack(1).

-t --test   Test. Check the compressed file integrity.

-v --verbose

> Verbose. Display the name and percentage reduction for each file compressed or decompressed.

-V --version

> Version. Display the version number and compilation options, then quit.

-# --fast --best

> Regulate the speed of compression with the specified digit #, where -1 or --fast indicates the fastest compression method (less compression) and -9 or --best indicates the slowest compression method (best compression). The default compression level is -6 (that is, biased toward high compression at the expense of speed).

Advanced Usage

Multiple compressed files can be concatenated. In this case, `gunzip` extracts all members at once. For example:

```
gzip -c file1 > foo.gz
gzip -c file2 >> foo.gz
```

Then

```
gunzip -c foo
```

is equivalent to

```
cat file1 file2
```

When one member of a `.gz` file is damaged, you can still recover other members if you remove the damaged member. However, you can get better compression by compressing all members at once, as shown in the following example.

```
cat file1 file2 | gzip > foo.gz
```

compresses better than

```
gzip -c file1 file2 > foo.gz
```

To recompress concatenated files for better compression, use the following syntax.

```
gzip -cd old.gz | gzip > new.gz
```

When a compressed file consists of several members, the uncompressed size and CRC reported by the `--list` option applies only to the last member. If you need the uncompressed size for all members, you can use the following command.

```
gzip -cd file.gz | wc -c
```

To create a single archive file with multiple members so that members can later be extracted independently, use an archiver such as `tar` or `zip`. GNU `tar` supports the `-z` option to invoke `gzip` transparently. `gzip` is designed as a complement to `tar`, not as a replacement.

Environment

The environment variable `GZIP` can hold a set of default options for `gzip`. These options are interpreted first and can be overwritten by explicit command-line parameters, as shown in the following examples.

For `sh`	`GZIP="-8v --name"; export GZIP`
For `csh`	`setenv GZIP "-8v --name"`
For MS-DOS	`set GZIP=-8v --name`

On VAX/VMS, the name of the environment variable is `GZIP_OPT` to avoid a conflict with the symbol set for invocation of the program.

Attributes

See `attributes`(5) for descriptions of the following attributes.

Attribute Type	Attribute Value
Availability	SUNWgzip

See Also

`compress`(1), `gzcmp`(1), `gzexe`(1), `gzforce`(1), `gzmore`(1), `gznew`(1), `pack`(1), `unzip`(1)

Diagnostics

Exit status is normally 0; if an error occurs, exit status is 1. If a warning occurs, exit status is 2.

`Usage: gzip [-cdfhlLnNrtvV19] [-S suffix] [file ...]`

       Invalid options were specified on the command line.

`file: not in gzip format`

       The file specified to `gunzip` has not been compressed.

`file: Corrupt input. Use gzcat to recover some data.`

       The compressed file has been damaged. The data up to the point of failure can be recovered with `gzcat file > recover`.

`file: compressed with xx bits, can only handle yy bits`

       File was compressed (with LZW) by a program that could deal with more bits than the decompress code on this machine. Recompress the file with `gzip`, which compresses better and uses less memory.

`file: already has .gz suffix -- no change`

       The file is assumed to be already compressed. Rename the file and try again.

`file already exists; do you wish to overwrite (y or n)?`

       Respond **y** if you want the output file to be replaced; **n** if not.

`gunzip: corrupt input`

       A `SIGSEGV` violation was detected, which usually means that the input file has been corrupted.

`xx.x%`   Percentage of the input saved by compression. (Relevant only for `-v` and `-l`.)

`-- not a regular file or directory: ignored`

       When the input file is not a regular file or directory (for example, a symbolic link, socket, FIFO, or device file), it is left unaltered.

```
-- has xx other links: unchanged
```
> The input file has links; it is left unchanged. See ln(1) for more
> information. Use the -f option to force compression of multiply linked
> files.

Copyright

Copyright (C) 1987, 88, 89, 90, 91, 92, 1993 Free Software Foundation, Inc.

This program is free software; you can redistribute it and/or modify it under the terms of the GNU General Public License as published by the Free Software Foundation; either version 2, or (at your option) any later version.

This program is distributed in the hope that it will be useful, but WITHOUT ANY WARRANTY; without even the implied warranty of MERCHANTABILITY or FITNESS FOR A PARTICULAR PURPOSE. See the GNU General Public License for more details.

You should have received a copy of the GNU General Public License along with this program; if not, write to the Free Software Foundation, 59 Temple Place, Suite 330, Boston, MA 02111, USA.

Caveats

When writing compressed data to a tape, gzip generally needs to pad the output with zeros up to a block boundary. When the data is read and the whole block is passed to gunzip for decompression, gunzip detects that there is extra trailing garbage after the compressed data and emits a warning by default. You have to use the --quiet option to suppress the warning. This option can be set in the GZIP environment variable as shown in the following examples.

For sh   `GZIP="-q" tar -xfz --block-compress /dev/rst0`

For csh   `setenv GZIP -q; tar -xfz --block-compr /dev/rst0`

In the above examples, gzip is invoked implicitly by the -z option of GNU tar. Be sure to use the same block size (-b option of tar) for reading and writing compressed data on tapes. (This example assumes you are using the GNU version of tar.)

Bugs

The --list option reports incorrect sizes if they exceed 2 gigabytes. The --list option reports sizes as -1 and CRC as ffffffff if the compressed file is on a nonseekable media.

In some rare cases, the --best option provides worse compression than the default compression level (-6). On some highly redundant files, compress compresses better than gzip.

gzmore — File Filter for Viewing of Compressed Text   *New!*

Synopsis

```
/bin/gzmore [name...]
```

Description

Use the gzmore command, new in the Solaris 8 Operating Environment, as a filter that enables you to examine compressed or plain-text files one screenful at a time on a soft-copy terminal. gzmore works on files compressed with compress, pack, or gzip as well as on uncompressed files. If a file does not exist, gzmore looks for a file of the same name with the addition of a .gz, .z, or .Z suffix.

gzmore usually pauses after each screenful, printing --More-- at the bottom of the screen. When you press Return, one more line is displayed. When you press the space bar, another screenful is displayed. Other possibilities are enumerated later.

gzmore looks in the /etc/termcap file to determine terminal characteristics and to determine the default window size. On a terminal capable of displaying 24 lines, the default window size is 22 lines. To use a pager other than the default more, set environment variable PAGER to the name of the desired program, such as less.

Other sequences that you can type when gzmore pauses are shown below. *i* is an optional integer argument. The default value of *i* is 1.

! *command*	Invoke a shell with *command*. The character ! in *command* is replaced with the previous shell command. The sequence \! is replaced by !.
. (dot)	Repeat the previous command.
:q or :Q	Quit reading the current file; go on to the next (if any) (same as q or Q).
=	Display the current line number.
d	Same as ^D (Control-D).
e or q	Exit when the prompt --More-- (Next file: *file*) is printed.
i/ *expr*	Search for the *i*-th occurrence of the regular expression *expr*. If the pattern is not found, gzmore goes to the next file (if any). Otherwise, a screenful is displayed, starting two lines before the place where the expression was found. You can use your erase and kill characters to edit the regular expression. Erasing back past the first column cancels the search command.
i<space>	Display *i* more lines (or another screenful if you specify no argument).
*i*f	Skip *i* screenfuls, and print a screenful of lines.
*i*n	Search for the *i*-th occurrence of the last regular expression entered.
*i*s	Skip *i* lines, and print a screenful of lines.
*i*z	Same as typing a space except that *i*, if present, becomes the new window size. Note that the window size reverts to the default at the end of the current file.
q or Q	Quit reading the current file; go on to the next (if any).
s	When the prompt --More-- (Next file: *file*) is printed, this command skips the next file and continues.
^D	Display 11 more lines (a "scroll"). When you specify *i*, the scroll size is set to *i*.

The commands take effect immediately; that is, you do not need to press Return. Up to the time you type the command character, you can press the line kill character to cancel the numerical argument. In addition, you can press the erase character to redisplay the --More-- message.

At any time output is being sent to the terminal, you can press the quit key (normally Control-\). gzmore stops sending output and displays the usual --More-- prompt. You can then enter one of the above commands in the normal manner. Unfortunately, some output is lost when you do this because any characters waiting in the terminal's output queue are flushed when the quit signal occurs.

The terminal is set to noecho mode by gzmore so that the output can be continuous. What you type does not show on your terminal except for the / and ! commands.

If the standard output is not a teletype, gzmore acts just like zcat except that a header is printed before each file.

Files

/etc/termcap

Terminal database.

Attributes

See attributes(5) for descriptions of the following attributes.

Attribute Type	Attribute Value
Availability	SUNWgzip

See Also

gzdiff(1), gzexec(1), gzforce(1), gzgrep(1), gzip(1), gznew(1), more(1)

New! **gznew** — Recompress .Z Files to .gz Files

Synopsis

/bin/gznew [-ftv9PK] [*name*.Z...]

Description

Use the gznew command, new in the Solaris 8 Operating Environment, to recompress
files from .Z (compress) format to .gz (gzip) format. To recompress a file already in
gzip format, rename the file to force a .Z extension and then apply gznew.

Options

-9	Use the slowest compression method (optimal compression).
-f	Force recompression from .Z to .gz format even if a .gz file already exists.
-K	Keep a .Z file when it is smaller than the .gz file.
-P	Use pipes for the conversion to reduce disk space use.
-t	Test the new files before deleting originals.
-v	Display the name and percentage reduction for each file compressed.

Attributes

See attributes(5) for descriptions of the following attributes.

Attribute Type	Attribute Value
Availability	SUNWgzip

See Also

compress(1), gzdiff(1), gzexe(1), gzforce(1), gzgrep(1), gzip(1),
gzmore(1)

Bugs

gznew does not maintain the timestamp with the -P option if cpmod(1) is not available
and touch(1) does not support the -r option.

H

hash, rehash, unhash, hashstat — Evaluate the Internal Hash Table of the Contents of Directories

Synopsis

```
/usr/bin/hash [name]
/usr/bin/hash [- r]
```

sh
```
hash [- r] [name...]
```

csh
```
rehash
unhash
hashstat
```

ksh
```
hash [name...]
```

Description

Hashing is a method of indexing information by using an algorithm that generates an index of values indicating the ordered position of each item. For example, when the C shell starts, it finds all of the commands in directories specified by the path environment variable and builds an internal hash table of full path names. Then, when you execute a command, the C shell uses the hash table instead of searching directly for the path. This hashing technique is designed to improve performance. However, if you change your path or add a command to one of the directories, the C shell does not find the command unless you force it to rebuild its hash table with the rehash command.

/usr/bin/hash

The /usr/bin/hash command affects the way the current shell environment remembers the locations of commands found. Depending on the arguments specified, it adds command locations to its list of remembered locations or it purges the contents of the list. When you specify no arguments, hash reports on the contents of the list, as shown in the following example.

```
$ hash
hits    cost    command
2       3       /bin/touch
1       3       /bin/ps
0       3       /bin/grep
3       3       /bin/ls
0       3       /bin/env
$
$ hash
hits    cost    command
$
```

The hits column of output shows the number of times a command has been invoked by the shell process. The cost column of output is a measure of the work required to locate a command in the search path. If a command is found in a relative directory in the search path, after hash changes to that directory, the stored location of that command is recalculated. Commands for which this is done are indicated by an asterisk (*) adjacent to the hits information. cost is incremented when the recalculation is done.

hash does not report on shell built-in commands.

Bourne Shell

For each command *name*, the shell determines and remembers the location in the search path. When you use the -r option to the hash built-in, the shell forgets all remembered locations. If you specify no arguments, hash provides information about remembered commands.

C Shell

rehash recomputes the internal hash table of the contents of directories listed in the path environmental variable to account for new commands added.

unhash disables the internal hash table.

hashstat prints a statistics line indicating how effective the internal hash table has been at locating commands (and avoiding execs), as shown in the following example.

```
castle% hashstat
6 hits, 1 misses, 85%
castle%
```

An exec is attempted for each component of the path where the hash function indicates a possible hit and in each component that does not begin with a /.

Korn Shell

For each command *name*, the shell determines and remembers the location in the search path. If you specify no arguments, hash provides information about remembered commands.

Operands

command   The name of a command to be searched for and added to the list of
            remembered locations.

Output

When you specify no arguments, the standard output of hash is used. Its format is
unspecified but includes the path name of each command in the list of remembered
locations for the current shell environment. This list consists of those commands named
in previous hash invocations that have been invoked, and the list may contain those
invoked and found through the normal command search process.

Environment Variables

See environ(5) for descriptions of the following environment variables that affect the
execution of hash: LC_CTYPE, LC_MESSAGES, and NLSPATH.

PATH   Determine the location of command.

Exit Status

0   Successful completion.

>0   An error occurred.

Attributes

See attributes(5) for descriptions of the following attributes:

Attribute Type	Attribute Value
Availability	SUNWcsu

See Also

csh(1), ksh(1), sh(1), attributes(5), environ(5)

hashcheck, hashmake — Report Spelling Errors

Synopsis

/usr/lib/spell/hashmake
/usr/lib/spell/hashcheck *spelling-list*

Description

See spell(1).

hashstat — Evaluate the Internal Hash Table of the Contents of Directories

Synopsis

csh
```
hashstat
```

Description

See hash(1).

head — Display First Few Lines of Files

Synopsis

```
/usr/bin/head [-number | -n number] [filename...]
```

Description

The head command copies the first *number* of lines of each *filename* to the standard output. If you specify no file name, head copies lines from the standard input. The default value of *number* is 10 lines.

When you specify more than one *filename*, the start of each file displays the file name between two arrows, as shown below.

```
==> filename <==
```

The following example shows a common way to display a set of short files, identifying each one by name.

```
castle% head -9999 kookaburra1 kookaburra2
==> kookaburra1 <==
Kookaburra sits in the old gum tree
Merry merry king of the bush is he
Laugh, kookaburra, laugh, kookaburra
Gay your life must be.

Kookaburra sits in the old gum tree
Eating all the gumdrops he can see
Stop, kookaburra, stop, kookaburra
Leave some there for me.

==> kookaburra2 <==
Kookaburra sits in the old gum tree
Merry merry king of the bush is he
Laugh, kookaburra, laugh, kookaburra
Glad your life must be.

Kookaburra sits in the old gum tree
```

```
Eating all the gumdrops he can see
Stop, kookaburra, stop, kookaburra
Leave some there for me.
castle%
```

Options

-n *number*   Copy the first *number* lines of each input file to standard output.
               Specify the *number* option argument as a positive decimal integer.

-*number*   Specify the *number* of lines as a positive decimal integer with the same
               effect as the -n *number* option.

If you specify no options, head uses a default of -n 10.

Operands

file   A path name of an input file. If you specify no file operands, use the
               standard input.

Usage

See largefile(5) for the description of the behavior of head when encountering files
greater than or equal to 2 Gbytes (2**31 bytes).

Examples

The following example writes the first 10 lines of all files (except those with a leading
period) in the directory.

example% **head ***

Environment Variables

See environ(5) for descriptions of the following environment variables that affect the
execution of head: LC_CTYPE, LC_MESSAGES, and NLSPATH.

Exit Status

0   Successful completion.

>0   An error occurred.

Attributes

See attributes(5) for descriptions of the following attributes:

Attribute Type	Attribute Value
Availability	SUNWcsu
CSI	Enabled

See Also

cat(1), more(1), pg(1), tail(1), attributes(5), environ(5), largefile(5)

help, sccs-help — Ask for Help Regarding SCCS Error or Warning Messages

Synopsis

```
/usr/ccs/bin/help [argument]...
```

Description

See sccs-help(1).

---

history, fc — Process Command History List

Synopsis

sh

```
/usr/bin/fc [first[last]]
/usr/bin/fc -l [-nr] [first[last]]
/usr/bin/fc -s [old=new] [first]
```

csh

```
history [-hr] [n]
```

ksh

```
fc -e - [old=new] [command]
fc [-e editor] [-nlr] [first[last]]
```

Description

Command history creates a numbered list of the most recent commands that you have used. You can display these commands and reuse them as originally issued. You can also change a command by editing it. The syntax and arguments for history commands differ for each shell.

/usr/bin/fc

The fc command lists or edits and reexecutes commands previously entered to an interactive sh.

The command history list references commands by number. The first number in the list is chosen arbitrarily. The relationship of a number to its command does not change except when you log in and no other process is accessing the list, at which time the system may reset the numbering to start the oldest retained command at another number (usually 1). When the number reaches the value in HISTSIZE or 128 (whichever is greater), the shell may wrap the numbers, starting the next command with a lower number (usually 1). However, despite this optional wrapping of numbers, fc maintains the time-ordering sequence of the commands. For example, if four commands in sequence are given the numbers 32766, 32767, 1 (wrapped), and 2 as they are executed, command 32767 is considered the command previous to 1, even though its number is higher.

When you edit commands and you did not specify the -l option, the resulting lines are entered at the end of the history list and then reexecuted by sh. The fc editing command is not entered into the history list. If the editor returns a non-zero exit status, this status suppresses the entry into the history list and the command reexecution. Any command-line variable assignments or redirection operators used with fc affect both the fc command itself as well as the command that results. For example, the following command reinvokes the previous command, suppressing standard error for both fc and the previous command.

```
$ fc -s -- -1 2>/dev/null
$
```

C Shell
Use the history command to display the history list; if you specify the number n, display only the n most recent events.

-h   Display the history list without leading numbers. Use this option to produce files suitable for sourcing with the -h option to the csh built-in source(1) command.

-r   Reverse the order of printout to be most recent first instead of oldest first.

If you use any of the options together with n, specify the options first.

History Substitution
History substitution enables you to use words from previous command lines in the command line you are typing. This substitution simplifies spelling corrections and the repetition of complicated commands or arguments. Command lines are saved in the history list, the size of which is controlled by the history variable. You can set the history shell variable to specify the maximum number of command lines that are saved in the history file; for example, the following command enables the history list to keep track of the most recent 200 command lines.

```
castle% set history = 200
```

If the history variable is not set, the C shell saves only the most recent command.
Begin a history substitution with a ! (although you can change this character with the histchars variable). The ! can occur anywhere on the command line; history substitutions do not nest. You can escape the ! with a backslash (\) to suppress its special meaning.
Input lines containing history substitutions are echoed on the terminal after being expanded but before any other substitutions take place or the command is executed.

Event Designators
An event designator is a reference to a command-line entry in the history list.

!   Start a history substitution, except when followed by a space character, Tab, newline, =, or (.

!!   Refer to the previous command. By itself, this substitution repeats the previous command.

!n Refer to command line n.

!-n Refer to the current command line minus n.

!str Refer to the most recent command starting with str.

!?*str*?   Refer to the most recent command containing *str*.

!?*str*? *additional*

Refer to the most recent command containing *str*, and append *additional* to that referenced command.

!{*command*} *additional*

Refer to the most recent command beginning with *command*, and append *additional* to that referenced command.

^*previous-word*^*replacement*^

Repeat the previous command line, replacing the string *previous-word* with the string *replacement*. This syntax is equivalent to the history substitution !:s/*previous-word*/*replacement*/

To reexecute a specific previous command *and* make such a substitution, say, reexecuting command #6

!:6s/*previous-word*/*replacement*/

Word Designators

A colon (:) separates the event specification from the word designator. You can omit the colon if the word designator begins with a ^, $, *, -, or %. If the word is to be selected from the previous command, you can omit the second ! character from the event specification. For instance, !!:1 and !:1 both refer to the first word of the previous command, while !!$ and !$ both refer to the last word in the previous command. Word designators include:

#	The entire command line typed so far.
0	The first input word (command).
n	The *n*-th argument.
^	The first argument, that is, 1.
$	The last argument.
%	The word matched by the most recent ?*s* search.
x-y	A range of words; -*y* abbreviates 0 -*y*.
*	All the arguments, or a null value if there is just one word in the event.
*x**	Abbreviates *x*-$.
x-	Like *x** but omitting word *$*.

Modifiers

After the optional word designator, you can add a sequence of one or more of the following modifiers, each preceded by a colon (:).

h	Remove a trailing path-name component, leaving the head.
r	Remove a trailing suffix of the form .*xxx*, leaving the basename.
e	Remove all but the suffix, leaving the extension.

s/*oldchars*/replacements/

      Substitute replacements for *oldchars*. *oldchars* is a string that may contain embedded blank spaces, whereas *previous-word* in the event designator `^oldchars^replacements^` may not.

t   Remove all leading path-name components, leaving the tail.

&   Repeat the previous substitution.

g   Apply the change to the first occurrence of a match in each word by prefixing the above modifiers (for example, g&).

p   Print the new command, but do not execute it.

q   Quote the substituted words, escaping further substitutions.

x   Like q, but break into words at each space character, Tab, or newline.

Unless preceded by a g, the modification is applied only to the first string that matches *oldchars*; an error results if no string matches.

The left-hand side of substitutions are character strings, not regular expressions. You can use any character as the delimiter in place of /. A backslash escapes the delimiter character. The character & in the right-hand side is replaced by the text from the left-hand side. You can escape the & with a backslash. A null *oldchars* uses the previous string either from *oldchars* or from a contextual scan string *s* from !?s. You can omit the rightmost delimiter if a newline immediately follows replacements; similarly, you can omit the rightmost ? in a context scan.

Without an event specification, a history reference refers either to the previous command or to a previous history reference on the command line (if any).

Korn Shell

When you use the form fc -e - [*old=new*] [*command*], the *command* is reexecuted after the substitution *old=new* is performed. If you specify no command argument, the most recent command typed at this terminal is executed.

When you use the form fc [-e *editor*] [-nlr] [*first* [*last*]], a range of commands from *first* to *last* is selected from the last HISTSIZE commands that were typed at the terminal. You can specify the arguments *first* and *last* as a number or as a string. A string is used to locate the most recent command starting with the given string. A negative number is used as an offset to the current command number. If you use the -l flag, the commands are listed on standard output. Otherwise, the editor program -e *editor* is invoked on a file containing these keyboard commands. If you do not specify *editor*, then the value of the variable FCEDIT (default /bin/ed) is used as the editor. When editing is complete, the edited command(s) is executed. If you do not specify *last*, then the value is set to *first*. If you do not specify *first*, the default is the previous command for editing and -16 for listing. The -r option reverses the order of the commands, and the -n option suppresses command numbers when listed. (See ksh(1) for more information about command-line editing.)

HISTFILE   If this variable is set when the shell is invoked, then the value is the path name of the file that is used to store the command history.

HISTSIZE   If this variable is set when the shell is invoked, then the number of previously entered commands that are accessible by this shell is greater than or equal to this number. The default is 128.

Command Reentry
The text of the last HISTSIZE (default 128) commands entered from a terminal device is saved in a history file. The file $HOME/.sh_history is used if the HISTFILE variable is not set or if the file it names is not writable. A shell can access the commands of all interactive shells that use the same named HISTFILE. The special command fc is used to list or edit a portion of this file. You can select the portion of the file to be edited or listed by number or by giving the first character or characters of the command. You can specify a single command or a range of commands. If you do not specify an editor program as an argument to fc, then the value of the variable FCEDIT is used. If FCEDIT is not defined, then /bin/ed is used. The edited command(s) is printed and reexecuted on leaving the editor. The editor name - is used to skip the editing phase and to reexecute the command. In this case, you can use a substitution parameter of the form *old=new* to modify the command before execution. For example, if r is aliased to fc -e -, then **r bad=good c** reexecutes the most recent command that starts with the letter c, replacing the first occurrence of the string bad with the string good.

Using the fc built-in command within a compound command removes the whole command from the history file.

Options

-e *editor*	Use the editor named by *editor* to edit the commands. The *editor* string is a command name, subject to searching the PATH variable. The value in the FCEDIT variable is used as a default when you do not specify -e. If FCEDIT is null or unset, ed is used as the editor.
-h	Display the history list without leading numbers. Use this option to produce files suitable for sourcing with the -h option to the csh built-in source(1) command.
-l	List the commands instead of invoking an editor on them. Write the commands in the sequence indicated by the *first* and *last* operands, as affected by -r, with each command preceded by the command number.
-n	Suppress command numbers when listing with -l.
-r	Reverse the order of the commands listed (with -l) or edited.
-s	Reexecute the command without invoking an editor.

Operands

first last Choose the commands to list or edit. The number of previous commands that can be accessed is determined by the value of the HISTSIZE variable. The value of *first* or *last* or both is one of the following:

[+]number	A positive number representing a command number; you can display command numbers with the -l option.
-number	A negative decimal number representing the command that was executed *number* of commands previously. For example, -1 is the previous command.

string　　　　A string indicating the most recently entered command that begins with that string. If you do not also specify the *old=new* operand with -s, the string form of the *first* operand cannot contain an embedded equal sign.

old=new　　Replace the first occurrence of string *old* in the commands to be reexecuted by the string *new*.

When you use the synopsis form with -s:

- If you omit *first*, use the previous command. For the synopsis, forms without -s.

- If you omit *last*, *last* defaults to the previous command when -1 is specified; otherwise, it defaults to *first*.

- If you omit both *first* and *last*, list the previous 16 commands or edit the previous single command (based on the -1 option).

- If you specify both *first* and *last*, edit or list all of the commands from *first* to *last*. When editing multiple commands, the editor presents all of the commands at one time, each command starting on a new line. If *first* represents a newer command than *last*, the commands are listed or edited in reverse sequence, equivalent to using -r. For example, the following commands on the first line are equivalent to the corresponding commands on the second:

```
fc -r 10 20
fc
30 40
fc 20 10
fc -r
40 30
```

When you use a range of commands, you can specify *first* or *last* values that are not in the history list; fc substitutes the value representing the oldest or newest command in the list, as appropriate. For example, if the history list has only 10 commands, numbered 1 to 10, the following command lists and edits all 10 commands.

```
fc -l
fc 1 99
```

Output

When you use the -1 option to list commands, the format of each command in the list is as follows:

line-number command

If you specify both the -1 and -n options, the format of each command is:

`"\t%s\n"`, *command*

If the command consists of more than one line, the lines after the first are displayed as:

`"\t%s\n"`, *continued-command*

Examples

C Shell
The following C shell examples show various ways to use the history event designators.

```
castle% history
      1  cd /etc
      2  vi passwd
      3  date
      4  cd
      5  du .
      6  ls -t
      7  history
castle% !da
date
Mon Jan 18 17:53:28 WST 1999
castle% !!
date
Mon Jan 18 17:53:34 WST 1999
castle% !5
du .
262    ./SCCS
336    .
castle% !ls ma*
ls -t malloc.c
malloc.o
malloc.c
```

Korn Shell
The following example shows the various ways to use the fc event designators.

```
$ fc -l
1    cd /etc
2    vi passwd
3    date
4    cd
5    du .
6    ls -t
7    fc -l
$ fc -e - d
du .
262    ./SCCS
336    .
$ fc -e - da
date
Mon Jan 18 17:59:52 WST 1999
$ !!
ksh: !!: not found
$ alias \!='fc -e -'
$ !
alias ='fc -e -'
$ !5
ksh: !5: not found
du .
```

```
262   ./SCCS
336   .
```

```
$ ! ls ma*
malloc.o
malloc.c
$
```

Environment Variables

See environ(5) for descriptions of the following environment variables that affect the execution of fc: LC_CTYPE, LC_MESSAGES, and NLSPATH.

FCEDIT   When expanded by the shell, this variable determines the default value for the e *editor* argument. If FCEDIT is null or unset, use ed as the editor.

HISTFILE   Determine a path name naming a command history file. If the HISTFILE variable is not set, the shell may try to access or create a file .sh_history in the user's home directory. If the shell cannot obtain both read and write access to, or create, the history file, it uses an unspecified mechanism that enables the history to operate properly. (References to history file in this section are understood to mean this unspecified mechanism in such cases.) fc may choose to access this variable only when initializing the history file. This initialization occurs when fc or sh first tries to retrieve entries from, or add entries to, the file as the result of commands issued by the user, the file named by the ENV variable, or a system startup file such as /etc/profile. (The initialization process for the history file can depend on the system startup files in that they can contain commands that effectively preempt the user's settings of HISTFILE and HISTSIZE. For example, function definition commands are recorded in the history file unless you set the set -o nolog option. If the system administrator includes function definitions in some system startup file called before the ENV file, the history file is initialized before the user gets a chance to influence its characteristics.) The variable HISTFILE is accessed initially when the shell is invoked. Any changes to HISTFILE do not take effect until another shell is invoked.

HISTSIZE   Determine a decimal number representing the limit to the number of previous commands that are accessible. If this variable is unset, an unspecified default greater than or equal to 128 is used. The variable HISTSIZE is accessed initially when the shell is invoked. Any changes to HISTSIZE do not take effect until another shell is invoked.

Exit Status

0   Successful completion of the listing.

>0   An error occurred.

Otherwise, the exit status is that of the commands executed by fc.

Attributes

See attributes(5) for descriptions of the following attributes:

Attribute Type	Attribute Value
Availability	SUNWcsu

See Also

csh(1), ed(1), ksh(1), set(1), sh(1), source(1), set(1F), attributes(5), environ(5)

---

hostid — Print the Numeric Identifier of the Current Host

Synopsis

/usr/bin/hostid

Description

Use the hostid command to print the identifier of the current host in hexadecimal.

Example

The following example displays the host ID for the system castle.

```
castle% hostid
727014d0
castle%
```

Attributes

See attributes(5) for descriptions of the following attributes:

Attribute Type	Attribute Value
Availability	SUNWcsu

See Also

sysinfo(2), gethostid(3C), attributes(5)

---

hostname — Set or Print Name of Current Host System

Synopsis

/usr/bin/hostname [*name-of-host*]

Description

Use the `hostname` command to print the name of the current host, as given before the login prompt. The superuser can set the host name by giving an argument.

Example

The following example uses `hostname` with no arguments to display the host name.

```
$ hostname
castle
$
```

Attributes

See `attributes`(5) for descriptions of the following attributes:

Attribute Type	Attribute Value
Availability	SUNWcsu

See Also

`uname(1)`, `attributes(5)`

---

hp7221plot, hpplot — Graphics Filters for Various Plotters

Synopsis

`/usr/ucb/plot [-Tterminal]`

Description

See `plot(1)`.

I

iconv — Code Set Conversion Utility

Synopsis

```
/usr/bin/iconv -f fromcode -t tocode [file...]
```

Description

The iconv command converts the characters or sequences of characters in *file* from one code set to another and writes the results to standard output. Should no conversion exist for a particular character, then it is converted to the underscore (_) in the target code set.

The list of supported conversions and the locations of the associated conversion tables are provided in the iconv(5) manual page.

The iconv command can use conversion modules (/usr/lib/iconv/*.so) or conversion tables (/usr/lib/iconv/*.t). If both a conversion module and a conversion table exist for a particular code set conversion, iconv uses the conversion module.

Refer to the /usr/share/man/man5/iconv_locale.5 manual page in the Asian localized releases for information on supported code sets. For example, the following command displays the manual page describing the code set conversions that are supported for the Japanese locale.

```
% man -s 5 iconv_ja
```

Note — The iconv_locale.5 manual page may not exist in every localized release. Also, the iconv_locale.5 manual page does not exist in the U. S. (nonlocalized) release.

Options

-f *fromcode*

> Identify the input code set.

-t *tocode*   Identify the output code set.

Operands

file   A path name of the input file to be translated. If you omit *file*, use the standard input.

Examples

The following example converts the contents of file mail1 from code set 8859 to 646fr and stores the results in the file mail.local.

```
castle% iconv -f 8859 -t 646fr mail1 > mail.local
castle%
```

Environment Variables

See environ(5) for descriptions of the following environment variables that affect the execution of iconv: LC_CTYPE, LC_MESSAGES, and NLSPATH.

Exit Status

0   Successful completion.

1   An error has occurred.

Files

/usr/lib/iconv/*.so

> Conversion modules.

/usr/lib/iconv/*.t

> Conversion tables.

New! /usr/lib/iconv/geniconvtbl/binarytables/*.bt

> Conversion binary tables. New in the Solaris 8 release.

/usr/lib/iconv/iconv_data

> List of conversions supported by conversion tables.

Attributes

See attributes(5) for descriptions of the following attributes:

Attribute Type	Attribute Value
Availability	SUNWcsu

See Also

New! geniconvtbl(1), iconv(3), geniconvtbl(4), attributes(5), environ(5), iconv(5), iconv_unicode(5)

implot — Graphics Filters for Various Plotters

Synopsis

`/usr/ucb/plot [-T`*terminal*`]`

Description

See `plot`(1).

indxbib — Create an Inverted Index to a Bibliographic Database

Synopsis

`/usr/bin/indxbib` *database-file...*

Description

A bibliographic reference is a set of lines constituting fields of bibliographic information. Each field starts on a line beginning with a %, followed by a key letter, then a blank, and finally the contents of the field that may continue until the next line starting with %. A database contains bibliographic references (or other kinds of information) separated by blank lines.

`indxbib` makes an inverted index to the named *database-file* (that must reside within the current directory), typically for use by `lookbib`(1) and `refer`(1). As output, `indxbib` creates an entry file (with a `.ia` suffix), a posting file (`.ib`), and a tag file (`.ic`), in the working directory.

`indxbib` is a shell script that calls two programs: `/usr/lib/refer/mkey` and `/usr/lib/refer/inv.mkey`, truncates words to 6 characters, and maps upper case to lower case. It also discards words shorter than 3 characters, words among the 100 most common English words, and numbers (dates) < 1000 or > 2099. You can change these parameters.

Bugs

All dates should probably be indexed because many disciplines refer to literature written in the 1800s or earlier.

`indxbib` does not recognize path names.

Examples

The following example runs the `indxbib` command on a bibliographic database named `bibliography` and shows the contents of the output files.

```
castle% indxbib bibliography
castle% more bibliography.*
::::::::::::::
bibliography.ia
::::::::::::::
(((((((((((((((((((((((((((,<<<<<<<<<<<<<<<<<<<<<<<<<<<@PPPPPPPPPPP
  PPPPPPPPPPTdddddddddddd
```

```
: : : : : : : : : : : : : : :
bibliography.ib
: : : : : : : : : : : : : : :
ÿÿÿÿ(>ÿÿÿÿ(>ÿÿÿÿ(>ÿÿÿÿ(>ÿÿÿÿ(>ÿÿÿÿ(>ÿÿÿÿ(>ÿÿÿÿ(>ÿÿÿÿ(>ÿÿÿÿ(>ÿÿÿÿ(>ÿÿÿÿ(
    >ÿÿÿÿ(>ÿÿÿÿ
: : : : : : : : : : : : : : :
bibliography.ic
: : : : : : : : : : : : : : :
bibliography:0,721
bibliography:721,720
bibliography:1441,720
bibliography:2161,720
castle%
```

Files

/usr/lib/refer/mkey

> Use to map the bibliographic database.

/usr/lib/refer/inv

> Use to invert the bibliographic database.

x.ia   Entry file.

x.ib   Posting file.

x.ic   Tag file.

x.ig   Reference file.

Attributes

See attributes(5) for descriptions of the following attributes:

Attribute Type	Attribute Value
Availability	SUNWdoc

See Also

addbib(1), lookbib(1), refer(1), roffbib(1), sortbib(1), attributes(5)

install — Install Commands

Synopsis

```
/usr/sbin/install -c dira [-m mode] [-u user] [-g group] [-o] [-s] file
/usr/sbin/install -f dirb [-m mode] [-u user] [-g group] [-o] [-s] file
/usr/sbin/install -n dirc [-m mode] [-u user] [-g group] [-o] [-s] file
/usr/sbin/install -d|-i [-m mode] [-u user] [-g group] [-o] [-s] dirx...
/usr/sbin/install [-m mode] [-u user] [-g group] [-o] [-s] file
    [dirx...]
```

Description

The install command is most commonly used in makefiles (see make(1S)) to install a file in a specific location or to create directories within a file system. Each file is installed by being copied into the appropriate directory.

install uses no special privileges to copy files from one place to another. The implications of this are:

- You must have permission to read the files to be installed.
- You must have permission to copy into the destination directory.
- You must have permission to change the modes on the final copy of the file if you want to use the -m option.
- You must be superuser if you want to specify the ownership of the installed file with the -u or -g options. If you are not the superuser, the installed file is owned by you, regardless of who owns the original.

install prints messages telling you exactly what files it is replacing or creating and where they are going.

If you specify no options or directories (*dirx*...), install searches a set of default directories (/bin, /usr/bin, /etc, /lib, and /usr/lib, in that order) for a file with the same name as *file*. When it finds the first occurrence, install issues a message saying that it is overwriting that file with *file* and proceeds to do so. If the file is not found, the program states this and exits.

If you specify one or more directories (*dirx*...) after *file*, those directories are searched before the default directories.

Options

-c *dira*	Install *file* in the directory specified by *dira* if *file* does not yet exist. If it is found, issue a message saying that the file already exists and exit without overwriting it.
-d	Create a directory. Missing parent directories are created as required as in mkdir -p. If the directory already exists, set the owner, group, and mode to the values given on the command line.
-f *dirb*	Force *file* to be installed in the given directory, even if the file already exists. If the file being installed does not already exist, set the mode to 755 and the owner to bin. If the file already exists, the mode and owner are those of the already existing file.
-g *group*	Set the group ID of the new file to *group*. Only available to the superuser. Set to bin by default.
-i	Ignore default directory list, searching only through the given directories (*dirx*...).
-m *mode*	Set the mode of the new file to *mode*. Set to 0755 by default.
-n *dirc*	If *file* is not found in any of the searched directories, put it in the directory specified in *dirc*. Set the mode of the new file to 755 and the owner to bin.

-o   If *file* is found, save the found file by copying it to OLDFILE in the
            directory in which it was found. This option is useful for installing a
            frequently used file, such as /bin/sh or /lib/saf/ttymon, from which
            you cannot remove the existing file.

-s   Suppress printing of messages other than error messages.

-u *user*   Set the owner of the new file to *user*. Only available to the superuser.
            Set to bin by default.

Usage

See largefile(5) for the description of the behavior of install when encountering files
greater than or equal to 2 Gbytes (2**31 bytes).

Attributes

See attributes(5) for descriptions of the following attributes:

Attribute Type	Attribute Value
Availability	SUNWcsu

See Also

chgrp(1), chmod(1), chown(1), cp(1), mkdir(1), chown(1M), make(1S),
attributes(5), largefile(5)

Intro, intro — Introduction to Commands and Application Programs

Synopsis

This section describes, in alphabetical order, commands available with this operating
system.
    Pages of special interest are categorized as follows:

1B   Commands found only in the SunOS/BSD Compatibility Package. Refer
            to the *Source Compatibility Guide* for more information.

1C   Commands for communicating with other systems.

1F   Commands associated with Form and Menu Language Interpreter
            (FMLI).

1S   Commands specific to the SunOS system.

Note — This book does not include the FMLI commands.

Other Sections

The following other sections of the manual pages provide more information.

Section 1M   System maintenance commands.

Section 4   Information on file formats.

Section 5   Descriptions of publicly available files and miscellaneous information pages.

Section 6   Computer demonstrations.

For tutorial information about these commands and procedures, see:
Solaris Advanced User's Guide
Programming Utilities Guide

Manual Page Command Syntax

Unless otherwise noted, commands described in the Synopsis section of a manual page accept options and other arguments according to the following syntax and should be interpreted as explained below.

name [-*option*...] [*cmdarg*...]

where

[ ]	Surround an *option* or *cmdarg* that is not required.
...	Indicate multiple occurrences of the *option* or *cmdarg*.
name	Specify the name of an executable file.
{ }	Indicate interdependent options and/or arguments, so that everything enclosed is treated as a unit.
option	Always preceded by a dash (-) *noargletter*... or *argletter optarg*[,...].
noargletter	A single letter represents an option without an option-argument. Note that you can group more than one *noargletter* option after one dash (-) (Rule 5, below).
argletter	A single letter represents an option that requires an option-argument.
optarg	An option-argument (character string) that satisfies a preceding *argletter*. Note that groups of *optargs* following an *argletter* must be separated by commas or separated by a Tab or space character and quoted (Rule 8, below).
cmdarg	Specify a path name (or other command argument) not beginning with a dash (-) or - by itself, indicating the standard input.

Command Syntax Standard: Rules

These command syntax rules are not followed by all current commands, but all new commands obey them. All shell procedures should use getopts(1) to parse positional parameters and to check for legal options. getopts supports Rules 3–10 below. The enforcement of the other rules must be done by the command itself.

1. Command names (*name* above) must be between two and nine characters long.
2. Command names must include only lowercase letters and digits.

3. Option names (*option* above) must be one character long.

4. All options must be preceded by a dash (-).

5. Options with no arguments may be grouped after a single dash (-).

6. The first option-argument (*optarg* above) following an option must be preceded by a Tab or space character.

7. Option-arguments cannot be optional.

8. Groups of option-arguments following an option must either be separated by commas or separated by Tab or space character and quoted (-o xxx,z,yy or -o "xxx z yy").

9. All options must precede operands (*cmdarg* above) on the command line.

10. You can use a double dash (--) to indicate the end of the options.

11. The order of the options relative to one another should not matter.

12. The relative order of the operands (*cmdarg* above) may affect their significance in ways determined by the command.

13. Use a dash preceded and followed by a space character (-) only to mean standard input.

Attributes

See `attributes`(5) for a discussion of the attributes listed in this section.

See Also

`getopts(1)`, `wait(1)`, `exit(2)`, `wait(3B)`, `getopt(3C)`, `attributes(5)`

Diagnostics

On termination, each command returns two bytes of status, one supplied by the system and giving the cause for termination, and (in the case of "normal" termination) one supplied by the program [see `wait`(3B) and `exit`(2)]. The former byte is 0 for normal termination; the latter is customarily 0 for successful execution and non-zero to indicate troubles such as erroneous parameters, or bad or inaccessible data. It is called variously "exit code," "exit status," or "return code," and is described only when special conventions are involved. In this book, the Exit Status section for each command describes the values returned on command termination.

Warnings

Some commands produce unexpected results when processing files containing null characters. These commands often treat text input lines as strings and therefore become confused on encountering a null character (the string terminator) within a line.

List of Commands

New!

An asterisk (*) next to a command name indicates that the command is new or revised in the Solaris 7 release. New commands in the Solaris 8 and Solaris 9 releases are marked with a New icon in the margin and the release is indicated in the description. A dagger next to a command name indicates that the command is not included in this book.

`acctcom(1)`	Search and print process accounting files.
`adb(1)`*	General-purpose debugger.
`addbib(1)`	Create or extend a bibliographic database.

admin(1)	See sccs-admin(1).
aedplot(1B)	See plot(1B).
alias(1)	Create or remove a pseudonym or shorthand for a command or series of commands.
allocate(1)	Device allocation. New in the Solaris 9 release.
amt(1)	Run abstract machine test. New in the Solaris 9 release.
answerbook2(1)*	Online documentation system.
appcert(1)	Examine application-level products for unstable use of Solaris interfaces. New in the Solaris 9 release.
apptrace(1)	Trace application function calls to Solaris shared libraries. New in the Solaris 8 release.
apropos(1)	Locate commands by keyword lookup.
ar(1)	Maintain portable archive or library.
arch(1)	Display the architecture of the current host.
as(1)*	Assembler.
asa(1)	Convert FORTRAN carriage control output to printable form.
at(1)	Execute commands at a later time.
atoplot(1B)	See plot(1B).
atq(1)	Display the jobs queued to run at specified times.
atrm(1)	Remove jobs spooled by at or batch.
audioconvert(1)	Convert audio file formats.
audioplay(1)	Play audio files.
audiorecord(1)	Record an audio file.
auths(1)	Print authorizations granted to a user. New in the Solaris 8 release.
awk(1)	Pattern scanning and processing language.
banner(1)	Make posters.
basename(1)	Deliver portions of path names.
basename(1B)	Display portions of path names.
batch(1)	See at(1).
bc(1)	Arbitrary precision arithmetic language.
bdiff(1)	Big diff.
bfs(1)	Big file scanner.
bg(1)	See jobs(1).
bgplot(1B)	See plot(1B).
biff(1B)	Give notice of incoming mail messages.

break(1)		Shell built-in functions to escape from or advance within a controlling `while`, `for`, `foreach`, or `until` loop.
cal(1)		Display a calendar.
calendar(1)		Reminder service.
cancel(1)		Cancel print request.
cat(1)		Concatenate and display files.
cc(1B)		C compiler.
cd(1)		Change working directory.
cdc(1)		See sccs-cdc(1).
chdir(1)		See cd(1).
cdrw(1)		CD read and write. New in the Solaris 8 release, bundled in the Solaris 9 release.
checkeq(1)		See eqn(1).
checknr(1)		Check `nroff` and `troff` input files; report possible errors.
chgrp(1)		Change file group ownership.
chkey(1) *		Change user's secure RPC key pair.
chmod(1)		Change the permissions mode of a file.
chown(1) *		Change file ownership.
chown(1B)		Change owner.
ckdate(1) †		Prompt for and validate a date.
ckgid(1) †		Prompt for and validate a group ID.
ckint(1) †		Display a prompt; verify and return an integer value.
ckitem(1) †		Build a menu; prompt for and return a menu item.
ckkeywd(1) †		Prompt for and validate a keyword.
ckpath(1) †		Display a prompt; verify and return a path name.
ckrange(1) †		Prompt for and validate an integer.
ckstr(1) †		Display a prompt; verify and return a string answer.
cksum(1)		Write file checksums and sizes.
cktime(1) †		Display a prompt; verify and return a time of day.
ckuid(1) †		Prompt for and validate a user ID.
ckyorn(1) †		Prompt for and validate yes/no.
clear(1)		Clear the terminal screen.
cmp(1)		Compare two files.
cocheck(1F) †		See coproc(1F).
cocreate(1F) †		See coproc(1F).
codestroy(1F) †		See coproc(1F).

New!

col(1)	Reverse linefeeds filter.
comb(1)	See sccs-comb(1).
comm(1)	Select or reject lines common to two files.
command(1)	Execute a simple command.
compress(1)	Compress, uncompress files or display expanded files.
continue(1)	See break(1).
coproc(1F) †	Communicate with a process.
coreceive(1F) †	See coproc(1F).
cosend(1F) †	See coproc(1F).
cp(1)	Copy files.
cpio(1)	Copy file archives in and out.
cpp(1) *	The C-language preprocessor.
cputrack(1)	Monitor process and LPW behavior with CPU performance counters. New in the Solaris 8 release. *New!*
crle(1)	Configure runtime linking environment. New in the Solaris 8 release. *New!*
crontab(1)	Edit or display user crontab file.
crtplot(1B)	See plot(1B).
crypt(1)	Encrypt or decrypt a file.
csh(1)	Shell command interpreter with a C-like syntax.
csplit(1)	Split files based on context.
ct(1C)	Spawn login to a remote terminal.
ctags(1)	Create a tags file for use with ex and vi.
cu(1C)	Call another UNIX system.
cut(1)	Cut out selected fields of each line of a file.
date(1)	Write the date and time.
dc(1)	Desk calculator.
deallocate(1)	Device deallocation. New in the Solaris 9 release. *New!*
delta(1)	See sccs-delta(1).
deroff(1)	Remove nroff/troff, tbl, and eqn constructs.
df(1B)	Display status of disk space on file systems.
dhcpinfo(1)	Display value of parameters received through DHCP.
diff(1)	Display line-by-line differences between pairs of text files.
diff3(1)	Three-way differential file comparison.
diffmk(1)	Mark differences between versions of a troff input file.
digestp(1)	See mailp(1). *New!*

`dircmp(1)`	Directory comparison.
`dirname(1)`	See `basename`(**1**).
`dirs(1)`	See `cd`(**1**).
`dis(1)*`	Object code disassembler.
`disable(1)`	See `enable`(**1**).
`dispgid(1)`	Display a list of all valid group names.
`dispuid(1)`	Display a list of all valid user names.
`dos2unix(1)`	Convert text file from DOS format to ISO format.
`download(1)`	Host-resident PostScript font downloader.
`dpost(1)`	`troff` postprocessor for PostScript printers.
`du(1B)`	Display the number of disk blocks used per directory or file.
`dumbplot(1B)`	See `plot`(**1B**).
`dump(1)`	Dump selected parts of an object file.
`dumpcs(1)`	Show codeset table for the current locale.
`dumpkeys(1)`	Dump keyboard translation tables.
`echo(1)`	Echo arguments.
`echo(1B)`	Echo arguments to standard output.
`echo(1F)`†	Put string on virtual output.
`ed(1)`	Text editor.
`edit(1)`	Text editor (variant of `ex` for casual users).
`egrep(1)`	Search a file for a pattern, using full regular expressions.
`eject(1)`	Eject media such as CD-ROM and diskette from drive.
`elfdump(1)*`	Dump selected parts of an object file.
`enable(1)`	Enable/disable LP printers.
`env(1)`	Set environment for command invocation.
`eqn(1)`	Typeset mathematics test.
`errange(1)`†	See `ckrange`(**1**).
`errdate(1)`†	See `ckdate`(**1**).
`errgid(1)`†	See `ckgid`(**1**).
`errint(1)`†	See `ckint`(**1**).
`erritem(1)`†	See `ckitem`(**1**).
`error(1)`†	Insert compiler error messages at right source lines.
`errpath(1)`†	See `ckpath`(**1**).
`errstr(1)`†	See `ckstr`(**1**).
`errtime(1)`†	See `cktime`(**1**).
`erruid(1)`†	See `ckuid`(**1**).

erryorn(1)†	See ckyorn(1).
eval(1)	See exec(1).
ex(1)	Text editor.
exec(1)	Shell built-in functions to execute other commands.
exit(1)	Shell built-in functions to enable the execution of the shell to advance beyond its sequence of steps.
expand(1)	Expand Tab characters to space characters, and vice versa.
export(1)	See set(1).
exportfs(1B)	Translate exportfs options to share/unshare commands.
expr(1)	Evaluate arguments as an expression.
expr(1B)	Evaluate arguments as a logical, arithmetic, or string expression.
exstr(1)	Extract strings from source files.
face(1)†	Executable for the Framed Access Command Environment Interface.
factor(1)	Obtain the prime factors of a number.
false(1)	See true(1).
fastboot(1B)	Reboot or halt the system without checking the disks.
fasthalt(1B)	See fastboot(1B).
fc(1)	See history(1).
fdformat(1)*	Format diskette or PCMCIA memory card.
fg(1)	See jobs(1).
fgrep(1)	Search a file for a fixed character string.
file(1)	Determine file type.
file(1B)	Determine the type of a file by examining its contents.
filep(1)	See mailp(1).
filesync(1)*	Synchronize ordinary, directory, or special files.
filofaxp(1)	See mailp(1).
find(1)*	Find files.
finger(1)	Display information about local and remote users.
fmlcut(1F)†	Cut out selected fields of each line of a file.
fmlexpr(1F)†	Evaluate arguments as an expression.
fmlgrep(1F)†	Search a file for a pattern.
fmli(1)†	Invoke the Form and Menu Language Interpreter.
fmt(1)	Simple text formatters.
fmtmsg(1)	Display a message on stderr or system console.

	fnattr(1)	Update and examine attributes associated with a Federated Naming Service (FNS) named object.
	fnbind(1)	Bind a reference to an FNS name.
	fnlist(1)	Display the names and references bound in an FNS context.
	fnlookup(1)	Display the reference bound to an FNS name.
	fnrename(1)	Rename the binding of an FNS name.
	fnsearch(1)	Search for FNS objects with specified attributes.
	fnunbind(1)	Unbind the reference from an FNS name.
	fold(1)	Filter for folding lines.
New!	franklinp(1)	See mailp(1).
	from(1B)	Display the sender and date of newly arrived mail messages.
	ftp(1)	File transfer program.
New!	ftpcount(1)	Show current number of users in each FTP server class. New in the Solaris 9 release.
New!	ftpwho(1)	Show current process information for each FTP server user. New in the Solaris 9 release.
	function(1)	Shell built-in command to define a function that is usable within this shell.
	gcore(1)*	Get core images of running processes.
	gencat(1)	Generate a formatted message catalog.
New!	geniconvtbl(1)	Generate iconv code conversion tables. New in the Solaris 8 release.
New!	genlayouttbl(1)	Generate layout table for complex text layout. New in the Solaris 9 release.
	genmsg(1)	Generate a message source file by extracting messages from source files.
	get(1)*	See sccs-get(1).
	getconf(1)*	Get configuration values.
	getfacl(1)	Display discretionary file information.
	getfrm(1F)†	Return the current frame ID number.
	getitems(1F)†	Return a list of currently marked menu items.
	getopt(1)	Parse command options.
	getoptcvt(1)	Convert to getopts to parse command options.
	getopts(1)	Parse command options.
	gettext(1)	Retrieve a text string from message database.
	gettxt(1)	Retrieve a text string from a message database.
	gigiplot(1B)	See plot(1B).

glob(1)	Shell built-in function to expand a word list.
goto(1)	See exit(1).
gprof(1)*	Display call-graph profile data.
graph(1)	Draw a graph.
grep(1)	Search a file for a pattern.
groups(1)	Print group membership of user.
groups(1B)	Display a user's group memberships.
grpck(1B)	Check group database entries.
gunzip(1)	Compress or expand files. New in the Solaris 8 release.
gzcat(1)	Compress or expand files. New in the Solaris 8 release.
gzcomp(1)	Compare compressed files. New in the Solaris 8 release.
gzdiff(1)	Compare compressed files. New in the Solaris 8 release.
gzexec(1)	Compare compressed files. New in the Solaris 8 release.
gzexec(1)	Compress executable files in place. New in the Solaris 8 release.
gzforce(1)	Force a .gz extension on all gzip files. New in the Solaris 8 release.
gzip(1)	Compress or expand files. New in the Solaris 8 release.
gzmore(1)	File filter for viewing of compressed text. New in the Solaris 8 release.
gznew(1)	Recompress .Z files to .gz files. New in the Solaris 8 release.
hash(1)	Evaluate the internal hash table of the contents of directories.
hashcheck(1)	See spell(1).
hashmake(1)	See spell(1).
hashstat(1)	See hash(1).
head(1)	Display first few lines of files.
help(1)*	See sccs-help(1).
helpdate(1)†	See ckdate(1).
helpgid(1)†	See ckgid(1).
helpint(1)†	See ckint(1).
helpitem(1)†	See ckitem(1).
helppath(1)†	See ckpath(1).
helprange(1)†	See ckrange(1).
helpstr(1)†	See ckstr(1).
helptime(1)†	See cktime(1).
helpuid(1)†	See ckuid(1).
helpyorn(1)†	See ckyorn(1).

history(1)	Process command history list.
hostid(1)	Print the numeric identifier of the current host.
hostname(1)	Set or print name of current host system.
hp7221plot(1B)	See plot(1B).
hpplot(1B)	See plot(1B).
iconv(1)	Convert code set.
implot(1B)	See plot(1B).
indicator(1F) †	Display application-specific alarms and/or the "working" indicator.
indxbib(1)	Create an inverted index to a bibliographic database.
install(1B)	Install files.
Intro(1) *	Introduction to commands and application programs,
ipcrm(1)	Remove a message queue, semaphore set, or shared memory ID.
ipcs(1) *	Report interprocess communication facilities status.
isainfo(1) *	Describe instruction set architecture.
isalist(1)	Display the native instruction sets executable on this platform.
jobs(1)	Control process execution.
join(1)	Relational database operator.
jsh(1)	See sh(1).
kbd(1)	Manipulate the state of keyboard or display the type of keyboard or change the default keyboard abort sequence effect.
kdestroy(1)	Destroy Kerberos tickets.
keylogin(1) *	Decrypt and store secret key with keyserv.
keylogout(1)	Delete stored secret key with keyserv.
kill(1)	Terminate or signal processes.
kinit(1)	Kerberos login command.
klist(1)	List currently held Kerberos tickets.
New! kpasswd(1)	Change a user's Kerberos password. New in the Solaris 8 release.
ksh(1) *	Korn shell, a standard/restricted command and programming language.
New! ktutil(1)	Kerberos keytab maintenance command. New in the Solaris 8 release.
last(1)	Display login and logout information about users and terminals.
lastcomm(1)	Display the last commands executed, in reverse order.
ld(1) *	Link editor for object files.
ld(1B)	Link editor, dynamic link-editor.

ldap(1)	LDAP as a naming repository. New in the Solaris 8 release. _New!_
ldapadd(1)*	See ldapmodify(1).
ldapdelete(1)*	Delete entry tool for ldap.
ldaplist(1)	Search and list naming information from an LDAP directory _New!_ service. New in the Solaris 8 release.
ldapmodify(1)*	Addition and modification tool for ldap.
ldapmodrdn(1)*	Modify entry RDN tool for ldap.
ldapsearch(1)*	Search tool for ldap.
ldd(1)	List dynamic dependencies of executable files or shared objects.
ld.so.1(1)*	Runtime linker for dynamic objects.
let(1)	Shell built-in function to evaluate one or more arithmetic expressions.
lex(1)	Generate programs for lexical tasks.
limit(1)*	Set or get limitations on the system resources available to the current shell and its descendants.
line(1)	Read one line.
lint(1B)	Verify C programs.
list_devices(1)	List allocatable devices. New in the Solaris 9 release. _New!_
listusers(1)	List user login information.
llc2_autoconfig(1)	_New!_
	Generate LLC2 configuration files. New in the Solaris 8 release.
llc2_config(1)	Configure LLC2 interface parameters. New in the Solaris 8 _New!_ release.
llc2_stats(1)	LLC2 station, SAP, and connection statistics. New in the Solaris _New!_ 8 release.
ln(1)	Make hard or symbolic links to files.
ln(1B)	Make hard or symbolic links to files.
loadkeys(1)	Dump keyboard translation tables.
locale(1)	Get locale-specific information.
localedef(1)*	Define locale environment.
logger(1)	Add entries to the system log.
logger(1B)	Add entries to the system log.
login(1)*	Sign on to the system.
logname(1)	Return user's login name.
logout(1)	Shell built-in function to exit from a login session.
longline(1F)†	See readfile(1F).
look(1)	Find words in the system dictionary or lines in a sorted list.

	lookbib(1)	Find references in a bibliographic database.
	lorder(1)	Find ordering relation for an object or library archive.
	lp(1)*	Submit print request.
	lpc(1B)	Line printer control program.
	lpq(1B)	Display the content of a print queue.
	lpr(1B)	Submit print requests.
	lprm(1B)	Remove print requests from the print queue.
	lpstat(1)	Print information about the status of the print service.
	lptest(1B)	Generate line printer ripple pattern.
	ls(1)	List contents of a directory.
	ls(1B)	List contents of a directory.
	m4(1)	Macro processor.
	mach(1)	Display the processor type of the current host.
	machid(1)	Get processor type truth value.
	mail(1)	Read mail or send mail to users.
	Mail(1)	See mailx(**1**).
	mail(1B)	See mailx(**1**).
	mailcompat(1)	Provide SunOS compatibility for Solaris mailbox format.
New!	mailp(1)	Front ends to the mp text to PDL pretty print filter. New in the Solaris 8 release.
	mailq(1)*	Print the mail queue.
	mailstats(1)*	Print statistics collected by sendmail.
	mailx(1)	Interactive message processing system.
	make(1)	Maintain, update, and regenerate related programs and files.
	man(1)	Find and display reference manual pages.
	mconnect(1)	Connect to SMTP mail server socket.
	mcs(1)	Manipulate the comment section of an object file.
New!	mdb(1)	Modular debugger. New in the Solaris 8 release.
	mesg(1)	Permit or deny messages.
	message(1F) †	Put arguments on the Form and Menu Language Interpreter message line.
New!	mixerctl(1)	Audio mixer control command-line application. New in the Solaris 8 release.
	mkdir(1)	Make directories.
	mkmsgs(1)	Create message files for use by gettxt.
	mkstr(1B)	Create an error message file by massaging C source files.

more(1)	Browse or page through a text file.
mp(1)	Text to PDL pretty print filter. New in the Solaris 8 release. *New!*
mpss.so.1(1)	Shared object for setting preferred page size. New in the Solaris 9 release.
msgfmt(1)	Create a message object from a message file.
mt(1)	Control magnetic tapes.
mv(1)*	Move files.
nawk(1)	Pattern scanning and processing language.
nca(1)	The Solaris network cache and accelerator (NCA). New in the *New!* Solaris 8 release.
ncab2clf(1)	Convert binary log file to common log file format. New in the *New!* Solaris 8 release.
ncakmod(1)	Start or stop the NCA kernel module. New in the Solaris 8 *New!* release.
neqn(1)	See eqn(1).
nctscape(1)	Start Netscape Communicator for Solaris. New in the Solaris 8 *New!* release.
newaliases(1)*	Rebuild the database for the mail aliases file.
newform(1)	Change the format of a text file.
newgrp(1)	Log in to a new group.
news(1)	Print news items.
newsp(1)	See mailp(1). *New!*
newtask(1)	Create new task. New in the Solaris 9 release. *New!*
nice(1)	Invoke a command with an altered scheduling priority.
nis+(1)*	A new version of the Network Information Name Service.
nis(1)	See nis+(1).
niscat(1)	Display NIS+ tables and objects.
nischgrp(1)	Change the group owner of an NIS+ object.
nischmod(1)	Change access rights on an NIS+ object.
nischown(1)	Change the owner of an NIS+ object.
nischttl(1)	Change the time-to-live value of an NIS+ object.
nisdefaults(1)	Display NIS+ default values.
niserror(1)	Display NIS+ error messages.
nisgrep(1)*	See nismatch(1).
nisgrpadm(1)*	NIS+ group administration command.
nisln(1)	Symbolically link NIS+ objects.
nisls(1)	List the contents of an NIS+ directory.

	`nismatch(1)*`	Command for searching NIS+ tables.
	`nismkdir(1)`	Create NIS+ directories.
New!	`nisopaccess(1)`	NIS+ operation access control administration command. New in the Solaris 8 release.
	`nispasswd(1)*`	Change NIS+ password information.
	`nisrm(1)`	Remove NIS+ objects from the namespace.
	`nisrmdir(1)`	Remove NIS+ directories.
	`nistbladm(1)`	Administer NIS+ tables.
	`nistest(1)*`	Return the state of the NIS+ namespace, using a conditional expression.
	`nl(1)`	Filter line numbers.
	`nm(1)`	Print name list of an object file.
	`nohup(1)`	Run a command immune to hangups.
	`notify(1)`	See `jobs(1)`.
	`nroff(1)*`	Format documents for display or line printer.
	`od(1)`	Octal dump.
	`on(1)`	Execute a command on a remote system, but with the local environment.
	`onintr(1)`	See `trap(1)`.
	`optisa(1)`	Determine which variant instruction set is optimal to use.
	`pack(1)`	Compress and expand files.
	`page(1)`	See `more(1)`.
	`pagesize(1)`	Display the size of a page of memory.
	`passwd(1)`	Change login password and password attributes.
	`paste(1)`	Merge corresponding or subsequent lines of files.
	`patch(1)`	Apply changes to files.
	`pathchk(1)`	Check path names.
	`pathconv(1F)†`	Search Form and Menu Language Interpreter criteria for file name.
	`pax(1)`	Portable archive interchange.
	`pargs(1)`	See `proc(1)`.
	`pcat(1)`	See `pack(1)`.
	`pcred(1)*`	See `proc(1)`.
	`pdp11(1)`	See `machid(1)`.
New!	`perl(1)`	Practical extraction and report language. New in the Solaris 8 release.
New!	`pfcsh(1)`	Execute a command in a profile. New in the Solaris 8 release.

pfexec(1)	Execute a command in a profile. New in the Solaris 8 release. *New!*
pfiles(1)*	See proc(1).
pfksh(1)	Execute a command in a profile. New in the Solaris 8 release. *New!*
pflags(1)*	See proc(1).
pfsh(1)	Execute a command in a profile. New in the Solaris 8 release. *New!*
pg(1)	Files perusal filter for CRTs.
pgrep(1)*	Find or signal processes by name and other attributes.
pkginfo(1)	Display software package information.
pkgmk(1)	Produce an installable package.
pkgparam(1)	Display package parameter values.
pkgproto(1)	Generate prototype file entries for input to pkgmk command.
pkgtrans(1)	Translate package format.
pkill(1)*	See pgrep(1)
pldd(1)*	See proc(1).
plimit(1)	Get or set the resource limits of running processes.
plot(1B)	Graphics filters for various plotters.
plottoa(1B)	See plot(1B).
pmap(1)*	See proc(1).
popd(1)	See cd(1).
postdaisy(1)	PostScript translator for Diablo 630 daisy-wheel files.
postdmd(1)	PostScript translator for DMD bitmap files.
postio(1)	Serial interface for PostScript printers.
postmd(1)	Matrix display program for PostScript printers.
postplot(1)	PostScript translator for plot(4) graphics files.
postprint(1)	PostScript translator for text files.
postreverse(1)	Reverse the page order in a PostScript file.
posttek(1)	PostScript translator for Tektronix 4014 files.
ppgsz(1)	Set preferred stack and/or heap page size. New in the Solaris 9 release. *New!*
pr(1)	Print files.
praliases(1)	Display system mail aliases. New in the Solaris 8 release. *New!*
prctl(1)	Get or set the resource controls of running processes, tasks, and projects. New in the Solaris 9 release. *New!*
preap(1)	Force a defunct process to be reaped by its parent. New in the Solaris 9 release. *New!*
prex(1)*	Control tracing in a process or the kernel.

	print(1)	Shell built-in function to output characters to the screen or window.
	printenv(1B)	Display environment variables currently set.
	printf(1)	Write formatted output.
	priocntl(1)	Display or set scheduling parameters of specified process(es).
	proc(1)*	proc tools.
	prof(1)*	Display profile data.
New!	profiles(1)	Print execution profiles for a user. New in the Solaris 8 release.
New!	projects(1)	Print project membership of user. New in the Solaris 9 release.
	prs(1)*	See sccs-prs(1).
	prt(1)	See sccs-prt(1).
	prun(1)*	See proc(1).
	ps(1)*	Report process status.
	ps(1B)	Display the status of current processes.
	psig(1)*	See proc(1).
	pstack(1)*	See proc(1).
	pstop(1)*	See proc(1).
	ptime(1)*	See proc(1).
	ptree(1)*	See proc(1).
	pushd(1)	See cd(1).
	pvs(1)	Display the internal version information of dynamic objects.
	pwait(1)*	See proc(1).
	pwd(1)	Return working directory name.
	pwdx(1)*	See proc(1).
	ranlib(1)	Convert archives to random libraries.
	rcp(1)	Remote file copy.
	rdist(1)	Remote file distribution program.
	read(1)	Read a line from standard input.
	readfile(1F)†	Read file; get longest line.
	readonly(1)	Shell built-in function to protect the value of the given variable from reassignment.
	red(1)	See ed(1).
	refer(1)	Expand and insert references from a bibliographic database.
	regcmp(1)	Regular expression compile.
	regex(1F)†	Match patterns against a string.
	rehash(1)	See hash(1).

reinit(1F)†	Run an initialization file.
remote_shell(1)	See rsh(1).
remsh(1)	See rsh(1).
renice(1)	Alter priority of running processes.
reset(1B)	See tset(1B).
reset(1F)†	Reset the current form field to its default values.
return(1)	See exit(1).
rksh(1)*	See ksh(1).
rlogin(1)	Remote login.
rm(1)	Remove directory entries.
rmail(1)	See mail(1).
rmdel(1)	See sccs-rmdel(1).
rmdir(1)	See rm(1).
rmformat(1)	Removable rewritable media format command. New in the Solaris 9 release.
roffbib(1)	Format and print a bibliographic database.
roles(1)	Print roles granted to a user. New in the Solaris 8 release.
rpcgen(1)	An RPC protocol compiler.
rpm2cpio(1)	Convert Red Hat Package (RPM) to cpio archive. New in the Solaris 9 release.
rsh(1)	Remote shell.
run(1F)†	Run an executable.
runat(1)	Execute command in extended attribute name space. New in the Solaris 9 release.
rup(1)	Show host status of remote machines (RPC version).
rup(1C)	Show host status of remote machines (RPC version).
ruptime(1)	Show host status of local machines.
rusage(1B)	Print resource usage for a command.
rusers(1)	Report who is logged in on remote machines.
rwho(1)	Report who is logged in on local machines.
sact(1)	See sccs-sact(1).
sag(1)*	Graph system activity.
sar(1)	System activity reporter.
sccs(1)*	Front end for the Source Code Control System (SCCS).
sccs-admin(1)	Create and administer SCCS history files.
sccs-cdc(1)	Change the delta commentary of an SCCS delta.

	`sccs-comb(1)`	Combine SCCS deltas.
	`sccs-delta(1)`	Make a delta to an SCCS file.
	`sccsdiff(1)`	See `sccs-sccsdiff(1)`.
	`sccs-get(1)*`	Retrieve a version of an SCCS file.
	`sccs-help(1)*`	Ask for help regarding SCCS error or warning messages.
	`sccs-prs(1)*`	Display selected portions of an SCCS history.
	`sccs-prt(1)`	Display delta table information from an SCCS file.
	`sccs-rmdel(1)`	Remove a delta from an SCCS file.
	`sccs-sact(1)*`	Show editing activity status of an SCCS file.
	`sccs-sccsdiff(1)`	Compare two versions of an SCCS file.
	`sccs-unget(1)`	Undo a previous get of an SCCS file.
	`sccs-val(1)`	Validate an SCCS file.
New!	`snca (1)`	The Solaris network cache and accelerator (NCA). New in the Solaris 8 release.
New!	`scp(1)`	Secure copy (remote file copy program). New in the Solaris 9 release.
	`script(1)`	Make record of a terminal session.
	`sdiff(1)`	Print differences between two files side-by-side.
	`sed(1)*`	Stream editor.
	`sed(1B)`	Stream editor.
	`set(1)`	Shell built-in functions to determine the characteristics for environmental variables of the current shell and its descendants.
	`set(1F)†`	Set and unset local or global environment variables.
	`setcolor(1F)†`	Redefine or create a color.
	`setenv(1)`	See `set(1)`.
	`setfacl(1)*`	Modify the Access Control List (ACL) for a file or files.
New!	`setpgrp(1)`	Set process group ID. New in the Solaris 9 release.
	`settime(1)*`	See `touch(1)`.
New!	`sftp(1)`	Secure file transfer program. New in the Solaris 9 release.
	`sh(1)`	Standard and job control shell and command interpreter.
	`shell(1F)†`	Run a command, using shell.
	`shell_builtins(1)`	Shell command interpreter built-in functions.
	`shift(1)`	Shell built-in function to traverse either a shell's argument list or a list of field-separated words.
	`shutdown(1B)`	Close down the system at a given time.
	`size(1)`	Print section sizes in bytes of object files.

sleep(1)	Suspend execution for an interval.
soelim(1)	Resolve and eliminate .so requests from nroff or troff input.
solregis(1)	Solaris user registration.
sort(1)	Sort, merge, or sequence-check text files.
sortbib(1)	Sort a bibliographic database.
sotruss(1)	Trace shared library procedure calls.
source(1)	See exec(**1**).
sparc(1)	See machid(**1**).
spell(1)	Report spelling errors.
spellin(1)	See spell(**1**).
spline(1)	Interpolate smooth curve.
split(1)	Split a file into pieces.
srchtxt(1)	Display contents of, or search for a text string in, message databases.
ssh(1)	Open SSH secure shell client (remote login program). New in the Solaris 9 release.
ssh-add(1)	Add RSA or DSA identities for the authentication agent. New in the Solaris 9 release.
ssh-agent(1)	Authentication agent. New in the Solaris 9 release.
ssh-http-proxy-connect(1)	
	Secure shell proxy for HTTP. New in the Solaris 9 release.
ssh-keygen(1)	Authentication key generation. New in the Solaris 9 release.
ssh-socks5-proxy-connect(1)	
	Secure shell proxy for SOCKS5. New in the Solaris 9 release.
stop(1)	See jobs(**1**).
strchg(1)	Change or query stream configuration.
strconf(1)	See strchg(**1**).
strings(1)	Find printable strings in an object or binary file.
strip(1)	Strip symbol table, debugging, and line number information from an object file.
stty(1)	Set the options for a terminal.
stty(1B)	Set the options for a terminal.
sum(1)	Print checksum and block count for a file.
sum(1B)	Calculate a checksum for a file.
sun(1)	See machid(**1**).
symorder(1)	Rearrange a list of symbols.
sysV-make(1) *	Maintain, update, and regenerate groups of programs.

t300(1)	See tplot(1).
t300(1B)	See plot(1B).
t300s(1)	See tplot(1).
t300s(1B)	See plot(1B).
t4013(1B)	See plot(1B).
t4014(1)	See tplot(1).
t450(1)	See tplot(1).
t450(1B)	See plot(1B).
tabs(1)	Set Tabs on a terminal.
tail(1)	Deliver the last part of a file.
talk(1)	Talk to another user.
tar(1)*	Create tape archives and add or extract files.
tbl(1)	Format tables for nroff or troff.
tcopy(1)	Copy a magnetic tape.
tee(1)	Replicate the standard output.
tek(1)	See tplot(1).
tek(1B)	See plot(1B).
telnet(1)*	User interface to a remote system, using the TELNET protocol.
test(1)	Test for conditions.
test(1B)	Condition evaluation command.
test(1F)†	Condition evaluation command.
tftp(1)	Trivial file transfer program.
time(1)	Time a simple command.
timemanp(1)	See mailp(1).
times(1)	Shell built-in function to report time usages of the current shell.
timesysp(1)	See mailp(1).
timex(1)	Time a command; report process data and system activity.
tip(1)	Connect to remote system.
tnfdump(1)	Convert binary Trace Normal Form file to ASCII.
tnfxtract(1)	Extract kernel probes output into a trace file.
touch(1)*	Change file access and modification times.
touch(1B)	Change file access and modification times.
tplot(1)	Graphics filters for various plotters.
tput(1)	Initialize a terminal or query terminfo database.
tr(1)	Translate characters.
tr(1B)	Translate characters.

New! (timemanp(1) row)

New! (timesysp(1) row)

trap(1)	Shell built-in functions to respond to hardware signals.
troff(1)*	Typeset or format documents.
true(1)	Provide truth values.
truss(1)*	Trace system calls and signals.
tset(1B)	Establish or restore terminal characteristics.
tsort(1)	Topological sort.
tty(1)	Return user's terminal name.
type(1)	Write a description of command type.
typeset(1)	Shell built-in functions to set/get attributes and values for shell variables and functions.
u370(1)	See machid(**1**).
u3b(1)	See machid(**1**).
u3b15(1)	See machid(**1**).
u3b2(1)	See machid(**1**).
u3b5(1)	See machid(**1**).
ucblinks(1B)	Add /dev entries to give SunOS 4.x compatible names to SunOS 5.x devices.
ul(1)	Underline text.
ulimit(1)*	See limit(**1**).
umask(1)	Get or set the file-mode creation mask.
unalias(1)	See alias(**1**).
uname(1)	Print name of current system.
uncompress(1)	See compress(**1**).
unexpand(1)	See expand(**1**).
unget(1)	See sccs-unget(**1**).
unhash(1)	See hash(**1**).
unifdef(1)	Resolve and remove ifdef'ed lines from C program source.
uniq(1)	Report or filter out repeated lines in a file.
units(1)	Convert quantities expressed in standard scales to other scales.
unix2dos(1)	Convert text file from ISO format to DOS format.
unlimit(1)*	See limit(**1**).
uname(1)	Print name of current system.
unpack(1)	See pack(**1**).
unset(1)	See set(**1**).
unset(1F)†	See set(**1F**).
unsetenv(1)	See set(**1**).

unzip(1)	List, test, and extract compressed files from a ZIP archive.
uptime(1)	Show how long the system has been up.
users(1B)	Display a compact list of users logged in.
uucp(1C)	UNIX-to-UNIX system copy.
uudecode(1C)	See uuencode(1C).
uuencode(1C)	Encode a binary file, or decode its encoded representation.
uuglist(1C)	Print the list of service grades that are available on this UNIX system.
uulog(1C)	See uucp(1C).
uuname(1C)	See uucp(1C).
uupick(1C)	See uuto(1C).
uustat(1C)	UUCP status inquiry and job control.
uuto(1C)	Public UNIX-to-UNIX system file copy.
uux(1C)	UNIX-to-UNIX system command execution.
vacation(1)	Reply to mail automatically.
val(1)	See sccs-val(1).
vax(1)	See machid(1).
vc(1)	Version control.
vedit(1) *	See vi(1).
ver(1)	See tplot(1).
vgrind(1) *	Format program listings.
vi(1) *	Screen-oriented (visual) display editor based on ex.
view(1) *	See vi(1).
vipw(1B)	Edit the password file.
volcancel(1)	Cancel user's request for removable media that is not currently in drive.
volcheck(1)	Check for media in a drive, and, by default, check all floppy media.
volmissing(1)	Notify user that volume requested is not in the CD-ROM or diskette drive.
volrmmount(1)	Call rmmount to mount or unmount media.
vplot(1B)	See plot(1B).
vsig(1F) †	Synchronize a coprocess with the controlling Form and Menu Language Interpreter application.
w(1)	Display information about currently logged-in users.
wait(1) *	Await process completion.
wc(1)	Display a count of lines, words, and characters in a file.

what(1)	Extract SCCS version information from a file.
whatis(1)	Display a one-line summary about a keyword.
whence(1)	See typeset(1).
whereis(1B)	Locate the binary, source, and manual page files for a command.
which(1)	Locate a command; display its path name or alias.
who(1)	Report who is on the system.
whoami(1B)	Display the effective current user name.
whocalls(1)	Report on the calls to a specific procedure.
whois(1)	Internet user name directory service.
write(1)	Write to another user.
xargs(1)	Construct argument lists and invoke command.
xgettext(1)	Extract gettext call strings from C programs.
xstr(1)	Extract strings from C programs to implement shared strings.
yacc(1)	Yet another compiler-compiler.
yes(1)	Generate repetitive affirmative output. New in the Solaris 9 release.
ypcat(1)	Print values in an NIS database.
ypmatch(1)	Print the value of one or more keys from an NIS map.
yppasswd(1)	Change your network password in the NIS database.
ypwhich(1)	Return name of NIS server or map master.
zcat(1)	See compress(1).
zip(1)	Package and compress (archive) files. New in the Solaris 9 release.
zipcloak(1)	See zip(1).
zipinfo(1)	List detailed information about a ZIP archive.
zipnote(1)	See zip(1).
zipsplit(1)	See zip(1).

ipcrm — Remove a Message Queue, Semaphor Set, or Shared Memory ID

Synopsis

```
/usr/bin/ipcrm [-m shmid] [-q msqid] [-s semid] [-M shmkey] [-Q msgkey]
    [-S semkey]
```

Description

ipcrm removes one or more messages, semaphores, or shared memory identifiers.
If you specify either the -C or -N flag, the real and effective UID/GID is set to the real UID/GID of the user invoking ipcs.

Options

-m *shmid*   Remove the shared memory identifier *shmid* from the system. Destroy the shared memory segment and data structure associated with it after the last detach.

-q *msqid*   Remove the message queue identifier *msqid* from the system, and destroy the message queue and data structure associated with it.

-s *semid*   Remove the semaphore identifier *semid* from the system, and destroy the set of semaphores and data structure associated with it.

-M *shmkey*   Remove the shared memory identifier, created with key *shmkey*, from the system. Destroy the shared memory segment and data structure associated with it after the last detach.

-Q *msgkey*   Remove the message queue identifier, created with key *msgkey*, from the system, and destroy the message queue and data structure associated with it.

-S *semkey*   Remove the semaphore identifier, created with key *semkey*, from the system, and destroy the set of semaphores and data structure associated with it.

The details of the removals are described in msgctl(2), shmctl(2), and semctl(2). Use the ipcs command to find the identifiers and keys.

Attributes

See attributes(5) for descriptions of the following attributes:

Attribute Type	Attribute Value
Availability	SUNWipc

See Also

ipcs(1), msgctl(2), msgget(2), msgrcv(2), msgsnd(2), semctl(2), semget(2), semop(2), shmctl(2), shmget(2), shmop(2), attributes(5)

ipcs — Report Interprocess Communication Facilities Status

Synopsis

New!

/usr/bin/ipcs [-aAbcimopqst] [-D *mtype*]

Description

The `ipcs` command prints information about active interprocess communication facilities. The information that is displayed is controlled by the options you supply. Without options, information is printed in short format for message queues, shared memory, and semaphores that are currently active in the system, as shown in the following example.

```
castle% ipcs
IPC status from <running system> as of Tue Jan 19 17:16:05 1999
Message Queue facility not in system.
T         ID      KEY          MODE        OWNER     GROUP
Shared Memory:
m          0     0x50018325 --rw-r--r--     root      root
Semaphores:
castle%
```

> **Note** — Things can change while `ipcs` is running; the information it gives is guaranteed to be accurate only when it was retrieved.

Options

-a	Use all XCU5 print options. (A shorthand notation for -b, -c, -o, -p, and -t.)
-A	Use all print options. (A shorthand notation for -b, -c, -i, -o, -p, and -t.)
-b	Print information on biggest allowable size: maximum number of bytes in messages on queue for message queues, size of segments for shared memory, and number of semaphores in each set for semaphores.
-c	Print creator's login name and group name.
-D *mtype*	Display, in hexadecimal and ASCII, the contents of all messages of type *mtype* found on any message queue that the user invoking `ipcs` has permission to read. If *mtype* is 0, display all messages. If *mtype* is negative, display all messages with type less than or equal to the absolute value of *mtype*. (See `msgrcv`(2) and `msgsnap`(2)). New in the Solaris 9 release.
-i	Print number of ISM attaches to shared memory segments.
-m	Print information about active shared memory segments.
-o	Print information on outstanding usage: number of messages on queue, total number of bytes in messages on queue for message queues, and number of processes attached to shared memory segments.
-p	Print process number information: process ID of last process to send a message, process ID of last process to receive a message on message queues, process ID of creating process, and process ID of last process to attach or detach on shared memory segments.
-q	Print information about active message queues.
-s	Print information about active semaphores.

New!

If you specify -m, -q, or -s, print information about only those indicated. If you specify none of these options, print information about all three, subject to the following options: -a, -A, -b, -c, -o, -i, -p, and -t.

-t   Print time information: time of the last control operation that changed the access permissions for all facilities, time of last msgsnd(2) and last msgrcv(2) on message queues, time of last shmat(2) and last shmdt(2) on shared memory (see shmop(2)), time of last semop(2) on semaphores.

The column headings and the meaning of the columns in an ipcs listing are shown below; the letters in parentheses indicate the options that display the corresponding heading; (all) means that the heading is always shown.

Note — These options determine only what information is provided for each facility; they do not determine what facilities are listed.

T   (all) Type of the facility:

     q   Message queue.

     m   Shared memory segment.

     s   Semaphore.

ID   (all) The identifier for the facility entry.

KEY   (all) The key used as an argument to msgget(2), semget(2), or shmget(2) to create the facility entry. (Note: The key of a shared memory segment is changed to IPC_PRIVATE when the segment has been removed until all processes attached to the segment detach it.)

MODE   (all) The facility access modes and flags: The mode consists of 11 characters that are interpreted as follows. The first two characters are any two of the following:

     R   A process is waiting on a msgrcv(2).

     S   A process is waiting on a msgsnd(2).

     D   Remove the associated shared memory segment. It is removed when the last process attached to the segment detaches it. (Note: If the shared memory segment identifier is removed by an IPC_RMID call to shmctl(2) before the process has detached from the segment with shmdt(2), the segment is no longer visible to ipcs and it does not appear in the ipcs output.)

     C   Clear the associated shared memory segment when the first attach is executed.

     -        The corresponding special flag is not set.

The next nine characters are interpreted as three sets of three bits each. The first set refers to the owner's permissions; the next, to permissions of others in the user group of the facility entry; and the last, to all others. Within each set, the first character indicates permission to read, the second character indicates permission to write or alter the facility entry, and the last character is currently unused.

The permissions are indicated as follows:

r   Read permission is granted.

w   Write permission is granted.

a   Alter permission is granted.

–   The indicated permission is not granted.

OWNER   (all) The login name of the owner of the facility entry.

GROUP   (all) The group name of the group of the owner of the facility entry.

CREATOR   (a, A, c) The login name of the creator of the facility entry.

CGROUP   (a, A, c) The group name of the group of the creator of the facility entry.

CBYTES   (a, A, o) The number of bytes in messages currently outstanding on the associated message queue.

QNUM   (a, A, o) The number of messages currently outstanding on the associated message queue.

QBYTES   (a, A, b) The maximum number of bytes allowed in messages outstanding on the associated message queue.

LSPID   (a, p) The process ID of the last process to send a message to the associated queue.

LRPID   (a, A, p) The process ID of the last process to receive a message from the associated queue.

STIME   (a, A, t) The time the last message was sent to the associated queue.

RTIME   (a, A, t) The time the last message was received from the associated queue.

CTIME   (a, A, t) The time when the associated entry was created or changed.

ISMATTCH   (a, i) The number of ISM attachments to the associated shared memory segments.

NATTCH   (a, A, o) The number of processes attached to the associated shared memory segment.

SEGSZ   (a, A, b) The size of the associated shared memory segment.

CPID   (a, A, p) The process ID of the creator of the shared memory entry.

LPID   (a, A, p) The process ID of the last process to attach or detach the shared memory segment.

ATIME   (a, A, t) The time the last attach to the associated shared memory segment was completed.

DTIME   (a, A, t) The time the last detach on the associated shared memory segment was completed.

NSEMS   (a, A, b) The number of semaphores in the set associated with the semaphore entry.

OTIME   (a, A, t) The time the last semaphore operation on the set associated with the semaphore entry was completed.

Environment Variables

See environ(5) for descriptions of the following enviornment variables that affect the execution of ipcs: LANG, LC_ALL, LC_CTYPE, LC_MESSAGES, and NLSPATH.

TZ   Determine the time zone for the time strings written by ipcs.

Files

/etc/group   Group names.

/etc/passwd   User names.

Attributes

See attributes(5) for descriptions of the following attributes:

Attribute Type	Attribute Value
Availability	SUNWcsu (32-bit)
	SUNWipcx (64-bit)

See Also

New!

ipcrm(1), msgget(2), msgids(2), msgrcv(2), msgsnap(2), msgsnd(2), semget(2), semids(2), semop(2), shmctl(2), shmget(2), shmids(2), shmop(2), attributes(5), environ(5)

isainfo — Describe Instruction Set Architectures

Synopsis

New!

/usr/bin/isainfo [-v] [-b | -n | -k]

Description

Use the isainfo command to identify various attributes of the instruction set architectures supported on the currently running system. Among the questions isainfo can answer are whether 64-bit applications are supported, or whether the running kernel uses 32-bit or 64-bit device drivers.

When invoked with no options, isainfo prints the name(s) of the native instruction sets for applications supported by the current version of the operating system. These names are a subset of the list returned by isalist(1). The subset corresponds to the basic applications environments supported by the currently running system.

Options

-b   Print the number of bits in the address space of the native instruction set.

-k   Print the name of the instruction set(s) used by the operating system kernel components such as device drivers and STREAMS modules.

-n   Print the name of the native instruction set used by portable
            applications supported by the current version of the operating system.

-v   Print more detailed information about the other options.

Examples

The following are examples of invoking the isainfo command on different operating
systems.

On a system running the 32-bit operating system on a 64-bit SPARC processor,

```
% isainfo -n
sparc
% isainfo -v
32-bit sparc applications
% isainfo -kv
32-bit sparc kernel modules
%
```

On a system running the 64-bit operating system on a 64-bit SPARC processor,

```
% isainfo
sparcv9 sparc
% isainfo -n
sparcv9
% isainfo -v
64-bit sparcv9 applications
32-bit sparc applications
% isainfo -vk
64-bit sparcv9 kernel modules
%
```

Exit Status

Non-zero   Options are either not specified correctly, or the command is
            unable to recognize attributes of the system on which it is running.
            An error message is printed to standard error.

Attributes

See attributes(5) for descriptions of the following attributes:

Attribute Type	Attribute Value
Availability	SUNWcsu

See Also

isalist(1), uname(1), psrinfo(1M), sysinfo(2), attributes(5),
isalist(5)

isalist — Display the Native Instruction Sets for This Platform

Synopsis

```
/usr/bin/isalist
```

Description

`isalist` prints the names of the native instruction sets executable on this platform on the standard output, as returned by the `SI_ISALIST` command of `sysinfo`(2).

The names are space-separated and are ordered in the sense of best performance. That is, earlier-named instruction sets may contain more instructions than later-named instruction sets; a program that is compiled for an earlier-named instruction set most likely runs faster on this machine than does the same program compiled for a later-named instruction set.

Programs compiled for instruction sets that do not appear in the list most likely experience performance degradation or do not run at all on this machine.

The instruction set names known to the system are listed in `isalist`(5). These names may or may not match predefined names or compiler options in the C-language compilation system.

Example

The following example runs `isalist` on a SPARCstation 10.

```
castle% isalist
sparcv8 sparcv8-fsmuld sparcv7 sparc
castle%
```

Attributes

See `attributes`(5) for descriptions of the following attributes:

Attribute Type	Attribute Value
Availability	SUNWcsu

See Also

`optisa`(1), `uname`(1), `sysinfo`(2), `attributes`(5), `isalist`(5)

J

jobs, fg, bg, stop, notify — Control Process Execution

Synopsis

jsh
```
jobs [-p | -l] [%job-id...]
jobs -x command [arguments]
fg [%job-id...]
bg [%job-id...]
stop %job-id...
stop pid...
```

csh
```
jobs[-l]
fg [%job-id]
bg [%job-id]...
notify [%job-id]...
stop %job-id...
stop pid...
```

ksh
```
jobs [-lnp] [%job-id...]
fg [%job-id...]
bg [%job-id...]
stop %job-id...
stop pid...
```

Description

Job control enables you to move currently executing commands into the foreground or background and to stop, suspend, or restart them as needed. There is always one job in the foreground, which is the job that accepts your keyboard input. The foreground job may be a shell or another command such as an editor that accepts keyboard input.

When you execute a command line or start a job in the foreground, input to the terminal window is blocked and you cannot enter additional commands until that job completes. You can use the job control commands to push that job into the background to regain control of your terminal window. Similarly, you can bring a background job back to the foreground so that you can control it or enter data from the terminal window. Job control enables you to perform these actions within the current layer or window.

Each command or pipeline that you enter at a terminal window is assigned a positive numeric *job-id* The shell keeps track of current and previous jobs. The current job is the most recent job to be started or restarted. The previous job is the first noncurrent job.

All jobs exist in one of the following states.

- A *foreground* job has read and write access to the controlling terminal.
- A *background* job is denied read access and has conditional write access to the *controlling* terminal (see stty(1)).
- A stopped job is a job that has been placed in a suspended state, usually as a result of a SIGTSTP signal (see signal(5)).

The Korn and C shells and the jsh job control shell of the Bourne shell all support job control.

Output

For all of the shells, if you specify no options, the output is a series of lines of the following form.

```
[%d] %c %s %s\n, job-number, current, state, command
```

The fields are described below.

job-number	A number used to identify the process group to the wait, fg, bg, and kill commands. With these commands, you can identify the job by prefixing the job number with %.
current	The + character identifies the job that would be used as a default for the fg or bg commands; you can also specify this job with *job-id* %+ or %% . The - character identifies the job that would become the default if the current default job were to exit; you can also specify this job with *job-id* %-. For other jobs, this field is a space character. You can identify one job with + and one job with -. If there is any suspended job, then the current job is a suspended job. If there are at least two suspended jobs, then the previous job is also a suspended job.
state	One of the following strings (in the POSIX locale):

	Running	The job has not been suspended by a signal and has not exited.
	Done	The job completed and returned exit status 0.

Done(*code*)   The job completed normally and it exited with the specified non-zero exit status, *code*, expressed as a decimal number.

Stopped
Stopped (SIGTSTP)

The job was suspended by the SIGTSTP signal.

Stopped (SIGSTOP)

The job was suspended by the SIGSTOP signal.

Stopped (SIGTTIN)

The job was suspended by the SIGTTIN signal.

Stopped (SIGTTOU)

The job was suspended by the SIGTTOU signal.

The implementation may substitute the string Suspended in place of Stopped. If the job was terminated by a signal, the format of *state* is unspecified, but it is visibly distinct from all of the other state formats shown here and indicates the name or description of the signal that terminated the job.

command   The associated command that was given to the shell.

If you specify the -l option, a field containing the process group ID is inserted before the state field. Also, more processes in a process group may be output on separate lines, using only the process ID and command fields.

For jsh and ksh, if you specify the -p option, the output consists of one line for each process ID.

The following jsh example lists two jobs.

```
$ jobs
[1] - Running                  spider
[2] + Done(0)                  find . -name core -print
$
```

Bourne Job Control Shell

jsh is the Bourne job control shell. jsh provides all of the functionality of sh in addition to the built-in job control commands. Typically, you use jsh only as an interactive shell; noninteractive shells typically do not benefit from the added functionality of job control.

The jsh built-in jobs command reports all jobs that are stopped or executing in the background. If you omit %*job-id*, the jobs command reports all jobs that are stopped or running in the background. The following options modify or enhance the output of jobs.

-l   Report the process group ID and the working directory of the jobs.

-p   Report only the process group ID of the jobs.

-x   Replace any *job-id* found in command or arguments with the corresponding process group ID, and then execute *command*, passing it arguments.

The acceptable syntax for a job identifier is of the form:

%*job-id*

You can specify *job-id* in any of the following formats:

% or +	The current job.
-	The previous job.
?*string*	The job for which the command line uniquely contains *string*.
n	Job number *n*, where *n* is a job number.
pref	A unique prefix of the command name (for example, if the command `ls -l` *name* were running in the background, it could be referred to as %`ls`); *pref* cannot contain blanks unless you quote it.

The `fg` (foreground) command resumes the execution of a stopped job in the foreground and moves an executing background job into the foreground. If you omit %*job-id*, the current job is assumed.

The `bg` (background) command resumes the execution of a stopped job in the background. If you omit %*job-id*, the current job is assumed.

The `stop` command stops the execution of a background job(s) by using its *job-id*, or of any process by using its *pid*; see ps(1).

C Shell

The C shell built-in `jobs` command without an argument lists the active jobs under job control.

The following option modifies or enhances the output of `jobs`.

-l	List process IDs, in addition to the normal information.

The shell associates a numbered *job-id* with each command sequence to keep track of those commands that are running in the background or have been stopped with TSTP signals (typically Control-Z). When you start a command or command sequence (semicolon-separated list) in the background by using the & metacharacter at the end of the command line, the shell displays a line with the job number in brackets and a list of associated process numbers:

[1] 567

Note — To see the current list of jobs, use the `jobs` built-in command. The job most recently stopped (or put into the background if none are stopped) is referred to as the current job and is indicated with a plus sign (+). The previous job is indicated with a dash (-); when the current job is terminated or moved to the foreground, this job takes its place (becomes the new current job).

To manipulate jobs, use the `bg`, `fg`, `kill`, `stop`, and % built-in commands.

A reference to a job begins with a percent sign (%). By itself, the percent sign refers to the current job.

% %+ %%	The current job.
%-	The previous job.

%*j*   Refer to job *j* as in: `kill -9 %j`. *j* can be a job number or a string that
                uniquely specifies the command line that started it; for example, `fg`
                `%vi` might bring a stopped `vi` job to the foreground.

%?*string*   Specify the command-line job that uniquely contains *string*.

A job running in the background stops when it tries to read from the terminal.
Background jobs can normally produce output, but you can suppress this feature with
the `stty tostop` command.

The following list describes the additional C shell built-in job control commands.

`fg`   Bring the current or specified *job-id* into the foreground.

`bg`   Run the current or specified jobs in the background.

`stop`   Stop the execution of a background job(s) by using its *job-id*, or of
                any process by using its *pid*; see ps(1).

`notify`   Notify you asynchronously when the status of the current job or
                specified jobs changes.

Korn Shell

The Korn shell built-in `jobs` command displays the status of the jobs that were started
in the current shell environment. When `jobs` reports the termination status of a job, the
shell removes its process ID from the list of those known in the current shell execution
environment.

The following options modify or enhance the output of `jobs`.

`-l`   (The letter ell.) Provide more information about each job listed. This
                information includes the job number, current job, process group ID,
                state, and the command that formed the job.

`-n`   Display only jobs that have stopped or exited since you were last
                notified.

`-p`   Display only the process IDs for the process group leaders of the
                selected jobs.

By default, `jobs` displays the status of all the stopped jobs, running background jobs,
and any job whose status has changed and has not been reported by the shell.

If the `monitor` option of the `set` command is turned on, an interactive shell associates
a job with each pipeline. It keeps a table of current jobs, printed by the `jobs` command,
and assigns them small integer numbers. When a job is started asynchronously with &,
the shell prints a line that looks like [1] 567, indicating that the job that was started
asynchronously was job number 1 and has one (top-level) process, whose process ID is
567.

If you are running a job and want to do something else, you can use the ^Z (Control-Z)
key combination to send a STOP signal to the current job. The shell normally indicates
that the job has been stopped and displays another prompt. You can then manipulate
the state of this job, putting it in the background with the `bg` command, or you can run
some other commands and then eventually bring the job back into the foreground with
the `fg` command. A ^Z takes effect immediately and is like an interrupt in that pending
output and unread input are discarded.

You can refer to jobs in the shell by their process ID or by any of the following.

%*number*   The job with the given number.

`%`*string*	Any job whose command line begins with *string*. This syntax works only in the interactive mode when the history file is active.
`%?`*string*	Any job whose command line contains *string*. This syntax works only in the interactive mode when the history file is active.
`%%`	Current job.
`%+`	Equivalent to `%%`.
`%-`	Previous job.

The shell learns immediately whenever a process changes state. It normally informs you whenever a job becomes blocked so that no further progress is possible, but only just before it displays a prompt. The warning is done in this way so that it does not otherwise disturb your work. When the `monitor` mode is on, each background job that completes triggers any trap set for CHLD. When you try to leave the shell while jobs are running or stopped, you are warned `You have stopped (running) jobs`. You can use the `jobs` command to see what the stopped jobs are. If you do this or immediately try to exit again, the shell does not warn you a second time, and the stopped jobs are terminated.

The following list describes the additional Korn shell job control commands.

`fg`	Move a background job from the current environment into the foreground. Using `fg` to place a job in the foreground removes its process ID from the list of those known in the current shell execution environment. The `fg` command is available only on systems that support job control. If you do not specify a *job-id*, the current job is brought into the foreground.
`bg`	Resume suspended jobs from the current environment by running them as background jobs. If the job specified by *job-id* is already a running background job, `bg` has no effect and exits successfully. Using `bg` to place a job into the background makes its process ID known in the current shell execution environment as if it had been started as an asynchronous list. The `bg` command is available only on systems that support job control. If you do not specify *job-id*, the current job is placed in the background.
`stop`	Stop the execution of a background job(s) by using its *job-id*, or of any process by using its *pid*; see ps(1).

Environment Variables

See environ(5) for descriptions of the following environment variables that affect the execution of jobs, fg, and bg: LC_CTYPE, LC_MESSAGES, and NLSPATH.

Exit Status

0	Successful completion.
>0	An error occurred.

Attributes

See attributes(5) for descriptions of the following attributes:

Attribute Type	Attribute Value
Availability	SUNWcsu

See Also

csh(1), kill(1), ksh(1), ps(1), sh(1), shell_builtins(1), stop(1), stty(1), wait(1), attributes(5), environ(5), signal(5)

join — Relational Database Operator

Synopsis

```
/usr/bin/join [-a filenumber | -v filenumber] [-1 fieldnumber]
    [-2 fieldnumber] [-o list] [-e string] [-t char] file1 file2
/usr/bin/join [-a filenumber] [-j fieldnumber] [-j1 fieldnumber]
    [-j2 fieldnumber] [-o list] [-e string] [-t char] file1 file2
```

Description

The join command forms a join of the two relations specified by the lines of *file1* and *file2* and displays the result on standard output.

The output has one line for each pair of lines in *file1* and *file2* that have identical join fields. The output line normally consists of the common field, then the rest of the line from *file1*, then the rest of the line from *file2*. You can change this format with the -o option. Use the -a option to add unmatched lines to the output. Use the -v option to output only unmatched lines.

The default input field separators are blank, Tab, or newline. Multiple separators count as one field separator, and leading separators are ignored. The default output field separator is a blank.

If the input files are not in the appropriate collating sequence, the results are unspecified.

> **Note** — With default field separation, the collating sequence is that of sort -b; with -t, the sequence is that of a plain sort.
>
> The conventions of the join, sort, comm, uniq, and awk commands are wildly incongruous.

Options

Some of the options below use the argument *filenumber*. This argument should be a 1 or a 2 referring to either *file1* or *file2*, respectively.

-a *filenumber*

> In addition to the normal output, produce a line for each unpairable line in file *filenumber*, where *filenumber* is 1 or 2. If you specify both -a 1 and -a 2, output all unpairable lines.

-e *string*   Replace empty output fields with *string*.

-j *fieldnumber*

> Equivalent to -1 *fieldnumber* -2 *fieldnumber*.

-j1 *fieldnumber*

> Equivalent to -1 *fieldnumber*.

-j2 *fieldnumber*

> Equivalent to -2 *fieldnumber*. Fields are numbered starting with 1.

-o *list*   Include the fields specified in *list* in each output line. Fields selected by *list* that do not appear in the input are treated as empty output fields. (See the -e option.) Each element has either the form *filenumber.fieldnumber* or 0, which represents the join field. Do not print the common field unless specifically requested.

-t *char*   Use character *char* as a separator. Every appearance of *char* in a line is significant. Use the character *char* as the field separator for both input and output. When you specify this option, the collating term should be the same as sort without the -b option.

-v *filenumber*

> Instead of the default output, produce a line only for each unpairable line in *filenumber*, where *filenumber* is 1 or 2. If you specify both -v 1 and -v 2, output all unpairable lines.

-1 *fieldnumber*

> Join on the *fieldnumber*-th field of *file1*. Fields are decimal integers starting with 1.

-2 *fieldnumber*

> Join on the *fieldnumber*-th field of *file2*. Fields are decimal integers starting with 1.

Operands

file1   A path name of a file to be joined. If either of the *file1* or *file2*
file2   operands is -, use the standard input in its place.

    file1 and *file2* must be sorted in increasing collating sequence as determined by LC_COLLATE on the fields on which they are to be joined, normally, the first in each line (see sort(1)).

Usage

See `largefile(5)` for the description of the behavior of `join` when encountering files greater than or equal to 2 Gbytes (2**31 bytes).

Examples

The following command line joins the password file and the group file, matching on the numeric group ID and outputting the login name, the group name, and the login directory. It is assumed that the files have been sorted in ASCII collating sequence on the group ID fields.

```
castle% join -j1 4 -j2 3 -o 1.1 2.1 1.6 -t: /etc/passwd /etc/group
root:other:/
daemon:other:/
bin:bin:/usr/bin
sys:sys:/
adm:adm:/var/adm
lp:lp:/usr/spool/lp
nuucp:nuucp:/var/spool/uucppublic
```

The `-o 0` field essentially selects the union of the join fields. For example, given file `phone`:

!Name	Phone Number
Don	+1 123-456-7890
Hal	+1 234-567-8901
Yasushi	+2 345-678-9012

and file `fax`:

!Name	Fax Number
Don	+1 123-456-7899
Keith	+1 456-789-0122
Yasushi	+2 345-678-9011

(where the large expanses of white space are meant to each represent a single Tab character), the command

```
example% join -t "<tab>" a 1 -a 2 -e '(unknown)' o 0,1.2,2.2 phone ax
```

produces

!Name	Phone Number	Fax Number
Don	+1 123-456-7890	+1 123-456-7899
Hal	+1 234-567-8901	(unknown)
Keith	(unknown)	+1 456-789-0122
Yasushi	+2 345-678-9012	+2 345-678-9011

Environment Variables

See `environ(5)` for descriptions of the following environment variables that affect the execution of `join`: LC_CTYPE, LC_MESSAGES, LC_COLLATE, and NLSPATH.

Exit Status

0	All input files were output successfully.
>0	An error occurred.

Attributes

See attributes(5) for descriptions of the following attributes:

Attribute Type	Attribute Value
Availability	SUNWcsu
CSI	Enabled

See Also

awk(1), comm(1), sort(1), uniq(1), attributes(5), environ(5),
largefile(5)

---

jsh — Standard and Job Control Shell and Command Interpreter

Synopsis

/usr/bin/jsh [-acefhiknprstuvx] [*argument*...]

Description

See jobs(1) and sh(1).

K

---

kbd — Keyboard Command

Synopsis

```
/usr/bin/kbd [-r] [-t] [-a enable | disable | alternate] [-c on | off]
    [-d keyboard device]
/usr/bin/kbd -i [-d keyboard device]
```

Description

Use the kbd command to manipulate the state of the keyboard, display the keyboard
type, or change the effect of the default keyboard abort sequence. The abort sequence
also applies to serial console devices. By default, this command operates on the
/dev/kbd device.

The -i option reads and processes default values for the keyclick and keyboard abort
settings from the keyboard default file, /etc/default/kbd, shown below.

```
mopoke% more /etc/default/kbd
#pragma ident    "@(#)kbd.dfl    1.3     99/05/04 SMI"
#
# Copyright 1996, 1999 by Sun Microsystems, Inc.
# All Rights Reserved.
#
# /etc/default/kbd
#
# kbd default settings processed via kbd(1).
#
# KEYBOARD_ABORT affects the default behavior of the keyboard abort
# sequence, see kbd(1) for details. The default value is "enable". The
```

551

```
# optional values are "disable" or "alternate". Any other value is ignored.
# If you choose "alternate" it will affect the serial console drivers ONLY.
# The keyboard BREAK (sequence and plug/unplug) won't be affected by this.
# If "alternate" is in effect any protocol (PPP, SLIP... etc) should not be
# run over the serial console port.
#
# KEYCLICK affects the default keyclick behavior. Possible values are
# 'on' and 'off'. Any other value is ignored. The default behavior is
# to leave the current keyclick setting unchanged.
#
# Uncomment the following line to disable keyboard or serial device
# abort sequences:
#KEYBOARD_ABORT=disable

# Uncomment the following line to enable a non-BREAK alternate
# serial input device abort sequence:
#KEYBOARD_ABORT=alternate

# Uncomment the following line to change the keyclick behavior:
#KEYCLICK=off
mopoke%
```

Only keyboards that support a clicker respond to the -c option. You can change the keyclick setting for a session with the -c option from the command line.

To turn clicking on by default, edit the /etc/default/kbd file, remove the comment (#) from the beginning of the KEYCLICK variable line, and change the default value to on, as shown below.

KEYCLICK=on

Then, run the command kbd -i to change the current setting. Valid settings for the KEYCLICK variable are the values on and off. Other values are ignored. If the variable is not specified in the default file, the setting is unchanged.

On most systems, the default effect of the keyboard abort sequence is to suspend the operating system and enter the debugger or the monitor. The abort sequence on most systems is L1-A or STOP-A on the keyboard and Break on the serial console input device.

A Break condition that originates from an erroneous electrical signal cannot be distinguished from one deliberately set by remote DCE. As a remedy, superuser can use the -a alternate option (Alternate Break)—new in the Solaris 8 release—to switch break interpretation. Because of the risk of incorrect sequence interpretation, binary protocols such as PPP, SLIP, and others should not be run over the serial console port when Alternate Break sequence is in effect. The Alternate Break sequence has no effect on the keyboard abort. See zs(7D), se(7D), and asy(7D) for more information on the Alternate Break Sequence.

Note — Some systems have key switches with a secure position. On these systems, the key switch in the secure position overrides any software default set with the kbd command.

There is no way to determine the state of the keyboard click setting when set from a command line.

Only superuser can use the -a option to change the keyboard abort sequence. Superuser can change the keyboard abort sequence from the command line. The system can be configured to ignore the keyboard abort sequence or trigger on the standard or alternate sequence.

To permanently change the software default effect of the keyboard abort sequence, as superuser, edit the /etc/default/kbd file, remove the comment (#) from the beginning of the KEYBOARD_ABORT line, and change the default value to disable, as shown below.

KEYBOARD_ABORT=disable

Then, run the command kbd -i to change the current setting. Valid settings for the KEYBOARD_ABORT variable are the values enable and disable. Other values are ignored. If the variable is not specified in the default file, the setting is unchanged.

To set the abort sequence to the hardware Break, set the value of the KEYBOARD_ABORT variable in the /etc/default/kbd file to enable, as shown below.

KEYBOARD_ABORT=enable

To change the current setting, run the kbd -i command. To set the abort sequence to the Alternate Break character sequence, first set the current value of the KEYBOARD_ABORT variable in the /etc/default/kbd file to alternate, as shown below.

KEYBOARD_ABORT=alternate

Next, run the kbd -i command to change the setting. When the Alternate Break sequence is in effect, only serial console devices are affected.

Options

-a enable/disable/alternate *state*

Enable or disable the keyboard abort sequence effect. By default, a keyboard abort sequence (typically, Stop-A or L1-A on the keyboard and BREAK on the serial console device) suspends the operating system on most systems. This option can be used only by the superuser.

alternate	Enable the alternate effect of the keyboard abort sequences—suspend the operating system and enter the debugger or the monitor—on receiving the Alternate Break character sequence on the console. The Alternate Break sequence is defined by the zs(7D), se(7d), and asy(7D) drivers. Because of a risk of incorrect sequence interpretation, binary protocols cannot be run over the serial console port when you use this value. New in the Solaris 8 release.
enable	Enable the default effect of the keyboard abort sequence, which is to suspend the operating system and enter the debugger or the monitor.
disable	Disable the default effect, and ignore keyboard abort sequences.

-c on/off *state*

Turn the clicking of the keyboard on or off.

on   Enable clicking.

off   Disable clicking.

-d *keyboard device*

Specify the keyboard device being set. The default is /dev/kbd.

-i   Set keyboard defaults from the keyboard default file. This option is
              mutually exclusive with all other options except for the -d keyboard
              device option. This option instructs the keyboard command to read and
              process keyclick and keyboard abort default values from the
              /etc/default/kbd file. This option can be used only by the superuser.

-r   Reset the keyboard as if power-up.

-t   Return the type of the keyboard being used.

Examples

The following example displays the keyboard type.

```
castle% kbd -t
Type 4 Sun keyboard
castle%
```

The following example sets keyboard defaults as specified in the keyboard default
file.

```
castle% kbd -i
castle%
```

The following example turns clicking on from the command line.

```
castle% kbd -c on
castle%
```

Files

/dev/kbd   Keyboard device file.

/etc/default/kbd

              Keyboard default file containing software defaults for keyboard
              configurations.

/etc/rcS   Shell script containing commands to put the system in single-user
              mode.

Attributes

See attributes(5) for descriptions of the following attributes:

Attribute Type	Attribute Value
Architecture	SPARC
Availability	SUNWcsu

See Also

loadkeys(1), kadb(1M), keytables(4), attributes(5), asy(7D), se(7D),
zs(7d), kb(7M)

kdestroy — Destroy Kerberos Tickets

Synopsis

/usr/bin/kdestroy [-q] [-c *cache_name*]

New!

Description

Kerberos is an authentication system that uses Data Encryption Standard (DES) to authenticate a user logging in to the system. Authentication is based on the capability of the sending system to use a common key to encrypt a ticket containing the current time that the receiving system can decrypt and check against its current time.

You destroy Kerberos tickets by using the kdestroy command. You should destroy Kerberos tickets when the session is over so that an unauthorized user cannot gain access to them.

kdestroy destroys the user's active Kerberos authorization tickets by writing zeros to the file that contains them. If you do not specify the credentials cache, the default credentials cache is destroyed. If the credentials cache does not exist, kdestroy displays a message to that effect.

New!

After overwriting the cache, kdestroy removes the cache from the system. The command displays a message indicating the success or failure of the operation. If kdestroy is unable to destroy the cache, it warns you by making your terminal beep.

You can put the kdestroy command in your .logout file so that your tickets are destroyed automatically when you log out.

> **Note —** For file systems that are mounted with Secure NFS, when you put kdestroy in your .logout file, NFS operations done on your behalf fail after you log out.

Bugs

Only the tickets in the user's current ticket file are destroyed. Separate ticket files are used to hold root instance and password-changing tickets. These files should probably be destroyed too, or all of a user's tickets should be kept in a single ticket file.

Options

-c *cache_name*

New!

Use *cache_name* as the credentials (ticket) cache name and location. If you do not specify this option, kdestroy uses the default cache name and location.

-q   Do not make your terminal beep if kdestroy fails to destroy the tickets.

Environment Variables

New!

KRB5CCNAME   Location of the credentials (ticket) cache.

Examples

The following example shows how to destroy Kerberos tickets. After the tickets are destroyed, if the user tries to change to or list a Secure NFS file system mount point that is being treated as a Kerberos service, the ticket server denies access.

```
castle% kdestroy
Tickets destroyed
castle% ls /mntkrb
Can't get Kerberos key: No ticket file (tf_util)
NSF getattr failed for server castle: RPC: Authentication error
cannot access directory /mntkrb.
castle%
```

Files

New!

/tmp/krb5cc_*uid*

Default credentials cache (*uid* is the decimal UID of the user).

Attributes

See attributes(5) for descriptions of the following attributes:

Attribute Type	Attribute Value
Availability	SUNWkrbu

New!

See Also

New!

kinit(1), klist(1), attributes(5), SEAM(5)

Authors

Steve Miller, MIT Project Athena/Digital Equipment Corporation; Clifford Neuman, MIT Project Athena; Bill Sommerfeld, MIT Project Athena

---

keylogin — Decrypt and Store Secret Key with keyserv

Synopsis

/usr/bin/keylogin [-r]

Description

The keylogin command is part of the set of Secure RPC commands. Before you can use keylogin, a system administrator must use the newkey(1M), nisaddcred(1M), or nisclient(1M) commands to generate a public and secret key. Each user has a unique public key and secret key. The key can be found in the /etc/publickey file (see publickey(4)) in the NIS map publickey.byname, or in the NIS+ table cred.org_dir in the user's home domain. The sources and their lookup order are specified in the /etc/nsswitch.conf file (see nsswitch.conf(4)).

The keylogin command prompts for a password and uses it to decrypt the user's secret key. Once decrypted, the secret key is stored by the local key server process, keyserv(1M). This stored key is used when requests are issued to any secure RPC services, such as NFS or NIS+. You can delete the key stored by keyserv with the keylogout(1) command.

keylogin fails if it cannot get the caller's key or if the password is incorrect. For a new user or host, a new key can be added with newkey(1M), nisaddcred(1M), or nisclient(1M).

When multiple authentication mechanisms are configured for a system, each of the configured mechanism's secret keys is decrypted and stored by keyserv(1M). See nisauthconf(1M) for information on configuring multiple authentication mechanisms.

Options

-r   Update the /etc/.rootkey file. This file holds the unencrypted secret key of the superuser. Only the superuser can use this option. Processes running as superuser can issue authenticated requests without requiring that the administrator explicitly run keylogin as superuser at system startup time (see keyserv(1M)). The administrator should use the -r option when the host's entry in the publickey database has changed and the /etc/.rootkey file has become out of date with the actual key pair stored in the publickey database. The permissions on the /etc/.rootkey file are read and write by the superuser but by no other user on the system.

           If multiple authentication mechanisms are configured for the system, the /etc/.rootkey file stores each of the secret keys.

Files

/etc/.rootkey

       Superuser's secret key.

Attributes

See attributes(5) for descriptions of the following attributes:

Attribute Type	Attribute Value
Availability	SUNWcsu

See Also

chkey(1), keylogout(1), login(1), keyserv(1M), newkey(1M), nisaddcred(1M), nisauthconf(1M), nisclient(1M), nsswitch.conf(4), publickey(4), attributes(5)

keylogout — Delete Stored Secret Key with keyserv

Synopsis

/usr/bin/keylogout [-f]

Description

The keylogout command is part of the set of Secure RPC commands. keylogout deletes the key stored by the key server process keyserv(1M). Further access to the key is revoked; however, current session keys may remain valid until they expire or are refreshed.

When you delete the keys stored by keyserv, any background jobs or scheduled at(1) jobs that need secure RPC services fail. Because only one copy of the key is kept on a system, it is a bad idea to place a call to this command in your .logout file because it affects other sessions on the same machine.

Options

-f   Force keylogout to delete the secret key for superuser. By default, keylogout by superuser is disallowed because it would break all RPC services, such as NFS, that are started by superuser.

Attributes

See attributes(5) for descriptions of the following attributes:

Attribute Type	Attribute Value
Availability	SUNWcsu

See Also

at(1), chkey(1), login(1), keylogin(1), keyserv(1M), newkey(1M), publickey(4), attributes(5)

kill — Terminate or Signal Processes

Synopsis

```
/usr/bin/kill -s signal pid...
/usr/bin/kill -l [exit-status]
/usr/bin/kill [-signal_name] pid...
/usr/bin/kill [-signal_number] pid...
```

sh, csh, and ksh
```
kill [-sig] [pid] [%job]...
kill -l
```

Description

At times, you may need to eliminate a process entirely because you want to stop a large job before it completes or you detect a process that is hung or not working properly. To delete a process, use the kill command. The kill command sends a signal to the process or processes specified by each *pid* operand. Use the ps(1) command to find the process ID for the process you want to kill.

When you kill a process, you are actually telling the system to send the process a signal. There are 36 numbered signals and 4 unnumbered ones. Refer to the signal(5) manual page for the complete list.

You can specify a signal either by its number or by its logical signal name as listed in the signal(5) manual page, with the SIG part removed. The following example specifies signal 15 by number and then by name.

```
castle% kill -15 456
castle% kill -TERM 457
```

When you specify no signal, the kill command sends signal 15 (SIGTERM) by default. Signal 15 terminates the process if it can and is the preferred method for killing a process. Sometimes processes do not die when you use the kill command. The three most common cases are:

- The process is waiting for a device, such as a tape drive, to complete an operation before exiting.
- The process is waiting for resources that are unavailable because of NFS problems. For such processes, use signal 3 (SIGQUIT).
- The process is a zombie, as shown by the message defunct in the ps report. A zombie process is one that has had all its resources freed but has not received an acknowledgment from a parent process, receipt of which would ordinarily remove its entry from the process table. The next time a system is booted, zombie processes are cleared. Zombies do not affect system performance, and you do not need to remove them.

When a process does not die with a signal 15, use signal 9 (SIGKILL) to force the process to die.

```
castle% kill -9 458
castle% kill -KILL 459
```

Built-in Shell kill Commands

The Bourne shell, the Korn shell, and the C shell have built-in versions of kill that provide the functionality of the kill command for processes identified with a *job.*

The csh kill built-in sends the TERM (terminate) signal by default or the signal specified to the specified process ID, the job indicated, or the current job. Specify signals either by number or by name. There is no default. Typing kill does not send a signal to the current job. If the signal being sent is TERM (terminate) or HUP (hangup), then the job or process is sent a CONT (continue) signal as well.

The syntax of the ksh kill command is shown below.

The Korn shell kill sends either the TERM (terminate) signal or the specified signal to the specified jobs or processes. Specify signals either by number or by names (as given in signal(5) but stripped of the prefix SIG). If the signal being sent is TERM (terminate) or HUP (hangup), then the job or process is sent a CONT (continue) signal if it is stopped. The *job-id* argument can be the process ID of a process that is not a member of one of the active jobs.

Options

-l   (The letter ell.) Write all values of *signal* supported by the
                 implementation for jsh, ksh, and csh. For /usr/bin/kill, write all
                 values of *signal* if you do not specify the *exit-status* operand. If you
                 specify an *exit-status* operand and it has a value of the ? shell
                 special parameter and a wait corresponding to a process that was
                 terminated by a signal, write the *signal* corresponding to the signal
                 that terminated the process. If you give an *exit-status* operand and
                 it is the unsigned decimal integer value of a signal number, write the
                 signal corresponding to that signal. Otherwise, the results are
                 unspecified.

-s *signal*   Send the specified signal to the process or job ID, using either the
                 signal number or the symbolic name as defined in the signal(5)
                 manual page. Values of *signal* are case independent, without the SIG
                 prefix. In addition, the symbolic name 0 is recognized, representing the
                 signal value 0. Typical values used with the kill command are –15
                 (TERM)—the default—and 9 (KILL).

Operands

pid   One of the following:

                 • A decimal integer specifying a process or process group to be
                   signaled. The process or processes selected by positive, negative, and
                   0 values of the *pid* operand are as described for the kill command.
                   If you specify process number 0, then all processes in the process
                   group are signaled. If the first *pid* operand is negative, precede it
                   with -- to keep it from being interpreted as an option.

                 • A job control job ID that identifies a background process group to be
                   signaled. The job control job ID notation is applicable only for
                   invocations of kill in the current shell execution environment.

exit-status

                 A decimal integer specifying a signal number or the exit status of a
                 process terminated by a signal.

Note — The job control job ID type of *pid* is available only on systems
supporting the job control option.

Usage

You can find process ID numbers with the ps(1) command.

The job control job ID notation is not required to work as expected when kill is
operating in its own command execution environment. For example, in both of the
following examples, kill operates in a different environment and does not share the
shell's understanding of job numbers.

```
nohup kill %1 &
system( "kill %1");
```

Output

When you do not specify the -1 option, the standard output is not used. When you specify the -1 option, the symbolic name of each signal is written in the following format:

%s%c, *signal, separator*

where the *signal* is in upper case, without the SIG prefix, and the *separator* is either a newline or a space. For the last signal written, *separator* is a newline.

When you specify both the -1 option and *exit-status* operand for /usr/bin/kill, the symbolic name of the corresponding signal is written in the following format.

%s\n, *signal*

Examples

The following example uses the -1 option to list the available signals for /usr/bin/kill.

```
castle% /usr/bin/kill -l
EXIT HUP INT QUIT ILL TRAP ABRT EMT FPE KILL BUS SEGV SYS PIPE ALRM TERM
    USR1 USR2 CLD PWR WINCH URG POLL STOP TSTP CONT TTIN TTOU VTALRM PROF
    XCPU XFSZ WAITING LWP FREEZE THAW CANCEL LOST RTMIN RTMIN+1 RTMIN+2
    RTMIN+3 RTMAX-3 RTMAX-2 RTMAX-1 RTMAX
castle%
```

If the sending process has permission to send the signal, any of the following commands sends the SIGKILL signal to an existing process whose process ID is 100 and to all existing processes whose process group ID is 165.

```
# kill -9 100 -165
# kill -s kill 100 -165
# kill -s KILL 100 -165
```

To avoid an ambiguity of an initial negative number argument specifying either a signal number or a process group, the signal number is always specified. Therefore, to send the default signal to a process group (for example, 123), an application should use a command similar to one of the following:

```
# kill -TERM -123
# kill -- -123
```

The following example uses the ps command to find the process ID for the game spider and then uses the kill command to kill it by process ID.

```
castle% ps -ef | grep spider
  winsor   544   419  0 15:45:42 pts/3     0:00 grep spider
  winsor   542   419  1 15:45:35 pts/3     0:00 spider.exe
castle% kill 542
[1]    Exit 1              spider
castle%
```

The following example uses the jobs command to find the job number for the game spider and then uses the kill command to kill it by job ID.

```
castle% jobs
[2]  + Running             spider
castle% kill %2
```

```
castle%
[2]    Exit 1              spider
castle%
```

Environment Variables

See environ(5) for descriptions of the following environment variables that affect the execution of kill: LC_CTYPE, LC_MESSAGES, and NLSPATH.

Exit Status

0	At least one matching process was found for each *pid* operand, and the specified signal was successfully processed for at least one matching process.
>0	An error occurred.

Attributes

See attributes(5) for descriptions of the following attributes:

Attribute Type	Attribute Value
Availability	SUNWcsu

See Also

csh(1), jobs(1), ksh(1), ps(1), sh(1), shell_builtins(1), wait(1), kill(2), signal(3C), signal(3HEAD), attributes(5), environ(5)

kinit — Kerberos Login Command

Synopsis

/usr/bin/kinit [-fpRv] [-c *cache_name*] [-k [-t *keytab_file*]]
    [-l *lifetime*] [-r *renewable_life*] [-s *start_time*] [-S *service_name*]
    [*principal*]

Description

The kinit command is used to log in to the Kerberos authentication and authorization system. Note that only registered Kerberos users can use the Kerberos system. For information about Kerberos principals, see the SEAM(5) manual page.

When you use kinit without options, the command prompts for the password of the Kerberos principal that has the same name as your UNIX login name. A single user can have multiple Kerberos principals. If you have an alternative principal name created for you by the Kerberos administrator and want to get a ticket for it instead of your default principal name, you can specify that name as an option to kinit.

If Kerberos authenticates the login attempt, kinit retrieves your initial ticket (that is, the ticket-granting ticket) and puts it in the ticket cache—changed from ticket file starting with the Solaris 8 release. By default the ticket is stored in the /tmp/krb5cc_*uid*, where *uid* specifies your user identification number. Tickets expire after a specified lifetime, after which you must run `kinit` again to refresh the tickets. Any existing contents of the cache are destroyed by `kinit`.

Use the `kdestroy(1)` command to destroy any active tickets before you end your login session.

Configuration File

You must configure the system on which you plan to run `kinit` as a Kerberos client by making the appropriate modifications to the `/etc/krb5/krb5.conf` file. The default `krb5.conf` file is shown below.

```
#
#pragma ident    "@(#)krb5.conf    1.2    99/07/20 SMI"
# Copyright (c) 1999, by Sun Microsystems, Inc.
# All rights reserved.
#

# krb5.conf template
# In order to complete this configuration file
# you will need to replace the __<name>__ placeholders
# with appropriate values for your network.
#
[libdefaults]
        default_realm = ___default_rcalm___

[realms]
        ___default_realm___ = {
                kdc = ___master_kdc___
                ___slave_kdcs___
                admin_server = ___master_kdc___
        }

[domain_realm]
        ___domain_mapping___

[logging]
        default = FILE:/var/krb5/kdc.log
        kdc = FILE:/var/krb5/kdc.log
    kdc_rotate = {

# How often to rotate kdc.log. Logs will get rotated no more
# often than the period, and less often if the KDC is not used
# frequently.

    period = 1d

# how many versions of kdc.log to keep around (kdc.log.0, kdc.log.1,
  ...)

    versions = 10
    }

[appdefaults]
    kinit = {
        renewable = true
```

```
            forwardable= true
      }
   gkadmin = {
         help_url =
   http://docs.sun.com:80/ab2/coll.384.1/SEAM/@AB2PageView/1195
      }
```

The following example shows a file configured for the gmarler.com domain.

```
# Configuration file for a Kerberos 5 client
# This client is in the gmarler.com DNS domain and the Kerberos 5 realm
# is named after the DNS domain
# Thus, this client's default Kerberos realm is GMARLER.COM
[libdefaults]
        default_realm = GMARLER.COM

# For the GMARLER.COM realm, we have a primary and secondary Key
# Distribution Center (KDC):  kdc.gmarler.com and kdc2.gmarler.com
# kdc.gmarler.com also doubles as the Kerberos admin server
[realms]
        GMARLER.COM = {
                kdc = kdc.gmarler.com
                kdc = kdc2.gmarler.com
                admin_server = kdc.gmarler.com
        }

# This section maps any host in the .gmarler.com DNS domain into the
# GMARLER.COM Kerberos realm
[domain_realm]
        .gmarler.com = GMARLER.COM

# This section defines defaults for applications that are Kerberos
# aware.  See the Sun Online Blueprint concerning Kerberos for more
# details:  http://www.sun.com/blueprints/online.html
[appdefaults]
        gkadmin = {
                help_url = http://localhost:8888/ab2/coll.384.2/SEAM
        }
        kinit = {
                renewable = true
                forwardable= true
                proxiable = false
        }
        rlogin = {
                renewable = true
                forwardable= true
                encrypt = true
        }
        rsh = {
                renewable = true
                forwardable= true
                encrypt = true
        }
        rcp = {
```

```
                encrypt = true
        }
        telnet = {
                autologin = true
                renewable = true
                forwardable= true
        }
        login = {
                krb5_get_tickets = true
        }
```

Options

-c *cache_name*

> Use *cache_name* as the credentials (ticket) cache name and location. If you do not specify this option, kinit uses the default cache name and location.

-f

> Request forwardable tickets.

-k [-t *keytab_file*]

> Request a host ticket, obtained from a key in the local host keytab file. You can specify the name and location of the keytab file with the -t *keytab_file* option. Otherwise, kinit uses the default name and location.

-l *lifetime*

> Request a ticket with the *lifetime* lifetime. If you do not specify the -l option, the default ticket lifetime (configured by each site) is used. Specifying a ticket lifetime longer than the maximum ticket lifetime configured for each site results in a ticket with the maximum lifetime. See "Time Formats" on page 566 for the valid time duration formats you can specify for *lifetime*.

-p

> Request proxyable tickets.

-r *renewable_life*

> Request renewable tickets with a total lifetime of *renewable_life*. See "Time Formats" on page 566 for the valid time duration formats that you can specify for *renewable_life*.

-R

> Request renewal of the ticket-granting ticket. Notice that you cannot renew an expired ticket even if the ticket is still within its renewable life.

-s *start_time*

> Request a postdated ticket, valid starting at *start_time*. Postdated tickets are issued with the invalid flag set and need to be fed back to the KDC before use. See "Time Formats" on page 566 for either the valid absolute time or time duration formats that you can specify for *start_time*. kinit tries to match an absolute time first before trying to match a time duration.

-S *service_name*

> Specify an alternate service name to use when getting initial
> tickets.

-v

> Request that the ticket-granting ticket in the cache (with the
> invalid flag set) be passed to the KDC for validation. If the ticket
> is within its requested time range, the cache is replaced with the
> validated ticket.

New! *Time Formats*

The following absolute time formats can be used for the -s *start_time* option. The
examples are based on the date and time of July 2, 2002, 1:35:30 p.m.

Absolute Time Format	Example
yymmddhhmm[ss]	020702133530
hhmm[ss]	133530
yy:mm:dd:hh:mm:ss	02:07:02:13:35:30
hh:mm[:ss]	13:35:30
ldate:ltime	07-07-99:13:35:30
dd-month-yyyy:hh:mm[:ss]	02-july-2002:13:35:30

Variable	Description
dd	Day.
hh	Hour (24-hour clock).
mm	Minutes.
ss	Seconds.
yy	Year within century (0-68 is 2000 to 2068; 69-99 is 1969 to 1999)
yyyy	Year including century.
month	Locale's full or abbreviated month name.
ldate	Locale's appropriate date representation.
ltime	Locale's appropriate time representation.

The following time duration formats can be used for the -l *lifetime*,
-r *renewable_life*, and -s *start_time* options. The examples are based on the time
duration of 14 days, 7 hours, 5 minutes, and 30 seconds.

Time Duration Format	Example
#d	14d
#h	7h
#m	5m

Time Duration Format	Example
#s	30s
#d#h#m#s	14d7h5m30s
#h#m[#s]	7h5m30s
days-hh:mm:ss	14-07:05:30
hours:mm[:ss]	7:05:30

Delimiter	Description
d	Number of days.
h	Number of hours.
m	Number of minutes.
s	Number of seconds.

Variable	Description
#	Number.
days	Number of days.
hours	Number of hours.
hh	Hour (24-hour clock).
mm	Minutes.
ss	Seconds.

Examples

The following example uses the kinit command to get the Ticket-Granting Ticket (TGT) *New!*
for the user gmarler in the Kerberos realm gmarler.com.

Note — The user is already logged in under the user name gmarler.

```
$ kinit
Password for gmarler@GMARLER.COM: <principal password>
$
$ klist
Ticket cache: /tmp/krb5cc_1067
Default principal: gmarler@GMARLER.COM

Valid starting                 Expires
   Service principal
Tue Feb 26 08:09:12 2002  Tue Feb 26 16:09:12 2002
   krbtgt/GMARLER.COM@GMARLER.COM
         renew until Tue Mar 05 08:09:12 2002
$
```

New!

In the following example, user `gmarler` in the Kerberos realm `gmarler.com` wants to use his `gmarler/admin` principal to administer some aspect of the Kerberos KDC. To do this, he needs to obtain the TGT for the principal `gmarler/admin`.

```
$ kinit gmarler/admin
Password for gmarler/admin@GMARLER.COM: <principal password>
$ klist
Ticket cache: /tmp/krb5cc_1067
Default principal: gmarler/admin@GMARLER.COM

Valid starting                     Expires
  Service principal
Tue Feb 26 08:11:44 2002  Tue Feb 26 16:11:44 2002
  krbtgt/GMARLER.COM@GMARLER.COM
          renew until Tue Mar 05 08:11:44 2002
$
```

New! ## Environment Variables

KRB5CCNAME   Location of the credentials (ticket) cache.

New! ## Files

/etc/krb5/krb5.keytab

Default location for the local host's `keytab` file.

/etc/krb5/krb5.conf

Kerberos configuration file.

/tmp/krb5cc_*uid*

Default credentials cache (*uid* is the decimal UID of the user).

Attributes

See `attributes`(5) for descriptions of the following attributes:

Attribute Type	Attribute Value
Availability	SUNWkrbu

New!

See Also

New!

kdestroy(1), klist(1), attributes(5), SEAM(5)

Authors

Steve Miller, MIT Project Athena/Digital Equipment Corporation; Clifford Neuman, MIT Project Athena

klist — List Currently Held Kerberos Tickets

Synopsis

```
/usr/bin/klist [-e] [[-c] [cache_name] [-f] [-s]]
    [-k [-t] [keytab_file] [-K]]
```

New!

Description

Use the klist command to print the name of the credentials cache and the identity of *New!*
the principal that the tickets are for (as listed in the ticket file). The command also lists
the principal names of all Kerberos tickets currently held by the user along with the
issue and expiration time for each authenticator. Principal names are listed in the form
name/instance@realm, with the slash (/) omitted if the instance is not included and the
at sign (@) omitted if the realm is not included.

If you do not specify *cache_file* or *keytab_name*, klist displays the credentials in
the default credentials cache or keytab files as appropriate. By default, your ticket is
stored in the /tmp/krb5cc_*uid* file, where *uid* is the current user ID. The above changes
are new in the Solaris 8 release.

Bugs

When a file is read as a service key file, very little error checking is performed.

Options

New!

-c [*cache_name*]

> List tickets held in a credentials cache. This option is the default if you
> specify neither -c nor -k.

-e

> Display the encryption types of the session key and the ticket for each
> credential in the credential cache, or each key in the keytab file.

-f

> Show the flags present in the credentials, using the following
> abbreviations.

> | | |
> |---|---|
> | F | Forwardable. |
> | f | Forwarded. |
> | P | Proxyable. |
> | p | Proxy. |
> | D | Postdateable. |
> | d | Postdated. |
> | R | Renewable. |
> | I | Initial. |
> | i | Invalid. |

-k [*keytab_file*]

> List keys held in a keytab file.

-K

> Display the value of the encryption key in each keytab entry in the
> keytab file.

-s   Run silently (produce no output), but still set the exit status according to whether it finds the credentials cache. The exit status is 0 if klist finds a credentials cache, and 1 if it does not.

-t   Display the time entry timestamps for each keytab entry in the keytab file.

Examples

The following example lists a Kerberos ticket for user ray.

```
castle% klist
Ticket file: /tmp/tkt8765
Principal: ray@Castle.Abc.COM
  Issued             Expires           Principal
  Oct 10 15:15:56   Oct 10:16:15:56  krbtgt.Castle.Abc.COM@Castle.Abc.com
castle%
```

The following invocation of klist shows the encryption types of the session key for the principal gmarler/admin.

```
$ klist -e
Ticket cache: /tmp/krb5cc_1067
Default principal: gmarler/admin@GMARLER.COM

Valid starting                       Expires
    Service principal
Tue Feb 26 08:11:44 2002  Tue Feb 26 16:11:44 2002
    krbtgt/GMARLER.COM@GMARLER.COM
          renew until Tue Mar 05 08:11:44 2002, Etype (skey, tkt):
    DES-CBC-MD5, DES-CBC-CRC
$
```

The following invocation of klist shows the flags associated with the credentials for the principal gmarler/admin.

```
$ klist -f
Ticket cache: /tmp/krb5cc_1067
Default principal: gmarler/admin@GMARLER.COM

Valid starting                       Expires
    Service principal
Tue Feb 26 08:11:44 2002  Tue Feb 26 16:11:44 2002
    krbtgt/GMARLER.COM@GMARLER.COM
          renew until Tue Mar 05 08:11:44 2002, Flags: FRI
$
```

The flags are FRI, which means that these credentials are Forwardable, Renewable, and the Initial set of credentials for this principal.

ksh, rksh — Korn Shell, a Standard/Restricted Command and Programming Language

Synopsis

```
/usr/bin/ksh [± abCefhikmnoprstuvx] [± o option]... [arg...]
/usr/bin/ksh -c [± abCefhikmnoprstuvx] [± o option]... command-string
    [command-name [arg...]]
/usr/xpg4/bin/sh [± abCefhikmnoprstuvx] [± o option]... [arg...]
/usr/xpg4/bin/sh -c [± abCefhikmnoprstuvx] [± o option]...
    command-string [command-name [arg...]]
/usr/bin/ksh [± abCefhikmnoprstuvx] [± o option]... [arg...]
/usr/bin/ksh -c [± abCefhikmnoprstuvx] [± o option]... command-string
    [command-name [arg...]]
```

Description

The Korn shell, written by David Korn of AT&T Bell Laboratories, was designed to be compatible with the Bourne shell and to offer interactive features comparable to the C shell. The Korn shell includes convenient programming features such as built-in integer arithmetic, arrays, and string-manipulation facilities. The Korn shell runs faster than the C shell and runs virtually all scripts that are written for the Bourne shell.

The Korn shell command is /usr/bin/ksh or /usr/xpg4/bin/ksh. These two commands are identical.

/usr/bin/rksh is a restricted version of the command interpreter ksh; it is used to set up login names and execution environments whose capabilities are more controlled than those of the standard shell.

The default prompt for the Korn shell is a dollar sign ($). The root prompt is a pound sign (#).

The Korn shell discussion uses the following definitions.

- A *metacharacter* is one of the following characters: ; & ( ) | < > newline space Tab.
- A *blank* is a Tab or a space.
- An *identifier* is a sequence of letters, digits, or underscores starting with a letter or underscore. Identifiers are used as names for functions and variables.
- A *word* is a sequence of characters separated by one or more nonquoted metacharacters.
- A *command* is a sequence of characters in the syntax of the shell language. The shell reads each command and carries out the desired action either directly or by invoking separate commands.
- A *special command* is a command that is carried out by the shell without creating a separate process. Except for documented side effects, most special commands can be implemented as separate commands.

Initialization

If the shell is invoked by exec(2) and the first character of argument 0 ($0) is -, then the shell is assumed to be a login shell and it reads commands in the following sequence:

1. Execute commands in /etc/profile.

2. Execute commands from either .profile in the current directory or
$HOME/.profile if either file exists.

3. Read commands from the file named by performing parameter substitution on the
value of the environment variable ENV if the file exists. If the -s option is not
present and *arg* is -, then perform a path search on the first *arg* to determine the
name of the script to execute. The script *arg* must have read permission, and any
setuid and setgid settings are ignored. If the script is not found in the path,
process *arg* as if it named a built-in command or function. Commands are then
read as described.

The following options are interpreted by the shell when it is invoked.

-c   Read commands from the *command-string* operand. Set the value of
            the special parameter 0 from the value of the *command-name* operand
            and the positional parameters ($1, $2, and so on) in sequence from the
            remaining *arg* operands. Read no commands from the standard input.

-i   If you specify -i or if the shell input and output are attached to a
            terminal (as told by ioctl(2)), this shell is interactive. In this case,
            ignore TERM (so that kill 0 does not kill an interactive shell), and catch
            and ignore INTR (so that wait is interruptible). In all cases, ignore QUIT.

-r   Specify a restricted shell.

-s   If you specify the -s option or if no arguments remain, read commands
            from the standard input. Write shell output, except for the output of
            the special commands, to file descriptor 2.

Restricted Korn Shell
Use the restricted Korn shell, rksh, to set up login names and execution environments
with more controlled capabilities than those of the standard shell. The actions of rksh
are identical to those of ksh, except that the following actions are not enabled.

- Changing directory (see cd(1)).
- Setting the value of SHELL, ENV, or PATH.
- Specifying path or command names containing /.
- Redirecting output (>, >|, <>, and >>).
- Changing group (see newgrp(1)).

The restrictions above are enforced after the .profile and ENV files are interpreted.
When a command to be executed is found to be a shell procedure, rksh invokes ksh to
execute it. Thus, you can provide shell procedures that have access to the full power of
the standard shell while imposing a limited menu of commands; this scheme assumes
that the user does not have write and execute permissions in the same directory.

The net effect of these rules is that the writer of the .profile has complete control
over user actions, by performing guaranteed setup actions and leaving the user in an
appropriate directory (probably not the login directory).

The system administrator often sets up a directory of commands (that is, /usr/rbin)
that can be safely invoked by rksh.

Interactive Operation

After startup processing is complete, an interactive Korn shell begins reading commands from the terminal. The default prompts are a dollar sign ($) for normal use or a pound sign (#) for superuser.

The following list describes some of the key features of using ksh as an interactive shell.

- *Command-line editing.* ksh provides an emacs-like and a vi-like interface that you can use to edit the current line. You can use the same interface to make changes to previous commands, which ksh keeps in a history file.

- *Command history mechanism.* ksh uses a history file to store the commands that you enter. You can access the history file with emacs or vi editor directives or by using the built-in fc command. The history file is maintained across login sessions and can be shared by several simultaneous instances of ksh.

- *Aliasing.* You can customize command name and option combinations by defining shorthand names, called aliases, for frequently used commands.

- *Job control.* ksh can display a completion message at the prompt after a background job terminates. You can stop jobs and move them to and from background processing.

- *Tilde expansion.* You can symbolically refer to the home directory of any user and the last directory that you were in. You do not need to know the name of the directory or type it in.

When you use the Korn shell interactively, it prompts with the parameter expanded value of PS1 before reading a command. If at any time you type a newline and the shell needs further input to complete a command, then the secondary prompt (that is, the value of PS2) is displayed.

Programming Language Operation

The Korn shell programming language provides the following benefits.

- *I/O mechanism.* You can simultaneously open and read more than one file. You can specify the number of columns printed for each item of information.

- *Arithmetic evaluation.* ksh can perform integer arithmetic in any base from 2 through 36 by using constants and ksh variables.

- *Substring operators.* ksh can generate substrings derived from the values of shell variables.

- *Array variables and attributes.* You can convert strings to lower case or upper case. You can use one-dimensional arrays of strings or numbers.

- *Function facility.* You can define local variables within functions to enable you to write recursive procedures. You can specify code to be executed whenever the function terminates.

- *Coprocessing facility.* You can run one or more programs in the background and send queries to and receive responses from it. This capability enables you to use shell scripts as a front end to another application such as a database management system.

Warning — The use of setuid shell scripts is strongly discouraged because of potential security risks.

Commands

A simple command is a sequence of blank-separated words that can be preceded by a variable assignment list. The first word specifies the name of the command to be executed. Except as specified below, the remaining words are passed as arguments to the invoked command. The command name is passed as argument 0 (see exec(2)). The value of a simple command is its exit status if it terminates normally or (octal) 200+ status if it terminates abnormally (see signal(3C) for a list of status values).

A pipeline is a sequence of one or more commands separated by |. The standard output of each command but the last is connected by a pipe(2) to the standard input of the next command. Each command is run as a separate process; the shell waits for the last command to terminate. The exit status of a pipeline is the exit status of the last command.

A list is a sequence of one or more pipelines separated by ;, &, &&, or ||, and optionally terminated by ;, &, or |&. Of these five symbols, ;, &, and |& have equal precedence, which is lower than that of && and ||. The symbols && and || also have equal precedence. A semicolon (;) sequentially executes the preceding pipeline; an ampersand (&) asynchronously executes the preceding pipeline (that is, the shell does not wait for that pipeline to finish). The symbol |& asynchronously executes the preceding command or pipeline with a two-way pipe established to the parent shell.

The standard input and output of the spawned command can be written to and read from by the parent shell with the -p option of the special commands read and print described in "Special Commands" on page 607. The symbol && (||) executes the list following it only if the preceding pipeline returns 0 (or a non-zero) value. You can use an arbitrary number of newlines instead of a semicolon in a list to delimit a command.

A command is either a simple command or one of the following. Unless otherwise stated, the value returned by a command is that of the last simple command executed in the command.

for *identifier* [in *word*...] ; do *list* ; done

> Each time a for command is executed, set *identifier* to the next word taken from the in *word* list. If you omit in *word*..., execute the do *list* once for each positional parameter that is set. Execution ends when there are no more words in the list.

select *identifier* [in *word*...] ; do *list* ; done

> Print to standard error (file descriptor 2) the set of words, each preceded by a number. If you omit in *word*..., use the positional parameters instead (see Parameter Substitution). Print the PS3 prompt, and read a line from the standard input. If this line consists of the number of one of the listed words, then set the value of the variable identifier to the word corresponding to this number. If this line is empty, print the selection list again. Otherwise, set the value of the variable identifier to null. Save the contents of the line read from standard input in the shell variable REPLY. Execute the list for each selection until a break or EOF is encountered. If the REPLY variable is set to null by the execution of list, then print the selection list before displaying the PS3 prompt for the next selection.

```
case word in [pattern [| pattern] ) list ;;]... esac
```
> A case command executes the *list* associated with the first pattern that matches *word.* The form of the patterns is the same as that used for file-name generation.

```
if list ; then list ; [elif list ; then list;...][else list ;] fi
```
> Execute the *list* following if and, if it returns an exit status of 0, execute the *list* following the first then. Otherwise, execute the *list* following elif, and, if its value is 0, execute the *list* following the next then. Failing that, execute the else *list.* If no else *list* or then *list* is executed, then return 0 exit status.

```
while list ; do list ; done
until list ; do list ; done
```
> Repeatedly execute the while *list,* and, if the exit status of the last command in the list is 0, execute the do *list;* otherwise, terminate the loop. If no commands in the do list are executed, then return 0 exit status; you can use until in place of while to negate the loop termination test.

`(list)`
> Execute *list* in a separate environment. Note that if two adjacent open parentheses are needed for nesting, you must insert a space to avoid arithmetic evaluation.

`{list}`
> Execute *list.* Note that unlike the metacharacters (and), { and } are reserved words and must occur at the beginning of a line or after a semicolon to be recognized.

`[[expression]]`
> Evaluate *expression* and return 0 exit status when *expression* is true. See "Conditional Expressions" on page 603 for a description of *expression.*

```
function identifier { list ;} identifier() { list ;}
```
> Define a function that is referenced by *identifier.* The body of the function is the list of commands between { and }. (See Functions.)

```
time pipeline
```
> Execute the pipeline and print the elapsed time as well as the user and system time to standard error.

The following reserved words are recognized only as the first word of a command and when not quoted.

```
! if then else elif fi esac ASIC for while until do done { } function
    select time [[]]
```

Inline Editing Option

Normally, you simply type each command line from a terminal device followed by a newline (Return or linefeed). However, if the emacs, gmacs, or vi option is active, you can edit the command line. To be in one of these edit modes, you must set the corresponding option. An editing option is automatically selected each time the VISUAL or EDITOR variable is assigned a value ending with one of the editing option names.

The editing features require that your terminal accept Return as Return without linefeed and that a space must overwrite the current character on the screen. The editing modes implement the concept that you are looking through a window at the current line. The window width is the value of COLUMNS if it is defined; otherwise, it is 80 characters. If the window width is too small to display the prompt and leaves at least 8 columns for input, the prompt is truncated from the left. If the line is longer than the window width minus 2, a mark is displayed at the end of the window. As the cursor moves and reaches the window boundaries, the window is centered about the cursor. The mark is a > if the line extends on the right side of the window, < if the line extends on the left, and * if the line extends on both sides of the window. The search commands in each edit mode provide access to the history file. Only strings are matched, not patterns, although a leading ^ in the string restricts the match to begin at the first character in the line.

emacs Editing Mode

You enter emacs editing mode by enabling either the emacs or gmacs option. The only difference between these two modes is the way they handle ^T. To edit, move the cursor to the point needing correction and then insert or delete characters or words as needed. All the editing commands are control characters or escape sequences. The notation for control characters is a caret (^) followed by the control character.

For example, ^F is the notation for Control-F. You enter this key sequence by holding down the Control key and typing f. Do not press the Shift key. (The notation ^? indicates the Delete key.)

The notation for escape sequences is M- followed by a character. For example, enter M-f (pronounced Meta f) by pressing Escape (ASCII 033) followed by f. (M-F would be the notation for Escape followed by Shift (capital) F.)

All edit commands operate from any place on the line (not just at the beginning).

Note — Do not press either the Return or the linefeed key after edit commands except when noted.

^F	Move cursor forward (right) one character.
M-f	Move cursor forward one word. (The emacs editor considers a word to be a string of characters consisting of only letters, digits, and underscores.)
^B	Move cursor backward (left) one character.
M-b	Move cursor backward one word.
^A	Move cursor to start of line.
^E	Move cursor to end of line.
^] char	Move cursor forward to character *char* on current line.
M-^] char	Move cursor backward to character *char* on current line.
^X^X	Interchange the cursor and mark.
erase	Delete previous character. The user-defined erase character, usually ^H or #, is defined by the stty(1) command.
^D	Delete current character.
M-d	Delete current word.
M-^H	(Meta-backspace) Delete previous word.

M-h	Delete previous word.
M-^?	(Meta-Delete) Delete previous word (if your interrupt character is ^? (Delete, the default), then this command does not work).
^T	Transpose current character with next character in emacs mode. Transpose two previous characters in gmacs mode.
^C	Capitalize current character.
M-c	Capitalize current word.
M-l	Change the current word to lower case.
^K	Delete from the cursor to the end of the line. If preceded by a numerical parameter whose value is less than the current cursor position, then delete from given position up to the cursor. If preceded by a numerical parameter whose value is greater than the current cursor position, then delete from cursor up to given cursor position.
^W	Kill from the cursor to the mark.
M-p	Push the region from the cursor to the mark on the stack.
kill	Kill the entire current line. If you enter two kill characters in succession, all kill characters from then on insert a linefeed (useful when using paper terminals). The user-defined kill character, usually ^G or @, is defined by the stty(1) command.
^Y	Restore last item removed from line. (Yank item back to the line.)
^L	Linefeed, and print current line.
^@	(Null character) Set mark.
M-space	(Meta-space) Set mark.
J	(Newline) Execute the current line.
M	(Return) Execute the current line.
eof	Process end-of-file character, normally ^D, as an End-of-File only if the current line is null.
^P	Fetch previous command. Each time you enter ^P, access the previous command back in time. Move back one line when not on the first line of a multiline command.
M-<	Fetch the least recent (oldest) history line.
M->	Fetch the most recent (youngest) history line.
^N	Fetch next command line. Each time you enter ^N, access the next command line forward in time.
^R*string*	Reverse search history for a previous command line containing *string*. If you give a parameter of 0, search forward. Terminate *string* with a Return or newline. If you precede *string* with a ^, the matched line must begin with *string*. If you omit *string*, then access the next command line containing the most recent string. In this case, a parameter of 0 reverses the direction of the search.

^O   Execute the current line, and operate on the next line relative to the
                 current line from the history file.

M-*digits*   Define numeric parameter for Escape. The digits are taken as a
                 parameter to the next command. The commands that accept a
                 parameter are ^F, ^B, erase, ^C, ^D, ^K, ^R, ^P, ^N, ^], M-., M-^],
                 M-_, M-b, M-c, M-d, M-f, M-h, M-l, and M-^H.

M-*letter*   Search your alias list for an alias with the name _*letter*, and if an alias
                 of this name is defined, insert its value on the input queue. The letter
                 must not be one of the above metafunctions.

M-[*letter*   Search your alias list for an alias with the name __*letter*, and if an
                 alias of this name is defined, insert its value on the input queue. You
                 can use this option to program functions keys on many terminals.

M-.   Insert the last word of the previous command on the line. If preceded by
                 a numeric parameter, the value of this parameter determines what
                 word to insert instead of the last word.

M-_   Same as M-.

M-*   Append an asterisk to the end of the word, and try a file-name
                 expansion.

M-Escape   Complete file name by replacing the current word with the longest
                 common prefix of all file names matching the current word with an
                 asterisk appended. If the match is unique, append a / if the file is a
                 directory and a space if the file is not a directory.

M-=   List files matching current word pattern if an asterisk is appended.

^U   Multiply parameter of next command by 4.

\   Escape next character. You can enter editing characters and erase, kill,
                 and interrupt (normally ^?) characters in a command line or in a search
                 string if you precede them with a \. The \ removes the next character's
                 editing features (if any).

^V   Display version of the shell.

M-#   Insert a # at the beginning of the line and execute it. This command also
                 inserts a comment in the history file.

vi Editing Mode

vi has an input mode and a control mode. Initially, when you enter a command, you are
in input mode. To edit, press Escape (033) to enter control mode, move the cursor to the
point that needs correction, and then insert or delete characters or words as needed.
Most control commands accept an optional repeat count to the command.

In vi mode on most systems, canonical processing is initially enabled. The command
is echoed again if the speed is 1200 baud or greater and it contains any control
characters or if less than one second has elapsed since the prompt was printed. The
Escape character terminates canonical processing for the remainder of the command,
and you can then modify the command line. This scheme has the advantages of
canonical processing with the type-ahead echoing of raw mode.

If the option `viraw` is also set, the terminal always has canonical processing disabled. This mode is implicit for systems that do not support two alternate end-of-line delimiters and may be helpful for certain terminals.

vi Input Edit Commands

By default the editor is in input mode.

erase	Delete previous character. The user-defined erase character, usually ^H or #, is defined by the `stty`(1) command.
^W	Delete the previous blank-separated word.
^D	Terminate the shell.
^V	Escape the next character. You can enter editing characters and the erase or kill characters in a command line or in a search string if preceded by a ^V. The ^V removes the next character's editing features (if any).
\	Escape the next erase or kill character.

vi Motion Edit Commands

The following commands move the cursor.

[*count*]l	Move cursor forward (right) one character.
[*count*]w	Move cursor forward one alphanumeric word.
[*count*]W	Move cursor to the beginning of the next word that follows a blank.
[*count*]e	Move cursor to end of word.
[*count*]E	Move cursor to end of the current blank delimited word.
[*count*]h	Move cursor backward (left) one character.
[*count*]b	Move cursor backward one word.
[*count*]B	Move cursor to preceding blank-separated word.
[*count*]|	Move cursor to column *count*.
[*count*]f*c*	Find the next character *c* in the current line.
[*count*]F*c*	Find the previous character *c* in the current line.
[*count*]t*c*	Equivalent to f followed by h.
[*count*]T*c*	Equivalent to F followed by l.
[*count*];	Repeat *count* times, the last, single-character find command, f, F, t, or T.
[*count*],	Reverse the last single-character find command *count* times.
0	Move cursor to start of line.
^	Move cursor to first nonblank character in line.
$	Move cursor to end of line.

%   Move to balancing (,), {, }, [, or]. If the cursor is not on one of the above characters, first search the remainder of the line for the first occurrence of one of the above characters.

vi Search Edit Commands

Use these commands to access your command history.

[*count*] k   Fetch previous command. Each time you enter k, access the previous command back in time.

[*count*] -   Equivalent to k.

[*count*] j   Fetch next command. Each time you enter j, access the next command forward in time.

[*count*] +   Equivalent to j.

[*count*] G   Fetch the command number *count*. The default is the least recent history command.

/*string*   Search backward through history for a previous command containing *string*. Terminate *string* with a Return or newline. If you precede *string* with a ^, the matched line must begin with *string*. If *string* is null, use the previous string.

?*string*   Same as / except search forward.

n   Search for next match of the last pattern to / or ? commands.

N   Search for next match of the last pattern to / or ?, but in reverse direction. Search history for the *string* entered by the previous / command.

vi Text Modification Edit Commands

Use these commands to modify the line.

a   Enter input mode, and enter text after the current character.

A   Append text to the end of the line. Equivalent to $a.

[*count*] c*motion* c[*count*]*motion*

     Delete current character through the character that *motion* would move the cursor to, and enter input mode. If *motion* is c, delete the entire line and enter input mode.

C   Delete the current character through the end of line, and enter input mode. Equivalent to c$.

[*count*] s   Delete *count* characters, and enter input mode.

S   Delete entire line, and enter input mode. Equivalent to cc.

[*count*] d*motion* d[*count*]*motion*

     Delete current character through the character that *motion* would move to. If *motion* is d, delete the entire line.

D   Delete the current character through the end of line. Equivalent to d$.

i	Enter input mode, and insert text before the current character.
I	Insert text before the beginning of the line. Equivalent to 0i.
[*count*]P	Put the previous text modification before the cursor.
[*count*]p	Put the previous text modification after the cursor.
R	Enter input mode, and replace, in overlay fashion, characters on the screen with characters you type.
[*count*]r*c*	Replace the *count* character(s) starting at the current cursor position with *c*, and advance the cursor.
[*count*]x	Delete current character.
[*count*]X	Delete preceding character.
[*count*].	Repeat the previous text modification command.
[*count*]~	Invert the case of the *count* character(s) starting at the current cursor position, and advance the cursor.
[*count*]_	Append the *count* word of the previous command, and enter input mode. If you omit *count*, use the last word.
*	Append an asterisk (*) to the current word, and try file-name generation. If no match is found, ring the bell. Otherwise, replace the word with the matching pattern, and enter input mode.
\	Perform file-name completion by replacing the current word with the longest common prefix of all file names matching the current word with an asterisk appended. If the match is unique, append a / if the file is a directory and a space if the file is not a directory.

vi Other Edit Commands

Miscellaneous commands.

[*count*]y*motion* y[*count*]*motion*

Yank current *character* through *character* that *motion* would move the cursor to, and put them into the delete buffer. Leave the text and cursor unchanged.

Y	Yank from current position to end of line. Equivalent to y$.
u	Undo the last text-modifying command.
U	Undo all the text-modifying commands performed on the line.
[*count*]v	Return the command fc -e ${VISUAL:-${EDITOR:-vi}} *count* in the input buffer. If you omit *count*, then use the current line.
^L	Linefeed, and print current line. Has effect only in control mode.
J	(Newline) Execute the current line, regardless of mode.
M	(Return) Execute the current line, regardless of mode.

#	If the first character of the command is a #, then delete this # and each # that follows a newline. Otherwise, send the line after inserting a # in front of each line in the command. Useful for inserting the current line in the history as a comment and removing comments from previous comment commands in the history file.
=	List the file names that match the current word if an asterisk is appended to it.
@*letter*	Search your alias list for an alias by the name *_letter*, and if an alias of this name is defined, insert its value on the input queue for processing.

Command History

Commands you enter from a terminal device are saved in a history file. The HISTSIZE environment variable determines the number of commands that are saved. The default is 128. If the HISTFILE variable is not set or if the file it names is not writable, ksh uses the file $HOME/.sh_history to store the history list. A shell can access the commands of all interactive shells that use the same named HISTFILE. Use the special command fc to list or edit a portion of this file. You can specify the portion of the file to be edited or listed by the number assigned in the history list or by specifying the first character or characters of the command. You can specify a single command or a range of commands. If you do not specify an editor program as an argument to fc, then the value of the variable FCEDIT is used. If FCEDIT is not defined, then /bin/ed is used as the editor. The edited commands are printed and reexecuted on leaving the editor. Use the editor name - to skip the editing phase and to reexecute the command. In this case, you can use a substitution parameter of the form *old=new* to modify the command before execution. For example, if r is aliased to fc -e -, then typing r bad=good c reexecutes the most recent command that starts with the letter c, replacing the first occurrence of the string bad with the string good. For more details, see history(1).

> **Note —** Using the fc built-in command within a compound command removes the whole command from the history file.

Aliasing

If you have defined an alias for a word, the first word of each command is replaced by the text of the alias. An alias name consists of any number of characters, excluding metacharacters, quoting characters, file-expansion characters, parameter and command-substitution characters, and =. The replacement string can contain any valid shell script including the metacharacters listed above. The first word of each command in the replaced text, other than any that are in the process of being replaced, is tested for aliases. If the last character of the alias value is a blank, then the word following the alias is also checked for alias substitution. You can use aliases to redefine special built-in commands, but you cannot use them to redefine the reserved words.

Create, list, and export aliases with the alias command. Remove them with the unalias command. Exported aliases remain in effect for scripts invoked by name but must be reinitialized for separate invocations of the shell. To prevent infinite loops in recursive aliasing, if the shell is not currently processing an alias of the same name, the word is replaced by the value of the alias; otherwise, it is not replaced.

Aliasing is performed when scripts are read, not while they are executed. Therefore, for an alias to take effect, the alias definition command has to be executed before the command that references the alias is read. Aliases are frequently used as a shorthand for full path names. An option to the aliasing facility enables the value of the alias to be automatically set to the full path name of the corresponding command. These aliases are called *tracked aliases*. The value of a tracked alias is defined the first time the corresponding command is looked up and becomes undefined each time the PATH variable is reset. These aliases remain tracked so that the next subsequent reference redefines the value. Several tracked aliases are compiled into the shell. The -h option of the set command makes each referenced command name into a tracked alias. The following exported aliases are compiled into (and built into) the shell, but you can unset or redefine them.

```
autoload='typeset -fu'
false='let 0'
functions='typeset -f'
hash='alias -t'
history='fc -l'
integer='typeset -i'
nohup='nohup '
r='fc -e -'
true=':'
type='whence -v'
```

The following example shows a problem involving trailing blank characters and reserved words. If you type the commands

```
$ alias foo="/bin/ls "
$ alias while="/"
```

then the effect of executing the following commands is a never-ending sequence of Hello, World strings.

```
$ while true
> do
> echo "Hello, World"
> done
```

If, however, you type the following command, the result is an ls listing of /.

```
$ foo while
```

Because the alias substitution for foo ends in a space character, the next word is checked for alias substitution. The next word, while, has also been aliased, so it is substituted as well. Because it is not in the proper position as a command word, it is not recognized as a reserved word.

If you type

```
$ foo; while
```

while retains its normal reserved-word properties.

Note — If a command that is a tracked alias is executed, and then a command with the same name is installed in a directory in the search path before the directory where the original command was found, the shell continues to execute the original command. Use the -t option of the alias command to correct this situation.

Tilde Substitution

After alias substitution is performed, each word is checked to see if it begins with an unquoted tilde (~). If it does, then the word up to a / is checked to see if it matches a user name. If a match is found, the ~ and the matched login name are replaced with the login directory of the matched user. This action is called a *tilde substitution*. If no match is found, the original text is left unchanged. A ~ by itself or in front of a / is replaced by $HOME. A ~ followed by a + or - is replaced by $PWD and $OLDPWD, respectively. In addition, tilde substitution is attempted when the value of a variable assignment begins with a ~.

Job Control

Job control enables you to move currently executing commands into the foreground or background and to stop, suspend, or restart them as needed. There is always one job in the foreground, which is the job that accepts your keyboard input. The foreground job may be a shell or another command such as an editor that accepts keyboard input.

When you execute a command line or start a job in the foreground, input to the terminal window is blocked and you cannot enter additional commands until that job completes. You can use the job control commands to push that job into the background to regain control of your terminal window. Similarly, you can bring a background job back to the foreground so that you can control it or enter data from the terminal window. Job control enables you to perform these actions within the current layer or window.

When the monitor option of the set command is turned on, an interactive shell associates a job with each pipeline. Each command or pipeline that you enter at a terminal window is then assigned a positive numeric *job-id*. The shell keeps track of current and previous jobs. The current job is the most recent job to be started or restarted. The previous job is the first noncurrent job.

When a job is started asynchronously with &, the shell prints a line that looks like [1] 567, indicating that the job that was started asynchronously was job number 1 and has one (top-level) process whose process ID is 567.

All jobs exist in one of the following states.

- A *foreground* job has read and write access to the controlling terminal.
- A *background* job is denied read access and has conditional write access to the *controlling* terminal (see stty(1)).
- A *stopped* job has been placed in a suspended state, usually as a result of a SIGTSTP signal (see signal(5)).

If you specify no options, the output is a series of lines of the following form.

    [%d] %c %s %s\n, *job-number*, *current*, *state*, *command*

The following example lists two jobs.

```
$ jobs
[1] - Running                    spider
[2] + Done(0)                    find . -name core -print
$
```

The fields are described below.

job-number   A number used to identify the process group to the wait, fg, bg, and kill commands. Using these commands, you can identify the job by prefixing the job number with %.

current   The character + identifies the job that would be used as a default for the fg or bg commands; this job can also be specified with the *job-id* %+ or %%. The character – identifies the job that would become the default if the current default job were to exit; this job can also be specified with the *job-id* %-. For other jobs, this field is a space character. One job can be identified with +, and one job can be identified with –. If there is any suspended job, then the current job is a suspended job. If there are at least two suspended jobs, then the previous job is also a suspended job.

state   One of the following strings (in the POSIX locale):

Running   The job has not been suspended by a signal and has not exited.

Done   The job completed and returned exit status 0.

Done(*code*)   The job completed normally and exited with the specified non-zero exit status, *code*, expressed as a decimal number.

Stopped
Stopped (SIGTSTP)
                The job was suspended by the SIGTSTP signal.

Stopped (SIGSTOP)
                The job was suspended by the SIGSTOP signal.

Stopped (SIGTTIN)
                The job was suspended by the SIGTTIN signal.

Stopped (SIGTTOU)
                The job was suspended by the SIGTTOU signal.

The implementation may substitute the string Suspended in place of Stopped. If the job was terminated by a signal, the format of state is unspecified, but it is visibly distinct from all of the other state formats shown here and indicates the name or description of the signal that terminated the job.

command   The associated command that was given to the shell.

If you specify the –l option, a field containing the process group ID is inserted before the state field. Also, more processes in a process group can be output on separate lines, using only the process ID and command fields.

If you specify the –p option, the output consists of one line for each process ID.

The built-in jobs command displays the status of the jobs that were started in the current shell environment. When jobs reports the termination status of a job, the shell removes its process ID from the list of those known in the current shell execution environment.

The following options modify or enhance the output of `jobs`.

-l   (The letter ell.) Provide more information about each job listed. This information includes the job number, current job, process group ID, state, and command that formed the job.

-n   Display only jobs that have stopped or exited since last notified.

-p   Display only the process IDs for the process group leaders of the selected jobs.

By default, `jobs` displays the status of all the stopped jobs, running background jobs, and all jobs whose status has changed and have not been reported by the shell.

If you are running a job and want to do something else, you can use the ^Z (Control-Z) key combination to send a STOP signal to the current job. The shell normally indicates that the job has been stopped and displays another prompt. You can then manipulate the state of this job, putting it in the background with the `bg` command, or run some other commands and then eventually bring the job back into the foreground with the `fg` command. A ^Z takes effect immediately and is like an interrupt in that pending output and unread input are discarded.

You can refer to jobs in the shell by their process ID or by any of the following.

%*number*   The job with the given number.

%*string*   Any job whose command line begins with *string*. This syntax works only in the interactive mode when the history file is active.

%?*string*   Any job whose command line contains *string*. This syntax works only in the interactive mode when the history file is active.

%%   Current job.

%+   Equivalent to %%.

%-   Previous job.

The following list describes the additional Korn shell job control commands.

fg   Move a background job from the current environment into the foreground. Using `fg` to place a job in the foreground removes its process ID from the list of those known in the current shell execution environment. The `fg` command is available only on systems that support job control. If you do not specify a *job-id*, the current job is brought into the foreground.

bg   Resume suspended jobs from the current environment by running them as background jobs. If the job specified by *job-id* is already a running background job, `bg` has no effect and exits successfully. Using `bg` to place a job into the background makes its process ID known in the current shell execution environment as if it had been started as an asynchronous list. The `bg` command is available only on systems that support job control. If you do not specify *job-id*, the current job is placed in the background.

stop   Stop the execution of a background job(s) by using its *job-id*, or of any process by using its *pid*; see ps(1).

The shell learns immediately whenever a process changes state. It normally informs you whenever a job becomes blocked so that no further progress is possible, but only just before it displays a prompt. The warning is done in this way so that it does not otherwise disturb your work. When the monitor mode is on, each background job that completes triggers any trap set for CHLD.

When you try to leave the shell while jobs are running or stopped, you are warned that You have stopped(running) jobs. You can use the jobs command to see what they are. If you do this or immediately try to exit again, the shell does not warn you a second time, and the stopped jobs are terminated. If you have nohup'ed jobs running when you attempt to log out, you are warned with the message

```
You have jobs running.
```

You then need to log out a second time to actually log out; however, your background jobs continue to run.

Signals

The INT and QUIT signals for an invoked command are ignored if the command is followed by & and the monitor option is not active. Otherwise, signals have the values inherited by the shell from its parent (but see also the trap special command).

Tilde Expansion

A tilde-prefix consists of an unquoted tilde character (~) at the beginning of a word, followed by all of the characters preceding the first unquoted slash in the word, or all the characters in the word if there is no slash. In an assignment, you can use multiple tilde-prefixes at the beginning of the word (that is, following the equal sign of the assignment), following any unquoted colon, or both. A tilde-prefix in an assignment is terminated by the first unquoted colon or slash. If none of the characters in the tilde-prefix are quoted, the characters in the tilde-prefix following the tilde are treated as a possible login name from the user database.

A portable login name cannot contain characters outside the set given in the description of the LOGNAME environment variable. If the login name is null (that is, the tilde-prefix contains only the tilde), the tilde-prefix is replaced by the value of the variable HOME. If HOME is unset, the results are unspecified. Otherwise, the tilde-prefix is replaced by a path name of the home directory associated with the login name obtained with the getpwnam function. If the system does not recognize the login name, the results are undefined.

Tilde expansion generally occurs only at the beginning of words, but an exception based on historical practice has been included:

```
PATH=/posix/bin:~dgk/bin
```

is eligible for tilde expansion because the tilde follows a colon and none of the relevant characters are quoted. Consideration was given to prohibiting this behavior because any of the following are reasonable substitutes.

```
PATH=$(printf %s ~karels/bin : ~bostic/bin)
for Dir in ~maart/bin ~srb/bin...
do
  PATH=${PATH:+$PATH:}$Dir
done
```

With the first command, explicit colons are used for each directory. In all cases, the shell performs tilde expansion on each directory because all are separate words to the shell.

Note — Expressions in operands such as:

```
make -k mumble LIBDIR=~chet/lib
```

do not qualify as shell variable assignments, and tilde expansion is not performed (unless the command does so itself, which make does not). The special sequence $~ has been designated for future implementations to evaluate as a means of forcing tilde expansion in any word.

Because of the requirement that the word not be quoted, the following are not equivalent; only the last does tilde expansion.

```
\~hlj/ ~h\lj/ ~"hlj"/ ~hlj\/ ~hlj/
```

The results of specifying a tilde with an unknown login name are undefined because the Korn shell ~+ and ~- constructs make use of this condition. In general it is an error to give an incorrect login name with a tilde. The results of having HOME unset are unspecified because some historical shells treat this as an error.

Command Substitution

The standard output from a command enclosed in parentheses preceded by a dollar sign $(*command*) or a pair of grave accents (` `) can be used as part or all of a word; trailing newlines are removed. In the second (archaic) form, the string between the quotes is processed for special quoting characters before the command is executed. (See "Quoting (Escaping) Characters" on page 602.) The command substitution $(cat *file*) can be replaced by the equivalent but faster (<file). Command substitution of most special commands that do not perform input/output redirection are carried out without creating a separate process. Command substitution enables the output of a command to be substituted in place of the command name itself. Command substitution occurs when the command is enclosed as follows:

$(*command*)

or (backquoted version):

` *command* `

The shell expands the command substitution by executing *command* in a subshell environment and replacing the command substitution (the text of *command* plus the enclosing $( ) or backquotes) with the standard output of the command, removing sequences of one or more newline characters at the end of the substitution. Embedded newline characters before the end of the output are not removed; however, they can be treated as field delimiters and eliminated during field splitting, depending on the value of IFS and quoting that is in effect.

Within the backquoted style of command substitution, backslash retains its literal meaning, except when followed by $ ` \ (dollar sign, backquote, backslash). The search for the matching backquote is satisfied by the first backquote found without a preceding backslash; during this search, if a nonescaped backquote is encountered within a shell comment, a here-document, an embedded command substitution of the $(*command*) form, or a quoted string, then undefined results occur. A single- or double-quoted string that begins but does not end within the ` ... ` sequence produces undefined results.

With the $(*command*) form, all characters following the opening parenthesis to the matching closing parenthesis constitute the command. Any valid shell script can be used for command; however,

- A script consisting solely of redirections produces unspecified results.
- See the restriction on single subshells described below.

The result of command substitution is that field splitting and path-name expansion are processed for further tilde expansion, parameter expansion, command substitution, or arithmetic expansion. If a command substitution occurs inside double quotes, it is not performed on the results of the substitution.

Command substitution can be nested. To specify nesting within the backquoted version, precede the inner backquotes with backslashes; for example:

```
`\`command\``
```

The `$( )` form of command substitution solves a problem of inconsistent behavior when backquotes are used. For example:

Command	Output
`echo '\$x'`	`\$x`
`echo `echo '\$x'``	`$x`
`echo $(echo '\$x')`	`\$x`

Additionally, the backquoted syntax has historical restrictions on the contents of the embedded command. Whereas the new `$( )` form can process any kind of valid embedded script, the backquoted form cannot handle some valid scripts that include backquotes. For example, these otherwise valid embedded scripts do not work in the left column, but do work in the right:

`echo ``	`echo $(`
`cat <<eeof`	`cat <<eeof`
`a here-doc with ``	`a here-doc with )`
`eof`	`eof`
`` ` ``	`)`
`echo ``	`echo $(`
`echo abc # a comment with ``	`echo abc # a comment with )`
`` ` ``	`)`
`echo ``	`echo $(`
`echo '`'`	`echo ')'`
`` ` ``	`)`

Because of these inconsistent behaviors, the backquoted variety of command substitution is not recommended for new applications that nest command substitutions or attempt to embed complex scripts.

If the command substitution consists of a single subshell, such as:

```
$( (command) )
```

a portable application must separate the $(and (into two tokens (that is, separate them with white space). This space is required to avoid any ambiguities with arithmetic expansion.

Input/Output

Before a command is executed, you can redirect its input and output by using a special notation interpreted by the shell. The following syntax can be used anywhere in a simple command or can precede or follow a command without being passed on to the invoked command. Command and parameter substitution occur before *word* or *digit* is used except as noted below. File-name generation occurs only if the pattern matches a single file, and blank interpretation is not performed.

<word	Use file *word* as standard input (file descriptor 0).
>word	Use file *word* as standard output (file descriptor 1). If the file does not exist, then create it. If the file exists and the `noclobber` option is on, an error occurs; otherwise, truncate it to 0 length.
>| word	Same as >, except override the `noclobber` option.
>>word	Use file *word* as standard output. If the file exists, then seek to the EOF and append output to it; otherwise, create the file.
<>word	Open file *word* for reading and writing as standard input.
<< [-] word	Read the shell input up to a line that is the same as *word* or to an end-of-file. Perform no parameter substitution, command substitution, or file-name generation on *word*. The resulting document, called a *here-document*, becomes the standard input. If any character of *word* is quoted, then put no interpretation on the characters of the document; otherwise, parameter and command substitution occur, \newline is ignored, and \ must be used to quote the characters \, $, `, and the first character of *word*. If you append - to <<, then strip all leading tabs from *word* and from the document.
<&digit	Duplicate the standard input from file descriptor *digit* (see dup(2)). Similarly for the standard output using >&*digit*.
<&-	Close the standard input. Similarly for the standard output using >&-.
<&p	Move the input from the coprocess to standard input.
>&p	Move the output to the coprocess to standard output.

If one of the above is preceded by a digit, then the file descriptor number referred to is that specified by the digit (instead of the default 0 or 1). For example, . . . 2>&1 means file descriptor 2 is to be opened for writing as a duplicate of file descriptor 1.

The specified order of redirections is significant. The shell evaluates each redirection in terms of the (file descriptor, file) association at the time of evaluation. For example, . . . 1>fname 2>&1 first associates file descriptor 1 with file fname. It then associates file descriptor 2 with the file associated with file descriptor 1 (that is, fname). If the order of redirections is reversed, file descriptor 2 is associated with the terminal (assuming file descriptor 1 had been) and then file descriptor 1 is associated with file fname. If a command is followed by & and job control is not active, then the default standard input for the command is the empty file /dev/null. Otherwise, the environment for the execution of a command contains the file descriptors of the invoking shell as modified by input/output specifications.

Execution

Each time a command is executed, the above substitutions are carried out in the following sequence.

- If the command name matches one of the special commands, it is executed within the current shell process.
- The command name is checked to see if it matches one of the user-defined functions. If it does, the positional parameters are saved and then reset to the arguments of the function call. When the function completes or issues a return, the positional parameter list is restored and any trap set on EXIT within the function is executed. The value of a function is the value of the last command executed. A function is also executed in the current shell process.
- If a command name is not a special command or a user-defined function, a process is created and an attempt is made to execute the command with exec(2). The shell variable PATH defines the search path for the directory containing the command. Alternative directory names are separated by a colon (:). The default path is /bin:/usr/bin:. (specifying /bin, /usr/bin, and the current directory, in that order). The current directory can be specified by two or more adjacent colons or by a colon at the beginning or end of the path list. If the command name contains a /, then the search path is not used. Otherwise, each directory in the path is searched for an executable file. If the file has execute permission but is not a directory or an a.out file, it is assumed to be a file containing shell commands. A subshell is spawned to read it. All nonexported aliases, functions, and variables are removed in this case. A parenthesized command is executed in a subshell without removing nonexported quantities.

Arithmetic Expansion

An arithmetic expression enclosed in double parentheses preceded by a dollar sign $((arithmetic-expression)) is replaced by the value of the arithmetic expression within the double parentheses. Arithmetic expansion provides a mechanism for evaluating an arithmetic expression and substituting its value. The format for arithmetic expansion is as follows:

$((*expression*))

The expression is treated as if it were in double quotes, except that a double-quote inside the expression is not treated specially. The shell expands all tokens in the expression for parameter expansion, command substitution, and quote removal.

Next, the shell treats the expression as an arithmetic expression and substitutes the value of the expression. The arithmetic expression is processed according to the rules of the ISO C with the following exceptions:

- Only integer arithmetic is required.
- The sizeof() operator and the prefix and postfix ++ and -- operators are not required.

- Selection, iteration, and jump statements are not supported. As an extension, the shell may recognize arithmetic expressions beyond those listed. If the expression is invalid, the expansion fails and the shell writes a message to standard error indicating the failure.

The following simple example uses arithmetic expansion.

```
# repeat a command 100 times
x=100
while [$x -gt 0]
do
command
x=$(($x-1))
done
```

Process Substitution

Note — Process substitution is available in SunOS and only on versions of the UNIX operating system that support the `/dev/fd` directory for naming open files.

Each command argument of the form `<(`*list*`)` or `>(`*list*`)` runs process *list* asynchronously connected to some file in `/dev/fd`. The name of this file becomes the argument to the command. If you use the form with >, then writing to this file provides input for *list*. If you use <, then the file passed as an argument contains the output of the list process. For example,

```
paste <(cut -f1 file1) <(cut -f3 file2) |
tee >( process1) >( process2)
```

cuts fields 1 and 3 from the files *file1* and *file2* respectively, pastes the results together, and sends it to the processes *process1* and *process2*, as well as putting it onto the standard output.

Note — The file passed as an argument to the command is a UNIX pipe(2), so programs that expect to execute lseek(2) on the file do not work.

Parameter Substitution

A parameter is an identifier of one or more digits or any of the characters *, @, #, ?, -, $, and !. A variable (a parameter denoted by an identifier) has a value and zero or more attributes. You can assign values and attributes to variables by using the typeset special command. The attributes supported by the shell are described with the typeset special command. Exported variables pass values and attributes to the environment.

The shell supports a one-dimensional array facility. An element of an array variable is referenced by a subscript. A subscript is denoted by a [, followed by an arithmetic expression followed by a]. To assign values to an array, use

```
set -A name value....
```

The value of all subscripts must be in the range of 0 through 1023. Arrays need not be declared. Any reference to a variable with a valid subscript is legal, and an array is created if necessary. Referencing an array without a subscript is equivalent to referencing the element 0. If you use an array identifier with subscript * or @, then the value for each of the elements is substituted (separated by a field separator character).

You can assign the value of a variable in the following way:

name=value [*name=value*]...

If the integer attribute, `-i`, is set for *name*, the value is subject to arithmetic evaluation as described below. Positional parameters, parameters denoted by a number, may be assigned values with the `set` special command. Parameter `$0` is set from argument `0` when the shell is invoked. If parameter is one or more digits, then it is a positional parameter. You must enclose a positional parameter of more than one digit in braces.

Parameter Expansion

The format for parameter expansion is as follows:

`${`*expression*`}`

where expression consists of all characters until the matching `}`. Any `}` escaped by a backslash or within a quoted string, characters in embedded arithmetic expansions, command substitutions, and variable expansions are not examined in determining the matching `}`.

The simplest form for parameter expansion is:

`${`*parameter*`}`

The value, if any, of *parameter* is substituted.

You can enclose the parameter name or symbol in braces, which are optional except for positional parameters with more than one digit or when parameter is followed by a character that could be interpreted as part of the name. The matching closing brace is determined by counting brace levels, skipping over enclosed quoted strings and command substitutions.

If you do not enclose the parameter name or symbol in braces, the expansion uses the longest valid name whether or not the symbol represented by that name exists. When the shell is scanning its input to determine the boundaries of a name, it is not bound by its knowledge of what names are already defined. For example, if `F` is a defined shell variable, the following command does not echo the value of `$F` followed by `red`.

`echo $Fred`

Instead, it selects the longest possible valid name, `Fred`, which might be unset. If a parameter expansion occurs inside double-quotes:

- Path name expansion is not performed on the results of the expansion.
- Field splitting is not performed on the results of the expansion, with the exception of `@`.

In addition, a parameter expansion can be modified by one of the following formats. In each case that a value of *word* is needed (based on the state of parameter, as described below), *word* is subjected to tilde expansion, parameter expansion, command substitution, and arithmetic expansion. If *word* is not needed, it is not expanded.

The `}` character that delimits the following parameter expansion modifications is determined as described previously in this section. (For example, `${foo-bar}xyz}` results in the expansion of `foo` followed by the string `xyz}` if `foo` is set; otherwise, the expanded string is `barxyz}`.)

`${`*parameter*`:-`*word*`}`

> Use default values. If *parameter* is unset or null, substitute the expansion of *word*; otherwise, substitute the value of *parameter*.

${parameter:=word}

> Assign default values. If parameter is unset or null, assign the
> expansion of *word* to *parameter*. In all cases, substitute the final
> value of *parameter*. You can assign only variables in this way, not
> positional parameters or special parameters.

${parameter:?[word]}

> Indicate error if null or unset. If *parameter* is unset or null, write
> to standard error the expansion of *word* (or a message indicating it
> is unset if you omit *word*) and exit with a non-zero exit status.
> Otherwise, substitute the value of *parameter*. An interactive shell
> need not exit.

${parameter:+[word]}

> Use alternative value. If *parameter* is unset or null, substitute
> null; otherwise, substitute the expansion of *word*.

In the above parameter expansions, use of the colon in the format results in a test for
a parameter that is unset or null; omitting the colon results in a test for a parameter
that is only unset. The following table summarizes the effect of the colon:

Format	Parameter set and not null	Parameter set but null	Parameter unset
${parameter:-word}	Substitute *parameter*.	Substitute *word*.	Substitute *word*.
${parameter-word}	Substitute *parameter*.	Substitute null.	Substitute *word*.
${parameter:=word}	Substitute *parameter*.	Assign *word*.	Assign *word*.
${parameter=word}	Substitute *parameter*.	Substitute *parameter*.	Assign null.
${parameter:?word}	Substitute *parameter*.	Error; exit.	Error; exit.
${parameter?word}	Substitute *parameter*.	Substitute null.	Error; exit.
${parameter:+word}	Substitute *word*.	Substitute null.	Substitute null.
${parameter+word}	Substitute *word*.	Substitute *word*.	Substitute null.

All cases shown with Substitute replace the expression with the value shown. All
cases shown with Assign assign *parameter* that value, which also replaces the
expression.

${#*parameter*}

>   String length. Specify the length, in characters, of the value of *parameter*. If *parameter* is * or @, then substitute all the positional parameters, starting with $1 separated by a field separator character.

The following four varieties of parameter expansion provide for substring processing. In each case, pattern-matching notation (see patmat), instead of regular expression notation, is used to evaluate the patterns. If *parameter* is * or @, then all the positional parameters, starting with $1, are substituted (separated by a field separator character). Enclosing the full parameter expansion string in double quotes does not cause the following four varieties of pattern characters to be quoted, whereas quoting characters within the braces does have this effect.

${*parameter*%*word*}

>   Remove smallest suffix pattern. Expand *word* to produce a pattern. The parameter expansion then results in *parameter*, with the smallest portion of the suffix matched by the pattern deleted.

${*parameter*%%*word*}

>   Remove largest suffix pattern. Expand *word* to produce a pattern. The parameter expansion then results in *parameter*, with the largest portion of the suffix matched by the pattern deleted.

${*parameter*#*word*}

>   Remove smallest prefix pattern. Expand *word* to produce a pattern. The parameter expansion then results in *parameter*, with the smallest portion of the prefix matched by the pattern deleted.

${*parameter*##*word*}

>   Remove largest prefix pattern. Expand *word* to produce a pattern. The parameter expansion then results in *parameter*, with the largest portion of the prefix matched by the pattern deleted.

Pattern Expansion Examples

The following examples illustrate each of the pattern expansion forms.

   In the first example, 1s is executed only if x is null or unset. (The $(1s) command substitution notation is explained in "Command Substitution" on page 590.)

${*parameter*:-*word*}

```
       ${x:-$(ls)}
```

${*parameter*:=*word*}

```
       unset X
       echo ${X:=abc}
       abc
```

${*parameter*:?*word*}

```
       unset posix
       echo ${posix:?}
       sh: posix: parameter null or not set
```

${*parameter*:+*word*}

```
set a b c
echo ${3:+posix}
posix
```

${#*parameter*}

```
HOME=/usr/posix
echo ${#HOME}
10
```

${*parameter*%v}

```
x=file.c
echo ${x%.c}.o
file.o
```

${*parameter*%%*word*}

```
x=posix/src/std
echo ${x%%/*}
posix
```

${*parameter*#*word*}

```
x=$HOME/src/cmd
echo ${x#$HOME}
/src/cmd
```

${*parameter*##*word*}

```
x=/one/two/three
echo ${x##*/}
three
```

Parameters Set by Shell

The shell automatically sets the following parameters.

#	The number of positional parameters in decimal.
-	Options supplied to the shell on invocation or by the set command.
?	The decimal value returned by the last executed command.
$	The process number of this shell.
_	Initially, the value of _ is an absolute path name of the shell or script being executed as passed in the environment. Subsequently, it is assigned the last argument of the previous command. This parameter is not set for commands that are asynchronous. This parameter is also used to hold the name of the matching MAIL file when checking for mail.
!	The process number of the last background command invoked.
ERRNO	The value of errno as set by the most recently failed system call. This value is system dependent and is intended for debugging purposes.
LINENO	The line number of the current line within the script or function being executed.
OLDPWD	The previous working directory set by the cd command.

OPTARG	The value of the last option argument processed by the getopts special command.
OPTIND	The index of the last option argument processed by the getopts special command.
PPID	The process number of the parent of the shell.
PWD	The present working directory set by the cd command.
RANDOM	Each time this variable is referenced, generate a random integer, uniformly distributed between 0 and 32767. You can initialize the sequence of random numbers by assigning a numeric value to RANDOM.
REPLY	This variable is set by the select statement and by the read special command when you supply no arguments.
SECONDS	Each time this variable is referenced, return the number of seconds since shell invocation. If this variable is assigned a value, then the value returned on reference is the value that was assigned plus the number of seconds since the assignment.

Variables Used by Shell

The shell gives default values to PATH, PS1, PS2, PS3, PS4, MAILCHECK, FCEDIT, TMOUT, and IFS, whereas HOME, SHELL ENV, and MAIL are not set at all by the shell (although HOME is set by login(1)). On some systems MAIL and SHELL are also set by login. The shell uses the following variables.

CDPATH	Specify the search path for the cd command.
COLUMNS	If this variable is set, use the value to define the width of the edit window for the shell edit modes and for printing select lists.
EDITOR	If the value of this variable ends in emacs, gmacs, or vi and the VISUAL variable is not set, then turn on the corresponding option (see the set special command).
ENV	When the shell is invoked, subject this variable to parameter expansion by the shell and use the resulting value as a path name of a file containing shell commands to execute in the current environment. The file need not be executable. If the expanded value of ENV is not an absolute path name, the results are unspecified. ENV is ignored if the user's real and effective user IDs or real and effective group IDs are different. You can use this variable to set aliases and other items local to the invocation of a shell. The file referred to by ENV differs from $HOME/.profile so that .profile is typically executed at session startup, whereas the ENV file is executed at the beginning of each shell invocation. The ENV value is interpreted in a manner similar to a dot script, in that the commands are executed in the current environment and the file needs to be readable but not executable. However, unlike dot scripts, no PATH searching is performed as a guard against Trojan horse security breaches.
FCEDIT	Specify the default editor for the fc command.

FPATH	Specify the search path for function definitions. By default, search the FPATH directories after the PATH variable. If an executable file is found, then read and execute it in the current environment. FPATH is searched before PATH when a function with the –u attribute is referenced. The autoload preset alias creates a function with the –u attribute.
IFS	Specify the internal field separators, normally space, Tab, and newline, used to separate command words that result from command or parameter substitution and for separating words with the read special command. The first character of the IFS variable is used to separate arguments for the $* substitution.
HISTFILE	If this variable is set when the shell is invoked, use the value as the file to store the command history.
HISTSIZE	If this variable is set when the shell is invoked, specify the number of commands to store in the history file. The default is 128.
HOME	Specify the default argument (home directory) for the cd command.
LC_ALL	A default value for the LC_* variables.
LC_COLLATE	Determine the behavior of range expressions, equivalence classes, and multibyte character-collating elements within pattern matching.
LC_CTYPE	Determine how the shell handles characters. When LC_CTYPE is set to a valid value, the shell can display and handle text and file names containing valid characters for that locale. If LC_CTYPE (see environ(5)) is not set in the environment, the operational behavior of the shell is determined by the value of the LANG environment variable. If LC_ALL is set, its contents override both the LANG and the other LC_* variables.
LC_MESSAGES	Determine the language for messages.
LANG	Provide a default value for the internationalization variables that are unset or null. If any of the internationalization variables contains an invalid setting, the command behaves as if none of the variables are defined.
LINENO	Set by the shell to a decimal number representing the current sequential line number (numbered starting with 1) within a script or function before it executes each command. If the user unsets or resets LINENO, the variable may lose its special meaning for the life of the shell. If the shell is not currently executing a script or function, the value of LINENO is unspecified.
LINES	If this variable is set, use the value to determine the column length for printing select lists. Select lists print vertically until about two-thirds of LINES' lines are filled.
MAIL	If this variable is set to the name of a mail file and the MAILPATH variable is not set, then inform the user of arrival of mail in the specified file.

MAILCHECK	Specify how often (in seconds) the shell checks for changes in the modification time of any of the files specified by the MAILPATH or MAIL variables. The default value is 600 seconds. When the time has elapsed, the shell checks before issuing the next prompt.
MAILPATH	A colon-separated list of file names. If this variable is set, then inform the user of any modifications to the specified files that have occurred within the last MAILCHECK seconds. Each file name can be followed by a ? and a message that is printed. The message undergoes parameter substitution with the variable $_ defined as the name of the file that has changed. The default message is you have mail in $_.
NLSPATH	Determine the location of message catalogs for the processing of LC_MESSAGES.
PATH	Specify the search path for commands. The user cannot change PATH if executing under rksh (except in .profile).
PPID	Set by the shell to the decimal process ID of the process that invoked the shell. In a subshell, PPID is set to the same value as that of the parent of the current shell. For example, echo $PPID and (echo $PPID) would produce the same value.
PS1	Expand the value of this variable for parameter substitution to define the primary prompt string, by default, $. Replace the character ! in the primary prompt string by the command number. Two successive occurrences of ! produce a single ! when the prompt string is printed.
PS2	Specify the secondary prompt string, by default, >.
PS3	Specify the selection prompt string used within a select loop, by default, #?.
PS4	Expand the value of this variable for parameter substitution and use that value to precede each line of an execution trace. If omitted, the execution trace prompt is +.
SHELL	Store the path name of the shell in the environment. At invocation, if the basename of this variable is rsh, rksh, or krsh, then the shell becomes restricted.
TMOUT	If set to a value greater than 0, terminate if a command is not entered within the prescribed number of seconds after the PS1 prompt is issued. (Note that the shell can be compiled with a maximum bound for this value which cannot be exceeded.)
VISUAL	If the value of this variable ends in emacs, gmacs, or vi, then turn on the corresponding option.

Blank Interpretation

After parameter and command substitution, the results of substitutions are scanned for the field separator characters (those found in IFS) and split into distinct arguments when such characters are found. Explicit null arguments (" ") or (' ') are retained. Implicit null arguments (those resulting from parameters that have no values) are removed.

File-Name Generation

Following substitution, each command word is scanned for the characters *, ?, and [unless you specify the -f option. If one of these characters appears, the word is regarded as a pattern. The word is replaced with lexicographically sorted file names that match the pattern. If no file name that matches the pattern is found, the word is left unchanged. When a pattern is used for file-name generation, the character dot (.) at the start of a file name or immediately following a /, as well as the character / itself, must be matched explicitly. A file name beginning with a dot is not matched with a pattern with the dot inside parentheses; that is, ls .@(r*) would locate a file named .restore, but ls @(.r*) would not.

In other instances of pattern matching, the / and . are not treated specially.

*	Match any string, including the null string.
?	Match any single character.
[...]	Match any one of the enclosed characters. A pair of characters separated by - matches any character lexically between the pair, inclusive. If the first character following the opening square bracket ([) is an exclamation mark (!), then any character not enclosed is matched. You can include a dash (-) in the character set by putting it as the first or last character.

A *pattern-list* is a list of one or more patterns separated from each other with a |. You can form composite patterns with one or more of the following.

?(*pattern-list*)

> Optionally match any one of the given patterns.

*(*pattern-list*)

> Match zero or more occurrences of the given patterns.

+(*pattern-list*)

> Match one or more occurrences of the given patterns.

@(*pattern-list*)

> Match exactly one of the given patterns.

!(*pattern-list*)

> Match anything except one of the given patterns.

Quoting (Escaping) Characters

Each of the metacharacters has a special meaning to the shell. To remove the normal meaning, you can quote it. (Note that in other contexts, the term *escape* is used to describe this action.) You can quote a single character (that is, make it stand for itself) by preceding it with a backslash. The pair \newline is removed.

To quote a string of characters, you can enclose them in quotes.

- All characters enclosed between a pair of single quote marks (' ') are quoted. A single quote cannot appear within single quotes.
- Inside double-quote marks (""), parameter and command substitution occurs, and \ quotes the characters \, `, ", and $. The meaning of $* and $@ is identical when not quoted or when used as a parameter assignment value or as a file name.

However, when used as a command argument, $* is equivalent to $1d$2d..., where d is the first character of the IFS variable, whereas $@ is equivalent to $1 $2....

- Inside grave quote marks (``), \ quotes the characters \, `, and $. If the grave quotes occur within double quotes, then \ also quotes the character ".

You can remove the special meaning of reserved words or aliases by quoting any character of the reserved word. You cannot alter the recognition of function names or special command names by quoting them.

Arithmetic Evaluation

The let special command provides the capability of performing integer arithmetic. Evaluations are performed using long arithmetic. Constants are of the form [*base*#] *n*, where *base* is a decimal number between 2 and 36 representing the arithmetic base and *n* is a number in that base. If you omit base, then base 10 is used. An arithmetic expression uses the same syntax, precedence, and associativity of expression as the C language. All the integral operators, other than ++, --, ?:, and , are supported. You can reference variables by name within an arithmetic expression without using the parameter substitution syntax. When you reference a variable, its value is evaluated as an arithmetic expression.

You can specify an internal integer representation of a variable with the -i option of the typeset special command. Arithmetic evaluation is performed on the value of each assignment to a variable with the -i attribute. If you do not specify an arithmetic base, the first assignment to the variable determines the arithmetic base. This base is used when parameter substitution occurs. Because many of the arithmetic operators require quoting, an alternative form of the let command is provided. For any command that begins with a ((, all the characters until a matching)) are treated as a quoted expression. More precisely, ((...)) is equivalent to let "...".

Conditional Expressions

Use conditional expressions with the [[compound command to test attributes of files and to compare strings.

Word splitting and file-name generation are not performed on the words between [[and]]. Each expression can be constructed from one or more of the following unary or binary expressions.

-a *file*	true if *file* exists.	
-b *file*	true if *file* exists and is a block special file.	
-c *file*	true if *file* exists and is a character special file.	
-d *file*	true if *file* exists and is a directory.	
-e *file*	true if *file* exists.	
-f *file*	true if *file* exists and is an ordinary file.	
-g *file*	true if *file* exists and has its setgid bit set.	
-k *file*	true if *file* exists and has its sticky bit set.	
-n *string*	true if length of *string* is non-zero.	
-o *option*	true if option named *option* is on.	
-p *file*	true if *file* exists and is a fifo special file or a pipe.	
-r *file*	true if *file* exists and is readable by current process.	

-s *file*   true if *file* exists and has size greater than 0.

-t *fildes*   true if file descriptor number *fildes* is open and associated with a
                 terminal device.

-u *file*   true if *file* exists and has its setuid bit set.

-w *file*   true if *file* exists and is writable by current process.

-x *file*   true if *file* exists and is executable by current process. If *file* exists
                 and is a directory, then the current process has permission to search in
                 the directory.

-z *string*   true if length of *string* is 0.

-L *file*   true if *file* exists and is a symbolic link.

-O *file*   true if *file* exists and is owned by the effective user ID of this process.

-G *file*   true if *file* exists and its group matches the effective group ID of this
                 process.

-S *file*   true if *file* exists and is a socket.

file1 -nt *file2*

                 true if *file1* exists and is newer than *file2*.

file1 -ot *file2*

                 true if *file1* exists and is older than *file2*.

file1 -ef *file2*

                 true if *file1* and *file2* exist and refer to the same file.

string   true if the string *string* is not the null string.

string = *pattern*

                 true if *string* matches *pattern*.

string != *pattern*

                 true if *string* does not match *pattern*.

string1 = *string2*

                 true if the strings *string1* and *string2* are identical.

string1 ! = *string2*

                 true if the strings *string1* and *string2* are not identical.

string1 < *string2*

                 true if *string1* comes before *string2* based on strings interpreted as
                 appropriate to the locale setting for category LC_COLLATE.

string1 > *string2*

                 true if *string1* comes after *string2* based on strings interpreted as
                 appropriate to the locale setting for category LC_COLLATE.

exp1 -eq *exp2*

                 true if *exp1* is equal to *exp2*.

exp1 -ne *exp2*

true if *exp1* is not equal to *exp2*.

exp1 -lt *exp2*

true if *exp1* is less than *exp2*.

exp1 -gt *exp2*

true if *exp1* is greater than *exp2*.

exp1 -le *exp2*

true if *exp1* is less than or equal to *exp2*.

exp1 -ge *exp2*

true if *exp1* is greater than or equal to *exp2*.

In each of the above expressions, if *file* is of the form /dev/fd/*n*, where *n* is an integer, then the test is applied to the open file whose descriptor number is *n*.

You can construct a compound expression from these primitives by using any of the following, listed in decreasing order of precedence.

(*expression*)

true if *expression* is true. Use to group expressions.

! *expression*

true if *expression* is false.

expression1 && *expression2*

true if *expression1* and *expression2* are both true.

expression1 || *expression2*

true if either *expression1* or *expression2* is true.

Environment Variables

The environment (see environ(5)) is a list of name-value pairs that is passed to an executed program in the same way as a normal argument list. The names must be identifiers, and the values are character strings. The shell interacts with the environment in several ways. On invocation, the shell scans the environment and creates a variable for each name found, giving it the corresponding value and marking it export. Executed commands inherit the environment. If the user modifies the values of these variables or creates new ones by using the export or typeset -x commands, they become part of the environment. The environment seen by any executed command is thus composed of any name-value pairs originally inherited by the shell, whose values may be modified by the current shell, plus any additions that must be noted in export or typeset -x commands.

You can augment the environment for any simple command or function by prefixing it with one or more variable assignments. A variable assignment argument is a word of the form *identifier=value*. Thus:

TERM=450 *cmd args*

and

(export TERM; TERM=450; *cmd args*)

are equivalent (as far as the above execution of *cmd* is concerned except for special commands listed in "Special Commands" on page 607 that are preceded with an asterisk).

If the -k option is set, all variable assignment arguments are placed in the environment, even if they occur after the command name. The following example first prints a=b c and then c:

```
$ echo a=b c
a=b c
$ set -k
$ echo a=b c
c
$
```

Note — Because this feature is intended for use with scripts written for early versions of the shell, its use in new scripts is strongly discouraged. The feature is likely to disappear someday.

Functions

Use the function reserved word to define shell functions. Shell functions are read in and stored internally. Alias names are resolved when the function is read. Functions are executed like commands with the arguments passed as positional parameters.

Functions execute in the same process as the caller and share all files and present working directory with the caller. Traps caught by the caller are reset to their default action inside the function. A trap condition that is not caught or ignored by the function terminates the function and passes the condition on to the caller. A trap on EXIT set inside a function is executed after the function completes in the environment of the caller. Ordinarily, variables are shared between the calling program and the function. However, the typeset special command used within a function defines local variables whose scope includes the current function and all functions it calls.

Use the return special command to return from function calls. Errors within functions return control to the caller.

typeset +f lists the names of all functions. typeset -f lists all function names as well as the text of all functions. typeset -f *function-names* lists the text of the named functions only. You can undefine functions with the -f option of the unset special command.

Ordinarily, functions are unset when the shell executes a shell script. The -xf option of the typeset command enables you to export a function to scripts that are executed without a separate invocation of the shell. Specify functions that need to be defined across separate invocations of the shell in the ENV file with the -xf option of typeset.

Function Definition Command

A function is a user-defined name that is used as a simple command to call a compound command with new positional parameters. A function is defined with a function definition command. The format of a function definition command is as follows:

fname() *compound-command*[*io-redirect...*]

The function is named *fname*; it must be a name. An implementation may allow other characters in a function name as an extension. The implementation maintains separate name spaces for functions and variables. The () in the function definition command consists of two operators. Therefore, intermixing blank characters with the *fname*, (, and) is allowed, but unnecessary. The argument *compound-command* represents a compound command.

When you declare a function, none of the expansions in wordexp are performed on the text in *compound-command* or *io-redirect*; all expansions are performed as normal each time you call the function. Similarly, the optional *io-redirect* redirections and any variable assignments within *compound-command* are performed during the execution of the function itself, not the function definition.

When a function is executed, it has the syntax-error and variable-assignment properties described for the special built-in commands.

The *compound-command* is executed whenever the function name is specified as the name of a simple command. The operands to the command temporarily become the positional parameters during the execution of the *compound-command*; the special parameter # is also changed to reflect the number of operands. The special parameter 0 is unchanged. When the function completes, the values of the positional parameters and the special parameter # are restored to the values they had before the function was executed. If the special built-in return is executed in the *compound-command*, the function completes and execution resumes with the next command after the function call.

The following example shows how you can use a function definition wherever a simple command is allowed.

```
# If variable i is equal to "yes",
# define function foo to be ls -l
#
["$i" = yes] && foo() {
  ls -l
}
```

The exit status of a function definition is 0 if the function was declared successfully; otherwise, it is greater than 0. The exit status of a function invocation is the exit status of the last command executed by the function.

Special Commands

The following simple commands are executed in the shell process. Input/output redirection is permitted. Unless otherwise indicated, the output is written on file descriptor 1 and the exit status, when there is no syntax error, is 0.

Commands that are preceded by one or two asterisks (*) are treated specially in the following ways.

- Variable assignment lists preceding the command remain in effect when the command completes.
- I/O redirections are processed after variable assignments.
- Errors abort a script that contains them.
- Words following a command preceded by ** that are in the format of a variable assignment are expanded with the same rules as a variable assignment. This means that tilde substitution is performed after the equal sign and word splitting and file-name generation are not performed.

* : [*arg*...]

        Expand only parameters.

* . *file* [*arg*...]

> Read the complete file, then execute the commands. Execute the commands in the current shell environment. Use the search path specified by PATH to find the directory containing *file*. If you specify any arguments *arg*, they become the positional parameters. Otherwise, the positional parameters are unchanged. The exit status is the exit status of the last command executed.

** alias [-tx] [*name*[=*value*]]...

> With no arguments, print the list of aliases in the form *name*=*value* on standard output. An alias is defined for each *name* whose *value* is given. A trailing space in value checks the next word for alias substitution. With the -t option, set and list tracked aliases. The value of a tracked alias is the full path name corresponding to the given name. The value becomes undefined when the value of PATH is reset, but the aliases remained tracked. Without the -t option, for each name in the argument list for which no value is given, print the name and value of the alias. With the -x option, set or print exported aliases. An exported alias is defined for scripts invoked by name. The exit status is non-zero if you specify a *name* but no *value* and if no alias has been defined for the *name*.

bg [%*job*...]

> Available only on systems that support job control. Put each specified job into the background. If you specify no *job*, put the current job in the background. See "Job Control" on page 586 for a description of the format of *job*.

* break [*n*]   Exit from the enclosed for, while, until, or select loop, if any. If you specify *n*, then break *n* levels.

* continue [*n*]

> Resume the next iteration of the enclosed for, while, until, or select loop. If you specify *n*, then resume at the *n*-th enclosed loop.

cd [*arg*]   In the first form, change the current directory to *arg*. If *arg* is -,
cd *old new*   change the directory to the previous directory. The shell variable HOME is the default *arg*. The variable PWD is set to the current directory. The shell variable CDPATH defines the search path for the directory containing *arg*. Alternative directory names are separated by a colon (:). The default path is null (specifying the current directory). Note that the current directory is specified by a null path name, which can appear immediately after the equal sign or between the colon delimiters anywhere else in the path list. If *arg* begins with a /, do not use the search path. Otherwise, search each directory in the path for *arg*. The second form substitutes the string *new* for the string *old* in the current directory name, PWD, and tries to change to this new directory. The cd command may not be executed by rksh.

```
command [-p] [command-name] [argument...]
command [-v -V] command-name
```

>   The command command treats the arguments as a simple command,
>   suppressing the shell function lookup. The -p option performs the
>   command search, using a default value for PATH that is guaranteed to
>   find all of the standard commands. The -v option writes a string to
>   standard output that indicates the path name or command used by the
>   shell, in the current shell execution environment, to invoke
>   command-name. The -V option writes a string to standard output that
>   indicates how the name given in the command-name operand is
>   interpreted in the current shell execution environment.

```
echo [arg...]
```

>   See echo(1) for usage and description.

```
* eval [arg...]
```

>   Read the arguments as input to the shell and execute the resulting
>   command(s).

```
* exec [arg...]
```

>   If you specify arg, execute the command specified by the arguments in
>   place of this shell without creating a new process. Input/output
>   arguments can appear and affect the current process. If you specify no
>   arguments, modify file descriptors as prescribed by the input/output
>   redirection list. In this case, any file descriptor numbers greater than
>   2 that are opened with this mechanism are closed when another
>   program is invoked.

```
* exit [n]
```
Exit the calling shell or shell script with the exit status specified by n.
The value is the least significant 8 bits of the specified status. If you
omit n, then the exit status is that of the last command executed. When
exit occurs when executing a trap, the last command refers to the
command that executed before the trap was invoked. An EOF exits the
shell except for a shell that has the ignoreeof option turned on.

```
** export [name[=value]]...
```

>   Mark the given names for automatic export to the environment of
>   subsequently executed commands.

```
fc [-e ename] [-nlr] [first [last]]
fc -e - [old=new] [command]
```

>   In the first form, choose a range of commands from first to last from
>   the last HISTSIZE commands that were typed at the terminal. You can
>   specify the arguments first and last as a number or as a

string. Use a string to locate the most recent command starting with the given string. Use a negative number as an offset to the current command number. If you use the -1 option, list the command on standard output. Otherwise, invoke the editor program *ename* on a file containing these keyboard commands. If you do not supply *ename*, use the value of the variable FCEDIT (default /bin/ed) as the editor. When editing is complete, execute the edited command(s). If you do not specify *last*, then the command is set to *first*. If you do not specify *first*, the default is the previous command for editing and -16 for listing. The -r option reverses the order of the commands, and the -n option suppresses command numbers when listing. In the second form, the command is reexecuted after it performs the substitution *old=new*. If you specify no command argument, execute the most recent command typed at this terminal.

fg [%*job*...]

On systems that support job control only, bring each job specified to the foreground. Otherwise, bring the current job into the foreground. See "Job Control" on page 586 for a description of the format of *job*.

getopts *optstring name* [*arg*...]

Check *arg* for legal options. If you omit *arg*, use the positional parameters. Begin an option argument with a + or a -. An option not beginning with + or - or the argument -- ends the options. *optstring* contains the letters that getopts recognizes. If you follow a letter by a :, that option is expected to have an argument. You can separate the options from the argument by blanks. getopts places the next option letter it finds inside variable *name* each time it is invoked with a + prepended when *arg* begins with a +. The index of the next *arg* is stored in OPTIND. The option argument, if any, is stored in OPTARG. A leading : in *optstring* stores the letter of an invalid option in OPTARG and sets name to ? for an unknown option and to : when a required option is missing. Otherwise, getopts prints an error message. The exit status is non-zero when there are no more options. See getoptcvt(1) for usage and description.

hash [*name*...]

For each *name*, determine the location in the search path of the command specified by *name*, and remember it. The -r option forgets all remembered locations. If you give no arguments, present information about remembered commands. In the hash output, Hits is the number of times a command has been invoked by the shell process. Cost is a measure of the work required to locate a command in the search path. If a command is found in a relative directory in the search path, after changing to that directory, recalculate the stored location of that command. Recalculated commands are indicated by an asterisk (*) adjacent to the Hits information. Cost is incremented when the recalculation is done.

jobs [-lnp] [%*job*...]

> List information about each given job; or, if you omit *job*, list all active
> jobs. The -1 option lists process IDs in addition to the normal
> information. The -n option displays only jobs that have stopped or
> exited since last notified. The -p option lists only the process group.
> See "Job Control" on page 586 and jobs(1) for a description of the
> format of *job*.

kill [-*sig*] %*job*...
kill [-*sig*] *pid*...
kill -1

> Send either the TERM (terminate) signal or the specified signal to the
> specified jobs or processes. You can specify signals either by number or
> by name (as given in signal(5) stripped of the prefix SIG, with the
> exception that SIGCHD is named CHLD). If you send TERM (terminate) or
> HUP (hangup), then the job or process is sent a CONT (continue) signal if
> it is stopped. The argument *job* can be the process ID of a process that
> is not a member of one of the active jobs. See "Job Control" on page 586
> for a description of the format of *job*. The third form, kill -1, lists the
> signal names.

let *arg*... Each *arg* is a separate arithmetic expression to be evaluated. The exit
> status is 0 if the value of the last expression is non-zero, and 1
> otherwise.

login *argument*...

> Equivalent to exec login *argument*.... See login(1) for usage and
> description.

* newgrp [*arg*...]

> Equivalent to exec /bin/newgrp *arg*....

print [-Rnprsu[n]] [*arg*...]

> The shell output mechanism. With no options or with option - or --,
> print the arguments on standard output as described by echo(1). The
> exit status is 0, unless the output file is not open for writing.

-n   Suppress newline from being added to the output.

-R | -r   Ignore the escape conventions of echo. The -R option prints all
> subsequent arguments and options other than -n.

-p   Write the arguments to the pipe of the process spawned with |&
> instead of standard output.

-s   Write the arguments to the history file instead of standard output.

-u [*n*]   Specify a one-digit file descriptor unit number *n* on which the output is
> placed. The default is 1.

pwd   Equivalent to print -r - $PWD.

Read   Read one line.

read [-prsu[*n*]] [*name?prompt*] [*name*...]

> Break up the shell input into fields, using the characters in IFS as separators. Use the escape character (\) to remove any special meaning for the next character and for line continuation. In raw mode, -r, the \ character is not treated specially. Assign the first field to the first *name*, the second field to the second *name*, and so on, with leftover fields assigned to the last *name*. The -p option takes the input line from the input pipe of a process spawned by the shell using |&.
>
> If you specify the -s option, save the input as a command in the history file. Use the -u option to specify a one-digit file descriptor unit *n* to read from. The file descriptor can be opened with the exec special command. The default value of *n* is 0. If you omit *name*, then use REPLY as the default name. The exit status is 0 unless the input file is not open for reading or an end-of-file is encountered. An end-of-file with the -p option cleans up for this process so that another can be spawned. If the first argument contains a ?, use the remainder of this word as a prompt on standard error when the shell is interactive. The exit status is 0 unless an end-of-file is encountered.

** readonly [*name*[=*value*]]...

> Mark the given names read-only. You cannot change these names by subsequent assignment.

* return [*n*]

> Return the invoking script for a shell function or . script with the return status specified by *n*. The value is the least significant 8 bits of the specified status. If you omit *n*, then the return status is that of the last command executed. If you invoke return while not in a function or a . script, then it is the same as an exit.

set [± abCefhkmnopstuvx] [± o *option*]... [± A *name*] [*arg*...]

> The options for this command have meaning as follows.
>
> -A   Unset the variable name, and assign array values sequentially from the list *arg*. If you use +A, do not first unset the variable name.
>
> -a   Automatically export all subsequent variables that are defined.
>
> -b   Notify the user asynchronously of background job completions. The following message is written to standard error:
>
> "[%d]%c %s%s\n", *job-number*, *current*, *status*, *job-name*
>
> where the fields are as follows:

current   The + character identifies the job that would be used as a
             default for the fg or bg commands. You can also specify this
             job with the *job-id*%+ or %%. The - character identifies the
             job that would become the default if the current default job
             were to exit. You can also specify this job with the *job-id*
             %-. For other jobs, this field is a space character. At most one
             job can be identified with +, and at most one job can be
             identified with -. If there is any suspended job, then the
             current job is a suspended job. If there are at least two
             suspended jobs, then the previous job is also a suspended
             job.

job-name

             Unspecified. When the shell notifies the user that a job has
             been completed, it may remove the job's process ID from the
             list of those known in the current shell execution
             environment. Asynchronous notification is not enabled by
             default.

job-number

             A number used to identify the process group to the wait, fg,
             bg, and kill commands. Using these commands, you can
             identify the job by prefixing the job number with %.

status   Unspecified.

-C   Prevent existing files from being overwritten by the shell's >
             redirection operator; the > | redirection operator overrides
             this noclobber option for an individual file.

-e   If a command has a non-zero exit status, execute the ERR
             trap if set, and exit. This mode is disabled while profiles are
             read.

-f   Disable file-name generation.

-h   Make each command a tracked alias when first
             encountered.

-k   Put all variable assignment arguments in the environment
             for a command, not just those that precede the command
             name.

-m   Run background jobs in a separate process group, and print
             a line on completion. Report the exit status of background
             jobs in a completion message. On systems with job control,
             this option is turned on automatically for interactive shells.

-n   Read commands, and check them for syntax errors, but do
             not execute them. Ignored for interactive shells.

-o   The argument for this option can be one of the following
             names:

             allexport   Same as -a.

errexit	Same as -e.
bgnice	Run all background jobs at a lower priority. This mode is the default.
emacs	Put you in an emacs-style inline editor for command entry.
gmacs	Put you in a gmacs-style inline editor for command entry.
ignoreeof	Do not exit on end-of-file. You must use the exit command.
keyword	Same as -k.
markdirs	Append a trailing / to all directory names resulting from file-name generation.
monitor	Same as -m.
noclobber	Prevent redirection > from truncating existing files. Require >| to truncate a file when turned on. Equivalent to -C.
noexec	Same as -n.
noglob	Same as -f.
nolog	Do not save function definitions in history file.
notify	Equivalent to -b.
nounset	Same as -u.
privileged	Same as -p.
verbose	Same as -v.
trackall	Same as -h.
vi	Put you in insert mode of a vi-style inline editor until you press escape character 033 to enter control mode. A Return sends the line.
viraw	Process each character as it is typed in vi mode.
xtrace	Same as -x.

If you supply no option name, then print the current option settings.

-p   Disable processing of the $HOME/.profile file, and use the file /etc/suid_profile instead of the ENV file. This mode is on whenever the effective UID is not equal to the real UID, or when the effective GID is not equal to the real GID. Turning this option off sets the effective UID and GID to the real UID and GID.

-s		Sort the positional parameters lexicographically.
-t		Exit after reading and executing one command.
-u		Treat unset parameters as an error when substituting.
-v		Print shell input lines as they are read.
-x		Print commands and their arguments as they are executed.
-		Turn off -x and -v options, and stop examining arguments for options.
--		Do not change any of the options; useful in setting $1 to a value beginning with -. If no arguments follow this option, unset the positional parameters. Using + instead of - turns these options off. You can also use these options on invocation of the shell. The current set of options can be found in $-. Unless you specify -A, assign the remaining arguments as positional parameters, in order, to $1 $2.... If you specify no arguments, print the names and values of all variables on the standard output.

* shift [*n*] Rename the positional parameters from $n+1 $n+1... as $1..., default *n* is 1. The parameter *n* can be any arithmetic expression that evaluates to a nonnegative number less than or equal to $#.

stop %*job-id*...
stop *pid*...

>Stop the execution of a background job(s) by using its *job-id*, or of any process by using its *pid* (see ps(1)).

suspend Stop the execution of the current shell (but not if it is the login shell).

test *expression*

>Evaluate conditional expressions. See "Conditional Expressions" on page 603 and test(1) for usage and description.

* times Print the accumulated user and system times for the shell and for processes run from the shell.

* trap [*arg sig*...] *arg*

>Read and execute the command when the shell receives signal(s) *sig*. Scan *arg* once when the trap is set and once when the trap is taken. You can specify *sig* as a signal number or signal name. Execute trap commands in order of signal number. Any attempt to set a trap on a signal number that was ignored on entry to the current shell is ineffective. If *arg* is -, reset each *sig* to the default value. If *arg* is null (' '), ignore each specified *sig* if it arises. Otherwise, read and execute *arg* when one of the corresponding *sig*s arises.
>
>The action of the trap overrides a previous action (either default action or one explicitly set). The value of $? after the trap action completes is the value it had before the trap was invoked. *sig* can be EXIT, 0 (equivalent to EXIT) or a signal specified by a symbolic name, without

the SIG prefix, for example, HUP, INT, QUIT, TERM. If *sig* is 0 or EXIT and the trap statement is executed inside the body of a function, execute the command *arg* after the function completes. If *sig* is 0 or EXIT for a trap set outside any function, execute the command *arg* on exit from the shell. If *sig* is ERR. execute *arg* whenever a command has a non-zero exit status. If *sig* is DEBUG, execute *arg* after each command. The environment in which the shell executes a trap on EXIT is identical to the environment immediately after the last command executed before the trap on EXIT was taken. Each time the trap is invoked, process *arg* in a manner equivalent to eval "$*arg*" .

You cannot trap or reset signals that were ignored on entry to a noninteractive shell, although no error need be reported when an attempt is made to do so. An interactive shell may reset or catch signals ignored on entry. Traps remain in place for a given shell until explicitly changed with another trap command. When a subshell is entered, traps are set to the default *args*. This does not imply that you cannot use the trap command within the subshell to set new traps. The trap command with no arguments writes to standard output a list of commands associated with each *sig*. The format is:

trap -- %s %s... *arg, sig*...

The shell formats the output, including the proper use of quoting, so that it is suitable for reinput to the shell as commands that achieve the same trapping results. For example:

save_traps=$(trap)
...
eval "$save_traps"

If the trap name or number is invalid, return a non-zero exit status; otherwise, return 0. For both interactive and noninteractive shells, invalid signal names or numbers are not considered a syntax error and do not abort the shell. Traps are not processed while a job is waiting for a foreground process. Thus, a trap on CHLD won't be executed until the foreground job terminates.

type *name*...

For each *name*, indicate how it would be interpreted if used as a command name.

** typeset [± HLRZfilrtux[*n*]] [*name*[=*value*]]...

Set attributes and values for shell variables and functions. When you invoke typeset inside a function, create a new instance of the variable *name*. Restore the variables *value* and *type* when the function completes. You can specify the following attributes.

-H   Provide UNIX to host-name file mapping on non-UNIX machines.

-L   Left-justify, and remove leading blanks from *value*. If *n* is non-zero, it defines the width of the field; otherwise, determine it by the width of the value of first assignment. When the variable is assigned, it is filled on the right with blanks or truncated, if necessary, to fit into the field. Leading 0s are removed if the -Z option is also set. The -R option is turned off.

-R   Right-justify, and fill with leading blanks. If *n* is non-zero, it defines the width of the field; otherwise, determine it by the width of the value of first assignment. The field is left-filled with blanks or truncated from the end if the variable is reassigned. The -L option is turned off.

-Z   Right-justify, and fill with leading zeros if the first non-blank character is a digit and you have not used the -L option. If *n* is non-zero, it defines the width of the field; otherwise, determine it by the width of the value of first assignment.

-f   The names refer to function names instead of variable names. No assignments can be made, and the only other valid options are -t, -u, and -x.

-i   Parameter is an integer. This makes arithmetic faster. If *n* is non-zero, it defines the output arithmetic base; otherwise, the first assignment determines the output base.

-l   Convert all uppercase characters to lower case. The -u uppercase option is turned off.

-r   Mark the given names read-only. You cannot change these names by subsequent assignment.

-t   Tag the variables. Tags are user definable and have no special meaning to the shell.

-u   Convert all lowercase characters to uppercase characters. The -l lowercase option is turned off.

-x   Mark the given names for automatic export to the environment of subsequently executed commands.

You cannot specify the -l attribute along with -R, -L, -Z, or -f.

Using + instead of - turns these options off. If you specify no *name* arguments but specify options, print a list of names (and optionally the values) of the variables that have these options set. (Using + instead of - keeps the values from being printed.) If you specify no names or if options are given, print the names and attributes of all variables.

ulimit [-HSacdfnstv] [*limit*]

Set or display a resource limit. The available resources limits are listed below. Many systems do not contain one or more of these limits. When you specify a limit for a specific resource, it is set. The value of *limit* can be a number in the unit specified below with each resource, or the value unlimited. The H and S options specify whether the hard limit or the soft limit for the given resource is set. Once a hard limit is set, you cannot increase it. You can increase a soft limit up to the value of the hard limit. If you specify neither the H nor S option, the limit applies to both. Print the current resource limit when you omit *limit*. In this case, print the soft limit unless you specified H. When you specify more than one resource, print the limit name and unit before the value.

-a   List all of the current resource limits.

-c   The number of 512-byte blocks on the size of core dumps.

-d   The number of kilobytes on the size of the data area.

-f   The number of 512-byte blocks on files written by child processes (files of any size may be read).

-n   The number of file descriptors plus 1.

-s   The number of kilobytes on the size of the stack area.

-t   The number of seconds to be used by each process.

-v   The number of kilobytes for virtual memory. If you specify no option, assume -f.

umask [-S] [*mask*]

Set the user file-creation mask to *mask* (see umask(2)). *mask* can be either an octal number or a symbolic value as described in chmod(1). If you specify a symbolic value, the new umask value is the complement of the result of applying *mask* to the complement of the previous umask value. If you omit *mask*, print the current value of the mask. The -S option produces symbolic output.

unalias *name*...

Remove the aliases given by the list of names from the alias list.

unset [-f] *name*...

Unassign the variables given by the list of names, that is, erase their values and attributes. You cannot unset read-only variables. If you specify the -f option, the names refer to function names. Unsetting ERRNO, LINENO, MAILCHECK, OPTARG, OPTIND, RANDOM, SECONDS, TMOUT, and _ removes their special meaning even if they are subsequently assigned.

* wait [*job*]

Wait for the specified job, and report its termination status. If you do not specify *job*, wait for all currently active child processes. The exit status from this command is that of the process waited for. See "Job Control" on page 586 for a description of the format of *job*.

```
whence [-pv] name...
```

> For each *name*, indicate how it would be interpreted if used as a
> command name. The -v option produces a more verbose report. The -p
> option does a path search for *name* even if *name* is an alias, a function,
> or a reserved word.

Errors

Errors detected by the shell, such as syntax errors, return a non-zero exit status.
Otherwise, the shell returns the exit status of the last command executed (see also the
`exit` command). If the shell is being used noninteractively, then execution of the shell
file is abandoned. Runtime errors detected by the shell are reported by printing the
command or function name and the error condition. If the line number at which the
error occurred is greater than 1, then the line number is also printed in square brackets
(`[]`) after the command or function name. For a noninteractive shell, an error condition
encountered by a special built-in or other type of command writes a diagnostic message
to standard error and exits as shown in the following table.

Error	Special Built-in	Other Utilities
Shell language syntax error	Exit	Exit.
Utility syntax error (option or operand error)	Exit	Do not exit.
Redirection error	Exit	Do not exit.
Variable assignment error	Exit	Do not exit.
Expansion error	Exit	Exit.
Command not found	N/A	May exit.
Dot script not found	Exit	N/A.

An expansion error is one that occurs when the shell expansions are carried out (for
example, `${x!y}`, because ! is not a valid operator); an implementation can treat these
as syntax errors if it is able to detect them during tokenization instead of during
expansion.

If any of the errors shown as (may) exit occur in a subshell, the subshell (may) exit
with a non-zero status, but the script containing the subshell does not exit because of the
error.

In all of the cases shown in the table, an interactive shell writes a diagnostic message
to standard error without exiting.

Notes

Some very old shell scripts contain a ^ as a synonym for the pipe character |.

The built-in command . *file* reads the whole file before executing any commands.
Therefore, `alias` and `unalias` commands in the file do not apply to any functions
defined within the file.

When the shell executes a shell script that tries to execute a nonexistent command
interpreter, the shell returns an erroneous diagnostic message that the shell script file
does not exist.

Usage

See largefile(5) for the description of the behavior of ksh and rksh when encountering files greater than or equal to 2 Gbytes (2**31 bytes).

Exit Status

Each command has an exit status that can influence the behavior of other shell commands. The exit status of commands that are not treated as commands is documented in this section. The exit status of the standard commands is documented in their respective sections.

If a command is not found, the exit status is 127. If the command name is found, but the command is not executable, the exit status is 126. Applications that invoke commands without using the shell should use these exit status values to report similar errors.

If a command fails during word expansion or redirection, its exit status is greater than 0.

When reporting the exit status with the special parameter ?, the shell reports the full 8 bits of exit status available. The exit status of a command that terminated because it received a signal is reported as greater than 128.

Files

/etc/profile

/etc/suid_profile

$HOME/.profile

/tmp/sh*

/dev/null

Attributes

See attributes(5) for descriptions of the following attributes:

/usr/bin/ksh, /usr/bin/rksh

Attribute Type	Attribute Value
Availability	SUNWcsu
CSI	Enabled

/usr/xpg4/bin/ksh

Attribute Type	Attribute Value
Availability	SUNWxcu4
CSI	Enabled

See Also

cat(1), cd(1), chmod(1), cut(1), echo(1), env(1), getoptcvt(1), jobs(1), login(1), newgrp(1), paste(1), ps(1), shell_builtins(1), stty(1), test(1), vi(1), dup(2), exec(2), fork(2), ioctl(2), lseek(2), pipe(2), ulimit(2), umask(2), wait(2), rand(3C), signal(3C), a.out(4), profile(4), attributes(5), environ(5), largefile(5), signal(5), xpg4(5)

Morris I. Bolsky and David G. Korn, *The Korn Shell Command and Programming Language*, Prentice Hall, 1989.

ktutil — Kerberos Keytab Maintenance Command   *New!*

Synopsis

```
/usr/bin/ktutil
```

Description

You can use the ktutil interactive command-line interface command, new in the Solaris 8 release, to manage the keylist in keytab files. You must read in a keytab's keylist before you can manage it. Also, the user running the ktutil command must have read/write permissions on the keytab. For example, if a keytab is owned by root, as it is typically, you must run ktutil as root to gain the appropriate permissions.

Commands

clear_list, clear
> Clear the current keylist.

read_kt file, rkt *file*
> Read a keytab into the current keylist. You must specify a keytab file to read.

write_kt file, wkt *file*
> Write the current keylist to a keytab file. You must specify a keytab file to write. If the keytab file already exists, append the current keylist to the existing keytab file.

delete_entry *number*, delent *number*
> Delete an entry from the current keylist. Specify the entry by the keylist slot number.

list, l   List the current keylist.

list_request, lr
> List available requests (commands).

quit, exit, q
> Exit command.

Examples

The following example deletes the host/denver@ACME.com principal from the /etc/krb5/krb5.keytab file. Notice that if you want to delete an entry from an existing keytab, you must first write the keylist to a temporary keytab and then overwrite the existing keytab with the temporary keytab. The reason for this requirement is that the wkt command actually appends the current keylist to an existing keytab, so you can't use it to overwrite a keytab.

```
example# /usr/krb5/bin/ktutil
ktutil: rkt /etc/krb5/krb5.keytab
ktutil: list
slot KVNO Principal
---- ---- -------------------------------------
1    8    host/vail@ACME.COM
2    5    host/denver@ACME.COM
ktutil:delent 2
ktutil:l
slot KVNO Principal
---- ---- -------------------------------------
1    8    host/vail@ACME.COM
ktutil:wkt /tmp/krb5.keytab
ktutil:q
example# mv /tmp/krb5.keytab /etc/krb5/krb5.keytab
example#
```

Files

/etc/krb5/krb5.keytab

keytab file for Kerberos clients.

/etc/krb5/krb5.conf

Kerberos configuration file.

Attributes

See attributes(5) for descriptions of the following attributes:

Attribute Type	Attribute Value
Availability	SUNWkrbu

New!

See Also

SEAM(5)

L

last — Display Login and Logout Information

Synopsis

/usr/bin/last [-a] [-n *number* | -*number*] [-f *filename*] [*name* | *tty*]... *New!*

Description

Use the last command to display login and logout information about users and terminals. The last command looks in the /var/adm/wtmpx file, which records all logins and logouts. You can use the arguments to specify names of users or terminals of interest. If you specify multiple arguments, the information applicable to the arguments is printed. For example, last root console lists all of root's sessions, as well as all sessions on the console terminal. last displays the sessions of the specified users and terminals, most recent first, indicating the times at which the session began, the duration of the session, and the terminal on which the session took place. last also indicates whether the session is continuing or was cut short by a reboot.

The pseudo-user reboot logs in when the system reboots. Thus, the following example shows the mean time between reboots.

```
castle% last reboot
reboot     system boot              Thu Mar  4 11:10
reboot     system boot              Thu Mar  4 07:35
reboot     system boot              Wed Mar  3 18:40

wtmp begins Wed Mar  3 18:40
castle%
```

last with no arguments displays a record of all logins and logouts, in reverse order, as shown in the following example.

```
castle% last
winsor    console       :0      Thu Mar   4 11:13    still logged in
reboot    system boot           Thu Mar   4 11:10
winsor    console       :0      Thu Mar   4 07:38 - 08:46  (01:07)
reboot    system boot           Thu Mar   4 07:35
root      console       :0      Wed Mar   3 19:55 - 19:55  (00:00)
winsor    console       :0      Wed Mar   3 19:52 - 19:54  (00:02)
winsor    console       :0      Wed Mar   3 19:51 - 19:52  (00:00)
root      console       :0      Wed Mar   3 18:44 - 19:51  (01:06)
root      console               Wed Mar   3 18:43 - 18:43  (00:00)
reboot    system boot           Wed Mar   3 18:40

wtmp begins Wed Mar   3 18:40
castle%
```

If last is interrupted, it indicates how far the search has progressed in /var/adm/wtmpx. If interrupted with a quit signal (generated by a Control-\), last indicates how far the search has progressed and then continues the search.

Options

New!

-a   Display the host name in the last column.

-n *number*|-*number*

Limit the number of entries displayed to that specified by *number*. These options are identical; the -*number* option is provided as a transition tool only and will be removed in future releases.

-f *filename*

Use *filename* as the name of the accounting file instead of /var/adm/wtmpx.

Environment Variables

Date and time format is based on locale specified by the LC_ALL, LC_TIME, or LANG environments, in that order of priority.

Files

/var/adm/wtmpx

Accounting file.

Attributes

See attributes(5) for descriptions of the following attributes:

Attribute Type	Attribute Value
Availability	SUNWesu

See Also

utmpx(4), attributes(5)

lastcomm — Display the Last Commands Executed, in Reverse Order

Synopsis

/usr/bin/lastcomm [-f *file*] [-x] [*command-name*]... [*user-name*]...
   [*terminal-name*]...

Description

The lastcomm command shows information about previously executed accounting commands that are stored in the /var/adm/pacct file. lastcomm with no arguments displays information about all the commands recorded during the current accounting file's lifetime. If you specify arguments, lastcomm displays only accounting entries with a matching *command-name*, *user-name*, or *terminal-name*.

If extended process accounting is active (see acctadm(1M)) and is recording the appropriate data items, lastcomm tries to take data from the current extended process accounting file. If standard process accounting is active, lastcomm takes data from the current standard accounting file (see acct(2)).

New!

If *terminal-name* is - -, there was no controlling TTY for the process. The process was probably executed during boot time. If *terminal-name* is ??, the controlling TTY could not be decoded into a printable name.

For each process entry, lastcomm displays the following information:

- The command name under which the process was called.
- One or more flags indicating special information about the process. The flags have the following meanings:

   F   The process performed a fork but not an exec.

   S   The process ran as a setuid program.

- The name of the user who ran the process.
- The terminal where the user was logged in at the time (if applicable).
- The amount of CPU time used by the process (in seconds).
- The date and time the process exited.

Options

New!

-f *file*   Use *file* as the source of accounting data. *file* can be either an extended process accounting file or a standard process accounting file. New in the Solaris 8 release.

-x   Use the currently active extended process accounting file. If extended process accounting is inactive, lastcomm produces no output. New in the Solaris 8 release.

Examples

The following command lists all the executions of commands named a.out by user root while using the terminal term/01.

castle% **lastcomm a.out root term/01**

The following command lists all of the commands executed by user root.

example% **lastcomm root**

Files

/var/adm/pacct

Accounting file.

New! /var/adm/exacct/proc

Extended accounting file.

Attributes

See attributes(5) for descriptions of the following attributes:

Attribute Type	Attribute Value
Availability	SUNWesu

See Also

New! last(1), acctadm(1m), acct(2), acct(3HEAD), sigvec(3UCB), core(4), attributes(5)

ld — Link-Editor for Object Files

Synopsis

New! /usr/ccs/bin/ld [-64] [-a|-r] [-b] [-c *name*] [-C] [-G] [-i] [-m] [-s]
        [-t] [-V] [-B direct] [-B dynamic | static] [-B group] [-B local]
        [-B eliminate] [-B reduce] [-B symbolic] [-d y|n] [-D *token*]
        [-e *epsym*] [-F *name* | -f *name*] [-h *name*] [-I *name*] [-L *path*] [-l *x*]
        [-M *mapfile*] [-N *string*] [-o *outfile*] [-p *auditlib*] -P *auditlib*]
        [-Q y| n] [-R *path*] [-S *supportlib*] [-u *symname*] [-Y P,*dirlist*]
        [-z *absexec*] [-z allextract | defaultextract | weakextract]
        [-z combreloc] [-z defs | nodefs] [-z endfiltee]
        [-z finiarray=*function*] [-z groupperm | nogroupperm]
        [-z ignore | record] [-z initarray=function] [-z initfirst]
        [-z interpose] [-z lazyload | nolazyload] [-z ld32=*arg1,arg2,...*]
        [-z ld64=*arg1,arg2,...*][-z loadfltr] [-z muldefs] [-z nodefaultlib]
        [-z nodelete] [-z nodlopen] [-z nodump] [-z nopartial] [-z noversion]
        [-z now] [-z origin] [-z preinitarray=*function*] [-z redlocsym]
        [-z rescan] [-z text | textwarn | textoff] [-z verbose] *filename*...

Description

The ld command is the link-editor for object files. It is often automatically invoked by compiler commands such as cc.

The ld command combines relocatable object files, performs relocation, and resolves external symbols. ld operates in two modes, static or dynamic, as governed by the -d option. Specify -dn for static mode and -dy for dynamic mode. In all cases, the output of ld is left in a.out by default.

Note — Default options applied by ld are maintained for historic reasons. In today's programming environment where dynamic objects dominate, alternative defaults would often make more sense. However, historic defaults must be maintained to ensure compatibility with existing program development environments. Historic defaults are called out whenever possible. For a description of the current recommended options, see the "Link-Editor Quick Reference" in *Linker and Libraries Guide*.

New!

If the file being created by ld already exists, it is truncated after all input files have been processed and is overwritten by the new file contents. ld does not create a temporary file as part of the link-edit because multiple instances of large output files frequently exhaust system resources. The drawback of overwriting an existing file occurs if the file is in use by a running process. In this case, the process may be prematurely terminated as the output file image is created. You can avoid this situation by removing the output file before performing the link-edit. This removal is not detrimental to the running process, because it frees up the file system namespace, not the actual disk space, for the new output file creation. The disk space of a removed file is freed when the last process referencing the file terminates.

In -dn static mode, relocatable object files specified as arguments are combined to produce an executable object file. If you specify the -r option, relocatable object files are combined to produce one relocatable object file.

In -dy dynamic mode (the default), relocatable object files you specify as arguments are combined to produce an executable object file that is linked at execution with any shared object files you specify as arguments. If you specify the -G option, relocatable object files are combined to produce a shared object. In all cases, the output of ld is left in a.out by default.

If any argument is a library, ld searches exactly once at the point it encounters the library in the argument list. The library can be either a relocatable archive (see ar(3HEAD)) or a shared object.

For an archive library, ld loads only those routines that define an unresolved external reference. ld searches the archive library symbol table sequentially with as many passes as are needed to resolve external references that can be satisfied by library members. Thus, the order of members in the library is functionally unimportant unless multiple library members exist that define the same external symbol. Archive libraries that have interdependencies may require multiple command-line definition or use of the -z rescan option, which is new in the Solaris 9 release.

New!

A shared object consists of an indivisible, whole unit that has been generated by a previous link-edit of one or more input files. When the link-editor processes a shared object, the entire contents of the shared object become a logical part of the resulting output file image. The shared object is not physically copied during the link-edit because its actual inclusion is deferred until process execution. This logical inclusion means that all symbol entries defined in the shared object are made available to the link-editing process.

New!   No command-line option is required to distinguish 32-bit or 64-bit objects. The link-editor uses the ELF class of the first input relocatable file it sees to govern the mode in which it operates. Intermixing 32-bit and 64-bit objects is not permitted. See also the -64 option, new in the Solaris 8 release, and the LD_NOEXEC_64 environment variable, new in the Solaris 9 release.

Options

New!   -64   Create a 64-bit object. By default, the class of the object being generated is determined from the first ELF object processed from the command line. This option is useful when creating an object directly with ld whose input is solely from a mapfile (see the -M option) or an archive library. New in the Solaris 8 release.

      -a   In static mode only, produce an executable object file. Display errors for undefined references (the default for static mode). You cannot use -a with the -r option.

      -b   In dynamic mode only, when creating an executable, do not do special processing for relocations that reference symbols in shared objects. Without the -b option, create special position-independent relocations for references to functions defined in shared objects, and arrange for data objects defined in shared objects to be copied into the memory image of the executable by the runtime linker.

New!   The -b option is intended for specialized dynamic objects and is not recommended for general use. Its use suppresses all specialized processing required to ensure an object's shareability and may even prevent the relocation of 64-bit executables. New in the Solaris 8 release.

New!   -B direct   Establish direct binding information by recording the relationship between each symbol reference and the dependency that provides the definition. The runtime linker uses this information to search directly for the symbol in the associated object instead of carrying out its default symbol search. Direct binding information can be established only to dependencies specified with the link-editor. Thus, you should use the -z defs option. Objects that want to interpose on symbols in a direct binding environment should identify themselves as interposers with the -z interpose option. The use of -B direct enables -z lazyload for all dependencies. New in the Solaris 8 release.

    -B dynamic | static

        Options governing library inclusion. -B dynamic is valid in dynamic mode only. You can specify these options any number of times on the command line as toggles: if you use the -B static option, no shared objects are accepted until -B dynamic is seen. See also the -l option.

    -B eliminate

        Do not assign any global symbols to a version definition to be eliminated from the symbol table. This option achieves the same symbol elimination as the auto-elimination directive available as part of a mapfile version definition.

-B group   Establish a shared object and its dependencies as a group. Objects within the group are bound to other members of the group at runtime. The runtime processing of an object containing this option mimics what happens if the object is added to a process by dlopen(3DL) with the RTLD_GROUP mode. Because the group must be self-contained, use of the -B group option also asserts the -z defs option.

-B local   Reduce any global symbols not assigned to a version definition to local. You can supply version definitions from a mapfile and indicate the global symbols that should remain visible in the generated object. This option achieves the same symbol reduction as the auto-reduction directive available as part of a mapfile version definition and can be useful when combining versioned and nonversioned relocatable objects.

-B reduce   When generating a relocatable object, reduce the symbolic information defined by any version definitions. You can supply version definitions from a mapfile to indicate the global symbols that should remain visible in the generated object. When a relocatable object is generated, version definitions are by default recorded only in the output image. The actual reduction of symbolic information is carried out when the object itself is used in the construction of a dynamic executable or shared object. This option is applied automatically when a dynamic executable or shared object is created.

-B symbolic

            In dynamic mode only. When building a shared object, bind references to global symbols to their definitions, if available, within the object. Normally, references to global symbols within shared objects are not bound until runtime even if definitions are available, so that definitions of the same symbol in an executable or other shared object can override the object's own definition. ld issues warnings for undefined symbols unless -z defs overrides.

            The -B symbolic option is intended for specialized dynamic objects and is not recommended for general use. To reduce the runtime relocation overhead of an object, the creation of a version definition is recommended. New in the Solaris 8 release.

-c name   Record the configuration file name for use at runtime. You can use configuration files to alter default search paths, provide a directory cache, and provide alternative object dependencies. See crle(1). New in the Solaris 8 release.

-C   Demangle C++ symbol names displayed in diagnostic messages. New in the Solaris 8 release.

-dy | n   When you specify -dy (the default), use dynamic linking; when you specify -dn, use static linking. See also -B dynamic|static.

-D token, ...

            Print debugging information to the standard error as specified by each token. The special token help shows the full list of available tokens.

-e *epsym*	Set the entry point address for the output file to be that of the symbol *epsym*.
-f *name*	Useful only when building a shared object. Specify that the symbol table of the shared object is used as an auxiliary filter on the symbol table of the shared object specified by *name*. You can use multiple instances of this option. You cannot combine this option with the -F option.
-F *name*	Useful only when building a shared object. Specify that the symbol table of the shared object is used as a filter on the symbol table of the shared object specified by *name*. You can use multiple instances of this option. You cannot combine this option with the -f option.
-G	In dynamic mode only, produce a shared object. Allow undefined symbols.
-h *name*	In dynamic mode only, when building a shared object, record *name* in the object's dynamic section. *name* is recorded in executables that are linked with this object instead of the object's UNIX system file name. Accordingly, *name* is used by the runtime linker as the name of the shared object to search for at runtime.
-i	Ignore LD_LIBRARY_PATH setting. This option is useful when an LD_LIBRARY_PATH setting is in effect to influence the runtime library search, which would interfere with performing link-editing.
-I *name*	When building an executable, use *name* as the path name of the interpreter to be written into the program header. The default in static mode is no interpreter; in dynamic mode, the default is the name of the runtime linker, ld.so.1(1). You can override either case by -I *name*. exec(2) loads this interpreter when it loads a.out and passes control to the interpreter instead of directly to a.out.
-l *x*	Search a library lib*x*.so or lib*x*.a, the conventional names for shared object and archive libraries, in that order. In dynamic mode, unless you use the -B static option, search each directory specified in the library search path for a lib*x*.so or lib*x*.a file. Stop the directory search at the first directory containing either. Choose the file ending in .so if -l *x* expands to two files with names of the form lib*x*.so and lib*x*.a. If no lib*x*.so is found, accept lib*x*.a. In static mode or when the -B static option is in effect, choose only the file ending in .a. ld searches a library when it encounters its name, so the placement of -l is significant.
-L *path*	Add *path* to the library search directories. Search for libraries first in any directories specified by the -L options and then in the standard directories. This option is useful only if it precedes the -l options to which it applies. You can use the environment variable LD_LIBRARY_PATH to supplement the library search path.
-m	Produce a memory map or listing of the input/output sections, together with any nonfatal, multiply defined symbols, on the standard output.

-M *mapfile*	Read *mapfile* as a text file of directives to ld. You can specify this option multiple times. If *mapfile* is a directory, then process all regular files within the directory, as defined by stat(2). See *Linker and Libraries Guide* for description of mapfiles.

Mapfiles in /usr/lib/ld show the default layout of programs and link *New!* 64-bit programs above or below 4 gigabytes. New in the Solaris 8 release.

-N *string*	Add a DT_NEEDED entry to the .dynamic section of the object being built. The value of the DT_NEEDED string is the string specified on the command line. This option is position dependent, and the DT_NEEDED .dynamic entry is relative to the other dynamic dependencies discovered on the link-edit line.
-o *outfile*	Produce an output object file named *outfile*. The name of the default object file is a.out.
-p *auditlib*	*New!*

Identify an audit library, *auditlib*, used to audit this object at runtime. Any object specifying this shared object as a dependency inherits this requirement from any shared object that requires auditing of itself. New in the Solaris 8 release.

-P *auditlib*	*New!*

Identify an audit library, *auditlib*, used to audit this object's dependencies at runtime. Dependency auditing can also be inherited from dependencies identified as requiring auditing (see the -p option). New in the Solaris 8 release.

-Q y|n	For -Qy, add an ident string to the .comment section of the output file to identify the version of the link-editor used to create the file. When there are multiple linking steps, such as when using ld -r, multiple ld idents result. This option is identical to the default action of the cc command. For -Qn, suppress version identification.
-r	Combine relocatable object files to produce one relocatable object file. Do not complain about unresolved references. You cannot use this option in dynamic mode or with -a.
-R *path*	Specify a colon-separated list of directories used as library search directories by the runtime linker. If present and not null, *path* is recorded in the output object file and passed to the runtime linker. Multiple instances of this option are concatenated, with each path separated by a colon.
-s	Strip symbolic information from the output file. Remove any debugging information, that is, .debug, .line, and .stab sections, and their associated relocation entries. Except for relocatable files or shared objects, also remove the symbol table and string table sections from the output object file.

-S *supportlib*

> Load the shared object *supportlib* with the link-editor and give information regarding the linking process. Support shared objects can also be supplied with the SGS_SUPPORT environment variable. See *Linker and Libraries Guide* for more details.

-t

> Turn off the warning about multiply defined symbols that are not the same size.

-u *symname*

> Enter *symname* as an undefined symbol in the symbol table. This option is useful for loading entirely from an archive library because initially the symbol table is empty and an unresolved reference is needed to force the loading of the first routine. The placement of this option on the command line is significant; put it before the library that defines the symbol.

-V

> Display a message giving information about the version of ld being used.

-Y P, *dirlist*

> Change the default directories used for finding libraries. *dirlist* is a colon-separated path list.

-z absexec

> Useful only when building a dynamic executable. Resolve references to external absolute symbols immediately instead of leaving them for resolution at runtime. In very specialized circumstances, this option removes text relocations that can result in excessive swap space demands by an executable. New in the Solaris 8 release.

-z allextract | defaultextract | weakextract

> Alter the extraction criteria of objects from any archives that follow. By default, extract archive members to satisfy undefined references and to promote tentative definitions with data definitions. Weak symbol references do not trigger extraction. For -z allextract, extract all archive members from the archive. For -z weakextract, weak references trigger archive extraction. -z defaultextract provides a way of returning to the default following use of the former extract options.

-z combreloc

> Combine multiple relocation sections. Historically, relocation sections are maintained in a one-to-one relationship with the sections to which the relocations are applied. When building an executable or shared object, ld sorts the entries of data relocation sections by their symbol reference to reduce runtime symbol lookup. Combining multiple data relocation sections enables optimal sorting and, hence, the least relocation overhead when objects are loaded into memory.

-z defs | nodefs

> The -z defs option forces a fatal error if any undefined symbols remain at the end of the link. This option is the default when an executable is built but, for historic reasons, is not the default when a shared object

is built. Use of the -z defs option is recommended, because it ensures that the object being built is self-contained, that is, that all its symbolic references are resolved internally.

The - z nodefs option permits undefined symbols. For historic reasons, this option is the default when a shared object is built. When used with executables, the behavior of references to such undefined symbols is unspecified. Use of the -z nodefs option is not recommended. New in the Solaris 8 release.

-z endfiltee

New!

Mark a filtee so that, when processed by a filter, it terminates any further filtee searches by the filter. New in the Solaris 8 release.

-z finiarray=*function*

New!

Append an entry to the .finiarray section of the object being built. If no .finiarray section is present, create one. The new entry is initialized to point to the function. See *Linker and Libraries Guide* for more information. New in the Solaris 8 release.

-z groupperm | nogroupperm

New!

Assign or deassign each dependency that follows to a unique group. Assigning a dependency to a group has the same effect as if the dependency was built with the -B group option. New in the Solaris 8 release.

-z ignore | record

Ignore or record dynamic dependencies that are not referenced as part of the link-edit. -z record is the default.

-z initarray=*function*

New!

Append an entry to the .initarray section of the object being built. If no .initarray section is present, create one. The new entry is initialized to point to the function. See *Linker and Libraries Guide* for more information. New in the Solaris 8 release.

-z initfirst

Mark the object so that its runtime initialization occurs before the runtime initialization of any other objects brought into the process at the same time. In addition, the object runtime finalization occurs after the runtime finalization of any other objects removed from the process at the same time. This option is meaningful only when building a shared object.

-z interpose

New!

Mark the object as an interposer. When direct bindings are in effect (see -B direct) the runtime linker searches for symbols in any interposers before the object associated to the direct binding. New in the Solaris 8 release.

-z lazyload | nolazyload

> Enable or disable the marking of dynamic dependencies to be lazily loaded. Dynamic dependencies that are marked lazyload are not loaded at initial process startup but instead are delayed until the first binding to the object is made.

New!

-z ld32=*arg1*,*arg2*,...
-z ld64=*arg1*,*arg2*,...

> The class of the link-editor is affected by the class of the output file being created and by the capabilities of the underlying operating system. This option provides a way to define any link-editor argument so that it is interpreted only by either the 32- or 64-bit class of the link-editor.
>
> For example, support libraries are class specific, so the correct class of support library can be ensured with the following syntax.
>
> ld ... -s ld32=-Saudit32.so.1 -z ld64=Saudit64.so1 ...
>
> Note that the class of link-editor invoked is, in part, determined from the ELF class of the first input relocatable file seen on the command line. This determination is carried out before any -z ld [32 | 64] processing. New in the Solaris 9 release.

-z loadfltr

> Mark the object to require that when a filter is built, filtered objects are processed immediately at runtime. Normally, filter processing is delayed until a symbol reference is bound to the filter. The runtime processing of an object that contains this flag mimics that which occurs if the LD_LOADFLTR environment variable is in effect. See ld.so.1(1).

-z muldefs   Enable multiple symbol definitions. By default, multiple symbol definitions that occur between relocatable objects result in a fatal error. This option suppresses the error condition and enables the first symbol definition to be taken.

-z nodefs   Enable undefined symbols. This option is the default when a shared object is built. When used with executables, the behavior of references to such undefined symbols is unspecified.

-z nodelete

> Mark the object as nondeletable at runtime. The runtime processing of an object that contains this flag mimics that which occurs if the object is added to a process by dlopen(3X) with the RTLD_NODELETE mode.

New!

-z nodefaultlib

> Mark the object so that the runtime default library search path (used after any LD_LIBRARY_PATH or run paths) is ignored. This option implies that all dependencies of the object can be satisfied from its run path. New in the Solaris 8 release.

-z nodlopen

> Mark the object as not available to dlopen(3DL), either as the object specified by the dlopen() or as any form of dependency required by the object specified by dlopen(). This option is meaningful only when building a shared object.

-z nodump   Mark the object as not available to dldump(3DL). New in the Solaris 8 *New!* release.

-z nopartial

> Expand the partially initialized symbols when the output file is generated if any exist in the input relocatable object files.

-z noversion

> Do not record any versioning sections. Any version sections or associated .dynamic section entries are not generated in the output image.

-z now   Mark the object to override the runtime linker's default mode and to require nonlazy runtime binding. This option is similar to adding the object to the process by using dlopen(3X) with the RTLD_NOW mode or by setting the LD_BIND_NOW environment variable. See ld.so.1(1).

-z origin   Mark the object as requiring immediate $ORIGIN processing at runtime.

-z preinitarray=*function*   *New!*

> Append an entry to the .preinitarray section of the object being built. If no .preinitarray section is present, create one. The new entry is initialized to point to the function. See *Linker and Libraries Guide* for more information. New in the Solaris 8 release.

-z redlocsym

> Eliminate all local symbols except for the SECT symbols from the symbol table SHT_SYMTAB. Update all relocations that refer to local symbols to now refer to the corresponding SECT symbol.

-z rescan   Rescan the archive files provided to the link-edit. By default, archives *New!* are processed once as they appear on the command line. Archives are traditionally specified at the end of the command line so that their symbol definitions resolve any preceding references. However, you often need to specify the archives multiple times to satisfy their own interdependencies.

> The -z rescan option reprocesses the entire archive list to try to locate additional archive members that resolve symbol references. This archive rescanning continues until a pass over the archive list occurs in which no new members are extracted. New in the Solaris 9 release.

-z text   In dynamic mode only, force a fatal error if any relocations against nonwritable, allocatable sections remain.

-z textoff   In dynamic mode only, allow relocations against all allocatable sections including nonwritable ones. This option is the default when building a shared object.

-z textwarn

In dynamic mode only, list a warning if any relocations against nonwritable, allocatable sections remain. This option is the default when building an executable.

New!   -z verbose   Provide additional warning diagnostics during a link-edit. The present implementation displays suspicious use of displacement relocations. In the future, it may be enhanced to provide additional diagnostics deemed too noisy to be generated by default. New in the Solaris 9 release.

Environment Variables

LD_LIBRARY_PATH

A list of directories to search for libraries specified with the -l option. Separate multiple directories with a colon. In the most general case, the variable contains two directory lists separated by a semicolon:

dirlist1; *dirlist2*

If ld is called with any number of occurrences of -L, as in

ld... -L*path1*... -L*pathn*...

then the search path ordering is

dirlist1 path1... pathn dirlist2 LIBPATH

When the list of directories does not contain a semicolon, it is interpreted as *dirlist2*.

The LD_LIBRARY_PATH environment variable also affects the runtime linkers searching for dynamic dependencies.

New! You can specify LD_LIBRARY_PATH with a _32 or _64 suffix to make it specific to 32-bit or 64-bit processes. This specification overrides any nonsuffixed version of the environment variable that may be in effect. New in the Solaris 8 release.

New! LD_NOEXEC_64

Suppress the automatic execution of the 64-bit link-editor. By default, the link-editor executes its 64-bit version when the ELF class of the first input relocatable file it reads identifies it as a 64-bit object. New in the Solaris 9 release.

LD_OPTIONS   A default set of options to ld. LD_OPTIONS is interpreted by ld just as though its value had been placed on the command line, immediately following the name used to invoke ld, as in:

ld $LD_OPTIONS... *other-arguments*...

LD_RUN_PATH   An alternative mechanism for specifying a run path to the link-editor (see -R option). If both LD_RUN_PATH and the -R option are specified, -R supersedes.

SGS_SUPPORT   Provide a colon-separated list of shared objects that are loaded with the link-editor and given information regarding the linking process. *New!*

You can specify this environment variable with a _32 or _64 suffix, which makes the environment variable specific to either the 32- or 64-bit class of ld and overrides any nonsuffixed version of the environment variable that may be in effect.

See also the -S option. New in the Solaris 8 release.

Note — Environment-variable names beginning with the characters LD_ are reserved for possible future enhancements to ld and ld.so.1(1).

Files

libx.so   Libraries.

libx.a   Libraries.

a.out   Output file.

LIBPATH   Usually /usr/lib or /usr/lib/64 for 64-bit libraries. New in the Solaris 8 release. *New!*

/usr/lib/ld/map.default

    Mapfile showing default layout of 32-bit programs.

/usr/lib/ld/map.noexstk   *New!*

    Mapfile showing a nonexecutable stack definition. New in the Solaris 9 release.

/usr/lib/ld/sparcv9/map.default

    Mapfile showing default layout of 64-bit SPARC V9 programs.

/usr/lib/ld/sparcv9.map.above4G

    Mapfile showing suggested layout above 4 Gbytes of 64-bit SPARC V9 programs.

/usr/lib/ld/sparcv9/map.below4G

    Mapfile showing suggested layout below 4 Gbytes of 64-bit SPARC V9 programs.

Attributes

See attributes(5) for descriptions of the following attributes:

Attribute Type	Attribute Value
Availability	SUNWtoo

See Also

New! as(1), crle(1), gprof(1), ld.so.1(1), pvs(1), exec(2), stat(2),
dlopen(3DL), dldump(3DL), elf(3ELF), ar(3HEAD), a.out(4), attributes(5)
Linker and Libraries Guide
Binary Compatibility Guide

New! ldap — LDAP as a Naming Repository

Description

LDAP refers to the Lightweight Directory Access Protocol, new in the Solaris 8
Operating Environment, which is emerging as an industry standard for accessing
directory servers. Changes in the Solaris 9 release are shown with the New icon in the
margin. By initializing the client with the ldapclient(1M) command and using the
ldap keyword in the /etc/nsswitch.conf name service switch file, Solaris clients can
obtain naming information from an LDAP server. Information such as user names, host
names, and passwords are stored on the LDAP server in the form of a tree called
Directory Information Tree or DIT. The DIT contains entries that, in turn, are composed
of attributes. Each attribute has a type and one or more values.

Solaris LDAP clients use the LDAP v3 protocol to access naming information from
LDAP servers. The LDAP server must support the object classes and attributes defined
in *RFC2307bis* (draft), that maps the Naming Information Service model onto LDAP.

New! As an alternative to using the schema defined in RFC2307bis (draft), you can
configure the system to use other schema setsl; the schema mapping feature is
configured to map between the two. Refer to the *System Administration Guide: Naming
and Directory Services (DNS, NIS, and LDAP)* for more details.

New! ### Configuration Information

You can use the ldapclient(1M) command to set up the appropriate directories and
configuration information to make a Solaris machine an LDAP client. The LDAP clients
cache this configuration information in local cache files. This configuration information
is accessed with the ldap_cachemgr(1M) daemon. This daemon also refreshes the
information in the configuration files from the LDAP server, providing better
performance and security than that of other nameservices. The ldap_cachemgr must
run at all times for the proper operation of the naming services.

LDAP uses two kinds of configuration information: the information available
through a profile and the information configured per client. The profile contains all the
information about how the client accesses the directory. The credential information for
a proxy user is configured for each client and is not downloaded through the profile.

The profile contains server-specific parameters that are required by all clients to
locate the servers for the desired LDAP domain. This information could be the server's
IP address and the search base Distinguished Name (DN), for example. The profile is
configured on the client from the default profile during client initialization, and the
ldap_cachemgr daemon updates the profile when the expiration time has elapsed.

A client profile is stored in the LDAP server, and the ldapclient command uses the
profile to initialize an LDAP client. The client profile provides the easiest way to
configure a client machine. See ldapclient(1M).

Credential Information

Credential information includes client-specific parameters that are used by a client. This information could get the Bind DN (LDAP "login" name) of the client and the password. If these parameters are required, they are manually defined during the initialization through ldapclient(1M).

Naming Information

The naming information is stored in containers on the LDAP server. A container is a nonleaf entry in the DIT that contains naming service information. Containers are similar to maps in NIS and tables in NIS+. The mapping between the Network Information Service (NIS) databases and the containers in LDAP is shown below. The location of these containers as well as their names can be overridden through the use of service SearchDescriptors. For more information see ldapclient(1M).

Database	Object Class	Container	
alias	mailGroup	ou=Aliases,dc=...	
audit_attr	SolarisAuditAttr	ou=people,dc=...	*New!*
auth_attr	SolarisAuthAttr	ou=SolarisAuthAttr,dc=...	*New!*
bootparams	bootableDevice	ou=Ethers,dc=...	
ethers	ieee802Device	ou=Ethers,dc=...	
exec_attr	SolarisExecAttr	ou=SolarisExecAttr,dc=...	*New!*
generic	nisObject	nisMapName=...,dc=...	
group	posixGroup	ou=Group,dc=...	
hosts	ipHost	ou=Hosts,dc=...	
ipnodes			
netgroup	nisNetgroup	ou=Netgroup,dc=...	
netmasks	ipNetwork	ou=Networks,dc=...	
networks	ipNetwork	ou=Networks,dc=...	
passwd	posixAccount	ou=people,dc=...	
	shadowAccount		
printers	printerService	ou=Printers,dc=...	*New!*
prof_attr	SolarisProfAttr	ou=SolarisProfAttr,dc=...	*New!*
protocols	ipProtocol	ou=Protocols,dc=...	
publickey	nisKeyObject		*New!*
rpc	oncRpc	ou=Rpc,dc=...	
service	ipService	ou=Services,dc=...	
user_attr	SolarisUserAttr	ou=people,dc=...	*New!*

Client Authentication

The security model for clients is defined by a combination of the credential level to be used, the authentication method, and the PAM module to be used—that is, pam_unix or pam_ldap. The credential level defines what credentials the client should use to authenticate to the directory server. The authentication method defines the method by which authentication is accomplished. Both can be set with multiple values. The Solaris LDAP client supports the following values for credential level.

- anonymous
- proxy

The Solaris LDAP client supports the following values for authentication method.

- none
- simple
- sasl/CRAM-MD5
- sasl/DIGEST-MD5
- tls:simple
- tls:sasl/CRAM-MD5
- tls:sasl/DIGEST-MD5

The form of access control provides different levels of protection, enabling the server to grant access for certain containers and/or entries. You specify access control in the form of access control lists (ACLs). Each ACL specifies one or more directory objects (for example, the cn attribute in a specific container), one or more clients to which you grant or deny access, and one or more access rights that determine what the clients can do to or with the objects. Clients can be either users or applications. You can specify access rights as read and write, for example. Refer to the *System Administration Guide: Naming and Directory Services (DNS, NIS, and LDAP)* for restrictions on ACLs when using LDAP as a naming repository.

The Network Switch File

A sample nsswitch.conf(4) file named nsswitch.ldap is available in the /etc directory. This file is copied to /etc/nsswitch.conf by the ldapclient(1M) command. The nsswitch.ldap file uses ldap as a repository for the different databases in the nsswitch.conf file. The default nsswitch.ldap file is shown below.

New!

```
#
# /etc/nsswitch.ldap:
#
# An example file that could be copied over to /etc/nsswitch.conf; it
# uses LDAP in conjunction with files.
#
# "hosts:" and "services:" in this file are used only if the
# /etc/netconfig file has a "-" for nametoaddr_libs of "inet" transports.

# the following two lines obviate the "+" entry in /etc/passwd and /etc/group.
passwd:     files ldap
group:      files ldap

# consult /etc "files" only if ldap is down.
hosts:      ldap [NOTFOUND=return] files
ipnodes:    files
# Uncomment the following line and comment out the above to resolve
# both IPv4 and IPv6 addresses from the ipnodes databases. Note that
# IPv4 addresses are searched in all of the ipnodes databases before
# searching the hosts databases. Before turning this option on, consult
# the Network Administration Guide for more details on using IPv6.
```

```
#ipnodes:     ldap [NOTFOUND=return] files

networks:     ldap [NOTFOUND=return] files
protocols:    ldap [NOTFOUND=return] files
rpc:          ldap [NOTFOUND=return] files
ethers:       ldap [NOTFOUND=return] files
netmasks:     ldap [NOTFOUND=return] files
bootparams:   ldap [NOTFOUND=return] files
publickey:    ldap [NOTFOUND=return] files

netgroup:     ldap

automount:    files ldap
aliases:      files ldap

# for efficient getservbyname() avoid ldap
services:     files ldap
sendmailvars:    files

printers:          user files ldap

auth_attr: files ldap
prof_attr: files ldap

project:      files ldap
```

User Commands

The user commands related to ldap are listed below.

idsconfig(1M)   *New!*

> Prepare an iPlanet directory server to be ready to support Solaris LDAP clients.

ldapaddent(1M)   *New!*

> Create LDAP entries from corresponding /etc files.

ldapclient(1M)

> Initialize ldap clients.

ldaplist(1)

> List the contents of the ldap naming space.

Files

/var/ldap/ldap_client_cred   *New!*
/var/ldap/ldap_client_file

> Files that contain the LDAP configuration of the client. Do not manually modify these files. Their content is not guaranteed to be human readable. Use the ldapclient(1M) command to update them.

`/etc/nsswitch.conf`

> Configuration file for the name-service switch
> `/etc/nsswitch.ldap` configuration file for the name-service
> switch configured with `ldap`.

New! `/etc/nsswitch.ldap`

> Sample configuration file for the name-service switch configured
> with LDAP and `files`.

New! `/etc/pam.conf`

> PAM framework configuration files.

See Also

New! `ldaplist(1)`, `idsconfig(1M)`, `ldap_cachemgr(1M)`, `ldapaddent(1M)`,
`ldapclient(1M)`, `nsswitch.conf(4)`, `pam.conf(4)`, `pam_ldap(5)`
    System Administration Guide: Naming and Directory Services (DNS, NIS, and LDAP)

---

ldapadd — ldap Entry Addition and Modification Tools

Synopsis

`/opt/SUNWconn/ldap/bin/ldapadd [-b] [-c] [-n] [-v] [-F] [-d` *debuglevel*`]`
  `[-D` *binddn*`] [-w` *passwd*`] [-h` *ldaphost*`] [-p` *ldapport*`] [-f` *file*`]`
  `[-l` *nb-ldap-connections*`]`

Description

See `ldapmodify`(1).

---

ldapdelete — ldap Delete Entry Tool

Synopsis

New! `/usr/bin/ldapdelete [-n] [-o] [-v] [-c] [-d` *debuglevel*`] [-f` *file*`]`
  `[-D` *binddn*`] [-w` *passwd*`] [-h` *ldaphost*`] [-M` *authentication*`]`
  `[-p` *ldapport*`] [`*dn*`...]`

Description

`ldapdelete` opens a connection to an LDAP server and binds and deletes one or more
entries. If you specify one or more *dn* arguments, entries with those distinguished names
are deleted. If you specify no *dn* arguments, a list of distinguished names (DNs) is read
from *file*, if you specify the `-f` option, or from standard input.

Options

-c   Continuous operation mode. Report errors but continue with
                      deletions. The default is to exit after reporting an error.

-d *debuglevel*
                      Set the LDAP debugging level. Useful levels of debugging for
                      ldapdelete are:

1   Trace.

2   Packets.

4   Arguments.

32   Filters.

128   Access control.

                      To request more than one category of debugging information, add the
                      masks. For example, to request trace and filter information, specify a
                      debug level of 33.

-D *binddn*   Use the distinguished name *binddn* to bind to the directory.

-f *file*   Read the entry deletion information from *file* instead of from
                      standard input.

-h *ldaphost*
                      Specify an alternative host on which the slapd server is running.

-M *authentication*
                      Specify the authentication mechanism used to bind to the directory.
                      This option can have the value CRAM-MD5. The bind DN and bind
                      password are mandatory with this option.

-n   Show what would be done, but don't actually delete entries. Useful in
                      conjunction with -v and -d for debugging.

-o   Specify the security layer for the mechanism (none, integrity,
                      privacy). New in the Solaris 9 release.

-p *ldapport*
                      Specify an alternative TCP port where the slapd server is listening.

-v   Use verbose mode and write diagnostics to standard output.

-w *passwd*   Use *passwd* as the password for authentication to the directory.

Operands

dn   Specify one or several distinguished names of entries to delete.

Examples

The following example deletes the entry named with commonName "Delete Me" directly
below the XYZ Corporation organizational entry.

```
castle% ldapdelete "cn=Delete Me, o=XYZ, c=US" -D "cn=Administrator,
   o=XYZ, c=US" -w password
```

Exit Status

0   No errors occurred.

non-zero   Errors result and a diagnostic message is written to standard error.

Attributes

See `attributes`(5) for descriptions of the following attributes:

Attribute Type	Attribute Value
Availability	`SUNW11dap` (32-bit)
	`SUNW1dapx` (64-bit)
Stability Level	`Evolving`

See Also

New!   `ldapadd(1)`, `ldapmodify(1)`, `ldapmodrdn(1)`, `ldapsearch(1)`,
`ldap_get_option(3LDAP)`, `ldap_set_option(3LDAP)`

New! **ldaplist** — Search and List Naming Information from an LDAP Directory Service

Synopsis

```
/usr/bin/ldaplist [-dlv] [database [key]...]
/usr/bin/ldaplist -h
```

Description

Use the `ldaplist` command, new in the Solaris 8 Operating Environment, to search for
and list the naming information from the LDAP directory service defined in the
`/var/ldap/LDAP_CLIENT_CACHE` file that is generated by `ldapclient`(1M) during the
client initialization phase.

New!   **Note** — The Solaris LDAP client must be set up before you can use this
command.

The database is either a container name or a database name. The `nsswitch.conf`(4)
file specifies the kind of name-service database to search for a particular type of
information. A container is a nonleaf entry in the Directory Information Tree (DIT) that
contains naming-service information. The container name is the LDAP Relative

New!   Distinguished Name (RDN) of the container relative to the `defaultSearchBase` as
defined in the configuration files (new in the Solaris 9 release). For example, for a
container named `ou=people`, the database name is the database specified in
`nsswitch.conf`. This database is mapped to a container (for example, `passwd` maps to
`ou=people`). When an invalid database is specified, the database is mapped to a generic
container to be searched for in the database (for example, `nisMapName=name`).
The *key* is the attribute value to be searched in the database. You can specify more
than one key to be searched in the same database. You can specify the key either as
attribute=*value* or as *value*. In the first case, `ldaplist` passes the search key to the

server. In the latter case, an attribute is assigned, depending on how the database is specified. When the database is a container name, then the ldaplist command uses the cn attribute type. When the database is a valid database name as defined in the nsswitch.conf file, then the ldaplist command uses a predefined attribute type, as specified in the following table. When the database name is invalid, the ldaplist command uses cn as the attribute type.

The ldaplist command relies on the Schema defined in RFC 2307bis.

Note — RFC 2307bis is an IETF experimental document, in draft stage, that defines an approach for using LDAP as a Network Information Service.

The data stored on the LDAP server must be stored in accordance with this Schema *New!* unless the profile contains schema mapping definitions (new in the Solaris 9 release). The following table lists the mapping from the database names to the container, the LDAP object class, and the attribute type used if not defined in the key. Databases new in the Solaris 9 release are shown with the New icon in the margin.

Database	Object Class	Attr Type	Container	
aliases	mailGroup	cn	ou=Aliases	
audit_attr	SolarisAuditUser	uidT	ou=people	*New!*
auth_attre	SolarisAuthAttr	nameT	ou=SolarisAuthAttr	*New!*
automount	nisObject	cn	nisMapName=auto_* 1	
bootparams	bootableDevice	cn	ou=Ethers	
ethers	ieee802Device	cn	ou=Ethers	
exec_attrt	SolarisExecAttr	name%T	ou=SolarisExecAttr	*New!*
group	posixgroup	cn	ou=Group	
hosts	ipHost	cn	ou=Hosts	
ipnodes	ipHost	cn	ou=Hosts	
netgroup	ipNetgroup	cn	ou=Netgroup	
netmasks	ipNetwork	ipnetworknumber	ou=Networks	
networks	ipNetwork	ipnetworknumber	ou=Networks	
passwd	posixAccount	uid	ou=People	
printers	printerService	printer-uri	ou=printers	*New!*
prof_attr	SolarisProfAttr	nameT	ou=SolarisProfAttr	*New!*
protocols	ipProtocol	cn	ou=Protocols	
publickey	nisKeyObject	uidnumber	ou=People 2	
		cn	ou=Hosts 3	
rpc	oncRpc	cn	ou=Rpc	
services	ipService	cn	ou=Services	
user_attr	SolarisUserAttr	uidT	ou=people	*New!*

- auto_* represents auto_home, auto_direct,...
- When the key starts with a digit, it is interpreted as a UID number.
- When the key starts with a nondigit, it is interpreted as a host name.

The ldaplist command supports substring search with the * wild-card in the key. For example, my* matches any strings that begin with my. In some shell environments, you may need to quote keys containing the wild-card.

When you specify no key, all the containers in the current search baseDN are listed.

Options

-d	List the attributes for the specified database, rather than the entries. By default, the entries are listed.
-h	List the database mapping.
-l	List all the attributes for each entry matching the search criteria. By default, ldaplist lists only the Distinguished Name of the entries found.
-v	Set verbose mode. The ldaplist command also prints the filter used to search for the entry. The filter is prefixed with +++.

Examples

The following example lists all entries in the hosts database.

```
example% lpdalist hosts
```

The following example lists all entries in a nonstandard database ou=new.

```
example% ldaplist ou=new
```

The following example finds user1 in the passwd database.

```
example% ldaplist passwd user1
```

The following example finds the entry with service port of 4045 in the services database.

```
example% ldaplist services ipserviceport=4045
```

The following example finds all users with a user name starting with new in the passwd database.

```
example% ldaplist passwd 'new*'
```

The following example lists the attributes for the hosts database.

```
example% ldaplist -d hosts
```

Exit Status

0	Successfully matched some entries.
1	Successfully searched the table and no matches were found.
2	An error occurred. An error message is displayed.

Files

`/var/ldap/ldap_client_file`   *New!*
`/var/ldap/ldap_client_cache`

> Files that contain the LDAP configuration of the client. Do not manually modify these files. Their content is not guaranteed to be human readable. To update these files, use ldapclient(1M). New in the Solaris 9 release.

Attributes

See `attributes`(5) for descriptions of the following attributes:

Attribute Type	Attribute Value
Availability	SUNWnisu
Interface Stability	Evolving

New!

See Also

`ldap(1)`, `ldapadd(1)`, `ldapdelete(1)`, `ldapmodify(1)`, `ldapmodrdn(1)`,   *New!*
`ldapsearch(1)`, `idsconfig(1M)`, `ldap_cachemgr(1M)`, `ldapaddent(1M)`,
`ldapclient(1M)`, `suninstall(1M)`, `resolve.conf(4)`, `attributes(5)`

---

ldapmodify, ldapadd — ldap Entry Addition and Modification Tools

Synopsis

```
/usr/bin/ldapmodify [-a] [-c] [-r] [-n] [-v] [-F] [-d debuglevel]
    [-D binddn] [-w passwd] [-h ldaphost] [-M authentication]
    [-p ldapport] [-f file] [-l nb-ldap-connections]
/opt/SUNWconn/ldap/bin/ldapadd [-b] [-n] [-v] [-F] [-d debuglevel]
    [-D binddn] [-w passwd] [-h ldaphost] [-p ldapport] [-f file]
    [-l nb-ldap-connections]
```

Description

ldapmodify opens a connection to an LDAP server and binds, modifies, or adds entries. The entry information is read from standard input or from *file*, specified with the -f option. ldapadd is implemented as a hard link to ldapmodify. When invoked as ldapadd, the -a (add new entry) option is turned on automatically.

Both ldapadd and ldapmodify reject duplicate attribute-name/value pairs for the same entry.

Options

Note — The -b option was removed in the Solaris 9 release.

-a   Add new entries. The default for ldapmodify is to modify existing entries. If invoked as ldapadd, this option is always set.

-c   Continuous operation mode. Report errors and continue with modifications. The default is to exit after reporting an error.

-d *debuglevel*

Set the LDAP debugging level. Useful levels of debugging for ldapmodify and ldapadd are:

1   Trace.

2   Packets.

4   Arguments.

32   Filters.

128   Access control.

To request more than one category of debugging information, add the masks. For example, to request trace and filter information, specify a debug level of 33.

-D *binddn*   Use the distinguished name *binddn* to bind to the directory.

-f *file*   Read the entry modification information from *file* instead of from standard input.

-F   Force application of all changes regardless of the content of input lines that begin replica:. By default, replica: lines are compared against the LDAP server host and port in use to decide whether to apply a replog record.

-h *ldaphost* Specify an alternative host on which the slapd server is running.

-l *nb-ldap-connections*

Specify the number of LDAP connections ldappadd or ldapmodify opens to process the modifications in the directory. The default is one connection.

-M *authentication*

Specify the authentication mechanism used to bind to the directory. This option can have the value CRAM-MD5. Bind DN and bind password are mandatory with this option.

-n   Preview modifications but make no changes to entries. Useful in conjunction with -v and -d for debugging.

-p *ldapport*

Specify an alternative TCP port on which the slapd server is listening.

Specify the number of LDAP connections that ldapadd or ldapmodify opens to process the modifications in the directory. The default is one connection.

-r   Replace existing value with the specified value (the default for ldapmodify). When you call ldapadd or if you specify the -a option, the -r option is ignored.

-v   Use verbose mode, and write diagnostics to standard output.

-w *passwd*   Use *passwd* as the password for authentication to the directory.

Examples

The format of the content of file (or standard input if you specify no -f option) is shown in the following examples.

The file /tmp/entrymods contains the following modification instructions:

```
dn: cn=Modify Me, o=XYZ, c=US
changetype: modify
replace: mail
mail: modme@atlanta.xyz.com
-
add: title
title: System Manager
-
add: jpegPhoto
jpegPhoto: /tmp/modme.jpeg
-
delete: description
-
```

The following command modifies the Modify Me entry as described below.

castle% **ldapmodify -r -f /tmp/entrymods**

1. Replace the current value of the mail attribute with the value modme@atlanta.xyz.com.
2. Add a title attribute with the value System Manager.
3. Add a jpegPhoto attribute using the contents of the file /tmp/modme.jpeg as the attribute value.
4. Remove the description attribute.

In the following example, the file /tmp/newentry contains the information for creating a new entry:

```
dn: cn=Ann Jones, o=XYZ, c=US
objectClass: person
cn: Ann Jones
cn: Annie Jones
sn: Jones
title: Director of Research and Development
mail: ajones@londonrd.xyz.us.com
uid: ajones
```

The following command uses the information in the newentry file to add a new entry for Ann Jones.

castle% **ldapadd -f /tmp/newentry**

In the following example, the file /tmp/badentry contains the information about an entry to be deleted.

dn: cn=Ann Jones, o=XYZ, c=US
changetype: delete

The following command removes Ann Jones' entry.

castle% **ldapmodify -f /tmp/badentry**

Exit Status

0   No errors.

non-zero   Errors occur and a diagnostic message is written to standard error.

Attributes

See attributes(5) for descriptions of the following attributes:

Attribute Type	Attribute Value
Availability	SUNWllldap (32-bit)
	SUNWldapx (64-bit)
Stability Level	Evolving

See Also

New!

ldapdelete(1), ldapmodrdn(1), ldapsearch(1), ldap_get_option(3LDAP), ldap_set_option(3LDAP)

ldapmodrdn — ldap Modify Entry RDN Tool

Synopsis

/usr/bin/ldapmodrdn [-r] [-n] [-v] [-c] [-d *debuglevel*] [-D *binddn*]
[-w *passwd*] [-h *ldaphost*] [-M *authentication*] [-p *ldapport*] [-f *file*]
[*dn rdn*]

Description

ldapmodrdn opens a connection to an LDAP server and binds and modifies the relative distinguished name (RDN) of entries. The entry information is read from standard input, from *file* with the -f option, or from the command-line pair *dn* and *rdn*.

Options

-c   Continuous operation mode. Report errors and continue with modifications. The default is to exit after reporting an error.

-d *debuglevel*

>Set the LDAP debugging level. Useful values of debug level for ldapmodrdn are:

>1   Trace.

>2   Packets.

>4   Arguments.

>32   Filters.

>128   Access control.

>To request more than one category of debugging information, add the masks. For example, to request trace and filter information, specify a debug level of 33.

-D *binddn*   Use the distinguished name *binddn* to bind to the directory.

-f *file*   Read the entry modification information from *file* instead of from standard input or the command line.

-h *ldaphost*

>Specify an alternative host on which the slapd server is running.

-M *authentication*

>Specify the authentication mechanism used to bind to the directory. This option can have the value CRAM-MD5. The bind DN and bind password are mandatory with this option.

-n   Show what would be done, but don't actually change entries. Useful in conjunction with -v for debugging.

-p *ldapport*

>Specify an alternative TCP port where the slapd server is listening.

-r   Remove old RDN values from the entry. By default, keep the old values.

-v   Use verbose mode, and write diagnostics to standard output.

-w *passwd*   Use *passwd* as the password for authentication to the directory.

Input Format
If you specify the command-line arguments *dn* and *rdn*, *rdn* replaces the relative distinguished name (RDN) of the entry specified by the distinguished name (DN), *dn*.

Otherwise, the contents of *file* (or standard input if you do not specify the -f option) must consist of one or more pairs of lines:

```
Distinguished Name (DN)
Relative Distinguished Name (RDN)
```

Use one or more blank lines to separate each DN/RDN pair.

Examples
In the following example, the file /tmp/entrymods contains the following lines:

```
cn=Modify Me, o=XYZ, c=US
cn=The New Me
```

The following command changes the RDN of the Modify Me entry from Modify Me to The New Me and removes the old cn, Modify Me.

example% **ldapmodify -r -f /tmp/entrymods**

Exit Status

0   No errors occurred.

non-zero   Errors result and a diagnostic message is written to standard error.

Attributes

See attributes(5) for descriptions of the following attributes:

Attribute Type	Attribute Value
Availability	SUNW11dap (32-bit)
	SUNW1dapx (64-bit)
Stability Level	Evolving

See Also

ldapadd(1), ldapdelete(1), ldapmodify(1), ldapsearch(1), attributes(5)

ldapsearch — ldap Search Tool

Synopsis

```
/usr/bin/ldapsearch [-n] [-u] [-v] [-t] [-A] [-B] [-L] [-R]
    [-d debuglevel] [-F sep] [-S attribute] [-f file] [-D binddn]
    [-w passwd] [-h ldaphost] [-M authentication] [-p ldapport]
    [-b searchbase] [-s scope] [-a deref] [-l time limit] [-z size limit]
    filter [attrs...]
```

Description

ldapsearch opens a connection to an LDAP server and binds and performs a search by using the *filter* filter.

If ldapsearch finds one or more entries, the attributes specified by *attrs* are retrieved and the entries and values are printed to standard output. If no *attrs* are listed, all attributes are returned.

Options

-a *deref*   Specify how aliases dereferencing is done. The possible values for *deref* are never, always, search, or find to specify that aliases are never dereferenced, always dereferenced, dereferenced when searching, or dereferenced only when finding the base object for the search. The default is to never dereference aliases.

-A   Retrieve attributes only (no values). This option is useful when you just want to see whether an attribute is present in an entry and are not interested in the specific value.

-b *searchbase*

Use *searchbase* as the starting point for the search instead of the default.

-B   Do not suppress display of non-ASCII values. This option is useful when dealing with values that appear in alternative character sets such as ISO-8859.1. This option is automatically set by the -L option.

-d *debuglevel*

Set the LDAP debugging level. Useful levels of debugging for ldapsearch are:

1   Trace.

2   Packets.

4   Arguments.

32   Filters.

128   Access control.

To request more than one category of debugging information, add the masks. For example, to request trace and filter information, specify a debug level of 33.

-D *binddn*   Use the distinguished name *binddn* to bind to the directory.

-f *file*   Read a series of lines from *file*, performing one LDAP search for each line. In this case, treat the filter given on the command line as a pattern where the first occurrence of %s is replaced with a line from *file*. If *file* is a single - character, then read the lines from standard input.

-F *sep*   Use *sep* as the field separator between attribute names and values. The default separator is =. If you specify the -L option, this option is ignored.

-h *ldaphost*

Specify an alternative host on which the slapd server is running.

-l *timelimit*

Wait at most *timelimit* seconds for a search to complete.

-L   Display search results in a modified format. Turn on the -B option, and ignore the -F option.

-M *authentication*

Specify the authentication mechanism used to bind to the directory. This option can have the value CRAM-MD5. The bind DN and bind password are mandatory with this option.

-n	Show what would be done, but don't actually perform the search. Useful in conjunction with -v and -d for debugging.
-p *ldapport*	
	Specify an alternative TCP port where the slapd server is listening.
-R	Do not automatically follow referrals returned while searching.
-s *scope*	Specify the scope of the search. The possible values of *scope* are base, one, or sub to specify a base object, one-level, or subtree search. The default is sub.
-S *attribute*	
	Based on *attribute*, sort the entries returned. If *attribute* is a zero-length string (" "), sort the entries by the components of their Distinguished Name. Note that ldapsearch normally prints entries as it receives them. Retrieve, then sort, then print all entries. The default is not to sort entries returned.
-t	Write retrieved values to a set of temporary files. This option is useful for dealing with non-ASCII values such as jpegPhoto or audio.
-u	Include the user-friendly form of the Distinguished Name (DN) in the output.
-v	Run in verbose mode and write diagnostics to standard output.
-w *passwd*	Use *passwd* as the password for authentication to the directory.
-z *sizelimit*	
	Retrieve at most *sizelimit* entries for a search to complete.

Output Format

If one or more entries are found, each entry is written to standard output in the form:

```
Distinguished Name (DN)
User Friendly Name (if you specify the -u option)
attributename=value
attributename=value
attributename=value
. . .
```

Multiple entries are separated with a single blank line. If you use the -F option to specify a different separator character, this character is used instead of the = character. If you use the -t option, the name of a temporary file is returned in place of the actual value. If you use the -A option, only the *attributename* is returned and not the attribute value.

Examples

The following command performs a subtree search (using the default search base) for entries with a commonName of mark smith. The commonName and telephoneNumber values are retrieved and printed to the standard output.

```
castle% ldapsearch "cn=mark smith' cn telephoneNumber
cn=Mark D Smith, ou=Sales, ou=Atlanta, ou=People, o=XYZ, c=US
cn=Mark Smith
```

```
cn=Mark David Smith
cn=Mark D Smith 1
cn=Mark D Smith
telephoneNumber=+1 123 456-7890
cn=Mark C Smith, ou=Distribution, ou=Atlanta, ou=People, o=XYZ, c=US
cn=Mark Smith
cn=Mark C Smith 1
cn=Mark C Smith
telephoneNumber=+1 123 456-9999
castle%
```

The following command performs a substring search, using the default search base for entries with user ID of mcs. The user-friendly form of the entry's DN is output after the line that contains the DN itself, and the jpegPhoto and audio values are retrieved and written to temporary files. The output might look like this if one entry with one value for each of the requested attributes is found.

```
castle% ldapsearch -u -t "uid=mcs" jpegPhoto audio
cn=Mark C Smith, ou=Distribution, ou=Atlanta, ou=People, o=XYZ, c=US
Mark C Smith, Distribution, Atlanta, People, XYZ, US
audio=/tmp/ldapsearch-audio-a19924
jpegPhoto=/tmp/ldapsearch-jpegPhoto-a19924
castle%
```

The following command performs a one-level search at the c=US level for all organizations whose organizationName begins with XY. Search results are displayed in the LDIF format. The organizationName and description attribute values are retrieved and printed to standard output, resulting in output similar to this.

```
castle% ldapsearch -L -s one -b "c=US" "o=XY*" o description
dn: o=XYZ, c=US
o: XYZ
description: XYZ Corporation
dn: o="XY Trading Company", c=US
o: XY Trading Company
description: Import and export specialists

dn: o=XYInternational, c=US
o: XYInternational
o: XYI
o: XY International
castle%
```

Exit Status

0	No errors occurred.
non-zero	Errors result and a diagnostic message is written to standard error.

Attributes

See attributes(5) for descriptions of the following attributes:

Attribute Type	Attribute Value
Availability	SUNW11dap (32-bit)
	SUNWldapx (64-bit)
Stability Level	Evolving

See Also

ldapadd(1), ldapdelete(1), ldapmodify(1), ldapmodrdn(1)

ldd — List Dynamic Dependencies of Executable Files or Shared Objects

Synopsis

New!

/usr/bin/ldd [-d | -r] [-c] [-e *envar*] [-f] [-i] [-l] [-L] [-s] [-u]
[-v] *filename*...

Description

Use the ldd (list dynamic dependencies) command to list the dynamic dependencies of executable files or shared objects.

New!

ldd uses the runtime linker, ld.so.1, to generate the diagnostics because it prepares the object being inspected as it would a running process. By default, ldd triggers the loading of any lazy dependencies.

If *filename* is an executable file, ldd lists the path names of all shared objects that would be loaded when *filename* is loaded.

If *filename* is a shared object, ldd lists the path names of all shared objects that would be loaded when *filename* is loaded. ldd expects shared objects to have execute permission. and if they don't, ldd issues a warning before trying to process the file.

ldd processes its input one file at a time. For each input file ldd performs one of the following:

- Lists the object dependencies if they exist.
- Succeeds quietly if dependencies do not exit.
- Prints an error message if processing fails.

Note — ldd does not list shared objects explicitly attached with dlopen(3X).

Using the -d or -r option with shared objects can give misleading results. ldd does a worst-case analysis of the shared object. However, in practice, some or all of the symbols reported as unresolved can be resolved by the executable file referencing the shared object.

ldd uses the same algorithm as the runtime linker to locate shared objects.

Options

ldd can also check the compatibility of *filename* with the shared objects it uses. With each of the following options, ldd prints warnings for any unresolved symbol references that would occur if *filename* were executed.

-c   Disable any configuration file in use. Configuration files can be used to alter default search paths, provide a directory cache, and provide alternative object dependencies. See crle(1). New in the Solaris 8 release.

-d   Check references to data objects. You cannot use -d with -r.

-e *envar*   Set the environment variable to *envar*. This option is useful for experimenting with runtime linker environment variables that can adversely affect ldd itself. New in the Solaris 8 release.

-f   Force a check for an executable file that is not secure. When ldd is invoked by a superuser, by default, it does not process any executable that it finds not secure. An executable is considered not secure if the interpreter it specifies does not reside in /usr/lib or /etc/lib or if the interpreter cannot be determined.

-i   Display the order of execution of initialization sections.

-l   Force the immediate processing of any filters so that all filtered objects and their dependencies are listed.

             The immediate processing of filters is the default for ldd starting in the Solaris 8 release. However, under this default, any auxiliary filtered objects that cannot be found are silently ignored. Any missing auxiliary filtered objects generate an error message.

-L   Enable lazy loading. This mode is the default when the object under inspection is loaded as part of a process. In this case, any lazy dependencies or filters are loaded into the process only when reference is made to a symbol that is defined within the lazy object. You can use the -d or -r options, together with the -l option, to inspect the dependencies and their order of loading because they occur in a running process. New in the Solaris 8 release.

-r   Check references to both data objects and functions. You cannot use -r with -d.

-s   Display the search path used to locate shared object dependencies.

-u   Display any unused dependencies. When a symbol reference is bound to a dependency, that dependency is deemed used. This option is useful, therefore, only when checking symbol references. If the -r option is not in effect, the -d option is disabled. New in the Solaris 8 release.

             Objects that are found to be unused with the -r option should be removed as dependencies. They provide no references but result in unnecessary overhead when *filename* is loaded. Objects are found to be unused with the -d option when not immediately required when *filename* is loaded, and they are, therefore, candidates for lazy loading. See "Lazy Loading."

-v   Display all dependency relationships incurred when processing
                filename. This option also displays any dependency version
                requirements. See pvs(1).

Usage

Security
Superuser should use the -f option only if the executable to be examined is known to be
trustworthy, because use of -f on an untrustworthy executable by superuser can
compromise system security. If you do not know whether the executable to be examined
is trustworthy, temporarily become a regular user and invoke ldd as that regular user.

You can safely examine untrustworthy objects with dump(1) and with adb(1) as long
as you do not use the :r subcommand. In addition, a non-superuser can use either the
:r subcommand of adb or truss(1) to examine an untrustworthy executable without too
much risk of compromise. To minimize risk when using ldd, adb :r, or truss on an
untrustworthy executable, use the user ID nobody.

New!
Lazy Loading
Objects that use lazy loading techniques—new in the Solaris 8 release—either by
directly specified lazy dependencies (see the -z lazyload option of ld(1)) or by filters
(see the -f and -F options of ld(1)) can experience variations in ldd output because of
the options they use. If an object expresses all its dependencies as lazy, the default
operation of ldd lists all dependencies in the order in which they are recorded in that
object, as shown in the following example.

```
example% ldd main
    libelf.so.1 =>    /usr/lib/libelf.so.1
    libnsl.so.1 =>    /usr/lib/libnsl.so.1
    libc.so.1 =>      /usr/lib/libc.so.1
```

With the -L option, you can enable the lazy loading behavior that occurs when this
object is used at runtime. In this mode, lazy dependencies are loaded when reference is
made to a symbol that is defined within the lazy object. Therefore, combining the -L
option with the -d and -r options reveals the dependencies needed to satisfy the data
and function references.

```
example% ldd -L main
example% ldd -d main
    libc.so.1 =>       /usr/lib/libc.so.1
example% ldd -r main
    libc.so.1 =>      /usr/lib/libc.so.1
    libelf.so.1 =>    /usr/lib/libelf.so.1
```

In this example, the order of the dependencies listed is not the same as those
displayed from ldd with no options. Even with the -r option, the function reference to
dependencies may not occur in the same order as it does in a running program.

Observing lazy loading can also reveal objects that are not required to satisfy any
references. These objects (in this example, libnsl.so.1) are candidates for removal
from the link-line used to build the object being inspected.

Initialization Order

New!

Objects that do not explicitly define their required dependencies can observe variations in the initialization section order displayed by ldd because of the options they use. The following example shows a simple application of ldd.

```
example% ldd -i main
  libA.so.1 =>       ./libA.so.1
  libc.so.1 =>       /usr/lib/libc.so.1
  libB.so.1 =>       ./libB.so.1

  init object=./libB.so.1
  init object=./libA.so.1
  init object=/usr/lib/libc.so.1
```

When relocations are applied, however, the following initialization order results.

```
example% ldd -ir main
  .........
  init object=/usr/lib/libc.so.1
  init object=./libB.so.1
  init object=./libA.so.1
```

In this case, libB.so.1 references a function in /usr/lib/libc.so.1. However, it has no explicit dependency on this library. Only after a relocation is discovered is a dependency established, which in turn affects the initialization section sort order.

Typically, the initialization section sort order established when an application is executed is equivalent to ldd with the -d option. You can obtain the optimum order if all objects fully define their dependencies. Use of the ld(1) -zdefs and -zignore options when building dynamic objects is recommended.

Cyclic dependencies can result when one or more dynamic objects reference each other. Avoid cyclic dependencies because a unique initialization sort order for these dependencies cannot be established.

Users who prefer a more static analysis of object files can inspect dependencies with tools such as dump(1) and elfdump(1).

Examples

The following example uses the -s option to display the search path used to locate shared object dependencies. Because the file is not an executable, a warning message is also displayed.

```
castle% ldd -s /usr/lib/adb/adbsub.o
warning: ldd: /usr/lib/adb/adbsub.o: is not executable
    search path=/usr/lib (default)
    trying path=/usr/lib/libld.so.2
    search path=/usr/lib (default)
    trying path=/usr/lib/libc.so.1

  find library=libdl.so.1; required by /usr/lib/libc.so.1
    search path=/usr/lib (default)
    trying path=/usr/lib/libdl.so.1

  find library=/usr/platform/SUNW,SPARCstation-10/lib/libc_psr.so.1;
  required by /usr/lib/libc.so.1
    search path=/usr/lib (default)
```

```
      trying path=/usr/lib/libelf.so.1
castle%
```

Files

/usr/lib/lddstub

Fake executable loaded to check the dependencies of shared objects.

Attributes

See attributes(5) for descriptions of the following attributes:

Attribute Type	Attribute Value
Availability	SUNWtoo

See Also

New!

adb(1), crle(1), dump(1), elfdump(1), ld(1), ld.so.1(1), pvs(1),
truss(1), dlopen(3DL), attributes(5)
Linker and Libraries Guide

Diagnostics

ldd prints the record of shared object path names to standard output. The optional list
of symbol resolution problems is printed to standard error. If *filename* is not an
executable file or a shared object or if it cannot be opened for reading, a non-zero exit
status is returned.

ld.so.1 — Runtime Linker for Dynamic Objects

Synopsis

```
/usr/lib/ld.so.1
/etc/lib/ld.so.1
```

Description

Dynamic applications consist of one or more dynamic objects, typically a dynamic
executable and its shared object dependencies. As part of the initialization and
execution of a dynamic application, an interpreter is called to complete the binding of
the application to its shared object dependencies. In Solaris, this interpreter is referred
to as the runtime linker.

During the link-editing of a dynamic executable, a special .interp section is created
along with an associated program header. This section contains a path name specifying
the program's interpreter. When the executable is being constructed, you can specify the
path name to the interpreter with the -I option to ld(1), the link-editor. The default
name supplied by the link-editor is that of the runtime linker, /usr/lib/ld.so.1.

During the process of executing a dynamic executable, the kernel maps the file and
locates the required interpreter. See exec(2) and mmap(2). The kernel maps this
interpreter and transfers control to it, passing sufficient information to enable the
interpreter to continue binding the application and then to run it.

In addition to initializing an application, the runtime linker provides services that enable the application to extend its address space by mapping additional shared objects and binding to symbols within them.

The runtime linker performs the following functions:

- Opens and processes any application configuration file. You can use configuration *New!* files to alter default search paths, provide a directory cache, and provide alternative dependencies. See crle(1). By default, the /var/ld/ld.config file is used for 32-bit objects and /var/ld/64/ld.config for 64-bit objects. You can specify alternative configuration files with the LD_CONFIG environment variable or encode them within a dynamic executable with the -c option of ld(1). New in the Solaris 8 release.

- Analyzes the application's dynamic information section (.dynamic) and determines which shared object dependencies are required.

- Locates and maps in these dependencies, then analyzes their dynamic information sections to determine if any additional shared object dependencies are required.

- Once all shared object dependencies are located and mapped, performs any necessary relocations to bind these shared objects in preparation for process execution.

- Calls any initialization functions provided by the shared object dependencies. By default, these functions are called in the reverse order of the topologically sorted dependencies. Should cyclic dependencies exist, the initialization functions are called, using the sorted order with the cycle removed. ldd(1) can be used to display the initialization order of shared object dependencies. See also LD_BREADTH.

- Passes control to the application.

- During the application's execution, the runtime linker can be called on to perform any delayed function binding.

- Calls any finalization functions on deletion of shared objects from the process. By default, these functions are called in the order of the topologically sorted dependencies.

- The application can also call on the runtime linker's services to acquire additional shared objects by dlopen(3X) and bind to symbols within these objects with dlsym(3X).

You can find further details on each of the above topics in the *Linker and Libraries Guide*.

The runtime linker uses a prescribed search path for locating the dynamic dependencies of an object. The default search paths are the run path recorded in the object, followed by /usr/lib. You specify the run path when the dynamic object is constructed with the -R option to ld(1). You can use LD_LIBRARY_PATH to indicate directories to be searched before the default directories.

Note — The user compatibility library /usr/lib/0@0.so.1 provides a mechanism that establishes a value of 0 at location 0. Some applications erroneously assume that a null character pointer should be treated the same as a pointer to a null string. Such applications produce a segmentation violation when they access a null character pointer. If this library is added to such an application at runtime, with LD_PRELOAD, it provides an environment that is sympathetic to this errant behavior.

However, the user compatibility library is intended neither to enable the generation of such applications nor to endorse this particular programming practice.

Environment Variables

LD_AUDIT   Specify a colon-separated list of objects that are loaded by the runtime linker. As each object is loaded, it is examined for Link-Auditing interfaces. The routines that are present are called as specified in the Link-Auditing interface described in the *Linker and Libraries Guide*.

LD_BIND_NOW   Override the runtime linker's default mode of performing lazy binding by setting the environment variable LD_BIND_NOW to any non-null value. With this setting, the runtime linker performs both data reference and function reference relocations during process initialization before transferring control to the application. Also see the -z now option of ld(1).

LD_CONFIG   Provide an alternative configuration file. You can use configuration files to alter default search paths, provide a directory cache, and provide alternative object dependencies. See crle(1). New in the Solaris 8 release.

LD_DEBUG   Specify a comma-separated list of tokens so that the runtime linker can print debugging information to the standard error. The help special token supplies the full list of tokens available. You can also supply the environment variable LD_DEBUG_OUTPUT to specify a file to which the debugging information is sent. The file name is suffixed with the process ID of the application generating the debugging information.

LD_DEMANGLE

     Show any symbol name used as part of a diagnostic message as it is defined within an ELF file. When you set LD_DEMANGLE to a non-null value, the runtime linker tries to decode (demangle) any C++ symbol names. New in the Solaris 8 release.

LD_FLAGS   An alternative way to supply environment variable information. You can specify any of the LD_*XXX* environment variables as an *xxx* token. Separate multiple tokens with commas. New in the Solaris 8 release.

LD_LIBRARY_PATH

     Enhance the search path that the runtime linker uses to find dynamic dependencies. LD_LIBRARY_PATH specifies a colon-separated list of directories that are to be searched before the default directories. Also note that LD_LIBRARY_PATH adds additional semantics to ld(1).

LD_LOADFLTR   Set to any non-null value to process filters immediately when they are loaded. Filters are a form of shared object. They enable an alternative shared object to be selected at runtime and provide the implementation for any symbols defined within the filter. See the -f

New! (margin marker beside LD_CONFIG)

New! (margin marker beside LD_DEMANGLE)

New! (margin marker beside LD_FLAGS)

and -F options of ld(1). By default, defer the alternative shared object processing until symbol resolution occurs against the filter. Also see the -z loadfltr option of ld(1).

LD_NOAUDIT   When you set LD_NOAUDIT to any non-null value, the runtime linker ignores any local auditing libraries. Local auditing libraries can be defined within applications and shared objects. See the -p and -P options of ld(1). New in the Solaris 8 release.   *New!*

LD_NOAUXFLTR

Set to any non-null value to disable alternative shared lookup. Auxiliary filters are a form of shared object. They enable an alternative shared object to be selected at runtime and provide the implementation for any symbols defined within the filter. See the -f option of ld(1).

LD_NOCONFIG   *New!*

When you set LD_NOCONFIG to any non-null value, the runtime linker disables configuration file processing. By default, the runtime linker tries to open and process a configuration file. New in the Solaris 8 release.

LD_NODIRCONFIG   *New!*

A subset of LD_NOCONFIG that ignores any directory cache information provided in a configuration file. New in the Solaris 8 release.

LD_NODIRECT   *New!*

When you set LD_NODIRECT to any non-null value, the runtime linker ignores any direct binding information. Direct binding information instructs the runtime linker to search directly for a symbol in an associated object instead of carrying out the default symbol model. See the -B direct option of ld(1). New in the Solaris 8 release.

LD_NOENVCONFIG   *New!*

Provide a subset of LD_NOCONFIG in that any environment variables provided in a configuration file are ignored. New in the Solaris 9 release.

LD_NOLAZYLOAD   *New!*

When you set LD_NOLAZYLOAD to any non-null value, the runtime linker ignores a dependency's lazy loading label and loads it immediately. Dependencies labeled for lazy loading are not loaded into memory until explicit references have been made to them. See the -z lazyload option of ld(1). New in the Solaris 8 release.

LD_NOOBJALTER   *New!*

A subset of LD_NOCONFIG that ignores any alternative object dependencies provided in a configuration file. New in the Solaris 8 release.

LD_NOVERSION

> Set to any non-null value to disable the runtime linker version checking. By default, the runtime linker verifies version dependencies for the primary executable and all of its dependencies.

LD_ORIGIN
> Trigger the immediate processing of $ORIGIN by setting the environment variable LD_ORIGIN to any non-null value.

New!
> Before the Solaris 9 release, this environment variable was useful for applications that invoked chdir(2) before loading dependencies that use the $ORIGIN string token. The establishment of the current working directory by the runtime linker is now the default and thus makes this option redundant.

New! LD_PRELOAD
> Provide a white-space-separated list of shared objects that are loaded after the program being executed but before any other shared objects that the program references. Symbol definitions provided by the preloaded objects interpose on references made by the shared object that the program references but do not interpose on the program itself.

LD_PROFILE
> Define a shared object that is profiled by the runtime linker. When profiling is enabled, create and map a profiling buffer file. The name of the buffer file is the name of the shared object being profiled with a .profile extension. By default, this buffer is placed in /var/tmp. You can also use the environment variable LD_PROFILE_OUTPUT to indicate an alternative directory in which to place the profiling buffer.

> This buffer contains profil(2) and call count information similar to the gmon.out information generated by programs that have been linked with the –xpg option of cc(1). Any applications that use the named shared object and that run while this environment variable is set accumulate data in the profile buffer. You can use gprof(1) to examine the profile buffer information.

New!
> Note that this profiling technique is an alternative to any that may be provided by the compilation system. The shared object being profiled does not have to be instrumented in any way, and LD_PROFILE should not be combined with a profile-instrumented application. See the *Linker and Libraries Guide* for more information on profiling shared objects.

New!
> Take care when using LD_PROFILE in combination with other process monitoring techniques (for example users of proc(4)) because deadlock conditions can result that leave the profile buffer locked. A locked buffer blocks any processes that try to record profiling information. To reduce this likelihood, the runtime linker's profile implementation determines whether the process is being monitored at startup and, if so, silently disables profiling of the process. However, this mechanism cannot catch monitoring processes that attach to the process during its execution.

You can specify each environment variable with a _32 or _64 suffix that makes the environment variable specific to 32-bit or 64-bit processes and overrides any nonsuffixed version of the environment variable that may be in effect. New in the Solaris 8 release.

Note — Environment-variable names beginning with the characters LD_ are reserved for possible future enhancements to ld and ld.so.1(1).

Security

For the prevention of malicious dependency substitution or symbol interposition, some restrictions may apply to the evaluation of the dependencies of secure processes.

The runtime linker categorizes a process as secure if the user is not a superuser and either the real user and effective user identifiers are not equal or the real group and effective group identifiers are not equal. See getuid(2), geteuid(2), getgid(2), and getegid(2).

The default trusted directory known to the runtime linker is /usr/lib/secure for 32-bit objects and /usr/lib/secure/64 for 64-bit objects. You can use the crle(1) command to specify additional trusted directories applicable to secure applications. Administrators who use this technique should ensure that the target directories are suitably protected from malicious intrusion. New in the Solaris 8 release.

If an LD_LIBRARY_PATH environment variable is in effect for a secure process, only the trusted directories specified by this variable are used to augment the runtime linker's search rules. Presently, the only trusted directory known to the runtime linker is /usr/lib, or /usr/lib/sparcv9 for 64-bit SPARC V9 objects.

In a secure process, any run-path specifications provided by the application or any of its dependencies are used, provided they are full path names; that is, the path name starts with a /.

In a secure process, the expansion of the $ORIGIN string is allowed only if it expands to a trusted directory. New in the Solaris 8 release.

You can load additional objects with a secure process by using the LD_PRELOAD or LD_AUDIT environment variables. You can specify these objects as full path names or simple file names. Full path names are restricted to known trusted directories. Simple file names with no / in the name are located subject to the search path restrictions previously described and, thus, resolve only to known trusted directories. New in the Solaris 8 release.

In a secure process, any dependencies that consist of simple file names are processed with the path-name restrictions previously described. Dependencies that are expressed as full or relative path names are used as is. Therefore, the developer of a secure process should ensure that the target directory referenced as a full or relative path-name dependency is suitably protected from malicious intrusion. New in the Solaris 8 release.

When creating a secure process, it is recommended that you not use relative path names to express dependencies or to construct dlopen(3DL) path names. This restriction should be applied to the application and all dependencies. New in the Solaris 8 release.

Examples

The following example uses the LD_FLAGS environment variable to group environment variable information.

```
example% LD_FLAGS_32=bind_now,library_path=lib/one:/lib/two
example% LD_FLAGS_64=library_path=/lib/one/64,preload=foo.so
```

These examples are equivalent to setting the individual environment variables LD_BIND_NOW and LD_LIBRARY_PATH for 32-bit applications and LD_LIBRARY_PATH and LD_PRELOAD for 64-bit applications.

Files

/usr/lib/ld.so.1

> Default runtime linker.

/etc/lib/ld.so.1

> Alternative runtime linker.

/usr/lib/libc.so.

> Alternative interpreter for SVID ABI compatibility.

/usr/lib/ld.so

> AOUT(BCP) runtime linker.

/usr/lib/0@0.so.1

> Null character pointer compatibility library.

New! /usr/lib/secure

> LD_PRELOAD location for secure applications. New in the Solaris 8 release.

New! /usr/lib/secure/64

> LD_PRELOAD location for secure 64-bit applications. New in the Solaris 8 release.

New! /usr/lib/64/ld.so.1

> Default runtime linker for 64-bit applications. New in the Solaris 8 release.

New! /usr/lib/64/0@0.so.1

> Null character pointer compatibility library for 64-bit applications. New in the Solaris 8 release.

New! /var/ld/ld.config

> Default configuration file for 32-bit applications. New in the Solaris 8 release.

New! /var/ld/64/ld.config

> Default configuration file for 64-bit applications. New in the Solaris 8 release.

Attributes

See attributes(5) for descriptions of the following attributes:

Attribute Type	Attribute Value
Availability	SUNWcsu

See Also

crle(1), gprof(1), ld(1), ldd(1), exec(2), getegid(2), geteuid(2),
getuid(2), mmap(2), profil(2), dladdr(3DL), dlclose(3DL), dldump(3DL),
dlerror(3DL), dlopen(3DL), dlsym(3DL), proc(4), attributes(5)

New!

Linker and Libraries Guide

let — Shell Built-in Function to Evaluate One or More Arithmetic Expressions

Synopsis

ksh

let "*arg*"...

Description

ksh

Use the let command to perform integer arithmetic as specified by one or more
arguments. Each *arg* can contain numbers, operators, constants, and shell variables
that define a separate arithmetic expression to be evaluated. Use double quotes with
any arguments that contain spaces or other special characters. You can also use double
parentheses ((...)) instead of double quotes for arguments that contain white space.

The exit status is 0 if the value of the last expression is non-zero, and 1 otherwise.

Examples

The following example sets the variable X to the sum of 1 + 1.

```
$ let "X=1 + 1"
$ print $X
2
$
```

Attributes

See attributes(5) for descriptions of the following attributes:

Attribute Type	Attribute Value
Availability	SUNWcsu

See Also

ksh(1), set(1), typeset(1), attributes(5)

lex — Generate Programs for Lexical Tasks

Synopsis

/usr/ccs/bin/lex [-cntv] [-e | -w] [-V -Q [y | n]] [*file*]...

Description

The lex command generates C programs to be used in lexical processing of character input that can also be used as an interface to yacc. The C programs are generated from lex source code and conform to the ISO C standard. Usually, the lex command writes the program it generates to the file lex.yy.c; the state of this file is unspecified if lex exits with a non-zero exit status.

Options

-c	Indicate C-language action (default option).
-e	Generate a program that can handle EUC characters (cannot be used with the -w option). yytext[] is of type unsigned char[].
-n	Suppress the summary of statistics usually written with the -v option. If no table sizes are specified in the lex source code and you do not specify the -v option, then -n is implied.
-Q[y|n]	Print version information to output file lex.yy.c by using -Qy. The -Qn option does not print out version information and is the default.
-t	Write the resulting program to standard output instead of lex.yy.c.
-v	Write a summary of lex statistics to the standard error. If table sizes are specified in the lex source code and you do not specify the -n option, the -v option can be enabled.
-w	Generate a program that can handle EUC characters (cannot be used with the -e option). Unlike the -e option, yytext[] is of type wchar_t[].
-V	Print version information on standard error.

Operands

file	A path name of an input file. If you specify more than one such file, concatenate all files to produce a single lex program. If you specify no *file* operands or if a *file* operand is -, use the standard input.

Output

Standard Output

If you specify the -t option, the text file of C source code output of lex is written to standard output.

Standard Error

If you specify the -t option, then informational, error, and warning messages concerning the contents of lex source code input are written to the standard error.

If you do not specify the -t option:

- Informational error and warning messages concerning the contents of lex source code input are written to either the standard output or standard error.

- If you specify the -v option and do not specify the -n option, lex statistics are also written to standard error. These statistics may also be generated if table sizes are specified with a % operator as long as you do not specify the -n option.

Output Files

A text file containing C source code is written to lex.yy.c or to the standard output if you use the -t option.

Extended Description

Each input file contains lex source code, which is a table of regular expressions with corresponding actions in the form of C-program fragments.

When lex.yy.c is compiled and linked with the lex library (by use of the -1 1 operand with c89 or cc), the resulting program reads character input from the standard input and partitions it into strings that match the given expressions.

When an expression is matched, the following actions occur.

- The input string that was matched is left in yytext as a null-terminated string; yytext is either an external character array or a pointer to a character string. You can explicitly select the type with the %array or %pointer declarations. The default is %array.

- The external int yyleng is set to the length of the matching string.

- The expression's corresponding program fragment, or action, is executed.

During pattern matching, lex searches the set of patterns for the single longest possible match. The rule given first is chosen from the rules that match the same number of characters.

The general format of lex source is:

```
Definitions %%
Rules %%
User Subroutines
```

The first %% is required to mark the beginning of the rules (regular expressions and actions); the second %% is required only if user subroutines follow.

Any line in the Definitions section beginning with a blank character is assumed to be a C-program fragment and is copied to the external definition area of the lex.yy.c file. Similarly, anything in the Definitions section included between delimiter lines containing only %{ and %} is also copied unchanged to the external definition area of the lex.yy.c file.

Any such input (beginning with a blank character or within %{ and %} delimiter lines) appearing at the beginning of the Rules section before any rules are specified is written to lex.yy.c after the declarations of variables for the yylex function and before the first line of code in yylex. Thus, user variables local to yylex can be declared here, as can application code to execute on entry to yylex.

The action taken by lex is undefined when lex encounters any input beginning with a blank character or within %{ and %} delimiter lines appearing in the Rules section but coming after one or more rules. The presence of such input may result in an erroneous definition of the `yylex` function.

Definitions in lex

Definitions in `lex` appear before the first `%%` delimiter. Any line in this section not contained between `%{` and `%}` lines and not beginning with a blank character is assumed to define a `lex` substitution string. The format of these lines is:

name substitute

If *name* does not meet the requirements for identifiers in the ISO C standard, the result is undefined. The string substitute replaces the string { *name*} when it is used in a rule. The *name* string is recognized in this context only when the braces are provided and when it does not appear within a bracket expression or within double quotes.

In the `Definitions` section, any line beginning with a `%` (percent sign) character and followed by an alphanumeric word beginning with either `s` or `S` defines a set of start conditions. Any line beginning with a `%` followed by a word beginning with either `x` or `X` defines a set of exclusive start conditions. When the generated scanner is in a `%s` state, patterns with no state specified are also active; in a `%x` state, such patterns are not active. The rest of the line after the first word is considered to be one or more blank-character-separated names of start conditions. Start condition names are constructed in the same way as definition names. Start conditions can be used to restrict the matching of regular expressions to one or more states.

Implementations accept either of the following two mutually exclusive declarations in the `Definitions` section.

%array   Declare the type of `yytext` to be a null-terminated character array.

%pointer   Declare the type of `yytext` to be a pointer to a null-terminated character string.

Note — When using the `%pointer` option, you cannot use the `yyless` function to alter `yytext`.

`%array` is the default. If you specify `%array` (or do not specify either `%array` or `%pointer`), the correct way to make an external reference to `yytext` is with a declaration of the following form.

```
extern char yytext[]
```

If you specify `%pointer`, the correct way to make an external reference to `yytext` is with a declaration of the following form.

```
extern char *yytext;
```

`lex` accepts declarations in the `Definitions` section for setting certain internal table sizes. The declarations are shown in the following table.

Declaration	Description	Default
%p n	Number of positions.	2500
%n n	Number of states.	500
%a n	Number of transitions.	2000

Declaration	Description	Default
%e n	Number of parse tree nodes.	1000
%k n	Number of packed character classes.	10000
%o n	Size of the output array.	3000

Programs generated by lex need either the -e or -w option to handle input that contains EUC characters from supplementary codesets. If you specify neither of these options, yytext is of the type char [], and the generated program can handle only ASCII characters.

When you use the -e option, yytext is of the type unsigned char [] and yyleng gives the total number of bytes in the matched string. With this option, the macros input(), unput(c), and output(c) should do a byte-based I/O in the same way as with the regular ASCII lex. Two more variables are available with the -e option—yywtext and yywleng—which behave the same as would yytext and yyleng under the -w option.

When you use the -w option, yytext is of the type wchar_t [] and yyleng gives the total number of characters in the matched string. If you supply your own input(), unput(c), or output(c) macros with this option, they must return or accept EUC characters in the form of wide character (wchar_t). This enables a different interface between your program and the lex internals to expedite some programs.

Rules in lex

The Rules source files are a table in which the left column contains regular expressions and the right column contains actions (C-program fragments) to be executed when the expressions are recognized.

```
ERE action
ERE action
. . .
```

The extended regular expression (ERE) portion of a row is separated from action by one or more blank characters. A regular expression containing blank characters is recognized under one of the following conditions:

- The entire expression appears within double quotes.
- The blank characters appear within double quotes.
- Each blank character is preceded by a backslash character.

User Subroutines in lex

Anything in the user subroutines section is copied to lex.yy.c following yylex.

Regular Expressions in lex

The lex command supports the set of Extended Regular Expressions (EREs) described in regex(5) with the following additions and exceptions to the syntax.

> . . . Any string enclosed in double quotes represents the characters within the double quotes as themselves, except that backslash escapes (which appear in the following table) are recognized. Any backslash-escape sequence is terminated by the closing quote. For example, "\01""1" represents a single string: the octal value 1 followed by the character 1.

<state>r <state1, state2,...>r

> Match the regular expression *r* only when the program is in one of the start conditions indicated by *state*, *state1*, and so forth. (As an exception to the typographical conventions of the rest of this document, in this case *<state>* does not represent a metavariable, but the literal angle-bracket characters surrounding a symbol.) The start condition is recognized as such only at the beginning of a regular expression.

r/x

> Match the regular expression *r* only if it is followed by an occurrence of regular expression *x*. The token returned in yytext matches only *r*. If the trailing portion of *r* matches the beginning of *x*, the result is unspecified. The *r* expression cannot include further trailing context or the $ (match-end-of-line) operator; *x* cannot include the ^ (match-beginning-of-line) operator, or trailing context, or the $ operator. That is, only one occurrence of trailing context is allowed in a lex regular expression, and you can use the ^ operator only at the beginning of such an expression.

{name}

> When *name* is one of the substitution symbols from the Definitions section, replace the string, including the enclosing braces, with the substitute value. Treat the substitute value in the extended regular expression as if it were enclosed in parentheses. No substitution occurs if *{name}* occurs within a bracket expression or within double quotes.

Within an ERE, a backslash character (\\, \a, \b, \f, \n, \r, \t, \v) is considered to begin an escape sequence. In addition, the escape sequences in the following table are recognized.

You cannot use a literal newline character within an ERE; you cannot use the \n escape sequence to represent a newline character. A newline character cannot be matched by a period operator.

Escape Sequences in lex

Sequence	Description	Meaning
\digits	A backslash character followed by the longest sequence of one, two, or three octal-digit characters (01234567). If all of the digits are 0, (that is, representation of the null character), the behavior is undefined.	The character whose encoding is represented by the one-, two-, or three-digit octal integer. Multibyte characters require multiple concatenated escape sequences of this type, including the leading \ for each byte.

Sequence	Description	Meaning
\x*digits*	A backslash character followed by the longest sequence of hexadecimal-digit characters (01234567 abcdefABCDEF). If all of the digits are 0, (that is, representation of the null character), the behavior is undefined.	The character whose encoding is represented by the hexadecimal integer.
c	A backslash character followed by any character not described in this table (\\\\, \a, \b, \f, \n, \r, \t, \v).	The character *c*, unchanged.

ERE Precedence in lex

The order of precedence given to extended regular expressions for lex is as shown in the following table, from high to low.

> **Note —** The escaped characters entry is not meant to imply that these are operators. They are included in the table to show their relationships to the true operators. The start condition, trailing context, and anchoring notations have been omitted from the table because of the placement restrictions described in this section; they can only appear at the beginning or ending of an ERE.

[= =] [: :] [. .]	Collation-related bracket symbols.
\\<*special character*>	Escaped characters.
[]	Bracket expression.
"..."\grouping ( )	Quoting.
{*name*}	Definition.
* + ?	Single-character RE duplication concatenation.
{*m*, *n*}	Interval expression.
|	Alternation.

The ERE anchoring operators (^ and $) do not appear in the table. With lex regular expressions, use of these operators is restricted. You can use the ^ operator only at the beginning of an entire regular expression and the $ operator only at the end. The operators apply to the entire regular expression. Thus, for example, the pattern (^abc)|(def$) is undefined. Instead, you can write it as two separate rules, one with the regular expression ^abc and one with def$, that share a common action via the special | action. If you write the pattern ^abc|def$, it would match either of abc or def on a line by itself.

Unlike the general ERE rules, embedded anchoring is not allowed by most historical lex implementations. An example of embedded anchoring is for patterns such as (^)foo($) to match foo when it exists as a complete word. You can achieve this functionality with existing lex features, as shown below.

```
^foo/[\n] |
" foo"/[\n]   /* found foo as a separate word */
```

Note also that $ is a form of trailing context (it is equivalent to /\n) and as such you cannot use it with regular expressions containing another instance of the operator.

You can use the additional regular expressions trailing-context operator / as an ordinary character if presented within double quotes, "/"; preceded by a backslash, \/; or within a bracket expression, [/]. The start-condition < and > operators are special only in a start condition at the beginning of a regular expression; elsewhere in the regular expression they are treated as ordinary characters.

The following examples clarify the differences between lex regular expressions and regular expressions appearing elsewhere in this document. For regular expressions of the form r/x, the string matching r is always returned; confusion may arise when the beginning of x matches the trailing portion of r. For example, given the regular expression a*b/cc and the input aaabcc, yytext would contain the string aaab on this match. But, given the regular expression x*/xy and the input xxxy, the token xxx, not xx, is returned by some implementations because xxx matches x*.

In the rule ab*/bc, the b* at the end of r extends r's match into the beginning of the trailing context, so the result is unspecified. If this rule were ab/bc, however, the rule matches the text ab when it is followed by the text bc. In this latter case, the matching of r cannot extend into the beginning of x, so the result is specified.

Actions in lex

The action to be taken when an ERE is matched can be a C-program fragment or the special actions described below. The program fragment can contain one or more C statements and can also include special actions. The empty C statement ; is a valid action; any string in the lex.yy.c input that matches the pattern portion of such a rule is effectively ignored or skipped. However, the absence of an action is not valid, and the action lex takes in such a condition is undefined.

The specification for an action, including C statements and special actions, can extend across several lines if you enclose them in braces.

```
ERE <one or more blanks> { program statement program statement }
```

The default action is to copy the string to the output when a string in the input to a lex.yy.c program is not matched by any expression. Because the default behavior of a program generated by lex is to read the input and copy it to the output, a minimal lex source program that has just %% generates a C program that simply copies the input to the output unchanged.

Four special actions are available: | ECHO; REJECT; BEGIN.

| | The action for the next rule is the action for this rule. Unlike the other three actions, you cannot enclose | in braces or terminate it with a semicolon. You must specify it alone with no other actions. |

ECHO;   Write the contents of the string yytext on the output.

REJECT;   Usually only a single expression is matched by a given string in the input. REJECT means continue to the next expression that matches the current input and execute whatever rule was the second choice after the current rule for the same input. Thus, you can match and execute multiple rules for one input string or overlapping input strings. For example, given the regular expressions xyz and xy and the input xyz, usually only the regular expression xyz would match. The next attempted match would start after z. If the last action in the xyz rule is REJECT, both this rule and the xy rule would be executed. The REJECT action can be implemented so that flow of control does not continue after it, as if it were equivalent to a goto to another part of yylex. Using REJECT can result in somewhat larger and slower scanners.

BEGIN   The action BEGIN *newstate;* switches the state (start condition) to *newstate.* If you have not previously declared the string *newstate* as a start condition in the Definitions, the results are unspecified. The initial state is indicated by the digit 0 or the token INITIAL.

The functions or macros described below are accessible to user code included in the lex input. It is unspecified whether they appear in the C code output of lex or are accessible only through the -l l operand to c89 or cc (the lex library).

int yylex(void)

Perform lexical analysis on the input; this is the primary function generated by the lex command. The function returns 0 when the end of input is reached; otherwise it returns non-zero values (tokens) determined by the actions that are selected.

int yymore(void)

When called, indicate that when the next input string is recognized, and append it to the current value of yytext instead of replacing it; adjust the value in yyleng accordingly.

int yyless(int *n*)

Retain *n* initial characters in yytext, null terminated, and treat the remaining characters as if they had not been read; adjust the value in yyleng accordingly.

int input(void)

Return the next character from the input or 0 on end-of-file. Obtain input from the stream pointer yyin, although possibly through an intermediate buffer. Thus, once scanning has begun, the effect of altering the value of yyin is undefined. Remove the character read from the input stream of the scanner without any processing by the scanner.

int unput(int *c*)

Return the character *c* to the input; yytext and yyleng are undefined until the next expression is matched. The result of using unput for more characters than have been input is unspecified.

The following functions appear only in the `lex` library, accessible through the `-l 1` operand. They can, therefore, be redefined by a portable application.

`int yywrap(void)`

> Called by `yylex` at end-of-file; the default `yywrap` always returns 1. If the application requires `yylex` to continue processing with another source of input, then the application can include a function `yywrap`, which associates another file with the external variable `FILE *yyin` and returns a value of 0.

`int main(int argc, char *argv[])`

> Call `yylex` to perform lexical analysis, then exit. The user code can contain `main` to perform application-specific operations, calling `yylex` as applicable.

These functions are broken into two lists because only those functions in `libl.a` can be reliably redefined by a portable application.

Except for `input`, `unput`, and `main`, all external and static names generated by `lex` begin with the prefix `yy` or `YY`.

Usage

Portable applications are warned that in the `Rules` section, an ERE without an action is not acceptable but need not be detected as erroneous by `lex`. This may result in compilation or runtime errors.

The purpose of `input` is to take characters off the input stream and discard them as far as the lexical analysis is concerned. A common use is to discard the body of a comment once the beginning of a comment is recognized.

The `lex` command is not fully internationalized in its treatment of regular expressions in the `lex` source code or generated lexical analyzer. It would seem desirable to have the lexical analyzer interpret the regular expressions given in the `lex` source according to the environment specified when the lexical analyzer is executed, but this is not possible with the current `lex` technology. Furthermore, the very nature of the lexical analyzers produced by `lex` must be closely tied to the lexical requirements of the input language being described, which frequently are locale specific anyway. (For example, writing an analyzer that is used for French text is not automatically useful for processing other languages.)

Note — If routines such as `yyback()`, `yywrap()`, and `yylock()` in `.1` (ell) files are to be `extern` C functions, the command line to compile a C++ program must define the `__EXTERN_C__` macro, for example:

```
castle% CC -D__EXTERN_C__ ... file
```

Examples

The following example of a `lex` program implements a rudimentary scanner for a Pascal-like syntax.

```
%{
/* need this for the call to atof() below */
#include <math.h>
/* need this for printf(), fopen() and stdin below */
#include <stdio.h>
%}
```

```
DIGIT [0-9]
ID [a-z] [a-z0-9]*
%%
{DIGIT}+ {
    printf("An integer: %s (%d)\n", yytext,
    atoi(yytext));
    }
{DIGIT}+"."{DIGIT}*  {
    printf("A float: %s (%g)\n", yytext,
    atof(yytext));
    }
if|then|begin|end|procedure|function  {
    printf("A keyword: %s\n", yytext);
    }
{ID} printf("An identifier: %s\n", yytext);
"+"|"-"|"*"|"/"    printf("An operator: %s\n", yytext);
"{"[^}\n]*"}"  /* eat up one-line comments */
[\t\n]+ /* eat up white space */
    printf("Unrecognized character: %s\n", yytext);
%%
int main(int argc, char *argv[])
{
    ++argv, --argc;  /* skip over program name */
    if (argc > 0)
    yyin = fopen(argv[0], "r");
    else
    yyin = stdin;
    yylex();
}
```

Environment Variables

See environ(5) for descriptions of the following environment variables that affect the execution of lex: LC_COLLATE, LC_CTYPE, LC_MESSAGES, and NLSPATH.

Exit Status

0	Successful completion.
>0	An error occurred.

Attributes

See attributes(5) for descriptions of the following attributes:

Attribute Type	Attribute Value
Availability	SUNWbtool

See Also

yacc(1), attributes(5), environ(5), regex(5)

limit, ulimit, unlimit — Set or Get Limitations on Available System Resources

Synopsis

```
/usr/bin/ulimit [-f] [blocks]
```

sh
```
ulimit [-[HS] [a | cdfnstv]]
ulimit [-[HS]] c | d | f | n | s | t | v]] limit
```

csh
```
limit [-h] [resource [limit]]
unlimit [-h] [resource]
```

ksh
```
ulimit [-HSacdfnstv] [limit]
```

Description

/usr/bin/ulimit

The ulimit command sets or reports the file-size writing limit imposed on files written by the shell and its child processes (files of any size can be read). Only a process with appropriate privileges can increase the limit.

Bourne Shell

The Bourne shell built-in function, ulimit, prints or sets hard or soft resource limits. These limits are described in getrlimit(2).

If you specify limit, ulimit prints the specified limits. You can print any number of limits at one time. The -a option prints all limits, as shown in the following example.

```
$ ulimit -a
time(seconds) unlimited
file(blocks) unlimited
data(kbytes) unlimited
stack(kbytes) 8192
coredump(blocks) unlimited
nofiles(descriptors) 64
memory(kbytes) unlimited
$
```

If limit is present, ulimit sets the specified limit to limit. The string unlimited requests the largest valid limit. You can set limits for only one resource at a time. Any user can set a soft limit to any value below the hard limit. Any user can lower a hard limit. Only superuser can raise a hard limit; see su(1M).

The -H option specifies a hard limit. The -S option specifies a soft limit. If you specify neither option, ulimit sets both limits and prints the soft limit.

The following options specify the resource whose limits are to be printed or set. If you specify no option, the file size limit is printed or set.

-c	Maximum corefile size (in 512-byte blocks).
-d	Maximum size of data segment or heap (in kilobytes).

-f	Maximum file size (in 512-byte blocks).
-n	Maximum file descriptor plus 1.
-s	Maximum size of stack segment (in kilobytes).
-t	Maximum CPU time (in seconds).
-v	Maximum size of virtual memory (in kilobytes).

C Shell

The C shell `limit` built-in function limits the consumption by the current process or any process it spawns, each not to exceed *limit* on the specified resource. If you omit *limit*, the current limit is displayed. If you omit *resource*, all limits are displayed. (Run the sysdef(1M) command to obtain the maximum possible limits for your system. The values reported are in hexadecimal, but you can translate them into decimal numbers with the bc(1) command).

-h	Use hard limits instead of the current limits. Hard limits impose a ceiling on the values of the current limits. Only superuser can raise the hard limits.

resource is one of the following:

cputime	Maximum CPU seconds per process.
filesize	Largest single file allowed; limited to the size of the file system (see df(1M)).
datasize	The maximum size of a process's heap in bytes.
stacksize	Maximum stack size for the process (see swap(1M)).
coredumpsize	Maximum size of a core dump (file). This value is limited to the size of the file system.
descriptors	Maximum number of file descriptors. (Run sysdef().)
memorysize	Maximum size of virtual memory.

limit is a number, with an optional scaling factor, as follows:

nh	Hours (for cputime).
nk	n kilobytes (the default for all but cputime).
nm	n megabytes or minutes (for cputime).
mm:ss	Minutes and seconds (for cputime).

`unlimit` removes a limitation on resources. If you specify no resource, all resource limitations are removed. See the description of the `limit` command for the list of resource names.

-h	Remove corresponding hard limits. Only superuser can use this option.

Korn Shell

The Korn shell built-in function, `ulimit`, sets or displays a resource limit. The available resources limits are listed below. Many systems do not contain one or more of these limits. The limit for a specified resource is set when you specify *limit*. The value of *limit* can be a number in the unit specified below with each resource, or the value unlimited. The -H and -S flags specify whether to set the hard limit or the soft limit for the given resource. Once you set a hard limit, you cannot increase it. You can increase a soft limit up to the value of the hard limit. If you specify neither the -H nor -S option, the limit applies to both. When you omit *limit*, the current resource limit is printed.

In this case, the soft limit is printed unless you specify -H. When you specify more than one resource, the limit name and unit are printed before the value.

-a	List all of the current resource limits.
-c	The number of 512-byte blocks on the size of core dumps.
-d	The number of kilobytes on the size of the data area.
-f	The number of 512-byte blocks on files written by child processes (files of any size can be read).
-n	The number of file descriptors plus 1.
-s	The number of kilobytes on the size of the stack area.
-t	The number of seconds (CPU time) to be used by each process.
-v	The number of kilobytes for virtual memory.

If you specify no option, -f is assumed.

Options

-f	Set (or report, if no *blocks* operand is present), the file-size limit in blocks. The -f option is also the default case.

Operands

blocks	The number of 512-byte blocks to use as the new file-size limit.

Examples

/usr/bin/ulimit
The following example limits the stack size to 512 kilobytes.

```
castle% ulimit -s 512
castle% ulimit -a
time(seconds) unlimited
file(blocks) 100
data(kbytes) 523256
stack(kbytes) 512
coredump(blocks) 200
nofiles(descriptors) 64
memory(kbytes) unlimited
castle%
```

Bourne and Korn Shells

The following example limits the number of file descriptors to 12.

```
$ ulimit -n 12
$ ulimit -a
time(seconds) unlimited
file(blocks) 41943
data(kbytes) 523256
stack(kbytes) 8192
coredump(blocks) 200
nofiles(descriptors) 12
vmemory(kbytes) unlimited
$
```

C Shell

The following example limits the size of a core dump file size to 0 kilobytes.

```
castle% limit coredumpsize 0
castle% limit
cputime          unlimited
filesize         unlimited
datasize         unlimited
stacksize        8192 kbytes
coredumpsize     0 kbytes
descriptors      64
memorysize       unlimited
castle%
```

The following example removes the above limitation for the corefile size.

```
castle% unlimit coredumpsize
castle% limit
cputime          unlimited
filesize         unlimited
datasize         unlimited
stacksize        8192 kbytes
coredumpsize     unlimited
descriptors      64
memorysize       unlimited
castle%
```

Environment Variables

See environ(5) for descriptions of the following environment variables that affect the execution of ulimit: LC_CTYPE, LC_MESSAGES, and NLSPATH.

Exit Status

0	Successful completion.
>0	A request for a higher limit was rejected or an error occurred.

Attributes

See attributes(5) for descriptions of the following attributes:

Attribute Type	Attribute Value
Availability	SUNWcsu

See Also

bc(1), csh(1), ksh(1), sh(1), df(1M), su(1M), swap(1M), sysdef(1M), getrlimit(2), attributes(5), environ(5)

line — Read One Line

Synopsis

/usr/bin/line

Description

The line command copies one line (up to and including a newline) from the standard input and writes it on the standard output. It returns an exit status of 1 on end-of-file and always prints at least a newline. It is often used within shell files to read from the user's terminal.

Examples

When you invoke the line command, it enters a newline and waits for you to type a line. When you press Return, the line is echoed to standard output, as shown in the following example.

```
castle% line
This is a line
This is a line
castle%
```

Exit Status

0	Successful completion.
>0	End-of-file on input.

Attributes

See attributes(5) for descriptions of the following attributes:

Attribute Type	Attribute Value
Availability	SUNWcsu

See Also

sh(1), read(2), attributes(5)

lint — C Program Verifier

Synopsis

/usr/ucb/lint [*options*]

Description

Use the lint command to detect portability problems, bugs, and other potential errors in C programs. /usr/ucb/lint is the interface to the BSD Compatibility Package C program verifier. It is a script that looks for the link /usr/ccs/bin/ucblint to the C program verifier. /usr/ccs/bin/ucblint is available only with the SPROcc package, whose default location is /opt/SUNWspro. /usr/ucb/lint is identical to /usr/ccs/bin/ucblint, except that BSD headers are used and BSD libraries are linked before base libraries. The /opt/SUNWspro/man/man1/lint.1 manual page is available only with the SPROcc package.

Options

/usr/ucb/lint accepts the same options as /usr/ccs/bin/ucblint, with the following exceptions.

-I*dir*   Search *dir* for included files whose names do not begin with a slash (/) before searching the usual directories. Search the directories for multiple -I options in the order specified. The preprocessor first searches for #include files in the directory containing a source file, and then in directories named with -I options (if any), then /usr/ucbinclude, and finally, /usr/include.

-L*dir*   Add *dir* to the list of directories searched for libraries by /usr/ccs/bin/ucblint. This option is passed to /usr/ccs/bin/ld. Directories specified with this option are searched before /usr/ucblib and /usr/lib.

-Y P, *dir*   Change the default directory used for finding libraries.

Exit Status

0   Successful completion.

>0   An error occurred.

Files

/usr/lint/bin/ld

            Link editor.

/usr/lib/libc

            C library.

/usr/ucbinclude

            BSD compatibility directory for header files.

/usr/ucblib   BSD compatibility directory for libraries.

/usr/ucblib/libucb

> BSD compatibility C library.

/usr/lib/libsocket

> Library containing socket routines.

/usr/lib/libnsl

> Library containing network functions.

/usr/lib/libelf

> Library containing routines to process ELF object files.

/usr/lib/libaio

> Library containing asynchronous I/O routines.

Attributes

See attributes(5) for descriptions of the following attributes:

Attribute Type	Attribute Value
Availability	SUNWscpu

See Also

ld(1), a.out(4), attributes(5)

New! list_devices — List Allocatable Devices

Synopsis

```
/usr/sbin/list_devices [-s] [-U uid] -l [device]
/usr/sbin/list_devices [-s] [-U uid] -n [device]
/usr/sbin/list_devices [-s] [-U uid] -u [device]
```

Description

Use the list_devices command, new in the Solaris 9 Operating Environment, to list the allocatable devices in the system according to specified qualifications.

> **Note —** The functionality described in this manual page is available only if the Basic Security Module (BSM) has been enabled. See bsmconv(1M) for more information.

The Solaris 9 Operating Environment provides a device-allocation method—with the allocate(1), deallocate(1), dminfo(1M), and list_devices(1) commands—that fulfills the Trusted Computer System Evaluation Criteria (TCSEC) object-reuse requirement for computing systems at C2 level and above. The device allocation mechanism prevents simultaneous access to a device, prevents one user from reading media written to by another user, and prevents one user from accessing any information from the device or driver internal storage after another user is finished with the device.

The device and all device special files associated with the device are listed. The device argument is optional, and if it is not present, all relevant devices are listed.

Options

-l [*device*]

List the path name(s) of the device special files associated with the device that are allocatable to the current process. If *device* is given, list only the files associated with the specified device.

-n [*device*]

List the path name(s) of device special files associated with the device that are allocatable to the current process but are not currently allocated. If you specify *device*, list_devices lists only the files associated with that device.

-s   Silent. Suppress any diagnostic output.

-u [*device*]

List the path name(s) of device special files associated with the device that are allocated to the owner of the current process. If you specify *device*, list_devices lists only the files associated with that device.

-U *uid*   Use the user ID *uid* instead of the real user ID of the current process when performing the list_devices operation. Only a user with the solaris.devices.revoke authorization can use this option.

Examples

The following example shows the long listing for the list_devices command.

```
mopoke% list_devices -l
device: audio type: audio files: /dev/audio /dev/audioctl /dev/sound/0
  /dev/sound/0ctl
device: fd0 type: fd files: /dev/diskette /dev/rdiskette /dev/fd0a
  /dev/rfd0a /dev/fd0 /dev/fd0b /dev/rfd0b /dev/fd0c /dev/rfd0c
  /dev/rfd0
device: sr0 type: sr files: /dev/sr0 /dev/rsr0 /dev/dsk/c1t1d0s0
  /dev/dsk/c1t1d0s1 /dev/dsk/c1t1d0s2 /dev/dsk/c1t1d0s3
  /dev/dsk/c1t1d0s4 /dev/dsk/c1t1d0s5 /dev/dsk/c1t1d0s6
  /dev/dsk/c1t1d0s7 /dev/rdsk/c1t1d0s0 /dev/rdsk/c1t1d0s1
  /dev/rdsk/c1t1d0s2 /dev/rdsk/c1t1d0s3 /dev/rdsk/c1t1d0s4
  /dev/rdsk/c1t1d0s5 /dev/rdsk/c1t1d0s6 /dev/rdsk/c1t1d0s7
mopoke%
```

Diagnostics

list_devices returns a non-zero exit status in the event of an error.

Files

/etc/security/device_allocate

Mandatory access control information about each device.

```
/etc/security/device_maps
```
> Access control information about each physical device.

```
/etc/security/dev/*
```
> Lock files that must exist for each allocatable device.

```
/etc/security/lib/*
```
> Device allocate files.

Attributes

See `attributes`(5) for descriptions of the following attributes:

Attribute Type	Attribute Value
Availability	SUNWcsu

See Also

```
allocate(1), deallocate(1), bsmconv(1M), device_allocate(4),
device_maps(4), attributes(5)
```

listusers — List User Login Information

Synopsis

```
/usr/bin/listusers [-g groups][-l logins]
```

Description

Executed without any options, the `listusers` command lists all user logins sorted by login. The output shows the login ID and the account field value from the system's password database as specified by `/etc/nsswitch.conf`, as shown in the following example.

```
castle% listusers
des
noaccess        No Access User
nobody          Nobody
nobody4         SunOS 4.x Nobody
ray
rob
winsor
castle%
```

A user login is one that has a UID of 100 or greater.

You can combine the -l and -g options. User logins are listed only once, even if they belong to more than one of the selected groups.

Options

-g *groups*   List all user logins belonging to *groups*, sorted by login. You can specify multiple groups as a comma-separated list.

-l *logins*   List the user login or logins specified by *logins*, sorted by login. You can specify multiple logins as a comma-separated list.

Attributes

See attributes(5) for descriptions of the following attributes:

Attribute Type	Attribute Value
Availability	SUNWcsu

See Also

nsswitch.conf(4), attributes(5)

llc2_autoconfig — Generate LLC2 Configuration Files

New!

Synopsis

/usr/lib/llc2/llc2_autoconfig [-f]

Description

Use the llc2_autoconfig command, new in the Solaris 8 Operating Environment, to automatically generate LLC2 configuration files (/etc/llc2/default/llc2.*). If no configuration file is present in the /etc/llc2/default/ directory, the llc2_autoconfig command detects all the available interfaces in the system and generates corresponding default configuration files.

If configuration files are present in /etc/llc2/default/, the llc2_config command checks to make sure those interfaces defined in the files still exist. If they do not exist in the system, the command sets llc2_on in those files to 0. After this, the command detects any new interfaces in the system and generates configuration files for them.

Options

-f   Erase all configuration files in /etc/llc2/default/. Then detect all the available interfaces in the system and generate corresponding default configuration files. Use this option with caution.

Files

/etc/llc2/default/llc2.*

LLC2 configuration files.

Attributes

See attributes(5) for descriptions of the following attributes.

Attribute Type	Attribute Value
Availability	SUNWllc

See Also

llc2_config(1), llc2(4), attributes(5), llc2(7D)

New! llc2_config — Configure LLC2 Interface Parameters

Synopsis

/usr/lib/llc2/llc2_config [-P | -U | -d | -q | -i ppa| -r ppa]

Description

Use the llc2_config command, new in the Solaris 8 Operating Environment, to start
and stop the LLC2 subsystem and to configure LLC2 interface parameters.

Options

-d	Turn on debug mode to print extra debugging information.
-i ppa	Initialize the corresponding interface using the file /etc/llc2/default/llc2.ppa.
-P	Read in all /etc/llc2/default/llc2.* configuration files, open those devices defined in the files, and set up the streams needed for LLC2 to use those devices. Before you use this command, llc2_config -q shows nothing.
-q	Query the LLC2 subsystem. Information similar to that shown in the following example is printed for all PPAs (Physical Point of Attachment) available under the LLC2 module.

PPA State ID MACAddr Type MaxSDU MinSDU Mode

0 up 0000 00208a217e ethernet 1500 0

The fields are described below:

PPA	The relative logical position of the interface.
State	The state of the interface.

up	The interface is initialized and operational.
down	The interface was discovered by the LLC2 driver, has passed its boot diagnostics, and is awaiting initialization.

| | bad | The interface is known to the LLC2 driver and failed one or more of the integrity checks performed at boot time. This failure might include detecting Interrupt Request and shared memory conflicts or failures detected during the execution of the level 0 diagnostics. |

| ID | The interface ID. |

| MACAddr | The MAC address currently in effect for the interface. |

| Type | The MAC type. Current types supported are listed below. |

	csma/cd	10-megabit Ethernet.
	ethernet	Ethernet type device.
	tkn-ring	4/16-megabit Token Ring.
	fddi	100-megabit Fiber Distributed Data Interface.

| MaxSDU | The Maximum Service Data Unit size transmitted on this interface. |

| Mode | The Service Modes supported by this interface. This field consists of the bitwise logical-ORing of the supported modes, also defined in /usr/include/sys/dlpi.h. |

-r *ppa*   Uninitializes the corresponding interface. With this option in combination with the -i option, you can change the parameters associated with an interface.

-U   Destroy all streams used by the LLC2 subsystem. This option is the reverse of the -P option. After you execute this option, llc2_config -q shows nothing.

Files

/etc/llc2/default/llc2.*

LLC2 configuration files.

Attributes

See attributes(5) for descriptions of the following attributes.

Attribute Type	Attribute Value
Availability	SUNWllc

See Also

llc2_autoconfig(1), llc2(4), attributes(5), llc2(7D)

llc2_stats — LLC2 Station, SAP, and Connection Statistics

Synopsis

/usr/lib/llc2/llc2_stats *ppa* [-r][-s *sap*][-c *connection*]

Description

Use the llc2_stats command, new in the Solaris 8 Operating Environment, to retrieve statistical information from the Host-based Logical Link Control Class 2 component of the LLC2 Driver. Statistics are kept for the station, SAP (Service Access Point), and connection components.

> **Note** — For further information on the LLC2 components, states and flags, refer to the International Standards Organization document, ISO 8802-2: 1994, Section 7.

Options

-c *connection*

Specify the connection of interest. Enter the value in hexadecimal notation with no leading 0x.

-r

Reset the specified counters to zero after reading them. This option is valid only when the root user is executing the command.

-s *sap*

Specify the SAP for this request. Specify a single-byte value, expressed in hexadecimal notation with no leading 0x. For example, you would enter the NetBIOS sap, 240 (0xf0) as -s f0.

Operands

ppa

The logical number used to address the adapter. The PPA (Physical Point of Attachment) must be the first argument.

Examples

The following command displays the station statistics for PPA 4.

```
example% /usr/lib/llc2/llc2_stats 4
Station values received.
ppa                = 0x00000004
clearFlag          = 0x00
# of saps (hex)    = 0x0002
saps (hex)         = 02 aa
state              = 0x01
nullSapXidCmdRcvd  = 0x00000000
nullSapXidRspSent  = 0x00000000
nullSapTestCmdRcvd = 0x00000000
nullSapTestRspSent = 0x00000000
outOfState         = 0x00000000
allocFail          = 0x00000000
```

```
protocolError      = 0x00000000
example%
```

The fields in the output are described below.

ppa	The logical number used to address the adapter.
clearFlag	Whether the statistics are reset to zero after reading (set to 1) or if the statistics are read-only (set to 0).
# of saps	The number of Service Access Points currently bound on this station.
saps	The array of the station's Service Access Point (SAP) logical interface values between the LLC and its adjacent layers.
state	A number indicating the current state of the station component (0 = down, 1 = up).

nullSapXidCmdRcvd

> The number of XID command Protocol Data Units (PDUs) received for the null SAP address (sap = 0x00).

nullSapXidRspSent

> The number of XID response PDUs sent in response to XID command PDUs received for the null SAP address.

nullSapTestCmdRcvd

> The number of TEST command PDUs received for the null SAP address.

nullSapTestRspSent

> The number of TEST response PDUs sent in response to TEST command PDUs received for the null SAP address.

outOfState	The number of events received in an invalid state.
allocFail	The number of buffer allocation failures.

protocolError

> The number of LLC protocol errors, that is, the receipt of malformed PDUs or the receipt of frame X when frame Y was expected.

In the previous example, two SAPs are active: 0x02 and 0xaa. The following example retrieves the statistics for SAP 02.

```
example% /usr/lib/llc2/llc2_stats 4 -s 02

Sap values received.
ppa                 = 0x00000004
clearFlag           = 0x00
sap                 = 0x02
state               = 0x01
# of cons (hex)     = 0x0000000a
connections (hex) = 0000 0001 0002 0003 0004 0005 0006 0007 0008 0009
xidCmdSent          = 0x00000000
xidCmdRcvd          = 0x00000000
xidRspSent          = 0x00000000
```

```
xidRspRcvd        = 0x00000000
testCmdSent       = 0x00000000
testCmdRcvd       = 0x00000000
testRspSent       = 0x00000000
testRspRcvd       = 0x00000000
uiSent            = 0x00000000
uiRcvd            = 0x00000000
outOfState        = 0x00000000
allocFail         = 0x00000000
protocolError     = 0x00000000
example%
```

The fields in the output are described below.

ppa	The logical number used to address the adapter.
clearFlag	Whether the statistics are reset to zero after reading (set to 1) or if the statistics are read-only (set to 0).
sap	The specified Service Access Point (SAP) logical interface value for the station.
state	A number indicating the current state of the SAP component (0 = inactive, 1 = active).
# of cons	The number of active connections on this SAP.
connections	The array of active connection indexes.
xidCmdSent	The number of XID command PDUs sent (Source SAP = this SAP).
xidCmdRcvd	The number of XID command PDUs received (Destination SAP = this SAP).
xidRspSent	The number of XID response PDUs sent (Source SAP = this SAP).
xidRspRcvd	The number of XID response PDUs received (Source SAP = this SAP).
testCmdSent	The number of TEST command PDUs sent (Source SAP = this SAP).
testCmdRcvd	The number of TEST command PDUs received (Destination SAP = this SAP).
testRspSent	The number of TEST response PDUs sent (Source SAP = this SAP).
testRspRcvd	The number of TEST response PDUs received (Source SAP = this SAP).

`uiSent`	The number of Unnumbered Information Frames sent.
`uiRcvd`	The number of Unnumbered Information Frames received.
`outOfState`	The number of events received in an invalid state.

`state.allocFail`

> The number of buffer allocation failures.

`protocolError`

> The number of LLC protocol errors, that is, the receipt of malformed PDUs or the receipt of frame X when frame Y was expected.

In the following example, 10 established connections are associated with this SAP. The following command retrieves the statistics for connection 1.

`example% `**`/usr/lib/llc2/llc2_stats 4 -s 2 -c 1`**

```
Connection values received.
ppa             = 0x0004
clearFlag       = 0x00
sap             = 0x02
con             = 0x0001
sid             = 0x0201
stateOldest     = 0x00
stateOlder      = 0x00   stateOld  = 0x01
state           = 0x08
dl_nodeaddr     = 0x0080d84008c2
dl_sap          = 0x04
flag            = 0x50
dataFlag        = 0x00
timerOn         = 0x18
vs              = 0x29
vr              = 0x1e
nrRcvd          = 0x29  k = 0x14
retryCount      = 0x000
numToBeAcked    = 0x0000 numToResend = 0x0000
macOutSave      = 0x0000
macOutDump      = 0x0000
iSent           = 0x0ba9
iRcvd           = 0x001e
frmrSent        = 0x0000
frmrRcvd        = 0x0000
rrSent          = 0x016a
rrRcvd          = 0x00c1
rnrSent         = 0x0000
rnrRcvd         = 0x06fb
rejSent         = 0x0000
rejRcvd         = 0x0000
sabmeSent       = 0x0000
sabmeRcvd       = 0x0001
uaSent          = 0x0001
uaRcvd          = 0x0000
discSent        = 0x0000
outOfState      = 0x0000
```

```
allocFail        = 0x0000
protocolError    = 0x0000
localBusy        = 0x0000
remoteBusy       = 0x00b5
maxRetryFail     = 0x0000
ackTimerExp      = 0x0000
pollTimerExp     = 0x0000
rejTimerExp      = 0x0000
remBusyTimerExp  = 0x0000
inactTimerExp    = 0x0000
sendAckTimerExp  = 0x0000
example%
```

The fields in the output are described below.

ppa
: The logical number used to address the adapter.

clearFlag
: Whether the statistics are reset to zero after reading (set to 1) or if the statistics are read-only (set to 0).

sap
: The specified Service Access Point (SAP) logical interface value for the station.

con
: The specified connection index value for the SAP.

stateOldest

: A number representing the state of the connection component before stateOlder.

stateOlder

: A number representing the state of the connection component before stateOld.

stateOld
: A number representing the state of the connection component before state.

state
: A number representing the most current state of the connection component. See "LLC2 States" on page 696.

sid
: The Station Identifier composed of the SAP (upper byte) and connection index (lower byte).

dl_nodeaddr

: The Data Link Node Address. This is the destination node's MAC address.

dl_sap
: The destination node's SAP.

flag
: The connection component processing flag. See "LLC2 Flags" on page 697.

dataFlag
: A number representing the status of the data units from received I-frame PDUs (0 = not discarded, 1 = discarded, 2 = busy state entered with REJ PDU outstanding).

timerOn   A number representing the timer activity flag, with each bit representing an active timer for this connection. See "timersOn" on page 697 for timer definitions.

vs   The sequence number of the next I-frame PDU to send.

vr   The expected sequence number of the next I-frame PDU to be received.

nrRcvd   The sequence number plus 1 of the last sent I-frame PDU acknowledged by the remote node.

k   The transmit window size.

retryCount

                The retryCount is incremented whenever a timer expiration occurs. These timers protect outbound frames.

numToBeAcked

                The number of outbound I-frames awaiting acknowledgement.

numToResend

                The number of outbound I-frames to be retransmitted.

macOutSave

                No longer used.

macOutDump

                No longer used.

iSent   The number of I-frames sent.

iRcvd   The number of I-frames received.

frmrSent   The number of Frame Reject PDUs (FRMR)

sent.frmrRcvd

                The number of Frame Reject PDUs (FRMR) received.

rrSent   The number of Receiver Ready PDUs (RR) sent.

rrRcvd   The number of Receiver Ready PDUs (RR) received.

rnrSent   The number of Receiver Not Ready PDUs (RNR) sent.

rnrRcvd   The number of Receiver Not Ready PDUs (RNR) received.

rejSent   The number of Reject PDUs (REJ) sent.

rejRcvd   The number of Reject PDUs (REJ) received.

sabmeSent   The number of Set Asynchronous Balanced Mode Extended PDUs (SABME) sent.

sabmeRcvd   The number of Set Asynchronous Balanced Mode Extended PDUs (SABME) received.

uaSent   The number of Unnumbered Acknowledgment PDUs (UA) sent.

uaRcvd   The number of Unnumbered Acknowledgment PDUs (UA) received.

discSent   The number of Disconnect PDUs (DISC) sent.

outOfState   The number of events received in an invalid state.

allocFail   The number of buffer allocation failures.

protocolError

         The number of LLC protocol errors, that is, the receipt of malformed PDUs or the receipt of frame X when frame Y was expected.

localBusy   The number of times this component was in local busy state and could not accept I-frames.

remoteBusy

         The number of times the remote connection component was busy and could not accept I-frames.

maxRetryFail

         The number of failures that occurred because maxRetry was reached.

ackTimerExp

         The number of expirations of the Acknowledgement timer.

pollTimerExp

         The number of expirations of the Poll timer.

rejTimerExp

         The number of expirations of the Reject timer.

remBusyTimerExp

         The number of expirations of the Remote Busy timer.

inactTimerExp

         The number of expirations of the Inactivity timer.

sendAckTimerExp

         The number of expirations of the Send Acknowledgement timer.

LLC2 States

STATION

~~DOWN   0x00

~~UP   0x01

SAP

~~INACTIVE   0x00

~~ACTIVE   0x01

CONNECTION

~~ADM   0x00

~~CONN   0x01

~~RESET_WAIT   0x02

~~RESET_CHECK   0x03

~~SETUP	0x04
~~RESET	0x05
~~D_CONN	0x06
~~ERROR	0x07
~~NORMAL	0x08
~~BUSY	0x09
~~REJECT	0x0a
~~AWAIT	0x0b
~~AWAIT_BUSY	0x0c
~~AWAIT_REJECT	0x0d

timersOn

Acknowledgement	0x80
Poll	0x40
Reject	0x20
Remove Busy	0x10
Inactivity	0x08
Send Acknowledgement	0x04

LLC2 Flags

P_FLAG	0x80
F_FLAG	0x40
S_FLAG	0x20
REMOTE_BUSY	0x10
RESEND_PENDING	0x08

Attributes

See attributes(5) for descriptions of the following attributes.

Attribute Type	Attribute Value
Availability	SUNWllc

Files

/dev/llc2   Clone device.

See Also

attributes(5)

ln — Make Hard or Symbolic Links to Files

Synopsis

```
/usr/bin/ln [-fns] source-file [target]
/usr/bin/ln [-fns] source-file... target
/usr/xpg4/bin/ln [-fs] source-file [target]
/usr/xpg/bin/ln [-fs] source-file... target
```

Description

At times it is useful to have one file accessible from several directories. Linking a file can reduce the amount of disk space used and make it easier to maintain consistency in files used by several people. Use the ln (link) command to create links between directory entries in a single file system to make a single file accessible at two or more locations in the directory hierarchy.

Symbolic links (-s) can link files across file systems. A symbolic link has a name and a location in the directory tree but has no contents. It simply points to another file or directory.

Use the ln command to create both hard links and symbolic links. A hard link is a pointer to a file and is indistinguishable from the original directory entry. Any changes to a file are effective independently of the name used to reference the file. Hard links cannot span file systems and cannot refer to directories.

By default, ln creates hard links. *source-file* is linked to *target*. If *target* is a directory, another file named *source-file* is created in *target* and linked to the original *source-file*.

In the first synopsis form, the ln command creates a new directory entry (link) for the file specified by *source-file*, at the destination path specified by *target*. If you do not specify *target*, the link is made in the current directory. This first synopsis form is assumed when the final operand does not name an existing directory; if you specify more than two operands and the final operand is not an existing directory, an error results.

In the second synopsis form, the ln command creates a new directory entry for each file specified by a *source-file* operand at a destination path in the existing directory named by *target*.

/usr/bin/ln

If *target* is a file, its contents are overwritten. If /usr/bin/ln determines that the mode of *target* forbids writing, it prints the mode (see chmod(1)), asks for a response, and reads the standard input for one line. If the response is affirmative, the link occurs if permissible; otherwise, the command exits.

/usr/xpg4/bin/ln

If *target* is a file and you do not specify the -f option, /usr/xpg4/bin/ln writes a diagnostic message to standard error, does nothing more with the current *source-file*, and goes on to any remaining *source-files*. A symbolic link is an indirect pointer to a file; its directory entry contains the name of the file to which it is linked. Symbolic links can span file systems and can refer to directories.

When you create a hard link and the source file is, itself, a symbolic link, the *target* is a hard link to the file referenced by the symbolic link, not to the symbolic link object itself (*source_file*).

File permissions for *target* can differ from those displayed with a -l listing of the ls(1) command. To display the permissions of *target*, use ls -lL. See stat(2) for more information.

Notes

A symbolic link to a directory behaves differently than you might expect in certain cases. While an ls(1) on such a link displays the files in the pointed-to directory, an ls -1 displays information about the link itself, as shown in the following example.

```
castle% ln -s dir link
castle% ls link
file1 file2 file3 file4
castle% ls -l link
lrwxrwxrwx  1 user           7 Jan 11 23:27 link -> dir
castle%
```

When you use cd(1) to change to a directory through a symbolic link, you wind up in the pointed-to location within the file system. This means that the parent of the new working directory is not the parent of the symbolic link but, rather, the parent of the pointed-to directory. For instance, in the following case, the final working directory is /usr and not /home/user/linktest.

```
castle% pwd
/home/user/linktest
castle% ln -s /usr/tmp symlink
castle% cd symlink
castle% cd ..
castle% pwd
/usr
castle%
```

C shell users can avoid any resulting navigation problems by using the pushd and popd built-in commands instead of cd.

Options

The following options are supported for both /usr/bin/ln and /usr/xpg4/bin/ln.

-f   Link files without questioning even if the mode of *target* forbids writing (the default if the standard input is not a terminal).

-s   Create a symbolic link.

If you use the -s option with two arguments, *target* can be an existing directory or a nonexistent file. If *target* already exists and is not a directory, an error is returned. *source-file* can be any path name and need not exist. If it exists, it can be a file or directory and can reside on a different file system from *target*. If *target* is an existing directory, a file is created in directory *target* whose name is *source-file* or the last component of *source-file*. This file is a symbolic link that references *source-file*. If *target* does not exist, a file with name *target* is created and is a symbolic link that references *source-file*.

If you use the -s option with more than two arguments, *target* must be an existing directory or an error is returned. For each *source-file*, a link is created in *target* whose name is the last component of *source-file*, each new *source-file* is a symbolic link to the original *source-file*. The files and *target* can reside on different file systems.

/usr/bin/ln

-n　　　　　　If the link is an existing file, do not overwrite the contents of the file. The -f option overrides this option. This behavior is the default for /usr/xpg4/bin/ln and is silently ignored.

Operands

source-file

A path name of a file to be linked. This file can be either a regular or special file. If you specify the -s option, *source-file* can also be a directory.

target　　　The path name of the new directory entry to be created or of an existing directory in which the new directory entries are to be created.

Usage

See largefile(5) for the description of the behavior of ln when encountering files greater than or equal to 2 Gbytes (2**31 bytes).

Environment Variables

See environ(5) for descriptions of the following environment variables that affect the execution of ln: LC_CTYPE, LC_MESSAGES, and NLSPATH.

Exit Status

0　　　　　　All the specified files were linked successfully.

>0　　　　　　An error occurred.

Attributes

See attributes(5) for descriptions of the following attributes:

/usr/bin/ln

Attribute Type	Attribute Value
Availability	SUNWcsu
CSI	Enabled

/usr/xpg4/bin/ln

Attribute Type	Attribute Value
Availability	SUNWxcu4
CSI	Enabled

See Also

chmod(1), ls(1), stat(2), attributes(5), environ(5), largefile(5), XPG4(5)

loadkeys, dumpkeys — Load and Dump Keyboard Translation Tables

Synopsis

```
/usr/bin/loadkeys [filename]
/usr/bin/dumpkeys
```

Description

loadkeys reads the file specified by *filename* and modifies the keyboard streams module's translation tables. If you specify no file and the keyboard is a Type-4 keyboard, a default file for the layout indicated by the DIP switches on the keyboard is used. The file is in the format specified by keytables(4).

By default, loadkeys loads the file

```
/usr/share/lib/keytables/type_tt/layout_dd
```

where *tt* is the value returned by the KIOCTYPE ioctl and *dd* is the value returned by the KIOCLAYOUT ioctl (see kb(7M)). On self-identifying keyboards, the value returned by the KIOCLAYOUT ioctl is set from the DIP switches. These files specify only the entries that change between the different Type-4 keyboard layouts.

dumpkeys writes to standard output the current contents of the keyboard streams module's translation tables in the format specified by keytables(4).

Examples

The following example shows the first few lines output by the dumpkeys command for a Type-4 keyboard.

```
castle% dumpkeys
key 0     all hole
key 1     all buckybits+systembit up buckybits+systembit
key 2     all hole
key 3     all lf(2)
key 4     all hole
key 5     all tf(1)
key 6     all tf(2)
key 7     all tf(10)
key 8     all tf(3)
key 9     all tf(11)
key 10    all tf(4)
key 11    all tf(12)
key 12    all tf(5)
...
```

Files

```
/usr/share/lib/keytables/layout_dd
```

Default keytable files.

Attributes

See attributes(5) for descriptions of the following attributes:

Attribute Type	Attribute Value
Architecture	SPARC, IA
Availability	SUNWcsu

See Also

kbd(1), keytables(4), attributes(5), kb(7M), usbkbm(7M)

locale — Get Locale-Specific Information

Synopsis

```
/usr/bin/locale [-a | -m]
/usr/bin/locale [-ck] name...
```

Description

The locale command writes information to standard output about the current locale environment or all public locales. For the purposes of this command, a public locale is one provided by the implementation that is accessible to the application.

When you use the locale command without any arguments, it summarizes the current locale environment for each locale category as determined by the settings of the environment variables. If the LANG environment variable is set with the following format

```
LANG=locale_x LC_COLLATE=locale_y
```

locale displays the results in the following format.

```
LANG=locale_x
LC_CTYPE=locale_x
LC_NUMERIC=locale_x
LC_TIME=locale_x
LC_COLLATE=locale_y
LC_MONETARY=locale_x
LC_MESSAGES=locale_x
LC_ALL=
```

When you specify operands, locale writes values that have been assigned to the keywords in the locale categories, as follows:

- Specifying a keyword name selects the named keyword and the category containing that keyword.
- Specifying a category name selects the named category and all keywords in that category.

> **Note —** If you specify LC_CTYPE or keywords in the category LC_CTYPE, only the values in the range 0x00-0x7f are displayed.
>
> If you specify LC_COLLATE or keywords in the category LC_COLLATE, no actual values are written.

Options

-a   Write information about all available public locales. The available locales include POSIX, representing the POSIX locale.

-c   Write the names of selected locale categories. The -c option increases readability when you specify more than one category (for example, with more than one keyword name or a category name). It is valid both with and without the -k option.

-k   Write the names and values of selected keywords. The implementation can omit values for some keywords.

-m   Write names of available charmaps; see localedef(1).

Operands

name   Specify the name of a locale category (such as LC_NUMERIC), the name of a keyword in a locale category (such as decimal_point), or the reserved name charmap. The named category or keyword is used for output. If a single name represents both a locale category name and a keyword name in the current locale, the results are unspecified; otherwise, you can specify both category and keyword names as *name* operands, in any sequence.

Examples

The following example shows the output of the locale command with no arguments for an Australian locale.

```
castle% locale
LANG=en_AU
LC_CTYPE=en_AU
LC_NUMERIC=en_AU
LC_TIME=en_AU
LC_COLLATE=en_AU
LC_MONETARY=en_AU
LC_MESSAGES=C
LC_ALL=
castle%
```

If LC_ALL is set to POSIX, the following example shows the first few lines of the values for the LC_ALL environment variable.

```
castle% setenv LC_ALL=POSIX
castle% locale -ck LC_ALL
LC_CTYPE
lower="a";"b";"c";"d";"e";"f";"g";"h";"i";"j";"k";"l";"m";"n";"o";"p";
    "q";"r";"s";"t";"u";"v";"w";"x";"y";"z"
```

```
upper="A";"B";"C";"D";"E";"F";"G";"H";"I";"J";"K";"L";"M";"N";"O";"P";
   "Q";"R";"S";"T";"U";"V";"W";"X";"Y";"Z"
alpha="A";"B";"C";"D";"E";"F";"G";"H";"I";"J";"K";"L";"M";"N";"O";"P";
   "Q";"R";"S";"T";"U";"V";"W";"X";"Y";"Z";"a";"b";"c";"d";"e";"f";"g";
   "h";"i";"j";"k";"l";"m";"n";"o";"p";"q";"r";"s";"t";"u";"v";"w";"x";
   "y";"z"
digit="0";"1";"2";"3";"4";"5";"6";"7";"8";"9"
space="\x09";"\x0a";"\x0b";"\x0c";"\x0d";" "
...
```

The following example displays the values for the LC_NUMERIC category.

```
castle% locale -ck LC_NUMERIC
LC_NUMERIC
decimal_point="."
thousands_sep=""
grouping=-1
castle%
```

You can check for the value of specific elements within an environment variable by specifying the keyword as arguments to the `locale` command. The following example displays the `decimal_point` value of the LC_NUMERIC category.

```
castle% locale -ck decimal_point
LC_NUMERIC
decimal_point="."
castle%
```

The following example uses the `locale` command to determine whether a user-supplied response is affirmative.

```
if printf "%s\n" "$response" | /usr/xpg4/bin/grep -Eq "$(locale yesexpr)"
then
 affirmative processing goes here
else
  non-affirmative processing goes here
fi
```

Environment Variables

See environ(5) for the descriptions of LANG, LC_ALL, LC_CTYPE, LC_MESSAGES, and NLSPATH.

The LANG, LC_*, and NLSPATH environment variables must specify the current locale environment to be written; they are used if you do not specify the -a option.

Exit Status

0	All the requested information was found and output successfully.
>0	An error occurred.

Attributes

See attributes(5) for descriptions of the following attributes:

Attribute Type	Attribute Value
Availability	SUNWloc
CSI	Enabled

See Also

localedef(1), attributes(5), charmap(5), environ(5), locale(5)

localedef — Define Locale Environment

Synopsis

```
localedef [-c] [-C compiler-options [-f charmap] [-i sourcefile]
    [-L linker-options] [-m model] [-W cc, arg] [-x extensions-file]
    localename
```

Description

The localedef command converts source definitions for locale categories into a format usable by the functions and commands whose operational behavior is determined by the setting of the locale environment variable (see environ(5)).

The command reads source definitions for one or more locale categories belonging to the same locale from the file named in the -i option (if specified) or from standard input.

Each category source definition is identified by the corresponding environment variable name and terminated by an END category-name statement. The following categories are supported.

LC_CTYPE   Define character classification and case conversion.

LC_COLLATE   Define collation rules.

LC_MONETARY

         Define the format and symbols used in the formatting of monetary information.

LC_NUMERIC   Define the decimal delimiter, grouping, and grouping symbol for nonmonetary numeric editing.

LC_TIME   Define the format and content of date and time information.

LC_MESSAGES

         Define the format and values of affirmative and negative responses.

Options

-c   Create permanent output even if warning messages have been issued.

-C *compiler-options*

Pass the *compiler-options* to the C compiler (cc). If you specify more than one option, you must enclose all of them in quotes (" ").

New!   This option is old starting with the Solaris 8 release. Instead, use the -W cc,*arg* option.

-f *charmap*   Specify the path name of a file containing a mapping of character symbols and collating element symbols to actual character encodings. You must specify this option if you use symbolic names (other than collating symbols defined in a collating-symbol keyword). If you do not use the -f option, use the default character mapping.

-i *sourcefile*

Specify the path name of a file containing the source definitions. If you do not use this option, read source definitions from standard input.

-L *linker-options*

Pass the *linker-options* to the C compiler (cc) that follows the C source file name. If you specify more than one option, you must enclose all of them in quotes (" ").

New!   This option is old starting with the Solaris 8 release. Instead, use the -W cc,*arg* option.

-m *model*   Specify whether localedef generates a 64-bit or a 32-bit locale object. To generate a 32-bit object, specify model as ilp32. To generate a 64-bit locale object, specify lp64. The default is -m ilp32.

-W cc,*arg*   Pass *arg* options to the C compiler. Separate each argument from the preceding with just a comma. (You can make a comma part of an argument by immediately preceding it with a backslash character to escape it. The backslash is removed from the resulting argument.)

New!   Use this option instead of the -C and -L options, starting with the Solaris 8 release.

-x *extensions-file*

Specify the name of an extension file where various localedef options are listed. See locale(5).

If you specify the -c option and warnings occur, permanent output is created. The following conditions issue warning messages.

- If you use a symbolic name not found in the charmap file for the descriptions of the LC_CTYPE or LC_COLLATE categories (for other categories, this is an error condition).

- If optional keywords not supported by the implementation are present in the source.

Operands

localename   Identify the locale. If the name contains one or more slash characters, interpret *localename* as a path name where the created locale definitions are stored. This capability can be restricted to users with appropriate privileges. (You can process one category by specifying just one *localename*, although you can process several categories in one execution.)

Output

localedef creates a temporary C source file that represents the locale's data. localedef then calls the C compiler to compile this C source file into a shared object. This object is named localename.so.1. localedef also creates a text file named localename that is for information only.

If you specify the -m ilp32 option, localedef calls the C compiler for generating 32-bit objects and it generates a 32-bit locale object. If you specify the -m lp64 option, localedef calls the C compiler for generating 64-bit objects and it generates a 64-bit locale object.   *New!*

If you do not specify the -m option, localedef calls the C compiler for generating 32-bit objects and it generates a 32-bit object locale. If you specify no options other than -c, -f, and -i, and if the system running localedef supports the 64-bit environment, localedef additionally calls the C compiler for generating 64-bit objects and it generates a 64-bit locale object.   *New!*

If you do not explicitly specify an option to the C compiler with the -W, -C, or -L option, localedef calls the C compiler with appropriate C compiler options to generate a locale object or objects.   *New!*

If you specify the -m ilp32 option, localedef generates a 32-bit locale object named *localename*.so.*version_number*.   *New!*

If you specify the -m lp64 option, localedef generates a 64-bit locale object named *localename*.so.*version_number*.   *New!*

If you do not specify the -m option, localedef generates a 32-bit locale object named *localename*.so.*version_number* and, if appropriate, generates a 64-bit locale object named 64-*bit_architecture_name*/*localename*.so.*version_number*.   *New!*

You must move the shared object for the 32-bit environment to:

/usr/lib/locale/*localename*/*localename*.so.*version_number*

You must move the shared object for the 64-bit environment to:

/usr/lib/locale/*localename*/sparcv9/*localename*.so.*version_number*

localedef also generates a text file named localename that is used for information only.   *New!*

Environment Variables

See environ(5) for definitions of the following environment variables that affect the execution of localedef: LC_CTYPE, LC_MESSAGES, and NLSPATH.

Exit Status

0	No errors occurred, and the locales were successfully created.
1	Warnings occurred, and the locales were successfully created.
2	The locale specification exceeded implementation limits or the coded character set or sets used were not supported by the implementation, and no locale was created.
3	The capability to create new locales is not supported by the implementation.
>3	Warnings or errors occurred, and no output was created.

If an error is detected, no permanent output is created.

Files

/usr/lib/localedef/generic_eucbc.*x*

Describes what a generic EUC locale uses in the system (the default).

/usr/lib/localedef/single_byte.*x*

Describes a generic single-byte file used in the system.

/usr/lib/locale/*localename*/*localename*.so.*version_number*

The shared object for the 32-bit environment.

/usr/lib/locale/*localename*/sparcv9/*localename*.so.*version_number*

The shared object for the 64-bit environment on SPARC.

Attributes

See attributes(5) for descriptions of the following attributes:

Attribute Type	Attribute Value
Availability	SUNWcsu

See Also

locale(1), nl_langinfo(3C), strftime(3C), attributes(5), charmap(5), environ(5), extensions(5), locale(5)

logger — Add Entries to the System Log

Synopsis

/usr/bin/logger [-i] [-f *file*] [-p *priority*] [-t *tag*] [*message*]...

Description

The logger command provides a method for adding one-line entries to the system log file from the command line. You can specify one or more message arguments on the command line, in which case each is logged immediately. If you specify no command-line arguments, either the file indicated with -f or the standard input is added to the log. Otherwise, you can specify a file with a set of lines to be logged. If you specify no options, logger reads and logs messages on a line-by-line basis from the standard input.

Options

-f *file*   Use the contents of file as the message to log.

-i   Log the process ID of the logger process with each line.

-p *priority*

Enter the message with the specified priority. The message priority can be specified numerically or as a *facility.level* pair. For example, -p local3.info assigns the message priority to the information level in the local3 facility. The default priority is user.notice.

-t *tag*   Mark each line added to the log with the specified tag.

Operands

message   One of the string arguments whose contents are concatenated in the order specified, separated by single-space characters.

Examples

The following example logs the message System rebooted to the default priority-level notice to be treated by syslogd in the same way as other messages to the facility user.

```
castle% logger System rebooted
castle%
```

The following example reads from the file /dev/idmc and logs each line in that file as a message with the tag HOSTIDM at priority-level notice to be treated by syslogd in the same way as other messages to the facility local0.

```
castle% logger -p local0.notice -t HOSTIDM -f /dev/idmc
```

Environment Variables

See environ(5) for descriptions of the following environment variables that affect the execution of logger: LC_CTYPE, LC_MESSAGES, and NLSPATH.

Exit Status

0   Successful completion.

>0   An error occurred.

Attributes

See attributes(5) for descriptions of the following attributes:

Attribute Type	Attribute Value
Availability	SUNWcsu

See Also
mailx(1), write(1), syslogd(1M), syslog(3), attributes(5), environ(5)

login — Sign On to the System

Synopsis
/usr/bin/login [-p] [-d *device*] [-h *hostname* [*terminal*]] | -r *hostname*]
[*name* [*environ*...]]

Description
Use the login command at the beginning of each terminal session to identify yourself to the system. login is invoked by the system when a connection is first established and after the previous user has terminated the login shell by issuing the exit command.

If you invoke login as a command, it must replace the initial command interpreter. To invoke login in this way, from the initial shell, type:

exec login

The C shell and Korn shell have their own built-in login commands. See ksh(1) and csh(1) for descriptions of login built-ins and usage.

login asks for your user name if it is not supplied as an argument and for your password if appropriate. Where possible, echoing is turned off while you type your password so that it does not appear on the written record of the session.

If you make any mistake in the login procedure, the following message is displayed and a new login prompt is displayed.

Login incorrect

If you make five incorrect login attempts, all five may be logged in /var/adm/loginlog if it exists. The TTY line is dropped.

If password aging is turned on and the password has aged (see passwd(1) for more information), you are forced to change the password. In this case, the /etc/nsswitch.conf file is consulted to determine password repositories (see nsswitch.conf(4)). The password update configurations supported are limited to the following five cases.

- passwd: files
- passwd: files nis
- passwd: files nisplus
- passwd: compat (==> files nis)
- passwd: compat (==> files nisplus) passwd_compat: nisplus

Failure to comply with these configurations prevents you from logging in to the system because passwd(1) fails. If you do not complete the login successfully within a certain period of time, it is likely that you will be silently disconnected.

After a successful login, accounting files are updated. Device owner, group, and permissions are set according to the contents of the /etc/logindevperm file, and the time you last logged in is printed (see logindevperm(4)).

The user ID, group ID, supplementary group list, and working directory are initialized, and the command interpreter specified in your password file is started.

The basic environment is initialized to:

```
HOME=your-login-directory
LOGNAME=your-login-name
PATH=/usr/bin:
SHELL=last-field-of-passwd-entry
MAIL=/var/mail/your-login-name
TZ=timezone-specification
```

For Bourne shell and Korn shell logins, the shell executes /etc/profile and $HOME/.profile if it exists. For C shell logins, the shell executes /etc/.login, $HOME/.cshrc, and $HOME/.login. The default /etc/profile and /etc/.login files check quotas (see quota(1M)), print /etc/motd, and check for mail. None of the messages are printed if the file $HOME/.hushlogin exists. The name of the command interpreter is set to - (dash), followed by the last component of the interpreter's path name, for example, -sh.

If the login-shell field in the password file (see passwd(4)) is empty, then the default command interpreter, /usr/bin/sh, is used. If this field is * (asterisk), then the named directory becomes the root directory. At that point, login is reexecuted at the new level, which must have its own root structure.

You can expand or modify the environment (except for PATH and SHELL) by supplying additional arguments to login, either at execution time or when login requests your login name. The arguments can take either the form xxx or xxx=yyy. Arguments without an equal sign (=) are put into the environment as:

L*n*=*xxx*

where *n* is a number starting at 0 that is incremented each time a new variable name is required. Variables containing an = (equal sign) are put into the environment without modification. If these variables already appear in the environment, then they replace the older values.

You cannot change the PATH and SHELL environment variables to prevent people who are logged in to restricted shell environments from spawning secondary shells that are not restricted. login understands simple single-character quoting conventions. Typing a backslash (\) in front of a character quotes it and allows you to include characters such as spaces and tabs.

Alternatively, you can pass the current environment by supplying the -p option to login. This option indicates that login should pass all currently defined environment variables, if possible, to the new environment. This option does not bypass any environment variable restrictions mentioned above. Environment variables specified on the login line take precedence if a variable is passed by both methods.

To enable remote logins by root, edit the /etc/default/login file and insert a pound sign (#) before the CONSOLE=/dev/console entry.

Security

login uses pam(3PAM) for authentication, account management, session management, and password management. The PAM configuration policy, listed through /etc/pam.conf, specifies the modules to be used for login. Below is a partial pam.conf file with entries for the login command and using the UNIX authentication, account management, session management, and password management module.

```
login   auth      required    /usr/lib/security/pam_unix.so.1

login   account   required    /usr/lib/security/pam_unix.so.1
```

```
login session    required    /usr/lib/security/pam_unix.so.1

login password   required    /usr/lib/security/pam_unix.so.1
```

If the login service has no entries, then the entries for the other service are used. If multiple authentication modules are listed, then the user may be prompted for multiple passwords.

When login is invoked through rlogind or telnetd, the service name used by PAM is rlogin or telnet.

Warnings

Users with a UID greater than 76695844 are not subject to password aging and the system does not record their last login time.

If you use the CONSOLE setting to disable root logins, you should arrange that remote command execution by root is also disabled. See rsh(1), rcmd(3N), and hosts.equiv(4) for further details.

Options

-d *device*   Specify the path name of the TTY port login is to operate on. The device option can improve login performance because login does not need to call ttyname(3C). The -d option is available only to users whose UID and effective UID are root. Any other attempt to use -d exits quietly.

-h *hostname* [*terminal*]

Pass information about the remote host and terminal type from in.telnetd(1M).

-p   Pass environment variables to the login shell.

-r *hostname*

Pass information about the remote host from in.rlogind(1M).

Exit Status

0   Successful operation.

non-zero   Error.

Files

$HOME/.cshrc

Initial commands for each csh.

$HOME/.hushlogin

Suppress login messages.

$HOME/.login

User's login commands for csh.

$HOME/.profile

User's login commands for sh and ksh.

`$HOME/.rhosts`

> Private list of trusted host name/user name combinations.

`/etc/.login`

> Systemwide `csh` login commands.

`/etc/logindevperm`

> Login-based device permissions.

`/etc/motd`   Message-of-the-day.

`/etc/nologin`

> Message displayed to users attempting to log in during system shutdown.

`/etc/passwd`   Password file.

`/etc/profile`

> Systemwide `sh` and `ksh` login commands.

`/etc/shadow`   List of users' encrypted passwords.

`/usr/bin/sh`

> User's default command interpreter.

`/var/adm/lastlog`

> Time of last login.

`/var/adm/loginlog`

> Record of failed login attempts.

`/var/adm/utmpx`

> Accounting.

`/var/adm/wtmpx`

> Accounting.

`/var/mail/`*your-name*

> Mailbox for user *your-name*.

`/etc/default/login`

> Default value that can be set for the flags in `/etc/default/login`. For example, `TIMEZONE=EST5EDT`.

The following list describes the variables that can be set in `/etc/default/login`.

ALTSHELL   Determine if `login` should set the SHELL environment variable.

CONSOLE   If set, root can log in on that device only. This setting does not prevent execution of remote commands with `rsh`(1). Comment out this line to enable login by root.

New!   DISABLETIME

If present and greater than zero, specify the number of seconds that login waits after RETRIES failed attempts or the PAM framework returns PAM_ABORT. Another login attempt is permitted provided that RETRIES has not been reached or the PAM framework has not returned PAM_MAXTRIES. Default is 4 seconds, Minimum is 0 seconds. Maximum is 5 seconds. New in the Solaris 9 release.

HZ   Set the HZ environment variable of the shell.

PASSREQ   Determine if login requires a password.

PATH   Set the initial shell PATH variable.

New!   RETRIES   Removed in the Solaris 9 release. See DISABLETIME.

SLEEPTIME   If present, set the number of seconds to wait before login failure is printed to the screen and another login attempt is allowed. Default is 4 seconds. Minimum is 0 seconds. Maximum is 5 seconds.

SUPATH   Set the initial shell PATH variable for root.

SYSLOG   Determine whether the syslog(3C) LOG_AUTH facility should be used to log all root logins at level LOG_NOTICE and multiple failed login attempts at LOG_CRIT.

New!   SYSLOG_FAILED_LOGINS

Determine how many failed login tries are allowed by the system before a failed login message is logged with the syslog(3C) LOG_NOTICE facility. For example, if the variable is set to 0, login logs all failed login attempts. New in the Solaris 8 release.

TIMEOUT   Set the number of seconds (between 0 and 900) to wait before abandoning a login session.

TIMEZONE   Set the TZ environment variable of the shell (see environ(5)).

ULIMIT   Set the file-size limit for the login. Units are disk blocks. Default is 0 (no limit).

UMASK   Set the initial shell file-creation mode mask. See umask(1).

Attributes

See attributes(5) for descriptions of the following attributes:

Attribute Type	Attribute Value
Availability	SUNWcsu

See Also

New!   csh(1), exit(1), ksh(1), mail(1), mailx(1), newgrp(1), passwd(1), rlogin(1), rsh(1), sh(1), shell_builtins(1), telnet(1), umask(1), in.rlogind(1M), in.telnetd(1M), logins(1M), quota(1M), su(1M), syslogd(1M), useradd(1M), userdel(1M), syslog(3C), ttyname(3C), rcmd(3SOCKET), pam(3PAM), auth_attr(4), exec_attr(4), hosts.equiv(4), `logindevperm(4)`, `loginlog(4)`, `nologin(4)`, `nsswitch.conf(4)`, `pam.conf(4)`, `passwd(4)`, `profile(4)`, `shadow(4)`, `user_attr(4)`, `utmpx(4)`, `wtmpx(4)`, `attributes(5)`, `environ(5)`, `pam_unix(5)`, `termio(7I)`

Diagnostics

`Login incorrect`

>   The user name or the password cannot be matched.

`Not on system console`

>   Root login denied. Check the CONSOLE setting in `/etc/default/login`.

`No directory! Logging in with home=/`

>   The user's home directory named in the `passwd(4)` database cannot be found or has the wrong permissions. Contact your system administrator.

`No shell`   Cannot execute the shell named in the `passwd(4)` database. Contact your system administrator.

`NO LOGINS: System going down in N minutes`

>   The system is in the process of being shut down and logins have been disabled.

logname — Return User's Login Name

Synopsis

`/usr/bin/logname`

Description

The `logname` command writes your login name to standard output as shown in the following example.

```
castle% logname
winsor
castle%
```

The login name is the string returned by the `getlogin(3C)` function. Under the conditions where `getlogin()` would fail, `logname` writes a diagnostic message to standard error and exits with a non-zero exit status.

Environment Variables

See `environ(5)` for descriptions of the following environment variables that affect the execution of `logname`: LC_CTYPE, LC_MESSAGES, and NLSPATH.

Exit Status

0   Successful completion.

>0   An error occurred.

Files

/etc/profile

Environment for user at login time.

/var/adm/utmpx

User and accounting information.

Attributes

See attributes(5) for descriptions of the following attributes:

Attribute Type	Attribute Value
Availability	SUNWesu

See Also

env(1), login(1), getlogin(3C), utmpx(4), attributes(5), environ(5)

---

logout — Shell Built-in Function to Exit from a Login Session

Synopsis

csh

logout

Description

The logout command terminates a login C shell. If the shell is not a login shell, the message Not login shell is displayed.

Attributes

See attributes(5) for descriptions of the following attributes:

Attribute Type	Attribute Value
Availability	SUNWcsu

See Also

csh(1), login(1), attributes(5)

look — Find Words in the System Dictionary or Lines in Sorted List

Synopsis

/usr/bin/look [-d] [-f] [-t*c*] *string* [*filename*]

Description

The look command consults a sorted *filename* and prints all lines that begin with *string*. If you specify no file name, look uses /usr/share/lib/dict/words with collating sequence -df.

look limits the length of a search to 256 characters.

Options

-d	Dictionary order. Use only letters, digits, Tabs, and space characters in comparisons.
-f	Fold case. Do not distinguish uppercase letters from lowercase letters in comparisons.
-t*c*	Set termination character. Ignore all characters to the right of *c* in *string*.

Examples

The following example uses the default dictionary to list all lines that begin with the string sun.

```
castle% look sun
sun
sunbeam
sunbonnet
sunburn
sunburnt
Sunday
sunder
sundew
sundial
sundown
sundry
sunfish
sunflower
sung
sunglasses
sunk
sunken
sunlight
sunlit
sunny
Sunnyvale
sunrise
sunscreen
```

```
sunset
sunshade
sunshine
sunshiny
sunspot
suntan
suntanned
suntanning
SUNY
castle%
```

Files

/usr/share/lib/dict/words

Spelling list.

Attributes

See attributes(5) for descriptions of the following attributes:

Attribute Type	Attribute Value
Availability	SUNWesu

See Also

grep(1), sort(1), attributes(5)

lookbib — Find References in a Bibliographic Database

Synopsis

/usr/bin/lookbib *database*

Description

A bibliographic reference is a set of lines, constituting fields of bibliographic information. Each field starts on a line beginning with a percent sign (%), followed by a key letter, then a blank, and finally the contents of the field, which may continue until the next line starting with %.

lookbib uses an inverted index made by indxbib to find sets of bibliographic references. It reads keywords typed after the > prompt on the terminal and retrieves records containing all these keywords. If nothing matches, nothing is returned except another > prompt.

You can search multiple databases as long as they have a common index made by indxbib(1). In that case, only the first argument given to indxbib is specified to lookbib.

If lookbib does not find the index files (the .i[abc] files), it looks for a reference file with the same name as the argument without the suffixes. It creates a file with an .ig suffix, suitable for use with fgrep (see grep(1)). lookbib then uses this fgrep file to find references. This method is simpler to use, but the `.ig` file is slower to use than the `.i[abc]` files and does not allow the use of multiple reference files.

Bugs

All dates should probably be indexed because many disciplines refer to literature written in the 1800s or earlier.

Examples

The following example accesses the bibliographic file named `bibliography`, displays instructions, and searches for references to the keyword `dreams`.

```
castle% lookbib bibliography
Instructions? y

Type keywords (such as author and date) after the > prompt.
References with those keywords are printed if they exist;
        if nothing matches you are given another prompt.
To quit lookbib, press CTRL-d after the > prompt.

> dreams
%A Janice Winsor
%T Opening the Dream Door
%P 153
%I Merrill-West Publishing
%C Carmel, California
%D 1998
%K dreams, psychic development
%X Not just another dream interpretation book! Opening the Dream Door
is a practical guide to psychic development. Written in a
friendly, personal style, Opening the Dream Door does not
attempt to interpret dream symbology. It is the author's belief
that each person has their own personal myths and symbols that
cannot be deciphered in a collective fashion. By using her own
dreams as an example, Janice Winsor makes practical suggestions
for expanding the subconscious life and connecting to other realms.
Processes for remembering and accessing dreams are taught in an
easy to understand style.
~
~
~
"bibliography" 27 lines, 946 characters
> ^D
castle%
```

To exit `lookbib`, press Control-D at the > prompt.

Files

x.ia	
x.ib	
x.ic	Index files.
x.ig	Reference file.

Attributes

See attributes(5) for descriptions of the following attributes:

Attribute Type	Attribute Value
Availability	SUNWdoc

See Also

addbib(1), grep(1), indxbib(1), refer(1), roffbib(1), sort bib(1), attributes(5)

lorder — Find Ordering Relation for an Object or Library Archive

Synopsis

/usr/ccs/bin/lorder *filename...*

Description

Use the lorder command to search a list of object file names and display a list of related pairs. The input is one or more object or library archive file names (see ar(1)). The standard output is a list of pairs of object file or archive member names; the first file of the pair refers to external identifiers defined in the second.

lorder accepts as input any object or archive file regardless of its suffix, provided there is more than one input file. If there is a single input file, its suffix must be .o.

You can process the output by tsort(1) to find an ordering of a library suitable for one-pass access by ld.

Note — The link-editor ld is capable of multiple passes over an archive in the portable archive format (see ar(4)) and does not require that you use lorder when building an archive. The use of the lorder command may, however, allow for a more efficient access of the archive during the link-edit process.

The following example builds a new library from existing .o files.

```
castle% ar -cr library `lorder *.o | tsort`
```

Files

TMPDIR/*symref

    Temporary files.

TMPDIR/*symdef

    Temporary files.

TMPDIR   Usually /var/tmp, but you can redefine by setting the environment variable TMPDIR (see tempnam() in tmpnam(3S)). The length of the file name for TMPDIR is limited to whatever sed allows.

Attributes

See attributes(5) for descriptions of the following attributes:

Attribute Type	Attribute Value
Availability	SUNWbtool

See Also

ar(1), ld(1), tsort(1), tmpnam(3S), ar(4), attributes(5)

lp — Submit Print Request

Synopsis

```
/usr/bin/lp [-c] [-m] [-p] [-s] [-w] [-d destination] [-f form-name]
    [-H special-handling] [-n number] [-o option] [-P page-list]
    [-q priority-level] [-S character-set|print-wheel] [-t title]
    [-T content-type [-r]] [-y mode-list] [file...]
/usr/bin/lp -i request-ID... [-c] [-m] [-p] [-s] [-w] [-d destination]
    [-f form-name] [-H special-handling] [-n number] [-o option]
    [-P page-list] [-q priority-level] [-S character-set|print-wheel]
    [-t title] [-T content-type [-r]] [-y mode-list]
```

Description

lp submits print requests to a destination. The lp command has two formats.

- The first form of lp prints files (*file*) and associated information (collectively called a print request). If you do not specify *file*, lp assumes the standard input. Use a dash (-) with *file* to specify the standard input. Files are printed in the order you specify them on the command line.

- The second form of lp changes print request options. You can use this form of lp only in a Solaris 2.6 operating environment or compatible versions of the LP print server. The print request identified by *request-ID* is changed according to the printing options specified. The printing options available are the same as those with the first form of the lp. If the request has finished printing when the lp command is executed, the change is rejected. If the request is in the process of printing, it is stopped and restarted from the beginning (unless you specify the -P option).

The print client commands locate destination information in a specific order. See printers(4) and printers.conf(4) for details.

Note — Print jobs are assumed to contain one type of data. That type of data is either specified on the command line or autodetected (simple, PostScript) according to the contents of the first file in the job.

Options

Printers that have a 4.x- or BSD-based print server are not configured to handle BSD protocol extensions. lp handles print requests sent to such printers in the following ways.

- Print requests with more than 52 file names are truncated to 52 files. lp displays a warning message.
- The -f, -H, -o, -P, -p, -q, -S, -T, and -y options may require a protocol extension to pass to a print server. If lp cannot handle the print request, it displays the following warning message.

```
LP administrators enable protocol extensions by setting a printer's
bsdaddr entry in /etc/printers.conf. Changing the bsdaddr entry in
/etc/printers.conf to:
```

destination:bsdaddr=*server*,*destination*,Solaris

```
generates a set of BSD print protocol extensions that can be processed
by a Solaris print server. lp supports only Solaris protocol
extensions at this time.
```

-c   Copy *file* before printing. Unless you specify -c, you should not remove any file before the print request has completely printed. Changes made to *file* after the print request is made but before it is printed are reflected in the printed output. *file* is linked (as opposed to copied).

-d *destination*

Print *file* on a specific *destination. destination* can be either a printer or a class of printers, (see lpadmin(1M)). Specify destination using atomic, POSIX-style (*server.destination*) or Federated Naming Service (FNS) (...*/service/printer/*...) names. See printers.conf(4) for information regarding the naming conventions for atomic and FNS names, and standards(5) for information regarding POSIX.

-f *form-name*

Print file on *form-name*. The LP print service ensures that the form is mounted on the printer. The print request is rejected if the printer does not support *form-name*, if *form-name* is not defined for the system, or if the user is not allowed to use *form-name* (see lpforms(1M)).

-H *special-handling*

Print the print request according to the value of *special-handling*. The following *special-handling* values are acceptable:

hold	Do not print the print request until notified. If printing has already begun, stop it. Other print requests go ahead of a request that has been put on hold (held print request) until the print request is resumed.
resume	Resume a held print request. If the print request had begun to print when held, it is the next print request printed unless it is superseded by an immediate print request.
immediate	Print the print request next. If more than one print request is assigned, print the most recent print request next. If a print request is currently printing on the desired printer, you must issue a hold request to enable the immediate request to print. The immediate request is available only to LP administrators.

-i *request-ID*

New!

Change options for the print request identified by *request-ID*. There must be a space between -i and *request-ID*. This option applies only to jobs that are in a local queue on a print server.

-m

Send mail after file has printed (see mail(1)). By default, send no mail on normal completion of a print request.

-n *number*

Print a specific number of copies of *file*. Specify *number* as a digit. The default for *number* is 1.

-o *option*

Specify printer-dependent options. Specify several options by specifying -o *option* multiple times (-o *option* -o *option* -o *option*). You can also specify printer-dependent options by using the -o key letter once followed by a list of options enclosed in double quotes (o "*option option option*"). The following options are valid.

nobanner	Do not print a banner page with the request. This option can be disallowed by the LP administrator.
nofilebreak	Print multiple files without inserting a formfeed between them.
length=*number*i | *number*c | *number*	
	Print the print request with pages of a specific length. Specify length in inches, centimeters, or number of lines. Use *number* to specify the number of inches, centimeters, or lines. Indicate inches or centimeters by appending to *number* the letter i for inches, c for centimeters. Indicate the number of lines by specifying *number* alone. length=66 indicates a page length of 66 lines. length=11i

indicates a page length of 11 inches. length=27.94c indicates a page length of 27.94 centimeters. You cannot use this option with the -f option.

width=*numberi* | *numberc* | *number*

Print the print request with pages of a specific width. Specify width in inches, centimeters, or number of columns. Use *number* to specify the number of inches, centimeters, or lines. Indicate inches or centimeters by appending to *number* the letter i for inches, c for centimeters. Indicate the number of lines by specifying *number* alone. width=65 indicates a page width of 65 columns. width=6.5i indicates a page width of 6.5 inches. width=10c indicates a page width of 10 centimeters. You cannot use this option with the -f option.

lpi=*number*

Print the print request with the line pitch set to *number* lines in an inch. Use *number* to specify the number of lines in an inch. You cannot use this option with the -f option.

cpi=*number* | pica | elite | compressed

Print the print request with the character pitch set to *number* characters in an inch. Use *number* to specify the number of characters in an inch. Use pica to set character pitch to pica (10 characters per inch), or elite to set character pitch to elite (12 characters per inch). Use compressed to set character pitch to as many characters as the printer can handle. There is no standard number of characters per inch for all printers; see the terminfo database (see terminfo(4)) for the default character pitch for your printer. You cannot use this option with the -f option.

stty=*stty-option-list*

Print the request, using a list of options valid for the stty command (see stty(1)). Enclose the list in single quotes (' ') if it contains blanks.

-p   Enable notification on completion of the print request. Delivery of the notification is dependent on additional software.

-P *page-list*

Print the pages specified in *page-list* in ascending order. Specify *page-list* as a range of numbers, single-page number, or a combination of both. You can use -P only if a filter is available to handle it; otherwise, the print request is rejected.

-q *priority-level*

               Assign the print request a priority in the print queue. Specify *priority-level* as an integer between from 0 and 39. Use 0 to indicate the highest priority; 39 to indicate the lowest priority. If you specify no priority, the default priority for a print service is assigned by the LP administrator. The LP administrator can also assign a default priority to individual users.

-s   Suppress the display of messages sent from lp.

-S *character-set|print-wheel*

               Print the request using the *character-set* or *print-wheel*. If a form was requested and requires a character set or print wheel other than the one specified with the -S option, reject the request. Printers using mountable print wheels or font cartridges use the print wheel or font cartridge mounted at the time of the print request unless you specify the -S option.

               Printers using print wheels: If *print-wheel* is not one listed by the LP administrator as acceptable for the printer, the request is rejected unless the print wheel is already mounted on the printer.

               Printers using selectable or programmable character sets: If you do not specify the -S option, lp uses the standard character set. If *character-set* is not defined in the terminfo database for the printer (see terminfo(4)) or is not an alias defined by the LP administrator, the request is rejected.

-t *title*   Print a title on the banner page of the output. Enclose *title* in quotes if it contains blanks. If you do not specify *title*, print the name of the file on the banner page.

-T *content-type* [-r]

               Print the request on a printer that can support the specified *content-type*. If no printer accepts this type directly, use a filter to convert the content into an acceptable type. If you specify the -r option, use no filter. If you specify -r and no printer accepts the *content-type* directly, reject the request. If the *content-type* is not acceptable to any printer, either directly or with a filter, the request is rejected.

-w   Write a message on the user's terminal after the files have been printed. If the user is not logged in, then send mail instead.

-y *mode-list*

               Print the request according to the printing modes listed in *mode-list*. The allowed values for *mode-list* are locally defined. You can use this option only if a filter is available to handle it; otherwise, the print request is rejected.

Operands

file   The name of the file to be printed. Specify *file* as a path name or as a
                 dash (–) to indicate the standard input. If you do not specify *file*, use
                 the standard input.

Usage

See largefile(5) for the description of the behavior of lp when encountering files
greater than or equal to 2 Gbytes (2**31 bytes).

Exit Status

0   Successful completion.

non-zero   An error occurred.

Files

/var/spool/lp/*

                 LP print queue.

$HOME/.printers

                 User-configurable printer database.

/etc/printers.conf

                 System printer configuration database.

fns.ctx_dir.domain

                 NIS+ version of /etc/printers.conf.

Attributes

See attributes(5) for descriptions of the following attributes:

Attribute Type	Attribute Value
Availability	SUNWpcu
CSI	Enabled

Note — CSI capability assumes that printer names are composed of ASCII
characters.

See Also

cancel(1), enable(1), lpstat(1), mail(1), postprint(1), pr(1), stty(1),
lpq(1B), lpr(1B), lprm(1B), accept(1M), lpadmin(1M), lpfilter(1M),
lpforms(1M), lpmove(1M), lpsched(1M), lpshut(1M), lpsystem(1M),
lpusers(1M), nsswitch.conf(4), printers(4), printers.conf(4),
terminfo(4), attributes(5), environ(5), largefile(5), standards(5)

lpc — Line Printer Control Program

Synopsis

/usr/ucb/lpc [*command* [*parameter*...]]

Description

Use the lpc (line printer control) command to control the operation of printers. lpc performs the following functions.

- Starts or stops a printer.
- Disables or enables a printer's spooling queue.
- Rearranges the order of jobs in a print queue.
- Displays the status of a printer print queue and printer daemon

You can run lpc from the command line or interactively. Specifying lpc with the optional *command* and *parameter* arguments interprets the first argument as an lpc command and all other arguments as parameters to that command. Specifying lpc without arguments runs it interactively, prompting for lpc commands with lpc>. If you redirect the standard input, lpc can read commands from a file.

Usage

You can type lpc commands in their entirety or abbreviate them to an unambiguous substring. Some lpc commands are available to all users; others are available only to superusers.

All users can execute the following lpc commands.

? [*command*...] | help [*command*...]

> Display a short description of *command*. *command* is an lpc command. If *command* is not specified, display a list of lpc commands.

exit | quit **Exit from** lpc.

restart [all | *printer*...]

> Try to start a new printer daemon. restart is useful when a print daemon dies unexpectedly and leaves jobs in the print queue. all performs this command on all locally attached printers.
>
> *printer* performs this command on specific printers. Specify *printer* as an atomic name. See printers.conf(4) for information regarding naming conventions for atomic names.

status [all | *printer*...]

> Display the status of print daemons and print queues. all performs this command on all locally attached printers. *printer* performs this command on specific printers. Specify *printer* as an atomic name. See printers.conf(4) for information regarding naming conventions for atomic names.

Only superuser can execute the following lpc commands.

abort [all | *printer*...]

> Terminate an active spooling daemon. Disable printing (by preventing new daemons from being started by lpr(1B)) for *printer*. all performs this command on all locally attached printers. *printer* performs this command on specific printers. Specify *printer* as an atomic name. See printers.conf(4) for information regarding naming conventions for atomic names.

clean [all | *printer*...]

> Remove files created in the print spool directory by the print daemon from *printer*'s print queue. all performs this command on all locally attached printers. *printer* performs this command on specific printers. Specify *printer* as an atomic name. See printers.conf(4) for information regarding naming conventions for atomic names.

disable [all | *printer*...]

> Turn off the print queue for *printer*. Prevent new printer jobs from being entered into the print queue for *printer* by lpr(1B). all performs this command on all locally attached printers. *printer* performs this command on specific printers. Specify *printer* as an atomic name. See printers.conf(4) for information regarding naming conventions for atomic names.

down [all | *printer*...] [*message*]

> Turn off the queue for *printer*, and disable printing on *printer*. Insert *message* in the printer status file. You do not need to quote *message*; treat multiple arguments to *message* in the same way as arguments to echo(1). Use down to take a printer down and inform users. all performs this command on all locally attached printers. *printer* performs this command on specific printers. Specify *printer* as an atomic name. See printers.conf(4) for information regarding naming conventions for atomic names.

enable [all | *printer*...]

> Enable lpr(1B) to add new jobs to the spool queue. all performs this command on all locally attached printers. *printer* performs this command on specific printers. Specify *printer* as an atomic name. See printers.conf(4) for information regarding naming conventions for atomic names.

start [all | *printer*...]

> Enable printing. Start a spooling daemon for the printer. all performs this command on all locally attached printers. *printer* performs this command on specific printers. Specify *printer* as an atomic name. See printers.conf(4) for information regarding naming conventions for atomic names.

stop [all | *printer*...]

> Stop a spooling daemon after the current job is complete. Disable printing at that time. all performs this command on all locally attached printers. *printer* performs this command on specific printers. Specify *printer* as an atomic name. See printers.conf(4) for information regarding naming conventions for atomic names.

topq printer [*request-ID*...] [*user*...]

> Move *request-ID* or print jobs belonging to *user* on *printer* to the beginning of the print queue. Specify *user* as a user's login name. Specify *printer* as an atomic name. See printers.conf(4) for information regarding naming conventions for atomic names.

up [all | *printer*...]

> Turn the queue on for *printer*, and enable printing. Delete the message in the printer status file (inserted by down). Use up to undo the effects of down. all performs this command on all locally attached printers. *printer* performs this command on specific printers. Specify *printer* as an atomic name. See printers.conf(4) for information regarding naming conventions for atomic names.

Exit Status

0	Successful completion.
non-zero	An error occurred.

Files

/var/spool/lp/*

> LP print queue.

/var/spool/lp/system/pstatus

> Printer status information file.

Attributes

See attributes(5) for descriptions of the following attributes:

Attribute Type	**Attribute Value**
Availability	SUNWscplp

See Also

echo(1), lpstat(1), lpq(1B), lpr(1B), lprm(1B), lpsched(1M), lpshut(1M), printers.conf(4), attributes(5)   *New!*

Diagnostics

Ambiguous command

> The lpc command or abbreviation matches more than one command.

?Invalid command

> The lpc command or abbreviation is not recognized.

?Privileged command

> The lpc command or abbreviation can be executed only by superuser.

lpc: printer: unknown printer to the print service

> That printer does not exist in the LP database. Check that printer was correctly specified. Use lpstat -p or the status command (see lpstat(1)) to check the status of printers.

lpc: error on opening queue to spooler

> The connection to lpsched failed. Usually means that the printer server has died or is hung. Use /usr/lib/lp/lpsched to check if the printer spooler daemon is running.

lpc: Can't send message to LP print service
lpc: Can't receive message from LP print service

> The LP print service stopped. Contact the LP administrator.

lpc: Received unexpected message from LP print service

> A problem with the software. Contact the LP administrator.

lpq — Display the Contents of a Print Queue

Synopsis

/usr/ucb/lpq [-P *destination*] [-l] [+ [*interval*]] [*request-ID*] [*user*]

Description

The lpq command displays the information about the contents of a print queue. A print queue comprises print requests that are waiting in the process of being printed.

lpq displays the following information to the standard output.

- The user name of the person associated with a print request.
- The position of a print request in the print queue.
- The name of file or files comprising a print request.
- The job number of a print request.
- The size of the file requested by a print request. File size is reported in bytes.

Normally, only as much information as fits on one line is displayed. If the name of the input file associated with a print request is not available, the input file field indicates the standard input.

The print client commands locate destination information in a specific order. See `nsswitch.conf(4)`, `printer.conf(4)` and `printers(4)` for details.

Options

-P *destination*

> Display information about printer or class of printers (see `lpadmin(1M)`). Specify *destination* using atomic, POSIX-style (*server*: *destination*) or Federated Naming Service (FNS) (*.../service/printer/...*) names. See `printers.conf(4)` for information regarding the naming conventions for atomic and FNS names, and `standards(5)` for information regarding POSIX.

-l

> Display information in long format. Long format includes the name of the host from which a print request originated.

+ [*interval*]

> Display information at specific time intervals. Stop displaying information when the print queue is empty. Clear the screen before displaying the print queue. Specify *interval* as the number of seconds between displays. If *interval* is not specified, execute only once.

Operands

request-ID   The job number associated with a print request.

user   The name of the user about whose jobs `lpq` reports information. Specify *user* as a valid user name.

Exit Status

0   Successful completion.

non-zero   An error occurred.

Files

/var/spool/print/[cd]f*

> Spooling directory and request files for jobs awaiting transfer.

Attributes

See `attributes(5)` for descriptions of the following attributes:

Attribute Type	Attribute Value
Availability	SUNWscplo

See Also

`lp(1)`, `lpstat(1)`, `lpc(1B)`, `lpr(1B)`, `lprm(1B)`, `lpadmin(1M)`, `nsswitch.conf(4)`, `printers(4)`, `printers.conf(4)`, `attributes(5)`, `standards(5)`

lpr — Submit BSD Print Requests

Synopsis

```
/usr/ucb/lpr [-P destination] [-# number] [-C class] [-J job]
    [-T title] [-i [indent]] [-1|-2|-3|-4 font] [-w cols] [-m] [-h] [-s]
    [-filter-option] [file...]
```

Description

The lpr command submits print requests to a destination. lpr prints files (*file*) and associated information, collectively called a print request. If you do not specify *file*, lpr assumes the standard input.

The print client commands locate destination information in a specific order. See printers(4) and printers.conf(4) for details.

Print requests with more than 52 files specified are truncated to 52 files. lpr displays a warning message.

New!

> **Note** — Print jobs are assumed to contain one type of data. That type of data is either specified on the command line or autodetected (simple, PostScript) according to the contents of the first file in the job.

Options

-# *number*	Print a specific number of copies. Specify *number* as a positive integer. The default for number is 1.
-1|-2|-3|-4 *font*	
	Mount the specified font in the font position 1, 2, 3, or 4. Specify *font* as a valid font name.
-C *class*	Print *class* as the job classification on the banner page of the output. Enclose *class* in double quotes if it contains blanks. If you do not specify *class*, print the name of the system (as returned by hostname) as the job classification. See hostname(1).
-h	Suppress printing of the banner page of the output.
-i [*indent*]	
	Indent the output a specific number of space characters. Use *indent* to indicate the number of space characters to be indented. Specify *indent* as a positive integer. Eight space characters is the default. The -i option is ignored unless you specify it with the -p *filter* option.
-J *job*	Print *job* as the job name on the banner page of the output. Enclose *job* in double quotes if it contains blanks. If you do not specify *job*, print *file* (or in the case of multiple files, the first file specified on the command line) as the job name on the banner page of the output.
-m	Send mail after *file* has printed (see mail(1)). By default, send no mail on normal completion of a print request.

New!

-P *destination*

> Print file on a specific printer or class of printers (see lpadmin(1M)). Specify *destination* using atomic, POSIX-style (*server*:*destination*) or Federated Naming Service (FNS) (*.../service/printer/*...) names. See printers.conf(4) for information regarding the naming conventions for atomic and FNS names, and standards(5) for information regarding POSIX.

-s

> Use full path names (as opposed to symbolic links) to *file* instead of trying to copy them. File should not be modified or removed until it has completed printing. -s prevents only copies of local files from being made on the local system. -s works only with specified files. If the lpr command is at the end of a pipeline, *file* is copied to the spool.

-T *title*   Print a title on the banner page of the output. Enclose *title* in double quotes if it contains blanks. If you do not specify *title*, print file name on the banner page.

-w *cols*   Print *file* with pages of a specific width. *cols* indicates the number of columns.

- *filter-options*

> Notify the print spooler that *file* is not a standard text file. Enable the spooling daemon to use the appropriate filters to print *file*. *filter-options* offers a standard user interface. All options may not be available for, or applicable to, all printers. Specify *filter-options* as a single character. If you do not specify *filter-options* and the printer can interpret PostScriptO, inserting %! as the first two characters of *file* interprets the file as PostScript. The following *filter-options* are supported.

c   File contains data produced by cifplot.

d   File contains tex data from in DVI format from Stanford.

f   Interpret the first character of each line as a standard FORTRAN carriage control character.

g   File contains standard plot data produced by plot(1B) routines.

l   Print control characters and suppress page breaks.

n   File contains ditroff data from device-independent troff.

p   Use pr to format the files.

t   File contains troff (cat phototypesetter) binary data.

v   File contains a raster image. *printer* must support an appropriate imaging model such as PostScript to print the image.

Operands

file The name of the file to be printed. Specify *file* as a path name. If you do not specify *file*, use the standard input.

Usage

See largefile(5) for the description of the behavior of lpr when encountering files greater than or equal to 2 Gbytes (2**31 bytes).

Exit Status

0 Successful completion.

non-zero An error occurred.

Files

/var/spool/print/.seq

File containing the sequence numbers for job ID assignment.

/var/spool/print/[cd]f*

Spooling directories and files.

Attributes

See attributes(5) for descriptions of the following attributes:

Attribute Type	Attribute Value
Availability	SUNWscplp
CSI	Enabled

Note — lpr is CSI enabled except for the printer name.

See Also

hostname(1), lp(1), lpstat(1), mail(1), pr(1), troff(1), lpc(1B), lpq(1B), lprm(1B), plot(1B), lpadmin(1M), nsswitch.conf(4), printers(4), printers.conf(4), attributes(5), largefile(5), standards(5)

Diagnostics

lpr: *destination* |: unknown destination

destination was not found in the LP configuration database. Usually this error results from a typing mistake; however, it may indicate that the destination does not exist on the system. Use lpstat -p to display information about the status of the print service.

lprm — Remove Print Requests from the Print Queue

Synopsis

/usr/ucb/lprm [-P *destination*] [-] [*request-ID*...] [*user*...]

Description

Use the lprm command to remove print requests (*request-ID*) from the print queue.
Without arguments, lprm deletes the current print request. lprm reports the name of the file associated with print requests that it removes. lprm is silent if there are no applicable print requests to remove.

You can only remove print requests associated with your own user name. If a superuser executes lprm and specifies the *user* operand, lprm removes all print requests belonging to the specified user.

The print client commands locate destination information in a specific order. See nsswitch.conf(4), printers(4), and printers.conf(4) for details.

Note — You can only remove print requests associated with your own user name. By default, you can only remove print requests on the host from which the print request was submitted. If a superuser has set user-equivalence=true in /etc/printers.conf on the print server, you can remove print requests associated with your user name on any host. Superusers can remove print requests on the host from which the print request was submitted. Superusers can also remove print requests from the print server.

Options

-P *destination*

Specify the name of the printer or class of printers (see lpadmin(1M)) from which to remove print requests. Specify *destination*, using atomic, POSIX-style (*server*: *destination*) or Federated Naming Service (FNS) (.../ *service*/ *printer*/...) names. See printers.conf(4) for information regarding the naming conventions for atomic and FNS names, and standards(5) for information regarding POSIX.

-

Remove all print requests owned by the user. If a superuser specifies this option, remove all requests in the print queue. Job ownership is determined by the user's login name and host name on the system from which lpr was executed.

Operands

user

Remove print requests associated with a specific user. Specify *user* as a valid user name. Only superuser can use this option.

request-ID

Remove a specific print request. Specify *request-ID* as the job number associated with a print request and reported by lpq. See lpq(1B).

Examples

The following example removes *request-ID* 385 from destination killtree.

```
castle% lprm -P killtree 385
```

Exit Status

0	Successful completion.
non-zero	An error occurred.

Files

/var/spool/print/[cd]f*

Spooling directories and files.

Attributes

See attributes(5) for descriptions of the following attributes:

Attribute Type	Attribute Value
Availability	SUNWscplp

See Also

New!

lp(1), lpstat(1), lpc(1B), lpq(1B), lpr(1B), lpadmin(1M),
nsswitch.conf(4), printers(4), printers.conf(4), attributes(5),
standards(5)

---

lpstat — Display Information About the Status of the Print Service

Synopsis

```
/usr/bin/lpstat [-d] [-r] [-R] [-s] [-t] [-a [list]] [-c [list]]
    [-f [list] [-l]] [-o [list]] [-p [list] [-D] [-l]] [-S [list] [-l]]
    [-u [login-ID-list]] [-v [list]]
```

Description

lpstat displays information about the current status of the LP print service to standard output.

If you specify no options, lpstat prints the status of all your print requests made by lp (see lp(1)). Any arguments that are not options are assumed to be *request-ID*s as returned by lp. The lpstat command prints the status of such requests. You can specify options in any order and can repeat and intermix them with other arguments. You can follow some key letters with an optional list that can be in one of two forms: a list of items separated from one another by a comma, or a list of items separated from one another by spaces enclosed in quotes. For example:

```
castle% lpstat -u "user1 user2 user3"
```

Specifying all after any key letter that takes *list* as an argument prints all information relevant to the key letter. For example, the following command prints the status of all output requests.

castle% **lpstat -o all**

Omitting a list following such key letters prints all information relevant to the key letter. For example, the following command prints the status of all output requests.

castle% **lpstat -o**

The print client commands locate printer information in a specific order. See nsswitch.conf(4), printers.conf(4), and printers(4) for details. *New!*

Options

-d	Print the default destination for output requests.
-o [*list*]	Print the status of output requests. *list* is a list of intermixed printer names, class names, and *request-ID*s. You can omit the key letter -o. Specify printer and class names using atomic, POSIX-style (*server*:*destination*) or Federated Naming Service (FNS) (.../*service*/*printer*/...) names. See printers.conf(4) for information regarding the naming conventions for atomic and FNS names, and standards(5) for information regarding POSIX.
-r	Print the status of the LP request scheduler.
-R	Print a number showing the position of each request in the print queue.
-s	Print a status summary, including the status of the LP scheduler, the default destination, a list of printers and their associated devices, a list of the systems sharing print services, a list of all forms currently mounted, and a list of all recognized character sets and print wheels.
-t	Print all status information. This includes all the information obtained with the -s option, plus the acceptance and idle/busy status of all printers.
-u [*login-ID-list*]	Print the status of output requests for users. The *login-ID-list* argument can include any or all of the following constructs:

login-ID	A user on any system.
system-name!*login-ID*	A user on system *system-name*.
system-name!all	All users on system *system-name*.
all!*login-ID*	A user on all systems.

-v [*list*]	Print the names of printers and the path names of the devices associated with them or remote system names for network printers. *list* is a list of printer names.

The following options return accurate results only if they are issued from a Solaris 2.x LP print server.

-a [*list*]   Report whether print destinations are accepting requests. *list* is a list of intermixed printer names and class names.

-c [*list*]   Print the name of all classes and their members. *list* is a list of class names.

-d   Print the default destination for output requests.

-f [*list*] [-1]
                     Print a verification that the forms in *list* are recognized by the LP print service. *list* is a list of forms; the default is all. The -1 option lists the form descriptions.

-o [*list*]   Print the status of output requests. *list* is a list of intermixed printer names, class names, and request IDs. You can omit the key letter -o.

-p [*list*] [-D] [-1]
                     Print the status of printers. *list* is a list of printer names. If you specify the -D option, print a brief description for each printer in *list*. If you specify the -1 option and the printer is on the local system, return a full description of each printer's configuration, including the form mounted, the acceptable content and printer types, a printer description, and the interface used.

-r   Print the status of the LP request scheduler.

-R   Print a number showing the position of each request in the print queue.

-s   Print a status summary, including the status of the LP scheduler, the default destination, a list of printers and their associated devices, a list of the systems sharing print services, a list of all forms currently mounted, and a list of all recognized character sets and print wheels.

-S [*list*] [-1]
                     Print a verification that the character sets or the print wheels specified in *list* are recognized by the LP print service. Items in *list* can be character sets or print wheels; the default for the list is all. If you specify the -1 option, append to each line a list of printers that can handle the print wheel or character set. The list also shows whether the print wheel or character set is mounted or specifies the built-in character set into which it maps.

-t   Print all status information, including all the information obtained with the -s option, plus the acceptance and idle/busy status of all printers.

-u [*login-ID-list*]
                     Print the status of output requests for users. The *login-ID-list* argument can include any or all of the following constructs:

                     login-ID   A user on any system.

	system-name! *login-I*	A user on system *system-name*.
	system-name! all	All users on system *system-name*.
	all! *login-ID*	A user on all systems.
	all	All users on all systems.
-v [*list*]	Print the names of printers and the path names of the devices associated with them or remote system names for network printers. *list* is a list of printer names.	

Exit Status

0	Successful completion.
non-zero	An error occurred.

Files

/var/spool/print/*

> LP print queue.

$HOME/.printers

> User-configurable printer database.

/etc/printers.conf

> System configuration database.

printers.conf.byname

> NIS version of /etc/printers.conf. New in the Solaris 9 release.

New!

printers.org

> NIS+ version of /etc/printers.conf. New in the Solaris 9 release.

New!

fns.ctx_dir.org

> FNS version of /etc/printers.conf. New in the Solaris 9 release.

New!

Attributes

See attributes(5) for descriptions of the following attributes:

Attribute Type	**Attribute Value**
Availability	SUNWpcu

See Also

cancel(1), lp(1), lpq(1B), lpr(1B), lprm(1B), nsswitch.conf(4), printers(4), printers.conf(4), attributes(5), standards(5)

New!

lptest — Generate Line Printer Ripple Pattern

Synopsis

```
/usr/ucb/lptest [length [count]]
```

Description

lptest writes the traditional ripple test pattern to the standard output. In 96 lines, the ripple test pattern prints all 96 printable ASCII characters in each position. The ripple test pattern was originally created to test printers. It is also useful for testing terminals, driving terminal ports, debugging, and performing tasks that require a quick supply of random data.

Note — This command is obsolete.

Options

length	Specify the length of the output line in characters. The default is 79 characters.
count	Specify the number of output lines. The default is 200 lines. If you specify count, you must also specify length.

Exit Status

0	Successful completion.
non-zero	An error occurred.

Attributes

See attributes(5) for descriptions of the following attributes:

Attribute Type	Attribute Value
Availability	SUNWscplp

See Also

attributes(5)

ls — List Contents of Directory

Synopsis

New!

```
/usr/bin/ls [-aAbcCdfFgilLmnopqrRstux1@] [file...]
/usr/xpg4/bin/ls [-aAbcCdfFgilLmnopqrRstux1@] [file...]
/usr/ucb/ls [-aAcCdfFgilLqrRstu1] file...
```

Description

Use the ls command to list the contents of a directory and display permissions, links, ownership, group, size (in bytes), modification date and time, and file name for files.

For each file that is a directory, ls lists the contents of the directory; for each file that is an ordinary file, ls repeats its name and any other information requested. The output is sorted alphabetically by default. When you specify no arguments, ls lists the contents of the current directory. When you specify several arguments, the arguments are first sorted appropriately, with file arguments before directories and their contents.

ls has three major listing formats.

- The default format for output directed to a terminal is multicolumn with entries sorted down the columns.
- The -1 option displays single-column output.
- The -m option displays stream output format. Files are listed all on the same line separated by a comma and a space.

To determine output formats for the -C, -x, and -m options, ls uses an environment variable, COLUMNS, to determine the number of character positions available on one output line. If this variable is not set, the terminfo(4) database is used to determine the number of columns, based on the environment variable TERM. If this information cannot be obtained, 80 columns are assumed.

The mode printed with the -1 option consists of ten characters. The first character is one of the following.

d	The entry is a directory.
D	The entry is a door.
l	The entry is a symbolic link.
b	The entry is a block special file.
c	The entry is a character special file.
p	The entry is a FIFO (or named pipe) special file.
s	The entry is an AF_UNIX address family socket.
–	The entry is an ordinary file.

The next nine characters are interpreted as three sets of three bits each. The first set refers to the owner's permissions; the next, to permissions of others in the user-group of the file; and the last, to all others. Within each set, the three characters indicate permission to read, to write, and to execute the file as a program. For a directory, execute permission is interpreted as permission to search the directory for a specified file.

For user and group permissions, the third position can be occupied by x (execute), – (deny access), or s (set user ID). The s permission designation refers to the state of the set-ID bit, whether it be the user's or the group's. For example, the ability to assume the same ID as the user during execution is used during login where you begin the process as root but then assume the identity of your user login.

For group permissions, l can occupy the third position. l refers to mandatory file and record locking. This permission describes a file's ability to allow other files to lock its reading or writing permissions during access.

For others permissions, the third position can be occupied by t or T. These refer to the state of the sticky bit and execution permissions.

The permissions are indicated as follows.

r	The file is readable.
w	The file is writable.
x	The file is executable.
–	The indicated permission is not granted.
s	The setuid or setgid bit is on, and the corresponding user or group execution bit is also on.
S	Undefined bit-state (the setuid bit is on, and the user execution bit is off).
t	The 1000 (octal) bit, or sticky bit, is on (see chmod(1)), and execution is on.
T	The 1000 bit is on, and execution is off (undefined bit state).
l	Mandatory locking occurs during access (the setgid bit is on, and the group execution bit is off) (/usr/bin/ls).
L	Mandatory locking occurs during access (the setgid bit is on and the group execution bit is off) (/usr/xpg4/bin/ls).

ls -l (the long list) prints its output as follows for the POSIX locale:

```
-rwxrwxrwx+  1 winsor   staff    10876  May 16 9:42 part2
```

Reading from right to left, the current directory holds one file, named part2. The last time that file's contents were modified was 9:42 a.m. on May 16. The file contains 10,876 characters or bytes. The owner of the file, or the user, belongs to the group staff, and the login name is winsor. The number, in this case, 1, indicates the number of links to file part2 (see cp(1)). The plus sign indicates that there is an access control list (ACL) associated with the file.

New!

Note — If you specify the -@ option—new in the Solaris 9 release to display extended attributes of a file—the presence of extended attributes supersedes the presence of an ACL and the + sign is replaced with an at sign (@).

Finally, the dash and letters tell you that user, group, and others have permissions to read, write, and execute part2.

Note — Unprintable characters in file names may confuse the columnar output options.

The total block count is incorrect if there are hard links among the files.

Options

New!

-@	The same as -l except that extended attribute information supersedes ACL information. An at sign (@) is displayed after the file permission bits for files that have extended attributes. New in the Solaris 9 release.

-a	List all entries, including those that begin with a dot (.), which are normally not listed.
-A	List all entries, including those that begin with a dot (.) with the exception of the working directory (.) and the parent directory (..).
-b	Force printing of nonprintable characters to be in the octal *ddd* notation.
-c	Use time of last modification of the inode (file created, mode changed, and so forth) for sorting (-t) or printing (-l or -n).
-C	Display multicolumn output, and sort entries down the columns. This format is the default.
-d	If an argument is a directory, list only its name (not its contents); often used with -l to get the status of a directory.
-f	Force each argument to be interpreted as a directory, and list the name found in each slot. This option turns off -l, -t, -s, and -r, and turns on -a; the order is the order in which entries appear in the directory.
-F	Mark directories with a trailing slash (/), doors with a trailing greater-than sign (>), executable files with a trailing asterisk (*), FIFOs with a trailing vertical bar (|), symbolic links with a trailing at-sign (@), and AF_UNIX address family sockets with a trailing equal sign (=).
-g	The same as -l, except do not print the owner.
-i	For each file, print the inode number in the first column of the report.
-l	List in long format, giving mode, ACL indication, number of links, owner, group, size in bytes, and time of last modification for each file. If the file is a special file, the size field contains the major and minor device numbers. If the time of last modification is greater than six months ago, it is shown in the format *month date year* for the POSIX locale. When the LC_TIME locale category is not set to the POSIX locale, a different format of the time field can be used. Files modified within six months show *month date time*. If the file is a symbolic link, the file name is printed, followed by -> and the path name of the referenced file.
-L	If an argument is a symbolic link, list the file or directory the link references instead of the link itself.
-m	Stream output format; list files across the page, separated by commas and spaces.
-n	The same as -l, except print the owner UID and group GID numbers instead of the associated character strings.
-o	The same as -l, except do not print the group.
-p	Put a slash (/) after each file name if the file is a directory.
-q	Force printing of nonprintable characters in file names as the character question mark (?).

-r	Reverse the order of sort to get reverse alphabetic or oldest first as appropriate.
-R	Recursively list subdirectories.
-s	Give size in blocks, including indirect blocks, for each entry.
-t	Sort by timestamp (latest first) instead of by name. The default is the last modification time. (See -u and -c.)
-u	Use time of last access instead of last modification for sorting (with the -t option) or printing (with the -l option).
-x	Display multicolumn output, and sort entries across instead of down the page.
-1	Print one entry per line of output.

Specifying more than one of the options in the following mutually exclusive pairs is not considered an error: -C and -1 (one), -c and -u. The last option specified in each pair determines the output format.

/usr/bin/ls

Specifying more than one of the options in the following mutually exclusive pairs is not considered an error: -C and -1 (ell), -m and -1 (ell), -x and -1 (ell), -@ and -1 (ell). The -1 option overrides the other option specified in each pair.

/usr/xpg4/bin/ls

Specifying more than one of the options in the following mutually exclusive pairs is not considered an error: -C and -1 (ell), -m and -1 (ell), -x and -1 (ell), -@ and -1 (ell). The last option specified in each pair determines the output format.

Operands

file	A path name of a file to be listed. If the specified file is not found, display a diagnostic message on standard error.

Usage

See largefile(5) for the description of the behavior of ls when encountering files greater than or equal to 2 Gbytes (2**31 bytes).

Examples

The following example of file permissions describes a file that is readable, writable, and executable by the user and readable by the group and others.

```
-rwxr--r--
```

The following example describes a file that is readable, writable, and executable by the user, readable and executable by the group and others, and enables its user ID to be assumed, during execution, by the user presently executing it.

```
-rwsr-xr-x
```

The following example describes a file that is readable and writable only by the user and the group and that can be locked during access.

```
-rw-rwl---
```

The following command displays the names of all files in the current directory, including those that begin with a dot (.), which normally are not displayed.

```
castle% ls -a
```

The following example provides information on all files, including those that begin with a dot (the -a option), the i-number—the memory address of the inode associated with the file—printed in the left-hand column (the -i option); the size (in blocks) of the files, printed in the column to the right of the i-numbers (the -s option); finally, the report is displayed in the numeric version of the long list (the -n option), printing the UID (instead of user name) and GID (instead of group name) numbers associated with the files.

```
castle% ls -aisn
total 10272
   297874    2 drwxr-xr-x   6 1001    10       512 Mar  9 13:50 .
   296220    2 drwxr-xr-x   6 0        1       512 Mar  3 18:49 ..
   297877    2 -rw-r--r--   1 1001    10       411 Mar  3 19:05 .cshrc
   407708    2 drwxr-xr-x  14 1001    10       512 Mar  9 13:15 .dt
   297878   10 -rwxr-xr-x   1 1001    10      5111 Mar  3 19:52 .dtprofile
    41663    2 drwxr-xr-x   2 1001    10       512 Mar  4 07:42 .hotjava
    81587    2 drwxrwxrwx   2 1001    10       512 Mar  4 11:22 .jetadmin
   297875    2 -rw-r--r--   1 1001    10       581 Mar  3 18:48 .login
   297884    2 -rw-------   1 1001    10        36 Mar  6 16:52 .sh_history
    36679    2 drwx------   2 1001    10       512 Mar  9 13:15 .solregis
   297890    2 -rw-------   1 1001    10       100 Mar  9 13:15 .Xauthority
   297880    8 -rw-r--r--   1 1001    10      3985 Mar  4 11:26 .Xdefaults
   297885    0 -rw-r--r--   1 1001    10         0 Mar  8 12:55 a.out
   297888    2 -rw-r--r--   1 1001    10       783 Mar  8 18:08 bibliography
   297881  240 -rw-------   1 1001    10    111560 Mar  5 10:33 core
   297879    4 -rw-------   1 1001    10      1068 Mar  8 18:11 examples
   297887    2 -rw-r--r--   1 1001    10       265 Mar  8 18:00 kookaburra-1
   297876 9984 -rw-r--r--   1 1001    10   5097472 Mar  3 19:03 SOLd515.pkg
castle%
```

When the sizes of the files in a directory are listed, a total count of blocks, including indirect blocks, is printed.

The following scenario shows how you can list files that have unprintable or white space in their file names: Very handy when you want to delete a file that has embedded white space or control characters in the file name.

New!

If a file has been created with control characters or spaces in its name, the -b option to ls can show you exactly which characters are in the file name so that you can rename or delete the file. For example, if you see the following in your ls listing:

```
$ ls
tfile
$
```

and when you receive the following message when you try to remove the file, the file name probably contains invisible control characters.

```
$ rm tfile
tfile: No such file or directory
$
```

Then, you can use the -b option to display the real file-name characters, as shown in the following example.

```
$ ls -b tfile
test\010\010\010file
$
```

In this case, the actual file name is

```
test[BACKSPACE][BACKSPACE][BACKSPACE]file
```

The backspaces are printed by the -b option as octal 010.
One way to remove the file, now that you know the actual characters in the file name, is shown below.

```
$ rm test*file
$
```

New! The following example enables you to get a helpful listing that indicates directories, symbolic links, sockets and executable files.

```
$ ls -F /
./              .kshrc         .wastebasket/   export/         opt/          var/
../             .lsof_ns1      a/              home/           platform/     vol/
.TTauthority    .netscape/     bin@            kernel/         prefs_v3      xfn/
.Xauthority     .profile       cdrom/          lib@            proc/
.cpan/          .rnd           db/             log             sbin/
.dt/            .sh_history    dev/            lost+found/     tftpboot/
.dtprofile*     .ssh/          devices/        mnt/            tmp/
.fm/            .ssh2/         etc/            net/            usr/
$
```

Directories have a / appended, symbolic links have an @ appended, and executables have an * appended.

Environment Variables

See environ(5) for descriptions of the following environment variables that affect the execution of ls: LC_COLLATE, LC_CTYPE, LC_TIME, LC_MESSAGES, NLSPATH, and TZ.

COLUMNS   Determine the preferred column position width for writing multiple text-column output. If this variable contains a string representing a decimal integer, the ls command calculates how many path-name text columns to write (see -C) based on the width provided. If COLUMNS is not set or is invalid, use 80. The column width chosen to write the names of files in any given directory is constant. File names are not truncated to fit into the multiple text column output.

New! **Note** — The sort order of ls output is affected by the locale and can be overrridden by the LC_COLLATE environment variable. For example, if LC_COLLATE equals C, dot files are displayed first, followed by names beginning with uppercase letters, and then, followed by names beginning with lowercase letters. But, if LC_COLLATE equals en_US.ISO8859-1, then leading dots as well as case are ignored in determining the sort order.

Exit Status

0	All information was written successfully.
>0	An error occurred.

Files

/etc/group   Group IDs for ls -l and ls -g.

/etc/passwd User IDs for ls -l and ls -o.

/usr/share/lib/terminfo/?/*

Terminal information database.

Attributes

See attributes(5) for descriptions of the following attributes:

/usr/bin/ls

Attribute Type	Attribute Value
Availability	SUNWcsu
CSI	Enabled
Interface Stability	Stable

New!

/usr/xpg4/bin/ls

Attribute Type	Attribute Value
Availability	SUNWcsu
CSI	Enabled
Interface Stability	Standard

New!

See Also

chmod(1), cp(1), setfacl(1), terminfo(4), attributes(5), environ(5), largefile(5), XPG4(5)

M

---

m4 — Macro Processor

Synopsis

```
/usr/ccs/bin/m4 [-e] [-s] [-B int] [-H int] [-S int] [-T int]
   [-Dname [=val]]...[-U name]... [file...]
/usr/xpg4/bin/m4 [-e] [-s] [-B int] [-H int] [-S int] [-T int] [-Dname
   [=val]]... [-U name]... [file...]
```

Description

The m4 command is a macro processor front end for C, assembler, and other languages.
Each of the argument files is processed in order; if there are no files or if a file is -, the
standard input is read. The processed text is written to the standard output.

Macro Syntax

Macro calls have the form:

name(arg1,arg2,..., argn)

The (must immediately follow the name of the macro. If the name of a defined macro is
not followed by a (, it is considered to be a call of that macro with no arguments.
Potential macro names consist of alphanumeric characters and underscore (_), where
the first character is not a digit.

Leading unquoted blanks, Tabs, and newlines are ignored while arguments are
collected. Left and right single quotes are used to quote strings. The value of a quoted
string is the string stripped of the quotes.

Macro Processing

When a macro name is recognized, its arguments are collected by a search for a matching right parenthesis. If fewer arguments are supplied than are in the macro definition, the trailing arguments are taken to be null. Macro evaluation proceeds normally during the collection of the arguments, and any commas or right parentheses that happen to turn up within the value of a nested call are as effective as those in the original input text. After argument collection, the value of the macro is pushed back onto the input stream and rescanned.

Options

-e	Operate interactively. Ignore interrupts, and buffer the output.
-s	Enable line sync output for the C preprocessor (#line...).
-B *int*	Change the size of the push-back and argument-collection buffers from the default of 4,096.
-H *int*	Change the size of the symbol table hash array from the default of 199. The size should be prime.
-S *int*	Change the size of the call stack from the default of 100 slots. Macros take three slots, and nonmacro arguments take one.
-T *int*	Change the size of the token buffer from the default of 512 bytes.

To be effective, put the above options before any file names and before any -D or -U options.

-D *name*[=*val*]	
	Define *name* to *val* or to null in *val*'s absence.
-U *name*	Undefine *name*.

Operands

file	A path name of a text file to be processed. If you specify no file or if it is -, read the standard input.

Usage

The m4 command makes the following built-in macros available. You can redefine these macros, but if you do so, you lose their original meaning. Macro values are null unless otherwise stated.

changequote	
	Change quote symbols to the first and second arguments. The symbols can be up to five characters long. changequote without arguments restores the original values (that is, ').
changecom	Change left and right comment markers from the default # and newline. With no arguments, the comment mechanism is effectively disabled. With one argument, the left marker becomes the argument and the right marker becomes newline. With two arguments, both markers are affected. Comment markers can be up to five characters long.

decr | Return the value of the argument decremented by 1.

define | The second argument is installed as the value of the macro whose name is the first argument. Replace each occurrence of $n in the replacement text, where n is a digit, with the n-th argument. Argument 0 is the name of the macro. Replace missing arguments with the null string. Replace $# with the number of arguments. Replace $* with a list of all the arguments separated by commas. $@ is like $* but quotes each argument with the current quotes.

defn | Return the quoted definition of the argument(s). This macro is useful for renaming macros, especially built-ins.

divert | Change the current output stream to the (*digit-string*) argument. m4 maintains 10 output streams, numbered 0–9. The final output is the concatenation of the streams in numerical order; initially, stream 0 is the current stream. Output diverted to a stream other than 0 through 9 is discarded.

divnum | Return the value of the current output stream.

dnl | Read and discard characters up to and including the next newline.

dumpdef | Print current names and definitions for the named items or for all if you specify no arguments.

errprint | Print the argument on the diagnostic output file.

/usr/ccs/bin/m4

eval | Evaluate the argument as an arithmetic expression, using 32-bit signed-integer arithmetic. The following operators are supported: parentheses, unary -, unary +, !, ~, *, /, %, +, -, relationals, bitwise &, |, &&, and | |. You can specify octal and hex numbers as in C. The second argument specifies the radix for the result; the default is 10. You can use the third argument to specify the minimum number of digits in the result.

/usr/xpg4/bin/m4

eval | Evaluate the argument as an arithmetic expression using 32-bit signed-integer arithmetic. The following operators are supported: parentheses, unary -, unary +, !, ~, *, /, %, +, -, <<, >>, relationals, bitwise &, |, &&, and | |. Precedence and associativity are as in C. You can also specify octal and hex numbers as in C. The second argument specifies the radix for the result; the default is 10. You can use the third argument to specify the minimum number of digits in the result.

ifdef | If the first argument is defined, use the value of the second argument; otherwise, use the third. If there is no third argument, the value is null. The word unix is predefined.

ifelse	This macro has three or more arguments. If the first argument is the same string as the second, then use the value of the third argument. If not and if there are more than four arguments, repeat the process with arguments 4, 5, 6, and 7. Otherwise, the value is either the fourth string or, if it is not present, `null`.
include	Return the contents of the file named in the argument.
incr	Return the value of the argument incremented by 1. The value of the argument is calculated by interpretation of an initial digit-string as a decimal number.
index	Return the position in the first argument where the second argument begins (0 origin), or `-1` if there is no second argument.
len	Return the number of characters in the argument.
m4exit	Exit from m4. Argument 1, if specified, is the exit code; the default is 0.
m4wrap	Push back argument 1 at final EOF; for example, `m4wrap('cleanup()')`.
maketemp	Fill in a string of X characters in the argument with the current process ID.
popdef	Remove current definition of the argument(s), exposing the previous one, if any.
pushdef	Like `define`, but save any previous definition.
shift	Return all but the first argument. Quote and push back the other arguments with commas in between. The quoting nullifies the effect of the extra scan that is subsequently performed.
sincludd	Identical to `include`, except say nothing if the file is inaccessible.
substr	Return a substring of the first argument. The second argument is a 0-origin number selecting the first character; the third argument specifies the length of the substring. A missing third argument is taken to be large enough to extend to the end of the first string.
syscmd	Execute the command given in the first argument. Return no value.
sysval	Return the return code from the last call to `syscmd`.
translit	Transliterate the characters in the first argument from the set given by the second argument to the set given by the third. Permit no abbreviations.
traceon	Turn on tracing for all macros (including built-ins) with no arguments. Otherwise, turn on tracing for named macros.
traceoff	Globally turn off `traceand` for any macros specified. Macros specifically traced by `traceon` can be untraced only by specific calls to `traceoff`.
undefine	Remove the definition of the macro named in the argument.
undivert	Immediately output the text from diversions named as arguments, or all diversions if you specify no argument. Text can be undiverted into another diversion. Undiverting discards the diverted text.

Examples

An example of a single `m4` input file capable of generating two output files follows. The file `file1.m4` could contain lines such as the following.

```
if(VER, 1, do_something)
if(VER, 2, do_something)
```

The makefile for the program could include the following lines.

```
file1.1.c :        file1.m4
                   m4 -D VER=1 file1.m4 > file1.1.c...
file1.2.c :        file1.m4
                   m4 -D VER=2 file1.m4 > file1.2.c
                   ...
```

You can use the `-U` option to undefine `VER`. If `file1.m4` contains the following statements,

```
if(VER, 1, do_something)
if(VER, 2, do_something)
ifndef(VER, do_something)
```

then the makefile would contain

```
file1.0.c :        file1.m4
                   m4 -U VER file1.m4 > file1.0.c
                   ...
file1.1.c :        file1.m4
                   m4 -D VER=1 file1.m4 > file1.1.c
                   ...
file1.2.c :        file1.m4
                   m4 -D VER=2 file1.m4 > file1.2.c
                   ...
```

Environment Variables

See `environ(5)` for descriptions of the following environment variables that affect the execution of m4: LC_CTYPE, LC_MESSAGES, and NLSPATH.

Exit Status

0	Successful completion.
>0	An error occurred.

If you use the `m4` `exit` macro, the exit value can be specified by the input file.

Attributes

See `attributes(5)` for descriptions of the following attributes:

/usr/ccs/bin/m4

Attribute Type	Attribute Value
Availability	SUNWcsu

/usr/xpg4/bin/m4

Attribute Type	Attribute Value
Availability	SUNWcsu

See Also

as(1), attributes(5), environ(5), xpg4(5)

---

mach — Display the Processor Type of the Current Host

Synopsis

/usr/bin/mach

Description

The mach command displays the processor type of the current host.

> **Note —** mach and uname -p return equivalent values. Independent software vendors and others who need to ascertain processor type are encouraged to use uname with the -p option instead of the mach command. The mach command is provided for compatibility with previous releases, but generally its use is discouraged.

Attributes

See attributes(5) for descriptions of the following attributes:

Attribute Type	Attribute Value
Availability	SUNWcsu

See Also

arch(1), uname(1), attributes(5)

---

machid — Get Processor Type Truth Value

Synopsis

/usr/bin/sun
/usr/bin/pdp11
/usr/bin/sparc
/usr/bin/u3b
/usr/bin/u3b2
/usr/bin/u3b5
/usr/bin/u3b15

```
/usr/bin/vax
/usr/bin/u370
```

Description

> **Note** — The machid family of commands is obsolete. Use uname -p and uname -m instead.

The following commands return a true value (exit code of 0) if you are using an instruction set that the command name indicates.

sun	true if you are on a Sun system.
pdp11	true if you are on a PDP-11/45 or PDP-11/70.
sparc	true if you are on a computer using a SPARC family processor.
u3b	true if you are on a 3B20 computer.
u3b2	true if you are on a 3B2 computer.
u3b5	true if you are on a 3B5 computer.
u3b15	true if you are on a 3B15 computer.
vax	true if you are on a VAX-11/750 or VAX11/780.
u370	true if you are on an IBM (Reg.) System/370 computer.

The commands that do not apply return a false (non-zero) value. These commands are often used within make files (see make(1S)) and shell scripts (see sh(1)) to increase portability.

Attributes

See attributes(5) for descriptions of the following attributes:

Attribute Type	Attribute Value
Availability	SUNWcsu

See Also

sh(1), test(1), true(1), uname(1), make(1S), attributes(5)

---

mail, rmail — Read Mail or Send Mail to Users

Synopsis

Sending Mail

```
/usr/bin/mail [-tw] [-m message-type] recipient...
/usr/bin/rmail [-tw] [-m message-type] recipient...
```

Reading Mail

/usr/bin/mail [-ehpPqr] [-f *file*]

Debugging

/usr/bin/mail [-x *debug-level*] [*other-mail-options*] *recipient*...

Description

A *recipient* is usually a user name recognized by login(1). When you specify
recipients, mail assumes a message is being sent. It reads from the standard input up
to an end-of-file (Control-D) or, if reading from a terminal device, until it reads a line
consisting of just a period. When either of those indicators is received, mail adds the
letter to the mail file for each recipient.

A letter is composed of some header lines followed by a blank line followed by the
message content. The header lines section of the letter consists of one or more UNIX
postmarks:

From *sender date-and-time* [remote from *remote-system-name*]

followed by one or more standardized message header lines of the form:

keyword-name: [*printable text*]

where *keyword-name* consists of any printable, non-white-space characters other than
colon (:). A Content-Length: header line indicating the number of bytes in the message
content is always present unless the letter consists of only header lines with no message
content. A Content-Type: header line that describes the type of the message content
(such as text, binary, or multipart) is also present unless the letter consists of only
header lines with no message content. Header lines can be continued on the following
line if that line starts with white space.

Options

Sending Mail

-m *message-type*

        Add a Message-Type: line to the message header with the value of
        message-type.

-t

        Add a To: line to the message header for each of the intended
        recipients.

-w

        Send a letter to a remote recipient without waiting for the completion of
        the remote transfer program.

If a letter is found to be undeliverable, it is returned to the sender with diagnostics
that indicate the location and nature of the failure. If mail is interrupted during input,
the message is saved in the file dead.letter to enable editing and resending.
dead.letter is always appended to, thus preserving any previous contents. The initial
attempt to append to (or create) dead.letter is in the current directory. If this attempt
fails, dead.letter is appended to (or created in) the user's login directory. If the second
attempt also fails, no dead.letter processing is done.

rmail permits only the sending of mail; uucp(1C) uses rmail as a security precaution. Any application programs that generate mail messages should be sure to invoke rmail instead of mail for message transport and/or delivery.

If the local system has the Basic Networking Utilities installed, you can send mail to a recipient on a remote system. There are numerous ways to address mail to recipients on remote systems, depending on the transport mechanisms available to the local system. The two most prevalent addressing schemes are domain style and UUCP style. Consult your local system administrator for details on which addressing conventions are available on the local system.

Domain-Style Addressing

For domain-style addressing, you specify remote recipients by appending an @ and domain (and possibly subdomain) information to the recipient name (such as *user*@sf.att.com).

UUCP-Style Addressing

For UUCP-style addressing, you specify remote recipients by prefixing the recipient name with the remote system name and an exclamation point, such as sysa!user. If csh(1) is the default shell, use sysa\!user. You can use a series of system names separated by exclamation points to direct a letter through an extended network (such as sysa!sysb!sysc!*user* or sysa\!sysb\!sysc\!*user*).

Reading Mail

-e	Do not print mail. Return an exit status of 0 if the user has mail; otherwise, return an exit status of 1.
-f *file*	Use *file* (such as mbox) instead of the default mail file.
-h	Initially display a window of headers instead of the latest message. The display is followed by the ? prompt.
-p	Print all messages without prompting for disposition.
-P	Print all messages with all header lines displayed instead of the default selective header line display.
-q	Terminate mail after interrupts. Normally, an interrupt terminates only the message being printed.
-r	Print messages in first-in, first-out order.

mail, unless otherwise influenced by command-line arguments, prints mail messages in last-in, first-out order. The default mode for printing messages is to display only those header lines of immediate interest. These include, but are not limited to, the UNIX From and >From postmarks, From:, Date:, Subject:, and Content-Length: header lines, and any recipient header lines such as To:, Cc:, Bcc:, and so forth. After the header lines have been displayed, mail displays the contents (body) of the message only if it contains no unprintable characters. Otherwise, mail issues a warning statement about the message having binary content and does not display the content. (You can override this feature with the p command.)

For each message, you are prompted with a ? and a line is read from the standard input. The following commands are available to determine the disposition of the message.

#	Print the number of the current message.
-	Print previous message.
newline | + | n	
	Print the next message.
! *command*	Escape to the shell to execute *command*.
a	Print message that arrived during the mail session.
d | dp	Delete the current message, and print the next message.
d *n*	Delete message number *n*. Do not go on to next message.
dq	Delete message and quit mail.
h	Display a window of headers around current message.
h *n*	Display a window of headers around message number *n*.
h a	Display headers of all messages in your mail file.
h d	Display headers of messages scheduled for deletion.
m [*persons*]	
	Mail (and delete) the current message to the named persons.
n	Print message number *n*.
p	Print current message, again overriding any indications of binary (that is, unprintable) content.
P	Override default brief mode, and print current message, again displaying all header lines.
q | Control-D	
	Put undeleted mail back in the mail file, and quit mail.
r [*users*]	Reply to the sender and other users, then delete the message.
s [*files*]	Save message in the named files (mbox is the default), and delete the message.
u [*n*]	Undelete message number *n* (default is last read).
w [*files*]	Save message content without any header lines in the named *files* (mbox is the default), and delete the message.
x	Put all mail back in the mail file unchanged, and exit mail.
y [*files*]	Same as the -w option.
?	Print a command summary.

When you log in, mail informs you if you have any mail. It also notifies you if new mail arrives while you are using mail.

You can manipulate the permissions of the mail file with chmod(1) in two ways to alter the function of mail. The permissions of the file for others can be read-write (0666), read-only (0664), or neither read nor write (0660) to permit different levels of privacy. If you change others permissions to anything besides the default (mode 0660), the file is preserved even when empty to perpetuate the desired permissions. (The administrator can override this file preservation with the DEL_EMPTY_MAILFILE option of mailcnfg.)

The group ID of the mail file must be mail to enable new messages to be delivered, and the mail file must be writable by group mail.

Debugging

The following command-line argument provides mail debugging information.

-x *debug-level*

> Create a trace file containing debugging information.

The -x option creates a file named /tmp/MLDBGprocess_id that contains debugging information relating to how mail processed the current message. The absolute value of *debug-level* controls the verboseness of the debug information. 0 implies no debugging. If *debug-level* is greater than 0, the debug file is retained only if mail encountered some problem while processing the message. If *debug-level* is less than 0 the debug file is always retained. The *debug-level* specified with -x overrides any specification of DEBUG in /etc/mail/mailcnfg. The information provided by the -x option is esoteric and is probably useful only to system administrators.

Delivery Notification

mail provides several forms of notification, including one of the following lines in the message header:

Transport-Options: [/*options*]
Default-Options: [/*options*]
>To: recipient [/*options*]

where the /*options* can be one or more of the following.

/delivery	Inform the sender that the message was successfully delivered to the recipient's mailbox.
/nodelivery	Do not inform the sender of successful deliveries.
/ignore	Do not inform the sender of failed deliveries.
/return	Inform the sender if mail delivery fails. Return the failed message to the sender.
/report	Same as /return except that the original message is not returned.

The default is /nodelivery/return. If you use contradictory options, the first is recognized and any later, conflicting, terms are ignored.

Notes

The interpretation and resulting action taken because of the header lines described in the Delivery Notification section occur only if this version of mail is installed on the system on which the delivery (or failure) happens. Earlier versions of mail may not support any types of delivery notification.

Conditions sometimes result in a failure to remove a lock file.

After an interrupt, the next message may not be printed; you can force printing by typing p.

Operands

    recipient   A user login name.

Usage

See `largefile`(5) for the description of the behavior of `mail` and `rmail` when encountering files greater than or equal to 2 Gbytes (2**31 bytes).

Environment Variables

See `environ`(5) for descriptions of the following environment variables that affect the execution of `mail`: `LC_CTYPE`, `LC_MESSAGES`, and `NLSPATH`.

    `TZ`   Determine the time zone used with date and time strings.

Exit Status

    `0`   Successful completion when the user had mail.

    `1`   The user had no mail or an initialization error occurred.

    `>1`   An error occurred after initialization.

Files

    `dead.letter` Unmailable text.

    `/etc/passwd` Used to identify sender and locate recipients.

    `$HOME/mbox` Saved mail.

    `$MAIL`   Variable containing path name of mail file.

    `/tmp/ma*`   Temporary file.

    `/tmp/MLDBG*` Debug trace file.

    `/var/mail/*.lock`

            Lock for mail directory.

    `/var/mail/:saved`

            Directory for holding temp files to prevent loss of data in the event of a system crash.

    `/var/mail/user`

            Incoming mail for user; that is, the mail file.

Attributes

See `attributes`(5) for descriptions of the following attributes:

Attribute Type	Attribute Value
Availability	SUNWcsu

See Also

`chmod`(1), `csh`(1), `login`(1), `mailx`(1), `vacation`(1), `write`(1), `uucp`(1C), `uuencode`(1C), `attributes`(5), `environ`(5), `largefile`(5)

Solaris Advanced User's Guide

mailcompat — Provide Compatibility for Solaris Mailbox

Format

/usr/bin/mailcompat

Description

The mailcompat command provides SunOS 4.x compatibility for the Solaris mailbox format. You typically run mailcompat to be able to read mail on a workstation running 4.x when your mail server is running Solaris.

Enabling mailcompat creates an entry in an existing .forward file in your home directory. If the .forward file does not exist, mailcompat creates it. Disabling mailcompat removes the entry from the .forward file and, if this was the only entry, removes the entire file.

To execute mailcompat, log in to the Solaris mail server and enter mailcompat on the command line. Answer the queries provided by the program.

Usage

See largefile(5) for the description of the behavior of mailcompat when encountering files greater than or equal to 2 Gbytes (2**31 bytes).

Examples

The following example enables the mailcompat feature and displays the contents of the .forward file.

```
castle% mailcompat
This program can be used to store your mail in a format
that you can read with SunOS 4.X based mail readers
To enable the mailcompat feature a ".forward" file is created.
Would you like to enable the mailcompat feature? y
Mailcompat feature ENABLED.Run mailcompat with no arguments to remove it
castle% more .forward
"|/usr/bin/mailcompat winsor"
castle%
```

The following example disables the mailcompat feature for user winsor.

```
castle% mailcompat
This program can be used to store your mail in a format
that you can read with SunOS 4.X based mail readers
You have a .forward file in your home directory containing:
    "|/usr/bin/mailcompat winsor"
Would you like to remove it and disable the mailcompat feature? y
Back to normal reception of mail.
castle%
```

Files

~/.forward   List of recipients for forwarding messages.

Attributes

See attributes(5) for descriptions of the following attributes:

Attribute Type	Attribute Value
Availability	SUNWcsu

See Also

mailx(1), attributes(5), largefile(5)

New! **mailp** — Front Ends to the mp Text to PDL Pretty Print Filter

Synopsis

```
/bin/mailp [options] filename...
/bin/newsp [options] filename...
/bin/digestp [options] filename...
/bin/filep [options] filename...
/bin/filofaxp [options] filename...
/bin/franklinp [options] filename...
/bin/timemanp [options] filename...
/bin/timesysp [options] filename...
```

Description

The mailp command, new in the Solaris 8 Operating Environment, is a front end to the mp(1) program. The mailp command has different names to provide various mp options, as described below.

mailp	Print mail messages.
newsp	Print USENET news articles.
digestp	Print USENET digest files.
filep	Print ordinary ASCII files.
filofaxp	Print in Filofax personal organizer format.
franklinp	Print in Franklin Planner personal organizer format.
timemanp	Print in Time Manager personal organizer format.
timesysp	Print in Time/System International personal organizer format.

mailp and the associated programs read each file name in sequence and generate a prettified version of the contents. If you provide no file-name arguments, mailp reads the standard input. mailp works in the following two ways.

- With the -D option, it acts as an X print server client to produce the PDL of the target printer and spool it.
- With the -d or -P option, it generates and spools PostScript output.

Options

-d *printer*   Send output to the named printer. Otherwise, send output to the printer named in the PRINTER environment variable.

-D   Generate the PDL for the target printer, and spool it to the printer.

-F   Instead of printing the name of the recipient of the mail article, the top header displays the name of the sender of the mail article. This option is useful for people with their own personal printer.

-h   Disable banner printing. Most of the information that typically appears on the banner sheet is output in the mp banners.

-l   Format output in landscape mode, and print two pages of text per sheet of paper.

-P *printer*   Same as the -d option. For backward compatibility, the -P option—which spools the PDL directly to the target printer in mp(1)—produces PostScript when used in mailp.

-s *subject*   Use *subject* as the new subject for the printout. When printing ordinary ASCII files that have been specified on the command line, the subject defaults to the name of each file.

Operands

filename   The name of the file to be read.

Environment Variables

If you do not specify the -d, -D, or -P option, mailp uses the PRINTER environment variable to determine the printer to receive the output from the mp(1) program. If the PRINTER variable is not found, the default destination is the PostScript printer.

Exit Status

0   Successful completion.

1   An error occurred.

Attributes

See attributes(5) for descriptions of the following attributes.

Attribute Type	Attribute Value
Availability	SUNWmp

See Also

mp(1), attributes(5)

mailq — Print the Mail Queue

Synopsis

New!

`/usr/bin/mailq [-q subarg] [-v]`

Description

`mailq` displays a summary of the mail messages queued for future delivery.

The first line displayed for each mail message shows the internal identifier used on this host for the message, the size of the message in bytes, the date and time the message was accepted into the queue, and the envelope sender of the message. The second line of the display shows the error message that retained this message in the queue. This line is not displayed if the message is being processed for the first time.

New!

The `mailq` command used to be identical to `sendmail -bp`. Starting in the Solaris 9 release, it checks for the authorization attribute, `solaris.mail.mailq`. If the check for the invoking user succeeds, `sendmail -bp` is executed with the remaining argument vector. Otherwise, an error message is printed. This authorization attribute is, by default, enabled for all users. You can disable it by modifying the Basic Solaris User entry in `prof_attr(4)`.

Options

New!

`-qp[time]`   Similar to `-qtime`, except that instead of periodically forking a child to process the queue, `sendmail` forks a single persistent child for each queue that alternates between processing the queue and sleeping. Specify the sleep time as the argument. The sleep time default is 1 second. The process always sleeps at least 5 seconds if the queue was empty in the previous queue run. New in the Solaris 9 release.

New!

`-qf`   Process saved messages in the queue once and do not `fork()` but run in the foreground. New in the Solaris 9 release.

New!

`-qG name`   Process jobs only in the queue group called *name*.

New!

`-q[!]I substr`

     Limit processed jobs to those containing *substr* as a substring of the queue ID. Specify ! to negate the *substr* argument. New in the Solaris 9 release.

New!

`-q[!]R substr`

     Limit processed jobs to those containing *substr* as a substring of one of the recipients. Specify ! to negate the *substr* argument. New in the Solaris 9 release.

New!

`-q[!]S substr`

     Limit processed jobs to those containing *substr* as a substring of the sender. Specify ! to negate the *substr* argument. New in the Solaris 9 release.

-v	Print verbose information. This option adds the priority of the message and a single character indicator (+ or blank) on the first line of the message indicating whether a warning message has been sent. Additionally, extra lines can be intermixed with the recipients indicating the "controlling user"; this information shows who owns any programs that are executed on behalf of this message and the name of the alias this command is expanded from, if any.

Exit Status

0	Successful completion.
>0	An error occurred.

Attributes

See attributes(5) for descriptions of the following attributes:

Attribute Type	Attribute Value
Availability	SUNWsndmu

See Also

sendmail(1M), prof_attr(4), attributes(5)   *New!*

mailstats — Print Statistics Collected by sendmail

Synopsis

```
/usr/bin/mailstats [-o] [-c configfile | -C configfile]
    [-f statisticsfile] [-p] [-P]
```
New!

Description

The mailstats command prints the statistics collected by the sendmail(1M) program on mailer usage. These statistics are collected if the file indicated by the StatusFile configuration option of sendmail (defined in /etc/mail/sendmail.cf) exists. The StatusFile configuration option is new in the Solaris 9 release. Starting with the Solaris 9 release, the default statistics file is /etc/mail/statistics.   *New!*

The mailstats command first prints the time that the statistics file was created and the last time it was modified. It then prints a table with statistics for each mailer displayed on a single line, each with the following whitespace-separated fields.

M	The mailer number.
msgsfr	Number of messages from the mailer.
bytes_from	Kilobytes from the mailer.
msgsto	Number of messages to the mailer.
bytes_to	Kilobytes to the mailer.

New!

msgsrej   Number of messages rejected by the mailer.

msgsdis   Number of messages discarded by the mailer.

Mailer   The name of the mailer.

New!   After this display, a line totaling the values for all of the mailers is displayed, separated from the previous information by a line containing only equal sign (=) characters.

New!   To reinitialize the statistics file once a night, add the following entry to the root crontab(1).

```
mailstats -p > /dev/null
```

Options

-c *configfile*
-C *configfile*

        Specify a sendmail configuration file. The -C option is new in the Solaris 9 release.

-f *statisticsfile*

        Specify a sendmail statistics file.

New!   -o   Don't display the name of the mailer in the output. New in the Solaris 8 release.

New!   -p   Output information in program-readable mode, and clear statistics. New in the Solaris 9 release.

New!   -P   Output information in program-readable mode without clearing statistics. New in the Solaris 9 release.

Examples

The following example shows the output for a system that uses the ESMTP and Cyrus mailers.

```
$ mailstats
Statistics from Fri Jul 20 14:23:08 2001
 M   msgsfr bytes_from   msgsto   bytes_to  msgsrej msgsdis  Mailer
 5     1501     33183K      302     10612K       57       0  esmtp
 9      290     23568K     1523     44588K        1       0  cyrus
===============================================================
 T     1791     56751K     1825     55200K       58       0
 C     1791              1825                58
Statistics from Sun Mar 14 12:16:39 1999
 M   msgsfr bytes_from   msgsto   bytes_to  msgsrej msgsdis  Mailer
 3        1         1K        0         0K        0       0  local
===============================================================
 T        1         1K        0         0K        0       0
$
```

Usage

See largefile(5) for the description of the behavior of mailstats when encountering files greater than or equal to 2 Gbytes (2**31 bytes).

Files

/dev/null   Zero-lined file.

/etc/mail/statistics

> Default sendmail statistics file. Changed from
> /etc/mail/sendmail.st in the Solaris 9 release.

/etc/mail/sendmail.cf

> Default sendmail configuration file.

Attributes

See attributes(5) for descriptions of the following attributes:

Attribute Type	Attribute Value
Availability	SUNWsndmu

See Also

crontab(1), cron(1M), sendmail(1M), attributes(5), largefile(5)

---

mailx, mail, Mail — Interactive Message Processing System

Synopsis

```
mailx [-BdeHiInNUvV~] [-f [file|+folder]] [-T file] [-u user]
mailx [-BdFintUv~] [-b bcc] [-c cc] [-h number] [-r address]
   [-s subject] recipient...
/usr/ucb/mail...
/usr/ucb/Mail...
```

Description

The mail commands listed above provide a comfortable, flexible environment for sending and receiving mail messages electronically.

When mail is being read, the mail commands facilitate saving, deleting, and responding to messages. When mail is being sent, the mail commands enable editing, reviewing, and other modification of the message as you enter it.

Incoming mail for each user is stored in a standard file, called the mailbox. When the mail commands are called to read messages, the mailbox is the default place to find them. As messages are read, they are marked to be moved to a secondary file for storage, unless specific action is taken, so that the messages need not be seen again. This secondary file is called the mbox and is normally located in the user's HOME directory. You can save messages in other secondary files with names you specify. Messages remain in a secondary file until forcibly removed.

You can access a secondary file by using the -f option. You can then read or otherwise process messages in the secondary file, using the same commands you use for the primary mailbox. When you access a secondary file with the -f option, that file is considered the current mailbox.

Options

On the command line, options start with a dash (-). Any other arguments are taken to be destinations (recipients). If you specify no recipients, mailx tries to read messages from the mailbox.

-b *bcc*	Set the blind carbon copy list to *bcc*. Enclose *bcc* in quotes if it contains more than one name.
-B	Do not buffer standard input or standard output.
-c *cc*	Set the carbon copy list to *cc*. Enclose *cc* in quotes if it contains more than one name.
-d	Turn on debugging output. (Neither particularly interesting nor recommended.)
-e	Test for the presence of mail. mailx prints nothing and exits with a successful return code if there is mail to read.
-f [*file*]	Read messages from *file* instead of mailbox. If you specify no file, use the mbox.
-f [+*folder*]	
	Use the file *folder* in the folder directory (same as the folder command). The name of this directory is listed in the *folder* variable.
-F	Record the message in a file named after the first recipient. Override the record variable if set.
-h *number*	The number of network hops made so far. This option is provided for network software to avoid infinite delivery loops. This option and its argument are passed to the delivery program.
-H	Print header summary only.
-i	Ignore interrupts.
-I	Include the newsgroup and article ID header lines when printing mail messages. This option requires that you also specify the -f option.
-n	Do not initialize from the system default mailx.rc or Mail.rc file.
-N	Do not print initial header summary.
-r *address*	Use *address* as the return address when invoking the delivery program. Disable all tilde commands. This option and its argument are passed to the delivery program.
-s *subject*	Set the Subject header field to *subject*. You must enclose *subject* in quotes if it contains embedded white space.
-t	Scan the input for To:, Cc:, and Bcc: fields. Ignore any recipients on the command line.
-T *file*	Record message ID and article ID header lines in *file* after the message is read. This option also sets the -I option.
-u *user*	Read *user*'s mailbox. This option is effective only if *user*'s mailbox is not read protected.

-U	Convert UUCP-style addresses to Internet standards. Override the `conv` environment variable.
-v	Pass the -v flag to `sendmail`(1M).
-V	Print the `mailx` version number and exit.
-~	Interpret tilde escapes in the input even if not reading from a TTY.

Operands

recipient   Addressee of message.

Usage

Starting Mail

At startup time, `mailx` executes the system startup file `/etc/mail/mailx.rc`. If invoked as `mail` or `Mail`, the system startup file `/etc/mail/Mail.rc` is used instead.

The system startup file sets up initial display options and alias lists and assigns values to some internal variables. These variables are flags and valued parameters that are set and cleared with the `set` and `unset` commands. See "Internal Variables" on page 781. If `mailx` is started with the -n option, the mail commands do not execute the system startup file.

Regular commands are legal inside startup files except for the following commands: !, Copy, edit, followup, Followup, hold, mail, preserve, reply, Reply, shell, and visual. When the startup file contains an error, the remaining lines are ignored.

After executing the system startup file, the mail commands execute the optional personal startup file `$HOME/.mailrc`, which you can use to override the values of the internal variables as set by the system startup file.

Many system administrators include the following commands in the system startup files (to be compatible with past Solaris behavior), but these commands do not meet standards requirements for `mailx`.

```
set appenddeadletter
unset replyall
unset pipeignore
```

To get standard behavior for `mailx`, either use the -n option or include the following commands in a personal startup file.

```
unset appenddeadletter
set replyall
set pipeignore
```

When mail is being read, the mail commands are in command mode. A header summary of the first several messages is displayed, followed by a prompt indicating that mail commands can accept regular commands (see "Commands" on page 771). When mail is being sent, the mail commands are in input mode. If you specify no subject on the command line and the `asksub` variable is set, you are prompted for the subject.

As you type the message, the mail commands read the message and store it in a temporary file. You can enter commands by beginning a line with the tilde (~) escape character followed by a single command letter and optional arguments. See "Tilde Escapes" on page 779 for a summary of these commands.

Reading Mail

Note — To read mail on a workstation running Solaris 1.x when your mail server is running Solaris 2.x, first execute the mailcompat(1) program.

Each message is assigned a sequential number. The current message is marked by a right angle bracket (>) in the header summary. Many commands take an optional list of messages (*message-list*) to operate on. In most cases, the current message is set to the highest-numbered message in the list after the command is finished executing.

The default for *message-list* is the current message. A *message-list* is a list of message identifiers separated by spaces, which may include the following.

n	Message number *n*.
.	The current message.
^	The first undeleted message.
$	The last message.
*	All messages.
+	The next undeleted message.
−	The previous undeleted message.
n-m	An inclusive range of message numbers.
user	All messages from *user*.
/*string*	All messages with *string* in the Subject line (case ignored).
:*c*	All messages of type *c*, where *c* is one of the following.

d	Deleted messages.
n	New messages.
o	Old messages.
r	Read messages.
u	Unread messages.

Note — The context of the command determines whether the type of message specification makes sense.

Other arguments are usually arbitrary strings whose usage depends on the command involved. File names, where expected, are expanded according to the normal shell conventions (see sh(1)). Special characters are recognized by certain commands and are documented with the commands listed in "Commands" on page 771.

Sending Mail

Recipients listed on the command line can be of three types:

- Login names.
- Shell commands.
- Alias groups.

Login names can be any network address, including mixed network addressing. If mail is found to be undeliverable, an attempt is made to return it to the sender's mailbox. If the recipient name begins with a pipe symbol (|), the rest of the name is taken to be a shell command to pipe the message through. This provides an automatic interface with any program that reads the standard input, such as lp(1), for recording outgoing mail on paper. Alias groups are set by the alias command or in a system startup file (for example, $HOME/.mailrc). Aliases are lists of recipients of any type.

Note — Full Internet addressing is not fully supported by mailx. The new standards need some time to settle down.

Replies do not always generate correct return addresses. Try resending the errant reply with onehop set.

Forwarding Mail

To forward a specific message, include it in a message to the desired recipients with the ~f or ~m tilde escapes. See "Tilde Escapes" on page 779. To forward mail automatically, add a comma-separated list of addresses for additional recipients to the .forward file in your home directory. This format is different from the format of the alias command, which takes a space-separated list instead.

Note — Forwarding addresses must be valid or the messages bounce. For example, you cannot reroute your mail to a new host by forwarding it to your new address if it is not yet listed in the NIS aliases domain.

Commands

Regular commands are of the form

```
[command] [message-list] [arguments]
```

In input mode, commands are recognized by the escape character, tilde (~), and lines not treated as commands are taken as input for the message.
    If you specify no command in command mode, next is assumed.
    The following is a complete list of mailx commands.

!*shell-command*

> Escape to the shell. Note that where *shell-command* is valid, arguments are not always allowed. Experimentation is recommended.

comment   Null command (comment). Useful in mailrc files.

=   Print the current message number.

?   Print a summary of commands.

alias *alias name*...
group *alias name*...

> Declare an alias for the given *names*. Substitute names when you use *alias* as a recipient. This command is useful in the mailrc file. With no arguments, display the list of defined aliases.

alternates *name*...

> Declare a list of alternative names for your login. When responding to a message, remove these names from the list of recipients for the response. With no arguments, print the current list of alternative names. See also allnet in "Internal Variables" on page 781.

cd [*directory*] chdir [*directory*]

> Change directory. If you specify no *directory*, use $HOME.

copy [*file*]
copy [*message-list*] *file*

> Copy messages to the file without marking the messages as saved.
> Otherwise, equivalent to the save command.

Copy [*message-list*]

> Save the specified messages in a file whose name is derived from the
> author of the message to be saved without marking the messages as
> saved. Otherwise, equivalent to the Save command.

delete [*message-list*]

> Delete messages from the mailbox. If autoprint is set, print the next
> message after the last one (see "Internal Variables" on page 781).

discard [*header-field*...]
ignore [*header-field*...]

> Suppress printing of the specified header fields when displaying
> messages on the screen. Examples of header fields to ignore are Status
> and Received. Include the fields when the message is saved unless the
> alwaysignore variable is set. The More, Page, Print, and Type
> commands override this command. If you specify no header, print the
> current list of header fields being ignored. See also the undiscard and
> unignore commands.

dp [*message-list*]
dt [*message-list*]

> Delete the specified messages from the mailbox and print the next
> message after the last one is deleted. Roughly equivalent to a delete
> command followed by a print command.

echo *string*...

> Echo the given strings. (Like echo(1).)

edit [*message-list*]

> Edit the given messages. Put each message in a temporary file, and
> invoke the program named by the EDITOR variable to edit it. Default
> editor is ed(1).

exit
xit

> Exit from mailx without changing the mailbox. Save no messages in
> the mbox (see also quit).

field [*message-list*] *header-file*

> Display the value of the header field in the specified message.

```
file [file]
folder [file]
```

> Quit from the current file of messages, and read in the specified file.
> The following special characters are recognized when used as file
> names.
>
> % is the current mailbox.
>
> %*user* is the mailbox for *user*.
>
> # is the previous mail file.
>
> & is the current mbox.
>
> +*file* is the named file in the folder directory (listed in the folder
> variable).
>
> With no arguments, print the name of the current mail file and the
> number of messages and characters it contains.

folders
> Print the names of the files in the directory set by the folder variable
> (see "Internal Variables" on page 781).

Followup [*message*]

> Respond to a message, recording the response in a file whose name is
> derived from the author of the message. Override the record variable
> if set. If the replyall variable is set, reverse the actions of Followup
> and followup. See also the followup, Save, and Copy commands,
> outfolder in "Internal Variables" on page 781, and "Starting Mail" on
> page 769.

followup [*message-list*]

> Respond to the first message in the *message-list*, sending the
> message to the author of each message in the *message-list*. Using the
> subject line from the first message, record the response in a file whose
> name is derived from the author of the first message. If the replyall
> variable is set, reverse the actions of followup and Followup. See also
> the Followup, Save, and Copy commands, outfolder in "Internal
> Variables" on page 781, and "Starting Mail" on page 769.

from [*message-list*]

> Print the header summary for the specified messages. If you specify no
> messages, print the header summary for the current message.

group *alias name*...
alias *alias name*...

> Declare an alias for the given names. The names are substituted when
> *alias* is used as a recipient. Useful in the mailrc file.

headers [*message*]

> Print the page of headers that include the message specified. The
> screen variable sets the number of headers per page (see "Internal
> Variables" on page 781). See also the z command.

help   Print a summary of commands.

hold [*message-list*]
preserve [*message-list*]

Hold the specified messages in the mailbox.

if s | r | t
mail-commands
else
mail-commands
endif

Conditional execution, where s executes following *mail-commands* up
to an else or endif if the program is in send mode. r executes the
mail-commands only in receive mode. t executes the *mail-commands*
only if mailx is being run from a terminal. Useful in the mailrc file.

ignore [*header-field*...]
discard [*header-field*...]

Suppress printing of the specified header fields when displaying
messages on the screen. Examples of header fields to ignore are Status
and Cc. Include all fields when the message is saved. The More, Page,
Print, and Type commands override this command. If you specify no
header, print the current list of header fields being ignored. See also the
undiscard and unignore commands.

inc   Incorporate messages that arrive while you are reading the system
mailbox. Add the new messages to the message list in the current mail
session. This command does not commit changes made during the
session and does not renumber prior messages.

list   Print all commands available. No explanation is given.

load [*message*] *file*

Replace the specified message by the message in the named file. *file*
should contain a single mail message including mail headers (as saved
by the save command).

mail *recipient*...

Mail a message to the specified recipients.

Mail *recipient*...

Mail a message to the specified recipients and record it in a file whose
name is derived from the author of the message. Override the record
variable if set. See also the Save and Copy commands and outfolder in
"Internal Variables" on page 781.

mbox [*message-list*]

Arrange for the given messages to end up in the standard mbox save file
when mailx terminates normally. See MBOX in "Environment Variables"
on page 785 for a description of this file. See also the exit and quit
commands.

more [*message-list*]
page [*message-list*]

> Print the specified messages. If crt is set, page through the messages
> that are longer than the number of lines specified by the crt variable,
> using the command specified by the PAGER variable. The default
> command is pg(1), or if the bsdcompat variable is set, the default is
> more(1). See "Environment Variables" on page 785. Same as the print
> and type commands.

More [*message-list*]
Page [*message-list*]

> Print the specified messages on the screen, including all header fields.
> Override suppression of fields by the ignore command. Same as the
> Print and Type commands.

new [*message-list*]
New [*message-list*]
unread [*message-list*]
Unread [*message-list*]

> Mark each message in a message list as not having been read.

next [*message*]

> Go to the next message matching *message*. If you do not supply
> *message*, find the next message that was not deleted or saved. If you
> specify a *message-list*, the first valid message in the list is the only
> one used. This command is useful for jumping to the next message from
> a specific user because, otherwise, the name would be taken as a
> command in the absence of a real command. See the discussion of
> *message-list* above for a description of possible message
> specifications.

pipe [*message-list*] [*shell-command*]
| [*message-list*] [*shell-command*]

> Pipe the message through the given *shell-command*. Treat the
> message as if it were read. If you specify no arguments, pipe the current
> message through the command specified by the value of the cmd
> variable. If the page variable is set, insert a formfeed character after
> each message (see "Internal Variables" on page 781).

preserve [*message-list*]
hold [*message-list*]

> Preserve the specified messages in the mailbox.

print [*message-list*]
type [*message-list*]

> Print the specified messages. If crt is set, page through the messages
> that are longer than the number of lines specified by the crt variable,
> using the command specified by the PAGER variable. The default
> command is pg(1), or if the bsdcompat variable is set, the default is

more(1). See "Environment Variables" on page 785. Same as the more and page commands.

Print [*message-list*]
Type [*message-list*]

Print the specified messages on the screen, including all header fields. Override suppression of fields by the ignore command. Same as the More and Page commands.

put [*file*]
put [*message-list*] *file*

Save the specified message in the given file. Use the same conventions as the print command for which header fields are ignored.

Put [*file*]
Put [*message-list*] *file*

Save the specified message in the given file. Override suppression of fields by the ignore command.

quit   Exit from mailx, storing messages that were read in mbox and unread messages in the mailbox. Delete messages that have been explicitly saved in a file unless the keepsave variable is set.

reply [*message-list*]
respond [*message-list*]
replysender [*message-list*]

Send a response to the author of each message in the *message-list*. Take the subject line from the first message. If record is set to a file, add a copy of the reply to that file. If the replyall variable is set, reverse the actions of Reply/Respond and reply/respond. The replysender command is not affected by the replyall variable but sends each reply only to the sender of each message. See "Starting Mail" on page 769.

Reply [*message*]
Respond [*message*]
replyall [*message*]

Reply to the specified message, including all other recipients of that message. If the variable record is set to a file, add a copy of the reply to that file. If the replyall variable is set, reverse the actions of Reply/Respond and reply/respond. The replyall command is not affected by the replyall variable but always sends the reply to all recipients of the message. See "Starting Mail" on page 769.

retain   Add the list of header fields named to the retained list. Show only the header fields in the retain list on your terminal when you print a message. Suppress all other header fields. Override any list of ignored fields specified by the ignore command. You can use the Type and Print commands to print a message in its entirety. If you execute retain with no arguments, it lists the current set of retained fields.

Save [*message-list*]

> Save the specified messages in a file whose name is derived from the author of the first message. The name of the file is taken to be the author's name with all network addressing stripped off. See also the Copy, followup, and Followup commands, and outfolder in "Internal Variables" on page 781.

save [*file*]
save [*message-list*] *file*

> Save the specified messages in the given file. Create the file if it does not exist. The file defaults to mbox. Delete the message from the mailbox when mailx terminates unless keepsave is set (see also "Internal Variables" on page 781 and the exit and quit commands).

set
set *variable*
set *variable=string*
set *variable=number*

> Define a variable. To assign a value to variable, separate the variable name from the value by an equal sign (=). Do not follow the equal sign with a space. You can give a null, string, or numeric value. To embed space characters within a value, enclose the value in quotes.
>
> With no arguments, set displays all defined variables and any values they might have. See "Internal Variables" on page 781 for a description of all predefined mail variables.

shell   Invoke an interactive shell. See also SHELL in "Environment Variables" on page 785.

size [*message-list*]

> Print the size in characters of the specified messages.

source *file*

> Read commands from the given file and return to command mode.

top [*message-list*]

> Print the top few lines of the specified messages. If the toplines variable is set, take it as the number of lines to print (see "Internal Variables" on page 781). The default is 5.

touch [*message-list*]

> Touch the specified messages. If any message in *message-list* is not specifically saved in a file, on normal termination, put it in the mbox or in the file specified in the MBOX environment variable. See exit and quit.

Type [*message-list*]
Print [*message-list*]

> Print the specified messages on the screen, including all header fields. Override suppression of fields by the ignore command.

type [*message-list*]
print [*message-list*]

> Print the specified messages. If crt is set, use the command specified by the PAGER variable to page through the messages that are longer than the number of lines specified by the crt variable. The default command is pg(1).

unalias [alias]...
ungroup [alias]...

> Remove the definitions of the specified aliases.

undelete [*message-list*]

> Restore the specified deleted messages. Restore only messages deleted in the current mail session. If autoprint is set, print the last message of those restored (see "Internal Variables" on page 781).

undiscard [*header-field*...]
unignore [*header-field*...]

> Remove the specified header fields from the list being ignored. If you specify no header fields, remove all header fields from the list being ignored.

unread [*message-list*]
Unread [*message-list*]

> Same as the new command.

unretain [*header-field*...]

> Remove the specified header fields from the list being retained. If you specify no header fields, remove all header fields from the list being retained.

unset variable...

> Erase the specified variables. If the variable was imported from the environment (that is, an environment variable or exported shell variable), you cannot unset it from within mailx.

version   Print the current version and release date of the mailx command.

visual [*message-list*]

> Edit the given messages with a screen editor. Put each message in a temporary file, and invoke the program named by the VISUAL variable to edit it (see "Environment Variables" on page 785). Note that the default visual editor is vi.

write [*message-list*] file

> Write the given messages on the specified file, minus the header and trailing blank line. Otherwise, equivalent to the save command.

xit   Exit from mailx, without changing the mailbox. Save no messages in
exit   the mbox (see also quit).

z[+|-]   Scroll the header display forward or backward by one full screen. The
           number of headers displayed is set by the screen variable (see "Internal
           Variables" on page 781).

Tilde Escapes

You can use the following tilde escape commands when composing mail to send. You can
enter them only from input mode by beginning a line with the tilde escape character (~).
See escape in "Internal Variables" on page 781 for information on how to change this
special character. You can enter the escape character as text by typing it twice.

~!*shell-command*

           Escape to the shell. If present, run *shell-command*.

~.   Simulate end-of-file (terminate message input).

~:*mail-command*
~_*mail-command*

           Perform the command-level request. Valid only when sending a
           message while reading mail.

~?   Print a summary of tilde escapes.

~a   Insert the autograph string sign into the message (see "Internal
           Variables" on page 781).

~A   Insert the autograph string Sign into the message (see "Internal
           Variables" on page 781).

~b *name*... Add the names to the blind carbon copy (Bcc) list. This escape is like
           the carbon copy (Cc) list, except that the names in the Bcc list are not
           shown in the header of the mail message.

~c *name*... Add the names to the carbon copy (Cc) list.

~d   Read in the dead-letter file. See DEAD in "Environment Variables" on
           page 785 for a description of this file.

~e   Invoke the editor on the partial message. See also EDITOR in
           "Environment Variables" on page 785.

~f [*message-list*]

           Forward the specified message or the current message being read.
           Valid only when sending a message while reading mail. The messages
           are inserted into the message without alteration (as opposed to ~m
           escape).

~F [*message-list*]

           Forward the specified message or the current message being read,
           including all header fields. Override the suppression of fields by the
           ignore command.

~h   Prompt for Subject line and To, Cc, and Bcc lists. If the field is
           displayed with an initial value, you can edit it as if you had just
           typed it.

~i *variable*

> Insert the value of the named *variable* into the text of the message. For example, ~A is equivalent to ~i Sign. Environment variables set and exported in the shell are also accessible with ~i.

~m [*message-list*]

> Insert the listed messages or the current message being read into the letter. Valid only when sending a message while reading mail. Shift the text of the message to the right and insert the string contained in the indentprefix variable as the leftmost characters of each line. If indentprefix is not set, insert a Tab character into each line.

~M [*message-list*]

> Insert the listed messages or the current message being read, including the header fields, into the letter. Valid only when sending a message while reading mail. Shift the text of the message to the right, and insert the string contained in the indentprefix variable as the leftmost characters of each line. If indentprefix is not set, insert a Tab character into each line. Override the suppression of fields by the ignore command.

~p   Print the message being entered.

~q   Quit from input mode by simulating an interrupt. If the body of the message is not null, save the partial message in deadletter. See DEAD in "Environment Variables" on page 785 for a description of this file.

~R   Mark message for return receipt.

~r *file* ~< *file* ~< ! *shell-command*

> Read in the specified file. If the argument begins with an exclamation point (!), interpret the rest of the string as an arbitrary shell command and execute it with the standard output inserted into the message.

~s *string*...

> Set the subject line to string.

~t *name*...   Add the given names to the To list.

~v   Invoke a preferred screen editor on the partial message. The default visual editor is vi(1). See also VISUAL in "Environment Variables" on page 785.

~w *file*   Write the message, without the header, into the specified file.

~x   Exit as with ~q, except do not save the message in deadletter.

~| *shell-command*

> Pipe the body of the message through the given *shell-command*. If the *shell-command* returns a successful exit status, replace the message with the output of the command.

Internal Variables

The following variables are internal variables. You can import them from the execution environment or set them by using the set command at any time. You can use the unset command to erase variables.

Note — You cannot unset internal variables that are imported from the execution environment.

---

allnet　　　　　Treat all network names whose last component (login name) matches as identical. The *message-list* message specifications behave similarly. Disabled by default. See also the alternates command and the metoo variable.

alwaysignore

　　　　　　　Ignore header fields with ignore everywhere, not just during print or type. Affects the save, Save, copy, Copy, top, pipe, and write commands and the ~m and ~f tilde escapes. Enabled by default.

append　　　　On termination, append messages to the end of the mbox file instead of prepending them. Although disabled by default, append is set in the system startup file (which you can suppress with the -n command-line option).

appenddeadletter

　　　　　　　Append to the deadletter file instead of overwriting it. Although disabled by default, appenddeadletter is frequently set in the system startup file. See "Starting Mail" on page 769.

askbcc　　　　Prompt for the Bcc list after you enter the Subject if it is not specified on the command line with the -b option. Disabled by default.

askcc　　　　　Prompt for the Cc list after you enter the Subject if it is not specified on the command line with the -c option. Disabled by default.

asksub　　　　Prompt for Subject if it is not specified on the command line with the -s option. Enabled by default.

autoinc　　　　Automatically incorporate new messages into the current session as they arrive. This variable has an effect similar to that of issuing the inc command every time the command prompt is displayed. Disabled by default, but autoinc is set in the default system startup file for mailx; it is not set for /usr/ucb/mail or /usr/ucb/Mail.

autoprint　　　Enable automatic printing of messages after delete and undelete commands. Disabled by default.

bang　　　　　Enable the special casing of exclamation points (!) in shell escape command lines as in vi(1). Disabled by default.

bsdcompat　　Set automatically if mailx is invoked as mail or Mail. Use /etc/mail/Mail.rc as the system startup file. Change the default pager to more(1).

cmd=*shell-command*

　　　　　　　Set the default command for the pipe command. No default value.

conv=*conversion*

> Convert uucp addresses to the specified address style, which can be either of the following values:
>
> internet: Require a mail delivery program conforming to the RFC822 standard for electronic mail addressing.
>
> optimize: Remove loops in uucp(1C) address paths (typically generated by the reply command). Perform no rerouting; mail has no knowledge of UUCP routes or connections.
>
> Conversion is disabled by default. See also sendmail(1M) and the -U command-line option.

crt[=*number*]

> Pipe messages having more than *number* lines through the command specified by the value of the PAGER variable (pg(1) or more(1) by default). If you do not specify *number*, use the current window size. Disabled by default.

debug
> Enable verbose diagnostics for debugging. Do not deliver messages. Disabled by default.

dot
> Take a period on a line by itself, or EOF during input from a terminal, as end-of-file. Disabled by default, but dot is set in the system startup file (which you can suppress with the -n command line option).

escape=*c*
> Substitute *c* for the ~ escape character. Takes effect with the next message sent.

flipr
> Reverse the effect of the followup/Followup and reply/Reply command pairs. If both flipr and replyall are set, the effect is as if neither was set.

folder=*directory*

> The directory for saving standard mail files. Expand user-specified file names beginning with a plus (+) by preceding the file name with this directory name to obtain the real file name. If *directory* does not start with a slash (/), prepend $HOME to it. There is no default for the folder variable. See also outfolder.

header
> Enable printing of the header summary when entering mailx. Enabled by default.

hold
> Preserve all messages that are read in the mailbox instead of putting them in the standard mbox save file. Disabled by default.

ignore
> Ignore interrupts while entering messages. Handy for noisy dial-up lines. Disabled by default.

ignoreeof
> Ignore end-of-file during message input. Input must be terminated by a period (.) on a line by itself or by the ~. command. See also dot above. Disabled by default.

indentprefix=*string*

> Use *string* to mark indented lines from messages included with ~m.
> The default is a Tab character.

iprompt=*string*

> Display the specified prompt string before each line on input when
> sending a message.

keep

> When the mailbox is empty, truncate it to 0 length instead of removing
> it. Disabled by default.

keepsave

> Keep messages that have been saved in other files in the mailbox
> instead of deleting them. Disabled by default.

makeremote

> When replying to all recipients of a message, if an address does not
> include a machine name, assume it to be relative to the sender of the
> message. Normally not needed when dealing with hosts that support
> RFC 822.

metoo

> If your login appears as a recipient, do not delete it from the list.
> Disabled by default.

mustbang

> Force all mail addresses to be in bang format.

onehop

> Disable alteration of the recipients' addresses, improving efficiency in a
> network where all machines can send directly to all other machines
> (that is, those that are one hop away). When responding to a message
> that was originally sent to several recipients, the other recipient
> addresses are normally forced to be relative to the originating author's
> machine for the response. Disabled by default.

outfolder

> Locate the files used to record outgoing messages in the directory
> specified by the folder variable unless the path name is absolute.
> Disabled by default. See folder and the Save, Copy, followup, and
> Followup commands.

page

> Used with the pipe command to insert a formfeed after each message
> sent through the pipe. Disabled by default.

pipeignore

> Omit ignored header when outputting to the pipe command. Although
> disabled by default, pipeignore is frequently set in the system startup
> file. See "Starting Mail" on page 769.

postmark

> Include your real name in the From line of messages you send. By
> default this value is derived from the comment field in your passwd(4)
> file entry.

prompt=*string*

> Set the command mode prompt to *string*. Default is ? unless the
> bsdcompat variable is set; then, the default is &.

quiet

> Refrain from printing the opening message and version when entering
> mailx. Disabled by default.

record=*file*

> Record all outgoing mail in *file*. Disabled by default. See also
> outfolder. Note that mailx does not lock your record file. So, if you use
> a record file and send two or more messages simultaneously, lines from
> the messages may be interleaved in the record file.

replyall

> Reverse the effect of the reply and Reply and followup and Followup
> commands. Although set by default, replyall is frequently unset in
> the system startup file. See flipr and "Starting Mail" on page 769.

save

> Enable saving of messages in deadletter on interrupt or delivery
> error. See DEAD in "Environment Variables" on page 785 for a
> description of this file. Enabled by default.

screen=*number*

> Set the number of lines in a full screen of headers for the headers
> command. *number* must be a positive number. The default is set
> according to baud rate or window size. With a baud rate less than 1200,
> *number* defaults to 5; if the baud rate is exactly 1200, it defaults to 10.
> If you are in a window, *number* defaults to the default window size
> minus 4. Otherwise, the default is 20.

sendmail=*shell-command*

> Alternative command for delivering messages. Note that, in addition to
> the expected list of recipients, mail also passes the -i and -m options to
> the command. Because these options are not appropriate for other
> commands, you may have to use a shell script that strips them from the
> arguments list before invoking the desired command. Default is
> /usr/bin/rmail.

sendwait

> Wait for background mailer to finish before returning. Disabled by
> default.

showname

> Show the sender's real name (if known) in the message header instead
> of the mail address. Disabled by default, but showname is set in the
> /etc/mail/mailx.rc system startup file for mailx.

showto

> When displaying the header summary and the message is from you,
> print the recipient's name instead of the author's name.

sign=*string*

> Insert the variable into the text of a message when the ~a (autograph)
> command is used. No default (see also ~i in "Tilde Escapes" on
> page 779).

Sign=*string*

> Insert the variable into the text of a message when the ~A command is
> used. No default (see also ~i in "Tilde Escapes" on page 779).

toplines=*number*

> Set the number of lines of header to print with the top command.
> Default is 5.

verbose	Invoke sendmail(1M) with the –v flag.
translate	Use the translate program to translate mail addresses. The program receives mail addresses as arguments. It produces, on the standard output, lines containing the following data, in this order:

- The postmark for the sender (see the postmark variable).

- Translated mail addresses, one per line, corresponding to the program's arguments. Each translated address replaces the corresponding address in the mail message being sent.

- A line containing only y or n. If the line contains y, you are asked to confirm that the message should be sent.

The translate program is invoked for each mail message to be sent. If the program exits with a non-zero exit status or fails to produce enough output, the message is not sent.

Usage

See largefile(5) for the description of the behavior of mailx when encountering files greater than or equal to 2 Gbytes (2**31 bytes).

Environment Variables

See environ(5) for descriptions of the following environment variables that affect the execution of mailx: HOME, LANG, LC_CTYPE, LC_TIME, LC_MESSAGES, NLSPATH, and TERM.

DEAD	The name of the file used to save partial letters in case of untimely interrupt. Default is $HOME/dead.letter.
EDITOR	The command to run when the edit or ~e command is used. Default is ed(1).
LISTER	The command (and options) to use when listing the contents of the folder directory. The default is ls(1).
MAIL	The name of the initial mailbox file to read (in lieu of the standard system mailbox).The default is /var/mail/*username*.
MAILRC	The name of the startup file. Default is $HOME/.mailrc.
MAILX_HEAD	Include the specified string at the beginning of the body of each message that is sent.
MAILX_TAIL	Include the specified string at the end of the body of each message that is sent.
MBOX	The name of the file in which to save messages that have been read. The exit command overrides this function, as does saving the message explicitly in another file. Default is $HOME/mbox.
PAGER	The command to use as a filter for paginating output. You can also use this variable to specify the options to be used. Default is pg(1), or if the bsdcompat variable is set, the default is more(1). See "Internal Variables" on page 781.
SHELL	The name of a preferred command interpreter. Default is sh(1).
VISUAL	The name of a preferred screen editor. Default is vi(1).

Exit Status

When you specify the -e option, the following exit values are returned:

0   Mail was found.

>0   Mail was not found or an error occurred.

Otherwise, the following exit values are returned:

0   Successful completion. Note that this status implies that all messages
             were sent, but it gives no assurances that any of them were actually
             delivered.

>0   An error occurred.

Files

$HOME/.mailrc

             Personal startup file.

$HOME/mbox   Secondary storage file.

$HOME/.Maillock

             Lock file to prevent multiple writers of system mailbox.

/etc/mail/mailx.rc

             Optional system startup file for mailx only.

/etc/mail/Mail.rc

             BSD compatibility systemwide startup file for /usr/ucb/mail and
             /usr/ucb/Mail.

/tmp/R[emqsx]*

             Temporary files.

/usr/share/lib/mailx/mailx.help*

             Help message files.

/var/mail/* Post office directory.

Attributes

See attributes(5) for descriptions of the following attributes:

Attribute Type	Attribute Value
Availability	SUNWcsu

See Also

echo(1), ed(1), ex(1), fmt(1), lp(1), ls(1), mail(1), mailcompat(1),
more(1), newaliases(1), pg(1), sh(1), vacation(1), vi(1), biff(1B),
uucp(1C), sendmail(1M), aliases(4), passwd(4), attributes(5), environ(5),
largefile(5), standards(5)

make — Maintain, Update, and Regenerate Related Programs and Files

Synopsis

```
/usr/ccs/bin/make [-d] [-dd] [-D] [-DD] [-e] [-i] [-k] [-n] [-p] [-P]
    [-q] [-r] [-s] [-S] [-t] [-V] [-f makefile]...[-K statefile]...
    [target] [macro=value]
/usr/xpg4/bin/make [-d] [-dd] [-D] [-DD] [-e] [-i] [-k] [-n] [-p] [-P]
    [-q] [-r] [-s] [-S] [-t] [-V] [-f makefile]...[target] [macro=value]
```

Description

Use the make command to reduce the compilation time for large projects. You use a *makefile* to specify a list of dependencies between source files and the target application. The make command uses *makefile* to determine the minimum recompilation needed to rebuild the application. make uses file-system modification dates to determine which files are newer than their dependents. Then, make rebuilds the modules and reconstructs the application.

The make command executes a list of shell commands associated with each *target*, typically to create or update a file of the same name. *makefile* contains entries that describe how to bring a *target* up-to-date with its dependencies. Because each dependency is a *target*, it can have dependencies of its own. Targets, dependencies, and subdependencies constitute a tree structure that make traces when deciding whether or not to rebuild a *target*.

The make command recursively checks each *target* against its dependencies, beginning with the first target entry in *makefile* if you supply no *target* argument on the command line. If, after processing all of its dependencies, a target file is either missing or older than any of its dependencies, make rebuilds it. Optionally, with this version of make, you can treat a *target* as out-of-date when the commands used to generate it have changed since the last time the target was built.

To build a given target, make executes the list of commands, called a rule. You can list this rule explicitly in the target's *makefile* entry, or it can be supplied implicitly by make.

If you specify no *target* on the command line, make uses the first target defined in *makefile*.

If a target has no *makefile* entry or if its entry has no rule, make tries to derive a rule by each of the following methods, in turn, until a suitable rule is found. Each method is described under "Reading Makefiles and the Environment" on page 789.

1. Pattern matching rules.

2. Implicit rules read in from a user-supplied *makefile*.

3. Standard implicit rules (also known as suffix rules), typically read in from the file /usr/share/lib/make/make.rules.

4. SCCS retrieval. make retrieves the most recent version from the SCCS history file (if any). See the description of the .SCCS_GET: special-function target for details.

5. The rule from the .DEFAULT: target entry if there is such an entry in the *makefile*.

6. If the target has no *makefile* entry for a target, if no rule can be derived for building it, and if no file by that name is present, make issues an error message and halts.

Options

-d	Display the reasons why make chooses to rebuild a target. Display any and all dependencies that are newer. In addition, display options read in from the MAKEFLAGS environment variable.
-dd	Display the dependency check and processing in vast detail.
-D	Display the text of the makefiles read in.
-DD	Display the text of the makefiles, make.rulesfile, the state file, and all hidden dependency reports.
-e	Specify that environment variables override assignments within makefiles.

-f *makefile*

Use the description file *makefile*. A - as the *makefile* argument denotes the standard input. The contents of *makefile*, when it is present, override the standard set of implicit rules and predefined macros. When you specify more than one -f *makefile* argument pair, use the concatenation of those files in order of appearance.

When you specify no *makefile*, /usr/ccs/bin/make tries the following in sequence, except when in POSIX mode (see the "Special-Function Targets" on page 793).

- If there is a file named *makefile* in the working directory, use that file. If an SCCS history file (SCCS/s.makefile) is newer, try to retrieve and use the most recent version.

- In the absence of the above file(s), if a file named Makefile is present in the working directory, try to use it. If an SCCS history file (SCCS/s.Makefile) is newer, try to retrieve and use the most recent version.

When you specify no *makefile*, /usr/ccs/bin/make in POSIX mode and /usr/xpg4/bin/make try the following files in sequence:

- ./makefile, ./Makefiles

- .makefile, SCCS/s.makefile

- s.Makefile, SCCS/s.Makefile

-i	Ignore error codes returned by commands. Equivalent to the special-function target .IGNORE:.
-k	When a non-zero error status is returned by a rule or when make cannot find a rule, abandon work on the current target but continue with other dependency branches that do not depend on it.

-K *statefile*

Use the state file *statefile*. A dash (-) as the *statefile* argument denotes the standard input. The contents of *statefile*, when present, override the standard set of implicit rules and predefined macros. When you specify more than one -K *statefile* argument pair, use the

concatenation of those files, in order of appearance. (See also
.KEEP_STATE and .KEEP_STATE_FILE in "Special-Function Targets" on
page 793).

-n Print commands, but do not execute them. Print lines beginning with an
@. However, if a command line contains a reference to the $(MAKE)
macro, always execute that line (see the discussion of MAKEFLAGS in
"Reading Makefiles and the Environment" on page 789). When in
POSIX mode, execute lines beginning with a plus (+).

-p Print the complete set of macro definitions and target descriptions.

-P Merely report dependencies instead of building them.

-q Return a 0 or non-zero status code depending on whether the target file
is up-to-date. When in POSIX mode, execute lines beginning with a plus
(+).

-r Do not read the default makefile /usr/share/lib/make/make.rules.

-s Do not print command lines before executing them. Equivalent to the
special function target .SILENT:.

-S Undo the effect of the -k option. Stop processing when a command
returns a non-zero exit status.

-t Touch the target files (bringing them up-to-date) instead of performing
their rules. This option can be dangerous when files are maintained by
more than one person. When the .KEEP_STATE: target appears in the
makefile, update the state file just as if the rules had been performed.
When in POSIX mode, execute lines beginning with a plus (+).

-V Put make into SysV mode. Refer to sysVmake(1) for details.

Operands

target Target names.

macro=value

Macro definition. This definition overrides any regular definition for
the specified macro within the *makefile* itself or in the
environment. However, you can still override this definition with
conditional macro assignments.

Usage

Refer to make in *Programming Utilities Guide* for tutorial information.

Reading Makefiles and the Environment

When make first starts, it reads the MAKEFLAGS environment variable to obtain any of the
following options specified present in its value: -d, -D, -e, -i, -k, -n, -p, -q, -r, -s, -S, or
-t. Because of the implementation of POSIX.2 (see POSIX.2(5), the MAKEFLAGS values

contain a leading – character. The make command then reads the command line for additional options, which also take effect.

Next, make reads in a default makefile that typically contains predefined macro definitions, target entries for implicit rules, and additional rules such as the rule for retrieving SCCS files. If present, make uses the file make.rules in the current directory; otherwise it reads the file /usr/share/lib/make/make.rules, which contains the standard definitions and rules. Use the following directive in your local make.rules file to include them.

```
include /usr/share/lib/make/make.rules
```

Next, make imports variables from the environment (unless you specify the –e option), and treats them as defined macros. Because make uses the most recent definition it encounters, a macro definition in the makefile normally overrides an environment variable of the same name. When you specify –e, however, environment variables are read in after all makefiles have been read. In that case, the environment variables take precedence over definitions in the makefile.

Next, make reads any makefiles you specify with –f or one of makefile or Makefile, as described above, and then the state file in the local directory if it exists. If the makefile contains a .KEEP_STATE_FILE: target, then make reads the state file that follows the target. Refer to special target .KEEP_STATE_FILE: for details.

Next (after reading the environment if you specify –e), make reads in any macro definitions supplied as command-line arguments. These macro definitions override macro definitions both in the makefile and the environment, but only for the make command itself.

make exports environment variables, using the most recently defined value. Macro definitions supplied on the command line are not normally exported unless the macro is also an environment variable.

make does not export macros defined in the makefile. If an environment variable is set and you define a macro with the same name on the command line, make exports its value as defined on the command line. Unless you specify –e, macro definitions within the makefile take precedence over those imported from the environment.

The macros MAKEFLAGS, MAKE, SHELL, HOST_ARCH, HOST_MACH, and TARGET_MACH are special cases. See "Special-Purpose Macros" on page 795 for details.

Makefile Target Entries

A target entry has the following format:

target... [:|::] [*dependency*]... [; *command*]... [*command*]

The first line contains the name of a target or a space-separated list of target names terminated with a colon or double colon. A list of targets is equivalent to having a separate entry of the same form for each target. The colon(s) can be followed by a dependency or a dependency list. make checks this list before building the target. You can terminate the dependency list with a semicolon (;), which in turn can be followed by a single Bourne shell command. Subsequent lines in the target entry begin with a Tab and contain Bourne shell commands. These commands constitute the rule for building the target.

You can continue shell commands across input lines by escaping the newline with a backslash (\). The continuing line must also start with a Tab.

To rebuild a target, make expands macros, strips off initial Tab characters, and either executes the command directly (if it contains no shell metacharacters) or passes each command line to a Bourne shell for execution.

The first line that does not begin with a Tab or # begins another target or macro definition.

Special Characters

This section lists global special characters and targets and dependencies.

Global

Start a comment. The comment ends at the next newline. If the # follows the Tab in a command line, pass that line to the shell (which also treats # as the start of a comment).

include *filename*

If the word include appears as the first seven letters of a line and is followed by a space or Tab, take the string that follows as a file name to interpolate at that line. You can nest include files to a depth of no more than about 16. If *filename* is a macro reference, expand it.

Targets and Dependencies

:   Target list terminator. Add words following the colon to the dependency list for the target or targets. If you name a target in more than one colon-terminated target entry, add the dependencies for all its entries to form that target's complete dependency list.

::   Target terminator for alternative dependencies. When used in place of a :, the double colon enables a target to check and update from alternative dependency lists. When the target is out-of-date with dependencies listed in the first alternative, build it according to the rule for that entry. When out-of-date with dependencies in another alternative, build it according to the rule in that other entry. Implicit rules do not apply to double-colon targets; you must supply a rule for each entry. If you specify no dependencies, the rule is always performed.

target [+ *target*...] :

Use the rule in the target entry to build all the indicated targets as a group. It is normally performed only once per make run but is checked for command dependencies every time a target in the group is encountered in the dependency scan.

%   Match any string of zero or more characters in a target name or dependency, in the target portion of a conditional macro definition, or within a pattern-replacement macro reference. (Like the * shell wild-card.) Note that a target, dependency name, or pattern-replacement macro reference can have only one %.

./pathname   Ignore the leading ./ characters from targets with names given as path names relative to dot (the working directory).

Macros

=	Macro definition. The word to the left of this character is the macro name; words to the right constitute its value. Strip leading and trailing white space characters from the value. A word break following the = is implied.
$	Macro reference. Interpret the following character or the parenthesized or bracketed string as a macro reference. Expand the reference (including the $) by replacing it with the macro's value.
( ) { }	Macro-reference name delimiters. Take a parenthesized or bracketed word appended to a $ as the name of the macro being referred to. Without the delimiters, make recognizes only the first character as the macro name.
$$	A reference to the dollar sign macro, the value of which is the character $. Used to pass variable expressions beginning with $ to the shell, to refer to environment variables that are expanded by the shell, or to delay processing of dynamic macros within the dependency list of a target until that target is actually processed.
\$	Escaped dollar sign character. Interpreted as a literal dollar sign within a rule.
+=	When used in place of =, append a string to a macro definition (must be surrounded by white space, unlike =).
:=	Conditional macro assignment. When preceded by a list of targets with explicit target entries, the macro definition that follows takes effect when processing only those targets and their dependencies.
:sh =	Define the value of a macro to be the output of a command (see "Command Substitutions" on page 808).
:sh	In a macro reference, execute the command stored in the macro and replace the reference with the output of that command (see "Command Substitutions" on page 808).

Rules

+	Always execute the commands preceded by a plus (+), even when you specify -n.
–	Ignore any non-zero error code returned by a command line for which the first non-Tab character is a dash (–). This character is not passed to the shell as part of the command line. make normally terminates when a command returns non-zero status unless you specify the -i or -k options or the .IGNORE: special-function target.
@	If the first non-Tab character is an @, do not print the command line before executing it. This character is not passed to the shell.
?	Escape command-dependency checking. Do not subject command lines starting with this character to command-dependency checking.

!   Force command dependency checking. Apply command dependency checking to command lines for which it would otherwise be suppressed. This checking is normally suppressed for lines that contain references to the ? dynamic macro (for example, $?).

When any combinations of +, -, @, ?, or ! are the first characters after the Tab, all that are present apply. None are passed to the shell.

Special-Function Targets

When incorporated in a makefile, the following target names perform special functions.

.DEFAULT: If it has an entry in the makefile, use the rule for this target to process a target when there is no other entry for it, no rule for building it, and no SCCS history file from which to retrieve a current version. make ignores any dependencies for this target.

.DONE: If defined in the makefile, process this target and its dependencies after all other targets are built. This target is also performed when make halts with an error unless the .FAILED: target is defined.

.FAILED: Perform this target along with its dependencies instead of .DONE: when defined in the makefile and halt with an error.

.GET_POSIX: Retrieve the current version of an SCCS file from its history file in the current working directory. Use this rule when running in POSIX mode.

.IGNORE: Ignore errors. When this target appears in the makefile, ignore non-zero error codes returned from commands. When used in POSIX mode, .IGNORE: can be followed only by target names for which the errors are ignored.

.INIT: If defined in the makefile, build this target and its dependencies before processing any other targets.

.KEEP_STATE:

                This target has no effect if used in POSIX mode. If this target is in effect, update the .make.state state file in the current directory. Also activate command dependencies and hidden dependency checks. If either the .KEEP_STATE: target is in the makefile or the environment variable KEEP_STATE is set ("setenv KEEP_STATE"), rebuild everything to collect dependency information even if all the targets were up-to-date because of previous make runs. See also "Environment Variables" on page 809.

.KEEP_STATE_FILE:

                This target has no effect if used in POSIX mode. This target implies .KEEP_STATE:. If the target is followed by a file name, use it as the state file. If the target is followed by a directory name, look for a .make.state file in that directory. If the target is not followed by any name, look for a .make.state file in the current working directory.

.MAKE_VERSION:

                A target-entry of the form

.MAKE_VERSION: VERSION-*number*

enables version checking. If the version of make differs from the version indicated, make issues a warning message.

.NO_PARALLEL:

Reserved for future use.

.PARALLEL: Reserved for future use.

.POSIX: Enable POSIX mode.

.PRECIOUS: Specify a list of files not to delete. Do not remove any of the files listed as dependencies for this target when interrupted. make normally removes the current target when it receives an interrupt. When used in POSIX mode, if the target is not followed by a list of files, assume all the files are precious.

.SCCS_GET: Contain the rule for retrieving the current version of an SCCS file from its history file. To suppress automatic retrieval, add an entry for this target with an empty rule to your makefile.

.SCCS_GET_POSIX:

Contain the rule for retrieving the current version of an SCCS file from its history file. make uses this rule when it is running in POSIX mode.

.SILENT: Run silently. Do not echo commands before executing them. When used in POSIX mode, it could be followed by target names, and only those are executed silently.

.SUFFIXES: Specify the suffixes list for selecting implicit rules.

.WAIT: Reserved for future use.

Clearing Special Targets

In this version of make, you can clear the definition of the following special targets by supplying entries for them with no dependencies and no rule. .DEFAULT:, .SCCS_GET:, and .SUFFIXES:.

Command Dependencies

When the .KEEP_STATE: target is in effect, make checks the command for building a target against the state file. If the command has changed since the last make run, make rebuilds the target.

Hidden Dependencies

When the .KEEP_STATE: target is in effect, make reads reports from cpp(1) and other compilation processors for any "hidden: files, such as #include files. If the target is out-of-date with any of these files, make rebuilds it.

Macros

Entries of the following form define macros.

```
macro=value
```

macro is the name of the macro, and *value*, which consists of all characters up to a comment character or unescaped newline, is the value. make strips both leading and trailing white space in accepting the value.

Subsequent references to the macro, of the forms $(name) or ${name} are replaced by *value*. You can omit the parentheses or brackets in a reference to a macro with a single-character name.

Macro references can contain references to other macros, in which case nested references are expanded first.

Suffix Replacement Macro References

Substitutions within macros can be made as follows,

```
$(name:string1=string2)
```

where *string1* is either a suffix or a word to be replaced in the macro definition and *string2* is the replacement suffix or word. Words in a macro value are separated by space, Tab, and escaped newline characters.

Pattern-Replacement Macro References

Pattern-matching replacements can also be applied to macros, with a reference of the following form,

```
$(name: op%os= np%ns)
```

where *op* is the existing (old) prefix, and *os* is the existing (old) suffix, *np* and *ns* are the new prefix and new suffix, and the pattern matched by % (a string of zero or more characters) is carried forward from the value being replaced. For example, the following statements set the value of DEBUG to tmp/fabricate-g.

```
PROGRAM=fabricate
DEBUG= $(PROGRAM:%=tmp/%-g)
```

Note — You cannot use pattern-replacement macro references in the dependency list of a pattern-matching rule; the % characters are not evaluated independently. Also, any number of % metacharacters can appear after the equal sign.

Appending to a Macro

You can append words to macro values as shown below.

```
macro += word...
```

Special-Purpose Macros

When the MAKEFLAGS variable is present in the environment, make takes options from it in combination with options entered on the command line. make retains this combined value as the MAKEFLAGS macro and exports it automatically to each command or shell it invokes.

Flags passed by way of MAKEFLAGS are only displayed when you use the -d or -dd options.

The MAKE macro is another special case. It has the value make by default and temporarily overrides the -n option for any line in which it is referred to. The following

syntax enables you to write nested invocations of make to run recursively with the -n
flag in effect for all commands but make.

```
$ (MAKE) ...
```

You can use make -n to test an entire hierarchy of makefiles.

For compatibility with the 4.2 BSD make, the MFLAGS macro is set from the MAKEFLAGS
variable by prepending a -. MFLAGS is not automatically exported.

The SHELL macro, when set to a single-word value such as /usr/bin/csh, indicates
the name of an alternative shell to use. The default is /bin/sh. Note that make executes
commands that contain no shell metacharacters. Built-in commands, such as dirs in
the C shell, are not recognized unless the command line includes a metacharacter (for
instance, a semicolon). This macro is neither imported from, nor exported to, the
environment, regardless of -e. To be sure it is set properly, you must define this macro
within every makefile that requires it.

The following macros are provided for use with cross-compilation.

HOST_ARCH
The machine architecture of the host system. By default, the output of
the arch(1) command prepended with -. In normal circumstances, you
should never alter this value.

HOST_MACH
The machine architecture of the host system. By default, the output of
the mach(1), prepended with -. In normal circumstances, you should
never alter this value.

TARGET_ARCH

The machine architecture of the target system. By default, the output of
mach, prepended with -.

Dynamic Macros

Several dynamically maintained macros are useful as abbreviations within rules. They
are shown here as references. If you define them, make simply overrides the definition.

$*
The basename of the current target, derived as if selected for use with
an implicit rule.

$<
The name of a dependency file, derived as if selected for use with an
implicit rule.

$@
The name of the current target. This macro is the only one whose value
is strictly determined when used in a dependency list (in which case, it
takes the form $$@).

$?
The list of dependencies that are newer than the target. Command
dependency checking is automatically suppressed for lines that contain
this macro just as if you had prefixed the command with a ?. See the
description of ?. You can force this check with the ! command-line
prefix.

$%
The name of the library member being processed. (See "Library
Maintenance" on page 807.)

To refer to the $@ dynamic macro within a dependency list, precede the reference with an
additional $ character (as in, $$@). Because make assigns $< and $* as it would for
implicit rules (according to the suffixes list and the directory contents), they may be
unreliable when used within explicit target entries.

You can modify these macros to apply either to the file-name part (F) or the directory part (D) of the strings they stand for, by adding an uppercase F or D and enclosing the resulting name in parentheses or braces. Thus, $(@D) refers to the directory part of the string $@; if there is no directory part, . is assigned. $(@F) refers to the file-name part.

Conditional Macro Definitions

A macro definition of the following form indicates that when processing any of the targets listed and their dependencies, *macro* is to be set to the value supplied.

```
target-list := macro = value
```

Note — If a conditional macro is referred to in a dependency list, the $ must be delayed (use $$ instead). Also, *target-list* can contain a % pattern, in which case the macro is conditionally defined for all targets encountered that match the pattern. You can use a pattern-replacement reference within the value.

You can temporarily append to a macro's value with a conditional definition of the following form.

```
target-list := macro += value
```

Predefined Macros

make supplies the macros shown in the following table for compilers and their options, host architectures, and other commands. Unless these macros are read in as environment variables, their values are not exported by make. If you run make with any of these macros set in the environment, it is a good idea to add commentary to the makefile to indicate what value each is expected to take. If you use the -r option, make does not read the default makefile (./make.rules or /usr/share/lib/make/make.rules) in which these macro definitions are supplied.

The following table lists the predefined macros and shows their default values.

Table of Predefined Macros

Use	Macro	Default Value
Library archives	AR	ar
	ARFLAGS	rv
Assembler commands	AS	as
	ASFLAGS	$(AS) $(ASFLAGS)
	COMPILE.s	$(CC) $(ASFLAGS) $(CPPFLAGS) -c
	COMPILE.S	
C compiler commands	CC	cc
	CFLAGS	
	CPPFLAGS	$(CC) $(CFLAGS) $(CPPFLAGS) -c
	COMPILE.c	$(CC) $(CFLAGS) $(CPPFLAGS) $(LDFLAGS)
	LINK.c	

Use	Macro	Default Value
C++ compiler commands	CCC	CC
	CCFLAGS	CFLAGS
	CPPFLAGS	$(CCC) $(CCFLAGS) $(CPPFLAGS) -c
	COMPILE.cc	$(CCC) $(CCFLAGS) $(CPPFLAGS) $(LDFLAGS)
	LINK.cc	$(CCC) $(CCFLAGS) $(CPPFLAGS) -c
	COMPILE.C	$(CCC) $(CCFLAGS) $(CPPFLAGS) $(LDFLAGS)
	LINK.C	
FORTRAN 77 compiler commands	FC	f77
	FFLAGS	$(FC) $(FFLAGS) -c
	COMPILE.f	$(FC) $(FFLAGS) $(LDFLAGS)
	LINK.f	$(FC) $(FFLAGS) $(CPPFLAGS) -c
	COMPILE.F	$(FC) $(FFLAGS) $(CPPFLAGS) $(LDFLAGS)
	LINK.F	
FORTRAN 90 compiler commands	FC	f90
	F90FLAGS	$(F90C) $(F90FLAGS) -c
	COMPILE.f90	$(F90C)
	LINK.f90	$(F90C) $(F90FLAGS) $(CPPFLAGS) -c
	COMPILE.ftn	$(F90C) $(F90FLAGS) $(CPPFLAGS)
	LINK.ftn	$(LDFLAGS)
lex command	LEX	lex
	LFLAGS	$(LEX) $(LFLAGS) -t
	LEX.l	
Link editor command	LD	ld
	LDFLAGS	
lint command	LINT	lint
	LINTFLAGS	$(LINT) $(LINTFLAGS) $(CPPFLAGS)
	LINT.c	
Modula 2 commands	M2C	m2c
	M2FLAGS	
	MODFLAGS	$(M2C) $(M2FLAGS) $(DEFFLAGS)
	DEFFLAGS	$(M2C) $(M2FLAGS) $(MODFLAGS)
	COMPILE.def	
	COMPILE.mod	
Pascal compiler commands	PC	pc
	PFLAGS	$(PC) $(PFLAGS) $(CPPFLAGS) -c
	COMPILE.p	$(PC) $(PFLAGS) $(CPPFLAGS) $(LDFLAGS)
	LINK.p	
Ratfor compilation commands	RFLAGS	
	COMPILE.r	$(FC) $(FFLAGS) $(RFLAGS) -c
	LINK.r	$(FC) $(FFLAGS) $(RFLAGS) $(LDFLAGS)
rm command	RM	rm -f

Use	Macro	Default Value
sccs command	SCCSFLAGS	
	SCCSGETFLAGS	-s
yacc command	YACC	yacc
	YFLAGS	$(YACC) $(YFLAGS)
	YACC.y	
Suffixes list	SUFFIXES	.o .c .c~ .cc .cc~ .y .y~ .l .l~ .s .s~
		.sh .sh~ .S .S~ .ln .h .h~ ..f .f~ .F
		.F~ .mod .mod~ .sym .def .def~ .p .p~ .r
		.r~ .cps .cps~ .C .C~ .Y .Y~ .L .L .f90
		.f90~ .ftn .ftn~

Implicit Rules

When a target has no entry in the makefile, make tries to determine its class (if any) and apply the rule for that class. An implicit rule describes how to build any target of a given class from an associated dependency file. The class of a target determines, either by a pattern or by a suffix, the corresponding dependency file (with the same basename) from which such a target might be built. In addition to a predefined set of implicit rules, make enables you to define your own rules, either by pattern or by suffix.

Pattern-Matching Rules

A target entry of the following form is a pattern-matching rule where tp is a target prefix, ts is a target suffix, dp is a dependency prefix, and ds is a dependency suffix (any of which can be null).

tp%ts: *dp%ds*   *rule*

The % stands for a basename of zero or more characters that is matched in the target and is used to construct the name of a dependency. When make encounters a match in its search for an implicit rule, it uses the rule in that target entry to build the target from the dependency file. Pattern-matching implicit rules typically make use of the $@ and $< dynamic macros as placeholders for the target and dependency names. Other, regular dependencies can occur in the dependency list; however, none of the regular dependencies can contain %. An entry of the following form is a valid pattern-matching rule.

tp%ts: [*dependency...*] *dp%ds* [*dependency...*] *rule*

Suffix Rules

When no pattern-matching rule applies, make checks the target name to see if it ends with a suffix in the known suffixes list. If so, make checks for any suffix rules, as well as a dependency file with the same root and another recognized suffix, from which to build it.

The target entry for a suffix rule takes the following form:

DsTs: *rule*

where Ds is the suffix of the dependency file, Ts is the suffix of the target, and *rule* is the rule for building a target in the class. Both Ds and Ts must appear in the suffixes list. (A suffix need not begin with a . to be recognized.)

A suffix rule with only one suffix describes how to build a target having a null (or no) suffix from a dependency file with the indicated suffix. For instance, you could use the .c rule to build an executable program named *file* from a C source file named *file*.c. If a target with a null suffix has an explicit dependency, make omits the search for a suffix rule.

The following table lists the standard implicit (suffix) rules.

Use	Implicit Rule Name	Command Line
Assembly files	.s.o	$(COMPILE.s) -o $@ $<
	.s.a	$(COMPILE.s) -o $% $<
		$(AR) $(ARFLAGS) $@ $%
		$(RM) $%
	.s~.o	$(-s1GET) $(-s1GFLAGS) -p $< > $*.s
		$(-s1COMPILE.s) -o $@ $*.s
	.S.o	$(COMPILE.S) -o $@ $<
	.S.a	$(COMPILE.S) -o $% $<
		$(AR) $(ARFLAGS) $@ $%
		$(RM) $%
	.S~.o	$(GET) $(GFLAGS) -p $< > $*.S
		$(COMPILE.S) -o $@ $*.S
	.S~.a	$(GET) $(GFLAGS) -p $< > $*.S
		$(COMPILE.S) -o $% $*.S
		$(AR) $(ARFLAGS) $@ $%
		$(RM) $%
C files	.c	$(LINK.c) -o $@ $< $(LDLIBS)
	.c.ln	$(LINT.c) $(OUTPUT_OPTION) -i $<
	.c.o	$(COMPILE.c) $(OUTPUT_OPTION) $<
	.c.a	$(COMPILE.c) -o $% $<
		$(AR) $(ARFLAGS) $@ $%
		$(RM) $%
	..c~	$(GET) $(GFLAGS) -p $< > $*.c
		$(CC) $(CFLAGS) $(LDFLAGS) -o $@ $*.c
	..c~.o	$(GET) $(GFLAGS) -p $< > $*.c
		$(CC) $(CFLAGS) -c $*.c
	..c~.ln	$(GET) $(GFLAGS) -p $< > $*.c
		$(LINT.c) $(OUTPUT_OPTION) -c $*.c
	..c~.a	$(GET) $(GFLAGS) -p $< > $*.c

Use	Implicit Rule Name	Command Line
		`$(COMPILE.c) -o $% $*.c`
		`$(AR) $(ARFLAGS) $@ $%`
		`$(RM) $%`
C++ files	.cc	`$(LINK.cc) -o $@ $< $(LDLIBS)`
	.cc.o	`$(COMPILE.cc) $(OUTPUT_OPTION) $<`
	.cc.a	`$(COMPILE.cc) -o $% $<`
		`$(AR) $(ARFLAGS) $@ $%`
		`$(RM) $%`
	.cc~	`$(GET) $(GFLAGS) -p $< > $*.cc`
		`$(LINK.cc) -o $@ $*.cc $(LDLIBS)`
	.cc.o	`$(COMPILE.cc) $(OUTPUT_OPTION) $<`
	.cc~.o	`$(GET) $(GFLAGS) -p $< > $*.cc`
		`$(COMPILE.cc) $(OUTPUT_OPTION) $*.cc`
	.cc.a	`$(COMPILE.cc) -o $% $<`
		`$(AR) $(ARFLAGS) $@ $%`
		`$(RM) $%`
	.cc~.a	`$(GET) $(GFLAGS) -p $< > $*.cc`
		`$(COMPILE.cc) -o $% $*.cc`
		`$(AR) $(ARFLAGS) $@ $%`
		`$(RM) $%`
	.C	`$(LINK.C) -o $@ $< $(LDLIBS)`
	.C~	`$(GET) $(GFLAGS) -p $< > $*.C`
		`$(LINK.C) -o $@ $*.C $(LDLIBS)`
	.C.o	`$(COMPILE.C) $(OUTPUT_OPTION) $<`
	.C~.o	`$(GET) $(GFLAGS) -p $< > $*.C`
		`$(COMPILE.C) $(OUTPUT_OPTION) $*.C`
	.C.a	`$(COMPILE.C) -o $% $<`
		`$(AR) $(ARFLAGS) $@ $%`
		`$(RM) $%`
	.C~.a	`$(GET) $(GFLAGS) -p $< > $*.C`
		`$(COMPILE.C) -o $% $*.C`
		`$(AR) $(ARFLAGS) $@ $%`
		`$(RM) $%`

Use	Implicit Rule Name	Command Line
FORTRAN 77 files	.f	`$(LINK.f) -o $@ $< $(LDLIBS)`
	.f.o	`$(COMPILE.f) $(OUTPUT_OPTION) $<`
	.f.a	`$(COMPILE.f) -o $% $<`
		`$(AR) $(ARFLAGS) $@ $%`
		`$(RM) $%`
	.f	`$(LINK.f) -o $@ $< $(LDLIBS)`
	.f~	`$(GET) $(GFLAGS) -p $< > $*.f`
		`$(FC) $(FFLAGS) $(LDFLAGS) -o $@ $*.f`
	.f~.o	`$(GET) $(GFLAGS) -p $< > $*.f`
		`$(FC) $(FFLAGS) -c $*.f`
	.f~.a	`$(GET) $(GFLAGS) -p $< > $*.f`
		`$(COMPILE.f) -o $% $*.f`
		`$(AR) $(ARFLAGS) $@ $%`
		`$(RM) $%`
	.F	`$(LINK.F) -o $@ $< $(LDLIBS)`
	.F.o	`$(COMPILE.F) $(OUTPUT_OPTION) $<`
	.F.a	`$(COMPILE.F) -o $% $<`
		`$(AR) $(ARFLAGS) $@ $%`
		`$(RM) $%`
	.F~	`$(GET) $(GFLAGS) -p $< > $*.F`
		`$(FC) $(FFLAGS) $(LDFLAGS) -o $@ $*.F`
	.F~.o	`$(GET) $(GFLAGS) -p $< > $*.F`
		`$(FC) $(FFLAGS) -c $*.F`
	.F~.a	`$(GET) $(GFLAGS) -p $< > $*.F`
		`$(COMPILE.F) -o $% $*.F`
		`$(AR) $(ARFLAGS) $@ $%`
		`$(RM) $%`
FORTRAN 90 files	.f90	`$(LINK.f90) -o $@ $< $(LDLIBS)`
	.f90~	`$(GET) $(GFLAGS) -p $< > $*.f90`
		`$(LINK.f90) -o $@ $*.f90 $(LDLIBS)`
	.f90.o	`$(COMPILE.f90) $(OUTPUT_OPTION) $<`
	.f90~.o	`$(GET) $(GFLAGS) -p $< > $*.f90`

Use	Implicit Rule Name	Command Line
		`$(COMPILE.f90) $(OUTPUT_OPTION) $*.f90`
	.f90.a	`$(COMPILE.f90) -o $% $<`
		`$(AR) $(ARFLAGS) $@ $%`
		`$(RM) $%`
	.f90~.a	`$(GET) $(GFLAGS) -p $< > $*.f90`
		`$(COMPILE.f90) -o $% $*.f90`
		`$(AR) $(ARFLAGS) $@ $%`
		`$(RM) $%`
	.ftn	`$(LINK.ftn) -o $@ $< $(LDLIBS)`
	.ftn~	`$(GET) $(GFLAGS) -p $< > $*.ftn`
		`$(LINK.ftn) -o $@ $*.ftn $(LDLIBS)`
	.ftn.o	`$(COMPILE.ftn) $(OUTPUT_OPTION) $<`
	.ftn~.o	`$(GET) $(GFLAGS) -p $< > $*.ftn`
		`$(COMPILE.ftn) $(OUTPUT_OPTION) $*.ftn`
	.ftn.a	`$(COMPILE.ftn) -o $% $<`
		`$(AR) $(ARFLAGS) $@ $%`
		`$(RM) $%`
	.ftn~.a	`$(GET) $(GFLAGS) -p $< > $*.ftn`
		`$(COMPILE.ftn) -o $% $*.ftn`
		`$(AR) $(ARFLAGS) $@ $%`
		`$(RM) $%`
lex files	.l	`$(RM) $*.c`
		`$(LEX.l) $< > $*.c`
		`$(LINK.c) -o $@ $*.c $(LDLIBS)`
		`$(RM) $*.c`
	.l.c	`$(RM) $@`
		`$(LEX.l) $< > $@`
	.l.ln	`$(RM) $*.c`
		`$(LEX.l) $< > $*.c`
		`$(LINT.c) -o $@ -i $*.c`
		`$(RM) $*.c`
	.l.o	`$(RM) $*.c`
		`$(LEX.l) $< > $*.c`

Use	Implicit Rule Name	Command Line
		`$(COMPILE.c) -o $@ $*.c`
		`$(RM) $*.c`
	.l~	`$(GET) $(GFLAGS) -p $< > $*.l`
		`$(LEX) $(LFLAGS) $*.l`
		`$(CC) $(CFLAGS) -c lex.yy.c`
		`rm -f lex.yy.c`
		`mv lex.yy.c $@`
	.l~.c	`$(GET) $(GFLAGS) -p $< > $*.l`
		`$(LEX) $(LFLAGS) $*.l`
		`mv lex.yy.c $@`
	.l~.ln	`$(GET) $(GFLAGS) -p $< > $*.l`
		`$(RM) $*.c`
		`$(LEX.l) $*.l > $*.c`
		`$(LINT.c) -o $@ -i $*.c`
		`$(RM) $*.c`
	.l~.o	`$(GET) $(GFLAGS) -p $< > $*.l`
		`$(LEX) $(LFLAGS) $*.l`
		`$(CC) $(CFLAGS) -c lex.yy.c`
		`rm -f lex.yy.c`
		`mv lex.yy.c $@`
Modula 2 files	.mod	`$(COMPILE.mod) -o $@ -e $@ $<`
	.mod.o	`$(COMPILE.mod) -o $@ $<`
	.def.sym	`$(COMPILE.def) -o $@ $<`
	.def~.sym	`$(GET) $(GFLAGS) -p $< > $*.def`
		`$(COMPILE.def) -o $@ $*.def`
	.mod~	`$(GET) $(GFLAGS) -p $< > $*.mod`
		`$(COMPILE.mod) -o $@ -e $@ $*.mod`
	.mod~.o	`$(GET) $(GFLAGS) -p $< > $*.mod`
		`$(COMPILE.mod) -o $@ $*.mod`
	.mod~.a	`$(GET) $(GFLAGS) -p $< > $*.mod`
		`$(COMPILE.mod) -o $% $*.mod`
		`$(AR) $(ARFLAGS) $@ $%`

Use	Implicit Rule Name	Command Line
		`$(RM) $%`
NeWS files	`.cps.h`	`cps $*.cps`
	`.cps~.h`	`$(GET) $(GFLAGS) -p $< > $*.cps`
		`$(CPS) $(CPSFLAGS) $*.cps`
Pascal files	`.p`	`$(LINK.p) -o $@ $< $(LDLIBS)`
	`.p.o`	`$(COMPILE.p) $(OUTPUT_OPTION) $<`
	`.p~`	`$(GET) $(GFLAGS) -p $< > $*.p`
		`$(LINK.p) -o $@ $*.p $(LDLIBS)`
	`.p~.o`	`$(GET) $(GFLAGS) -p $< > $*.p`
		`$(COMPILE.p) $(OUTPUT_OPTION) $*.p`
	`.p~.a`	`$(GET) $(GFLAGS) -p $< > $*.p`
		`$(COMPILE.p) -o $% $*.p`
		`$(AR) $(ARFLAGS) $@ $%`
		`$(RM) $%`
Ratfor files	`.r`	`$(LINK.r) -o $@ $< $(LDLIBS)`
	`.r.o`	`$(COMPILE.r) $(OUTPUT_OPTION) $<`
	`.r.a`	`$(COMPILE.r) -o $% $<`
		`$(AR) $(ARFLAGS) $@ $%`
		`$(RM) $%`
	`.r~`	`$(GET) $(GFLAGS) -p $< > $*.r`
		`$(LINK.r) -o $@ $*.r $(LDLIBS)`
	`.r~.o`	`$(GET) $(GFLAGS) -p $< > $*.r`
		`$(COMPILE.r) $(OUTPUT_OPTION) $*.r`
	`.r~.a`	`$(GET) $(GFLAGS) -p $< > $*.r`
		`$(COMPILE.r) -o $% $*.r`
		`$(AR) $(ARFLAGS) $@ $%`
		`$(RM) $%`
SCCS files	`.SCCS_GET`	`sccs $(SCCSFLAGS) get $(SCCSGETFLAGS) $@ -G$@`
	`.SCCS_GET_POSIX`	`sccs $(SCCSFLAGS) get $(SCCSGETFLAGS) $@`
	`.GET_POSIX`	`$(GET) $(GFLAGS) s.$@`
Shell scripts	`.sh`	`cat $< >$@`
		`chmod +x $@`
	`.sh~`	`$(GET) $(GFLAGS) -p $< > $*.sh`

Use	Implicit Rule Name	Command Line
		cp $*.sh $@
		chmod a+x $@
yacc files	.y	$(YACC.y) $<
		$(LINK.c) -o $@ y.tab.c $(LDLIBS)
		$(RM) y.tab.c
	.y.c	$(YACC.y) $<
		mv y.tab.c $@
	.y.ln	$(YACC.y) $<
		$(LINT.c) -o $@ -i y.tab.c
		$(RM) y.tab.c
	.y.o	$(YACC.y) $<
		$(COMPILE.c) -o $@ y.tab.c
		$(RM) y.tab.c
	.y~	$(GET) $(GFLAGS) -p $< > $*.y
		$(YACC) $(YFLAGS) $*.y
		$(COMPILE.c) -o $@ y.tab.c
		$(RM) y.tab.c
	.y~.c	$(GET) $(GFLAGS) -p $< > $*.y
		$(YACC) $(YFLAGS) $*.y
		mv y.tab.c $@
	.y~.ln	$(GET) $(GFLAGS) -p $< > $*.y
		$(YACC.y) $*.y
		$(LINT.c) -o $@ -i y.tab.c
		$(RM) y.tab.c
	.y~.o	$(GET) $(GFLAGS) -p $< > $*.y
		$(YACC) $(YFLAGS) $*.y
		$(CC) $(CFLAGS) -c y.tab.c
		rm -f y.tab.c
		mv y.tab.o $@

make reads in the standard set of implicit rules from the file
/usr/share/lib/make/make.rules unless -r is in effect or there is a make.rules file
in the local directory that does not include that file.

The Suffixes List

The suffixes list is given as the list of dependencies for the .SUFFIXES: special-function target. The default list is contained in the SUFFIXES macro (see "Table of Predefined Macros" on page 797 for the standard list of suffixes). You can define additional .SUFFIXES: targets; a .SUFFIXES: target with no dependencies clears the list of suffixes. Order is significant within the list; make selects a rule that corresponds to the target's suffix and the first dependency-file suffix found in the list. To put suffixes at the head of the list, clear the list and replace it with the new suffixes followed by the default list, as shown below.

```
.SUFFIXES:
.SUFFIXES: suffixes $(SUFFIXES)
```

A tilde (~) indicates that if a dependency file with the indicated suffix (minus the ~) is under SCCS, its most recent version should be retrieved, if necessary, before the target is processed.

Library Maintenance

A target name of the following form refers to a member or a space-separated list of members in an ar(1) library.

```
lib(member...)
```

You must give the dependency of the library member on the corresponding file as an explicit entry in the makefile. This entry can be handled with a pattern-matching rule of the following form:

```
lib(%.s): %.s
```

where .s is the suffix of the member; this suffix is typically .o for object libraries.

A target name of the following form refers to the member of a randomized object library that defines the entry point named symbol.

```
lib((symbol))
```

Command Execution

Command lines are executed one at a time, each by its own process or shell. Shell commands, notably cd, are ineffectual across an unescaped newline in the makefile. A line is printed (after macro expansion) just before being executed. This printing is suppressed if the line starts with a @, if there is a .SILENT: entry in the makefile, or if you run make with the -s option. Although the -n option specifies printing without execution, lines containing the macro $(MAKE) are executed regardless, and lines containing the @ special character are printed. The -t (touch) option updates the modification date of a file without executing any rules. This behavior can be dangerous when sources are maintained by more than one person.

make invokes the shell with the -e (exit-on-errors) argument. Thus, with semicolon-separated command sequences, execution of the later commands depends on the success of the former. This behavior can be overridden by starting the command line with a - or by writing a shell script that returns a non-zero status only as appropriate.

Bourne Shell Constructs

To use the Bourne shell if control structure for branching, use a command line of the following form.

```
if expression ; \
    then command ; \
        ... ; \
    else command ; \
        ... ; \
    fi
```

Although composed of several input lines, the escaped newline characters ensure that make treats them all as one (shell) command line.

To use the Bourne shell for control structure for loops, use a command line of the following form.

```
for var in list ; \
  do command; \
    ... ; \
  done
```

To refer to a shell variable, use a double dollar sign ($$). This syntax prevents expansion of the dollar sign by make.

Command Substitutions

To incorporate the standard output of a shell command in a macro, use a definition of the following form.

MACRO:sh =*command*

The *command* is executed only once, standard error output is discarded, and newline characters are replaced with spaces. If the command has a non-zero exit status, make halts with an error.

To capture the output of a shell command in a macro reference, use a reference of the following form:

$(*MACRO*:sh)

where *MACRO* is the name of a macro containing a valid Bourne shell command line. In this case, the command is executed whenever the reference is evaluated. As with shell command substitutions, the reference is replaced with the standard output of the command. If the command has a non-zero exit status, make halts with an error.

In contrast to commands in rules, the command is not subject to macro substitution; therefore, you do not need to replace a dollar sign ($) with a double dollar sign ($$).

Signals

INT, SIGTERM, and QUIT signals received from the keyboard halt make and remove the target file being processed unless that target is in the dependency list for .PRECIOUS:.

Examples

The following makefile says that pgm depends on two files, a.o and b.o, and that they in turn depend on their corresponding source files (a.c and b.c) along with a common file incl.h.

```
pgm: a.o b.o
    $(LINK.c) -o $@ a.o b.o
a.o: incl.h a.c
    cc -c a.c
```

```
b.o: incl.h b.c
     cc -c b.c
```

The following makefile uses implicit rules to express the same dependencies:

```
pgm: a.o b.o
     cc a.o b.o -o pgm
a.o b.o: incl.h
```

Environment Variables

See environ(5) for descriptions of the following environment variables that affect the execution of make: LC_CTYPE, LC_MESSAGES, and NLSPATH.

KEEP_STATE
Produce the same effect as the .KEEP_STATE: special-function target. Enable command dependencies, hidden dependencies, and writing of the state file.

USE_SVR4_MAKE

Invoke the generic System V version of make (/usr/ccs/lib/svr4.make). See sysV-make(1).

MAKEFLAGS
Specify a character string representing a series of option characters to be used as the default options. The implementation accepts both of the following formats (but need not accept them when intermixed).

- The characters are option letters without the leading dashes or blank-character separation used on a command line.

- The characters are formatted in a manner similar to a portion of the make command line: options are preceded by dashes and are blank-character separated. The *macro=name* macro definition operands can also be included. The difference between the contents of MAKEFLAGS and the command line is that the contents of the variable are not subject to the word expansions (see wordexp(3C)) associated with parsing the command-line values.

When you use the command-line options -f or -p, they take effect regardless of whether they also appear in MAKEFLAGS. If they otherwise appear in MAKEFLAGS, the result is undefined.

The MAKEFLAGS variable is accessed from the environment before the makefile is read. At that time, all of the options (except -f and -p) and command-line macros not already included in MAKEFLAGS are added to the MAKEFLAGS macro. The MAKEFLAGS macro is passed into the environment as an environment variable for all child processes. If the MAKEFLAGS macro is subsequently set by the makefile, it replaces the MAKEFLAGS variable currently found in the environment.

Exit Status

When you specify the -q option, the make command exits with one of the following values.

0	Successful completion.
1	The target was not up-to-date.
>1	An error occurred.

When you do not specify the -q option, the make command exits with one of the following values.

0   Successful completion.

>0   An error occurred.

Files

makefile
Makefile   Current version(s) of the make description file.

s.makefile   SCCS history files for the above makefile(s) in the current directory.
s.Makefile

SCCS/s.makefile

                SCCS history files for the above makefile(s).

make.rules   Default file for user-defined targets, macros, and implicit rules.

/usr/share/lib/make/make.rules

                Makefile for standard implicit rules and macros (not read if make.rules is read).

.make.state State file in the local directory.

Attributes

See attributes(5) for descriptions of the following attributes:

/usr/ccs/bin/make

Attribute Type	Attribute Value
Availability	SUNWsprot

/usr/xpg4/bin/make

Attribute Type	Attribute Value
Availability	SUNWxcu4t

See Also

ar(1), cd(1), lex(1), sccs-get(1), sh(1), sysV-make(1) yacc(1), passwd(4), attributes(5), POSIX.2(5)

Solaris Advanced User's Guide and *Programming Utilities Guide*

Diagnostics

Don't know how to make target *target*

                There is no makefile entry for *target*, and none of make's implicit rules apply (there is no dependency file with a suffix in the suffixes list, or the target's suffix is not in the list).

```
*** target removed
```

> make was interrupted while building *target*. Instead of leaving a partially completed version that is newer than its dependencies, make removes the file named *target*.

```
*** target not removed
```

> make was interrupted while building *target*, and *target* was not present in the directory.

```
*** target could not be removed, reason
```

> make was interrupted while building *target*, which was not removed for the stated *reason*.

```
Read of include file file failed
```

> The makefile specified in an include directive was not found or was inaccessible.

```
Loop detected when expanding macro value macro
```

> A reference to the macro being defined was found in the definition.

```
Could not write state file file
```

> You used the .KEEP_STATE: target, but you do not have write permission on the state file.

```
*** Error code n
```

> The previous shell command returned a non-zero error code.

```
*** signal message
```

> The previous shell command was aborted because of a signal. If - core dumped appears after the message, a corefile was created.

```
Conditional macro conflict encountered
```

> Displayed only when -d is in effect, this message means that two or more parallel targets currently being processed depend on a target that is built differently for each by virtue of conditional macros. Because the target cannot simultaneously satisfy both dependency relationships, it is conflicted.

Bugs

Some commands return non-zero status inappropriately; to overcome this difficulty, prefix the offending command line in the rule with a -.

File names with the characters =, :, or @ do not work.

You cannot build *file*.o from *lib*(*file*.o).

Options supplied by MAKEFLAGS should be reported for nested make commands. Use the -d option to find out what options the nested command picks up from MAKEFLAGS.

This version of make is incompatible with previous versions in the following ways.

- The -d option output is much briefer in this version. -dd now produces the equivalent voluminous output.

- `make` tries to derive values for the dynamic macros $*, $<, and $? while processing explicit targets. It uses the same method as for implicit rules; in some cases, this can lead either to unexpected values or to an empty value being assigned. (Actually, this was true for earlier versions as well, even though the documentation stated otherwise.)
- `make` no longer searches for SCCS history (`s.`) files.
- Suffix replacement in macro references is now applied after the macro is expanded.

There is no guarantee that makefiles created for this version of `make` work with earlier versions.

If there is no `make.rules` file in the current directory and the file `/usr/share/lib/make/make.rules` is missing, `make` stops before processing any targets. To force `make` to run anyway, create an empty `make.rules` file in the current directory.

Once a dependency is made, `make` assumes the dependency file is present for the remainder of the run. If a rule subsequently removes that file and future targets depend on its existence, unexpected errors may result.

When hidden dependency checking is in effect, the `$?` macro's value includes the names of hidden dependencies. This can lead to improper file-name arguments to commands when `$?` is used in a rule.

Pattern-replacement macro references cannot be used in the dependency list of a pattern-matching rule.

Unlike previous versions, this version of `make` strips a leading `./` from the value of the `$@` dynamic macro.

With automatic SCCS retrieval, this version of `make` does not support tilde suffix rules.

The only dynamic macro whose value is strictly determined when used in a dependency list is `$@` (takes the form `$$@`).

`make` invokes the shell with the `-e` argument, which cannot be inferred from the syntax of the rule alone.

man — Find and Display Reference Manual Pages

Synopsis

```
/usr/bin/man [-] [-adFlrt] [-M path] [-T macro-package] [-s section]
    name...
/usr/bin/man [-M path] -k keyword...
/usr/bin/man [-M path] -f file...
```

Description

Use the `man` command to display information from the online reference manuals. `man` displays complete manual pages that you specify by name or one-line summaries that you specify either with keyword (`-k`) or with the name of an associated file (`-f`). If no manual page is located, `man` prints an error message.

Source Format

Reference manual pages are marked up with either nroff(1) or sgml(5) (Standard Generalized Markup Language) tags. The man command recognizes the type of markup and processes the file accordingly. The various source files are kept in separate directories depending on the type of markup.

Location of Manual Pages

The online reference manual page directories are conventionally located in /usr/share/man. The nroff sources are located in the /usr/share/man/man* directories. The SGML sources are located in the /usr/share/man/sman* directories. Each directory corresponds to a section of the manual. Because these directories are optionally installed, they may not reside on your host; you may have to mount /usr/share/man from a host on which they do reside.

If there are preformatted, up-to-date versions in the corresponding cat* or fmt* directories, man displays or prints those versions. If the preformatted version of interest is out-of-date or missing, man reformats it before displaying it and stores the preformatted version if cat* or fmt* is writable. The windex database is not updated. See catman(1M). If directories for the preformatted versions are not provided, man reformats a page whenever it is requested; it uses a temporary file to store the formatted text during display.

If the standard output is not a terminal or if you specify the – option, man pipes its output through cat(1); otherwise, man pipes its output through more(1) to handle paging and underlining on the screen.

Options

–	Pipe output through cat(1) instead of more(1).
-a	Show all manual pages in the order found matching *name* within the MANPATH search path.
-d	Display what a section-specifier evaluates to, method used for searching, and paths searched by man.
-f *file*...	Locate manual pages related to any of the given files. Strip the leading path-name components from each file and print one-line summaries containing the resulting basename or names. This option uses the windex database.
-F	Force man to search all directories specified by MANPATH or the man.cf file instead of using the windex lookup database. This option is useful if the database is not up-to-date. If the windex database does not exist, this option is assumed.
-k *keyword*...	Print one-line summaries from the windex database (table of contents) that contain any of the given keywords. The windex database is created with catman(1M).
-l	List all manual pages found matching *name* within the search path.

-M *path*	Specify an alternative search path for manual pages. *path* is a colon-separated list of directories that contain manual page directory subtrees. For example, if path is /usr/share/man:/usr/local/man, man searches for *name* in the standard location and then in /usr/local/man. When used with the -k or -f options, the -M option must be first. Each directory in the path is assumed to contain subdirectories of the form man*, one for each section. This option overrides the MANPATH environment variable.
-r	Reformat the manual page, but do not display it. This option replaces the man - -t *name* combination.

-s *section*...

Specify sections of the manual for man to search. The directories searched for *name* are limited to those specified by *section*. *section* can be a digit (perhaps followed by one or more letters), a word (for example: local, new, old, public), or a letter. To specify multiple sections, separate each section with a comma. This option overrides the MANPATH environment variable and the man.cf file.

-t	Process with troff, and send specified manual pages to a suitable raster output device (see troff(1). If you use both the - and -t flags, man updates the troffed versions of each named *name* (if needed) but does not display the names.

-T *macro-package*

Format manual pages, using *macro-package* instead of the standard -man macros defined in /usr/share/lib/tmac.

Note — The -f and -k options use the windex database, which is created by catman(1M).

Operands

name	A keyword or the name of a standard command.

Usage

Manual Page Sections

Entries in the reference manuals are organized into sections. A section name consists of a major section name, typically a single digit, optionally followed by a subsection name, typically one or more letters. For example, the command lpr(1B) is in Section (1), User Commands, and belongs to the BSD Compatibility Package subsection. An unadorned major section name acts as an abbreviation for the section of the same name along with all of its subsections. Each section contains descriptions appropriate to a particular reference category, with subsections refining these distinctions. See the intro manual pages for an explanation of the classification used in this release.

Search Path

Before searching for a given name, man constructs a list of candidate directories and sections. man searches for *name* in the directories specified by the MANPATH environment variable. If this variable is not set, /usr/share/man is searched by default.

Within the manual page directories, man confines its search to the sections specified, in the following order:

- Sections specified on the command line with the -s option.
- Sections embedded in the MANPATH environment variable.
- Sections specified in the man.cf file for each directory specified in the MANPATH environment variable

If none of the above exist, man searches each directory in the manual page path and displays the first matching manual page found.

The man.cf file has the following format:

MANSECTS=*section*[,*section*]...

Lines beginning with # and blank lines are considered comments and are ignored. Each directory specified in MANPATH can contain a manual page configuration file specifying the default search order for that directory.

Formatting Manual Pages

Manual pages are marked up in nroff(1) or sgml(5). nroff manual pages are processed by nroff(1) or troff(1) with the -man macro package. Please refer to man(5) for information on macro usage. SGML-tagged manual pages are processed by an SGML parser and are passed to the formatter.

Preprocessing nroff Manual Pages

When formatting an nroff manual page, man examines the first line to determine whether it requires special processing. If the first line is a string of the following form,

'\" *X*

where *X* is separated from the " by a single space and consists of any combination of characters in the following list, then man pipes its input to troff(1) or nroff(1) through the corresponding preprocessors.

e   eqn(1), or neqn for nroff.

r   refer(1).

t   tbl(1).

v   vgrind(1).

If eqn or neqn is invoked, man automatically reads the file /usr/pub/eqnchar (see eqnchar(5)). If nroff(1) is invoked, col(1) is automatically used.

Referring to Other nroff Manual Pages

If the first line of the nroff manual page is a reference to another manual page entry fitting the following pattern, man processes the indicated file in place of the current one.

`.so man*/ `*`sourcefile`*

You must express the reference as a path name relative to the root of the manual page directory subtree.

When the second or any subsequent line starts with `.so`, man ignores it; `troff(1)` or `nroff(1)` processes the request in the usual manner.

Processing SGML Manual Pages

Manual pages are identified as being marked up in SGML by the presence of the string `<!DOCTYPE`. If the file also contains the string `SHADOW_PAGE`, the file refers to another manual page for the content. The reference is made with a file entity reference to the manual page that contains the text. This mechanism is similar to the `.so` mechanism used in the `nroff`-formatted manual pages.

Bugs

The manual is supposed to be reproducible either on a phototypesetter or on an ASCII terminal. However, on a terminal, some information (indicated by font changes, for instance) is lost.

Some dumb terminals cannot process the vertical motions produced by the e (see `eqn(1)`) preprocessing flag. To prevent garbled output on these terminals, when you use e also use t to invoke `col(1)` implicitly. This workaround has the disadvantage of eliminating superscripts and subscripts even on those terminals that can display them. Use Control-Q to clear a terminal that gets confused by `eqn(1)` output.

Environment Variables

See `environ(5)` for descriptions of the following environment variables that affect the execution of man: `LC_CTYPE`, `LC_MESSAGES`, and `NLSPATH`.

MANPATH	A colon-separated list of directories; each directory can be followed by a comma-separated list of sections. If set, its value overrides `/usr/share/man` as the default directory search path and the `man.cf` file as the default section search path. The `-M` and `-s` options, in turn, override these values.
PAGER	A program to use for interactively delivering man's output to the screen. If not set, `more -s` is used. See `more(1)`.
TCAT	The name of the program to use to display `troff`ed manual pages.
TROFF	The name of the formatter to use when you specify the `-t` option. If not set, `troff(1)` is used.

Exit Status

0	Successful completion.
>0	An error occurred.

Files

`/usr/share/man`

Root of the standard manual page directory subtree.

/usr/share/man/man?/*

> Unformatted nroff manual entries.

/usr/share/man/sman?/*

> Unformatted SGML manual entries.

/usr/share/man/cat?/*

> nroffed manual entries.

/usr/share/man/fmt?/*

> troffed manual entries.

/usr/share/man/windex

> Table of contents and keyword database.

/usr/share/lib/tmac/an

> Standard -man macro package.

/usr/share/lib/sgml/locale/C/dtd/*

> SGML document type definition files.

/usr/share/lib/sgml/locale/C/solbook/*

> SGML style sheet and entity definitions directories.

/usr/share/lib/pub/eqnchar

> Standard definitions for eqn and neqn.

man.cf   Default search order by section.

Attributes

See attributes(5) for descriptions of the following attributes:

Attribute Type	Attribute Value
Availability	SUNWdoc
CSI	Enabled

Note — The man command is CSI capable. However, some commands invoked by the man command, namely, troff, eqn, neqn, refer, tbl, and vgrind, are not verified to be CSI capable. Because of this, the man command with the -t option may not handle non-EUC data. Also, if the man command is used to display manual pages that require special processing through eqn, neqn, refer, tbl, or vgrind, man may not be CSI capable.

See Also

apropos(1), cat(1), col(1), eqn(1), more(1), nroff(1), refer(1), tbl(1), troff(1), vgrind(1), whatis(1), catman(1M), attributes(5), environ(5), eqnchar(5), man(5), sgml(5)

mconnect — Connect to SMTP Mail Server Socket

Synopsis

/usr/bin/mconnect [-p *port*] [-r] [*hostname*]

Description

mconnect opens a connection to the mail server on a given host so that the mail server can be tested independently of all other mail software. If no host is given, the connection is made to the local host. Servers expect to speak the Simple Mail Transfer Protocol (SMTP) on this connection. Exit by typing the quit command. Typing EOF sends an end-of-file to the server. An interrupt closes the connection immediately and exits.

Options

-p *port*   Specify the port number instead of the default SMTP port (number 25) as the next argument.

-r   Disable the default line buffering and input handling to operate in raw mode. This option produces an effect similar to telnet to port number 25.

Files

/etc/mail/sendmail.hf

Help file for SMTP commands.

Attributes

See attributes(5) for descriptions of the following attributes:

Attribute Type	Attribute Value
Availability	SUNWcsu

See Also

New!

telnet(1), sendmail(1M), attributes(5), IP6(7P)

Postel, Jonathan B., *Simple Mail Transfer Protocol*, RFC 821, Information Sciences Institute, University of Southern California, August 1982.

mcs — Manipulate the Comment Section of an Objectfile

Synopsis

/usr/ccs/bin/mcs { -c | -d | -p | -V | -a *string* | -n *name* }... *file*...

Description

Use the mcs command to manipulate a section in an ELF objectfile. The default section is .comment. mcs is used to add to, delete, print, and compress the contents of a section in an ELF objectfile and print only the contents of a section in a Common Object File Format (COFF) objectfile. COFF is an objectfile format that preceded ELF on some computer architectures. mcs cannot add, delete, or compress the contents of a section that is contained within a segment.

If the input file is an archive (see ar(4)), the archive is treated as a set of individual files. For example, if you specify the -a option, the string is appended to the comment section of each ELF objectfile in the archive; if the archive member is not an ELF objectfile, then it is left unchanged.

Note — When mcs deletes a section with the -d option, it tries to bind together sections of type SHT_REL and target sections pointed to by the sh_info section header field. If one is to be deleted, mcs tries to delete the other of the pair.

Options

You must specify one or more of the options described below. Each specified option is applied, in order, to each file.

-a *string*   Append *string* to the comment section of the ELF objectfiles. If *string* contains embedded blanks, enclose it in quotation marks.

-c   Compress the contents of the comment section of the ELF objectfiles. Remove all duplicate entries. The ordering of the remaining entries is not disturbed.

-d   Delete the contents of the comment section from the ELF objectfiles. Also remove the section header for the comment section.

-n *name*   Specify the name of the comment section to access if other than .comment. By default, mcs deals with the section named .comment. You can use this option to specify another section. You can specify multiple -n options to specify multiple section comments.

-p   Print the contents of the comment section on standard output. Tag each section printed with the name of the file from which it was extracted, using the format file[*member_name*] : for archive files and file: for other files.

-V   Print on standard error the version number of mcs.

Examples

The following example prints the comments section from elf.file.

```
castle% mcs -p elf.file
```

The following example appends string xyz to the comment section of elf.file.

```
castle% mcs -a xyz elf.file
```

Files

/tmp/mcs*   Temporary files.

Attributes

See attributes(5) for descriptions of the following attributes:

Attribute Type	Attribute Value
Availability	SUNWbtool

See Also

ar(1), as(1), ld(1), elf(3E), tmpnam(3S), a.out(4), ar(4), attributes(5)

New! **mdb** — Modular Debugger

Synopsis

New!

```
/bin/mdb [-fkmuwyAFMS] [-o option] [-p pid] [-s distance] [-I path]
    [-L path] [-P prompt] [-R root] [-V dis-version]
    [object [core] | core| suffix]
```

Description

Introduction

The mdb command, new in the Solaris 8 Operating Environment, is an extensible command you can use for low-level debugging and editing of the following targets.

- Live operating systems.
- Operating system crash dumps.
- User processes.
- User process core dumps.
- Objectfiles.

For a more detailed description of mdb features, see the *Solaris Modular Debugger Guide*. For a more detailed description of targets, see "Definitions" on page 821. Enhancements to mdb in the Solaris 9 release are marked with the New icon in the margin.

Debugging is the process of analyzing the execution and state of a software program to remove defects. Traditional debugging tools provide a way to control execution so that you can reexecute programs in a controlled environment. With a debugger you can display the current state of program data or evaluate expressions in the source language used to develop the program.

Unfortunately, these techniques are often inappropriate for debugging complex software systems such as the following scenarios.

- An operating system in which bugs may not be reproducible and program state is massive and distributed.
- Programs that are highly optimized, have had their debug information removed, or are themselves low-level debugging tools.
- Customer situations in which the developer can access only postmortem information.

mdb provides a completely customizable environment for debugging these types of programs and scenarios, including a dynamic module facility that you can use to implement your own debugging commands to perform program-specific analysis. You can use each mdb module to examine the program in several different contexts, including live and postmortem.

Definitions

The *target* is the program being inspected by the debugger. mdb currently supports the following types of targets.

- User processes.
- User process corefiles.
- The live operating system (through /dev/kmem and /dev/ksyms).
- Operating system crash dumps.
- User process images recorded inside an operating system crash dump.
- ELF objectfiles.

Each target exports a standard set of properties, including one or more address spaces, one or more symbol tables, a set of load objects, and a set of threads that can be examined with the debugger commands described below.

A debugger command, or *dcmd* (pronounced dee-command) in mdb terminology, is a routine in the debugger that can access any of the properties of the current target. mdb parses commands from standard input and then executes the corresponding dcmds. Each dcmd can also accept a list of string or numerical arguments, as shown in "Syntax" on page 821. mdb contains a set of built-in dcmds, described in "Commands" on page 822, that are always available. You can also extend the capabilities of mdb itself by writing your own dcmds, as described in the *Solaris Modular Debugger Guide.*

A *walker* is a set of routines that describe how to walk—or iterate—through the elements of a particular program data structure. A walker encapsulates the data structure's implementation from dcmds and from mdb itself. You can use walkers interactively or as primitives to build other dcmds or walkers. As with dcmds, you can extend mdb by implementing your own walkers as part of a debugger module.

A *debugger module*, or *dmod* (pronounced dee-mod), is a dynamically loaded library that contains a set of dcmds and walkers. During initialization, mdb tries to load dmods corresponding to the load objects present in the target. You can subsequently load or unload dmods at any time while running mdb. mdb ships with a set of standard dmods for debugging the Solaris kernel. The *Solaris Modular Debugger Guide* contains more information on developing your own debugger modules.

A *macro file* is a text file that contains a set of commands to execute. Macro files are typically used to automate the process of displaying a simple data structure. mdb provides complete backward compatibility for the execution of macro files written for adb(1), and the Solaris installation includes a set of macro files for debugging the Solaris kernel that you can use with either tool.

Syntax

The debugger processes commands from standard input. If standard input is a terminal, mdb provides terminal editing capabilities. mdb can also process commands from macro files and from dcmd pipelines, as described in "dcmd Pipelines" on page 828. The language syntax is designed around the concept of computing the value of an expression (typically, a memory address in the target) and then applying a dcmd to that address. The current address location is referred to as dot (.), and its value is referenced with the . character.

A metacharacter is one of the following characters.

```
[ ] | ! / \ ? = > $ : ; Newline Space Tab
```

A *blank* is a *Tab* or a *Space*. A *word* is a sequence of characters separated by one or more nonquoted metacharacters. Some of the metacharacters function as delimiters only in certain contexts, as described below. An *identifier* is a sequence of letters, digits, underscores, periods, or backquotes beginning with a letter, underscore, or period. Identifiers are used as the names of symbols, variables, dcmds, and walkers. Commands are delimited by a *newline* or semicolon (;).

A dcmd is denoted by one of the following words or metacharacters.

```
/ \ ? = > $character :character ::identifier
```

dcmds named by metacharacters or prefixed by a single $ or : are provided as built-in operators and implement complete compatibility with the command set of the legacy adb(1) command. Once a dcmd has been parsed, the /, \, ?, =, >, $, and : characters are not recognized as metacharacters until the termination of the argument list.

A simple-command is a dcmd followed by a sequence or zero or more blank-separated words. The words are passed as arguments to the invoked dcmd, except as specified in "Arithmetic Expansion" on page 823 and "Quoting" on page 825. Each dcmd returns an exit status that indicates it was either successful, failed, or invoked with invalid arguments.

A *pipeline* is a sequence of one or more simple-commands separated by |. Unlike the shell, dcmds in mdb pipelines are not executed as separate processes. After the pipeline has been parsed, each dcmd is invoked in order from left to right. The output of each dcmd is processed and stored as described in "dcmd Pipelines" on page 828. Once the left-hand dcmd is complete, its processed output is used as input for the next dcmd in the pipeline. If any dcmd does not return a successful exit status, the pipeline is aborted.

An expression is a sequence of words that is evaluated to compute a 64-bit unsigned integer value. The words are evaluated by the rules described in "Arithmetic Expansion" on page 823.

Commands

pipeline [! *word*...] [;]

> You can optionally suffix a simple-command or pipeline with the ! character, indicating that the debugger should open a pipe(2) and send the standard output of the last dcmd in the mdb pipeline to an external process created by executing $SHELL -c followed by the string formed by concatenating the words after the ! character. For more details, refer to "Shell Escapes" on page 826.

expression pipeline [! *word*...] [;]

> You can prefix a simple-command or pipeline with an expression. Before execution of *pipeline*, the value of dot (the variable denoted by .) is set to the value of *expression*.

expression , expression pipeline [! *word*...] [;]

> You can prefix a simple-command or pipeline with two expressions. The first is evaluated to determine the new value of dot, and the second is evaluated to determine a repeat count for the first dcmd in the pipeline. This dcmd is executed *count* times before the next dcmd in the pipeline is executed. The repeat count applies only to the first dcmd in the pipeline.

, *expression pipeline* [! *word*...] [;]

> If you omit the initial *expression*, dot is not modified but the first dcmd in the pipeline is repeated according to the value of the *expression*.

expression [! *word*...] [;]

> A command can consist of only an arithmetic expression. The *expression* is evaluated and the dot variable is set to its value; the previous dcmd and arguments are then executed with the new value of dot.

expression, expression [! *word*...] [;]

> A command can consist only of a dot expression and repeat count expression. After dot is set to the value of the first expression, the previous dcmd and arguments are repeatedly executed the number of times specified by the value of the second expression.

, *expression* [! *word*...] [;]

> If the initial expression is omitted, dot is not modified and the previous dcmd and arguments are repeatedly executed the number of times specified by the value of the *count* expression.

! *word*... [;]

> If the command begins with the ! character, no dcmds are executed and the debugger simply executes $SHELL -c followed by the string formed by concatenating the words after the ! character.

Comments

When a word begins with //, that word and all the subsequent characters up to a newline are ignored.

Arithmetic Expansion

Arithmetic expansion is performed when you precede an mdb command with an optional expression representing a start address, or a start address and a repeat count. Arithmetic expansion can also be performed to compute a numerical argument for a dcmd. An arithmetic expression can appear in an argument list enclosed in square brackets preceded by a dollar sign ($ [*expression*]) and is replaced by the value of the expression.

Expressions can contain any of the following special words.

integer   The specified integer value. You can prefix integer values with 0i or 0I to indicate binary values, 0o prefixed with 0i or 0I to indicate binary values, 0o or 0O to indicate octal values, 0t or 0T to indicate decimal values, and 0x or 0X to indicate hexadecimal values (the default).

0[tT] [0-9]+.[0-9]+

The specified decimal floating-point value, converted to its IEEE double-precision floating-point representation.

'*cccccccc*'   The integer value computed by converting each character to a byte equal to its ASCII value. You can specify up to eight characters in a character constant. Characters are packed into the integer in reverse order (right-to-left) beginning at the least significant byte.

<*identifier*

The value of the variable named by *identifier*.

identifier

The value of the symbol named by *identifier*.

(*expression*)

The value of *expression*.

.   The value of dot.

&   The most recent value of dot used to execute a dcmd.

+   The value of dot incremented by the current increment.

^   The value of dot decremented by the current increment.

The increment is a global variable that stores the total bytes read by the last formatting dcmd. For more information on the increment, see "Formatting dcmds" on page 830.

Unary operators are right associative and have higher precedence than binary operators. The unary operators are listed below.

#*expression*

Logical negation.

~*expression*

Bitwise complement.

-*expression*

Integer negation.

%*expression*

The value of a pointer-sized quantity at the objectfile location corresponding to virtual address expression in the target's virtual address space.

%/[csil]/*expression*

> The value of a char-, short-, int-, or long-sized quantity at the objectfile location corresponding to virtual address expression in the target's virtual address space.

%/[1248]/*expression*

> The value of a 1-, 2-, 4-, or 8-byte quantity at the objectfile location corresponding to virtual address expression in the target's virtual address space.

*expression

> The value of a pointer-sized quantity at virtual address expression in the target's virtual address space.

*/[csil]/*expression*

> The value of a char-, short-, int-, or long-sized quantity at virtual address expression in the target's virtual address space.

*/[1248]/*expression*

> The value of a 1-, 2-, 4-, or 8-byte quantity at virtual address expression in the target's virtual address space.

Binary operators are left associative and have lower precedence than unary operators. The binary operators, in order of precedence from highest to lowest, are listed below.

*	Integer multiplication.
%	Integer division.
#	Left-hand side rounded up to next multiple of right-hand side.
+	Integer addition.
−	Integer subtraction.
<<	Bitwise shift left.
>>	Bitwise shift right.
==	Logical equality.
!=	Logical inequality.
&	Bitwise AND.
^	Bitwise exclusive OR.
|	Bitwise inclusive OR.

Quoting

Each metacharacter described in "Syntax" on page 821 terminates a word unless quoted. Characters can be quoted (forcing mdb to interpret each character as itself without any special significance) by enclosure in a pair of single (') or double (") quote marks. You cannot quote a single quote within single quotes. Inside double quotes, mdb recognizes the C-language character escape sequences.

Shell Escapes

You can use the ! character to create a pipeline between an mdb command and the user's shell. If the $SHELL environment variable is set, mdb forks and execs this program for shell escapes; otherwise, mdb uses /bin/sh. The shell is invoked with the -c option followed by a string formed by concatenating the words after the ! character. The ! character takes precedence over all other metacharacters except semicolon (;) and newline. Once a shell escape is detected, the remaining characters up to the next semicolon or newline are passed, as is, to the shell. The output of shell commands cannot be piped to mdb dcmds. Output of commands executed by a shell escape is sent directly to the terminal, not to mdb.

Variables

A variable is a variable name, a corresponding integer value, and a set of attributes. A variable name is a sequence of letters, digits, underscores, or periods. You can assign a variable a value with the > dcmd or ::typeset dcmd and manipulate its attributes with the ::typeset dcmd. Each variable's value is represented as a 64-bit unsigned integer. A variable can have one or more of the following attributes.

- Read-only (cannot be modified by the user).
- Persistent (cannot be unset by the user).
- Tagged (user-defined indicator).

The following variables are defined as persistent.

0	The most recent value printed using the /, \, ?, or = dcmd.
9	The most recent count used with the $< dcmd.
b	The virtual address of the base of the data section.
d	The size of the data section in bytes.
e	The virtual address of the entry point.
m	The initial bytes (magic number) of the target's primary objectfile, or zero if no objectfile has been read yet.
t	The size of the text section in bytes.
hits	The count of the number of times the matched software event specifier has been matched. See "Event Callbacks" on page 834. New in the Solaris 9 release.
thread	The thread identifier of the current representative thread. The value of the identifier depends on the threading model used by the current target. See "Thread Support" on page 834. New in the Solaris 9 release.

New! (hits)

New! (thread)

In addition, the mdb kernel and process targets export the current values of the representative thread's register set as named variables. The names of these variables depend on the target's platform and instruction set architecture.

Symbol Name Resolution

As explained in "Syntax" on page 821, a symbol identifier present in an expression context evaluates to the value of this symbol. The value typically denotes the virtual address of the storage associated with the symbol in the target's virtual address space. A target can support multiple symbol tables including, but not limited to, a primary executable symbol table, a primary dynamic symbol table, a runtime link-editor symbol table, and standard and dynamic symbol tables for each of a number of load objects (such as shared libraries in a user process, or kernel modules in the Solaris kernel). The target typically searches the primary executable's symbol tables first, and then one or more of the other symbol tables. Notice that ELF symbol tables contain entries only for external, global, and static symbols; automatic symbols do not appear in the symbol tables processed by mdb.

Additionally, mdb provides a private user-defined symbol table that is searched before any of the target symbol tables. The private symbol table is initially empty; it can be manipulated with the ::nmadd and ::nmdel dcmds. You can use the ::nm -P option to display the contents of the private symbol table. The private symbol table enables you to create symbol definitions for program functions or data that either were missing from the original program or stripped out. These definitions are then used when mdb converts a symbolic name to an address, or an address to the nearest symbol.

Because targets contain multiple symbol tables and each symbol table can include symbols from multiple objectfiles, different symbols with the same name can exist. mdb uses the backquote (` ) character as a symbol name scoping operator to enable you to obtain the value of the desired symbol in this situation. You can specify the scope used to resolve a symbol name as either *object*`*name*, or *file*`*name*, or *object*`*file*`*name*. The *object* identifier refers to the name of a load object. The *file* identifier refers to the basename of a source file that has a symbol of type STT_FILE in the specified object's symbol table. The object identifier's interpretation depends on the target type.

The mdb kernel target expects *object* to specify the basename of a loaded kernel module. For example, the symbol name specfs`_init evaluates to the value of the _init symbol in the specfs kernel module.

The mdb process target expects *object* to specify the name of the executable or of a loaded shared library. It can take any of the following forms.

1. An exact match (that is, a full path name): /usr/lib/libc.so
2. An exact basename match: libc.so.1
3. An initial basename match up to a . suffix: libc.so or libc
4. The literal string a.out is accepted as an alias for the executable.

Starting in the Solaris 9 release, the process target also accepts any of the four forms *New!* described above preceded by an optional link-map ID (lmid). The lmid prefix is specified by an initial LM followed by the link-map ID in hexadecimal followed by an additional backquote. For example, the symbol name

```
LM0`libc.so.1`_init
```

evaluates to the value of the _init symbol in the libc.so.1 library that is loaded on link-map 0 (LM_ID_BASE). You may need to use the link-map specifier to resolve symbol naming conflicts if the same library is loaded on more than one link map. For more information on link maps, refer to the *Linker and Libraries Guide* and dlopen(3DL). Link-map identifiers are displayed when symbols are printed according to the setting of the showlmid option, as described in "Options" on page 852.

When names conflict between symbols and hexadecimal integer values, mdb evaluates an ambiguous token first as a symbol before evaluating it as an integer value. For example, the token f can refer to either the decimal integer value 15 specified in hexadecimal (the default base) or to a global variable named f in the target's symbol table. When a symbol with an ambiguous name is present, you can specify the integer value with an explicit 0x or 0X prefix.

dcmd and Walker Name Resolution

As described earlier, each mdb dmod provides a set of dcmds and walkers. dcmds and walkers are tracked in two distinct, global namespaces. mdb also keeps track of a dcmd and walker namespace associated with each dmod. Identically named dcmds or walkers within a given dmod are not allowed: a dmod with this type of naming conflict fails to load. Name conflicts between dcmds or walkers from different dmods are allowed in the global namespace. In the case of a conflict, the first dcmd or walker with that particular name to be loaded is given precedence in the global namespace. Alternative definitions are kept in a list in load order. You can use the backquote character (`` ` ``) in a dcmd or walker name as a scoping operator to select an alternative definition. For example, if dmods m1 and m2 each provide a dcmd d and m1 is loaded before m2, then

::d	Execute m1's definition of d.
::m1`d	Execute m1's definition of d.
::m2`d	Execute m2's definition of d.

If module m1 is now unloaded, the next dcmd on the global definition list (m2`d) is promoted to global visibility. You can determine the current definition of a dcmd or walker with the ::which dcmd, described in "Built-in dcmds" on page 834. You can display the global definition list with the ::which -v option.

dcmd Pipelines

You can compose dcmds into a pipeline with the | operator. A pipeline passes a list of values, typically virtual addresses, from one dcmd or walker to another. You might use pipeline stages to map a pointer from one type of data structure to a pointer to a corresponding data structure, to sort a list of addresses, or to select the addresses of structures with certain properties.

mdb executes each dcmd in the pipeline in order from left to right. The leftmost dcmd is executed with the current value of dot or with the value specified by an explicit expression at the start of the command. When mdb encounters a | operator, it creates a pipe (a shared buffer) between the output of the dcmd to its left and the mdb parser, and an empty list of values. As the dcmd executes, its standard output is placed in the pipe and then consumed and evaluated by the parser as if mdb were reading this data from standard input. Each line must consist of an arithmetic expression terminated by a newline or semicolon (;). The value of the expression is appended to the list of values associated with the pipe. If a syntax error is detected, the pipeline is aborted.

When the dcmd to the left of a | operator completes, the list of values associated with the pipe is then used to invoke the dcmd to the right of the | operator. For each value in the list, dot is set to this value and the right-hand dcmd is executed. Only the rightmost dcmd in the pipeline has its output printed to standard output. If any dcmd in the pipeline produces output to standard error, these messages are printed directly to standard error and are not processed as part of the pipeline.

Signal Handling

The debugger ignores the PIPE and QUIT signals. The INT signal aborts the command that is currently executing. The debugger intercepts and provides special handling for the ILL, TRAP, EMT, FPE, BUS, and SEGV signals. If any of these signals are generated asynchronously (that is, delivered from another process with kill(2)), mdb restores the signal to its default disposition and dumps core. However, if any of these signals are generated synchronously by the debugger process itself, if a dcmd from an externally loaded dmod is currently executing, or if standard input is a terminal, mdb provides a menu of choices enabling you to force a core dump, quit without producing a core dump, stop for attach by a debugger, or attempt to resume. The resume option aborts all active commands and unloads the dmod whose dcmd was active at the time the fault occurred. You can subsequently reload the dmod. The resume option provides limited protection against buggy dcmds. See "Use of the Error Recovery Mechanism" on page 850 for information about the risks associated with the resume option.

Command Reentry

The text of the last HISTSIZE (default 128) commands entered from a terminal device are saved in memory. The inline editing facility, described next, provides key mappings for searching and fetching elements from the history list.

Inline Editing

When standard input is a terminal device, mdb provides some simple Emacs-style facilities for editing the command line. The search, previous, and next commands in edit mode provide access to the history list. Only strings, not patterns, are matched when searching. As shown below, the notation for control characters is caret (^) followed by a character shown in upper case. The notation for escape sequences is M followed by a character. For example, you enter M-f (pronounced metaeff) by pressing the Escape key and then f or by pressing the Meta key then f on keyboards that support a Meta key. A command line is committed and executed when you press Return or newline. The edit commands are listed below.

^F	Move cursor forward (right) one character.
M-f	Move cursor forward one word.
^B	Move cursor backward (left) one character.
M-b	Move cursor backward one word.
^A	Move cursor to start of line.
^E	Move cursor to end of line.
^D	Delete current character if the current line is not empty. If the current line is empty, ^D denotes EOF and the debugger exits.
^K	Delete from the cursor to the end of the line.
^L	Reprint the current line.
^T	Transpose current character with next character.
^N	Fetch the next command from the history. Each time you enter ^N, the next command forward in time is retrieved.
^P	Fetch the previous command from the history. Each time you enter ^P, the next command backward in time is retrieved.
^R[*string*]	Search backward in the history for a previous command line containing *string*. The string should be terminated by a Return or newline. If you omit *string*, the previous history element containing the most recent string is retrieved.

The editing mode also interprets the following user-defined sequences as editing commands. You can read or modify user-defined sequences with the stty(1) command.

erase	User-defined erase character (usually ^H or ^?). Delete previous character.

intr   User-defined interrupt character (usually ^C). Abort the current
              command, and print a new prompt.

kill   User-defined kill character (usually ^U). Kill the entire current
              command line.

quit   User-defined quit character (usually ^\). Quit the debugger.

suspend   User-defined suspend character (usually ^Z). Suspend the debugger.

On keyboards that support an extended keypad with arrow keys, mdb interprets the
following keystrokes as editing commands.

up-arrow   Fetch the previous command from the history (same as ^P).

down-arrow

              Fetch the next command from the history (same as ^N).

left-arrow

              Move cursor backward one character (same as ^B).

right-arrow

              Move cursor forward one character (same as ^F).

Output Pager

mdb provides a built-in output pager. The output pager is enabled when the debugger's
standard output is a terminal device. Each time a command is executed, mdb pauses
after one screenful of output and displays a pager prompt, as shown below.

```
>> More [<space>, <cr>, q, n, c, a] ?
```

The following key sequences are recognized by the pager.

Space   Display the next screenful of output.

a, A   Abort the current top-level command, and return to the prompt.

c, C   Continue displaying output without pausing at each screenful until the
              current top-level command is complete.

n, N, Newline, Return

              Display the next line of output.

q, Q, ^C, ^\

              Quit (abort) only the current dcmd.

Formatting dcmds

The /, \, ?, and = metacharacters are used to denote the special output-formatting
dcmds. Each of these dcmds accepts an argument list consisting of one or more format
characters, repeat counts, or quoted strings. A format character is one of the ASCII
characters shown below. Format characters are used to read and format data from the
target. A repeat count is a positive integer preceding the format character that is always
interpreted in base 10 (decimal). You can also specify a repeat count as an expression
enclosed in square brackets preceded by a dollar sign ($[ ]). A string argument must be
enclosed in double quotes (" "). No blanks are needed between format arguments.

The formatting dcmds are listed below.

/   Display data from the target's virtual address space starting at the virtual address specified by dot.

\   Display data from the target's physical address space starting at the physical address specified by dot.

?   Display data from the target's primary objectfile starting at the objectfile location corresponding to the virtual address specified by dot.

=   Display the value of dot itself in each of the specified data formats. The = dcmd is useful for converting between bases and performing arithmetic.

In addition to dot, mdb keeps track of another global value called the *increment*. The increment represents the distance between dot and the address following all the data read by the last formatting dcmd. For example, if a formatting dcmd is executed with dot equal to address A and displays a 4-byte integer, then after this dcmd completes, dot is still A, but the increment is set to 4. The + character (described in "Arithmetic Expansion" on page 823) would now evaluate to the value A + 4 and could be used to reset dot to the address of the next data object for a subsequent dcmd.

Most format characters increase the value of the increment by the number of bytes corresponding to the size of the data format, shown below. You can display the list of format characters from within mdb with the ::formats dcmd. The format characters are listed below.

+   Increment dot by the count (variable size).

–   Decrement dot by the count (variable size).

B   Hexadecimal integer (1 byte).

C   Character with C character notation (1 byte).

D   Decimal signed integer (4 bytes).

E   Decimal unsigned long long (8 bytes).

F   Double (8 bytes).

G   Octal unsigned long long (8 bytes).

H   Swap bytes and shorts (4 bytes).

I   Address and disassembled instruction (variable size).

J   Hexadecimal long long (8 bytes).

K   Hexadecimal uintptr_t (4 or 8 bytes).

N   Newline. New in the Solaris 9 release.   *New!*

O   Octal unsigned integer (4 bytes).

P   Symbol (4 or 8 bytes).

Q   Octal signed integer (4 bytes).

R   Binary integer (8 bytes). New in the Solaris 9 release.   *New!*

S   String using C string notation (variable size).

T   Horizontal Tab. New in the Solaris 9 release.   *New!*

U	Decimal unsigned integer (4 bytes).
V	Decimal unsigned integer (1 byte).
W	Default radix unsigned integer (4 bytes).
X	Hexadecimal integer (4 bytes).
Y	Decoded time32_t (4 bytes).
Z	Hexadecimal long long (8 bytes).
^	Decrement dot by increment * count (variable size).
a	Dot as symbol+offset.
b	Octal unsigned integer (1 byte).
c	Character (1 byte).
d	Decimal signed short (2 bytes).
e	Decimal signed long long (8 bytes).
f	Float (4 bytes).
g	Octal signed long long (8 bytes).
h	Swap bytes (2 bytes).
i	Disassembled instruction (variable size).
n	Newline.
o	Octal unsigned short (2 bytes).
p	Symbol (4 or 8 bytes).
q	Octal signed short (2 bytes).
r	White space.
s	Raw string (variable size).
t	Horizontal tab.
u	Decimal unsigned short (2 bytes).
v	Decimal signed integer (1 byte).
w	Default radix unsigned short (2 bytes).
x	Hexadecimal short (2 bytes).
y	Decoded time64_t (8 bytes).

You can also use the /, \, and ? formatting dcmds to write to the target's virtual address space, physical address space, or objectfile by specifying one of the following modifiers as the first format character and then specifying a list of words that are either immediate values or expressions enclosed in square brackets preceded by a dollar sign ($[ ]).

The write modifiers are listed below.

New!

v	Write the lowest byte value of each expression to the target beginning at the location specified by dot. Changed in the Solaris 9 release. In the Solaris 8 release, v and w were identical.

w   Write the lowest 2 bytes of the value of each expression to the target, beginning at the location specified by dot.

W   Write the lowest 4 bytes of the value of each expression to the target, beginning at the location specified by dot.

Z   Write the complete 8 bytes of the value of each expression to the target, beginning at the location specified by dot.

You can also use the /, \, and ? formatting dcmds to search for a particular integer value in the target's virtual address space, physical address space, and objectfile, respectively, by specifying one of the following modifiers as the first format character and then specifying a value and optional mask. The value and mask are each specified as either immediate values or expressions enclosed in square brackets preceded by a dollar sign. If you specify only a value, mdb reads integers of the appropriate size and stops at the address containing the matching value. If you specify a value V and mask M, mdb reads integers of the appropriate size and stops at the address containing a value X where (X & M) == V. At the completion of the dcmd, dot is updated to the address containing the match. If no match is found, dot is left at the last address that was read.

The search modifiers are listed below.

l   Search for the specified 2-byte value.

L   Search for the specified 4-byte value.

M   Search for the specified 8-byte value.

Note that for both user and kernel targets, an address space is typically composed of a set of discontiguous segments. It is not legal to read from an address that does not have a corresponding segment. If a search reaches a segment boundary without finding a match, it aborts when the read past the end of the segment boundary fails.

Execution Control

Starting in the Solaris 9 release, mdb provides facilities for controlling and tracing the execution of a live, running program. Currently, only the user process target provides support for execution control. mdb provides a simple model of execution control.

A target process can be started from within the debugger with ::run, or mdb can attach to an existing process with :A, ::attach, or the -p command-line option.

You can specify a list of traced software events. Each time a traced event occurs in the target process, all threads in the target stop, the thread that triggered the event is chosen as the representative thread, and control returns to the debugger. Once the target program is running, you can return asynchronous control to the debugger by typing the user-defined interrupt character (typically ^C).

A software event is a state transition in the target program that is observed by the debugger. For example, the debugger may observe the transition of a program counter register to a value of interest (a breakpoint) or the delivery of a particular signal.

A software event specifier is a description of a class of software events that is used by the debugger to instrument the target program to observe these events. Use the ::events dcmd to list the software event specifiers. A set of standard properties is associated with each event specifier, as described in the following paragraph.

The debugger can observe a variety of different software events, including breakpoints, watchpoints, signals, machine faults, and system calls. You can create new specifiers with ::bp, ::fltbp, ::sigbp, ::sysbp, or ::wp. Each specifier has an associated callback (an mdb command string to execute as if it had been typed at the command prompt) and a set of properties. You can create any number of specifiers for the same event, each with different callbacks and properties. The current list of traced events and the properties of the corresponding event specifiers can be displayed with the ::events dcmd. The event specifier properties are defined as part of the description of the ::events and ::evset dcmds in the following section.

The execution control built-in dcmds, described in "Built-in dcmds" on page 834, are always available but issue an error message indicating they are not supported if applied to a target that does not support execution control. For more information about the interaction of exec, attach, release, and job control with debugger execution control, see "Interaction with exec" on page 851.

New! ## Event Callbacks

Starting in the Solaris 9 release, the ::evset dcmd and event tracing dcmds enable you to associate an event callback (with the -c option) with each event specifier. The event callbacks are strings that represent mdb commands to execute when the corresponding event occurs in the target. These commands are executed as if they had been typed at the command prompt. Before each callback is executed, the dot variable is set to the value of the representative thread's program counter and the hits variable is set to the number of times this specifier has been matched, including the current match.

If the event callbacks themselves contain one or more commands to continue the target (for example, ::cont or ::step), these commands do not immediately continue the target and wait for it to stop again. Instead, inside an event callback, the continue dcmds note that a continue operation is now pending and then return immediately. Therefore, if multiple dcmds are included in an event callback, the step or continue dcmd should be the last command specified. Following the execution of all event callbacks, the target immediately resumes execution if all matching event callbacks requested a continue. If conflicting continue operations are requested, the operation with the highest precedence determines what type of continue occurs. The order of precedence from highest to lowest is step, step-over (next), step-out, continue.

New! ## Thread Support

Starting in the Solaris 9 release, mdb provides facilities to examine the stacks and registers of each thread associated with the target. The persistent thread variable contains the current representative thread identifier. The format of the thread identifier depends on the target. You can use the ::regs and ::fpregs dcmds to examine the register set of the representative thread or of another thread if its register set is currently available. In addition, the register set of the representative thread is exported as a set of named variables. You can modify the value of one or more registers by applying the > dcmd to the corresponding named variable.

The mdb kernel target exports the virtual address of the corresponding internal thread structure as the identifier for a given thread. The *Solaris Modular Debugger Guide* provides more information on debugging support for threads in the Solaris kernel. The mdb process target provides proper support for examination of multithreaded user processes that use the native lwp_* interfaces, /usr/lib/libthread.so or /usr/lib/lwp/libthread.so. When debugging a live user process, mdb detects when a single-threaded process dlopens or closes libthread and automatically adjusts its view of the threading model on-the-fly. The process target thread identifiers correspond to either the lwpid_t, thread_t, or pthread_t of the representative thread, depending on the threading model used by the application.

Built-in dcmds

mdb provides a set of built-in dcmds that are always defined. Some of these dcmds are applicable only to certain targets: if a dcmd is not applicable to the current target, it fails and prints a message saying command is not supported by current target. In many cases, mdb provides a mnemonic equivalent (::*identifier*) for the legacy adb(1) dcmd names. For example, ::quit is the equivalent of $q. Programmers who are experienced with adb(1) or who appreciate brevity or arcana may prefer the $ or : forms of the built-in commands. Programmers who are new to mdb may prefer the more verbose :: form. The built-in commands are listed in alphabetical order. If a $ or : form has a ::*identifier* equivalent, it is shown below the ::*identifier* form.

> *variable-name*
>/*modifier*/ *variable-name*

> Assign the value of dot to the specified named variable. Some variables are read-only and cannot be modified. If the > is followed by a modifier character surrounded by //, then the value is modified as part of the assignment. The modifier characters are listed below.

> c   Unsigned char quantity (1-byte).

> s   Unsigned short quantity (2-byte).

> i   Unsigned integer quantity (4-byte).

> l   Unsigned long quantity (4-byte in 32-bit, 8-byte in 64-bit).

Notice that these operators do not perform a cast; instead, they fetch the specified number of low-order bytes (on little-endian architectures) or high-order bytes (big-endian architectures). Modifiers are provided for backward compatibility; you should instead use the mdb */*modifier*/ and %/*modifier*/ syntax.

$< *macro-name*

> Read and execute commands from the specified macro file. You can specify the file name as an absolute or relative path. If the file name is a simple name (that is, if it does not contain a /), mdb searches for it in the macro file include path. If another macro file is currently being processed, this file is closed and replaced with the new file.

$<< *macro-name*

> Read and execute commands from the specified macro file (as with $<), but do not close the current open macro file.

$?   Print the process-ID and current signal of the target if it is a user process or corefile, and then print the general register set of the representative thread.

[*address*] $C [*count*]

> Print a C stack backtrace including stack frame pointer information. If the dcmd is preceded by an explicit address, display a backtrace beginning at this virtual memory address. Otherwise, display the stack of the representative thread. Specifying an optional *count* value displays no more than *count* arguments for each stack frame in the output.

[*base*] $d

> Get or set the default output radix. If the dcmd is preceded by an explicit expression, the default output radix is set to the given base; otherwise, the current radix is printed in base 10 (decimal). The default radix is base 16 (hexadecimal).

$e

> Print a list of all known external (global) symbols of type `object` or `function`, the value of the symbol, and the first four (32-bit mdb) or eight (64-bit mdb) bytes stored at this location in the target's virtual address space. The ::nm dcmd provides more flexible options for displaying symbol tables.

$P *prompt-string*

> Set the prompt to the specified *prompt-string*. The default prompt is >. You can also set the prompt with ::set -P or with the -P command-line option.

distance $s

> Get or set the symbol matching distance for address-to-symbol-name conversions. The symbol-matching distance modes are discussed along with the -s command-line option in "Options" on page 852. You can also modify the symbol-matching distance with the ::set -s option. If you specify no distance, display the current setting.

$v

> Print a list of the named variables that have non-zero values. The ::vars dcmd provides other options for listing variables.

width $w

> Set the output page width to the specified value. Typically, you do not need this command because mdb queries the terminal for its width and handles resize events.

$W

> Reopen the target for writing as if mdb had been executed with the -w option on the command line. You can also enable write with the ::set -w option.

[*pid*] ::attach [*core* | *pid*]
[*pid*] :A [*core* | *pid*]

> If the user process target is active, attach to and debug the specified process-ID or corefile. You specify the corefile path name as a string argument. You can specify the process-ID as the string argument or as the value of the expression preceding the dcmd. The default base is hexadecimal, so precede decimal PIDs obtained with pgrep(1) or ps(1) with 0t when you specify them as expressions.

New!

[*address*] ::bp [+/-dDesT] [-c *cmd*] [-n *count*] *sym*...
address :b [*cmd*...]

> Set a breakpoint at the specified locations. The ::bp dcmd sets a breakpoint at each address or symbol specified, including an optional address specified by an explicit expression preceding the dcmd and each string or immediate value following the dcmd. The arguments can be either symbol names or immediate values denoting a particular virtual

address of interest. If you specify a symbol name, it can refer to a symbol that cannot yet be evaluated in the target process. That is, it can consist of an object name and function name in a load object that has not yet been opened. In this case, the breakpoint is deferred and it is not active in the target until an object matching the given name is loaded. The breakpoint is automatically enabled when the load object is opened. The -d, -D, -e, -s, -t, -T, -c, and -n options have the same meaning as they do for the ::evset dcmd. If you use the :b form of the dcmd, a breakpoint is set only at the virtual address specified by the expression preceding the dcmd. The arguments following the :b dcmd are concatenated to form the callback string. If this string contains metacharacters, you must quote it. New in the Solaris 9 release.

::cat *filename*...

Concatenate and display files. You can specify each file name as a relative or absolute path name. The file contents are printed to standard output but are not be passed to the output pager. Use this dcmd with the | operator; you can initiate a pipeline with a list of addresses stored in an external file.

::cont [*SIG*]
:c [*SIG*]

Suspend the debugger, continue the target program, and wait for it to terminate or stop following a software event of interest. If the target is already running because the debugger was attached to a running program with the -o nostop option enabled, this dcmd simply waits for the target to terminate or stop after an event of interest. If you specify the optional signal name or number (see signal(3HEAD)) as an argument, the signal is immediately delivered to the target as part of resuming its execution. If the SIGINT signal is traced, you can asynchronously return control to the debugger by typing the user-defined interrupt character (usually ^C). This SIGINT signal is cleared automatically and is not observed by the target the next time it is continued. If no target program is currently running, ::cont starts a new program running as if by ::run. New in the Solaris 9 release.

address ::context
address $p

Switch context to the specified process. A context switch operation is valid only with the kernel target. You specify the process context by the address of its proc structure in the kernel's virtual address space. Use the special context address 0 to denote the context of the kernel itself.

mdb can perform a context switch only when examining a crash dump if the dump contains the physical memory pages of the specified user process (as opposed to just kernel pages). The kernel crash dump can be configured with dumpadm(1M) to dump all pages.

You can use the ::status dcmd to display the contents of the current crash dump.

When you request a context switch from the kernel target, mdb constructs a new target representing the specified user process. Once the switch occurs, the new target interposes its dcmds at the global level: thus, the / dcmd now formats and displays data from the virtual address space of the user process, the ::mappings dcmd displays the mappings in the address space of the user process, and so on. You can restore the kernel target by executing 0::context.

::dcmds   List the available dcmds and print a brief description for each one.

[*address*] ::delete [*id* | all]
[*address*] :d [*id* | all]

Delete the event specifiers with the given ID number. The ID number argument is interpreted in decimal by default. If you specify an optional address preceding the dcmd, all event specifiers that are associated with the given virtual address are deleted (for example, all breakpoints or watchpoints affecting that address). If you specify the special argument all, all event specifiers are deleted except those that are marked sticky (T flag). The ::events dcmd displays the current list of event specifiers. New in the Solaris 9 release.

[*address*] ::dis [-fw] [-n *count*] [*address*]

Disassemble, starting at or around the address specified by either the final argument or the current value of dot. If the address matches the start of a known function, the entire function is disassembled; otherwise, a "window" of instructions before and after the specified address is printed to provide context. By default, instructions are read from the target's virtual address space; specifying the -f option reads instructions from the target's objectfile instead. You can use the -w option to force "window" mode, even if the address is the start of a known function. The size of the window defaults to 10 instructions; you can explicitly specify the number of instructions with the -n option.

::disasms   List the available disassembler modes. When a target is initialized, mdb tries to select the appropriate disassembler mode. The user can change the mode to any of the modes listed with the ::dismode dcmd.

::dismode [*mode*]
$V [*mode*]

Get or set the disassembler mode. Specifying no argument prints the current disassembler mode. Specifying a mode argument switches the disassembler to the specified mode. You can display the list of available disassemblers with the ::disasms dcmd.

::dmods [-l] [*module-name*]

List the loaded debugger modules. Specifying the -l option prints the list of the dcmds and walkers associated with each dmod below its name. You can restrict the output to a particular dmod by specifying its name as an additional argument.

[*address*] ::dump [-eqrstu] [-f|-p] [-g *bytes*] [-w *paragraphs*]   *New!*

Print a hexadecimal and ASCII memory dump of the 16-byte-aligned region of memory containing the address specified by dot. If a repeat count is specified for ::dump, this is interpreted as a number of bytes to dump rather than a number of iterations. The ::dump dcmd also recognizes the following options.

-e   Adjust for endianness. The -e option assumes 4-byte words. You can use the -g option to change the default word size.

-f   Read data from the objectfile location corresponding to the given virtual address instead of from the target's virtual address space. The -f option is enabled by default if the debugger is not currently attached to a live process, corefile, or crash dump.

-g *bytes*

Display bytes in groups of *bytes*. The default group size is 4 bytes. The group size must be a power of 2 that divides the line width.

-p   Interpret address as a physical address location in the target's address space instead of a virtual address.

-q   Do not print an ASCII decoding of the data.

-r   Number lines relative to the start address instead of with the explicit address of each line. This option implies the -u option.

-s   Elide repeated lines.

-t   Read from and display only the contents of the specified addresses instead of reading and printing entire lines.

-u   Unalign output instead of aligning the output at a paragraph boundary.

-w *paragraphs*

Display *paragraphs* at 16-byte paragraphs per line. The default number of paragraphs is 1. The maximum accepted value for *paragraphs* is 16.

This dcmd is new in the Solaris 9 release and replaces the Solaris 8 ::dump dcmd.

::echo [*string* | *value*...]

Print the arguments separated by blanks and terminated by a newline to standard output. Expressions enclosed in $[ ] are evaluated to a value and printed in the default base.

::eval *command*

Evaluate and execute the specified string as a command. When the command contains metacharacters or white space, enclose it in double or single quotes.

```
::events [ -av ]
$b [ -av ]
```

Display the list of software event specifiers. Each event specifier is assigned a unique ID number that you can use to delete or modify the event specifier at a later time. The debugger can also have its own internal events enabled for tracing. These events are displayed only when you specify the -a option. Specifying the -v option shows a more verbose display, including the reason for any specifier inactivity. New in the Solaris 9 release. The following example shows some sample output.

```
> ::events
ID S TA HT LM Description                         Action
----- - -- -- -- ---------------------------- ------
[ 1 ] - T 1 0 stop on SIGINT                      -
[ 2 ] - T 0 0 stop on SIGQUIT                     -
[ 3 ] - T 0 0 stop on SIGILL                      -
...
[ 11] - T 0 0 stop on SIGXCPU                     -
[ 11] - T 0 0 stop on SIGXCPU                     -
[ 12] - T 0 0 stop on SIGXFSZ                     -
[ 13] -   2 0 stop at libc`printf                 ::echo
printf
>
```

The following list explains the meaning of each column. You can display a summary of this information with ::help events.

ID   The event specifier identifier. The identifier is in square brackets [] if the specifier is enabled, in parentheses () if the specifier is disabled, or in angle brackets < > if the target program is currently stopped on an event that matches the given specifier.

S   The event specifier state. The state is shown with one of the following symbols.

-     The event specifier is idle. When no target program is running, all specifiers are idle. When the target program is running, a specifier can be idle if it cannot be evaluated (for example, a deferred breakpoint in a shared object that is not yet loaded).

+   The event specifier is active. When the target is continued, events of this type are detected by the debugger.

*   The event specifier is armed. This state means that the target is currently running with instrumentation for this type of event. This state is visible only if the debugger is attached to a running program with the -o nostop option.

!   The event specifier was not armed because of an operating system error. You can use the ::events -v option to display more information about the reason the instrumentation failed.

TA   The Temporary, Sticky, and Automatic event specifier properties.
     One or more of the following symbols can be shown.

   t   The event specifier is temporary and is deleted the next time
     the target stops, regardless of whether it is matched.

   T   The event specifier is sticky and is not deleted by `::delete`
     `all` or `:z`. You can delete the specifier by explicitly specifying
     its ID number to `::delete`.

   d   The event specifier is automatically disabled when the hit
     count is equal to the hit limit.

   D   The event specifier is automatically deleted when the hit
     count is equal to the hit limit.

   s   The target stops automatically when the hit count is equal to
     the hit limit.

HT   The current hit count. This column displays the number of times
     the corresponding software event has occurred in the target since
     the creation of this event specifier.

LM   The current hit limit. This column displays the limit on the hit
     count at which the autodisable, autodelete, or autostop behavior
     takes effect. You can configure these behaviors with the `::evset`
     dcmd.

Description

A description of the type of software event that is matched by the
given specifier.

Action

The callback string to execute when the corresponding software
event occurs. This callback is executed as if it had been typed at
the command prompt.

`[id]` `::evset` `[+/-dDestT]` `[-c cmd]` `[-n count]` `id...`   *New!*

Modify the properties of one or more software event specifiers. The
properties are set for each specifier identified by the optional expression
preceding the dcmd and an optional list of arguments following the
dcmd. The argument list is interpreted as a list of decimal integers
unless you specify an explicit radix. New in the Solaris 9 release. The
`::evset` dcmd recognizes the following options.

`-c cmd`

Execute the specified *cmd* string each time the corresponding
software event occurs in the target program. You can display the
current callback string with `::events`.

-d   Disable the event specifier when the hit count reaches the hit limit. When you specify the +d form of the option, this behavior is disabled. Once you disable an event specifier, the debugger removes any corresponding instrumentation and ignores the corresponding software events until the specifier is subsequently reenabled. If the −n option is not present, the specifier is disabled immediately.

-D   Delete the event specifier when the hit count reaches the hit limit. Specifying the +D form of the option disables this behavior. The −D option takes precedence over the −d option. You can configure the hit limit with the −n option.

-e   Enable the event specifier. When you specify the +e form of the option, the specifier is disabled.

-n *count*

    Set the current value of the hit limit to *count*. If no hit limit is currently set and the −n option does not accompany −s or D, the hit limit is set to 1.

-s   Stop the target program when the hit count reaches the hit limit. Specifying the +s form of the option disables this behavior. The −s behavior tells the debugger to act as if the ::cont were issued following each execution of the specifier's callback, except for the *n*-th execution, where *n* is the current value of the specifier's hit limit. The −s option takes precedence over both the −D and −d options.

-t   Mark the event specifier as temporary. Temporary specifiers are automatically deleted the next time the target stops, regardless of whether it stopped as the result of a software event corresponding to the given specifier. Specifying the +t form of the option removes the temporary marker. The −t option takes precedence over the −T option.

-T   Mark the event specifier as sticky. Sticky specifiers are not deleted by ::delete all or :z. You can delete them by specifying the corresponding specifier ID as an explicit argument to ::delete. Specifying the +T form of the option removes the sticky property. The default set of event specifiers are all initially marked sticky.

You can display a summary of this information with ::help evset.

::files   Print a list of the known source files (symbols of type STT_FILE present
$f   in the various target symbol tables).

New!

[*flt*] ::fltbp [+/−dDestT] [−c *cmd*] [−n *count*] *flt*...

    Trace the specified machine faults. The faults are identified with an optional fault number preceding the dcmd, or a list of fault names or numbers (see <sys/fault.h>) following the dcmd. The −d, −D, −e, −s, −t,−T, −c, and −n options have the same meaning as they do for the ::evset dcmd. New in the Solaris 9 release.

[*thread*] ::fpregs   *New!*
[*thread*] $x, $X, $y, $Y

> Print the floating-point register set of the representative thread. When
> you specify *thread*—new in the Solaris 9 release—the floating-point
> registers of that thread are displayed. The thread expression should be
> one of the thread identifiers described in "Thread Support" on page 834.

::formats   List the available output format characters for use with the /, \, ?, and
                = formatting dcmds. The formats and their use are described in
                "Formatting dcmds" on page 830.

::grep *command*

> Evaluate the specified command string and then print the old value of
> dot if the new value of dot is non-zero. When the command contains
> whitespace or metacharacters, you must quote it. You can use the
> ::grep dcmd in pipelines to filter a list of addresses.

::help [*dcmd-name*]

> With no arguments, the ::help dcmd prints a brief overview of the help
> facilities available in mdb. When you specify *dcmd-name*, mdb prints a
> usage summary for that dcmd.

signal :i   If the target is a live user process, ignore the specified signal and allow   *New!*
            it to be delivered transparently to the target. Delete all event specifiers
            that are tracing delivery of the specified signal from the list of traced
            events. By default, the set of ignored signals is initialized to the
            complement of the set of signals that dump core by default (see
            signal(3HEAD)), except for SIGINT, which is traced by default. New in
            the Solaris 9 release.

$i   Display the list of signals that are ignored by the debugger and that are   *New!*
        handled directly by the target. You can obtain more information on
        traced signals with the ::events dcmd. New in the Solaris 9 release.

::kill   Forcibly terminate the target if it is a live user process. The target is also   *New!*
:k   forcibly terminated when the debugger exits if it was created by the
        debugger with ::run. New in the Solaris 9 release.

$l   Print the LWPID of the representative thread if the target is a user   *New!*
        process. New in the Solaris 9 release.

$L   Print the LWPIDs of each SPW in the target if the target is a user   *New!*
        process. New in the Solaris 9 release.

::load [-s] *module-name*   *New!*

> Load the specified dmod. You can specify the module name as an
> absolute or relative path. If *module-name* is a simple name (that is, does
> not contain a /), mdb searches for it in the module library path. You
> cannot load modules with conflicting names; you must first unload the
> existing module. When you specify the -s option—new in the Solaris 9
> release—mdb remains silent and does not issue any error messages if the
> module is not found or could not be loaded.

```
::log [-d | [-e] filename]
$> [filename]
```

> Enable or disable the output log. mdb provides an interactive logging facility where you can log both the input commands and standard output to a file while the debugger is still interacting with you. The -e option enables logging to the specified file, or reenables logging to the previous log file if you specify no file name. The -d option disables logging. The $> dcmd enables logging if you specify a *filename* argument; otherwise, logging is disabled. If the specified log file already exists, mdb appends any new log output to the file.

```
::map command
```

> Map the value of dot to a corresponding value with the command specified as a string argument, and then print the new value of dot. When the command contains white space or metacharacters, you must quote it. You can use the ::map dcmd in pipelines to transform the list of addresses into a new list of addresses.

```
[address] ::mappings [name]
[address] $m [name]
```

> Print a list of each mapping in the target's virtual address space, including the address, size, and description of each mapping. If you precede the dcmd by an address, mdb shows only the mapping that contains the given address. Specifying a string name argument shows only the mapping matching that description.

New!
```
::next [SIG]
:e [SIG]
```

> Step the target program one instruction, but step over subroutine calls. If you specify an optional signal name or number (see signal (3HEAD)), the signal is immediately delivered to the target as part of resuming its execution. If no target program is currently running, ::next starts a new program running as if by ::run and stops it at the first instruction. New in the Solaris 9 release.

New!
```
[address] ::nm [-DPdghnopuvx] [object]
```

> Print the symbol tables associated with the current target. When you specify an optional address preceding the dcmd—new in the Solaris 9 release—mdb displays the symbol table entry only for the symbol corresponding to the address. When you specify an object name argument, the symbol table only for this load object is displayed. The ::nm dcmd also recognizes the following options.
>
> -d   Print value and size fields in decimal.
>
> -D   Print .dynsym (dynamic symbol table) instead of .symtab.
>
> -P   Print the private symbol table instead of .symtab.
>
> -g   Print only global symbols.
>
> -h   Suppress the header line.

-n   Sort symbols by name.

-o   Print value and size fields in octal.

-p   Print symbols as a series of ::nmadd commands. You can use this
      option with -P to produce a macro file that you can subsequently
      read into the debugger with $<.

-u   Print only undefined symbols.

-v   Sort symbols by value.

-x   Print value and size fields in hexadecimal.

value ::nmadd [-fo] [-e *end*] [-s *size*] *name*

Add the specified symbol *name* to the private symbol table. mdb provides
a private, configurable symbol table that can be used to interpose on the
target's symbol table, as described in "Symbol Name Resolution" on
page 826. The ::nmadd dcmd also recognizes the following options.

-e *end*

Set the size of the symbol to the value of *end*.

-f   Set the type of the symbol to STT_FUNC.

-o   Set the type of the symbol to STT_OBJECT.

-s *size*

Set the size of the symbol to *size*.

::nmdel *name*

Delete the specified symbol name from the private symbol table.

::objects   Print a map of the target's virtual address space, showing only those
             mappings that correspond to the primary mapping (usually the text
             section) of each of the known load objects.

::offsetof *type member*

Print the offset of the specified member of the specified type. The type
should be the name of a C structure. The offset is printed in bytes, unless
the member is a bit field, in which case the offset can be printed in bits.
The output is always suffixed with the appropriate units for clarity. The
type name can use the backquote (`) scoping operator described in
"Symbol Name Resolution" on page 826. You can use the ::offsetof
dcmd only with objects that contain symbolic debugging information
designed for use with mdb. See "Symbolic Debugging Information" on
page 852 for more information. New in the Solaris 9 release.

address ::print [-aCLtx] [-c *lim*] [-l *lim*] [*type*]

Print the data structure at the specified virtual address, using the given
type information. The type parameter can name a C struct, union, enum,
fundamental integer type, or a pointer to any of these types. If the type
is a structured type, the ::print dcmd recursively prints each member

of the struct or union. If the *type* argument is not present and a static or global STT_OBJECT symbol matches the address, ::print infers the appropriate type automatically. You can use ::print dcmd only with objects that contain symbolic debugging information designed for use with mdb. Refer to "Symbolic Debugging Information" on page 852 for more information.

-a   Display the address of each member.

-c   Limit the number of characters in a character array that are read and displayed as a string.

-C   Enforce no limit on the number of characters in a character array that are read and displayed as a string.

-l   Limit the number of elements in a standard array that are read and displayed.

-L   Enforce no limit on the number of elements in a standard array that are read and displayed.

-t   Display the type of each member.

-x   Display all integers in hexadecimal. By default, a heuristic is used to determine if the value should be displayed in decimal or hexadecimal.

You can modify the default values for -c and -l with ::set or the -o command-line option as described in "Options" on page 852. New in the Solaris 9 release.

::quit   Quit the debugger.
$q

New!

[*thread*] ::regs
[*thread*] $r

Print the general-purpose register set of the representative thread. When you specify *thread*—new in the Solaris 9 release—the general-purpose register of that thread is displayed. The *thread* expression should be one of the thread identifiers described in "Thread Support" on page 834.

New!

::release [-a]
:R [-a]

Release the previously attached process or corefile. When you specify the -a option—new in the Solaris 9 release—the process is released and left stopped and abandoned. You can subsequently continue it with prun(1) (see proc(1)) or resume it by applying mdb or another debugger. By default, a released process is forcibly terminated if it was created by mdb with ::run, or it is released and set running if it was attached to by mdb with the -p option or with the ::attach or :A dcmds.

[path] *[-P prompt]*
::set *[-wF]* *[+/-o option]* *[- s distance]* *[I path]* *[-L]*

>Get or set miscellaneous debugger properties. Specifying no options, displays the current set of debugger properties. The ::set dcmd recognizes the following options.

>-F   Forcibly take over the next user process that ::attach is applied to as if mdb was executed with the -F option on the command line.

>-I *path*

>>Set the default path for locating macro files. The *path* argument can contain any of the special tokens described for the -I command-line option in "Options" on page 852.

>-L   Set the default path for locating debugger modules. The path argument can contain any of the special tokens described for the -I command-line option in "Options" on page 852.

>-o *option*

>>Enable the specified debugger option. If you use the +o form, the option is disabled. The option strings are described along with the -o command-line option in "Options" on page 852.

>-P   Set the command prompt to the specified prompt string.

>-s *distance*

>>Set the symbol-matching distance to the specified distance. Refer to the description of the -s command-line option in "Options" on page 852 for more information.

>-w   Reopen the target for writing, as if mdb had been executed with the -w option on the command line.

[signal] ::sigbp *[+/-dDestT]* *[-c cmd]* *[-n count]* *SIG*...   **New!**
[signal] :t *[+/-dDestT]* *[-c cmd]* *[-n count]* *SIG*...

>Trace delivery of the specified signals. You identify signals with an optional signal number preceding the dcmd or with a list of signal names or numbers (see signal (3HEAD)) following the dcmd. The -d, -D, -e, -s, -t, -T, -c, and -n options have the same meaning as for the ::evset dcmd on page 833. Initially, the set of signals for the process that dumped core by default (see signal(3HEAD)) and SIGINT are traced. New in the Solaris 9 release.

::sizeof *type*   **New!**

>Print the size of the specified type in bytes. The *type* parameter can name a C struct, union, enum, fundamental integer type, or a pointer to any of these types. The type name can use the backquote (`) scoping operator described in "Symbol Name Resolution" on page 826. The ::sizeof dcmd can be used only with objects that contain symbolic debugging information designed for use with mdb. See "Symbolic Debugging Information" on page 852 for more information. New in the Solaris 9 release.

[*address*] ::stack [*count*]
[*address*] $c [*count*]

> Print a C stack backtrace. If the dcmd is preceded by an explicit address, display a backtrace beginning at this virtual memory address. Otherwise, display the stack of the representative thread. Specifying an optional *count* value as an argument displays no more than *count* arguments for each stack frame in the output.

::status Print a summary of information related to the current target.

New! :step [over | out] [*SIG*]
:s [*SIG*]
:u [*SIG*]

> Step the target program one instruction. If you specify an optional signal name or number (see signal(3HEAD)), the signal is immediately delivered to the target as part of resuming its execution. When you specify the optional over argument, ::step steps over subroutine calls. The ::step over argument is the same as the ::next dcmd. When you specify the optional out argument, the target program continues until the representative thread returns from the current function. If no target program is currently running, ::step out starts a new program running as if by ::run and stops at the first instruction. The :s dcmd is the same as ::step. The :u dcmd is the same as ::step out. New in the Solaris 9 release.

New! [syscall] ::sysbp [+/-dDestT] [-io] [-c *cmd*] [-n *count*] *syscall*...

> Trace entry to or exit from the specified system calls. Identify system calls as an optional system call number preceding the dcmd or a list of system call names or numbers (see <sys/syscall.h>) following the dcmd. When you specify the -i option (the default), the event specifiers trigger on entry into the kernel for each system call. When you specify the -o option, the event specifiers trigger on exit from the kernel. The -d, -D, -e, -s, -t, -T, -c, and -n options have the same meaning as for the ::evset dcmd on page 833. New in the Solaris 9 release.

::typeset [+/-t] *variable-name*...

> Set attributes for named variables. Specifying one or more variable names defines them and sets them to the value of dot. Specifying the -t option sets the user-defined tag associated with each variable. Specifying the +t option clears the tag. Specifying no variable names prints the list of variables and their values.

::unload *module-name*

> Unload the specified dmod. You can print the list of active dmods with the ::dmods dcmd. Built-in modules cannot be unloaded. Modules that are busy (that is, provide dcmds that are currently executing) cannot be unloaded.

`::unset` *variable-name*...

> Unset (remove) the specified variable(s) from the list of defined variables. Some variables exported by mdb are marked as persistent and you cannot unset those variables.

`::vars` [-npt]

> Print a listing of named variables. Specifying the -n option restricts the output to variables that currently have non-zero values. Specifying the -p option prints the variables in a form suitable for reprocessing by the debugger with the $< dcmd. You can use this option to record the variables to a macro file and then restore these values later. Specifying the -t option prints only the tagged variables. You can tag variables with the -t option of the `::typeset` dcmd.

`::version` Print the debugger version number.

address `::vtop`

> Print the physical address mapping for the specified virtual address, if possible. The `::vtop` dcmd is available only when examining a kernel target or when examining a user process inside a kernel crash dump (after issuing a `::context` dcmd).

[*address*] `::walk` *walker-name* [*variable-name*]

> Walk through the elements of a data structure with the specified walker. You can list the available walkers with the `::walkers` dcmd. Some walkers operate on a global data structure and do not require a starting address. For example, walk the list of proc structures in the kernel.
>
> Other walkers operate on a specific data structure whose address you must explicitly specify. For example, given a pointer to an address space, walk the list of segments. When used interactively, the `::walk` dcmd prints the address of each element of the data structure in the default base. You can also use this dcmd to provide a list of addresses for a pipeline. You can use the backquote (`) scoping operator described in "dcmd and Walker Name Resolution" on page 828 with *walker-name*. Specifying the optional *variable-name* assigns the specified variable the value returned at each step of the walk when mdb invokes the next stage of the pipeline.

`::walkers` List the available walkers, and print a brief description of each one.

`::whence` [-v] *name*...
`::which` [-v] *name*...

> Print the dmod that exports the specified dcmds and walkers. You can use these dcmds to determine which dmod is currently providing the global definition of the given dcmd or walker. See "dcmd and Walker Name Resolution" on page 828 for more information on global name resolution. Specifying the -v option prints the alternative definitions of each dcmd and walker in order of precedence.

```
addr [,len] ::wp [+/-dDestT] [-rwx] [-c cmd] [-n count]
addr [,len] :a [-c cmd...]
addr [,len] :p [-c cmd...]
addr [,len] :w [-c cmd...]
```

Set a watchpoint at the specified address. You can set the length of the watched region in bytes by specifying an optional repeat count preceding the dcmd. If you set no explicit length, the default is one byte. The ::wp dcmd enables you to configure the watchpoint to trigger on any combination of read (-r), write (-w), or execute (-x) access. The -d, -D, -e, -s, -t, -T, -c, and -n options have the same meaning as for the ::evset dcmd on page 833. The :a dcmd sets a read access watchpoint at the specified address. The :p dcmd sets an execute access watchpoint at the specified address. The :w dcmd sets a write access watchpoint at the specified address. The arguments following the :a, :p, and :w dcmds are concatenated to form the callback string. If this string contains metacharacters, you must quote it. New in the Solaris 9 release.

::xdata
List the external data buffers exported by the current target. External data buffers represent information associated with the target that cannot be accessed through standard target facilities (that is, an address space, symbol table, or register set). These buffers can be consumed by dcmds; for more information, refer to the *Solaris Modular Debugger Guide*.

:z
Delete all event specifiers from the list of traced software events. You can also delete event specifiers with ::delete. New in the Solaris 9 release.

Warnings

Use of the Error Recovery Mechanism

The debugger and its dmods execute in the same address space, and it is quite possible that a buggy dmod can dump core or otherwise misbehave. The mdb resume capability, described in "Signal Handling" on page 828, provides a limited recovery mechanism for these situations. However, mdb cannot know definitively whether the dmod in question has corrupted only its own state or the debugger's global state. Therefore, a resume operation cannot be guaranteed to be safe or to prevent a subsequent crash of the debugger. The safest course of action following a resume is to save any important debug information and then quit and restart the debugger.

Use of the Debugger to Modify the Live Operating System

The use of the debugger to modify (that is, write to) the address space of a live, running operating system is extremely dangerous and can panic a system if the user damages a kernel data structure.

Notes

Limitations on Examining Process Corefiles

mdb does not provide support for examining process corefiles that were generated by a release of Solaris before Solaris 2.6. If a corefile from one operating system release is examined on a different operating system release, the runtime link-editor debugging interface (librtld_db) may not be able to initialize. In this case, symbol information for shared libraries is not available. Furthermore, because shared mappings are not present in user corefiles, the text section and read-only data of shared libraries may not match the data that was present in the process at the time it dumped core. Core files from Solaris Intel systems cannot be examined on Solaris SPARC systems, and vice versa.

Limitations on Examining Crash Dump Files   *New!*

mdb does not provide support for examining process corefiles that were generated by a release of Solaris preceding Solaris 2.6. If a corefile from one operating system release is examined on a different operating system release, the runtime link-editor debugging interface (librtld_db) may not be able to initialize. In this case, symbol information for shared libraries is not available. Furthermore, because shared mappings are not present in user corefiles, the text section and read-only data of shared libraries may not match the data that was present in the process at the time it dumped core. Core files from Solaris Intel systems cannot be examined on Solaris SPARC systems, and vice versa.

Relationship Between 32-bit and 64-bit Debugger

mdb provides support for debugging both 32-bit and 64-bit programs. Once it has examined the target and determined its data model, mdb automatically reexecutes the mdb binary that has the same data model as the target if necessary. This approach simplifies the task of writing debugger modules, because the modules that are loaded use the same data model as the primary target. You can use the 64-bit debugger only to debug 64-bit target programs. The 64-bit debugger can be used only on a system that is running the 64-bit operating environment.

The debugger may also need to reexecute itself when debugging a 32-bit process that   *New!* executes a 64-bit process, or vice versa. The handling of this situation is discussed in more detail in the next section.

Interaction with exec   *New!*

When a controlled process performs a successful exec(2), the behavior of the debugger is controlled by the ::set -o follow_exec_mode option. If the debugger and victim process have the same data model, then the stop and follow modes determine whether mdb automatically continues the target or returns to the debugger prompt following the execution. If the debugger and victim process have a different data model, then the follow behavior automatically reexecutess the mdb binary with the appropriate data model and reattaches to the process, still stopped on return from the exec. Not all debugger state is preserved across this reexecution.

If a 32-bit victim process executes a 64-bit program, then stop returns to the command prompt but the debugger is no longer able to examine the process because it is now using the 64-bit data model. To resume debugging, execute the ::release -a dcmd, quit mdb, and then execute mdb -p *pid* to reattach the 64-bit debugger to the process.

If a 64-bit victim process execs a 32-bit program, then stop returns to the command prompt, but the debugger provides only limited capabilities for examining the new process. All built-in dcmds work as advertised, but loadable dcmds do not because they do not perform data model conversion of structures. Release and reattach the debugger as described in the previous paragraph to restore full debugging capabilities.

New!

Interaction with Job Control

If the debugger is attached to a process that is stopped by job control (that is, it stopped in response to SIGTSTP, SIGTTIN, or SIGTTOU, the process may not be able to be set running again when it is continued by a continue dcmd. If the victim process is a member of the same session (that is, it shares the same controlling terminal as mdb), mdb tries to bring the associated process group to the foreground and to continue the process with SIGCONT to resume it from job control stop. When mdb is detached from such a process, it restores the process group to the background before exiting. If the victim process is not a member of the same session, mdb cannot safely bring the process group to the foreground, so it continues the process with respect to the debugger, but the process remains stopped by job control. mdb prints a warning in this case, and you must issue an fg command from the appropriate shell to resume the process.

New!

Process Attach and Release

When mdb attaches to a running process, the process is stopped and remains stopped until one of the continue dcmds is applied or the debugger quits. If you enable the -o nostop option before attaching the debugger to a process with -p or before issuing an ::attach or :A command, mdb attaches to the process but does not stop it. While the process is still running, you can inspect it as usual (albeit with inconsistent results) and enable breakpoints or other tracing flags. If you execute the :c or ::cont dcmds while the process is running, the debugger waits for the process to stop. If no traced software events occur, you can send an interrupt (^C) after :c or ::cont to force the process to stop and return control to the debugger.

   mdb releases the current running process (if any) when you execute the :R, ::release, :r, ::run, $q, or ::quit dcmds or when the debugger terminates as the result of an EOF or signal. If the process was originally created by the debugger with :r or ::run, it is forcibly terminated as if by SIGKILL when it is released. If the process was already running before mdb was attached to it, the process is set running again when it is released. A process can be released and left stopped and abandoned with the ::release -a option.

New!

Symbolic Debugging Information

The ::offsetof, ::print, and ::sizeof dcmds require that one or more load objects contain compressed symbolic debugging information suitable for use with mdb. This information is currently available only for certain Solaris kernel modules.

Developer Information

The *Solaris Modular Debugger Guide* provides a more detailed description of mdb features, as well as information for debugger module developers.

New!

   Starting in the Solaris 9 release, the header file <sys/mdb_modapi.h> contains prototypes for the functions in the MDB Module API, and the SUNWmdbdm package provides source code for an example module in the /usr/demo/mdb directory.

Options

-A   Disable automatic loading of mdb modules. By default, mdb tries to load
               debugger modules corresponding to the active shared libraries in a user
               process or corefile or to the loaded kernel modules in the live operating
               system or an operating system crash dump.

-f   Force raw file debugging mode. By default, mdb tries to infer whether the
              object and corefile operands refer to a user executable and core dump or
              to a pair of operating system crash dump files. If mdb cannot infer the file
              type, it defaults to examining the files as plain binary data. The -f
              option forces mdb to interpret the arguments as a set of raw files to
              examine. New in the Solaris 9 release.

-F   Forcibly take over the specified user process, if necessary. By default,
              mdb refuses to attach to a user process that is already under the control
              of another debugging tool such as truss(1). With the -F option, mdb
              attaches to these processes anyway. This option can produce unexpected
              interactions between mdb and the other tools trying to control the
              process.

-I *path*   Set the default path for locating macro files. Macro files are read by the
              $< or $<< dcmds. The path is a sequence of directory names delimited by
              colon (:) characters. The -I include path and -L library path can also
              contain any of the following tokens.

              %i   Expand to the current instruction set architecture (ISA)
                        name (sparc or sparcv9).

              %o   Expand to the old value of the path being modified. This
                        token is useful for appending or prepending directories to
                        an existing path.

              %p   Expand to the current platform string (either uname -i or
                        the platform string stored in the process corefile or crash
                        dump).

              %r   Expand to the path name of the root directory. You can
                        specify an alternative root directory with the -R option. If
                        you specify no -R option, the root directory is derived
                        dynamically from the path to the mdb executable itself.

                        For example, if you execute /bin/mdb, the root directory
                        is /. If you execute /net/*hostname*/bin/mdb, the root
                        directory is derived as /net/*hostname*.

              %t   Expand to the name of the current target. This name is
                        either the literal string proc (a user process or user
                        process corefile) or kvm (a kernel crash dump or the live
                        operating system).

              The default include path for 32-bit mdb is

              %r/usr/platform/%p/lib/adb:%r/usr/lib/adb

              The default include path for 64-bit mdb is

              %r/usr/platform/%p/lib/adb/%i:%r/usr/lib/adb/%i

-k   Force kernel debugging mode. By default, mdb tries to infer whether the object and corefile operands refer to a user executable and core dump or to a pair of operating system crash dump files. The -k option forces mdb to assume these files are operating system crash dump files. If you specify no object or core operand and specify the -k option, mdb defaults to an objectfile of /dev/ksyms and a corefile of /dev/kmem. Access to /dev/kmem is restricted to group sys.

-L *path*   Set the default path for locating debugger modules. Modules are loaded automatically on startup or with the ::load dcmd. *path* is a sequence of directory names delimited by colon (:) characters. The -L library path can also contain any of the tokens for the -I option.

-m   Disable demand-loading of kernel module symbols. By default, mdb processes the list of loaded kernel modules and performs demand loading of per-module symbol tables. Specifying the -m option prevents mdb from trying to process the kernel module list or provide per-module symbol tables. As a result, mdb modules corresponding to active kernel modules are not loaded on startup.

-M   Preload all kernel module symbols. By default, mdb performs demand-loading for kernel module symbols: the complete symbol table for a module is read when an address that is that module's text or data section is referenced. With the -M option, mdb loads the complete symbol table of all kernel modules during startup.

-o *option*   Enable the specified debugger option. Specifying the +o form of the option disables the debugger option. Unless noted below, each option is off by default. mdb recognizes the following option arguments.

         adb   Enable stricter adb(1) compatibility. The prompt is set to the empty string, and many mdb features, such as the output pager, are disabled.

         array_mem_limit=*limit*

                Set the default limit on the number of array members that ::print displays. If *limit* is the special token none, mdb displays all array members by default. New in the Solaris 9 release.

         array_str_limit=*limit*

                Set the default limit on the number of array members that ::print displays. If *limit* is the special token none, mdb displays the entire char array as a string by default. New in the Solaris 9 release.

         follow_exec_mode=*mode*

                Set the debugger behavior for following an exec(2) system call. New in the Solaris 9 release. *mode* should be one of the following named constants.

ask
If standard out is a terminal device, mdb stops after the exec(2) system call has returned and then prompts you to decide whether to follow the exec or stop. If standard out is not a terminal device, the ask mode defaults to stop.

follow
Follow the exec by automatically continuing the target process and resetting all of its mappings and symbol tables in accordance with the new executable. The follow behavior is discussed in more detail in "Interaction with exec" on page 851.

stop
Stop following return from the exec system call. The stop behavior is discussed in more detail in "Interaction with exec" on page 851.

follow_fork_mode=*mode*

New!

Set the behavior for following a fork(2), fork1(2), or vfork(2) system call. New in the Solaris 9 release. *mode* should be one of the following named constants.

ask
If standard out is a terminal device, mdb stops after the fork(2) system call has returned and then prompts you to decide whether to follow the parent or child. If standard out is not a terminal device, the ask mode defaults to parent.

parent
Follow the parent process, detach from the child process, and set it running.

child
Follow the child process, detach from the parent process, and set it running.

ignoreeof
Do not exit the debugger when an EOF sequence (^D) is entered at the terminal. You must use the ::quit dcmd to quit.

nostop
Do not stop a user process when attaching to it when you specify the -p option or when you apply the ::attach or :A dcmds. The nostop behavior is described in more detail in "Process Attach and Release" on page 852. New in the Solaris 9 release.

New!

pager
The output pager is enabled (default).

repeatlast
If you enter a newline as the complete command at the terminal, mdb repeats the previous command with the current value of dot. This option is implied by -o adb.

showlmid   mdb provides support for symbol naming and identifications in user applications that make use of link maps other than LM_ID_BASE and LM_ID_LDSO, as described in "Process Attach and Release" on page 852. Symbols on link maps other than LM_ID_BASE or LM_ID_LDSO are shown as LM*lmid*`library`symbol, where *lmid* is the link-map ID in the default output radix (16). You can optionally configure mdb to show the link-map ID scope of all symbols and objects, including those associated with LM_ID_BASE and LM_ID_LDSO, by enabling the showlmid option. Built-in dcmds that deal with objectfile names display link-map IDs according to the value of showlmid, including ::nm, ::mappings, $m, and ::objects. New in the Solaris 9 release.

-p *pid*   Attach to and stop the specified process-ID. mdb uses the /proc/pid/object/a.out file as the executable file path name.

-P *prompt*   Set the command prompt. The default prompt is >.

-R   Set root directory for path-name expansion. By default, the root directory is derived from the path name of the mdb executable itself. The root directory is substituted in place of the %r token during path-name expansion.

-s *distance*

   Set the symbol-matching distance for address-to-symbol-name conversions to the specified *distance*. By default, mdb enables a smart-matching mode by setting the distance to zero. Each ELF symbol table entry includes a value V and size S, representing the size of the function or data object in bytes. In smart mode, mdb matches an address A with the given symbol if A is in the range [v, V + v]. If you specify any non-zero distance, the same algorithm is used but v in the expression above is always the specified absolute distance and the symbol size is ignored.

-S   Suppress processing of the user's ~/.mdbrc file. By default, mdb reads and processes the .mdbrc macro file if one is present in the user's home directory, as defined by $HOME. Specifying the -S option prevents this file from being read.

-u   Force user debugging mode. By default, mdb tries to infer whether the object and corefile operands refer to a user executable and core dump or to a pair of operating system crash dump files. The -u option forces mdb to assume these files are not operating system crash dump files.

-V *dis-version*

   Set the disassembler version. By default, mdb tries to infer the appropriate disassembler version for the debug target. You can explicitly set the disassembler with the -V option. The ::disasms dcmd lists the available disassembler versions.

-w   Open the specified object and corefiles for writing.

-y
Send explicit terminal initialization sequences for TTY mode. Some terminals, such as cmdtool(1), require explicit initialization sequences to switch into a TTY mode. Without this initialization sequence, terminal features such as standout mode may not be available to mdb.

Operands

object
Specify an ELF format objectfile to examine. With mdb you can examine and edit ELF format executables (ET_EXEC), ELF dynamic library files (ET_DYN), ELF relocatable objectfiles (ET_REL), and operating system unix.*X* symbol table files.

core
Specify an ELF process corefile (ET_CORE) or an operating system crash dump vmcore.*X* file. If you provide an ELF corefile operand without a corresponding objectfile, mdb tries to infer the name of the executable file that produced the core with several different algorithms. If mdb finds no executable, it still executes but some symbol information may be unavailable.

suffix
Specify the numerical suffix representing a pair of operating system crash dump files. For example, if the suffix is 3, mdb infers that it should examine the files unix.3 and vmcore.3. The string of digits is not interpreted as a suffix if an actual file of the same name is present in the current directory.

Exit Status

0
Debugger completed execution successfully.

1
A fatal error occurred.

2
Invalid command-line options were specified.

Environment Variables

HISTSIZE
Determine the maximum length of the command history list. If this variable is not present, the default length is 128.

HOME
Determine the path name of the user's home directory, where a .mdbrc file can reside. If this variable is not present, no .mdbrc processing is done.

SHELL
Determine the path name of the shell used to process shell escapes requested by the ! metacharacter. If this variable is not present, /bin/sh is used.

Files

$HOME/.mdbrc

User mdb initialization file. The .mdbrc file, if present, is processed after the debug target has been initialized but before module autoloading is performed or before any commands have been read from standard input.

/dev/kmem   Kernel virtual memory image device. This device special file is used as the corefile when the live operating system is examined.

/dev/ksyms   Kernel symbol table device. This device special file is used as the objectfile when the live operating system is examined.

/proc/pid/*   Process information files that are read during examination and control of user processes.

/usr/lib/adb/usr/platform/*platform-name*/lib/adb

Default directories for macro files that are read with the $< and $<< dcmds. *platform-name* is the name of the platform, derived either from information in a corefile or crash dump, or from the current machine as by uname -i (see uname(1)).

/usr/lib/mdb/usr/platform/*platform-name*/lib/mdb

Default directories for debugger modules that are loaded with the ::load dcmds. *platform-name* is the name of the platform, derived either from information in a corefile or crash dump, or from the current machine as by uname -i (see uname(1)).

Attributes

See attributes(5) for descriptions of the following attributes.

Attribute Type	Attribute Value
Availability	SUNWmdb (32 bit)
	SUNWmdbx (64 bit)
Interface stability	Evolving

See Also

New!

adb(1), cmdtool(1), gcore(1), proc(1), pgrep(1), ps(1), stty(1), truss(1), uname(1), coreadm(1M), dumpadm(1M), savecore(1M), exec(2), fork(2), _lwp_self(2), pipe(2), vfork(2), dlopen(3DL), elf(3ELF), signal(3C), signal(3HEAD), libkvm(3LIB), libthread(3LIB), libthread_db(3LIB), signal(3HEAD), thr_self(3THR), threads(3THR), core(4), proc(4), attributes(5), largefile(5), ksyms(7D), mem(7D)
Linker and Libraries Guide
Solaris Modular Debugger Guide

mesg — Permit or Deny Messages

Synopsis

/usr/bin/mesg [-n | -y | n | y]

Description

The mesg command controls whether other users can send messages to a terminal device by using write(1), talk(1), or other commands. The terminal device affected is determined from a search for the first terminal in the sequence of devices associated with standard input, standard output, and standard error. With no arguments, mesg reports the current state without changing it. Processes with appropriate privileges may be able to send messages to the terminal independently of the current state.

Options

-n | n   Deny permission to other users to send message to the terminal. See write(1).

-y | y   Grant permission to other users to send messages to the terminal.

Examples

The following example uses the mesg command with no arguments to display the current state, and first turns off, then turns on, the ability to receive messages from another terminal.

```
castle% mesg
is y
castle% mesg -n
castle% mesg
is n
castle% mesg -y
castle% mesg
is y
castle%
```

Environment Variables

See environ(5) for descriptions of the following environment variables that affect the execution of mesg: LC_CTYPE, LC_MESSAGES, and NLSPATH.

Exit Status

0   Messages are receivable.

1   Messages are not receivable.

2   Error.

Files

/dev/tty*   Terminal devices.

/dev/pts*   Terminal devices.

Attributes

See attributes(5) for descriptions of the following attributes:

Attribute Type	Attribute Value
Availability	SUNWcsu

See Also

talk(1), write(1), attributes(5), environ(5)

mixerctl — Audio Mixer Control Command-Line Application

Synopsis

/usr/sbin/mixerctl [-a | -d *dev*] [-iv] [-e | -o]

Description

Some audio devices support the audio mixer functionality. See mixer(7I) for a complete description of the audio mixer. Use the mixerctl command, new in the Solaris 8 Operating Environment, to control the mode of the audio mixer and to get information about the audio mixer and the audio device. See audio(7I) for details.

Options

If you specify no options, option -i is assumed.

-a	Apply the command to all audio devices.
-d *dev*	The *dev* argument specifies an alternative audio control device for the command to use.
-e	Enable the audio mixer function if the audio device supports it. If supported, you can enable the audio mixer at any time. If the audio mixer is already enabled, the command silently ignores the enable option.
-i	Print the audio device type information for the device and indicate whether the audio device uses the audio mixer. If the device does use the audio mixer, this option displays the audio mixer's mode.
-o	Turn off the audio mixer function if the audio device supports it. You can turn off the audio mixer, if supported, only if one process has the device opened with the O_RDWR flag or if two different processes have the device opened, one with the O_RDONLY flag and the other with the O_WRONLY flag. The command silently ignores the disable option if the audio mixer function is already disabled.
-v	Verbose mode. Print the audio_info_t structure for the device, along with the device type information. This option implies the -i option.

Examples

The following example turns off the audio mixer function.

```
mopoke% mixerctl -o
Audio mixer for /dev/audioctl is disabled

mopoke%
```

The following example enables the audio mixer function.

```
mopoke% mixerctl -e
Audio mixer for /dev/audioctl is enabled

mopoke%
```

The following example prints information for the audio device.

```
mopoke% mixerctl -i
Device /dev/audioctl:
  Name    = SUNW,audiots
  Version = a
  Config  = onboard1

Audio mixer for /dev/audioctl is enabled

mopoke%
```

The following example prints the audio_info_t structure for the device along with the device type information. This option implies the -i option.

```
mopoke% mixerctl -v
Device /dev/audioctl:
  Name    = SUNW,audiots
  Version = a
  Config  = onboard1

Audio mixer for /dev/audioctl is enabled
Sample Rate
  Play        48000
  Record      48000
Channels
  Play        2
  Record      2
Precision
  Play        16
  Record      16
Encoding
  Play        3 (linear)
  Record      3 (linear)
Gain
  Play        191
  Record      127
Balance
  Play        32
  Record      32
Port
  Play        0x00000003 (SPKR|HDPHONE)
  Record      0x00000001 (MIC)
Avail Ports
  Play        0x00000007 (SPKR|HDPHONE|LINE)
  Record      0x00000043 (MIC|LINE|CODEC LOOPBACK)
Mod Ports
  Play        0x00000005 (SPKR|LINE)
  Record      0x00000043 (MIC|LINE|CODEC LOOPBACK)
```

```
Samples
   Play          0
   Record        0
Active
   Play          0
   Record        0
Pause
   Play          0
   Record        0
Error
   Play          0
   Record        0
EOF Count
   Play          0
Waiting
   Play          0
   Record        0
Open
   Play          0
   Record        0
HW Features                 0x0000001d
   PLAY
   RECORD
   DUPLEX
   INPUT TO OUTPUT LOOPBACK
SW Features                 0x00000001
   MIXER
SW Features Enabled         0x00000001
   MIXER

mopoke%
```

Environment Variables

AUDIODEV   If you do not specify the -d and -a options, the AUDIODEV environment
             variable is consulted. If set, AUDIODEV contains the full path name of the
             user's default audio device. The default audio device is converted into a
             control device and then used. If the AUDIODEV variable is not set,
             /dev/audioctl is used.

Files

/dev/audioctl/dev/sound/{0...n}ctl

Attributes

See attributes(5) for descriptions of the following attributes.

Attribute Type	Attribute Value
Architecture	SPARC, IA
Availability	SUNWauda
Stability level	Evolving

See Also

audioconvert(1), audioplay(1), audiorecord(1), open(2), attributes(5),
usb_ac(7D), audio(7I), audio_support(7I), mixer(7I)

New!

mkdir — Make Directories

Synopsis

/usr/bin/mkdir [-m *mode*] [-p] *dir*...

Description

Use the mkdir command to create new directories. If you specify a complete path name, the new directory is created at the bottom of the specified path. If you specify a directory name, the new directory is created as a subdirectory of the current directory. You must have write permission for the parent directory. When a new directory is created, standard entries in a directory (for instance, the files . for the directory itself and .. for its parent) are made automatically.

By default, new directories are created with mode 777 permissions. These permissions are altered by the file-mode creation mask (see umask(1)).

The owner ID and group ID of the new directories are set to the effective user-ID and group-ID of the process. mkdir calls the mkdir(2) system call.

setgid and mkdir

To change the setgid bit on a newly created directory, you must use chmod g+s or chmod g-s.

The setgid bit setting is inherited from the parent directory.

Options

-m *mode*	Specify the mode to be used for new directories. Choices for modes can be found in chmod(1).
-p	Create *dir* by first creating all the nonexisting parent directories. The mode given to intermediate directories is the difference between 777 and the bits set in the file-mode creation mask. The difference must be at least 300 (write and execute permission for the user).

Operands

dir	A path name of a directory to be created.

Usage

See largefile(5) for the description of the behavior of mkdir when encountering files greater than or equal to 2 Gbytes (2**31 bytes).

Examples

The following example creates the subdirectory structure ltr/jw/jan.

```
castle% mkdir -p ltr/jw/jan
castle% ls -lsa
```

```
total 6
    2 drwxr-xr-x   3 winsor   staff      512 Mar 15 15:30 .
    2 drwxr-xr-x  10 winsor   staff      512 Mar 15 15:30 ..
    2 drwxr-xr-x   3 winsor   staff      512 Mar 15 15:30 ltr
castle% cd ltr
castle% ls -lsa
total 6
    2 drwxr-xr-x   3 winsor   staff      512 Mar 15 15:30 .
    2 drwxr-xr-x   3 winsor   staff      512 Mar 15 15:30 ..
    2 drwxr-xr-x   3 winsor   staff      512 Mar 15 15:30 jw
castle% cd jw
castle% ls -lsa
total 6
    2 drwxr-xr-x   3 winsor   staff      512 Mar 15 15:30 .
    2 drwxr-xr-x   3 winsor   staff      512 Mar 15 15:30 ..
    2 drwxr-xr-x   2 winsor   staff      512 Mar 15 15:30 jan
castle% cd jan
castle% ls -lsa
total 4
    2 drwxr-xr-x   2 winsor   staff      512 Mar 15 15:30 .
    2 drwxr-xr-x   3 winsor   staff      512 Mar 15 15:30 ..
castle%
```

Environment Variables

See environ(5) for descriptions of the following environment variables that affect the execution of mkdir: LC_CTYPE, LC_MESSAGES, and NLSPATH.

Exit Status

0	All the specified directories were created successfully, or the -p option was specified and all the specified directories now exist.
>0	An error occurred.

Attributes

See attributes(5) for descriptions of the following attributes:

Attribute Type	Attribute Value
Availability	SUNWcsu
CSI	Enabled

See Also

rm(1), sh(1), umask(1), intro(2), mkdir(2), attributes(5), environ(5), largefile(5)

mkmsgs — Create Message Files for Use by gettxt

Synopsis

/usr/bin/mkmsgs [-o] [-i *locale*] *input-strings msgfile*

Description

Use the mkmsgs command to create a file of text strings that can be accessed by the text retrieval tools (see gettxt(1), srchtxt(1), exstr(1), and gettxt(3C)). mkmsgs takes as input a file of text strings for a particular geographic locale (see setlocale(3C)) and creates a file of text strings in a format that can be retrieved by both gettxt(1) and gettxt(3C). By using the -i option, you can install the created file under the /usr/lib/locale/*locale*/LC_MESSAGES directory (*locale* corresponds to the language in which the text strings are written).

   input-strings is the name of the file that contains the original text strings. *msgfile* is the name of the output file where mkmsgs writes the strings in a format that is readable by gettxt(1) and gettxt(3C). The name of *msgfile* can be up to 14 characters in length but cannot contain either \0 (null) or the ASCII code for slash (/) or colon (:).

   The input file contains a set of text strings for the particular geographic locale. Separate text strings with a newline character. Represent nongraphic characters as alphabetic escape sequences. Messages are transformed and copied sequentially from *input-strings* to *msgfile*. To generate an empty message in *msgfile*, leave an empty line at the correct place in *input-strings*.

   You can change strings by editing the *input-strings* file. Add new strings only at the end of the file; then, create a new *msgfile* file and install it in the correct place. If you do not follow this procedure, the retrieval function retrieves the wrong string and software compatibility will be broken.

Options

-o   Overwrite *msgfile* if it exists.

-i *locale*   Install *msgfile* in the /usr/lib/locale/*locale*/LC_MESSAGES directory. Create directories under /usr/lib/locale if they do not exist. Only someone who is superuser or a member of group bin can create or overwrite files in this directory.

Examples

The following example shows an input message source file C.str.

```
File %s:\t cannot be opened\n
%s: Bad directory\n
.
.
.
write error\n
.
.
```

   The following command uses the input strings from C.str to create text strings in the appropriate format in the file UX in the current directory.

```
castle% mkmsgs C.str UX
```

The following command uses the input strings from FR.str to create text strings in the appropriate format in the file UX in the directory /usr/lib/locale/fr/LC_MESSAGES.

```
castle% mkmsgs -i fr FR.str UX
```

You would be able to access these text strings if you had set the environment variable LC_MESSAGES=fr and then invoked one of the gettxt(1), srchtxt(1), or exstr(1) text retrieval tools.

Files

/usr/lib/locale/locale/LC_MESSAGES/*

Message files created by mkmsgs.

Attributes

See attributes(5) for descriptions of the following attributes:

Attribute Type	Attribute Value
Availability	SUNWloc

See Also

exstr(1), gettxt(1), srchtxt(1), gettxt(3C), setlocale(3C), attributes(5)

mkstr — Create an Error Message File by Massaging C Source Files

Synopsis

/usr/ucb/mkstr [-] *messagefile prefix filename*...

Description

mkstr creates files of error messages. You can use mkstr to make smaller programs from those that have a large numbers of error diagnostics. You reduce system overhead in running such programs because the error messages do not have to be constantly swapped in and out.

mkstr processes each of the specified file names, placing a massaged version of the input file in a file with a name consisting of the specified prefix and the original source file name. A typical example of using mkstr is

```
mkstr pistrings processed *.c
```

This command puts all the error messages from the C source files in the current directory in the file pistrings and puts processed copies of the source for these files into files whose names are prefixed with processed.

To process the error messages in the source to the message file, mkstr keys on the string error(" ' in the input stream. Each time it occurs, the C string starting at the " ' is placed in the message file, followed by a null character and a newline character. The null character terminates the message so it can be easily used when retrieved. The newline character makes it possible to sensibly use cat on the error message file to see its contents. The massaged copy of the input file then contains an lseek pointer into the file that can be used to retrieve the message.

```
char efilname[] = "/usr/lib/pi_strings";
      int efil = -1;
error(a1, a2, a3, a4)
      {
      char
            buf[256];
            if (efil < 0) {
efil = open(efilname, 0);
      if (efil < 0) {
oops:
      perror (efilname);
      exit (1);
            }
      }
      if (lseek(efil, (long) a1, 0) || read(efil, buf, 256) <= 0)
            goto oops;
      printf(buf, a2, a3, a4);
}
```

Notes

/usr/bin/more
Skipping backward is slow on large files.

usr/xpg4/bin/more
This command does not behave correctly if the terminal is not set up properly.

Options

- Put error messages at the end of the specified message file for recompiling part of a large mkstred program.

Attributes
See attributes(5) for descriptions of the following attributes:

Attribute Type	Attribute Value
Availability	SUNWscpu

See Also
xstr(1), attributes(5)

more, page — Browse or Page Through a Text File

Synopsis

```
/usr/bin/more [-cdflrsuw] [-lines] [+linenumber] [+/pattern] [file...]
/usr/bin/page [-cdflrsuw] [-lines] [+linenumber] [+/pattern] [file...]
/usr/xpg4/bin/more [-cdeisu] [-nnumber] [-p command] [-t tagstring]
   [file...]
/usr/xpg4/bin/more [-cdeisu] [-nnumber] [+command] [-t tagstring]
   [file...]
```

Description

The more command is a filter that displays the contents of a text file on the terminal, one screen at a time. It normally pauses after each screen. /usr/bin/more prints --More-- and /usr/xpg4/bin/more prints *file* at the bottom of the screen. If more is reading from a file instead of a pipe, the percentage of characters displayed so far is also shown.

Press Return to scroll one more line. Press the space bar to display another screen. Other commands are listed below.

The page command clears the screen before displaying the next screen of text; it provides only a one-line overlap between screens.

The more command sets the terminal to NOECHO mode so that the output can be continuous. Commands that you type do not normally show up on your terminal except for the / and ! commands.

The /usr/bin/more command exits after displaying the last specified file; /usr/xpg4/bin/more prompts for a command at the last line of the last specified file.

If the standard output is not a terminal, more acts just like cat(1), except that a header is printed before each file in a series.

Options

The following options are supported for both /usr/bin/more and /usr/xpg4/bin/more.

-c	Clear before displaying. Redraw the screen instead of scrolling for faster displays. Ignore this option if the terminal does not have the ability to clear to the end of a line.
-d	Display error messages instead of ringing the terminal bell if you use an unrecognized command. This option is helpful for inexperienced users.
-s	Replace multiple blank lines with a single blank line. This squeezing is helpful when viewing nroff(1) output.

/usr/bin/more

-f	Do not fold long lines. This option is useful when lines contain nonprinting characters or escape sequences, such as those generated when nroff(1) output is piped through ul(1).
-l	Do not treat formfeed characters (Control-L) as page breaks. If you do not use -l, more pauses to accept commands after any line containing a ^L character (Control-L). Also, if a file begins with a formfeed, clear the screen before printing the file.

-r   Display control characters such as $^\wedge C$, where C stands for any control character. Normally, more ignores control characters that it does not interpret in some way.

-u   Suppress generation of underlining escape sequences. Normally, more handles underlining, such as that produced by nroff(1), in a manner appropriate to the terminal. If the terminal can perform underlining or has a standout mode, supply appropriate escape sequences as called for in the text file.

-w   Prompt, and wait for any key to be pressed before exiting. Normally, more exits when it comes to the end of its input.

-*lines*   Display the indicated number of lines in each screen instead of the default (the number of lines in the terminal screen less 2).

+*linenumber*

     Start at *linenumber*.

+/*pattern*   Start two lines above the line containing the regular expression *pattern*. Note that, unlike editors, this construct should not end with a slash (/). If it does, then take the trailing slash as a character in the search pattern.

/usr/xpg4/bin/more

-e   Exit immediately after writing the last line of the last file in the argument list.

-i   Perform pattern matching in searches without regard to case.

-n *number*   Specify the number of lines per screen. The *number* argument is a positive decimal integer. The -n option overrides any values obtained from the environment.

-p *command*   For each file examined, initially execute the more command in the
+*command*   *command* argument. If *command* is a positioning command such as a line number or a regular expression search, set the current position to represent the final results of the command without writing any intermediate lines of the file. For example, the two commands:

```
more -p 1000j file
```

```
more -p 1000G file
```

     are equivalent and start the display with the current position at line 1000, bypassing the lines that j would write and scroll off the screen if it had been issued during the file examination. If the positioning command is unsuccessful, the first line in the file is the current position.

-t *tagstring*   Write the screen of the file containing the tag named by the *tagstring* argument. See the ctags(1) command.

-u   Treat a backspace character as a printable control character, displayed
                as a ^H (Control-H), suppressing backspacing and the special handling
                that produces underlined or standout-mode text on some terminal
                types. Also, do not ignore a Return character at the end of a line.

If you specify both the -t *tagstring* and -p *command* (or the obsolescent +*command*)
options, the -t *tagstring* is processed first.

Usage

Environment

more uses the terminfo(4) entry for the terminal to determine its display
characteristics.

more looks in the environment variable MORE for any preset options. For instance, to
page through files using the -c mode by default, set the value of this variable to -c.
(Normally, the command sequence to set up this environment variable is put in the
.login or .profile file).

Commands

The commands take effect immediately. It is not necessary to press Return unless the
command requires a file, command, tagstring, or pattern. Up to the time you type the
command character itself, you can type the line-kill character to cancel the numerical
argument. In addition, you can type the erase character to redisplay the
--More--(*xx%*) or *file* message.

In the following commands, i is a numerical argument (1 by default).

$i$space	Display another screen or i more lines if i is specified.
iReturn	Display another line, or i more lines, if specified.
ib | i^B	(Control-B) Skip back i screens, and then print a screen.
id | i^D	(Control-D) Scroll forward half a screen or i more lines. If i is specified, the count becomes the default for subsequent d and u commands.
if	Skip i screens, and then print a screen.
h	Give a description of all the more commands.
^L	(Control-L) Refresh.
in	Search for the i-th occurrence of the last pattern entered.
q | Q	Exit from more.
is	Skip i lines and then print a screen.
v	Drop into the vi editor at the current line of the current file.
iz	Same as space except that i, if present, becomes the new default number of lines per screen.
=	Display the current line number.

i/*pattern*	Search forward for the *i*-th occurrence of the regular expression *pattern*. Display the screen, starting two lines before the line that contains the *i*-th match for the regular expression pattern or the end of a pipe, whichever comes first. If more is displaying a file and there is no match, its position in the file remains unchanged. You can edit regular expressions by using the erase and kill characters. Erasing back past the first column cancels the search command.
! *command*	Invoke a shell to execute *command*. Replace the characters % and !, when used within *command*, with the current file name and the previous shell command. If there is no current file name, do not expand %. Prepend a backslash to these characters to escape expansion.
:f	Display the current file name and line number.
i:n	Skip to the *i*-th next file name given in the command line or to the last file name in the list if *i* is out of range.
i:p	Skip to the *i*-th previous file name given in the command line or to the first file name if *i* is out of range. If used while more is positioned within a file, go to the beginning of the file. If more is reading from a pipe, ring the terminal bell.
:q | :Q	Exit from more (same as q or Q).

/usr/bin/more
The following commands are available only in /usr/bin/more.

'	Single quote. Go to the point from which the last search started. If no search has been performed in the current file, go to the beginning of the file.
.	Repeat the previous command.
^\	Halt a partial display of text. Stop sending output and display the usual --More- prompt. Some output is lost as a result.

/usr/xpg4/bin/more
The following commands are available only in /usr/xpg4/bin/more.

i^F	(Control-F) Skip *i* full screens, and print a screen. (Same as *i*f.)
^G	(Control-G) Display the current line number (same as =).
*i*g	Go to line number *i* with the default of the first line in the file.
*i*G	Go to line number *i* with the default of the last line in the file.
*i*j	Display another line or *i* more lines if specified. (Same as *i*Return.)
*i*k	Scroll backward one or *i* lines if specified.
m*letter*	Mark the current position with the name letter.
N	Reverse direction of search.
r	Refresh the screen.
R	Refresh the screen, discarding any buffered input.

| *i*u | (Control-U) Scroll backward half a screen of *i* lines if specified. If you |
| *i*^U | specify *i*, the count becomes the new default for subsequent d and u commands. |

| ZZ | Exit from more (same as q). |

| :e *file* | Examine (display) a new file. If you specify no file, redisplay the current file. |

:t *tagstring*

> Go to the tag named by the *tagstring* argument, and scroll/rewrite the screen with the tagged line in the current position. See the ctags command.

| ' *letter* | Return to the position that was previously marked with the name *letter*. |

| ' ' | Return to the position from which the last move of more than a screen was made. Default to the beginning of the file. |

i?[!]*pattern*

> Search backward in the file for the *i*-th line containing *pattern*. The ! specifies to search backward for the *i*-th line that does not contain *pattern*.

| *i*/!*pattern* | Search forward in the file for the *i*-th line that does not contain the *pattern*. |

| ![*command*] | Invoke a shell or the specified command. |

Usage

See largefile(5) for the description of the behavior of more and page when encountering files greater than or equal to 2 Gbytes (2**31 bytes).

Environment Variables

See environ(5) for descriptions of the following environment variables that affect the execution of more: LC_COLLATE.

For /usr/xpg4/bin/more only: LC_CTYPE, LC_MESSAGES, NLSPATH, and TERM.

/usr/xpg4/bin/more

The following environment variables also affect the execution of /usr/xpg4/bin/more.

| COLUMNS | Override the system-selected horizontal screen size. |

| EDITOR | Used by the v command to select an editor. |

| LINES | Override the system-selected vertical screen size. The -n option has precedence over LINES in determining the number of lines in a screen. |

| MORE | A string specifying options. As in a command line, separate the options with blank characters, and start each option specification with a -. Process any command-line options after those specified in MORE as though the command line were: |

more $MORE *options operands*

Exit Status

0	Successful completion.
>0	An error occurred.

Files

/usr/lib/more.help

> Help file for /usr/bin/more and /usr/bin/page.

Attributes

See attributes(5) for descriptions of the following attributes:

/usr/bin/more /usr/bin/page

Attribute Type	Attribute Value
Availability	SUNWcsu
CSI	Not enabled

/usr/xpg4/bin/more

Attribute Type	Attribute Value
Availability	SUNWxcu4
CSI	Enabled

See Also

cat(1), csh(1), ctags(1), man(1), nroff(1), script(1), sh(1), ul(1), environ(4), terminfo(4), attributes(5), environ(5), largefile(5)

/usr/bin/more /usr/bin/page

regcomp(3C)

/usr/xpg4/bin/more

regex(5), xpg4(5)

---

mp — Text to PDL Pretty Print Filter

New!

Synopsis

/usr/openwin/bin/mp [-A4] [-C] [-D *target_printer_name*] [-F]
    [-L *localename*] [-P *target_spool_printer*] [-PS] [-US] [-a] [-c *chars*]
    [-d] [-e] [-ff] [-fp] [-l] [-m] [-o] [-p *prologue*] [-s *subject*] [-tm]
    [-ts] [-u *config_file_path*] [-v] [-w *words*] [-?] [*filename...*]

Description

The mp program is new in the Solaris 8 Operating Environment. When you call mp without the -D or -P option, it reads each file name in sequence and sends a prettified version of the contents in PostScript format to standard output. If you specify no *filename* argument, mp reads the standard input. If the standard input is a terminal, input is terminated by an EOF signal, usually Control-D.

The -D and -P options require the target printer name as an argument and produce the Printer Description Language (PDL) of the target printer. The -D option outputs the PDL to standard output. The -P option spools the PDL directly to the printer. In the absence of these options, mp produces default PostScript output.

The mp program accepts international text files of various Solaris locales and produces the output that is proper for the specified locale. The output also contains proper text layout. For example, because the complex text layout (CTL) is supported in mp, the output may contain bidirectional text rendering and shaping.

Mail items, news articles, ordinary ASCII files, complete mail folders, and digests are all acceptable input formats for mp. The output format includes grayscale lozenges or the outline of the same dimensions as the lozenges, containing banner information at the top and bottom of every page.

Options

-a	Format the file as a news article. The top banner contains the text Article from newsgroup, where *newsgroup* is the first news group found on the Newsgroups: line.
-A4	Use A4 paper size (8.26 x 11.69 inches).
-c *chars*	Specify the maximum number of characters to extract from the gecos field of the user's /etc/passwd entry. The default is 18.
-C	Instead of using \nFrom to denote the start of new mail messages, look for (and use) the value of the Content-Length mail header. If the Content-Length doesn't take you to the next \nFrom, then it is wrong, and mp looks for the next \nFrom in the mail folder.
-d	Format the file as a digest.
-D *target_printer_name*	
	Produce the PDL for the target printer. Requires X Print Server connection.
-e	Assume the ELM mail front-end intermediate file format. Used when printing messages from within ELM (with the p command), especially for printing tagged messages. You must specify this option in your ELM option setup.
-ff	Format the file for use with a Filofax personal organizer.
-fp	Format the file for use with a Franklin Planner personal organizer.
-F	Instead of printing the name of the recipient of the mail article, the top header displays the sender of the mail article. A useful option for people with their own personal printer.
-l	Format output in landscape mode. Two pages of text are printed per sheet of paper.

-L *localename*

> Provide the locale of the file to be printed. If this command-line option is not present, then mp looks for the MP_LANG environment variable. If that is not present, then the LANG environment variable is used. If none of these options are present, then mp tries to determine the locale it is running in, and if it cannot, then it assumes it is running in the C locale.

-m Format the file as a mail folder, printing multiple messages.

-o Format the file as an ordinary ASCII file.

-p *prologue*

> Use the *prologue* file as the PostScript/Xprt prologue file, overriding any previously defined file names. This file specifies the format of the print output. For PostScript output, the prologue file has a .ps extension; for Xprt clients (when you specify the -D option), this file has an .xpr extension. These files are defined in "Supplied Prologue Files" on page 876.

-P *target_spool_printer*

> Spool the PDL to the target printer. No output is sent to standard output. Requires X Print Server connection.

-PS If the mail or digest message has just PostScript as the text of the message, then this is normally just passed straight through. Specifying this option prints PostScript as text.

-s *subject*

> Use *subject* as the new subject for the printout. If you are printing ordinary ASCII files that have been specified on the command line, the subject defaults to the name of each of these files.

-tm Format the file for use with the Time Manager personal organizer.

-ts Format the file for use with the Time/System International personal organizer.

-US Use U.S. paper size (8.5 x 11 inches). U.S. is the default paper size.

-u *config_file_path*

> Specify an alternative configuration file to the default file /usr/lib/lp/locale/*locale_name*/mp/mp.conf. You must use the absolute file path name.

-v Print the version number of this release of mp.

-w *words* The maximum number of words to extract from the gecos field of the user's /etc/passwd entry. The default is 3.

-? Print the usage line for mp (notice that the ? character must be escaped if you use csh(1)).

Operands

filename   The name of the file to be read.

Environment Variables

XPDISPLAY   Used with option -D or -P to determine the X Print Display to which the client connects.

MP_PROLOGUE

Used to determine the directory in which the page formatting files (.xpr or .ps) are kept. These files determine characteristics such as page decorations, number of logical pages per physical page, and landscape or portrait format. In the absence of MP_PROLOGUE, the default location of the directory is /usr/lib/lp/locale/C/mp.

MP_LANGLANG

If you specify neither the -D nor -P option, a prologue file called /usr/openwin/lib/locale/*localename*/print/prolog.ps or /usr/lib/lp/locale/*localename*/mp/prolog.ps, where *localename* is the value of the MP_LANG or LANG environment variable, if present, is prepended to the output to be printed. If both are present, then prolog.ps is given preference for backward compatibility. If either of these files is not present and you do not specify the -D option, a configuration file of the locale called /usr/lib/lp/locale/*localename*/mp/mp.conf is used as the source of the configuration information that substitutes the prologue information for printing. The presence of prolog.ps disables mp.conf for backward compatibility.

Exit Status

0   Successful completion.

1   An error occurred.

Supplied Prologue Files

The following prologue files are provided. Files with .ps extensions are for the PostScript output; files with .xpr extensions are for the X Print Server client. .xpr files are created for 300dpi printers and scale to other resolution values.

mp.common.ps

Common prologue file for all other .ps files in this directory.

mp.pro.psmp.pro.xpr

Used by default.

mp.pro.ff.psmp.pro.ff.xpr

Used with the -ff option.

mp.pro.fp.psmp.pro.fp.xpr

Used with the -fp option.

`mp.pro.tm.ps` `mp.pro.tm.xpr`

> Used with the -tm option.

`mp.pro.ts.ps` `mp.pro.ts.xpr`

> Used with the -ts option.

`mp.pro.alt.ps` `mp.pro.alt.xpr`

> An alternative modification of the default prologue file that outputs the page number in the right corner of the bottom banner.

`mp.pro.l.ps` `mp.pro.l.xpr`

> Prologue file used for landscape outputs.

`mp.pro.altl.ps` `mp.pro.altl.xpr`

> Alternative prologue file used for landscape outputs.

Files

`.cshrc`   Initialization file for csh(1).

`.mailrc`   Initialization file for mail(1).

`/usr/bin/mp`

> Executable.

`/usr/lib/lp/locale/C/mp/mp.conf`

> Default configuration file.

`/usr/lib/lp/locale/C/mp/mp.common.ps`

> Common prologue file for all other .ps files in this directory. Not for .xpr files.

`/usr/lib/lp/locale/C/mp/mp.pro.ps`
`/usr/lib/lp/locale/C/mp/mp.pro.xpr`

> Default prologue files for mail printing.

`/usr/lib/lp/locale/C/mp/mp.pro.l.ps`
`/usr/lib/lp/locale/C/mp/mp.pro.l.xpr`

> Default prologue files for landscape format.

`/usr/lib/lp/locale/C/mp/mp.pro.altl.ps`
`/usr/lib/lp/locale/C/mp/mp.pro.altl.xpr`

> Alternative prologue files for landscape format.

`/usr/lib/lp/locale/C/mp/mp.pro.alt.ps`
`/usr/lib/lp/locale/C/mp/mp.pro.alt.xpr`

> Alternative "default" prologue files. Inserts page numbers in the bottom-right corner of each page.

`/usr/lib/lp/locale/C/mp/mp.pro.ff.ps`
`/usr/lib/lp/locale/C/mp/mp.pro.ff.xpr`

> Default prologue files for Filofax format.

/usr/lib/lp/locale/C/mp/mp.pro.fp.ps
/usr/lib/lp/locale/C/mp/mp.pro.fp.xpr

> Default prologue files for Franklin Planner format.

/usr/lib/lp/locale/C/mp/mp.pro.tm.ps
/usr/lib/lp/locale/C/mp/mp.pro.tm.xpr

> Default prologue files for Time Manager format.

/usr/lib/lp/locale/C/mp/mp.pro.ts.ps
/usr/lib/lp/locale/C/mp/mp.pro.ts.xpr

> Default prologue files for Time/System International format.

/usr/openwin/lib/locale/localename/print/prolog.ps
/usr/lib/lp/locale/localename/mp/prolog.ps

> Default locale-specific prologue file as an alternative to the mp.conf file. See "Environment Variables" on page 876 for more detail on the relationship. The structure and format for mp.conf and .xpr files are documented in the *International Language Environments Guide*. Refer to this document if you need to use alternative fonts, including Printer Resident Fonts, or if you want to make changes to output format.

Attributes

See attributes(5) for descriptions of the following attributes.

Attribute Type	Attribute Value
Availability	SUNWmp

See Also

csh(1), mail(1), attributes(5)
International Language Environments Guide

New! mpss.so.1 — Shared Object for Setting Preferred Page Size

Synopsis

/usr/lib/mpss.so.1

Description

Use the mpss.so.1 shared object, new in the Solaris 9 Operating Environment, to selectively configure the preferred stack and/or heap page size for launched processes and their descendants. For mpss.so.1 to be enabled, the following string must be present in the environment (see ld.so.1(1)) along with one or more MPSS (Multiple Page Size Support) environment variables.

LD_PRELOAD=$LD_PRELOAD:mpss.so.1

Notes

Because of resource constraints, setting the preferred page size does not necessarily guarantee that the target process(es) get the preferred page size.

Large pages are required to be mapped at addresses that are multiples of the size of the large page. Given that the heap is typically not large-page aligned, the starting portions of the heap—below the first large-page aligned address—are mapped with the system memory page size (see getpagesize(3C)).

The heap and stack preferred page sizes are inherited. A child process has the same preferred page sizes as its parent. On exec() (see exec(2)), the preferred page sizes are set back to the default system page size unless a preferred page size has been configured through the mpss shared object.

You can also use ppgsz(1), a proc tool, to set the preferred stack and/or heap page sizes. It cannot selectively configure the page size for descendants on the basis of name matches.

Environment Variables

If the mpss.so.1 shared object is specified in the LD_PRELOAD list, the following environment variables are read by the mpss shared object to determine to which created process(es) the specified preferred page size(s) should be applied.

MPSSHEAP=*size*
MPSSSTACK=*size*

> MPSSHEAP and MPSSSTACK specify the preferred page sizes for the heap and stack. The specified page size(s) are applied to all created processes.
>
> *size* must be a supported page size (see pagesize(1)) or 0, in which case the system selects an appropriate page size (see memcntl(2)).
>
> *size* can be qualified with K, M, G, or T to specify kilobytes, megabytes, gigabytes, or terabytes.

MPSSCFGFILE=*config-file*

> *config-file* is a text file that contains one or more mpss configuration entries of the following form.
>
> *exec-name*: *heap-size*: *stack-size*
>
> *exec-name* specifies the name of an application or executable. The corresponding preferred page size(s) are set for newly created processes (see getexecname(3C)) that match the first *exec-name* found in the file.
>
> *exec-name* can be a full path name, a base name, or a pattern string. See "File Name Generation" in sh(1) for a discussion of pattern matching.
>
> If *heap-size* and/or *stack-size* are not specified, the corresponding preferred page size(s) are not set.
>
> MPSSCFGFILE takes precedence over MPSSHEAP and MPSSSTACK.

MPSSERRFILE=*pathname*

> By default, error messages are logged with syslog(3C), using level LOG_ERR and facility LOG_USER. If MPSSERRFILE contains a valid path name (such as /dev/stderr), error messages are logged there instead.

Examples

The following example configures preferred page sizes with MPSSCFGFILE.

The following Bourne shell commands (see sh(1)) configure the preferred page sizes to a select set of applications with exec names that begin with foo, using the MPSSCFGFILE environment variable. The MPSS configuration file, mpsscfg, is assumed to have been previously created with a text editor such as vi(1). The cat(1) command is only dumping out the contents.

```
example$ LD_PRELOAD=$LD_PRELOAD:mpss.so.1
example$ MPSSCFGFILE=mpsscfg
example$ export LD_PRELOAD MPSSCFGFILE
example$ cat $MPSSCFGFILE
foo*:512K:64K
example$
```

Once the application has been started, you can use pmap (see proc(1)) to view the actual page sizes configured.

```
example$ foobar &
example$ pmap -s `pgrep foobar`
```

If the desired page size is not configured (shown in the pmap output), it may be because of errors in the MPSS configuration file or environment variables. Check the error log (by default: /var/adm/messages) for errors.

If no errors can be found, resource or alignment constraints may be responsible.

The following example configures preferred page sizes with MPSSHEAP and MPSSTACK.

The following Bourne shell commands configure 512K heap and 64K stack preferred page sizes for all applications with the MPSSHEAP and MPSSTACK environment variables.

```
example$ LD_PRELOAD=$LD_PRELOAD:mpss.so.1
example$ MPSSHEAP=512K
example$ MPSSTACK=64K
example$ export LD_PRELOAD MPSSHEAP MPSSTACK
example$
```

The preferred page size configuration in MPSSCFGFILE overrides MPSSHEAP and MPSSTACK. Appending the following commands to those in the previous example would configure all applications with 512K heap and 64K stack preferred page sizes with the exception of the ls command and all applications beginning with ora, in the configuration file.

```
example$ MPSSCFGFILE=mpsscfg2
example$ export MPSSCFGFILE
example$ cat $MPSSCFGFILE
ls::
ora*:4m:4m
example$
```

Attributes

See attributes(5) for descriptions of the following attributes.

Attribute Type	Attribute Value
Availability	SUNWesu (32 bit)
	SUNWesxu (64 bit)
Interface Stability	Evolving

See Also

cat(1), ld.so.1(1), pagesize(1), ppgsz(1), proc(1), sh(1), vi(1), exec(2), fork(2), memcntl(2), getexecname(3C), getpagesize(3C), syslog(3C), proc(4), attributes(5)

msgfmt — Create a Message Object from a Message File

Synopsis

/usr/bin/msgfmt [-D *dir* | --directory=*dir*] [-f | --use-fuzzy] [-g]
    [-v] [-o *output-file* | --output-file=*output-file*] [-s] [--strict]
    [-v] [--verbose] *filename*.po...

New!

Description

msgfmt creates message objectfiles from portable objectfiles (*filename*.po), without changing the portable objectfiles.

The .po file contains messages displayed to users by system commands or by application programs. You can edit .po files and rewrite the messages in them in any language supported by the system.

You can use the xgettext(1) command to create .po files from scripts or programs.

msgfmt interprets data as characters according to the current setting of the LC_CTYPE locale category.

Note — Neither msgfmt nor any gettext() routine imposes a limit on the total length of a message. However, each line in the *.po file is limited to MAX_INPUT (512) bytes.

Installing message catalogs under the C locale is pointless because they are ignored for the sake of efficiency.

Portable Objectfiles

Formats for all .po files are the same. Each .po file contains one or more lines, with each line containing either a comment or a statement. Comments start the line with a pound sign (#) and end with the newline character. All comments (except special comments described later) and empty lines are ignored. The format of a statement is:

New!

directive value

Each *directive* starts at the beginning of the line and is separated from *value* by white space such as one or more spaces or Tab characters. *value* consists of one or more quoted strings separated by white space. Use any of the following types of directives for the Solaris message file.

```
domain domainname
msgid message_identifier
msgstr message_string
```

New!

Starting with the Solaris 9 release, for a GNU-compatible message file, use any of the following types of directives.

```
domain domainname
msgid message_identifier
msgid_plural untranslated_string_plural
msgstr message_string
msgstr[n] message_string
```

New!

The behavior of the domain directive is affected by the options used. See "Options" on page 884 for the behavior when you specify the -o or --output-file option. (The --output-file option is new in the Solaris 9 release.) If you do not specify the -o or --output-file option, the behavior of the domain directive is as follows.

New!

- If you use the Solaris Message catalog file format—new in the Solaris 9 release—to generate the message objectfile or specify the --strict option, then put all *msgids* from the beginning of each .po file to the first domain directive into a default message objectfile, messages.mo. Otherwise, the default objectfile is named messages.

New!

- When msgfmt encounters a domain *domainname* directive in the .po file, put all following *msgids* until the next domain directive into the message objectfile *domainname*.mo if you use the Solaris message catalog file format—new in the Solaris 9 release—to generate the message objectfile or if you specify the --strict option. Otherwise, put the *msgids* into the message objectfile named *domainname*.

- Define duplicate *msgids* in the scope of each domain. That is, a *msgid* is considered a duplicate only if the identical *msgid* exists in the same domain.

- Ignore all duplicate *msgids*.

New!

The msgid directive specifies the value of a message identifier associated with the directive that follows it. The msgid_plural directive—new in the Solaris 9 release—specifies the plural form message specified to the plural message handling functions ngettext(), dngettext(), or dcngettext(). The *message_identifier* string identifies a target string to be used at retrieval time. Each statement containing a *msgid* directive must be followed by a statement containing a msgstr directive or msgstr[n] directives.

The msgstr directive specifies the target string associated with the *message_identifier* string declared in the immediately preceding msgid directive.

New!

The msgstr[n] directive—new in the Solaris 9 release—where n = 0, 1, 2, ..., specifies the target string to be used with plural form handling functions ngettext(), dngettext(), and dcngettext().

Message strings can contain the escape sequences \n for newline, \t for Tab, \v for vertical Tab, \b for backspace, \r for Return, \f for formfeed, \\ for backslash, \" for double quote, *ddd* for octal bit pattern, and \x*DD* for hexadecimal bit pattern.

GNU-Compatible Message Files

New!

Use one of the following formats for comments for a GNU-compatible message file (the msgfmt command ignores these comments when processing Solaris message files).

```
# translator-comments
#. automatic-comments
#: reference...
#, flag
```

The `#:` comments indicate the location of the mesgid string in the source files in *filename*: *line* format. The `#`, `#.`, and `#,` comments are informative only and are silently ignored by the msgfmt command. The `#,` comments require one or more flags separated by the comma character. You can specify the following flags.

fuzzy
: The translator can insert fuzzy to show that the msgstr string might not be a correct translation (anymore). Only the translator can judge if the translation requires further modification or is acceptable as is. Once satisfied with the translation, the translator removes the fuzzy flag. If this flag is specified, msgfmt does not generate the entry for the immediately following msgid in the output message catalog.

c-format
no-c-format

: The c-format flag indicates that the msgid string is used as a format string by printf-like functions. When the c-format flag is given for a string, the msgfmt command does some more tests to check the validity of the translation.

In the GNU-compatible message file, the msgid entry with empty string ("") is called the header entry and treated specially. If the message string for the header entry contains nplurals=*value*, the *value* indicates the number of plural forms. For example, nplurals=4 means that there are four plural forms. If nplurals is defined, the same line should contain plural=*expression*, separated by a semicolon character. The *expression* is a C language expression to determine which version of msgstr[n] is to be used, based on the value of n, the last argument of ngettext(), dngettext(), or dcngettext(). For example,

```
nplurals=2; plural= n == 1 ? 0 : 1
```

indicates that there are two plural forms in the language. msgstr[0] is used if n == 1; otherwise, msgstr[1] is used. In another example,

```
nplurals=3; plural= n == 1 ? 0 : n == 2 ? 1 : 2
```

indicates that there are three plural forms in the language. msgstr[0] is used if n == 1, and msgstr[1] is used if n == 2; otherwise, msgstr[2] is used.

If the header entry contains a charset=*codeset* string, *codeset* specifies the codeset to be used to encode the message strings. If the output string's codeset is different from the message string's codeset, codeset conversion from the message string's codeset to the output string's codeset is performed on the call of gettext(), dgettext(), dcgettext(), ngettext(), dngettext(), and dcngettext() for the GNU-compatible message catalogs. The output string's codeset is determined by the current locale's codeset (the return value of `nl_langinfo(CODESET)`) by default and can be changed by the call of `bind_textdomain_codeset()`.

Message Catalog File Formats

Starting with the Solaris 9 release, the `msgfmt` command can generate the message object both in Solaris message catalog file format and in GNU-compatible message catalog file format. If you specify the `-s` option and the input file is a Solaris `.po` file, the `msgfmt` command generates the message object in Solaris message catalog file format. If you specify the `-g` option and the input file is a GNU `.po` file, the `msgfmt` command generates the message object in GNU-compatible message catalog file format. If you specify neither the `-s` nor the `-g` option, the `msgfmt` command determines the message catalog file format as follows.

- If the `.po` file contains a valid GNU header entry (having an empty string for `msgid`), the `msgfmt` command uses the GNU-compatible message catalog file format.
- Otherwise, the `msgfmt` command uses the Solaris message catalog file format.

If the `msgfmt` command determined that the Solaris message catalog file format is used, as above, but found that the `.po` file contains directives that are specific to the GNU-compatible message catalog file format, such as `msgid_plural` and `msgstr[n]`, the `msgfmt` command handles those directives as invalid specifications.

Options

`-D `*`dir`*
`--directory=`*`dir`*

        Add *dir* to the list for input files search. New in the Solaris 9 release.

`-f`
`--use-fuzzy`

        Use fuzzy entries in output. If you do not specify this option, fuzzy entries are not included into the output. These options are ignored if Solaris message catalogs are processed. New in the Solaris 9 release.

`-g`   Generate the GNU-compatible message catalog file. You cannot specify this option with the `-s` option. New in the Solaris 9 release.

`-o `*`output-file`*
`--output=`*`output-file`*

        Specify the output file name as *output-file*. All domain directives and duplicate *msgid*s in the `.po` file are ignored. The `--output` option is new in the Solaris 9 release.

`-s`   Generate the Solaris message catalog file. You cannot specify this option with the `-g` option. New in the Solaris 9 release.

`--strict`   Append the `.mo` suffix to the generating message objectfile name if it doesn't have this suffix. This option is ignored if Solaris message catalogs are processed. New in the Solaris 9 release.

`-v--verbose`

        List duplicate message identifiers if Solaris message catalog files are processed. Message strings are not redefined.

If GNU-compatible message files are processed, this option detects and diagnoses input file anomalies that might represent translation errors. The msgid and msgstr strings are studied and compared. It is considered abnormal if one string starts or ends with a newline and the other does not. Also, if the string represents a format string used in a printf-like function, both strings should have the same number of % format specifiers, with matching types. If the flag c-format appears in the special comment # for this entry, a check is performed.

Examples

In the following example, module1.po and module2.po are portable message objects files.

```
castle% cat module1.po
# default domain "messages.mo"
msgid "msg 1"
msgstr "msg 1 translation"
#
domain "help_domain"
msgid "help 2"
msgstr "help 2 translation"
#
domain "error_domain"
msgid "error 3"
msgstr "error 3 translation"
castle% cat module2.po
# default domain "messages.mo"
msgid "mesg 4"
msgstr "mesg 4 translation"
#
domain "error_domain"
msgid "error 5"
msgstr "error 5 translation"
#
domain "window_domain"
msgid "window 6"
msgstr "window 6 translation"
castle%
```

The following command produces the output files, messages.mo, help_domain.mo, and error_domain.mo.

```
castle% msgfmt module1.po
```

The following command produces the output files, messages.mo, help_domain.mo, error_domain.mo, and window_domain.mo.

```
castle% msgfmt module1.po module2.po
```

The following example produces the output file hello.mo.

```
castle% msgfmt -o hello.mo module1.po module2.po
```

Environment Variables

See environ(5) for descriptions of the following environmental variables that affect the execution of msgfmt: LC_CTYPE, LC_MESSAGES, and NLSPATH.

Attributes

See attributes(5) for descriptions of the following attributes:

Attribute Type	Attribute Value
Availability	SUNWloc

See Also

xgettext(1), gettext(3C), setlocale(3C), attributes(5), environ(5)

mt — Magnetic Tape Control

Synopsis

/usr/bin/mt [-f *tapename*] *command*... [*count*]

Description

mt sends commands to a magnetic tape drive. If you do not specify -f *tapename*, the environment variable TAPE is used. If TAPE does not exist, mt uses the device /dev/rmt/0*n*.

Bugs

Not all devices support all options. Some options are hardware dependent. Refer to the corresponding device manual page.

mt is architecture sensitive. Heterogeneous operation (that is, Sun-3 to Sun-4 or the reverse) is not supported.

Options

-f *tapename*

Specify the raw tape device.

Operands

count   The number of times that the requested operation is to be performed. By default, mt performs *command* once; you can specify multiple operations of *command* with *count*.

command   Available commands that can be sent to a magnetic tape drive. You need specify only as many characters as are required to uniquely identify a command.

eof, weof   Write *count* EOF marks at the current position on the tape.

`fsf`	Forward space over *count* EOF marks. Position the tape on the first block of the file.
`fsr`	Forward space *count* records.
`bsf`	Backspace over *count* EOF marks. Position the tape on the beginning-of-tape side of the EOF mark.
`bsr`	Backspace *count* records.
`nbsf`	Backspace *count* files. Position the tape on the first block of the file. Equivalent to *count*+1 `bsf` followed by one `fsf`.
`asf`	Absolute space to *count* file number. This is equivalent to a `rewind` followed by an `fsf`.

If *count* is specified with any of the following commands, ignore the count and perform the command only once.

`eom`	Space to the end of recorded material on the tape. Useful for appending files onto previously written tapes.
`rewind`	Rewind the tape.
`offline,` `rewoffl`	Rewind the tape and, if appropriate, take the drive unit off-line by unloading the tape. The drive unit cycles through all four tapes.
`status`	Print status information about the tape unit.
`retension`	Rewind the cartridge tape completely, then wind it forward to the end of the reel and back to beginning-of-tape to smooth out tape tension.
`reserve`	Allow the tape drive to remain reserved after closing the device. The drive must then be explicitly released.
`release`	Reestablish the default behavior of releasing at close.
`forcereserve`	
	Break the reservation of the tape drive held by another host, and then reserve the tape drive. This command can be executed only with superuser privileges.
`erase`	Erase the entire tape. Erasing a tape may take a long time, depending on the device and/or tape. Refer to the device-specific manual for time details.

Exit Status

0	All operations were successful.
1	Command was unrecognized or `mt` was unable to open the specified tape drive.
2	An operation failed.

Files

/dev/rmt/*   Magnetic tape interface.

Attributes

See attributes(5) for descriptions of the following attributes:

Attribute Type	Attribute Value
Availability	SUNWcsu

See Also

tar(1), tcopy(1), ar(4), attributes(5), environ(5), mtio(7I), st(7D)

---

mv — Move Files

Synopsis

```
/usr/bin/mv [-fi] source target-file
/usr/bin/mv [-fi] source... target-dir
/usr/xpg4/bin/mv [-fi] source target-file
/usr/xpg4/bin/mv [-fi] source... target-dir
```

Description

Use the mv command to move files from one place to another or to change the name of a file.

In the first synopsis form, the mv command moves the file named by the *source* operand to the destination specified by *target-file*. *source* and *target-file* cannot have the same name. If *target-file* does not exist, mv creates a file named *target-file*. If *target-file* exists, its contents are overwritten. This first synopsis form is assumed when the final operand does not name an existing directory.

In the second synopsis form, mv moves each file named by a *source* operand to a destination file in the existing directory named by the *target-dir* operand. The destination path for each source is the concatenation of the target directory, a single slash character (/), and the last path-name component of the source. This second form is assumed when the final operand names an existing directory.

If mv determines that the mode of *target-file* forbids writing, it prints the mode (see chmod(2)), asks for a response, and reads the standard input for one line. If the response is affirmative, the move occurs if permissible; otherwise, the command exits.

Note that the mode displayed may not fully represent the access permission if the target is associated with an access control list (ACL). When the parent directory of source is writable and has the sticky bit set, one or more of the following conditions must be true:

- The user must own the file.
- The user must own the directory.
- The file must be writable by the user.
- The user must be a privileged user.

If *source* is a file and *target-file* is a link to another file with links, the other links remain and *target-file* becomes a new file.

If *source* and *target-file* or *target-dir* are on different file systems, mv copies the source and deletes the original; any hard links to other files are lost. mv tries to duplicate the source file characteristics to the target, that is, the owner and group ID, permission modes, modification and access times, and ACLs, and extended attributes—new in the Solaris 9 release—if applicable. For symbolic links, mv preserves only the owner and group of the link itself.

If unable to preserve owner and group ID, mv clears the setuid and setgid bits in the target. mv prints a diagnostic message to standard error if unable to clear these bits, though the exit code is not affected. mv may be unable to preserve extended attributes if the target file system does not have extended attribute support. /usr/xpg4/bin/mv prints a diagnostic message to standard error for all other failed attempts to duplicate file characteristics; the exit code is not affected.

To preserve the source file characteristics, you must have the appropriate file access permissions, including being superuser or having the same owner ID as the destination file.

Note — You can use -- to explicitly mark the end of any command-line options, enabling mv to recognize file-name arguments that begin with a -. As an aid to BSD migration, mv accepts - as a synonym for --. This migration aid may disappear in a future release. If a -- and a - both appear on the same command line, the second is interpreted as a file name.

Options

-f   Move the file(s) without prompting even if it is writing over an existing target. Note that this is the default if the standard input is not a terminal.

-i   Prompt for confirmation whenever the move would overwrite an existing target. An affirmative answer means that the move should proceed. Any other answer prevents mv from overwriting the target.

usr/bin/mv
Specifying both the -f and the -i options is not considered an error. The -f option overrides the -i option.

/usr/xpg4/bin/mv
Specifying both the -f and the -i options is not considered an error. The last option specified determines the behavior of mv.

Operands

source   A path name of a file or directory to be moved.

target-file
                A new path name for the file or directory being moved.

target-dir   A path name of an existing directory into which to move the input files.

Usage

See largefile(5) for the description of the behavior of mv when encountering files greater than or equal to 2 Gbytes (2**31 bytes).

Environment Variables

See environ(5) for descriptions of the following environment variables that affect the execution of mv: LC_CTYPE, LC_MESSAGES, and NLSPATH.

Exit Status

0	All input files were moved successfully.
>0	An error occurred.

Attributes

See attributes(5) for descriptions of the following attributes:

Attribute Type	Attribute Value
Availability	SUNWcsu
CSI	Enabled
Interface Stability	Stable

/usr/xpg4/bin/mv

Attribute Type	Attribute Value
Availability	SUNWxcu4
CSI	Enabled
Interface Stability	Standard

See Also

cp(1), cpio(1), ln(1), rm(1), setfacl(1), chmod(2), attributes(5), environ(5), fsattr(5), largefile(5), XPG4(5)

N

---

nawk — New Pattern Scanning and Processing Language

Synopsis

```
/usr/bin/nawk [-F ERE] [-v assignment] 'program' | -f progfile
    [argument...]
/usr/xpg4/bin/awk [-F ERE] [-v assignment 'program' |   -f progfile
    [argument...]
```

Description

The awk command is a complete programming language that is very useful for computation and pattern matching. The name awk is an acronym composed of the last initials of the three developers of the language: Aho, Weinberger, and Kernighan. The nawk (new awk) command is a greatly enhanced and optimized version of awk.

The /usr/bin/nawk and /usr/xpg4/bin/awk commands execute programs written in the nawk programming language, which is specialized for manipulating textual data. A nawk program is a sequence of patterns and corresponding actions. You must enclose the string specifying *program* in single quotes (') to protect it from interpretation by the shell. You can specify the sequence of pattern-action statements in the command line as *program* or in one or more files that you specify with the -f *progfile* option. When input that matches a pattern is read, the action associated with the pattern is performed.

Input is interpreted as a sequence of records. By default, a record is a line, but you can change this default by using the RS built-in variable. Each record of input is matched to each pattern in the program. For each pattern matched, the associated action is executed.

The nawk command interprets each input record as a sequence of fields where, by default, a field is a string of nonblank characters. You can change this default white-space field delimiter (blanks and/or tabs) by using the FS built-in variable or the -F *ERE* option. The nawk command denotes the first field in a record as $1, the second $2, and so forth. The symbol $0 refers to the entire record; setting any other field reevaluates $0. Assigning to $0 resets the values of all fields and the NF built-in variable.

Notes

nawk is a new version of awk that provides capabilities unavailable in previous versions. This version becomes the default version of awk in the next major release.

Input white space is not preserved on output if fields are involved.

There are no explicit conversions between numbers and strings. To force an expression to be treated as a number, add 0 to it; to force it to be treated as a string, concatenate the null string (" ") to it.

Options

-F *ERE*   Define the input field separator to be the extended regular expression *ERE*, before any input is read (can be a character).

-f *progfile*

Specify the path name of the file *progfile* containing a nawk program. If you specify multiple instances of this option, process the concatenation of the files in the order specified in *progfile*. Alternatively, you can specify the nawk program in the command line as a single argument.

-v *assignment*

The *assignment* argument must be in the same form as an *assignment* operand. The assignment is of the form *var*=*value*, where *var* is the name of one of the variables described below. The specified assignment occurs before the nawk program is executed including the actions associated with BEGIN patterns (if any). You can specify this option multiple times.

Operands

program   If you specify no -f option, the first operand to nawk is the text of the nawk program. The application supplies the *program* operand as a single argument to nawk. If the text does not end in a newline character, nawk interprets the text as if it did.

argument   You can intermix either of the following two types of arguments.

file   A path name of a file that contains the input to be read, which is matched against the set of patterns in the program. If you specify no file operands or if a file operand is -, use the standard input.

assignment   An operand that begins with an underscore or
             alphabetic character from the portable character set,
             followed by a sequence of underscores, digits, and
             alphabetics from the portable character set, followed by
             the = character specifies a variable assignment instead
             of a path name. The characters before the = represent
             the name of a nawk variable; if that name is a nawk
             reserved word, the behavior is undefined. The
             characters following the equal sign are interpreted as if
             they appeared in the nawk program preceded and
             followed by a double-quote (") character, as a STRING
             token. When the last character is an unescaped
             backslash, it is interpreted as a literal backslash
             instead of as the first character of the sequence "\". The
             variable is assigned the value of that STRING token. If
             the value is considered a numeric string, the variable is
             assigned its numeric value. Each such variable
             assignment is performed just before the processing of
             the following file (if any). Thus, an assignment before
             the first file argument is executed after the BEGIN
             actions (if any), whereas an assignment after the last
             file argument is executed before the END actions (if any).
             If there are no file arguments, execute assignments
             before processing the standard input.

Input Files

Input files to the nawk program can come from any of the following sources:

- Any file operands or their equivalents, achieved by modifying the nawk variables ARGV and ARGC.
- Standard input in the absence of any file operands.
- Text file arguments to the getline function. Whether the variable RS is set to a value other than a newline character, for these files, implementations support records terminated with the specified separator up to {LINE_MAX} bytes and can support longer records.
- Text file arguments to the -f *progfile* option containing a nawk program.
- The standard input when you specify no file operands or if a file operand is -.

Extended Description

A nawk program is composed of pairs of the form:

pattern { action }

You can omit either the *pattern* or the *action*, including the enclosing brace characters. Separate pattern-action statements by a semicolon or by a newline.

A missing pattern matches any record of input, and a missing action is equivalent to an action that writes the matched record of input to standard output.

Execution of the nawk program is done as follows.

1. The actions associated with all BEGIN patterns are executed in the order they occur in the program.
2. Each file operand (or standard input if no files were specified) is processed by reading data from the file until a record separator is seen (a newline character by default).
3. The current record is split into fields, using the current value of FS, evaluating each pattern in the program in the order of occurrence and executing the action associated with each pattern that matches the current record.
4. The action for a matching pattern is executed before evaluating subsequent patterns.
5. The actions associated with all END patterns are executed in the order they occur in the program.

Expressions in nawk

Expressions describe computations used in patterns and actions. The following table lists valid expression operations from highest to lowest precedence. In expression evaluation where the grammar is formally ambiguous, higher precedence operators are evaluated before lower precedence operators. In the table, *expr, expr1, expr2,* and *expr3* represent any expression, and *lvalue* represents any entity that can be assigned to (that is, on the left side of an assignment operator).

Syntax	Name	Type of Result	Associativity
(*expr*)	Grouping	Type of *expr*	N/A
$*expr*	Field reference	String	N/A
++ *lvalue*	Preincrement	Numeric	N/A
-- *lvalue*	Predecrement	Numeric	N/A
lvalue ++	Postincrement	Numeric	N/A
lvalue --	Postdecrement	Numeric	N/A
expr ^ *expr*	Exponentiation	Numeric	Right
! *expr*	Logical NOT	Numeric	N/A
+ *expr*	Unary plus	Numeric	N/A
- *expr*	Unary minus	Numeric	N/A
expr * *expr*	Multiplication	Numeric	Left
expr / *expr*	Division	Numeric	Left
expr % *expr*	Modulus	Numeric	Left
expr + *expr*	Addition	Numeric	Left
expr - *expr*	Subtraction	Numeric	Left
expr *expr*	String concatenation	String	Left
expr < *expr*	Less than	Numeric	None

Syntax	Name	Type of Result	Associativity
expr <= *expr*	Less than or equal to	Numeric	None
expr != *expr*	Not equal to	Numeric	None
expr == *expr*	Equal to	Numeric	None
expr > *expr*	Greater than	Numeric	None
expr >= *expr*	Greater than or equal to	Numeric	None
expr ~ *expr*	ERE match	Numeric	None
expr !~ *expr*	ERE nonmatch	Numeric	None
expr in array	Array membership	Numeric	Left
(*index*) in *array*	Multidimension array membership	Numeric	Left
expr && *expr*	Logical AND	Numeric	Left
expr || *expr*	Logical OR	Numeric	Left
expr1 ? *expr2* : *expr3*	Conditional *expression*	Type of selected *expr2* or *expr3*	Right
lvalue ^= *expr*	Exponentiation assignment	Numeric	Right
lvalue %= *expr*	Modulus assignment	Numeric	Right
lvalue *= *expr*	Multiplication assignment	Numeric	Right
lvalue /= *expr*	Division assignment	Numeric	Right
lvalue += *expr*	Addition assignment	Numeric	Right
lvalue -= *expr*	Subtraction assignment	Numeric	Right
lvalue = *expr*	Assignment	Type of *expr*	Right

Each expression has a string value, a numeric value, or both. Except as stated for specific contexts, the value of an expression is implicitly converted to the type needed for the context in which it is used. A string value is converted to a numeric value by the equivalent of the following calls.

```
setlocale(LC_NUMERIC, ""); numeric_value = atof(string_value);
```

A numeric value that is exactly equal to the value of an integer is converted to a string by the equivalent of a call to the sprintf function, with the string %d as the *fmt* argument and the numeric value being converted as the first and only *expr* argument. Any other numeric value is converted to a string by the equivalent of a call to the sprintf function, with the value of the variable CONVFMT as the *fmt* argument and the numeric value being converted as the first and only *expr* argument.

A string value is considered to be a numeric string in the following cases.

- Any leading and trailing blank characters are ignored.
- If the first unignored character is a + or -, it is ignored.
- If the remaining unignored characters would be lexically recognized as a NUMBER token, the string is considered a numeric string.
- If a - character is ignored in the above steps, the numeric value of the numeric string is the negation of the numeric value of the recognized NUMBER token. Otherwise the numeric value of the numeric string is the numeric value of the recognized NUMBER token. Whether a string is a numeric string is relevant only in contexts where that term is used in this section.
- When an expression is used in a Boolean context, if it has a numeric value, a value of 0 is treated as false and any other value is treated as true. Otherwise, a string value of the null string is treated as false, and any other value is treated as true. A Boolean context is one of the following.
  - The first subexpression of a conditional expression.
  - An expression operated on by logical NOT, logical AND, or logical OR.
  - The second expression of a for statement.
  - The expression of an if statement.
  - The expression of the while clause in either a while or do...while statement.
  - An expression used as a pattern (as in Overall Program Structure).

The nawk language supplies arrays that are used for storing numbers or strings. Arrays need not be declared. They are initially empty and their sizes change dynamically. The subscripts or element identifiers are strings, providing a type of associative array capability. You can use an array name followed by a subscript within square brackets as an *lvalue* and as an expression, as described in the grammar. Unsubscripted array names are used only in the following contexts.

- A parameter in a function definition or function call.
- The NAME token following any use of the keyword in.

A valid array index consists of one or more comma-separated expressions, similar to the way that multidimensional arrays are indexed in some programming languages. Because nawk arrays are really one dimensional, nawk converts such a comma-separated list to a single string by concatenating the string values of the separate expressions, each separated from the other by the value of the SUBSEP variable. Thus, the following two index operations are equivalent.

```
var[expr1, expr2,... exprn]
var[expr1 SUBSEP expr2 SUBSEP... SUBSEP exprn]
```

You must enclose in parentheses a multidimensioned index used with the in operator. The in operator, which tests for the existence of a particular array element, does not create the element if it does not exist. Any other reference to a nonexistent array element automatically creates it.

Variables and Special Variables

You can use variables in a nawk program by referencing them. With the exception of function parameters, variables are not explicitly declared. Uninitialized scalar variables and array elements have both a numeric value of 0 and a string value of the empty string.

Field variables are designated by a $ followed by a number or numerical expression. The effect of the field number expression evaluating to anything other than a nonnegative integer is unspecified. You do not need to convert uninitialized variables or string values to numeric values in this context. Create new field variables by assigning a value to them. References to nonexistent fields (that is, fields after $NF) produce the null string. However, assigning to a nonexistent field (for example, $(NF+2) = 5) increases the value of NF, creates any intervening fields with the null string as their values, and recomputes the value of $0 with the fields separated by the value of OFS. Each field variable has a string value when created. When the decimal-point character from the current locale is changed to a period character, the string is considered a *numeric string*; the field variable also has the numeric value of the *numeric string*.

nawk sets the following special variables.

ARGC   The number of elements in the ARGV array.

ARGV   An array of command-line arguments excluding options and the program argument, numbered from 0 to ARGC-1.

You can modify or add to the arguments in ARGV. You can alter ARGC. As each input file ends, nawk treats the next non-null element of ARGV, up to the current value of ARGC-1, inclusive, as the name of the next input file. Setting an element of ARGV to null means that it is not treated as an input file. The name - indicates the standard input. If an argument matches the format of an assignment operand, this argument is treated as an assignment instead of a file argument.

/usr/xpg4/bin/awk

CONVFMT   The printf format for converting numbers to strings (except for output statements, where OFMT is used); %.6g by default.

ENVIRON   The variable ENVIRON is an array representing the value of the environment. The indices of the array are strings consisting of the names of the environment variables, and the value of each array element is a string consisting of the value of that variable. If the value of an environment variable is considered a numeric string, the array element also has its numeric value.

In all cases where nawk behavior is affected by environment variables (including the environment of any commands that nawk executes via the system function or via pipeline redirections with the print statement, the printf statement, or the getline function), the environment used is the environment at the time nawk began executing.

FILENAME   A path name of the current input file. Inside a BEGIN action, the value is undefined. Inside an END action, the value is the name of the last input file processed.

FNR   The ordinal number of the current record in the current file. Inside a BEGIN action, the value is 0. Inside an END action, the value is the number of the last record processed in the last file processed.

FS   Input field separator regular expression; by default, a space character.

NF
: The number of fields in the current record. Inside a BEGIN action, the use of NF is undefined unless a getline function without a var argument is executed previously. Inside an END action, NF retains the value it had for the last record read unless a subsequent, redirected getline function without a var argument is performed before entering the END action.

NR
: The ordinal number of the current record from the start of input. Inside a BEGIN action, the value is 0. Inside an END action, the value is the number of the last record processed.

OFMT
: The printf format for converting numbers to strings in output statements; by default, "%.6g". The result of the conversion is unspecified if the value of OFMT is not a floating-point format specification.

OFS
: The print statement output field separator; by default, a space character.

ORS
: The print output record separator; by default, a newline character.

LENGTH
: The length of the string matched by the match function.

RS
: The first character of the string value of RS is the input record separator; by default, a newline character. If RS contains more than one character, the results are unspecified. If RS is null, records are separated by sequences of one or more blank lines: leading or trailing blank lines do not produce empty records at the beginning or end of input, and the field separator is always newline, no matter what the value of FS.

RSTART
: The starting position of the string matched by the match function, numbering from 1. This value is always equivalent to the return value of the match function.

SUBSEP
: The subscript separator string for multidimensional arrays; the default value is 1.

Regular Expressions

The nawk command uses the extended regular expression notation (see regex(5)) except that it allows the use of C-language conventions to escape special characters within the EREs, namely, \\, \a, \b, \f, \n, \r, \t, \v, and those specified in the following table. These escape sequences are recognized both inside and outside bracket expressions.

> **Note** — You do not need to separate records with newline characters, and string constants can contain newline characters, so even the \n sequence is valid in nawk EREs. Using a slash character within the regular expression requires escaping as shown in the table below.

Escape Sequence	Description	Meaning
\"	Backslash quotation mark.	Quotation mark character.

Escape Sequence	Description	Meaning
\/	Backslash slash.	Slash character.
ddd	A backslash character followed by the longest sequence of one-, two-, or three-digit octal characters (01234567). If all of the digits are 0 (null character), the behavior is undefined.	The character encoded by the one-, two-, or three-digit octal integer. Multibyte characters require multiple concatenated escape sequences, including the leading \ for each byte.
\c	A backslash character followed by any character not described in this table or the special characters \\, \a, \b, \f, \n, \r, \t, \v.	Undefined.

A regular expression can be matched against a specific field or string by one of the two regular expression matching operators, ~ and !~. These operators interpret their right-hand operand as a regular expression and their left-hand operand as a string. If the regular expression matches the string, the ~ expression evaluates to the value 1, and the !~ expression evaluates to the value 0. If the regular expression does not match the string, the ~ expression evaluates to the value 0, and the !~ expression evaluates to the value 1. If the right-hand operand is any expression other than the lexical token ERE, the string value of the expression is interpreted as an extended regular expression, including the escape conventions described above. Note that these same escape conventions also are applied in determining the value of a string literal (the lexical token STRING) and are applied a second time when a string literal is used in this context.

When an ERE token appears as an expression in any context other than as the right-hand side of the ~ or !~ operator or as one of the built-in function arguments described below, the value of the resulting expression is the equivalent of $0 ~ /ere/.

The *ere* argument to the gsub, match, and sub functions and the *fs* argument to the split function (see "String Functions" on page 903) are interpreted as extended regular expressions. These ERE tokens or arbitrary expressions are interpreted in the same manner as the right-hand side of the ~ or !~ operator.

An extended regular expression can separate fields by using the -F *ERE* option or by assigning a string containing the expression to the built-in variable FS. The default value of the FS variable is a single-space character.

FS behaves in the following way.

1. If FS is a single character,
   - Skip leading and trailing blank characters; fields are delimited by sets of one or more blank characters.
   - Otherwise, if FS is any other character *c*, fields are delimited by each single occurrence of *c*.

2. Otherwise, the string value of FS is considered to be an extended regular expression. Each occurrence of a sequence matching the extended regular expression delimits fields.

Except in the gsub, match, split, and sub built-in functions, regular expression matching is based on input records; that is, record separator characters (the first character of the value of the variable RS, a newline character by default) cannot be embedded in the expression, and no expression matches the record separator character. If the record separator is not a newline character, newline characters embedded in the expression can be matched. In those four built-in functions, regular expression matching is based on text strings. So, any character (including the newline character and the record separator) can be embedded in the pattern, and an appropriate pattern matches any character. However, in all nawk regular expression matching, the use of one or more null characters in the pattern, input record, or text string produces undefined results.

Patterns

A pattern is any valid expression, a range specified by two expressions separated by a comma, or one of the two special patterns, BEGIN or END.

Special Patterns

The nawk command recognizes two special patterns, BEGIN and END. Each BEGIN pattern is matched once and its associated action executed before the first record of input is read (except possibly by use of the getline function in a prior BEGIN action) and before command-line assignment is done. Each END pattern is matched once, and its associated action is executed after the last record of input has been read. These two patterns have associated actions.

BEGIN and END do not combine with other patterns. Multiple BEGIN and END patterns are allowed. The actions associated with the BEGIN patterns are executed in the order specified in the program, as are the END actions. An END pattern can precede a BEGIN pattern in a program.

If a nawk program consists of only actions with the pattern BEGIN and the BEGIN action contains no getline function, nawk exits without reading its input when the last statement in the last BEGIN action is executed. If a nawk program consists of only actions with the pattern END or only actions with the patterns BEGIN and END, the input is read before the statements in the END actions are executed.

Expression Patterns

An expression pattern is evaluated as if it were an expression in a Boolean context. If the result is true, the pattern is considered to match and the associated action (if any) is executed. If the result is false, the action is not executed.

Pattern Ranges

A pattern range consists of two expressions separated by a comma. In this case, the action is performed for all records between a match of the first expression and the following match of the second expression, inclusive. At this point, the pattern range can be repeated, starting at input records subsequent to the end of the matched range.

Actions

An action is a sequence of statements. A statement can be one of the following.

```
if ( expression ) statement [else statement]
while ( expression ) statement
do statement while ( expression )
for ( expression ; expression ; expression ) statement
for ( var in array ) statement
delete array[subscript]          #delete an array element
break
continue
```

```
{ [statement]... }
expression              # commonly, variable = expression
print [expression-list] [>expression]
printf format [, expression-list] [>expression]
next                    # skip remaining patterns on this input line
exit [expr]             # skip the rest of the input; exit status is expr
return [expr]
```

You can replace any single statement with a statement list enclosed in braces. Terminate statements with newline characters or semicolons. Statements are executed sequentially in the order in which they appear.

The next statement abandons all further processing of the current input record. The behavior is undefined if a next statement appears or is invoked in a BEGIN or END action.

The exit statement invokes all END actions in the order in which they occur in the program source and then terminates the program without reading further input. An exit statement inside an END action terminates the program without further execution of END actions. If an expression is specified in an exit statement, its numeric value is the exit status of nawk unless subsequent errors are encountered or a subsequent exit statement with an expression is executed.

Output Statements

Both print and printf statements write to standard output by default. The output is written to the location specified by output redirection if one is supplied, as follows.

```
>  expression
>> expression
|  expression
```

In all cases, the expression is evaluated to produce a string that is used as a full path name to write into (for > or >>) or as a command to be executed (for |). Using the first two forms, if the file of that name is not currently open, it is opened. If necessary, it is created. With the first form, the file is truncated. The output then is appended to the file. As long as the file remains open, subsequent calls in which expression evaluates to the same string value simply append output to the file. The file remains open until the close function is called with an expression that evaluates to the same string value.

The third form writes output onto a stream piped to the input of a command. The stream is created if no stream is currently open, with the value of expression as its command name. The stream created is equivalent to one created by a call to the popen(3S) function, with the value of expression as the command argument and a value of w as the mode argument. As long as the stream remains open, subsequent calls, in which expression evaluates to the same string value, write output to the existing stream. The stream remains open until the close function is called with an expression that evaluates to the same string value. At that time, the stream is closed as if by a call to the pclose function.

These output statements take a comma-separated list of expressions referred to in the grammar by the nonterminal symbols expr_list, print_expr_list, or print_expr_list_opt. This list is referred to here as the expression list, and each member is referred to as an expression argument.

The print statement writes the value of each expression argument onto the indicated output stream separated by the current output field separator (see variable OFS) and terminated by the output record separator (see variable ORS). All expression arguments are taken as strings, converted if necessary; with the exception that the printf format in OFMT is used instead of the value in CONVFMT. An empty expression list stands for the whole input record ($0).

The `printf` statement produces output based on a notation similar to the File Format Notation used to describe file formats in this document. Output is produced as specified, with the first expression argument as the string format and subsequent expression arguments as the strings `arg1` to `argn`, inclusive, with the following exceptions.

- The format is an actual character string instead of a graphical representation. Therefore, it cannot contain empty character positions. The space character in the format string, in any context other than a flag of a conversion specification, is treated as an ordinary character
- If the character set contains a / \ character and that character appears in the format string, it is treated as an ordinary character that is copied to the output.
- The escape sequences beginning with a backslash character are treated as sequences of ordinary characters that are copied to the output. Note that these same sequences are interpreted lexically by `nawk` when they appear in literal strings, but they are not treated specially by the `printf` statement.
- A field width or precision can be specified as the * character instead of a digit string. In this case, the next argument from the expression list is fetched, and its numeric value is taken as the field width or precision.
- The implementation does not precede or follow output from the `d` or `u` conversion specifications with blank characters not specified by the format string.
- The implementation does not precede output from the `o` conversion specification with leading `0`s not specified by the format string.
- For the `c` conversion specification: if the argument has a numeric value, the character whose encoding is that value is output. If the value is 0 or is not the encoding of any character in the character set, the behavior is undefined. If the argument does not have a numeric value, the first character of the string value is output; if the string does not contain any characters, the behavior is undefined.
- For each conversion specification that consumes an argument, the next expression argument is evaluated. With the exception of the `c` conversion, the value is converted to the appropriate type for the conversion specification.
- If there are insufficient expression arguments to satisfy all the conversion specifications in the format string, the behavior is undefined.
- If any character sequence in the format string begins with a `%` character but does not form a valid conversion specification, the behavior is unspecified.

Both `print` and `printf` can output at least {LINE_MAX} bytes.

Functions

The `nawk` language has a variety of built-in functions: arithmetic, string, input/output, and general.

Arithmetic Functions

The arithmetic functions, except for `int`, are based on the ISO C standard. The behavior is undefined in cases where the ISO C standard specifies that an error be returned or that the behavior is undefined. Although the grammar permits built-in functions to appear with no arguments or parentheses, unless the argument or parentheses are indicated as optional in the following list (by being displayed within the [] brackets), such use is undefined.

atan2(*y*, *x*)	Return arctangent of *y*/*x*.
cos(*x*)	Return cosine of *x*, where *x* is in radians.
sin(*x*)	Return sine of *x*, where *x* is in radians.
exp(*x*)	Return the exponential function of *x*.
log(*x*)	Return the natural logarithm of *x*.
sqrt(*x*)	Return the square root of *x*.
int(*x*)	Truncate its argument to an integer. Truncate toward 0 when $x > 0$.
rand()	Return a random number *n*, such that $0 < n < 1$.
srand([*expr*])	

Set the seed value for rand to *expr*, or use the time of day if *expr* is omitted. Return the previous seed value.

String Functions

The string functions in the following list are supported. Although the grammar permits built-in functions to appear with no arguments or parentheses, unless the argument or parentheses are indicated as optional in the following list (by being displayed within the [] brackets), such use is undefined.

gsub(*ere*, *repl*[, *in*])

Behave like sub (see below), except replace all occurrences of the regular expression (like the ed command global substitute) in $0 or in the *in* argument, when specified.

index(*s*, *t*)

Return the position, in characters, numbering from 1, in string *s* where string *t* first occurs, or 0 if it does not occur at all.

length[([*s*])]

Return the length, in characters, of its argument taken as a string, or of the whole record, $0, if there is no argument.

match(*s*, *ere*)

Return the position, in characters, numbering from 1, in string *s* where the extended regular expression *ere* occurs, or 0 if it does not occur at all. Set RSTART to the starting position (which is the same as the returned value), 0 if no match is found; set RLENGTH to the length of the matched string, –1 if no match is found.

split(*s*, *a*[, *fs*])

Split the string *s* into array elements *a*[1], *a*[2],..., *a*[*n*], and return *n*. Do the separation with the extended regular expression *fs* or with the field separator FS if you do not specify *fs*. Each array element has a string value when created. When any occurrence of the decimal-point character from the current locale is changed to a period character, a string assigned to any array element is considered a numeric string; the array element also has the numeric value of the numeric string. The effect of a null string as the value of *fs* is unspecified.

sprintf(fmt, *expr, expr,* ...)

Format the expressions according to the printf format given by fmt, and return the resulting string.

sub(*ere, repl*[,*in*])

Substitute the string *repl* in place of the first instance of the extended regular expression *ere* in string *in*, and return the number of substitutions. Replace an ampersand (&) in the string *repl* with the string from *in* that matches the regular expression. For each occurrence of backslash (\) encountered when scanning the string *repl* from beginning to end, take the next character literally and lose its special meaning (for example, interpret \& as a literal ampersand character). Except for & and \, it is unspecified what the special meaning of any such character is. If you specify *in* and it is not an *lvalue*, the behavior is undefined. If you omit *in*, substitute the current record ($0).

substr(*s, m*[,*n*])

Return at most the *n*-character substring of *s* that begins at position *m*, numbering from 1. If *n* is missing, limit the length of the substring by the length of the string *s*.

tolower(*s*)   Return a string based on the string *s*. In the returned string, replace each character in *s* that is an uppercase letter specified to have a tolower mapping by the LC_CTYPE category of the current locale with the lowercase letter specified by the mapping. Other characters in *s* are unchanged in the returned string.

toupper(*s*)   Return a string based on the string *s*. In the returned string, replace each character in *s* that is a lowercase letter specified to have a toupper mapping by the LC_CTYPE category with the uppercase letter specified by the mapping. Other characters in *s* are unchanged in the returned string.

All of the preceding functions that take *ERE* as a parameter expect a pattern or a string-valued expression that is a regular expression as defined below.

Input/Output and General Functions

The input/output and general functions are listed below.

close(*expression*)

Close the file or pipe opened by a print or printf statement or a call to getline with the same string-valued expression. If the close was successful, return 0; otherwise, return non-zero.

expression | getline [*var*]

> Read a record of input from a stream piped from the output of a command. If no stream is currently open, create the stream with the value of *expression* as its command name. The stream created is equivalent to one created by a call to the popen function with the value of *expression* as the command argument and a value of *r* as the mode argument. As long as the stream remains open, subsequent calls in which expression evaluates to the same string value read subsequent records from the file. The stream remains open until the close function is called with an expression that evaluates to the same string value. At that time, the stream is closed as if by a call to the pclose function. If *var* is missing, $0 and NF are set; otherwise, *var* is set.

> The getline operator can form ambiguous constructs when there are operators that are not in parentheses (including concatenate) to the left of the | (to the beginning of the expression containing getline). In the context of the $ operator, | behaves as if it had a lower precedence than $. The result of evaluating other operators is unspecified, and all such uses of portable applications must be put in parentheses properly.

getline   Set $0 to the next input record from the current input file. This form of getline sets the NF, NR, and FNR variables.

getline *var*   Set variable *var* to the next input record from the current input file. This form of getline sets the FNR and NR variables.

getline [*var*] < *expression*

> Read the next record of input from a named file. The expression is evaluated to produce a string that is used as a full path name. If the file of that name is not currently open, open it. As long as the stream remains open, subsequent calls in which *expression* evaluates to the same string value read subsequent records from the file. The file remains open until the close function is called with an expression that evaluates to the same string value. If *var* is missing, $0 and NF are set; otherwise, *var* is set.

> The getline operator can form ambiguous constructs when there are binary operators that are not in parentheses (including concatenate) to the right of the < (up to the end of the expression containing the getline). The result of evaluating such a construct is unspecified, and all such uses of portable applications must be put in parentheses properly.

system(*expression*)

> Execute the command given by *expression* in a manner equivalent to the system(3S) function, and return the exit status of the command.

All forms of getline return 1 for successful input, 0 for end-of-file, and –1 for an error.

Where strings are used as the name of a file or pipeline, the strings must be textually identical. The terminology "same string value" implies that "equivalent strings," even those that differ only by space characters, represent different files.

User-Defined Functions

The nawk language also provides user-defined functions. You can define such functions with the following syntax.

```
function name(args,...) { statements }
```

You can refer to a function anywhere in a nawk program; in particular, you can use it before it is defined. The scope of a function is global.

Function arguments can be either scalars or arrays; the behavior is undefined if an array name is passed as an argument that the function uses as a scalar or if a scalar expression is passed as an argument that the function uses as an array. Function arguments are passed by value if scalar, and by reference if array name. Argument names are local to the function; all other variable names are global. The same name is not used both as an argument name and as the name of a function or a special nawk variable. The same name must not be used both as a variable name with global scope and as the name of a function. The same name must not be used within the same scope both as a scalar variable and as an array.

The number of parameters in the function definition need not match the number of parameters in the function call. Excess formal parameters can be used as local variables. If fewer arguments are supplied in a function call than are in the function definition, the extra parameters that are used in the function body as scalars are initialized with a string value of the null string and a numeric value of 0 and the extra parameters that are used in the function body as arrays are initialized as empty arrays. If more arguments are supplied in a function call than are in the function definition, the behavior is undefined.

When invoking a function, put no white space between the function name and the opening parenthesis. You can nest function calls and make recursive calls on functions. On return from any nested or recursive function call, the values of all of the calling function's parameters are unchanged except for array parameters passed by reference. You can use the return statement to return a value. If a return statement appears outside a function definition, the behavior is undefined.

In the function definition, newline characters are optional before the opening brace and after the closing brace. Function definitions can appear anywhere in the program where a pattern-action pair is allowed.

Usage

Do not confuse the index, length, match, and substr functions with similar functions in the ISO C standard; the nawk versions deal with characters, whereas the ISO C standard deals with bytes.

Because the concatenation operation is represented by adjacent expressions instead of an explicit operator, you often need to use parentheses to enforce the proper evaluation precedence.

See largefile(5) for the description of the behavior of nawk when encountering files greater than or equal to 2 Gbytes ($2**31$ bytes).

Examples

The nawk program specified in the command line is most easily specified within single quotes (for example, 'program') for applications using sh, because nawk programs commonly contain characters that are special to the shell, including double quotes. In the cases where a nawk program contains single-quote characters, it is usually easiest to specify most of the program as strings within single quotes concatenated by the shell with quoted single-quote characters. The following example prints all lines from the standard input containing a single quote character prefixed with quote:.

```
awk '/'\''/ { print "quote:", $0 }'
```

The rest of the examples show simple nawk programs.

The following example writes to the standard output all input lines for which field 3 is greater than 5.

```
$3 > 5
```

The following example writes every tenth line.

```
(NR % 10) == 0
```

The following example writes any line with a substring matching the regular expression.

```
/(G|D)(2[0-9] [[:alpha:]]*)/
```

The following example prints any line with a substring containing a G or D, followed by a sequence of digits and characters. It uses character classes digit and alpha to match language-independent digit and alphabetic characters.

```
/(G|D)([[:digit:] [:alpha:]]*)/
```

The following example writes any line in which the second field matches the regular expression and the fourth field does not.

```
$2 ~ /xyz/ && $4 !~ /xyz/
```

The following example writes any line in which the second field contains a backslash.

```
$2 ~ /\\/
```

The following example writes any line in which the second field contains a backslash. Note that backslash escapes are interpreted twice, once in lexical processing of the string and once in processing the regular expression.

```
$2 ~ "\\\\"
```

The following example writes the penultimate and the last field in each line with fields separated by colons.

```
{OFS=":";print $(NF-1), $NF}
```

The following example writes the line number and number of fields in each line. The three strings representing the line number, the colon, and the number of fields are concatenated and that string is written to standard output.

```
{print NR ":" NF}
```

The following example writes lines longer than 72 characters.

```
{length($0) > 72}
```

The following example writes the first two fields in opposite order, separated by the OFS.

```
{ print $2, $1 }
```

The following example writes the first two fields in opposite order, with input fields separated by comma, or space and Tab characters, or both.

```
BEGIN { FS = ",[\t]*|[\t]+" }
  { print $2, $1 }\
```

The following example adds up the first column and prints the sum and average.

```
{s += $1 }
END {print "sum is ", s, " average is", s/NR}
```

The following example writes the fields in reverse order, one per line (many lines out for each line in).

```
{ for (i = NF; i > 0; --i) print $i }
```

The following example writes all lines between occurrences of the strings start and stop.

```
/start/, /stop/
```

The following example writes all lines whose first field is different from the previous one.

```
$1 != prev { print; prev = $1 }
```

The following example simulates the echo command.

```
BEGIN {
  for (i = 1; i < ARGC; ++i)
  printf "%s%s", ARGV[i], i==ARGC-
  1?"\n":""
}
```

The following example writes the path prefixes contained in the PATH environment variable, one per line.

```
BEGIN {
  n = split (ENVIRON["PATH"], path, ":")
  for (i = 1; i <= n; ++i)
  print path[i]
}
```

In the following example, if a file named input contains page headers of the following form

```
Page#
```

and a file named program contains the following lines

```
/Page/{ $2 = n++; }
  { print }
```

then the following command prints the file input, filling in page numbers starting at 5.

```
nawk -f program n=5 input
```

Environment Variables

See environ(5) for descriptions of the following environment variables that affect execution of nawk: LC_COLLATE, LC_CTYPE, LC_MESSAGES, and NLSPATH.

LC_NUMERIC   Determine the radix character used when interpreting numeric input, performing conversions between numeric and string values and formatting numeric output. Regardless of locale, the period character (the decimal-point character of the POSIX locale) is the decimal-point character recognized in processing awk programs, including assignments in command-line arguments.

Exit Status

0   All input files were processed successfully.

>0   An error occurred.

You can alter the exit status within the program by using an exit expression.

Attributes

See attributes(5) for descriptions of the following attributes:

/usr/bin/nawk

Attribute Type	Attribute Value
Availability	SUNWcsu

/usr/xpg4/bin/awk

Attribute Type	Attribute Value
Availability	SUNWxcu4

See Also

awk(1), ed(1), egrep(1), grep(1), lex(1), sed(1), popen(3C), printf(3C), system(3C), attributes(5), environ(5), largefile(5), regex(5), XPG4(5)

Aho, A. V., B. W. Kernighan, and P. J. Weinberger, *The AWK Programming Language*, Addison-Wesley, 1988.

Diagnostics

If any file operand is specified and the named file cannot be accessed, nawk writes a diagnostic message to standard error and terminates without any further action.

If the program specified by either the *program* operand or a *progfile* operand is not a valid nawk program, the behavior is undefined.

[New!] **nca, snca** — Solaris Network Cache and Accelerator (NCA)

Description

The Solaris Network Cache and Accelerator (NCA), new in the Solaris 8 Operating Environment, is a kernel module that provides improved Web server performance. The kernel module, ncakmod, services HTTP requests.

To improve the performance of servicing HTTP requests, the NCA kernel module maintains an in-kernel cache of Web pages. If the NCA kernel module cannot service the request itself, it passes the request to the HTTP daemon (httpd). The NCA kernel uses either a sockets interface, with family type designated PF_NCA, or a private Solaris doors interface based on the Solaris doors RPC mechanism, to pass the request.

To use the sockets interface, the Web server must open a socket of family type PF_NCA. The PF_NCA family supports only SOCK_STREAM and protocol 0; otherwise, an error occurs.

The following features are presently not supported.

- You cannot initiate a connection from a PF_NCA type socket. The connect(3SOCKET) interface on PF_NCA fails.

[New!]
- System calls associated with type SO_DGRAM, such as send(), sendto(), sendmsg(), recv(), recvfrom(), and recvmsg() fail. New in the Solaris 9 release.

- You cannot set TCP or IP options on a PF_NCA type socket through setsockopt(3SOCKET).

- The NCA cache consistency is maintained by honoring HTTP headers that deal with a given content type and expiration date, much the same way as a proxy cache is handled.

- For configuration information, see *System Administration Guide*, Volume 3

- When native PF_NCA socket support does not exist in the Web server, you must use the ncad_addr(4) interface to provide NCA support on that Web server.

- NCA is intended to be run on a dedicated Web server. Running other large processes while running NCA can result in undesirable behavior.

[New!]   Starting with the Solaris 9 release, NCA supports the logging of in-kernel cache hits. See ncalogd.conf(4). NCA stores logs in a binary format. Use the ncab2clf(1) command to convert the log from a binary format to the Common Log File format.

Files

/etc/nca/ncakmod.conf

Configuration parameters for NCA.

/etc/nca/ncalogd.conf

Configuration parameters for NCA logging.

/etc/nca/nca.if

The physical interfaces on which NCA runs.

/etc/hostname.{}{0-9}

All physical interfaces configured on the server.

/etc/hosts

All host names associated with the server. Entries in this file must match entries in /etc/hostname.{}{0-9} for NCA to function.

Attributes

See attributes(5) for descriptions of the following attributes.

Attribute Type	Attribute Value
Availability	SUNWncar (32 bit)
	SUNWncarx (64 bit)
Interface stability	Evolving

See Also

ncab2clf(1), ncakmod(1), close(2), read(2), sendfilev(2), write(2), door_bind(3DOOR), door_call(3DOOR), door_create(3DOOR), sendfileev(3EXT), socket(3HEAD), accept(3SOCKET), bind(3SOCKET), connect(3SOCKET), getsockopt(3SOCKET), listen(3SOCKET), setsockopt(3SOCKET), shutdown(3SOCKET), socket(3SOCKET), ncad_addr(4), nca.if(4), ncakmod.conf(4), ncalogd.conf(4), attributes(5)
System Administration Guide, Volume 3

ncab2clf — Convert Binary Log File to Common Log File Format

Synopsis

/usr/bin/ncab2clf [-Dhv] [-i *input-file*] [-o *output-file*] [-b *size*]

Description

Use the ncab2clf command, new in the Solaris 8 Operating Environment, to convert the log file generated by the Solaris Network Cache and Accelerator (NCA) from binary format, to Common Log File (CLF) format. If you specify no *input-file*, ncab2clf uses standard input. If you specify no *output-file*, the output goes to standard output.

Note — The binary log files generated by NCA can become quite large. When converting large binary files, use the -b option to the ncab2clf command to improve performance.

Direct I/O is a benefit if the data being written does not come in as large chunks. However, if you want to convert the log file in large chunks with the -b option, then you should disable direct I/O with the -D option.

Options

-b *size* Specify the binary-log-file blocking in kilobytes; the default is 64 kilobytes.

-D   Disable direct I/O.

-h   Print a usage message.

-i *input-file*

                Specify the input file.

-o *output-file*

                Specify the output file.

-v   Provide verbose output.

Examples

The following example converts the binary file /var/nca/logs/nca.blf to a file /var/nca/logs/nca.clf, which is in Common Log File format.

```
example% ncab2clf -D -i /var/nca/logs/nca.blf -o /var/nca/logs/nca.clf
```

You can use the following script to convert multiple log files. The directory designated by * must contain only log files.

```
!/bin/ksh
for filename in *
do
  ncab2clf -D < $filename > $filename.clf
done
```

Exit Status

0   The file converted successfully.

>0   An error occurred.

Attributes

See attributes(5) for descriptions of the following attributes.

Attribute Type	Attribute Value
Availability	SUNWncau
Interface Stability	Evolving

See Also

attributes(5)
    System Administration Guide, Volume 3

New! **ncakmod** — Start or Stop the NCA Kernel Module

Synopsis

/etc/init.d/ncakmod start | stop

Description

Use the ncakmod command, new in the Solaris 8 Operating Environment, to start or stop the Solaris Network Cache and Accelerator (NCA) kernel module.

When you specify the start option on the command line, the NCA kernel module is activated for all physical interfaces listed in the nca.if file. When you invoke the ncakmod command with the stop option, the NCA kernel warns you that you must restart the system to stop NCA functionality.

Note — To properly stop NCA on your system, you must first edit the ncakmod.conf(4) file and set the status field to disable, then reboot the system. By default, the status field is set to disable.

Options

start   Start the NCA kernel module.

stop   Describe the current method for stopping the NCA feature.

Examples

The following command starts NCA functionality.

```
mopoke% su
Password:
# /etc/init.d/ncakmod start
#
```

The following command stops NCA functionality.

```
# /etc/init.d/ncakmod stop
System reset is required to stop NCA functionality
#
```

Files

/etc/init.d/ncakmod

The NCA kernel module startup script.

/etc/nca/ncakmod.conf

Specify configuration options for the NCA kernel module.

Attributes

See attributes(5) for descriptions of the following attributes.

Attribute Type	Attribute Value
Availability	SUNWncar
Interface Stability	Evolving

See Also

nca(1), ncab2clf(1), ncak_addr(4), nca.if(4), ncakmod.conf(4), ncalogd.conf(4), attributes(5)

New!

neqn — Typeset Mathematics Test

Synopsis

`/usr/bin/neqn [file] ...`

Description

See eqn(1).

New! netscape — Start Netscape Communicator for Solaris

Synopsis

`/usr/dt/bin/netscape [options] [arguments]`

Description

Netscape Communicator for Solaris is a comprehensive set of components that integrates browsing, e-mail, Web-based word processing, chat, and group scheduling to enable users to easily communicate, share, and access information. The `netscape` command is new in the Solaris 8 Operating Environment.

Options

Any argument that is not a switch is interpreted as either a file or URL.

`-component-bar`

> Show only the Component Bar.

`-composer`   Open all command-line URLs in Composer.

`-discussions`

> Show Collabra Discussions.

`-display dpy`

> Specify the X server to use for display.

`-dont-force-window-stacking`

> Ignore the `alwaysraised`, `alwayslowered`, and `z-lock` JavaScript `window.open()` attributes.

`-dont-save-geometry-prefs`

> Do not save window geometry preferences for the session.

`-edit`   See `-composer`.

`-geometry =WxH+X+Y`

> Position and size the Netscape window.

`-help`   Show the command-line options for Netscape.

`-iconic`   Minimize Netscape after startup.

-id *window-id*

> Identify an X window to receive -remote commands. If you do not specify a window, the first window found is used.

-ignore-geometry-prefs

> Ignore saved window geometry preferences for the current session.

-install   Install private colormap.

-irix-session-management

> Enable IRIX session management. On SGI systems, IRIX session management is enabled by default. IRIX session management is available on other platforms and may work with session managers other than the IRIX desktop. See -no-irix-session-management.

-mail   Same as -messenger.

-messenger

> Show the Messenger Mailbox (Inbox).

-mono   Force a 1-bit-deep image display.

-ncols N   Set the maximum number of colors to allocate for images when not using -install.

-nethelp   Start NetHelp, Netscape's online help system.

-news   Same as -discussions.

-no-about-splash

> Bypass the startup license page.

-no-install

> Use the default colormap.

-no-irix-session-management

> Disable IRIX session management. See -irix-session-management.

-no-session-management

> Disable session management. Session management is enabled by default. See -session-management.

-noraise   Do not display the remote window on top when using -remote commands. See -raise and -remote.

-raise   Display the remote window on top when using -remote commands. See -noraise and -remote.

-remote *remote-command*

> Connect to and control an existing process. You can issue multiple -remote options on the same command line. The commands are executed sequentially unless a command fails. If no Netscape process is currently running, this command fails.

New!

If the command fails, an error message is reported to standard error and the command exits with a nonzero status. See "Remote Actions" for more information. New in the Solaris 9 release.

The following options exist for finer-grained control of the -remote commands.

-id *X_window_ID*

If more than one Netscape Navigator window is open, select the window to control. If you do not use this option, the first window found is controlled.

-raise   Control whether the -remote command raises/does not raise the
-noraise   Netscape window to the top. The default is -raise. You can use -raise
             and -noraise options with the addBookmark and openURL arguments.

-session-management

Enable session management. Session management is enabled by default. See -no-session-management.

-version   Display the version number and build date.

-visual *id-or-number*

Use the specified server visual.

-xrm *resource-spec*

Set the specified X resource.

New! Remote Actions

When you invoke Netscape Navigator with the -remote argument, it does not open a window. Instead, it connects to and controls an already existing process. The argument to -remote is to invoke an Xt action with optional arguments. Remote control is implemented with X properties, so the two processes need not be running on the same system and need not share a file system. For more information, see http://home.netscape.com/newsref/std/x-remote.html.

All of Netscape's action names are the same as its resource names. For example, if you want to know the name of the action that corresponds to the Add Bookmark menu item, you could look in Netscape for Add Bookmark and see that the resource that is set to that string is addBookmark. That name is also the name of the action.

Note — To find the Netscape file, use the full default path name:
/usr/dt/appconfig/netscape/lib/locale/C/appdefaults/Netscape

You can use actions in Translation tables in the usual Xt manner, and you can also invoke them directly with the remote option, as shown in the following example.

```
netscape -remote 'addBookmark()'
```

This command adds the current URL to bookmarks for the existing Netscape Navigator process just as if you had selected that menu item.

Use the following command to open a document.

```
netscape -remote 'openURL(http://home.netscape.com)'
```

Arguments

Invoking an action with no arguments is the same as selecting the corresponding menu item. However, with some actions you can pass the following arguments.

addBookmark( )

> Add the current document to the Bookmark list.

addBookmark(URL)

> Add the specified document to the Bookmark list. See "Examples" on page 917.

addBookmark(URL, title)

> Add the specified document and title to the Bookmark list.

mailto( ) Open the mail dialog box with an empty To: field.

mailto(a, b. c)

> Insert the specified address(es) in the default To: field.

openFile( )

> Open a dialog box that prompts for a file.

openFile(*filename*)

> Open the specified file.

openURL( ) Open a dialog box that prompts for a URL.

openURL(URL)

> Open the specified document. See "Examples."

openURL(*URL*, new window)

> Open a new window displaying the specified document.

saveAs( ) Open a dialog box that prompts for a URL.

saveAs(*output_file*)

> Write HTML to the specified file.

saveAs(*output_file*, *type*)

> Write the type to the specified file (HTML, text, or PostScript).

Exit Status

If a command fails, an error message is reported to standard error and the command exits with a non-zero status.

Examples

The following examples all use the -remote command option. For more information and examples, see:

```
http://home.netscape.com/newsref/std/x-remote.html
```

The following example selects among open Netscape windows.

```
example% netscape -id 0x3c00124 -remote 'openURL(http://www.sun.com)'
example%
```

The following example adds a bookmark without raising a window, then opens a URL and raises the window.

```
example% netscape -noraise -remote 'adBookmark(http://www.sun.com)'
  -raise -remote 'openURL(http://home.netscape.com)'
example%
```

The following example adds a specified document to the Bookmark list.

```
example% netscape -remote 'addBookmark(http://www.sun.com)'
example%
```

The following example opens a specified document.

```
example% netscape -remote 'openURL(http://www.sun.com)'
example%
```

Attributes

See attributes(5) for descriptions of the following attributes.

Attribute Type	Attribute Value
Availability	NSCPcom

See Also

attributes(5)

Refer to the Netscape Communicator online help for more information.

---

newaliases — Rebuild the Database for the Mail Aliases File

Synopsis

/usr/bin/newaliases

Description

The newaliases command rebuilds the random access database for the mail aliases file /etc/mail/aliases.

newaliases accepts all the flags that sendmail(1M) accepts. However, most of these flags have no effect, except for the -C option and three of the processing options that can be set from a configuration file with the -o option.

-C /path/to/alt/config/file

Use an alternative configuration file.

-oA*file*   Specify possible alias *file*(s).

-oL*n*	Set the default log level to *n*. Default is 9.
-o*n*	Validate the RHS of aliases when rebuilding the aliases(4) database.

newaliases automatically runs in verbose mode (-v option).

Examples

To run newaliases on an alias file different from the /etc/mail/aliases default in sendmail(1M):

castle% **newaliases -oA/path/to/alternate/alias/file**

Exit Status

newaliases returns an exit status describing what it did. The codes are defined in /usr/include/sysexits.h.

EX_OK	Successful completion on all addresses.
EX-NOUSER	User name not recognized.
EX_UNAVAILABLE	
	Necessary resources were not available. This exit status is a catchall.
EX_SYNTAX	Syntax error in address.
EX_SOFTWARE	
	Internal software error including bad arguments.
EX-OSERR	Temporary operating system error such as cannot fork.
EX-NOHOST	Host name not recognized.
EX_TEMPFAIL	
	Message could not be sent immediately but was queued.

Files

/etc/aliases

Symbolic link to /etc/mail/aliases.

/etc/mail/aliases.pag

/etc/mail/aliases.dir

ndbm files maintained by newaliases.

/etc/mail/aliases.db

New!

Berkeley database file maintained by newaliases. New in the Solaris 9 release.

Attributes

See attributes(5) for descriptions of the following attributes:

Attribute Type	Attribute Value
Availability	SUNWsndmu

New!

See Also
newform(1), sendmail(1M), aliases(4), attributes(5)

---

newform — Change the Format of a Text File

Synopsis
/usr/bin/newform [-s] [-i*tabspec*] [-o*tabspec*] [-b*n*] [-e*n*] [-p*n*] [-a*n*]
  [-f] [-c*char*] [-l*n*] [*filename*...]

Description
Use the newform command to reformat files according to the specified options. newform reads lines from the named file names, or the standard input if you specify no input file, and reproduces the lines on the standard output. Lines are reformatted in accordance with the specified command-line options.

Except for -s, you can specify options in any order, repeat them, and intermingle them with optional file names. Command-line options are processed in the order specified. This means that option sequences such as -e15 -l60 yield results different from -l60 -e15. Options are applied to all file names on the command line.

Notes
newform normally keeps track only of physical characters; however, for the -i and -o options, newform keeps track of backspaces to be able to line up Tabs in the appropriate logical columns.

newform does not prompt you if a *tabspec* is to be read from the standard input (by use of -i-- or -o--).

If you use the -f option and the last -o option specified was -o-- and it was preceded by either a -o-- or a -i--, the Tab specification format line is incorrect.

Options

-a*n*	Same as -p*n*, except append characters to the end of a line.
-b*n*	Truncate *n* characters from the beginning of the line when the line length is greater than the effective line length (see -l*n*). Default is to truncate the number of characters necessary to obtain the effective line length. The default value is used when you specify -b with no *n*. You can use this option to delete the sequence numbers from a COBOL program as follows: newform -l1 -b7 *filename*
-c*char*	Change the prefix/append character to *char*. Default character for *char* is a space.
-e*n*	Same as -b*n*, except truncate characters from the end of the line.
-f	Write the Tab specification format line on the standard output before any other lines are output. The Tab specification format line that is printed corresponds to the format specified in the last -o option. If you specify no -o option, the line that is printed contains the default specification of -8.

-i *tabspec*	Expand Tabs to spaces according to the Tab specifications given. *tabspec* recognizes all Tab specification forms described in tabs(1). In addition, *tabspec* can be --, in which case, newform assumes that the Tab specification is to be found in the first line read from the standard input (see fspec(4)). If you specify no *tabspec*, *tabspec* defaults to -8. A *tabspec* of -0 expects no Tabs; if any are found, they are treated as -1.
-l*n*	Set the effective line length to *n* characters. If you do not specify *n*, -l defaults to 72. The default line length without the -l option is 80 characters. Note that Tabs and backspaces are considered to be one character (use -i to expand Tabs to spaces). You must use -l1 to set the effective line length shorter than any existing line in the file so that the -b option is activated.
-o *tabspec*	Replace spaces with Tabs according to the Tab specifications given. The Tab specifications are the same as for -i *tabspec*. If you specify no *tabspec*, *tabspec* defaults to -8. A *tabspec* of -0 means that no spaces are converted to Tabs on output.
-p*n*	Prefix *n* characters (see -c *char*) to the beginning of a line when the line length is less than the effective line length. Default is to prefix the number of characters necessary to obtain the effective line length.
-s	Shear off leading characters on each line up to the first Tab, and put up to eight of the sheared characters at the end of the line. If more than eight characters (not counting the first Tab) are sheared, replace the eighth character with an * and discard any characters to the right of it. Always discard the first Tab.
	Save the characters sheared off internally until all other options specified are applied to that line. Then, add the characters at the end of the processed line.
	For example, you have a file with leading digits, one or more Tabs, and text on each line. You want to convert that file to a file beginning with the text, all Tabs after the first expanded to spaces, padded with spaces out to column 72 (or truncated to column 72), and the leading digits placed starting at column 73. The command is:
	`newform -s -i -l -a -e` *filename*
	If you use this option on a file without a Tab on each line, newform displays an error message and exits.

Operands

filename	Input file.

Examples

The following example first uses the cat command to display a file with leading numbers and Tabs. Then it uses the newform -s command to strip the numbers and Tabs from the beginning of each line and append the numbers to the end of the line. The first Tab is always discarded.

```
castle% cat kookaburra-1
1.      Kookaburra sits in the old gum tree
2.      Merry merry king of the bush is he.
3.      Laugh, kookaburra, laugh, kookaburra
4.      Gay your life must be.
5.
6.      Kookaburra sits in the old gum tree
7.      Eating all the gumdrops he can see.
8.      Stop, kookaburra, stop, kookaburra
9.      Leave some there for me.
castle% newform -s kookaburra-1
Kookaburra sits in the old gum tree1.
Merry merry king of the bush is he.2.
Laugh, kookaburra, laugh, kookaburra3.
Gay your life must be.4.
5.
Kookaburra sits in the old gum tree6.
Eating all the gumdrops he can see.7.
Stop, kookaburra, stop, kookaburra8.
Leave some there for me.9.
castle%
```

Exit Status

0	Successful operation.
1	Operation failed.

Attributes

See attributes(5) for descriptions of the following attributes:

Attribute Type	Attribute Value
Availability	SUNWesu

See Also

csplit(1), tabs(1), fspec(4), attributes(5)

Diagnostics

All diagnostics are fatal.

usage:...

> newform was called with a bad option.

"not -s format"

> There was no Tab on one line.

"can't open file"

> Self-explanatory.

`"internal line too long"`

> A line exceeds 512 characters after being expanded in the internal work buffer.

`"tabspec in error"`

> A Tab specification is incorrectly formatted, or specified Tab stops are not ascending.

`"tabspec indirection illegal"`

> A *tabspec* read from a file (or standard input) may not contain a *tabspec* referencing another file (or standard input).

newgrp — Log In to a New Group

Synopsis

`/usr/bin/newgrp [- | -l] [group]`

sh

`newgrp [argument]`

ksh

`*`

`newgrp [argument...]`

Description

Use the `newgrp` command to log in to a new group by changing your real and effective group ID. You remain logged in and the current directory is unchanged. The execution of `newgrp` always replaces the current shell with a new shell even if the command terminates with an error (unknown group).

Any variable that is not exported is reset to `null` or its default value. Exported variables retain their values. System variables (such as `PS1`, `PS2`, `PATH`, `MAIL`, and `HOME`) are reset to default values unless they have been exported by the system or the user. For example, when you have a primary prompt string (`PS1`) other than $ (default) and have not exported `PS1`, your `PS1` is set to the default prompt string $, even if `newgrp` terminates with an error.

> **Note —** The shell command `export` (see sh(1) and set(1)) is the method to export variables so that they retain their assigned value when invoking new shells.

With no operands and options, `newgrp` changes your group IDs (real and effective) back to the group specified in your password file entry. This way, you can exit the effect of an earlier `newgrp` command.

A password is demanded if the group has a password and you are not listed in `/etc/group` as being a member of that group.

> **Note —** The only way to create a password for a group is to use passwd(1), then cut and paste the encrypted password from `/etc/shadow` to `/etc/group`. Group passwords are antiquated and not often used.

Bourne Shell

Equivalent to exec newgrp *argument*, where *argument* represents the options or operand of the newgrp command.

Korn Shell

Equivalent to exec /bin/newgrp *argument* where *argument* represents the options or operand of the newgrp command.

For the newgroup command, ksh(1) commands that are preceded by one or two asterisks (*) are treated specially in the following ways.

- Variable assignment lists preceding the command remain in effect when the command completes.
- I/O redirections are processed after variable assignments.
- Errors cause a script that contains them to abort.
- Words that follow a command preceded by ** and that are in the format of a variable assignment are expanded with the same rules as a variable assignment. This means that tilde substitution is performed after the = sign, and word splitting and file-name generation are not performed.

Options

-l | -   Change the environment to what would be expected if the user actually logged in again as a member of the new group.

Operands

group   A group name from the group database or a nonnegative numeric group ID. Specify the group ID used to set the real and effective group IDs. If group is a nonnegative numeric string and exists in the group database as a group name (see getgrnam(3C)), use the numeric group ID associated with that group name as the group ID.

argument   sh and ksh only. Options and/or operand of the newgrp command.

Environment Variables

See environ(5) for descriptions of the following environment variables that affect the execution of newgrp: LC_CTYPE, LC_MESSAGES, and NLSPATH.

Exit Status

If newgrp succeeds in creating a new shell execution environment, whether or not the group identification was changed successfully, the exit status is the exit status of the shell. Otherwise, the following exit value is returned.

>0   An error occurred.

Files

/etc/group   System group file.

/etc/passwd   System password file.

Attributes

See attributes(5) for descriptions of the following attributes:

Attribute Type	Attribute Value
Availability	SUNWcsu

See Also

ksh(1), login(1), set(1), sh(1), intro(2), getgrnam(3C), group(4), passwd(4), attributes(5), environ(5)

news — Print News Items

Synopsis

/usr/bin/news [-a] [-n] [-s] [*items*]

Description

Use news to keep informed of current events. The news command consults the /var/news directory for information about current events. By convention, these events are described by files in the directory /var/news.

When invoked without arguments, news prints the contents of all current files in /var/news, most recent first, with each preceded by an appropriate header. news stores the currency time as the modification date of a file named .news_time in the user's home directory (the identity of this directory is determined by the environment variable $HOME); only files more recent than this currency time are considered current.

Options

-a   Print all items, regardless of currency. In this case, the stored time is not changed.

-n   Report the names of the current items without printing their contents and without changing the stored time.

-s   Report how many current items exist, without printing their names or contents and without changing the stored time. It is useful to include such an invocation of news in your .profile file or in the system's /etc/profile.

All other arguments are assumed to be specific news items that are to be printed.

If you press the Delete key during the printing of a news item, printing stops and the next item is started. Another delete within one second of the first terminates the program.

Examples

The following example displays one news item.

```
castle% news

stocknews (root) Thu Mar 18 14:46:34 1999
```

```
    Today the U.S. Stock Market broke the 10,000 barrier.

castle%
```

When all news items have been read, typing news simply returns the prompt, as shown in the following example.

```
castle% news
castle%
```

You can display all news items by using the -a option, as shown in the following example.

```
castle% news -a

stocknews (root) Thu Mar 18 14:46:34 1999
    Today the U.S. Stock Market broke the 10,000 barrier.

castle%
```

You can display individual news items by name by typing the name of the article as an argument to news, as shown in the following example.

```
castle% news stocknews

stocknews (root) Thu Mar 18 14:46:34 1999
    Today the U.S. Stock Market broke the 10,000 barrier.

castle%
```

New! **newsp** — Front Ends to the mp Text to PDL Pretty Print Filter

Synopsis
/bin/newsp [*options*] *filename*...

Description
See mailp(1).

New! **newtask** — Create New Task

Synopsis
/bin/newtask [-Flv] [-p *project*] [*command*...]

Description
The newtask command, new in the Solaris 8 Operating Environment, is a part of the new project management capability that you can administer with the Solaris Management Console (SMC) 2.1 Projects tool, which is new in the Solaris 9 release. The project management tools enable you to track and manage system resource use with the

/etc/projects database in a files environment or the project tables in an NIS or LDAP environment.

Use the newtask command to execute the user's default shell or a specified command placing the executed command in a new task owned by the specified project.

The user's default shell is the one specified in the passwd database and is determined by getpwnam().

When extended accounting is active, the newtask command may additionally create a task accounting record marking the completion of the preceding system task.

Options

-F	Create a finalized task within which further newtask or settaskid(2) invocations fail. Finalized tasks can be useful at some sites for simplifying the attribution of resource consumption.
-l	Change the environment to what would be expected if the user actually logged in again as a member of the new project.
-p	Change the project ID of the new task to that associated with the given project name. The invoking user must be a valid member of the requested project for the command to succeed. If you specify no project name, start the new task in the invoking user's current project.
-v	Display the system task ID as the new system task is begun.

Operands

project	The project that is charged the resource usage by the created task. The requested project must be defined in the project databases defined in nsswitch.conf(4).
command	The command to be executed as the new task. If you specify no command, the user's login shell is invoked. (If the login shell is not available, /bin/sh is invoked.)

Examples

The following example creates a new shell in the canada project, displaying the task ID.

```
example$ id -p uid=565(gh) gid=10(staff) projid=10(default)
example$ newtask -v -p canada
38
example$ id -p
uid=565(gh) gid=10(staff) projid=82(canada)
example$
```

The following example runs the date command in the russia project.

```
example$ newtask -p russia date
Tue Aug 31 11:12:10 PDT 1999
example$
```

Exit Status

0	Successful execution.

1	A fatal error occurred during execution.
2	Invalid command-line options were specified.

Files

/etc/project

Local database containing valid project definitions for this machine.

Attributes

See attributes(5) for descriptions of the following attributes.

Attribute Type	Attribute Value
Availability	SUNWcsu

See Also

id(1M), execvp(2), settaskid(2), nsswitch.conf(4), project(4), attributes(5)

---

nice — Invoke a Command with an Altered Scheduling Priority

Synopsis

```
/usr/bin/nice [-increment | -n increment] command [argument...]
/usr/xpg4/bin/nice [-increment | -n increment] command [argument...]
```

csh Built-in

```
nice [-increment | +increment] [command]
```

Description

Use the nice command to raise or lower the priority of a command or a process. When you use the nice command without an argument, the default is to increase the nice number by 10 units, thus lowering the priority of the process.

The priocntl(1) command is a more general interface to scheduler functions.

The invoking process (generally, the user's shell) must be in a scheduling class that supports nice.

If you use the C shell (see csh(1)), you must specify the full path of the nice command; otherwise, the csh built-in version of nice is invoked. See C Shell Built-in below.

/usr/bin/nice

If nice executes commands with arguments, it uses the default shell /usr/bin/sh (see sh(1)).

/usr/xpg4/bin/nice

If nice executes commands with arguments, it uses /usr/xpg4/bin/sh, which is equivalent to /usr/bin/ksh (see ksh(1)).

C Shell Built-in

nice is also a csh built-in command with behavior different from the command versions. See csh(1) for a description.

Options

-increment | -n *increment*

> *increment* must be in the range 1-19; if not specified, assume an increment of 10. An increment greater than 19 is equivalent to 19.

The superuser can run commands with priority higher than normal by using a negative increment such as --10. A negative increment assigned by an unprivileged user is ignored.

Operands

command   The name of a command that is to be invoked. If *command* names any of the special built-in commands (see shell_builtins(1)), the results are undefined.

argument   Any string to be supplied as an argument when invoking command.

Examples

The following example lowers the priority of a command by four units (the default).

castle% **/usr/bin/nice** *command*

The following example lowers the priority of a command by increasing the nice number by 10 units.

castle% **/usr/bin/nice +1-** *command*

Note — The plus sign is optional for positive numbers. The minus sign is required for negative numbers.

The following example raises the priority of a command by lowering the nice number by 10 units. The first minus sign is the option sign, and the second minus sign indicates a negative number.

/usr/bin/nice - -10 *command*

Environment Variables

See environ(5) for descriptions of the following environment variables that affect the execution of nice: LC_CTYPE, LC_MESSAGES, PATH, and NLSPATH.

Exit Status

If *command* is invoked, the exit status of nice is the exit status of *command*; otherwise, nice exits with one of the following values.

1-125   An error occurred.

126   *command* was found but could not be invoked.

127   *command* could not be found.

Attributes

See attributes(5) for descriptions of the following attributes:

/usr/bin/nice

Attribute Type	Attribute Value
Availability	SUNWcsu
CSI	Enabled

/usr/xpg4/bin/nice

Attribute Type	Attribute Value
Availability	SUNWxcu4
CSI	Enabled

See Also

csh(1), ksh(1), nohup(1), priocntl(1), sh(1), shell_builtins(1), nice(2), attributes(5), environ(5), XPG4(5)

nis+, NIS+, nis — New Version of the Network Information Name Service

Description

NIS+ is a new version of the network information name service. This version differs in several significant ways from Version 2, which is referred to as NIS or YP in earlier releases. Specific areas of enhancement include the ability to scale to larger networks, security, and the administration of the service.

The manual pages for NIS+ are divided into three basic categories. Section 1 manual pages describe the user commands that are most often executed from a shell script or directly from the command line. Section 1M manual pages describe commands that can be used by the network administrator to administer the service itself. Section 3N manual pages describe the NIS+ programming API.

All commands and functions that use NIS Version 2 are prefixed by the letters yp as in ypmatch(1), ypcat(1), yp_match(3NSL), and yp_first(3NSL). Commands and functions that use the new replacement software NIS+ are prefixed by the letters nis as in nismatch(1), nischown(1), nis_list(3NSL), and nis_add_entry(3NSL). See "List of Commands" on page 940 for a complete list of NIS+ commands.

These pages introduce the NIS+ terminology. It also describes the NIS+ namespace, authentication, and authorization policies.

NIS+ Namespace

The naming model of NIS+ is based on a tree structure. Each node in the tree corresponds to an NIS+ object. NIS+ has six types of objects:

- Directory
- Table
- Group

- Link
- Entry
- Private

NIS+ Directory Object

Each NIS+ namespace has at least one NIS+ directory object. An NIS+ directory is like a UNIX file-system directory that contains other NIS+ objects, including NIS+ directories. The NIS+ directory that forms the root of the NIS+ namespace is called the root directory. NIS+ has two special directories.

- `org_dir` consists of all the systemwide administration tables such as `passwd`, `hosts`, and `mail_aliases`.
- `groups_dir` holds NIS+ group objects that are used for access control.

The collection of `org_dir`, `groups_dir`, and their parent directory is referred to as an NIS+ domain. You can arrange NIS+ directories in a treelike structure so that the NIS+ namespace can match the organizational or administrative hierarchy.

NIS+ Table Object

NIS+ tables (not files) contained within NIS+ directories store the actual information about some particular type. For example, the `hosts` system table stores information about the IP address of the hosts in that domain. NIS+ tables are multicolumn, and you can search the tables through any of the searchable columns. Each table object defines the schema for its table. The NIS+ tables consist of NIS+ entry objects. For each entry in the NIS+ table, there is an NIS+ entry object. NIS+ entry objects conform to the schema defined by the NIS+ table object.

NIS+ Group Object

NIS+ group objects are used for access control at group granularity. NIS+ group objects, contained within the `groups_dir` directory of a domain, contain a list of all the NIS+ principals within a certain NIS+ group. An NIS+ principal is a user or a machine making NIS+ requests.

NIS+ Link Object

NIS+ link objects are like UNIX symbolic file-system links. They are typically used for shortcuts in the NIS+ namespace.

Refer to `nis_objects`(3NSL) for more information about the NIS+ objects.

NIS+ Names

The NIS+ service defines two forms of names.

- Simple names identify NIS+ objects contained within the NIS+ namespace.
- Indexed names identify NIS+ entries contained within NIS+ tables.

Furthermore, entries within NIS+ tables are returned to the caller as NIS+ objects of type entry. NIS+ objects are implemented as a union structure that is described in the file `rpcsvc/nis_object.x`. The differences between the various types and the meanings of the components of these objects are described in `nis_objects`(3NSL).

Simple Names

Simple names consist of a series of labels that are separated by the dot (.) character. Each label is composed of printable characters from the ISO Latin-1 set. Each label can

be of any non-zero length provided that the fully qualified name is fewer than
NIS_MAXNAMELEN octets including the separating dots. (See rpcsvc/nis.h for the actual
value of NIS_MAXNAMELEN in the current release.) Labels that contain special characters
(see "Grammar" on page 932) must be quoted. The NIS+ namespace is organized as a
singly rooted tree. Simple names identify nodes within this tree. These names are
constructed so that the leftmost label in a name identifies the leaf node and all of the
labels to the right of the leaf identify the parent node of the object. The parent node is
referred to as the leaf's directory. The leaf directory is a naming directory and should not
be confused with a file-system directory.

For example, the name example.simple.name. is a simple name with three labels,
where example is the leaf node in this name. The directory of this leaf is simple.name.
which by itself is a simple name, the leaf of which is simple, and its directory is simply
name.

The function nis_leaf_of(3NSL) returns the first label of a simple name. The
function nis_domain_of(3NSL) returns the name of the directory that contains the leaf.
Iterative use of these two functions can break a simple name into each of its label
components.

The name dot (.) is reserved to name the global root of the namespace. For systems
that are connected to the Internet, this global root is served by a Domain Name Service.
When an NIS+ server is serving a root directory whose name is not dot (.), this directory
is referred to as a local root.

NIS+ names are said to be fully qualified when the name includes all of the labels
identifying all of the directories, up to the global root. Names without the trailing dot are
called partially qualified.

Indexed Names

Indexed names are compound names that are composed of a search criteria and a simple
name. The search criteria component is used to select entries from a table; the simple
name component is used to identify the NIS+ table that is to be searched. The search
criteria is a series of column names and their desired values enclosed in bracket
characters ([]). This criteria takes the following form.

```
[column_name=value, column_name=value,...]
```

A search criteria is combined with a simple name to form an indexed name by
concatenating the two parts, separated by a comma as follows.

```
[search-criteria],table.directory.
```

When multiple column name/value pairs are present in the search criteria, only those
entries in the table that have the appropriate value in all columns specified are
returned. When no column name/value pairs are specified in the search criteria, [], all
entries in the table are returned.

Grammar

The following text represents a context-free grammar that defines the set of legal NIS+
names. The terminals in this grammar are the characters dot (.), open bracket ([), close
bracket (]), comma (,), equal (=), and white space. Use the vertical bar (|) character to
separate alternate productions. Read this syntax as "this production OR this
production."

```
name              ::=   . | simple-name | indexed-name

simple name       ::=   string. | string.simple-name
```

indexed name	::=	*search-criteria, simple-name*
search criteria	::=	*[attribute-list]*
attribute list	::=	*attribute* | *attribute, attribute-list*
attribute	::=	*string = string*
string	::=	ISO Latin-1 character set except the character slash (/). The initial character cannot be a terminal character or the characters at (@), plus (+), or dash (-).

Terminals that appear in strings must be quoted with double quote ("). You can quote the " character by quoting it with itself (" ").

Name Expansion

The NIS+ service accepts only fully qualified names. However, because such names can be unwieldy, the NIS+ commands in section 1 use a set of standard expansion rules that try to fully qualify a partially qualified name. This expansion is actually done by the NIS+ library function nis_getnames(3NSL), which generates a list of names by using the default NIS+ directory search path or the NIS_PATH environment variable. The default NIS+ directory search path includes all the names in its path. nis_getnames() is invoked by the functions nis_lookup(3NSL) and nis_list(3NSL) when the EXPAND_NAME flag is used.

The NIS_PATH environment variable contains an ordered list of simple names. The names are separated by the colon (:) character. If any name in the list contains colons, the colon should be quoted as described in the Grammar section. When the list is exhausted, the resolution function returns the error NIS_NOTFOUND. This error message may mask the fact that the name existed but a server for it was unreachable. If the name presented to the list or lookup interface is fully qualified, the EXPAND_NAME flag is ignored. In the list of names from the NIS_PATH environment variable, the dollar sign ($) character is treated specially. Simple names that end with the label $ have this character replaced by the default directory (see nis_local_directory(3NSL)). Using $ as a name in this list results in this name being replaced by the list of directories between the default directory and the global root that contain at least two labels.

Below is an example of this expansion. With a default directory of some.long.domain.name. and the NIS_PATH variable set to fred.bar.:org_dir.$:$, the path is initially broken up into the following list.

```
1 fred.bar.
2 org_dir.$
3 $
```

The dollar sign in the second component is replaced with the default directory. The dollar sign in the third component is replaced with the names of the directories between the default directory and the global root that have at least two labels in them. The effective path values become:

```
1 fred.bar.
2a org_dir.some.long.domain.name.
3a some.long.domain.name.
3b long.domain.name.
3c domain.name.
```

Each of these simple names is appended to the partially qualified name that was passed to the `nis_lookup`(3NSL) or `nis_list`(3NSL) interface. Each is tried in turn until `NIS_SUCCESS` is returned or the list is exhausted.

If the `NIS_PATH` variable is not set, the path $ is used.

The library function `nis_getnames`(3NSL) can be called from user programs to generate the list of names that would be attempted. The program `nisdefaults`(1) with the `-s` option can also be used to show the fully expanded path.

Concatenation Path

Normally, all the entries for a certain type of information are stored within the table itself. However, at times it is desirable for the table to point to other tables where entries can be found. For example, you may want to store all the IP addresses in the `host` table for their own domain and want to still be able to resolve hosts in some other domain without explicitly specifying the new domain name. NIS+ provides a mechanism for concatenating different but related tables with an NIS+ concatenation path. With a concatenation path, you can create a sort of flat namespace from a hierarchical structure. You can also create a table with no entries and just point the hosts or any other table to its parent domain. Note that with such a setup, you are moving the administrative burden of managing the tables to the parent domain. The concatenation path slows down the request response time because more tables and more servers are searched. It also decreases the availability of tables if all the servers are incapacitated for a particular directory in the table path.

The NIS+ concatenation path is also referred to as the *table path*. This path is set up at table creation time with `nistbladm`(1). You can specify more than one table to be concatenated, and the tables are searched in the given order. Note that the NIS+ client libraries, by default, do not follow the concatenation path set in site-specific tables. Refer to `nis_list`(3NSL) for more details.

Namespaces

The NIS+ service defines two additional disjoint namespaces for its own use. These namespaces are:

- The NIS+ principal namespace.
- The NIS+ group namespace.

The names associated with the group and principal namespaces are syntactically identical to simple names. However, the information they represent cannot be obtained by direct presentation of these names to the NIS+ interfaces. Instead, special interfaces are defined to map these names into NIS+ names so that they can then be resolved.

Principal Names

NIS+ principal names are used to uniquely identify users and machines that are making NIS+ requests. These names have the following form.

principal.domain

Here, domain is the fully qualified name of an NIS+ directory where the named principal's credentials can be found. See "Directories and Domains" on page 936 for more information on domains. Note that this name, *principal*, is not a leaf in the NIS+ namespace.

Credentials are used to map the identity of a host or user from one context, such as a process UID, into the NIS+ context. They are stored as records in an NIS+ table named `cred`, which always appears in the `org_dir` subdirectory of the directory named in the principal name.

This mapping can be expressed as a replacement function with the following syntax.

principal.domain ->[cname=*principal.domain*],cred.org_dir.*domain*

This replacement name is an NIS+ name that can be presented to the nis_list(3NSL) interface for resolution. NIS+ principal names are administered with the nisaddcred(1M) command.

The cred table contains five columns named cname, auth_name, auth_type, public_data, and private_data. This table contains one record for each identity mapping for an NIS+ principal. The current service supports three types of mappings.

LOCAL   Map from the UID of a given process to the NIS+ principal name associated with that UID. If no mapping exists, return the name nobody. When the effective UID of the process is 0 (for example, the superuser), return the NIS+ name associated with the host. Note that UIDs are sensitive to the context of the machine on which the process is executing.

DES   Map to and from a Secure RPC netname into an NIS+ principal name. See secure_rpc(3NSL) for more information on netnames. Note that because netnames contain the notion of a domain, they span NIS+ directories.

DH*nnn-m*   Map netnames and NIS+ principal names for extended Diffie-Hellman keys, for example, DH640-0, DH1024-0. See nisauthconf(1M) for further information.

The NIS+ client library function nis_local_principal(3NSL) uses the cred.org_dir table to map the UNIX notion of an identity, a process UID, into an NIS+ principal name. Shell programs can use the program nisdefaults(1) with the -p option to return this information.

Mapping from UIDs to an NIS+ principal name is accomplished by constructing a query of the following form.

[auth_type=LOCAL, auth_name=*uid*],cred.org_dir.*defaultdomain*.

This query returns a record containing the NIS+ principal name associated with this UID, in the machine's default domain.

The NIS+ service uses the Data Encryption Standard (DES) mapping to map the names associated with Secure RPC requests into NIS+ principal names. RPC requests that use Secure RPC include the netname of the client making the request in the RPC header. This netname has the following form.

unix.*UID@domain*

The service constructs a query by using this name of the following form where the *domain* part is extracted from the netname instead of being the default domain.

[auth_type=DES, auth_name=*netname*],cred.org_dir.*domain*.

This query looks up the mapping of this netname into an NIS+ principal name in the domain where it was created.

This mechanism of mapping UID and netnames into an NIS+ principal name guarantees that a client of the NIS+ service has only one principal name. This principal name is used as the basis for authorization described below. All objects in the NIS+

namespace and all entries in NIS+ tables must have an owner specified for them. This owner field always contains an NIS+ principal name.

Group Names
Like NIS+ principal names, NIS+ group names take the following form.

`group_name.`*`domain`*

All objects in the NIS+ namespace and all entries in NIS+ tables can optionally have a group owner specified for them. This group owner field, when filled in, always contains the fully qualified NIS+ group name.

The NIS+ client library defines several interfaces (`nis_groups`(3NSL)) for dealing with NIS+ groups. These interfaces internally map NIS+ group names into an NIS+ simple name that identifies the NIS+ group object associated with that group name. This mapping can be shown as follows.

`group.``domain -> `*`group.`*`groups_dir.`*`domain`*

This mapping eliminates collisions between NIS+ group names and NIS+ directory names. For example, without this mapping, a directory with the name `engineering.foo.com.` would make it impossible to have a group named `engineering.foo.com` because of the restriction that within the NIS+ namespace, a name unambiguously identifies a single object. With this mapping, the NIS+ group name `engineering.foo.com.` maps to the NIS+ object name `engineering.groups_dir.foo.com.`

The contents of a group object are a list of NIS+ principal names and the names of other NIS+ groups. See `nis_groups`(3NSL) for a more complete description of their use.

NIS+ Security
NIS+ defines a security model to control access to information managed by the service. The service defines access rights that are selectively granted to individual clients or groups of clients. Principal names and group names define clients and groups of clients that may be granted or denied access to NIS+ information. These principals and groups are associated with NIS+ domains as defined below.

The security model also uses the notion of a class of principals, called `nobody`, that contains all clients whether or not they have authenticated themselves to the service. The class `world` includes any client who has been authenticated.

Directories and Domains
Some directories within the NIS+ namespace are referred to as NIS+ domains. Domains are those NIS+ directories that contain the subdirectories `groups_dir` and `org_dir`. Further, the subdirectory `org_dir` should contain the table named `cred`. NIS+ group names and NIS+ principal names always include the NIS+ domain name after their first label.

Authentication
The NIS+ name service uses Secure RPC for the integrity of the NIS+ service. Secure RPC requires that users of the service and their machines must have a Secure RPC key pair associated with them. This key is initially generated with either the `nisaddcred`(1M) or `nisclient`(1M) commands and modified with the `chkey`(1) or `nispasswd`(1) commands.

The use of Secure RPC enables private information that is not available to untrusted machines or users on the network to be stored in the name service.

In addition to the Secure RPC key, users need a mapping of their UID into an NIS+ principal name. This mapping is created by the system administrator, using the nisclient(1M) or nisaddcred(1M) commands.

Users that are using machines in several NIS+ domains must ensure that they have a local credential entry in each of those domains. This credential should be created with the NIS+ principal name of the user in their "home" domain. For the purposes of NIS+ and Secure RPC, the home domain is defined to be the one where the user's Secure RPC key pair is located.

Although extended Diffie-Hellman keys use an alternative to Secure RPC, administration is done through the same commands. See nisauthconf(1M).

Authorization

The NIS+ service defines four access rights that can be granted or denied to clients of the service. These rights are:

- Read
- Modify
- Create
- Destroy

These access rights are specified in the object structure at creation time and can be modified later with the nischmod(1) command. In general, the rights granted for an object apply only to that object. However, for purposes of authorization, rights granted to clients reading directory and table objects are granted to those clients for all of the objects "contained" by the parent object. This notion of containment is abstract. The objects do not actually contain other objects within them. Note that group objects do contain the list of principals within their definition.

Access rights are interpreted as follows.

read
: Grant read access to an object. For directory and table objects, having read access on the parent object conveys read access to all of the objects that are direct children of a directory or to entries within a table.

modify
: Grant modification access to an existing object. Read access is not required for modification. However, in many applications, one needs to read an object before modifying it. Such modify operations fail unless read access is also granted.

create
: Grant a client permission to create new objects where one had not previously existed. create is used only in conjunction with directory and table objects. Having create access for a table enables a client to add additional entries to the table. Having create access for a directory enables a client to add new objects to an NIS+ directory.

destroy
: Grant a client permission to destroy or remove an existing object or entry. When a client tries to destroy an entry or object by removing it, the service first checks to see if the table or directory containing that object grants the client destroy access. If it does, the operation proceeds; if the containing object does not grant this right, then the object itself is checked to see if it grants this right to the client. If the object grants the right, then the operation proceeds; otherwise, the request is rejected.

Each of these rights can be granted to any one of four different categories.

owner
Grant a right to the owner of an object. The owner is the NIS+ principal identified in the owner field. The owner can be changed with the nischown(1) command. Note that if the owner does not have modification access rights to the object, he cannot change any access rights to the object unless he has modification access rights to its parent object.

group owner
Grant a right to the group owner of an object. This grants the right to any principal that is identified as a member of the group associated with the object. The group owner can be changed with the nischgrp(1) command. The object owner need not be a member of this group.

world
Grant a right to everyone in the world. This grants the right to all clients who have authenticated themselves with the service.

nobody
Grant a right to the nobody principal. This has the effect of granting the right to any client that makes a request of the service, regardless of whether the client is authenticated.

Note that for bootstrapping reasons, directory objects that are NIS+ domains, the org_dir subdirectory, and the cred table within that subdirectory must grant read access to the nobody principal. This permission makes navigation of the namespace possible when a client is in the process of locating its credentials. Granting this access does not enable the contents of other tables within org_dir to be read (such as the entries in the password table) unless the table itself gives "real" access rights to the nobody principal.

Directory Authorization

Additional capabilities grant access rights to clients for directories. These rights are contained within the object access rights (OAR) structure of the directory. This structure enables the NIS+ service to grant rights that are not granted by the directory object for objects contained by the directory of a specific type.

An example of this capability is a directory object that does not grant create access to all clients but does grant create access in the OAR structure for objects of type group to clients who are members of the NIS+ group associated with the directory. In this example, the only objects that could be created as children of the directory would have to be of the type group.

Another example is a directory object that grants create access only to the owner of the directory and then additionally grants create access through the OAR structure for objects of type table, link, group, and private to any member of the directory's group. The group thus gains nearly complete create access to the group with the exception of creating subdirectories. The creation of new NIS+ domains are restricted because creating a domain requires creating both a groups_dir and org_dir subdirectory.

> **Note** — There is currently no command-line interface to set or change the OAR of the directory object.

Table Authorization

As with directories, additional capabilities are provided for granting access to entries within tables. Rights granted to a client by the access rights field in a table object apply to the table object and all of the entry objects "contained" by that table. If an access right is not granted by the table object, it can be granted by an entry within the table. This authorization holds for all rights except create.

For example, a table cannot grant read access to a client performing an nis_list(3NSL) operation on the table. However, the access rights field of entries within that table can grant read access to the client. Note that access rights in an entry are granted to the owner and group owner of the entry and not the owner or group of the table. When the list operation is performed, all entries to which the client has read access are returned. Those entries that do not grant read access are not returned. If none of the entries that match the search criteria grant read access to the client making the request, no entries are returned and the result status contains the NIS_NOTFOUND error code.

Access rights that are granted by the rights field in an entry are granted for the entire entry. However, in the table object, an additional set of access rights is maintained for each column in the table. These rights apply to the equivalent column in the entry. The rights are used to grant access when neither the table nor the entry itself grants access. The access rights in a column specification apply to the owner and group owner of the entry instead of the owner and group owner of the table object.

When a read operation is performed, if read access is not granted by the table and is not granted by the entry but is granted by the access rights in a column, that entry is returned with the correct values in all columns that are readable and the string *NP* (No Permission) in columns where read access is not granted.

As an example, consider a client who has performed a list operation on a table that does not grant read access to that client. Each entry object that satisfied the search criteria specified by the client is examined to see if it grants read access to the client. If it does, it is included in the returned result. If it does not, then each column is checked to see if it grants read access to the client. If any columns grant read access to the client, data in those columns is returned. Columns that do not grant read access have their contents replaced by the string *NP*. If none of the columns grant read access, then the entry is not returned.

Protocol Operation Authorization

Most NIS+ operations have implied access control through the permissions on the objects that they manipulate. For example, to read an entry in a table, you must have read permission on that entry. However, some NIS+ operations by default perform no access checking at all and so are allowed for everyone.

Operation	Example of Commands That Use the Operation
NIS_CHECKPOINT	nisping -C
NIS_CPTIME	nisping, rpc.nisd
NIS_MKDIR	nismkdir
NIS_PING	nisping, rpc.nisd
NIS_RMDIR	nisrmdir
NIS_SERVSTATE	nisbackup, nisrestore
NIS_STATUS	nisstat, rpc.nispasswdd

See nisopaccess(1) for a description of how to enforce access control to these NIS+ operations. The nisopaccess(1) command is new in the Solaris 8 release.

List of Commands

The following list shows all commands and programming functions related to NIS+.

NIS+ User Commands

nisaddent(1M)

> Add /etc files and NIS maps into their corresponding NIS+ tables.

niscat(1)   Display NIS+ tables and objects.

nischgrp(1)   Change the group owner of an NIS+ object.

nischmod(1)   Change access rights on an NIS+ object.

nischown(1)   Change the owner of an NIS+ object.

nischttl(1)   Change the time-to-live value of an NIS+ object.

nisdefaults(1)

> Display NIS+ default values.

niserror(1)   Display NIS+ error messages.

nisgrep(1)   Search NIS+ tables.

nisgrpadm(1)

> Administer NIS+ groups.

nisln(1)   Symbolically link NIS+ objects.

nisls(1)   List the contents of an NIS+ directory.

nismatch(1)   Search NIS+ tables.

nismkdir(1)   Create NIS+ directories.

New! nisopaccess(1)

> Control operation access to NIS+. New in the Solaris 8 release.

nispasswd(1)

> Change NIS+ password information.

nisrm(1)   Remove NIS+ objects from the namespace.

nisrmdir(1)   Remove NIS+ directories.

nisshowcache(1M)

> Print the contents of the shared cache file.

nistbladm(1)

> Administer NIS+ tables.

nistest(1)   Return the state of the NIS+ namespace, using a conditional expression.

NIS+ Administrative Commands

aliasadm(1M)

> Manipulate the NIS+ aliases map.

`nis_cachemgr(1M)`

> Cache location information about NIS+ servers.

`nisaddcred(1M)`

> Create NIS+ credentials.

`nisaddent(1M)`

> Create NIS+ tables from corresponding /etc files or NIS maps.

`nisauthconf(1M)`

> Configure extended Diffie-Hellman keys.

`nisbackup(1)`   *New!*

> Back up NIS+ credentials for NIS+ principals. New in the Solaris 8 release.

`nisclient(1M)`

> Initialize NIS+ credentials for NIS+ principals.

`nisd(1M)`   NIS+ service daemon.

`nisd_resolv(1M)`

> NIS+ service daemon.

`nisinit(1M)`   Initialize NIS+ clients and servers.

`nislog(1M)`   Display the contents of the NIS+ transaction log.

`nisping(1M)`   Send `ping` to NIS+ servers.

`nispopulate(1M)`

> Populate the NIS+ tables in an NIS+ domain.

`nisprefadm(1M)`   *New!*

> Set server preferences for NIS+ clients. New in the Solaris 8 release.

`nisrestore(1M)`   *New!*

> Restore NIS+ directory backup. New in the Solaris 8 release.

`nisserver(1M)`

> Set up NIS+ servers.

`nissetup(1M)`

> Initialize an NIS+ domain.

`nisshowcache(1M)`

> Print the contents of the shared cache file.

`nisstat(1M)`   Report NIS+ server statistics.

`nisupdkeys(1M)`

> Update the public keys in an NIS+ directory object.

`rpc.nisd(1M)`

> NIS+ service daemon.

rpc.nisd_resolv(1M)

>NIS+ service daemon.

sysidnis(1M)

>System configuration.

NIS+ Programming API

nis_add(3NSL)

>NIS+ namespace functions.

nis_add_entry(3NSL)

>NIS+ table functions.

nis_addmember(3NSL)

>NIS+ group-manipulation functions.

nis_checkpoint(3NSL)

>Miscellaneous NIS+ log administration functions.

nis_clone_object(3NSL)

>NIS+ subroutines.

nis_creategroup(3NSL)

>NIS+ group-manipulation functions.

nis_destroy_object(3NSL)

>NIS+ subroutines.

nis_destroygroup(3NSL)

>NIS+ group manipulation functions.

nis_dir_cmp(3NSL)

>NIS+ subroutines.

nis_domain_of(3NSL)

>NIS+ subroutines.

nis_error(3NSL)

>Display NIS+ error messages.

nis_first_entry(3NSL)

>NIS+ table functions.

nis_freenames(3NSL)

>NIS+ subroutines.

nis_freeresult(3NSL)

>NIS+ namespace functions.

nis_freeservlist(3NSL)

>Miscellaneous NIS+ functions.

nis_freetags(3NSL)

> Miscellaneous NIS+ functions.

nis_getnames(3NSL)

> NIS+ subroutines.

nis_getservlist(3NSL)

> Miscellaneous NIS+ functions.

nis_groups(3NSL)

> NIS+ group manipulation functions.

nis_ismember(3NSL)

> NIS+ group manipulation functions.

nis_leaf_of(3NSL)

> NIS+ subroutines.

nis_lerror(3NSL)

> Display some NIS+ error messages.

nis_list(3NSL)

> NIS+ table functions.

nis_local_directory(3NSL)

> NIS+ local names.

nis_local_group(3NSL)

> NIS+ local names.

nis_local_host(3NSL)

> NIS+ local names.

nis_local_names(3NSL)

> NIS+ local names.

nis_local_principal(3NSL)

> NIS+ local names.

nis_lookup(3NSL)

> NIS+ namespace functions.

nis_mkdir(3NSL)

> Miscellaneous NIS+ functions.

nis_modify(3NSL)

> NIS+ namespace functions.

nis_modify_entry(3NSL)

> NIS+ table functions.

nis_name_of(3NSL)

> NIS+ subroutines.

nis_names(3NSL)

>   NIS+ namespace functions.

nis_next_entry(3NSL)

>   NIS+ table functions.

nis_objects(3NSL)

>   NIS+ object formats.

nis_perror(3NSL)

>   Display NIS+ error messages.

nis_ping(3NSL)

>   Miscellaneous NIS+ log administration functions.

nis_print_group_entry(3NSL)

>   NIS+ group-manipulation functions.

nis_print_object(3NSL)

>   NIS+ subroutines.

nis_remove(3NSL)

>   NIS+ namespace functions.

nis_remove_entry(3NSL)

>   NIS+ table functions.

nis_removemember(3NSL)

>   NIS+ group-manipulation functions.

nis_rmdir(3NSL)

>   Miscellaneous NIS+ functions.

nis_server(3NSL)

>   Miscellaneous NIS+ functions.

nis_servstate(3NSL)

>   Miscellaneous NIS+ functions.

nis_sperrno(3NSL)

>   Display NIS+ error messages.

nis_sperror(3NSL)

>   Display NIS+ error messages.

nis_sperror_r(3NSL)

>   Display NIS+ error messages.

nis_stats(3NSL)

>   Miscellaneous NIS+ functions.

nis_subr(3NSL)

>   NIS+ subroutines.

nis_tables(3NSL)

> NIS+ table functions.

nis_verifygroup(3NSL)

> NIS+ group-manipulation functions.

NIS+ Files and Directories

nisfiles(4)　NIS+ database files and directory structure.

Files

rpcsvc/nis_object.x

> Protocol description of an NIS+ object.

rpcsvc/nis.x

> Defines the NIS+ protocol, using the RPC language as described in the *ONC+ Developer's Guide*.

rpcsvc/nis.h

> Should be included by all clients of the NIS+ service.

See Also

nischown(1), nisdefaults(1), nismatch(1), nisopaccess(1), nispasswd(1), **New!**
newkey(1M), nisaddcred(1M), nisauthconf(1M). nisclient(1M),
nispopulate(1M), nisserver(1M), nis_add_entry(3NSL),
nis_domain_of(3NSL), nis_getnames(3NSL), nis_groups(3NSL),
nis_leaf_of(3NSL), nis_list(3NSL), nis_local_directory(3NSL),
nis_lookup(3NSL), nis_objects(3NSL)

ONC+ Developer's Guide

> Describes the application programming interfaces for networks including NIS+.

System Administration Guide: Naming and Directory Services (DNS, NIS, and LDAP) **New!**

> Describes how to transition from NIS to NIS+ and plan for and configure an NIS+ namespace. New in the Solaris 9 release.

System Administration Guide, Volume 3 **New!**

> Describes IPv6 extensions to Solaris nameservices, new in the Solaris 9 release.

niscat — Display NIS+ Tables and Objects

Synopsis

```
/usr/bin/niscat [-AhLMv] [-s sep] tablename...
/usr/bin/niscat [-ALMP] -o name...
```

Description

Use the niscat command to display information in NIS+ tables and objects. In the first synopsis, niscat displays the contents of the NIS+ tables named by *tablename*. In the second synopsis, niscat displays the internal representation of the NIS+ objects named by *name*.

Note — Columns without values in a table are displayed by two adjacent separator characters.

Options

-A	Display the data within the table and all of the data in tables in the initial table's concatenation path.
-h	Display the header line before displaying the table. The header consists of the hash (#) character followed by the name of each column. The column names are separated by the table separator character.
-L	If *tablename* or *name* names an object of type LINK, follow the link and display the object or table named by the link.
-M	Master server only. Send the request to the master server of the named data. This option guarantees that the most up-to-date information is seen, at the possible expense of increasing the load on the master server and increasing the possibility of the NIS+ server being unavailable or busy for updates.
-o *name*	Display the internal representation of the named NIS+ object(s). If *name* is an indexed name (see nismatch(1)), then display each of the matching entry objects. Use this option to display access rights and other attributes of individual columns.
-P	Follow the concatenation path of a table if the initial search is unsuccessful. This option is useful only when using an indexed name for *name* and the -o option.
-s *sep*	Specify the character used to separate the table columns. If you specify no character, use the default separator (a space) for the table.
-v	Display columns containing binary data on the standard output. Without this option, display binary data as the string *BINARY*.

Examples

The following example displays the contents of the `hosts` table.

```
castle% niscat -h hosts.org_dir
# cname name addr comment
client1 client1 129.144.201.100 Joe Smith
crunchy crunchy 129.144.201.44 Jane Smith
crunchy softy 129.144.201.44
castle%
```

The string `*NP*` is returned in those fields where the user has insufficient access rights.

The following example displays `passwd.org_dir` on the standard output.

```
castle% niscat passwd.org_dir
```

The following example displays the contents of table `frodo` and the contents of all tables in its concatenation path.

```
castle% niscat -A frodo
```

The following example displays the entries in the table `groups.org_dir` as NIS+ objects. Note that the brackets are protected from the shell by single quotes.

```
castle% niscat -o '[]groups.org_dir'
```

The following example displays the table object of the `passwd.org_dir table`.

```
castle% niscat -o passwd.org_dir
```

The previous example displays the `passwd` table object and not the `passwd` table. The table object includes information such as the number of columns, column type, searchable or not searchable, separator, access rights, and other defaults.

The following example displays the directory object for `org_dir`, which includes information such as the access rights and replica information.

```
castle% niscat -o org_dir
```

Environment Variables

NIS_PATH   If this variable is set and the NIS+ name is not fully qualified, search each directory specified until the object is found (see `nisdefaults`(1)).

Exit Status

0   Successful completion.

1   An error occurred.

Attributes

See `attributes`(5) for descriptions of the following attributes:

Attribute Type	Attribute Value
Availability	SUNWnisu

See Also

nis+(1), nisdefaults(1), nismatch(1), nistbladm(1), nis_objects(3NSL), nis_tables(3NSL), attributes(5)

nischgrp — Change the Group Owner of an NIS+ Object

Synopsis

/usr/bin/nischgrp [-AfLP] *group name*...

Description

Use the nischgrp command to change the group owner of the NIS+ objects or entries specified by *name* to the specified NIS+ *group*. Specify entries, using indexed names (see nismatch(1)). If *group* is not a fully qualified NIS+ group name, it is resolved by means of the directory search path (see nisdefaults(1)).

The only restriction on changing an object's group owner is that you must have modify permissions for the object.

This command fails if the master NIS+ server is not running.

Note — The NIS+ server checks the validity of the group name before making the change.

Options

-A	Modify all entries in all tables in the concatenation path that match the search criteria specified in *name*. This option implies the -P option.
-f	Force the operation, and fail silently if it does not succeed.
-L	Follow links, and change the group owner of the linked object or entries instead of the group owner of the link itself.
-P	Follow the concatenation path within a named table. This option makes sense only when either name is an indexed name or when you also specify the -L option and the named object is a link pointing to entries.

Examples

The following examples show how to change the group owner of an object to a group in a different domain and how to change the group owner in the local domain.

```
castle% nischgrp newgroup.remote.domain. object
castle% nischgrp my-buds object
```

The following example shows how to change the group owner for a password entry. admins is an NIS+ group in the same domain.

```
castle% nischgrp admins '[uid=99],passwd.org_dir'
```

The following two examples change the group owner of the object or entries pointed to by a link, and the group owner of all entries in the hobbies table.

```
castle% nischgrp -L my-buds linkname
castle% nischgrp my-buds '[],hobbies'
```

Environment Variables

NIS_PATH   If this variable is set and the NIS+ name is not fully qualified, search
             each specified directory until the object is found (see nisdefaults(1)).

Exit Status

0   Success.

1   Failure.

Attributes

See attributes(5) for descriptions of the following attributes:

Attribute Type	Attribute Value
Availability	SUNWnisu

See Also

nis+(1), nischmod(1), nischown(1), nisdefaults(1), nisgrpadm(1),
nis_objects(3NSL), attributes(5)

nischmod — Change Access Rights on an NIS+ Object

Synopsis

/usr/bin/nischmod [-AfLP] *mode name*...

Description

Use the nischmod command to change the access rights (mode) of the NIS+ objects or
entries specified by *name* to *mode*. Specify entries, using indexed names (see
nismatch(1)). Only principals with modify access to an object can change its mode.
   mode has the following form.

rights [, *rights*]...

rights has the form:

[*who*] *op permission* [*op permission*]...

   who is a combination of the following identities.

n   Nobody's permissions.

o   Owner's permissions.

g   Group's permissions.

w   World's permissions.

a   All or owg.

   If you omit *who*, the default is a.

op is one of the following operators.

+	To grant the permission.
–	To revoke the permission.
=	To set the permissions explicitly.

permission is any combination of the following permissions.

r	Read.
m	Modify.
c	Create.
d	Destroy.

Note — Unlike the system chmod(1) command, the nischmod command does not accept an octal notation.

Options

-A	Modify all entries in all tables in the concatenation path that match the search criteria specified in *name*. This option implies the -P option.
-f	Force the operation, and fail silently if it does not succeed.
-L	Follow links, and change the permission of the linked object or entries instead of the permission of the link itself.
-P	Follow the concatenation path within a named table. This option is applicable only when either *name* is an indexed name or you specify the -L option and the named object is a link pointing to an entry.

Examples

The following example gives everyone read access to an object (that is, access for owner, group, and all).

```
castle% nischmod a+r object
```

The following example denies create and modify privileges to group and unauthenticated clients (nobody).

```
castle% nischmod gn-cm object
```

The following example sets a complex set of permissions for an object.

```
castle% nischmod o=rmcd,g=rm,w=rc,n=r object
```

The following example sets the permissions of an entry in the password table so that the group owner can modify them.

```
castle% nischmod g+m '[uid=55],passwd.org_dir'
```

The following example changes the permissions of a linked object.

```
castle% nischmod -L w+mr linkname
```

Environment Variables

NIS_PATH   If this variable is set and the NIS+ name is not fully qualified, search each specified directory until the object is found (see nisdefaults(1)).

Exit Status

0   Success.

1   Failure.

Attributes

See attributes(5) for descriptions of the following attributes:

Attribute Type	Attribute Value
Availability	SUNWnisu

See Also

chmod(1), nis+(1), nischgrp(1), nischown(1), nisdefaults(1), nis_objects(3NSL), attributes(5)

nischown — Change the Owner of an NIS+ Object

Synopsis

/usr/bin/nischown [-AfLP] *owner name*...

Description

Use the nischown command to change the owner of the NIS+ objects or entries specified by *name* to *owner*. Specify entries, using indexed names (see nismatch(1)). If *owner* is not a fully qualified NIS+ principal name (see nisaddcred(1M)), the default domain (see nisdefaults(1)) is appended to it.

The only restriction on changing an object's owner is that you must have modify permissions for the object.

Note — If you are the current owner of an object and you change ownership, you may not be able to regain ownership unless you have modify access to the new object.

The NIS+ server checks the validity of the name before making the modification. The nischown command fails if the master NIS+ server is not running.

Options

-A   Modify all entries in all tables in the concatenation path that match the search criteria specified in *name*. This option implies the -P option.

-f   Force the operation, and fail silently if it does not succeed.

-L   Follow links, and change the owner of the linked object or entries
                instead of the owner of the link itself.

-P   Follow the concatenation path within a named table. This option is
                meaningful only when either *name* is an indexed name or you also
                specify the -L option and the named object is a link pointing to entries.

Examples

The following two examples show how to change the owner of an object to a principal in
a different domain and how to change it to a principal in the local domain.

```
castle% nischown bob.remote.domain. object
castle% nischown skippy object
```

The following example shows how to change the owner of an entry in the passwd
table.

```
castle% nischown bob.remote.domain. '[uid=99],passwd.org_dir'
```

The following example shows how to change the object or entries pointed to by a link.

```
castle% nischown -L skippy linkname
```

Environment Variables

NIS_PATH   If this variable is set and the NIS+ name is not fully qualified, search
                each specified directory until the object is found (see nisdefaults(1)).

Exit Status

0   Success.

1   Failure.

Attributes

See attributes(5) for descriptions of the following attributes:

Attribute Type	Attribute Value
Availability	SUNWnisu

See Also

nis+(1), nischgrp(1), nischmod(1), nischttl(1), nisdefaults(1),
nisaddcred(1M), nis_objects(3NSL), attributes(5)

nischttl — Change the Time-to-Live Value of an NIS+ Object

Synopsis

```
nischttl [-AfLP] time name...
```

Description

Use the nischttl command to change the time-to-live value (ttl) of the NIS+ objects or entries specified by *name* to *time*. Specify entries using indexed names (see nismatch(1)).

The time-to-live value is used by object caches to set the expiration time of objects within their cache. When an object is read into the cache, this value is added to the current time in seconds, yielding the time when the cached object would expire. The object can be returned from the cache while the current time is earlier than the calculated expiration time. When the expiration time has been reached, the object is flushed from the cache.

You can specify the time-to-live time in seconds or in days, hours, minutes, seconds format. The latter format uses a suffix letter of d, h, m, or s to identify the units of time. The command fails if the master NIS+ server is not running.

Note — Setting a high ttl value enables objects to persist in caches for a longer period and can improve performance. However, when an object changes, in the worst case, the number of seconds in this attribute must pass before that change is visible to all clients. Setting a ttl value of 0 does not cache the object at all.

A high ttl value is a week, a low value is less than a minute. Password entries should have ttl values of about 12 hours (easily allowing one password change a day), entries in the RPC table can have ttl values of several weeks (this information is effectively unchanging). Only directory and group objects are cached in this implementation.

Options

-A	Modify all tables in the concatenation path that match the search criteria specified in *name*. This option implies the -P option.
-f	Force the operation, and fail silently if it does not succeed.
-L	Follow links, and change the time-to-live of the linked object or entries instead of the time-to-live of the link itself.
-P	Follow the concatenation path within a named table. This option makes sense only when either *name* is an indexed name or you also specify the -L option and the named object is a link pointing to entries.

Examples

The following example changes the ttl of an object, using the seconds format and the days, hours, minutes, seconds format. The ttl of the second object is set to 1 day and 12 hours.

```
castle% nischttl 184000 object
castle% nischttl 1d12h object
```

The following example changes the ttl for a password entry.

```
castle% nischttl 1h30m '[uid=99],passwd.org_dir'
```

The next two examples change the ttl of the object or entries pointed to by a link and the ttl of all entries in the hobbies table.

```
castle% nischttl -L 12h linkname
castle% nischttl 3600 '[],hobbies'
```

Environment Variables

NIS_PATH   If this variable is set and the NIS+ name is not fully qualified, search
             each specified directory until the object is found (see nisdefaults(1)).

Exit Status

0   Success.

1   Failure.

Attributes

See attributes(5) for descriptions of the following attributes:

Attribute Type	Attribute Value
Availability	SUNWnisu

See Also

nis+(1), nischgrp(1), nischmod(1), nischown(1), nisdefaults(1),
nis_objects(3NSL), attributes(5)

---

nisdefaults — Display NIS+ Default Values

Synopsis

/usr/bin/nisdefaults [-adghprstv]

Description

Use the nisdefaults command to print the default values that are returned by calls to
the NIS+ local name functions (see nis_local_names(3NSL)). When you specify no
options, all defaults are printed in a verbose format. With options, information for that
option only is displayed in a terse form suitable for shell scripts.

Options

-a   Print all defaults in a terse format.

-d   Print the default domain name.

-g   Print the default group name.

-h   Print the default host name.

-p   Print the default principal name.

-r   Print the default access rights with which new objects are created.

-s   Print the default directory search path.

-t   Print the default time-to-live value.

-v   Print the defaults in a verbose format. This option prepends an
identifying string to the output.

Examples

The following example prints the NIS+ defaults for a root process on machine `castle` in
the `foo.bar.` domain.

```
castle% nisdefaults
Principal Name : castle.foo.bar
Domain Name : foo.bar
Host Name : castle.foo.bar
Group Name :
Access Rights : ----rmcdr---r---
Time to live : 12:00:00
Search Path : foo.bar.
```

The following example sets a variable in a shell script to the default domain.

```
DOMAIN=`nisdefaults -d`
```

The following example prints out the default time-to-live in a verbose format.

```
castle% nisdefaults -tv
Time to live : 12:00:00
```

The following example prints out the time-to-live in the terse format.

```
castle% nisdefaults -t
43200
```

Environment Variables

Several environment variables affect the defaults associated with a process.

NIS_DEFAULTS

Specify a defaults string that overrides the NIS+ standard defaults. The
defaults string is a series of tokens separated by colons. These tokens
represent the default values to be used for the generic object properties.
All of the legal tokens are described below.

ttl=*time*   Set the default time-to-live for objects that are created.
Specify the *time* value in the format defined by the
`nischttl(1)` command. The default value is 12 hours.

owner=*ownername*

Specify that the NIS+ principal *ownername* should own
created objects. The default for this value is the principal
who is executing the command.

group=*groupname*

Specify that the group *groupname* should be the group
owner for created objects. The default is `null`.

access=*rights*

> Specify the set of access rights that are to be granted for created objects. Specify the *rights* value in the format defined by the nischmod(1) command. The default value is ----rmcdr---r---.

NIS_GROUP   The name of the local NIS+ group. If the name is not fully qualified, append the default domain to it.

NIS_PATH   Override the default NIS+ directory search path. Specify an ordered list of directories separated by colons. The dollar sign character ($) is treated specially. Append the default domain to directory names that end in $. Replace a $ by itself with the list of directories between the default domain and the global root that are at least two levels deep. The default NIS+ directory search path is $.

> Refer to the Name Expansion subsection in nis+(1) for more details.

Attributes

See attributes(5) for descriptions of the following attributes:

Attribute Type	Attribute Value
Availability	SUNWnisu

See Also

nis+(1), nis_local_names(3NSL), attributes(5)

---

niserror — Display NIS+ Error Messages

Synopsis

/usr/bin/niserror *error-num*

Description

Use the niserror command to print the NIS+ error associated with status value *error-num* on the standard output. This command is used in shell scripts to translate returned NIS+ error numbers into text messages.

Examples

The following example prints the error associated with the error number 20.

```
castle% niserror 20
Not Found, no such name
castle%
```

The following example prints the error associated with the error number 21.

```
castle% niserror 21
Name/entry isn't unique
castle%
```

Attributes

See attributes(5) for descriptions of the following attributes:

Attribute Type	Attribute Value
Availability	SUNWnisu

See Also

nis+(1), nis_error(3NSL), attributes(5)

---

nisgrep — Search NIS+ Tables

Synopsis

```
/usr/bin/nisgrep [-AchiMov] [-s sep] keypat tablename
/usr/bin/nisgrep [-AchiMov] [-s sep] colname=keypat... tablename
```

Description

See nismatch(1).

---

nisgrpadm — NIS+ Group Administration Command

Synopsis

```
/usr/bin/nisgrpadm -a| -r| -t [-s] group principal...
/usr/bin/nisgrpadm -d| -l [-M] [-s] group
/usr/bin/nisgrpadm -c [-D defaults] [-M] [-s] group
```

Description

Use the nisgrpadm command to administer NIS+ groups and the membership lists for groups. nisgrpadm can create, destroy, or list NIS+ groups and can be used to administer a group's membership list. It can add or delete principals to the group or test principals for membership in the group.

The names of NIS+ groups are syntactically similar to names of NIS+ objects, but they occupy a separate namespace. A group named a.b.c.d. is represented by an NIS+ group object named a.groups_dir.b.c.d.; the functions described here all expect the name of the group, not the name of the corresponding group object.

There are three types of group members.

- An explicit member is just an NIS+ principal name, for example, wickedwitch.west.oz..

- An implicit ("domain") member, written `*.west.oz.`, means that all principals in the given domain belong to this member. No other forms of wild-carding are allowed: `wickedwitch.*.oz.` is invalid, as is `wickedwitch.west.*.`. Note that principals in subdomains of the given domain are not included.
- A recursive ("group") member, written `@cowards.oz.`, refers to another group; all principals that belong to that group are considered to belong here.

You can make any member negative by prefixing it with a minus sign (-). A group can thus contain explicit, implicit, recursive, negative explicit, negative implicit, and negative recursive members.

A principal is considered to belong to a group if it belongs to at least one nonnegative group member of the group and belongs to no negative group members.

Note — Principal names must be fully qualified, whereas groups can be abbreviated on all operations except `create`.

Options

`-a`	Add the list of NIS+ principals specified to group. The principal name should be fully qualified.
`-c`	Create *group* in the NIS+ namespace. The NIS+ group name should be fully qualified.
`-d`	Destroy (remove) *group* from the namespace.
`-D defaults`	

Specify a different set of defaults to be used when creating objects. The *defaults* string is a series of colon-separated tokens that represent the default values to be used for the generic object properties. All of the legal tokens are described below.

`ttl=time`   Set the default time-to-live for objects created with this command. You specify the *time* value in the format as defined by the `nischttl(1)` command. The default value is 12 hours.

`owner=ownername`

Specify that the NIS+ principal *ownername* owns the created object. Normally, this value is the same as the principal who is executing the command.

`group=groupname`

Specify that the group *groupname* is the group owner for the created object. The default value is `null`.

`access=rights`

Specify the set of access rights that are to be granted for the given object. You specify the *rights* value in the format defined by the `nischmod(1)` command. The default value is `----rmcdr---r---`.

`-l`	List the membership list of the specified group. (see `-M`.)

-M	Master server only. Send the lookup to the master server of the named data. This option guarantees that the most up-to-date information is seen, at the possible expense that the master server may be busy. Note that the -M option is applicable only with the -l option.
-r	Remove the list of principals specified from group. The principal name should be fully qualified.
-s	Work silently. Return results, using the exit status of the command. This status can be translated into a text string by the niserror(1) command.
-t	Display whether the principals specified are members in *group*.

Examples

Administering Groups
The following example creates a group in the foo.com. domain.

castle% **nisgrpadm -c my_buds.foo.com.**

The following example removes the group from the current domain.

castle% **nisgrpadm -d freds_group**

Administering Members
The following example shows how you would add two principals, bob and betty, to the group my_buds.foo.com..

castle% **nisgrpadm -a my_buds.foo.com. bob.bar.com. betty.foo.com.**

The following example removes betty from freds_group.

castle% **nisgrpadm -r freds_group betty.foo.com.**

Environment Variables

NIS_DEFAULTS

Specify a default string that overrides the NIS+ standard defaults.

NIS_PATH   If this variable is set and the NIS+ name is not fully qualified, search each specified directory until the object is found (see nisdefaults(1)).

Attributes

See attributes(5) for descriptions of the following attributes:

Attribute Type	Attribute Value
Availability	SUNWnisu

See Also

nis+(1), nischgrp(1), nischmod(1), nischttl(1), nisdefaults(1), niserror(1), nis_groups(3NSL), attributes(5)

Diagnostics

NIS_SUCCESS

> On success, return an exit status of 0.

NIS_PERMISSION

> This error is returned when you do not have the needed access right to change the group.

NIS_NOTFOUND

> This error is returned when the group does not exist.

NIS_TRYAGAIN

> This error is returned when the server for the group's domain is currently checkpointing or otherwise in a read-only state. Retry the command at a later date.

NIS_MODERROR

> This error is returned when the group was modified by someone else during the execution of the command. Reissue the command and optionally recheck the group membership list.

nisln — Symbolically Link NIS+ Objects

Synopsis

/usr/bin/nisln [-L] [-D *defaults*] *name linkname*

Description

Use the nisln command to link an NIS+ object named *name* to an NIS+ *linkname*. If *name* is an indexed name (see nismatch(1)), the link points to entries within an NIS+ table. Clients who want to look up information in the name service can use the FOLLOW_LINKS flag to force the client library to follow links to the name they point to. Further, all of the NIS+ administration commands accept the -L option indicating they should follow links (see nis_names(3NSL) for a description of the FOLLOW_LINKS flag).

Note — When creating the link, nisln verifies that the linked object exists. Once the link is created, you can delete or replace the linked object without affecting the link. At that time the link becomes invalid and attempts to follow it return NIS_LINKNAMEERROR to the client. When the path attribute in tables specifies a link instead of another table, the link is followed if the flag FOLLOW_LINKS was present in the call to nis_list() (see nis_tables(3NSL)) and ignored if the flag is not present. If the flag is present and the link is no longer valid, a warning is sent to the system logger and the link is ignored.

Options

-D *defaults*

> Specify a different set of defaults to be used for the creation of the link object. The defaults string is a series of tokens separated by colons. These tokens represent the default values to be used for the generic object properties. All of the legal tokens are described below.

> > ttl=*time* Set the default time-to-live for objects created with this command. You specify the *time* value in the format as defined by the nischttl(1) command. The default value is 12 hours.

> > owner=*ownername*

> > > Specify that the NIS+ principal *ownername* owns the created object. Normally, this value is the same as the principal who is executing the command.

> > group=*groupname*

> > > Specify that the group *groupname* is the group owner for the created object. The default value is null.

> > access=*rights*

> > > Specify the set of access rights that are to be granted for the given object. You specify the *rights* value in the format defined by the nischmod(1) command. The default value is ----rmcdr---r---.

-L If *name* is itself a link, follow it to the linked object that it points to. The new link points to that linked object instead of to *name*.

Examples

The following example creates a link in the domain foo.com. named hosts that points to the hosts.bar.com. object.

```
castle% nisln hosts.bar.com. hosts.foo.com.
```

The following example makes a link example.sun.com. that points to an entry in the hosts table in eng.sun.com..

```
castle% nisln '[name=example],hosts.eng.sun.com.' example.sun.com.
```

Environment Variables

NIS_PATH If this variable is set and the NIS+ name is not fully qualified, search each specified directory until the object is found (see nisdefaults(1)).

Exit Status

0 Success.

1 Failure.

Attributes

See attributes(5) for descriptions of the following attributes:

Attribute Type	Attribute Value
Availability	SUNWnisu

See Also

nisdefaults(1), nismatch(1), nisrm(1), nistbladm(1), nis_names(3NSL), nis_tables(3NSL), attributes(5)

nisls — List the Contents of an NIS+ Directory

Synopsis

/usr/bin/nisls [-dglLmMR] [*name...*]

Description

Use the nisls command to list the contents of NIS+ directories or objects. For each *name* that is an NIS+ directory, nisls lists the contents of the directory. For each *name* that is an NIS+ object other than a directory, nisls simply echoes *name*. If you specify no *name*, the first directory in the search path (see nisdefaults(1)) is listed.

Options

-d Treat NIS+ directories like other NIS+ objects instead of listing their contents.

-g Display group owner instead of owner when listing in long format.

-l List in long format, displaying additional information about the objects such as their type, creation time, owner, and access rights. List the access rights in the following order in long mode: nobody, owner, group owner, and world.

-L Follow links. If *name* actually points to a link, follow it to the linked object.

-m Display modification time instead of creation time when listing in long format.

-M Master only. Return information from the master server of the named object. This option guarantees that the most up-to-date information is seen, at the possible expense that the master server may be busy.

-R List directories recursively. This option reiterates the list for each subdirectory found in the process of listing each name.

Environment Variables

NIS_PATH If this variable is set and the NIS+ name is not fully qualified, search each specified directory until the object is found (see nisdefaults(1)).

Exit Status

0	Success.
1	Failure.

Attributes

See `attributes(5)` for descriptions of the following attributes:

Attribute Type	Attribute Value
Availability	SUNWnisu

See Also

nisdefaults(1), nisgrpadm(1), nismatch(1), nistbladm(1),
nis_objects(3NSL), attributes(5)

---

nismatch, nisgrep — Search NIS+ Tables

Synopsis

```
/usr/bin/nismatch [-AchMoPv] [-s sep] key tablename
/usr/bin/nismatch [-AchMoPv] [-s sep] colname=key... tablename
/usr/bin/nismatch [-AchMoPv] [-s sep] indexedname
/usr/bin/nisgrep [-AchiMov] [-s sep] keypat tablename
/usr/bin/nisgrep [-AchiMov] [-s sep] colname=keypat... tablename
```

Description

Use the `nismatch` and `nisgrep` commands to search NIS+ tables. The `nisgrep` command differs from the `nismatch` command in its ability to accept regular expressions *keypat* for the search criteria instead of simple text matches.

Because `nisgrep` uses a callback function, it is not constrained to searching only those columns that are specifically made searchable at the time of table creation. It is slower but more flexible than `nismatch`.

With `nismatch`, the server does the searching; with `nisgrep`, the server returns all the readable entries and then the client does the pattern matching.

With both commands, the parameter *tablename* is the NIS+ name of the table to be searched. If you specify only one key or key pattern without the column name, then the first column is searched. You can search specific named columns by using the *colname=key* syntax. When you search multiple columns, only entries that match in all columns are returned. This result is the equivalent of a logical join operation.

`nismatch` accepts an additional form of search criteria, *indexedname*, which is an NIS+ indexed name of the form:

```
[colname=value,...],tablename
```

Options

-A	Return all data within the table and all of the data in tables in the initial table's concatenation path.

-c   Print only a count of the number of entries that matched the search criteria.

-h   Display a header line before the matching entries that contains the names of the table's columns.

-i   Ignore upper/lowercase distinction during comparisons.

-M   Master server only. Send the lookup to the master server of the named data. This option guarantees that the most up-to-date information is seen, at the possible expense that the master server may be busy.

-o   Display the internal representation of the matching NIS+ object(s).

-P   Follow concatenation path. Specify that the lookup should follow the concatenation path of a table if the initial search is unsuccessful.

-s *sep*   Specify the character used to separate the table columns. If you specify no character, use the default separator (a space) for the table.

-v   Do not suppress the output of binary data when displaying matching entries. Without this option, display binary data as the string *BINARY*.

Examples

The following example searches a table named passwd in the org_dir subdirectory of the zotz.com. domain. It returns the entry that has the user name of skippy. In the following example, all the work is done on the server.

castle% **nismatch name=skippy passwd.org_dir.zotz.com.**

The following example is similar to the one above except that it uses nisgrep to find all users in the table named passwd that are using either ksh(1) or csh(1).

castle% **nisgrep 'shell=[ck]sh' passwd.org_dir.zotz.com.**

Environment Variables

NIS_PATH   If this variable is set and the NIS+ name is not fully qualified, search each specified directory until the object is found (see nisdefaults(1)).

Exit Status

0   Successfully matched some entries.

1   Successfully searched the table and no matches were found.

2   An error condition occured. An error message is also printed.

Attributes

See attributes(5) for descriptions of the following attributes:

Attribute Type	Attribute Value
Availability	SUNWnisu

See Also

niscat(1), nisdefaults(1), nisls(1), nistbladm(1), nis_objects(3NSL), attributes(5)

Diagnostics

No memory   An attempt to allocate memory for the search failed.

tablename is not a table

> The object with the name *tablename* was not a table object.

Can't compile regular expression

> The regular expression in *keypat* was malformed.

column not found: *colname*

> The column named *colname* does not exist in the table named *tablename*.

nismkdir — Create NIS+ Directories

Synopsis

/usr/bin/nismkdir [-D *defaults*] [-m *hostname*] [-s *hostname*] *dirname*

Description

Use the nismkdir command to create new NIS+ subdirectories within an existing domain. You can also use it to create replicated directories. Without options, this command creates a subdirectory with the same master and the replicas as its parent directory.

It is advisable to use nisserver(1M) to create an NIS+ domain that consists of the specified directory along with the org_dir and groups_dir subdirectories.

The two primary aspects that are controlled when making a directory are its access rights and its degree of replication.

> **Note** — A host that serves an NIS+ directory must be an NIS+ client in a directory above the one it is serving. The exceptions to this rule are the root NIS+ servers, which are both clients and servers of the same NIS+ directory.
>
> When the host's default domain is different from the default domain on the client where the command is executed, the host name supplied as an argument to the -s or -m options must be fully qualified.
>
> Special per-server and per-directory access restrictions may apply when this command updates the serving lists of the affected NIS+ servers. See nisopaccess(1), new in the Solaris 8 release.

New!

Options

-D *defaults* Specify a different set of defaults to be used when creating new directories. The defaults string is a series of tokens separated by colons. These tokens represent the default values to be used for the generic object properties. All of the legal tokens are described below.

        ttl=*time*   Set the default time-to-live for objects that are created by this command. Specify the *time* value in the format defined by the nischttl(1) command. The default value is 12 hours.

        owner=*ownername*

                Specify that the NIS+ principal *ownername* should own the created object. The default for this value is the principal who is executing the command.

        group=*groupname*

                Specify that the group *groupname* should be the group owner for the object that is created. The default value is null.

        access=*rights*

                Specify the set of access rights that are to be granted for the given object. Specify the *rights* value in the format defined by the nischmod(1) command. The default value is ----rmcdr---r---.

-m *hostname* If the directory named by *dirname* does not exist, then create a new directory that is not replicated with host *hostname* as its master server. If the directory name by *dirname* does exist, then the host named by *hostname* is made its master server.

-s *hostname* Specify that the host *hostname* is a replica for an existing directory named *dirname*.

Operands

dirname   The fully qualified NIS+ name of the directory to be created.

Examples

The following example creates a new directory bar under the foo.com. domain that shares the same master and replicas as the foo.com. directory.

castle% **nismkdir bar.foo.com.**

The following example creates a new directory bar.foo.com. that is not replicated under the foo.com. domain.

castle% **nismkdir -m myhost.foo.com. bar.foo.com.**

The following example adds a replica server of the bar.foo.com. directory.

castle% **nismkdir -s replica.foo.com. bar.foo.com.**

Environment Variables

NIS_DEFAULTS

>Specify a defaults string that overrides the NIS+ standard defaults. If you use the -D option, then those values override both the NIS_DEFAULTS variable and the standard defaults.

NIS_PATH

>If this variable is set and the NIS+ directory name is not fully qualified, *New!* each directory specified is searched until the directory is found. See nisdefaults(1).

Exit Status

0   Success.

1   Failure.

Attributes

See attributes(5) for descriptions of the following attributes:

Attribute Type	Attribute Value
Availability	SUNWnisu

See Also

nis+(1), nischmod(1), nischttl(1), nisdefaults(1), nisls(1),   *New!*
nisopaccess(1), nisrmdir(1), nisserver(1M), attributes(5)

---

nisopaccess — NIS+ Operation Access Control   *New!*
Administration Command

Synopsis

```
/usr/lib/nis/nisopaccess [-v] directory operation rights
/usr/lib/nis/nisopaccess [-v] [-r] directory operation
/usr/lib/nis/nisopaccess [-v] [-l] directory [operation]
```

Description

Use the nisopaccess command, new in the Solaris 8 Operating Environment, to control operation access to NIS+.

Most NIS+ operations have implied access control through the permissions on the objects that they manipulate. For example, to read an entry in a table, you must have read permission on that entry. However, some NIS+ operations by default perform no access checking at all and are allowed to all, as described below.

Operation	Example of Commands That Use the Operation

NIS_CHECKPOINT

>nisping -C

Operation	Example of Commands That Use the Operation
NIS_CPTIME	nisping, rpc.nisd
NIS_MKDIR	nismkdir
NIS_PING	nisping, rpc.nisd
NIS_RMDIR	nisrmdir
NIS_SERVSTATE	
	nisbackup, nisrestore
NIS_STATUS	nisstat, rpc.nispasswdd

You can use the nisopaccess command to enforce access control on these operations by an NIS+ directory.

Specify the *directory* argument as a fully qualified name, including the trailing dot, of the NIS+ directory to which nisopaccess is applied. As a shorthand, if the directory name does not end in a trailing dot, for example, org_dir, then the domain name is appended. The domain name is also appended to partial paths such as org_dir.xyz.

You can use upper or lower case for the *operation* argument; however, you cannot mix cases. You can omit the NIS_ prefix. For example, you can specify NIS_PING as NIS_PING, nis_ping, PING, or ping.

Specify the *rights* argument in the format defined by the nischmod(1) command. Because only the read (r) rights are used to determine who has the right to perform the operation, you can use the modify and delete rights to control who can change access to the operation.

Note — The access control is implemented by an NIS+ table called proto_op_access created in each NIS+ directory to which access control should be applied. You can manipulate this table with normal NIS+ commands. However, nisopaccess is the only supported interface for NIS+ operation access control.

The access checking performed for each operation is as follows. When an operation requires that access be checked on all directories served by its rpc.nisd(1M), access is denied if even one of the directories prohibits the operation.

NIS_CHECKPOINT

> Check the specified directory or all directories if there is no directory argument (as is the case when NIS_CHECKPOINT is issued by the nisping -Ca command). Return NIS_PERMISSION when access is denied.

NIS_CPTIME Check the specified directory. Return 0 when access is denied.

NIS_MKDIR Check the parent of the specified directory. Return NIS_PERMISSION when access is denied.

> If the parent directory is not available locally, that is, it is not served by this rpc.nisd(1M), NIS_MKDIR access is allowed, though the operation is executed only if this rpc.nisd is a known replica of the directory.

> Note that the NIS_MKDIR operation does not create an NIS+ directory; it adds a directory to the serving list for this rpc.nisd if appropriate.

NIS_PING	Check specified directory. No return value.
NIS_RMDIR	Check specified directory. Return NIS_PERMISSION when access denied.
	The NIS_RMDIR operation does not remove an NIS+ directory; it deletes the directory from the serving list for this rpc.nisd if appropriate.
NIS_SERVSTATE	
	Check access on all directories served by this rpc.nisd. If access is denied for a tag, return <permission denied> instead of the tag value.
NIS_STATUS	Same as for NIS_SERVSTATE.

Note — Older clients may not supply authentication information for some of the operations listed above. These clients are treated as nobody when access checking is performed.

Options

-l	List the access control for a single operation or for all operations that have access control enabled.
-r	Remove access control for a certain operation on the specified directory.
-v	Verbose mode.

Examples

The following example enables access control for the NIS_PING operation on org_dir.`domainname`. so that only the owner of the directory can perform a NIS_PING or change the NIS_PING rights.

```
example% nisopaccess org_dir
NIS_PING o=rmcd,g=,w=,n=
example%
```

The following example lists the access to the NIS_PING operation for org_dir.

```
example% nisopaccess -l org_dir NIS_PING
NIS_PING ----rmcd-------- owner.dom.ain. group.dom.ain.
example%
```

The following example removes access control for NIS_PING on org_dir.

```
example% nisopaccess -r org_dir NIS_PING
example%
```

Exit Status

0	Successful operation.
Other	Operation failed. The status is usually the return status from an NIS+ command such as nistbladm.

Attributes

See attributes(5) for descriptions of the following attributes.

Attribute Type	Attribute Value
Availability	SUNWnisu

See Also

nis+(1), nischmod(1), nistbladm(1), rpc.nisd(1M), attributes(5)

---

nispasswd — Change NIS+ Password Information

Synopsis

```
/usr/bin/nispasswd [-ghs] [-D domainname] [username]
/usr/bin/nispasswd -a
/usr/bin/nispasswd -D domainname [-d [username]]
/usr/bin/nispasswd [-l] [-f] [-n min] [-x max] [-w warn] [-D domainname]
    username
```

Description

New!

Warning — Use the passwd(1) command with the -r nisplus option instead of nispasswd. The passwd command operates consistently across all available name services. passwd -r nisplus is the recommended way to change the password in NIS+.

The use of nispasswd is *strongly* discouraged. Even though it is a hard link to the passwd(1) command, its operation is subtly different and not desirable in a modern NIS+ domain.

In particular, nispasswd does not try to contact the rpc.nispasswdd daemon running on the NIS+ master. Instead, it tries to do the updates itself through the NIS+ API. For this to work, the permissions on the password data need to be modified from the default as set up by the nisserver setup script. See nisserver(1M).

Note — The login program, file access display programs (for example, ls -l), and network programs that require user passwords (such as rlogin(1) and ftp(1)) use the standard getpwnam(3C) and getspnam(3C) interfaces to get password information. These programs get the NIS+ password information that is modified by nispasswd only if the passwd: entry in the /etc/nsswitch.conf file includes nisplus. See nsswitch.conf(4) for more details.

Use the nispasswd command to change a password, comment (finger) field (-g option), home directory (-h option), or login shell (-s option) associated with the *username* (invoker by default) in the NIS+ passwd table.

Additionally, if you have the right NIS+ privileges, you can use the command to view or modify aging information associated with the specified user.

nispasswd uses secure RPC to communicate with the NIS+ server and, therefore, never sends unencrypted passwords over the communication medium.

nispasswd does not read or modify the local password information stored in the /etc/passwd and /etc/shadow files.

When used to change a password, nispasswd prompts nonprivileged users for their old password. It then prompts for the new password twice to forestall typing mistakes. When you enter the old password, nispasswd checks to see if it has "aged" sufficiently. If aging is insufficient, nispasswd terminates; see getspnam(3C).

The old password is used to decrypt the user-name's secret key. If the password does not decrypt the secret key, nispasswd prompts for the old secure-RPC password. It uses this password to decrypt the secret key. If this fails, it gives the user one more chance. The old password is also used to ensure that the new password differs from the old by at least three characters. Assuming aging is sufficient, a check is made to ensure that the new password meets construction requirements, described below. When you enter the new password a second time, the two copies of the new password are compared. If the two copies are not identical, the cycle of prompting for the new password is repeated twice. The new password is used to reencrypt the user's secret key. Hence, it also becomes the user's secure-RPC password, and the secure-RPC is no longer a different password from the user's password.

Construct passwords to meet the following requirements.

- Each password must have at least six characters. Only the first eight characters are significant.

- Each password must contain at least two alphabetic characters and at least one numeric or special character. In this case, "alphabetic" refers to all upper- or lowercase letters.

- Each password must differ from the login user name and any reverse or circular shift of that login username. For comparison purposes, an uppercase letter and its corresponding lowercase letter are equivalent.

- New passwords must differ from the old by at least three characters. For comparison purposes, an uppercase letter and its corresponding lowercase letter are equivalent.

Network administrators who own the NIS+ password table can change any password attributes if they establish their credentials (see keylogin(1)) before invoking nispasswd. nispasswd does not prompt these privileged users for the old password, and they are not forced to comply with password aging and password construction requirements.

Any user can use the -d option to display password attributes for his or her own login name. The format of the display is:

username status mm/dd/yy min max warn

or, if password aging information is not present,

username status

where

username　　　The login ID of the user.

status　　　The password status of *username*. PS means the password exists or is locked, LK means locked, and NP means no password.

mm/dd/yy	The date password was last changed for *username*. (Note that all password aging dates are determined from Greenwich Mean Time (Universal Time) and, therefore, may differ by as much as a day in other time zones.)
min	The minimum number of days required between password changes for *username*.
max	The maximum number of days the password is valid for *username*.
warn	The number of days, relative to *max*, before the password expires that the *username* is warned.

Options

-a	Show the password attributes for all entries. This option shows only the entries in the NIS+ passwd table in the local domain that the invoker is authorized to read.
-d [*username*]	Display password attributes for the caller or the user specified if the invoker has the right privileges.
-D *domainname*	Consult the passwd.org_dir table in *domainname*. If you do not specify this option, use the default *domainname* returned by nis_local_directory(). This *domainname* is the same as that returned by domainname(1M).
-f	Force the user to change password at the next login by expiring the password for *username*.
-g	Change the comment (finger) information.
-h	Change the home directory.
-l	Lock the password entry for *username*. Subsequently, login(1) disallows logins with this NIS+ password entry.
-n *min*	Set minimum field for *username*. The *min* field contains the minimum number of days between password changes for *username*. If *min* is greater than *max*, the user cannot change the password. Always use this option with the -x option, unless *max* is set to -1 (aging turned off). In that case, *min* need not be set.
-s	Change the login shell. By default, only the NIS+ administrator can change the login shell. Users are prompted for the new login shell.
-w *warn*	Set *warn* field for *username*. The *warn* field contains the number of days before the password expires that the user is warned when logging in.
-x *max*	Set maximum field for *username*. The *max* field contains the number of days that the password is valid for *username*. The aging for *username* is turned off immediately if *max* is set to -1. If it is set to 0, then the user is forced to change the password at the next login session and aging is turned off.

Exit Status

0	Success.
1	Permission denied.
2	Invalid combination of options.
3	Unexpected failure. NIS+ passwd table unchanged.
4	NIS+ passwd table missing.
5	NIS+ was busy. Try again later.
6	Invalid argument to option.
7	Aging was disabled.

Attributes

See attributes(5) for descriptions of the following attributes:

Attribute Type	Attribute Value
Availability	SUNWnisu

See Also

keylogin(1), login(1), nis+(1), nistbladm(1), passwd(1), rlogin(1), domainname(1M), getpwnam(3C), getspnam(3C), nis_local_directory(3NSL), nsswitch.conf(4), passwd(4), shadow(4), attributes(5)

nisrm — Remove NIS+ Objects from the Namespace

Synopsis

/usr/bin/nisrm [-if] *name*...

Description

Use the nisrm command to remove NIS+ objects named *name* from the NIS+ namespace. This command fails if the NIS+ master server is not running.

Note — This command does not remove directories (see nisrmdir(1)), nor does it remove tables that are not empty (see nistbladm(1)).

Options

-f	Attempt a forced removal, and if it fails for permission reasons, try an nischmod(1) operation and retry the removal. If the command fails, it fails silently.
-i	Like the system rm(1) command, interactively ask for confirmation before removing an object. If the name specified by *name* is not a fully qualified name, force this option on. This option prevents the removal of unexpected objects.

Examples

The following example removes the objects foo, bar, and baz from the namespace.

castle% **nisrm foo bar baz**

Environment Variables

NIS_PATH   If this variable is set and the NIS+ name is not fully qualified, search
           each specified directory until the object is found (see nisdefaults(1)).

Exit Status

0   Success.

1   Failure.

Attributes

See attributes(5) for descriptions of the following attributes:

Attribute Type	Attribute Value
Availability	SUNWnisu

See Also

nis+(1), nischmod(1), nisdefaults(1), nisrmdir(1), nistbladm(1), rm(1),
attributes(5)

---

nisrmdir — Remove NIS+ Directories

Synopsis

/usr/bin/nisrmdir [-if] [-s *hostname*] *dirname*

Description

Use the nisrmdir command to delete existing NIS+ subdirectories. You can remove a
directory outright or simply remove replicas from serving a directory.

This command modifies the object that describes the directory *dirname* and then
notifies each replica to remove the directory named *dirname*. If the notification of any of
the affected replicas fails, the directory object is returned to its original state unless you
specify the -f option.

This command fails if the NIS+ master server is not running.

New!

Note — Special per-server and per-directory access restrictions may apply
when this command updates the serving lists of the affected NIS+ servers.
For more information, see nisopaccess(1).

Options

-f
Force the command to succeed even though it may not be able to contact the affected replicas. Use this option when a replica is known to be down and is not able to respond to the removal notification. When the replica is finally rebooted, it reads the updated directory object, notes that it is no longer a replica for that directory, and stops responding to lookups on that directory. You can manually clean up the files that held the now removed directory by removing the appropriate files in the /var/nis directory (see nisfiles(4) for more information).

-i
Like the system rm(1) command, interactively ask for confirmation before removing a directory. If the name specified by *dirname* is not a fully qualified name, force this option on. This option prevents the removal of unexpected directories.

-s *hostname*
Remove the host *hostname* as a replica for the directory named *dirname*. If this option is not present, remove all replicas and the master server for a directory and remove the directory from the namespace.

Operands

dirname
An existing NIS+ directory.

Examples

The following example removes a directory bar under the foo.com. domain.
castle% **nisrmdir bar.foo.com.**

The following example removes a replica that is serving the bar.foo.com. directory.
castle% **nisrmdir -s replica.foo.com. bar.foo.com.**

The following example forces the removal of the bar.foo.com. directory from the namespace.
castle% nisrmdir **-f bar.foo.com.**

Environment Variables

NIS_PATH
If this variable is set and the NIS+ name is not fully qualified, search each specified directory until the object is found (see nisdefaults(1)).

Exit Status

0
Success.

1
Failure.

Attributes

See attributes(5) for descriptions of the following attributes:

Attribute Type	Attribute Value
Availability	SUNWnisu

See Also

New!

nis+(1), nisdefaults(1), nisopaccess(1), nisrm(1), nisfiles(4), attributes(5)

nistbladm — Administer NIS+ Tables

Synopsis

```
/usr/bin/nistbladm -a|-A [-D defaults] colname=value... tablename
/usr/bin/nistbladm -a|-A [-D defaults] indexedname
/usr/bin/nistbladm -c [-D defaults] [-p path] [-s sep] type
   colname=[flags] [,access]... tablename
/usr/bin/nistbladm -d tablename
/usr/bin/nistbladm -e|-E colname=value... indexedname
/usr/bin/nistbladm -m colname=value... indexedname
/usr/bin/nistbladm -r|-R [colname=value...] tablename
/usr/bin/nistbladm -r|-R indexedname
/usr/bin/nistbladm -u [-p path] [-s sep] [-t type] [colname=access...]
   tablename
```

Description

Use the nistbladm command to administer NIS+ tables. It performs five primary operations:

- Creating tables.
- Deleting tables.
- Adding entries to tables.
- Modifying entries within tables.
- Removing entries from tables.

Although NIS+ does not place restrictions on the size of tables or entries, the size of data has an impact on the performance and the disk space requirements of the NIS+ server. NIS+ is not designed to store huge pieces of data such as files.

NIS+ design is optimized to support 10,000 objects with a total size of 10 megabytes. If the requirements exceed the above, it is suggested that you create the domain hierarchy or store pointers to the data in the tables instead of storing the data itself.

When creating tables, you must specify a table type, *type*, and a list of column definitions.

type is a string that is stored in the table and later used by the service to verify that entries being added to it are of the correct type. Column definitions use the following syntax.

colname=[*flags*] [,*access*]

flags is a combination of:

S	Searches can be done on the column's values (see nismatch(1)).
I	Searches ignore case (makes sense only in combination with S).
C	Encrypt column values.
B	Binary data (does not make sense in combination with S). If not set, the column's values are expected to be null-terminated ASCII strings.
X	XDR encode data (makes sense only in combination with B).

access is specified in the format as defined by the nischmod(1) command.

When manipulating entries, this command takes two forms of entry name. The first uses a series of space-separated *colname=value* pairs that specify column values in the entry. The second is an NIS+ indexed name, *indexedname*, of the following form.

[*colname=value*, . . .], *tablename*

Options

-a | A	Add entries to an NIS+ table. The difference between the lowercase a and the uppercase A is in the treatment of preexisting entries. The entry's contents are specified by the *column=value* pairs on the command line. Note that you must specify values for all columns when adding entries to a table.
	Normally, NIS+ reports an error if you try to add an entry to a table that would overwrite an entry that already exists. This feature prevents multiple parties from adding duplicate entries and having one of them get overwritten. The uppercase A specifies that the entry is to be added even if it already exists. This option is analogous to a modify operation on the entry.
-c	Create a table named *tablename* in the namespace. The table that is created must have at least one column, and at least one column must be searchable.
-d *tablename*	
	Destroy the table named *tablename*. The table that is being destroyed must be empty. First delete the table's contents with the -R option.
-D *defaults*	
	When creating objects, specify a different set of defaults to be used during this operation. The *defaults* string is a series of tokens separated by colons. These tokens represent the default values to be used for the generic object properties. All of the legal tokens are described below.

ttl=*time*

> Set the default time-to-live for objects that are created by this command. Specify the *time* value in the format defined by the nischttl(1) command. The default value is 12 hours.

owner=*ownername*

> Specify that the NIS+ principal *ownername* should own the created object. Normally, this value is the same as the principal who is executing the command.

group=*groupname*

> Specify that the group *groupname* should be the group owner for the object that is created. The default value is null.

access=*rights*

> Specify the set of access rights that are to be granted for the given object. Specify the *rights* value in the format defined by the nischmod(1) command. The default value is ----rmcdr---r---.

-e|E
Edit the entry in the table that is specified by *indexedname*. *indexedname* must uniquely identify a single entry. It is possible to edit the value in a column that would change the indexed name of an entry.

The change (*colname=value*) can affect other entries in the table if the change results in an entry whose indexed name is different from *indexedname* and matches that of another existing entry. In this case, the -e option fails and an error is reported. The -E option forces the replacement of the existing entry by the new entry (effectively removing two old entries and adding a new one).

-m
A synonym for -E. This option has been superseded by the -E option.

-p *path*
When creating or updating a table, specify the table's search path. When you invoke an nis_list() function, you can specify the flag FOLLOW_PATH to tell the client library to continue searching tables in the table's path if the search criteria used do not yield any entries. The path consists of an ordered list of table names, separated by colons. The names in the path must be fully qualified.

When creating or updating a table, specify the table's separator character. The separator character is used by niscat(1) when displaying tables on the standard output. Its purpose is to separate column data when the table is in ASCII form. The default value is a space.

-r|R	Remove entries from a table. Specify the entry by either a series of *column=value* pairs on the command line or an indexed name that is specified as *entryname*. The difference between the interpretation of the lowercase r and the uppercase R is in the treatment of nonunique entry specifications. Normally, the NIS+ server disallows an attempt to remove an entry when the search criteria specified for that entry resolves to more than one entry in the table. However, you sometimes want to be able to remove more than one entry, for example, when you are trying to remove all of the entries from a table. In this case, using the uppercase R forces the NIS+ server to remove all entries matching the passed search criteria. If that criteria is null and no column values are specified, then all entries in the table are removed.
-t *type*	When updating a table, specify the table's *type* string.
-u	Update attributes of a table. This option enables the concatenation path (-p), separation character specified with the (-s), column access rights, and table type string (-t) of a table to be changed. Neither the number of columns nor the columns that are searchable can be changed.

Examples

The following example creates a table named hobbies in the directory foo.com. of the type hobby_tbl with two searchable columns, name and hobby.

```
castle% nistbladm -c hobby_tbl name=S,a+r,o+m hobby=S,a+r
    hobbies.foo.com.
```

The column name has read access for all (that is, owner, group, and world) and modify access for only the owner. The column hobby is readable by all but not modifiable by anyone.

In the following example, if the access rights had not been specified, the table's access rights would have come from either the standard defaults or the NIS_DEFAULTS variable.

The following examples add entries to this table.

```
castle% nistbladm -a name=bob hobby=skiing hobbies.foo.com.
castle% nistbladm -a name=sue hobby=skiing hobbies.foo.com.
castle% nistbladm -a name=ted hobby=swimming hobbies.foo.com.
```

The following example adds to the concatenation path.

```
castle% nistbladm -u -p hobbies.bar.com.:hobbies.baz.com. hobbies
```

The following example deletes the skiers from the list.

```
castle% nistbladm -R hobby=skiing hobbies.foo.com.
```

> **Note** — The previous example uses the -R option. Using the -r option would fail because there are two entries with the value of skiing.

To create a table with a column that is named with no flags set, you supply only the name and the equal (=) sign as follows.

```
castle% nistbladm -c notes_tbl name=S,a+r,o+m note= notes.foo.com.
```

The following example created a table, named `notes.foo.com.`, of type `notes_tbl`, with two columns `name` and `note`. The `note` column is not searchable.

When entering data for columns in the form of a value string, protect the characters equal (`=`), comma (`,`), left bracket (`[`), right bracket (`]`), and space ( ) with single or double quotes. These characters are parsed by NIS+ within an indexed name. Protect these characters by enclosing the entire value in double quote (`"`) characters as follows.

```
castle% nistbladm -a fullname="Joe User" nickname=Joe nicknames
```

If there is any doubt about how the string is parsed, it is best to enclose it in quotes.

Environment Variables

NIS_DEFAULTS

This variable contains a defaults string that overrides the NIS+ standard defaults. If you use the `-D` option, those values then override both the NIS_DEFAULTS variable and the standard defaults.

NIS_PATH

If this variable is set and the NIS+ table name is not fully qualified, search each specified directory until the table is found (see `nisdefaults(1)`).

Exit Status

0	Success.
1	Failure.

Attributes

See `attributes(5)` for descriptions of the following attributes:

Attribute Type	Attribute Value
Availability	SUNWnisu

See Also

`nis+(1)`, `niscat(1)`, `nischmod(1)`, `nischown(1)`, `nisdefaults(1)`, `nismatch(1)`, `nissetup(1M)`, `attributes(5)`

Warnings

To modify one of the entries, say, for example, from `bob` to `robert`, the following command is incorrect.

```
castle% nistbladm -m name=robert [name=bob],hobbies
```

`[name=bob],hobbies` is an indexed name and the characters `[` (open bracket) and `]` (close bracket) are interpreted by the shell. When typing entry names in the form of NIS+ indexed names, you must protect the name by using single quotes, as shown below.

```
castle% nistbladm -m name=robert '[name=bob],hobbies'
```

It is possible to specify a set of defaults so that you cannot read or modify the table object later.

nistest — Return the State of the NIS+ Namespace with Conditional Expression

Synopsis

```
/usr/bin/nistest [-ALMP] [-a rights | -t type] object
/usr/bin/nistest [-ALMP] [-a rights] indexedname
/usr/bin/nistest -c dir1 op dir2
```

Description

Use the nistest command as a way for shell scripts and other programs to test for the existence, type, and access rights of objects and entries. Entries are named using indexed names (see nismatch(1)). With the -c option, you can compare directory names to test where they lie in relation to each other in the namespace.

Options

-a *rights*	Verify that the current process has the desired or required access rights on the named object or entries. The access rights are specified in the same way as the nischmod(1) command.
-A	Return all data within the table and all of the data in tables in the initial table's concatenation path. This option is valid only when using indexed names or following links.

-c *dir1 op dir2*

Test whether two directory names have a certain relationship to each other; for example, higher than (ht) or lower than (lt). You can display the complete list of values for *op* by using the -c option with no arguments. The complete list of *op* values is shown below.

<	Lower than.
lt	Lower than.
<=	Lower than or equal.
le	Lower than or equal.
=	Equal.
eq	Equal.
>	Higher than.
ht	Higher than.
gt	Higher than.
>=	Higher than or equal.
he	Higher than or equal.
ge	Higher than or equal.
!=	Not equal.

	ne	Not equal.
	ns	Not sequential.

-L	If the object named by object or the *tablename* component of *indexedname* names a LINK type object, follow the link.
-M	Master server only. Send the lookup to the master server of the named data. This option guarantees that the most up-to-date information is seen, at the possible expense that the master server may be busy.
-P	Follow the concatenation path of a table if the initial search is unsuccessful. This option is valid only when using indexed names or following links.
-t *type*	Test the type of object. The value of *type* can be one of the following:

	D	Return true if the object is a directory object.
	G	Return true if the object is a group object.
	L	Return true if the object is a link object.
	P	Return true if the object is a private object.
	T	Return true if the object is a table object.

Examples

When testing for access rights, nistest returns success (0) if the specified rights are granted to the current user. Thus, the following test for access rights tests that all authenticated NIS+ clients have read and modify access to the skippy.domain object.

```
castle% nistest -a w=mr skippy.domain
```

You can test for access on a particular entry in a table by using the indexed name syntax. The following example tests to see if an entry in the password table can be modified.

```
castle% nistest -a o=m '[uid=99],passwd.org_dir'
```

The following example tests whether a directory lies higher in the namespace than another directory by using the -c option with an *op* of ht (higher than). The test returns true.

```
castle% nistest -c dom.com. ht lower.dom.com.
```

Environment Variables

NIS_PATH	If this variable is set and the NIS+ name is not fully qualified, search each specified directory until the object is found (see nisdefaults(1)).

Exit Status

0	Success.
1	Failure because the object was not present, not of specified type, and/or no such access.
2	Failure because of illegal usage.

Attributes

See attributes(5) for descriptions of the following attributes:

Attribute Type	Attribute Value
Availability	SUNWnisu

See Also

nis+(1), nischmod(1), nisdefaults(1), nismatch(1), attributes(5)

---

nl — Line-Numbering Filter

Synopsis

```
/usr/bin/nl [-p] [-b[type]] [-d[delim]] [-f[type]] [-h[type]] [-i[incr]]
    [-l[num]] [-n[format]] [-s[sep]] [-w[width]] [-v[startnum]] [file]
/usr/xpg4/bin/nl [-p] [-b type] [-d delim] [-f type] [-h type] [-i incr]
    [-l num] [-n format] [-s sep] [-w width] [-v startnum] [file]
```

Description

Use the nl command to number the lines of a file. The nl command divides pages into logical segments and restarts the line numbering at the top of each new page. A logical page consists of a header, a body, and a footer section. Empty sections are valid.

The nl command reads lines from the named file, or the standard input if no file is named, and reproduces the lines on the standard output. Lines are numbered on the left in accordance with the specified command options.

Different line-numbering options are independently available for header, body, and footer. For example, -bt (the default) numbers nonblank lines in the body section and does not number any lines in the header and footer sections.

The start of logical page sections is signaled by input lines containing nothing but the following delimiter character(s).

Line contents	Start of
\:\:\:	Header.
\:\:	Body.
\:	Footer.

Unless optioned otherwise, nl assumes the text being read is in a single logical page body.

Notes

Internationalized Regular Expressions are used in the POSIX and C locales. In other locales, Internationalized Regular Expressions are used if the following two conditions are met:

- /usr/lib/locale/*locale*/LC_COLLATE/CollTable is present, and
- /usr/lib/locale/*locale*/LC_COLLATE/coll.so is not present;

otherwise, Simple Regular Expressions are used. Internationalized Regular Expressions are explained in regex(5). Simple Regular Expressions are explained in regexp(5).

Options

You can specify options in any order and intermingle them with an optional file name. You can name only one file. The specified default is used when the option is not entered on the command line. /usr/xpg4/bin/nl options require option arguments. A space character can separate options from option arguments. /usr/bin/nl options can have arguments. If you do not specify arguments for /usr/bin/nl, the default options are used.

-b*type*   Specify which logical page body lines are to be numbered. Recognized types and their meanings are:

        a   Number all lines.

        t   Number all nonempty lines.

        n   No line numbering.

        p*exp*   Number only lines that contain the regular expression specified in *exp*. Default type for logical page body is t (text lines numbered).

-f*type*   Same as -b*type* except for footer. Default type for logical page footer is n (no lines numbered).

-d*delim*   Change the two delimiter characters specifying the start of a logical page section from the default characters (\:) to two user-specified characters. If you enter only one character, the second character remains the default character (:). Do not include a space between the -d and the delimiter characters. To enter a backslash, use two backslashes.

-h*type*   Same as -b*type* except for header. Default type for logical page header is n (no lines numbered).

-i*incr*   Specify the increment value used to number logical page lines. Default *incr* is 1.

-l*num*   Specify the number of blank lines to be considered as one. For example, -l2 results in only the second adjacent blank being numbered (if the appropriate -ha, -ba, or -fa option is set). Default *num* is 1.

-n*format*   Specify the line numbering format. Recognized values are:

        ln   Left-justified, leading zeros suppressed.

        rn   Right-justified, leading zeros suppressed.

        rz   Right-justified, leading zeros kept. Default format is rn (right-justified).

-p   Do not restart numbering at logical page delimiters.

-s*sep*   Specify the character(s) used in separating the line number and the corresponding text line. Default *sep* is a Tab.

-v*startnum*   Specify the initial value used to number logical page lines. Default *startnum* is 1.

-w*width*   Specify the number of characters to be used for the line number. Default width is 6.

Operands

file   A path name of a text file to be line numbered.

Examples

The following example uses the default options to add line numbers to the file kookaburra-1.

```
castle% nl kookaburra-1
     1  Kookaburra sits in the old gum tree
     2  Merry merry king of the bush is he.
     3  Laugh, kookaburra, laugh, kookaburra
     4  Gay your life must be.
     5
     6  Kookaburra sits in the old gum tree
     7  Eating all the gumdrops he can see.
     8  Stop, kookaburra, stop, kookaburra
     9  Leave some there for me.
castle%
```

The following command numbers the first line of the page body 10, the second line of the page body, 20, the third 30, and so forth. The logical page delimiters are ++.

```
castle% nl -v10 -i10 -d++ kookaburra-2
    10  Kookaburra sits in the old gum tree
    20  Merry merry king of the bush is he.
    30  Laugh, kookaburra, laugh, kookaburra
    40  Gay your life must be.
    50
    60  Kookaburra sits in the old gum tree
    70  Eating all the gumdrops he can see.
    80  Stop, kookaburra, stop, kookaburra
    90  Leave some there for me.

castle%
```

Environment Variables

See environ(5) for descriptions of the following environment variables that affect the execution of nl: LC_COLLATE, LC_CTYPE, LC_MESSAGES, and NLSPATH.

Exit Status

0   Successful completion.

>0   An error occurred.

Files

/usr/lib/locale/*locale*/LC_COLLATE/CollTable

Collation table generated by localedef.

/usr/lib/locale/*locale*/LC_COLLATE/coll.so

Shared object containing string transformation library routines.

Attributes

See attributes(5) for descriptions of the following attributes:

/usr/bin/nl

Attribute Type	**Attribute Value**
Availability	SUNWesu

/usr/xpg4/bin/nl

Attribute Type	**Attribute Value**
Availability	SUNWxcu4

See Also

pr(1), attributes(5), environ(5), regex(5), regexp(5)

nm — Print Name List of an Object File

Synopsis

/usr/ccs/bin/nm [-ACDhlnPprRsTuVv] [-efox] [-g | -u] [-t *format*] *file*...
/usr/xpg4/bin/nm [-ACDhlnPprRsTuVv] [-efox] [-g | -u] [-t *format*]
   file...

Description

The nm command displays the symbol table of each ELF object file that is specified by *file*.

If no symbolic information is available for a valid input file, the nm command reports that fact but does not consider it an error condition.

Options

You can specify options in any order, either singly or in combination, and can put them anywhere on the command line. When you specify conflicting options (such as -v and -n; and -o and -x) the first is taken and the second ignored with a warning message. (See -R for exception.)

-A   Write the full path name or library name of an object on each line.

-C   Demangle C++ symbol names before printing them.

-D	Display the SHT_DYNSYM symbol table used by ld.so.1 that is present even in stripped dynamic executables. By default, the SHT_SYMTab symbol table is displayed.
-g	Write only external (global) symbol information.
-h	Do not display the output heading data.
-l	Distinguish between WEAK and GLOBAL symbols by appending an asterisk (*) to the key letter for WEAK symbols.
-n	Sort external symbols by name before they are printed.
-o	Print the value and size of a symbol in octal instead of decimal. (equivalent to -t o).
-p	Produce easy-to-parse, terse output. Precede each symbol name by its value (blanks if undefined) and one of the letters:

A	Absolute symbol.
B	bss (uninitialized data space) symbol.
C	COMMON symbol. New in the Solaris 9 release.
D	Data object symbol.
F	File symbol.
L	Thread-Local storage symbol. New in the Solaris 9 release.
N	Symbol has no type.
S	Section symbol.
T	Text symbol.
U	Undefined.

If the symbol's binding attribute is:

LOCAL	The key letter is lower case.
WEAK	The key letter is upper case; if you specify the -l modifier, the uppercase key letter is followed by *.
GLOBAL	The key letter is upper case.

-P	Write information in a portable output format, as specified in "Standard Output" on page 988.
-r	Prepend the name of the object file or archive to each output line.
-R	Print the archive name (if present), followed by the object file and symbol name. If you also specify the -r option, ignore this option.
-s	Print section name instead of section index.
-t *format*	Write each numeric value in the specified format. The format is dependent on the single character used as the format option argument.

d	Write the offset in decimal (default).
o	Write the offset in octal.

x   Write the offset in hexadecimal.

The following options are obsolete because of changes to the object file format and will be deleted in a future release.

-e   Print only external and static symbols. The symbol table now contains only static and external symbols. Automatic symbols no longer appear in the symbol table. They do appear in the debugging information produced by cc -g, which you can examine by using dump(1).

-f   Produce full output. Redundant symbols (such as .text and .data) that existed previously no longer exist. Producing full output is identical to the default output.

-T   By default, nm prints the entire name of the symbols listed. Because symbol names have been moved to the last column, the problem of overflow is removed; truncating the symbol name is no longer necessary.

/usr/ccs/bin/nm

-u   Print undefined symbols only.

/usr/xpg4/bin/nm

-u   Print long listing for each undefined symbol.

-v   Sort external symbols by value before they are printed.

-V   Print the version of the nm command executing on the standard error output.

-x   Print the value and size of a symbol in hexadecimal instead of decimal (equivalent to -t x).

Operands

file   A path name of an object file, executable file, or object-file library.

Output

Standard Output

For each symbol, the following information is printed:

Index   The index of the symbol. (The index appears in brackets.)

Value   The value of the symbol is one of the following.

- A section offset for defined symbols in a relocatable file.

- Alignment constraints for symbols whose section index is SHN_COMMON.

- A virtual address in executable and dynamic library files.

Size   The size in bytes of the associated object.

Type   A symbol is of one of the following types.

NOTYPE   No type was specified.

OBJECT	A data object such as an array or variable.
FUNC	A function or other executable code.
REGI	A register symbol (SPARC only). New in the Solaris 8 release.
SECTION	A section symbol.
FILE	Name of the source file.
COMMON	An unallocated common block. New in the Solaris 9 release.
TLS	A variable associated with Thread-Local storage. New in the Solaris 9 release.

Bind   The symbol's binding attributes.

LOCAL	Limit scope to the object file containing their definition.
GLOBAL	Visible to all object files being combined.
WEAK	Specify that global symbols have a lower precedence than GLOBAL.

Other   Reserved for future use, currently contains 0.

Shndx   Except for three special values, this is the section header table index in relation to which the symbol is defined. The following special values exist.

ABS	The symbol's value does not change through relocation.
COMMON	An unallocated block and the value provides alignment constraints.
UNDEF	An undefined symbol.

Name   The name of the symbol.

Object Name The name of the object or library if you specify -A.

If you specify the -P option, the previous information is displayed, using the following portable format. The three versions differ depending on whether you specify -t d, -t o or -t x.

```
%s%s %s %d %d\n, library/object-name, name, type, value, size
%s%s %s %o %o\n, library/object-name, name, type, value, size
%s%s %s %x %x\n, library/object-name, name, type, value, size
```

where *library/object-name* is formatted as follows.

- If you specify -A, *library/object-name* is an empty string.
- If you specify -A and the corresponding file operand does not name a library: `%s:`
  `, file`
- If you specify -A and the corresponding file operand names a library. In this case, *object-file* names the object file in the library containing the symbol being described: `%s[%s]: , file, object-file`

If you do not specify -A, if you specify more than one file operand, or if you specify only one file operand and it names a library, nm writes a line identifying the object containing the following symbols before the lines containing those symbols, in one of the following forms.

- If the corresponding file operand does not name a library: %s:\n, *file*
- If the corresponding file operand names a library; in this case, *object-file* is the name of the file in the library containing the following symbols: %s[%s]:\n, *file*, *object-file*

If you specify -P but not -t, the format is as if you had specified -t x.

Examples

The following example shows the first few lines of output from the zipinfo command.

```
castle% /usr/ccs/bin/nm /bin/zipinfo
```

[Index]	Value	Size	Type	Bind	Other	Shndx	Name
[20]	216572	0	SECT	LOCL	0	19	
[2]	65748	0	SECT	LOCL	0	1	
[3]	65768	0	SECT	LOCL	0	2	
[4]	67380	0	SECT	LOCL	0	3	
[5]	70420	0	SECT	LOCL	0	4	
[6]	73532	0	SECT	LOCL	0	5	
[7]	73564	0	SECT	LOCL	0	6	
[8]	73588	0	SECT	LOCL	0	7	
[9]	73624	0	SECT	LOCL	0	8	
[10]	74296	0	SECT	LOCL	0	9	
[11]	148616	0	SECT	LOCL	0	10	
[12]	148672	0	SECT	LOCL	0	11	
[13]	148728	0	SECT	LOCL	0	12	
[14]	148732	0	SECT	LOCL	0	13	
[15]	148924	0	SECT	LOCL	0	14	
[16]	215644	0	SECT	LOCL	0	15	
[17]	215648	0	SECT	LOCL	0	16	
[18]	216372	0	SECT	LOCL	0	17	
[19]	216540	0	SECT	LOCL	0	18	
[21]	232300	0	SECT	LOCL	0	20	
[39]	0	0	NOTY	LOCL	0	UNDEF	
[22]	233152	0	SECT	LOCL	0	21	
[23]	0	0	SECT	LOCL	0	22	
[24]	0	0	SECT	LOCL	0	23	
[25]	0	0	SECT	LOCL	0	24	
[26]	0	0	SECT	LOCL	0	25	
[27]	0	0	SECT	LOCL	0	26	
[28]	0	0	SECT	LOCL	0	27	
[38]	0	0	NOTY	LOCL	0	UNDEF	
[566]	215996	0	FUNC	GLOB	0	UNDEF	.div
[473]	216008	0	FUNC	GLOB	0	UNDEF	.rem
[565]	216188	0	FUNC	GLOB	0	UNDEF	.udiv
[471]	216116	0	FUNC	GLOB	0	UNDEF	.urem
[484]	216608	4	OBJT	GLOB	0	19	___Argv
[522]	216604	4	OBJT	GLOB	0	19	__cg89_used
[523]	216604	4	OBJT	GLOB	0	19	__cg92_used

...

Environment Variables

See environ(5) for descriptions of the following environment variables that affect the execution of nm: LC_COLLATE, LC_CTYPE, LC_MESSAGES, and NLSPATH.

Exit Status

| 0 | Successful completion. |
| >0 | An error occurred. |

Attributes

See attributes(5) for descriptions of the following attributes:

/usr/ccs/bin/nm

Attribute Type	**Attribute Value**
Availability	SUNWbtool

/usr/xpg4/bin/nm

Attribute Type	**Attribute Value**
Availability	SUNWxcu4

See Also

ar(1), as(1), dump(1), ld(1), ld.so.1(1), a.or(3HEAD), a.out(4), attributes(5), environ(5), XPG4(5)

New!

nohup — Run a Command Immune to Hangups

Synopsis

```
/usr/bin/nohup command [argument...]
/usr/xpg4/bin/nohup command [argument...]
```

Description

Use the nohup command to run background jobs that keep running even if you log out. The nohup command invokes the named command with the arguments supplied. When the command is invoked, nohup arranges for the SIGHUP signal to be ignored by the process.

When a shell exits, the system sends its children SIGHUP signals which, by default, kill them. You can, however, use the nohup command when you know that *command* takes a long time to run and you want to be able to log out of the terminal without interrupting the command. When you precede a command invocation with the nohup command (or if the process programmatically has chosen to ignore SIGHUP), all stopped, running, and background jobs ignore SIGHUP and continue running.

nohup automatically sends command output, including standard error, to the nohup.out file.

/usr/bin/nohup
Processes run by /usr/bin/nohup are immune to SIGHUP (hangup) and SIGQUIT (quit) signals.

/usr/xpg4/bin/nohup
Processes run by /usr/xpg4/bin/nohup are immune to SIGHUP.

The nohup command does not arrange to make processes immune to a SIGTERM (terminate) signal, so they receive it unless you arrange for the processes to be immune to SIGTERM or unless the shell makes them immune to SIGTERM.

If nohup.out is not writable in the current directory, output is redirected to $HOME/nohup.out. If a file is created, the file has read and write permission (600, see chmod(1)). If the standard error is a terminal, output is redirected to the standard output; otherwise, it is not redirected. The priority of the process run by nohup is not altered.

Warnings
If you are running the Korn shell (ksh(1)) as your login shell and have nohup'ed jobs running when you attempt to log out, you are warned with the message

```
You have jobs running.
```

You then need to log out a second time to actually log out; however, your background jobs continue to run.

Notes
The C shell (csh(1)) has a built-in nohup command that provides immunity from SIGHUP but does not redirect output to nohup.out. Commands executed with & are automatically immune to HUP signals while in the background.

nohup does not recognize command sequences. In the case of the following command, the nohup command applies only to *command1*.

```
$ nohup command1; command2
```

The following command is syntactically incorrect.

```
$ nohup (command1; command2)
```

Operands

command	The name of a command that is to be invoked. If the *command* operand names any of the special shell_builtins(1) commands, the results are undefined.
argument	Any string to be supplied as an argument when invoking the command operand.

Examples
It is frequently desirable to apply nohup to pipelines or lists of commands. You can do this only by placing pipelines and command lists in a single file, called a shell script. If you run the script with the following command, then nohup applies to everything in the file.

```
$ nohup sh file
```

If the shell script file is to be executed often, you can eliminate the need to type sh by giving *file* execute permission.

When you add an ampersand, the contents of *file* are run in the background with interrupts also ignored (see sh(1)).

```
$ nohup file &
```

Environment Variables

See environ(5) for descriptions of the following environment variables that affect the execution of nohup: LC_CTYPE, LC_MESSAGES, PATH, and NLSPATH.

HOME   Determine the path name of the user's home directory. If the output file nohup.out cannot be created in the current directory, the nohup command uses the directory named by HOME to create the file.

Exit Status

126   Command was found but could not be invoked.

127   An error occurred in nohup, or command could not be found.

Otherwise, the exit values of nohup are those of the *command* operand.

Files

nohup.out   The output file of the nohup execution if standard output is a terminal and if the current directory is writable.

$HOME/nohup.out

         The output file of the nohup execution if standard output is a terminal and if the current directory is not writable.

Attributes

See attributes(5) for descriptions of the following attributes:

/usr/bin/nohup

Attribute Type	Attribute Value
Availability	SUNWcsu
CSI	Enabled

/usr/xpg4/bin/nohup

Attribute Type	Attribute Value
Availability	SUNWxcu4
CSI	Enabled

See Also

batch(1), chmod(1), csh(1), ksh(1), nice(1), sh(1), shell_builtins(1), signal(3C), attributes(5), environ(5), xpg4(5)

notify — Control Process Execution

Synopsis

csh

```
notify [%job-id] ...
```

Description

See jobs(1).

nroff — Format Documents for Display or Line Printer

Synopsis

```
/usr/bin/nroff [-ehiq] [-mname] [-nM] [-opagelist] [-raM] [-sM] [-Tname]
```

Description

nroff formats text in the named files for typewriter-like devices. See also troff(1).

If you specify no *file* argument, nroff reads the standard input. An argument consisting of a dash (-) is taken to be a file name corresponding to the standard input.

Notes

Previous documentation incorrectly described the numeric register yr as being the "Last two digits of current year". yr is in actuality the number of years since 1900. To correctly obtain the last two digits of the current year through the year 2099, you can include the following definition of string register yy in a document to display a two-digit year. Note that you can substitute any other available one- or two-character register name for yy.

```
.\" definition of new string register yy--last two digits of year
.\" use yr (# of years since 1900) if it is < 100
.ie \n(yr<100 .ds yy \n(yr
.el \{            .\" else, subtract 100 from yr, store in ny
.nr ny \n(yr-100
.ie \n(ny>9 \{    .\" use ny if it is two digits
.ds yy \n(ny
.\" remove temporary number register ny
.rr ny \}
.el \{.ds yy 0
.\" if ny is one digit, append it to 0
.as yy \n(ny
.rr ny \} \}
```

Options

You can specify options in any order as long as they appear before the files.

-e	Produce equally spaced words in adjusted lines, using full terminal resolution.
-h	Use output Tab characters during horizontal spacing to speed output and reduce output character count. Tab settings are assumed to be every eight nominal character widths.
-i	Read the standard input after the input files are exhausted.
-m*name*	Prepend the macro file `/usr/share/lib/tmac/tmac.`*name* to the input files.
-n*N*	Number the first generated page *N*.
-o*pagelist*	Print pages whose page numbers appear only in the comma-separated list of numbers and ranges. A range *N-M* means pages *N* through *M*, an initial *-N* means from the beginning to page *N*, and a final *N-* means from *N* to the end.
-q	Do not print output that was read from an `.rd` request. Changed in the Solaris 9 release.
-ra*N*	Set register a (one-character) to *N*.
-s*N*	Stop every *N* pages (default N=1) to allow paper loading or changing. Resume on receipt of a newline.
-T*name*	Prepare output for a device of the specified name. Known names are:

37	Teletype Corporation Model 37 terminal (the default).
lp | tn300	GE Any line printer or terminal without half-line capability.
300	DASI-300.
300-12	DASI-300–12-pitch.
300S	DASI-300S.
300S-12	DASI-300S.
382	DASI-382 (fancy DTC 382).
450	DASI-450 (Diablo Hyterm).
450-12	DASI-450 (Diablo Hyterm)–12pitch.
832	AJ 832.

-u*N*	Set the emboldening factor for the fonts mounted in position 3 to *N*. If you do not specify *N*, then set the emboldening factor to 0. New in the Solaris 9 release.

Examples

The following example formats `user.guide`, using the -me macro package and stopping every four pages.

```
castle% nroff -s4 -me users.guide
```

Environment Variables

See environ(5) for descriptions of the following environment variables that affect the execution of nroff: LC_CTYPE, LC_MESSAGES, and NLSPATH.

Files

/usr/tmp/trtmp*

> Temporary file.

/usr/share/lib/tmac/tmac.*

> Standard macro files.

/usr/share/lib/nterm/*

> Terminal driving tables for nroff.

/usr/share/lib/nterm/README

> Index to terminal description files.

Note — /usr/tmp is currently a symbolic link to /var/tmp.

Attributes

See attributes(5) for descriptions of the following attributes:

Attribute Type	Attribute Value
Availability	SUNWdoc
CSI	Enabled

See Also

checknr(1), col(1), eqn(1), man(1), tbl(1), troff(1), attributes(5), environ(5), me(5), ms(5), term(5)

O

od — Octal Dump

Synopsis

```
/usr/bin/od [-bcCDdFfOoSsvXx] [-] [file] [offset_string]
/usr/bin/od [-bcCDdFfOoSsvXx] [-A address-base] [-j skip] [-N count]
   [-t type-string...] [-] [file]
/usr/xpg4/bin/od [-bcCDdFfOoSsvXx] [-] [file] [offset-string]
/usr/xpg4/bin/od [-bcCDdFfOoSsvXx] [-A address-base] [-j skip]
   [-N count] [-t type-string...] [-] [file...]
```

Description

The od command sequentially copies each input file to standard output and transforms the input data according to the output types specified with the -t or -bcCDdFfOoSsvXx options. If you specify no output type, the default output is as if you specified -t o2. You can specify multiple types by using multiple -bcCDdFfOoSstvXx options. Output lines are written for each type specified in the order in which the types are specified. If you specify no file, the standard input is used. The [offset-string] operand is mutually exclusive from the -A, -j, -N, and -t options. For the purposes of this description, the following terms are used:

word   A 16-bit unit, independent of the word size of the system.

long word   A 32-bit unit.

double long word

                A 64-bit unit.

Options

-A *address-base*

        Specify the input offset base. The *address-base* argument must be a character. The characters d, o, or x specify that the offset base is written in decimal, octal, or hexadecimal. The character n specifies that the offset is not written. Unless you specify -A, the output line is preceded by the input offset, cumulative across input files, of the next byte to be written. In addition, the offset of the byte following the last byte written is displayed after all the input data has been processed. Without the -A *address-base* option and the [*offset-string*] operand, the input offset base is displayed in octal.

-b

        Interpret bytes in octal. This option is equivalent to -t o1.

/usr/bin/od

-c

        Display single-byte characters. Certain nongraphic characters appear as C-language escapes:

        \0   Null.

        \b   Backspace.

        \f   Formfeed.

        \n   Newline.

        \r   Return.

        \t   Tab.

        Others appear as 3-digit octal numbers. For example:

```
echo "hello world" | od -c
0000000 h e l l o   w o r l d \n
0000014
```

/usr/xpg4/bin/od

-c

        Interpret bytes as single- or multibyte characters according to the current setting of the LC_CTYPE locale category. Write printable multibyte characters in the area corresponding to the first byte of the character; write the two-character sequence ** in the area corresponding to each remaining byte in the character as an indication that the character is continued. Nongraphic characters appear the same as they would with the -C option.

-C

        Interpret bytes as single- or multibyte characters according to the current setting of the LC_CTYPE locale category. Write printable multibyte characters in the area corresponding to the first byte of the character; write the two-character sequence ** in the area corresponding to each remaining byte in the character as an indication that the character is continued. Certain nongraphic characters appear as C escapes.

\0	Null.
\b	Backspace.
\f	Formfeed.
\n	Newline.
\r	Return.
\t	Tab.

Other nonprintable characters appear as one 3-digit octal number for each byte in the character.

-d   Interpret words in unsigned decimal. This option is equivalent to -t u2.

-D   Interpret long words in unsigned decimal. This option is equivalent to -t u4.

-f   Interpret long words in floating point. This option is equivalent to -t f4.

-F   Interpret double-long words in extended precision. This option is equivalent to -t f8.

-j *skip*   Jump over *skip* bytes from the beginning of the input. The od command reads or seeks past the first *skip* bytes in the concatenated input files. If the combined input is not at least *skip* bytes long, write a diagnostic message to standard error and exit with a non-zero exit status.

By default, the *skip* argument is interpreted as a decimal number. With a leading 0x or 0X, the offset is interpreted as a hexadecimal number; otherwise, with a leading 0, the offset is interpreted as an octal number. Appending the character b, k, or m to offset interprets it as a multiple of 512, 1,024 or 1,048,576 bytes. If the *skip* number is hexadecimal, consider any appended b to be the final hexadecimal digit. Display the address starting at 0000000, and do not imply its base by the base of the *skip* argument.

-N *count*   Format no more than *count* bytes of input. By default, *count* is interpreted as a decimal number. With a leading 0x or 0X, *count* is interpreted as a hexadecimal number; otherwise, with a leading 0, it is interpreted as an octal number. If *count* bytes of input (after successfully skipping if -j *skip* is specified) are not available, it is not considered an error; the od command formats the input that is available. The base of the address displayed is not implied by the base of the *count* argument.

-o   Interpret words in octal. This option is equivalent to -t o2.

-O   Interpret long words in unsigned octal. This option is equivalent to -t o4.

-s   Interpret words in signed decimal. This option is equivalent to -t d2.

-S   Interpret long words in signed decimal. This option is equivalent to -t d4.

-t *type-string*

> Specify one or more output types. The *type-string* argument must be a string specifying the types to be used when writing the input data. The string must consist of the type specification characters.

> a Interpret bytes as named characters. Use only the least significant seven bits of each byte for this type specification. Bytes with the values listed in the following table are written using the corresponding names of those characters.

Value	Name	Value	Name	Value	Name	Value	Name
\000	nul	\001	soh	\002	stx	\003	etx
\004	eot	\005	enq	\006	ack	\007	bel
\010	bs	\011	ht	\012	lf	\013	vt
\014	ff	\015	cr	\016	so	\017	si
\020	dle	\021	dc1	\022	dc2	\023	dc3
\024	dc4	\025	nak	\026	syn	\027	etb
\030	can	\031	em	\032	sub	\033	esc
\034	fs	\035	gs	\036	rs	\037	us
\040	sp	\177	del				

> c Interpret bytes as single- or multibyte characters specified by the current setting of the LC_CTYPE locale category. Write printable multibyte characters in the area corresponding to the first byte of the character; write the two-character sequence ** in the area corresponding to each remaining byte in the character, as an indication that the character is continued. Certain nongraphic characters appear as C escapes: \0, \a, \b, \f, \n, \r, \t, \v. Other nonprintable characters appear as one 3-digit octal number for each byte in the character.

> You can follow the type specification characters d, f, o, u, and x with an optional, unsigned decimal integer that specifies the number of bytes to be transformed by each instance of the output type.

> f Can be followed by an optional F, D, or L, applying the conversion to an item of type float, double, or long double.

> d, o, u, and x

> Signed decimal, octal, unsigned decimal, and hexadecimal. Can be followed by an optional C, S, I, or L, applying the conversion to an item of type char, short, int, or long.

You can concatenate multiple types within the same *type-string* and specify multiple -t options. Write output lines for each type specified in the order in which the type specification characters are specified.

-v   Show all input data (verbose). Without the -v option, replace all groups of output lines that would be identical to the immediately preceding output line (except for byte offsets) with an asterisk (*).

-x   Interpret words in hex. This option is equivalent to -t x2.

-X   Interpret long words in hex. This option is equivalent to -t x4.

Operands

The following operand is supported for both /usr/bin/od and /usr/xpg4/bin/od.

–   Use the standard input in addition to any files specified. When you do not specify this operand, use the standard input only if no file operands are specified.

/usr/bin/od

The following operands are supported for /usr/bin/od only.

file   A path name of a file to be read. If you specify no *file* operands, use the standard input. If there are no more than two operands, none of the -A, -j, -N, or -t options are specified and any of the following are true, then the corresponding operand is assumed to be an offset operand instead of a file operand.

- The first character of the last operand is a plus sign (+).

- The first character of the second operand is numeric.

- The first character of the second operand is x, and the second character of the second operand is a lowercase hexadecimal character or digit.

- The second operand is named x.

- The second operand is named ..

Without the -N *count* option, the display continues until an end-of-file is reached.

```
[+] [0] offset [.] [b|B]
[+] [0] [offset] [.]
[+] [0x|x] [offset]
[+] [0x|x] offset[B]
```

The *offset-string* operand specifies the byte offset in the file where dumping is to commence. The *offset* is interpreted in octal bytes by default. If *offset* begins with 0, interpret it in octal. If offset begins with x or 0x, interpret it in hexadecimal and consider any appended b to be the final hexadecimal digit. If . is appended, interpret the offset in decimal. If b or B is appended, interpret the offset in units of 512 bytes. If you omit the *file* argument, the offset argument must be preceded by a plus sign (+). Display the address starting at the given offset. The radix of the address is the same as the radix of the offset if specified; otherwise, it is octal. Decimal overrides octal, and it is an error to specify both hexadecimal and decimal conversions in the same *offset* operand.

/usr/xpg4/bin/od

The following operands are supported for /usr/xpg4/bin/od only.

file   Same as /usr/bin/od, except only one of the first two conditions must be true.

```
[+] [0] offset [.] [b|B]
+ [offset] [.]
[+] [0x] [offset]
[+] [0x] offset[B]
+x [offset]
+xoffset [B]
```

Description of *offset-string* is the same as for /usr/bin/od.

Environment Variables

See environ(5) for descriptions of the following environment variables that affect the execution of od: LC_CTYPE, LC_MESSAGES, LC_NUMERIC, and NLSPATH.

Exit Status

0   Successful completion.

>0   An error occurred.

Attributes

See attributes(5) for descriptions of the following attributes:

/usr/bin/od

Attribute Type	Attribute Value
Availability	SUNWtoo
CSI	Enabled

/usr/xpg4/bin/od

Attribute Type	Attribute Value
Availability	SUNWxcu4
CSI	Enabled

See Also

sed(1), attributes(5), environ(5), XPG4(5)

on — Execute a Command on a Remote System, Using the Local Environment

Synopsis

/usr/bin/on [-i] [-d] [-n] *host command* [*argument*] ...

Description

Use the on command to execute commands on another system in an environment similar to that invoking the program. All environment variables are passed through, and the current working directory is preserved. For the working directory to be preserved, the working file system must either be already mounted on the host or be exported to it. Relative path names work only if they are within the current file system; absolute path names may cause problems.

The standard input is connected to the standard input of the remote command, and the standard output and the standard error from the remote command are sent to the corresponding files for the on command.

Bugs

When the working directory is remote mounted over NFS, a Control-Z hangs the window.

Root cannot use on.

Options

-i   Use remote echoing and special character processing. This option is needed for programs that expect to be talking to a terminal. All terminal modes and window size changes are propagated.

-d   Print debugging messages as work is being done.

-n   Get end-of-file when on reads from the standard input instead of passing the standard input from the standard input of the on program. For example, you need to use the -n option when running commands in the background with job control.

Attributes

See attributes(5) for descriptions of the following attributes:

Attribute Type	Attribute Value
Availability	SUNWnfscu

New!

See Also

chkey(1), rlogin(1), rsh(1), telnet(1), attributes(5)

Diagnostics

unknown host

Host name not found.

```
cannot connect to server
```
Host down or not running the server.

```
can't find
```
Problem finding the working directory.

```
can't locate mount point
```
Problem finding current file system.

```
RPC: Authentication error
```
The server requires DES authentication and you do not have a secret key registered with keyserv. Perhaps you logged in without a password. Try to use keylogin. If that fails, try to set your public key with chkey.

Other diagnostic messages may be passed back from the server.

onintr — Shell Built-in Functions to Respond to (Hardware) Signals

Synopsis

csh
onintr [-| *label*]

Description
See trap(1).

optisa — Determine Which Variant Instruction Set Is Optimal

Synopsis
/usr/bin/optisa *instruction-set*...

Description
optisa prints the instruction set out of the ones specified in the command that performs best on this machine. Best is defined by the order in which instruction set names are returned by isalist(1). Possible values for *instruction-set* are given in isalist(5).

> **Note** — optisa is preferable to uname -p or uname -m in determining which of several binary versions of a given program should be used on the given machine.

Examples
The following example displays the isalist instruction set and then uses the optisa command to find the command that performs best on a SPARCstation 10.

```
castle% isalist
sparcv8 sparcv8-fsmuld sparcv7 sparc
castle% optisa sparcv8 sparcv8-fsmuld sparcv7 sparc
sparcv8
castle%
```

Attributes

See attributes(5) for descriptions of the following attributes:

Attribute Type	Attribute Value
Availability	SUNWcsu

Exit Status

0	One of the *instruction-set* values you specified is printed.
1	No output; that is, this system cannot use any *instruction-set* that you specified with the optisa command.

See Also

isalist(1), uname(1), attributes(5), isalist(5)

Diagnostics

Exit status is 0 if one of the *instruction-set* values you specified is printed by this command. Exit status is 1 if there is no output; that is, this machine cannot use any *instruction-set* that you specified with the optisa command.

P

---

pack, pcat, unpack — Compress and Expand Files

Synopsis

```
/usr/bin/pack  [-f]  [-]  file...
/usr/bin/pcat  file...
/usr/bin/unpack  file...
```

Description

pack

The pack command stores the specified files in a compressed form. Wherever possible (and useful), each specified input file is replaced by a packed file named *file*.z with the same access modes, access and modified dates, and owner as those of *file*. When the pack is successful, the original file is removed.

The size of the input file and the character frequency distribution determine the amount of compression. Because a decoding tree forms the first part of each .z file, it is usually not worthwhile to pack files smaller than three blocks. You may find it worthwhile, however, to pack small files such as printer plots or pictures in which the character frequency distribution is very skewed.

Text files are typically reduced to 60–75 percent of their original size. Load modules, which use a larger character set and have a more uniform distribution of characters, show little compression. The packed versions are usually about 90 percent of the original size.

pack returns a value that is the number of files that it failed to compress.

No packing is done under the following conditions.

1007

- The file is already packed.
- The file name has more than 14 bytes.
- The file has links.
- The file is a directory.
- The file cannot be opened.
- The file is empty.
- No disk storage blocks are saved by packing.
- A file named *file*.z already exists.
- The .z file cannot be created.
- An I/O error occurs during processing.

The file name must contain no more than 14 bytes to allow space to append the .z extension. You cannot compress directories.

pcat

Use the pcat command on packed files in the same way that you use the cat(1) command on ordinary files. You cannot use pcat as a filter. The specified files are unpacked and written to the standard output.

pcat returns the number of files it was unable to unpack. Unpacking can fail in the following conditions.

- The file cannot be opened.
- The file is not output from the pack command.

unpack

The unpack command expands files created by pack. For each file specified in the command, a search is made for a file called *file*.z (or just *file*, if *file* ends in .z). If this file appears to be a packed file, it is replaced by its expanded version. The new file has the .z suffix stripped from its name and has the same access modes, access and modification dates, and owner as those of the packed file.

unpack returns a value that is the number of files it was unable to unpack. Unpacking can fail under the following conditions.

- The file cannot be opened.
- The file is not output from the pack command.
- A file with the unpacked name already exists.
- The unpacked file cannot be created.
- The file name (excluding the .z extension) has more than 14 bytes.

Options

    –   pack uses Huffman (minimum redundancy) codes on a byte-by-byte basis. With the – argument, set an internal flag that prints to standard output the number of times each byte is used, the relative frequency, and the code for the bytes. Additional use of – in place of *file* sets and resets the internal flag.

-f   Force packing of file. This option is useful for packing entire directories even if some of the files do not save disk storage blocks. You can restore packed files to their original form with either the unpack or pcat commands.

Operands

file   A path name of a file to be packed, packed with pcat, or unpacked. *file* can either include or omit the .z suffix.

Examples

In the following example, the passwd file is too small to save any disk storage blocks by packing. The termcap file is big enough to compress, and it is compressed 29.8 percent.

```
castle% pack passwd
pack: passwd: no saving - file unchanged
castle% pack termcap
pack: termcap: 29.8% Compression
castle%
```

In the following example, the pcat command displays the contents of the compressed termcap.z file and pipes the output through the more command. To save space, only the first line of the output is shown here.

```
castle% pcat termcap.z | more
#ident "@(#)termcap 1.13 93/03/27 SMI" /* SunOS 4,1,3 termcap */
...
```

The following example unpacks the termcap.z file.

```
castle% unpack termcap.z
unpack: termcap: unpacked
castle%
```

Environment Variables

See environ(5) for descriptions of the following environment variables that affect the execution of pack, pcat, and unpack: LC_CTYPE, LC_MESSAGES, and NLSPATH.

Exit Status

0   Successful completion.

>0   The number of files the command failed to pack or unpack.

Attributes

See attributes(5) for descriptions of the following attributes:

Attribute Type	Attribute Value
Availability	SUNWcsu
CSI	Enabled

See Also

cat(1), compress(1), zcat(1), attributes(5), environ(5), largefile(5)

page — Browse or Page through a Text File

Synopsis

```
/usr/bin/page [-cdflrsuw] [-lines] [+linenumber] [+/pattern] [file...]
```

Description

See more(1).

pagesize — Display the Size of a Page of Memory

Synopsis

New!
```
/usr/bin/pagesize [-a]
```

Description

Use the pagesize command to print the size of a page of memory, in bytes, as returned by getpagesize(3C). This program is useful in constructing portable shell scripts.

New! Options

-a   Print all possible hardware address translation sizes supported by the system. New in the Solaris 9 release.

Example

```
mopoke% /usr/bin/pagesize
8192
mopoke%
```

New!   The following example shows the output of the pagesize -a command.

```
mopoke% pagesize -a
8192
65536
524288
4194304
mopoke%
```

Attributes

See attributes(5) for descriptions of the following attributes:

Attribute Type	Attribute Value
Availability	SUNWcsu

See Also

New!   getpagesize(3C), getpagesizes(3C), attributes(5)

pargs — Print Command Arguments, Environment Variables, or Auxiliary Vector

Synopsis
```
/usr/bin/pargs [-aeFx] [pid | core]...
```

Description
New in the Solaris 9 release. See proc(1).

passwd — Change Login Password and Password Attributes

Synopsis
```
/usr/bin/passwd [-r files | -r nis| -r nisplus] [name]
/usr/bin/passwd [-r files | -r ldap | -r nis | -r nisplus] [name]     New!
/usr/bin/passwd [-r files] [-egh] [name]                              New!
/usr/bin/passwd [-r files] -s [-a]
/usr/bin/passwd [-r files] -s [name]
/usr/bin/passwd [-r files] [-d | -l] [-f] [-min] [-w warn] [-x max] name
/usr/bin/passwd -r ldap [-egh] [name]                                 New!
/usr/bin/passwd -r nis [-egh] [name]
/usr/bin/passwd -r nisplus [-egh] [-D domainname] [name]
/usr/bin/passwd -r nisplus -s [-a]
/usr/bin/passwd -r nisplus [-D domainname] -s [name]
/usr/bin/passwd -r nisplus [-l] [-f] [-n min] [-w warn] [-x max]
    [-D domainname] name
```

Description

> **Note** — The passwd command replaces the nispasswd and yppasswd commands and should be used in their place.

Use the passwd command to change the password or list password attributes associated with the user's login name. Additionally, superuser can use passwd to install or change passwords and attributes associated with any login name.

When used to change a password, passwd prompts for the old password if any. It then prompts again for the new password. When you type the old password, passwd checks to see if it has aged sufficiently. If aging is insufficient, passwd terminates. See pwconv(1M), nistbladm(1), and shadow(4) for additional information.

When LDAP (new in the Solaris 8 release), NIS, or NIS+ is in effect on a system,   New! passwd changes the LDAP, NIS, or NIS+ database. The LDAP, NIS, or NIS+ password can be different from the password on the local machine. If NIS or NIS+ is running, use passwd -r to change password information on the local machine.

The pwconv command creates and updates /etc/shadow with information from /etc/passwd. pwconv relies on a special value of x in the password field of the /etc/passwd file. The value of x indicates that the password for the user is already in /etc/shadow and should not be modified.

If aging is sufficient, a check is made to ensure that the new password meets construction requirements. When you type the new password a second time, the two copies of the new password are compared. If the two copies are not identical, the cycle of prompting for the new password is repeated for, at most, two more times.

Passwords must be constructed to meet the following requirements.

- Each password must have at least PASSLENGTH characters, where PASSLENGTH is defined in /etc/default/passwd and is set to 6. Only the first eight characters are significant.

- Each password must contain at least two alphabetic characters and at least one numeric or special character. In this case, alphabetic refers to all upper- or lowercase letters.

- Each password must differ from the user's login name and any reverse or circular shift of that login name. For comparison purposes, an uppercase letter and its corresponding lowercase letter are equivalent.

- New passwords must differ from the old by at least three characters. For comparison purposes, an uppercase letter and its corresponding lowercase letter are equivalent.

If all requirements are met, by default, the passwd command consults /etc/nsswitch.conf to determine which repositories to update. It searches the passwd and passwd_compat entries. The sources (repositories) associated with these entries are updated. However, the password update configurations supported are limited to the following five cases. Failure to comply with the configurations prevents users from logging in to the system.

- passwd: files
- passwd: files ldap
- passwd: files nis
- passwd: files nisplus
- passwd: compat (==> files nis)
- passwd: compat (==> files ldap)
- passwd: compat: ldap
- passwd: compat (==> files nisplus)
- passwd_compat: nisplus

Network administrators who own the NIS+ password table can change any password attributes.

In the case of files, superuser (anyone with real and effective UID equal to 0, see id(1M) and su(1M)) can change any password. passwd does not prompt superuser for the old password. Superuser is not forced to comply with password aging or password construction requirements.

Superuser can create a null password by pressing Return in response to the prompt for a new password. (This procedure differs from passwd -d because the password prompt is still displayed.) If NIS is in effect, superuser on the root master can change any password without being prompted for the old NIS password and is not forced to comply with password construction requirements.

Normally, passwd with no arguments changes the password of the current user. When a user logs in and then invokes su(1M) to become superuser or another user, passwd changes the original user's password, not the password of the superuser or the new user.

Users can use the -s option to show password attributes for their own login name provided they use the -r nisplus argument. Otherwise, the -s argument is restricted to the superuser.

The format of the display is:

name status mm/dd/yy min max warn

or, if password aging information is not present,

name status

	name is the login ID of the user. *status* is the password status of *name*. PS means having a password or locked, LK means locked, and NP means no password.
mm/dd/yy	The date the password was last changed for *name*. Note that all password aging dates are determined from Greenwich Mean Time (Universal Time) and, therefore, can differ by as much as a day in other time zones.
min	The minimum number of days required between password changes for name. MINWEEKS is found in /etc/default/passwd and is set to null.
max	The maximum number of days the password is valid for *name*. MAXWEEKS is found in /etc/default/passwd and is set to null.
warn	The number of days relative to *max* before the password expires and *name* is warned.

Security

passwd uses pam(3) for password management. The PAM configuration policy, listed in /etc/pam.conf, specifies the password modules to be used for passwd. Here is the passwd entry from a pam.conf file and using the UNIX password module.

```
passwd    password required    /usr/lib/security/pam_unix.so.1
```

If there are no entries for the passwd service, then the entries for the other service, shown below, are used.

```
# Password management
#
other    password required        /usr/lib/security/pam_unix.so.1
```

If multiple password modules are listed, then the user may be prompted for multiple passwords.

Options

-a	Show password attributes for all entries. Use only with the -s option; you must not specify *name*. For the nisplus repository, this option shows only the entries in the NIS+ password table in the local domain that the invoker is authorized to read. For the files repository, this option is restricted to superuser.

-D *domainname*

Consult the `passwd.org_dir` table in *domainname*. If you do not specify this option, the default *domainname* returned by `nis_local_directory`(3NSL) is used. This domain name is the same as that returned by `domainname`(1M).

-e
Change the login shell. For the `files` repository, this option works only for superuser. Normal users can change the `nis` or `nisplus` repositories.

-g
Change the comment (`finger`) information. For the `files` repository, this option works only for superuser. Normal users can change the `nis` or `nisplus` repositories.

-h
Change the home directory.

-r
Specify the repository to which an operation is applied. The supported repositories are `files`, `nis`, and `nisplus`.

-s *name*
Show password attributes for the login *name*. For the `nisplus` repository, this option works for everyone. However, for the `files` repository, this option works only for superuser. It does not work at all for the `nis` repository, which does not support password aging.

Superuser Options

Only superuser can use the following options.

-d
Delete password for *name*. The login name is not prompted for password. It is only applicable to the `files` repository.

-f
Force the user to change password at the next login by expiring the password for *name*.

-l
Lock password entry for *name*.

-n *min*
Set minimum field for *name*. The *min* field contains the minimum number of days between password changes for *name*. If *min* is greater than *max*, the user cannot change the password. Always use this option with the -x option, unless *max* is set to -1 (aging turned off). In that case, *min* need not be set.

-w *warn*
Set *warn* field for *name*. The *warn* field contains the number of days before the password expires and the user is warned. This option is not valid if password aging is disabled.

-x *max*
Set maximum field for *name*. The *max* field contains the number of days that the password is valid for *name*. The aging for *name* is turned off immediately if *max* is set to -1. If it is set to 0, then the user is forced to change the password at the next login session and aging is turned off.

Operands

name
User login name.

Environment Variables

If any of the LC_* variables (LC_CTYPE, LC_MESSAGES, LC_TIME, LC_COLLATE, LC_NUMERIC, and LC_MONETARY) (see environ(5)) are not set in the environment, the operational behavior of passwd for each corresponding locale category is determined by the value of the LANG environment variable. If LC_ALL is set, its contents are used to override both the LANG and the other LC_* variables. If none of the above variables are set in the environment, the C (U.S. style) locale determines how passwd behaves.

LC_CTYPE   Determine how passwd handles characters.When LC_CTYPE is set to a valid value, passwd can display and handle text and file names containing valid characters for that locale. passwd can display and handle Extended Unix Code (EUC) characters in which any individual character can be 1, 2, or 3 bytes. passwd can also handle EUC characters of 1, 2, or more column widths. In the C locale, only characters from ISO 8859-1 are valid.

LC_MESSAGES

Determine how diagnostic and informative messages are presented. This presentation includes the language and style of the messages and the correct form of affirmative and negative responses. In the C locale, the messages are presented in the default form found in the program itself (in most cases, U.S. English).

Exit Status

0	Success.
1	Permission denied.
2	Invalid combination of options.
3	Unexpected failure. Password file unchanged.
4	Unexpected failure. Password file(s) missing.
5	Password file(s) busy. Try again later.
6	Invalid argument to option.
7	Aging option was disabled.

Files

/etc/oshadow
/etc/passwd

Password files.

/etc/shadow

Shadow password file.

/etc/shells

File containing a list of valid shells on the system.

New!

```
/etc/default/passwd
```

> Default values can be set for the following flags in
> `/etc/default/passwd`. For example, `MAXWEEKS=26`.

MAXWEEKS	Maximum time period that password is valid.
MINWEEKS	Minimum time period before the password can be changed.
PASSLENGTH	Minimum length of password, in characters.
WARNWEEKS	Time period until warning of date of password's pending expiration.

Attributes

See `attributes(5)` for descriptions of the following attributes:

Attribute Type	Attribute Value
Availability	SUNWcsu
CIS	Enabled

See Also

finger(1), login(1), nispasswd(1), nistbladm(1), yppasswd(1),
domainname(1M), eeprom(1M), id(1M), passmgmt(1M), pwconv(1M), su(1M),
useradd(1M), userdel(1M), usermod(1M), pam(3PAM), crypt(3C),
getpwnam(3C), getspnam(3C), nis_local_directory(3NSL), loginlog(4),
nsswitch.conf(4), pam.conf(4), passwd(4), shadow(4), attributes(5),
environ(5), pam_ldap(5), pam_unix(5)

New!

paste — Merge Corresponding or Subsequent Lines of Files

Synopsis

```
/usr/bin/paste [-s] [-d list] file...
```

Description

Use the `paste` command to join files together line by line, writing the output to standard output. You can use `paste` to create new tables by pasting together fields or columns from between 1 and 12 files. Each line of each input file is considered to be one field for the output line. By default, `paste` adds a Tab character as the delimiter between the contributions of each file. `paste` takes one or more file names as arguments, reads a line from each file, and combines the lines into a single line. If some of the files have fewer lines than others, `paste` simply puts in the delimiters and leaves the field empty. You can specify a dash (–) as one or more of the file names to read standard input.

Options

-d *list*   Unless you use a backslash character (\) in *list*, specify each character in *list* as a delimiter character. If you use a backslash character, specify it and one or more characters following it as a delimiter character, as described below. These elements specify one or more delimiters to use instead of the default Tab character that replaces the newline character of each of the input lines. The elements in *list* are used circularly; that is, when the list is exhausted, the first element from the list is reused.

When you specify the -s option:

- Do not modify the last newline character in a file.
- Reset the delimiter to the first element of *list* after each *file* operand is processed.

When you do not specify the -s option:

- Do not modify the newline characters in the file specified by the last *file*.
- Reset the delimiter to the first element of *list* each time a line is processed from each file.

If a backslash character appears in *list*, use it and the character following it to represent the following delimiter characters.

\n   Newline character.

\t   Tab character.

\\   Backslash character.

\0   Empty string (not a null character). If \0 is immediately followed by the character x, the character X, or any character defined by the LC_CTYPE digit keyword, the results are unspecified.

If any other characters follow the backslash, the results are unspecified.

-s   Concatenate all of the lines of each separate input file in command-line order. Replace the newline character of every line except the last line in each input file with the Tab character unless otherwise specified by the -d option.

Operands

file   A path name of an input file. If you specify - for one or more of the files, use the standard input; read the standard input one line at a time, circularly, for each instance of -. Implementations support pasting of at least 12 file operands.

Usage

See largefile(5) for the description of the behavior of paste when encountering files greater than or equal to 2 Gbytes (2**31 bytes).

Examples

The following example uses the `paste` command to list the files in a directory in one column, using a space character as the delimiter.

```
castle% ls | paste -d" " -
085X01.DOC
085X02.DOC
085X03~1.DOC
085X042.DOC
085X08R.DOC
085X09E.RTF
085XDOCS.ZIP
085XFILE.ZIP
085XINTR.ZIP
a.out
bibliography
bibliography.ig
C.str
DeadLetters
examples
file1
kookaburra-1
ltr
Mail
new
castle%
```

The following example lists the contents of a directory in four columns, using the default Tab delimiter.

```
castle% ls | paste - - - -
085X01.DOC      085X02.DOC      085X03~1.DOC    085X042.DOC
085X08R.DOC     085X09E.RTF     085XDOCS.ZIP    085XFILE.ZIP
085XINTR.ZIP    a.out   bibliography    bibliography.ig
C.str   DeadLetters     examples        file1
kookaburra-1    ltr     Mail    new
castle%
```

The following example combines pairs of lines from one file into single lines. The lines in the file `kookaburra-1` are numbered to make it easier for you to see the results.

```
castle% paste -s -d"\t\n" kookaburra-1
   1  Kookaburra sits in the old gum tree          2  Merry merry king
of the bush is he.
   3  Laugh, kookaburra, laugh, kookaburra         4  Gay your life
must be.
   5          6  Kookaburra sits in the old gum tree
   7  Eating all the gumdrops he can see.          8  Stop,
kookaburra, stop, kookaburra
   9  Leave some there for me.               10
  11  Kookaburra sits in the old gum tree         12  Merry merry king
of the bush is he.
  13  Laugh, kookaburra, laugh, kookaburra        14  Gay your life
must be.
          15  Kookaburra sits in the old gum tree
```

```
16  Eating all the gumdrops he can see.      17  Stop,
kookaburra, stop, kookaburra
   18  Leave some there for me.
castle%
```

Environment Variables

See environ(5) for descriptions of the following environment variables that affect the execution of paste: LC_CTYPE and LC_MESSAGES.

Exit Status

0	Successful completion.
>0	An error occurred.

Attributes

See attributes(5) for descriptions of the following attributes:

Attribute Type	**Attribute Value**
Availability	SUNWesu
CSI	Enabled

See Also

cut(1), grep(1), pr(1), attributes(5), environ(5), largefile(5)

Diagnostics

"line too long"

Output lines are restricted to 511 characters.

"too many files"

Except with the -s option, you can specify no more than 12 input files.

"no delimiters"

The -d option was specified with an empty list.

"cannot open file"

The specified file cannot be opened.

patch — Apply Changes to Files

Synopsis

/usr/bin/patch [-blNR] [-c | -e | -n | -u] [-d *dir*] [-D *define*]
[-i *patchfile*] [-o *outfile*] [-p *num*] [-r *rejectfile*] [*file*]

New!

Description

Use the patch command to edit text files created by diff(1). patch reads a source (patch) file containing any of the three forms of difference (diff) listings produced by the diff(1) command (normal, context, or in the style of ed(1)) and applies those differences to a file. By default, patch reads from the standard input.

patch tries to determine the type of the diff listing unless overruled by a -c, -e, or -n option.

If the patch file contains more than one patch, patch tries to apply each patch as if it came from a separate patch file. (In this case, the name of the patch file must be determinable for each diff listing.)

Options

-b   Before applying the differences, save a copy of the original contents of each modified file in a file of the same name with the suffix .orig appended to it. If the file already exists, overwrite it; if multiple patches are applied to the same file, write the .orig file only for the first patch. When you also specify the -o *outfile* option, do not create *file*.orig; if *outfile* already exists, create *outfile*.orig.

-c   Interpret the patch file as a context difference (the output of the command diff when you specify the -c or -C option).

-d *dir*   Change the current directory to *dir* before processing.

-D *define*   Mark changes with the C preprocessor construct.

              #ifdef *define*

              . . .

              #endif

              Use *define* as the differentiating symbol.

-e   Interpret the patch file as an ed script instead of a diff script.

-i *patchfile*
              Read the patch information from the file named by the path name *patchfile* instead of from the standard input.

-l   Match any sequence of blank characters in the difference script with any sequence of blank characters in the input file. Match other characters exactly.

-n   Interpret the script as a normal difference.

-N   Ignore patches where the differences have already been applied to the file; by default, reject already applied patches.

-o *outfile* Instead of modifying the files (specified by the *file* operand or the difference listings) directly, write a copy of the file referenced by each patch to *outfile* with the appropriate differences applied. Apply multiple patches for a single file to the intermediate versions of the file created by any previous patches, and write multiple, concatenated versions of the file to *outfile*.

-p *num*   For all path names in the patch file that indicate the names of files to be patched, delete *num* path-name components from the beginning of each path name. If the path name in the patch file is absolute, consider any leading slashes as the first component (that is, -p 1 removes the leading slashes). Specifying -p 0 uses the full path name. If you do not specify -p, use only the basename (the final path-name component).

-R   Reverse the sense of the patch script; that is, assume that the difference script was created from the new version to the old version. You cannot use the -R option with ed scripts; patch tries to reverse each portion of the script before applying it. Save rejected differences in swapped format. If you do not specify this option and until a portion of the patch file is successfully applied, patch tries to apply each portion in its reversed sense as well as in its normal sense. If the attempt is successful, prompt the user to determine if the -R option should be set.

-r *rejectfile*

                    Override the default reject file name. In the default case, the reject file has the same name as the output file, with the suffix .rej appended to it.

-u   Interpret the patch file as a unified context difference, that is, the output of the diff command when the -u or -U option is specified. New in the Solaris 9 release.

Operands

file   A path name of a file to patch.

Usage

The -R option does not work with ed scripts because there is too little information to reconstruct the reverse operation.

The -p option makes it possible to customize a *patchfile* to local user directory structures without manually editing the *patchfile*. For example, if the file name in the patch file was

/curds/whey/src/blurfl/blurfl.c

then setting -p 0 results in the entire path name unmodified. Setting -p 1 returns the following path.

curds/whey/src/blurfl/blurfl.c

Without the leading slash, -p 4 returns the following path.

blurfl/blurfl.c

Not specifying -p at all returns the following path.

blurfl.c.

When using -b in some file-system implementations, the saving of a .orig file can produce unwanted results. With 12-, 13- or 14-character file names on file systems supporting 14-character maximum file names, the .orig file overwrites the new file.

Environment Variables

See environ(5) for descriptions of the following environment variables that affect the execution of patch: LC_CTYPE, LC_MESSAGES, LC_TIME, and NLSPATH.

Output Files

The output of patching the save files (.orig suffixes) and the reject files (.rej suffixes) is text files.

Extended Description

A *patchfile* can contain patching instructions for more than one file. When you specify the -b option, for each patched file, the original is saved in a file of the same name with the suffix .orig appended to it.

For each patched file, a reject file can also be created, as noted in "Patch Application" on page 1023. In the absence of a -r option, the name of this file is formed by appending the suffix .rej to the original file name.

Patch-file Format

The patch file must contain zero or more lines of header information followed by one or more patches. Each patch must contain zero or more lines of file-name identification in the format produced by diff -c and one or more sets of diff output, which are customarily called hunks.

patch recognizes the following expression in the header information.

Index: *pathname*   The file to be patched is named *pathname*.

If all lines (including headers) within a patch begin with the same leading sequence of blank characters, patch removes this sequence before proceeding. Within each patch, if the type of difference is context, patch recognizes the following expressions.

*** *filename timestamp* The patches arose from *filename*.
--- *filename timestamp* The patches should be applied to *filename*.

Each hunk within a patch must be the diff output to change a line range within the original file. The line numbers for successive hunks within a patch must occur in ascending order.

File-name Determination

If you specify no *file* operand, patch performs the following steps to obtain a path name.

1. If the patch contains the strings *** and ---, patch strips components from the beginning of each path name (depending on the presence or value of the -p option) and then tests for the existence of both files in the current directory (or directory specified with the -d option).

2. If both files exist, patch assumes that no path name can be obtained from this step. If the header information contains a line with the string Index:, patch strips components from the beginning of the path name (depending on -p) and then tests for the existence of this file in the current directory (or directory specified with the -d option).

3. If an SCCS directory exists in the current directory, patch tries to perform a get -e SCCS/s.*filename* command to retrieve an editable version of the file.

4. If no path name can be obtained by applying the previous steps or if the path names obtained do not exist, patch writes a prompt to standard output and requests a file name interactively from standard input.

Patch Application

If you specify the -c, -e, -n or -u options, patch interprets information within each hunk as a context difference, an ed difference, or a normal difference. In the absence of any of these options, patch determines the type of difference on the basis of the format of information within the hunk.

For each hunk, patch begins to search for the place to apply the patch at the line number at the beginning of the hunk plus or minus any offset used in applying the previous hunk. If lines matching the hunk context are not found, patch scans both forward and backward at least 1,000 bytes for a set of lines that match the hunk context.

If no such place is found and it is a context difference, then patch does another scan, ignoring the first and last line of context. If that fails, the first two and last two lines of context are ignored and another scan is made. Implementations can search more extensively for installation locations.

If no location can be found, patch appends the hunk to the reject file. The rejected hunk is written in context-difference format regardless of the format of the patch file. If the input was a normal or ed style difference, the reject file can contain differences with zero lines of context. The line numbers on the hunks in the reject file can be different from the line numbers in the patch file because they reflect the approximate locations for the failed hunks in the new file instead of the old one.

If the type of patch is an ed diff, the implementation can accomplish the patching by invoking the ed command.

Examples

diff(1) compares two text files and creates a third text file containing the differences. The output file created by diff contains lines that look like ed(1) commands. You can use the output to make file1 look like file2 by running the patch command.

The following example shows the contents of file1 and file2.

```
# cat file1
bill
tom
pete
joe
mike
# cat file2
patti
bill
tom
pete
joe
mike
glenda
#
```

Then, running diff redirects the output to file3, as shown below.

```
# diff file1 file2 > file3
```

The file3 output from diff is shown below.

```
# cat file3
0a1
> patti
5a7
> glenda
#
```

Now you can use the `patch` command on `file3` to make it look like `file1`.

```
# patch -i file3 file1
  Looks like a normal diff.
done
#
```

The following example shows the contents of `file2`.

```
# cat file1
bill
tom
pete
joe
mike
#
```

Exit Status

0	Successful completion.
1	One or more lines were written to a reject file.
>1	An error occurred.

Attributes

See `attributes`(5) for descriptions of the following attributes:

Attribute Type	Attribute Value
Availability	SUNWcsu

See Also

`ed(1)`, `diff(1)`, `attributes(5)`, `environ(5)`

pathchk — Check Path Names

Synopsis

```
/usr/bin/pathchk [-p] path...
```

Description

The `pathchk` command checks that one or more path names are valid (that is, they could be used to access or create a file without causing syntax errors) and that they are portable (that is, no file-name truncation results). More extensive portability checks are provided by the -p option.

By default, pathchk checks each component of each *path* operand based on the underlying file system. A diagnostic is written for each *path* operand that:

- Is longer than PATH_MAX bytes.
- Contains any component longer than NAME_MAX bytes in its containing directory.
- Contains any component in a directory that is not searchable.
- Contains any character in any component that is not valid in its containing directory.

The format of the diagnostic message is not specified but indicates the error detected and the corresponding path operand.

It is not considered an error if one or more components of a *path* operand do not exist as long as a file that matches the path name specified by the missing components could be created and that such a file does not violate any of the checks specified above.

Options

-p   Instead of performing checks based on the underlying file system, write a diagnostic for each path operand that:

- Is longer than _POSIX_PATH_MAX bytes.
- Contains any component longer than _POSIX_NAME_MAX bytes.
- Contains any character in any component that is not in the portable file-name character set.

Operands

path   A path to be checked.

Usage

See largefile(5) for the description of the behavior of pathchk when encountering files greater than or equal to 2 Gbytes (2**31 bytes).

Examples

The following example verifies that all paths in an imported data interchange archive are legitimate and unambiguous on the current system.

```
pax -f archive | sed -e '/ == .*/s///' | xargs pathchk
  if [$? -eq 0]
    then
      pax -r -f archive
    else
      echo Investigate problems before importing files.
    exit 1
  fi
```

The following example verifies that all files in the current directory hierarchy could be moved to any system conforming to the X/Open specification that also supports the pax(1) command.

```
find . -print | xargs pathchk -p
  if [$? -eq 0]
```

```
        then
          pax -w -f archive .
        else
          echo Portable archive cannot be created.
          exit 1
    fi
```

The following example verifies that a user-supplied path specifies a readable file and that the application can create a file extending the given path without truncation and without overwriting any existing file.

```
case $- in
  *C*)      reset="";;
  *)        reset="set +C"
    set -C;;
esac
test -r "$path" && pathchk "$path.out" &&
  rm "$path.out" > "$path.out"
if [$? -ne 0]; then
  printf "%s: %s not found or %s.out fails \
  creation checks.\n" $0 "$path" "$path"
    $reset      # reset the noclobber option in case a trap
                # on EXIT depends on it
    exit 1
fi
$reset
PROCESSING < "$path" > "$path.out"
```

The following assumptions are made in the previous example.

- PROCESSING represents the code that is used by the application to use $path once it is verified that $path.out works as intended.
- The state of the noclobber option is unknown when this code is invoked and should be set on exit to the state it was in when this code was invoked. (The reset variable is used in this example to restore the initial state.)
- Note the usage of rm "$path.out" > "$path.out".
  - The pathchk command has already verified, at this point, that $path.out is not truncated.
  - With the noclobber option set, the shell verifies that $path.out does not already exist before invoking rm.
  - If the shell succeeded in creating $path.out, rm removes it so that the application can create the file again in the PROCESSING step.
  - If the PROCESSING step expects the file to exist already when it is invoked, replace rm "$path.out" > "$path.out" with > "$path.out", which verifies that the file did not already exist but leaves $path.out in place for use by PROCESSING.

Environment Variables

See environ(5) for descriptions of the following environment variables that affect the execution of pathchk: LC_CTYPE, LC_MESSAGES, and NLSPATH.

Exit Status

0	All path operands passed all of the checks.
>0	An error occurred.

Attributes

See attributes(5) for descriptions of the following attributes:

Attribute Type	Attribute Value
Availability	SUNWcsu

See Also

pax(1), test(1), attributes(5), environ(5), largefile(5)

---

pax — Portable Archive Interchange

Synopsis

```
/usr/bin/pax [-cdnv] [-f archive] [-s replstr]...[pattern...]
/usr/bin/pax -r [-cdiknuv] [-f archive] [-o options]...[-p string]...
    [-s replstr]... [pattern...]
/usr/bin/pax -w [-dituvX@] [-b blocksize] [-a] [-f archive]         New!
    [-o options]... [-s replstr]... [-x format] [v...]
/usr/bin/pax -r -w [-diklntuvX@] [-p string]...[-s replstr]... [file...]   New!
    directory
```

Description

The pax (portable archive exchange) command provides better portability for POSIX-compliant systems than do the tar or cpio commands. Use the pax command to copy files, special files, file systems that require multiple tape volumes, or files that you want to copy to and from POSIX-compliant systems. Disadvantages of the pax command are that it is not aware of file-system boundaries and that the full path-name length cannot exceed 255 characters.

pax reads, writes, and writes lists of the members of archive files and copies directory hierarchies. A variety of archive formats are supported; see the -x format option.

Modes of Operations

The action to be taken depends on the presence of the -r (read) and -w (write) options. The four combinations of -r and -w are referred to as the four modes of operation: list, read, write, and copy modes, which correspond to the four forms shown in the Synopsis.

list	When you specify neither -r nor -w, write to the standard output the names of the members of the archive file read from the standard input with path names matching the specified patterns. If a named file is of type *directory*, write the file hierarchy rooted at that file as well.

read | When you specify -r but not -w, extract the members of the archive file read from the standard input with path names matching the specified patterns. If an extracted file is of type *directory*, extract the file hierarchy rooted at that file as well. Create the extracted files relative to the current file hierarchy. The ownership, access and modification times, and file mode of the restored files are discussed under the -p option.

write | When you specify -w but not -r, write the contents of the file operands to the standard output in an archive format. If you specify no file operands, read a list of files to copy, one per line, from the standard input. A file of type *directory* includes all of the files in the file hierarchy rooted at the file.

copy | When you specify both -r and -w, copy the *file* operands to the destination *directory*.

If you specify no *file* operands, read a list of files to copy, one per line, from the standard input. A file of type *directory* includes all of the files in the file hierarchy rooted at the file.

The effect of the copy is as if the copied files were written to an archive file and then subsequently extracted, except that there may be hard links between the original and the copied files. If the destination *directory* is a subdirectory of one of the files to be copied, the results are unspecified. It is an error if *directory* does not exist, is not writable by the user, or is not a directory.

In read or copy modes, if intermediate directories are needed to extract an archive member, pax performs actions equivalent to the mkdir(2) function, called with the following arguments.

- Use the intermediate directory as the *path* argument.

- Use the octal value of 777 or rwx (read, write, and execute permissions) as the mode argument (see chmod(1)).

If any specified *pattern* or *file* operands are not matched by at least one file or archive member, pax writes a diagnostic message to standard error for each one that did not match and exits with a non-zero exit status.

The supported archive formats are automatically detected on input. The default output archive format is tar(1).

If the selected archive format supports the specification of linked files, it is an error if these files cannot be linked when the archive is extracted. Any of the various names in the archive that represent a file can be used to select the file for extraction.

Options

-r | Read an archive file from standard input.

-w | Write files to the standard output in the specified archive format.

-a   Append files to the end of the archive. This option does not work for some archive devices, such as 1/4-inch streaming tapes and 8mm tapes.

-b *blocksize*

Block the output at a positive, decimal-integer number of bytes per write to the archive file. Devices and archive formats can impose restrictions on blocking. Blocking is automatically determined on input. Portable applications must not specify a blocksize value larger than 32,256. Default blocking when creating archives depends on the archive format. (See the -x option.)

-c   Match all file or archive members except those specified by the *pattern* or *file* operands.

-d   Copy files of type *directory* or archive members of type *directory* being extracted to match only the file or archive member itself and not the file hierarchy rooted at the file.

-f *archive*   Specify the path name of the input or output archive, overriding the default standard input (in list or read modes) or the standard output (write mode).

-i   Interactively rename files or archive members. For each archive member matching a *pattern* operand or file matching a *file* operand, write a prompt to the file /dev/tty. The prompt contains the name of the file or archive member. Then, read a line from /dev/tty. If the line is blank, skip the file or archive member. If the line consists of a single period, process the file or archive member with no modification to its name. Otherwise, replace its name with the contents of the line. Exit immediately with a non-zero exit status if an end-of-file is encountered when reading a response or if /dev/tty cannot be opened for reading and writing.

-k   Prevent the overwriting of existing files.

-l   Link files. In copy mode, make hard links between the *source* and *destination* file hierarchies whenever possible.

-n   Use the first archive member that matches each *pattern* operand. Match no more than one archive member for each *pattern* (although members of type directory still match the file hierarchy rooted at that file).

-o *options*   Reserved for special format-specific options.

-p *string*   Specify one or more file characteristic options (privileges). The string argument must be a string specifying file characteristics to be retained or discarded on extraction. The string consists of the specification characters a, e, m, o, and p. You can concatenate multiple characteristics within the same string and specify multiple -p options. The meaning of the specification characters is as follows.

                a   Do not preserve file access times.

                e   Preserve the user ID, group ID, file-mode bits, access time, and modification time.

m	Do not preserve file-modification times.
o	Preserve the user ID and group ID.
p	Preserve the file-mode bits. Other, implementation-dependent file-mode attributes can be preserved.

In the preceding list, p indicates that an attribute stored in the archive is given to the extracted file, subject to the permissions of the invoking process; otherwise, the attribute is determined as part of the normal file creation action.

If you specify neither the e nor the o character or the user ID and group ID are not preserved for any reason, pax does not set the setuid and setgid bits of the file mode.

If the preservation of any of these items fails for any reason, pax writes a diagnostic message to standard error. Failure to preserve these items affects the final exit status but does not delete the extracted file.

If file-characteristic letters in any of the *string* arguments are duplicated or conflict with each other, the ones given last take precedence. For example, if you specify -p eme, file-modification times are preserved.

-s *replstr* Modify file or archive member names named by *pattern* or *file* operands according to the substitution expression *replstr*, which is based on the ed(1) s (substitution) command, using the regular expression syntax on the regex(5) manual page. The concepts of address and line are meaningless in the context of the pax command and must not be supplied. The format is:

-s / *old*/*new*/ [gp]

where, as in ed, *old* is a basic regular expression and *new* can contain an ampersand (&) or a *n* backreference, where *n* is a digit. The *old* string also is permitted to contain newline characters.

You can use any non-null character as a delimiter (/ shown here). You can specify multiple -s expressions; the expressions are applied in the order specified, terminating with the first successful substitution. The optional trailing g is as defined in the ed command. The optional trailing p writes successful substitutions to standard error. File or archive member names that substitute to the empty string are ignored when archives are read and written.

-t Reset the access times of the archived files to the same values they had before being read by pax.

-u Ignore files that are older (having a less recent file-modification time) than a preexisting file or archive member with the same name.

read mode Extract an archive member with the same name as a file in the file system if the archive member is newer than the file.

write mode Supersede an archive file member with the same name as a file in the file system if the file is newer than the archive member.

copy mode   Replace the file in the destination hierarchy by the file in the source hierarchy or by a link to the file in the source hierarchy if the file in the source hierarchy is newer.

-v   In list mode, produce a verbose table of contents. Otherwise, write archive member path names to standard error.

-x *format*   Specify the output archive format. The pax command recognizes the following formats.

cpio   The extended cpio interchange format; see the IEEE 1003.1(1990) specifications. The default blocksize for this format for character special archive files is 5,120. Implementations support all blocksize values less than or equal to 32,256 that are multiples of 512.

This archive format allows files with UIDs and GIDs up to 262,143 to be stored in the archive. Files with UIDs and GIDs greater than this value are archived with the UID and GID of 60001.

ustar   The extended tar interchange format; see the IEEE 1003.1(1990) specifications. The default blocksize for this format for character special archive files is 10,240. Implementations support all blocksize values less than or equal to 32,256 that are multiples of 512.

Any attempt to append to an archive file in a format different from the existing archive format exits immediately with a non-zero exit status.

This archive format allows files with UIDs and GIDs up to 2,097,151 to be stored in the archive. Files with UIDs and GIDs greater than this value are archived with the UID and GID of 60001.

-X   When traversing the file hierarchy specified by a path name, pax does not descend into directories that have a different device ID (st_dev, see stat(2)).

-@   When traversing the file hierarchy specified by a path name, pax descends into the attribute directory for any file with extended attributes. Extended attributes go into the archive as special files. When you use this option during file extraction, any extended attributes associated with a file being extracted are also extracted. Extended attribute files can be extracted from an archive only as part of normal file extracts. Attempts to explicitly extract attribute records are ignored. New in the Solaris 9 release.

The options that operate on the names of files or archive members (-c, -i, -n, -s, -u, and -v) interact as follows.

- In read mode, the archive members are selected on the basis of user-specified pattern operands as modified by the -c, -n, and -u options. Then, any -s and -i options modify, in that order, the names of the selected files. The -v option writes names resulting from these modifications.
- In write mode, the files are selected on the basis of user-specified path names as modified by the -n and -u options. Then, any -s and -i options, in that order, modify the names of these selected files. The -v option writes names resulting from these modifications.
- If you specify both the -u and -n options, pax does not consider a file selected unless it is newer than the file to which it is compared.

Operands

directory	The destination directory path name for copy mode.
file	A path name of a file to be copied or archived.
pattern	A pattern matching one or more path names of archive members. A pattern must conform to the pattern-matching notation found on the fnmatch(5) manual page. The default, if no pattern is specified, is to select all members in the archive.

Output

Standard Output

In write mode, if you do not specify -f, the standard output is the archive formatted according to cpio or ustar. (See -x *format*.)

In list mode, the table of contents of the selected archive members is written to standard output, using the following format.

"%s\n" *pathname*

If you specify the -v option in list mode, the table of contents of the selected archive members is written to standard output, using the following formats for path names. For path names representing hard links to previous members of the archive:

"%s/\==/\%s\n" ls -1 *listing*, *linkname*

For all other path names:

pathname "%s\n" ls -1 *listing*

where ls -1 *listing* is the format specified by the ls command with the -1 option. When path names are written in this format, it is unspecified what is written for fields for which the underlying archive format does not have the correct information, although the correct number of blank-separated fields is written.

In list mode, standard output is not buffered more than a line at a time.

Standard Error

If you specify -v in read, write, or copy modes, pax writes the path names it processes to the standard error output, using the following format.

"%s\n" *pathname*

These path names are written as soon as processing is begun on the file or archive member and are flushed to standard error. The trailing newline character, which is not buffered, is written when the file has been read or written.

If you specify the -s option and the replacement string has a trailing p, substitutions are written to standard error in the following format.

`"%s/\>>/\%s\n"` *original-pathname, new-pathname*

In all operating modes of pax, optional messages of unspecified format concerning the input archive format and volume number, the number of files, blocks, volumes, and media parts, as well as other diagnostic messages can be written to standard error.

In all formats for both standard output and standard error, it is unspecified how nonprintable characters in path names or link names are written.

Errors

If pax cannot create a file or a link when reading an archive; cannot find a file when writing an archive; or cannot preserve the user ID, group ID, or file mode when you specify the -p option, processing continues, a diagnostic message is written to standard error, and a non-zero exit status is returned. When pax cannot create a link to a file, pax does not, by default, create a second copy of the file.

If the extraction of a file from an archive is prematurely terminated by a signal or error, pax may have only partially extracted the file or (if you did not specify the -n option) may have extracted a file of the same name as that specified but that is not the file you wanted. Additionally, the file modes of extracted directories may have additional bits from the read, write, execute mask set, as well as incorrect modification and access times.

Usage

The -p (privileges) option was invented to reconcile differences between historical tar(1) and cpio(1) implementations. In particular, the two commands use -m in diametrically opposed ways. The -p option also provides a consistent means of extending the ways in which future file attributes can be addressed, such as for enhanced security systems or high-performance files. Although it may seem complex, the following two modes are most commonly used.

-p e   Preserve everything. Superuser can use this option to preserve all aspects of the files as they are recorded in the archive. The e flag is the sum of o, p, and other implementation-dependent attributes.

-p p   Preserve the file-mode bits. Users with regular privileges can use this option to preserve aspects of the file other than the ownership. The file times are preserved by default, but two other flags are offered to disable these and to use the time of extraction.

See largefile(5) for the description of the behavior of pax when encountering files greater than or equal to 2 Gbytes (2**31 bytes).

Examples

The following example copies the contents of the current directory to tape drive 1, medium density (assuming historical System V device naming procedures. The historical BSD device name would be /dev/rmt9).

```
castle% pax -w -f /dev/rmt/1m .
castle%
```

The following example copies the olddir directory hierarchy to newdir.

```
castle% mkdir newdir
castle% pax -rw olddir newdir
castle%
```

The following example reads the archive a.pax with all files rooted in /usr in the archive extracted relative to the current directory.

```
castle% pax -r -s ',^//*usr//*,,' -f a.pax
castle%
```

Environment Variables

See environ(5) for descriptions of the following environment variables that affect the execution of pax: LC_CTYPE, LC_MESSAGES, LC_TIME, and NLSPATH.

LC_COLLATE   Determine the locale for the behavior of ranges, equivalence classes, and multicharacter collating elements used in the pattern-matching expressions for the *pattern* operand, the basic regular expression for the -s option, and the extended regular expression defined for the yesexpr locale keyword in the LC_MESSAGES category.

Exit Status

0   All files were processed successfully.

>0   An error occurred.

Attributes

See attributes(5) for descriptions of the following attributes:

Attribute Type	Attribute Value
Availability	SUNWcsu
Interface Stability	Stable

New!

See Also

New!

chmod(1), cpio(1), ed(1), tar(1), mkdir(2), stat(2), attributes(5), environ(5), fnmatch(5), fsattr(5), largefile(5), regex(5)

pcat — Compress and Expand Files

Synopsis

/usr/bin/pcat *file*...

Description

See pack(1).

pcred — Proc Tools

Synopsis

/usr/proc/bin/pcred *pid*...

Description

See proc(1).

pdp11 — Get Processor Type Truth Value

Synopsis

/usr/bin/pdp11

Description

See machid(1).

perl — Practical Extraction and Report Language   *New!*

Synopsis

```
/bin/perl [-sTuU] [-hv] [-V[:configvar]] [-cw] [-d[:debugger]]
    [-D[number/list]] [-pna] [-Fpattern] [-l[octal]] [-0[octal]] [-Idir]
    [-m[-]module] [-M[-]'module...'] [-P] [-S] [-x[dir]] [-i[extension]]
    [-e 'command'] [--] [programfile] [argument]...
```

Description

The perl command is new in the Solaris 8 Operating Environment. The Perl manual
pages are provided with the programming modules. To view the manual pages for the
Perl modules with the man command, add /usr/perl5/man to the MANPATH environment
variable. See man(1) for more information. Running catman(1M) on the Perl manual
pages is not supported.

For ease of access, the Perl manual has been split up into a number of sections, as
described below.

perl   Perl overview (this section).

perldelta   Perl changes since previous version.

perl5004delta

                Perl changes in version 5.004.

perlfaq   Perl frequently asked questions.

perltoc   Perl documentation table of contents.

`perldata`	Perl data structures.
`perlsyn`	Perl syntax.
`perlop`	Perl operators and precedence.
`perlre`	Perl regular expressions.
`perlrun`	Perl execution and options.
`perlfunc`	Perl built-in functions.
`perlopentut`	Perl `open()` tutorial.
`perlvar`	Perl predefined variables.
`perlsub`	Perl subroutines.
`perlmod`	Perl modules: how they work.
`perlmodlib`	Perl modules: how to write and use.
`perlmodinstall`	
	Perl modules: how to install from CPAN.
`perlform`	Perl formats.
`perllocale`	Perl locale support.
`perlref`	Perl references.
`perlreftut`	Perl references: short introduction.
`perldsc`	Perl data structures: introduction.
`perllol`	Perl data structures: lists of lists.
`perltoot`	Perl OO tutorial.
`perlobj`	Perl objects.
`perltie`	Perl objects hidden behind simple variables.
`perlbot`	Perl OO tricks and examples.
`perlipc`	Perl interprocess communication.
`perlthrtut`	Perl threads tutorial.
`perldebug`	Perl debugging.
`perldiag`	Perl diagnostic messages.
`perlsec`	Perl security.
`perltrap`	Perl traps for the unwary.
`perlport`	Perl portability guide.
`perlstyle`	Perl style guide.
`perlpod`	Perl plain old documentation.
`perlbook`	Perl book information.
`perlembed`	Perl ways to embed Perl in your C or C++ application.
`perlapio`	Perl internal IO abstraction interface.
`perlxs`	Perl XS application programming interface.

`perlxstut`	Perl XS tutorial.
`perlguts`	Perl internal functions for those doing extensions.
`perlcall`	Perl calling conventions from C.
`perlhist`	Perl history records. (If you intend to read these straight through for the first time, the suggested order reduces the number of forward references.)

By default, all of the above manual pages are installed in the `/usr/local/man/` directory.

Extensive additional documentation for Perl modules is available. The default configuration for Perl puts this additional documentation in the `/usr/perl5/lib/man` directory (or else in the `/usr/local/lib/perl5/man` directory). Some of this additional documentation is distributed standard with Perl and you can also find documentation for third-party modules there.

You should be able to view Perl's documentation with the `man(1)` command by including the proper directories in the appropriate startup files or in the `MANPATH` environment variable. To find out where the configuration has installed the manual pages, type **perl -V:man.dir**.

If the directories have a common stem, such as `/usr/local/man/man1` and `/usr/local/man/man3`, you need only add that stem (`/usr/local/man`) to your `man(1)` configuration files or your `MANPATH` environment variable. If they do not share a stem, you need to add both stems.

If that doesn't work for some reason, you can still use the supplied `perldoc` script to view module information. You might also look into getting a replacement `man` command.

If something strange has gone wrong with your program and you're not sure where you should look for help, first try the `-w` option. It often points out exactly where the trouble is.

Perl is a language optimized for scanning arbitrary text files, extracting information from those text files, and printing reports based on that information. It's also a good language for many system management tasks. The language is intended to be practical (easy to use, efficient, complete) instead of beautiful (tiny, elegant, minimal).

Perl combines (in the Perl author's opinion, anyway) some of the best features of C, `sed`, `awk`, and `sh`, so people familiar with those languages should have little difficulty with it. (Language historians note that Perl also has some vestiges of `csh`, Pascal, and even BASIC-PLUS.) Expression syntax corresponds quite closely to C expression syntax. Unlike most UNIX commands, Perl does not arbitrarily limit the size of your data—if you've got the memory, Perl can slurp in your whole file as a single string. Recursion is of unlimited depth. And the tables used by hashes (sometimes called "associative arrays") grow as necessary to prevent degraded performance. Perl can use sophisticated pattern-matching techniques to scan large amounts of data very quickly. Although optimized for scanning text, Perl can also deal with binary data and can make `dbm` files look like hashes. Setuid Perl scripts are safer than C programs through a dataflow tracing mechanism that prevents many security holes.

Suppose you have a problem that you would ordinarily solve with `sed`, `awk`, or `sh`, but it exceeds their capabilities or must run a little faster, and you don't want to write a C solution, then Perl may be for you. Translators are also available that you can use to turn your `sed` and `awk` scripts into Perl scripts.

Perl Version 5 is nearly a complete rewrite, and provides the following additional benefits.

- Many usability enhancements.

  You can now write much more readable Perl code (even within regular expressions). You can replace formerly cryptic variable names with mnemonic identifiers. Error messages are more informative, and the optional warnings catch many of the mistakes a novice might make. Whenever you observe mysterious behavior, try the -w option. Whenever the behavior isn't mysterious, try -w anyway.

- Simplified grammar.

  The new yacc grammar is half the size of the old one. Many of the arbitrary grammar rules have been regularized. The number of reserved words has been cut by two-thirds. Despite this, nearly all old Perl scripts continue to work unchanged.

- Lexical scoping.

  You can now declare Perl variables within a lexical scope, like auto variables in C. Not only is this lexical scoping more efficient, it contributes to better privacy for programming in the large. Anonymous subroutines exhibit deep binding of lexical variables (closures).

- Arbitrarily nested data structures.

  Any scalar value, including any array element, can now contain a reference to any other variable or subroutine. You can easily create anonymous variables and subroutines. Perl manages your reference counts for you.

- Modularity and reusability.

  The Perl library is now defined in terms of modules that can be easily shared among various packages. A package can choose to import all or a portion of a module's published interface. Pragmas (that is, compiler directives) are defined and used by the same mechanism.

- Object-oriented programming.

  A package can function as a class. Dynamic multiple inheritance and virtual methods are supported in a straightforward manner and with very little new syntax. File handles can now be treated as objects.

- Embeddable and extensible.

  You can now easily embed Perl in your C or C++ application, and Perl can either call or be called by your routines through a documented interface. The XS preprocessor is provided to make it easy to glue your C or C++ routines into Perl. Dynamic loading of modules is supported, and Perl itself can be made into a dynamic library.

- POSIX compliant.

  The major new POSIX module provides access to all available POSIX routines and definitions, through object classes where appropriate.

- Package constructors and destructors.

  The new BEGIN and END blocks provide a way to capture control as a package is being compiled and after the program exits. As a degenerate case they work just like awk's BEGIN and END when you use the -p or -n options.

- Multiple simultaneous DBM implementations.

  A Perl program can now access DBM, NDBM, SDBM, GDBM, and Berkeley DB files from the same script simultaneously. In fact, the old dbmopen interface has been generalized to allow any variable to be tied to an object class that defines its access methods.

- Subroutine definitions can now be autoloaded.

  In fact, the AUTOLOAD mechanism also enables you to define any arbitrary semantics for undefined subroutine calls. It's not just for autoloading.

- Regular expression enhancements.

  You can now specify nongreedy quantifiers. You can now do grouping without creating a back reference. You can now write regular expressions with embedded whitespace and comments for readability. A consistent extensibility mechanism has been added that is upwardly compatible with all old regular expressions.
- Innumerable unbundled modules.

  The Comprehensive Perl Archive Network described in the `perlmodlib` manual page contains hundreds of plug-and-play modules full of reusable code. See `http://www.perl.com/CPAN` for a site near you.
- Compilability.

  While not yet in full production mode, a working Perl-to-C compiler does exist. It can generate portable bytecode, simple C, or optimized C code.

Diagnostics

The `-w` option produces some lovely diagnostics.

See the `-w` manual page for explanations of all Perl diagnostics. The use diagnostics pragma automatically turns Perl's normally terse warnings and errors into these longer forms.

Compilation errors tell you the line number of the error, with an indication of the next token or token type that was to be examined. (In the case of a script passed to Perl by `-e` options, each `-e` is counted as one line.)

Setuid scripts have additional constraints that can produce error messages such as `Insecure dependency`. See the `perlsec` manual pages.

Did we mention that you should definitely consider using the `-w` option?

Notes

The Perl motto is "There's more than one way to do it." Divining how many more is left as an exercise to the reader.

The three principal virtues of a programmer are Laziness, Impatience, and Hubris. See the Camel Book for why.

Bugs

The `-w` option is not mandatory.

Perl is at the mercy of your machine's definitions of various operations such as type casting, `atof()`, and floating-point output with `sprintf()`.

If your standard input/output requires a seek or EOF between reads and writes on a particular stream, so does Perl. (This doesn't apply to `sysread()` and `syswrite()`.)

While none of the built-in data types have any arbitrary size limits (apart from memory size), a few arbitrary limits still remain: a given variable name cannot be longer than 251 characters. Line numbers displayed by diagnostics are internally stored as short integers, so they are limited to a maximum of 65,535 (higher numbers usually are affected by wrap around).

You can mail your bug reports (be sure to include full configuration information as output by the `myconfig` program in the Perl source tree or by `perl -V`) to <perlbug@perl.com>. If you've succeeded in compiling Perl, you can use the `perlbug` script in the `utils/` subdirectory to help mail in a bug report.

Perl actually stands for Pathologically Eclectic Rubbish Lister, but don't tell anyone I said that.

Availability

Perl is available for the vast majority of operating system platforms, including most UNIX-like platforms. The following situation is as of February 1999 and Perl 5.005_03.

The following platforms can build Perl from the standard source code distribution available at `http://www.perl.com/CPAN/src/index.html`.

- A/UX
- AIX
- BeOS
- BSD/OS
- DG/UX
- DomainOS
- DOS DJGPP
- DYNIX/ptx
- FreeBSD
- HP-UX
- Hurd
- IRIX
- Linux
- MachTen
- MPE/iX
- NetBSD
- NeXTSTEP
- NT
- OpenBSD
- OPENSTEP
- OS/2
- OS390 (formerly known as MVS)
- PowerMAX
- QNX
- SCO ODT/OSR
- Solaris
- SunOS
- SVR4
- Tru64 UNIX (formerly known as Digital UNIX and, before that, DEC OSF/1)
- Ultrix
- UNICOS (in DOS mode you can use either the DOS or OS/2 ports)
- VMS
- VOS
- Windows
- Windows 3.1
- Windows 95 (compilers; Borland, Cygwin32, Mingw32 EGCS/GCC, VC++)
- Windows 98

The following platforms have been known to build Perl from the source but for the Perl release 5.005_03 we haven't been able to verify them, either because the hardware/software platforms are rather rare or because we don't have an active champion on these platforms, or both.

- 3b1
- AmigaOS
- ConvexOS
- CX/UX
- DC/OSx
- DDE SMES
- DOS EMX
- DYNIX
- EP/IX
- Esix
- FPS
- GENIX
- Greenhills
- ISC
- MachTen 68k
- MiNT
- MPC
- NEWS-OS
- Opus
- Plan 9
- PowerUX
- RISC/OS
- Stellar
- SVR2
- TIl500
- TitanOS
- UNICOS/mk
- Unisys Dynix
- Unixware

The following platforms are planned to be supported in the standard source code distribution of the Perl release 5.006 but are not supported in the Perl release 5.005_03.

- BS2000
- NetWare
- Rhapsody
- VM/ESA

The following platforms have their own source code distributions and binaries available at http://www.perl.com/CPAN/ports/index.html.

- AS/400, Perl release 5.003
- MacOS, Perl release 5.004
- NetWare, Perl release 5.003_07

- Tandem Guardian, Perl release 5.004

The following platforms have only binaries available from http://www.perl.com/CPAN/ports/index.html.

- Acorn RISCOS, Perl release 5.005_02
- AOS, Perl release 5.002
- LynxOS, Perl release 5.004_02

Environment

See the perlrun manual page.

Author

Larry Wall <larry@wall.org>, with the help of oodles of other folks.

If your Perl success stories and testimonials can be of help to others who want to advocate the use of Perl in their applications, or if you simply want to express your gratitude to Larry and the Perl developers, please write to <perl-thanks@perl.org>.

Files

@INC   Locations of Perl libraries.

Attributes

See attributes(5) for descriptions of the following attributes:

Attribute Type	Attribute Value
Availability	SUNWpl5u
	SUNWpl5p
	SUNWpl5m

See Also

a2p, awk to perl translators2p, sed to perl translator

New! **pfcsh** — Execute a Command in a Profile

Synopsis

/bin/pfcsh [*options*] *filename*...

Description

New in the Solaris 8 release. See pfexec(1).

pfexec, pfsh, pfcsh, pfksh — Execute a Command in a Profile New!

Synopsis

```
/usr/bin/pfexec command
/usr/bin/pfsh [options] [argument...]
/usr/bin/pfcsh [options] [argument...]
/usr/bin/pfksh [options] [argument...]
```

Description

The pfexec program, new in the Solaris 8 Operating Environment, executes commands with the attributes specified by the user's profiles in the exec_attr(4) database. It is invoked by the profile shells, pfsh, pfcsh, and pfksh, which are linked to the Bourne shell, C shell, and Korn shell.

Profiles are searched in the order specified in the user's entry in the user_attr(4) database. If the same command appears in more than one profile, the profile shell uses the first matching entry.

Usage

pfexec is used to execute commands with predefined process attributes, such as specific user or group IDs.

Refer to the sh(1), csh(1), and ksh(1) manual pages for complete usage descriptions of the profile shells.

Exit Status

0	Successful completion.
1	An error occurred.

Attributes

See attributes(5) for descriptions of the following attributes.

Attribute Type	Attribute Value
Availability	SUNWcsu

See Also

csh(1), ksh(1), profiles(1), sh(1), exec_attr(4), prof_attr(4), user_attr(4), attributes(5)

pfiles, pflags — Proc Tools

Synopsis
```
/usr/proc/bin/pfiles pid...
/usr/proc/bin/pflags pid...
```

Description
See proc(1).

New! pfksh — Execute a Command in a Profile

Synopsis
```
/bin/pfksh [options] filename...
```

Description
New in the Solaris 8 release. See pfexec(1).

New! pfsh — Execute a Command in a Profile

Synopsis
```
/bin/pfsh [options] filename...
```

Description
New in the Solaris 8 release. See pfexec(1).

pg — File Perusal Filter

Synopsis
```
/usr/bin/pg [-number] [-p string] [-cefnrs] [+linenumber] [+/pattern/]
   [filename...]
```

Description
The pg command is a filter that enables you to examine files one screen at a time. If you press Return, another page is displayed; other possibilities are listed below.

This command is different from previous paginators in that it enables you to back up and review something that has already moved off the screen. The method for backing up is explained below.

To determine terminal attributes, pg scans the terminfo(4) database for the terminal type specified by the environment variable TERM. If TERM is not defined, the terminal type dumb is assumed.

Notes

While waiting for terminal input, pg responds to BREAK, Control-C, and Control-\ by terminating execution. Between prompts, however, these signals interrupt the current task and display the prompt. Use these key combinations with caution when input is being read from a pipe because an interrupt is likely to terminate the other commands in the pipeline.

If terminal Tabs are not set every eight positions, undesirable results may occur.

When pg is used as a filter with another command that changes the terminal I/O options, terminal settings may not be restored correctly.

Options

-number   Specify the size (in lines) of the window that pg is to use instead of the default. (On a terminal containing 24 lines, the default window size is 23).

+linenumber

                 Start at *linenumber*.

+/pattern/   Start at the first line containing the regular expression *pattern*.

-c   Home the cursor and clear the screen before displaying each page. This option is ignored if clear_screen is not defined for this terminal type in the terminfo(4) database.

-e   Do not pause at the end of each file.

-f   Inhibit split lines. Without this option, pg splits lines longer than the screen width but some sequences of characters in the text being displayed (for instance, escape sequences for underlining) generate undesirable results.

-n   Normally, commands must be terminated by a newline character. This option automatically ends the command as soon as a command letter is entered.

-p *string*   Use *string* as the prompt. If the prompt string contains a %d, the first occurrence of %d in the prompt is replaced by the current page number when the prompt is issued. The default prompt string is a colon (:).

-r   Disallow the shell escape. Print an error message but do not exit.

-s   Print all messages and prompts in the standard output mode (usually inverse video).

Operands

filename   A path name of a text file to be displayed. If no file name is given or if it is -, read the standard input.

Usage

Commands

When pg pauses, you can respond with three types of commands:

- Those enabling further perusal.
- Those that search.
- Those that modify the perusal environment.

Commands that enable further perusal normally take a preceding address, which is an optionally signed number indicating the point from which further text should be displayed. This address is interpreted in either pages or lines, depending on the command. A signed address specifies a point relative to the current page or line, and an unsigned address specifies an address relative to the beginning of the file. Each command has a default address that is used if none is provided.

The perusal commands and their defaults are as follows.

(+1)newline | blank

> Display one page. The address is specified in pages.

(+1) l
> With a relative address, scroll the screen forward or backward the number of lines specified. With an absolute address, print a screen beginning at the specified line.

(+1) d
^D
> Scroll a half-screen forward or backward.

*i*f
> Skip *i* screens of text.

*i*z
> Same as newline except that *i*, if present, becomes the new default number of lines per screen.

The following perusal commands take no address.

. |^L
> Redisplay the current page of text.

$
> Display the last screen in the file. Use with caution when the input is a pipe.

The following commands are available for searching for text patterns in the text. The regular expressions are described on the regex(5) manual page. They must always be terminated by a newline even if you specify the −n option.

i/*pattern*/
> Search forward for the *i*-th (default *i*=1) occurrence of *pattern*. Begin searching immediately after the current page and continue to the end of the current file without wrap around.

i^*pattern*^
i?*pattern*?
> Search backward for the *i*-th (default *i*=1) occurrence of *pattern*. Begin searching immediately before the current page and continue to the beginning of the current file without wrap around. The ^ notation is useful for Adds 100 terminals that do not properly handle the ?.

Note — You can omit the final /, ^, or ? from the searching commands.

After searching, pg normally displays the line found at the top of the screen. You can modify this behavior by appending m or b to the search command to leave the line found in the middle or at the bottom of the window from now on. Use the t suffix to restore the original situation.

You can modify the perusal environment with the following commands.

*i*n   Begin perusing the *i*-th next file in the command line. The *i* is an unsigned number; default is 1.

*i*p   Begin perusing the *i*-th previous file in the command line. *i* is an unsigned number; default is 1.

*i*w   Display another window of text. If *i* is present, set the window size to *i*.

s *filename*   Save the input in the named file. Save only the current file being perused. The white space between the s and *filename* is optional. You must always terminate this command with a newline, even if you specify the -n option.

h   Help by displaying an abbreviated summary of available commands.

q or Q   Quit.

! *command*   Pass *command* to the shell specified in the SHELL environment variable. If this shell is not available, use the default shell. You must always terminate this command with a newline, even if you specify the -n option.

You can use the quit key (normally Control-\) or the interrupt (BREAK) key at any time to stop sending output and display the prompt. You can then enter one of the above commands in the normal manner. Unfortunately, some output is lost when this is done because any characters waiting in the terminal's output queue are flushed when the quit signal occurs.

If the standard output is not a terminal, then pg acts just like cat(1), except that a header is printed before each file (if there is more than one).

Large File Behavior

See largefile(5) for the description of the behavior of pg when encountering files greater than or equal to 2 Gbytes (2**31 bytes).

Examples

The following example uses pg to read the system news.

```
castle% news | pg -p "(Page %d):"
```

Environment Variables

See environ(5) for descriptions of the following environment variables that affect the execution of pg: LC_CTYPE, LC_MESSAGES, and NLSPATH.

The following environment variables also affect the execution of pg.

COLUMNS   Determine the horizontal screen size. If unset or null, use the value of TERM, the window size, baud rate, or some combination of these, to indicate the terminal type for the screen size calculation.

LINES   Determine the number of lines to be displayed on the screen. If unset or null, use the value of TERM, the window size, baud rate, or some combination of these, to indicate the terminal type for the screen size calculation.

SHELL   Determine the name of the command interpreter executed for a
! *command*.

TERM   Determine terminal attributes. Optionally, try to search a
system-dependent database, keyed on the value of the TERM
environment variable. If no information is available, assume a terminal
incapable of cursor-addressable movement.

Exit Status

0   Successful completion.

>0   An error occurred.

Files

/tmp/pg*   Temporary file when input is from a pipe.

/usr/share/lib/terminfo/*?*/*

Terminal information database.

Attributes

See attributes(5) for descriptions of the following attributes:

Attribute Type	Attribute Value
Availability	SUNWcsu
CSI	Enabled

See Also

cat(1), grep(1), more(1), terminfo(4), attributes(5), environ(5),
largefile(5), regex(5)

---

pgrep, pkill — Find or Signal Processes

Synopsis

New!
```
/usr/bin/pgrep [-flnvx] [-d delim] [-P ppidlist] [-g pgrplist]
    [-s sidlist] [-u euidlist] [-U uidlist] [-G gidlist] [-J projidlist]
    [-t termlist] [-T taskidlist] [pattern]
```

New!
```
/usr/bin/pkill [-signal] [-fnvx] [-P ppidlist] [-g pgrplist]
    [-s sidlist] [-u euidlist] [-U uidlist] [-G gidlist] [-J projidlist]
    [-t termlist] [-T taskidlist] [pattern]
```

Description

The pgrep command examines the active processes on the system and reports the
process IDs of the processes whose attributes match the criteria specified on the
command line. Each process ID is printed as a decimal value and is separated from the
next ID by a delimiter string, which is a newline by default. For each attribute option,
you can specify a comma-separated set of possible values on the command line. For

example, the following command matches processes whose real group ID is other or daemon.

```
castle% pgrep -G other,daemon
120
castle%
```

If you specify multiple criteria options, pgrep matches processes whose attributes match the logical AND of the criteria options. For example, the following command matches processes whose attributes are (real group ID is other OR daemon) AND (real user ID is root OR daemon).

```
castle% pgrep -G other,daemon -U root,daemon
120
castle%
```

pkill functions identically to pgrep except that each matching process is signaled as if by kill(1) instead of displaying its process ID. You can specify a signal name or number as the first command-line option to pkill.

Both commands match the ERE pattern argument against either the pr_fname or pr_psargs fields of the /proc/*nnnnn*/psinfo files. The lengths of these strings are limited according to definitions in sys/procfs.h. Patterns that can match strings longer than the current limits may fail to match the intended set of processes.

If the pattern argument contains ERE metacharacters that are also shell metacharacters, you may need to enclose the pattern with appropriate shell quotes.

Defunct processes are never matched by either pgrep or pkill.

The current pgrep or pkill process never considers itself a potential match.

Options

-d *delim* Specify the output delimiter to be printed between each matching process ID. If you specify no -d option, the default is a newline character. The -d option is valid only when specified as an option to pgrep.

-f Match the regular expression pattern against the full process argument string (obtained from the pr_psargs field of the /proc/*nnnnn*/psinfo file). If you specify no -f option, match the expression only against the name of the executable file (obtained from the pr_fname field of the /proc/*nnnnn*/psinfo file).

-g *pgrplist*

Match only processes whose process group ID is in the given list. If you include group 0 in the list, interpret it as the process group ID of the pgrep or pkill process.

-G *gidlist* Match only processes whose real group ID is in the given list. You can specify each group ID as either a group name or a numerical group ID.

-J *projidlist*

Match only processes whose project ID is in the given list. You can specify each project ID as either a project name or a numerical project ID. New in the Solaris 8 release.

-l
Print the process name along with the process ID of each matching process. The process name is obtained from the pr_psargs or pr_fname field, depending on whether you specified the -f option. The -l option is valid only when specified as an option to pgrep.

-n
Match only the newest (most recently created) process that meets all other specified matching criteria.

-P *ppidlist*
Match only processes whose parent process ID is in the given list.

-s *sidlist*
Match only processes whose process session ID is in the given list. If you include ID 0 in the list, interpret it as the session ID of the pgrep or pkill process.

-t *termlist*
Match only processes that are associated with a terminal in the given list. Each terminal is specified as the suffix following /dev/ of the terminal's device path name in /dev, for example, term/a or pts/0.

New! -T *taskidlist*
Match only processes whose task ID is in the given list. If you include ID 0 in the list, it is interpreted as the task ID of the pgrep or pkill process. New in the Solaris 8 release.

-u *euidlist*
Match only processes whose effective user ID is in the given list. You can specify each user ID either as a login name or as a numerical user ID.

-U *uidlist*
Match only processes whose real user ID is in the given list. You can specify each user ID either as a login name or as a numerical user ID.

-v
Reverse the sense of the matching. Match all processes except those that meet the specified matching criteria.

-x
Consider only processes to be matching whose argument string or executable file name exactly matches the specified pattern. The pattern match is considered to be exact when all characters in the process argument string or executable file name match the pattern.

-*signal*
Specify the signal to send to each matched process. If no signal is specified, send SIGTERM by default. The value of *signal* can be one of the symbolic names defined in signal(5) without the SIG prefix, or the corresponding signal number as a decimal value. The -*signal* option is valid only when specified as the first option to pkill.

Operands

pattern
Specify an Extended Regular Expression (ERE) pattern to match against either the executable file name or full process argument string. See regex(5) for a complete description of the ERE syntax.

Examples

The following example obtains the process ID of sendmail.

```
castle% pgrep -x -u root sendmail
336
castle%
```

The following example terminates the most recently created xterm.

```
castle% pkill -n xterm
castle%
```

Exit Status

0	One or more processes were matched.
1	No processes were matched.
2	Invalid command-line options were specified.
3	A fatal error occurred.

Files

/proc/*nnnnn*/psinfo

Process information files.

Attributes

See attributes(5) for descriptions of the following attributes:

Attribute Type	**Attribute Value**
Availability	SUNWcsu

See Also

kill(1), proc(1), ps(1), truss(1), kill(2), signal(3HEAD), proc(4), attributes(5), regex(5)

pkginfo — Display Software Package Information

Synopsis

```
/usr/bin/pkginfo [-q | -x | -l] [-p | -i] [-r] [-a arch] [-v version]
    [-c category ...] [pkginst...]
/usr/bin/pkginfo [-d device] [-R root-path] [-q | -x | -l] [-a arch]
    [-v version] [-c category...] [pkginst...]
```

Description

Use the pkginfo command to check which packages are installed on a system (with the first synopsis). By default, pkginfo displays information about currently installed packages. You can also use the pkginfo command to display packages that are on mounted distribution media or that reside in a particular directory (with the second synopsis).

Without options, pkginfo lists the primary category, package instance, and the names of all completely installed and partially installed packages. It displays one line for each package selected.

Options

Note — The -p and -i options are meaningless if used in conjunction with the -d option. The options -q, -x, and -l are mutually exclusive.

-a *arch*	Specify the architecture of the package as *arch*.
-c *category*	
	Display packages that match *category*. Categories are defined with the CATEGORY parameter in the pkginfo(4) file. If you supply more than one *category*, the package needs to match only one category in the list. The match is not case specific.
-d *device*	Define a device, *device*, on which the software resides. *device* can be an absolute directory path name or the identifiers for tape, diskette, removable disk, and so forth. You can use the special token spool to indicate the default installation spool directory (/var/spool/pkg).
-i	Display information only for fully installed packages.
-l	Specify long format, which includes all available information about the designated package(s).
-p	Display information only for partially installed packages.
-q	Do not list any information. Use from a program to check whether or not a package has been installed.
-r	List the installation base for relocatable packages.
-R *root-path*	
	Define the full path name of a directory to use as the *root-path*. All files, including package system information files, are relocated to a directory tree starting in the specified *root-path*.
-v *version*	Specify the version of the package as *version*. You define the version with the VERSION parameter in the pkginfo(4) file. You can request all compatible versions by preceding the version name with a tilde (~). Replace multiple white spaces with a single white space during version comparison.
-x	Designate an extracted listing of package information. The listing contains the package abbreviation, package name, package architecture (if available), and package version (if available).

Operands

pkginst	Specify a package designation by its instance. An instance can be the package abbreviation or a specific instance (for example, inst.1 or inst.2). You can request all instances of a package with inst.*.

The asterisk character (*) is a special character to some shells and may need to be escaped. In the C shell, * must be surrounded by single quotes (') or preceded by a backslash (\).

Examples

The following example shows the first few packages from a system.

```
castle% pkginfo
application HPNP         JetAdmin for Unix
ALE         SUNW5xmft   Chinese/Taiwan BIG5 X Windows Platform minimum
     required Fonts Package
system      SUNWab2m    Solaris Documentation Server Lookup
system      SUNWaccr    System Accounting, (Root)
system      SUNWaccu    System Accounting, (Usr)
system      SUNWadmap   System administration applications
system      SUNWadmc    System administration core libraries
system      SUNWadmfw   System & Network Administration Framework
system      SUNWadmr    System & Network Administration Root
system      SUNWapppr   PPP/IP Asynchronous PPP daemon configuration files
system      SUNWapppu   PPP/IP Asynchronous PPP daemon and PPP login service
system      SUNWarc     Archive Libraries
...
```

Exit Status

0	Successful completion.
>0	An error occurred.

Files

/var/spool/pkg

Default installation spool directory.

Attributes

See attributes(5) for descriptions of the following attributes:

Attribute Type	Attribute Value
Availability	SUNWcsu

See Also

pkgtrans(1), pkgadd(1M), pkgask(1M), pkgchk(1M), pkgrm(1M), pkginfo(4), attributes(5)

Application Packaging Developer's Guide

pkgmk — Produce an Installable Package

Synopsis

```
/usr/bin/pkgmk [-o] [-a arch] [-b base-src-dir] [-d device]
    [-f prototype] [-l limit] [-p pstamp] [-r root-path] [-v version]
    [variable=value ...] [pkginst]
```

Description

Use the pkgmk command to produce an installable package to be used as input to the pkgadd(1M) command. The package contents are in directory structure format.

The command uses the package prototype(4) file as input and creates a pkgmap(4) file. The contents for each entry in the prototype file are copied to the appropriate output location. Information concerning the contents (checksum, file size, modification date) is computed and stored in the pkgmap file along with attribute information specified in the prototype file.

You can provide architecture information on the command line with the -a option or in the prototype(4) file. If you supply no architecture information, pkgmk uses the output of uname -m.

You can provide version information on the command line with the -v option or in the pkginfo(4) file. If you supply no version information, a default based on the current date is provided.

Command-line definitions for both architecture and version override the prototype(4) definitions.

New!

pkgmk searches for the files listed in the prototype(4) file as described in the following conditions.

Note — If a prototype file contains the explicit location of the file to include in the package, then the following search explanations do not apply.

---

1. If you specify neither -b nor -r, the file-name component of each file path listed in the prototype(4) is expected to be found in the same directory as the prototype(4) file.

2. If you specify -b as a relative path (without a leading /), then *base_src_dir* is prepended to the relative file paths from the prototype(4) file. The resulting path is searched for in the *root_path* directories. If you do not specify a *root_path*, the default is /.

3. If you specify -b as an absolute path (with a leading /), then *base_src_dir* is prepended to the relative paths from the prototype(4) file and the result is the location of the file. *root_path* is not searched.

4. If you specify -r, then full file paths are used from the prototype(4) file. Relative paths have *base_src_dir* prepended. If you do not specify *base_src_dir*, the default is " ". The resulting path is searched for in each directory of the *root_path*.

If you create your prototype file with pkgproto *a/relative/path* or pkgproto *a/relative/path=install/path*, use the -r *root_path* option to specify the location of *a/relative/path* so that pkgmk can correctly locate your source files.

Options

-a *arch*   Override the architecture information provided in the pkginfo(4) file with *arch*.

-b *base_src_dir*

Prepend the indicated *base-src-dir* to locate relocatable objects on the source machine.

Use this option to search for all objects in the prototype file. pkgmk expects to find the objects in /*base_src_dir* or to locate the objects with the -b and -r options. New in the Solaris 9 release.

-d *device*   Create the package on *device*. *device* can be an absolute directory path name or the identifiers for a diskette or removable disk (for example, /dev/diskette). The default device is the installation spool directory (/var/spool/pkg).

-f *prototype*

Use the file *prototype* as input to the command. The default prototype file name is Prototype or prototype.

-l *limit*   Specify the maximum size in 512-byte blocks of the output device as *limit*. By default, if the output file is a directory or a mountable device, pkgmk uses the df(1M) command to dynamically calculate the amount of available space on the output device. This option is useful in conjunction with pkgtrans(1) to create a package with a datastream format.

-o   Overwrite the same instance of the package if it already exists.

-p *pstamp*   Override the production stamp definition in the pkginfo(4) file with *pstamp*.

-r *root-path*

Ignore destination paths in the prototype(4) file. Instead, use the indicated *root-path* with the source path name appended to locate objects on the source machine.

If you specify this option, pkgmk looks for the full destination path in each of the specified directories. If you specify neither -b nor -r, pkgmk looks for the leaf file name in the current directory. New in the Solaris 9 release.

-v *version*   Override the version information provided in the pkginfo(4) file with *version*.

variable=value

Place the indicated variable in the packaging environment. (See prototype(4) for definitions of variable specifications.)

Operands

    pkginst   A package designation by its instance. An instance can be the package abbreviation or a specific instance (for example, `inst.1` or `inst.2`). You can request all instances of a package with `inst.*`.

        The asterisk character (`*`) is a special character to some shells and may need to be escaped. In the C shell, you must surround `*` with single quotes (`'`) or precede it with a backslash (`\`).

Exit Status

    0   Successful completion.

    >0   An error occurred.

Attributes

See `attributes`(5) for descriptions of the following attributes:

Attribute Type	Attribute Value
Availability	SUNWcsu

See Also

    `pkgparam(1)`, `pkgproto(1)`, `pkgtrans(1)`, `uname(1)`, `df(1M)`, `pkgadd(1M)`, `pkginfo(4)`, `pkgmap(4)`, `prototype(4)`, `attributes(5)`
        Application Packaging Developer's Guide

pkgparam — Display Package Parameter Values

Synopsis

    `/usr/bin/pkgparam [-v] [-d device] [-R root-path] pkginst [param...]`
    `/usr/bin/pkgparam -f filename [-v] [param...]`

Description

Use the `pkgparam` command to display the value associated with the parameter or parameters requested on the command line. The values are located in either the `pkginfo`(4) file for *pkginst* or from the specific file named with the `-f` option.

    One parameter value is shown per line. Only the value of a parameter is given unless you use the `-v` option. With the `-v` option, the output of the command is in the following format.

```
parameter1='value1'
parameter2='value2'
parameter3='value3'
```

    The following example shows the output of the `-v` option for the SUNWdthj package.

```
castle% pkgparam -v SUNWdthj
CLASSES='base docs runtime'
BASEDIR='/usr'
```

```
TZ='Australia/West'
PATH='/sbin:/usr/sbin:/usr/bin:/usr/sadm/install/bin'
OAMBASE='/usr/sadm/sysadm'
ARCH='sparc'
PKG='SUNWdthj'
NAME='HotJava Browser for Solaris'
VERSION='1.0.1,REV=1998.02.13'
PRODNAME='HotJava'
PRODVERS='1.0.1'
SUNW_PKGTYPE='usr'
MAXINST='1000'
CATEGORY='system'
DESC='HotJava Browser for Solaris'
VENDOR='Sun Microsystems, Inc.'
HOTLINE='Please contact your local service provider'
EMAIL=''
HOTJAVA='dt/appconfig/hotjava'
PSTAMP='pavoni980213183227'
PKGINST='SUNWdthj'
PKGSAV='/var/sadm/pkg/SUNWdthj/save'
INSTDATE='Feb 15 1999 09:33'
castle%
```

If you specify no parameters on the command line, values for all parameters associated with the package are shown.

Options

-d *device*   Specify the device on which a *pkginst* is stored. *device* can be a directory path name or the identifiers for tape, diskette, or removable disk (for example, /var/tmp, /dev/diskette, and /dev/dsk/c1d0s0). You can use the special token spool to represent the default installation spool directory (/var/spool/pkg).

-f *filename*

    Read *filename* for parameter values. *filename* should be in the same format as a pkginfo(4) file. For example, you might create such a file during package development and use it for testing.

-R *root-path*

    Define the full path name of a subdirectory to use as the *root-path*. Relocate all files, including package system information files, to a directory tree starting in the specified *root-path*.

-v   Display the name of *param* and its value.

Operands

pkginst   Define a specific package instance for which to display parameter values.

param   Define a specific parameter whose value should be displayed.

Examples

The following example lists the information for the SUNWdthj package.

```
castle% pkgparam SUNWdthj
base docs runtime
/usr
Australia/West
/sbin:/usr/sbin:/usr/bin:/usr/sadm/install/bin
/usr/sadm/sysadm
sparc
SUNWdthj
HotJava Browser for Solaris
1.0.1,REV=1998.02.13
HotJava
1.0.1
usr
1000
system
HotJava Browser for Solaris
Sun Microsystems, Inc.
Please contact your local service provider

dt/appconfig/hotjava
pavoni980213183227
SUNWdthj
/var/sadm/pkg/SUNWdthj/save
Mar 03 1999 17:51
castle%
```

Exit Status

0	Successful completion.
>0	An error occurred.

If parameter information is not available for the indicated package, the command exits with a non-zero status.

Attributes

See attributes(5) for descriptions of the following attributes:

Attribute Type	Attribute Value
Availability	SUNWcsu

See Also

pkgmk(1), pkgproto(1), pkgtrans(1), pkginfo(4), attributes(5)
Application Packaging Developer's Guide

pkgproto — Generate Prototype File Entries for Input to pkgmk Command

Synopsis

```
/usr/bin/pkgproto [-i] [-c class] [path1]
/usr/bin/pkgproto [-i] [-c class] [path1=path2...]
```

Description

The pkgproto command scans the indicated paths and generates prototype(4) file entries that can be used as input to the pkgmk(1) command.

If you specify no paths on the command line, standard input is assumed to be a list of paths. If the path name listed on the command line is a directory, the contents of the directory are searched. However, if input is read from the standard input, a directory specified as a path name is not searched.

By default, pkgproto creates symbolic link entries for any symbolic link encountered (ftype=s). When you use the -i option, pkgproto creates a file entry for symbolic links (ftype=f). You would have to edit the prototype(4) file to assign such file types as v (volatile), e (editable), or x (exclusive directory). pkgproto detects linked files. If multiple files are linked together, the first path encountered is considered the source of the link.

By default, pkgproto prints prototype entries to the standard output. However, you should save the output in a file (named Prototype or prototype) to be used as input to the pkgmk(1) command.

Options

-i	Ignore symbolic links, and record the paths as ftype=f (a file) or ftype=s (a symbolic link).
-c class	Map the class of all paths to class.

Operands

path1	Path name where objects are located.
path2	Path name that should be substituted on output for path1.

Examples

The following examples show uses of pkgproto and a partial listing of the output produced.

```
castle% pkgproto /bin=bin /usr/bin=usrbin /etc=etc
f none bin/sed=/bin/sed 0775 bin bin
f none bin/sh=/bin/sh 0755 bin daemon
f none bin/sort=/bin/sort 0755 bin bin
f none usrbin/sdb=/usr/bin/sdb 0775 bin bin
f none usrbin/shl=/usr/bin/shl 4755 bin bin
d none etc/master.d 0755 root daemon
f none etc/master.d/kernel=/etc/master.d/kernel 0644 root daemon
f none etc/rc=/etc/rc 0744 root daemon
```

```
castle% find / -type d -print | pkgproto
d none / 755 root root
d none /bin 755 bin bin
d none /usr 755 root root
d none /usr/bin 775 bin bin
d none /etc 755 root root
d none /tmp 777 root root
castle%
```

Exit Status

0	Successful completion.
>0	An error occurred.

Attributes

See attributes(5) for descriptions of the following attributes:

Attribute Type	**Attribute Value**
Availability	SUNWcsu

See Also

pkgmk(1), pkgparam(1), pkgtrans(1), prototype(4), attributes(5)
Application Packaging Developer's Guide

---

pkgtrans — Translate Package Format

Synopsis

/usr/bin/pkgtrans [-inos] *device1 device2* [*pkginst...*]

Description

The pkgtrans command translates an installable package from one format to another.
It performs the following translations.

- A file-system format to a datastream.
- A datastream to a file-system format.
- One file-system format to another file-system format.

Device specifications can be either the special node name (for example,
/dev/diskette) or a device alias (for example, diskette1). The device spool indicates
the default spool directory. Source and destination devices cannot be the same.

By default, pkgtrans does not translate any instance of a package if any instance of
that package already exists on the destination device. Using the -n option creates a new
instance if an instance of this package already exists. Using the -o option overwrites an
instance of this package if it already exists. Neither of these options is useful if the
destination device is a datastream.

Options

-i	Copy only the pkginfo(4) and pkgmap(4) files.
-n	Create a new instance of the package on the destination device if any instance of this package already exists, up to the number specified by the MAXINST variable in the pkginfo(4) file.
-o	Overwrite the same instance on the destination device if it already exists.
-s	Write the package to *device2* as a datastream instead of as a file system. The default behavior is to write a file-system format on devices that support both formats.

Operands

device1	The source device. The package or packages on this device are translated and placed on *device2*.
device2	The destination device. Translated packages are placed on this device.
pkginst	Specify which package instance or instances on *device1* should be translated. You can use the token all to indicate all packages. You can use *pkginst.** to indicate all instances of a package. If no packages are defined, a prompt shows all packages on the device and asks which to translate.

The asterisk character (*) is a special character to some shells and may need to be escaped. In the C shell, you must surround * with single quotes (') or precede it with a backslash (\).

Examples

The following example translates all packages on the diskette drive /dev/diskette and places the translations on /tmp.

```
castle% pkgtrans /dev/diskette /tmp all
```

The following example translates packages pkg1 and pkg2 on /tmp and puts their translations (that is, a datastream) on the 9track1 output device.

```
castle% pkgtrans /tmp 9track1 pkg1 pkg2
```

The following example translates pkg1 and pkg2 on /tmp and puts them on the diskette in a datastream format.

```
castle% pkgtrans -s /tmp /dev/diskette pkg1 pkg2
```

Environment Variables

The MAXINST variable is set in the pkginfo(4) file and declares the maximum number of package instances.

Exit Status

0	Successful completion.
>0	An error occurred.

Attributes

See attributes(5) for descriptions of the following attributes:

Attribute Type	Attribute Value
Availability	SUNWcsu

See Also

pkginfo(1), pkgmk(1), pkgparam(1), pkgproto(1), installf(1M), pkgadd(1M), pkgask(1M), pkgrm(1M), removef(1M), pkginfo(4), pkgmap(4), attributes(5)
Application Packaging Developer's Guide

pkill — Find or Signal Processes

Synopsis

/usr/bin/pkill [-*signal*] [-fnvx] [-P *ppidlist*] [-g *pgrplist*]
[-s *sidlist*] [-u *euidlist*] [-U *uidlist*] [-G *gidlist*] [-t *termlist*]
[*pattern*]

Description

See pgrep(1).

pldd — Proc Tools

Synopsis

/usr/proc/bin/pldd *pid*...

Description

See proc(1).

plimit — Get or Set the Resource Limits of Running Processes

Synopsis

/usr/bin/plimit [-km] *pid*...
/usr/bin/plimit -cdfnstv *soft*,*hard*... *pid*...

Description

With no arguments, plimit reports the resource limits of the processes identified by *pid*. When you specify one or more of the cdfnstv options, plimit sets the *soft* (current) limit and/or the *hard* (maximum) limit of the indicated resource(s) in the processes identified by *pid*.

Only the owner of a process or the superuser is permitted either to get or to set the resource limits of a process. Only the superuser can increase the *hard* limit.

Options

-k   Show file sizes in kilobytes (1,024 bytes) instead of in 512-byte blocks.

-m   Show file and memory sizes in megabytes (1,024*1,024 bytes).

The following options change specified resource limits. They each accept an argument of the form:

soft,hard

where *soft* specifies the soft (current) limit and *hard* specifies the hard (maximum) limit. If you do not specify a hard limit, you can omit the comma. If the soft limit is an empty string, only the hard limit is set. Each limit is either the literal string unlimited or a number with an optional scaling factor, as follows:

*n*k   *n* kilobytes.

*n*m   *n* megabytes (minutes for CPU time).

*n*h   *n* hours (for CPU time only).

mm:*ss*   Minutes and seconds (for CPU time only).

The soft limit cannot exceed the hard limit.

-c *soft,hard*

Set corefile size limits (default unit is 512-byte blocks).

-d *soft,hard*

Set data segment (heap) size limits (default unit is kilobytes).

-f *soft,hard*

Set file-size limits (default unit is 512-byte blocks).

-n *soft,hard*

Set file-descriptor limits (no default unit).

-s *soft,hard*

Set stack segment size limits (default unit is kilobytes).

-t *soft,hard*

Set CPU time limits (default unit is seconds).

-v *soft,hard*

Set virtual memory size limits (default unit is kilobytes).

Operands

pid   Process ID list.

Examples

The following example shows the current settings for the Volume Management daemon, vold.

```
# plimit 213
213:    /usr/sbin/vold
   resource              current          maximum
   time(seconds)         unlimited        unlimited
   file(blocks)          unlimited        unlimited
   data(kbytes)          unlimited        unlimited
   stack(kbytes)         8192             2097148
   coredump(blocks)      unlimited        unlimited
   nofiles(descriptors)  1024             1024
   vmemory(kbytes)       unlimited        unlimited
#
```

Exit Status

0	Success.
non-zero	Failure such as no such process, permission denied, or invalid option.

Files

/proc/pid/* Process information and control files.

Attributes

See attributes(5) for descriptions of the following attributes:

Attribute Type	Attribute Value
Availability	SUNWesu

See Also

proc(1), ulimit(1), getrlimit(2), setrlimit(2), proc(4), attributes(5)

plot — Graphics Filters for Various Plotters

Synopsis

/usr/ucb/plot [-T*terminal*]

Description

The plot command reads plotting instructions (see plot(4B)) from the standard input and produces on the standard output plotting instructions suitable for a particular terminal.

If you do not specify a terminal, the environment variable TERM is used. The default terminal is tek.

Environment Variables

Except for ver, you can use the following terminal types with lpr -g (see lpr) to produce plotted output.

2648 | 2648a | h8 | hp2648 | hp2648a

> Hewlett-Packard 2648 graphics terminal.

hp7221 | hp7 | h7

> Hewlett-Packard 7221 plotter.

300   DASI 300 or GSI terminal (Diablo mechanism).

300s | 300S

> DASI 300s terminal (Diablo mechanism).

450   DASI Hyterm 450 terminal (Diablo mechanism).

4013   Tektronix 4013 storage scope.

4014 | tek   Tektronix 4014 and 4015 storage scope with Enhanced Graphics Module. (Use 4013 for Tektronix 4014 or 4015 without the Enhanced Graphics Module).

aed   AED 512 color graphics terminal.

bgplot | bitgraph

> BBN bitgraph graphics terminal.

crt   Any CRT terminal capable of running vi(1).

dumb | un | unknown

> Dumb terminals without cursor addressing or line printers.

gigi | vt125

> DEC vt125 terminal.

implot   Imagen plotter.

var   Benson Varian printer-plotter

ver   Versatec D1200A printer-plotter. The output is scan converted and suitable input to lpr -v.

Files

/usr/ucb/aedplot

/usr/ucb/atoplot

/usr/ucb/bgplot

/usr/ucb/crtplot

/usr/ucb/dumbplot

/usr/ucb/gigiplot

/usr/ucb/hp7221plot

/usr/ucb/hpplot

```
/usr/ucb/implot

/usr/ucb/plot

/usr/ucb/plottoa

/usr/ucb/t300

/usr/ucb/t300s

/usr/ucb/t4013

/usr/ucb/t450

/usr/ucb/tek

/usr/ucb/vplot
```

Attributes

See attributes(5) for descriptions of the following attributes:

Attribute Type	Attribute Value
Availability	SUNWscpu

See Also

graph(1), tplot(1), vi(1), lpr(1B), plot(4B), attributes(5)

pmap — Proc Tools

Synopsis

/usr/proc/bin/pmap [-r] *pid*...

Description

See proc(1).

popd — Change Working Directory

Synopsis

/usr/bin/cd [*directory*]

sh

popd [+*n*]

Description

See cd(1).

postdaisy — PostScript Translator for Diablo 630 Daisy-Wheel Files

Synopsis

```
/usr/lib/lp/postdaisy [-c num] [-f num] [-h num] [-m num] [-n num]
    [-o list] [-p mode] [-r num] [-s num] [-v num] [-x num] [-y num]
    [file...]
/usr/lib/lp/postscript/postdaisy
```

Description

The postdaisy filter translates Diablo 630 daisy-wheel files into PostScript and writes the results to the standard output. If you specify no files or if - is one of the input files, the standard input is read.

Options

-c *num*	Print *num* copies of each page. By default, only one copy is printed.
-f *name*	Print files, using font *name*. You can use any PostScript font, although the best results are obtained with constant-width fonts. The default font is Courier.
-h *num*	Set the initial horizontal motion index to *num*. Determine the character advance and the default point size unless you use the -s option. The default is 12.
-m *num*	Magnify each logical page by the factor *num*. Scale pages uniformly about the origin, which is located near the upper-left corner of each page. The default magnification is 1.0.
-n *num*	Print *num* logical pages on each piece of paper, where *num* can be any positive integer. By default, *num* is set to 1.
-o *list*	Print pages whose numbers are given in the comma-separated list. The *list* contains single numbers *N* and ranges *N1* - *N2*. A missing *N1* means the lowest-numbered page, a missing *N2* means the highest. The page range is an expression of logical pages instead of physical sheets of paper. For example, if you are printing two logical pages to a sheet and you specified a range of 4, then two sheets of paper containing four page layouts would print. If you specified a page range of 3-4 when requesting two logical pages to a sheet, then only page 3 and page 4 layouts would print, and they would appear on one physical sheet of paper.
-p *mode*	Print files in either p (portrait) or 1 (landscape) mode. Only the first character of *mode* is significant. The default mode is portrait.
-r *num*	Choose Return and linefeed behavior. If *num* is 1, a linefeed generates a Return. If *num* is 2, a Return generates a linefeed. Setting *num* to 3 enables both modes.

`-s num`	Use point size *num* instead of the default value set by the initial horizontal motion index.
`-v num`	Set the initial vertical motion index to *num*. The default is 8.
`-x num`	Translate the origin *num* inches along the positive x axis. The default coordinate system has the origin fixed near the upper-left corner of the page, with positive x to the right and positive y down the page. Positive *num* moves everything right. The default offset is 0.25 inches.
`-y num`	Translate the origin *num* inches along the positive y axis. Positive *num* moves text up the page. The default offset is -0.25 inches.

Exit Status

0	Successful completion.
non-zero	An error occurred.

Files

/usr/lib/lp/postscript/forms.ps

/usr/lib/lp/postscript/ps.requests

Attributes

See `attributes`(5) for descriptions of the following attributes:

Attribute Type	Attribute Value
Availability	SUNWpsf

See Also

download(1), dpost(1), postdmd(1), postio(1), postmd(1), postprint(1), postreverse(1), posttek(1), attributes(5)

---

postdmd — PostScript Translator for DMD Bitmap Files

Synopsis

/usr/lib/lp/postdmd [-b *num*] [-c *num*] [-f] [-m *num*] [-n *num*] [-o *list*]
  [-p *mode*] [-x *num*] [-y *num*] [*file*...]
/usr/lib/lp/postscript/postdmd

Description

The `postdmd` command translates Digital Media Distribution (DMD) bitmap files produced by `dmdps` or files written in the Ninth Edition `bitfile`(9.5) format into PostScript and writes the results to the standard output. If no files are specified or if - is one of the input files, the standard input is read.

Options

-b *num*	Pack the bitmap in the output file, using *num* byte patterns. A value of 0 turns off all packing of the output file. By default, *num* is 6.
-c *num*	Print *num* copies of each page. By default, only one copy is printed.
-f	Flip the sense of the bits in files before printing the bitmaps.
-m *num*	Magnify each logical page by the factor *num*. Scale pages uniformly about the origin which, by default, is located at the center of each page. The default magnification is 1.0.
-n *num*	Print *num* logical pages on each piece of paper where *num* can be any positive integer. By default, *num* is set to 1.
-o *list*	Print pages whose numbers are given in the comma-separated list. The *list* contains single numbers *N* and ranges *N1*–*N2*. A missing *N1* means the lowest-numbered page, a missing *N2* means the highest. The page range is an expression of logical pages instead of physical sheets of paper. For example, if you are printing two logical pages to a sheet and you specified a range of 4, then two sheets of paper containing four page layouts would print. If you specified a page range of 3-4 when requesting two logical pages to a sheet, then only page 3 and page 4 layouts would print and they would appear on one physical sheet of paper.
-p *mode*	Print files in either p (portrait) or 1 (landscape) mode. Only the first character of *mode* is significant. The default mode is portrait.
-x *num*	Translate the origin *num* inches along the positive x axis. The default coordinate system has the origin fixed at the center of the page, with positive x to the right and positive y up the page. Positive *num* moves everything right. The default offset is 0 inches.
-y *num*	Translate the origin *num* inches along the positive y axis. Positive *num* moves everything up the page. The default offset is 0.

Only one bitmap is printed on each logical page, and each of the input files must contain complete descriptions of at least one bitmap. Decreasing the pattern size with the -b option may help throughput on printers with fast processors (such as PS-810s), while increasing the pattern size often is the right move on older models (such as PS-800s).

Exit Status

0	Successful completion.
non-zero	An error occurred.

Files

/usr/lib/lp/postscript/forms.ps

/usr/lib/lp/postscript/ps.requests

Attributes

See `attributes`(5) for descriptions of the following attributes:

Attribute Type	Attribute Value
Availability	SUNWpsf

See Also

`download`(1), `dpost`(1), `postdaisy`(1), `postio`(1), `postmd`(1), `postprint`(1), `postreverse`(1), `posttek`(1), `attributes`(5)

postio — Serial Interface for PostScript Printers

Synopsis

```
/usr/lib/lp/postio -l line [-D] [-i] [-q] [-t] [-S] [-b speed] [-B num]
    [-L file] [-P string] [-R num] [file...]
/usr/lib/lp/postscript/postio
```

Description

The `postio` command sends files to the PostScript printer attached to *line*. If you specify no files, the standard input is sent.

Notes

The input files are handled as a single PostScript job. Sending several different jobs, each with its own internal end-of-job mark (^D) is not guaranteed to work properly. `postio` can quit before all the jobs have completed and could be restarted before the last one finishes.

All the capabilities described below may not be available on every machine or even across the different versions of the UNIX system that are currently supported by the program.

There may be no default line, so using the -l option is strongly recommended. If you omit the -l option, `postio` may try to connect to the printer using the standard output. If Datakit is involved, the -b option may be ineffective and attempts by `postio` to impose flow control over data in both directions may not work. The -q option can help if the printer is connected to RADIAN. The -S option is not generally recommended and should be used only if all other attempts to establish a reliable connection fail.

Options

The following group of options should be sufficient for most applications.

-b *speed*	Transmit data over line at baud rate *speed*. Recognized baud rates are 1200, 2400, 4800, 9600, and 19200. The default speed is 9600 baud.
-B *num*	Set the internal buffer size for reading and writing files to *num* bytes. By default, *num* is 2048 bytes.
-D	Enable debug mode. Guarantee that everything read on *line* is added to the log file (standard error by default).

-l *line*   Connect to the printer attached to *line*. In most cases, there is no default and postio must be able to read and write *line*. If the line does not begin with a /, it may be treated as a Datakit destination.

-L *file*   Put data received on line in *file*. The default log file is standard error. Printer or status messages that don't show a change in state are not normally written to *file* but can be forced with the -D option.

-P *string*   Send *string* to the printer before any of the input files. The default string is simple PostScript code that disables timeouts.

-R *num*   Run postio as a single process if *num* is 1 or as separate read and write processes if *num* is 2. By default, postio runs as a single process.

-q   Prevent status queries while files are being sent to the printer. When status queries are disabled, append a dummy message to the log file before each block is transmitted.

The next two options are for users who expect to run postio on their own. Neither is suitable for use in spooler interface programs.

-i   Run the program in interactive mode. First, send any files, followed by the standard input. Force separate read and write processes and override many other options. To exit interactive mode, use your interrupt or quit character. To get a friendly interactive connection with the printer, type executive on a line by itself.

-t   Write data received on *line* and not recognized as printer or status information to the standard output. Force separate read and write processes. Convenient if you have a PostScript program that is returning useful data to the host.

The following option is not generally recommended and should be used only if all else fails to provide a reliable connection.

-S   Slow the transmission of data to the printer. Severely limit throughput, run as a single process, disable the -q option, limit the internal buffer size to 1,024 bytes. This option can use an excessive amount of CPU time and does nothing in interactive mode.

You usually obtain the best performance by using a large internal buffer (the -B option) and by running the program as separate read and write processes (the -R 2 option). Inability to fork the additional process continues as a single read/write process. When one process is used, only data sent to the printer is flow controlled.

The options are not all mutually exclusive. The -i option always wins, selecting its own settings for whatever is needed to run interactive mode independently of anything else found on the command line. Interactive mode runs as separate read and write processes, and few of the other options accomplish anything in the presence of the -i option. The -t option needs a reliable two-way connection to the printer and therefore tries to force separate read and write processes. The -S option relies on the status query mechanism, so -q is disabled and the program runs as a single process.

In most cases, postio starts by making a connection to *line* and then tries to force the printer into the IDLE state by sending an appropriate sequence of ^T (status query), ^C (interrupt), and ^D (end-of-job) characters. When the printer goes IDLE, files are transmitted along with an occasional ^T (unless you used the -q option). After all the files are sent, the program waits until it is likely that the job is complete.

Printer-generated error messages received at any time except while establishing the initial connection (or when running interactive mode) exit postio with a non-zero status. In addition to being added to the log file, printer error messages are also echoed to standard error.

Examples

The following example runs as a single process at 9600 baud and sends file1 and file2 to the printer attached to /dev/tty01.

```
castle% postio -l /dev/tty01 file1 file2
```

The following example is the same as the previous one except that two processes are used, the internal buffer is set to 4,096 bytes, and data returned by the printer gets put in file log.

```
castle% postio -R 2 -B 4096 -l/dev/tty01 -L log file1 file2
```

The following example establishes an interactive connection with the printer at Datakit destination my/printer.

```
castle% postio -i -l my/printer
```

The following example sends file program to the printer connected to /dev/tty22, recovers any data in file results, and puts log messages in file log.

```
castle% postio -t -l /dev/tty22 -L log program >results
```

Exit Status

0	Successful completion.
non-zero	An error occurred.

Attributes

See attributes(5) for descriptions of the following attributes:

Attribute Type	Attribute Value
Availability	SUNWpsf

See Also

download(1), dpost(1), postdaisy(1), postdmd(1), postmd(1), postprint(1), postreverse(1), posttek(1), attributes(5)

postmd — Matrix Display Program for PostScript Printers

Synopsis

/usr/lib/lp/postmd [-b num] [-c num] [-d dimen] [-g list] [-i list]
    [-m num] [-n num] [-o list] [-p mode] [-w window] [-x num] [-y num]
    [file...]
/usr/lib/lp/postscript/postmd

Description

The postmd filter reads a series of floating-point numbers from files, translates them into a PostScript grayscale image, and writes the results to the standard output. In a typical application the numbers might be the elements of a large matrix written in row major order, while the printed image could help locate patterns in the matrix. If you specify no files or if – is one of the input files, the standard input is read.

Notes

The largest matrix that can be adequately displayed is a function of the interval and grayscale lists, the printer resolution, and the paper size. A 600 by 600 matrix is an optimistic upper bound for a two-element interval list (that is, five regions) using 8.5- by 11-inch paper on a 300 dpi printer.

Using white (that is, 255) in a grayscale list is not recommended. It does not show in the legend and bar graph that postmd displays below each image.

Options

-b *num*   Pack the bitmap in the output file, using *num* byte patterns. A value of 0 turns off all packing of the output file. By default, *num* is 6.

-c *num*   Print *num* copies of each page. By default, only one copy is printed.

-d *dimen*   Set the default matrix dimensions for all input files to *dimen*. You can give the *dimen* string as rows or rows times columns. If you omit the columns value, set it to rows. By default, postmd assumes each matrix is square and sets the number of rows and columns to the square root of the number of elements in each input file.

-g *list*   Use *list*, a comma- or space-separated string of integers each lying between 0 and 255 inclusive, to assign PostScript grayscales to the regions of the real line chosen by the -i option. 255 corresponds to white, and 0, to black. The postmd filter assigns a default grayscale that omits white (that is, 255) and gets darker as the regions move from left to right along the real line.

-i *list*   Use *list*, a comma-, space- or slash- (/) separated string of *N* floating-point numbers to partition the real line into $2N+1$ regions. Specify the list in increasing numerical order. The partitions are used to map floating-point numbers read from the input files into grayscale integers that are either assigned automatically by postmd or that are arbitrarily chosen by using the -g option. The default interval list is -1,0,1, which partitions the real line into seven regions.

-m *num*   Magnify each logical page by the factor *num*. Scale pages uniformly about the origin which, by default, is located at the center of each page. The default magnification is 1.0.

-n *num*   Print *num* logical pages on each piece of paper, where *num* can be any positive integer. By default, *num* is set to 1.

-o *list*   Print pages whose numbers are given in the comma-separated list. The *list* contains single numbers *N* and ranges *N1–N2*. A missing *N1* means the lowest-numbered page, a missing *N2* means the highest. The page range is an expression of logical pages instead of physical sheets of paper. For example, if you are printing two logical pages to a sheet and you specified a range of 4, then two sheets of paper containing four page layouts would print. If you specified a page range of 3–4 when requesting two logical pages to a sheet, then only page 3 and page 4 layouts would print and they would appear on one physical sheet of paper.

-p *mode*   Print files in either p (portrait) or l (landscape) mode. Only the first character of *mode* is significant. The default mode is portrait.

-w *window*   Use *window*, a comma- or space-separated list of four positive integers, to choose the upper-left and lower-right corners of a submatrix from each of the input files. Row and column indices start at 1 in the upper-left corner and the numbers in the input files are assumed to be written in row major order. By default, the entire matrix is displayed.

-x *num*   Translate the origin *num* inches along the positive x axis. The default coordinate system has the origin fixed at the center of the page with positive x to the right and positive y up the page. Positive *num* moves everything right. The default offset is 0 inches.

-y *num*   Translate the origin *num* inches along the positive y axis. Positive *num* moves everything up the page. The default offset is 0.

One matrix only is displayed on each logical page, and each of the input files must contain complete descriptions of exactly one matrix. Matrix elements are floating-point numbers arranged in row major order in each input file. White space, including newlines, is not used to determine matrix dimensions. By default, postmd assumes each matrix is square and sets the number of rows and columns to the square root of the number of elements in the input file. Supplying default dimensions on the command line with the -d option overrides this default behavior, and in that case, the dimensions apply to all input files.

You can supply an optional header with each input file that is used to set the matrix dimensions, the partition of the real line, the grayscale map, and a window into the matrix. The header consists of keyword/value pairs, each on a separate line. It begins on the first line of each input file and ends with the first unrecognized string, which should be the first matrix element. Values set in the header take precedence but apply only to the current input file. Recognized header keywords are dimension, interval, grayscale, and window. The syntax of the value string that follows each keyword parallels what is accepted by the -d, -i, -g, and -w options.

Examples

Suppose file initially contains the 1,000 numbers in a 20 x 50 matrix. Then, you can produce exactly the same output by completing three steps. First, issue the following command.

```
castle% postmd -d20x50 -i"-100 100" -g0,128,254,128,0 file
```

Next, prepend the following header to file.

```
dimension 20x50
interval -100.0 .100e+3
grayscale 0 128 254 128 0
```

Then, issue the following command.

```
castle% postmd file
```

The interval list partitions the real line into five regions, and the grayscale list maps numbers less than –100 or greater than 100 into 0 (that is, black), numbers equal to –100 or 100 into 128 (that is, 50 percent black), and numbers between –100 and 100 into 254 (that is, almost white).

Files

```
/usr/lib/lp/postscript/forms.ps
```

```
/usr/lib/lp/postscript/ps.requests
```

Exit Status

0	Successful completion.
non-zero	An error occurred.

Attributes

See attributes(5) for descriptions of the following attributes:

Attribute Type	Attribute Value
Availability	SUNWpsf

See Also

dpost(1), postdaisy(1), postdmd(1), postio(1), postprint(1), postreverse(1), posttek(1), attributes(5)

postplot — PostScript Translator for plot(4) Graphics Files

Synopsis

```
/usr/lib/lp/postplot [-c num] [-f name] [-m num] [-n num] [-o list]
    [-p mode] [-w num] [-x num] [-y num] [filename...]
/usr/lib/lp/postscript/postplot
```

Description

The postplot filter translates plot(1B) graphics file names into PostScript and writes the results to the standard output. If you specify no file names or if - is one of the input file names, the standard input is read.

Note — The default line width is too small for write-white print engines such as the one used by the PS-2400.

Options

-c *num*	Print *num* copies of each page. By default, only one copy is printed.
-f *name*	Print text, using font *name*. You can use any PostScript font, although the best results are obtained with constant-width fonts. The default font is Courier.
-m *num*	Magnify each logical page by the factor *num*. Scale pages uniformly about the origin which, by default, is located at the center of each page. The default magnification is 1.0.
-n *num*	Print *num* logical pages on each piece of paper, where *num* can be any positive integer. By default, *num* is set to 1.
-o *list*	Print pages whose numbers are given in the comma-separated *list*. The list contains single numbers *N* and ranges *N1*–*N2*. A missing *N1* means the lowest-numbered page, a missing *N2* means the highest.
-p *mode*	Print file names in either p (portrait) or 1 (landscape) mode. Only the first character of *mode* is significant. The default mode is landscape.
-w *num*	Set the line width used for graphics to *num* points, where a point is approximately 1/72 of an inch. By default, *num* is set to 0 points, which forces lines to be one pixel wide.
-x *num*	Translate the origin *num* inches along the positive x axis. The default coordinate system has the origin fixed at the center of the page with positive x to the right and positive y up the page. Positive *num* moves everything right. The default offset is 0.0 inches.
-y *num*	Translate the origin *num* inches along the positive y axis. Positive *num* moves everything up the page. The default offset is 0.0.

Files

/usr/lib/lp/postscript/forms.ps

/usr/lib/lp/postscript/postplot.ps

/usr/lib/lp/postscript/ps.requests

Attributes

See attributes(5) for descriptions of the following attributes:

Attribute Type	Attribute Value
Availability	SUNWlps

See Also

download(1), dpost(1), postdaisy(1), postdmd(1), postio(1), postmd(1), postprint(1), postreverse(1), plot(1B), attributes(5)

Diagnostics

An exit status of 0 is returned if file names were successfully processed.

postprint — PostScript Translator for Text Files

Synopsis

```
/usr/lib/lp/postprint [-c num] [-f name] [-l num] [-m num] [-n num]
   [-o list] [-p mode] [-r num] [-s num] [-t num] [-x num] [-y num]
   [file...]
/usr/lib/lp/postscript/postprint
```

Description

The postprint filter translates text files into PostScript and writes the results to the standard output. If you specify no files or if - is one of the input files, the standard input is read.

Options

-c *num*	Print *num* copies of each page. By default, print only one copy.
-f *name*	Print files, using font *name*. You can use any PostScript font, although the best results are obtained with constant-width fonts. The default font is Courier.
-l *num*	Set the length of a page to *num* lines. By default, *num* is 66. Setting *num* to 0 is allowed, and postprint guesses a value, based on the point size.
-m *num*	Magnify each logical page by the factor *num*. Scale pages uniformly about the origin, which is located near the upper-left corner of each page. The default magnification is 1.0.
-n *num*	Print *num* logical pages on each piece of paper where *num* can be any positive integer. By default, *num* is set to 1.
-o *list*	Print pages whose numbers are given in the comma-separated *list*. The *list* contains single numbers *N* and ranges *N1-N2*. A missing *N1* means the lowest-numbered page, a missing *N2* means the highest. The page range is an expression of logical pages instead of physical sheets of paper. For example, if you are printing two logical pages to a sheet and you specified a range of 4, then two sheets of paper containing four page layouts would print. If you specified a page range of 3-4 when requesting two logical pages to a sheet, then only page 3 and page 4 layouts would print and they would appear on one physical sheet of paper.
-p *mode*	Print files in either p (portrait) or l (landscape) mode. Only the first character of *mode* is significant. The default mode is portrait.
-r *num*	Choose Return behavior. Ignore Returns if *num* is 0, go to column 1 if *num* is 1, and generate a newline if *num* is 2. The default *num* is 0.

-s *num*   Print files, using point size *num.* When printing in landscape mode, scale *num* by a factor that depends on the imaging area of the device. The default size for portrait mode is 10. Note that increasing point size increases virtual image size, so you either need to load larger paper or use the -10 option to scale the number of lines per page.

-t *num*   Assume Tabs are set every *num* columns, starting with the first column. By default, Tabs are set every 8 columns.

-x *num*   Translate the origin *num* inches along the positive x axis. The default coordinate system has the origin fixed near the upper-left corner of the page, with positive x to the right and positive y down the page. Positive *num* moves everything to the right. The default offset is 0.25 inches.

-y *num*   Translate the origin *num* inches along the positive y axis. Positive *num* moves text up the page. The default offset is -0.25 inches.

A new logical page is started after 66 lines have been printed on the current page or whenever an ASCII formfeed character is read. You can change the number of lines per page with the -l option. Unprintable ASCII characters are ignored, and lines that are too long are silently truncated by the printer.

Examples

The following example prints file1 and file2 in landscape mode.

```
castle% postprint -pland file1 file2
```

The following example prints three logical pages on each physical page in portrait mode.

```
castle% postprint -n3 file
```

Exit Status

0   Successful completion.

non-zero   An error occurred.

Files

/usr/lib/lp/postscript/forms.ps

/usr/lib/lp/postscript/ps.requests

Attributes

See attributes(5) for descriptions of the following attributes:

Attribute Type	Attribute Value
Availability	SUNWpsf

See Also

download(1), dpost(1), postdaisy(1), postdmd(1), postio(1), postmd(1), postreverse(1), posttek(1), attributes(5)

postreverse — Reverse the Page Order in a PostScript File

Synopsis

```
/usr/lib/lp/postreverse [-o list] [-r] [file]
/usr/lib/lp/postscript/postreverse
```

Description

The postreverse filter reverses the page order in files that conform to Adobe's Version 1.0 or Version 2.0 file structuring conventions and writes the results to the standard output. Only one input file is allowed, and, if you specify no file, the standard input is read.

The postreverse filter can handle a limited class of files that violate page independence, provided all global definitions are bracketed by %%BeginGlobal and %%EndGlobal comments. In addition, files that mark the end of each page with %%EndPage: label ordinal comments also reverse properly, provided the prologue and trailer sections can be located. If postreverse fails to find an %%EndProlog or %%EndSetup comment, the entire file is copied, unmodified, to the standard output.

Because global definitions are extracted from individual pages and put in the prologue, the output file can be minimally conforming even if the input file was not.

Note — No attempt has been made to deal with redefinitions of global variables or procedures. If standard input is used, the input file is read three times before being reversed.

Options

-o *list*   Print pages whose numbers are given in the comma-separated list. The *list* contains single numbers *N* and ranges *N1* - *N2*. A missing *N1* means the lowest-numbered page, a missing *N2* means the highest. The page range is an expression of logical pages instead of physical sheets of paper. For example, if you are printing two logical pages to a sheet and you specified a range of 4, then two sheets of paper containing four page layouts would print. If you specified a page range of 3-4 when requesting two logical pages to a sheet, then only page 3 and page 4 layouts would print and they would appear on one physical sheet of paper.

-r   Do not reverse the pages in *file*.

Examples

The following example reverses pages 1 to 100 from file.

castle% **postreverse -o1-100 file**

The following example prints four logical pages on each physical page and reverses all the pages.

example% **postprint -n4 file | postreverse**

The following example produces a minimally conforming file from output generated by dpost without reversing the pages.

```
example% dpost file | postreverse -r
```

Exit Status

0	Successful completion.
non-zero	An error occurred.

Attributes

See attributes(5) for descriptions of the following attributes:

Attribute Type	Attribute Value
Availability	SUNWpsf

See Also

download(1), dpost(1), postdaisy(1), postdmd(1), postio(1), postmd(1), postprint(1), posttek(1), attributes(5)

---

posttek — PostScript Translator for Tektronix 4014 Files

Synopsis

/usr/lib/lp/posttek [-c *num*] [-f *name*] [-m *num*] [-n *num*] [-o *list*]
   [-p *mode*] [-w *num*] [-x *num*] [-y *num*] [*file*...]
/usr/lib/lp/postscript/posttek

Description

The posttek filter translates Tektronix 4014 graphics files into PostScript and writes the results to the standard output. If you specify no files or if - is one of the input files, the standard input is read.

Note — The default line width is too small for write-white print engines such as the one used by the PS-2400.

Options

-c *num*	Print *num* copies of each page. By default, only one copy is printed.
-f *name*	Print text, using font *name*. You can use any PostScript font, although the best results are obtained with constant-width fonts. The default font is Courier.
-m *num*	Magnify each logical page by the factor *num*. Scale pages uniformly about the origin which is located near the upper-left corner of each page. The default magnification is 1.0.
-n *num*	Print *num* logical pages on each piece of paper, where *num* can be any positive integer. By default, *num* is set to 1.

-o *list*   Print pages whose numbers are given in the comma-separated list. The *list* contains single numbers *N* and ranges *N1*–*N2*. A missing *N1* means the lowest-numbered page, a missing *N2* means the highest. The page range is an expression of logical pages instead of physical sheets of paper. For example, if you are printing two logical pages to a sheet and you specified a range of 4, then two sheets of paper containing four page layouts would print. If you specified a page range of 3–4 when requesting two logical pages to a sheet, then only page 3 and page 4 layouts would print and they would appear on one physical sheet of paper.

-p *mode*   Print files in either p (portrait) or 1 (landscape) mode. Only the first character of *mode* is significant. The default mode is portrait.

-w *num*   Set the line width used for graphics to *num* points, where a point is approximately 1/72 of an inch. By default, *num* is set to 0 points, which forces lines to be 1 pixel wide.

-x *num*   Translate the origin *num* inches along the positive x axis. The default coordinate system has the origin fixed at the center of the page, with positive x to the right and positive y up the page. Positive *num* moves everything right. The default offset is 0.0 inches.

-y *num*   Translate the origin *num* inches along the positive y axis. Positive *num* moves everything up the page. The default offset is 0.0.

Exit Status

0   Successful completion.

non-zero   An error occurred.

Files

/usr/lib/lp/postscript/forms.ps

/usr/lib/lp/postscript/ps.requests

Attributes

See attributes(5) for descriptions of the following attributes:

Attribute Type	Attribute Value
Availability	SUNWpsf

See Also

download(1), dpost(1), postdaisy(1), postdmd(1), postio(1), postmd(1), postprint(1), postreverse(1), attributes(5)

New! ppgsz — Set Preferred Stack and/or Heap Page Size

Synopsis

/usr/bin/ppgsz [-F] -o *option*[,*option*] *cmd* |-p *pid*...

Description

Use the ppgsz command, new in the Solaris 9 Operating Environment, to set the preferred stack and/or heap page size for the target process(es), that is, the launched *cmd* or the process(es) in the *pid* list. ppgsz stops the target process(es) while changing the page size. See memcntl(2).

Because of resource constraints, setting the preferred page size does not necessarily guarantee that the target process(es) get the preferred page size. Use pmap(1) to view the actual heap and stack page sizes of the target process(es). See the pmap -s option.

You must map large pages at addresses that are multiples of the size of the large page. Given that the heap is typically not large-page aligned, the starting portions of the heap (below the first large page aligned address) are mapped with the system memory page size. See getpagesize(3C).

Options

-F
Force preferred page size for target process(es) even if controlled by other process(es). Exercise caution when using the -F option. See proc(1).

-p *pid*
Set the preferred page size option(s) for the target process(es) in the process-ID (*pid*) list following the -p option. The *pid* list can also consist of names in the /proc directory. Only the process owner or superuser is permitted to set page size.

cmd is interpreted if you do not specify -p. ppgsz launches *cmd* and applies page size option(s) to the new process.

The heap and stack preferred page sizes are inherited. Child process(es) created (see fork(2)) from the launched process or the target process(es) in the *pid* list after ppgsz completes inherit the preferred heap and stack page sizes. The preferred page sizes are set back to the default system page size (see getpagesize(3C)) on exec() (see exec(2)).

-o *option*[,*option*]
You must specify at least one of the following options

heap=*size*
Specify the preferred page size for the heap of the target process(es). heap is defined to be the bss (uninitialized data) and the brk area that immediately follows the bss (see brk(2)). The preferred heap page size is set for the existing heap and for any additional heap memory allocated in the future.

stack=*size*   Specify the preferred page size for the stack of the target process(es). The preferred stack page size is set for the existing stack and newly allocated parts of the stack as it expands.

size must be a supported page size (see pagesize(1)) or 0, in which case the system selects an appropriate page size (see memcntl(2)).

size defaults to bytes and can be specified in octal (0), decimal, or hexadecimal (0x). You can qualify the numeric value with K, M, G, or T to specify kilobytes, megabytes, gigabytes or terabytes. For example, you can specify 4 Megabytes as 4194304, 0x400000, 4096K, 0x1000K, or 4M.

Examples

The following example sets the preferred heap page size to 4M and the preferred stack page size to 512K for all ora-owned processes running commands that begin with ora.

example% **ppgsz -o heap=4M,stack=512K -p `pgrep -u ora '^ora'`**

Exit Status

0   Successful operation.

non-zero   An error occurred.

Files

/proc/*   Process files.

Attributes

See attributes(5) for descriptions of the following attributes:

Attribute Type	Attribute Value
Availability	SUNWesu (32 bit)
	SUNWesxu (64 bit)
Interface Stability	Evolving

See Also

pagesize(1), pgrep(1), pmap(1), proc(1), brk(2), exec(2), fork(2), memcntl(2), sbrk(2), getpagesize(3C), proc(4), attributes(5)

pr — Print Files

Synopsis

```
/usr/bin/pr [+page] [-column] [-adFmrt] [-e[char] [gap]] [-h header]
    [-i[char] [gap]] [-l lines] [-n[char] [width]] [-o offset] [-s[char]]
    [-w width] [-fp] [file...]
/usr/xpg4/bin/pr [+page] [-column | -c column] [-adFmrt] [-e[char]
    [gap]] [-h header] [-i[char] [gap]] [-l lines] [-n[char] [width]]
    [-o offset] [-s[char]] [-w width] [-fp] [file...]
```

Description

The pr command is a printing and pagination filter. If you specify multiple input files, each is read, formatted, and written to standard output. By default, the input is separated into 66-line pages, each with:

- A 5-line header that includes the page number, date, time, and the path name of the file.
- A 5-line trailer consisting of blank lines.

If standard output is associated with a terminal, diagnostic messages are deferred until the pr command has completed processing.

When you specify options for multicolumn output, output text columns are of equal width; input lines that do not fit into a text column are truncated. By default, text columns are separated with at least one blank character.

Options

In the following option descriptions, *column*, *lines*, *offset*, *page*, and *width* are positive decimal integers; *gap* is a nonnegative decimal integer. Some of the arguments are optional, and some of the arguments cannot be specified as arguments separate from the preceding option letter. In particular, the -s option requires that you keep the option letter with its argument, and the options -e, -i, and -n require that both arguments, if present, be kept with the option letter.

The following options are supported for both /usr/bin/pr and /usr/xpg4/bin/pr.

+*page*	Begin output at page number *page* of the formatted input.
-*column*	Produce multicolumn output that is arranged in *column* columns (default is 1) and is written down each column in the order in which the text is received from the input file. Do not use this option with -m. The -e and -i options are assumed for multiple text-column output. Whether text columns are produced with identical vertical lengths is unspecified, but a text column never exceeds the length of the page (see the -l option). When used with -t, use the minimum number of lines to write the output.
-a	Modify the effect of the -*column* option so that the columns are filled across the page in a round-robin order (for example, when *column* is 2, the first input line heads column 1, the second heads column 2, the third is the second line in column 1, and so forth).
-d	Produce output that is double spaced; append an extra newline character following every newline character found in the input.

-e[*char*] [*gap*]

> Expand each input Tab character to the next greater column position specified by the formula $n*gap+1$, where n is an integer >0. If *gap* is omitted or it is 0, it defaults to 8. Expand all Tab characters in the input into the appropriate number of space characters. If any nondigit character, *char*, is specified, use it as the input Tab character.

-f

> Use a formfeed character for new pages instead of the default behavior that uses a sequence of newline characters. Pause before beginning the first page if the standard output is associated with a terminal.

-h *header*

> Use the string *header* to replace the contents of the file operand in the page header.

-l *lines*

> Override the 66-line default, and reset the page length to *lines*. If *lines* is not greater than the sum of both the header and trailer depths (in lines), suppress both the header and trailer, as if the -t option were in effect.

-m

> Merge files. Format standard output to write one line from each file specified by *file*, side by side, into text columns of equal fixed widths in terms of the number of column positions. Implementations support merging of at least nine files.

-n[*char*] [*width*]

> Provide *width*-digit line numbering (default for *width* is 5). The number occupies the first *width* column positions of each text column of default output or each line of -m output. If you specify *char* (any nondigit character), append to the line number to separate it from whatever follows (default for *char* is a Tab character).

-o *offset*

> Precede each line of output by *offset* spaces. If you do not specify the -o option, the default offset is 0. The space taken is in addition to the output line width (see -w option).

-p

> Pause before beginning each page if the standard output is directed to a terminal (write an ALERT character to standard error and wait for a Return character to be read on /dev/tty).

-r

> Write no diagnostic reports on failure to open files.

-s[*char*]

> Separate text columns by the single character *char* instead of by the appropriate number of space characters (default for *char* is the Tab character).

-t

> Write neither the 5-line identifying header nor the 5-line trailer usually supplied for each page. Quit writing after the last line of each file without spacing to the end of the page.

-w *width*

> Set the width of the line to *width* column positions for multiple text-column output only. If you do not specify the -w or -s options, the default width is 72. If you do not specify the -w option and specify the -s option, the default width is 512. For single column output, input lines are not truncated.

/usr/bin/pr

The following options are supported for /usr/bin/pr only.

-F   Fold the lines of the input file. When used in multicolumn mode (with the -a or -m options), fold lines to fit the current column's width; otherwise, fold them to fit the current line width (80 columns).

-i[*char*] [*gap*]

In output, replace space characters with Tab characters wherever one or more adjacent space characters reach column positions *gap*+1, 2**gap+1, 3**gap+1, and so forth. If *gap* is 0 or is omitted, set default Tabs at every eighth column position. If you specify any nondigit character, *char*, use it as the output Tab character.

/usr/xpg4/bin/pr

The following options are supported for /usr/xpg4/bin/pr only.

-F   Use a formfeed character for new pages instead of the default behavior that uses a sequence of newline characters.

-i[*char*] [*gap*]

In output, replace multiple space characters with Tab characters wherever two or more adjacent space characters reach column positions *gap*+1, 2**gap+1, 3**gap+1, and so forth. If *gap* is 0 or is omitted, set default Tabs at every eighth column position. If any nondigit character, *char*, is specified, use it as the output Tab character.

Operands

file   A path name of a file to be written. If you specify no file operands or if a file operand is -, use the standard input.

Examples

The following example prints a numbered list of all files in the current directory.

```
$ ls -a | pr -n -h "Files in $(pwd)."
```

```
Mar 26 16:29 1999  Files in $(pwd). Page 1


    1    .
    2    ..
    3    .cshrc
    4    .dt
    5    .dtprofile
    6    .hotjava
    7    .jetadmin
    8    .login
    9    .news_time
   10    .sh_history
   11    .solregis
   12    .Xauthority
```

```
13    .Xdefaults
14    bibliography
15    DeadLetters
16    examples
17    file1
18    kookaburra-1
19    ltr
20    Mail
...  (extra linefeeds removed)
$
```

The following example prints kookaburra-1 and bibliography as a double-spaced, three-column listing headed by "file list".

$ pr -3d -h "file list" kookaburra-1 bibliography

```
Mar 25 16:52 1999   file list Page 1


    1  Kookaburra sits      8  Stop, kookaburr    14  Gay your life m

    2  Merry merry kin      9  Leave some ther

    3  Laugh, kookabur     10                     15  Kookaburra sits

    4  Gay your life m     11  Kookaburra sits    16  Eating all the

    5                      12  Merry merry kin    17  Stop, kookaburr

    6  Kookaburra sits     13  Laugh, kookabur    18  Leave some ther

    7  Eating all the

...  (extra linefeeds removed)

Mar 18 08:35 1999   file list Page 1


%A Janice Winsor        friendly, personal styl ~

%T Opening the Dream Do attempt to interpret dr ~

%P 153                  that each person has th %A Janice Winsor

%I Merrill-West Publish cannot be deciphered in %T Opening the Dream Do

%C Carmel, California   dreams as an example, J %P 153

%D 1998                 for expanding the subco %I Merrill-West Publish

%K dreams, psychic deve Processes for rememberi %C Carmel, California

%X Not just another dre easy to understand styl %D 1998
```

```
is a practical guide to                                    %K dreams, psychic deve
...
```

   The following example writes `file1` on `file2`, expanding Tabs to columns 10, 19, 28, and so on.

```
$ pr -e9 -t <file1 >file2
```

Environment Variables

See `environ`(5) for descriptions of the following environment variables that affect the execution of `pr`: `LC_CTYPE`, `LC_MESSAGES`, `LC_TIME`, `TZ`, and `NLSPATH`.

Exit Status

0	Successful completion.
>0	An error occurred.

Attributes

See `attributes`(5) for descriptions of the following attributes:

/usr/bin/pr

Attribute Type	Attribute Value
Availability	SUNWcsu
CSI	Enabled

/usr/xpg4/bin/pr

Attribute Type	Attribute Value
Availability	SUNWxcu4
CSI	Enabled

See Also

`expand(1)`, `lp(1)`, `attributes(5)`, `environ(5)`, `XPG4(5)`

New! **praliases** — Display System Mail Aliases

Synopsis

`/bin/praliases [-c configfile] [-f aliasfile] [key]`

Description

Use the `praliases` command, new in the Solaris 8 Operating Environment, to display system mail aliases. When you specify no *key*, `praliases` displays the current system aliases, one per line, in no particular order. The form is *key*: *value*. When you specify a *key*, only that key is looked up and the appropriate *key*: *value* is displayed if found.

Options

-c *configfile*

> Specify a sendmail configuration file.

-f *aliasfile*

> Reads the specified file *aliasfile* instead of the default sendmail system aliases file.

Operands

key   A specific alias key to look up.

Exit Status

0   Successful operation.

>0   An error occurred.

Files

/etc/mail/sendmail.cf

> The default sendmail configuration file.

/etc/mail/aliases

> The default sendmail system aliases file.

/etc/mail/aliases.dir
/etc/mail/aliases.pag

> The database versions of the /etc/mail/aliases file.

Attributes

See attributes(5) for descriptions of the following attributes:

Attribute Type	Attribute Value
Availability	SUNWsndmu

See Also

mailq(1), newaliases(1), sendmail(1M), attributes(5)

New! prctl — Get or Set the Resource Controls of Running
Processes, Tasks, and Projects

Synopsis

```
/bin/prctl [-t [basic | privileged| system]] [-e | -d action] [-rx]
    [-n name [-v value]] [-i idtype] [id...]
```

Description

Use the prctl command, new in the Solaris 9 Operating Environment, to examine and
modify the resource controls associated with an active process, task, or project on the
system. prctl enables access to the basic and privileged limits on the specified entity.

Options

-d | -e *action*

Disable (-d) or enable (-e) the specified action on the specified resource
control. The special token all is valid with the disable option to
deactivate all actions on the given resource control value.

The other defined actions for a resource are deny and signal=*signum*.
The deny action indicates that the resource control encountered tries to
deny granting the resource to the process, task, or project on a request
for resources in excess of the value provided by the -v option for the new
resource control. In the signal=*signum* action, *signum* is a signal
number (or string representation of a signal). You cannot activate or
deactivate deny actions when global flags indicate that the deny action
is unchangeable.

-i *idtype*
Specify the type of the ID operands. Valid *idtypes* are process, task,
or project. The default ID type is process.

-n *name*
Specify the name of the resource control to get or set. If you do not
specify *name*, prctl retrieves all resource controls.

-r
Replace the first resource control value (matching with the -t privilege)
with the new value specified by the -v option.

-t [basic| privileged | system]

Specify which resource control type to set. Unless the "lowerable" flag is
set for a resource control, only invocations by users (or setuid programs)
who have privileges equivalent to those of root can modify privileged
resource controls. See rctlblk_set_value(3C) for a description of the
RCTL_GLOBAL_LOWERABLE flag. If you do not specify the type, basic is
assumed. For a get operation, the values of all resource control types,
including system, are displayed if you specify no type.

-v *value*
Specify the value for the resource control for a set operation. If you
specify no value, then the modification (deletion, action enabling or
disabling) is carried out on the lowest-valued resource control with the
given type.

-x Delete the specified resource control value. If you do not provide the delete option, the default operation of prctl is to modify a resource control value of matching value and privilege or insert a new value with the given privilege. The matching criteria are discussed more fully in setrctl(2).

If you do not specify the -d, -e, -v, or -x option, the invocation is considered a get operation.

Operands

id The ID of the entity (process, task, or project) to interrogate. If the invoking user's credentials are unprivileged and the entity being interrogated possesses different credentials, the operation fails. If you specify no *id*, an error message is returned.

Examples

The following example displays current resource control settings for a specific process.

```
example$ pgrep sort
111759
example$ prctl 111759
111759: /usr/bin/sort
process.max-address-space          [ lowerable deny no-local-action ]
     18446744073709551615 privileged deny
     18446744073709551615 system      deny
process.max-file-descriptor        [ lowerable deny ]
              256 basic       deny
            65536 privileged deny
       2147483647 system      deny
process.max-core-size              [ lowerable deny no-local-action ]
           18446744073709551615 privileged deny
     18446744073709551615 system      deny
process.max-stack-size             [ lowerable deny no-local-action ]
          8388608 basic       deny
     9223372036854775807 privileged deny
     9223372036854775807 system      deny
process.max-data-size              [ lowerable deny no-local-action ]
     18446744073709551615 privileged deny
     18446744073709551615 system      deny
process.max-file-size              [ lowerable deny file-size ]
     9223372036854775807 privileged signal=XFSZ deny
     9223372036854775807 system      deny
process.max-cpu-time               [ lowerable no-deny cpu-time ]
     18446744073709551615 privileged signal=XCPU
     18446744073709551615 system      deny            [ infinite ]
task.max-cpu-time                  [ no-deny cpu-time ]
     18446744073709551615 system      deny            [ infinite ]
task.max-lwps
       2147483647 system      deny
project.cpu-shares                 [ no-basic no-local-action ]
           10 privileged none
            65535 system      deny
example$
```

The following example displays, replaces, and verifies the value of a specific control on a existing project.

```
# prctl -n project.cpu-shares -i project group.staff
111788: ksh
project.cpu-shares                      [ no-basic no-local-action]
        1 privileged none
            65535 system      deny
# prctl -n project.cpu-shares -v 10 -r -i project group.staff
# prctl -n project.cpu-shares -i project group.staff
111788: ksh
project.cpu-shares                      [ no-basic no-local-action ]
        10 privileged none
            65535 system      deny
#
```

Exit Status

0	Success.
1	Fatal error encountered.
2	Invalid command-line options were specified.

Files

/proc/pid/*

Process information and control files.

Attributes

See attributes(5) for descriptions of the following attributes.

Attribute Type	Attribute Value
Availability	SUNWesu

See Also

rctladm(1M), setrctl(2), rctlblk_get_local_action(3C), attributes(5)

New! preap — Force a Defunct Process to be Reaped by Its Parent

Synopsis

/bin/preap [-F] *pid*...

Description

Use the preap command, new in the Solaris 9 Operating Environment, to force a defunct process to be reaped by its parent.

A defunct (or zombie) process is one whose exit status has yet to be reaped by its parent. The exit status is reaped by the wait(2), waitid(2), or waitpid(2) system call. In the normal course of system operation, zombies can occur but are typically short-lived.

Zombies can result if a parent exits without having reaped the exit status of some or all of its children. In that case, those children are reparented to PID 1. See init(1M), which periodically reaps such processes.

An irresponsible parent process may not exit for a very long time and thus can leave zombies on the system. Because the operating system destroys nearly all components of a process before it becomes defunct, such defunct processes do not normally impact system operation. However, they do consume a small amount of system memory.

preap forces the parent of the process specified by *pid* to waitid(2) for *pid* if *pid* represents a defunct process.

preap tries to prevent the administrator from unwisely reaping a child process that might soon be reaped by the parent in the following conditions.

- The process is a child of init(1M).
- The parent process is stopped and might wait on the child when it is again allowed to run.
- The process has been defunct for less than one minute.

Warning — Apply preap sparingly and only in situations in which the administrator or developer has confirmed that defunct processes will not be reaped by the parent process. Otherwise, applying preap may damage the parent process in unpredictable ways.

Options

-F   Force the parent to reap the child, overriding safety checks.

Operands

pid   Process ID list.

Exit Status

The following exit values are returned by preap, which prints the exit status of each target process reaped.

0   Successful operation.

non-zero   Failure, such as no such process, permission denied, or invalid option.

Attributes

See attributes(5) for descriptions of the following attributes.

Attribute Type	Attribute Value
Availability	SUNWesu (32 bit)
	SUNWesxu (64 bit)

See Also

proc(1), init(1M), wait(2), waitid(2), waitpid(2), proc(4), attributes(5)

prex — Control Tracing in a Process or the Kernel

Synopsis

```
/usr/bin/prex [-o trace-file-name] [-l libraries] [-s kbytes-size] cmd
  [cmd-args...]
/usr/bin/prex [-o trace-file-name] [-l libraries] [-s kbytes-size]
  -p pid
/usr/bin/prex -k [-s kbytes-size]
```

Description

The prex command is the part of the Solaris tracing architecture that controls probes in a process or the kernel. See tracing(3TNF) for an overview of this tracing architecture and for example source code.

prex is the application used for external control of probes. It locates all the probes in a target executable or the kernel and provides an interface for you to manipulate them. prex enables you to turn on a probe for tracing, debugging, or both. Tracing generates a TNF (Trace Normal Form) trace file that you can convert to ASCII with tnfdump(1) and use for performance analysis. Debugging generates a line to standard error whenever the probe is hit at runtime.

Note — prex does not work on static executables. It works only on dynamic executables.

Invoking prex

You can invoke prex in three ways.

- Use prex to start the target application *cmd*. In this case, the target application need not be built with a dependency on libtnfprobe. See TNF_PROBE(3TNF). prex sets the environment variable LD_PRELOAD to load libtnfprobe into the target process. See ld(1). prex then uses the environment variable PATH to find the target application.

- Attach prex to a running application. In this case, the running target application should have libtnfprobe already linked in. Alternatively, you can manually set LD_PRELOAD to include libtnfprobe.so.1 before invoking the target.

- Use prex with the -k option to set it to kernel mode. You can then use prex to control probes in the Solaris kernel. In kernel mode, additional commands are defined and some commands that are valid in other modes are invalid.

Control File Format and Command Language

In a future release of prex, the command language may be moved to a syntax that is supported by an existing scripting language like ksh(1). In the meantime, the interface to prex is uncommitted.

- Specify commands in ASCII.
- Terminate each command with the newline character.
- Continue a command onto the next line by ending the previous line with the backslash (\) character.
- Separate tokens in a command by white space (one or more spaces or Tabs).

- Use the # character to indicate that the rest of the line is a comment.

Basic prex Commands

Command	Result
% **prex a.out**	Attach prex to your program, and start prex.
prex> **enable $all**	Enable all the probes.
prex> **quit resume**	Quit prex, and resume execution of the program.

Control File Search Path

You can communicate with prex in two different ways:

- By specifications in a control file. During startup, prex searches for a file named .prexrc in the directories specified below. prex does not stop at the first file it finds. You can use the control file to override any defaults. The search order is: $HOME/ ./.
- By typing commands at the prex prompt.

The command language for both methods is the same and is specified in "Usage" on page 1097. The commands that return output do not make sense in a control file. The output goes to standard output.

When prex is used on a target process, the target is in one of two states: running or stopped. You can detect the state by the presence or absence of the prex> prompt. If the prompt is absent, it means that the target process is running. Typing Control-C stops the target process and returns the prompt. There is no guarantee that Control-C returns to a prex prompt immediately. For example, if the target process is stopped on a job control stop (SIGSTOP), then Control-C in prex waits until the target has been continued (SIGCONT). See "Signals to Target Program" on page 1100 for more information on signals and the target process.

Notes

Currently, the only probe function that is available is the &debug function. When this function is executed, it prints the arguments sent to the probe as well as the value associated with the sunw%debug attribute in the detail field (if any) to standard error. For example, for the following probe point,

```
TNF_PROBE_2(input_values, "testapp main",
"sunw%debug 'have read input values successfully'",
tnf_long, int_input, x,
tnf_string, string_input, input);
```

if x was 100 and input was the string "success", then the output of the debug probe function would be

```
probe input_values; sunw%debug "have read input values successfully";
int_input=100; string_input="success";
```

Some non-SPARC hardware lacks a true high-resolution timer so that gethrtime() returns the same value multiple times in succession. As a result, some tools can have problems interpreting the trace file. You can improve this situation by interposing a version of gethrtime(), shown below, that artificially increments these successive values by one nanosecond.

```
hrtime_t
gethrtime()
{
    static mutex_t lock;
    static hrtime_t (*real_gethrtime)(void) = null;
    static hrtime_t last_time = 0;

    hrtime_t this_time;
    if (real_gethrtime == null) {
        real_gethrtime =
            (hrtime_t (*)(void)) dlsym(RTLD_NEXT, "gethrtime");
    }
    this_time = real_gethrtime();

    mutex_lock(&lock);
    if (this_time <= last_time)
        this_time = ++last_time;
    else
        last_time = this_time;
    mutex_unlock(&lock);
    return (this_time);
}
```

Of course, this workaround does not increase the resolution of the timer, so timestamps for individual events are still relatively inaccurate. However, this technique does maintain ordering so that if event A causes event B, B never seems to happen before or at the same time as A.

dbx is available with the Sun Workshop Products.

Options

-k   Control probes in the Solaris kernel. Kernel mode defines additional commands and invalidates commands valid in other modes. See "Kernel Mode" on page 1101.

-l *libraries*

Link *libraries*, a space-separated string of library names enclosed in double quotes, into the target application, using LD_PRELOAD (see ld(1)). You cannot use this option when attaching to a running process. Specify library names, following the LD_PRELOAD rules on how libraries should be specified and where they are found.

-o *trace-file-name*

Use *trace-file-name* to trace output. *trace-file-name* is assumed to be relative to the current working directory of prex (that is, the directory that you were in when you started prex).

If prex attaches to a process that is already tracing, do not use the new *trace-file-name* (if provided). If you specify no *trace-file-name*, the default is /$TMPDIR/trace-*pid*, where *pid* is the process ID of the target program. If TMPDIR is not set, use /tmp.

-s *kbytes-size*

>   Set the maximum size of the output trace file in kilobytes. The default
>   size of the trace *kbytes-size* is 4096 or 4 megabytes for normal usage
>   and 384 or 384 kilobytes in kernel mode. You can think of the trace file
>   as a least recently used circular buffer. Once the file has been filled,
>   newer events overwrite the older ones.

Usage

Grammar

Specify probes as a list of space-separated selectors. Selectors are of the form:

attribute=value

(see TNF_PROBE(3TNF)). The *attribute=* is optional. If you do not specify it, the default
is keys=.

The *attribute* or *value* (generically called spec) can be any of the following.

IDENT   Any sequence of letters, digits, _, \, ., % not beginning with a digit.
                 IDENT implies an exact match.

QUOTED_STR   Usually used to escape reserved words (any commands in the command
                 language). QUOTED_STR implies an exact match and must be enclosed in
                 single quotes (' ').

REGEXP   An ed(1) regular expression pattern match. Enclose REGEXP in slashes
                 (/ /). You can include a / in a REGEXP by escaping it with a backslash \.

The following grammar explains the syntax.

```
selector_list ::=     |                   /* empty */
                      selector_list selector
selector ::=          spec=spec |         /* white space around = opt */
                      spec
spec ::=              IDENT |
                      QUOTED_STR |
                      REGEXP
```

The terminals in the above grammar are shown below.

```
IDENT =               [a-zA-Z_\.%]{[a-zA-Z0-9_\.%]}+
QUOTED_STR =          '[^\n']*'           /* any string in single quotes */
REGEXP =              /[^\n/]*/           /* a regexp has to be in / / */
```

The following list shows the remaining grammar that is needed to understand the
syntax of the command language (defined in next subsection).

```
filename ::=          QUOTED_STR          /* QUOTED_STR defined above */
spec_list ::=         /* empty */ |
                      spec_list spec      /* spec defined above */
fcn_handle ::=        &IDENT              /* IDENT defined above */
set_name ::=          $IDENT              /* IDENT defined above */
```

Command Language

Set Creation and Set Listing

```
create $set_name selector_list
list    sets                      # list the defined sets
```

You can use `create` to define a set that contains probes that match the *selector_list*. The set `$all` is predefined as `/.*/`. It matches all the probes.

Function Listing

```
list    fcns                      # list the available fcn_handle
```

You can list the different functions that can be connected to probe points. Currently, only the `&debug` function is available.

Commands to Connect and Disconnect Probe Functions

```
connect &fcn_handle $set_name
connect &fcn_handle selector_list
clear $set_name
clear selector_list
```

Use the `connect` command to connect probe functions (which must be prefixed by `&`) to probes. You specify the probes either as a single set (with a `$`) or by explicitly listing the probe selectors in the command. The probe function has to be one that is listed by the `list fcns` command. This command does not enable the probes.

Use the `clear` command to disconnect all connected probe functions from the specified probes.

Commands to Toggle the Tracing Mode

```
trace $set_name
trace selector_list
untrace $set_name
untrace selector_list
```

Use the `trace` and `untrace` commands to toggle the tracing action of a probe point (that is, whether or not a probe emits a trace record if it is hit). This command does not enable the probes specified. Probes have tracing on by default. The most efficient way to turn off tracing is by using the `disable` command. `untrace` is useful if you want debug output but do no tracing. If so, set the state of the probe to `enabled`, `untraced`, and the debug function to `connected`.

Commands to Enable and Disable Probes

```
enable $set_name
enable selector_list
disable $set_name
disable selector_list
```

Use the `enable` and `disable` commands to control whether the probes perform the action for which they have been set up. To trace a probe, you must both enable and trace (using the `trace` command) the probe. Probes are disabled by default. Use the `list` history command to list the probe control commands issued: `connect`, `clear`, `trace`, `untrace`, `enable`, and `disable`. These commands are executed whenever a new shared object is brought in to the target program by `dlopen(3DL)`. See "dlopen'ed Libraries" on page 1100 for more information.

The following table shows the actions that result from specific combinations of tracing, enabling, and connecting.

New!

Enabled or Disabled	Tracing State (On/Off)	Debug State (Connected/Cleared)	Results in
Enabled	On	Connected	Tracing and debugging
Enabled	On	Cleared	Tracing only
Enabled	Off	Connected	Debugging only
Enabled	Off	Cleared	Nothing
Disabled	On	Connected	Nothing
Disabled	On	Cleared	Nothing
Disabled	Off	Connected	Nothing
Disabled	Off	Cleared	Nothing

List History

```
list history     # lists probe control command history
```

The `list` history command displays a list of the probe control commands previously issued in the tracing session, for example, `connect`, `clear`, `trace`, `disable`. Commands in the history list are executed whenever a new shared object is brought into the target program by `dlopen`(3DL).

Commands to List Probes or List Values

```
list spec_list probes $set_name          # list probes $all
list spec_list probes selector_list      # list name probes
                                         # file=test.c
list values spec_list                    # list values keys
list tracefile                           # list tracefile
```

New!

The first two commands list the selected attributes and values of the specified probes. You can use them to check the state of a probe. The third command lists the various values associated with the selected attributes. The fourth command lists the current tracefile.

New!

Help Command

```
help topic
```

Invoke the `help` command with no arguments to view a list of the available help topics. If a topic argument is specified, help is printed for that topic.

Source a File

```
source filename
```

You can use the `source` command to source a file of `prex` commands. `source` can be nested (that is, a file can source another file).

Process Control

```
continue          # resume the target process
quit kill         # quit prex, kill target
quit resume       # quit prex, continue target
quit suspend      # quit prex, leave target suspended
quit              # quit prex, continue or kill target
```

The default `quit` continues the target process if `prex` is attached to it. Instead, if `prex` had started the target program, `quit` kills the target process.

dlopen'ed Libraries

Probes in shared objects that are brought in by `dlopen`(3DL) are automatically set up according to the command history of `prex`. When a shared object is removed by a `dlclose`(3DL), `prex` again needs to refresh its understanding of the probes in the target program. This requirement implies that there is more work to do for `dlopen`(3DL) and `dlclose`(3DL), so they take slightly longer. If you are not interested in this feature and do not want to interfere with `dlopen`(3DL) and `dlclose`(3DL), detach `prex` from the target to inhibit this feature.

Signals to Target Program

`prex` does not interfere with signals that are delivered directly to the target program. However, `prex` receives all signals normally generated from the terminal, for example, Control-C (`SIGINT`), and Control-Z (`SIGSTOP`), and does not forward them to the target program. To signal the target program, use the `kill`(1) command from a shell.

Interactions with Other Applications

Process managing applications like `dbx`, `truss`(1), and `prex` cannot operate on the same target program simultaneously. `prex` is not able to attach to a target that is being controlled by another application. You can trace and debug a program serially by the following method: first, attach `prex` to target (or start target through `prex`), set up the probes by using the command language, and then type `quit suspend`. You can then attach `dbx` to the suspended process and debug it. You can also suspend the target by sending it a `SIGSTOP` signal, and then by typing `quit resume` to `prex`. In this case, you should also send a `SIGCONT` signal after invoking `dbx` on the stopped process, or else `dbx` hangs.

Failure of Event-Writing Operations

There are a few failure points, such as system call failures, that are possible when writing events to a trace file. These failures result in a failure code being set in the target process. The target process continues normally, but no trace records are written. Whenever you type Control-C to `prex` to get to a `prex` prompt, `prex` checks the failure code in the target and informs you if there was a tracing failure.

Target Executing a fork or exec

If the target program does a `fork`(2), any probes that the child encounters log events to the same trace file. Events are annotated with a process ID, so it is possible to determine which process a particular event came from. In multithreaded programs, a race condition results with a thread doing a `fork` while the other threads are still running. For the trace file not to be corrupted, either use `fork1`(2) or make sure that all other threads are quiescent when doing a `fork`(2),

If the target program itself (not any children it may fork) does an `exec`(2), `prex` detaches from the target and exits. You can reconnect `prex` with `prex -p` *pid*.

A vfork(2) is generally followed quickly by an exec(2) in the child and, in the interim, the child borrows the parent's process while the parent waits for the exec(2). Any events logged by the child from the parent process appear to have been logged by the parent.

Kernel Mode

Invoking prex with the -k flag runs prex in kernel mode. In kernel mode, prex controls probes in the Solaris kernel. See tnf_kernel_probes(4) for a list of available probes in the Solaris kernel. A few prex commands are unavailable in kernel mode; many other commands are valid only in kernel mode.

The -l, -o, and -p options are not valid in kernel mode (that is, you cannot combine them with the -k option).

The rest of this section describes the differences in the prex command language when prex runs in kernel mode.

prex Does Not Stop the Kernel

When prex attaches to a running user program, it stops the user program. Obviously, it cannot do so when attaching to the kernel. Instead, prex provides a tracing master switch: no probes have any effect unless the tracing master switch is on. This switch enables you to iteratively select probes to enable, then to enable them all at once by turning on the master switch.

Use the following command to inspect and set the value of the master switch.

```
ktrace [on | off]
```

Without an argument, prex reports the current state of the master switch.

Because prex does not stop or kill the kernel, the quit resume and quit kill commands are not valid in kernel mode.

No Functions Can Be Attached to Probes in the Kernel

The debug function is not available in kernel mode.

Trace Output is Written to an In-Core Buffer

In kernel mode, a trace output file is not generated directly to enable probes to be placed in time-critical code. Instead, trace output is written to an in-core buffer and copied out by a separate program, tnfxtract(1).

The in-core buffer is not automatically created. The following prex command controls buffer allocation and deallocation.

```
buffer [alloc [size] | dealloc]
```

Without an argument, the buffer command reports the size of the currently allocated buffer if any. With an argument of alloc [size], prex allocates a buffer of the given size in bytes, with an optional suffix of k or m specifying a multiplier of 1,024 or 1,048,576. If you specify no size, the size specified on the command line with the -s option is used as a default. If you do not use the -s option, the default is 384 kilobytes.

With an argument of dealloc, prex deallocates the trace buffer in the kernel.

prex rejects attempts to turn on the tracing master switch when no buffer is allocated and to deallocate the buffer when the tracing master switch is on. prex refuses to allocate a buffer when one is already allocated; use buffer dealloc first.

prex does not allocate a buffer larger than one-half of physical memory.

prex Supports Per-Process Probe Enabling in the Kernel

In kernel mode you can choose a set of processes for which probes are enabled. No trace output is written when other processes traverse these probe points. This mode is called "process filter mode." By default, process filter mode is off, and all processes generate trace records when they hit an enabled probe.

Some kernel events such as interrupts cannot be associated with a particular user process. By convention, these events are considered to be generated by process ID 0.

prex provides commands to turn process filter mode on and off, to get the current status of the process filter mode switch, to add and delete processes (by process ID) from the process filter set, and to list the current process filter set.

The process filter set is maintained even when process filter mode is off but has no effect unless process filter mode is on.

When a process in the process filter set exits, its process ID is automatically deleted from the process filter set.

The following command controls the process filter switch and process filter set membership.

```
pfilter [on | off | add pidlist | delete pidlist]
```

With no arguments, pfilter prints the current process filter set and the state of the process filter mode switch. on or off sets the state of the process filter mode switch.

```
add pidlist
delete pidlist
```

add or delete processes from the process filter set. pidlist is a comma-separated list of one or more process IDs.

Examples

See tracing(3TNF) for complete examples showing, among other things, the use of prex for simple probe control.

When either the process or kernel is started, all probes are disabled.

```
# Set creation and set listing
create $out name=/out/    # $out = probes with "out" in
                          #    value of "name" attribute
create $foo /page/ name=biodone    # $foo = union of
        # probes with "page" in value of keys attribute
        # probes with "biodone" as value of "name" attribute
list sets                 # list the defined sets
list fcns                 # list the defined probe fcns

# Commands to trace and connect probe functions

trace foobar='on'         # exact match on foobar attribute
trace $all                # trace all probes (predefined set $all)
connect &debug $foo       # connect debug func to probes in $foo

# Commands to enable and disable probes

enable $all               # enable all probes
enable /vm/ name=alloc    # enable the specified probes
disable $foo              # disable probes in set $foo
list history              # list probe control commands issued

# Process control

continue                  # resumes the target process
```

```
^C                              # stop target; give control to prex
quit resume                     # exit prex, leave process running

# Kernel mode

buffer alloc 2m                 # allocate a 2-megabyte buffer
enable $all                     # enable all probes
trace $all                      # trace all probes
ktrace on                       # turn tracing on
ktrace off                      # turn tracing off
pfilter on                      # turn process filter mode on
pfilter add 1379                # add pid 1379 to process filter
ktrace on                       # turn tracing on
                                # (only pid 1379 will be traced)
```

Files

.prexrc   Local prex initialization file.

~/.prexrc   User's prex initialization file.

/proc/*nnnnn*

            Process files.

Attributes

See attributes(5) for descriptions of the following attributes:

Attribute Type	Attribute Value
Availability	SUNWtnfs (32-bit)
	SUNWtnfcx (64-bit)

See Also

ed(1), kill(1), ksh(1), ld(1), tnfdump(1), tnfxtract(1), truss(1),
exec(2), fork(2), fork1(2), vfork(2), gethrtime(3C), dlclose(3DL),
dlopen(3DL), libtnfctl(3TNF), TNF_DECLARE_RECORD(3TNF), TNF_PROBE(3TNF),
tnf_process_disable(3TNF), tracing(3TNF), tnf_kernel_probes(4),
attributes(5)

New!

Bugs

prex should issue a notification when a process ID has been automatically deleted from
the filter set.

A known bug in prex can result in the following message:

```
Tracing shut down in target program due to an internal
error - Please restart prex and target
```

When you run prex as root, the target process is not root and you put the tracefile in
a directory where it cannot be removed and recreated (such as a directory like /tmp with
the sticky bit on), then the target process is not able to open the tracefile when it needs
to, thus disabling tracing.

Changing any of the circumstances listed above should fix the problem. Either don't
run prex as root, run the target process as root, or specify the tracefile in a directory
other than /tmp.

print — Shell Built-in Function to Output Characters to the Screen or Window

Synopsis

ksh

```
print [-Rnprsu[n]] [arg...]
```

Description

Korn Shell

The print built-in function is the mechanism used by the Korn shell to display *arg*. With no options or with - or --, the arguments are printed on standard output as described by echo(1). The exit status is 0 unless the output file is not open for writing.

Options

-n	Suppress newline from being added to the output.
-R | -r	Ignore the escape conventions of echo. The -R option prints all subsequent arguments and options other than -n.
-p	Write the arguments onto the pipe of the process spawned with |& instead of to standard output.
-s	Write the arguments into the history file instead of to standard output.
-u [n]	Use the *n* argument to specify a one-digit file descriptor unit number on which the output is placed. The default is 1.

Attributes

See attributes(5) for descriptions of the following attributes:

Attribute Type	**Attribute Value**
Availability	SUNWcsu

See Also

```
echo(1), ksh(1), attributes(5)
```

printenv — Display Current Environment Variable

Synopsis

```
/usr/ucb/printenv [variable]
```

Description

Use the `printenv` command to print the values of the variables in the environment. If a variable is specified, only its value is printed.

Examples

The following example displays the value for the EDITOR environment variable.

```
castle% printenv EDITOR
/usr/dt/bin/dtpad
castle%
```

Attributes

See `attributes`(5) for descriptions of the following attributes:

Attribute Type	Attribute Value
Availability	SUNWscpu

See Also

`csh(1)`, `echo(1)`, `sh(1)`, `stty(1)`, `tset(1B)`, `attributes(5)`, `environ(5)`

Diagnostics

If a variable is specified and it is not defined in the environment, `printenv` returns an exit status of 1.

printf — Write Formatted Output

Synopsis

`/usr/bin/printf` *format* [*argument...*]

Description

The `printf` command writes formatted operands to the standard output. The *argument* operands are formatted under control of the *format* operand.

Operands

format   A string describing the format used to write the remaining operands. Use the *format* operand as the format string described on the `formats`(5) manual page, with the following exceptions.

- In any context other than a flag of a conversion specification, treat a space character in the format string as an ordinary character that is copied to the output.

- Treat a delta character in the format string as a delta character, not as a space character.

- In addition to the escape sequences described on the formats(5) manual page (\\, \a, \b, \f, \n, \r, \t, \v), write \ *ddd*, where *ddd* is a one-, two- or three-digit octal number, as a byte with the numeric value specified by the octal number.

- Do not precede or follow output from the d or u conversion specifications with blank characters not specified by the *format* operand.

- Do not precede output from the o conversion specification with 0s not specified by the *format* operand.

- An additional conversion character, b, is supported as follows. Take the argument to be a string that can contain backslash-escape sequences. The following backslash-escape sequences are supported.

  - Convert the escape sequences listed on the formats(5) manual page (\\, \a, \b, \f, \n, \r, \t, \v) to the characters they represent.

  - Convert \0 *ddd*, where *ddd* is a zero-, one-, two-, or three-digit octal number to a byte with the numeric value specified by the octal number.

  - Write \c and ignore any remaining characters in the string operand containing it, any remaining string operands, and any additional characters in the format operand.

The interpretation of a backslash followed by any other sequence of characters is unspecified.

Write bytes from the converted string until reaching the end of the string or the number of bytes indicated by the precision specification. If the precision is omitted, take it to be infinite, so write all bytes up to the end of the converted string. For each specification that consumes an argument, evaluate the next argument operand and convert it to the appropriate type for the conversion, as specified below. Reuse the format operand as often as needed to satisfy the argument operands. Evaluate any extra c or s conversion specifications as if a null string argument were supplied; evaluate other extra conversion specifications as if a 0 argument were supplied. If the format operand contains no conversion specifications and argument operands are present, the results are unspecified. If a character sequence in the format operand begins with a % character but does not form a valid conversion specification, the behavior is unspecified.

argument Specify the strings to be written to standard output under the control of *format*. Treat the argument operands as strings if the corresponding conversion character is b, c, or s; otherwise, evaluate it as a C constant, as described by the ISO C standard, with the following extensions.

- Allow a leading + or – sign.

- If the leading character is a single or double quote, the value is the numeric value in the underlying codeset of the character following the single or double quote.

If an *argument* operand cannot be completely converted into an internal value appropriate to the corresponding conversion specification, write a diagnostic message to standard error, do not exit with a 0 exit status, continue processing any remaining operands, and write to standard output the value accumulated at the time the error was detected.

Usage

Note that the printf command, like the printf(3S) function on which it is based, makes no special provision for dealing with multibyte characters when using the %c conversion specification or when a precision is specified in a %b or %s conversion specification. Application programmers should be extremely cautious about using either of these features when there are multibyte characters in the character set.

You cannot specify field widths and precisions as *.

For compatibility with previous versions of SunOS 5.x, the $ format specifier is supported for formats containing only %s specifiers.

The %b conversion specification is not part of the ISO C standard; it has been added here as a portable way to process backslash escapes expanded in string operands as provided by the echo command. See also the echo(1) manual page for ways to use printf as a replacement for all of the traditional versions of the echo command.

If an argument cannot be parsed correctly for the corresponding conversion specification, the printf command reports an error. Thus, overflow and extraneous characters at the end of an argument being used for a numeric conversion are reported as errors.

It is not considered an error if an *argument* operand is not completely used for a c or s conversion or if a string operand's first or second character is used to get the numeric value of a character.

Examples

The following example alerts the user and then prints and reads a series of prompts.

```
printf "\aPlease fill in the following: \nName: "
read name
printf "Phone number: "
read phone
```

The following example reads a list of right and wrong answers from a file, calculates the percentages correctly, and prints them out. The numbers are right-justified and separated by a single Tab character. The percentage is written to one decimal place of accuracy.

```
while read right wrong ; do
  percent=$(echo "scale=1;($right*100)/($right+$wrong)" | bc)
  printf "%2d right\t%2d wrong\t(%s%%)\n" \
    $right $wrong $percent
done < database_file
```

The command

```
printf "%5d%4d\n" 1 21 321 4321 54321
```

produces

```
   1  21
3214321
54321   0
```

Note that the format operand is used three times to print all of the given strings and that a 0 was supplied by printf to satisfy the last %4d conversion specification.

The printf command tells the user when conversion errors are detected while producing numeric output; thus, the following results would be expected on an implementation with 32-bit twos-complement integers when %d is specified as the format operand.

Standard Argument	Output	Diagnostic Output
5a	5	printf: 5a not completely converted
9999999999	2147483647	printf: 9999999999: Results too large
-9999999999	-2147483648	printf: -9999999999: Results too large
ABC	0	printf: ABC expected numeric value

Note that the value shown on standard output is what would be expected as the return value from the function strtol(3C). A similar correspondence exists between %u and strtoul(3C), and %e, %f, %g and strtod(3C).

In a locale using the ISO/IEC 646:1991 standard as the underlying codeset, the command

```
printf "%d\n" 3 +3 -3 \'3 \"+3 "'-3"
```

produces:

3	Numeric value of constant 3.
3	Numeric value of constant 3.
-3	Numeric value of constant -3.
51	Numeric value of the character 3 in the ISO/IEC 646:1991 standard codeset.
43	Numeric value of the character + in the ISO/IEC 646:1991 standard codeset.
45	Numeric value of the character - in the SO/IEC 646:1991 standard codeset.

Note — In a locale with multibyte characters, the value of a character is intended to be the value of the equivalent of the wchar_t representation of the character.

If an *argument* operand cannot be completely converted into an internal value appropriate to the corresponding conversion specification, a diagnostic message is written to standard error and the command returns a 0 exit status, continues processing any remaining operands, and writes to standard output the value accumulated at the time the error was detected.

Environment Variables

See environ(5) for descriptions of the following environment variables that affect the execution of printf: LC_COLLATE, LC_CTYPE, LC_MESSAGES, LC_TIME, TZ, and NLSPATH.

Exit Status

0	Successful completion.
>0	An error occurred.

Attributes

See attributes(5) for descriptions of the following attributes:

Attribute Type	Attribute Value
Availability	SUNWloc
CSI	Enabled

See Also

awk(1), bc(1), echo(1), strtod(3C), strtol(3C), strtoul(3C), printf(3S), attributes(5), environ(5), formats(5)

priocntl — Display or Set Scheduling Parameters of Specified Process(es)

Synopsis

```
/usr/bin/priocntl -l
/usr/bin/priocntl -d [-i idtype] [idlist]
/usr/bin/priocntl -s [-c class] [class-specific options] [-i idtype]
    [idlist]
/usr/bin/priocntl -e [-c class] [class-specific options] command
    [argument(s)]
```

Description

Use the priocntl (priority control) command to assign processes to a priority class and to manage process priorities within a class. You can also use priocntl to display the current configuration information for the system process scheduler or to execute a command with specified scheduling parameters.

Processes fall into distinct classes with a separate scheduling policy applied to each class. The process classes currently supported are:

- Real-time.
- Timesharing.

- Interactive.

- Fair-share (new in the Solaris 9 release).

- Fixed-priority (new in the Solaris 9 release.

The characteristics of these classes and the class-specific options they accept are described below. With appropriate permissions, the priocntl command can change the class and other scheduling parameters associated with a running process.

The class-specific parameters to be set are specified by the class-specific options, as explained under the appropriate heading below. If you omit the -c *class* option, *idtype* and *idlist* must specify a set of processes that are all in the same class; otherwise, an error results. If you specify no class-specific options, the class-specific parameters of the process are set to the default values for the class specified by -c *class* (or to the default parameter values for the process's current class if you also omit the -c *class* option).

For the scheduling parameters of a process to be changed with priocntl, the real or effective user ID or group ID of the user invoking priocntl must match the real or effective user ID or group ID of the receiving process; otherwise, the effective user ID must be superuser. These are the minimum permission requirements enforced for all classes. An individual class can impose additional permissions requirements when setting processes to that class or when setting class-specific scheduling parameters.

When *idtype* and *idlist* specify a set of processes, priocntl acts on the processes in the set in an implementation-specific order. If priocntl encounters an error for one or more of the target processes, it may or may not continue through the set of processes, depending on the nature of the error.

If the error is related to permissions, priocntl prints an error message and then continues through the process set, resetting the parameters for all target processes for which the user has appropriate permissions. If priocntl encounters an error other than permissions, it does not continue through the process set but prints an error message and exits immediately.

Real-Time Class

The real-time class provides a fixed-priority, preemptive scheduling policy for those processes requiring fast and deterministic response and absolute user/application control of scheduling priorities. If the real-time class is configured in the system, it should have exclusive control of the highest range of scheduling priorities on the system. This control ensures that a runnable real-time process is given CPU service before any process belonging to any other class.

> **Note —** In the default configuration, a runnable real-time process runs before any other process. Therefore, inappropriate use of real-time processes can have a dramatic negative impact on system performance.

The real-time class has a range of real-time priority (*rtpri*) values that can be assigned to processes within the class. Real-time priorities range from 0 to *x*, where the value of *x* is configurable and can be displayed for a specific installation that has already configured a real-time scheduler, with the following command.

```
castle% priocntl -l
CONFIGURED CLASSES
==================

SYS (System Class)

TS (Time Sharing)
        Configured TS User Priority Range: -60 through 60
```

```
IA (Interactive)
      Configured IA User Priority Range: -60 through 60
castle%
```

The real-time scheduling policy is a fixed-priority policy. The scheduling priority of a real-time process never changes except as the result of an explicit request by the user/application to change the *rtpri* value of the process.

For processes in the real-time class, the *rtpri* value is, for all practical purposes, equivalent to the scheduling priority of the process. The *rtpri* value completely determines the scheduling priority of a real-time process relative to other processes within its class. Numerically higher *rtpri* values represent higher priorities. Because the real-time class controls the highest range of scheduling priorities in the system, it is guaranteed that the runnable real-time process with the highest *rtpri* value is always selected to run before any other process in the system.

In addition to controlling priority, priocntl can control the length of the time quantum allotted to processes in the real-time class. The time quantum value specifies the maximum amount of time a process can run, assuming that it does not complete or enter a resource or event wait state (sleep). Note that if another process becomes runnable at a higher priority, the currently running process can be preempted before receiving its full time quantum.

The following command displays the real-time priority and time quantum (in millisecond resolution) for each real-time process in the set specified by *idtype* and *idlist*.

```
priocntl -d [-i idtype] [idlist]
```

You can use any combination of the -p and -t options with priocntl -s or priocntl -e for the real-time class. If you omit an option and the process is currently real-time, the associated parameter is unaffected. If you omit an option when changing the class of a process to real-time from some other class, the associated parameter is set to a default value. The default value for *rtpri* is 0, and the default for the time quantum is dependent on the value of *rtpri* and on the system configuration; see rt_dptbl(4).

When using the -t *tqntm* option, you can optionally specify a resolution with the -r *res* option. (If you specify no resolution, millisecond resolution is assumed.) If you specify *res*, it must be a positive integer between 1 and 1,000,000,000 inclusive and the resolution used is the reciprocal of *res* in seconds. For example, specifying -t 10 -r 100 sets the resolution to one-hundredths of a second and the resulting time-quantum length to one-tenth of a second (10/100). Although you can specify very fine (nanosecond) resolution, the time-quantum length is rounded up by the system to the next integral multiple of the system clock's resolution. Requests for time quanta of 0 or quanta greater than the (typically very large) implementation-specific maximum quantum result in an error.

You can use the real-time quantum signal—new in the Solaris 9 release—to notify *New!* runaway real-time processes about the consumption of their time quantum. Those processes, which are monitored by the real-time quantum signal, receive the configured signal when the time quantum expires. The default value (0) of the time quantum signal *tqsig* denotes no signal delivery. A positive value denotes the delivery of the signal specified by the value. Like kill (1) and other commands operating on signals, the -q *tqsig* option is also able to handle symbolically named signals like XCPU or KILL.

To change the class of a process to real-time (from any other class), you must have superuser privileges. To change the *rtpri* value or time quantum of a real-time process, you either must be superuser or must currently be in the real-time class (shell running as a real-time process) with a real or effective user ID matching the real or effective user ID of the target process.

The real-time priority, time quantum, and time quantum signal are inherited across the fork(2) and exec(2) system calls. When you use the time quantum signal with a user-defined signal handler across the exec(2) system call, the new image must install an appropriate user-defined signal handler before the time quantum expires. Otherwise, unpredictable behavior results.

Timesharing Class

The timesharing scheduling policy provides for a fair and effective allocation of the CPU resource among processes with varying CPU consumption characteristics. The objectives of the timesharing policy are to provide good response time to interactive processes and good throughput to CPU-bound jobs while providing a degree of user or application control over scheduling.

The timesharing class has a range of timesharing user priority (*tsupri*) values that can be assigned to processes within the class. User priorities range from –*x* to +*x*, where the value of *x* is configurable. You can display the range for a specific installation with the priocntl -l command.

The user priority provides some degree of user or application control over the scheduling of processes in the timesharing class. Raising or lowering the *tsupri* value of a process in the timesharing class raises or lowers the scheduling priority of the process. However, it is not guaranteed that a timesharing process with a higher *tsupri* value runs before one with a lower *tsupri* value, because the *tsupri* value is just one factor used to determine the scheduling priority of a timesharing process. The system can dynamically adjust the internal scheduling priority of a timesharing process based on other factors such as recent CPU usage.

In addition to the systemwide limits on user priority (displayed with priocntl -l), a per-process user priority limit (*tsuprilim*) specifies the maximum *tsupri* value that can be set for a given process.

The priocntl -d [-i *idtype*] [*idlist*] command displays the user priority and the user priority limit for each timesharing process in the set specified by *idtype* and *idlist*.

Any timesharing process can lower its own *tsuprilim* (or that of another process with the same user ID). Only a timesharing process with superuser privilege can raise a *tsuprilim*. When changing the class of a process to timesharing from some other class, you must have superuser privilege to set the initial *tsuprilim* to a value greater than 0.

Any timesharing process can set its own *tsupri* (or that of another process with the same user ID) to any value less than or equal to the process's *tsuprilim*. Attempts to set the *tsupri* above the *tsuprilim* (and/or set the *tsuprilim* below the *tsupri*) set the *tsupri* equal to the *tsuprilim*.

You can use any combination of the –m and –p options with priocntl -s or priocntl -e for the timesharing class. If you omit an option and the process is currently timesharing, the associated parameter is normally unaffected. The exception is that you can omit the –p option and use –m to set a *tsuprilim* below the current *tsupri*. In this case, the *tsupri* is set equal to the *tsuprilim* that is being set. If you omit an option when changing the class of a process to timesharing from some other class, the associated parameter is set to a default value. The default value for *tsuprilim* is 0, and the default for *tsupri* is to be set equal to the *tsuprilim* value that is being set.

The timesharing user priority and user priority limit are inherited across the fork(2) and exec(2) system calls.

Interactive Class

The interactive scheduling policy provides for a fair and effective allocation of the CPU resource among processes with varying CPU consumption characteristics while providing good responsiveness for user interaction. The objectives of the interactive policy are to provide good response time to interactive processes and good throughput to CPU-bound jobs. You can change the priorities of processes in the interactive class in the same way as those in the timesharing class, although the modified priorities continue to be adjusted to provide good responsiveness for user interaction.

In the default configuration, a runnable real-time process runs before any other process. Therefore, inappropriate use of real-time processes can have a dramatic negative impact on system performance.

If an *idlist* is present, it must appear last on the command line and the elements of the list must be separated by white space. If no *idlist* is present, an *idtype* argument of pid, ppid, pgid, sid, class, uid, or gid specifies the process ID, parent process ID, process group ID, session ID, class, user ID, or group ID of the priocntl command itself.

The following command displays the class and class-specific scheduling parameters of the process(es) specified by *idtype* and *idlist*.

```
priocntl -d [-i idtype] [idlist]
```

The following example uses the –d option with no arguments.

```
castle% priocntl -d
INTERACTIVE CLASS PROCESSES:
    PID   IAUPRILIM   IAUPRI   IAMODE
    422       0          0        1
castle%
```

The following command sets the class and class-specific parameters of the specified processes to the values given on the command line.

```
# priocntl -s [-c class] [class-specific options] [-i idtype] [idlist]
```

The –c class option specifies the class to be set. (The valid class arguments are RT for real-time, TS for timesharing, or IA for interactive.)

The *iaupri* interactive user priority is equivalent to *tsupri*. The interactive per-process user priority limit, *iauprilim*, is equivalent to *tsuprilim*.

Interactive processes that have the *iamode* (interactive mode) bit set are given a priority boost value of 10, which is factored into the user mode priority of the process when that calculation is made, that is, every time a process's priority is adjusted. This feature is used by the X Window System, which sets this bit for those processes that run inside of the current active window to give them a higher priority.

Fair-Share Class

The fair-share scheduling policy—new in the Solaris 9 release—provides a fair allocation of system CPU resources among projects, independently of the number of processes they own. Projects are given "shares" to control their entitlement to CPU resources. Resource use is remembered over time, so that entitlement is reduced for heavy use and increased for light use with respect to other projects. CPU time is scheduled among processes according to their owner's entitlements, independently of the number of processes each project owns.

The FSS scheduling class supports the notion of per-process user priority and user priority limit for compatibility with the time-share scheduler. The fair-share scheduler tries to provide an evenly graded effect across the whole range of user priorities.

Processes with positive *fssupri* values receive time slices less frequently than is normal, whereas negative `nice` processes receive time slices more frequently than is normal. Notice that user priorities do not interfere with shares. That is, changing a *fssupri* value of a process is not going to affect its project's overall CPU use, which relates only to the amount of shares it is allocated compared to other projects.

You can change the priorities of processes in the fair-share class in the same way as those in the time-share class.

Fixed-Priority Class

The fixed-priority class—new in the Solaris 9 release—provides a fixed-priority preemptive-scheduling policy for those processes requiring that the scheduling priorities are not dynamically adjusted by the system and that the user or application has control of the scheduling priorities.

The fixed-priority class shares the same range of scheduling priorities as the timesharing class, by default. The fixed-priority class has a range of fixed-priority user priority (*fxupri*) values that can be assigned to processes within the class. User priorities range from 0 to x, where the value of x is configurable. You can display the range for a specific installation with the `priocntl -l` command.

The user priority provides user and application control over the scheduling of processes in the fixed-priority class. For processes in the fixed-priority class, the *fxupri* value is, for all practical purposes, equivalent to the scheduling priority of the process. The *fxupri* value completely determines the scheduling priority of a fixed-priority process relative to other processes within its class. Numerically higher *fxupri* values represent higher priorities.

In addition to the systemwide limits on user priority (displayed with the `priocntl` `-l` command, a per-process priority limit (*fxuprilim*) specifies the maximum *fxupri* value that can be set for a given process.

Any fixed-priority process can lower its own *fxuprilim* (or that of another process with the same user ID). Only a process with superuser privilege can raise a *fxuprilim*. When the class of a process is changed to fixed priority from some other class, superuser privilege is required to set the initial *fxuprilim* to a value greater than zero.

Any fixed-priority process can set its own *fxupri* (or that of another process with the same user ID) to any value less than or equal to the process's *fxuprilim*. Attempts to set the *fxupri* above the *fxuprilim* (or set the *fxuprilim* below the *fxupri*) set the *fxupri* equal to the *fxuprilim*.

In addition to providing control over priority, `priocntl` provides control over the length of the time quantum allotted to the processes in the fixed-priority class. The time quantum value specifies the maximum time a process can run before surrendering the CPU, assuming that it does not complete or enter a resource or event wait state (sleep). Notice that if another process becomes runnable at a higher priority, the currently running process can be preempted before receiving its full time quantum.

You can use any combination of the -m, -p, and -t options with `priocntl -s` or `priocntl -e` for the fixed-priority class. If you omit an option and the process is currently fixed-priority, the associated parameter is normally unaffected. The exception is that you can omit the -p option and use the -m option to set a *fxuprilim* below the current *fxupri*. In this case, the *fxupri* is set equal to the *fxuprilim* that is being set. If you omit an option when changing the class of a process to fixed-priority from some other class, the associated parameter is set to a default value. The default value for *fxuprilim* is 0. The default for *fxupri* is to set it equal to the *fxuprilim* value that is being set. The default for time quantum depends on the *fxupri* and on the system configuration. See fx-dptbl(4).

You can change the time quantum of processes in the fixed-priority class in the same way as those in the real-time class.

The fixed-priority user priority, user priority limit, and time quantum are inherited across the fork(2) and exec(2) system calls.

sys Scheduling Class

A special sys scheduling class exists to schedule the execution of certain special system processes (such as the swapper process). It is not possible to change the class of any process in the sys class. In addition, priocntl disregards any processes in the sys class that are included in the set of processes specified by *idtype* and *idlist*.

For example, if *idtype* were uid, an *idlist* consisting of a 0 would specify all processes with a UID of 0 except processes in the sys class and (if changing the parameters with the -s option) the init process.

The init process (process ID 1) is a special case. For the priocntl command to change the class or other scheduling parameters of the init process, *idtype* must be pid and *idlist* must consist of only a 1. The init process can be assigned to any class configured on the system, but the timesharing class is almost always the appropriate choice. (Other choices can be highly undesirable; see the *System Administration Guide* for more information.)

The following command executes the specified command with the class and scheduling parameters specified on the command line (*argument* is the arguments to the command).

```
priocntl -e [-c class] [class-specific options] command [argument...]
```

If you omit the -c *class* option, the command is run in the user's current class.

Options

-c *class*   Specify the *class* to be set. (The valid class arguments are RT for real-time, TS for timesharing, or IA for interactive.) If the specified class is not already configured, configure it automatically.

-d   Display the scheduling parameters associated with a set of processes.

-e   Execute a specified command with the class and scheduling parameters associated with a set of processes.

-i *idtype* Specify (together with the *idlist* arguments if any) one or more processes to which the priocntl command is to apply. The interpretation of *idlist* depends on the value of *idtype*. The valid *idtype* arguments and corresponding interpretations of *idlist* are as follows.

-i *pid*   A list of process IDs. The priocntl command applies to the specified processes.

-i *ppid*   A list of parent process IDs. The priocntl command applies to all processes whose parent process ID is in the list.

-i *pgid*   A list of process group IDs. The priocntl command applies to all processes in the specified process groups.

-i *sid*   A list of session IDs. The priocntl command applies to all processes in the specified sessions.

-i *taskid*   *idlist* is a list of task IDs. The priocntl command applies to all processes in the specified task. New in the Solaris 8 release.

-i *class*   A single class name (RT for real-time, TS for timesharing, or IA for interactive). The priocntl command applies to all processes in the specified class.

-i *uid*   A list of user IDs. The priocntl command applies to all processes with an effective user ID equal to an ID from the list.

-i *gid*   A list of group IDs. The priocntl command applies to all processes with an effective group ID equal to an ID from the list.

-i *projid*   *idlist* is a list of project IDs. The priocntl command applies to all processes with an effective project ID equal to an ID from the list. New in the Solaris 8 release.

-i all   All existing processes. No *idlist* should be specified (if one is, ignore it). The permission restrictions described below still apply.

If you omit the -i *idtype* option when using the -d or -s options, assume the default *idtype* of pid.

-l   Display a list of the classes currently configured in the system along with class-specific information about each class.

-s   Set the scheduling parameters associated with a set of processes.

The valid class-specific options for setting real-time parameters are:

-p *rtpri*   Set the real-time priority of the specified process(es) to *rtpri*.

-t *tqntm* [-r *res*]

Set the time quantum of the specified process(es) to *tqntm*. You can optionally specify a resolution as explained below.

-q *tqsig*   Set the real-time quantum signal of the specified process(es) to *tqsig*. New in the Solaris 9 release.

The valid class-specific options for setting timesharing parameters are:

-m *tsuprilim*

Set the user priority limit of the specified process(es) to *tsuprilim*.

-p *tsupri*   Set the user priority of the specified process(es) to *tsupri*.

The valid class-specific options for setting interactive parameters are:

-m *iauprilim*

Set the user priority limit of the specified process(es) to *iauprilim*.

-p *iaupri*

Set the user priority of the specified process(es) to *iaupri*.

The valid class-specific options for setting fair-share parameters—new in the Solaris *New!*
9 release—are shown below.

-m *fssuprilim*

Set the user priority limit of the specified process(es) to *fssuprilim*.

-p *fssupri*   Set the user priority of the specified process(es) to *fssupri*.

The valid class-specific options for setting fixed-priority parameters—new in the   *New!*
Solaris 9 release—are shown below.

-m *fxuprilim*

Set the user priority limit of the specified process(es) to *fxuprilim*.

-p *fxupri*   Set the user priority of the specified process(es) to *fxupri*.

-t *tqntm* [-r *res*]

Set the time quantum of the specified process(es) to *tqntm*. You can
optionally specify a resolution.

Examples

The following real-time class example sets the class of any non-real-time processes
selected by *idtype* and *idlist* to real-time and sets their real-time priority to the
default value of 0.

```
castle% priocntl -s -c RT -t 1 -r 10 -i idtype idlist
```

The real-time priorities of any processes currently in the real-time class are unaffected.
The time quanta of all of the specified processes are set to 1/10 second.

The following example executes *command* in the real-time class with a real-time
priority of 15 and a time quantum of 20 milliseconds.

```
castle% priocntl -e -c RT -p 15 -t 20 command
```

The following example executes a command in real time with a real-time priority of   *New!*
11 and a time quantum of 250 milliseconds and specifies the real-time quantum signal
as SIGXCPU.

```
mopoke% priocntl -e -c RT -p 11 -t 250 -qa XCPU command
```

The following timesharing class example sets the class of any non-timesharing
processes selected by *idtype* and *idlist* to timesharing and sets both their user
priority limit and user priority to 0. Processes already in the timesharing class are
unaffected.

```
castle% priocntl -s -c TS -i idtype idlist
```

The following example executes *command* with the *arguments* arguments in the timesharing class with a user priority limit of 0 and a user priority of -15.

castle% **priocntl -e -c TS -m 0 -p -15** *command* [*arguments*]

New!

The following example executes a command in the fixed-priority class with a user priority limit of 20, a user priority of 10, and a time quantum of 250 milliseconds.

mopoke% **priocntl -e -c FX -m 20 -p 10 -t 250** *command*

Exit Status

The following exit values are returned for the -d, -l, and -s options.

0   Successful operation.

1   Error condition.

The following exit values are returned for the -e option.

Exit status of executed command.

0   Successful operation.

1   Command could not be executed at the specified priority.

Attributes

See attributes(5) for descriptions of the following attributes:

Attribute Type	Attribute Value
Availability	SUNWcsu
CSI	Enabled

See Also

New!

kill(1), nice(1), ps(1), exec(2), fork(2), priocntl(2), fx_dptbl(4), rt_dptbl(4), attributes(5), FSS(7)
       System Administration Guide: Basic Administration

Diagnostics

Process(es) not found

              None of the specified processes exist.

Specified processes from different classes

              The -s option is being used to set parameters, the -c *class* option is not present, and processes from more than one class are specified.

Invalid option or argument

              An unrecognized or invalid option or option argument is used.

proc tools — Proc Tools

Synopsis

```
/usr/proc/bin/pflags [-r] pid | core...
/usr/proc/bin/pcred pid | core...
/usr/proc/bin/pmap [-srxlF] pid | core...
/usr/proc/bin/pldd [-F] pid | core...
/usr/proc/bin/psig [-n] pid...
/usr/proc/bin/pstack [-F] pid | core...
/usr/proc/bin/pfiles [-F] pid...
/usr/proc/bin/pwdx [-F] pid...
/usr/proc/bin/pstop pid...
/usr/proc/bin/prun pid...
/usr/proc/bin/pwait [-v] pid...
/usr/proc/bin/ptree [-a] [pid | user]...]
/usr/proc/bin/ptime command [arg...]
/usr/bin/pargs [-aeFx] [pid | core]
```

Note — Starting with the Solaris 8 release, all of the proc tools were moved from /usr/proc/bin to /usr/bin. The tools in /usr/proc/bin are now links to the tools in the /usr/bin directory.

Description

The proc tools are commands that exercise features of /proc (see proc(4)). Most of them take a list of process IDs (pid). The tools that take process IDs also accept /proc/nnn as a process ID, so you can use the shell expansion /proc/* to specify all processes in the system.

Starting in the Solaris 8 release, you can also apply some of the proc tools to corefiles (see core(4)). Those commands that can be applied to corefiles accept a list of either process IDs or names of corefiles, or both.

pargs	Print the command arguments (argv[]), environment variables, or auxiliary vector. New in the Solaris 9 release.
pflags	Print the /proc tracing flags, the pending and held signals, and other /proc status information for each lightweight process (lwp) in each process.
pcred	Print the credentials (effective, real, and saved UIDs and GIDs) of each process.
pfiles	Report fstat(2) and fcntl(2) information for all open files in each process.
pldd	List the dynamic libraries linked into each process, including shared objects explicitly attached by means of dlopen(3DL). See also ldd(1).
pmap	Print the address space map of each process.
prun	Set each process running (inverse of pstop).
psig	List the signal actions of each process. See signal(3HEAD).
pstack	Print a hex+symbolic stack trace for each lwp in each process.

pstop
: Stop each process (PR_REQUESTED stop).

ptime
: Time a command, such as the time(1) command, but using microstate accounting for reproducible precision.

ptree
: Print the process trees containing the specified *pids* or *users*, with child processes indented from their respective parent processes. Take an argument of all digits to be a process ID; otherwise, assume it is a user login name. Default is all processes.

pwait
: Wait for all of the specified processes to terminate.

pwdx
: Print the current working directory of each process.

The pfiles, pldd, pmap, pstack, and pwdx commands stop their target processes while inspecting them and reporting the results. While a process is stopped, it can do nothing.

Options

	-a	(ptree only) Include children of process 0.
New!	-a	(pargs only) Print process arguments as contained in argv[]. New in the Solaris 9 release.
New!	-e	(pargs only) Print process environment variables and values. New in the Solaris 9 release.
	-F	Force a grab of the target process even if another process has control.
	-l	(pmap only) Print unresolved dynamic linker map names.
New!	-n	(psig only) Display signal handler addresses instead of names. New in the Solaris 9 release.
	-r	(pflags only) If the process is stopped, display its machine registers.
	-r	(pmap only) Print the process's reserved addresses.
New!	-s	(pmap only) Print page size of hardware translations used. New in the Solaris 9 release.
	-v	(pwait only) Report each termination to standard output.
	-x	(pmap only) Print resident/shared/private mapping details.
New!	-x	(pargs only) Print process auxiliary vector. New in the Solaris 9 release.

New! Usage

The pfiles, pldd, pmap, and stack proc tools stop their target processes while inspecting them and reporting the results. A process can do nothing while it is stopped. Thus, for example, if the X server is inspected by one of these proc tools running in a window under the X server's control, the whole window system can become deadlocked because the proc tool would be trying to print its results to a window that cannot be refreshed. Logging in from another system with rlogin(1) and killing the offending proc tool would clear up the deadlock in this case.

Exercise caution when using the -F option. Imposing two controlling processes on one victim process can lead to chaos. Safety is assured only if the primary controlling process, typically a debugger, has stopped the victim process and the primary controlling process is doing nothing at the moment of application of the proc tool in question.

Starting with the Solaris 8 release, some of the proc tools can also be applied to corefiles. A corefile is a snapshot of a process's state and is produced by the kernel before terminating a process with a signal or with the gcore(1) command. Some of the proc tools may need to derive the name of the executable corresponding to the process that dumped core or the names of shared libraries associated with the process. These files are needed, for example, to provide symbol table information for pstack(1). If the proc tool in question is unable to locate the needed executable or shared library, some symbol information is unavailable for display. Similarly, if a corefile from one operating system release is examined on a different operating system release, the runtime link-editor debugging interface (librtld_db) may not be able to initialize. In this case, symbol information for shared libraries is not available.

Exit Status

0	Success.
non-zero	An error has occurred.

Files

/proc/*	Process files.
/usr/proc/lib/*	
	proc tools supporting files.

Attributes

See attributes(5) for descriptions of the following attributes:

Attribute Type	Attribute Value
Availability	SUNWesu (32-bit)
	SUNWesxu (64-bit)

See Also

gcore(1), ldd(1), pgrep(1), pkill(1), plimit(1), preap(1), ps(1), pwd(1), *New!*
rlogin(1), time(1), truss(1), wait(1), fcntl(2), fstat(2), dlopen(3DL),
signal(3HEAD), core(4), proc(4), attributes(5)

---

prof — Display Profile Data

Synopsis

/usr/ccs/bin/prof [-ChsVz] [-a | c | n | t] [-o | x] [-g | l] [-m *mdata*]
[*prog*]

Description

The prof command interprets a profile file produced by the monitor function. The symbol table in the object file prog (a.out by default) is read and correlated with a profile file (mon.out by default). For each external text symbol, the percentage of time spent executing between the address of that symbol and the address of the next is printed, together with the number of times that function was called and the average number of milliseconds per call.

Notes

The times reported in successive identical runs can vary because of varying cache-hit ratios that result from sharing the cache with other processes. Even if a program seems to be the only one using the system, hidden background or asynchronous processes can blur the data. In rare cases, the clock ticks initiating recording of the program counter may cycle with loops in a program, grossly distorting measurements. Call counts are always recorded precisely, however.

Only programs that call exit or return from main are guaranteed to produce a profile file unless a final call to monitor is explicitly coded.

The times for static functions are attributed to the preceding external text symbol if you do not use the -g option. However, the call counts for the preceding function are still correct; that is, the static function call counts are not added to the call counts of the external function.

If you specify more than one of the options -t, -c, -a, and -n, the last option specified is used and you are warned.

LD_LIBRARY_PATH must not contain /usr/lib as a component when a program is compiled for profiling. If LD_LIBRARY_PATH does contain /usr/lib, the program is not linked correctly with the profiling versions of the system libraries in /usr/lib/libp. See gprof(1).

Functions such as mcount(), _mcount(), moncontrol(), _moncontrol(), monitor(), and _monitor() can appear in the prof report. These functions are part of the profiling implementation and, thus, account for some amount of the runtime overhead. Because these functions are not present in an unprofiled application, time accumulated and call counts for these functions can be ignored when the performance of an application is evaluated.

64-bit Profiling

You can use 64-bit profiling freely with dynamically linked executables, and profiling information is collected for the share objects if the objects are compiled for profiling. Apply care in interpreting the profile output because it is possible for symbols from different shared objects to have the same name. If you see duplicate names in the profile output, it is better to use the -s (summary) option to prefix a module ID before each symbol that is duplicated. You can then map the symbols to the appropriate modules by looking at the module's information in the summary.

If you use the -a option with a dynamically linked executable, sorting is done on a per-shared-object basis. Because there is a high likelihood of symbols from different shared objects having the same value, this sorting results in an output that is more understandable. If you use the -s option, a blank line separates the symbols from different shared objects.

32-bit Profiling

You can use 32-bit profiling with dynamically linked executables, but you must be careful. In 32-bit profiling, you cannot use prof to profile shared objects. Thus, when you execute a profiled, dynamically linked program, only the main portion of the image is sampled. All time spent outside of the main object—time spent in a shared object—is not included in the profile summary. Consequently, the total time reported for the program can be less than the total time used by the program.

Because the time spent in a shared object cannot be accounted for, minimize the use of shared objects whenever you use prof to profile a program. You can link the program to the profiled version of a library (or to the standard archive version if no profiling version is available) instead of the shared object to get profile information on the functions of a library. Versions of profiled libraries can be supplied with the system in the /usr/lib/libp directory. Refer to compiler driver documentation on profiling.

Consider an extreme case. A profiled program dynamically linked with the shared C library spends 100 units of time in some libc routine, say, malloc(). Suppose malloc() is called only from routine B and B consumes only 1 unit of time. Suppose further that routine A consumes 10 units of time, more than any other routine in the main (profiled) portion of the image. In this case, prof concludes that most of the time is being spent in A and almost no time is being spent in B. From this, it is almost impossible to tell that the greatest improvement can be made by looking at routine B and not routine A. The value of the profiler in this case is severely degraded; the solution is to use archives as much as possible for profiling.

Options

The mutually exclusive options -a, -c, -n, and -t determine the type of sorting of the output lines.

-a	Sort by increasing symbol address.
-c	Sort by decreasing number of calls.
-n	Sort lexically by symbol name.
-t	Sort by decreasing percentage of total time (default).

The mutually exclusive options -o and -x specify the printing of the address of each symbol monitored.

-o	Print each symbol address (in octal) along with the symbol name.
-x	Print each symbol address (in hexadecimal) along with the symbol name.

The mutually exclusive options -g and -l control the type of symbols to be reported. Use the -l option with care; it applies the time spent in a static function to the preceding (in memory) global function instead of giving the static function a separate entry in the report. If all static functions are properly located, this feature can be very useful. If not, the resulting report can be misleading.

Assume that A and B are global functions and that only A calls static function S. If S is located immediately after A in the source code (that is, if S is properly located), then, with the -l option, the amount of time spent in A can easily be determined, including the time spent in S. If, however, both A and B call S, then, if you use the -l option, the report is misleading; the time spent during B's call to S is attributed to A, making it seem as if more time had been spent in A than really had been. In this case, function S cannot be properly located.

-g	List the time spent in static (nonglobal) functions separately. The -g option function is the opposite of the -l function.
-l	Suppress the printing of statically declared functions. Allocate time spent executing in a static function to the closest global function loaded before the static function in the executable. This option is the default. It is the opposite of the -g function and should be used with care.

The following options can be used in any combination.

-C	Demangle C++ symbol names before printing them.
-h	Suppress the heading normally printed on the report. This option is useful if the report is to be processed further.
-m *mdata*	Use file *mdata* instead of mon.out as the input profile file.
-s	Print a summary of several of the monitoring parameters and statistics on the standard error output.
-V	Print prof version information on the standard error output.
-z	Include all symbols in the profile range, even if associated with 0 number of calls and 0 time.

A program creates a profile file if it has been link edited with the -p option of cc(1B). This option to the cc(1B) command arranges for calls to monitor at the beginning and end of execution. The call to monitor at the end of execution writes a profile file. The number of calls to a function is tallied if you use the -p option when compiling the file containing the function.

A single function can be split into subfunctions for profiling by means of the MARK macro. See prof(5).

Environment Variables

PROFDIR — Specify the name of the file created by a profiled program. If PROFDIR is not set, produce mon.out in the directory current when the program terminates. If PROFDIR=*string*, *string*/*pid*.*progname* is produced, where *progname* consists of argv[0] with any path prefix removed and *pid* is the process ID of the program. If PROFDIR is set but null, produce no profiling output.

Files

mon.out	Default profile file.
a.out	Default name list (object) file.

Attributes

See attributes(5) for descriptions of the following attributes:

Attribute Type	Attribute Value
Availability	SUNWbtool

See Also

gprof(1), cc(1B), exit(2), profil(2), psample(2), malloc(3C), malloc(3MALLOC), monitor(3C), attributes(5), prof(5)

profiles — Print Execution Profiles for a User

New!

Synopsis

/bin/profiles [-l] [*user*...]

Description

Use the profiles command, new in the Solaris 8 Operating Environment, to print on standard output the names of the execution profiles that have been assigned to you or to the optionally specified user or role name. Profiles are a role-based access control (RBAC) bundling mechanism used to enumerate the commands and authorizations needed to perform a specific function. profile displays the process attributes for each listed executable, such as the effective user and group IDs with which the process runs when started by a privileged command interpreter. The profile shells are pfcsh, pfksh, and pfexec. See the pfexec(1) manual page. Profiles can contain other profiles defined *New!* in prof_attr(4).

You can combine multiple profiles to construct the appropriate access control. When profiles are assigned, the authorizations are added to the existing set. If the same command appears in multiple profiles, the first occurrence, as determined by the ordering of the profiles, is used for process-attribute settings. For convenience, you can specify a wild-card to match all commands.

When profiles are interpreted, the profile list is loaded from user_attr(4). Starting *New!* with the Solaris 9 release, if any default profile is defined in /etc/security/policy.conf (see policy.conf(4)), the list of default profiles is added to the list loaded from user_attr(4). Matching entries in prof_attr(4) provide the authorizations list, and matching entries in exec_attr(4) provide the commands list.

Options

-l   List the commands in each profile followed by the special process attributes such as user and group IDs.

Examples

The following example shows the output of the profiles command. With no options, the profiles command shows the profiles for the current user.

```
mopoke% profiles
Primary Administrator
Basic Solaris User
All
mopoke%
```

The following example shows the output of the profiles command for three users. User winsor has Primary Administrator rights, user ray has System Administrator rights, and user des has only the default Basic Solaris User and All rights. One way to determine where one set of rights stops and the next one starts is to look for the All right, which is always the last one in the list.

```
mopoke% profiles winsor ray des
Primary Administrator
Basic Solaris User
```

```
All
System Administrator
Audit Review
Printer Management
Cron Management
Device Management
File System Management
Mail Management
Maintenance and Repair
Media Backup
Media Restore
Name Service Management
Network Management
Object Access Management
Process Management
Software Installation
User Management
All
Basic Solaris User
Basic Solaris User
All
mopoke%
```

The following example uses the list option to display commands and attributes for a user with Primary Administrator rights.

```
mopoke% profiles -l winsor

    Primary Administrator:
        *    uid=0, gid=0
    All:
        *
mopoke%
```

The following example uses the list option to display commands and attributes for a user with System Administrator rights.

```
mopoke% profiles -l ray

    Audit Review:
        /usr/sbin/praudit      euid=0
        /usr/sbin/auditreduce     euid=0
        /usr/sbin/auditstat     euid=0
    Printer Management:
        /usr/sbin/accept      euid=lp
        /usr/ucb/lpq     euid=0
        /etc/init.d/lp      euid=0
        /usr/bin/lpstat      euid=0
        /usr/lib/lp/lpsched     uid=0
        /usr/sbin/lpfilter      euid=lp
        /usr/bin/lpset      egid=14
        /usr/sbin/lpadmin      egid=14
        /usr/sbin/lpsystem      uid=0
        /usr/sbin/lpmove      euid=lp
```

```
        /usr/sbin/lpshut      euid=lp
        /usr/bin/cancel       euid=0
        /usr/bin/disable      euid=lp
        /usr/sbin/reject      euid=lp
        /usr/sbin/lpforms     euid=lp
        /usr/ucb/lprm      euid=0
        /usr/bin/enable      euid=lp
        /usr/sbin/lpusers     euid=lp
Cron Management:
        /etc/init.d/cron      uid=0, gid=sys
        /usr/bin/crontab      euid=0
Device Management:
        /usr/sbin/allocate      uid=0
        /usr/sbin/deallocate      uid=0
File System Management:
        /usr/sbin/mount      uid=0
        /usr/sbin/dfshares      euid=0
        /usr/sbin/format      uid=0
        /usr/sbin/devinfo      euid=0
        /usr/sbin/mkfs      euid=0
        /etc/init.d/standardmounts      uid=0, gid=sys
        /usr/sbin/shareall      uid=0, gid=root
        /usr/sbin/clri      euid=0
        /usr/bin/rmdir      euid=0
        /usr/lib/autofs/automountd      euid=0
        /usr/sbin/unshareall      uid=0, gid=root
        /etc/init.d/buildmnttab      uid=0, gid=sys
        /usr/lib/fs/autofs/automount      euid=0
        /usr/sbin/share      uid=0, gid=root
        /usr/bin/mkdir      euid=0
        /usr/lib/fs/ufs/tunefs      uid=0
        /usr/sbin/fstyp      euid=0
        /usr/sbin/ff      euid=0
        /usr/sbin/fuser      euid=0
        /usr/sbin/fsck      euid=0
        /usr/bin/eject      euid=0
        /usr/sbin/umountall      uid=0
        /usr/sbin/mountall      uid=0
        /usr/sbin/unshare      uid=0, gid=root
        /etc/init.d/ufs_quota      uid=0, gid=sys
        /usr/sbin/fsdb      euid=0
        /usr/lib/fs/ufs/newfs      euid=0
        /usr/lib/fs/ufs/fsirand      euid=0
        /usr/sbin/swap      euid=0
        /usr/sbin/umount      uid=0
        /etc/init.d/autofs      uid=0, gid=sys
        /usr/lib/fs/nfs/showmount      euid=0
        /usr/sbin/mkfile      euid=0
        /usr/sbin/dfmounts      euid=0
Mail Management:
        /usr/bin/mconnect      euid=0
        /usr/lib/sendmail      uid=0
        /usr/bin/mailq      euid=0
        /usr/bin/newaliases      euid=0
```

```
        /etc/init.d/sendmail    uid=0, gid=sys
Maintenance and Repair:
        /etc/init.d/syslog     uid=0, gid=sys
        /usr/sbin/syslogd     euid=0
        /usr/sbin/init    euid=0
        /usr/sbin/halt     euid=0
        /usr/sbin/prtconf    euid=0
        /usr/sbin/poweroff    uid=0
        /usr/bin/ldd     euid=0
        /usr/sbin/eeprom    euid=0
        /usr/bin/adb     euid=0
        /usr/sbin/reboot    uid=0
        /usr/bin/date    euid=0
        /etc/init.d/sysetup    uid=0, gid=sys
        /usr/bin/vmstat    euid=0
        /usr/sbin/crash    euid=0
Media Backup:
        /usr/bin/mt    euid=0
        /usr/sbin/tar     euid=0
        /usr/lib/fs/ufs/ufsdump    euid=0, gid=sys
Media Restore:
        /usr/sbin/tar     euid=0
        /usr/bin/cpio    euid=0
        /usr/bin/mt    euid=0
        /usr/lib/fs/ufs/ufsrestore    euid=0
Name Service Management:
        /usr/lib/nis/nisping    euid=0
        /usr/lib/nis/nisshowcache    euid=0
        /usr/sbin/nscd    euid=0
        /usr/bin/nisln    euid=0
        /usr/lib/nis/nisctl    euid=0
        /usr/bin/nischttl    euid=0
        /usr/lib/nis/nisstat    euid=0
Network Management:
        /usr/sbin/in.named    uid=0
        /usr/sbin/snoop    uid=0
        /etc/init.d/nscd    uid=0, gid=sys
        /etc/init.d/inetsvc    uid=0, gid=sys
        /usr/bin/ruptime    euid=0
        /usr/sbin/spray    euid=0
        /usr/sbin/ifconfig    uid=0
        /usr/bin/rup    euid=0
        /etc/init.d/uucp    uid=0, gid=sys
        /etc/init.d/inetinit    uid=0, gid=sys
        /etc/init.d/rpc    uid=0, gid=sys
        /usr/bin/netstat    uid=0
        /etc/init.d/asppp    uid=0, gid=sys
        /etc/init.d/sysid.net    uid=0, gid=sys
        /usr/sbin/asppp2pppd    euid=0
        /etc/init.d/sysid.sys    uid=0, gid=sys
        /usr/sbin/route    uid=0
        /usr/bin/setuname    euid=0
Object Access Management:
        /usr/bin/chmod    euid=0
```

```
            /usr/bin/getfacl     euid=0
            /usr/bin/chgrp    euid=0
            /usr/bin/setfacl     euid=0
            /usr/bin/chown    euid=0
     Process Management:
            /usr/bin/crontab     euid=0
            /usr/bin/pmap    euid=0
            /usr/bin/truss    euid=0
            /usr/bin/psig    euid=0
            /etc/init.d/perf    uid=0, gid=sys
            /usr/bin/pstop    euid=0
            /usr/bin/prun    euid=0
            /usr/bin/nice    euid=0
            /usr/bin/renice    euid=0
            /etc/init.d/power     euid=0
            /etc/init.d/cvc    uid=0, gid=root
            /usr/bin/pfiles    euid=0
            /usr/bin/pstack    euid=0
            /usr/sbin/fuser    euid=0
            /usr/bin/pwdx    euid=0
            /usr/bin/pldd    euid=0
            /usr/bin/pcred    euid=0
            /usr/bin/pflags    euid=0
            /usr/bin/ps    euid=0
            /usr/bin/kill    euid=0
            /etc/init.d/cron    uid=0, gid=sys
            /usr/bin/pwait    euid=0
            /usr/bin/ptime    euid=0
            /usr/bin/ptree    euid=0
     Software Installation:
            /usr/bin/pkgparam    uid=0
            /usr/bin/pkgtrans    uid=0
            /usr/sbin/install    euid=0
            /usr/bin/pkgmk    uid=0
            /usr/sbin/pkgrm    uid=0, gid=bin
            /usr/bin/pkginfo    uid=0
            /usr/sbin/pkgadd    uid=0, gid=bin
            /usr/sbin/pkgmv    uid=0, gid=bin
            /usr/ccs/bin/make    euid=0
            /usr/sbin/pkgchk    uid=0
            /usr/bin/admintool    uid=0, gid=bin
            /usr/sbin/pkgask    uid=0
            /usr/bin/pkgproto    uid=0
            /usr/bin/ln    euid=0
     User Management:
            /usr/sbin/grpck    euid=0
            /usr/sbin/pwck    euid=0
            /etc/init.d/utmpd    uid=0, gid=sys
     All:
            *
mopoke%
```

Exit Status

0	Successful completion.
1	An error occurred.

Files

/etc/security/exec_attr

Execution profiles database.

New!   /etc/security/policy.conf

Configuration file for security policy. Consulted by profiles, starting with the Solaris 9 release.

/etc/security/prof_attr

Profile description database.

/etc/user_attr

Extended user attributes database.

Attributes

See attributes(5) for descriptions of the following attributes:

Attribute Type	**Attribute Value**
Availability	SUNWcsu

See Also

New!   auths(1), pfexec(1), roles(1), getprofattr(3SECDB), exec_attr(4), policy.conf(4), prof_attr(4), user_attr(4), attributes(5)

New! projects — Print Project Membership of User

Synopsis

/bin/projects [-dv] [*user*]

Description

The projects command was introduced in the Solaris 8 Operating Environment. Starting with the Solaris 9 Operating Environment, the projects command provides the same functionality as the Sun Resource Manager, which it replaces. The projects command is a part of the Solaris 9 project management capability that you can administer with the Solaris Management Console (SMC) 2.1 Projects tool. The project management tools enable you to track and manage system resource use with the /etc/projects database in a files environment or the project tables in an NIS or LDAP environment.

Use the projects command to print on standard output the projects to which the invoking user or an optionally specified user belongs. Each user belongs to some set of projects specified in the project(4) file and possibly in the associated NIS maps and LDAP databases for project information.

Options

-d   Print only default project.

-v   Print project descriptions along with project names.

Operands

user   Display project memberships for the specified user.

Examples

The following example displays project membership for user winsor.

```
mopoke% projects winsor
default group.staff pubs
mopoke%
```

The following example displays the default project for user winsor.

```
mopoke% projects -d winsor
group.staff
mopoke%
```

If you have not specified a primary project, the default project is group.staff. You can use the SMC Users tool to specify a different primary (default) project for each user.

Exit Status

0   Successful completion.

1   A fatal error occurred during execution.

2   Invalid command-line options were specified.

Files

/etc/project

          Local database containing valid project definitions for this machine.

Attributes

See attributes(5) for descriptions of the following attributes:

Attribute Type	Attribute Value
Availability	SUNWcsu

See Also

getdefaultproj(3PROJECT), getprojent(3PROJECT), project(4), attributes(5)

prs, sccs-prs — Display Selected Portions of an SCCS History

Synopsis
/usr/ccs/bin/prs [-ael] [-c*date-time*] [-d*dataspec*] [-r*sid*] s.*filename*...

Description
See sccs-prs(1).

prt, sccs-prt — Display Delta Table Information from an SCCS File

Synopsis
/usr/ccs/bin/prt [-abdefistu] [-c*date-time*] [-r*date-time*] [-y*sid*]
    s.*filename*...

Description
See sccs-prt(1).

prun — Proc Tools

Synopsis
/usr/proc/bin/prun *pid*...

Description
See proc(1).

ps — Report Process Status

Synopsis
/usr/bin/ps [-aAcdefjlLPy] [-g *grplist*] [-n *namelist* [[-o *format*]...]
    [-p *proclist*] [-s *sidlist*] [-t *term*] [-u *uidlist*] [-U *uidlist*]
    [-G *gidlist*]

Description
Use the ps command to determine process status and get detailed information about an individual process, such as:

- PID (process ID).
- UID (user ID).

- Priority.
- Control terminal.
- Memory use.
- CPU time.
- Current status.

The ps command takes a snapshot of system activity at the time you type the command. Some data printed for defunct processes is irrelevant. If you are monitoring system activity by time, be aware that the results are already slightly out-of-date by the time you read them.

When you type the ps command without options, ps prints information about processes associated with the controlling terminal. The output contains only the PID, terminal identifier, cumulative execution time, and the command name. The other information that you can access by using the ps command is controlled with the options.

If you use no options to select processes, ps reports all processes associated with the controlling terminal. If there is no controlling terminal, only the headers are printed.

Options

The most frequently used options for the ps command are listed below.

-a	List information about all processes most frequently requested: all those except process group leaders and processes not associated with a terminal.
-e	Report information about all processes now running.
-f	Show the owner of the process, by name instead of by UID, in the first column. This option turns off -1, -t, -s, and -r and turns on -a.
-1	Generate a long report that includes all fields except STIME.

Additional options for the ps command are listed below. Some options accept lists as arguments. You can separate items in a list either by using commas or by enclosing the entire argument in quotes and separating the items with commas or spaces. Many of the options are used to select processes to list. If you specify any processes, the default list is ignored and the ps command chooses the processes represented by the inclusive OR of all the selection-criteria options. Note that the *proclist* and *grplist* options require numeric values.

-A	List information for all processes. Identical to -e.
-c	Print information in a format that reflects scheduler properties as described in priocntl(1). The -c option affects the output of the -f and -1 options.
-d	List information about all processes except session leaders.
-g *grplist*	List only process data whose group leader's ID number(s) appears in *grplist*. (A group leader is a process whose process ID number is identical to its process group ID number.)
-G *gidlist*	List information for processes whose real group ID numbers are given in *gidlist*. The *gidlist* must be a single argument in the form of a blank or comma-separated list.
-j	Print session ID and process group ID.

-L   Print information about each lightweight process (lwp) in each selected process.

-n *namelist*

                Specify the name of an alternative system *namelist* file in place of the default. This option is accepted for compatibility but is ignored.

-o *format*   Print information according to the format specification given in *format*. This option is described fully in "Creating Custom Reports" on page 1137. You can specify multiple -o options; interpret the format specification as the space-character- separated concatenation of all the *format* arguments.

-p *proclist*

                List only process data whose process ID numbers are given in *proclist*.

-P   Print the number of the processor to which the process or lwp is bound, if any, under an additional column header, PSR.

-s *sidlist*   List information on all session leaders whose IDs appear in *sidlist*.

-t *term*   List only process data associated with *term*. You specify terminal identifiers as a device file name and an identifier. For example, term/a or pts/0.

-u *uidlist*   List only process data whose effective user ID number or login name is given in *uidlist*. Print the numerical user ID unless you specify the -f option to print the login name.

-U *uidlist*   List information for processes whose real user ID numbers or login names are given in *uidlist*. Specify *uidlist* as a single argument in the form of a blank- or comma-separated list.

-y   Under a long listing (-1), omit the obsolete F and ADDR columns and include an RSS column to report the resident set size of the process. Report both RSS and SZ in units of kilobytes instead of pages.

Note — ps -if or ps -o *stime* may report an earlier time when a getty was last respawned on the tty line instead of the actual start of a TTY login session.

Command Report Formats

The ps -e command displays a report that looks like the following:

```
castle% ps -e
   PID TTY       TIME CMD
     0 ?         0:01 sched
     1 ?         0:00 init
     2 ?         0:00 pageout
     3 ?         0:20 fsflush
   242 ?         0:01 vold
   186 ?         0:00 nscd
   302 ?         0:00 sac
   113 ?         0:00 rpcbind
```

```
     103 ?       0:00 in.route
     140 ?       0:00 inetd
     115 ?       0:00 keyserv
     162 ?       0:00 automoun
     145 ?       0:00 statd
     147 ?       0:00 lockd
     305 ?       0:00 listen
     166 ?       0:01 syslogd
     180 ?       0:00 cron
     196 ?       0:00 lpsched
     217 ?       0:00 sendmail
     205 ?       0:02 lp
     307 ?       0:14 Xsun
     214 ?       0:00 powerd
```
...(*More information not shown here*)

The columns are described below.

PID	Process identification number.
TTY	The terminal from which the process (or its parent) started. If the process has no controlling terminal, this column contains a question mark (?). Processes with question marks usually are system processes.
TIME	The cumulative amount of CPU time used by the process.
COMD	The name of the command that generated the process. Note that, for the ps -e command, only the first eight characters of the file name are displayed.

When you type ps -el and press Return, you get a listing that looks like the following example.

```
castle% ps -el
 F S   UID   PID  PPID  C PRI NI    ADDR    SZ    WCHAN TTY   TIME CMD
19 T     0     0     0  0   0 SY f0274e38    0           ?    0:01 sched
 8 S     0     1     0  0  41 20 f5b2d888    4 f5b2da80  ?    0:00 init
19 S     0     2     0  0   0 SY f5b2d1c8    0 f02886a4  ?     :00 pageout
19 S     0     3     0  1   0 SY f5b2cb08    0 f028aeb4  ?    0:21 fsflush
 8 S     0   242     1  0  59 20 f5b2b6c8  515 f5d387de  ?     01 vold
 8 S     0   186     1  0  46 20 f5b2c448  480 f5b2c640  ?     :00 nscd
 8 S     0   302     1  0  41 20 f5b2bd88  350 f5a81c78  ?    0:00 sac
 8 S     0   113     1  0  41 20 f5b2b008  445 f5d38f36  ?    0:00 rpcbind
 8 S     0   103     1  0  41 20 f5d2d890  340 f5d38f86  ?    0:00 in.route
 8 S     0   140     1  0  54 20 f5d2d1d0  446 f5d38e6e  ?    0:00 inetd
 8 S     0   115     1  0  57 20 f5d2cb10  461 f5d38ebe  ?    0:00 keyserv
 8 S     0   162     1  0  41 20 f5d2c450  560    3e39c  ?    0:00 automoun
 8 S     0   145     1  0  47 20 f5d2bd90  501 f5d38e96  ?    0:00 statd
 8 S     0   147     1  0  65 20 f5d2b6d0  409 f5d38df6  ?    0:00 lockd
 8 S     0   305   302  0  41 20 f5d2b010  352 f597e0ce  ?    0:00 listen
 8 S     0   166     1  0  46 20 f5e18898  702 f5d38c66  ?    0:01 syslogd
 8 S     0   180     1  0  51 20 f5e181d8  358 f5a81eb8  ?    0:00 cron
 8 S     0   196     1  0  67 20 f5e17b18  652 f5d38a5e  ?    0:00 lpsched
 8 S     0   217     1  0  41 20 f5e17458  448 f5d38a0e  ?    0:00 sendmail
 8 S     0   205     1  0  41 20 f5e16d98  462 f5e16f90  ?    0:02 lp
 8 S  1001   307   293  2  41 20 f5e166d8  343 f5d38586  ?    0:17 Xsun
 8 S     0   214     1  0  58 20 f5e16018  215 f5e16210  ?    0:00 powerd
```

```
8 S   0   227     1   0   41  20  f5e808a0    214  f5d38a36  ?    0:00  utmpd
8 S   0   232     1   0   40  20  f5e801e0    483  f5d3896e  ?    0:00  hpnpd
8 S   1   250     1   0   66  20  f5e7fb20   1429  f5e7fb90  ?    0:00  dwhttpd
8 S   0   310     1   0   40  20  f5e7f460    471  f5d38496  ?    0:00  fbconsol
8 S   1   251   250   0   41  20  f5e7eda0   1551  f5d38806  ?    0:01  dwhttpd
```
(*More information not shown here*)

The fields in a ps -el long listing report are described below.

F	Hexadecimal flags which, added together, indicate the process's current state. These flags are available for historical purposes only.
S	The current state of the process, as shown by one of the following letters:

O	Currently running on the processor.
S	Sleeping; waiting for an I/O event to complete.
R	Ready to run.
I	Idle; process is being created.
Z	Zombie. The process has terminated and the parent is not waiting, but the dead process is still in the process table.
T	Stopped because parent is tracing the process.
X	Waiting for more memory.

UID	The user ID of the owner of the process.
PID	The process ID number.
PPID	The parent process ID number.
C	The CPU use (that is, an estimate of the percentage of CPU time used by the process).
CLS	Scheduling class. Printed only when you use the -c option.
PRI	The scheduling priority. Higher numbers mean lower priority.
NI	The nice number, which contributes to the scheduling priority of the process. Making a process nicer means lowering its priority so it does not use as much CPU time.
ADDR	The memory address of the process.
SZ	The amount of virtual memory required by the process. This number indicates how much demand the process puts on system memory.
WCHAN	The address of an event for which the process is sleeping. If this column is blank, the process is running.
TTY	The terminal from which the process (or its parent) started or a question mark to indicate there is no controlling terminal (which usually indicates a system process).
TIME	The total amount of CPU time used by the process since it began.
COMD	The command that generated the process.

The fields in a ps -f report are listed below.

UID	The user ID of the owner of the process.
PID	The process ID number.
PPID	The parent process ID number.
C	The CPU use (that is, an estimate of the percentage of CPU time used by the process).
STIME	The starting time of the process in hours, minutes, and seconds. A process that began more than 24 hours before the ps command is executed is shown in months and days.
TTY	The terminal from which the process (or its parent) started or a question mark to indicate there is no controlling terminal (which usually indicates a system process).
TIME	The total amount of CPU time used by the process since it began.
CMD	The command that generated the process.

When you specify the -j option, the following two additional columns are printed.

PGID	The process ID of the process group leader.
SID	The process ID of the session leader.

When you specify the -L option, the following two additional columns are printed.

LWP	The lwp ID of the lightweight process being reported.
NLWP	The number of lwps in the process if you also specify the -f option.

When you use the -L option, one line is printed for each lwp in the process and the STIME and TIME fields show the values for the lwp, not for the process. A traditional single-threaded process contains only one lwp.

A process that has exited and has a parent but has not yet been waited for by the parent is marked <defunct>.

Creating Custom Reports

You can use the -o option to create your own custom reports that display only columns of information that are of interest to you. You specify the format by providing a list of the columns you want to view as a single argument. The names must be either a comma-separated list or a quoted list separated by spaces or by commas, as shown in the following examples.

```
castle% ps -o "user pcpu nice args"
   USER %CPU NI COMMAND
 winsor  0.0 20 /bin/csh
castle% ps -o user,pcpu,nice,args
   USER %CPU NI COMMAND
 winsor  0.0 20 /bin/csh
castle%
```

Each variable has a default header. You can overwrite the default header by appending an equal sign and the new text of the header as part of the argument to the -o option.

The report writes the fields in the order specified on the command line and arranges the output in columns. The width of the fields is chosen by the system to be at least as wide as the header text. If the header text is null (as specified by -o user=), the field is at least as wide as the default header text. If all header text fields are null, no header line is displayed.

The -o option has both a set of POSIX and Solaris format names. You can use names from either name set and combine them in the same argument. The following example shows the output for the Solaris environment.

```
castle% ps -o user,pid,ppid=MOM -o args
  USER  PID  MOM COMMAND
 winsor  413  401 /bin/csh
castle%
```

The following table shows an alphabetical list of the names recognized in the POSIX locale along with the default header.

Name	Default Header	Description
args	COMMAND	The command with all its arguments as a string. Applications cannot depend on being able to modify their argument list and having that modification be reflected in the output of the ps command. The Solaris implementation limits the string to 80 bytes; the string is the version of the argument list as it was passed to the command when it started.
comm	COMMAND	The name of the command being executed (argv[0] value) as a string.
etime	ELAPSED	The elapsed time since the process was started, in the form [[dd-]hh:]mm.ss where dd is the number of days, hh is the number of hours, mm is the number of minutes, and ss is the number of seconds.
group	GROUP	The effective group ID of the process displayed as text if it can be obtained and if the field width permits. Otherwise, the decimal GID value is displayed.
nice	NI	The decimal value of the system scheduling priority of the process. See nice(1).
pcpu	%CPU	The ratio of CPU time used recently to CPU time available in the same period expressed as a percentage. The meaning of "recently" in this context is not specified. The CPU time available is determined in an unspecified manner.
pgid	PGID	The decimal value of the process group ID.
pid	PID	The decimal value of the process ID.
ppid	PPID	The decimal value of the parent process ID.

Name	Default Header	Description
rgroup	RGROUP	The real group ID of the process displayed as text if it can be obtained and the field width permits. Otherwise, the decimal value is displayed.
ruser	RUSER	The real user ID of the process displayed as text if it can be obtained and the field width permits. Otherwise, the decimal value is displayed.
time	TIME	The cumulative CPU time of the process, in the form [*dd*-]*hh*:*mm*:*ss*.
TTY	TT	The name of the controlling terminal of the process (if any) in the same format used by the who(1) command.
user	USER	The effective user ID of the process displayed as text if it can be obtained and the field width permits. Otherwise, the decimal value is displayed.
vsz	VSZ	The total size of the process in virtual memory, in kilobytes.

The following table shows an alphabetical list of the names recognized by the Solaris implementation along with the default header.

Name	Default Header	Description
addr	ADDR	The memory address of the process.
c	C	Processor use for scheduling (obsolete).
class	CLS	The scheduling class of the process.
f	F	Flags (hexadecimal and additive) associated with the process.
fname	COMMAND	The first eight bytes of the basename of the process's executable file.
gid	GID	The effective group ID number of the process as a decimal integer.
lwp	LWP	The decimal value of the lwp ID. This option prints one line for each lightweight process.
nlwp	NLWP	The number of lwps in the process.
opri	PRI	The obsolete priority of the process. Lower numbers mean higher priority.
osz	SZ	The total size of the process in virtual memory, in pages.
pmem	%MEM	The ratio of the resident set size of the process to the physical memory on the machine, expressed as a percentage.

Name	Default Header	Description
pri	PRI	The priority of the process. Higher numbers mean higher priority.
psr	PSR	The number of the processor to which the process or lwp is bound.
pset	PSET	The ID of the processor set to which the process or LWP is bound. New in the Solaris 9 release.
rgid	RGID	The real group ID number of the process as a decimal integer.
projid	PROJID	The project ID number of the process as a decimal integer. New in the Solaris 8 release.
project	PROJECT	The project ID of the process as a text value if that value can be obtained; otherwise as a decimal integer. New in the Solaris 8 release.
rss	RSS	The resident set size of the process in kilobytes.
ru+id	RUID	The real user ID number of the process as a decimal integer. Changed from ruid in the Solaris 9 release.
s	S	The state of the process.
sid	SID	The process ID of the session leader.
stime	STIME	The starting time or date of the process, printed with no blanks.
taskid	TASKID	The task ID of the process. New in the Solaris 8 release.
uid	UID	The effective user ID number of the process as a decimal integer.
wchan	WCHAN	The address of an event for which the process is sleeping. If the process is running, - is displayed.

Using the ps Report

When you need to check on which processes or daemons are running, use the ps -e option. If you need more detailed information about a process, use the ps -el options. With experience, you will learn how the report should look and how to judge what is out of the ordinary.

Use the following guidelines to spot potential problems.

- Look for many identical jobs owned by the same user. This condition can result from someone running a script that starts a lot of background jobs without waiting for any of the jobs to terminate. Talk to the user to find out if that is the case. If necessary, use the kill command to terminate some of the processes. See kill(1) for more information on killing a process.

- Look at the TIME field for processes that have accumulated a large amount of CPU time. Such processes might be in an endless loop.

- Look at the C field to find unimportant processes that consume a large percentage of CPU time. If you do not think a process warrants so much attention, use the priocntl command to lower its priority. See the priocntl(1) manual page for more information.
- Look at the SZ field for processes that consume too large a percentage of memory. If a process is a memory hog, kill the process. If many processes are using lots of memory, the system may need more memory.
- Watch for a runaway process that progressively uses more and more CPU time. You can check this condition by using the -f option to see the start time (STIME) of the process and by watching the TIME field for the accumulation of CPU time.

Environment Variables

See environ(5) for descriptions of the following environment variables that affect the execution of ps: LC_CTYPE, LC_MESSAGES, LC_TIME, and NLSPATH. COLUMNS can override the system-selected horizontal screen size used to determine the number of text columns to display.

Exit Status

0	Successful completion.
>0	An error occurred.

Files

/dev/pts/*	Terminal (TTY) names searcher files.
/dev/term/*	
	Terminal (TTY) names searcher files.
/etc/passwd	
	UID information supplier.
/proc*	Process control files.
/tmp/ps_data	
	Internal data structure.

Attributes

See attributes(5) for descriptions of the following attributes:

Attribute Type	Attribute Value
Availability	SUNWcsu
CSI	Enabled

Note — ps is CSI enabled except for login names (user names).

See Also

kill(1), nice(1), pagesize(1), priocntl(1), who(1), getty(1M), proc(4), ttysrch(4), attributes(5), environ(5)

psig, pstack, pstop, ptime, ptree — Proc Tools

Synopsis

```
/usr/proc/bin/psig pid...
/usr/proc/bin/pstack pid...
/usr/proc/bin/pstop pid...
/usr/proc/bin/ptree [[pid|user]...]
/usr/proc/bin/ptime command [arg...]
```

Description

See proc(1).

pushd — Change Working Directory

Synopsis

csh

```
pushd [+n | dir]
```

Description

See cd(1).

pvs — Display the Internal Information of Dynamic Objects

Synopsis

New!   /usr/bin/pvs [-Cdlnorsv] [-N name] file...

Description

Use the pvs command to display any internal version information contained in an
executable and linking format (ELF) object file. Commonly, ELF files are dynamic
executables, shared objects, and possibly relocatable objects. This version information
can fall into one of two categories.

- Version definitions describe the interfaces made available by an ELF file. Each
  version definition is associated with a set of global symbols provided by the file.
  Version definitions can be assigned to a file during its creation by the link editor,
  using the -M option and the associated mapfile directives (see the *Linker and
  Libraries Guide* for more details).

- Version dependencies describe the binding requirements of dynamic objects on the
  version definitions of any shared object dependencies. When a dynamic object is
  built with a shared object, the link-editor records information within the dynamic

object, indicating that the shared object is a dependency. This dependency must be satisfied at runtime. If the shared object also contains version definitions, then those version definitions that satisfy the global symbol requirements of the dynamic object are also recorded in the dynamic object being created. At process initialization, the runtime linker uses any version dependencies as a means of validating the interface requirements of the dynamic objects used to construct the process.

Options

If you specify neither the -d nor -r option, both are enabled.

-C	Demangle C++ symbol names. New in the Solaris 8 release.
-d	Print version definition information.
-l	When used with the -s option, print any symbols that have been reduced from global to local binding because of versioning. By convention, these symbol entries are located in the .symtab section and fall between the FILE symbol representing the output file and the FILE symbol representing the first input file used to generate the output file.
	These reduced symbol entries are assigned the fabricated version definition _REDUCED_. No reduced symbols are printed if the file has been stripped (see strip(1)) or if the symbol entry convention cannot be determined.
-n	Normalize version definition information. By default, display all version definitions within the object. However, version definitions can inherit other version definitions and, under normalization, only the head of each inheritance list is displayed.
-N *name*	Print only the information for the given version definition *name* and any of its inherited version definitions (when used with the -d option) or for the given dependency file name (when used with the -r option).
-o	Create one-line version definition output. By default, file, version definitions, and any symbol output are indented to ease human inspection. This option prefixes each output line with the file and version definition name and may be more useful for analysis with automated tools.
-r	Print version dependency (requirements) information.
-s	Print the symbols associated with each version definition. Accompany any data symbols with the size, in bytes, of the data item.
-v	Show any weak version definitions and any version definition inheritance. When used with the -N and -d options, also show the inheritance of the base version definition. When used with the -s option, also show the version symbol definition.

Operands

file	The ELF file about which internal version information is displayed.

Examples

The following example displays the version definitions of `libelf.so.1`.

```
castle% pvs -d /usr/lib/libelf.so.1
        libelf.so.1;
        SUNW_1.2;
        SUNW_1.1;
        SUNW_0.7;
        SUNWprivate_1.1;
castle%
```

The following example uses the -n and -o options to produce a normalized, one-line display suitable for creating a mapfile version-control directive.

```
castle% pvs -don /usr/lib/libelf.so.1
/usr/lib/libelf.so.1 -  SUNW_1.2; /usr/lib/libelf.so.1 -
    SUNWprivate_1.1;
castle%
```

The following example displays the version requirements of `ldd` and pvs.

```
castle% pvs -r /usr/bin/ldd /usr/bin/pvs
/usr/bin/ldd:
        libelf.so.1 (SUNW_1.2);
        libc.so.1 (SUNW_1.1);
/usr/bin/pvs:
        libelf.so.1 (SUNW_1.2);
        libc.so.1 (SUNW_1.1);
castle%
```

Exit Status

If the requested version information is not found, a non-zero value is returned; otherwise, a 0 value is returned.

Version information is not found when any of the following is true:

- You specify the -d option, and no version definitions are found.
- You specify the -r option, and no version requirements are found.
- You specify neither the -d nor -r option, and no version definitions or version requirements are found.

Attributes

See attributes(5) for descriptions of the following attributes:

Attribute Type	Attribute Value
Availability	SUNWtoo

See Also

ld(1), ldd(1), strip(1), elf(3ELF), attributes(5)

Linker and Libraries Guide

pwait — Proc Tools

Synopsis

/usr/proc/bin/pwait [-v] *pid*...

Description

See proc(1).

pwck, grpck — Password/Group File Checkers

Synopsis

/usr/sbin/pwck [*filename*]
/usr/sbin/grpck [*filename*]

Description

The pwck command scans the password file and notes any inconsistencies. The checks include validation of the number of fields, login name, user ID, group ID, and whether the login directory and the program-to-use-as-shell exist. The default password grpck verifies all entries in the group file. This verification includes a check of the number of fields, group name, group ID, whether any login names belong to more than NGROUPS_MAX groups, and that all login names appear in the password file. The default group file is /etc/group.

> **Note** — If you specify no *filename* argument, grpck checks the local group file, /etc/group, and also makes sure that all login names encountered in the checked group file are known to the system getpwent(3C) routine. The login names may be supplied by a network nameservice.

Files

/etc/group

/etc/passwd

Attributes

See attributes(5) for descriptions of the following attributes:

Attribute Type	Attribute Value
Availability	SUNWcsu

See Also

getpwent(3C), group(4), passwd(4), attributes(5)

Diagnostics

Group entries in `/etc/group` with no login names are flagged.

```
Group file 'filename' is empty
```

The `/etc/passwd` or `/etc/group` file is an empty file.

```
cannot open file filename: No such file or directory
```

The `/etc/passwd` or `/etc/group` file does not exist.

pwd — Return Working Directory Name

Synopsis

```
/usr/bin/pwd
```

Description

Use the `pwd` (print working directory) command to display the absolute path name of the current working directory to standard output.

Both the Bourne shell, `sh(1)`, and the Korn shell, `ksh(1)`, also have a built-in `pwd` command.

Note — If you move the current directory or one above it, `pwd` may not give the correct response. Use the `cd(1)` command with a full path name to correct this situation.

Example

The following example displays the current directory, changes to another directory, and displays the new current directory.

```
castle% pwd
/export/home/winsor
castle% cd /etc
castle% pwd
/etc
castle%
```

Environment Variables

See `environ(5)` for descriptions of the following environment variables that affect the execution of `pwd`: `LC_MESSAGES` and `NLSPATH`.

Exit Status

0	Successful completion.
>0	An error occurred.

If an error is detected, output is not written to standard output, a diagnostic message is written to standard error, and the exit status is not 0.

Attributes

See attributes(5) for descriptions of the following attributes:

Attribute Type	Attribute Value
Availability	SUNWcsu
CSI	Enabled

See Also

cd(1), ksh(1), sh(1), shell_builtins(1), attributes(5), environ(5)

Diagnostics

Cannot open... and Read error in... indicate possible file-system trouble. Consult a UNIX system administrator if you see one of these error messages.

pwdx — Proc Tools

Synopsis

/usr/proc/bin/pwdx *pid*...

Description

See proc(1).

R

---

ranlib — Convert Archives to Random Libraries

Synopsis

/usr/ccs/bin/ranlib *archive*

Description

> **Note —** The `ranlib` command was used in SunOS 4.x to add a table of contents to archive libraries. It converted each archive to a form that could be linked more rapidly. This command is no longer needed because the `ar(1)` command automatically provides all the functionality of `ranlib`.

This command is provided as a convenience for software developers who need to maintain makefiles that are portable across a variety of operating systems.

Exit Status

`ranlib` has exit status 0.

Attributes

See `attributes`(5) for descriptions of the following attributes:

Attribute Type	Attribute Value
Availability	SUNWbtool

See Also
ar(1), ar(4), attributes(5)

---

rcp — Remote File Copy

Synopsis
```
/usr/bin/rcp [-p] filename1 filename2
/usr/bin/rcp [-pr] filename... directory
```

Description
Use the rcp command to copy files between systems. Each file name or directory argument is either a local file name (containing no colon (:) or backslash (\) characters) or a remote file name of the following form.

hostname:*path*

Or, starting with the Solaris 8 release, you can specify a local file name containing no colon (:) characters or backslashes (/) before any colon characters.

hostname can be an IPv4 or IPv6 address string. See inet(7P) and inet6(7P). Because IPv6 addresses already contain colons, enclose an IPv6 address in a pair of square brackets, as shown in the following example.

```
[1080::8:800:200C:417A]:/tmp/file
```

Otherwise, the first occurrence of a colon can be interpreted as the separator between *hostname* and *path*.

If a file name is not a full path name, it is interpreted relative to your home directory on *hostname*. You can quote a path on a remote host by using \, ", or ' so that the metacharacters are interpreted remotely.

rcp does not prompt for passwords; your current local user name must exist on *hostname* and must allow remote command execution by rsh(1).

rcp handles third-party copies where neither source nor target files are on the current system. Host names can also take the following form with *username* as the user name on the remote host instead of your current local user name.

username@*hostname*: *filename*

rcp also supports Internet domain addressing of the remote host; the following form specifies the *username*, the *hostname*, and the *domain* in which that host resides.

username@*host.domain*: *filename*

File names that are not full path names are interpreted relative to the home directory of the user named *username* on the remote host.

Notes
rcp is designed to copy between different hosts; trying to remotely copy a file onto itself, as with the following command, results in a severely corrupted file.

```
rcp tmp/file myhost:/tmp/file
```

rcp may not fail correctly when the target of a copy is a file instead of a directory.

rcp can become confused by output generated by commands in a $HOME/.profile on the remote host.

rcp requires that the source host have permission to execute commands on the remote host when doing third-party copies.

rcp does not properly handle symbolic links. Use tar (see tar(1)) or cpio (see cpio(1)) piped to rsh to obtain remote copies of directories containing symbolic links or named pipes.

If you forget to quote metacharacters intended for the remote host, you get an incomprehensible error message.

rcp fails if you copy access control lists (ACLs) to a file system that does not support them.

Options

-p	Try to give each copy the same modification times, access times, modes, and access control lists (ACLs) as the original file if applicable.
-r	Copy each subtree rooted at *filename*; the destination must be a directory.

Usage

See largefile(5) for the description of the behavior of rcp when encountering files greater than or equal to 2 Gbytes (2**31 bytes).

Files

$HOME/.profile

Attributes

See attributes(5) for descriptions of the following attributes:

Attribute Type	Attribute Value
Availability	SUNWrcmdc
CSI	Enabled

New!

Note — rcp is CSI enabled except for the handling of *username*, *hostname*, and *domain*.

See Also

cpio(1), ftp(1), rlogin(1), rsh(1), setfacl(1), tar(1), hosts.equiv(4), attributes(5), largefile(5), inet(7P), inet6(7P), ip6(7P)

New!

---

rdist — Remote File Distribution Program

Synopsis

/usr/bin/rdist [-b] [-D] [-h] [-i] [-n] [-q] [-R] [-v] [-w] [-y]
    [-d *macro=value*] [-f *distfile*] [-m *host*]...

/usr/bin/rdist [-b] [-D] [-h] [-i] [-n] [-q] [-R] [-v] [-w] [-y]
  -c *pathname*... [*login*@] *hostname* [:*destpath*]

Description

Use the rdist (remote distribution) command to maintain copies of files on multiple hosts. It preserves the owner, group, mode, and modification time of the master copies and can update programs that are executing.

Note — rdist does not propagate ownership or mode changes when the file contents have not changed.

Normally, a copy on a remote host is updated if its size or modification time differs from that of the original on the local host. rdist reads the indicated *distfile* for instructions on updating files and/or directories. With the -y option, (younger mode), only the modification times are checked, not the size.

The rdist command has two forms. The first form reads the indicated *distfile* for instructions on updating files and directories. If *distfile* is -, the standard input is used. If you do not specify the -f option, rdist first looks for instructions in its working directory for *distfile*, and then for Distfile. The second form uses the -c option and specifies paths as command-line options.

For rdist to be used across systems, each host system must have a /etc/host.equiv file or the user must have an entry in the .rhosts file in the home directory. See hosts.equiv(4) for more information.

Options

-b   Perform a binary comparison, and update files if they differ instead of merely comparing dates and sizes.

-c *pathname*... [*login*@]*hostname*[:*destpath*]

                Update each path name on the named host. (Take relative file names as relative to your home directory.) If you specify the *login*@ prefix, perform the update with the user ID of *login*. If you specify the :*destpath*, install the remote file, using that path name.

-d *macro=value*

                Define *macro* to have *value*. Use this option to define or override macro definitions in the *distfile*. *value* can be the empty string, one name, or a list of names surrounded by parentheses and separated by white space.

-D   Enable debugging.

-f *distfile*

                Use the description file *distfile*. A dash (-) as the *distfile* argument denotes the standard input.

-h   Follow symbolic links. Copy the file that the link points to instead of the link itself.

-i   Ignore unresolved links. rdist normally tries to maintain the link structure of files being transferred and warns you if all the links cannot be found.

-m *host*   Limit which systems are to be updated. You can specify multiple –m arguments to limit updates to a subset of the hosts listed in the *distfile*.

-n   Print the commands without executing them. This option is useful for debugging a *distfile*.

-q   Do not display the files being updated on the standard output.

-R   Remove extraneous files. If a directory is being updated, remove files on the remote host that do not correspond to those in the master (local) directory. This option is useful for maintaining truly identical copies of directories.

-v   Verify that the files are up-to-date on all the hosts. Display any files that are out-of-date, update no files, and send no mail.

-w   Append the whole file name to the destination directory name. Normally, only the last component of a name is used when files are renamed. This option preserves the directory structure of the files being copied instead of flattening it. For instance, renaming a list of files such as dir1/dir2 to dir3 would create files dir3/dir1 and dir3/dir2 instead of dir3 and dir3. When you use the –w option with a file name that begins with ~, append everything except the home directory to the destination name.

-y   Do not update remote copies that are younger than the master copy, but issue a warning message instead.

Usage

White-Space Characters
Newline, Tab, and space characters are all treated as white space; a mapping continues across input lines until the start of the next mapping: either a single file name followed by a -> or the opening parenthesis of a file-name list.

Comments
Comments begin with # and end with a newline.

Distfiles
The *distfile* contains a sequence of entries that specify the files to be copied, the destination for the files to be copied, the destination hosts, and the operations to perform to do the updating. Each entry has one of the following formats.

```
variable_name '=' name_list
[ label: ] source_list '->' destination_list command_list
[ label: ] source_list '::' time_stamp_file command_list
```

Use the first format to define variables. Use the second format to distribute files to other hosts. Use the third format to make lists of files that have been changed since some given date.

The source list specifies a list of files and/or directories on the local host that are to be used as the master copy for distribution.

The destination list is the list of hosts to which these files are to be copied. Each file in the source list is added to a list of changes if the file is out-of-date on the host that is being updated (second format) or if the file is newer than the timestamp file (third format).

Labels are optional. Use them to identify a command for partial updates. Use a colon (:) after an optional label, and use a double colon (::) for making lists of files that have been changed since a certain date (specified by the date/time of the *time_stamp* file). Typically, notify is used only with the '::' format of the command line.

Macros

rdist has a limited macro facility. Macros are expanded only in *filename* or *hostname* lists and in the argument lists of certain primitives. Macros cannot be used to stand for primitives or their options, or the -> or :: symbols.

A macro definition is a line of the following form.

macro = value

A macro reference is a string of the following form,

$*{macro}*

although (as with make(1S)) you can omit the braces if the macro name consists of just one character.

Metacharacters

The shell metacharacters [,], {, }, *, and ? are recognized and expanded (on the local host only) just as they are with csh(1). You can escape metacharacters by preceding them with a backslash.

The ~ character is also expanded in the same way as with csh; however, it is expanded separately on the local and destination hosts.

File Names

File names that do not begin with / or ~ are taken to be relative to user's home directory on each destination host; they are not relative to the current working directory. Enclose multiple file names within parentheses.

Primitives

You can use the following primitives to specify actions rdist is to take when updating remote copies of each file.

install [-b] [-h] [-i] [-R] [-v] [-w] [-y] [*newname*]

Copy out-of-date files and directories recursively. If you use no *newname* operand, give the name of the local file to the copy on the remote host. If absent from the remote host, create parent directories in the path of the file name. To help prevent disasters, do not replace a nonempty directory on a target host with a regular file or a symbolic link. However, when using the -R option, remove a nonempty directory if the corresponding file name is absent on the master host.

The options for install have the same semantics as their command-line counterparts but are limited in scope to a particular map. The login name used on the destination host is the same as the local host unless the destination name is of the format *login*@host. In that case, perform the update under the *username* login.

notify *address*...

> Send mail to the indicated TCP/IP address of the form:
>
> *user@host*
>
> listing the files updated and any errors that may have occurred. If an address does not contain an @*host* suffix, use the name of the destination host to complete the address.

except *filename*...

> Omit from updates the files named as arguments.

except_pat *pattern*...

> Omit from updates the file names that match each regular expression pattern (see ed(1) for more information on regular expressions). Note that you must escape \ and $ characters in the *distfile*. You can also use shell variables within a pattern; however, shell file-name expansion is not supported.

special [*filename*]... "*command-line*"

> Specify a Bourne shell, sh(1), command line to execute on the remote host after each named file is updated. If you provide no *filename* argument, the command line is performed for every updated file, with the shell variable FILE set to the name of the file on the local host.
>
> The quotation marks enable *command-line* to span input lines in the *distfile*, separate multiple shell commands by semicolons (;).
>
> The default working directory for the shell executing each command line is the user's home directory on the remote host.

IPv6

The rdist command is IPv6 enabled. See ip6(7P).

New!

Examples

The following sample *distfile* instructs rdist to maintain identical copies of a shared library, a shared library initialized data file, several include files, and a directory, on hosts named hermes and magus. On magus, commands are executed as superuser. rdist notifies merlin@druid whenever it discovers that a local file has changed relative to a timestamp file.

```
HOSTS = ( hermes root@magus )
FILES = ( /usr/local/lib/libcant.so.1.1
    /usrlocal/lib/libcant.sa.1.1 /usr/local/include/{*.h}
    /usr/local/bin )
(${FILES}) -> (${HOSTS})
    install -R ;
${FILES} :: /usr/local/lib/timestamp
    notify merlin@druid ;
```

Files

~/.rhosts   User's trusted hosts and users.

/etc/host.equiv

System trusted hosts and users.

/tmp/rdist*

Temporary file for update lists.

Attributes

See attributes(5) for descriptions of the following attributes:

Attribute Type	Attribute Value
Availability	SUNWrcmdc

See Also

csh(1), ed(1), sh(1), make(1S), stat(2), hosts.equiv(4), attributes(5), ip6(7P)

Diagnostics

A complaint about mismatch of rdist version numbers can really stem from some problem with starting your shell, for example, you are in too many groups.

Warnings

The superuser does not have the accustomed access privileges on NFS-mounted file systems. Using rdist to copy to such a file system may fail or the copies may be owned by user nobody.

Bugs

Source files must reside on or be mounted on the local host.

There is no easy way to have a special command executed only once after all files in a directory have been updated.

Variable expansion works only for name lists; there should be a general macro facility.

rdist aborts on files that have a negative modification time (before Jan. 1, 1970).

There should be a "force" option to enable replacement of nonempty directories by regular files or symbolic links. A means of updating file modes and owners of otherwise identical files is also needed.

read — Read a Line from Standard Input

Synopsis

/usr/bin/read [-r] *var*...

sh

read *name*...

csh

```
set variable = $<
```

ksh

```
read [-prsu[n]] [name?prompt] [name...]
```

Description

/usr/bin/read

The read command reads a single line from standard input.

By default, unless you specify the -r option, backslash (\) acts as an escape character. If standard input is a terminal device and the invoking shell is interactive, read prompts for a continuation line in the following cases:

- When the shell reads an input line ending with a backslash, unless you specify the -r option.
- When a here-document is not terminated after a newline character is entered.

The line is split into fields as in the shell; the first field is assigned to the first variable *var*, the second field to the second variable *var*, and so forth. If you specify fewer *var* operands than there are fields, the leftover fields and their intervening separators are assigned to the last *var*. If you specify fewer fields than *var*s, the remaining *var*s are set to empty strings.

The setting of variables specified by the *var* operands affect the current shell execution environment. If read is called in a subshell or separate command execution environment, such as one of the following, read does not affect the shell variables in the caller's environment.

```
(read foo)
       nohup read...
       find . -exec read... \;
```

The standard input must be a text file.

Bourne Shell

One line is read from the standard input and, using the IFS internal field separator (normally space or Tab) to delimit word boundaries, the first word is assigned to the first *name*, the second word to the second *name*, and so forth, with leftover words assigned to the last *name*. Lines can be continued with \newline. You can quote characters other than newline by preceding them with a backslash. These backslashes are removed before words are assigned to names, and no interpretation is done on the character that follows the backslash. The return code is 0 unless an end-of-file is encountered.

C Shell

The following notation loads one line of standard input as the value for a variable. (See *csh*(1)).

```
set variable = $<
```

Korn Shell

One line is read and is broken up into fields, using the characters in IFS as separators. The escape character (\) is used to remove any special meaning for the next character and for line continuation. In -r raw mode, the \ character is not treated specially. The first field is assigned to the first *name*, the second field to the second *name*, and so forth, with leftover fields assigned to the last *name*. The -p option takes the input line from the input pipe of a process spawned by the shell, using |&. If you specify the -s option, the input is saved as a command in the history file. You can use the -u option to specify a one-digit file descriptor unit *n* to read from. The file descriptor can be opened with the exec special command. The default value of *n* is 0. If you omit *name*, then REPLY is used as the default name. The exit status is 0 unless the input file is not open for reading or an end-of-file is encountered. An end-of-file with the -p option cleans up for this process so that another can be spawned. If the first argument contains a ?, the remainder of this word is used as a prompt on standard error when the shell is interactive. The exit status is 0 unless an end-of-file is encountered.

Options

-p	Read from the output of a |& process.
-r	Do not treat a backslash character in any special way. Consider each backslash to be part of the input line.
-s	Save input as a command in the history file.
-u[*n*]	Read input from file descriptor *n* (default is 0).

Operands

var	The name of an existing or nonexisting shell variable.

Examples

The following example for /usr/bin/read prints a file with the first field of each line moved to the end of the line.

```
while read -r xx yy
do
  printf "%s %s\n" "$yy" "$xx"
done < input_file
```

Environment Variables

See environ(5) for descriptions of the following environment variables that affect the execution of read: LC_CTYPE, LC_MESSAGES, and NLSPATH.

IFS	Determine the internal field separators used to delimit fields.
PS2	Provide the prompt string that an interactive shell writes to standard error when a line ending with a backslash is read and you did not specify the -r option or if a here-document is not terminated after you enter a newline character.

Exit Status

0	Successful completion.
>0	End-of-file was detected or an error occurred.

Attributes

See attributes(5) for descriptions of the following attributes:

Attribute Type	Attribute Value
Availability	SUNWcsu

See Also

csh(1), ksh(1), line(1), set(1), sh(1), attributes(5), environ(5)

readonly — Shell Built-in Function to Protect the Value of the Given Variable from Reassignment

Synopsis

sh

readonly [*name*...]

ksh

**

readonly [*name*[=*value*]]...

Description

Bourne Shell

The names you specify are marked readonly, and the values of the names cannot be changed by subsequent assignment. If you specify no arguments, a list of all readonly names is printed.

Korn Shell

The given names are marked readonly and cannot be changed by subsequent assignment.

For the readonly command, ksh(1) commands that are preceded by one or two asterisks (*) are treated specially in the following ways.

- Variable assignment lists preceding the command remain in effect when the command completes.

- I/O redirections are processed after variable assignments.

- Errors abort a script that contains them.

- Words following a command preceded by ** that are in the format of a variable assignment are expanded with the same rules as a variable assignment. This means that tilde substitution is performed after the equal sign and word splitting and file-name generation are not performed.

Attributes

See attributes(5) for descriptions of the following attributes:

Attribute Type	Attribute Value
Availability	SUNWcsu

See Also

ksh(1), sh(1), typeset(1), attributes(5)

---

red — Text Editor

Synopsis

/usr/bin/red [-s|-] [-p *string*] [-x] [-C] [*file*]

Description

See ed(1).

---

refer — Expand and Insert References from a Bibliographic Database

Synopsis

/usr/bin/refer [-ben] [-a*r*] [-c*string*] [-k*x*] [-l*m,n*] [-p *filename*]
    [-s*keys*] *filename*...

Description

The refer command is a preprocessor for nroff(1) or troff(1) that finds and formats references. The input files (by default, the standard input) are copied to the standard output, except for lines between . [and .] command lines. Such lines are assumed to contain keywords, as for lookbib(1), and are replaced by information from a bibliographic database. You can avoid the search, override fields from it, or add new fields. The reference data, from whatever source, is assigned to a set of troff strings. Macro packages such as ms(5) print the finished reference text from these strings. A flag is placed in the text at the point of reference. By default, the references are indicated by numbers.

When you use refer with eqn(1), neqn, or tbl(1), use refer first in the sequence, to minimize the volume of data passed through pipes.

Options

-a*r*	Reverse the first *r* author names (Jones, J. A. instead of J. A. Jones). If you omit *r*, reverse all author names.
-b	Do not put any flags in text (neither numbers nor labels).
-c*string*	Capitalize (with SMALL CAPS) the fields whose key letters are in *string*.
-e	Accumulate references instead of leaving the references where encountered until a sequence of the following form is encountered.

        . [
        $LIST$
        .]

        Then, write out all references collected so far. Collapse references to the same source.

-k*x*	Instead of numbering references, use labels as specified in a reference data line beginning with the characters %*x*, by default, *x* is L.

-l*m*, *n*   Instead of numbering references, use labels from the senior author's last name and the year of publication. Use only the first *m* letters of the last name and the last *n* digits of the date. If you omit either *m* or *n*, use the entire name or date.

-n   Do not search the default file.

-p *filename*   Take the next argument as a file of references to be searched. Search the default file last.

-s*keys*   Sort references by fields whose key letters are in the *keys* string and permute reference numbers in the text accordingly. Using this option also uses the -e option. You can follow the key letters in *keys* with a number indicating how many such fields are used. Use a + sign to indicate a very large number. The default is AD, which sorts on the senior author and date. For example, to sort on all authors and then the date, use the option sA+T.

Files

/usr/lib/refer

Directory of programs.

/usr/lib/refer/papers

Directory of default publication lists and indexes.

Attributes

See attributes(5) for descriptions of the following attributes:

Attribute Type	Attribute Value
Availability	SUNWdoc

See Also

addbib(1), eqn(1), indxbib(1), lookbib(1), nroff(1), roffbib(1), sortbib(1), tbl(1), troff(1), attributes(5)

regcmp — Compile Regular Expressions

Synopsis

/usr/ccs/bin/regcmp [-] *filename*...

Description

The regcmp command performs a function similar to the regcmp(3C) C language library function. In most cases, the regcmp(1) command precludes the need for calling the regcmp(3C) function from C programs. Bypassing regcmp(3C) saves on both execution time and program size. The regcmp command compiles the regular expressions in *filename* and puts the output in *filename*.i.

Options

- Put the output in *filename*.c. The format of entries in *filename* is a name (C variable), followed by one or more blanks, followed by one or more regular expressions, enclosed in double quotes. The output of regcmp is C source code. Compiled regular expressions are represented as extern char vectors. *filename*.i files can thus be #included in C programs, and *filename*.c files can be compiled and later loaded. In the C program that uses the regcmp output, regex(abc,line) applies the regular expression named abc to line. Diagnostics are self-explanatory.

Examples

In the following example, the three arguments to telno must all be entered on one line.

```
name    "([A-Za-z] [A-Za-z0-9_]*)$0"
telno   "\({0,1}([2-9] [01] [1-9])$0\){0,1} *"
        "([2-9] [0-9]{2})$1[-]{0,1}"
        "([0-9]{4})$2"
```

In the C program that uses the regcmp output, the following statement applies the regular expression named telno to line.

```
regex(telno, line, area, exch, rest)
```

Environment Variables

See environ(5) for a general description of the LC_* environment variables.

LC_CTYPE   Determine how regcmp handles characters. When LC_CTYPE is set to a valid value, regcmp can display and handle text and file names containing valid characters for that locale.

LC_MESSAGES

Determine how diagnostic and informative messages are presented, including the language and style of the messages and the correct form of affirmative and negative responses. In the C locale, the messages are presented in the default form found in the program itself (in most cases, U.S. English).

Attributes

See attributes(5) for descriptions of the following attributes:

Attribute Type	Attribute Value
Availability	SUNWtoo
CSI	Enabled

See Also

regcmp(3C), attributes(5), environ(5)

rehash — Evaluate the Internal Hash Table of the Contents of Directories

Synopsis

csh
rehash

Description

See hash(1).

remote_shell, remsh — Remote Shell

Synopsis

```
remsh [-n] [-l username] hostname command
remsh hostname [-n] [-l username] command hostname [-n] [-l username]
    command
```

Description

See rsh(1).

renice — Alter Priority of Running Processes

Synopsis

```
/usr/bin/renice [-n increment] [-i idtype] ID...
/usr/bin/renice [-n increment] [-g | -p | -u] ID... (This syntax is obsolete
    starting with the Solaris 9 release.)
/usr/bin/renice priority [-p] pid... [-g gid...] [-p pid...]
    [-u user...]
/usr/bin/renice priority -g gid... [-g gid...] [-p pid...] [-u user...]
/usr/bin/renice priority -u user [-g gid...] [-p pid...] [-u user...]
```

New!

Description

Note — The priocntl command subsumes the function of renice.

Use the renice command to alter the scheduling priority of one or more running processes. By default, specify the processes to be affected by their process IDs.

If the first operand is a number within the valid range of priorities (-20 to 20), renice treats it as a priority (as in all but the first synopsis form); otherwise, renice treats it as an ID (as in the first synopsis form).

Altering Process Priority

Users other than superuser can alter only the priority of processes they own and can monotonically increase only their nice value within the range 0 to 19. This limitation prevents you from overriding administrative fiats. Superuser can alter the priority of any process and set the priority to any value in the range -20 to 19. Useful priorities are:

- 19—Run the affected processes only when nothing else in the system wants to run.
- 0—The "base" scheduling priority.
- Any negative value—Make things go very fast.

20 is an acceptable nice value, but it is rounded down to 19.

Notes

If you make the priority very negative, then the process cannot be interrupted. To regain control you must make the priority greater than 0.

Users other than superuser cannot increase scheduling priorities of their own processes even if they were the ones that decreased the priorities in the first place.

Options

- The *priority* operand must precede the options and can be a multidigit option.
- The -g, -p, and -u options can each take multiple arguments.
- You can use the *pid* argument without its -p option.
- You can use the -i option to specify the ID type for the *ID* list. This option is preferred over the -g | -p | -u syntax, which is obsolete starting with the Solaris 9 release.

-g   Interpret all operands or just the *gid* arguments as unsigned decimal integer process group IDs.

-i *idtype*   This option, together with the *ID* list arguments, specifies a class of processes to which to apply the renice command. The interpretation of the *ID* list depends on the value of *idtype*. The valid *idtype* arguments are pid, pgid, uid, gid, sid, taskid, and projid. New in the Solaris 9 release.

-n *increment*
               Specify how to adjust the system scheduling priority of the specified process or processes. *increment* is a positive or negative decimal integer.

               Positive *increment* values schedule a lower system priority. Negative *increment* values can require appropriate privileges and schedule a higher system priority.

-p *pid*   Interpret all operands or just the *pid* arguments as unsigned decimal integer process IDs. The -p option is the default.

-u *user*   Interpret all operands or just the *user* argument as users. If a user exists with a user name equal to the operand, then use the user ID of that user in further processing. Otherwise, if the operand represents an unsigned decimal integer, use it as the numeric user ID of the user.

Operands

ID   A process ID, process group ID, or user name/user ID, depending on the option selected.

priority   The value specified is taken as the actual system scheduling priority instead of as an increment to the existing system scheduling priority. Specifying a scheduling priority higher than that of the existing process can require appropriate privileges.

Examples

The following example adjusts the system scheduling priority so that process IDs 987 and 32 have a lower scheduling priority.

```
castle% renice -n 5 -p 987 32
castle%
```

The following example adjusts the system scheduling priority so that group IDs 324 and 76 have a higher scheduling priority if the user has the appropriate privileges to raise the priority.

```
castle% renice -n -4 -g 324 76
castle%
```

The following example adjusts the system scheduling priority so that numeric user ID 1002 and user ray have a lower scheduling priority.

```
castle% renice -n 4 -u 1002 ray
castle%
```

Environment Variables

See environ(5) for descriptions of the following environment variables that affect the execution of renice: LC_CTYPE, LC_MESSAGES, and NLSPATH.

Exit Status

0   Successful completion.

>0   An error occurred.

Files

/etc/passwd

         Map user names to user IDs.

Attributes

See attributes(5) for descriptions of the following attributes:

Attribute Type	Attribute Value
Availability	SUNWcsu

See Also

nice(1), passwd(1), priocntl(1), attributes(5), environ(5)

reset — Establish or Restore Terminal Characteristics

Synopsis

```
/usr/ucb/reset [-] [-ec] [-I] [-kc] [-n] [-Q] [-r] [-s] [-m [indent]
    [test baudrate]: type]... [type]
```

Description

See tset(1B).

return — Shell Built-in Function to Advance Beyond a Sequence of Steps

Synopsis

sh
```
return [n]
```

csh
```
* return [n]
```

Description

See exit(1).

rksh — Korn Shell, a Standard/Restricted Command and Programming Language

Synopsis

```
/usr/bin/rksh [± abCefhikmnoprstuvx] [± o option]... [-c string]
    [arg...]
```

Description

See ksh(1).

rlogin — Remote Login

Synopsis

```
/usr/bin/rlogin [-8EL] [-ec] [-l username] hostname
```

Description

Use `rlogin` to establish a remote login session from your terminal to the remote system named *hostname*.

Host names are listed in the `hosts` database, which can be contained in the `/etc/hosts` file and `/etc/inet/ipnodes` file—new in the Solaris 8 release—the Network Information Service (NIS) `hosts` map, the Internet domain name server, or a combination of these. Each host has one official name (the first name in the database entry) and, optionally, one or more nicknames. You can specify either official host names or nicknames as *hostname*.

> **Note** — The Network Information Service (NIS) was formerly known as Sun Yellow Pages (YP). The functionality of the two remains the same; only the name has changed.

Each remote system can have a file named `/etc/hosts.equiv` containing a list of trusted host names with which it shares user names. Users with the same *username* on both the local and remote system can invoke `rlogin` from the systems listed in the remote `/etc/hosts.equiv` file without supplying a password. Individual users can set up a similar private equivalence list with the file `.rhosts` in their home directories. Each line in this file contains two names: a *hostname* and a *username* separated by a space. An entry in a remote user's `.rhosts` file permits the user named *username* who is logged into *hostname* to log in to the remote system as a remote user without supplying a password. If the name of the local host is not found in the `/etc/hosts.equiv` file on the remote system and the local *username* and *hostname* are not found in the remote user's `.rhosts` file, then the remote system prompts for a password. Host names listed in `/etc/hosts.equiv` and `.rhosts` files must be the official host names listed in the `hosts` database; nicknames cannot be used in either of these files.

> **Note** — When a system is listed in `hosts.equiv`, its security must be as good as local security. One insecure system listed in `hosts.equiv` can compromise the security of the entire system.

For security reasons, the `.rhosts` file must be owned either by the remote user or by root.

The remote terminal type is the same as your local terminal type (as given in your TERM environment variable). The terminal or window size is also copied to the remote system if the server supports the option, and changes in size are reflected as well. All echoing takes place at the remote site so that (except for delays) the remote login is transparent. Flow control with Control-S and Control-Q and flushing of input and output on interrupts are handled properly.

> **Note** — This implementation can use only the TCP network service.

Options

`-8`	Pass 8-bit data across the net instead of 7-bit data.
`-e`*c*	Specify a different escape character, *c*, for the line used to disconnect from the remote host.
`-E`	Stop any character from being recognized as an escape character.

-l *username*

> Specify a different *username* for the remote login. If you do not use this option, the remote *username* used is the same as your local *username*.

-L

> Run the rlogin session in litout mode.

Escape Sequences

Lines that you type that start with the tilde character are escape sequences (you can change the escape character with the -e option).

~.

> Disconnect from the remote host. This action is not the same as a logout because the local host breaks the connection with no warning to the remote end.

~*susp*

> Suspend the login session (only if you are using a shell with job control). *susp* is your suspend character, usually Control-Z; see tty(1).

~d*susp*

> Suspend the input half of the login, but output is still seen (only if you are using a shell with job control). d*susp* is your "deferred suspend" character, usually Control-Y; see tty(1).

Operands

hostname

> The name of the remote system on which rlogin establishes the remote login session.

Files

/etc/passwd

> Contains information about users' accounts.

/etc/hosts

> Hosts database for IPv4 hosts. Starting with the Solaris 8 release, it's also a symbolic link to /etc/inet/hosts.

/etc/hosts.equiv

> List of trusted host names with shared user names.

/etc/inet/ipnodes

> Hosts database for IPv6 hosts. New in the Solaris 8 release.

/etc/nologin

> Message displayed to users attempting to log in during system shutdown.

$HOME/.rhosts

> Private list of trusted *hostname/username* combinations.

/usr/hosts/*

> For host-name version of the command.

Attributes

See attributes(5) for descriptions of the following attributes:

Attribute Type	Attribute Value
Availability	SUNWrcmdc

New!

See Also

rsh(1), stty(1), tty(1), in.named(1M), hosts(4), hosts.equiv(4),
ipnodes(4), nologin(4), attributes(5)

New!

Diagnostics

NO LOGINS: System going down in *N* minutes

> The system is in the process of being shut down and logins have been
> disabled.

rm, rmdir — Remove Directory Entries

Synopsis

```
/usr/bin/rm [-f] [-i] file...
/usr/bin/rm -rR [-f] [-i] dirname...[file...]
/usr/xpg4/bin/rm [-fiRr] file...
/usr/bin/rmdir [-ps] dirname...
```

Description

/usr/bin/rm, /usr/xpg4/bin/rm

Use the rm command to remove files. The rm command removes the entry specified by
each *file* argument. If a file has no write permission and the standard input is a
terminal, the full set of permissions (in octal) for the file is printed, followed by a
question mark. The question mark is a prompt for confirmation. If your answer begins
with y (for yes), the file is deleted; otherwise, the file remains.

If *file* is a symbolic link, the link is removed but the file or directory to which it
refers is not deleted. You do not need write permission to remove a symbolic link
provided you have write permissions in the directory.

If you specify multiple files and removal of any file fails for any reason, rm writes a
diagnostic message to standard error, does nothing more to the current file, and goes on
to any remaining files.

If the standard input is not a terminal, the command operates as if you specified the
-f option.

Note — A - enables you to explicitly mark the end of any command-line
options, allowing rm to recognize file arguments that begin with a -. As an
aid to BSD migration, rm accepts - as a synonym for --. This migration aid
may disappear in a future release. If you use - twice in the same command
line, the second is interpreted as a file.

/usr/bin/rmdir

Use the rmdir command to remove empty directories.

Directories are processed in the order specified. If you specify a directory and a subdirectory of that directory in a single invocation of rmdir, then you must specify the subdirectory before the parent directory so that the parent directory is empty when rmdir tries to remove it.

Options

The following options are supported for /usr/bin/rm and /usr/xpg4/bin/rm.

-r   Recursively remove directories and subdirectories in the argument list. The directory is emptied of files and removed. You are normally prompted for removal of any write-protected files that the directory contains. If you specify the -f option, however, the write-protected files are removed without prompting. The write-protected files are also removed if the standard input is not a terminal and you do not use the -i option.

                 Do not traverse symbolic links that are encountered with this option.

                 If you try to remove a nonempty, write-protected directory, the command always fails (even if you use the -f option), resulting in an error message.

-R   Same as -r option.

The following options are supported for /usr/bin/rm only.

-f   Remove all files (whether write-protected or not) in a directory without prompting. In a write-protected directory, however, never remove files (whatever their permissions are) and display no messages. If you try to remove a write-protected directory, this option does not suppress an error message.

-i   Prompt for confirmation before removing any files. This option overrides the -f option and remains in effect even if the standard input is not a terminal.

The following options are supported for /usr/xpg4/bin/rm only.

-f   Do not prompt for confirmation. Do not write diagnostic messages or modify the exit status in the case of nonexistent operands. Ignore any previous occurrences of the -i option.

-i   Prompt for confirmation. Ignore the -f option.

The following options are supported for /usr/bin/rmdir only.

-p   Remove the directory *dirname* and its parent directories that become empty. Print a message on the standard error about whether the whole path is removed or part of the path remains for some reason.

-s   Suppress the message printed on the standard error when you also use the -p option.

Operands

file	A path name of a directory entry to be removed.
dirname	A path name of an empty directory to be removed.

Usage

See largefile(5) for the description of the behavior of rm and rmdir when encountering files greater than or equal to 2 Gbytes (2**31 bytes).

Examples

/usr/bin/rm, /usr/xpg4/bin/rm

The following example removes the files a.out and core.

```
castle% rm a.out core
castle%
```

   The following example removes the junk directory and all its contents without prompting.

```
castle% rm -rf junk
castle%
```

/usr/bin/rmdir

If directory a in the current directory is empty except that it contains a directory b, and a/b is empty except that it contains directory c, the following example removes all three directories.

```
castle% rmdir -p a/b/c
castle%
```

Environment Variables

See environ(5) for descriptions of the following environment variables that affect the execution of rm and rmdir: LC_COLLATE, LC_CTYPE, LC_MESSAGES, and NLSPATH.

Exit Status

0	If you do not specify the -f option, all the named directory entries are removed; otherwise, all the existing named directory entries are removed.
>0	An error occurred.

Attributes

See attributes(5) for descriptions of the following attributes:

/usr/bin/rm, /usr/bin/rmdir

Attribute Type	Attribute Value
Availability	SUNWcsu
CSI	Enabled

/usr/xpg4/bin/rm

Attribute Type	Attribute Value
Availability	SUNWxcu4
CSI	Enabled

See Also

rmdir(2), unlink(2), attributes(5), environ(5), largefile(5), XPG4(5)

Diagnostics

All messages are generally self-explanatory.

You cannot remove the files . and .. to avoid the consequences of inadvertently doing something like the following.

```
castle% rm -r .*
```

rmail — Read Mail or Send Mail to Users

Synopsis

```
/usr/bin/rmail [-tw] [-m message-type] recipient...
```

Description

See mail(1).

rmdel — Remove a Delta from an SCCS File

Synopsis

```
/usr/ccs/bin/rmdel -rsid s.filename...
```

Description

See sccs-rmdel(1).

rmdir — Remove Directory Entries

Synopsis

```
/usr/bin/rmdir [-ps] dirname...
```

Description

See rm(1).

rmformat — Removable Rewritable Media Format Command New!

Synopsis

```
/bin/rmformat [-DeHpU] [-b label] [-c blockno] [-F quick | long | force]
   [-R enable | disable] -s filename [-V read | write]
   [-w enable | disable] [-W enable | disable] [devname]
```

Description

The rmformat command, introduced in Solaris 8, was buggy. The bugs to rmformat command are fixed in the Solaris 9 Operating Environment. Use rmformat to format, label, partition, and perform other miscellaneous functions on removable, rewritable media that include diskette drives, Iomega Zip/Jaz products, and the PCMCIA memory and ata cards. You can also use this command for the verification, surface analysis, and repair of the bad sectors found during verification if the drive or the driver supports bad-block management.

rmformat provides functionality to read- or write-protect the media with or without a password. You can enable or disable password protection only with selective rewritable media such as the Iomega Zip/Jaz products.

After formatting, rmformat writes the label, which covers the full capacity of the media, as one slice on floppy and PCMCIA memory cards to maintain compatibility with the behavior of fdformat. On Zip/Jaz devices, the driver exports one slice covering the full capacity of the disk as default. rmformat does not write the label on Zip/Jaz media unless explicitly requested. You can change the partition information with the help of other rmformat options.

> **Note** — A rewritable medium or PCMCIA memory card or PCMCIA ata card containing a UFS file system created on a SPARC-based system (with newfs(1M)) is not identical to a rewritable medium or PCMCIA memory card containing a UFS file system created on an IA-based system. Do not interchange any removable media containing UFS between these platforms; use cpio(1) or tar(1) to transfer files on diskettes or memory cards between them. For interchangeable file systems refer to pcfs(7FS) and udfs(7FS).

Bugs

Bad sector mapping is currently not supported on floppy diskettes or PCMCIA memory cards. Therefore, a diskette or memory card is unusable if rmformat finds an error (bad sector).

Options

-b *label*   Label the media with a SUNOS label. A SUNOS volume label name is restricted to 8 characters. For writing a DOS Volume label, use mkfs_pcfs(1M).

-c *blockno* Correct and repair the given block. This correct and repair option may not be applicable to all devices supported by rmformat, because bad-block-management capability can be implemented in either the device or the driver. If the drive or driver supports bad block management, a best effort is made to rectify the bad block. If the bad block cannot be rectified, a message is displayed to indicate the failure to repair. You can specify the block in decimal, octal, or hexadecimal format.

The normal diskette and PCMCIA memory and ata cards do not support bad-block-management.

-D Format a 720KB (3.5-inch) double-density diskette. This option is the default for double-density type drives. You need to use this option if the drive is a high- or extended-density type.

-e Eject the medium on completion. This feature may not be available if the drive does not support motorized eject.

-F quick | long | force

Format the medium.

The quick option starts a format without certification or format with limited certification of certain tracks on the medium.

The long option starts a complete format. For some devices this might include the certification of the whole medium by the drive itself.

The force option starts a long format without user confirmation before the format is started. For drives that have a password protection mechanism, force clears the password while formatting. This feature is useful when a password is no longer available. On those medium that do not have such password protection, force starts a long format.

In legacy media such as diskette drives, all options start a long format depending on the mode (Extended-Density mode, High-Density mode, or Double-Density mode) with which the diskette drive operates by default. On PCMCIA memory cards, all options start a long format.

-H Format a 1.44 MB (3.5-inch) high-density diskette. This option is the default for high-density type drives. Use this option if the drive is the Extended-Density type.

-p Print the protection status of the medium. This option prints information about whether the medium is write, read, or password protected.

-R enable | disable

Enable read/write protection with a password or disable the password read/write protection. This option always works in interactive mode because the password is requested from the user in an interactive manner to maintain security.

A password length of 32 bytes (maximum) is allowed for the Iomega products that support this feature. This option is applicable only for Iomega products. Iomega products do not allow read/write protection without a password. On the devices that do not have such a software read/write protect facility, warnings indicating the nonavailability of this feature are provided.

-s *filename*

Enable the layout of partition information in the SUNOS label.

Provide *filename* as input with information about each slice in a format providing byte offset, size required, tags, and flags, in the following format.

```
slices: n = offset, size [, flags, tags]
```

where *n* is the slice number, *offset* is the byte offset at which the slice *n* starts, and *size* is the required size for slice *n*. Both *offset* and *size* must be a multiple of 512 bytes. You can represent these numbers as decimal, hexadecimal, or octal numbers. No floating-point numbers are accepted. You can obtain details about the maximum number of slices from the *System Administration Guide: Basic Administration*.

To specify the *size* or *offset* in kilobytes, megabytes, or gigabytes, add KB, MB, or GB. A number without a suffix is assumed to be a byte offset. The flags are described below.

wm = read-write, mountable.

wu = read-write, unmountable.

ru = read-only, unmountable.

The *tags* are unassigned, boot, root, swap, usr, backup, stand, var, home, alternates.

You can omit the *tags* and *flags* from the four tuple when you do not require finer control on those values. You must either omit both or include both. If you omit *tags* and *flags* from the four tuple for a particular slice, a default value for each is assumed. The default value for *flags* is wm, and for *tags* is unassigned.

You can use either full tag names or an abbreviation for the tags. The abbreviations can be the first two or more letters from the standard tag names. rmformat is case insensitive in handling the defined *tags* and *flags*.

Slice specifications are separated by a colon (:), as shown in the following example.

```
slices: 0 = 0, 30MB, "wm", "home" :
1 = 30MB, 51MB :
2 = 0, 100MB, "wm", "backup" :
6 = 81MB, 19MB
```

rmformat does the necessary checking to detect any overlapping partitions or illegal requests to addresses beyond the capacity of the medium under consideration. Only one slice of information entry is permitted for each slice n. If you provide multiple slice information entries for the same slice n, an appropriate error message is displayed. Slice 2 is the backup slice covering the whole disk capacity. You can use the pound-sign character (#) to describe a line of comments in the input file. If the line starts with #, then rmformat ignores all the characters following # until the end of the line.

You can partition some media with very small capacity, but be cautious in using this option on such devices.

-U   Perform umount on any file systems, and then format. See mount(1M). This option unmounts all the mounted slices and issues a long format on the device requested.

-V read | write

Verify each block of medium after format. The write verification is a destructive mechanism. You are queried for confirmation before the verification is started. The output of this option is a list of block numbers that are identified as bad.

The read verification verifies only the blocks and reports the blocks that are prone to errors.

You can use the list of block numbers with the -c option for repairing.

-w enable | disable

Enable or disable the write protection on medium. On devices that do not have a software write-protect facility, a message indicating nonavailability of this feature is displayed.

-W enable | disable

Enable or disable write protection with password. This option always works in interactive mode because a password is requested to maintain security.

A maximum password length of 32 bytes is allowed for Iomega products that support this feature. On devices that do not have the write protection with password, the software displays appropriate messages indicating the nonavailability of such features.

Operands

devname   An absolute or relative device path name for the device from the current working directory or the nickname as exported by the System Volume manager. See vold(1M).

For diskette devices, you can use /dev/rdiskette (for systems without volume management) or floppy0 (systems with volume management) to use the first drive. Specify /dev/rdiskette1 (for systems without volume management), or floppy1 (systems with volume management) to use the second drive.

For systems without volume management running, you can also provide the absolute device path name as /dev/rdsk/c?t?d?s? or the appropriate relative device path name from the current working directory.

Examples

The following example formats a diskette on a system without volume management.

```
mopoke% rmformat -F quick /dev/rdiskette
Formatting will erase all the data on the disk.
Do you want to continue? (y/n) y
mopoke%
```

The following example formats a diskette on a system running volume management.

```
mopoke% rmformat -F quick floppy0
Formatting will erase all the data on the disk.
Do you want to continue? (y/n) y
mopoke%
```

Note that running the rmformat with volume management takes substantially longer than running it without volume management.

Files

/vol/dev/diskette0

Directory providing block device access for the diskette in drive 0.

/vol/dev/rdiskette0

Directory providing character device access for the diskette in drive 0.

/vol/dev/aliases

Directory providing symbolic links to the character devices for the different medium under the control of volume management using appropriate alias.

/vol/dev/aliases/floppy0

Symbolic link to the character device for the diskette drive 0.

/vol/dev/aliases/zip0

Symbolic link to the character device for the medium in Zip drive 0.

/vol/dev/aliases/jaz0

Symbolic link to the character device for the medium in Jaz drive 0.

`/dev/rdiskette`
> Symbolic link providing character device access for the diskette in the primary diskette drive, usually drive 0.

`/vol/dev/dsk`
> Directory providing block device access for the PCMCIA memory and ata cards and removable media devices.

`/vol/dev/rdsk`
> Directory providing character device access for the PCMCIA memory and ata cards and removable media devices.

`/vol/dev/aliases/pcmem`S
> Symbolic link to the character device for the PCMCIA memory card in socket S, where S represents a PCMCIA socket number.

`/vol/dev/aliases/rmdisk0`
> Symbolic link to the generic removable medium device that is not a Zip, Jaz, CD-ROM, diskette, DVD-ROM, PCMCIA memory card, and so forth.

`/dev/rdsk`   Directory providing character device access for the PCMCIA memory and ata cards and other removable devices.

`/dev/dsk`   Directory providing block device access for the PCMCIA memory and ata cards and other removable media devices.

Attributes

See `attributes`(5) for descriptions of the following attributes:

Attribute Type	Attribute Value
Availability	SUNWcsu

See Also

`cpio`(1), `eject`(1), `fdformat`(1), `tar`(1), `volcancel`(1), `volcheck`(1), `volmissing`(1), `volrmmount`(1), `format`(1M), `mkfs_pcfs`(1M), `mount`(1M), `newfs`(1M), `prtvtoc`(1M), `rmmount`(1M), `rpc.smserved`(1M), `vold`(1M), `rmmount.conf`(4), `vold.conf`(4), `attributes`(5), `pcfs`(7FS), `udfs`(7FS)

---

roffbib — Format and Print a Bibliographic Database

Synopsis

```
/usr/bin/roffbib [-e] [-h] [-m filename] [-np] [-olist] [-Q] [-raM]
    [-sM] [-Tterm] [-V] [-x] [filename]...
```

Description

Use the roffbib command to print all records in a bibliographic database in bibliography format instead of as footnotes or endnotes. Generally, roffbib is used in conjunction with sortbib(1).

castle% **sortbib database | roffbib**

Options

roffbib accepts all options understood by nroff(1) except -i and -q.

-e	Produce equally spaced words in adjusted lines, using full terminal resolution.
-h	Use output Tabs during horizontal spacing to speed output and reduce output character count. Tab settings are assumed to be every 8 nominal character widths.
-m *filename*	Prepend the macro file /usr/share/lib/tmac/tmac.name to the input files. Leave a space between the -m and the macro *filename*. This set of macros replaces the ones defined in /usr/share/lib/tmac/tmac.bib.
-n*p*	Number the first generated page *p*.
-o*list*	Print only page numbers that appear in the comma-separated list of numbers and ranges. A range *N-M* means pages *N* through *M*; an initial -*N* means from the beginning to page *N*; a final *N-* means from page *N* to end.
-Q	Queue output for the phototypesetter. Set page offset to 1 inch.
-ra*N*	Set register a (single character) to *N*. The command-line argument -r*M* numbers the references starting at 1.
	Four command-line registers control formatting style of the bibliography, much like the number registers of ms(5). The flag -rV2 double-spaces the bibliography, whereas -rV1 double-spaces references and single-spaces annotation paragraphs. You can change the line length from the default 6.5 inches to 6 inches with the -rL6i argument, and you can set the page offset from the default of 0 to 1 inch by specifying -rO1i (capital O, not 0).
-s*N*	Halt before every *N* pages for paper loading or changing (default N=1). To resume, press newline or Return.
-T*term*	Specify *term* as the terminal type.
-V	Send output to the Versatec printer. Set page offset to 1 inch.
-x	If abstracts or comments are entered following the %X field key, roffbib formats them into paragraphs for an annotated bibliography. You can use several %X fields if you want several annotation paragraphs.

Files

/usr/share/lib/tmac/tmac.bib

File of macros used by nroff/troff.

Attributes

See attributes(5) for descriptions of the following attributes:

Attribute Type	Attribute Value
Availability	SUNWdoc

See Also

addbib(1), indxbib(1), lookbib(1), nroff(1), refer(1), sortbib(1), troff(1), attributes(5)

Bugs

Users must rewrite macros to create customized formats.

New! **roles** — Print Roles Granted to a User

Synopsis

/bin/roles [*user*...]

Description

Use the roles command, new in the Solaris 8 Operating Environment, to print on standard output the role-based access control (RBAC) roles that you or the optionally specified user have been granted. Roles are special accounts that correspond to a functional responsibility instead of to an actual person (referred to as a normal user).

Each user can have zero or more roles. Roles have most of the attributes of normal users and are identified like normal users in passwd(4) and shadow(4). Each role must have an entry in the user_attr(4) file that identifies it as a role. Roles can have their own authorizations and profiles. See auths(1) and profiles(1).

Roles cannot log in to a system as a primary user. Instead, a user must first log in as him or herself and then assume the role. The actions of a role are attributable to the normal user. When auditing is enabled, the audited events of the role contain the audit ID of the original user who assumed the role.

New! A role cannot assume itself or any other roles. Roles are not hierarchical. However, starting with the Solaris 9 release, rights profiles (see prof_attr(4)) are hierarchical, and you can use them to achieve the same effect as hierarchical roles.

Roles must have valid passwords and one of the shells that interprets profiles—either pfcsh, pfksh, or pfsh. See pfexec(1).

Users can assume roles with su(1M), rlogin(1), or some other service that supports the PAM_RUSER variable. To successfully assume a role, the user must be a member of the role and know the role password. Role assignments are specified in user_attr(4).

Examples

The following example shows the output of the `roles` command for three users.

```
mopoke% roles winsor ray des
winsor : printadm
ray : printadm
roles: des : No roles
mopoke%
```

The output shows that users `winsor` and `ray` are both members of the `printadm` role. User `des` is not assigned to any roles.

Exit Status

0	Successful completion.
1	An error occurred.

Files

`/etc/security/exec_attr`

Execution profiles database.

`/etc/security/prof_attr`

Profile description database.

`/etc/user_attr`

Extended user attributes database.

Attributes

See `attributes`(5) for descriptions of the following attributes.

Attribute Type	Attribute Value
Availability	SUNWcsu

See Also

`auths`(1), `pfexec`(1), `profiles`(1), `rlogin`(1), `su`(1M), `getauusernam`(3BSM), `auth_attr`(4), `passwd`(4), `shadow`(4), `user_attr`(4), `attributes`(5)

rpcgen — RPC Protocol Compiler

Synopsis

```
/usr/bin/rpcgen infile
/usr/bin/rpcgen [-a] [-A] [-b] [-C] [-Dname [= value]] [-i size]
    [-I [-K seconds]] [-L] [-M] [-N] [-T] [-v] [-Y pathname] infile
/usr/bin/rpcgen [-c | -h | -l | -m | -t | -Sc | -Ss | -Sm] [-o outfile]
    [infile]
```

/usr/bin/rpcgen [-s *nettype*] [-o *outfile*] [*infile*]
/usr/bin/rpcgen [-n *netid*] [-o *outfile*] [*infile*]

Description

The rpcgen command is a tool that generates C code to implement a Remote Procedure Call (RPC) protocol. The input to rpcgen is a C-like language known as RPC Language (Remote Procedure Call Language).

rpcgen is normally used as in the first synopsis where it takes an input file and generates output files. If the *infile* is named proto.x, then rpcgen generates a header in proto.h, XDR routines in proto_xdr.c, server-side stubs in proto_svc.c, and client-side stubs in proto_clnt.c. With the -T option, rpcgen also generates the RPC dispatch table in proto_tbl.i.

rpcgen can also generate sample client and server files that can be customized to suit a particular application. The -Sc, -Ss, and -Sm options generate sample client, server, and makefile. The -a option generates all files, including sample files. If the *infile* is proto.x, then the client-side sample file is written to proto_client.c, the server-side sample file to proto_server.c, and the sample makefile to makefile.proto.

The server created can be started both by the port monitors (for example, inetd or listen) or by itself. When the server is started by a port monitor, it creates servers only for the transport for which the file descriptor 0 was passed. You must specify the name of the transport by setting up the PM_TRANSPORT environment variable. When the server generated by rpcgen is executed, it creates server handles for all the transports specified in the NETPATH environment variable or, if it is unset, it creates server handles for all the visible transports from the /etc/netconfig file.

Note — The transports are chosen at runtime and not at compile time. When the server is self-started, it puts itself in background by default. You can use the special define symbol, RPC_SVC_FG, to run the server process in foreground.

The second synopsis provides special features that enable the creation of more sophisticated RPC servers. These features include support for user-provided #defines and RPC dispatch tables. The entries in the RPC dispatch table contain:

- Pointers to the service routine corresponding to that procedure.

- A pointer to the input and output arguments.

- The size of these routines.

A server can use the dispatch table to check authorization and then to execute the service routine; a client library can use the dispatch table to deal with the details of storage management and XDR data conversion.

The other three synopses are used when you want to generate a particular output file. See "Examples" on page 1185 for examples of rpcgen usage. When you execute rpcgen with the -s option, rpcgen creates servers for that particular class of transports. When you execute rpcgen with the -n option, it creates a server for the transport specified by netid. If you do not specify *infile*, rpcgen accepts the standard input.

You can use all the options mentioned in the second synopsis with the other three synopses, but the changes are made only to the specified output file.

The C preprocessor cc -E is run on the input file before it is actually interpreted by rpcgen. For each type of output file, rpcgen defines a special preprocessor symbol for use by the rpcgen programmer.

RPC_HDR   Defined when compiling into headers.

RPC_XDR   Defined when compiling into XDR routines.

RPC_SVC	Defined when compiling into server-side stubs.
RPC_CLNT	Defined when compiling into client-side stubs.
RPC_TBL	Defined when compiling into RPC dispatch tables.

Any line beginning with % is passed directly into the output file, uninterpreted by rpcgen except that the leading % is stripped off. To specify the path name of the C preprocessor, use the -Y option.

For every data type referred to in *infile*, rpcgen assumes that a routine exists with the string xdr_ prepended to the name of the data type. If this routine does not exist in the RPC/XDR library, you must provide it. Providing an undefined data type enables customization of XDR routines.

Options

-a	Generate all files, including sample files.
-A	Enable the Automatic MT mode in the server main program. In this mode, the RPC library automatically creates threads to service client requests. This option generates multithread-safe stubs by implicitly turning on the -M option. You can set server multithreading modes and parameters with the rpc_control(3N) call. rpcgen-generated code does not change the default values for the Automatic MT mode.
-b	Generate transport-specific RPC code for older versions of the operating system.
-c	Compile into XDR routines.
-C	Generate header and stub files that can be used with ANSI C compilers. You can also use headers generated with this option with C++ programs.
-D*name*[=*value*]	Define a symbol *name*. Equivalent to the #define directive in the source. If you specify no value, *value* is defined as 1. You can specify this option more than once.
-h	Compile into C data-definitions (a header). You can use this option together with the -T option to produce a header that supports RPC dispatch tables.
-i *size*	Specify the size at which to start generating inline code. This option is useful for optimization. The default size is 5.
-I	Compile support for inetd(1M) in the server-side stubs. Such servers can be self-started or can be started by inetd. When the server is self-started, it puts itself in background by default. You can use the special define symbol RPC_SVC_FG to run the server process in foreground, or you can simply compile without the -I option. If there are no pending client requests, the inetd servers exit after 120 seconds (default). You can change the default with the -K option. All of the error messages for inetd servers are always logged with syslog(3).

Note: This option is supported for backward compatibility only. You should always use it in conjunction with the -b option, which generates backward-compatible code. By default (that is, when you do not specify -b), rpcgen generates servers that can be invoked through port monitors.

-K *seconds*   Change the default 120-second time that services created by rpcgen and invoked through port monitors wait after servicing a request before exiting. To create a server that exits immediately on servicing a request, use -K 0. To create a server that never exits, use -K -1.

When monitoring for a server, some port monitors, like listen(1M), always spawn a new process in response to a service request. If you know that a server is used with such a monitor, the server should exit immediately on completion. For such servers, use rpcgen with -K 0.

-l   Compile into client-side stubs.

-L   When the servers are started in foreground, use syslog(3) to log the server errors instead of printing them on the standard error.

-m   Compile into server-side stubs, but do not generate a main routine. This option is useful for doing callback routines and for users who need to write their own main routine to do initialization.

-M   Generate multithread-safe stubs for passing arguments and results between rpcgen-generated code and user-written code. This option is useful if you want to use threads in your code.

-N   Enable procedures to have multiple arguments. This option uses a style of parameter passing that closely resembles C. So, when passing an argument to a remote procedure, you do not have to pass a pointer to the argument but can pass the argument itself. This behavior is different from the old style of rpcgen-generated code. To maintain backward compatibility, this option is not the default.

-n *netid*   Compile into server-side stubs for the transport specified by *netid*. The netconfig database should contain an entry for *netid*. You can specify this option more than once to compile a server that serves multiple transports.

-o *outfile*   Specify the name of the output file. If none is specified, use standard output (-c, -h, -l, -m, -n, -s, -Sc, -Sm, -Ss, and -t modes only).

-s *nettype*   Compile into server-side stubs for all the transports belonging to the class *nettype*. The supported classes are netpath, visible, circuit_n, circuit_v, datagram_n, datagram_v, tcp, and udp (see rpc(3N) for the meanings associated with these classes). You can specify this option more than once. Note that the transports are chosen at runtime and not at compile time.

-Sc   Generate sample client code that uses remote procedure calls.

-Sm   Generate a sample Makefile that can be used for compiling the application.

-Ss   Generate sample server code that uses remote procedure calls.

-t	Compile into RPC dispatch table.
-T	Generate the code to support RPC dispatch tables.
	Use the options -c, -h, -l, -m, -s, -Sc, -Sm, -Ss, and -t exclusively to generate a particular type of file. The options -D and -T are global and can be used with the other options.
-v	Display the version number. New in the Solaris 9 release.
-Y *pathname*	
	Specify the name of the directory where rpcgen starts looking for the C preprocessor.

New!

Operands

infile	Input file.

Examples

The following example generates all these five files: prot.h, prot_clnt.c, prot_svc.c, prot_xdr.c, and prot_tbl.i.

castle% **rpcgen -T prot.x**

The following example sends the C data-definitions (header) to the standard output.

castle% **rpcgen -h prot.x**

The following example sends the test version of the -DTEST, server-side stubs for all the transport belonging to the class datagram_n to standard output.

castle% **rpcgen -s datagram_n -DTEST prot.x**

The following example creates the server-side stubs for the transport indicated by *netid* tcp.

castle% **rpcgen -n tcp -o prot_svc.c prot.x**

Exit Status

0	Successful operation.
>0	An error occurred.

Attributes

See attributes(5) for descriptions of the following attributes:

Attribute Type	Attribute Value
Availability	SUNWcsu

See Also

cc(1B), inetd(1M), listen(1M), syslog(3), rpc(3NSL), rpc_control(3NSL), rpc_svc_calls(3NSL), netconfig(4), attributes(5)

The rpcgen chapter in the *ONC+ Developer's Guide.*

New! rpm2cpio — Convert Red Hat Package (RPM) to cpio Archive

Synopsis

/bin/rpm2cpio [*file*.rpm]

Description

Use the rpm2cpio command, new in the Solaris 9 Operating Environment, to convert the .rpm file specified as its sole argument to a cpio archive on standard output. If you specify no argument, an rpm stream is read from standard input. In both cases, rpm2cpio fails and prints a usage message if the standard output is a terminal. Therefore, you usually redirect output to a file or pipe it through the cpio(1) command.

Note — The rpm2cpio command handles versions 3 and 4 RPM files.

Examples

The following example converts an rpm file to a cpio archive.

```
example% rpm2cpio Device3Dfx-1.1-2.src.rpm | cpio -itv
CPIO archive found!
-rw-r--r--   1 root   root     2635 Sep 13 16:39 1998, 3dfx.gif
-rw-r--r--   1 root   root    11339 Sep 27 16:03 1998, Dev3Dfx.tar.gz
-rw-r--r--   1 root   root     1387 Sep 27 16:04 1998, Device3Dfx-1.1-2.spec
31 blocks
example%
```

The following example converts from standard input.

```
example% rpm2cpio < Device3Dfx-1.1-2.src.rpm | cpio -itv
CPIO archive found!
-rw-r--r--   1 root   root     2635 Sep 13 16:39 1998, 3dfx.gif
-rw-r--r--   1 root   root    11339 Sep 27 16:03 1998, Dev3Dfx.tar.gz
-rw-r--r--   1 root   root     1387 Sep 27 16:04 1998, Device3Dfx-1.1-2.spec
31 blocks
example%
```

Attributes

See attributes(5) for descriptions of the following attributes:

Attribute Type	Attribute Value
Availability	SUNWrpm

See Also

cpio(1), attributes(5)

rsh, remsh, remote_shell — Remote Shell

Synopsis

```
/usr/bin/rsh [-n] [-l username] hostname command
/usr/bin/rsh hostname [-n] [-l username] command
/usr/bin/remsh [-n] [-l username] hostname command
/usr/bin/remsh hostname [-n] [-l username] command
/usr/bin/hostname [-n] [-l username] command
```

Description

Use the rsh (remote shell) command to connect to the specified *hostname* and execute the specified *command.* rsh copies its standard input to the remote command, the standard output of the remote command to its standard output, and the standard error of the remote command to its standard error. Interrupt, quit, and terminate signals are propagated to the remote *command*, rsh normally terminates when the remote command does.

If you omit *command*, instead of executing a single command, rsh logs you in on the remote host, using rlogin(1).

rsh does not return the exit status code of *command.*

Shell metacharacters that are not quoted are interpreted on the local system, whereas quoted metacharacters are interpreted on the remote system.

If the initialization file of the login shell (.cshrc,...) for a particular user does not contain a locale setting, rsh always executes the command in the C locale instead of using the default locale of the remote system.

Notes

You cannot run an interactive command (such as vi(1)) with rsh; use rlogin if you want to run an interactive command.

Stop signals stop the local rsh process only; this is arguably wrong, but currently hard to fix.

The current local environment is not passed to the remote shell.

Options

-l *username*

> Use *username* as the remote *username* instead of your local *username.* If you do not specify this option, the remote *username* is the same as your local *username.*

-n

> Redirect the input of rsh to /dev/null. You sometimes need this option to avoid unfortunate interactions between rsh and the shell that invokes it. For example, if you are running rsh and invoke an rsh in the background without redirecting its input away from the terminal, it blocks even if no reads are posted by the remote command. The -n option prevents this behavior.
>
> The type of remote shell (sh, rsh, or other) is determined by the user's entry in the file /etc/passwd on the remote system.

Sometimes you need to use the -n option for reasons that are less than obvious. For example, the following command puts your shell into a strange state.

```
castle% rsh somehost dd if=/dev/nrmt0 bs=20b | tar xvpBf -
```

Evidently, what happens is that the `tar` terminates before the `rsh`. The `rsh` then tries to write into the broken pipe and, instead of terminating neatly, proceeds to compete with your shell for its standard input. Invoking `rsh` with the −n option avoids such incidents.

This bug occurs only when `rsh` is at the beginning of a pipeline and is not reading standard input. Do not use the −n option if `rsh` actually needs to read standard input. For example, the following command does not produce the bug.

```
castle% tar cf - . | rsh sundial dd of=/dev/rmt0 obs=20b
```

If you use the −n in a case like this, `rsh` incorrectly reads from `/dev/null` instead of from the pipe.

Operands

command	The command to be executed on the specified *hostname*.
hostname	The official host name or a nickname of the specified host system.

Usage

See `largefile(5)` for the description of the behavior of `rsh` and `remsh` when encountering files greater than or equal to 2 Gbytes (2**31 bytes).

The `rsh` and `remsh` commands are IPv6 enabled starting in the Solaris 8 release. See `ip6(7P)`.

Host names are specified in the `hosts` database, which may be contained in the `/etc/hosts` file, the Internet domain name database, or both. Each host has one official name (the first name in the database entry) and, optionally, one or more nicknames. You can specify official host names or nicknames as *hostname*.

If the name of the file from which you execute `rsh` is anything other than `rsh`, `rsh` takes this name as its *hostname* argument. This feature enables you to create a symbolic link to `rsh` in the name of a host that, when executed, invokes a remote shell on that host. By creating a directory and populating it with symbolic links in the names of commonly used hosts and then including the directory in your shell's search path, you can run `rsh` by typing *hostname* to your shell.

If you invoke `rsh` with the basename `remsh`, `rsh` checks for the existence of the file `/usr/bin/remsh`. If this file exists, `rsh` behaves as if `remsh` is an alias for `rsh`. If `/usr/bin/remsh` does not exist, `rsh` behaves as if `remsh` is a host name.

Each remote system can have a file named `/etc/hosts.equiv` containing a list of trusted host names with which it shares user names. Users with the same user name on both the local and remote system can run `rsh` from the systems listed in the remote system `/etc/hosts` file. Individual users can set up a similar private equivalence list with the file `.rhosts` in their home directories. Each line in this file contains two names: a *hostname* and a *username* separated by a space. The entry permits the user named *username* who is logged into *hostname* to use `rsh` to access the remote system as the remote user. If the name of the local host is not found in the `/etc/hosts.equiv` file on the remote system and the local *username* and *hostname* are not found in the remote user's `.rhosts` file, then the access is denied. The host names listed in the `/etc/hosts.equiv` and `.rhosts` files must be the official host names listed in the `hosts` database; nicknames cannot be used in either of these files.

> **Note** — When a system is listed in hosts.equiv, its security must be as good as local security. One insecure system listed in hosts.equiv can compromise the security of the entire system.

rsh does not prompt for a password if access is denied on the remote system unless you omit the *command* argument.

Examples

The following command appends the remote file lizard.file from the system called lizard to the file called castle.file on the system called castle.

```
castle% rsh lizard cat lizard.file >> castle.file
```

The following example appends the file lizard.file on the system called lizard to the file lizard.file2 which also resides on the system called lizard.

```
castle% rsh lizard cat lizard.file ">>" lizard.file2
```

Files

/etc/hosts   Internet host table.

/etc/hosts.equiv

       Trusted remote hosts and users.

/etc/passwd   System password file.

Exit Status

0	Successful completion.
1	An error occurred.

Attributes

See attributes(5) for descriptions of the following attributes:

Attribute Type	Attribute Value
Availability	SUNWrcmdc
CSI	Enabled

See Also

on(1), rlogin(1), telnet(1), vi(1), in.named(1M), hosts(4), hosts.equiv(4), ipnodes(4), attributes(5), largefile(5), ip6(7P)

runat — Execute Command in Extended Attribute Name Space

Synopsis

/usr/bin/runat *file* [*command*]

Description

Use the `runat` (run attributes) command, new in the Solaris 9 Operating Environment, to execute shell commands in a file's hidden attribute directory.

In the Solaris 9 Operating Environment, the UFS, NFS, and TMPFS file systems are enhanced to include extended file attributes. These file attributes enable application developers to associate specific attributes with a file. For example, a developer of a file management application for a windowing system might choose to associate a display icon with a file.

The `runat` command changes the current working directory to become the hidden attribute directory associated with the file argument and then executes the specified command in the Bourne shell (`/bin/sh`). If you specify no command argument, an interactive shell is spawned. The `$SHELL` environment variable defines the shell to be spawned. If this variable is undefined, the default shell `/bin/sh` is used.

The *file* argument can be any file, including a directory, that can support extended attributes. This file does not need to have any attributes (or be prepared in any way) before the `runat` command is invoked.

Note — It is not always obvious why a command fails in `runat` when the command is unable to determine the current working directory. The resulting errors can be confusing and ambiguous (see the `tcsh` and `zsh` examples).

Operands

file   Any file, including a directory, that can support extended attributes.

command   The command to be executed in an attribute directory.

Errors

A non-zero exit status is returned if `runat` cannot access the *file* argument or if the *file* argument does not support extended attributes.

Usage

See `fsattr(5)` for a detailed description of extended file attributes.

The process context created by the `runat` command has its current working directory set to the hidden directory containing the file's extended attributes. The parent of this directory (the `..` entry) always refers to the file provided on the command line. As such, it cannot be a directory. Therefore, commands (such as `pwd`) that depend on the parent entry being well formed (that is, referring to a directory) may fail.

In the absence of the command argument, `runat` spawns a new interactive shell with its current working directory set to be the provided file's hidden attribute directory. Notice that some shells (such as `zsh` and `tcsh`) are not well behaved when the directory parent is not a directory, as described above. Do not use these shells with `runat`.

Recommended methods for performing basic attribute operations are shown below.

Operation	Command
Display	runat *file* ls [*options*]
Read	runat *file* cat *attribute*

Operation	Command

Create/Modify

       runat *file* cp *absolute-file-path attribute*

Delete   runat *file* rm *attribute*

Change permissions

       runat *file* chmod *mode attribute*

       runat *file* chgrp *group attribute*

       runat *file* chown *owner attribute*

Interactive shell

       runat *file* /bin/sh

       or set your $SHELL to /bin/sh and type

       runat *file*

The above list of commands are known to work with *runat*. While many other commands may work, there is no guarantee that any beyond this list will work. Any command that relies on being able to determine its current working directory is likely to fail.

Examples

Before you use the runat command, you must first create the attributes file. See fsattr(5) for a detailed description of extended file attributes.

The following example shows two ways to use the runat command to add extended attributes already created in the /tmp/attrdata file to file.2.

```
example% runat file.2 cp /tmp/attrdata attr.1
example% runat file.2 cat /tmp/attrdata > attr.1
```

The following example shows how to list the attributes of a file.

```
example% runat file.2 ls -l
example% runat file.2 ls
```

The following example copies an attribute from one file to another.

```
example% runat file.2 cat attr.1 | runat file.1 "cat > attr.1"
```

The following example uses runat to spawn an interactive shell.

```
example% runat file.3 /bin/sh
```

This command spawns a new shell in the attribute directory for file.3. Notice that the shell cannot determine your current directory. To leave the attribute directory, either exit the spawned shell or change directory (cd) with an absolute path.

The remaining examples show commands that are likely to fail.

The following example runs man in an attribute directory.

```
example% runat file.1 man runat
getcwd: Not a directory
example%
```

The following example spawns a tcsh shell in an attribute directory.

```
example% runat file.3 /usr/bin/tcsh
tcsh: Not a directory
tcsh: Trying to start from "/home/user"
example%
```

A new tcsh shell has been spawned with the current working directory set to the user's home directory.

The following example spawns a zsh shell in an attribute directory.

```
example% runat file.3 /usr/bin/zsh
example%
```

While the command seems to have worked, zsh has actually just changed the current working directory to /. You can see this with the /bin/pwd command.

```
example% /bin/pwd
/
example%
```

Environment Variables

SHELL   Specify the command shell to be invoked by runat.

Exit Status

125   The attribute directory of the file referenced by the file argument cannot be accessed.

126   The exec of the provided command argument failed.

Otherwise, the exit status returned is the exit status of the shell invoked to execute the provided command.

Attributes

See attributes(5) for descriptions of the following attributes.

Attribute Type	Attribute Value
Availability	SUNWcsu
CSI	Enabled
Interface Stability	Evolving

See Also

open(2), attributes(5), fsattr(5)

rup — Show Host Status of Remote Systems (RPC Version)

Synopsis

```
/usr/bin/rup [-hlt]
/usr/bin/rup [host...]
```

Description

Use the rup command to find out how long a system has been up and to display the load average. rup gives a status similar to uptime for remote systems. It broadcasts on the local network and displays the responses it receives.

Normally, the listing is in the order that responses are received, but you can change this order by specifying one of the options listed below.

When you specify *host* arguments, instead of broadcasting, rup queries only the list of specified hosts.

A remote host responds only if it is running the rstatd daemon, which is normally started from inetd(1M).

Options

-h   Sort the display alphabetically by host name.

-l   Sort the display by load average.

-t   Sort the display by uptime.

Examples

The following example shows the uptime and load average for the system castle.

```
castle% rup castle
        castle      up            3:55,    load average: 0.06, 0.02, 0.01
castle%
```

Files

```
/etc/servers
```

Attributes

See attributes(5) for descriptions of the following attributes:

Attribute Type	Attribute Value
Availability	SUNWrcmdc

New!

See Also

```
ruptime(1), inetd(1M), attributes(5)
```
Solaris 9 Installation Guide

New!

Bugs

Broadcasting does not work through gateways.

ruptime — Show Host Status of Local Systems

Synopsis

New!

```
/usr/bin/ruptime [-ar] [-l | -t | -u]
```

Description

Use the `ruptime` command to view a status line like `uptime` for each system on the local network; these statistics are formed from packets broadcast by each host on the network once a minute.

Systems for which no status report has been received for 5 minutes are shown as being down.

Normally, the listing is sorted by host name, but you can change this order by specifying one of the options listed below.

Options

-a	Count even those users who have been idle for an hour or more.
-l	Sort the display by load average.
-r	Reverse the sorting order.
-t	Sort the display by uptime.
-u	Sort the display by number of users.

New!   The -l | -t | -u options are mutually exclusive. The use of one overrides the previous one(s).

Files

```
/var/spool/rwho/whod.*
```
                      Data files.

Attributes

See `attributes`(5) for descriptions of the following attributes:

Attribute Type	Attribute Value
Availability	SUNWrcmdc

New!

See Also

New!   `rwho(1)`, `uptime(1)`, `in.rwhod(1M)`, `attributes(5)`

rusage — Print Resource Usage for a Command

Synopsis

```
/usr/ucb/rusage command
```

Description

The rusage command is similar to time(1). It runs the given *command*, which you must specify; that is, *command* is not optional as it is in the C shell timing facility. When the command is complete, rusage displays the real (wall clock), the system CPU, and the user CPU times that elapsed during execution of the command, plus other fields in the rusage structure, all on one long line. Times are reported in seconds and hundredths of a second.

Examples

The following example shows the format of rusage output.

```
castle% rusage wc /kookaburra-1
        9       47       264 kookaburra-1
0.07 real 0.02 user 0.03 sys 0 pf 0 pr 0 sw 0 rb 0 wb 0 vcx 0 icx 0 mx 0
   ix 0 id 0 is
castle%
```

Each of the fields identified corresponds to an element of the rusage structure, described in getrusage(3C), as follows.

```
real                    elapsed real time
user     ru_utime       user time used
sys      ru_stime       system time used
pf       ru_majflt      page faults requiring physical I/O
pr       ru_minflt      page faults not requiring physical I/O
sw       ru_nswap       swaps
rb       ru_inblock     block input operations
wb       ru_oublock     block output operations
vcx      ru_nvcsw       voluntary context switches
icx      ru_nivcsw      involuntary context switches
mx       ru_maxrss      maximum resident set size
ix       ru_ixrss       currently 0
id       ru_idrss       integral resident set size
is       ru_isrss       currently 0
```

Attributes

See attributes(5) for descriptions of the following attributes:

Attribute Type	Attribute Value
Availability	SUNWscpu

See Also

csh(1), time(1), getrusage(3C), attributes(5)

Bugs

When the command being timed is interrupted, the timing values displayed may be inaccurate.

rusers — Display Who Is Logged In on Remote Systems

Synopsis

/usr/bin/rusers [-ahilu] *host*...

Description

The rusers command produces output similar to who(1), but for remote systems. The listing is in the order that responses are received, but you can change this order by specifying one of the options listed below.

The default is to print out the names of the users logged in. When you specify the -l option, additional information is printed for each user.

userid hostname:terminal login date login time idle time login host

If *hostname* and *login host* are the same value, the *login host* field is not displayed. Likewise, if *hostname* is not idle, the idle time is not displayed.

A remote host responds only if it is running the rusersd daemon, which can be started from inetd(1M) or listen(1M).

Options

-a	Report for a system even if no users are logged on.
-h	Sort alphabetically by host name.
-i	Sort by idle time.
-l	Display a longer listing in the style of who(1).
-u	Sort by number of users.

Examples

The following example shows the output of the rusers command for a small network.

```
castle% rusers
Sending broadcast for rusersd protocol version 3...
castle          winsor
seachild        ray
g3              des
castle%
```

The following example shows a longer listing for the system castle.

```
castle% rusers -l castle
winsor          castle:console            Mar 30 08:04            (:0)
castle%
```

Attributes

See attributes(5) for descriptions of the following attributes:

Attribute Type	Attribute Value
Availability	SUNWrcmdc

See Also

who(1), inetd(1M), listen(1M), pmadm(1M), sacadm(1M), attributes(5)

rwho — Display Who Is Logged In on Local Systems

Synopsis

/usr/bin/rwho [-a]

Description

Use the rwho command to display a list of the users logged in to all systems in your network with the login TTY port and the date and time. rwho is similar to who(1). If no report has been received from a system for 5 minutes, rwho assumes the system is down and does not report users last known to be logged in to that system.

If a user has not typed to the system for a minute or more, rwho reports this idle time. If a user has not typed to the system for an hour or more, the user is omitted from the output of rwho unless you specify the -a option.

Notes

rwho does not work through gateways.

The directory /var/spool/rwho must exist on the host from which you run rwho.

This service takes up progressively more network bandwith as the number of hosts on the local net increases. For large networks, the cost becomes prohibitive.

The rwho service daemon, in.rwhod(1M), must be enabled for this command to return useful results.

Options

-a   Report all users whether or not they have typed to the system in the past hour.

Files

/var/spool/rwho/whod.*

Information about other systems.

Attributes

See attributes(5) for descriptions of the following attributes:

Attribute Type	Attribute Value
Availability	SUNWrcmds

New!

See Also

finger(1), ruptime(1), who(1), in.rwhod(1M), attributes(5)

S

sact — Show Editing Activity Status of an SCCS File

Synopsis

/usr/ccs/bin/sact s.*filename*...

Description

See sccs-sact(1).

---

sag — System Activity Graph

Synopsis

/usr/sbin/sag [-e *time*] [-f *file*] [-i *sec*] [-s *time*] [-T *term*] [-x *spec*]
[-y *spec*]

Description

Use the sag command to graphically display the system activity data stored in a binary data file by a previous sar(1) run. You can plot any of the sar data items singly or in combination, as cross-plots or versus time. You can specify simple arithmetic combinations of data. sag invokes sar and finds the desired data by string-matching the data column header (run sar to see what is available). The sag command requires a graphic terminal to draw the graph, and uses tplot(1) to produce its output. When running Solaris 2.3 and OpenWindows, perform the following steps:

1199

1. As root, type **xterm -t** and press Return to run xterm as a Tektronics terminal.
2. In the xterm window, type **sag -T tek** *options* and press Return.

Options

The following options are passed through to sar.

-e *time*	Choose data up to *time*. Default is 18:00.
-f *file*	Use *file* as the data source for sar. Default is the current daily data file /usr/adm/sa/sadd.
-i *sec*	Choose data at intervals as close as possible to *sec* seconds.
-s *time*	Choose data later than *time* in the form *hh*[:*mm*]. Default is 08:00.

Other options:

-T *term*	Produce output suitable for terminal *term*. See tplot(1) for known terminals. Default for *term* is $TERM.
-x *spec*	Specify the x axis with *spec* in the form:

name[*op name*]...[*lo hi*]

name is either a string that matches a column header in the sar report with an optional device name in square brackets, for example, r+w/s[dsk-1], or an integer value. *op* is + - * or / surrounded by blank spaces. You can specify up to five names. Parentheses are not recognized. Contrary to custom, + and - have precedence over * and /. Evaluation is left-to-right. Thus, A / A + B * 100 is evaluated as (A/(A+B))*100, and A + B / C + D is (A+B)/(C+D). *lo* and *hi* are optional numeric scale limits. If unspecified, they are deduced from the data.

Enclose *spec* in double quotes ("") if it includes white space.

A single *spec* is permitted for the x axis. If unspecified, *time* is used.

-y *spec*	Specify the y axis with *spec* in the same form as for -x. You can specify up to five *spec* arguments separated by a semicolon (;). The default is:

-y "%usr 0 100; %usr + %sys 0 100; %usr + %sys + %wio 0 100"

Examples

The following example shows today's CPU use.

```
castle$ sag
```

The following example shows activity of all disk drives over 15 minutes.

```
$ TS=`date +%H:%M`
$ sar -o /tmp/tempfile 60 15

SunOS castle 5.7 Generic sun4m    03/31/99

11:49:38    %usr    %sys    %wio    %idle
11:50:38      4      29      48      18
```

```
11:51:38        4       20      45      32
11:52:38        0        1       0      99
11:53:38        0        0       0     100
11:54:38        0        0       0     100
11:55:38        0        0       0     100
11:56:38        0        0       0      99
11:57:38        0        0       0     100
11:58:38        0        0       0     100
11:59:38        0        0       0     100
12:00:38        0        0       0     100
12:01:38        0        0       0      99
12:02:38        5       30      51      14
12:03:38        3       15      38      44
12:04:39        0        0       0      99

Average         1        7      12      80
$ TE=`date +%H:%M`
$ sag -f /tmp/tempfile -s $TS -e $TE -y "r+w/s[dsk]"
terminal type not known
$
```

Files

/usr/adm/sa/sa*dd*

> Daily data file for day *dd*.

Attributes

See attributes(5) for descriptions of the following attributes:

Attribute Type	Attribute Value
Availability	SUNWaccu

See Also

sar(1), tplot(1), attributes(5)

---

sar — System Activity Reporter

Synopsis

```
/usr/sbin/sar [-aAbcdgkmpqruvwy] [-o filename] t [n]
/usr/sbin/sar [-aAbcdgkmpqruvwy] [-e time] [-f filename] [-i sec]
    [-s time]
```

Description

Use the sar command to view a complete profile of all system activity during an interval of time. In the first synopsis format, sar samples cumulative activity counters in the operating system at *n* intervals of *t* seconds, where *t* should be 5 or greater. If you specify *t* with more than one option, all headers are printed together and the output can be difficult to read. (If the sampling interval is less than 5, the activity of sar itself can affect the sample.) If you specify the -o option, sar saves the samples in *filename* in binary format. The default value of *n* is 1.

In the second synopsis format, you specify no sampling interval. Instead, sar extracts data from a previously recorded file name, either the one specified by the -f option or, by default, the standard, system-activity, daily data file /var/adm/sa/sa*dd* for the current day *dd*. You can bound the starting and ending times of the report with the -e and -s arguments with time specified in the form *hh*[:*mm*[:*ss*]]. The -i option selects records at *sec* second intervals. Otherwise, all intervals found in the data file are reported.

New!   **Note** — The sum of CPU use can vary slightly from 100 because of rounding errors in the production of a percentage figure.

Options

The following options modify the subsets of information reported by sar.

-a   Report use of file-access system routines iget/s, namei/s, dirblk/s.

-A   Report all data. Equivalent to -abcdgkmpqruvwy.

-b   Report buffer activity:

bread/s, bwrit/s

                         Transfers per second of data between system buffers and disk or other block devices.

lread/s, lwrit/s

                         Accesses to system buffers.

%rcache, %wcache

                         Cache hit ratios, that is, (1-bread/lread) as a percentage.

pread/s, pwrit/s

                         Transfers by raw (physical) device mechanism.

-c   Report system calls.

scall/s   System calls of all types.

sread/s, swrit/s, fork/s, exec/s

                         Specific system calls.

rchar/s, wchar/s

                         Characters transferred by read and write system calls. Report no incoming or outgoing exec(2) or fork(2) calls.

-d   Report activity for each block device (for example, disk or tape drive) with the exception of XDC disks and tape drives. The device specification dsk- is generally used to represent a disk drive. The device specification used to represent a tape drive is machine dependent. The activity data reported is:

%busy, avque

> Portion of time device was busy servicing a transfer request, average number of requests outstanding during that time.

read/s, write/s, blks/s

> Number of read/write transfers from or to device, number of bytes transferred in 512-byte units.

avseek   Number of milliseconds per average seek.

For more-general system statistics, use iostat(1M), sar(1M), or vmstat(1M). See *System Administration Guide: Basic Adminsitration* for naming conventions for disks.

-e *time*   Select data up to *time*. Default is 18:00.

-f *filename*

> Use *filename* as the data source for sar. Default is the current daily data file /usr/adm/sa/sa*dd*.

-g   Report paging activities:

pgout/s   Page-out requests per second.

ppgout/s   Pages paged out per second.

pgfree/s   Pages per second placed on the free list by the page-stealing daemon.

pgscan/s   Pages per second scanned by the page-stealing daemon.

%ufs_ipf   The percentage of UFS inodes that were taken off the free list by iget and that had reusable pages associated with them. These pages are flushed and cannot be reclaimed by processes. Thus, this value is the percentage of igets with page flushes.

-i *sec*   Select data at intervals as close as possible to *sec* seconds.

-k   Report kernel memory allocation (KMA) activities.

sml_mem, alloc, fail

> Information about the memory pool reserving and allocating space for small requests: the amount of memory in bytes that KMA has for the small pool, the number of bytes allocated to satisfy requests for small amounts of memory, and the number of requests for small amounts of memory that were not satisfied (failed).

lg_mem, alloc, fail

> Information for the large memory pool (analogous to the information for the small memory pool).

ovsz_alloc, fail

> The amount of memory allocated for oversize requests and the number of oversize requests that could not be satisfied (because oversized memory is allocated dynamically, there is not a pool).

-m   Report message and semaphore activities.

msg/s, sema/s

> Primitives per second.

-o *filename*

Save samples in *filename* in binary format.

-p   Report paging activities.

atch/s	Page faults per second that are satisfied by reclaiming a page currently in memory (attaches per second).
pgin/s	Page-in requests per second.
ppgin/s	Pages paged in per second.
pflt/s	Page faults from protection errors per second (illegal access to page) or "copy on writes."
vflt/s	Address translation page faults per second (valid page not in memory).
slock/s	Faults per second from software lock requests that require physical I/O.

-q   Report average queue length while occupied, and report percent of time occupied.

runq-sz, %runocc

> Run queue of processes in memory and runnable.

swpq-sz, %swpocc

> No longer reported by sar.

-r   Report unused memory pages and disk blocks.

freemem	Average pages available to user processes.
freeswap	Disk blocks available for page swapping.

-s *time*   Select data later than *time* in the form *hh*[:*mm*]. Default is 08:00.

-u   Report CPU use (the default).

%usr, %sys, %wio, %idle

> Portion of time running in user mode, running in system mode, idle with some process waiting for block I/O, and otherwise idle.

-v   Report status of process, inode, file tables.

proc-sz, inod-sz, file-sz, lock-sz

> Entries/size for each table, evaluated once at sampling point.

ov

> Overflows that occur between sampling points for each table.

-w   Report system swapping and switching activity.

swpin/s, swpot/s, bswin/s, bswot/s

> Number of transfers and number of 512-byte units transferred for swap-ins and swap-outs (including initial loading of some programs).

pswch/s   Process switches.

-y   Report TTY device activity.

rawch/s, canch/s, outch/s

> Input character rate, input character rate processed by canon, output character rate.

rcvin/s, xmtin/s, mdmin/s

> Receive, transmit, and modem interrupt rates.

Examples

The following example displays today's CPU activity.

```
castle% sar

SunOS castle 5.7 Generic sun4m     03/31/99

10:49:47    %usr    %sys    %wio    %idle
10:50:47      1       8      33      58
10:51:47      4      25      71       0
10:52:47      3      19      78       0
10:53:47      1       5      25      69
10:54:47      3      27      63       7
10:55:47      2       9      27      63
10:56:47      2      11      37      50
10:57:47      4      30      66       0
10:58:47      3      22      60      14
10:59:47      0       1      14      84
11:00:47      0       0       0      99
11:01:47      0       0       0     100
11:02:47      0       1       0      98
11:03:47      0       1       0      99
11:04:47      0       1       0      99

Average       2      11      32      56
castle%
```

The following example watches CPU activity evolve for 10 minutes and saves the data to a file named temp.

```
castle% sar -o temp 60 10

SunOS castle 5.7 Generic sun4m     03/31/99

12:30:27    %usr    %sys    %wio    %idle
12:31:27       0       1       0       99
12:32:27       0       0       0       99
12:33:27       0       0       0       99
12:34:27       0       0       0       99
12:35:27       0       0       0      100
12:36:27       0       0       0       99
12:37:27       0       1       0       99
12:38:27       0       0       0       99
12:39:27       0       0       0      100
12:40:27       0       0       0       99


Average        0       0       0       99
castle%
```

You can later review disk and tape activity from that period. The following example (truncated to save space) shows the results from the first two minutes.

```
castle% sar -d -f temp

SunOS castle 5.7 Generic sun4m     03/31/99

12:30:27    device       %busy   avque   r+w/s   blks/s   avwait   avserv

12:31:27    fd0             0      0.0      0        0       0.0      0.0
            nfs1            0      0.0      0        0       0.0      0.0
            sd0             0      0.0      0        4       0.0     90.8
            sd0,a           0      0.0      0        2       0.0     81.5
            sd0,b           0      0.0      0        0       0.0     30.6
            sd0,c           0      0.0      0        0       0.0      0.0
            sd0,d           0      0.0      0        0       0.0      0.0
            sd0,f           0      0.0      0        0       0.0     44.2
            sd0,g           0      0.0      0        2       0.0    119.8
            sd1             0      0.0      0        0       0.0     20.2
            sd1,a           0      0.0      0        0       0.0     20.2
            sd1,c           0      0.0      0        0       0.0      0.0
            sd2             0      0.0      0        1       0.0     23.8
            sd2,c           0      0.0      0        0       0.0      0.0
            sd2,h           0      0.0      0        1       0.0     23.8
            sd6             0      0.0      0        0       0.0      0.0
... (More information not shown)
castle%
```

Files

/var/adm/sa/sa*dd*

Daily data file, where *dd* is digits representing the day of the month.

Attributes

See attributes(5) for descriptions of the following attributes:

Attribute Type	Attribute Value
Availability	SUNWaccu

See Also

sag(1), iostat(1M), sar(1M), vmstat(1M), exec(2), fork(2), attributes(5)
System Administration Guide, Basic Administration

sccs — Front End for the Source Code Control System (SCCS)

Synopsis

```
/usr/ccs/bin/sccs [-r] [-drootprefix] [-psubdir] subcommand [option...]
    [file...]
/usr/xpg4/bin/sccs [-r] [-d rootprefix] [-p subdir] subcommand
    [option...] [file...]
```

Description

The sccs command is a comprehensive, straightforward front end to the various command programs of the Source Code Control System (SCCS).

The complete set of SCCS tools provides document management and version control for source code as well as for text documents. When you have a large project, managing the files and changes can be a difficult task. As documents change over time, it can be difficult to track and archive the original documents and all subsequent versions along with their dates and comments.

With SCCS, you administer a single history file that contains all changes to a document. You can add changed versions, called *deltas*, to the file at any time, without destroying older versions. Then, you can retrieve any version from the master file as needed with the SCCS get command.

SCCS keeps version numbers for each new delta that is added to the history file. When you create a file, it is assigned version number 1.1. When you get that version from the history file, make changes, and return the new version to the history file, it is marked as version 1.2, and so on.

The name of an SCCS history file is derived by addition of an s. prefix to the file name of a working copy. The sccs command normally expects these s. files to reside in an SCCS subdirectory. Thus, when you supply sccs with a file argument, it normally applies the subcommand to a file named s.*file* in the SCCS subdirectory. If *file* is a path name, sccs looks for the history file in the SCCS subdirectory of that file's parent directory. If *file* is a directory, however, sccs applies the subcommand to every s. file it contains. Thus, the following command applies the get subcommand to a history file named SCCS/s.program.c.

```
castle% sccs get program.c
```

By contrast, the following command applies the get subcommand to every s. file in the SCCS subdirectory.

```
castle% sccs get SCCS
```

You specify options for the sccs command itself before the subcommand argument.
Specify options for a given subcommand after the subcommand argument. These
options are specific to each subcommand and are described along with the subcommands
themselves.

Running Setuid

The sccs command also includes the capability to run setuid to provide additional
protection. However, this capability does not apply to subcommands such as
sccs-admin(1) because it would enable anyone to change the authorizations of the
history file. Commands that could change the history file are always run as the real user.

Options

New!   -d*rootprefix* (/usr/ccs/bin/sccs)
            -d *rootprefix* (/usr/xpg4/bin/sccs)

            Define the root portion of the path name for SCCS history files. The
            default root portion is the current directory. *rootprefix* is prepended
            to the entire file argument even if *file* is an absolute path name. -d
            overrides any directory specified by the PROJECTDIR environment
            variable.

New!   -p*subdir* (/usr/ccs/bin/sccs)
            -p *subdir* (/usr/xpg4/bin/sccs)

            Define the (sub)directory within which a history file is expected to
            reside. SCCS is the default.

      -r   (/usr/xpg4/bin/sccs only) Run sccs with the real user ID instead of
            setting it to the effective user ID.

Operands

    subcommand An SCCS command name or the name of one of the pseudo commands.

    options   An option or argument to be passed to *subcommand.*

    operands   An operand to be passed to *subcommand.*

Usage

Subcommands

Many of the following sccs subcommands invoke programs that reside in
/usr/ccs/bin. Many of these subcommands accept additional arguments that are
documented in the manual page for the command program the subcommand invokes.

    admin   Modify the flags or checksum of an SCCS history file. See
            sccs-admin(1) for more information about the admin command.
            Although you can use admin to initialize a history file, you may find
            that the create subcommand is simpler to use for this purpose.

```
cdc -rsid [-y[comment]] (/usr/ccs/bin/sccs)
cdc -rsid | -rsid [-y[comment]] (/usr/xpg4/bin/sccs)
```

> Annotate (change) the delta commentary. See sccs-cdc(1). You can use the fix subcommand to replace the delta instead of merely annotating the existing commentary.

> -rsid (/usr/ccs/bin/sccs)
> -r sid | -rsid (/usr/xpg4/bin/sccs)

>> Specify the SCCS delta ID (sid) to which the change notation is to be added. The sid for a given delta is a number, in Dewey decimal format, composed of two or four fields: the release and level fields and, for branch deltas, the branch and sequence fields. For instance, the sid for the initial delta is normally 1.1.

>> -y[comment] Specify the comment with which to annotate the delta commentary. If you omit -y, prompt for a comment. A null comment results in an empty annotation.

```
check [-b] [-u[username]] (/usr/ccs/bin/sccs)
check [-b] [-u [username] | -U] (/usr/xpg4/bin/sccs)
```

> Check for files currently being edited. Like info and tell, but return an exit code instead of producing a listing of files. check returns a non-zero exit status if anything is being edited.

> -b   Ignore branches.

> -u[username] (/usr/ccs/bin/sccs)

> -u [username]| -U (/usr/xpg4/bin/sccs)

>> Check only files being edited by you. When you specify username, check only files being edited by that user. For /usr/xpg4/bin/sccs, the -U option is equivalent to -u current-user.

clean [-b]   Remove everything in the current directory that can be retrieved from an SCCS history. Do not remove files that are being edited.

> -b   Do not check branches to see if they are being edited. clean -b is dangerous when branch versions are kept in the same directory.

comb   Generate scripts to combine deltas. See sccs-comb(1).

create   Create (initialize) history files. create performs the following steps.

- Renames the original source file to ,program.c in the current directory.

- Creates the history file called s.program.c in the SCCS subdirectory.

- Performs an sccs get on program.c to retrieve a read-only copy of the initial version.

`deledit [-s] [-y[`*`comment`*`]]`

> Equivalent to an `sccs delta` and then an `sccs edit`. The `deledit` subcommand checks in a delta and checks the file back out again but leaves the current working copy of the file intact.
>
> | | |
> |---|---|
> | `-s` | Do not report delta numbers or statistics. |
> | `-y[`*`comment`*`]` | Supply a comment for the `delta` commentary. If you omit `-y`, `delta` prompts for a comment. A `null` comment results in an empty comment field for the delta. |

`delget [-s] [-y[`*`comment`*`]]`

> Perform an `sccs delta` and then an `sccs get` to check in a delta and retrieve read-only copies of the resulting new version. See the `deledit` subcommand for a description of `-s` and `-y`. `sccs` performs a `delta` command on all the files specified in the argument list and then a `get` on all the files. If an error occurs during the `delta`, the `get` is not performed.

`delta [-s] [-y[`*`comment`*`]]`

> Check in pending changes. Record the line-by-line changes introduced while the file was checked out. The effective user ID must be the same as the ID of the person who has the file checked out. See `sccs-delta(1)`. See the `deledit` subcommand for a description of `-s` and `-y`.

`diffs [-C] [-I] [-c`*`date-time`*`] [-r`*`sid`*`]` *`diff-options`* `(/usr/ccs/bin/sccs)`

`diffs [-C] [-I] [-c`*`date-time`*` | -c `*`date-time`*`] [-r`*`sid`*` | -r `*`sid`*`]`
`diff-options` `(/usr/xpg4/bin/sccs)`

> Compare (in `diff(1)` format) the working copy of a file that is checked out for editing, with a version from the SCCS history. Use the most recent checked-in version by default. The `diffs` subcommand accepts the same options as `diff`.
>
> Any `-r`, `-c`, `-i`, `-x`, and `-t` options are passed to the `get` subcommand. Any `-l`, `-s`, `-e`, `-f`, `-h`, and `-b` options are passed to the `diff` command. A `-C` option is passed to `diff` as `-c`. An `-I` option is passed to `diff` as `-i`.
>
> `-c`*`date-time`* `(/usr/ccs/bin/sccs)`
>
> `-c `*`date-time`* ` | -c`*`date-time`* ` (/usr/xpg4/bin/sccs)`
>
> Use the most recent version checked in before the indicated date and time for comparison. `date-time` takes the form *`yy`*`[`*`mm`*`[`*`dd`*`[`*`hh`*`[`*`mm`*`[`*`ss`*`]]]]]`. Omitted units default to their maximum possible values; that is, `-c7502` is equivalent to `-c750228235959`.

> -r*sid* (/usr/ccs/bin/sccs)
>
> -r *sid* | -r*sid* (/usr/xpg4/bin/sccs)
>
> > Use the version corresponding to the indicated delta for comparison.

edit
: Retrieve a version of the file for editing. Extract a version of the file that is writable by you; create a p.*file* in the SCCS subdirectory as a lock on the history file so that no one else can check that version in or out. Retrieve ID keywords in unexpanded form. edit accepts the same options as get. See sccs-get(1) for a list of ID keywords and their definitions.

enter
: Similar to create, but omit the final sccs get. You can use this subcommand if you are performing an sccs edit immediately after initializing the history file.

fix -r*sid* (/usr/ccs/bin/sccs)

fix -r *sid* | -r*sid* (/usr/xpg4/bin/sccs)

> Revise a (leaf) delta. Remove the indicated delta from the SCCS history, but leave a working copy of the current version in the directory. This subcommand is useful for incorporating trivial updates for which you need no audit record or for revising the delta commentary. You must follow fix with a -r option to specify the *sid* of the delta to remove. The indicated delta must be the most recent (leaf) delta in its branch. Use fix with caution because it does not leave an audit trail of differences (although the previous commentary is retained within the history file).

get [-ekmps] [-G*newname*] [-c*date-time*] [-r[*sid*]] (/usr/ccs/bin/sccs)   **New!**

get [-ekmps] [-G *newname*] [-c *date-time* | -c*date-time*] [-r *sid* | **New!**
-r*sid*] (/usr/xpg4/bin/sccs)

> Retrieve a version from the SCCS history. By default, this copy is a read-only working copy of the most recent version; ID keywords are in expanded form. See sccs-get(1) for a list of ID keywords and their definitions.

> -e
> : Retrieve a version for editing. Same as sccs edit.

> -G *newname* | -G*newname*   **New!**
> : Use *newname* as the name of the retrieved version. New in the Solaris 9 release.

> -k
> : Retrieve a writable copy, but do not check out the file. ID keywords are unexpanded.

> -m
> : Precede each line with the *sid* of the delta in which it was added.

> -p
> : Produce the retrieved version to the standard output. Direct reports that would normally go to the standard output (delta IDs and statistics) to the standard error.

-s   Do not report version numbers or statistics.

-c*date-time* (/usr/ccs/bin/sccs)
-c *date-time* | -c*date-time* (/usr/xpg4/bin/sccs)

Retrieve the latest version checked in before the date
and time indicated by the *date-time* argument.
date-time takes the form *yy*[*mm*[*dd*
[*hh*[*mm*[*ss*]]]]].

-r[*sid*]   Retrieve the version corresponding to the indicated
sid. If you specify no *sid*, retrieve the latest *sid* for
the specified file.

-r *sid* | -r*sid*

Retrieve the version corresponding to the indicated
sid.

help *message-code*|*sccs-command*

help stuck   Supply more information about SCCS diagnostics. help displays a
brief explanation of the error when you supply the code displayed by an
SCCS diagnostic message. If you supply the name of an SCCS
command, help prints a usage line. help also recognizes the keyword
stuck. See sccs-help(1).

info [-b] [-u[*username*]] (/usr/ccs/bin/sccs)
info [-b] [-u [*username*] | -U] (/usr/xpg4/bin/sccs)

Display a list of files being edited, including the version number
checked out, the version to be checked in, the name of the user who
holds the lock, and the date and time the file was checked out.

-b   Ignore branches.

-u[*username*] (/usr/ccs/bin/sccs)
-u [*username*] | -U (usr/xpg4/bin/sccs)

List only files checked out by you. When you specify
username, list only files checked out by that user. For
/usr/xpg4/bin/sccs, the -U option is equivalent to -u
current-user.

print   Print the entire history of each named file. Equivalent to sccs prs -e
followed by sccs get -p -m.

prs [-el] [-c*date-time*] [-r*sid*] (/usr/ccs/bin/sccs)
prs [-el] [-c *date-time* | -c*date-time*] [-r *sid* | -r*sid*]
(/usr/xpg4/bin/sccs)

Peruse (display) the delta table or other portion of an s. file. See
sccs-prs(1).

-e   Display delta table information for all deltas earlier
than the one specified with -r (or all deltas if you
specify none).

<table>
<tr><td></td><td>-l</td><td>Display information for all deltas later than, and including, that specified by -c or -r.</td></tr>
</table>

        -c*date-time* (/usr/ccs/bin/sccs)
-c *date-time* | -c*date-time*

                    Specify the latest delta checked in before the indicated date and time. The *date-time* argument takes the form *yy*[*mm*[*dd* [*hh*[*mm*[*ss*]]]]].

        -r*sid* (/usr/ccs/bin/sccs)
-r *sid* | -r*sid* (/usr/xpg4/bin/sccs)

                    Specify a given delta by *sid*.

prt [-y]   Display the delta table, but omit the MR field (see sccsfile(4) for more information on this field). See sccs-prt(1).

                -y   Display the most recent delta table entry. The format is a single output line for each file argument; this format is convenient for use in a pipeline with awk(1) or sed(1).

rmdel -r*sid* (/usr/ccs/bin/sccs)
rmdel -r *sid* (/usr/xpg4/bin/sccs)

                    Remove the indicated delta from the history file. That delta must be the most recent (leaf) delta in its branch. See sccs-rmdel(1).

sact   Show editing activity status of an SCCS file. See sccs-sact(1).

sccsdiff -r*old-sid* -r*new-sid* *diff-options*

                    Compare two versions corresponding to the indicated *sid*s (deltas), using diff. See sccs-sccsdiff(1).

tell [-b] [-u[*username*]] (/usr/ccs/bin/sccs)
tell [-b] [-u [*username*] | -U] (/usr/xpg4/bin/sccs)

                    Display the list of files that are currently checked out, one file per line.

                -b   Ignore branches.

                -u[*username*] (/usr/ccs/bin/sccs)
                -u [*username*] | -U (/usr/xpg4/bin/sccs)

                        List only files checked out to you. When you specify *username*, list only files checked out to that user. For /usr/xpg4/bin/sccs, the -U option is equivalent to -u *current-user*.

unedit   Undo the last edit or get -e, and return the working copy to its previous condition. unedit backs out all pending changes made since the file was checked out.

unget   Same as unedit. See sccs-unget(1).

val   Validate the history file. See sccs-val(1).

what   Display any expanded ID keyword strings contained in a binary (object) or text file. See what(1) for more information.

Examples

The following example checks out a file, edits it, and checks it back in again.

```
castle% sccs edit program.c
1.1
new delta 1.2
14 lines
castle% vi program.c
your editing session
castle% sccs delget program.c
comments? clarified cryptic diagnostic
1.2
3 inserted
2 deleted
12 unchanged
1.2
15 lines
castle%
```

The following example defines the root portion of the command path name.

```
castle% sccs -d/usr/src/include get stdio.h
/usr/ccs/bin/get    /usr/src/include/SCCS/s.stdio.h
castle%
```

The following example redefines the resident subdirectory.

```
castle% sccs -pprivate get include/stdio.h
/usr/ccs/bin/get    include/private/s.stdio.h
castle%
```

The following example initializes the history file for a source file named program.c, creates the SCCS subdirectory, and then uses sccs create to create the history file.

```
castle% mkdir SCCS
castle% sccs create program.c
program.c:
1.1
14 lines
castle%
```

After verifying the working copy, you can remove the backup file that starts with a comma, as shown in the following example.

```
castle% diff program.c ,program.c
castle% rm ,program.c
castle%
```

The following two examples retrieve a file from another directory into the current directory.

```
castle% sccs get /usr/src/sccs/cc.c
castle% sccs -p/usr/src/sccs/ get cc.c
```

The following example checks out all files under SCCS in the current directory.

```
castle% sccs edit SCCS
```

The following example checks in all files currently checked out to you.

```
castle% sccs delta `sccs tell -u`
```

Environment Variables

See environ(5) for descriptions of the following environment variables that affect the execution of sccs: LC_CTYPE, LC_MESSAGES, and NLSPATH.

PROJECTDIR

Specify an absolute path name (beginning with a slash) for sccs to use to search for SCCS history files. If PROJECTDIR does not begin with a slash, take it as the name of a user and search the src or source subdirectory of that user's home directory for history files. If sccs finds such a directory, use it. Otherwise, use the value as a relative path name.

Exit Status

0	Successful completion.
>0	An error occurred.

Files

SCCS	SCCS subdirectory.
SCCS/d.*file*	
	Temporary file of differences.
SCCS/p.*file*	
	Lock (permissions) file for checked-out versions.
SCCS/q.*file*	
	Temporary file.
SCCS/s.*file*	
	SCCS history file.
SCCS/x.*file*	
	Temporary copy of the s. file.
SCCS/z.*file*	
	Temporary lock file.
/usr/ccs/bin/*	
	SCCS command programs.

Attributes

See attributes(5) for descriptions of the following attributes:

/usr/ccs/bin/sccs

Attribute Type	Attribute Value
Availability	SUNWsprot

/usr/xpg4/bin/sccs

Attribute Type	Attribute Value
Availability	SUNWxcu4t

See Also

awk(1), diff(1), sccs-admin(1), sccs-cdc(1), sccs-comb(1), sccs-delta(1),
sccs-get(1), sccs-help(1), sccs-prs(1), sccs-rmdel(1), sccs-sact(1),
sccs-sccsdiff(1), sccs-unget(1), sccs-val(1), sed(1), what(1),
sccsfile(4), attributes(5), XPG4(5)

sccs-admin, admin — Create and Administer SCCS History Files

Synopsis

/usr/ccs/bin/admin [-bhnz] [-a *username* | *groupid*]... [-d *flag*...
   [-e *username* | *groupid*]... [-f *flag value*]]... [-i [*filename*]]
   [-m *mr-list*] [-r *release*] [-t [*description-file*]] [-y[*comment*]]
   s.*filename*...

Description

Use the SCCS admin command to create or modify the flags and other parameters of
SCCS history files. File names of SCCS history files begin with the s. prefix and are
referred to as s. files, or history files.

The named s. file is created if it does not already exist. Its parameters are initialized
or modified according to the options you specify. Parameters not specified are given
default values when the file is initialized; otherwise, they remain unchanged.

If you use a directory name in place of the s. *filename* argument, the admin
command applies to all s. files in that directory. Unreadable s. files produce an error.
The use of a dash (-) as the s. *filename* argument indicates that the names of files are
to be read from the standard input, one s. file per line.

Options

-a *username* | *groupid*

        Add a user name or a numerical group ID to the list of users who can
        check deltas in or out. If the list is empty, any user is allowed to check
        deltas in or out.

-b   Force encoding of binary data. Files that contain ASCII `null` or other control characters or that do not end with a newline are recognized as binary data files. Store the contents of such files in the history file in encoded form. See uuencode(1C) for details about the encoding. This option is normally used in conjunction with -i to force admin to encode initial versions not recognized as containing binary data.

-d *flag*   Delete the indicated *flag* from the SCCS file. You can specify the -d option only for existing s. files. See -f for the list of recognized flags.

-e *username* | *groupid*

            Erase a user name or group ID from the list of users allowed to make deltas.

-f *flag* [*value*]

            Set the indicated *flag* to the (optional) value specified. The following flags are recognized.

         b   Enable branch deltas. When b is set, you can create branches with the -b option of the SCCS get command (see sccs-get(1)).

         c *ceil*   Set a ceiling on the releases that can be checked out. *ceil* is a number less than or equal to 9999. If you do not set c, the ceiling is 9999.

         f *floor*   Set a floor on the releases that can be checked out. The *floor* is a number greater than 0 but less than 9999. If you do not set f, the floor is 1.

         d *sid*   The default delta number (*sid*) to be used by an SCCS get command.

         i   Treat the No ID keywords (ge6) message issued by an SCCS get or delta command as an error instead of a warning.

         j   Allow concurrent updates.

         la *lrelease*[, *release*...]

            Lock the indicated list of releases against deltas. If you use a, lock out deltas to all releases. An SCCS get -e command fails when applied against a locked release.

         n   Create empty releases when releases are skipped. These null (empty) deltas serve as anchor points for branch deltas.

         q *value*   Supply a value to which the %Q% keyword is to expand when retrieving a read-only version with the SCCS get command.

         m *module*   Supply a value for the module name to which the %M% keyword is to expand. If you do not specify the m flag, the value assigned is the name of the SCCS file with the leading s. removed.

t *type*
: Supply a value for the module type to which the %Y% keyword is to expand.

v[*program*]
: Specify a validation program for the Modification Request (MR) numbers associated with a new delta. The optional *program* specifies the name of an MR number validity-checking program. If you set this flag when creating an SCCS file, you must also use the -m option, in which case the list of MRs can be empty.

-h
: Check the structure of an existing s. file (see sccsfile(4)), and compare a newly computed checksum with one stored in the first line of that file. -h inhibits writing to the file and, thus, nullifies the effect of any other options.

-i[*filename*]

Initialize the history file with text from the indicated file. This text constitutes the initial delta or set of checked-in changes. If you omit *filename*, obtain the initial text from the standard input. Omitting the -i option altogether creates an empty s. file. Using -i, you can initialize only one s. file with text. This option implies the -n option.

-m[*mr-list*]

Insert the indicated Modification Request (MR) numbers into the commentary for the initial version. When specifying more than one MR number on the command line, specify *mr-list* as a quoted, space-separated list. A warning results if you do not set the v flag or if the MR validation fails.

-n
: Create a new SCCS history file.

-r *release*
: Specify the release for the initial delta. You can use -r only in conjunction with -i. The initial delta is inserted into release 1 if you omit this option. The level of the initial delta is always 1; initial deltas are named 1.1 by default.

-t[*description-file*]

Insert descriptive text from the file *description-file*. When you use -t in conjunction with -n or -i to initialize a new s. file, you must supply the *description-file*. When modifying the description for an existing file, a -t option without a *description-file* removes the descriptive text if any; a -t option with a *description-file* replaces the existing text.

-y[*comment*]

Insert the indicated comment in the Comments: field for the initial delta. Valid only in conjunction with -i or -n. If you omit the -y option, insert a default comment line that notes the date and time the history file was created.

-z   Recompute the file checksum, and store it in the first line of the s. file. Caution: It is important to verify the contents of the history file (see sccs-val(1) and the print subcommand in sccs(1)) because using -z on a truly corrupted file can prevent detection of the error.

Exit Status

0   Successful completion.

1   An error occurred.

Files

s.*   History file.

SCCS/s.*   History file in SCCS subdirectory.

z.*   Temporary lock file.

Attributes

See attributes(5) for descriptions of the following attributes:

Attribute Type	Attribute Value
Availability	SUNWsprot

See Also

sccs(1), sccs-cdc(1), sccs-delta(1), sccs-get(1), sccs-help(1), sccs-rmdel(1), sccs-val(1), sccsfile(4), attributes(5)

Diagnostics

Use the SCCS help command for explanations (see sccs-help(1)).

Warnings

The last component of all SCCS file names must have the s. prefix. New SCCS files are given permission mode 444 (see chmod(1)). All writing done by admin is to a temporary file with an x. prefix, created with mode 444 for a new SCCS file or with the same mode as an existing SCCS file. After successful execution of admin, the existing s. file is removed and replaced with the x. file. This sequence ensures that changes are made to the SCCS file only when no errors have occurred.

It is recommended that directories containing SCCS files have permission mode 755 and that the s. files themselves have mode 444. The mode for directories allows only the owner to modify the SCCS files contained in the directories, and the mode of the s. files prevents all modifications except those performed with SCCS commands.

If you need to patch an SCCS file for any reason, the owner can change the mode to 644 to allow use of a text editor. However, take extreme care when editing an SCCS file. Always process the edited file with an admin -h to check for corruption, followed by an admin -z to generate a proper checksum. Another admin -h is recommended to ensure that the resulting s. file is valid.

admin also uses a temporary lock s. file, starting with the z. prefix, to prevent simultaneous updates to the s. file. See sccs-get(1) for further information about the z. file.

sccs-cdc, cdc — Change the Commentary of an SCCS Delta

Synopsis

`/usr/ccs/bin/cdc -rsid [-mmr-list] [-y [comment]] s.filename...`

Description

Use the SCCS cdc (change delta commentary) command to annotate the delta commentary for the SCCS delta ID (*sid*) specified by the -r option in each named s. file.

If the v flag is set in the s. file, you can also use cdc to update the Modification Request (MR) list.

If you checked in the delta or if you own the file and directory and have write permission, you can use cdc to annotate the commentary.

Instead of replacing the existing commentary, cdc inserts the new comment you supply, followed by a line of the following form above the existing commentary.

`*** CHANGED *** yy/mm/dd hh/mm/ss username`

If a directory is named as the s. *filename* argument, the cdc command applies to all s. files in that directory. Unreadable s. files produce an error; processing continues with the next file (if any). If you specify a dash (-) as the s. *filename* argument, each line of the standard input is taken as the name of an SCCS history file to be processed and you must also use the -m and -y options.

Options

-m*mr-list*   Specify one or more MR numbers to add or delete. When specifying more than one MR on the command line, specify *mr-list* as a quoted, space-separated list. To delete an MR number, precede it with a ! character (an empty MR list has no effect). Put a list of deleted MRs in the comment section of the delta commentary. If you do not use the -m option and the standard input is a terminal, cdc prompts with MRs? for the list (before issuing the comments? prompt). -m is useful only when the v flag is set in the s. file. If that flag has a value, take it to be the name of a program to validate the MR numbers. If that validation program returns a non-zero exit status, cdc terminates and the delta commentary remains unchanged.

-r*sid*   Specify the *sid* of the delta to change.

-y[*comment*]

                Use *comment* as the annotation in the delta commentary. Retain the previous comments; add the comment along with a notation that the commentary was changed. A null comment leaves the commentary unaffected. If you do not specify -y and the standard input is a terminal, cdc prompts with comments? for the text of the notation to be added. You terminate the annotation text with an unescaped newline character.

Examples

The following example produces annotated commentary for delta `1.6` in `s.program.c`.

```
castle% cdc -r1.6 -y"corrected commentary" s.program.c

D 1.6 88/07/05 23:21:07 username 9 0 00001/00000/00000
MRs:
COMMENTS:
corrected commentary
*** CHANGED *** 88/07/07 14:09:41 username
performance enhancements in main()
```

Files

    z.file   Temporary lock file.

Attributes

See `attributes`(5) for descriptions of the following attributes:

Attribute Type	Attribute Value
Availability	SUNWsprot

See Also

`sccs`(1), `sccs-admin`(1), `sccs-comb`(1), `sccs-delta`(1), `sccs-help`(1), `sccs-prs`(1), `sccs-prt`(1), `sccs-rmdel`(1), `what`(1), `sccsfile`(4), `attributes`(5)

Diagnostics

Use the SCCS `help` command for explanations (see `sccs-help`(**1**)).

sccs-comb, comb — Combine SCCS Deltas

Synopsis

`/usr/ccs/bin/comb` [-os] [-c*sid-list*] [-p*sid*] s.*filename* ...

Description

Use the SCCS `comb` command to generate a shell script (see `sh`(1)) that you can use to reconstruct the indicated s. files. This script is written to the standard output.

If you use a directory name in place of the s. *filename* argument, the `comb` command applies to all s. files in that directory. Unreadable s. files produce an error; processing continues with the next file (if any). The use of a dash (–) as the s. *filename* argument indicates that the names of files are to be read from the standard input, one s. file per line.

If you specify no options, `comb` preserves only the most recent (leaf) delta in a branch and the minimal number of ancestors needed to preserve the history.

Options

-c*sid-list*

Include the indicated list of deltas. Omit all other deltas. *sid-list* is a comma-separated list of SCCS delta IDs (*sids*). To specify a range of deltas, use a a dash (-) separator instead of a comma between two *sids* in the list.

-o

For each `get` -e generated, access the reconstructed file at the release of the delta to be created. Otherwise, access the reconstructed file at the most recent ancestor. Using -o can decrease the size of the reconstructed s. file. It can also alter the shape of the delta tree of the original file.

-p*sid*

Specify the *sid* of the oldest delta to be preserved.

-s

Generate scripts to gather statistics instead of combining deltas. When run, the shell scripts report the file name, size (in blocks) after combining, original size (in blocks), and the percentage size change, computed by the formula: `100 * (original - combined) / original`. You can use this option to calculate the space that is saved before actually doing the combining.

Files

s.COMB   Reconstructed SCCS file.

comb*?????*   Temporary file.

Attributes

See `attributes`(5) for descriptions of the following attributes:

Attribute Type	Attribute Value
Availability	SUNWsprot

See Also

sccs(1), sccs-admin(1), sccs-cdc(1), sccs-delta(1), sccs-help(1), sccs-prs(1), sccs-prt(1), sccs-rmdel(1), sccs-sccsdiff(1), what(1), sccsfile(4), attributes(5)

Diagnostics

Use the SCCS `help` command for explanations (see sccs-help(1)).

Bugs

comb can rearrange the shape of the tree of deltas. It may not save any space; in fact, it is possible for the reconstructed file to actually be larger than the original.

sccs-delta, delta — Make a Delta to an SCCS File

Synopsis

```
/usr/ccs/bin/delta [-dnps] [-g sid-list | -gsid-list] [-m mr-list |
    -mmr-list] [-r sid | -rsid] [-y[comment]] s.filename...
/usr/xpg4/bin/delta [-dnps] [-g sid-list | -gsid-list] [-m mr-list|
    -mmr-list] [-r sid | -rsid] [-y[comment]] s.filename...
```

Description

Use the SCCS delta command to check in a record of the line-by-line differences made to a checked-out version of a file under SCCS control. These changes are taken from the writable working copy that was retrieved with the SCCS get command (see sccs-get(1)). This working copy does not have the s. prefix and is also referred to as a g-file.

If you specify a directory name in place of the s.filename argument, the delta command applies to all s. files in that directory. Unreadable s. files produce an error; processing continues with the next file (if any). The use of a dash (-) as the s.filename argument indicates that the names of files are to be read from the standard input, one s. file per line (requires -y, and in some cases, -m).

delta can issue prompts to the standard output depending on the options specified, the flags that are set in the s. file (see sccs-admin(1), and the -m and -y options.

/usr/xpg4/bin/delta

The sid of the delta is not echoed to standard output.

Options

-d	Use the diff(1) command instead of bdiff(1). Return exit status 2 if you do not specify the s.filename argument.
-g sid-list | -gsid-list	
	Specify a list of deltas to omit when the file is accessed at the SCCS version ID (sid) created by this delta. sid-list is a comma-separated list of sids. To specify a range of deltas, use a hyphen (-) separator, instead of a comma, between two sids in the list.
-m mr-list| -mmr-list	
	If the SCCS file has the v flag set (see sccs-admin(1)), you must supply one or more Modification Request (MR) numbers for the new delta. When you specify more than one MR number on the command line, mr-list takes the form of a quoted, space-separated list. If you do not use -m and the standard input is a terminal, delta prompts with MRs? for the list (before displaying the comments? prompt). If the v flag in the s. file has a value, take it to be the name of a program to validate the MR numbers. If that validation program returns a non-zero exit status, terminate without checking in the changes.
-n	Retain the edited g-file that is normally removed at the completion of processing.

-p   Display line-by-line differences (in diff(1) format) to the standard
                        output.

-r *sid* | -r*sid*

                        When two or more versions are checked out, specify the version to check
                        in. This *sid* value can be either the *sid* specified on the get command
                        line or the *sid* of the new version to be checked in as reported by get. A
                        diagnostic results if the specified *sid* is ambiguous or if one is required
                        but not supplied.

-s   Do not display warning or confirmation messages. Do not suppress
                        error messages (which are written to standard error).

-y[*comment*]

                        Supply a comment for the delta table (version log). A null comment is
                        accepted and produces an empty commentary in the log. If you do not
                        specify -y and the standard input is a terminal, delta prompts with
                        comments?. You terminate the comment with an unescaped newline.

Exit Status

0   Successful completion.

1   An error occurred, and you did not specify the -d option.

2   An error occurred because you specified the -d option but did not
                        include the s.*filename* argument.

Files

d.*file*   Temporary file of differences.

p.*file*   Lock file for a checked-out version.

q.*file*   Temporary file.

s.*file*   SCCS history file.

x.*file*   Temporary copy of the s. file.

z.*file*   Temporary file.

Attributes

See attributes(5) for descriptions of the following attributes:

/usr/ccs/bin/delta

Attribute Type	Attribute Value
Availability	SUNWsprot

/usr/xpg4/bin/delta

Attribute Type	Attribute Value
Availability	SUNWxcu4t

See Also

bdiff(1), diff(1), sccs(1), sccs-admin(1), sccs-cdc(1), sccs-get(1),
sccs-help(1), sccs-prs(1), sccs-prt(1), sccs-rmdel(1), sccs-sccsdiff(1),
sccs-unget(1), what(1), sccsfile(4), attributes(5), XPG4(5)

Diagnostics

Use the SCCS help command for explanations (see sccs-help(1)).

Warnings

Lines beginning with an ASCII SOH character (binary 001) cannot be put into the SCCS
file unless you escape the SOH. This character has special meaning to SCCS (see
sccsfile(4)) and produces an error.

sccsdiff — Compare Two Versions of an SCCS File

Synopsis

/usr/ccs/bin/sccsdiff [-p] -r *sid* -r *sid* [*diff-options*]
   s.*filename*

Description

See sccs-sccsdiff(**1**).

sccs-get, get — Retrieve a Version of an SCCS File

Synopsis

/usr/ccs/bin/get [-begkmnpst] [-l[p]] [-a*sequence*] [-c *date-time* |
   -c*date-time*] [-G*g-file*] [-i *sid-list* | -i*sid-list*] [-r[*sid*]]
   [-x *sid-list* | -x*sid-list*] s.*filename*...
/usr/xpg4/bin/get [-begkmnpst] [-l[p]] [-a *sequence*] [-c *date-time* |
   -c*date-time*] [-G*g-file*] [-i *sid-list* | -i*sid-list*] [-r *sid* | -r*sid*]
   [-x *sid-list* | -x*sid-list*] s.*filename* ...

Description

Use the SCCS get command to retrieve a working copy from the SCCS history file, using
the specified options.

For each s.*filename* argument, get displays the SCCS delta ID (*sid*) and number of
lines retrieved.

If you use a directory name in place of the s.*filename* argument, the get command
applies to all s. files in that directory. Unreadable s. files produce an error; processing
continues with the next file (if any). The use of a dash (-) as the s.*filename* argument
indicates that the names of files are to be read from the standard input, one s. file per
line.

The retrieved file normally has the same file-name base as the s. file, less the prefix,
and is referred to as the g-file.

For each file processed, get responds (to the standard output) with the *sid* being
accessed and with the number of lines retrieved from the s. file.

Options

-a*sequence*

> Retrieve the version corresponding to the indicated delta sequence number. This option is used primarily by the SCCS comb command (see sccs-comb(1)); -r is an easier way for you to specify a version. -a supersedes -r when both are used.

-b

> Create a new branch. Use with the -e option to indicate that the new delta should have an *sid* in a new branch. Instead of incrementing the level for the version to be checked in, indicate in the p. file for the delta to be checked in to either initialize a new branch and sequence (if there is no existing branch at the current level) or to increment the branch component of the *sid* If the b flag is not set in the s. file, ignore this option.

-c *date-time* | -c*date-time*

> Retrieve the latest version checked in before the date and time indicated by the *date-time* argument. *date-time* takes the form *yy*[*mm*[*dd*[*hh*[*mm*[*ss*]]]]]. Units omitted from the indicated date and time default to their maximum possible values; that is, -c7502 is equivalent to -c750228235959. Any number of nonnumeric characters can separate the various 2-digit components. If white-space characters occur, you must quote the *date-time* specification.

-e

> Retrieve a version for editing. Put a lock on the s. file so that no one else can check in changes to the version you have checked out. If the j flag is set in the s. file, the lock is advisory: get issues a warning message. Concurrent use of get -e for different *sid*s is allowed; however, get does not check out a version of the file if a writable version is present in the directory. All SCCS file protections stored in the s. file, including the release ceiling, floor, and authorized user list, are honored by get -e.

-g

> Get the SCCS version ID without retrieving the version itself. Use to verify the existence of a particular *sid*

-G *g-file*   Use *g-file* as the name of the retrieved version.

-i *sid-list* | -i*sid-list*

> Specify a list of deltas to include in the retrieved version. The included deltas are noted in the standard output message. *sid-list* is a comma-separated list of *sid*s. To specify a range of deltas, use a hyphen (-) separator instead of a comma between two *sid*s in the list.

-k

> Suppress expansion of ID keywords. -k is implied by -e.

-l[p]

> Retrieve a summary of the delta table (version log), and write it to a listing file with the l. prefix (called l. file). When you use -lp, write the summary to the standard output.

-m

> Precede each retrieved line with the *sid* of the delta in which it was added to the file. The *sid* is separated from the line with a Tab.

-n   Precede each line with the %M% ID keyword and a Tab. When you use
            both the -m and -n options, the ID keyword precedes the *sid* and the
            line of text.

-p   Write the text of the retrieved version to the standard output. Write all
            messages that normally go to the standard output to the standard error
            instead.

-s   Suppress all output normally written to the standard output. However,
            fatal error messages (which always go to the standard error) are
            unaffected.

-t   Retrieve the most recently created (top) delta in a given release, for
            example, -r1.

/usr/ccs/bin/get

-r[*sid*]   Retrieve the version corresponding to the indicated *sid* (delta).

   The *sid* for a given delta is a number, in Dewey decimal format, composed of two or
four fields: the release and level fields and, for branch deltas, the branch and sequence
fields. For instance, if 1.2 is the *sid*, 1 is the release and 2 is the level number. If
1.2.3.4 is the *sid*, 3 is the branch and 4 is the sequence number.
   You need not specify the entire *sid* to retrieve a version with get. When you omit -r
altogether or when you omit both release and level, get normally retrieves the highest
release and level. If the d flag is set to an *sid* in the s. file and you omit the *sid*, get
retrieves the default version indicated by that flag.
   When you specify a release but omit the level, get retrieves the highest level in that
release. If that release does not exist, get retrieves the highest level from the
next-highest existing release.
   Similarly with branches, if you specify a release, level, and branch, get retrieves the
highest sequence in that branch.

/usr/xpg4/bin/get

-r *sid* | -r*sid*

            Same as for /usr/ccs/bin/get except that *sid* is mandatory.

-x *sid-list* | -x*sid-list*

            Exclude the indicated deltas from the retrieved version. The excluded
            deltas are noted in the standard output message. *sid-list* is a
            comma-separated list of *sid*s. To specify a range of deltas, use a hyphen
            (-) separator, instead of a comma, between two *sid*s in the list.

Output

/usr/ccs/bin/get
The /usr/ccs/bin/get command has the following output format.

"%s\n%d lines\n", *sid*, *number-of-lines*

/usr/xpg4/bin/get
The /usr/xpg4/bin/get command has the following output format.

"%s\n%d\n", *sid*, *number-of-lines*

Usage

ID Keywords

In the absence of -e or -k, get expands the following ID keywords by replacing them with the indicated values in the text of the retrieved source.

%A%	Shorthand notation for an ID line with data forwhat(1) in the format %Z%%Y% %M% %I%%Z%.
%B%	*sid* branch component.
%C%	Current line number. Intended for identifying messages output by the program such as "this shouldn't have happened" errors. It is not intended to be used on every line to provide sequence numbers.
%D%	Current date, in the format *yy/mm/dd*.
%E%	Date newest applied delta was created, in the format *yy/mm/dd*.
%F%	SCCS s. file name.
%G%	Date newest applied delta was created, in the format *mm/dd/yy*.
%H%	Current date, in the format *mm/dd/yy*.
%I%	*sid* of the retrieved version, in the format %R%.%L%.%B%.%S%.
%L%	*sid* level component.
%M%	Module name, either the value of the m flag in the s. file (see sccs-admin(1)) or the name of the s. file less the prefix.
%P%	Fully qualified s. file name.
%Q%	Value of the q flag in the s. file.
%R%	*sid* release component.
%S%	*sid* sequence component.
%T%	Current time, in the format *hh:mm:ss*.
%U%	Time the newest applied delta was created, in the format *hh:mm:ss*.
%W%	Shorthand notation for an ID line with data forwhat, in the format %Z%%M% %I%.
%Y%	Module type value of the t flag in the s. file.
%Z%	Four-character string: @(#) recognized by what.

ID String

The table below explains how the SCCS identification string is determined for retrieving and creating deltas.

SID(1) Specified	-b Option Used (2)	Other Conditions	SID Retrieved	SID of Delta to Be Created
none(3)	No	R defaults to mR	mR.mL	mR.(mL+1)
none(3)	Yes	R defaults to mR	mR.mL	mR.mL.(mB+1).1

SID(1) Specified	-b Option Used (2)	Other Conditions	SID Retrieved	SID of Delta to Be Created
R	No	R > mR	mR.mL	R.1(4)
R	No	R = mR	mR.mL	mR.(mL+1)
R	Yes	R > mR	mR.mL	mR.mL.(mB+1).1
R	Yes	R = mR	mR.mL	mR.mL.(mB+1).1
R	-	R < mR, and R does not exist	hR.mL(5)	hR.mL.(mB+1).1
R	-	Trunk succ.(6) in release > R, and R exists	R.mL	R.mL.(mB+1).1
R.L	No	No trunk succ.	RL	R.(L+1)
R.L	Yes	No trunk succ.	RL	R.L.(mB+1).1
R.L	-	Trunk succ. in release ≥ R	R.L	R.L.(mB+1).1
R.L.B	No	No branch succ.	R.L.B.mS	R.L.B.(mS+1)
R.L.B	Yes	No branch succ.	R.L.B.mS	R.L.(mB+1).1
R.L.B.S	No	No branch succ.	R.L.B.S	R.L.B.(S+1)
R.L.B.S	Yes	No branch succ.	R.L.B.S	R.L.(mB+1).1
R.L.B.S	-	Branch succ.	R.L.B.S	R.L.(mB+1).1

1. R, L, B, and S are the release, level, branch, and sequence components of the *sid*; m means maximum. Thus, for example, R.mL means the maximum level number within release R; R.L.(mB+1).1 means the first sequence number on the new branch (that is, maximum branch number plus 1) of level L within release R. Note that if the *sid* specified is of the form R.L, R.L.B, or R.L.B.S, each of the specified components must exist.

2. The -b option is effective only if the b flag is present in the file. An entry of a dash (-) means the -b option is not relevant.

3. This case applies if the d (default *sid*) flag is not present in the file. If the d flag is present in the file, the *sid* obtained from the d flag is interpreted as if it had been specified on the command line. Thus, one of the other cases in this table applies.

4. Force creation of the first delta in a new release.

5. hR is the highest existing release that is lower than the specified, nonexistent release R.

6. Successor.

Files

g-*file*	Version retrieved by get.
l.*file*	File containing extracted delta table information.
p.*file*	Permissions (lock) file.
z.*file*	Temporary copy of s. file.

Attributes

See attributes(5) for descriptions of the following attributes:

/usr/ccs/bin/get

Attribute Type	Attribute Value
Availability	SUNWsprot

/usr/ccs/bin/get

Attribute Type	Attribute Value
Availability	SUNWxcu4t

See Also

sccs(1), sccs-admin(1), sccs-delta(1), sccs-help(1), sccs-prs(1),
sccs-prt(1), sccs-sact(1), sccs-unget(1), what(1), sccsfile(4),
attributes(5), XPG4(5)

Diagnostics

Use the SCCS help command for explanations (see sccs-help(1)).

Bugs

If the effective user has write permission (either explicitly or implicitly) in the directory
containing the SCCS files but the real user does not, you can name only one file when
using -e.

sccs-help, help — Ask for Help Regarding SCCS Error or Warning Messages

Synopsis

/usr/ccs/bin/help [*argument*]...

Description

Use the SCCS help command to retrieve information to further explain errors,
messages, and warnings from SCCS commands. help also provides some information
about SCCS command usage. If you specify no arguments, help prompts for one.

An *argument* can be a message number (which normally appears in parentheses following each SCCS error or warning message) or an SCCS command name. `help` responds with an explanation of the message or a usage line for the command.

When all else fails, try `/usr/ccs/bin/help stuck`.

Files

`/usr/lib/help`

Directory containing files of message text.

Attributes

See `attributes`(5) for descriptions of the following attributes:

Attribute Type	Attribute Value
Availability	SUNWsprot

See Also

`sccs`(1), `sccs-admin`(1), `sccs-cdc`(1), `sccs-comb`(1), `sccs-delta`(1), `sccs-get`(1), `sccs-prs`(1), `sccs-prt`(1), `sccs-rmdel`(1), `sccs-sact`(1), `sccs-sccsdiff`(1), `sccs-unget`(1), `sccs-val`(1), `what`(1), `sccsfile`(4), `attributes`(5)

sccs-prs, prs — Display Selected Portions of an SCCS History

Synopsis

`/usr/ccs/bin/prs [-ael] [-c`*date-time*`] [-d`*dataspec*`] [-r`*sid*`] s.`*filename*`...`

Description

Use the SCCS `prs` (peruse) command to display part or all of the SCCS file (see `sccsfile`(4)) in a user-supplied format.

If you use a directory name in place of the `s.`*filename* argument, the `prs` command applies to all `s.` files in that directory. Unreadable `s.` files produce an error; processing continues with the next file (if any). The use of a dash (-) as the `s.`*filename* argument indicates that the names of files are to be read from the standard input, one `s.` file per line.

Options

In the absence of options, `prs` displays the delta table (version log). In the absence of `-d` or `-l`, `prs` displays the entry for each delta indicated by the other options.

`-a`	Include all deltas, including those marked as removed (see `sccs-rmdel`(1)).
`-e`	Request information for all deltas created earlier than, and including, the delta indicated with `-r` or `-c`.
`-l`	Request information for all deltas created later than, and including, the delta indicated with `-r` or `-c`.

-cdate-time

Display information on the latest delta checked in before the date and time indicated by the *date-time* argument. *date-time* takes the form *yy*[*mm*[*dd*[*hh*[*mm*[*ss*]]]]].

Units omitted from the indicated date and time default to their maximum possible values; that is, -c7502 is equivalent to -c750228235959. Any number of nonnumeric characters can separate the various 2-digit components. If white-space characters occur, you must quote the *date-time* specification.

-ddataspec

Produce a report according to the indicated data specification. Specify *dataspec* as a quoted text string that includes embedded data keywords of the form ': key:'. The prs command expands these keywords in the output it produces. To specify a Tab character in the output, use \t; to specify a newline in the output, use \n.

-rsid

Specify the SCCS delta ID (*sid*) of the delta for which you want information. If you specify no *sid*, use the most recently created delta.

Usage

Data Keywords

Data keywords specify which parts of an SCCS file are to be retrieved. All parts of an SCCS file (see sccsfile(4)) have an associated data keyword. A data keyword can appear any number of times in a data specification argument to -d. These data keywords are listed in the following table.

In the File Section column, B = body, D = delta table, F = flags, and U = user names. In the Format column, S = simple format and M = multiline format.

Keyword	Data Item	File Section	Value	Format
:A:	Format for the what string	N/A	:Z::Y: :M: :I::Z:	S
:B:	Branch number	D	*nnnn*	S
:BD:	Body	B	*text*	M
:BF:	Branch flag	F	yes or no	S
:CB:	Ceiling boundary	F	:R:	S
:C:	Comments for delta	D	*text*	M
:D:	Date delta created	D	:Dy:/:Dm:/:Dd:	S
:Dd:	Day delta created	D	*nn*	S
:Dg:	Deltas ignored (seq #)	D	:DS: :DS:...	S
:DI:	Seq # of deltas included	D	:Dn:/:Dx:/:Dg:	S excluded, ignored
:DL:	Delta line statistics	D	:Li:/:Ld:/:Lu:	S

Keyword	Data Item	File Section	Value	Format
:Dm:	Month delta created	D	*nn*	S
:Dn:	Deltas included (seq #)	D	:DS: :DS:...	S
:DP:	Predecessor delta seq #	D	*nnnn*	S
:Ds:	Default *sid*	F	:I:	S
:DS:	Delta seq #	D	nnnn	S
:Dt:	Delta information	D	:DT::I::D::T::P ::DS::DP: S	
:DT:	Delta type	D	D or R	S
:Dx:	Deltas excluded (seq #)	D	:DS: ...	S
:Dy:	Year delta created	D	*nn*	S
:F:	s.*filename*	N/A text	S	
:FB:	Floor boundary	F	:R:	S
:FD:	File descriptive text	C	*text*	M
:FL:	Flag list	F	*text*	M
:GB:	Gotten body	B	*text*	M
:I:	SCCS delta ID (*sid*)	D	:R:.:L:.:B:.:S:	S
:J:	Joint edit flag	F	yes **or** no	S
:KF:	Keyword error/warning flag	F	yes **or** no	S
:L:	Level number	D	*nnnn*	S
:Ld:	Lines deleted by delta	D	*nnnnn*	S
:Li:	Lines inserted by delta	D	*nnnnn*	S
:LK:	Locked releases	F	:R:...	S
:Lu:	Lines unchanged by delta	D	*nnnnn*	S
:M:	Module name	F	*text*	S
:MF: MR	Validation flag	F	yes **or** no	S
:MP: MR	Validation program	F	*text*	S
:MR: MR	Numbers for delta	D	*text*	M
:ND:	Null delta flag	F	yes **or** no	S

Keyword	Data Item	File Section	Value	Format
:Q:	User-defined keyword	F	*text*	S
:P:	User who created delta	D	*username*	S
:PN:	s. file path name	N/A text	S	
:R:	Release number	D	*nnnn*	S
:S:	Sequence number	D	*nnnn*	S
:T:	Time delta created	D	:Th:::Tm:::Ts:	S
:Th:	Hour delta created	D	*nn*	S
:Tm:	Minutes delta created	D	*nn*	S
:Ts:	Seconds delta created	D	*nn*	S
:UN:	User names	U	*text*	M
:W:	A form of what string	N/A	:Z::M:\t:I:	S
:Y:	Module type flag	F	*text*	S
:Z:	what string delimiter	N/A	@(#)	S

Examples

The following command:

```
castle% /usr/ccs/bin/prs -e -d":I:\t:P:" program.c
```

produces:

```
1.6   username
1.5   username
...
```

Files

/tmp/pr*?????*

Temporary file.

Attributes

See attributes(5) for descriptions of the following attributes:

Attribute Type	Attribute Value
Availability	SUNWsprot

See Also

sccs(1), sccs-cdc(1), sccs-delta(1), sccs-get(1), sccs-help(1), sccs-prt(1), sccs-sact(1), sccs-sccsdiff(1), what(1), sccsfile(4), attributes(5)

Diagnostics

Use the SCCS help command for explanations (see sccs-help(1)).

---

sccs-prt, prt — Display Delta Table Information from an SCCS File

Synopsis

/usr/ccs/bin/prt [-abdefistu] [-c *date-time*] [-r *date-time*] [-y *sid*]
   s.*filename*...

Description

Use the SCCS prt (print) command to print selected portions of an SCCS file. By default, prt prints the delta table (version log).

If you use a directory name in place of the s.*filename* argument, the prt command applies to all s. files in that directory. Unreadable s. files produce an error; processing continues with the next file (if any). The use of a dash (–) as the s.*filename* argument indicates that the names of files are to be read from the standard input, one s. file per line.

Options

If you supply any option other than -y, -c, or -r, the name of each file being processed (preceded by one newline and followed by two newline characters) appears above its contents.

If you use none of the -u, -f, -t, or -b options, -d is assumed. -s and -i are mutually exclusive, as are -c and -r.

-a   Display log entries for all deltas, including those marked as removed.

-b   Print the body of the s. file.

-c *date-time*

          Exclude delta table entries that have the specified cutoff date and time. Print each entry as a single line preceded by the name of the SCCS file. This format (also produced by -r and -y) makes it easy to sort multiple delta tables in chronological order. When you supply both -y and -c or both -y and -r, stop printing when the first of the two conditions is met.

-d   Print delta table entries (the default).

-e   Do everything. This option implies -d, -i, -u, -f, and -t.

-f   Print the flags of each named s. file.

-i   Print the serial numbers of included, excluded, and ignored deltas.

-r *date-time*

> Exclude delta table entries that are newer than the specified cutoff date and time.

-s   Print only the first line of the delta table entries; that is, only up to the statistics.

-t   Print the descriptive text contained in the s. file.

-u   Print the user names and/or numerical group IDs of users allowed to make deltas.

-y *sid*   Exclude delta table entries made before the specified *sid.* If no delta in the table has the specified *sid,* print the entire table. If you specify no *sid,* print the most recent delta.

Usage

Output Format

The following format is used to print those portions of the s. file that are specified by the various options.

- Newline.
- Type of delta (D or R).
- Space.
- SCCS delta ID (*sid*).
- Tab.
- Date and time of creation in the format *yy/mm/dd hh/mm/ss.*
- Space.
- User name of the delta's creator.
- Tab.
- Serial number of the delta.
- Space.
- Predecessor delta's serial number.
- Tab.
- Line-by-line change statistics in the format *inserted/deleted/unchanged.*
- Newline.
- List of included deltas followed by a newline (only if there were any such deltas and you used the -i option).
- List of excluded deltas followed by a newline (only if there were any such deltas and you used the -i option).
- List of ignored deltas followed by a newline (only if there were any such deltas and you used the -i option).
- List of Modification Requests (MRs) followed by a newline (only if you supplied any MR numbers).
- Lines of the delta commentary (if any) followed by a newline.

Examples

The following example produces a one-line display of the delta table entry for the most recent version.

```
castle% /usr/ccs/bin/prt -y program.c
s.program.c: D 1.6 88/07/06 21:39:39 username 5 4 00159/00080/00636...
```

Attributes

See attributes(5) for descriptions of the following attributes:

Attribute Type	Attribute Value
Availability	SUNWsprot

See Also

sccs(1), sccs-cdc(1), sccs-delta(1), sccs-get(1), sccs-help(1), sccs-prs(1), sccs-sact(1), sccs-sccsdiff(1), what(1), sccsfile(4), attributes(5)

Diagnostics

Use the SCCS help command for explanations (see sccs-help(1)).

---

sccs-rmdel, rmdel — Remove a Delta from an SCCS File

Synopsis

/usr/ccs/bin/rmdel -r*sid* s.*filename*...

Description

Use the SCCS rmdel command to remove the delta specified by the SCCS delta ID (*sid*) supplied with the -r option. The delta to be removed must be the most recent (leaf) delta in its branch. In addition, the *sid* must *not* be that of a version checked out for editing: it must not appear in any entry of the version lock file (p. file).

If you created the delta or if you own the file and directory and have write permission, you can remove it with rmdel.

If you use a directory name in place of the s.*filename* argument, the rmdel command applies to all s. files in that directory. Unreadable s. files produce an error; processing continues with the next file (if any). The use of a dash (-) as the s.*filename* argument indicates that the names of files are to be read from the standard input, one s. file per line.

Options

-r*sid*   Remove the version corresponding to the indicated *sid* (delta).

Files

p. file   Permissions file.

s. file   History file.

z. file   Temporary copy of the s. file.

Attributes

See attributes(5) for descriptions of the following attributes:

Attribute Type	Attribute Value
Availability	SUNWsprot

See Also

sccs(1), sccs-admin(1), sccs-cdc(1), sccs-comb(1), sccs-delta(1), sccs-help(1), sccs-prs(1), sccs-prt(1), sccs-sccsdiff(1), sccs-unget(1), what(1), sccsfile(4), attributes(5)

Diagnostics

Use the SCCS help command for explanations (see sccs-help(1)).

sccs-sact, sact — Show Editing Activity Status of an SCCS File

Synopsis

/usr/ccs/bin/sact s.*filename*...

Description

Use the SCCS sact command to list any SCCS files that are checked out for editing.
   The output for each named file consists of the following five fields separated by space characters.

- *sid* of a delta that currently exists in the SCCS file to which changes are made to create the new delta.
- *sid* for the new delta to be created.
- User name of the person who has the file checked out for editing.
- Date on which the version was checked out.
- Time at which the version was checked out.

If you use a directory name in place of the s. *filename* argument, the sact command applies to all s. files in that directory. Unreadable s. files produce an error; processing continues with the next file (if any). The use of a dash (-) as the s. *filename* argument indicates that the names of files are to be read from the standard input, one s. file per line.

Attributes

See attributes(5) for descriptions of the following attributes:

Attribute Type	Attribute Value
Availability	SUNWsprot

See Also

sccs(1), sccs-delta(1), sccs-get(1), sccs-help(1), sccs-prs(1),
sccs-prt(1), what(1), sccsfile(4), attributes(5)

Diagnostics

Use the SCCS help command for explanations (see sccs-help(1)).

Bugs

sact is not recognized as a subcommand of sccs(1).

sccs-sccsdiff, sccsdiff — Compare Two Versions of an SCCS File

Synopsis

/usr/ccs/bin/sccsdiff [-p] -r *sid* -r *sid* [*diff-options*] s.*filename*

Description

Use the SCCS sccsdiff command to compare two versions of an SCCS file and display
the differences between the two versions. You can specify any number of SCCS files; the
options specified apply to all named s. files.

Options

-p	Pipe output for each file through pr(1).
-r *sid*	Specify a version corresponding to the indicated SCCS delta ID (*sid*) for comparison. Versions are passed to diff(1) in the order given.
diff-options	Pass options to diff(1), including -b, -c, -C *number*, -D *string* -e, -f, -h, -u, and -U *number*.

Files

/tmp/get*?????*

Temporary files.

Attributes

See attributes(5) for descriptions of the following attributes:

Attribute Type	Attribute Value
Availability	SUNWsprot

See Also

diff(1), sccs(1), sccs-delta(1), sccs-get(1), sccs-help(1), sccs-prs(1),
sccs-prt(1), what(1), sccsfile(4), attributes(5)

Diagnostics

filename: No differences

The two versions are the same.

Use the SCCS `help` command for explanations of other messages (see `sccs-help`(1)).

---

sccs-unget, unget — Undo a Previous Get of an SCCS File

Synopsis

/usr/ccs/bin/unget [-ns] [-r *sid*] s.*filename*...

Description

Use the SCCS `unget` command to undo the effect of a `get` -e done before the creation of the pending delta.

If you use a directory name in place of the s.*filename* argument, the `unget` command applies to all s. files in that directory. Unreadable s. files produce an error; processing continues with the next file (if any). The use of a dash (-) as the s.*filename* argument indicates that the names of files are to be read from the standard input, one s. file per line.

Options

-n	Retain the retrieved version that would otherwise be removed.
-s	Suppress display of the SCCS delta ID (*sid*).
-r *sid*	When multiple versions are checked out, specify which pending delta to abort. A diagnostic results if the specified *sid* is ambiguous or if it is needed but you omit it from the command line.

Attributes

See `attributes`(5) for descriptions of the following attributes:

Attribute Type	Attribute Value
Availability	SUNWsprot

See Also

sccs(1), sccs-delta(1), sccs-get(1), sccs-help(1), sccs-prs(1), sccs-prt(1), sccs-rmdel(1), sccs-sact(1), sccs-sccsdiff(1), what(1), sccsfile(4), attributes(5)

Diagnostics

Use the SCCS `help` command for explanations (see `sccs-help`(1)).

sccs-val, val — Validate an SCCS File

Synopsis

```
/usr/ccs/bin/val -
/usr/ccs/bin/val [-s] [-m name] [-r sid] [-y type] s.filename...
```

Description

Use the SCCS val (validate) command to determine whether the specified s. files meet the characteristics specified by the indicated arguments. val can process up to 50 files on a single command line.

val has a special dash (-) argument that reads the standard input until the end-of-file condition is detected. Each line read is independently processed as if it were a command-line argument list.

val generates diagnostic messages to the standard output for each command line and file processed and also returns a single 8-bit code on exit as described below.

The 8-bit code returned by val is a disjunction of the possible errors, that is, it can be interpreted as a bit string where (moving from left to right) the bits set are interpreted as follows.

- Bit 0 = Missing file argument.
- Bit 1 = Unknown or duplicate option.
- Bit 2 = Corrupted s. file.
- Bit 3 = Cannot open file, or file not in s. file format.
- Bit 4 = The SCCS delta ID (*sid*) is invalid or ambiguous.
- Bit 5 = The *sid* does not exist.
- Bit 6 = Mismatch between %Y% and the -y argument.
- Bit 7 = Mismatch between %M% and the -m argument.

val can process two or more files on a given command line and, in turn, can process multiple command lines (when reading the standard input). In these cases, an aggregate code is returned that is the logical OR of the codes generated for each command line and file processed.

Options

-s	Suppress the normal error or warning messages.
-m *name*	Compare *name* with the %M% ID keyword in the s. file.
-r *sid*	Check to see if the indicated *sid* is ambiguous, invalid, or absent from the s. file.
-y *type*	Compare *type* with the %Y% ID keyword.

Attributes

See attributes(5) for descriptions of the following attributes:

Attribute Type	Attribute Value
Availability	SUNWsprot

See Also

sccs(1), sccs-admin(1), sccs-delta(1), sccs-get(1), sccs-help(1),
what(1), sccsfile(4), attributes(5)

Diagnostics

Use the SCCS help command for explanations (see sccs-help(1)).

New! **scp** — Secure Copy (Remote File Copy Program)

Synopsis

/bin/scp [-BpqrvC46] [-S *program*] [-P *port*] [-c *cipher*]
  [-i *identity_file*] [-o *option*] [[*user1*@] *host1*:] *file1* [[*user2*@]
host2:] *file2* [...]

Description

Use the scp command, new in the Solaris 9 Operating Environment, to copy files
between hosts on a network. The command uses ssh(1) for data transfer and uses the
same authentication and provides the same security as ssh(1). Unlike rcp(1), scp asks
for passwords or passphrases if they are needed for authentication.

    Any file name can contain a host and user specification to indicate that the file is to
be copied to or from that host. Copies between two remote hosts are permitted.

Options

-4	Use IPv4 addresses only.
-6	Use IPv6 addresses only.
-B	Select batch mode. (Prevents asking for passwords or passphrases.)
-c *cipher*	Specify the cipher to use for encrypting the data transfer. This option is directly passed to ssh(1).
-C	Enable compression. Passes the -C option to ssh(1) to enable compression.
-i *identity_file*	Specify the file from which to read the identity (private key) for RSA authentication. This option is passed directly to ssh(1).
-o *option*	Pass the given option directly to ssh(1).
-p	Preserve modification times, access times, and modes from the original file.
-P *port*	Specify the port to connect to on the remote host.
-q	Disable the progress meter.
-r	Recursively copy entire directories.
-S *program*	Specify the name of the program to use for the encrypted connection. The program must understand ssh(1) options.

-v   Print scp and ssh(1) debugging progress messages. This option is helpful in debugging connection, authentication, and configuration problems.

Operands

host1, host2,...

The name(s) of the host from or to which the file is to be copied.

file1, file2,...

The file(s) to be copied.

Examples

The following example copies the /etc/printcap file from the host named cardinal as the user gmarler, and puts it in the /tmp directory of the current login system.

```
$ scp gmarler@cardinal:/etc/printcap /tmp
gmarler@cardinal's password: <enter gmarler's password on cardinal>
printcap            100% |***************************|   681      00:00
$
```

The following example copies the /etc/group file from the current login system into the /tmp directory on the remote system named cardinal for the account of gmarler.

```
$ scp /etc/group gmarler@cardinal:/tmp
gmarler@cardinal's password: <enter gmarler's password on cardinal>
group               100% |**************************|   290      00:00
$
```

Exit Status

0   Successful completion.

1   An error occurred.

Attributes

See attributes(5) for descriptions of the following attributes:

Attribute Type	Attribute Value
Availability	SUNWsshu

See Also

rcp(1), ssh(1), ssh-add(1), ssh-agent(1), ssh-keygen(1), sshd(1M), attributes(5)

script — Make a Record of a Terminal Session

Synopsis

```
/usr/bin/script [-a] [filename]
```

Description

Use the script command to copy to a file everything that is displayed on your terminal, including your input and the system prompts and output. The record is written to *filename*. If you specify no file name, the record is saved in the file typescript.

The script command forks and creates a subshell, using the value of $SHELL, and records the text from this session. The script ends when the forked shell exits or when you type Control-D.

Options

-a   Append the session record to *filename* instead of overwriting it.

Examples

The following example starts script by using the default typescript file and then displays the comments of the typescript file.

```
castle% script
Script started, file is typescript
castle% who
winsor       console      Apr  1 07:53     (:0)
winsor       pts/3        Apr  1 07:54     (:0.0)
winsor       pts/4        Apr  1 07:54     (:0.0)
winsor       pts/5        Apr  1 07:54     (:0.0)
winsor       pts/6        Apr  1 07:54     (:0.0)
castle% ps -ef | grep script
  winsor    491    408  0 16:34:25 pts/6    0:00 script
  winsor    492    491  0 16:34:25 pts/6    0:00 script
  winsor    497    493  0 16:34:36 pts/7    0:00 grep script
castle% ^D Script done, file is typescript
castle% more typescript
Script started on Thu Apr 01 16:34:25 1999
castle% who
winsor       console      Apr  1 07:53     (:0)
winsor       pts/3        Apr  1 07:54     (:0.0)
winsor       pts/4        Apr  1 07:54     (:0.0)
winsor       pts/5        Apr  1 07:54     (:0.0)
winsor       pts/6        Apr  1 07:54     (:0.0)
castle% ps -ef | grep script
  winsor    491    408  0 16:34:25 pts/6    0:00 script
  winsor    492    491  0 16:34:25 pts/6    0:00 script
  winsor    497    493  0 16:34:36 pts/7    0:00 grep script
castle% ^D
script done on Thu Apr 01 16:34:38 1999
castle%
```

Attributes

See attributes(5) for descriptions of the following attributes:

Attribute Type	Attribute Value
Availability	SUNWcsu
CSI	Enabled

See Also

attributes(5)

---

sdiff — Print, Side-by-Side, Differences Between Two Files

Synopsis

/usr/bin/sdiff [-l] [-s] [-o *output*] [-w *n*] *filename1 filename2*

Description

The sdiff command uses the output of the diff command to produce a side-by-side listing of two files, indicating lines that are different.

Differences are shown in the following ways.

- A blank gutter is printed between the lines if they are identical.
- A < is shown in the gutter if the line appears only in *filename1*.
- A > is shown in the gutter if the line appears only in *filename2*.
- A ! is shown between the lines if they are different.

Options

-l	Print only the left side of any lines that are identical.
-s	Do not print identical lines.
-o *output*	Use the *output* argument as the name of a third file that is created as a merge of *filename1* and *filename2*. Copy identical lines of *filename1* and *filename2* to *output*. Print sets of differences as produced by diff when a set of differences share a common gutter character. After printing each set of differences, prompt with a *%* and wait for you to type one of the following commands.

l	Append the left column to the output file.
r	Append the right column to the output file.
s	Turn on silent mode; do not print identical lines.
v	Turn off silent mode.
e l	Call the editor with the left column.
e r	Call the editor with the right column.
e b	Call the editor with the concatenation of left and right.

e   Call the editor with a 0-length file.

q   Exit from the program. On exit from the editor, concatenate the
        resulting file to the end of the *output* file.

-w *n*   Use the argument *n* as the width of the output line. The default line
        length is 130 characters.

Usage

See largefile(5) for the description of the behavior of sdiff when encountering files
greater than or equal to 2 Gbytes (2** 31 bytes).

Examples

The following example shows output of sdiff.

```
x   |   y
a       a
b   <
c   <
d       d
    >   c
```

Environment Variables

If any of the LC_* variables (LC_CTYPE, LC_MESSAGES, LC_TIME, LC_COLLATE,
LC_NUMERIC, and LC_MONETARY) (see environ(5)) are not set in the environment, the
operational behavior of sdiff for each corresponding locale category is determined by
the value of the LANG environment variable. If LC_ALL is set, its contents are used to
override both the LANG and the other LC_* variables. If none of the above variables are
set in the environment, the C locale determines how sdiff behaves.

LC_CTYPE   Determine how sdiff handles characters. When LC_CTYPE is set
             to a valid value, sdiff can display and handle text and file names
             containing valid characters for that locale.

Attributes

See attributes(5) for descriptions of the following attributes:

Attribute Type	Attribute Value
Availability	SUNWesu
CSI	Enabled

See Also

diff(1), ed(1), attributes(5), environ(5), largefile(5)

sed — Stream Editor

Synopsis

```
/usr/bin/sed [-n] script [file...]
/usr/bin/sed [-n] [-e script]...[-f script-file]... [file...]
/usr/xpg4/bin/sed [-n] script [file...]
/usr/xpg4/bin/sed [-n] [-e script]...[-f script-file]... [file...]
```

Description

The sed command is a noninteractive stream editor that reads one or more text files, makes editing changes according to a script of editing commands, and writes the results to standard output. sed obtains the script from either the *script* operand string or a combination of the option-arguments from the -e *script* and -f *script-file* options.

sed is a text editor. It cannot edit binary files or files containing ASCII null (\0) characters or very long lines.

Options

-e *script*	*script* is an edit command for sed. See "Usage" for more information on the format of *script*. If there is just one -e option and no -f option, you can omit the -e option.
-f *script-file*	Take the script from *script-file*, which consists of editing commands, one per line.
-n	Suppress the default output.

You can specify multiple -e and -f options. All commands are added to the script in the order specified, regardless of their origin.

Operands

file	A path name of a file whose contents are read and edited. If you specify multiple file operands, read the named files in the order specified and edit the concatenation. If you specify no file operands, use the standard input.
script	A string to be used as the script of editing commands. The application must not present a *script* that violates the restrictions of a text file, except that the final character need not be a newline character.

Usage

A script consists of editing commands, one per line, of the following form.

[*address* [, *address*]] *command* [*arguments*]

Zero or more blank characters are accepted before the first address and before *command*. Any number of semicolons are accepted before the first *address*.

In normal operation, sed cyclically copies a line of input (less its terminating newline character) into a pattern space (unless there is something left after a D command), applies in sequence all commands whose addresses select that pattern space, copies the resulting pattern space to the standard output (except with the −n option), and deletes the pattern space. Whenever the pattern space is written to standard output or a named file, sed immediately follows it with a newline character.

Some of the commands use a hold space to save all or part of the pattern space for subsequent retrieval. The pattern and hold spaces are each able to hold at least 8,192 bytes.

sed Addresses

An *address* can have the following contents.

- Empty.
- A decimal number that counts input lines cumulatively across files.
- A $ that addresses the last line of input.
- A context address that consists of a /*regularexpression*/, as described on the regexp(5) manual page.

A command line with no addresses selects every pattern space.

A command line with one address selects each pattern space that matches the address.

A command line with two addresses selects the inclusive range from the first pattern space that matches the first address through the next pattern space that matches the second address. Thereafter, the process is repeated, looking again for the first address. (If the second address is a number less than or equal to the line number selected by the first address, only the line corresponding to the first address is selected.)

Typically, addresses are separated from each other by a comma (,). They can also be separated by a semicolon (;).

sed Regular Expressions

sed supports the basic regular expressions described on the regexp(5) manual page, with the following additions.

cREc	In a context address, the construction *cREc*, where *c* is any character other than a backslash or newline character, is identical to /*RE*/. If the character designated by *c* follows a backslash, then it is considered to be that literal character and does not terminate the *RE*. For example, in the context address \xabc\xdefx, the second x stands for itself, so that the regular expression is abcxdef.
\n	The escape sequence \n matches a newline character embedded in the pattern space. You must not use a literal newline character in the regular expression of a context address or in the substitute command.

Editing commands can be applied only to nonselected pattern spaces by use of the negation command ! (described below).

sed Editing Commands

The following list of editing commands indicates the maximum number of permissible addresses for each function.

The r and w commands take an optional *rfile* (or *wfile*) parameter, separated from the command letter by one or more blank characters.

You can specify multiple commands by separating them with a semicolon (;) on the same command line.

The *text* argument consists of one or more lines, all but the last of which end with \
to hide the newline. You must precede each embedded newline character in the text with
a backslash. Other backslashes in text are removed and the following character is
treated literally. Backslashes in text are treated like backslashes in the replacement
string of an s command and can be used to protect initial blanks and Tabs against the
stripping that is done on every script line. The *rfile* or *wfile* argument must terminate
the command line and must be preceded by exactly one blank. The use of the *wfile*
parameter creates that file initially if it does not exist or replaces the contents of an
existing file. There can be at most ten distinct *wfile* arguments.

Regular expressions match entire strings, not just individual lines, but a newline
character is matched by \n in a sed *RE*, a newline character is not allowed in an *RE*. Also
note that you cannot use \n to match a newline character at the end of an input line;
newline characters appear in the pattern space as a result of the N editing command.

Two of the commands take a command list that is a list of sed commands separated
by newline characters, as follows.

```
{ command
  command
}
```

You can precede the { with blank characters and follow it with white space. You can
precede the s command with white space. You must precede the terminating } with a
newline character and precede or follow it with blanks. You can precede or follow the
braces with blanks. You can precede the command with blanks but cannot follow it with
blanks.

The following table lists the editing commands.

Max. No. of Add-resses	Command	Description
2	{*command-list*}	Execute *command-list* only when the pattern space is selected.
1	a\ *text*	Append by executing N command or beginning a new cycle. Place *text* on the output before reading the next input line.
2	b *label*	Branch to the : command bearing the label. If *label* is empty, branch to the end of the script. Labels are recognized as unique up to eight characters.
2	c\ *text*	Change by deleting the pattern space. Put *text* on the output. Start the next cycle.
2	d	Delete the pattern space. Start the next cycle.
2	D	Delete the initial segment of the pattern space through the first newline. Start the next cycle. (See the N command.)
2	g	Replace the contents of the pattern space with the contents of the hold space.
2	G	Append the contents of the hold space to the pattern space.

Max. No. of Addresses	Command	Description
2	h	Replace the contents of the hold space with the contents of the pattern space.
2	H	Append the contents of the pattern space to the hold space.
1	i\ *text*	Insert *text* to the standard output.
2	l	/usr/bin/sed: List the pattern space to the standard output in an unambiguous form. Display nonprintable characters in octal notation, and fold long lines.
		/usr//xpg4/bin/sed: List the pattern space to the standard output in an unambiguous form. Display nonprintable characters in octal notation, and fold long lines. Write the characters (\\, \a, \b, \f, \r, \t, and \v) as the corresponding escape sequences. Write nonprintable characters not in that table as one 3-digit octal number (with a preceding backslash character) for each byte in the character (most significant byte first). If the size of a byte on the system is greater than 9 bits, the format used for nonprintable characters is implementation dependent.
		Fold long lines, with the point of folding indicated by writing a backslash followed by a newline character; the length at which folding occurs is unspecified but should be appropriate for the output device. Mark the end of each line with a $.
2	n	Copy the pattern space to the standard output if default is not suppressed. Replace the pattern space with the next line of input.
2	N	Append the next line of input to the pattern space with an embedded newline. (The current line number changes.) If the end of input is reached, the N command verb branches to the end of the script and quits without starting a new cycle.
2	p	Print the pattern space to the standard output.
2	P	Print the initial segment of the pattern space through the first newline to the standard output.
1	q	Quit by branching to the end of the script. Do not start a new cycle.
2	r *rfile*	Read the contents of *rfile*. Put them on the output before reading the next input line.

Max. No. of Addresses	Command	Description
2	t *label*	Test by branching to the : command bearing the label if any substitutions have been made since the most recent reading of an input line or execution of a t. If *label* is empty, branch to the end of the script.
2	w *wfile*	Write by appending the pattern space to *wfile*. The first occurrence of w clears *wfile*. Subsequent invocations of w append. Each time you use the sed command, *wfile* is overwritten.
2	x	Exchange the contents of the pattern and hold spaces.
2	! *command*	Apply the command (or group, if *command* is {}) only to lines not selected by the address(es).
0	: *label*	Hold a *label* for b and t commands to branch to.
1	=	Put the current line number to the standard output as a line.
2	{*command-list*}	Execute *command-list* only when the pattern space is selected.
0		Ignore an empty command.
0	#	If a # is the first character on a line of a script file, then treat that entire line as a comment with one exception: if a # is on the first line and the character after the # is an n, then suppress the default output. Also, ignore the rest of the line after #n. A script file must contain at least one noncomment line.

The following list describes the maximum command, using strings.

2   s/*regular expression*/*replacement*/*flags*

Substitute the *replacement* string for instances of the *regular expression* in the pattern space. You can use any character other than backslash or newline instead of a slash to delimit the *RE* and the replacement. Within the *RE* and the replacement, you can use the *RE* delimiter itself as a literal character if you precede it with a backslash.

Replace an ampersand (&) appearing in the *replacement* with the string matching the *RE*. You can suppress the special meaning of & in this context by preceding it with a backslash. Replace the characters \ *n*, where *n* is a digit, with the text matched by the corresponding backreference expression. For each backslash (\) encountered in scanning *replacement* from beginning to end, the character that follows loses its special meaning (if any). It is unspecified what special meaning is given to any character other than &, \, or digits.

You can split a line by substituting a newline character into it. The application must escape the newline character in *replacement* by preceding it with a backslash. A substitution is considered to have been performed even if the replacement string is identical to the string that it replaces. For a fuller description see ed(1). *flags* is zero or more of the following.

n	*n*= 1 - 512. Substitute for just the *n*-th occurrence of the *regular expression*.
g	Globally substitute all nonoverlapping instances of the *regular expression* instead of just the first one. If you use both g and *n*, the results are unspecified.
p	Print the pattern space if a replacement was made.
P	Print the initial segment of the pattern space through the first newline to the standard output.
w *wfile*	Write by appending the pattern space to *wfile* if a replacement was made. The first occurrence of w clears *wfile*. Subsequent invocations of w append to *wfile*. Each time you use the sed command, *wfile* is overwritten.

2 y/*string1*/*string2*/

Replace all occurrences of characters in *string1* with the corresponding characters in *string2*. *string1* and *string2* must have the same number of characters; otherwise, if any of the characters in *string1* appear more than once, the results are undefined. You can use any character other than backslash and newline instead of slash to delimit the strings. Within *string1* and *string2*, you can use the delimiter itself as a literal character if it is preceded with a backslash. For example, y/abc/ABC/ replaces a with A, b with B, and c with C.

See largefile(5) for the description of the behavior of sed when encountering files greater than or equal to 2 Gbytes (2** 31 bytes).

Examples

The following sed script simulates the BSD cat -s command by squeezing excess blank lines from standard input.

```
sed -n '
# Write nonempty lines.
/./     {
        p
        d
        }
# Write a single empty line, then look for more empty lines.
/^$/        p
# Get next line, discard the held newline (empty line),
```

```
# and look for more empty lines.
:Empty

    /^$/           {
        N
        s/.//
        b Empty
        }
# Write the nonempty line before going back to search
# for the first in a set of empty lines.
        p
    '
```

Environment Variables

See environ(5) for descriptions of the following environment variables that affect the execution of sed: LC_COLLATE, LC_CTYPE, LC_MESSAGES, and NLSPATH.

Exit Status

0	Successful completion.
>0	An error occurred.

Attributes

See attributes(5) for descriptions of the following attributes:

/usr/bin/sed

Attribute Type	Attribute Value
Availability	SUNWcsu
CSI	Not enabled

/usr/xpg4/bin/sed

Attribute Type	Attribute Value
Availability	SUNWxcu4
CSI	Enabled

See Also

awk(1), ed(1), grep(1), attributes(5), environ(5), largefile(5), regexp(5), XPG4(5)

set, unset, setenv, unsetenv, export — Shell Environment Variable Built-in Functions

Synopsis

sh

```
set [--aefhkntuvx [argument...]]
unset [name...]
export [name...]
```

csh

```
set [var [= value]]
set var[n] = word
unset pattern
setenv [VAR [word]]
unsetenv variable
```

ksh

```
set [±aefhkmnopstuvx] [±o option]... [±A name] [arg...]
unset [-f] name...
**
export [name[= value]]...
```

Description

Bourne Shell

The Bourne shell set command has the following options.

-a	Mark variables that are modified or created for export.
-e	Exit immediately if a command exits with a non-zero exit status.
-f	Disable file-name generation.
-h	Locate and remember function commands as you define functions (function commands are normally located when the function is executed).
-k	Put all keyword arguments in the environment for a command, not just those that precede the command name.
-n	Read commands, but do not execute them.
-t	Exit after reading and executing one command.
-u	Treat unset variables as an error when substituting.
-v	Print shell input lines as they are read.
-x	Print commands and their arguments as they are executed.
--	Do not change any of the options; useful in setting $1 to -.

Using + instead of - turns these options off. You can also use these options when invoking the shell. The current set of options is found in $-. The remaining arguments are positional parameters and are assigned, in order, to $1, $2, ... If you specify no arguments, the values of all names are printed.

For each name, unset removes the corresponding variable or function value. You cannot unset the variables PATH, PS1, PS2, MAILCHECK, and IF.

With the export built-in, the given names are marked for automatic export to the environment of subsequently executed commands. If you specify no arguments, variable names that have been marked for export during the current shell's execution are listed. Function names are not exported.

C Shell

With no arguments, set displays the values of all shell variables. Multiword values are displayed as a parenthesized list. With the *var* argument alone, set assigns an empty (null) value to the variable *var*. With arguments of the form *var* = *value*, set assigns *value* to *var*, where *value* is one of the following.

word   A single *word* (or quoted string).

(*wordlist*)   A space-separated list of words enclosed in parentheses.

Values are command- and file-name-expanded before being assigned. The form set *var*[*n*] = *word* replaces the *n*-th word in a multiword value with *word*.

unset removes variables whose names match (file-name substitution) *pattern*. All variables are removed by unset *; this command has noticeably distasteful side effects.

With no arguments, setenv displays all environment variables. With the *VAR* argument, setenv sets the environment variable *VAR* to an empty (null) value. (By convention, environment variables are normally given uppercase names.) When you specify both the *VAR* and *word* arguments, setenv sets *VAR* to *word*, which must be either a single word or a quoted string. The PATH variable can take multiple word arguments, separated by colons. The most commonly used environment variables, USER, TERM, and PATH, are automatically imported to and exported from the csh variables user, term, and path. Use setenv if you need to change these variables. In addition, the shell sets the PWD environment variable from the csh variable cwd whenever the latter changes.

The environment variables LC_CTYPE, LC_MESSAGES, LC_TIME, LC_COLLATE, LC_NUMERIC, and LC_MONETARY take immediate effect when changed within the C shell. See environ(5) for descriptions of these environment variables.

unsetenv removes *variable* from the environment. As with unset, pattern matching is not performed.

Korn Shell

The options for the set built-in command have the following meanings.

-A   Unset the variable name, and assign values sequentially from the list *arg*. If you use +A, do not first unset the variable name.

-a   Automatically export all subsequent variables that are defined.

-e   If a command has a non-zero exit status, execute the ERR trap if set, and exit. This mode is disabled while profiles are being read.

-f   Disable file-name generation.

-h   Interpret each command as a tracked alias when first encountered.

-k   Put all variable assignment arguments in the environment for a command, not just those that precede the command name.

-m   Run background jobs in a separate process group, and print a line on completion. Report the exit status of background jobs in a completion message. On systems with job control, this option is turned on automatically for interactive shells.

-n	Read commands and check them for syntax errors, but do not execute them. Ignored for interactive shells.
-o	Specify one of the following option names.

allexport	Same as -a.
errexit	Same as -e.
bgnice	Run all background jobs at a lower priority (the default).
emacs	Put you in an emacs-style line editor for command entry.
gmacs	Put you in a gmacs-style inline editor for command entry.
ignoreeof	Do not exit the shell on end-of-file. You must use the exit command.
keyword	Same as -k.
markdirs	Append a trailing slash (/) to all directory names resulting from file-name generation.
monitor	Same as -m.
noclobber	Prevent redirection > from truncating existing files. Require >| to truncate a file when turned on.
noexec	Same as -n.
noglob	Same as -f.
nolog	Do not save function definitions in history file.
nounset	Same as -u.
privileged	Same as -p.
verbose	Same as -v.
trackall	Same as -h.
vi	Put you in insert mode of a vi-style inline editor until you press escape character 033, which puts you in control mode. A Return sends the line.
viraw	Each character is processed as it is typed in vi mode.
xtrace	Same as -x. If you supply no option name, then print the current option settings.

-p	Disable processing of the $HOME/.profile file, and use the file /etc/suid_profile instead of the ENV file. This mode is on whenever the effective UID is not equal to the real UID or when the effective GID is not equal to the real GID. Turning this option off sets the effective UID and GID to the real UID and GID.
-s	Sort the positional parameters lexicographically.
-t	Exit after reading and executing one command.
-u	Treat unset parameters as an error when substituting.
-v	Print shell input lines as they are read.

-x	Print commands and their arguments as they are executed.
-	Turn off -x and -v options, and stop examining arguments for options.
--	Do not change any of the options; useful in setting $1 to a value beginning with -. If no arguments follow this option, then unset the positional parameters.

Using + instead of - turns these options off. You can also use these options on invocation of the shell. The current set of options is found in $-. Unless you specify -A, the remaining arguments are positional parameters and are assigned, in order, to $1, $2 . . . . If you specify no arguments, then the names and values of all variables are printed to the standard output.

The variables given by the list of names are unassigned; that is, their values and attributes are erased. You cannot unset read-only variables. If you use the -f option, then the names refer to function names. Unsetting ERRNO, LINENO, MAILCHECK, OPTARG, OPTIND, RANDOM, SECONDS, TMOUT, and _ removes their special meaning even if they are subsequently assigned.

With the export built-in, the given names are marked for automatic export to the environment of subsequently executed commands.

ksh(1) commands that are preceded by one or two asterisks (*) are treated specially in the following ways.

1. Variable assignment lists preceding the command remain in effect when the command completes.
2. I/O redirections are processed after variable assignments.
3. Errors abort a script that contains them.
4. Words following a command preceded by ** that are in the format of a variable assignment are expanded with the same rules as a variable assignment. This means that tilde substitution is performed after the equal sign and word splitting and file-name generation are not performed.

Examples

C Shell

The following example sets the PATH variable to search for files in the /bin, /usr/bin, /usr/bin, and /usr/bin directories, in that order.

```
castle% setenv PATH "/bin:/usr/bin:/usr/sbin:usr/ucb/bin"
castle%
```

Attributes

See attributes(5) for descriptions of the following attributes:

Attribute Type	Attribute Value
Availability	SUNWcsu

See Also

csh(1), ksh(1), read(1), sh(1), typeset(1), attributes(5), environ(5)

setfacl — Modify the Access Control List (ACL) for a File or Files

Synopsis

```
/usr/bin/setfacl [-r] -s acl-entries file...
/usr/bin/setfacl [-r] -md acl-entries file...
/usr/bin/setfacl [-r] -f acl-file file...
```

Description

Access Control Lists (ACLs) are extensions to standard UNIX file permissions. The ACL information is stored and associated with each file individually. Use the setfacl to set, add, modify, and delete ACL entries. For each file specified, setfacl either replaces its entire ACL, including the default ACL on a directory, or it adds, modifies, or deletes one or more ACL entries, including default entries on directories.

Setting an ACL on a file also modifies the file permission bits. The user entry modifies the file owner permission bits. If you do not specify a mask entry, the group entry modifies the file group owner permission bits. If you specify a mask entry, the group owner permission bits of the file are modified, based on the intersection (bitwise AND) of the group and mask entries. The other entry modifies the other permission bits.

If you use the chmod(1) command to change the group owner permissions on a file with ACL entries, both the group owner permissions and the ACL mask are changed to the new permissions. Be aware that the new ACL mask permissions can change the effective permissions for additional users and groups who have ACL entries on the file.

A directory can contain default ACL entries. If you create a file in a directory that contains default ACL entries, the newly created file has permissions generated according to the intersection of umask(1), the default ACL entries, and the permissions requested at creation time. If a default ACL is specified for a specific user (or users), the file has a regular ACL created; otherwise, only the mode bits are initialized according to the intersection described above. The default ACL should be thought of as the maximum discretionary access permissions that can be granted.

Syntax for acl-entries

For the -m and -s options, *acl-entries* is one or more comma-separated ACL entries. An ACL entry consists of the following fields separated by colons.

entry-type   Type of ACL entry on which to set file permissions. For example, *entry-type* can be user (the owner of a file) or mask (the ACL mask).

uid | gid   User name or user identification number. Or group name or group identification number.

perms   The permissions that are set on *entry-type*. You can indicate *perms* by the symbolic characters rwx or a number (the same permissions numbers used with the chmod(1) command).

The following list describes the valid ACL entries. (You can specify default entries only for directories.)

u[ser]::*perms*

File owner permissions.

g[roup]::*perms*

          Group owner permissions.

o[ther]:*perms*

          Permission for users other than the file owner or members of file group owner.

m[ask]:*perms*

          The ACL mask specifying the maximum permissions permitted for users (other than the owner) and for groups. The mask is a quick way to change permissions on all users and groups.

u[ser]:*uid*:*perms*

          Permissions for a specific user. For *uid*, use either a user name or a numeric ID.

g[roup]:*gid*:*perms*

          Permissions for a specific group. For *gid*, use either a group name or a numeric GID.

d[efault]:u[ser]::*perms*

          Default file owner permissions.

d[efault]:g[roup]::*perms*

          Default group owner permissions.

d[efault]:o[ther]:*perms*

          Default permissions for users other than the file owner or members of the file group owner.

d[efault]:m[ask]:*perms*

          Default ACL mask.

d[efault]:u[ser]:*uid*:*perms*

          Default permissions for a specific user. For *uid*, use either a user name or a numeric ID.

d[efault]:g[roup]:*gid*:*perms*

          Default permissions for a specific group. For *gid*, use either a group name or a numeric ID.

For the -d option, *acl-entries* is one or more comma-separated ACL entries without permissions, selected from the following Options list. Note that the entries for file owner, owning group, file group class, and others cannot be deleted.

Options

-s *acl-entries*

Set the ACL for a file. Remove all old ACL entries, and replace with the newly specified ACL. You can specify the entries in any order. They are sorted by the command before being applied to the file.

Required entries:

- Exactly one user entry specified for the owner of the file.
- Exactly one group entry for the owning group of the file.
- Exactly one other entry specified.

If there are additional user and group entries:

- Exactly one mask entry specified for the file group class of the file.
- Must not be duplicate user entries with the same *uid.*
- Must not be duplicate group entries with the same *gid.*

If file is a directory:

- Exactly one default:user entry for the owner of the file.
- Exactly one default:group entry for the owning group of the file.
- Exactly one default:mask entry for the file group class of the file.
- Exactly one default:other entry.

You can specify additional default:user entries and additional default:group entries, but there cannot be duplicate additional default:user entries with the same *uid* or duplicate default group entries with the same *gid.* The entries need not be in any specific order. They are sorted by the command before being applied to the file.

-m *acl-entries*

Add one or more new ACL entries to the file, and/or modify one or more existing ACL entries on the file. If an entry already exists for a specified *uid* or *gid,* replace the current permissions with the specified permissions. If an entry does not exist for the specified *uid* or *gid,* create it.

New!

The first time you use the -m option to modify a default ACL, you must specify a complete default ACL (user, group, other, mask, and any additional entries).

-d *acl-entries*

Delete one or more entries from the file. You cannot delete the entries for the file owner, the owning group, and others from the ACL. Note that deleting an entry does not necessarily have the same effect as removing all permissions from the entry.

-f *acl-file*

Set the ACL for a file, using the ACL entries contained in the file named *acl-file.* The same constraints on specified entries hold as with the -s option. The entries are not required to be in any specific order in the file.

You can use the # character in an *acl-file* to indicate a comment. Starting with the #, all characters until the end of the line are ignored. Note that if the *acl-file* has been created as the output of the getfacl(1) command, any effective permissions that follow a # are ignored.

-r   Recalculate the permissions for the group class entry, that is, the mask entry. Ignore the permissions specified in the group class entry, and replace them with the maximum permissions needed to grant the access in any additional user, owning group, and additional group entries in the ACL. Leave the permissions in the additional user, owning group, and additional group entries unchanged.

Examples

The following example lists the permissions on file foo. It then adds one ACL entry to file foo, giving user ray read permission only and lists the permissions again. The + at the end of the permission listing from the ls -l command shows that an ACL exists for the file. Then, the example uses the getfacl command to list the ACL information for the file.

```
castle% ls -l foo
-rw-r--r--   1 winsor    staff           0 Apr  2 14:23 foo
castle% setfacl -m user:ray:r-- foo
castle% ls -l foo
-rw-r--r--+  1 winsor    staff           0 Apr  2 14:23 foo
castle% getfacl foo

# file: foo
# owner: winsor
# group: staff
user::rw-
user:ray:r--            #effective:r--
group::r--              #effective:r--
mask:r--
other:r--
castle%
```

The following example replaces the entire ACL for the file foo, adding an entry for user ray allowing read/write access, an entry for the file owner allowing all access, an entry for the group allowing read access only, an entry for the group class allowing read/write, and an entry for others disallowing all access.

```
castle% setfacl -s user:ray:rw-,user::rwx,group::r--,mask:rw-,other:--- foo
castle% getfacl foo

# file: foo
# owner: winsor
# group: staff
user::rwx
user:ray:rw-            #effective:rw-
group::r--              #effective:r--
mask:rw-
other:---
castle%
```

> **Note** — Following this command, the file permission bits are set to
> rwxr-----.

Even though the file-owning group has only read permission, the maximum permissions available to all additional user ACL entries and all group ACL entries are read and write because the mask entry specifies these permissions.

The following example sets the same ACL on file bar as the file foo.

```
castle% getfacl foo | setfacl -f - bar
castle% getfacl bar

# file: bar
# owner: winsor
# group: staff
user::rwx
user:ray:rw-             #effective:rw-
group::r--               #effective:r--
mask:rw-
other:---
castle%
```

Files

/etc/passwd

Password file.

/etc/group   Group file.

Attributes

See attributes(5) for descriptions of the following attributes:

Attribute Type	Attribute Value
Availability	SUNWcsu

See Also

chmod(1), getfacl(1), umask(1), aclcheck(3), aclsort(3), group(4),
passwd(4), attributes(5)

New! **setpgrp** — Set Process Group ID

Synopsis

/bin/setpgrp *command* [*arg*...]

Description

Use the setgrp command, new in the Solaris 9 Operating Environment, to set the process group ID. If the current process is not already a session leader, the setpgrp command sets the process group ID and session ID to the current process ID and does an exec() of *command* and its argument(s) if any.

Operands

command	The name of a command to be invoked.
arg	An option or argument to *command*.

Exit Status

1	Error executing the setpgrp command or during exec() of *command*.

Otherwise, the exit status is that of *command*.

Attributes

See attributes(5) for descriptions of the following attributes:

Attribute Type	**Attribute Value**
Availability	SUNWcsu

See Also

exec(2), setpgrp(2), attributes(5)

settime — Change File Access and Modification Times

Synopsis

/usr/bin/settime [-f *ref-file*] *file*...

Description

See touch(1).

sftp — Secure File Transfer Program

New!

Synopsis

/bin/sftp [-vC] [-o *ssh_option*] [*hostname* | *user@hostname*]

Description

Use the sftp command, new in the Solaris 9 Operating Environment, as an interactive file transfer program with a user interface similar to ftp(1). sftp uses the ssh(1) command to create a secure connection to the server.

sftp implements the SSH File Transfer Protocol as defined in IETF draft-ietf-secsh-filexfer. There is no relationship between the protocol used by sftp and the FTP protocol (RFC959) provided by ftp(1).

Options

-C	Enable compression with the -C option in ssh(1).

-o *ssh_option*

> Specify an option to be directly passed to ssh(1).

-v   Raise logging level. This option is also passed to ssh(1).

Operands

hostname | user@hostname

> The name of the host sftp connects to and logs in to.

Interactive Commands

In interactive mode, sftp understands a set of commands similar to those of ftp(1). Commands are case insensitive, and you must enclose paths in quotes if they contain spaces.

cd *path*   Change remote directory to *path*.

lcd *path*   Change local directory to *path*.

chgrp *grp path*

> Change group of file *path* to *grp*. *grp* must be a numeric GID.

chmod *mode path*

> Change permissions of file *path* to *mode*.

chown *own path*

> Change owner of file *path* to *own*. *own* must be a numeric UID.

help   Display help text.

get [*flags*] *remote-path* [*local-path*]

> Retrieve the *remote-path*, and store it on the local machine. If you do not specify the local path name, the default is the same name it has on the remote machine. If you specify the -P option, sftp also copies the file's full permission and access time.

lls [*ls-options* [*path*]]

> Display local directory listing of either *path* or current directory if you do not specify *path*.

lmkdir *path*

> Create local directory specified by *path*.

lpwd   Print local working directory.

ls [*path*]   Display remote directory listing of either *path* or current directory if you do not specify *path*.

lumask umask

> Set local umask to *umask*.

mkdir *path*   Create remote directory specified by *path*.

put [*flags*] *local-path* [*local-path*]

>Upload *local-path*, and store it on the remote machine. If you do not specify the remote path name, the default is the same name it has on the local machine. If you specify the -P option, also copy the file's full permission and access time.

pwd — Display remote working directory.

exit — Quit.

quit — Quit.

rename *oldpath newpath*

>Rename remote file from *oldpath* to *newpath*.

rmdir *path* — Remove remote directory specified by *path*.

rm *path* — Delete remote file specified by *path*.

! command — Execute command in local shell.

! — Escape to local shell.

? — Synonym for help.

Examples

The following example uses sftp to download the /etc/printcap file from the cardinal system to /tmp/printcap on the local system.

```
$ sftp cardinal
Connecting to cardinal...
gmarler@cardinal's password:
sftp > lcd /tmp
sftp > get /etc/printcap
sftp > quit
$
```

Exit Status

0 — Successful completion.

1 — An error occurred.

Attributes

See attributes(5) for descriptions of the following attributes.

Attribute Type	Attribute Value
Availability	SUNWsshu

See Also

ftp(1), scp(1), ssh(1), ssh-add(1), ssh-keygen(1), sshd(1M), attributes(5)

sh, jsh — Standard and Job Control Shell and Command Interpreter

Synopsis

```
/usr/bin/sh [-acefhiknprstuvx] [argument...]
/usr/xpg4/bin/sh [± abCefhikmnoprstuvx] [± o option]... [-c string]
    [arg...]
/usr/bin/jsh [-acefhiknprstuvx] [argument...]
```

Description

The Bourne shell, written by Steve Bourne when he was at AT&T Bell Laboratories, is the original UNIX shell. This shell is preferred for shell programming because of its programming capabilities and its universal availability. It lacks features, such as built-in arithmetic, for interactive use. The Bourne shell is the default login shell for the root account, and it serves as the default user login shell if you do not specify another shell in your passwd file. The Bourne shell is used for all system-supplied administration scripts.

The Bourne shell command is /bin/sh. The default prompt is a dollar sign ($). The root prompt is a pound sign (#).

The /usr/bin/sh command is a command programming language that executes commands read from a terminal or a file.

New! The /usr/xpg4/bin/sh command is a standards compliant shell. This command provides all of the functionality of ksh(1) except in cases discussed in ksh(1) in which differences in behavior exist.

The jsh command is an interface to the shell that provides all of the functionality of sh and also enables job control (see "Job Control" on page 1279).

Arguments to the shell are listed in "Invocation" on page 1279.

Definitions

A *blank* is a Tab or a space. A *name* is a sequence of ASCII letters, digits, or underscores, beginning with a letter or an underscore. A *parameter* is a name, a digit, or any of the characters *, @, #, ?, -, $, and !.

Usage

Commands

A *simple command* is a sequence of nonblank words separated by blanks. The first word specifies the name of the command to be executed. Except as specified below, the remaining words are passed as arguments to the invoked command. The command name is passed as argument 0 (see exec(2)). The value of a command is its exit status if it terminates normally or (octal) 200+*status* if it terminates abnormally; see signal(3HEAD) for a list of status values.

A *pipeline* is a sequence of one or more commands separated by |. The standard output of each command but the last is connected by a pipe(2) to the standard input of the next command. Each command is run as a separate process; the shell waits for the last command to terminate. The exit status of a pipeline is the exit status of the last command in the pipeline.

A *list* is a sequence of one or more pipelines separated by ;, &, &&, or ||, and optionally terminated by ; or &. Of these four symbols, ; and & have equal precedence that is lower than that of && and ||. The symbols && and || also have equal precedence. A semicolon (;) sequentially executes the preceding pipeline (that is, the shell waits for the pipeline to finish before executing any commands following the semicolon); an ampersand (&) asynchronously executes the preceding pipeline (that is, the shell does not wait for that pipeline to finish). The symbol && (||) executes the list following it only if the preceding pipeline returns a 0 exit status. An arbitrary number of newlines can appear in a list instead of semicolons to delimit commands.

Note — Only the last process in a pipeline can be waited for.

A command is either a simple command or one of the following. Unless otherwise stated, the value returned by a command is that of the last simple command executed in the command.

for *name* [in *word...*] do *list* done

> Each time a for command is executed, set *name* to the next *word* taken from the in *word* list. If you omit in *word*..., then execute the do list once for each positional parameter that is set (see "Parameter Substitution" on page 1268). Execution ends when there are no more words in the list.

case *word* in [*pattern* [| *pattern*])*list*;;]... esac

> Execute the *list* associated with the first *pattern* that matches *word*. The form of the patterns is the same as that used for file-name generation (see "File-Name Generation" on page 1271) except that a slash, a leading dot, or a dot immediately following a slash need not be matched explicitly.

if *list* ; then *list* ; [elif *list* ; then *list* ;]

 [else *list* ;] fi

> Execute the *list* following if, and if it returns a 0 exit status, execute the *list* following the first then. Otherwise, execute the *list* following elif. If its value is 0, then execute the *list* following the next then. Failing that, execute the else *list*. If no else *list* or then *list* is executed, the if command returns a 0 exit status.

while *list*   Repeatedly execute the while *list* and, if the exit status of the last
do *list*   command in the list is 0, execute the do *list*; otherwise, the loop
done   terminates. If no commands in the do *list* are executed, then the
              while command returns a 0 exit status. You can use until in place of
              while to negate the loop termination test.

(*list*)   Execute *list* in a subshell.

{ *list*; }   Execute *list* in the current (that is, parent) shell. The { must be followed by a space.

name () { *list*; }

> Define a function that is referenced by *name*. The body of the function is the *list* of commands between { and }. The { must be followed by a space. Execution of functions is described in "Execution" on page 1273.

The { and } are not needed if the body of the function is a command as defined in "Commands" on page 1266.

The following words are recognized only as the first word of a command and when not quoted.

```
if then else elif fi case esac for while until do done { }
```

Note — Because commands in pipelines are run as separate processes, variables set in a pipeline have no effect on the parent shell.

Comments Lines

All characters following a word beginning with # are ignored up to a newline.

Command Substitution

The shell reads commands from the string between two grave accents (` ` `) and the standard output from these commands can be used as all or part of a word. Trailing newlines are removed from the standard output.

No interpretation is done on the string before the string is read except to remove backslashes (\) used to escape other characters. You can use backslashes to escape a grave accent (`) or another backslash (\). The leading backslashes are removed before the command string is read. Escaping grave accents enables nested command substitution. If the command substitution lies within a pair of double quotes (" ...` ...` ... "), a backslash used to escape a double quote (\") is removed; otherwise, it is left intact.

If you use a backslash to escape a newline character (\newline), both the backslash and the newline are removed (see "Quoting" on page 1272). In addition, backslashes used to escape dollar signs (\$) are removed. Because no parameter substitution is done on the command string before it is read, inserting a backslash to escape a dollar sign has no effect. Backslashes that precede characters other than \, `, ", newline, and $ are left intact when the command string is read.

Parameter Substitution

The $ character introduces substitutable parameters. The shell has two types of parameters: positional and keyword. If parameter is a digit, it is a positional parameter. Positional parameters can be assigned values by set. You can assign values to keyword parameters (also known as variables) by writing:

name= value [*name= value*] ...

Pattern matching is not performed on *value*. You cannot use a function and a variable with the same name.

${*parameter*}

Substitute the value, if any, of the parameter. The braces are required only when *parameter* is followed by a letter, digit, or underscore that is not to be interpreted as part of its name. If *parameter* is * or @, substitute all the positional parameters starting with $1 and separated by spaces. Parameter $0 is set from argument 0 when the shell is invoked.

${*parameter*:- *word*}

> If *parameter* is set and is non-null, substitute its value; otherwise substitute *word*.

${*parameter*:= *word*}

> If *parameter* is not set or is null, set it to *word*, otherwise, substitute the value of the parameter. You cannot assign positional parameters in this way.

${*parameter*:? *word*}

> If *parameter* is set and is non-null, substitute its value; otherwise, print *word* and exit from the shell. If you omit *word*, print the message `parameter null or not set`.

${*parameter*:+ *word*}

> If *parameter* is set and is non-null, substitute *word*, otherwise, substitute nothing. In the above, *word* is not evaluated unless it is to be used as the substituted string, so in the following example, pwd is executed only if d is not set or is null:
>
> ```
> echo ${d:-`pwd`}
> ```
>
> If you omit the colon (:) from the above expressions, the shell checks only whether parameter is set or not set.

The following parameters are automatically set by the shell.

#	The number of positional parameters in decimal.
-	Options supplied to the shell on invocation or by the set command.
?	The decimal value returned by the last synchronously executed command.
$	The process number of this shell.
!	The process number of the last background command invoked.

The following parameters are used by the shell. The parameters in this section are also referred to as environment variables.

HOME	The default argument (home directory) for the cd command, set to the user's login directory by login(1) from the password file (see passwd(4)).
PATH	The search path for commands (see "Execution" on page 1273).
CDPATH	The search path for the cd command.
MAIL	If this parameter is set to the name of a mail file and the MAILPATH parameter is not set, the shell informs you of the arrival of mail in the specified file.
MAILCHECK	Specify how often (in seconds) the shell checks for the arrival of mail in the files specified by the MAILPATH or MAIL parameters. The default value is 600 seconds (10 minutes). If set to 0, the shell checks before each prompt.

MAILPATH   A colon-separated list of file names. If this parameter is set, the shell
                informs the user of the arrival of mail in any of the specified files. Each
                file name can be followed by % and a message that is printed when the
                modification time changes. The default message is, you have mail.

PS1   Primary prompt string; by default, $.

PS2   Secondary prompt string; by default. >.

IFS   Internal field separators, normally space, Tab, and newline (see "Blank
                Interpretation" on page 1270).

SHACCT   If this parameter is set to the name of a file writable by the user, write
                an accounting record in the file for each shell procedure executed.

SHELL   When the shell is invoked, it scans the environment (see
                "Environment" on page 1272) for this name.

See environ(5) for descriptions of the following environment variables that affect the
execution of sh: LC_CTYPE and LC_MESSAGES.

The shell gives default values to PATH, PS1, PS2, MAILCHECK, and IFS. Default values
for HOME and MAIL are set by login(1).

Blank Interpretation

After parameter and command substitution, the results of substitution are scanned for
internal field separator characters (those found in IFS) and split into distinct arguments
where such characters are found. Explicit null arguments ("" or ' ') are retained.
Implicit null arguments (those resulting from parameters that have no values) are
removed.

Input/Output Redirection

You can redirect the input and output of a command by using a special notation
interpreted by the shell. The following constructs can appear anywhere in a command or
can precede or follow a command and are not passed on as arguments to the invoked
command.

Note — Parameter and command substitution occurs before *word* or *digit*
is used.

< *word*   Use file *word* as standard input (file descriptor 0).

> *word*   Use file *word* as standard output (file descriptor 1). If the file does not
                exist, create it; otherwise, truncate it to 0 length.

>> *word*   Use file *word* as standard output. If the file exists, append output to it
                (by first seeking to the end-of-file); otherwise, create the file.

<> *word*   Open file *word* for reading and writing as standard input.

<<[-] *word*   After parameter and command substitution is done on *word*, read the
                shell input up to the first line that literally matches the resulting word,
                or to an end-of-file. If, however, - is appended to <<:

                • Strip leading tabs from *word* before reading the shell input (but after
                  parameter and command substitution is done on *word*).

- Strip leading Tabs from the shell input as it is read and before each line is compared with *word*.

- Read shell input up to the first line that literally matches the resulting *word*, or to an end-of-file.

If any character of *word* is quoted, do no additional processing to the shell input. If no characters of *word* are quoted:

- Do parameter and command substitution.

- Remove (escaped) \newlines.

- Use \ to quote the characters \, $, and `.

The resulting document becomes the standard input.

    `<& digit`   Use the file associated with file descriptor *digit* as standard input. Similarly for the standard output, use `>& digit`.

    `<&-`   Close the standard input. Similarly for the standard output, use `>&-`.

If any of the above is preceded by a digit, the file descriptor that is associated with the file is that specified by the digit (instead of the default 0 or 1). For example, the following statement associates file descriptor 2 with the file currently associated with file descriptor 1.

```
... 2>&1
```

The order in which you specify redirections is significant. The shell evaluates redirections left-to-right. For example, the following statement first associates file descriptor 1 with file xxx. It associates file descriptor 2 with the file associated with file descriptor 1 (that is, xxx).

```
... 1> xxx 2>&1
```

If the order of redirections were reversed, file descriptor 2 would be associated with the terminal (assuming file descriptor 1 had been so associated) and file descriptor 1 would be associated with file xxx.

Using the terminology introduced under "Commands" on page 1266, if a command is composed of several simple commands, redirection is evaluated for the entire command before it is evaluated for each simple command. That is, the shell evaluates redirection for the entire list, then each pipeline within the list, then each command within each pipeline, then each list within each command.

If a command is followed by &, the default standard input for the command is the empty file /dev/null. Otherwise, the environment for the execution of a command contains the file descriptors of the invoking shell as modified by input/output specifications.

File-Name Generation

Before a command is executed, each command word is scanned for the characters *, ?, and [. If one of these characters is found, the word is regarded as a *pattern*. The word is replaced with alphabetically sorted file names that match the pattern. If no file name is found that matches the pattern, the word is left unchanged. The character . at the start of a file name or immediately following a /, as well as the character / itself, must be matched explicitly.

*	Match any string, including the `null` string.
?	Match any single character.
[...]	Match any one of the enclosed characters. A pair of characters separated by – matches any character lexically between the pair, inclusive. If the first character following the opening [is a !, match any character not enclosed.

Note — Words used for file names in input/output redirection are not interpreted for file-name generation. For example, `cat file1 > a*` creates a file named a*.

All quoted characters (see below) must be matched explicitly in a file name.

Quoting

The following characters have a special meaning to the shell and terminate a word unless quoted.

```
; & ( ) | ^ < > newline space tab
```

You can quote or escape a character (that is, make it stand for itself) by preceding it with a backslash (\) or by inserting it between a pair of quote marks (' ' or " "). During processing, the shell can quote certain characters to prevent them from taking on a special meaning. Backslashes used to quote a single character are removed from the word before the command is executed. The pair \newline is removed from a word before command and parameter substitution.

All characters enclosed between a pair of single quote marks (' ') except a single quote, are quoted by the shell. Backslash has no special meaning inside a pair of single quotes. You can quote a single quote inside a pair of double-quote marks (for example, " ' ") but you cannot quote a single quote inside a pair of single quotes.

Inside a pair of double quote marks (" "), parameter and command substitution occurs and the shell quotes the results to avoid blank interpretation and file-name generation. If $* is within a pair of double quotes, the positional parameters are substituted and quoted, separated by quoted spaces ("$1 $2 ..."); however, if $@ is within a pair of double quotes, the positional parameters are substituted and quoted, separated by unquoted spaces ("$1" "$2" ...). \ quotes the characters \, `, and $. The pair \newline is removed before parameter and command substitution. If a backslash precedes characters other than \, `, $, and newline, then the backslash itself is quoted by the shell.

Prompting

When used interactively, the shell prompts with the value of PS1 before reading a command. If at any time you press newline and further input is needed to complete a command, the secondary prompt (that is, the value of PS2) is displayed.

Environment

The environment (see environ(5)) is a list of name-value pairs that is passed to an executed program in the same way as a normal argument list. The shell interacts with the environment in several ways. On invocation, the shell scans the environment and creates a parameter for each name found, giving it the corresponding value. If you modify the value of any of these parameters or create new parameters, none of these affect the environment unless you use the export command to bind the shell's parameter to the environment (see also set -a). You can remove a parameter from the environment with the unset command. The environment seen by any executed command is thus composed of any unmodified name-value pairs originally inherited by the shell, minus any pairs removed by unset, plus any modifications or additions, all of which must be noted in export commands.

You can augment the environment for any command by prefixing it with one or more assignments to parameters. Thus:

TERM=450 *command*

and

(export TERM; TERM=450; *command*)

are equivalent as far as the execution of *command* is concerned if *command* is not a special command (see "Special Commands" on page 1274). If *command* is a special command, then

TERM=450 *command*

modifies the TERM variable in the current shell.

If the -k option is set, all keyword arguments are placed in the environment, even if they occur after the command name.

The following example first prints a=b c and c.

```
$ echo a=b c
a=b c
$ set -k
$ echo a=b c
c
$
```

Note — If a command is executed and a command with the same name is installed in a directory in the search path before the directory where the original command was found, the shell continues to execute the original command. Use the hash command to correct this situation.

Signals

The INTERRUPT and QUIT signals for an invoked command are ignored if the command is followed by &; otherwise, signals have the values inherited by the shell from its parent, with the exception of signal 11 (but see also the trap command).

Execution

Each time a command is executed, the command substitution, parameter substitution, blank interpretation, input/output redirection, and file-name generation listed above are carried out. If the command name matches the name of a defined function, the function is executed in the shell process (note how this differs from the execution of shell script files that require a subshell for invocation). If the command name does not match the name of a defined function but matches one of the special commands listed below, it is executed in the shell process. The positional parameters $1, $2, . . . are set to the arguments of the function. If the command name matches neither a special command nor the name of a defined function, a new process is created and an attempt is made to execute the command via exec(2).

The shell parameter PATH defines the search path for the directory containing the command. Alternative directory names are separated by a colon (:). The default path is /usr/bin. The current directory is specified by a null path name that can appear immediately after the equal sign, between two colon delimiters anywhere in the path list, or at the end of the path list. If the command name contains a /, the search path is not used. Otherwise, each directory in the path is searched for an executable file. If the file has execute permission but is not an a.out file, it is assumed to be a file containing shell commands. A subshell is spawned to read it. A parenthesized command is also executed in a subshell.

The location in the search path where a command was found is remembered by the shell (to help avoid unnecessary exec commands later). If the command was found in a relative directory, its location must be redetermined whenever the current directory changes. The shell forgets all remembered locations whenever the PATH variable is changed or the hash -r command is executed (see below).

Special Commands

Input/output redirection is now permitted for these commands. File descriptor 1 is the default output location. When job control is enabled, additional special commands are added to the shell's environment (see "Job Control" on page 1279).

:   Do nothing. Return a 0 exit code.

. *filename*   Read and execute commands from *filename*, and return. Use the search path specified by PATH to find the directory containing *filename*.

bg [%*jobid* ...]

When job control is enabled, add the bg command to your environment to manipulate jobs. Resume the execution of a stopped job in the background. If you omit %*jobid*, assume the current job. (See "Job Control" on page 1279 for more detail.)

break [*n*]   Exit from the enclosing for or while loop if any. If you specify *n*, break *n* levels.

cd [*argument*]

Change the current directory to *argument*. The shell parameter HOME is the default argument. The shell parameter CDPATH defines the search path for the directory containing *argument*. Separate alternative directory names with a colon (:). The default path is null (specifying the current directory). Note that the current directory is specified by a null path name that can appear immediately after the equal sign or between the colon delimiters

anywhere else in the path list. If *argument* begins with a /, do not use the search path. Otherwise, search each directory in the path for *argument*.

chdir [*dir*]

Change the shell's working directory to *dir*. If you specify no argument, change to your home directory. If *dir* is a relative path name not found in the current directory, check for it in those directories listed in the

CDPATH variable. If *dir* is the name of a shell variable whose value starts with a /, change to the directory named by that value.

continue [*n*]

> Resume the next iteration of the enclosing for or while loop. If *n* is specified, resume at the *n*-th enclosing loop.

echo [*arguments...*]

> Write the words in *arguments* to the standard output separated by space characters. See echo(1) for fuller usage and description.

eval [*argument...*]

> Read the argument(s) as input to the shell, and execute the resulting command(s).

exec [*argument...*]

> Execute the command specified by the arguments in place of this shell without creating a new process. Input/output arguments can appear, and if no other arguments are given, modify the shell input/output.

exit [*n*] Exit the calling shell or shell script with the exit status specified by *n*. If you omit n, use the exit status of the last command executed (an end-of-file also exits the shell.)

export [*name...*]

> Mark the given names for automatic export to the environment of subsequently executed commands. If you specify no arguments, list the variable names that have been marked for export during the current shell's execution. (Variable names exported from a parent shell are listed only if they have been exported again during the current shell's execution.) Function names are not exported.

fg [%*jobid...*]

> When job control is enabled, add the fg command to your environment to manipulate jobs. Resume the execution of a stopped job in the foreground; also move an executing background job into the foreground. If you omit %*jobid*, assume the current job. (See "Job Control" on page 1279 for more detail.)

getopts Use in shell scripts to support command syntax standards (see intro(1)); parse positional parameters, and check for legal options. See getoptcvt(1) for usage and description.

hash [-r] [*name ...*]

> For each *name*, determine the location in the search path of the command specified by *name* and remembered by the shell. The -r option forgets all remembered locations. If you specify no arguments, present information about remembered commands. Hits is the number of times a command has been invoked by the shell process. Cost is a measure of the work required to locate a command in the search path. If a command is found in a relative directory in the search path, then

after changing to that directory, recalculate the stored location of that command. Commands for which this are done are indicated by an asterisk (*) adjacent to the Hits information. Cost is incremented when the recalculation is done.

jobs [-p|-l] [%*jobid* ...]

jobs -x *command* [*arguments*]

> Report all jobs that are stopped or executing in the background. If you omit %*jobid*, report all jobs that are stopped or running in the background.

> -l   Report the process group ID and the working directory of the jobs.

> -p   Report only the process group ID of the jobs.

> -x   Replace any *jobid* found in *command* or *arguments* with the corresponding process group ID, and then execute *command*, passing it *arguments*.

kill [-*sig*] %*job* ...

kill -1   Send either the TERM (terminate) signal or the specified signal to the specified jobs or processes. Give signals either by number or by names (as given in signal(3HEAD) stripped of the SIG prefix, with the exception that SIGCHD is named CHLD). If the signal being sent is TERM (terminate) or HUP (hangup), then send the job or process a CONT (continue) signal if stopped. The *job* argument can be the process ID of a process that is not a member of one of the active jobs. See "Job Control" on page 1279 for a description of the format of *job*. In the second form, kill -1, list the signal numbers and names. (See kill(1)).

login [*argument*...]

> Equivalent to exec login *argument*. ... See login(1) for usage and description.

newgrp [*argument*]

> Equivalent to exec newgrp *argument*. See newgrp(1) for usage and description.

pwd   Print the current working directory. See pwd(1) for usage and description.

read *name*...

> Read one line from the standard input, and using the IFS internal field separator (normally space or Tab) to delimit word boundaries, assign the first *word* to the first *name*, the second *word* to the second *name*, and so forth, with leftover words assigned to the last *name*. You can continue lines with \newline. You can quote characters other than newline by preceding them with a backslash. These backslashes are removed before words are assigned to names, and no interpretation is done on the character that follows the backslash. The return code is 0 unless an end-of-file is encountered.

readonly [*name*...]

> Mark the given names read-only. You cannot change the values of these names by subsequent assignment. If you specify no arguments, print a list of all read-only names.

return [*n*]   Exit the function with the return value specified by *n*. If you omit *n*, the return status is that of the last command executed.

set [--aefhkntuvx [*argument*...]]

-a	Mark variables that are modified or created for export.
-e	Exit immediately if a command exits with a non-zero exit status.
-f	Disable file-name generation.
-h	Locate and remember function commands as functions are defined (function commands are normally located when the function is executed).
-k	Put all keyword arguments in the environment for a command, not just those that precede the command name.
-n	Read commands, but do not execute them.
-t	Exit after reading and executing one command.
-u	Treat unset variables as an error when substituting.
-v	Print shell input lines as they are read.
-x	Print commands and their arguments as they are executed.
--	Do not change any of the options; useful in setting $1 to -.

> Using + instead of - turns these options off. You can also use these options on invocation of the shell. The current set of options can be found in $-. The remaining arguments are positional parameters and are assigned, in order, to $1, $2, ... If you specify no arguments, print the values of all names.

shift [*n*]   The positional parameters from $*n*+1 ... are renamed $1 .... If you do not specify *n*, it is assumed to be 1.

stop *pid*...

> Halt execution of the process number *pid* (see ps(1)).

suspend   Stop the execution of the current shell (but not if it is the login shell).

test   Evaluate conditional expressions. See test(1) for usage and description.

times   Print the accumulated user and system times for processes run from the shell.

trap [*argument n* [*n* 2...]]

> Read and execute the command argument when the shell receives numeric or symbolic signal(s) (*n*). (Note that *argument* is scanned once when the trap is set and once when the trap is taken.) Trap commands

are executed in order of signal number or corresponding symbolic names. Any attempt to set a trap on a signal that was ignored on entry to the current shell is ineffective. An attempt to trap on signal 11 (memory fault) produces an error. If you do not specify *argument*, reset all trap(s) *n* to their original values. If *argument* is the null string, the shell and the commands it invokes ignore this signal. If *n* is 0, execute the command argument on exit from the shell. The trap command with no arguments prints a list of commands associated with each signal number.

type [*name*...]

For each *name*, indicate how it would be interpreted if used as a command name.

ulimit [-[HS] [a | cdfnstv]]

ulimit [-[HS] [c | d | f | n | s | t | v]] *limit*

Print or set hard or soft resource limits. These limits are described in getrlimit(2).

If *limit* is not present, print the specified limits. You can print any number of limits at one time. The -a option prints all limits.

If *limit* is present, set the specified limit to *limit*. The string unlimited requests the largest valid limit. You can set limits for only one resource at a time. Any user can set a soft limit to any value below the hard limit. Any user can lower a hard limit. Only a superuser can raise a hard limit; see su(1M).

The -H option specifies a hard limit. The -S option specifies a soft limit. If you specify neither option, ulimit sets both limits and prints the soft limit.

The following options specify the resource whose limits are to be printed or set. If you specify no option, print or set the file size limit.

-c   Maximum corefile size (in 512-byte blocks).

-d   Maximum size of data segment or heap (in kilobytes).

-f   Maximum file size (in 512-byte blocks).

-n   Maximum file descriptor plus 1.

-s   Maximum size of stack segment (in kilobytes).

-t   Maximum CPU time (in seconds).

-v   Maximum size of virtual memory (in kilobytes).

Run the sysdef(1M) command to obtain the maximum possible limits for your system. The values reported are in hexadecimal, but you can use the bc(1) command to translate them into decimal numbers. (See swap(1M).)

Example of ulimit: to limit the size of a corefile dump to 0 megabytes, type the following:

```
            ulimit -c 0
```

umask [*nnn*]

> Set the user file-creation mask to *nnn* (see umask(1)). If you omit *nnn*,
> print the current value of the mask.

unset [*name*...]

> For each *name*, remove the corresponding variable or function value.
> You cannot unset the variables PATH, PS1, PS2, MAILCHECK, and IFS.

wait [*n*]   Wait for your background process whose process ID is *n*, and report its
> termination status. If you omit *n*, wait for all your shell's currently
> active background processes. The return code is 0.

Invocation

If the shell is invoked through exec(2) and the first character of argument 0 is -,
commands are initially read from /etc/profile and from $HOME/.profile, if such files
exist. Thereafter, commands are read as described below, which is also the case when the
shell is invoked as /usr/bin/sh. The options below are interpreted by the shell on
invocation only.

Note — Unless you specify the -c or -s option, the first argument is
assumed to be the name of a file containing commands and the remaining
arguments are passed as positional parameters to that command file.

-c *string*   Read commands from *string*.

-i   If you specified the -i option or if the shell input and output are
> attached to a terminal, this shell is interactive. In this case, ignore
> TERMINATE (so that kill 0 does not kill an interactive shell), and
> catch and ignore INTERRUPT (so that wait is interruptible). In all
> cases, ignore QUIT.

-p   Do not set the effective user and group IDs to the real user and
> group IDs.

-r   Restrict the shell (see rsh(1M)).

-s   Read commands from the standard input. Any remaining
> arguments specify the positional parameters. Write shell output
> (except for special commands) to file descriptor 2.

The remaining options and arguments are described under the set command above.

Job Control

When you invoke the shell as jsh, job control is enabled in addition to all of the
functionality described previously for sh. Typically, job control is enabled only for the
interactive shell. Noninteractive shells typically do not benefit from the added
functionality of job control.

With job control enabled, every command or pipeline you enter at the terminal is
called a *job*. All jobs exist in one of the following states.

- Foreground jobs have read and write access to the controlling terminal.
- Background jobs are denied read access and have conditional write access to the controlling terminal (see tty(1)).
- Stopped jobs have been put in a suspended state, usually as a result of a SIGTSTP signal (see signal(3HEAD)).

Every job that the shell starts is assigned a positive integer, called a *job number*, that is tracked by the shell and is used as an identifier to indicate a specific job. Additionally the shell keeps track of the current and previous jobs. The current job is the most recent job to be started or restarted. The previous job is the first noncurrent job.

The acceptable syntax for a job identifier has the form

`%jobid`

where you can specify *jobid* in any of the following formats.

% or +	The current job.
-	The previous job.
? <string>	The job for which the command line uniquely contains *string*.
n	Job number *n*, where *n* is a job number.
pref	A unique prefix of the command name (for example, if the command ls −1 was running in the background, you could refer to it as %ls); *pref* cannot contain blanks unless it is quoted.

When job control is enabled, the following commands are added to your environment to manipulate jobs.

bg [%*jobid*...]

    Resume the execution of a stopped job in the background. If you omit %*jobid*, assume the current job.

fg [%*jobid*...]

    Resume the execution of a stopped job in the foreground, and also move an executing background job into the foreground. If you omit %*jobid*, assume the current job.

jobs [-p|-l] [%*jobid* ...]
jobs -x *command* [*arguments*]

    Report jobs that are stopped or executing in the background. If you omit %*jobid*, report all jobs that are stopped or running in the background. The following options modify or enhance the output of jobs.

-l	Report the process group ID and the working directory of the jobs.
-p	Report only the process group ID of the jobs.
-x	Replace any *jobid* found in *command* or *arguments* with the corresponding process group ID, and then execute *command*, passing it *arguments*.

kill [-*signal*] %*jobid*

> Built-in version of kill to provide the functionality of the kill command for processes identified with a *jobid*.

stop %*jobid*...

> Stop the execution of a background job(s).

suspend   Stop the execution of the current shell (but not if it is the login shell).

wait [%*jobid*...]

> Wait for the background process specified by %*jobid* and report its termination status. If you omit %*jobid*, wait behaves as described in "Special Commands" on page 1274.

Note — Because the shell implements both foreground and background jobs in the same process group, they all receive the same signals, which can lead to unexpected behavior. It is, therefore, recommended that you use other job control shells, especially in an interactive environment.

Large File Behavior

See largefile(5) for the description of the behavior of sh and jsh when encountering files greater than or equal to 2 Gbytes (2** 31 bytes).

Exit Status

Errors detected by the shell, such as syntax errors, return a non-zero exit status. If you are using the shell noninteractively, execution of the shell file is abandoned. Otherwise, the shell returns the exit status of the last command executed (see also the exit command).

jsh Only

If you invoke the shell as jsh and try to exit the shell while there are stopped jobs, the shell issues one warning.

There are stopped jobs.

> This is the only message. If you try to exit again and jobs are still stopped, the jobs are sent a SIGHUP signal from the kernel and the shell is exited.

Files

$HOME/.profile

/dev/null

/etc/profile

/tmp/sh*

Attributes

See attributes(5) for descriptions of the following attributes:

/usr/bin/sh /usr/bin/jsh

Attribute Type	Attribute Value
Availability	SUNWcsu
CSI	Enabled

/usr/xpg4/bin/sh

Attribute Type	Attribute Value
Availability	SUNWxcu4
CSI	Enabled

See Also

New!

bc(1), echo(1), getoptcvt(1), intro(1), kill(1), ksh(1), login(1), newgrp(1), ps(1), pwd(1), set(1), shell_builtins(1), stty(1), test(1), umask(1), wait(1), rsh(1M), su(1M), swap(1M), sysdef(1M), dup(2), exec(2), fork(2), getrlimit(2), pipe(2), ulimit(2), setlocale(3C), signal(3HEAD), passwd(4), profile(4), attributes(5), environ(5), largefile(5), XPG4(5)

Diagnostics

If you get the error message cannot fork, too many processes, try using the wait(1) command to clean up your background processes. If this doesn't help, the system process table is probably full or you have too many active foreground processes. (Your login has a limited number of process IDs, and the system can track a limited number.)

When the shell executes a shell script that tries to execute a nonexistent command interpreter, the shell returns an erroneous diagnostic message that the shell script file does not exist.

Warnings

For security reasons, the use of setuid shell scripts is strongly discouraged.

shell_builtins — Shell Command Interpreter Built-in Functions

Description

The sh(1), csh(1), and ksh(1) shell command interpreters have special built-in functions that are interpreted by the shell as commands. Many of these built-in commands are implemented by more than one of the shells, and some are unique to a particular shell. The commands are listed in the following table.

Command	Bourne Shell	Korn Shell	C Shell
alias		x	x
bg	x	x	x
break	x	x	x

Command	Bourne Shell	Korn Shell	C Shell
case	x	x	x
cd	x	x	x
chdir	x		x
continue	x	x	x
dirs			x
echo	x	x	x
eval	x	x	x
exec	x	x	x
exit	x	x	x
export	x	x	
fc		x	
fg	x	x	x
for	x	x	
foreach			x
function		x	
getopts	x	x	
glob			x
goto			x
hash	x	x	
hashstat			x
history			x
if	x	x	x
jobs	x	x	x
kill	x	x	x
let		x	
limit			x
login	x	x	x
logout	x	x	x
nice			x
newgrp	x	x	

Command	Bourne Shell	Korn Shell	C Shell
notify			x
onintr			x
popd			x
print		x	
pushd			x
pwd	x	x	
read	x	x	
readonly	x	x	
rehash			x
repeat			x
return	x	x	
select		x	
set	x	x	x
setenv			x
shift	x	x	x
source			x
stop	x	x	x
suspend	x	x	x
switch			x
test	x	x	
time			x
times	x	x	
trap	x	x	
type	x	x	
typeset		x	
ulimit	x	x	
umask	x	x	x
unalias		x	x
unhash			x
unlimit			x

Command	Bourne Shell	Korn Shell	C Shell
unset	x	x	x
unsetenv			x
until	x	x	
wait	x	x	x
whence		x	
while	x	x	x

Bourne Shell Special Commands

Input/output redirection is now permitted for these commands. File descriptor 1 is the default output location. When job control is enabled, additional special commands are added to the shell's environment.

In addition to these built-in reserved command words, sh also uses:

:   Do nothing. Return a 0 exit code.

. *filename*   Read and execute commands from *filename*, and return. Use the search path specified by PATH to find the directory containing *filename*.

C Shell

Built-in commands are executed within the C shell. If a built-in command occurs as any component of a pipeline except the last, it is executed in a subshell. In addition to these built-in reserved command words, csh also uses:

:   Interpret this command, but perform no action.

Korn Shell Special Commands

Input/output redirection is permitted. Unless otherwise indicated, the output is written on file descriptor 1, and the exit status, when there is no syntax error, is 0. Commands that are preceded by one or two asterisks (*) are treated specially in the following ways.

1. Variable assignment lists preceding the command remain in effect when the command completes.
2. I/O redirections are processed after variable assignments.
3. Errors abort a script that contains them.
4. Words following a command preceded by ** that are in the format of a variable assignment are expanded with the same rules as a variable assignment. This means that tilde substitution is performed after the equal sign and word splitting and file-name generation are not performed.

In addition to these built-in reserved command words, ksh also uses:

*: [*arg...*]

         Expand only parameters.

*

. *file* [*arg...*]

Read the complete file, then execute the commands in the current shell environment. Use the search path specified by PATH to find the directory containing *file*. If you specify any *arg* arguments, they become the positional parameters. Otherwise, leave the positional parameters unchanged. The exit status is the exit status of the last command executed: the loop termination test.

See Also

alias(1), break(1), cd(1), chmod(1), csh(1), echo(1), exec(1), exit(1),
find(1), getoptcvt(1), getopts(1), glob(1), hash(1), history(1),
intro(1), jobs(1), kill(1), ksh(1), let(1), limit(1), login(1),
logout(1), newgrp(1), nice(1), nohup(1), print(1), pwd(1), read(1),
readonly(1), set(1), sh(1), shift(1), suspend(1), time(1), times(1),
trap(1), typeset(1), umask(1), wait(1), test(1B), chdir(2), chmod(2),
creat(2), umask(2), getopt(3C), profile(4), environ(5)

shift — Shell Built-in Function to Traverse Either a Shell's Argument List or a List of Field-Separated Words

Synopsis

sh
shift [*n*]

csh
shift [*variable*]

ksh
```
*
```
shift [*n*]

Description

The shift command is a shell built-in command that traverses either the argument list of the shell or a list of field-separated words.

Bourne Shell

The positional parameters from $*n*+1 ... are renamed $1.... The default *n* is 1.

C Shell

The components of argv, or *variable*, if supplied, are shifted to the left, discarding the first component. It is an error for the variable not to be set or to have a null value.

Korn Shell

The positional parameters from $*n*+1 $*n*+1 ... are renamed $1.... The default *n* is 1. The parameter *n* can be any arithmetic expression that evaluates to a nonnegative number less than or equal to $#.

ksh(1) commands that are preceded by one or two asterisks (*) are treated specially in the following ways.

- Variable assignment lists preceding the command remain in effect when the command completes.
- I/O redirections are processed after variable assignments.
- Errors abort a script that contains them.
- Words following a command preceded by ** that are in the format of a variable assignment are expanded with the same rules as a variable assignment. This means that tilde substitution is performed after the equal sign and word splitting and file-name generation are not performed.

Attributes

See attributes(5) for descriptions of the following attributes:

Attribute Type	Attribute Value
Availability	SUNWcsu

See Also

csh(1), ksh(1), sh(1), attributes(5)

shutdown — Close Down the System at a Given Time

Synopsis

/usr/ucb/shutdown [-fhknr] *time* [*warning-message...*]

Description

Use the /usr/ucb/shutdown command as root when shutting down a system with multiple users. The shutdown command sends a warning message to all users who are logged in, waits 60 seconds (the default), and then shuts down the system to single-user state. You can choose a different default wait time and specify a different warning message.

Note — The default /usr/sbin/shutdown(1M) command has different options.

The shutdown command provides an automated procedure to notify users when the system is to be shut down. *time* specifies when shutdown brings the system down; you can specify the word now (indicating an immediate shutdown) or a future time in either the format +*number* or *hour*:*min*. The first form brings the system down in *number* minutes, and the second brings the system down at the time of day, indicated in 24-hour notation.

At intervals that get closer as the shutdown time approaches, warning messages are displayed at terminals of all logged-in users and of users who have remote mounts on that machine.

At shutdown time, a message is written to the system log daemon, syslogd(1M), containing the time of shutdown, the instigator of the shutdown, and the reason. Then, a terminate signal is sent to init; this action brings the system down to single-user mode.

Note — `/usr/ucb/shutdown` enables you to bring the system down between now and 23:59 only if you use the absolute time.

Options

As an alternative to the above procedure, you can specify the following options.

`-f`	Arrange, in the manner of `fastboot`(1B), that when the system is rebooted, the file systems are not checked.
`-h`	Execute `halt`(1M).
`-k`	Simulate shutdown of the system. Do not actually shut down the system.
`-n`	Prevent the normal `sync`(2) before stopping.
`-r`	Execute `reboot`(1M).

Examples

The following example uses the `-k` option to simulate the shutdown of a system.

```
# /usr/ucb/shutdown -k +1
Shutdown at 15:22 (in 1 minute) [pid 519]
#

        *** System shutdown message from winsor@castle ***

System going down in 60 seconds


        *** FINAL System shutdown message from winsor@castle ***

System going down in 30 seconds


        *** FINAL System shutdown message from winsor@castle ***

System going down IMMEDIATELY

System shutdown time has arrived
but you'll have to do it yourself

#
```

Files

`/etc/rmtab`   Remote mounted file-system table.

Attributes

See `attributes`(5) for descriptions of the following attributes:

Attribute Type	Attribute Value
Availability	SUNWscpu

See Also

`login(1)`, `fastboot(1B)`, `halt(1M)`, `reboot(1M)`, `syslogd(1M)`, `sync(2)`, `rmtab(4)`, `attributes(5)`

size — Print Section Sizes of Object Files in Bytes

Synopsis

`/usr/ccs/bin/size [-f] [-F] [-n] [-o] [-V] [-x]` *filename*`...`

Description

The `size` command produces segment or section size information in bytes for each loaded section in ELF object files. `size` prints out the size of the text, data, and bss (uninitialized data) segments (or sections) and their total.

   `size` processes ELF object files named on the command line. If an archive file name is input to the `size` command, the information for each object file in the archive is displayed.

   When calculating segment information, the `size` command prints the total file size of the nonwritable segments, the total file size of the writable segments, and the total memory size of the writable segments minus the total file size of the writable segments.

   If it cannot calculate segment information, `size` calculates section information. When calculating section information, `size` prints out the total size of sections that are allocatable, nonwritable, and not `NOBITS`; the total size of the sections that are allocatable, writable, and not `NOBITS`; and the total size of the writable sections of type `NOBITS`. `NOBITS` sections do not actually take up space in the file name.

   If `size` cannot calculate either segment or section information, it prints an error message and stops processing the file.

   Note — Because the size of bss sections is not known until link-edit time, the `size` command does not give the true total size of prelinked objects.

Options

`-f`	Print the size of each allocatable section, the name of the section, and the total of the section sizes. If there is no section data, print an error message and stop processing the file.
`-F`	Print the size of each loadable segment, the permission options of the segment, and the total of the loadable segment sizes. If there is no segment data, print an error message and stop processing the file.
`-n`	Print nonloadable segment or nonallocatable section sizes. If segment data exists, print the memory size of each loadable segment or file size of each nonloadable segment, the permission options, and the total size of the segments. If there is no segment data, then for each allocatable and nonallocatable section, print the memory size, the section name, and the total size of the sections. If there is no segment or section data, print an error message and stop processing.
`-o`	Print numbers in octal.

-V   Print the version information for the size command to the standard
            output.

-x   Print numbers in hexadecimal.

Examples

The following examples show typical size output.

```
castle% size /usr/ccs/bin/admin
44711 + 1972 + 12400 = 59083
castle% size -f /usr/ccs/bin/admin
17(.interp) + 1752(.hash) + 3600(.dynsym) + 3116(.dynstr) +
    64(.SUNW_version) + 24(.rela.ex_shared) + 60(.rela.bss) +
    912(.rela.plt) + 31460(.text) + 56(.init) + 56(.fini) +
    4(.exception_ranges) + 4(.rodata) + 3371(.rodata1) + 4(.got) +
    964(.plt) + 160(.dynamic) + 32(.ex_shared) + 188(.data) + 624(.data1)
    + 12396(.bss) = 58864
castle% size -F /usr/ccs/bin/admin
44711(r-x) + 14372(rwx) = 59243
castle%
```

Attributes

See attributes(5) for descriptions of the following attributes:

Attribute Type	Attribute Value
Availability	SUNWbtool

See Also

as(1), ld(1), cc(1B), a.out(4), ar(4), attributes(5)

sleep — Suspend Execution for an Interval

Synopsis

/usr/bin/sleep *time*

Description

The sleep command suspends execution for at least the integral number of seconds
specified by the *time* operand.

If the sleep command receives a SIGALRM signal, one of the following actions is
taken.

- Terminate normally with a 0 exit status.
- Effectively ignore the signal.

The sleep command takes the standard action for all other signals.

Operands

time   A nonnegative decimal integer specifying the number of seconds to suspend execution.

Examples

The following example executes a command after 105 seconds.

```
castle% (sleep 105; find . -name core -print)&
castle%
```

The following example executes a command every so often.

```
while true
 do
   command sleep 37
 done
```

Environment Variables

See environ(5) for descriptions of the following environment variables that affect the execution of sleep: LC_CTYPE, LC_MESSAGES, and NLSPATH.

Exit Status

0   The execution was successfully suspended for at least *time* seconds, or a SIGALRM signal was received.

>0   An error has occurred.

Attributes

See attributes(5) for descriptions of the following attributes:

Attribute Type	Attribute Value
Availability	SUNWcsu

See Also

wait(1), alarm(2), wait(3B), sleep(3C), attributes(5), environ(5)

snca — The Solaris Network Cache and Accelerator

Description

See nca(1).

soelim — Resolve and Eliminate .so Requests from nroff or troff Input

Synopsis

        /usr/bin/soelim [*filename*...]

Description

The soelim command is a preprocessor that reads nroff/troff input and performs the textual inclusion implied by the nroff(1) directives of the form .so *somefile* when they appear at the beginning of input lines. This command is useful because programs such as tbl(1) do not normally do this preprocessing. With the soelim command, you can place individual tables in separate files to be run as a part of a large document.

An argument consisting of a dash (-) is taken to be a file name corresponding to the standard input.

Note — You can suppress inclusion by using ' in place of ., for example, ' so /usr/share/lib/tmac/tmac.s

---

Examples

The following example shows a typical use of soelim.

        castle% **soelim exum?.n | tbl | nroff -ms | col | lpr**

Attributes

See attributes(5) for descriptions of the following attributes:

Attribute Type	Attribute Value
Availability	SUNWdoc

See Also

        more(1), nroff(1), tbl(1), attributes(5)

---

solregis — Solaris User Registration

Synopsis

        /usr/dt/bin/solregis [-dc]

Description

The solregis command initiates the Solaris user registration procedure, which enables you to register with Sun Microsystems and receive information about Solaris. Normally, solregis is executed in conditional mode as a part of desktop login so that you are prompted at desktop startup time to register unless you have already done so.

Options

-c   Exit without any dialog displayed if $HOME/.solregis/disable exists, DISABLE=1 is specified in /etc/default/solregis, or the user has already registered.

-d   Delay display of the initial screen until a window manager has asserted control of the X display.

Exit Status

0   Successful completion.

>0   An error occurred.

Usage

The following resources can control the behavior and appearance of solregis.

Name	Class	Value Type	Default
disable	Disable	Boolean	False
localeChoices	LocaleChoices	Int	1
action0	Action	String	/usr/dt/bin/hotjava
initialURL0	URL	String	file:///usr/dt/app-config/solregis/EReg.html
localeChoice$n$	LocaleChoice	String	null
action$n$	Action	String	null for $n>0$
initialURLn	URL	String	null for $n>0$
printContext	PrintContext	String	thisorgunit

disable   If true when executed in conditional mode, exit without displaying anything.

localeChoices

Specify the number of localeChoice$n$, action$n$, and initialURLn sets. The first set is 0, so if localeChoices is 1, localeChoice0, action0, and initialURL0 are the only active resources. If localeChoices is 1, display none of the localeChoice$n$ strings and use action0, and so forth. If localeChoices is greater than 1, make each localeChoice$n$ string an element in an exclusive choice list and apply the index of the selected item controls for the action$n$ and initialURLn resources.

localeChoice$n$

Specify the string presented to the user for this choice.

action*n* Specify the file name of the command to be executed (normally expected to be a World Wide Web browser) when you choose Register Now, or specify the special string print. If you specify print, the initialURL*n* string must be a file name on the local system naming a file that is to be printed after prompting for a print destination.

initialURL*n*

Specify the argument to be passed to action*n* for initial registration. This argument is normally the Uniform Resource Locator for the initial page to be displayed by the World Wide Web browser.

printContext

Specify the XFN naming context to be displayed if you choose the special print action. For example, if you use the default printContext thisorgunit, display the printers in thisorgunit/service/printer.

Environment Variables

See environ(5) for descriptions of the following environment variables that affect the execution of solregis: HOME, LANG, LC_MESSAGES, and NLSPATH.

Files

/etc/default/solregis

Default values.

/$HOME/.solregis/uprops

User registration information.

/$HOME/.solregis/disable

Users disabled from registration.

/usr/dt/app-defaults/C/Solregis

Default locale resources.

/usr/dt/app-defaults/$LANG/Solregis

Default localized resources.

/etc/dt/app-defaults/C/Solregis

Default installation resources.

/usr/dt/app-defaults/$LANG/Solregis

Localized installation resources.

Attributes

See attributes(5) for descriptions of the following attributes:

Attribute Type	Attribute Value
Availability	SUNWsregu

See Also

    attributes(5), environ(5)

sort — Sort, Merge, or Sequence-Check Text Files

Synopsis

    /usr/bin/sort [-bcdfimMnru] [-k *keydef*] [-o *output*] [-S *kmem*] [-t *char*]   *New!*
        [-T *directory*] [-y [*kmem*]] [-z *recsz*] [+*pos1* [-*pos2*]] [*file*...]
    /usr/xpg4/bin/sort [-bcdfimMnru] [-k *keydef*] [-o *output*] [-S *kmem*]   *New!*
        [-t *char*] [-T *directory*] [-y [*kmem*]] [-z *recsz*] [+*pos1* [-*pos2*]]
        [*file*...]

Description

Use the sort command to rearrange the lines in a file in alphabetic (the default) or numeric order and write the result to the standard output.

By default, the sort command uses the beginning of the line as the key field to sort on. However, you can specify any field in the file as the key field. Lines are sorted according to the collating sequence of the current locale. By default, sort uses the ASCII collating sequence, which sorts white space first, followed by most punctuation marks, followed by numbers, uppercase letters, and finally lowercase letters. When the first characters in the key field are identical, sort looks at each subsequent character up to the newline if needed to determine the correct sorting order.

For numeric sorts, numbers are not sorted in true numeric order unless you use the -n option. Instead, numerical sorted results could look like the following example.

    1
    10
    11
    2
    20
    21
    3
    30

You get this result because all of the lines starting with 1 are grouped together followed by all of the lines starting with 2, and so forth.

Note — When the last line of an input file is missing a newline character, sort appends one, prints a warning message, and continues. sort does not guarantee preservation of relative line ordering on equal keys.

Options

/usr/bin/sort

-c   Check that the single input file is ordered as specified by the arguments and the collating sequence of the current locale. Set the exit code, and produce no output unless the file is out of sort sequence.

/usr/xpg4/bin/sort

-c	Same as /usr/bin/sort, except produce no output under any circumstances.
-m	Merge only. Assume the input files are already sorted.
-u	Sort uniquely by suppressing all but one in each set of lines having equal keys. If used with the -c option, check that there are no lines with duplicate keys, in addition to checking that the input file is sorted.
-o *output*	Specify the name of an output file to be used instead of the standard output. This file can be the same as one of the input files.

New!

-S *kmem*   Specify the maximum amount of swap-based memory used for sorting, in kilobytes (the default unit). You can also specify *kmem* directly as a number of bytes (b), kilobytes (k), megabytes (m), gigabytes (g), or terabytes (t), or as a percentage (%) of the installed physical memory.

You can tune sort peformance for a specific scenario with the -S option. However, you should note in particular that sort has greater knowledge of how to use a finite amount of memory for sorting than does the virtual memory system. Thus, a sort invoked to request an extremely large amount of memory with the -S option performs extremely poorly. New in the Solaris 8 release.

-T *directory*

Specify the name of a directory to use for temporary files.

New!

-y *kmem*   (Obsolete starting with the Solaris 8 release.) Specify the amount of main memory used initially. Start using that number of kilobytes of memory unless the administrative minimum or maximum is exceeded, in which case use the corresponding extremum. Thus, -y 0 is guaranteed to start with minimum memory. -y with no *kmem* argument starts with maximum memory. If you omit this option, begin using a system default memory size and continue to use more space as needed.

-z *recsz*   (Obsolete). Use to prevent abnormal termination when lines longer than the system-dependent default buffer size are encountered. Because sort now automatically allocates buffers large enough to hold the longest line, this option has no effect.

Ordering Options

New!

The default sort order depends on the value of LC_COLLATE. If LC_COLLATE is set to C, sorting is in ASCII order. If LC_COLLATE is set to en_US, sorting is case insensitive except when the two strings are otherwise equal and one has an uppercase letter earlier than the other. Other locales have other sort orders.

The following options override the default ordering rules. When ordering options appear independently of any key field specifications, the requested field ordering rules are applied globally to all sort keys. When attached to a specific key, the specified ordering options override all global ordering options for that key. In the obsolescent forms, if one or more of these options follow a +*pos1* option, only the key field specified by that preceding option is affected.

-d	Sort in dictionary order. Consider only letters, digits, and blanks (spaces and Tabs) significant in comparisons.
-f	Fold lowercase letters into upper case.
-i	Ignore nonprintable characters.
-M	Compare as months. Fold the first three nonblank characters of the field to upper case, and compare. For example, in English the sorting order is JAN < FEB < ... < DEC. Compare invalid fields lower than JAN. Invalid fields beginning with one of the letters of the month confuse sort. The -M option implies the -b option.
-n	Restrict the sort key to an initial numeric string consisting of optional blank characters, optional minus sign, and zero or more digits with an optional radix character and thousands separators (as defined in the current locale), which is sorted by arithmetic value. An empty digit string is treated as 0. Leading 0s and signs on 0s do not affect ordering.
-r	Reverse the sense of comparisons.

Field Separator Options

You can alter the treatment of field separators by using the following options.

-b	Ignore leading blank characters when determining the starting and ending positions of a restricted sort key. If you specify the -b option before the first sort key option, apply it to all sort key options. Otherwise, you can attach the -b option independently to each -k *field-start*, *field-end*, or +*pos1* or -*pos2* argument.
-t *char*	Use *char* as the field separator character. *char* is not considered to be part of a field (although you can include it in a sort key). Each occurrence of *char* is significant (for example, *charchar* delimits an empty field). If you do not specify -t, use blank characters as default field separators; each maximal nonempty sequence of blank characters that follows a nonblank character is a field separator.

Sort Key Options

You can specify sort keys, using the following option.

-k *keydef*	Define a restricted sort key.

The format of this definition is:

-k *field-start* [*type*] [,*field-end* [*type*]]

where *field-start* and *field-end* define a key field restricted to a portion of the line. *type* is a modifier from the list of characters bdfiMnr. The b modifier behaves like the -b option but applies only to the *field-start* or *field-end* to which it is attached. Characters within a field are counted from the first nonblank character in the field. (This rule applies separately to *first-character* and *last-character*.) The other modifiers behave like the corresponding options but apply only to the key field to which they are attached. They have this effect if specified with *field-start*, *field-end*, or both. If any modifier is attached to a *field-start* or to a *field-end*, no option applies to either.

When there are multiple key fields, later keys are compared only after all earlier keys compare equal. Except when you specify the –u option, lines that otherwise compare equal are ordered as if none of the options –d, –f, –i, –n, or –k were present (but with –r still in effect if you specified it) and with all bytes in the lines significant to the comparison.

The following notation defines a key field that begins at *field-start* and ends at *field-end* inclusive, unless *field-start* falls beyond the end of the line or after *field-end*, in which case the key field is empty.

```
-k field-start[type] [,field-end[type]]
```

A missing *field-end* means the last character of the line.

A field comprises a maximal sequence of nonseparating characters and, in the absence of option –t, any preceding field separator.

The *field-start* portion of the *keydef* option argument has the form:

```
field-number[.first-character]
```

Fields and characters within fields are numbered starting with 1. *field-number* and *first-character*, interpreted as positive decimal integers, specify the first character to be used as part of a sort key. If you omit *.first-character*, the default is the first character of the field.

The *field-end* portion of the *keydef* option argument has the form

```
field-start[.last-character]
```

The *field-number* as described above for *field-start*. *last-character*, is interpreted as a nonnegative decimal integer and specifies the last character to be used as part of the sort key. If *last-character* evaluates to 0 or you omit *.last-character*, the default is the last character of the field specified by *field-number*.

If the –b option or b *type* modifier is in effect, characters within a field are counted from the first nonblank character in the field. (This applies separately to *first-character* and *last-character*.)

The following syntax is obsolete.

```
[+pos1[-pos2]]
```

It provides functionality equivalent to the –k *keydef* option.

pos1 and *pos2* each have the form *m.n* optionally followed by one or more of the options bdfiMnr. A starting position specified by +*m.n* is interpreted to mean the *n*+1st character in the *m*+1st field. A missing *.n* means *.0*, indicating the first character of the *m*+1st field. If the b option is in effect, *n* is counted from the first nonblank in the *m*+1st field; +*m.0b* refers to the first nonblank character in the *m*+1st field.

A last position specified by –*m.n* is interpreted to mean the *n*-th character (including separators) after the last character of the *m*-th field. A missing *.n* means *.0*, indicating the last character of the *m*-th field. If the b option is in effect, *n* is counted from the last leading blank in the *m*+1st field; –*m.1b* refers to the first nonblank in the *m*+1st field.

The fully specified +*pos1* –*pos2* form with type modifiers T and U

```
+w.xT -y.zU
```

is equivalent to:

```
undefined              (z==0 & U contains b & -t is present)
-k w+1.x+1T,y.0U       (z==0 otherwise)
-k w+1.x+1T,y+1.zU     (z > 0)
```

Implementations support at least nine occurrences of the sort keys (the -k option and obsolescent +*pos1* and -*pos2*) that are significant in command-line order. If you specify no sort key, a default sort key of the entire line is used.

Operands

file   A path name of a file to be sorted, merged, or checked. If you specify no file operands or if a file operand is -, use the standard input.

Usage

See largefile(5) for the description of the behavior of sort when encountering files greater than or equal to 2 Gbytes (2** 31 bytes).

Examples

The following example uses the sort -M command to sort a file by months. Notice that of the names in the list that are not months, those that begin with the same letters as the month confuse the sort command. They are sorted alphabetically with the months and are not pushed to the top of the list.

```
castle% cat sortmonth
Janice
Maris
March
July
February
December
June
April
January
Ray
Fred
Juno
castle% sort -M sortmonth
Fred
Ray
Janice
January
February
March
Maris
April
June
Juno
July
December
castle%
```

The following example shows the contents of the file named sortnum, sorts it without using the -n option, and then sorts it using the -n option.

```
castle% cat sortnum
2000
1998
1999
1
10
40
20
3
2

castle% sort sortnum
1
10
1998
1999
2
20
2000
3
40

castle% sort -n sortnum
1
2
3
10
20
40
1998
1999
2000
castle%
```

The following examples show both nonobsolescent and obsolescent ways of specifying sort keys as an aid to understanding the relationship between the two forms.

Either of the following commands sorts the contents of infile with the second field as the sort key.

```
castle% sort -k 2,2 infile
castle% sort +1 -2 infile

castle% sort -k 2,2 kookaburra-1
```

```
Eating all the gumdrops he can see.
Laugh, kookaburra, laugh, kookaburra
Stop, kookaburra, stop, kookaburra
Merry merry king of the bush is he.
Kookaburra sits in the old gum tree
Kookaburra sits in the old gum tree
Leave some there for me.
Gay your life must be
castle%
```

Either of the following commands sorts, in reverse order, the contents of `infile1` and `infile2`, placing the output in `outfile` and using the second character of the second field as the sort key (assuming that the first character of the second field is the field separator).

```
castle% sort -r -o outfile -k 2.2,2.2 infile1 infile2
castle% sort -r -o outfile +1.1 -1.2 infile1 infile2

castle% sort -r -o outfile -k 2.2,2.2 kookaburra-1 kookaburra-2
castle% cat outfile
Gay your life must be
Leave some there for me.
Kookaburra sits in the old gum tree
Kookaburra sits in the old gum tree
Merry merry king of the bush is he.
Stop, kookaburra, stop, kookaburra
Laugh, kookaburra, laugh, kookaburra
Eating all the gumdrops he can see.
        8  Leave some there for me.
        7  Stop, kookaburra, stop, kookaburra
        6  Eating all the gumdrops he can see.
        5  Kookaburra sits in the old gum tree
        4  Gay your life must be
        3  Laugh, kookaburra, laugh, kookaburra
        2  Merry merry king of the bush is he.
        1  Kookaburra sits in the old gum tree


castle%
```

Either of the following commands sorts the contents of `infile1` and `infile2`, using the second nonblank character of the second field as the sort key.

```
castle% sort -k 2.2b,2.2b infile1 infile2
castle% sort +1.1b -1.2b infile1 infile2

castle% sort -k 2.2b,2.2b kookaburra-1 kookaburra-2


        3  Laugh, kookaburra, laugh, kookaburra
        4  Gay your life must be
        6  Eating all the gumdrops he can see.
        2  Merry merry king of the bush is he.
        8  Leave some there for me.
Merry merry king of the bush is he.
Kookaburra sits in the old gum tree
Kookaburra sits in the old gum tree
Eating all the gumdrops he can see.
        1  Kookaburra sits in the old gum tree
        5  Kookaburra sits in the old gum tree
Gay your life must be
Laugh, kookaburra, laugh, kookaburra
Leave some there for me.
Stop, kookaburra, stop, kookaburra
        7  Stop, kookaburra, stop, kookaburra
castle%
```

Either of the following commands prints the passwd(4) file (user database) sorted by the numeric user ID (the third colon-separated field).

```
castle% sort -t : -k 3,3n /etc/passwd
castle% sort -t : +2 -3n /etc/passwd

castle% sort -t : -k 3,3n /etc/passwd
root:x:0:1:Super-User:/:/sbin/sh
daemon:x:1:1::/:
bin:x:2:2::/usr/bin:
sys:x:3:3::/:
adm:x:4:4:Admin:/var/adm:
uucp:x:5:5:uucp Admin:/usr/lib/uucp:
nuucp:x:9:9:uucp Admin:/var/spool/uucppublic:/usr/lib/uucp/uucico
listen:x:37:4:Network Admin:/usr/net/nls:
lp:x:71:8:Line Printer Admin:/usr/spool/lp:
winsor:x:1001:10::/export/home/winsor:/bin/csh
ray:x:1002:10::/export/home/ray:/bin/csh
des:x:1003:10::/esport/home/des:/bin/csh
rob:x:1004:10::/export/home/rob:/bin/csh
nobody:x:60001:60001:Nobody:/:
noaccess:x:60002:60002:No Access User:/:
nobody4:x:65534:65534:SunOS 4.x Nobody:/:
castle%
```

Either of the following commands prints the lines of the already sorted file infile, suppressing all but one occurrence of lines having the same third field.

```
castle% sort -um -k 3.1,3.0 infile
castle% sort -um +2.0 -3.0 infile

castle% sort -um -k 3.1,3.0 kookaburra-1
Kookaburra sits in the old gum tree
Merry merry king of the bush is he.
Laugh, kookaburra, laugh, kookaburra
Gay your life must be

Kookaburra sits in the old gum tree
Eating all the gumdrops he can see.
Stop, kookaburra, stop, kookaburra
Leave some there for me.
castle%
```

Environment Variables

See environ(5) for descriptions of the following environment variables that affect the execution of sort: LC_COLLATE, LC_MESSAGES, and NLSPATH.

LC_CTYPE   Determine the locale for the interpretation of sequences of bytes of text data as characters (for example, single- versus multibyte characters in arguments and input files) and the behavior of character classification for the -b, -d, -f, -i, and -n options.

LC_NUMERIC   Determine the locale for the definition of the radix character and thousands separator for the -n option.

Exit Status

0	All input files were output successfully, or you specified -c and the input file was correctly sorted.
1	With the -c option, the file was not ordered as specified or, if you specified both the -c and -u options, two input lines were found with equal keys.
>1	An error occurred.

Files

/var/tmp/stm*???*

Temporary files.

Attributes

See attributes(5) for descriptions of the following attributes:

/usr/bin/sort

Attribute Type	Attribute Value
Availability	SUNWesu
CSI	Enabled

/usr/xpg4/bin/sort

Attribute Type	Attribute Value
Availability	SUNWxcu4
CSI	Enabled

See Also

comm(1), join(1), uniq(1), passwd(4), attributes(5), environ(5), largefile(5), XPG4(5)

Diagnostics

The sort command comments and exits with non-zero status for various trouble conditions (for example, when input lines are too long) and for disorders discovered under the -c option.

sortbib — Sort a Bibliographic Database

Synopsis

/usr/bin/sortbib [-s *KEYS*] *database*...

Description

Use the sortbib command to sort files of records containing refer(1) key letters by keys you specify. Records can be separated by blank lines, or by . [and .] delimiters, but the two styles cannot be mixed together. This command reads through each database and pulls out key fields, which are sorted separately. The sorted key fields contain the file pointer, byte offset, and length of corresponding records. These records are delivered by disk seeks and reads, so `sortbib` cannot be used in a pipeline to read standard input.

The most common key letters and their meanings are given below.

`%A`	Author's name.
`%B`	Book containing article referenced.
`%C`	City (place of publication).
`%D`	Date of publication.
`%E`	Editor of book containing article referenced.
`%F`	Footnote number or label (supplied by `refer`).
`%G`	Government order number.
`%H`	Header commentary, printed before reference.
`%I`	Issuer (publisher).
`%J`	Journal containing article.
`%K`	Keywords to use in locating reference.
`%L`	Label field used by `-k` option of `refer`.
`%M`	Bell Labs memorandum (undefined).
`%N`	Number within volume.
`%O`	Other commentary printed at end of reference.
`%P`	Page number(s).
`%Q`	Corporate or foreign author (unreversed).
`%R`	Report, paper, or thesis (unpublished).
`%S`	Series title.
`%T`	Title of article or book.
`%V`	Volume number.
`%X`	Abstract. Used by `roffbib`, not by `refer`.
`%Y,Z`	Ignored by `refer`.

By default, `sortbib` alphabetizes by the first `%A` and the `%D` fields, which contain the senior author and date.

`sortbib` sorts on the last word on the `%A` line which is assumed to be the author's last name. A word in the final position, such as `jr.` or `ed.`, is ignored if the name before it ends with a comma. Authors with two-word last names or unusual constructions can be sorted correctly with the `nroff` convention `\0` in place of a blank. A `%Q` field is considered to be the same as `%A` except that sorting begins with the first, not the last, word. `sortbib` sorts on the last word of the `%D` line, usually the year. It also ignores leading articles (like `A` or `The`) when sorting by titles in the `%T` or `%J` fields; it ignores articles of any modern European language. If a sort-significant field is absent from a record, `%T` puts that record before other records containing that field.

No more than 16 databases can be sorted together at one time. Records longer than 4,096 characters are truncated.

Options

-s *KEYS*   Specify new *KEYS*. For instance, -sATD sorts by author, title, and date, whereas -sA+D sorts by all authors and date. Sort keys past the fourth are not meaningful.

Attributes

See attributes(5) for descriptions of the following attributes:

Attribute Type	Attribute Value
Availability	SUNWdoc

See Also

addbib(1), indxbib(1), lookbib(1), refer(1), roffbib(1), attributes(5)

Bugs

Records with missing author fields should probably be sorted by title.

sotruss — Trace Shared Library Procedure Calls

Synopsis

```
/usr/bin/sotruss [-f] [-F bindfromlist] [-T bindtolist]
  [-o outputfile] executable [executable arguments...]
```

Description

The sotruss command executes the specified command and produces a trace of the library calls that it performs. Each line of the trace output reports what bindings are occurring between dynamic objects as each procedure call is executed. sotruss traces all of the procedure calls that occur between dynamic objects through the Procedure Linkage Table, so only those procedure calls that are bound through the Procedure Linkage Table are traced. See *Linker and Libraries Guide*.

Options

-f   Follow all children created by fork(), and print truss output on each child process. This option also outputs a PID on each truss output line.

-F *bindfromlist*

Specify a colon-separated list of libraries that are to be traced. Trace only calls from these libraries. The default is to trace calls from the main executable only.

-o *outputfile*

Direct output to the *outputfile*. If you combine this option with the -f option, then the PID of the executing program is put at the end of the file name. By default, output goes to standard error.

-T *bindtolist*

>Specify a colon-separated list of libraries that are to be traced. Trace calls only to these libraries. The default is to trace all calls.

Examples

The following simple example shows the tracing of an `ls` command.

```
castle% sotruss ls | more
ls              ->      libc.so.1:*atexit(0xef7d9e8c, 0x24000, 0x0)
ls              ->      libc.so.1:*atexit(0x13bec, 0xef7d9e8c, 0xef674498)
ls              ->      libc.so.1:*setlocale(0x6, 0x13c2c, 0xef674490)
ls              ->      libc.so.1:*textdomain(0x13c30, 0x13c2c, 0xef674490)
ls              ->      libc.so.1:*time(0x0, 0xef671f98, 0xef674490)
ls              ->      libc.so.1:*isatty(0x1, 0xef671f98, 0x0)
ls              ->      libc.so.1:*getopt(0x1, 0xeffff46c, 0x13c40)
ls              ->      libc.so.1:*malloc(0x100, 0x0, 0x0)
ls              ->      libc.so.1:*malloc(0x9000, 0x0, 0x0)
ls              ->      libc.so.1:*lstat64(0x241b8, 0xeffff310, 0x0)
ls              ->      libc.so.1:*qsort(0x249d0, 0x1, 0x4)
ls              ->      libc.so.1:*opendir(0x241b8, 0xef7a1750, 0xef5cea9a)
ls              ->      libc.so.1:*readdir64(0x2dae0, 0x24480, 0xf000)
ls              ->      libc.so.1:*readdir64(0x2dae0, 0x0, 0xf000)
ls              ->      libc.so.1:*readdir64(0x2dae0, 0x0, 0xf000)
ls              ->      libc.so.1:*readdir64(0x2dae0, 0xb, 0x24d18)
ls              ->      libc.so.1:*readdir64(0x2dae0, 0xb, 0x24f58)
ls              ->      libc.so.1:*readdir64(0x2dae0, 0x6, 0x25198)
ls              ->      libc.so.1:*closedir(0x2dae0, 0x70, 0x25198)
ls              ->      libc.so.1:*qsort(0x249d4, 0x3, 0x4)
ls              ->      libc.so.1:*strcoll(0x24d18, 0x24f58, 0x8000)
ls              ->      libc.so.1:*.mul(0x1, 0xffffffff, 0x24f58)
ls              ->      libc.so.1:*strcoll(0x24d18, 0x25198, 0x8000)
ls              ->      libc.so.1:*.mul(0x1, 0xfffffff3, 0x25198)
ls              ->      libc.so.1:*strcoll(0x24d18, 0x24f58, 0x8000)
ls              ->      libc.so.1:*.mul(0x1, 0xffffffff, 0x24f58)
ls              ->      libc.so.1:*strcoll(0x24f58, 0x25198, 0x8000)
ls              ->      libc.so.1:*.mul(0x1, 0xfffffff3, 0x25198)
ls              ->      libc.so.1:*printf(0x13d24, 0x24d18, 0x241c0)
ls              ->      libc.so.1:*printf(0x13d24, 0x24f58, 0x241c0)
ls              ->      libc.so.1:*printf(0x13d24, 0x25198, 0x241c0)
ls              ->      libc.so.1:*exit(0x0, 0x244f8, 0x244f4)
addusr-1.rs
addusr-2.rs
newdir
castle%
```

Attributes

See `attributes`(5) for descriptions of the following attributes:

Attribute Type	Attribute Value
Availability	SUNWtoo

See Also

ld.so.1(1), truss(1), whocalls(1), fork(2), attributes(5)
Linker and Libraries Guide

---

source — Shell Built-in Function to Execute Other Commands

Synopsis

csh
source [-h] *name*

Description

See exec(1).

---

sparc — Get Processor Type Truth Value

Synopsis

/usr/bin/sparc

Description

See machid(1).

---

spell, hashmake, spellin, hashcheck — Report Spelling Errors

Synopsis

/usr/bin/spell [-bilvx] [+ *local-file*] [*file*]...
/usr/lib/spell/hashmake
/usr/lib/spell/spellin *n*
/usr/lib/spell/hashcheck *spelling-list*

Description

Use the spell command to check spelling in one or more files. The spell command collects words from the named files and looks them up in a spelling list. Words that neither occur among nor are derivable (by applying certain inflections, prefixes, or suffixes) from words in the spelling list are written to the standard output.

If you specify no *file* arguments, words to check are collected from the standard input. spell ignores most troff(1), tbl(1), and eqn(1) constructs. Copies of all output words are accumulated in the history file (spellhist), and a stop list filters out misspellings (for example, their=thy-y+ier) that would otherwise pass.

By default, spell (like deroff(1)) follows chains of included files (.so and .nx troff(1) requests) unless the names of such included files begin with /usr/lib.

The standard spelling list is based on many sources and, while more haphazard than an ordinary dictionary, it is also more effective for proper names and popular technical words. Coverage of the specialized vocabularies of biology, medicine, and chemistry is light.

Three programs help maintain and check the hash lists used by spell.

hashmake	Reads a list of words from the standard input and writes the corresponding nine-digit hash code to the standard output.
spellin	Reads n hash codes from the standard input and writes a compressed spelling list to the standard output.
hashcheck	Reads a compressed *spelling-list* and recreates the nine-digit hash codes for all the words in it. It writes these codes to the standard output.

You can monitor misspelled words by default by setting the H_SPELL variable in /usr/bin/spell to the name of a file that has permission mode 666.

spell works only on English words defined in the U.S. ASCII codeset.

> **Note —** Because copies of all output are accumulated in the spellhist file, spellhist can grow quite large and require purging.

Options

-b	Check British spelling. Besides preferring centre, colour, programme, speciality, travelled, and so forth, this option insists on -ise in words like standardise.
-i	Instruct deroff(1) to ignore .so and .nx commands. If deroff(1) is not present on the system, then this option is ignored.
-l	Follow the chains of all included files.
-v	Print all words not literally in the spelling list as well as plausible derivations from the words in the spelling list.
-x	Print every plausible stem, one per line, with = preceding each word.
+ *local-file*	
	Specify a set of words that are correct spellings (in addition to spell's own spelling list) for each job. *local-file* is the name of a user-provided file that contains a sorted list of words, one per line. Words found in *local-file* are removed from spell's output. Use sort(1) to order *local-file* in ASCII collating sequence. If this ordering is not followed, some entries in *local-file* may be ignored.

Operands

file	A path name of a text file to check for spelling errors. If you specify no files, collect words from the standard input.

Examples

The following example runs the spell command on the file kookaburra-1. Notice that both lowercase and uppercase spellings of kookaburra are listed in the output.

```
castle% spell kookaburra-1
Kookaburra
kookaburra
```

```
castle%
```

Environment Variables

See environ(5) for descriptions of the following environment variables that affect the execution of spell: LC_CTYPE, LC_MESSAGES, and NLSPATH.

Exit Status

| 0 | Successful completion. |
| >0 | An error occurred. |

Files

D_SPELL=/usr/lib/spell/hlist[ab]

>   Hashed spelling lists, American and British.

S_SPELL=/usr/lib/spell/hstop

>   Hashed stop list.

H_SPELL=/var/adm/spellhist

>   History file.

/usr/share/lib/dict/words

>   Master dictionary.

Attributes

See attributes(5) for descriptions of the following attributes:

Attribute Type	Attribute Value
Availability	SUNWesu

See Also

deroff(1), eqn(1), sort(1), tbl(1), troff(1), attributes(5), environ(5)

Bugs

The spelling list's coverage is uneven; new installations may want to monitor the output for several months to gather local additions.

British spelling was compiled by an American.

spline — Interpolate Smooth Curve

Synopsis

```
/usr/bin/spline [-aknpx]...
```

Description

The spline command takes pairs of numbers from the standard input as abscissas and ordinates of a function. It produces a similar set, which is approximately equally spaced and includes the input set, to the standard output. The cubic spline output has two continuous derivatives, and sufficient points to look smooth when plotted, for example, by graph(1).

Options

-a   Supply abscissas automatically (they are missing from the input); specify spacing by the next argument, or assume it is 1 if the next argument is not a number.

-k   Use the constant k in the boundary value computation. (2nd derivative at end) = k*(2nd derivative next to end) is set by the next argument. By default, k=0.

-n   Space output points so that approximately n intervals occur between the lower and upper x limits. (By default, n = 100.)

-p   Make output periodic, that is, match derivatives at ends. First and last input values should normally agree.

-x   Next 1 (or 2) arguments are lower (and upper) x limits. Normally, these limits are calculated from the data. Automatic abscissas start at the lower limit (default, 0).

Examples

The following example uses the plot and graph capabilities. The file named data contains the following data points.

```
castle% cat data
1       1.0
2       4.0
3       5.0
4       6.5     "Optional Label"
7       10.3
8       11.4
9       9.5
10      8.9
11      7.0
12      10.5
13      5.0
14      2.8
castle%
```

The following example displays the data in a shell tool, using the graph command.

```
castle% graph < data + plot -Tcrt
castle% **************************************************************************
   *                            *                       *                    *
   *                            *                       *                    *
   *                            *                       *                    *
   *                            *                       *                    *
   *                            *                       *                    *
   *                            *                       *                    *
   *                            *                       *                    *
   *                            *                 *     *                    *
   *                            *              *  *     *                    *
   *                            *            **    **   *         *          *
   ***********************************************************************************
   *                         *      **       **   *       *  *              *
   *                         *     **       **  *      *    *              *
   *                         * **                **     *    *             *
   *                         **                 **   *  *  *  *            *
   *                      ***                   *  **  *     *            *
   *                   ** *                     *    *  *   *            *
   *              *Optional Label               *         *            *
   *               *     *                      *            *          *
   *            **       *                      *            *          *
   *          *          *                      *             *         *
   ***********************************************************************************
   *        **          *                    *                *         *
   *       **           *                    *                  *       *
   *      *             *                    *                    *     *
   *    *               *                    *                      *   *
   *   *                *                    *                        * *
   *   *                *                    *                    *     *
   *  *                 *                    *                          *
   * *                  *                    *                          *
   *                    *                    *                          *
   *                    *                    *                          *
   ***********************************************************************************
 0 -x- 15   0 -y- 15
```

graph clears the screen and displays the graph, positioning the prompt at the the top
of the screen. Any subsequent commands you type are displayed on top of the graph. Use
the clear command to clear the screen after you display the plot.

To create a better, smoother, plot, the following example uses the spline command.

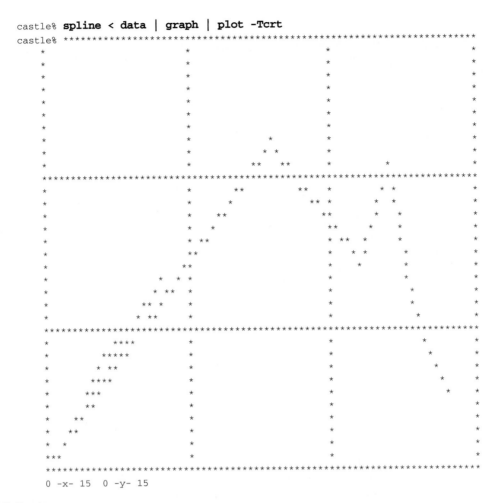

```
castle% spline < data | graph | plot -Tcrt
```

```
0 -x- 15   0 -y- 15
```

Attributes

See attributes(5) for descriptions of the following attributes:

Attribute Type	Attribute Value
Availability	SUNWesu

See Also

graph(1), attributes(5)

R. W. Hamming, *Numerical Methods for Scientists and Engineers*, 2nd ed., 1987, Dover Publications.

Diagnostics

When data is not strictly monotonic in x, spline reproduces the input without interpolating extra points.

Bugs

A limit of 1,000 input points is silently enforced.

split — Split a File into Pieces

Synopsis

```
/usr/bin/split [-linecount | -l linecount] [-a suffixlength] [file
    [name]]
/usr/bin/split [-b n | nk | nm] [-a suffixlength] [file [name]]
```

New!

Description

The split command reads *file* and writes it in *linecount*-line pieces into a set of output files. The name of the first output file is *name* with *aa* appended, and so on lexicographically, up to *zz* (a maximum of 676 files). The maximum length of *name* is two characters less than the maximum file-name length allowed by the file system. See statvfs(2). If you specify no output name, x is used as the default. Output files are named xaa, xab, and so forth.

Options

-*linecount* | -l *linecount*

Specify the number of lines in each piece. Default is 1000 lines.

-a *suffixlength*

Use *suffixlength* letters to form the suffix portion of the file names of the split file. If you do not specify -a, the default suffix length is 2. If the sum of the *name* operand and the *suffixlength* argument would create a file name exceeding NAME_MAX bytes, an error results; split exits with a diagnostic message and creates no files.

-b *n*   Split a file into pieces *n* bytes in size.

-b *n*k   Split a file into pieces *n**1024 bytes in size.

-b *n*m   Split a file into pieces *n**1048576 bytes in size.

Operands

file   The path name of the ordinary file to be split. If you specify no input file or *file* is -, use the standard input.

name   The prefix to be used for each of the files resulting from the split operation. If you specify no *name* argument, use x as the prefix of the output files. The combined length of the basename of the prefix and *suffixlength* cannot exceed NAME_MAX bytes.

Example

The following example splits a file into 50-line pieces.

```
castle% ls -l testfile
-rw-r--r--   1 winsor    staff      6452 Mar  3 08:58 testfile
```

```
castle% split -50 testfile
castle% ls -l x*
-rw-r--r--   1 winsor    staff        1933 Apr  5 12:16 xaa
-rw-r--r--   1 winsor    staff        1451 Apr  5 12:16 xab
-rw-r--r--   1 winsor    staff        1852 Apr  5 12:16 xac
-rw-r--r--   1 winsor    staff        1216 Apr  5 12:16 xad
castle%
```

Usage

See largefile(5) for the description of the behavior of split when encountering files greater than or equal to 2 Gbytes (2** 31 bytes).

Environment Variables

See environ(5) for descriptions of the following environment variables that affect the execution of split: LC_CTYPE, LC_MESSAGES, and NLSPATH.

Exit Status

0	Successful completion.
>0	An error occurred.

Attributes

See attributes(5) for descriptions of the following attributes:

Attribute Type	Attribute Value
Availability	SUNWesu
CSI	Enabled

See Also

csplit(1), statvfs(2), attributes(5), environ(5), largefile(5)

srchtxt — Display Contents of, or Search for, a Text String in Message Databases

Synopsis

/usr/bin/srchtxt [-s] [-l *locale*] [-m *msgfile*,...] [*text*]

Description

Use the srchtxt command to display all the text strings in message databases or to search for a text string in message databases (see mkmsgs(1)). These databases are files in the directory /usr/lib/locale/*locale*/LC_MESSAGES (see setlocale(3C)), unless a file name given with the -m option contains a /. The directory *locale* is the name of the language in which the text strings are written. If you do not specify the -l option, the file accessed is determined by the value of the environment variable LC_MESSAGES. If LC_MESSAGES is not set, the files accessed are determined by the value of the

environment variable LANG. If LANG is not set, the files accessed are in the directory
/usr/lib/locale//C/LC_MESSAGES, which contains default strings.

If you specify no *text* argument, then all the text strings in the files accessed are
displayed.

If you specify the -s option, the displayed text is prefixed by message sequence
numbers. The message sequence numbers are enclosed in angle brackets: <*msgfile:
msgnum*>.

msgfile	Name of the file where the displayed text occurred.
msgnum	Sequence number in *msgfile* where the displayed text occurred. This display is in the format used by gettxt(1) and gettxt(3C).

Options

-s	Suppress printing of the message sequence numbers of the messages being displayed.
-l *locale*	Access files in the directory /usr/lib/locale/*locale*/LC_MESSAGES. If you also specify -m *msgfile*, *locale* is ignored for *msgfiles* containing a /.
-m *msgfile*	Access files specified by one or more *msgfiles*. If *msgfile* contains a / character, then *msgfile* is interpreted as a path name; otherwise, it is assumed to be in the directory determined as described above. To specify more than one *msgfile*, separate the file names with commas.
text	Search for the text string specified by *text*, and display each one that matches. *text* can take the form of a regular expression; see regexp(5).

Examples

Note — A bug in srchtxt results in a segmentation error.

```
# srchtxt
<ibfirmware:1>
<ibfirmware:2>
<ibfirmware:3>
<ibfirmware:4>
<ibfirmware:5>
<ibfirmware:6>
<ibfirmware:7>
Segmentation Fault - core dumped
#
```

The following examples show uses of srchtxt.

If message files have been installed by mkmsgs(1) in a locale named french, then you
could display the entire set of text strings in the french locale
(/usr/lib/locale/french/LC_MESSAGES/*) by typing:

```
castle% srchtxt -l french
```

If a set of error messages associated with the operating system has been installed in
the file UX in the french locale (/usr/lib/locale/french/LC_MESSAGES/UX), then,
using the value of the LANG environment variable to determine the locale to be searched,
you could search that file in that locale for all error messages dealing with files.

```
castle% setenv LANG=french; export LANG
castle% srchtxt -m UX "[Ff]ichier"
```

If /usr/lib/locale/french/LC_MESSAGES/UX contained the following strings

```
Erreur E/S\n
Liste d'arguments trop longue\n
Fichier inexistant\n
Argument invalide\n
Trop de fichiers ouverts\n
Fichier trop long\n
Trop de liens\n
Argument hors du domaine\n
Identificateur supprim\n
Etreinte fatale\n
.
.
.
```

then the following strings would be displayed:

```
<UX:3>Fichier inexistant\n
<UX:5>Trop de fichiers ouverts\n
<UX:6>Fichier trop long\n
```

If a set of error messages associated with the operating system has been installed in the file UX and a set of error messages associated with the Ingress database product has been installed in the file ingress, both in the german locale, then you could search for the pattern [Dd]atei in both the files UX and ingress in the german locale with the following command.

```
castle% srchtxt -l german -m UX,ingress "[Dd]atei"
```

Environment Variables

See environ(5) for a description of the LC_CTYPE environment variable that affects the execution of srchtxt.

Files

/usr/lib/locale/C/LC_MESSAGES/*

Default files created by mkmsgs(1).

/usr/lib/locale/*locale*/LC_MESSAGES/*

Message files created by mkmsgs(1).

Attributes

See attributes(5) for descriptions of the following attributes:

Attribute Type	Attribute Value
Availability	SUNWloc

See Also

exstr(1), gettxt(1), locale(1), mkmsgs(1), gettxt(3C), setlocale(3C), attributes(5), environ(5), locale(5), regexp(5)

Diagnostics

The error messages produced by srchtxt are intended to be self-explanatory. They indicate an error in the command line or errors encountered while searching for a particular locale and/or message file.

ssh — Open SSH Secure Shell Client (Remote Login Program) New!

Synopsis

```
/bin/ssh [-l login_name] [hostname | user@hostname] [command]
/bin/ssh -afgknqtvxACNPTX246 [-c cipher_spec] [-e ch | ^ch | none]
  [-i identity_file] [-l login_name] [-o option] [-p port]
  [-L port:host:hostport] [-R port:host:hostport]
  [hostname | user@hostname] [command]
```

Description

Use the ssh (Secure Shell), new in the Solaris 9 Operating Environment, as a program for logging into a remote machine and for executing commands on a remote machine. ssh replaces rlogin and rsh and provides secure encrypted communications between two untrusted hosts over an insecure network. X11 connections and arbitrary TCP/IP ports can also be forwarded over the secure channel.

ssh connects and logs into the specified *hostname*. Users must prove their identity to the remote machine with one of several methods, depending on the protocol version used.

SSH Protocol Version 1

For the first authentication method, if the machine a user logs in from is listed in /etc/hosts.equiv or /etc/shosts.equiv on the remote machine and the user names are the same on both sides, the user is immediately permitted to log in. Then, if .rhosts or .shosts exists in the user's home directory on the remote machine and contains a line containing the name of the client machine and the name of the user on that machine, the user is permitted to log in. This form of authentication alone is normally not allowed by the server because it is not secure.

The second (and primary) authentication method is the rhosts or hosts.equiv method combined with RSA-based host authentication. It means that if the login would be permitted by $HOME/.rhosts, $HOME/.shosts, /etc/hosts.equiv or /etc/shosts.equiv, and if, additionally, the server can verify the client's host key (see /etc/ssh_known_hosts in "Exit Status" on page 1325), only then is login permitted. This authentication method closes security holes for IP spoofing, DNS spoofing, and routing spoofing.

> **Note** — /etc/hosts.equiv, $HOME/.rhosts, and the rlogin/rsh protocol in general, are inherently insecure and should be disabled if security is desired.

As a third authentication method, ssh supports RSA-based authentication. The scheme is based on public-key cryptography. Cryptosystems are available where encryption and decryption are done with separate keys, and it is not possible to derive the decryption key from the encryption key. RSA is one such system. The idea is that each user creates a public/private keypair for authentication purposes. The server knows the public key, and only the user knows the private key. The file $HOME/.ssh/authorized_keys lists the public keys that are permitted for logging in. When the user logs in, the ssh program tells the server which keypair it would like to use for authentication. The server checks whether this key is permitted, and if so, sends the user (actually the ssh program running on behalf of the user) a challenge in the form of a random number, encrypted by the user's public key. The challenge can be decrypted only with the proper private key. The user's client then decrypts the challenge with the private key, proving that the user knows the private key but without disclosing the private key to the server.

ssh implements the RSA authentication protocol automatically. The user creates his or her RSA keypair by running ssh-keygen(1). This command stores the private key in $HOME/.ssh/identity and the public key in $HOME/.ssh/identity.pub in the user's home directory. The user should then append the contents of the identity.pub to $HOME/.ssh/authorized_keys in his or her home directory on the remote machine (the authorized_keys file corresponds to the conventional $HOME/.rhosts file, and has one key per line, though the lines can be very long). After this, the user can log in without giving the password. RSA authentication is much more secure than rhosts authentication.

The most convenient way to use RSA authentication is with an authentication agent. See ssh-agent(1) for more information.

If other authentication methods fail, ssh prompts the user for a password. The password is sent to the remote host for checking. However, because all communications are encrypted, the password cannot be seen by someone listening on the network.

SSH Protocol Version 2

When a user connects with the protocol version 2, different authentication methods are available. At first, the client attempts to authenticate with the public key method. If this method fails, password authentication is tried.

The public key method is similar to RSA authentication, described in the previous section, except that the DSA algorithm is used instead of the patented RSA algorithm. The client uses the private DSA key $HOME/.ssh/id_dsa to sign the session identifier and sends the result to the server. The server checks whether the matching public key is listed in $HOME/.ssh/authorized_keys and grants access if both the key is found and the signature is correct. The session identifier is derived from a shared Diffie-Hellman value and is known only to the client and the server.

If public key authentication fails or is not available, a password can be sent encrypted to the remote host for proving the user's identity. This protocol 2 implementation does not yet support Kerberos or S/Key authentication.

Protocol 2 provides additional mechanisms for confidentiality (the traffic is encrypted with 3DES, Blowfish, CAST128, or Arcfour) and integrity (hmac-sha1, hmac-md5). Notice that protocol 1 lacks a strong mechanism for ensuring the integrity of the connection.

Login Session and Remote Execution

When the user's identity has been accepted by the server, the server either executes the given command or logs in to the machine and gives the user a normal shell on the remote machine. All communication with the remote command or shell is automatically encrypted.

If a pseudo terminal has been allocated (normal login session), the user can disconnect with ~. and suspend ssh with ~^Z. All forwarded connections can be listed with ~#. If the session blocks waiting for forwarded X11 or TCP/IP connections to terminate, ssh can be put in background with ~&, although you should not use this command while the user shell is active because it can hang the shell. All available escapes can be listed with ~?.

A single tilde character can be sent as ~~ (or by following the tilde with a character other than those described above). The escape character must always follow a newline to be interpreted as special. You can change the escape character in configuration files or on the command line.

If no pseudo TTY has been allocated, the session is transparent and can be used to reliably transfer binary data. On most systems, setting the escape character to none also makes the session transparent even if a TTY is used.

The session terminates when the command or shell in the remote machine exits and all X11 and TCP/IP connections have been closed. The exit status of the remote program is returned as the exit status of ssh.

X11 and TCP Forwarding

If the user is using X11 (the DISPLAY environment variable is set), the connection to the X11 display is automatically forwarded to the remote side so that any X11 programs started from the shell (or command) go through the encrypted channel and so that the connection to the real X server is made from the local machine. The user should not manually set DISPLAY. Forwarding of X11 connections can be configured on the command line or in configuration files.

The DISPLAY value set by ssh points to the server machine, but with a display number greater than zero. This behavior is normal, because ssh creates a "proxy" X server on the server machine for forwarding the connections over the encrypted channel.

ssh also automatically sets up Xauthority data on the server machine. For this purpose, it generates a random authorization cookie, stores it in Xauthority on the server, and verifies that any forwarded connections carry this cookie and replace it with the real cookie when the connection is opened. The real authentication cookie is never sent to the server machine (and no cookies are sent in plain text).

If the user is using an authentication agent, the connection to the agent is automatically forwarded to the remote side unless disabled on the command line or in a configuration file.

Forwarding of arbitrary TCP/IP connections over the secure channel can be specified either on the command line or in a configuration file. One possible application of TCP/IP forwarding is a secure connection to an electronic purse. Another possible application is going through firewalls.

Server Authentication

ssh automatically maintains and checks a database containing identifications for all hosts it has ever been used with. RSA host keys are stored in $HOME/.ssh/known_hosts in the user's home directory. Additionally, the file /etc/ssh_known_hosts is automatically checked for known hosts. Any new hosts are automatically added to the user's file. If a host's identification ever changes, ssh warns about this change and disables password authentication to prevent a Trojan horse from getting the user's password. Another purpose of this mechanism is to prevent man-in-the-middle attacks that could otherwise be used to circumvent the encryption. You can use the StrictHostKeyChecking option to prevent logins to machines whose host key is not known or has changed.

Options

-2   Force ssh to try protocol version 2 only.

-4   Force ssh to use IPv4 addresses only.

-6   Force ssh to use IPv6 addresses only.

-a   Disable forwarding of the authentication agent connection.

-A   Enable forwarding of the authentication agent connection. You can also specify this option on a per-host basis in a configuration file.

-c blowfish | 3des

                    Select the cipher to use for encrypting the session. 3des is used by default. It is believed to be secure. 3des (triple-des) is an encrypt-decrypt-encrypt triple with three different keys. It is presumably more secure than the des cipher, which is no longer fully supported in ssh. blowfish is a fast block cipher; it seems to be very secure and is much faster than 3des.

-c 3des-cbc,blowfish-cbc,aes-128-cbc

                    Additionally, for protocol version 2, specify a comma-separated list of ciphers in order of preference. Protocol version 2 supports 3DES, Blowfish, and AES 128 in CBC mode.

-C   Request compression of all data (including standard input, standard output, standard error, and data for forwarded X11 and TCP/IP connections). The compression algorithm is the same used by gzip(1). You can control the "level" with the CompressionLevel option. Compression is desirable on modem lines and other slow connections but only slows things down on fast networks. You can set the default value on a host-by-host basis in the configuration files.

-e ch | ^ch | none

                    Set the escape character for sessions with a PTY (default is ~). The escape character is recognized only at the beginning of a line. The escape character followed by a dot (.) closes the connection. If followed by Control-Z, the escape character suspends the connection. If followed by itself, the escape character sends itself once. Setting the character to none disables any escapes and makes the session fully transparent.

-f   Go to background just before command execution. This option is useful if ssh is going to ask for passwords or passphrases but the user wants ssh in the background. This option implies the -n option. The recommended way to start X11 programs at a remote site is with something like ssh -f *host* xterm.

-g   Allow remote hosts to connect to local forwarded ports.

-i *identity_file*

> Select the file from which the identity (private key) for RSA authentication is read. Default is $HOME/.ssh/identity in the user's home directory. You can also specify identity files on a per-host basis in the configuration file. You can have multiple -i options and multiple identities specified in configuration files.

-l *login_name*

> Specify the user to log in as on the remote machine. You can also specify this option on a per-host basis in the configuration file.

-L *port*:*host*:*hostport*

> Specify that the given port on the local (client) host is to be forwarded to the given host and port on the remote side. This option allocates a socket to listen to the port on the local side. Then, whenever a connection is made to this port, the connection is forwarded over the secure channel and a connection is made to host port *hostport* from the remote machine. You can also specify port forwarding in the configuration file. Only root can forward privileged ports. IPv6 addresses can be specified with an alternative syntax *port/host/hostport*.

-n

> Redirect standard input from /dev/null (actually, prevents reading from standard input). You must use this option when ssh is run in the background. A common trick is to use this option to run X11 programs on a remote machine. For example,

> ssh -n shadows.cs.hut.fi emacs &

> starts an emacs editor on shadows.cs.hut.fi, and the X11 connection is automatically forwarded over an encrypted channel. The ssh program is put in the background. This option does not work if ssh needs to ask for a password or passphrase. See also the -f option.

-N

> Do not execute a remote command. This option is useful if you just want to forward ports (protocol version 2 only).

-o *option*

> Specify options in the format used in the configuration file. This option is useful for specifying options for which there is no separate command-line option. The option has the same format as a line in the configuration file.

-p *port*

> Specify the port to connect to on the remote host. You can specify this option on a per-host basis in the configuration file.

-P

> Use a nonprivileged port for outgoing connections. You can use this option if your firewall does not permit connections from privileged ports. Notice that this option turns off RhostsAuthentication and RhostsRSAAuthentication.

-q

> Suppress all warning and diagnostic messages. Display only fatal errors.

-R *port*:*host*:*hostport*

>Specify that the given port on the remote (server) host is to be forwarded to the given host and port on the local side. This option allocates a socket to listen to the port on the remote side. Then, whenever a connection is made to this port, the connection is forwarded over the secure channel and a connection is made to host port *hostport* from the local machine. You can also specify port forwardings in the configuration file. Privileged ports can be forwarded only for root login on the remote machine.

-t

>Force pseudo-TTY allocation. You can use this option to execute arbitrary, screen-based programs on a remote machine. This option can be very useful, for example, for implementing menu services.

-T

>Disable pseudo-TTY allocation (protocol version 2 only).

-v

>Print debugging messages. This option is helpful in debugging connection, authentication, and configuration problems. The verbose mode is also used to display challenges if the user entered s/key as password. Multiple -v options increase the verbosity. Maximum is 3.

-x

>Disable X11 forwarding.

-X

>Enable X11 forwarding. You can also specify this option on a per-host basis in a configuration file.

Examples

The following example uses the verbose (-v) option of ssh to log in to the system cardinal. Before the login, an SSH v2 RSA keypair was created and stored in the default location of $HOME/.ssh/id_rsa. The public key in $HOME/.ssh/id_rsa.pub has been copied to the system cardinal and appended to the user's $HOME/.ssh/authorized_keys file. Note the bolded section where the public key authentication succeeds.

```
$ ssh -v cardinal
SSH Version Sun_SSH_1.0, protocol versions 1.5/2.0.
debug1: Reading configuration data /etc/ssh/ssh_config
debug1: Rhosts Authentication disabled, originating port will not be
   trusted.
debug1: ssh_connect: getuid 100 geteuid 100 anon 1
debug1: Connecting to cardinal [10.1.1.4] port 22.
debug1: Connection established.
debug1: identity file /home/gmarler/.ssh/identity type 0
debug1: Bad RSA1 key file /home/gmarler/.ssh/id_rsa.
debug1: identity file /home/gmarler/.ssh/id_rsa type 3
debug1: Bad RSA1 key file /home/gmarler/.ssh/id_dsa.
debug1: identity file /home/gmarler/.ssh/id_dsa type 3
debug1: Remote protocol version 1.99, remote software version
   OpenSSH_3.0.2p1
debug1: match: OpenSSH_3.0.2p1 pat ^OpenSSH
Enabling compatibility mode for protocol 2.0
debug1: Local version string SSH-2.0-Sun_SSH_1.0
debug1: sent kexinit: diffie-hellman-group1-sha1
debug1: sent kexinit: ssh-rsa,ssh-dss
```

```
debug1: sent kexinit: aes128-cbc,blowfish-cbc,3des-cbc,rijndael128-cbc
debug1: sent kexinit: aes128-cbc,blowfish-cbc,3des-cbc,rijndael128-cbc
debug1: sent kexinit: hmac-sha1,hmac-md5
debug1: sent kexinit: hmac-sha1,hmac-md5
debug1: sent kexinit: none
debug1: sent kexinit: none
debug1: sent kexinit:
debug1: sent kexinit:
debug1: send KEXINIT
debug1: done
debug1: wait KEXINIT
debug1: got kexinit:
   diffie-hellman-group-exchange-sha1,diffie-hellman-group1-sha1
debug1: got kexinit: ssh-rsa,ssh-dss
debug1: got kexinit:
   aes128-cbc,3des-cbc,blowfish-cbc,cast128-cbc,arcfour,aes192-cbc,aes25
   6-cbc,rijndael128-cbc,rijndael192-cbc,rijndael256-cbc,rijndael-cbc@ly
   sator.liu.se
debug1: got kexinit:
   aes128-cbc,3des-cbc,blowfish-cbc,cast128-cbc,arcfour,aes192-cbc,aes25
   6-cbc,rijndael128-cbc,rijndael192-cbc,rijndael256-cbc,rijndael-cbc@ly
   sator.liu.se
debug1: got kexinit:
   hmac-md5,hmac-sha1,hmac-ripemd160,hmac-ripemd160@openssh.com,hmac-sha
   1-96,hmac-md5-96
debug1: got kexinit:
   hmac-md5,hmac-sha1,hmac-ripemd160,hmac-ripemd160@openssh.com,hmac-sha
   1-96,hmac-md5-96
debug1: got kexinit: none,zlib
debug1: got kexinit: none,zlib
debug1: got kexinit:
debug1: got kexinit:
debug1: first kex follow: 0
debug1: reserved: 0
debug1: done
debug1: kex: server->client unable to decide common locale
debug1: kex: server->client aes128-cbc hmac-sha1 none
debug1: kex: client->server unable to decide common locale
debug1: kex: client->server aes128-cbc hmac-sha1 none
debug1: Sending SSH2_MSG_KEXDH_INIT.
debug1: bits set: 471/1024
debug1: Wait SSH2_MSG_KEXDH_REPLY.
debug1: Got SSH2_MSG_KEXDH_REPLY.
debug1: Host 'cardinal' is known and matches the RSA host key.
debug1: Found key in /home/gmarler/.ssh/known_hosts:1
debug1: bits set: 515/1024
debug1: ssh_rsa_verify: signature correct
debug1: Wait SSH2_MSG_NEWKEYS.
debug1: GOT SSH2_MSG_NEWKEYS.
debug1: send SSH2_MSG_NEWKEYS.
debug1: done: send SSH2_MSG_NEWKEYS.
debug1: done: KEX2.
debug1: send SSH2_MSG_SERVICE_REQUEST
debug1: service_accept: ssh-userauth
```

```
debug1: got SSH2_MSG_SERVICE_ACCEPT
debug1: authentications that can continue:
  publickey,password,keyboard-interactive
debug1: next auth method to try is publickey
debug1: userauth_pubkey_agent: trying agent key
  /home/gmarler/.ssh/id_rsa
debug1: ssh-userauth2 successfull: method publickey
debug1: channel 0: new [client-session]
debug1: send channel open 0
debug1: Entering interactive session.
debug1: client_init id 0 arg 0
debug1: channel request 0: shell
debug1: channel 0: open confirm rwindow 0 rmax 16384
Last login: Tue Mar 19 08:51:48 2002 from ns3

Sun Microsystems Inc.   SunOS 5.8      Generic February 2000
Sun Microsystems Inc.   SunOS 5.8      Generic February 2000
Agent pid 16936
[ns1.gmarler.com:/export/home/gmarler]
$ exit
Exiting
Killing SSH Agent
Agent pid 16936 killed
debug1: channel: 0 rcvd request for exit-status
debug1: cb_fn 2675c cb_event 91
debug1: channel 0: rcvd eof
debug1: channel 0: output open->drain
debug1: channel 0: rcvd close
debug1: channel 0: input open->closed
debug1: channel 0: close_read
debug1: channel 0: obuf empty
debug1: channel 0: output drain->closed
debug1: channel 0: close_write
debug1: channel 0: send close
debug1: channel 0: full closed2
debug1: channel_free: channel 0: status: The following connections are
  open:
  #0 client-session (t4 r0 i8/0 o128/0 fd -1/-1)

Connection to cardinal closed.
debug1: Transferred: stdin 0, stdout 0, stderr 32 bytes in 5.5 seconds
debug1: Bytes per second: stdin 0.0, stdout 0.0, stderr 5.9
debug1: Exit status -1
$
```

Environment Variables

ssh normally sets the following environment variables.

DISPLAY   The DISPLAY variable indicates the location of the X11 server. It is
               automatically set by ssh to point to a value of the form *hostname*: *n*,
               where *hostname* indicates the host on which the shell runs and *n* is an
               integer greater than or equal to 1. ssh uses this special value to forward

X11 connections over the secure channel. The user should normally not set DISPLAY explicitly, because doing so renders the X11 connection insecure (and requires the user to manually copy any required authorization cookies).

HOME   Set to the path of the user's home directory.

LOGNAME   Synonym for USER. Set for compatibility with systems that use this variable.

MAIL   Set to point to the user's mailbox.

PATH   Set to the default PATH, as specified when ssh is compiled.

SSH_AUTH_SOCK

The path of a UNIX-domain socket used to communicate with the agent.

SSH_CLIENT   The client end of the connection. The variable contains three space-separated values: *client ip-address*, *client port number*, and *server port number*.

SSH_TTY   Set to the name of the TTY (path to the device) associated with the current shell or command. If the current session has no TTY, this variable is not set.

TZ   Set to indicate the present time zone if it was set when the daemon was started, that is, the daemon passes the value on to new connections.

USER   Set to the name of the user logging in.

Additionally, ssh reads $HOME/.ssh/environment and adds lines of the format *VARNAME=value* to the environment.

Exit Status

0   Successful completion.

1   An error occurred.

Files

$HOME/.ssh/known_hosts

Records host keys for all hosts the user has logged in to that are not in /etc/ssh_known_hosts. See sshd(1M).

$HOME/.ssh/identity
$HOME/.ssh/id_dsa

Contains the RSA and the DSA authentication identity of the user. These files contain sensitive data and should be readable by the user but not accessible by others (read/write/execute). Notice that ssh ignores a private key file if it is accessible by others. It is possible to specify a passphrase when generating the key. The passphrase is used to encrypt the sensitive part of this file with 3DES.

`$HOME/.ssh/identity.pub`
`$HOME/.ssh/id_dsa.pub`

Contains the public key for authentication, that is, the public part of the identity file in human-readable form. The contents of the `$HOME/.ssh/identity.pub` file should be added to `$HOME/.ssh/authorized_keys` on all machines you want to log in to with RSA authentication. The contents of the `$HOME/.ssh/id_dsa.pub` file should be added to `$HOME/.ssh/authorized_keys` on all machines you want to log in to with DSA authentication. These files are not sensitive and can, but need not, be readable by anyone. These files are never used automatically and are not necessary. They are provided only for the convenience of the user.

`$HOME/.ssh/config`

The per-user configuration file. The format of this file is described above. This file is used by the ssh client. This file does not usually contain any sensitive information, but the recommended permissions are read/write for the user and not accessible by others.

`$HOME/.ssh/authorized_keys`

Lists the DSA keys that can be used for logging in as this user. This file is not highly sensitive, but the recommended permissions are read/write for the user and not accessible by others.

`/etc/ssh/ssh_known_hosts`

Systemwide list of known host keys. `/etc/ssh_known_hosts` contains RSA keys. This file should be prepared by the system administrator to contain the public host keys of all machines in the organization and should be world readable. The file contains public keys, one per line, in the following format, with fields separated by spaces: system name, number of bits in modulus, public exponent, modulus, and optional comment field. When different names are used for the same machine, all such names should be listed, separated by commas. See sshd(1M).

The canonical system name (as returned by name servers) is used by sshd(1M) to verify the client host when logging in. Other names are needed because ssh does not convert the user-supplied name to a canonical name before checking the key, to prevent someone with access to the name servers from being able able to fool host authentication.

`/etc/ssh/ssh_config`

Systemwide configuration file. This file provides defaults for those values that are not specified in the user's configuration file and for those users who do not have a configuration file. This file must be world readable.

$HOME/.rhosts

> This file is used in .rhosts authentication to list the host/user pairs
> that are permitted to log in. (Notice that this file is also used by rlogin
> and rsh,which makes use of this file insecure.) Each line of the file
> contains a host name (in the canonical form returned by name servers)
> and then a user name on that host, separated by a space. On some
> machines, this file may need to be world readable if the user's home
> directory is on an NFS partition, because sshd(1M) reads it as root.
> Additionally, this file must be owned by the user and must not have
> write permissions for anyone else. The recommended permission for
> most machines is read/write for the user and not accessible by others.

> Notice that, by default, sshd(1M) is installed so that it requires
> successful RSA host authentication before permitting .rhosts
> authentication. If your server machine does not have the client's host
> key in /etc/ssh_known_hosts, you can store it in
> $HOME/.ssh/known_hosts. The easiest way to do so is to connect back
> to the client from the server machine with ssh to automatically add the
> host key to $HOME/.ssh/known_hosts.

$HOME/.shosts

> Used exactly the same way as .rhosts. This file enables user hosts
> authentication with ssh without permitting login with rlogin(1) or
> rsh(1).

/etc/hosts.equiv

> Used during .rhosts authentication. The file contains canonical hosts
> names, one per line. (See sshd(1M) for the full format description.) If
> the client host is found in this file, login is automatically permitted,
> provided that client and server user names are the same. In addition,
> successful RSA host authentication is normally required. This file
> should be writable only by root.

/etc/ssh/shosts.equiv

> This file is processed exactly as /etc/hosts.equiv. This file can be
> useful to permit logins with ssh but not with rsh or rlogin.

/etc/ssh/sshrc

> Commands in this file are executed by ssh when the user logs in just
> before the user's shell or command is started. See sshd(1M) for more
> information.

$HOME/.ssh/rc

> Commands in this file are executed by ssh when the user logs in just
> before the user's shell or command is started. See sshd(1M) for more
> information.

$HOME/.ssh/environment

> Contains additional definitions for environment variables. See
> "Environment Variables" on page 1324.

Attributes

See attributes(5) for descriptions of the following attributes.

Attribute Type	Attribute Value
Availability	SUNWsshu

See Also

gzip(1), rlogin(1), rsh(1), ssh-add(1), sshagent(1), ssh-keygen(1), telnet(1), sshd(1M), ssh_config(4), attributes(5)

New! **ssh-add** — Add RSA or DSA Identities for the Authentication Agent

Synopsis

/bin/ssh-add [-1LdD] [*file*...]

Description

Use the ssh-add command, new in the Solaris 9 Operating Environment, to add RSA or DSA identities to the authentication agent, ssh-agent(1). When run without arguments, ssh-add tries to add all of the files $HOME/.ssh/identity (RSA v1), $HOME/.ssh/id_rsa (RSA v2), and $HOME/.ssh/id_dsa (DSA v2) that exist. If more than one of the private keys exist, an attempt to decrypt each with the same passphrase is made before reprompting for a different passphrase. The passphrase is read from the user's TTY or by running the program defined in SSH_ASKPASS.

The authentication agent must be running.

Options

-d	Instead of adding the identity, remove the identity from the agent.
-D	Delete all identities from the agent.
-1	List fingerprints of all identities currently represented by the agent.
-L	List public key parameters of all identities currently represented by the agent.

Examples

After you start your ssh-agent, you can decrypt and load the private portion of each keypair you use into the agent by using the ssh-add command.

The first example loads the private portion of the keypair located at $HOME/.ssh/work-keypair into your SSH agent.

```
$ ssh-add $HOME/.ssh/work-keypair
Enter passphrase for /home/gmarler/.ssh/work-keypair: Enter passphrase.
Identity added:
   /home/gmarler/.ssh/work-keypair(/home/gmarler/.ssh/work-keypair)
$
```

The following example examines the private keys currently loaded into the agent.

```
$ ssh-add -l
md5 1024 36:60:93:ee:6e:9a:31:9a:8b:0d:2b:aa:4a:d0:12:83
   /home/gmarler/.ssh/work-keypair(DSA)
$
```

The following example loads into the SSH agent all of the default private keys that exist. In this case, the user has the same passphrase for each private key, so they can all be loaded even though the passphrase for the first private key is entered.

```
$ ssh-add
Enter passphrase for A default SSH v1 RSA keypair: Enter passphrase.
Identity added: /home/gmarler/.ssh/identity(A default SSH v1 RSA keypair)
Identity added: /home/gmarler/.ssh/id_rsa(/home/gmarler/.ssh/id_rsa)
Identity added: /home/gmarler/.ssh/id_dsa(/home/gmarler/.ssh/id_dsa)
$
```

The following example examines the private keys currently loaded into the agent.

```
$ ssh-add -l
md5 1024 b3:eb:07:01:0d:af:1e:29:8e:f9:2a:6e:a1:04:8b:a9 A default SSH v1 RSA
   keypair(RSA1)
md5 1024 36:60:93:ee:6e:9a:31:9a:8b:0d:2b:aa:4a:d0:12:83
   /home/gmarler/.ssh/work-keypair(DSA)
md5 1024 d2:03:d0:1a:99:6f:c1:d9:e4:f8:32:58:e6:2b:4b:4a
   /home/gmarler/.ssh/id_rsa(RSA)
md5 1024 49:14:1b:ad:f5:0f:1d:ae:f3:7c:c6:ae:f6:db:a3:02
   /home/gmarler/.ssh/id_dsa(DSA)
$
```

The following example removes all of the default identities from the agent. These private keys are associated with the following files (if you've created them with ssh-keygen).

```
$HOME/.ssh/identity (for SSH v1 RSA private key)
$HOME/.ssh/id_rsa   (for SSH v2 RSA private key)
$HOME/.ssh/id_dsa   (for SSH v2 DSA private key)
```

```
$ ssh-add -d
Identity removed: /home/gmarler/.ssh/identity(A default SSH v1 RSA keypair)
Identity removed: /home/gmarler/.ssh/id_rsa(/home/gmarler/.ssh/id_rsa.pub)
Identity removed: /home/gmarler/.ssh/id_dsa(/home/gmarler/.ssh/id_dsa.pub)
$
```

Note that only the default private keys (if they existed and were loaded into the agent) are removed by the -d option; any other private keys that were loaded at the time are still inside the agent, as shown in the following example.

```
$ ssh-add -l
md5 1024 36:60:93:ee:6e:9a:31:9a:8b:0d:2b:aa:4a:d0:12:83
   /home/gmarler/.ssh/work-keypair(DSA)
$
```

You can remove these other private keys explicitly by referring to the file that holds these private keys, as shown in the following example.

```
$ ssh-add -d $HOME/.ssh/work-keypair
Identity removed:
   /home/gmarler/.ssh/work-keypair(/home/gmarler/.ssh/work-keypair.pub)
 $ ssh-add -l
The agent has no identities.
$
```

Alternatively, you can remove all keys with the –D option, as shown in the following example.

```
$ ssh-add
Enter passphrase for A default SSH v1 RSA keypair:
Identity added: /home/gmarler/.ssh/identity(A default SSH v1 RSA keypair)
Identity added: /home/gmarler/.ssh/id_rsa(/home/gmarler/.ssh/id_rsa)
Identity added: /home/gmarler/.ssh/id_dsa(/home/gmarler/.ssh/id_dsa)
$ ssh-add $HOME/.ssh/work-keypair
Enter passphrase for /home/gmarler/.ssh/work-keypair:
Identity added:
   /home/gmarler/.ssh/work-keypair(/home/gmarler/.ssh/work-keypair)
$ ssh-add -l
md5 1024 b3:eb:07:01:0d:af:1e:29:8e:f9:2a:6e:a1:04:8b:a9 A default SSH v1 RSA
   keypair(RSA1)
md5 1024 d2:03:d0:1a:99:6f:c1:d9:e4:f8:32:58:e6:2b:4b:4a
   /home/gmarler/.ssh/id_rsa(RSA)
md5 1024 49:14:1b:ad:f5:0f:1d:ae:f3:7c:c6:ae:f6:db:a3:02
   /home/gmarler/.ssh/id_dsa(DSA)
md5 1024 36:60:93:ee:6e:9a:31:9a:8b:0d:2b:aa:4a:d0:12:83
   /home/gmarler/.ssh/work-keypair(DSA)
$ ssh-add -D
All identities removed.
 $ ssh-add -l
The agent has no identities.
$
```

Environment Variables

DISPLAYS SH_ASKPASS	If ssh-add needs a passphrase, it reads the passphrase from the current terminal if the command was run from a terminal. If ssh-add does not have a terminal associated with it but DISPLAY and SSH_ASKPASS are set, ssh-add executes the program specified by SSH_ASKPASS and opens an X11 window to read the passphrase. This capability is particularly useful when ssh-add is called from a .Xsession or related script.

Exit Status

0	Successful completion.
1	An error occurred.

Files

Only the user should be able to read these files. Notice that ssh-add ignores a file if it is accessible by others. You can specify a passphrase when generating the key; that passphrase is used to encrypt the private part of this file.

If these files are stored on a network file system, it is assumed that either the protection provided in the files themselves or the transport layer of the network file system provides sufficient protection for the site policy. If not, then it is recommended that you store the key files on removable media or locally on the relevant hosts.

Recommended names for the DSA and RSA key files are listed below.

$HOME/.ssh/identity

> The RSA authentication identity of the user for protocol version 1.

$HOME/.ssh/identity.pub

> The public part of the RSA authentication identity of the user for protocol version 1.

$HOME/.ssh/id_dsa

> The private DSA authentication identity of the user.

$HOME/.ssh/id_dsa.pub

> The public part of the DSA authentication identity of the user.

$HOME/.ssh/id_rsa

> The private RSA authentication identity of the user.

$HOME/.ssh/id_rsa.pub

> The public part of the RSA authentication identity of the user.

Attributes

See attributes(5) for descriptions of the following attributes.

Attribute Type	Attribute Value
Availability	SUNWsshu

See Also

ssh(1), ssh-agent(1), ssh-keygen(1), sshd(1M), attributes(5)

ssh-agent — Authentication Agent

New!

Synopsis

/bin/ssh-agent [-c| -s] [-k] [*command* [*args*...]]

Description

Use the ssh-agent program, new in the Solaris 9 Operating Environment, to hold private keys used for public key authentication (RSA, DSA). ssh-agent is often started at the beginning of a login session. All other windows or programs are started as clients to the `ssh-agent` program. Through use of environment variables, the agent can be located and automatically used for authentication when you log in to other machines with `ssh`(1). (See "Using Secure Shell (Task Map)" in *System Administration Guide: Security Services*.)

If you specify a command, it is executed as a subprocess of the agent. When the command dies, so does the agent.

The agent initially does not have any private keys. Keys are added with `ssh-add`(1), which sends the identity to the agent. Several identities can be stored in the agent; the agent can automatically use any of these identities. Use the `ssh-add -l` option to display the identities currently held by the agent.

The agent is run in the user's local host. Authentication data need not be stored on any other machine, and authentication passphrases never go over the network. However, if the connection to the agent is forwarded over SSH remote logins, the user can use the privileges given by the identities anywhere in the network in a secure way.

You can set up an agent in two ways.

- You let the agent start a new subcommand into which some environment variables are exported.

- You let the agent print the needed shell commands (`sh`(1) or `csh`(1) syntax can be generated) that can be evaluated in the calling shell. Later, use `ssh`(1) to look at these variables, and use them to establish a connection to the agent.

A UNIX-domain socket is created (/tmp/ssh*XXXXXXXX*/agent.pid), and the name of this socket is stored in the `SSH_AUTH_SOCK` environment variable. The socket is made accessible only to the current user. This method is easily abused by root or another instance of the same user.

The `SSH_AGENT_PID` environment variable holds the agent's PID.

The agent exits automatically when the command given on the command line terminates.

Options

`-c`	Generate C-shell commands on standard output, the default if SHELL indicates a `csh`-style shell.
`-k`	Kill the current agent (given by the `SSH_AGENT_PID` environment variable).
`-s`	Generate Bourne shell commands on standard output, the default if SHELL does not indicate that it is a `csh`-style shell.

Examples

The following example invokes an `ssh-agent` with the Bourne, Korn, or BASH shells. You can later load your private keys into it with `ssh-add`(1).

```
$ eval `ssh-agent -s`
Agent pid 357
$
```

The following example invokes an `ssh-agent` with the C shell. You can later load your private keys into it with `ssh-add`(1).

```
% eval `ssh-agent -c`
Agent pid 25235
%
```

You can use this `eval` statement in your shell's `.profile` (Bourne/Korn/BASH shells) or `.login` (C shell) file to start up the agent when you log in.

Exit Status

0	Successful completion.
1	An error occurred.

Files

`/tmp/ssh-`*XXXXXXX*`/agent.pid`

UNIX-domain sockets used to contain the connection to the authentication agent. These sockets should be readable only by the owner. The sockets are removed when the agent exits.

Attributes

See `attributes`(5) for descriptions of the following attributes.

Attribute Type	Attribute Value
Availability	SUNWsshu

See Also

`ssh(1)`, `ssh-add(1)`, `ssh-keygen(1)`, `sshd(1M)`, `attributes(5)`
"Using Secure Shell (Task Map)" in *System Administration Guide: Security Services*

---

ssh-http-proxy-connect — Secure Shell Proxy for HTTP   *New!*

Synopsis

`/usr/lib/ssh/ssh-http-proxy-connect [-h` *http_proxy_host*`]`
`[-p` *http_proxy_port*`]` *connect_host connect_port*

Description

Use the `ssh-http-proxy-connect` command, new in the Solaris 9 Operating Environment, as a proxy command for `ssh(1)` that uses HTTP CONNECT. Typical use is for connections external to a network that are allowed only through a proxy Web server.

Options

-h *http_proxy_host*

Specify the proxy Web server through which to connect. Override the HTTPPROXY and http_proxy environment variables if they are set.

-p *http_proxy_port*

> Specify the port on which the proxy Web server runs. If not specified, assume port 80. Override the HTTPPROXYPORT and http_proxy environment variables if they are set.

Operands

http_proxy_host

> The host name or IP address (IPv4 or IPv6) of the proxy.

http_proxy_port

> The numeric port number to connect to on *http_proxy_host*.

connect_host

> The name of the remote host to which the proxy Web server is to connect.

connect_port

> The numeric port number of the proxy Web server to connect to on *http_proxy_host*.

Examples

The recommended way to use a proxy connection command is to configure ProxyCommand in ssh_config(4) as shown in the first two examples. The third example shows how the proxy command can be specified on the command line when you run ssh(1).

The following example configures ssh-http-proxy-connect in the /etc/ssh/ssh_config(4) file when the proxy is set from the environment.

```
Host playtime.foo.com
ProxyCommand /usr/lib/ssh/ssh-http-proxy-connect playtime.foo.com 22
```

The following example configures ssh-http-proxy-connect in the /etc/ssh/ssh_config(4) file to override (or, to set if not set) proxy environment variables.

```
Host playtime.foo.com
ProxyCommand /usr/lib/ssh/ssh-http-proxy-connect -h webcache -p 8080
   playtime.foo.com 22
```

The following example uses ssh-http-proxy-connect from the ssh(1) command line.

```
example$ ssh -o'ProxyCommand="/usr/lib/ssh/ssh-http-proxy-connect
   -h webcache -p 8080 playtime.foo.com 22"' playtime.foo.com
```

Environment Variables

HTTPPROXY   Use the *http_proxy_host* operand to specify the default proxy host. Override http_proxy if both are set.

HTTPPROXYPORT

>   Use the *http_proxy_port* operand to specify the default proxy port.
>   Ignored if HTTPPROXY is not set.

http_proxy   URL format for specifying proxy host and port.

Exit Status

0   Successful completion.

1   An error occurred.

Attributes

See attributes(5) for descriptions of the following attributes:

Attribute Type	Attribute Value
Availability	SUNWsshu

See Also

ssh(1), ssh-socks5-proxy-connect(1), ssh_config(4), attributes(5)

---

ssh-keygen — Authentication Key Generation   *New!*

Synopsis

```
/bin/ssh-keygen [-dq] [-b bits] [-N new_passphrase] [-C comment]
    [-f output_keyfile]
/bin/ssh-keygen -p [-P old_passphrase] [-N new_passphrase] [-f keyfile]
/bin/ssh-keygen -x [-f input_keyfile]
/bin/ssh-keygen -X [-f input_keyfile]
/bin/ssh-keygen -y [-f input_keyfile]
/bin/ssh-keygen -c [-P passphrase] [-C comment] [-f keyfile]
/bin/ssh-keygen -l [-f input_keyfile]
/bin/ssh-keygen -R
```

Description

Use the ssh-keygen command, new in the Solaris 9 Operating Environment, to
generate and manage authentication keys for ssh(1). ssh-keygen defaults to generating
an RSA key for use by protocol 2.0.

Each user wanting to use SSH with RSA or DSA authentication normally runs this
command once to create the authentication key in $HOME/.ssh/identity or
$HOME/.ssh/id_dsa. The system administrator can also use this command to generate
host keys.

Ordinarily, ssh-keygen generates the key and asks for a file in which to store the
private key. The public key is stored in a file with the same name but with the .pub
extension appended. The program also asks for a passphrase. The passphrase can be
empty to indicate no passphrase (host keys must have empty passphrases), or it can be
a string of arbitrary length. Good passphrases are 10–30 characters long and are not
simple sentences or otherwise easy to guess. (English prose has only 1–2 bits of entropy

per word and provides very poor passphrases.) You can change the passphrase later with the -p option.

There is no way to recover a lost passphrase. If the passphrase is lost or forgotten, you have to generate a new key and copy the corresponding public key to other machines.

For RSA, there is also a comment field in the key file that is only for convenience to the user to help identify the key. The comment can tell what the key is for or whatever is useful. The comment is initialized to *user@host* when the key is created but can be changed with the -c option.

After a key is generated, instructions below detail where to place the keys to activate them.

Options

-b *bits*   Specify the number of bits in the key to create. The minimum number is 512 bits. Generally, 1024 bits are considered sufficient. Key sizes above that no longer improve security but make things slower. The default is 1024 bits.

-c   Change the comment in the private and public key files. The command prompts for the file containing the private keys, for the passphrase if the key has one, and for the new comment.

-C *comment*   Specify the new comment.

-f *input_keyfile*

                   Specify the file name of the key file.

-l   Show the fingerprint of the specified private or public key file.

-N *new_passphrase*

                   Provide the new passphrase.

-p   Change the passphrase of a private key file instead of creating a new private key. The command prompts for the file containing the private key, for the old passphrase, and prompts twice for the new passphrase.

-P *passphrase*

                   Provide the (old) passphrase.

-q   Silence ssh-keygen. Used by /etc/rc when creating a new key.

-R   If RSA support is functional, immediately exit with code 0. If RSA support is not functional, exit with code 1. This option will be removed when the RSA patent expires.

-x   Read a private OpenSSH DSA format file, and print an SSH2-compatible public key to standard output.

-X   Read an unencrypted SSH2-compatible private (or public) key file, and print an OpenSSH compatible private (or public) key to standard output.

-y   Read a private OpenSSH DSA format file, and print an OpenSSH DSA public key to standard output.

Examples

The following example uses the ssh-keygen command with no options to create a key with a passphrase in the default location.

```
mopoke% ssh-keygen
Enter file in which to save the key(/home/winsor/.ssh/id_rsa):
Created directory '/home/winsor/.ssh'.
Generating public/private rsa key pair.
Enter passphrase(empty for no passphrase): Passphrase
Enter same passphrase again: Passphrase
Your identification has been saved in /home/winsor/.ssh/id_rsa.
Your public key has been saved in /home/winsor/.ssh/id_rsa.pub.
The key fingerprint is:
md5 1024 c6:8b:17:33:e5:d9:77:ef:bb:fe:2c:5e:5a:be:07:72 winsor@mopoke
mopoke%
```

The following example generates a default, 1024-bit SSH version 1 keypair.

```
$ ssh-keygen -b 1024 -t rsa1 -C "A default SSH v1 RSA keypair"
Enter file in which to save the key(/home/gmarler/.ssh/identity):
Generating public/private rsa1 key pair.
Enter passphrase(empty for no passphrase): Enter passphrase.
Enter same passphrase again: Enter passphrase again.
Your identification has been saved in /home/gmarler/.ssh/identity.
Your public key has been saved in /home/gmarler/.ssh/identity.pub.
The key fingerprint is:
md5 1024 b3:eb:07:01:0d:af:1e:29:8e:f9:2a:6e:a1:04:8b:a9 A default SSH
   v1 RSA keypair
$
```

The following example generates a default, 1024-bit SSH version 2 RSA keypair.

```
$ ssh-keygen -b 1024 -t rsa -C "A default SSH v2 RSA keypair"
Enter file in which to save the key(/home/gmarler/.ssh/id_rsa):
Generating public/private rsa key pair.
Enter passphrase(empty for no passphrase): Enter passphrase.
Enter same passphrase again: Enter passphrase again.
Your identification has been saved in /home/gmarler/.ssh/id_rsa.
Your public key has been saved in /home/gmarler/.ssh/id_rsa.pub.
The key fingerprint is:
md5 1024 d2:03:d0:1a:99:6f:c1:d9:e4:f8:32:58:e6:2b:4b:4a A default SSH
   v2 RSA keypair
$
```

The following example generates a default, 1024-bit SSH version 2 DSA keypair

```
$ ssh-keygen -b 1024 -t dsa -C "A default SSH v2 DSA keypair"
Enter file in which to save the key(/home/gmarler/.ssh/id_dsa):
Generating public/private dsa key pair.
Enter passphrase(empty for no passphrase): Enter passphrase.
Enter same passphrase again: Enter passphrase again.
Your identification has been saved in /home/gmarler/.ssh/id_dsa.
Your public key has been saved in /home/gmarler/.ssh/id_dsa.pub.
The key fingerprint is:
```

```
md5 1024 49:14:1b:ad:f5:0f:1d:ae:f3:7c:c6:ae:f6:db:a3:02 A default SSH
   v2 DSA keypair
$
```

The following example generates a custom, 1024-bit SSH version 2 DSA keypair for a particular use.

$ **ssh-keygen -b 1024 -t dsa -f $HOME/.ssh/work-keypair -C "Gordon's SSH v2 keypair for work"**
```
Generating public/private dsa key pair.
Enter passphrase(empty for no passphrase): Enter passphrase.
Enter same passphrase again: Enter passphrase again.
Your identification has been saved in /home/gmarler/.ssh/work-keypair.
Your public key has been saved in /home/gmarler/.ssh/work-keypair.pub.
The key fingerprint is:
md5 1024 36:60:93:ee:6e:9a:31:9a:8b:0d:2b:aa:4a:d0:12:83 Gordon's SSH v2
   keypair for work
$
```

The following example changes the passphrase associated with a private key located at $HOME/.ssh/work-keypair.

$ **ssh-keygen -p -f $HOME/.ssh/work-keypair**
```
Enter old passphrase: Enter old passphrase, or press Enter if there was none.
Key has comment 'dsa w/o comment'
Enter new passphrase(empty for no passphrase): Enter new passphrase.
Enter same passphrase again: Enter new passphrase again.
Your identification has been saved with the new passphrase.
$
```

Exit Status

0   Successful completion.

1   An error occurred.

Files

$HOME/.ssh/identity

Contains the RSA authentication identity of the user. This file should not be readable by anyone but the user. It is possible to specify a passphrase when generating the key; that passphrase is used to encrypt the private part of this file with 3DES. This file is not automatically accessed by ssh-keygen, but it is offered as the default file for the private key. sshd(1M) reads this file when a login attempt is made.

$HOME/.ssh/identity.pub

Contains the public key for authentication. The contents of this file should be added to $HOME/.ssh/authorized_keys on all systems where you want to log in with RSA authentication. You do not need to keep the contents of this file secret.

$HOME/.ssh/id_dsa

> Contains the DSA authentication identity of the user. This file should
> not be readable by anyone but the user. It is possible to specify a
> passphrase when generating the key; that passphrase is used to
> encrypt the private part of this file with 3DES. This file is not
> automatically accessed by ssh-keygen, but it is offered as the
> default file for the private key. sshd(1M) reads this file when a login
> attempt is made.

$HOME/.ssh/id_dsa.pub

> Contains the public key for authentication. The contents of this file
> should be added to $HOME/.ssh/authorized_keys on all machines
> where you want to log in with DSA authentication. You do not need to
> keep the contents of this file secret.

Attributes

See attributes(5) for descriptions of the following attributes:

Attribute Type	Attribute Value
Availability	SUNWsshu

See Also

ssh(1), ssh-add(1), ssh-agent(1), sshd(1M), attributes(5)

ssh-socks5-proxy-connect — Secure Shell Proxy for SOCKS5   *New!*

Synopsis

/usr/lib/ssh/ssh-socks5-proxy-connect [-h *socks5_proxy_host*]
   [-p *socks5_proxy_port*] *connect_host connect_port*

Description

Use the ssh-socks5-proxy-connect command, new in the Solaris 9 Operating
Environment, as a proxy command for ssh(1) that uses SOCKS5 (RFC 1928). Typical
use is for connections external to a network that are allowed only through a socks
gateway server.

   This proxy command does not provide any of the SOCKS5 authentication
mechanisms defined in RFC 1928. Only anonymous connections are possible.

Options

-h *socks5_proxy_host*

> Specify the proxy Web server through which to connect. Override the
> SOCKS5_SERVER environment variable.

-p *socks5_proxy_port*

> Specify the port on which the proxy Web server runs. If not specified, port 80 is assumed. Override the SOCKS5_PORT environment variable.

Operands

socks5_proxy_host

> The host name or IP address (IPv4 or IPv6) of the proxy.

socks5_proxy_port

> The numeric port number to connect to on *socks5_proxy_host*.

connect_host

> The name of the remote host to which the socks gateway is to connect.

connect_port

> The numeric port number of the socks gateway to connect to on *connect_host*.

Examples

The recommended way to use a proxy connection command is to configure the ProxyCommand in ssh_config(4), as shown in the first two examples.

The following example configures ssh-socks5-proxy-connect in the /etc/ssh/ssh_config(4) file when the proxy is set from the environment.

```
Host playtime.foo.com
ProxyCommand /usr/lib/ssh/ssh-socks5-proxy-connect playtime.foo.com 22
```

The following example configures ssh-socks5-proxy-connect in the /etc/ssh/ssh_config(4) file to override (or if not, to set) proxy environment variables.

```
Host playtime.foo.com
 ProxyCommand /usr/lib/ssh/ssh-socks5-proxy-connect -h socks-gw -p 1080
   -n 192.168.100.2 playtime.foo.com 22
```

The following example uses ssh-socks5-proxy-connect from the ssh(1) command line.

```
example$ ssh -o'ProxyCommand="/usr/lib/ssh/ssh-socks5-proxy-connect
   -h socks-gw -p 1080 playtime.foo.com 22"' playtime.foo.com
```

Environment Variables

SOCKS5_SERVER

> Use the *socks5_proxy_host* operand to specify the default proxy host.

SOCKS5_PORT

> Use the *socks5_proxy_port* operand to specify the default proxy port.

Exit Status

0   Successful completion.

    1   An error occurred.

Attributes

See attributes(5) for descriptions of the following attributes:

Attribute Type	Attribute Value
Availability	SUNWsshu
Interface Stability	Stable

See Also

ssh(1), ssh-http-proxy-connect(1), ssh_config(4), attributes(5)

stop — Control Process Execution

Synopsis

sh, csh, ksh
stop %*job-id*...
stop *pid*...

Description

See jobs(1).

strchg, strconf — Change or Query Stream Configuration

Synopsis

/usr/bin/strchg -h *module* 1[, *module* 2...]
/usr/bin/strchg -p [-a | -u *module*]
/usr/bin/strchg -f *filename*
/usr/bin/strconf [-m | -t *module*]

Description

Use these commands to alter or query the configuration of the stream associated with the standard input. The strchg command pushes modules on or pops modules off the stream. The strconf command queries the configuration of the stream. Only the superuser or owner of a STREAMS device can alter the configuration of that stream.

Invoked without any arguments, strconf prints a list of all the modules in the stream as well as the topmost driver. The list is printed with one name per line; the first name printed is the topmost module on the stream (if one exists), and the last item printed is the name of the driver.

If you are neither the owner of the stream nor superuser, the strchg command fails. If you do not have read permissions on the stream and are not superuser, the strconf command fails.

Note — If modules are pushed in the wrong order, you could end up with a stream that does not function as expected. For TTYs, if the line-discipline module is not pushed in the correct place, you could have a terminal that does not respond to any commands.

Options

The following options apply to strchg; -h, -f, and -p are mutually exclusive.

-a *module*   Pop all the modules above the topmost driver off the stream. This option requires the -p option.

-f *filename*

Specify a *filename* that contains a list of modules representing the desired configuration of the stream. Each module name must appear on a separate line; the first name represents the topmost module, and the last name represents the module that should be closest to the driver. strchg determines the current configuration of the stream and pops and pushes the necessary modules to achieve the desired configuration.

-h *module1* [, *module2*...]

Push modules onto a stream. Specify as arguments the names of one or more pushable streams modules. Push these modules in order; that is, push *module1* first, push *module2* second, and so forth.

-p   Pop modules off the stream. With the -p option alone, pop the topmost module from the stream.

-u *module*   Pop all modules above but not including *module* off the stream. This option requires the -p option.

The following options apply to strconf; -m and -t are mutually exclusive.

-m *module*   Determine if the named *module* is present on a stream. If it is, print the message yes and return 0. If not, print the message no and return a non-zero value. The -t and -m options are mutually exclusive.

-t *module*   Print only the topmost module (if one exists). The -t and -m options are mutually exclusive.

Examples

The following command pushes the module ldterm on the stream associated with the standard input.

castle% **strchg -h ldterm**

The following command pops the topmost module from the stream associated with /dev/term/24. You must be the owner of this device or the superuser.

castle% **strchg -p < /dev/term/24**

If the file `fileconf` contains the following lines

```
ttcompat
ldterm
ptem
```

then the following command configures the standard input stream so that the module `ptem` is pushed over the driver, followed by `ldterm` and `ttcompat` closest to the stream head.

```
castle% strchg -f fileconf
```

The `strconf` command with no arguments lists the modules and topmost driver on the stream; for a stream that has only the module `ldterm` pushed above the `zs` driver, you would get the following output.

```
castle% strconf
ldterm
zs
castle%
```

The following command asks if `ldterm` is on the stream and returns an exit status of 0.

```
castle% strconf -m ldterm
yes
castle%
```

Attributes

See `attributes`(5) for descriptions of the following attributes:

Attribute Type	Attribute Value
Availability	SUNWcsu

See Also

`attributes`(5), `streamio`(7I)

Diagnostics

`strchg` returns 0 on success. It prints an error message and returns non-zero status for various error conditions, including usage error, bad module name, too many modules to push, failure of an ioctl on the stream, or failure to open *filename* from the `-f` option.

`strconf` returns 0 on success (for the `-m` or `-t` option, success means the named or topmost module is present). It returns a non-zero status if invoked with the `-m` or `-t` option and the module is not present. It prints an error message and returns non-zero status for various error conditions, including usage error or failure of an ioctl on the stream.

strings — Find Printable Strings in an Object or Binary File

Synopsis

```
/usr/bin/strings [-a | -] [-t format | -o] [-n number | - number]
   [file...]
```

Description

The strings command looks for ASCII strings in a binary file. A string is any sequence of four or more printing characters ending with a newline or a null character.
strings is useful for identifying random object files and many other things.

Note — The algorithm for identifying strings is extremely primitive.

For backward compatibility, the -a and - options are interchangeable.

Options

-a | -	Look everywhere in the file for strings. If you omit this option, strings looks only in the initialized data space of object files.
-n number | -number	
	Use number as the minimum string length instead of the default, which is 4.
-o	Equivalent to -t d option.
-t format	Write each string preceded by its byte offset from the start of the file. The format is dependent on the single character used as the format argument.

d	Write the offset in decimal.
o	Write the offset in octal.
x	Write the offset in hexadecimal.

Operands

file	A path name of a regular file to be used as input. If you specify no file operand, read from the standard input.

Environment Variables

See environ(5) for descriptions of the following environment variables that affect the execution of strings: LC_CTYPE, LC_MESSAGES, and NLSPATH.

Exit Status

0	Successful completion.
>0	An error occurred.

Attributes

See attributes(5) for descriptions of the following attributes:

Attribute Type	Attribute Value
Availability	SUNWtoo
CSI	Enabled

See Also

od(1), attributes(5), environ(5)

strip — Strip Symbol Table, Debugging, and Line-Number Information from an Object File

Synopsis

/usr/ccs/bin/strip [-blrVx] *file*...

Description

Use the strip command to reduce the file storage overhead incurred by an object file. The strip command removes the symbol table, debugging information, and line-number information from ELF object files. Once this stripping process has been done, no symbolic debugging access is available for that file; therefore, you normally run this command only on production modules that have been debugged and tested.

If you execute strip on a common archive file (see ar(4)), then in addition to processing the members, strip removes the archive symbol table. You must restore the archive symbol table by executing the ar(1) command with the -s option before the archive can be linked with the ld(1) command. strip produces appropriate warning messages when this situation arises.

> **Note** — The symbol table section is not removed if it is contained within a segment or if the file is either a relocatable or dynamic shared object.
>
> The line number and debugging sections are not removed if they are contained within a segment or if their associated relocation section is contained within a segment.

Options

You can control the amount of information stripped from the ELF object with the following options.

-b   Same effect as the default behavior. This option is obsolete and will be removed in the next release.

-l   Strip line-number information only; do not strip the symbol table or debugging information.

-r   Same effect as the default behavior. This option is obsolete and will be removed in the next release.

-V	Print to standard error the version number of `strip`.
-x	Do not strip the symbol table; debugging and line-number information may be stripped.

Operands

file	A path name referring to an executable file.

Environment Variables

See `environ`(5) for descriptions of the following environment variables that affect the execution of `strip`: LC_CTYPE, LC_MESSAGES, and NLSPATH.

Exit Status

0	Successful completion.
>0	An error occurred.

Files

`/tmp/strp*`	Temporary files.

Attributes

See `attributes`(5) for descriptions of the following attributes:

Attribute Type	**Attribute Value**
Availability	SUNWbtool

See Also

`ar`(1), `as`(1), `ld`(1), `elf`(3E), `tmpnam`(3S), `a.out`(4), `ar`(4), `attributes`(5), `environ`(5)

stty — Set the Options for a Terminal

Synopsis

```
/usr/bin/stty [-a] [-g]
/usr/bin/stty [modes]
/usr/xpg4/bin/stty [-a | -g]
/usr/xpg4/bin/stty [modes]
```

Description

The `stty` command sets certain terminal I/O options for the device that is the current standard input; without arguments, it reports the settings of certain options.

In this section, if a character is preceded by a caret (^), then the value of that option is the corresponding control character (for example, ^h is Control-H; Control-H is the same as the backspace key.) The sequence ^ means that an option has a null value.

See `termio`(7I) for detailed information about the modes listed from "Control Modes through Local Modes." For detailed information about the modes listed under "Hardware Flow Control Modes" and "Clock Modes," see `termiox`(7I).

Operands described in the "Combination Modes" section are implemented by options described in the earlier sections. Note that many combinations of options make no sense, but no sanity checking is performed. Hardware flow control and clock modes options may not be supported by all hardware interfaces.

Options

-a   Write to standard output all of the option settings for the terminal.

-g   Report current settings in a form that can be used as an argument to another `stty` command. Emit termios-type output if the underlying driver supports it; otherwise, emit termio-type output.

Operands

Control Modes

parenb (-parenb)

Enable (disable) parity generation and detection.

parext (-parext)

Enable (disable) extended parity generation and detection for mark and space parity.

parodd (-parodd)

Select odd (even) parity, or mark (space) parity if parext is enabled.

cs5 cs6 cs7 cs8

Select character size (see `termio`(7I)).

0   Hang up line immediately.

110 300 600 1200 1800 2400 4800 9600 19200 38400 357600 76800 115200 153600 230400 307200 460800

Set terminal baud rate to the number given if possible. (All speeds are not supported by all hardware interfaces.)

ispeed 0 110 300 600 1200 1800 2400 4800 9600 19200 38400 57600 76800 115200 153600 230400 307200 460800

Set terminal input baud rate to the number given if possible. (Not all hardware supports split baud rates.) If the input baud rate is set to 0, use the value of the output baud rate to specify the input baud rate.

ospeed 0 110 300 600 1200 1800 2400 4800 9600 19200 38400 57600 76800 115200 153600 230400 307200 460800

Set terminal output baud rate to the number given if possible. (Not all hardware supports split baud rates.) If the output baud rate is set to 0, hang up the line immediately.

hupcl (-hupcl)

>   Hang up (do not hang up) connection on last close.

hup (-hup)   Same as hupcl (-hupcl).

cstopb (-cstopb)

>   Use two (one) stop bits per character.

cread (-cread)

>   Enable (disable) the receiver.

crtscts (-crtscts)

>   Enable output hardware flow control. Raise the RTS (Request to Send)
>   modem control line. Suspend output until the CTS (Clear to Send) line
>   is raised.

crtsxoff (-crtsxoff)

>   Enable (disable) input hardware flow control. Raise the RTS (Request
>   to Send) modem control line to receive data. Suspend input when RTS
>   is low.

clocal (-clocal)

>   Assume a line without (with) modem control.

loblk (-loblk)

>   Block (do not block) output from a noncurrent layer.

defeucw   Set the widths of multibyte Extended Unix Code (EUC) characters in
>   struct eucioc to default values for the current locale specified by
>   LC_CTYPE; width is expressed in terms of bytes per character, and
>   screen or display columns per character (see getwidth(3C) and
>   ldterm(7M)).

Input Modes

ignbrk (-ignbrk)

>   Ignore (do not ignore) break on input.

brkint (-brkint)

>   Signal (do not signal) interrupt (INTR) on break.

ignpar (-ignpar)

>   Ignore (do not ignore) parity errors.

parmrk (-parmrk)

>   Mark (do not mark) parity errors (see termio(7I)).

inpck (-inpck)

>   Enable (disable) input parity checking.

istrip (-istrip)

>   Strip (do not strip) input characters to seven bits.

inlcr (-inlcr)

> Map (do not map) NL to CR on input.

igncr (-igncr)

> Ignore (do not ignore) CR on input.

icrnl (-icrnl)

> Map (do not map) CR to NL on input.

iuclc (-iuclc)

> Map (do not map) uppercase alphabetics to lower case on input.

ixon (-ixon)

> Enable (disable) START/STOP output control. Stop output by sending STOP control character, and start it by sending the START control character.

ixany (-ixany)

> Allow any character (only DC1) to restart output.

ixoff (-ixoff)

> Request that the system send (not send) START/STOP characters when the input queue is nearly empty/full.

imaxbel (-imaxbel)

> Echo (do not echo) BEL when the input line is too long.

Output Modes

opost (-opost)

> Postprocess output (do not postprocess output; ignore all other output modes).

olcuc (-olcuc)

> Map (do not map) lowercase alphabetics to upper case on output.

onlcr (-onlcr)

> Map (do not map) NL to CR-NL on output.

ocrnl (-ocrnl)

> Map (do not map) CR to NL on output.

onocr (-onocr)

> Do not (do) output CRs at column 0.

onlret (-onlret)

> On the terminal, NL performs (does not perform) the CR function.

ofill (-ofill)

> Use fill characters (use timing) for delays.

ofdel (-ofdel)

>Fill characters are DELs (null).

cr0 cr1 cr2 cr3

>Select style of delay for Returns (see termio(7I)).

nl0 nl1 Select style of delay for linefeeds (see termio(7I)).

tab0 tab1 tab2 tab3

>Select style of delay for horizontal Tabs (see termio(7I)).

bs0 bs1 Select style of delay for backspaces (see termio(7I)).

ff0 ff1 Select style of delay for formfeeds (see termio(7I)).

vt0 vt1 Select style of delay for vertical Tabs (see termio(7I)).

Local Modes

isig (-isig)

>Enable (disable) the checking of characters against the special control characters INTR, QUIT, SWTCH, and SUSP.

icanon (-icanon)

>Enable (disable) canonical input (ERASE and KILL processing). Does not set MIN or TIME.

xcase (-xcase)

>Canonical (unprocessed) upper-/lowercase presentation.

echo (-echo)

>Echo back (do not echo back) every character typed.

echoe (-echoe)

>Echo (do not echo) ERASE character as a backspace-space-backspace string. Note that this mode erases the ERASEd character on many CRT terminals; however, it does not keep track of column position and, as a result, it can be confusing for escaped characters, Tabs, and backspaces.

echok (-echok)

>Echo (do not echo) NL after KILL character.

lfkc (-lfkc)

>The same as echok (-echok); obsolete.

echonl (-echonl)

>Echo (do not echo) NL.

noflsh (-noflsh)

>Disable (enable) flush after INTR, QUIT, or SUSP.

stwrap (-stwrap)

> Disable (enable) truncation of lines longer than 79 characters on a synchronous line.

tostop (-tostop)

> Send (do not send) SIGTTOU when background processes write to the terminal.

echoctl (-echoctl)

> Echo (do not echo) control characters as ^*char*; delete as ^?.

echoprt (-echoprt)

> Echo (do not echo) erase character as character is erased.

echoke (-echoke)

> BS-SP-BS erase (do not BS-SP-BS erase) entire line on line kill.

flusho (-flusho)

> Output is (is not) being flushed.

pendin (-pendin)

> Retype (do not retype) pending input at next read or input character.

iexten (-iexten)

> Enable (disable) special control characters not currently controlled by icanon, isig, ixon, or ixoff: VEOLZ, VSWTCH, VREPRINT, VDISCARD, VDSUSP, VWERASE, and VLNEXT.

stflush (-stflush)

> Enable (disable) flush on a synchronous line after every write(2).

stappl (-stappl)

> Use application mode (use line mode) on a synchronous line.

Hardware Flow Control Modes

rtsxoff (-rtsxoff)

> Enable (disable) RTS hardware flow control on input.

ctsxon (-ctsxon)

> Enable (disable) CTS hardware flow control on output.

dtrxoff (-dtrxoff)

> Enable (disable) DTR hardware flow control on input.

cdxon (-cdxon)

> Enable (disable) CD hardware flow control on output.

isxoff (-isxoff)

> Enable (disable) isochronous hardware flow control on input.

Clock Modes

xcibrg   Get transmit clock from internal baud rate generator.

xctset   Get the transmit clock from transmitter-signal-element timing (DCE source) lead, CCITT V.24 circuit 114, EIA-232-D pin 15.

xcrset   Get transmit clock from receiver-signal-element timing (DCE source) lead, CCITT V.24 circuit 115, EIA-232-D pin 17.

rcibrg   Get receive clock from internal baud rate generator.

rctset   Get receive clock from transmitter-signal-element timing (DCE source) lead, CCITT V.24 circuit 114, EIA-232-D pin 15.

rcrset   Get receive clock from receiver-signal-element timing (DCE source) lead, CCITT V.24 circuit 115, EIA-232-D pin 17.

tsetcoff   Transmitter-signal-element timing clock not provided.

tsetcrbrg   Output receive baud rate generator on transmitter-signal-element timing (DTE source) lead, CCITT V.24 circuit 113, EIA-232-D pin 24.

tsetctbrg   Output transmit baud rate generator on transmitter-signal-element timing (DTE source) lead, CCITT V.24 circuit 113, EIA-232-D pin 24.

tsetctset   Output transmitter-signal-element timing (DCE source) on transmitter-signal-element timing (DTE source) lead, CCITT V.24 circuit 113, EIA-232-D pin 24.

tsetcrset   Output receiver-signal-element timing (DCE source) on transmitter-signal-element timing (DTE source) lead, CCITT V.24 circuit 113, EIA-232-D pin 24.

rsetcoff   Receiver-signal-element timing clock not provided.

rsetcrbrg   Output receive baud rate generator on receiver-signal-element timing (DTE source) lead, CCITT V.24 circuit 128, no EIA-232-D pin.

rsetctbrg   Output transmit baud rate generator on receiver-signal-element timing (DTE source) lead, CCITT V.24 circuit 128, no EIA-232-D pin.

rsetctset   Output transmitter-signal-element timing (DCE source) on receiver-signal-element timing (DTE source) lead, CCITT V.24 circuit 128, no EIA-232-D pin.

rsetcrset   Output receiver-signal-element timing (DCE source) on receiver-signal-element timing (DTE source) lead, CCITT V.24 circuit 128, no EIA-232-D pin.

Control Assignments

control-character c

> Set *control-character* to *c*, where *control-character* is ctab, discard, dsusp, eof, eol, eol2, erase, intr, kill, lnext, quit, reprint, start, stop, susp, swtch, or werase (ctab is used with -stappl; see termio(7I)).

c	If *c* is a single character, set the control character to that character. In the POSIX locale, if *c* is preceded by a caret (^), indicating an escape from the shell, and is one of those listed in the ^c column of the following table, then use its value (in the Value column) as the corresponding control character (for example, ^d is a Control-D). ^? is interpreted as DEL, and ^- is interpreted as undefined.

^*c*	Value	^*c*	Value	^*c*	Value	^*c*	Value
a, A	<SOH>	l, L	<FF>	w, W	<ETB>		
b, B	<STX>	m, M	<CR>	x, X	<CAN>		
c, C	<ETX>	n, N	<SO>	y, Y	<EM>		
d, D	<EOT>	o, O	<SI>	z, Z	<SUB>		
e, E	<ENQ>	p, P	<DLE>	[	<ESC>		
f, F	<ACK>	q, Q	<DC1>	\	<FS>		
g, G	<BEL>	r, R	<DC2>	]	<GS>		
h, H	<BS>	s, S	<DC3>	^	<RS>		
i, I	<HT>	t, T	<DC4>	_	<US>		
j, J	<LF>	u, U	<NAK>	?	<DEL>		
k, K	<VT>	v, V	<SYN>				

min *number*

time *number*

      Set the value of min or time to *number*. MIN and TIME are used in noncanonical mode input processing (-icanon).

line *i*   Set line discipline to i (0<*i*<127).

Combination Modes

savedsettings

      Set the current terminal characteristics to the saved settings produced by the -g option.

evenp or parity

      Enable parenb and cs7, or disable parodd.

oddp   Enable parenb, cs7, and parodd.

spacep   Enable parenb, cs7, and parext.

markp   Enable parenb, cs7, parodd, and parext.

-parity or -evenp

      Disable parenb, and set cs8.

`-oddp`	Disable `parenb` and `parodd`, and set `cs8`.
`-spacep`	Disable `parenb` and `parext`, and set `cs8`.
`-markp`	Disable `parenb`, `parodd`, and `parext`, and set `cs8`.
`raw` (`-raw` or `cooked`)	
	Enable (disable) raw input and output. Raw mode is equivalent to setting:

```
stty cs8 -icanon min 1 time 0 -isig -xcase -inpck -opost
```

/usr/bin/stty

| `nl` (`-nl`) | Unset (set) `icrnl`, `onlcr`. In addition, `-nl` unsets `inlcr`, `igncr`, `ocrnl`, and `onlret`. |

/usr/xpg4/bin/stty

`nl` (`-nl`)	Set (unset) `icrnl`. In addition, `-nl` unsets `inlcr`, `igncr`, `ocrnl`, and `onlret`; `-nl` sets `onlcr`, and `nl` unsets `onlcr`.
`lcase` (`-lcase`)	
	Set (unset) `xcase`, `iuclc`, and `olcuc`.
`LCASE` (`-LCASE`)	
	Same as `lcase` (`-lcase`).
`tabs` (`-tabs` or `tab3`)	
	Preserve (expand to spaces) Tabs when printing.
`ek`	Reset `ERASE` and `KILL` characters back to normal # and @.
`sane`	Reset all modes to some reasonable values.
`term`	Set all modes suitable for the terminal type *term*, where *term* is one of `tty33`, `tty37`, `vt05`, `tn300`, `ti700`, or `tek`.
`async`	Set normal asynchronous communications, where clock settings are `xcibrg`, `rcibrg`, `tsetcoff`, and `rsetcoff`.

Window Size

`rows` *n*	Set window size to *n* rows.
`columns` *n*	Set window size to *n* columns.
`cols` *n*	Set window size to *n* columns. Note that `cols` is a shorthand alias for `columns`.
`ypixels` *n*	Set vertical window size to *n* pixels.
`xpixels` *n*	Set horizontal window size to *n* pixels.

Usage

The `-g` option is designed to facilitate the saving and restoring of terminal state from the shell level. For example, a program can do the following:

```
saveterm="$(stty -g)"          # save terminal state
stty (new settings)            # set new state
...                            # ...
stty $saveterm                 # restore terminal state
```

Because the -a format is so loosely specified, scripts that save and restore terminal settings should use the -g option.

Examples

The following example shows the output from the stty command when no options are specified.

```
castle% stty
ispeed 89376 baud; ospeed 89360 baud; -parity cstopb hupcl loblk
rows = 37; columns = 80; ypixels = 491; xpixels = 570;
quit = <undef>; erase = ^h; swtch = <undef>;
-inpck -istrip icrnl -ixany ixoff onlcr
echo echoe echok echoctl echoke iexten
castle%
```

Environment Variables

See environ(5) for descriptions of the following environment variables that affect the execution of stty: LC_CTYPE, LC_MESSAGES, and NLSPATH.

Exit Status

0	Successful completion.
>0	An error occurred.

Attributes

See attributes(5) for descriptions of the following attributes:

/usr/bin/stty

Attribute Type	Attribute Value
Availability	SUNWcsu

/usr/xpg4/bin/stty

Attribute Type	Attribute Value
Availability	SUNWxcu4

See Also

tabs(1), ioctl(2), write(2), getwidth(3C), attributes(5), environ(5), ldterm(7M), termio(7I), termiox(7I)

sum — Print Checksum and Block Count for a File

Synopsis

```
/usr/bin/sum [-r] [file...]
/usr/ucb/sum [file...]
```

Description

The sum command calculates and prints a 16-bit checksum for the named *file* and the number of 512-byte blocks in the file. It is typically used to look for bad spots or to validate a file communicated over some transmission line.

Portable applications should use cksum(1).

Note — sum and /usr/ucb/sum (see sum(1B)) return different checksums.

Options

-r   Use an alternative (machine-dependent) algorithm in computing the checksum.

Operands

file   A path name of a file. If you specify no files, use the standard input.

Examples

The following example displays a checksum for the file kookaburra-1.

```
castle% sum kookaburra-1
23823 1 kookaburra-1
castle%
```

Usage

See largefile(5) for the description of the behavior of sum when encountering files greater than or equal to 2 Gbytes (2** 31 bytes).

Environment Variables

See environ(5) for descriptions of the following environment variables that affect the execution of sum: LC_CTYPE, LC_MESSAGES, and NLSPATH.

Exit Status

0   Successful completion.

>0   An error occurred.

Attributes

See attributes(5) for descriptions of the following attributes:

Attribute Type	Attribute Value
Availability	SUNWesu
CSI	Enabled

See Also

cksum(1), sum(1B), wc(1), attributes(5), environ(5), largefile(5)

Diagnostics

Read error is indistinguishable from end-of-file on most devices; check the block count.

sun — Get Processor Type Truth Value

Synopsis

/usr/bin/sun

Description

See machid(1).

suspend — Shell Built-in Function to Halt the Current Shell

Synopsis

sh, csh, and ksh
suspend

Description

Bourne and Korn Shell
Stops the execution of the current shell (but not if it is the login shell).

C Shell
Stop the shell in its tracks much as if it had been sent a stop signal with ^Z. This function is most often used to stop shells started by su.

Attributes

See attributes(5) for descriptions of the following attributes:

Attribute Type	Attribute Value
Availability	SUNWcsu

See Also

csh(1), kill(1), ksh(1), sh(1), su(1M), attributes(5)

symorder — Rearrange a List of Symbols

Synopsis

/usr/ccs/bin/symorder [-s] *objectfile symbolfile*

Description

The symorder command was used in SunOS 4.x specifically to cut down on the overhead of getting symbols from vmunix. This command is no longer applicable because kernel symbol entries are dynamically obtained through /dev/ksyms.

This script is provided as a convenience for software developers who need to maintain scripts that are portable across a variety of operating systems.

Exit Status

symorder has exit status 0.

Attributes

See attributes(5) for descriptions of the following attributes:

Attribute Type	**Attribute Value**
Availability	SUNWbtool

See Also

nlist(3E), attributes(5), ksyms(7D)

sysV-make — Maintain, Update, and Regenerate Groups of Programs

Synopsis

/usr/lib/svr4.make [-f *makefile*] [-eiknpqrst] [*names*]

Description

The sysV-make command is the vanilla System V version of make. If the environment variable USE_SVR4_MAKE is set, then the make command invokes this version of make.

make enables the programmer to maintain, update, and regenerate groups of computer programs. make executes commands in *makefile* to update one or more target *names* (*names* are typically programs). If you do not specify the -f option, then makefile, Makefile, and the Source Code Control System (SCCS) files s.makefile, and s.Makefile are tried in order. If *makefile* is a dash (-), the standard input is taken. You can specify more than one -f *makefile* argument pair.

make updates a target only if its dependents are newer than the target. All prerequisite files of a target are added recursively to the list of targets. Missing files are deemed to be outdated.

You can include the directives from the following list in *makefile* to extend the options provided by make. The directives are used in *makefile* as if they were targets.

.DEFAULT: If a file must be made but there are no explicit commands or relevant built-in rules, use the commands associated with the name .DEFAULT if it exists.

.IGNORE: Same as the -i option.

.PRECIOUS: Do not remove dependents of the .PRECIOUS entry when quit or interrupt is pressed.

.SILENT: Same as the -s option.

Note — Some commands return status inappropriately; use -i or a dash (-) command-line prefix to overcome the difficulty.

File names containing the characters =, :, and @ do not work. Commands that are directly executed by the shell, notably cd(1), are ineffectual across newlines in make. The syntax lib(file1.o file2.o file3.o) is illegal. You cannot build lib(file.o) from file.o.

Options

-e Let environment variables override assignments within makefiles.

-f *makefile*

   Specify the name of a description file.

-i Ignore error codes returned by invoked commands.

-k Abandon work on the current entry if it fails, but continue on other branches that do not depend on that entry.

-n Print commands, but do not execute them. Print command lines even if they begin with an @.

-p Print the complete set of macro definitions and target descriptions.

-q Question whether the target file has been updated. make returns a 0 or non-zero status code.

-r Do not use the built-in rules.

-s Do not print command lines before executing.

-t Touch the target files (updating them) instead of issuing the usual commands.

Creating the makefile

The *makefile* invoked with the -f option is a carefully structured file of explicit instructions for updating and regenerating programs. It contains a sequence of entries that specify dependencies. The first line of an entry is a blank-separated, non-null list of targets, then a :, then a (possibly null) list of prerequisite files or dependencies. Text following a ; and all following lines that begin with a Tab are shell commands to be

executed to update the target. The first nonempty line that does not begin with a Tab or
begins a new dependency or macro definition. You can continue shell commands across
lines with a backslash-newline (\-newline) sequence. Everything printed by make
(except the initial Tab) is passed directly to the shell as is. Thus, the following sequence

```
echo a\
b
```

produces

```
ab
```

exactly as the shell would. Number sign (#) and newline surround comments including
contained \-newline sequences.

The following *makefile* says that pgm depends on two files, a.o and b.o, and that
they, in turn, depend on their corresponding source files (a.c and b.c) and a common file
incl.h.

```
pgm: a.o b.o
cc a.o b.o -o pgm
a.o: incl.h a.c
     cc -c a.c
b.o: incl.h b.c
     cc -c b.c
```

Command lines are executed one at a time, each by its own shell. You can use the
SHELL environment variable to specify which shell make should use to execute
commands. The default is /usr/bin/sh. The first one or two characters in a command
can be @, -, @-, or -@. If @ is present, printing of the command is suppressed. If a dash
(-) is present, make ignores an error. A line is printed when it is executed unless you
specify the -s option, the entry .SILENT: is included in *makefile*, or the initial
character sequence contains a @. The -n option specifies printing without execution;
however, if the command line has the string $(MAKE) in it, the line is always executed
(see the discussion of the MAKEOPTIONS macro in "make Environment" on page 1360).
The -t (touch) option updates the modified date of a file without executing any
commands.

Commands returning non-zero status normally terminate make. If you specify the -i
option, if the entry .IGNORE: is included in *makefile*, or if the initial character sequence
of the command contains a dash (-), the error is ignored. If you specify the -k option,
work is abandoned on the current entry but continues on other branches that do not
depend on that entry.

Interrupt and quit delete the target unless the target is a dependent of the directive
.PRECIOUS:.

make Environment

The environment is read by make. All variables are assumed to be macro definitions and
are processed as such. The environment variables are processed before any *makefile*
and after the internal rules; thus, macro assignments in a *makefile* override
environment variables. The -e option overrides the macro assignments in a *makefile*.
Suffixes and their associated rules in the *makefile* override any identical suffixes in the
built-in rules.

The MAKEFLAGS environment variable is processed by make as containing any legal
input option (except -f and -p) defined for the command line. Further, on invocation,
make "invents" the variable if it is not in the environment, puts the current options into
it, and passes it on to invocations of commands. Thus, MAKEFLAGS always contains the

current input options. This feature proves very useful for "supermakes." In fact, as noted above, when you use the -n option, the command $ (MAKE) is executed anyway; hence, you can perform a make -n recursively on a whole software system to see what would have been executed. This result is possible because the -n is put in MAKEFLAGS and passed to further invocations of $ (MAKE). This usage is one way of debugging all of the makefiles for a software project without actually doing anything.

Include Files

If the string include appears as the first seven letters of a line in a *makefile* and is followed by a blank or a Tab, the rest of the line is assumed to be a file name and is read by the current invocation after any macros are substituted.

Macros

Entries of the form *string1* = *string2* are macro definitions.

   string2 is defined as all characters up to a comment character or an unescaped newline. Subsequent appearances of $ (*string1* [: *subst1*= [*subst2*]]) are replaced by *string2*. The parentheses are optional if you use a single-character macro name and there is no substitute sequence. The optional : *subst1*= *subst2* is a substitute sequence. If you specify it, all nonoverlapping occurrences of *subst1* in the named macro are replaced by *subst2*. Strings (for the purposes of this type of substitution) are delimited by blanks, Tabs, newline characters, and beginnings of lines. An example of the use of the substitute sequence is shown in "Libraries" on page 1363.

Internal Macros

Five internally maintained macros are useful for writing rules for building targets.

$*   The file-name part of the current dependent with the suffix deleted. Evaluated only for inference rules.

$@   The full target name of the current target. Evaluated only for explicitly named dependencies.

$<   Evaluated only for inference rules or the . DEFAULT rule. It is the module that is outdated with respect to the target (the "manufactured" dependent file name). Thus, in the .c.o rule, the $< macro would evaluate to the .c file. An example for making optimized .o files from .c files is:

```
.c.o:
     cc -c -O $*.c
```

or

```
.c.o:
     cc -c -O $<
```

$?   Evaluated when explicit rules from the *makefile* are evaluated. It is the list of prerequisites that are outdated with respect to the target and, essentially, those modules that must be rebuilt.

$%   Evaluated only when the target is an archive library member of the form lib(file.o). In this case, $@ evaluates to lib and $% evaluates to the library member, file.o.

All macros except $? can have alternative forms. When you append an uppercase D or F to any of the four macros, the meaning is changed to "directory part" for D and "file part" for F. Thus, $(@D) refers to the directory part of the string $@. If there is no directory part, ./ is generated.

Suffixes

Certain names (for instance, those ending with .o) have inferable prerequisites such as .c, .s, and so forth. If no update commands for such a file appear in *makefile* and if an inferable prerequisite exists, that prerequisite is compiled to make the target. In this case, make has inference rules that enable it to build files from other files by examining the suffixes and determining an appropriate inference rule to use. The current default inference rules are:

.c	.c~	.f	.f~	.s	.s~	.sh	.sh~	.C	.C~
.c.a	.c.o	.c~.a	.c~.c	.c~.o	.f.a	.f.o	.f~.a	.f~.f	.f~.o
.h~.h	.l.c	.l.o	.l~.c	.l~.l	.l~.o	.s.a	.s.o	.s~.a	.s~.o
.s~.s	.sh~.sh	.y.c	.y.o	.y~.c	.y~.o	.y~.y	.C.a	.C.o	.C~.a
.C~.C	.C~.o	.L.C	.L.o	.L~.C	.L~.L	.L~.o	.Y.C	.Y.o	.Y~.C

The internal rules for make are contained in the source file make.rules for the make program. These rules can be locally modified. To print out the rules compiled into the make on any machine in a form suitable for recompilation, use the following command.

make -pf - 2>/dev/null </dev/null

A tilde in the above rules refers to an SCCS file (see sccsfile(4)). Thus, the rule .c~.o would transform an SCCS C source file into an object file (.o). Because the s. of the SCCS files is a prefix, it is incompatible with the make suffix point of view. Hence, the tilde is a way of changing any file reference into an SCCS file reference.

A rule with only one suffix (for example, .c:) is the definition of how to build x from x.c. In effect, the other suffix is null. This feature is useful for building targets from only one source file, for example, shell procedures and simple C programs.

Additional suffixes are given as the dependency list for .SUFFIXES. Order is significant: the first possible name for which both a file and a rule exist is inferred as a prerequisite. The default list is:

.SUFFIXES: .o .c .c~.y .y~ .l .l~ .s .s~ .sh .sh~ .h .h~ .f .f~ .C .C~
  .Y .Y~ .L .L~

Here again, the above command for printing the internal rules displays the list of suffixes implemented on the current machine. Multiple suffix lists accumulate; .SUFFIXES: with no dependencies clears the list of suffixes.

Inference Rules

The first example can be done more briefly.

```
pgm: a.o b.o
              cc a.o b.o -o pgm
a.o b.o: incl.h
```

This abbreviation is possible because make has a set of internal rules for building files. You can add rules to this list by simply putting them in the makefile.

Certain macros are used by the default inference rules to permit the inclusion of optional matter in any resulting commands. For example, CFLAGS, LFLAGS, and YFLAGS are used for compiler options to cc(1B). Again, the previous method for examining the current rules is recommended.

The inference of prerequisites can be controlled. The rule to create a file with suffix .o from a file with suffix .c is specified as an entry with .c.o: as the target and no dependents. Shell commands associated with the target define the rule for making a .o file from a .c file. Any target that has no slashes in it and starts with a dot is identified as a rule and not a true target.

Libraries

If a target or dependency name contains parentheses, it is assumed to be an archive library. The string within parentheses refers to a member within the library. Thus, lib(file.o) and $(LIB)(file.o) both refer to an archive library that contains file.o. (This example assumes the LIB macro has been previously defined.) The expression $(LIB)(file1.o file2.o) is not legal. Rules pertaining to archive libraries have the form .XX.a, where the XX is the suffix from which the archive member is to be made. An unfortunate byproduct of the current implementation requires the XX to be different from the suffix of the archive member. Thus, you cannot have lib(file.o) depend on file.o explicitly. The most common use of the archive interface follows. Here, we assume the source files are all C type source.

```
lib: lib(file1.o) lib(file2.o) lib(file3.o)
@echo lib is now up-to-date
.c.a:
        $(CC) -c $(CFLAGS) $<
        $(AR) $(ARFLAGS) $@ $*.o
        rm -f $*.o
```

In fact, the .c.a rule listed above is built into make and is unnecessary in this example. A more interesting but more limited example of an archive library maintenance construction is the following.

```
lib: lib(file1.o) lib(file2.o) lib(file3.o)
$(CC) -c $(CFLAGS) $(?:.o=.c)
        $(AR) $(ARFLAGS) lib $?
        rm $?
        @echo lib is now up-to-date
.c.a:;
```

Here, the substitution mode of the macro expansions is used. The $? list is defined to be the set of object file names (inside lib) whose C source files are outdated. The substitution mode translates the .o to .c. (Unfortunately, you cannot as yet transform to .c~; however, this transformation may become possible in the future.) Also note the disabling of the .c.a: rule, which would have created each object file, one by one. This particular construct speeds up archive library maintenance considerably. This type of construct becomes very cumbersome if the archive library contains a mix of assembly programs and C programs.

Environment Variables

USE_SVR4_MAKE

If this environment variable is set, then the make command invokes the System V version of make. If this variable is not set, then the default version of make(1S) is invoked.

You can set USE_SVR4_MAKE as follows (Bourne shell).

```
$ USE_SVR4_MAKE=""; export USE_SVR4_MAKE
```

The C shell syntax is as follows.

```
% setenv USE_SVR4_MAKE
```

Files

[Mm]akefile and s.[Mm]akefile

Default makefiles.

/usr/bin/sh

Default shell for make.

/usr/share/lib/make/make.rules

Default rules for make.

Attributes

See attributes(5) for descriptions of the following attributes:

Attribute Type	Attribute Value
Availability	SUNWsprot

See Also

cd(1), sh(1), cc(1B), make(1S), printf(3C), sccsfile(4), attributes(5)

T

---

t300, t300s, t4014, t450 — Graphics Filters for Various Plotters

Synopsis

    /usr/bin/tplot [-Tterminal]

Description

See tplot(1).

---

tabs — Set Tabs on a Terminal

Synopsis

    /usr/bin/tabs [-n | --file | [[-code] -a | -a2 | -c | -c2 | -c3 | -f |
       -p | -s | -u]] [+m[n]] [-T type]
    /usr/bin/tabs [-T type] [+m[n]] n1[,n2,...]

Description

Use the tabs command to clear any previous settings and reset the Tab stops on your terminal according to a Tab specification. Your terminal must have remotely settable hardware Tabs.

Different terminals are inconsistent in how they clear Tabs and set the left margin. tabs clears only 20 Tabs (on terminals requiring a long sequence), but it can set up to 64.

Note — The syntax for setting Tabs with the tabs command is slightly different from the one used with the newform command. For example, tabs -8 sets Tabs at every eighth position, whereas newform -i-8 sets Tabs at every eighth position.

Options

If you use a given option more than once, tabs uses the last value.

-T *type*   Set the Tabs and margins by specifying *type* as a name listed in term(5). If you do not specify the -T option, use the value of the environment variable TERM. If the value of TERM is null or TERM is not defined in the environment (see environ(5)), use ansi+tabs as the terminal type to provide a sequence that works for many terminals.

+m[*n*]   For some terminals, move all Tabs over *n* columns by making column *n*+1 the left margin. If you specify +m without a value of *n*, the default value is 10. For a TermiNet, the first value in the Tab list should be 1 or the margin moves even farther to the right. Specify the normal (leftmost) margin on most terminals with +m0. The margin for most terminals is reset only when you specify the +m option.

Tab Specification

The following four types of Tab specification are accepted.

- Canned.
- Repetitive (*-n*).
- Arbitrary (*n1,n2,...*).
- File (*--file*).

If you provide no Tab specification, the default value is -8, that is, UNIX system "standard" Tabs. The lowest column number is 1.

Note — For Tabs, column 1 always refers to the leftmost column on a terminal, even one whose column markers begin at 0, for example, the DASI 300, DASI 300s, and DASI 450.

Canned

Use one of the codes listed below to select a canned set of Tabs that you specify with the *-code* option. If you specify more than one *code*, the last code option is used. The legal codes and their meanings are shown below.

-a   1,10,16,36,72
          Assembler, IBM S/370, first format.

-a2   1,10,16,40,72
          Assembler, IBM S/370, second format.

-c   1,8,12,16,20,55
          COBOL, normal format.

-c2   1,6,10,14,49
                COBOL compact format (columns 1–6 omitted). When this code is used,
                the first typed character corresponds to card column 7, one space gets
                you to column 8, and a Tab reaches column 12. Files using this Tab
                setup should include a format specification as shown below (see
                fspec(4)).

                <:t-c2 m6 s66 d:>

-c3   1,6,10,14,18,22,26,30,34,38,42,46,50,54,58,62,67
                COBOL compact format (columns 1–6 omitted), with more Tabs than
                -c2. This format is recommended for COBOL. The appropriate format
                specification is shown below (see fspec(4)).

                <:t-c3 m6 s66 d:>

-f   1,7,11,15,19,23
                FORTRAN.

-p   1,5,9,13,17,21,25,29,33,37,41,45,49,53,57,61
                PL/I.

-s   1,10,55
                SNOBOL.

-u   1,12,20,44
                UNIVAC 1100 Assembler.

Repetitive

-*n*   A repetitive specification requests Tabs at columns $1+n$, $1+2*n$, and so
                forth, where n is a single-digit decimal number. Of particular
                importance is the value 8, which represents the UNIX system standard
                Tab setting and is the most likely Tab setting to be found at a terminal.
                When you use -0, the Tab stops are cleared and no new ones are set.

Arbitrary
See "Operands" on page 1368.

File

--*file*   If you specify the name of a file, tabs reads the first line of the file,
                searching for a format specification (see fspec(4)). If it finds one there,
                set the Tab stops according to it; otherwise, set them as -8. You can use
                this type of specification to make sure that a Tabbed file is printed with
                correct Tab settings. You would use it with the pr command, as shown
                in the following example.

                castle% **tabs** -- *file*; **pr** *file*

                The standard output sets Tabs and margins.

Operands

n1[,*n2*, ...]   The arbitrary format consists of Tab-stop values separated with commas or spaces. The Tab-stop values must be positive decimal integers in ascending order. Up to 40 numbers are allowed. If you precede any number (except the first one) by a plus sign, take it as an increment to be added to the previous value. Thus, the formats 1,10,20,30, and 1,10,+10,+10 are considered identical.

Examples

The following example uses the *-code* canned specification to set Tabs to the settings required by the IBM assembler, that is, columns 1, 10, 16, 36, 72.

```
castle% tabs -a
```

The following example uses the *-n* repetitive specification, where *n* is 8, to set Tabs every eight positions, that is, 1+(1*8), 1+(2*8),..., which evaluates to columns 9, 17,....

```
castle% tabs -8
```

The following example uses the *n1*,*n2*, . . . arbitrary specification to set Tabs at columns 1, 8, and 36.

```
castle% tabs 1,8,36
```

The following example uses the *-- file* file specification to set Tabs, using the first line of $HOME/fspec.list/att4425 (see fspec(4)).

```
castle% tabs --$HOME/fspec.list/att4425
```

Environment Variables

See environ(5) for descriptions of the following environment variables that affect the execution of tabs: LC_CTYPE, LC_MESSAGES, and NLSPATH.

TERM   Determine the terminal type. If this variable is unset or null and if you do not specify the -T option, use terminal type ansi+tabs.

Exit Status

0   Successful completion.

>0   An error occurred.

Attributes

See attributes(5) for descriptions of the following attributes:

Attribute Type	Attribute Value
Availability	SUNWcsu
CSI	Enabled

See Also

expand(1), newform(1), pr(1), stty(1), tput(1), fspec(4), terminfo(4), attributes(5), environ(5), term(5)

tail — Look at the Last Part of a File

Synopsis

```
/usr/bin/tail [±number [lbcr]] [file]
/usr/bin/tail [-lbcr] [file]
/usr/bin/tail [±number [lbcf]] [file]
/usr/bin/tail [-lbcf] [file]
/usr/xpg4/bin/tail [-f | -r] [-c number | -n number] [file]
/usr/xpg4/bin/tail [±number [l | b | c] [f]] [file]
/usr/xpg4/bin/tail [±number [l] [f | r]] [file]
```

Description

Use the `tail` command to look at the end of a file. By default, the last 10 lines are displayed. You can change the number of lines displayed by using the `-n` *number* option to specify the number of lines to be displayed. If you do not specify a file name, the standard input is used.

Lines are displayed to standard output beginning at a point in the file indicated by the `-c` *number*, `-n` *number*, or *±number* options (if you specify *+number*, the display begins at distance *number* from the beginning; if you specify *-number*, the count is done from the end of the input; if *number* is null, the value 10 is assumed). *number* is counted in units of lines or bytes according to the `-c` or `-n` options. Alternatively, you can append l, b, or c to the *number* to specify the count in lines, blocks, or bytes. When you specify no units, counting is by lines.

> **Note** — Piped tails relative to the end of the file are stored in a buffer and thus are limited in length. Various kinds of anomalous behavior can happen with character special files.

Options

The following options are supported for both `/usr/bin/tail` and `/usr/xpg4/bin/tail`. The `-r` and `-f` options are mutually exclusive. If you specify both, the `-f` option is ignored.

`-b`	Display units of blocks.
`-c`	Display units of bytes.
`-f`	If the input file is not a pipe, do not terminate after the line of the input file has been displayed; instead, enter an endless loop, sleep for a second, and then try to read and display further records from the input file. You can use this option to monitor the growth of a file that is being written by some other process.
`-l`	Display units of lines.
`-r`	Display lines from the specified starting point in the file in reverse order. The default is to display the entire file in reverse order.

/usr/xpg4/bin/tail
The following options are supported for /usr/xpg4/bin/tail only.

-c *number*   Specify *number* as a decimal integer whose sign affects the location in the file, measured in bytes, to begin the display.

+   Start the display relative to the beginning of the file.

-        Start the display relative to the end of the file.

none   Start the display relative to the end of the file.

The origin for counting is 1; that is, -c +1 represents the first byte of the file, -c -1 the last.

-n *number*   Equivalent to -c *number*, except measure the starting location in the file in lines instead of bytes. The origin for counting is 1; that is, -n +1 represents the first byte of the file, -n -1 the last.

Operands

file   A path name of an input file. If you specify no file operands, use the standard input.

Usage

See largefile(5) for the description of the behavior of tail when encountering files greater than or equal to 2 Gbytes (2**31 bytes).

Examples

The following command displays the last 10 lines of the file /var/adm/sulog followed by any lines that are appended to the file between the time you initiate tail and the time you kill it.

```
# tail -f /var/adm/sulog
SU 04/04 15:13 + pts/6 winsor-root
SU 04/04 17:25 + pts/6 winsor-root
SU 04/05 12:46 + pts/6 winsor-root
SU 04/05 12:48 + pts/6 winsor-root
SU 04/05 17:41 + pts/6 winsor-root
SU 04/06 09:46 + pts/3 winsor-root
SU 04/06 18:22 + pts/6 winsor-root
SU 04/07 08:56 + pts/6 winsor-root
SU 04/07 13:41 + pts/3 winsor-root
SU 04/07 16:17 + pts/6 winsor-root
SU 04/07 16:17 + pts/3 winsor-root
SU 04/07 16:17 + pts/3 winsor-root
SU 04/07 16:17 + pts/3 winsor-root
SU 04/07 16:18 + pts/3 winsor-root
^C#
```

The following example displays the last 15 bytes of the file /var/adm/sulog followed by any lines that are appended to it between the time you initiate tail and the time you kill it.

```
# tail -15cf /var/adm/sulog
/3 winsor-root
SU 04/07 16:22 + pts/5 winsor-root
```

```
SU 04/07 16:23 + pts/5 winsor-root
SU 04/07 16:24 + pts/5 winsor-root
^C#
```

The following example displays the contents of the file kookaburra-2 in reverse
order.

```
castle% tail -r kookaburra-2
    8  Leave some there for me.
    7  Stop, kookaburra, stop, kookaburra
    6  Eating all the gumdrops he can see.
    5  Kookaburra sits in the old gum tree

    4  Gay your life must be.
    3  Laugh, kookaburra, laugh, kookaburra
    2  Merry merry king of the bush is he.
    1  Kookaburra sits in the old gum tree
castle%
```

Environment Variables

See environ(5) for descriptions of the following environment variables that affect the
execution of tail: LC_CTYPE, LC_MESSAGES, and NLSPATH.

Exit Status

| 0 | Successful completion. |
| >0 | An error occurred. |

Attributes

See attributes(5) for descriptions of the following attributes:

/usr/bin/tail

Attribute Type	Attribute Value
Availability	SUNWcsu
CSI	Enabled

/usr/xpg4/bin/tail

Attribute Type	Attribute Value
Availability	SUNWxcu4
CSI	Enabled

See Also

cat(1), head(1), more(1), pg(1), dd(1M), attributes(5), environ(5),
largefile(5), XPG4(5)

talk — Talk to Another User

Synopsis

/usr/bin/talk *address* [*terminal*]

Description

The talk command is a two-way, screen-oriented communication program.

When you first invoke it, talk sends a message similar to the following to the specified address.

Message from TalkDaemon@ *her-system* at time...
 talk: connection requested by *your-address*
 talk: respond with: talk *your-address*

At this point, the recipient of the message can reply by typing:

talk *your-address*

Once communication is established, the two parties can type simultaneously with their output displayed in separate regions of the screen. Characters are processed as follows.

- The alert character alerts the recipient's terminal.
- Control-L refreshes the sender's screen regions.
- The erase and kill characters affect the sender's terminal in the manner described by the termios(3) interface.
- The interrupt or end-of-file characters terminate the local talk command. Once the talk session has been terminated on one side, the other side of the talk session is notified that the talk session has been terminated and is able to do nothing except exit.
- Typing characters from the print or space LC_CTYPE classifications sends those characters to the recipient's terminal.
- When and only when the stty iexten local mode is enabled, additional special control characters and multibyte or single-byte characters are processed as printable characters if their wide-character equivalents are printable.
- Typing other nonprintable characters writes them to the recipient's terminal as follows: control characters appear as a caret (^) followed by the appropriate ASCII character, and characters with the high-order bit set appear in "meta" notation. For example, \003 is displayed as ^C and \372 as M-z.

You can grant or deny permission to be a recipient of a talk message with the mesg(1) command. However, a user's privilege can further constrain the domain of accessibility of other user' terminals. Certain commands, such as pr(1), disallow messages to prevent interference with their output. talk fails when the user lacks the appropriate privileges to perform the requested action.

Certain block-mode terminals do not have all the capabilities necessary to support the simultaneous exchange of messages required for talk. When this type of exchange cannot be supported on such terminals, the implementation may support an exchange with reduced levels of simultaneous interaction, or it may report an error describing the terminal-related deficiency.

Note — Typing Control-L redraws the screen, whereas the erase, kill, and word-kill characters work in talk as normal. To exit, type an interrupt character; talk then moves the cursor to the bottom of the screen and restores the terminal to its previous state.

Operands

address
: Specify the recipient of the talk session. One form of address is the *username*, as returned by the who(1) command. If you want to talk to someone on your own system, then *username* is the person's login name. If you want to talk to a user on another host, then *username* is one of the following forms.

  host! *user*

  host. *user*

  host: *user*

  user@*host* (preferred)

terminal
: If the recipient is logged in more than once, you can use *terminal* to indicate the appropriate terminal name. If you do not specify *terminal*, display the talk message on one or more accessible terminals in use by the recipient. The format of *terminal* is the same as that returned by who.

Environment Variables

See environ(5) for descriptions of the following environment variables that affect the execution of talk: LC_CTYPE, LC_MESSAGES, and NLSPATH.

TERM
: Determine the name of the invoker's terminal type. If this variable is unset or null, use an unspecified terminal type.

Exit Status

0
: Successful completion.

>0
: An error occurred, or talk was invoked on a terminal incapable of supporting it.

Files

/etc/hosts   Host-name database.

/var/adm/utmpx
: User and accounting information for talk.

Attributes

See attributes(5) for descriptions of the following attributes:

Attribute Type	Attribute Value
Availability	SUNWrcmds

New!

See Also
mail(1), mesg(1), pr(1), stty(1), who(1), write(1), termios(3),
attributes(5), environ(5)

tar — Create Tape Archives and Add or Extract Files

Synopsis

New! /usr/bin/tar c [bBeEfFhiklnopPqvwX@ [0-7]] [*block*] [*tarfile*]
    [*exclude-file*] {-I *include-file* | -C *directory file* | *file*}...

New! /usr/bin/tar r [bBeEfFhiklnqvw@ [0-7]] [*block*]
    {-I *include-file* | -C *directory file* | *file*}...

/usr/bin/tar t [BefFhiklnqvX [0-7]] [*tarfile*] [*exclude-file*]
    {-I *include-file* | *file*}...

New! /usr/bin/tar u [bBeEfFhiklnqvw@ [0-7]] [*block*] [*tarfile*] *file*...

/usr/bin/tar x [BefFhiklmnopqvwX [0-7]] [*tarfile*] [*exclude-file*]
    [*file*...]

Description
Use the tar command to copy files and directory subtrees to a single tape. The advantages of the tar command are that it is available on most UNIX operating systems and that public domain versions are readily available. The disadvantages of the tar command are that tar is not aware of file-system boundaries, full path-name length cannot exceed 255 characters, it does not copy empty directories or special files such as device files, and it cannot be used to create multiple tape volumes.

The tar command archives and extracts files to and from a single file called a *tarfile*. A tarfile is usually a magnetic tape but it can be any file. You control tar with the key argument, which is a string of characters containing exactly one function letter—c (create), r (replace), t (table of contents), u (update), or x (extract)—and zero or more function modifiers (letters or digits), depending on the function letter used. The key string contains no space characters. Function modifier arguments are listed on the command line in the same order as their corresponding function modifiers appear in the key string.

The -I *include-file*, -C *directory file*, and *file* arguments specify which files or directories are to be archived or extracted. In all cases, appearance of a directory name refers to the files and (recursively) subdirectories of that directory. Arguments appearing within braces ({}) indicate that you must specify one of the arguments.

Notes
You cannot access the *n*-th occurrence of a file.

Tape errors are handled ungracefully.

When the Volume Management daemon is running, accesses to diskette devices through the conventional device names (for example, /dev/rdiskette) may not succeed. See vold(1M) for further details.

The tar archive format allows UIDs and GIDs up to 2097151 to be stored in the archive header. Files with UIDs and GIDs greater than this value are archived with the UID and GID of 60001 (nobody).

If you create an archive that contains files whose names are created by processes running in multiple locales, use a single locale with a full 8-bit codeset (for example, the en_US locale) both to create the archive and to extract files from it.

You cannot use the -r or -u option with quarter-inch archive tapes because these tape drives cannot backspace. *New!*

Options

-I *include-file*

> Open *include-file* containing a list of files, one per line, and treat as if each file appeared separately on the command line. Be careful of trailing white spaces. When you also specify excluded files (see the X function modifier), they take precedence over all included files. If a file is specified in both the *exclude-file* and the *include-file* (or on the command line), exclude it.

-C *directory file*

> Perform a change directory (see cd(1)) operation on *directory* and perform the c (create) or r (replace) operation on *file*. Use short relative path names for *file*. If *file* is dot (.), archive all files in *directory*. This option enables archiving files from multiple directories not related by a close common parent.

Operands

file

> A path name of a regular file or directory to be archived (when you specify the c, r, or u functions), extracted (x), or listed (t). When *file* is the path name of a directory, apply the action to all of the files and (recursively) subdirectories of that directory. The directory portion of file (see dirname(1)) cannot exceed 155 characters. The file-name portion (see basename(1)) cannot exceed 100 characters.
>
> When you archive a file and do not specify the E function modifier, the file name cannot exceed 256 characters. In addition, it must be possible to split the name between parent directory names so that the prefix is no longer than 155 characters and the name is no longer than 100 characters. With the E function modifier, you can specify a name of up to PATH_MAX characters.
>
> For example, you cannot archive a file whose basename is longer than 100 characters without using the E function modifier. You could archive a file whose directory portion is 200 characters and whose basename is 50 characters without using the E function modifier if the directory name contains a slash somewhere in character positions 151–156.

Function Letters

Specify the function portion of the key with one of the following letters.

c
> Create by writing at the beginning of *tarfile* instead of at the end.

r
> Replace by writing the named files at the end of *tarfile*.

t
List the table of contents of the specified files each time they occur in *tarfile*. If you specify no file argument, list the names of all files in *tarfile*. With the v function modifier, display additional information for the specified files.

u
Update by writing the named files at the end of *tarfile* if they are not already in *tarfile* or if they have been modified since last written to that tarfile. An update can be rather slow. You cannot update a tarfile created on a 5.x system on a 4.x system.

x
Extract or restore the named files from the tarfile and write them to the directory specified in *tarfile* relative to the current directory. Use the relative path names of files and directories to be extracted.

New!

Absolute path names contained in the tar archive are unpacked with the absolute path names; that is, the leading forward slash (/) is not stripped off.

If a named file matches a directory whose contents have been written to *tarfile*, extract this directory recursively. If possible, restore the owner, modification time, and mode; otherwise, you must be superuser to restore owner.

Only superuser can extract character special and block special devices (created by mknod(1M). If you specify no file argument, extract the entire contents of *tarfile*. If *tarfile* contains several files with the same name, write each file to the appropriate directory, overwriting the previous one. You cannot use file-name substitution wild-cards for extracting files from the archive; instead, use a command of the following form.

```
tar xvf... /dev/rmt/0 `tar tf... /dev/rmt/0 | grep 'pat-
tern'`
```

When tapes created with the r or u functions are extracted, directory modification times may not be set correctly. These same functions cannot be used with many tape drives because of tape drive limitations such as the absence of backspace or append capabilities.

When you use the r, u, or x functions or the X function modifier, the named files must exactly match the corresponding files in *tarfile*. For example, to extract ./thisfile, you must specify ./thisfile, and not thisfile. The t function displays how each file was archived.

Function Modifiers

You can use the characters below in conjunction with the letter that selects the desired function.

b
Blocking factor. Use when reading or writing to raw magnetic archives (see f). The block argument specifies the number of 512-byte tape blocks to be included in each read or write operation performed on *tarfile*. The minimum is 1, the default is 20. The maximum value is a function of the amount of memory available and the blocking

requirements of the specific tape device involved. (See mtio(7I) for details.)

When a tape archive is being read, its actual blocking factor is automatically detected provided that it is less than or equal to the nominal blocking factor (the value of the block argument or the default value if you do not specify the b modifier). If the actual blocking factor is greater than the nominal blocking factor, a read error results.

B   Block. Force tar to perform multiple reads (if necessary) to read exactly enough bytes to fill a block. This function modifier enables tar to work across the Ethernet because pipes and sockets return partial blocks even when more data is coming. When reading from standard input, -, the B function modifier is selected by default to ensure that tar can recover from short reads.

e   Error. Exit immediately with a positive exit status if any unexpected errors occur. The SYSV3 environment variable overrides the default behavior.

E   Write *tarfile* with extended headers. (Used with c, r, or u options; ignored with t or x options.) When *tarfile* is written with extended headers, maintain the modification time with a granularity of microseconds instead of seconds. In addition, support file names no longer than PATH_MAX characters that could not be archived without E and file sizes greater than 8 gigabytes. Require the E function modifier whenever archiving larger files, files with longer names, files whose UID/GID exceeds 2097151, or if you want time granularity of microseconds.

f   File. Use the *tarfile* argument as the name of the tarfile. If you specify f, do not search /etc/default/tar. If you omit f, use the device indicated by the TAPE environment variable if set; otherwise, use the default values defined in /etc/default/tar.

The number matching the archive*N* string is used as the output device with the blocking and space specifications for the file. The following example writes the output to the devices specified as archive2 in /etc/default/tar. New in the Solaris 9 release.

tar -c 2 /tmp/*

If the name of the tarfile is -, write to the standard output or read from the standard input, whichever is appropriate. You can use tar as the head or tail of a pipeline. You can also use tar to move hierarchies with the following command.

% cd fromdir; tar cf - . | (cd todir; tar xfBp -)

F   With one F argument, exclude all directories named SCCS and RCS from *tarfile*. With two arguments, FF, exclude all directories named SCCS and RCS, all files with .o as their suffix, and all files named errs, core, and a.out. The SYSV3 environment variable overrides the default behavior.

h   Follow symbolic links as if they were normal files or directories. Normally, `tar` does not follow symbolic links.

i   Ignore directory checksum errors.

k *size*   Use the *size* argument as the size of an archive in kilobytes. This option is useful when the archive is intended for a fixed-size medium such as a diskette. Large files are then split across volumes if they do not fit in the specified size.

l   Link. Output error message if unable to resolve all links to the files being archived. If you do not specify l, print no error messages.

m   Modify. Set the modification time of the file as the time of extraction. This function modifier is valid only with the x function.

n   Specify that the file being read is not a tape device. Reading of the archive is faster because `tar` can randomly seek around the archive.

o   Ownership. Assign to extracted files the user and group identifiers of the user running the program instead of those on *tarfile*. This behavior is the default for users other than root. If you do not set the o function modifier and the user is root, the extracted files take on the group and user identifiers of the files on *tarfile* (see chown(1) for more information). The o function modifier is valid only with the x function.

p   Restore the named files to their original modes and ACLs if applicable, ignoring the present umask(1). This behavior is the default if you invoke p as superuser with the x function letter. If superuser, also extract setuid and sticky bit information and restore files with their original owners and permissions instead of as being owned by root. When you use this function modifier with the c function, create ACLs in *tarfile* along with other information. Errors occur when a tarfile with ACLs is extracted by previous versions of `tar`.

P   Suppress the addition of a trailing / on directory entries in the archive.

q   Stop after extracting the first occurrence of the named file. `tar` normally continues reading the archive after finding an occurrence of a file.

v   Verbose. Output the name of each file preceded by the function letter. With the t function, v provides additional information about the tarfile entries. The listing is similar to the format produced by the -1 option of the ls(1) command.

w   What. Output the action to be taken and the name of the file, then await confirmation. If the response is affirmative, perform the action; otherwise, do not perform the action. You cannot use this function modifier with the t function.

X   Exclude. Use the *exclude-file* argument as a file containing a list of relative path names for files (or directories) to be excluded from *tarfile* when using the functions c, x, or t. Be careful of trailing white spaces. You can use multiple X arguments with one *exclude-file* per

argument. In the case where you also specify included files (see the
-I *include-file* option), the excluded files take precedence over all
included files. If you specify a file in both the *exclude-file* and the
include-file (or on the command line), tar excludes it.

@   Include extended attributes in archive. By default, tar does not put
          extended attributes in the archive. With this flag, tar looks for
          extended attributes on the files to be put in the archive and adds them
          to the archive. Extended attributes go into the archive as special files
          with a special type label. When you use this modifier with the x
          function, extended attributes are extracted from the tape along with
          the normal file data. You can extract extended attributes files only as
          part of a normal file extract. Attempts to explicitly extract attribute
          records are ignored. Extended attributes are new in the Solaris 9
          release.

[0-7]   Select an alternative drive on which the tape is mounted. The default
          entries are specified in /etc/default/tar. If you specify no digit or f
          function modifier, the default is the entry in /etc/default/tar with
          digit 0.

Usage

See largefile(5) for the description of the behavior of tar when encountering files
greater than or equal to 2 Gbytes (2**31 bytes).

The automatic determination of the actual blocking factor can be fooled when a pipe
or a socket (see the B function modifier) is read from.

Quarter-inch streaming tape has an inherent blocking factor of one 512-byte block.
You can read or write to it with any blocking factor.

The B function modifier works for archives on disk files and block special devices,
among others, but it is intended principally for tape devices.

For information on tar header format, see archives(4).

Examples

The following example uses tar to create an archive of your home directory on a tape
mounted on drive /dev/rmt/0.

```
castle% cd
castle% tar cvf /dev/rmt/0 .
messages from tar
```

The c function letter means create the archive; the v function modifier outputs messages
explaining what tar is doing; the f function modifier indicates the specified tarfile
(/dev/rmt/0 in this example). The dot (.) at the end of the command line means the
current directory and is the argument of the f function modifier.

The following example displays the table of contents of the tarfile. The output for the
POSIX locale is shown.

```
castle% tar tvf /dev/rmt/0
rw-r--r-- 1677/40 2123  Mar  7 18:15 1999    ./test.c...
castle%
```

The columns have the following meanings.

- Column 1 is the access permissions to ./test.c.
- Column 2 is the user ID/group ID of ./test.c.
- Column 3 is the size of ./test.c in bytes.
- Column 4 is the modification date of ./test.c. When the LC_TIME category is not set to the POSIX locale, a different format and date order field can be used.
- Column 5 is the name of ./test.c.

The following example extracts files from the archive.

```
castle% tar xvf /dev/rmt/0
messages from tar
castle%
```

If a tape has multiple archive files, each is separated from the following one by an end-of-file marker. To have tar read the first and second archives from a tape with multiple archives on it, you must use the non-rewinding version of the tape device name with the f function modifier, as shown in the following example. The first command reads the first archive on the tape; the second command reads the second archive.

```
castle% tar xvfp /dev/rmt/0n
messages from tar
castle% tar xvfp /dev/rmt/0n
messages from tar
castle%
```

> **Note —** In some earlier releases, the above scenario did not work correctly and intervention with mt(1) between tar invocations was required. To emulate the old behavior, use the nonrewind device name containing the letter b for BSD behavior. See the "Close Operations" section of the mtio(7I) manual page.

The following example archives files from /usr/include and from /etc to default tape drive 0.

```
castle% tar c -C /usr include -C /etc .
```

The table of contents from the resulting *tarfile* would produce output like

```
include/
include/a.out.h
```

and all the other files in /usr/include.

```
./chown
```

and all the other files in /etc.

The following example extracts all files in the `include` directory

```
castle% tar xv include
x include/, 0 bytes, 0 tape blocks
```

and all files under `include`...

The following example uses `tar` to transfer files across the Ethernet. First, you archive files from the local system (`castle`) to a tape on a remote system (`host`).

```
castle% tar cvfb - 20 files | rsh host dd of=/dev/rmt/0 obs=20b
messages from tar
castle%
```

The previous example creates a *tarfile* with the c key letter, asks for verbose output from `tar` with the v function modifier, specifies the name of the output *tarfile* with the f function modifier (the standard output is where the *tarfile* appears, as indicated by the – sign), and uses the b function modifier to specify the blocksize (20). If you want to change the blocksize, you must change the blocksize arguments both on the `tar` command and on the `dd` command.

The following example uses `tar` to retrieve files from a tape on the remote system back to the local system.

```
castle% rsh -n host dd if=/dev/rmt/0 bs=20b |tar xvBfb - 20 files
messages from tar
castle%
```

The previous example extracts from the tarfile with the x key letter, asks for verbose output from `tar` with the v function modifier, tells `tar` it is reading from a pipe with the B function modifier, specifies the name of the input tarfile with the f function modifier (the standard input is where the tarfile appears, as indicated by the – sign), and specifies the blocksize (20) with the b function modifier.

The following example creates an archive of the home directory on /dev/rmt/0 with an actual blocking factor of 19.

```
castle% tar cvfb /dev/rmt/0 19 $HOME
```

The following example recognizes the archive's actual blocking factor without using the b function modifier.

```
castle% tar tvf /dev/rmt/0
tar: blocksize = 19
...
```

The following example recognizes the archive's actual blocking factor, using a larger nominal blocking factor.

```
castle% tar tvf /dev/rmt/0 30
tar: blocksize = 19
...
```

The following example tries to recognize the archive's actual blocking factor, using a nominal blocking factor that is too small.

```
castle% tar tvf /dev/rmt/0 10
tar: tape read error
```

Environment Variables

SYSV3
    Override the default behavior of tar and provide compatibility with INTERACTIVE UNIX systems and SCO UNIX installation scripts. Do not use this environment variable in new scripts; it is intended for compatibility only. When set, the following options behave differently.

-F *filename*
    Use *filename* to obtain a list of command-line switches and files on which to operate.

-e
    Prevent files from being split across volumes. If there is insufficient room on one volume, prompt for a new volume. If the file does not fit on the new volume, exit with an error.

See environ(5) for descriptions of the following environment variables that affect the execution of tar: LC_CTYPE, LC_MESSAGES, LC_TIME, TZ, and NLSPATH.

Exit Status

0
    Successful completion.

>0
    An error occurred.

Files

```
/dev/rmt/[0-7] [b] [n]
/dev/rmt/[0-7]l[b] [n]
/dev/rmt/[0-7]m[b] [n]
/dev/rmt/[0-7]h[b] [n]
/dev/rmt/[0-7]u[b] [n]
/dev/rmt/[0-7]c[b] [n]
/etc/default/tar
```

Settings may look like this:

```
archive0=/dev/rmt/0
archive1=/dev/rmt/0n
archive2=/dev/rmt/1
archive3=/dev/rmt/1n
archive4=/dev/rmt/0
archive5=/dev/rmt/0n
archive6=/dev/rmt/1
archive7=/dev/rmt/1n
```

```
/tmp/tar*
```

Attributes

See `attributes`(5) for descriptions of the following attributes:

Attribute Type	Attribute Value
Availability	SUNWcsu
CSI	Enabled
Interface Stability	Stable

New!

See Also

`ar(1)`, `basename(1)`, `cd(1)`, `chown(1)`, `cpio(1)`, `csh(1)`, `dirname(1)`, `ls(1)`, `mt(1)`, `pax(1)`, `setfacl(1)`, `umask(1)`, `mknod(1M)`, `vold(1M)`, `attributes(5)`, `environ(5)`, `fsattr(5)`, `largefile(5)`, `mtio(7I)`

New!

Diagnostics

Diagnostic messages are output for bad key characters and tape read/write errors and for insufficient memory to hold the link tables.

tbl — Format Tables for nroff or troff

Synopsis

```
/usr/bin/tbl [-me] [-mm] [-ms] [filename]...
```

Description

The `tbl` command is a preprocessor for formatting tables for `nroff`(1) or `troff`(1). A table is a rectangular arrangement of entries. Using the right commands, you can create multicolumn tables and enclose them in boxes. The `tbl` command automatically produces the correct column positioning. The input file names are copied to the standard output, except that lines between `.TS` (table start) and `.TE` (table end) command lines are assumed to describe tables and are reformatted.

If you specify no arguments, `tbl` reads the standard input, so you can use `tbl` as a filter. When you use `tbl` with `eqn`(1) or `neqn`, put the `tbl` command first to minimize the volume of data passed through pipes.

You define the structure of a table by specifying global options, described below, as a comma-separated list on the second line of a table.

Option	Description
center	Center the table on the page.
expand	Expand the table width to the current line length.
box	Draw a box around the entire table.
doublebox	Draw a double-line box around the entire table.
allbox	Enclose each cell in the table in a box.
tab(x)	Use the character x as the data separator.

Option	Description
linesize(*n*)	
	Set all lines in *n* point type.

Within the table structure, you can specify formats for column entries as described in the following table.

Code	Result
^	Expand entry from previous row to this row.
a	Indent characters from left alignment by one em.
c	Center data.
l	Left-justify data.
n	Align numbers by decimal points or unit places.
r	Right-justify data.
s	Straddle columns by extending data in previous column to this column.
t	Span vertically with text on top of the column.

Options

-me	Copy the -me macro package to the front of the output file.
-mm	Copy the -mm macro package to the front of the output file.
-ms	Copy the -ms macro package to the front of the output file.

Examples

In the following example of tbl content, the at sign (@) represents a Tab that should be typed as an actual Tab character in the input file.

```
.TS
c s s
c c s
c c c
l n n.
Household Population
Town@Households
@Number@Size
Bedminster@789@3.26
Bernards Twp.@3087@3.74
Bernardsville@2018@3.30
Bound Brook@3425@3.04
Branchburg@1644@3.49
.TE
```

```
yields
Household Population
Town            Households Number    Size
 Bedminster          789    3.26
 Bernards Twp.      3087    3.74
 Bernardsville      2018    3.30
 Bound Brook        3425    3.04
 Branchburg         1644    3.49
```

Files

/usr/share/lib/tmac/e

> -me **macros.**

/usr/share/lib/tmac/m

> -mm **macros.**

/usr/share/lib/tmac/s

> -ms **macros.**

Attributes

See attributes(5) for descriptions of the following attributes:

Attribute Type	Attribute Value
Availability	SUNWdoc

See Also

eqn(1), nroff(1), troff(1), attributes(5)

tcopy — Copy a Magnetic Tape

Synopsis

/usr/bin/tcopy *source* [*destination*]

Description

Use the tcopy command to copy the magnetic tape mounted on the tape drive specified by the *source* argument. The only assumption made about the contents of a tape is that there are two tape marks at the end.

When you specify only a source drive, tcopy scans the tape and displays information about the sizes of records and tape files. If you specify a destination, tcopy copies the source tape onto the destination tape, with blocking preserved. As it copies, tcopy produces the same output as it does when only scanning a tape.

Note — tcopy runs only on systems supporting an associated set of ioctl(2) requests.

New!   You must use Berkeley-compatible device names with the tcopy command, as shown in the following example.

>   mopoke% **tcopy /dev/rmt/1b /dev/rmt/2b**

Attributes

See attributes(5) for descriptions of the following attributes:

Attribute Type	Attribute Value
Availability	SUNWesu

See Also

mt(1), ioctl(2), attributes(5)

---

tee — Replicate the Standard Output

Synopsis

/usr/bin/tee [-ai] [*file*...]

Description

The tee command is analogous to a tee joint in plumbing that splits an incoming stream of water. tee splits standard input into two or more output streams, sending one to standard output and the others to files you specify on the command line.

You can use the tee command to monitor a command to make sure it is doing what you want or to save an intermediate step in a pipeline sequence. tee does not buffer its output. The options determine whether the specified files are overwritten or appended to.

Options

-a   Append the output to the files instead of overwriting them.

-i   Ignore interrupts.

Operands

file   A path name of an output file. You can process at least 13 *file* operands.

Examples

The following example uses the file command to display information about files in the current directory and also saves a copy of the information in a file named filetypes.

```
castle% file * | tee filetypes
085XDOCS.zip:   data
Appletviewer.rs:        rasterfile, 511 x 180 x 8 standard format image
Mail:           directory
bibliography:   ascii text
core:           ELF 32-bit MSB core file SPARC Version 1, from 'srchtxt'
```

```
examples:        ascii text
find.zip:        ZIP archive
kookaburra-1:    ascii text
kookaburra-2:    ascii text
olddir:          directory
program.c:       c program text
tbltest:         [nt]roff, tbl, or eqn input text
temp:            data
xaa:             English text
castle%
```

The following example writes sar data into a file named /tmp/sardata and also displays the data to standard output. If you look in /tmp, you'll also see a file named sardata.

sar | tee /tmp/sardata

```
SunOS sun1 5.7 Generic sun4m    04/15/99

06:23:33    %usr    %sys    %wio    %idle
06:23:38     1       2       0       97
06:23:43     2       2       0       96
06:23:48     0       2       0       98
06:23:53    16       3       0       81
06:23:58     5       2       0       93
06:24:03     5       3       0       92
06:24:08     2       2       0       96
06:24:13     4       2       0       93
06:24:18     4       4       1       91
06:24:23     2       2       0       96

Average      4       2       0       93
#
```

If you want to append to a file instead of overwriting the contents, use the -a option.

Usage

See largefile(5) for the description of the behavior of tee when encountering files greater than or equal to 2 Gbytes (2**31 bytes).

Environment Variables

See environ(5) for descriptions of the following environment variables that affect the execution of tee: LC_CTYPE, LC_MESSAGES, and NLSPATH.

Exit Status

0	The standard input was successfully copied to all output files.
>0	The number of files that could not be opened or whose status could not be obtained.

Attributes

See attributes(5) for descriptions of the following attributes:

Attribute Type	Attribute Value
Availability	SUNWcsu
CSI	Enabled

See Also

cat(1), attributes(5), environ(5), largefile(5)

tek — Graphics Filters for Various Plotters

Synopsis

/usr/bin/plot [-T*terminal*]

Description

See tplot(1).

telnet — User Interface to a Remote System, Using the TELNET Protocol

Synopsis

New!

/usr/bin/telnet [-8ELcdr] [-e *escape-char*] [-l *user*] [-n *tracefile*]
[[[!] @*hop1*[@*hop2*...] @]*host* [*port*]]

Description

Use the telnet command to remotely log in to a system running some other operating system or a different version of UNIX. telnet communicates with another host, using the TELNET protocol. If you invoke telnet without arguments, it enters command mode and displays the telnet> prompt. In this mode, it accepts and executes its associated commands. (See "telnet Commands" on page 1390.) If you invoke telnet with arguments, it performs an open command with those arguments.

New!

If, for example, you specify a host as @*hop1*@*hop2*@*host*, the connection goes through hosts *hop1* and *hop2*, using loose source routing to end at *host*. If you use a leading !, the connection follows strict source routing.

New!

> **Note —** When telnet uses IPv6, it can use only loose source routing and the connection ignores the !.

Once a connection has been opened, telnet enters input mode. In this mode, text typed is sent to the remote host. The input mode entered depends on what the remote system supports. The three input modes are:

- *Line mode*: Character processing is done on the local system under the control of the remote system. When input editing or character echoing is to be disabled, the remote system relays that information. The remote system also relays changes to any special characters that happen on the remote system so that they can take effect on the local system.
- *Character-at-a-time mode*: Most text typed is immediately sent to the remote host for processing.
- *Old-line-by-line mode*: All text is echoed locally, and (normally) only completed lines are sent to the remote host. You can use the "local echo character" (initially, ^E) to turn off and on the local echo. (Use this feature mostly to enter passwords without the password being echoed.)

Note — On some remote systems, you must turn echo off manually when in "line-by-line" mode.

New!

In "old-line-by-line" mode, or LINEMODE, the terminal's end-of-file character is recognized (and sent to the remote system) only when it is the first character on a line.

If the line mode option is enabled or if the localchars toggle is true (the default in "old-line-by-line" mode), your quit, intr, and flush characters are trapped locally and sent as TELNET protocol sequences to the remote side. If "line mode" has ever been enabled, then your susp and eof are also sent as TELNET protocol sequences. quit is then sent as a TELNET ABORT instead of BREAK. The toggle autoflush and toggle autosynch options flush subsequent output to the terminal (until the remote host acknowledges the TELNET sequence) and flush previous terminal input in the case of quit and intr.

While connected to a remote host, you can enter telnet command mode by typing the telnet escape character (initially ^]). When in command mode, the normal terminal editing conventions are available. Pressing Return at the telnet command prompt exits command mode.

Options

-8   Specify an 8-bit data path. Negotiating the BINARY option is attempted for both input and output.

-c   Disable the reading of the user's telnetrc file. (See the toggle skiprc command.)

-d   Set the initial value of the debug toggle to true.

-e *escape-char*

    Set the initial escape character to *escape-char*. *escape-char* can also be a two-character sequence consisting of ^ followed by one character. If the second character is ?, select the DEL character. Otherwise convert the second character to a control character and use it as the escape character. If the escape character is the null string (that is, -e ' '), disable it.

-E   Stop any character from being recognized as an escape character.

-l *user*   When connecting to a remote system that understands the ENVIRON
              option, send *user* to the remote system as the value for the variable
              USER.

-L   Specify an 8-bit data path on output. This negotiates the BINARY option
              on output.

-n *tracefile*

              Open *tracefile* for recording trace information. See the set
              tracefile command.

-r   Specify a user interface similar to rlogin. In this mode, set the escape
              character to the tilde (~) character unless modified by the -e option. The
              rlogin escape character is recognized only when it is preceded by a
              Return. In this mode, you must still precede a telnet command with
              the telnet escape character, normally ^]. You can also follow the
              rlogin escape character by . \r or ^Z, like rlogin(1), to close or
              suspend the connection. This option is an uncommitted interface and
              may change in the future.

Usage

telnet Commands

The commands described in this section are available with telnet. You need to type only
enough of each command to uniquely identify it. (This is also true for arguments to the
mode, set, toggle, unset, environ, and display commands.)

close   Close any open TELNET session, and exit telnet. An end-of-file (in
              command mode) also closes a session and exits.

display [*argument*...]

              Display all or some of the set, and toggle values (see toggle
              arguments).

environ *arguments*...

              Use the environ command to manipulate variables that can be sent
              through the ENVIRON option. Take the initial set of variables from your
              environment. Only export the DISPLAY and PRINTER variables by
              default. Valid arguments for the environ command are as follows.

              define *variable value*

                          Define *variable* to have a value of *value*.
                          Automatically export any variables defined by this
                          command. You can enclose *value* in single or double
                          quotes so that you can include Tabs and spaces.

              export *variable*

                          Mark the variable to be exported to the remote side.

              list   List the current set of environment variables. Send
                          those marked with an asterisk (*) automatically. Send
                          other variables only if explicitly requested.

undefine *variable*

>Remove *variable* from the list of environment variables. Export *variable*.

unexport *variable*

>Mark the variable to not be exported unless explicitly requested by the remote side.

?
>Print help information for the environ command.

logout
: Send the telnet logout option to the remote side. This command is similar to a close command. However, nothing happens if the remote side does not support the logout option. If the remote side does support the logout option, this command should close the remote side of the TELNET connection. If the remote side also supports the concept of suspending a user's session for later reattachment, the logout argument indicates that the remote side should terminate the session immediately.

mode *type*
: The remote host is asked for permission to go into the requested mode. If the remote host is capable of entering that mode, enter the requested mode. *type* is one of the following.

character
>Disable the LINEMODE option, or, if the remote side does not understand the LINEMODE option, enter "character-at-a-time" mode.

edit (-edit)

>Try to enable (disable) the EDIT mode of the LINEMODE option. The LINEMODE option must be enabled.

isig (-isig)

>Try to enable (disable) the TRAPSIG mode of the LINEMODE option. The LINEMODE option must enabled.

line
>Enable the LINEMODE option, or, if the remote side does not understand the LINEMODE option, try to enter "old-line-by-line" mode.

litecho (-litecho)

>Try to enable (disable) the LIT_ECHO mode of the LINEMODE option. The LINEMODE option must be enabled.

softtabs (-softtabs)

>Try to enable (disable) the SOFT_TAB mode of the LINEMODE option. The LINEMODE option must be enabled.

?
>Print help information for the mode command.

New!   open [-l *user* [[!] @*hop1*[@*hop2*...]@*host* [*port*]

> Open a connection to the named host. If you specify no port number,
> telnet tries to contact a TELNET server at the default port. You can
> specify the host either as a host name (see hosts(4), ipnodes(4)), or as
> an Internet address specified in the dot notation (see inet(7P), or
> inet6(7P)). If you specify the host as @*hop1*@*hop2*@*host*, the connection
> goes through hosts *hop1* and *hop2*, using loose source routing to end at
> *host*. The @ symbol is required as a separator between the hosts
> specified. If you use a leading ! with IPv4, the connection follows strict
> source routing.
>
> The -l option passes to the remote system the *user* as the value of the
> ENVIRON variable USER. The hop operands are new in the Solaris 8
> release.

quit   Same as close.

send *arguments*

> Send one or more special character sequences to the remote host. You
> can specify one or more of the following arguments.
>
> | | |
> |---|---|
> | abort | Send the ABORT (abort process) sequence. |
> | ao | Send the AO (abort output) sequence to flush all output from the remote system to your terminal. |
> | ayt | Send the AYT (are you there) sequence. The remote system may or may not respond. |
> | brk or break | Send the BRK (break) sequence, which may have significance to the remote system. |
> | do *option* dont *option* will *option* wont *option* | Send the indicated protocol option negotiation. *option* can be the text name of the protocol option or the number corresponding to the option. The command is silently ignored if the indicated option negotiation is not valid in the current state. If you specify the help or ? option, list known option names. This command is useful mostly for unusual debugging situations. |
> | ec | Send the EC (erase character) sequence to erase the last character entered. |
> | el | Send the EL (erase line) sequence to erase the line currently being entered on the remote system. |
> | eof | Send the EOF (end-of-file) sequence. |
> | eor | Send the EOR (end-of-record) sequence. |
> | escape | Send the current telnet escape character (initially ^]). |
> | ga | Send the GA (go ahead) sequence, which probably has no significance for the remote system. |

getstatus	If the remote side supports the STATUS command, getstatus sends the subnegotiation to request that the server send its current option status.
ip	Send the IP (interrupt process) sequence to abort the currently running process on the remote system.
nop	Send the NOP (no operation) sequence.
susp	Send the SUSP (suspend process) sequence.
synch	Send the SYNCH sequence to discard all previously typed but not yet read input on the remote system. This sequence is sent as TCP urgent data and may not work if the remote system is a 4.2 BSD system. If it does not work, a lowercase r may be echoed on the terminal.
?	Print help information for the send command.

set *argument* [*value*]
unset *argument*

Set any one of a number of telnet variables to a specific value. The special value off turns off the function associated with the variable. You can interrogate the values of variables with the display command. If you omit *value*, take the value to be true or on. If you use the unset form, take the value to be false or off. You can specify the following variables.

ayt	Send an AYT sequence to the remote host when in localchars mode or LINEMODE is enabled and you type the status character. The initial value for ayt is the terminal status character.
echo	Set the value (initially, ^E) that "old-line-by-line" mode uses to toggle between local echoing of entered characters for normal processing and suppressed echoing of entered characters such as a password. Note that on some remote systems, you have to turn off echo manually when in "old-line-by-line" mode.
eof	When you enter the eof character as the first character on a line, send the eof character to the remote system when operating in "old-line-by-line" mode. Take the initial value of eof to be the terminal eof character.
erase	Send an ES sequence to the remote system when in localchars mode and operating in "character-at-a-time" mode. Take the initial value for the erase character to be the terminal erase character.
escape	Set the telnet escape character (initially, ^]) that enters telnet command mode when connected to a remote system.

flushoutput   Send an AO sequence to the remote host when in
               localchars mode and you type the flushoutput
               character. Take the initial value for the flush character
               to be the terminal flush character.

forw1   Forward partial lines to the remote system when
forw2   operating in LINEMODE (or "old-line-by-line" mode) and
               you type the forw1 or forw2 character. The initial
               values for the forwarding characters come from the
               terminal eol and eol2 characters.

interrupt   Set the interrupt sequence that is sent to the remote
               host when in localchars mode (see toggle
               localchars) and you type the interrupt character. Take
               the initial value for the interrupt character to be the
               terminal intr character.

kill   Send an EL sequence to the remote system when telnet
               is in localchars mode, operating in
               "character-at-a-time" mode, and you type the kill
               sequence. Take the initial value for the kill character
               to be the terminal kill character.

lnext   Assume the lnext character is the terminal lnext
               character when operating in LINEMODE or
               "old-line-by-line" mode. Take the initial value for the
               lnext character to be the terminal lnext character.

quit   Send a BRK sequence to the remote host when in
               localchars mode and you type the quit character. Take
               the initial value for the quit character to be the
               terminal quit character.

reprint   Assume the reprint character is the terminal's
               reprint character when operating in LINEMODE or
               "old-line-by-line" mode. Take the initial value for
               reprint to be the terminal reprint character.

rlogin   Set the rlogin escape character. Ignore the normal
               telnet escape character unless it is preceded by this
               character at the beginning of a line. Close the
               connection when the rlogin character followed by a . is
               at the beginning of a line. When followed by a ^Z,
               suspend the telnet command. The initial state is to
               disable the rlogin escape character.

start   If the TOGGLE-FLOW-CONTROL option has been enabled,
               take the start character to be the terminal start
               character. Take the initial value for the kill character
               to be the terminal start character.

stop	If the TOGGLE-FLOW-CONTROL option has been enabled, take the stop character to be the terminal stop character. Take the initial value for the kill character to be the terminal stop character.
susp	Send a SUSP sequence to the remote host when in localchars mode or LINEMODE is enabled and you type the suspend character. Take the initial value for the suspend character to be the terminal suspend character.
tracefile	Write the output to this file when the netdata or the debug option is true. If it is set to -, then write the tracing information to standard output (the default).
worderase	If operating in LINEMODE or "old-line-by-line" mode, take this character to be the terminal worderase character. Take the initial value for the worderase character to be the terminal worderase character.
?	Display the legal set and unset commands.

slc *state*   Set or change the state of special characters when the LINEMODE option has been enabled. Special characters are characters that get mapped to TELNET command sequences (like ip and quit) or line-editing characters (like erase and kill). By default, export the local special characters.

check	Verify the settings for the current special characters. The remote side is requested to send all the current special character settings. If there are any discrepancies with the local side, switch the local settings to the remote values.
export	Switch to the local defaults for the special characters. The local default characters are those of the local terminal at the time telnet was started.
import	Switch to the remote defaults for the special characters. The remote default characters are those of the remote system at the time the TELNET connection was established.
?	Print help information for the slc command.

toggle *arguments*...

Toggle between true and false the various flags that control how telnet responds to events. You can specify more than one argument. You can interrogate the state of these flags with the display command. Valid arguments are as follows.

autoflush
If autoflush and localchars are both true, then when the ao, intr, or quit characters are recognized (and transformed into TELNET sequences; see set for details), refuse to display any data on your terminal until the remote system acknowledges (using a TELNET Timing Mark option) that it has processed those TELNET sequences. The initial value for this toggle is true if you have not done an stty noflsh. Otherwise, the value is false (see stty(1)).

autosynch
If autosynch and localchars are both true, then when you type either the interrupt or quit characters (see set for descriptions of interrupt and quit), send the resulting TELNET sequence followed by the SYNCH sequence. This procedure should throw away all previously typed input on the remote system until both of the TELNET sequences have been read and acted on. The initial value is false.

binary
Enable or disable the BINARY option on both input and output.

crlf
Determine how Returns are sent. If the value is true, then send Returns as CR/LF. If the value is false, then send Returns as CRnull. The initial value is false.

crmod
Toggle Return mode. When this mode is enabled, most Return characters received from the remote host are mapped into a Return followed by a linefeed. This mode does not affect those characters you type, only those received from the remote host. This mode is useful only for remote hosts that send Return but never send a linefeed. The initial value is false.

debug
Toggle socket-level debugging (only available to the superuser). The initial value is false.

inbinary
Enable or disable the BINARY option on input.

localchars
If true, then recognize the flush, interrupt, quit, erase, and kill characters (see set) locally and transform them into the appropriate TELNET control sequences ao, ip, brk, ec, and el (see send). The initial value for this toggle is true in "old-line-by-line" mode and false in "character-at-a-time" mode. When the LINEMODE option is enabled, ignore the value of localchars and assume it is always true. If LINEMODE has ever been enabled, then quit is sent as abort, and eof and suspend are sent as eof and susp (see send).

netdata
Toggle the display of all network data (in hexadecimal format). The initial value is false.

options   Toggle the display of some internal TELNET protocol processing (having to do with `telnet` options). The initial value is `false`.

outbinary   Enable or disable the BINARY option on output.

prettydump   When the `netdata` toggle is enabled, if `prettydump` is enabled, format the output from the `netdata` command in a more user-readable format. Put spaces between each character in the output. The beginning of any TELNET escape sequence is preceded by an asterisk (*) to aid in locating it.

skiprc   When `true`, skip the reading of the `.telnetrc` file in your home directory when connections are opened. The initial value is `false`.

termdata   Toggle the display of all terminal data (in hexadecimal format). The initial value is `false`.

?   Display the legal toggle commands.

status   Show the current status of `telnet`, including the peer you are connected to and the current mode.

z   Suspend `telnet`. This command works only when you are using a shell that supports job control, such as sh(1).

? [*command*]

     Get help. With no arguments, print a help summary. If you specify *command*, print the help information just for that command.

Files

$HOME/.telnetrc

     Commands to be executed before a `telnet` session is initiated.

/etc/nologin

     Message displayed to users trying to log in during system shutdown.

Attributes

See `attributes`(5) for descriptions of the following attributes:

Attribute Type	Attribute Value
Availability	SUNWcsu

See Also

rlogin(1), sh(1), stty(1), hosts(4), ipnodes(4), nologin(4), telnetrc(4), *New!*
attributes(5), inet(7P), inet6(7P)

Diagnostics

NO LOGINS: System going down in *N* minutes

> The system is in the process of being shut down and logins have been disabled.

---

test — Evaluate Conditions

Synopsis

/usr/bin/test [*condition*]
[*condition*]

csh, ksh, sh

test *condition*
[[*condition*]]

Description

The test command evaluates the *condition* and indicates the result of the evaluation by its exit status. An exit status of 0 indicates that the condition evaluated as true, and an exit status of 1 indicates that the condition evaluated as false.

New!   In the test [*condition*] syntax, the square brackets denote that the condition is an optional operand. Do not enter the brackets on the command line.

In the [[*condition*]] form of the command, the first open square bracket is the required command name. *condition* is optional, as denoted by the inner pair of square brackets. The final close square bracket is a required operand.

See largefile(5) for the description of the behavior of test when encountering files greater than or equal to 2 Gbytes (2**31 bytes).

The test and [commands evaluate the *condition* condition and, if its value is true, they set exit status to 0. Otherwise a nonzero (false) exit status is set. test and [also set a nonzero exit status when you specify no arguments. When permissions are tested, the effective user ID of the process is used.

All operators, flags, and brackets (used as shown in the last Synopsis line) must be separate arguments to these commands. You normally separate these arguments with spaces.

Operands

New!   The primaries listed below are known as unary primaries. Unary primaries have the following form.

-primary_operator primary_operand

New!   Primaries with three elements are known as binary primaries and have the following form.

primary_operand -primary_operator primary_operand
primary_operand primary_operator primary_operand

New!   If any file operands except the -h and -L primaries refer to symbolic links, the symbolic link is expanded and the test is performed on the resulting file.

When you test a file you own (the -r, -w, or -x tests),but the permission tested does *New!* not have the owner bit set, a non-zero (false) exit status is returned even though the file may have the group or other bit set for that permission.

The = and != primaries have a higher precedence than the unary primaries. The = *New!* and != primaries always expect arguments; therefore, you cannot use = and != as an argument to the unary primaries.

You can use the following primaries to construct *condition*.

-a *file*   true if *file* exists.

-b *file*   true if *file* exists and is a block special *file*.

-c *file*   true if *file* exists and is a character special file.

-d *file*   true if *file* exists and is a directory.

-e *file*   true if *file* exists.

-f *file*   true if *file* exists and is a regular file.

          Alternatively, if /usr/bin/sh users specify /usr/ucb before /usr/bin *New!* in their PATH environment variable, then test returns true if *file* exists and is (not-a-directory). The csh test and [built-ins always use this alternative behavior.

          The not-a-directory alternative is a transition aid for BSD applications *New!* and may not be supported in future releases.

-g *file*   true if *file* exists and its set-group-ID flag is set.

-G *file*   true if *file* exists and its group matches the effective group ID of this process. (Not available in sh.) *New!*

-h   true if *file* exists and is a symbolic link. New in the Solaris 9 release. *New!*

-k *file*   true if *file* exists and its sticky bit is set.

-L *file*   true if *file* exists and is a symbolic link.

-n *string*   true if the length of string is non-zero.

-o *option*   true if option named *option* is on. (Not available in csh or sh.) *New!*

-O *file*   true if *file* exists and is owned by the effective user ID of this process. *New!* (Not available in sh.)

-p *file*   true if *file* is a named pipe (FIFO).

-r *file*   true if *file* exists and is readable.

-s *file*   true if *file* exists and has a size greater than 0.

-S *file*   true if *file* exists and is a socket. (Not available in sh.) *New!*

-t *file-descriptor*

          true if the *file* whose file descriptor number is *file-descriptor* is *New!* open and is associated with a terminal. If you do not specify *file-descriptor*, the default value is 1.

-u *file*   true if *file* exists and its set-user-ID flag is set.

-w *file*   true if *file* exists and is writable. true indicates only that the write flag is on. The file is not writable on a read-only file system even if this test indicates true.

-x *file*   true if *file* exists and is executable. true indicates only that the execute flag is on. If *file* is a directory, true indicates that *file* can be searched.

-z *string*   true if the length of string *string* is 0.

file1 -nt *file2*

New!   true if *file1* exists and is newer than *file2*. (Not available in sh.)

file1 -ot *file2*

New!   true if *file1* exists and is older than *file2*. (Not available in sh.)

file1 -ef *file2*

New!   true if *file1* and *file2* exist and refer to the same file. (Not available in sh.)

string   true if the string *string* is not the null string.

string1 = *string2*

                 true if the strings *string1* and *string2* are identical.

string1 != *string2*

                 true if the strings *string1* and *string2* are not identical.

n1 -eq *n2*   true if the integers *n1* and *n2* are algebraically equal.

n1 -ne *n2*   true if the integers *n1* and *n2* are not algebraically equal.

n1 -ge *n2*   true if the integer *n1* is algebraically greater than or equal to the integer *n2*.

n1 -gt *n2*   true if the integer *n1* is algebraically greater than the integer *n2*.

n1 -le *n2*   true if the integer *n1* is algebraically less than or equal to the integer *n2*.

n1 -lt *n2*   true if the integer *n1* is algebraically less than the integer *n2*.

New!   *condition1* -a *condition2*

                 true if both *condition1* and *condition2* are true. The -a binary primary is left associative and has higher precedence than the -o binary primary. New in the Solaris 9 release.

New!   *condition1* -o *condition2*

                 true if either *condition1* or *condition2* is true. The -o binary is left associative. New in the Solaris 9 release.

You can combine these primaries with the following operators.

New!   ! *condition*

                 true if *condition* is false.

(*condition*)

> true if *condition* is true. You can use the parentheses to alter the normal precedence and associativity. Notice also that parentheses are meaningful to the shell and therefore must be quoted.

The algorithm for determining the precedence of the operators and the return value generated is based on the number of arguments presented to test. (However, when you use the [...] form, the right-bracket final argument is not counted in this algorithm.) In the following list, $1, $2, $3, and $4 represent the arguments presented to test as a condition, *condition1* or *condition2*.

0 arguments   Exit false (1).

1 argument   Exit true (0) if $1 is not null; otherwise, exit false.

2 arguments   If $1 is !, exit true if $2 is null, false if $2 is not null.

> If $1 is a unary primary, exit true if the unary test is true, false if the unary test is false.

> Otherwise, produce unspecified results.

3 arguments   If $2 is a binary primary, perform the binary test of $1 and $3.

> If $1 is !, negate the two-argument test of $2 and $3.

> Otherwise, produce unspecified results.

4 arguments   If $1 is !, negate the three-argument test of $2, $3, and $4.

> Otherwise, the results are unspecified.

Usage

Be careful when you write scripts that deal with user-supplied input that could be confused with primaries and operators. Unless you, the application writer, know all the cases that produce input to the script, write invocations like

```
test "$1" -a "$2"
```

as follows to avoid problems if a user supplied values such as $1 set to ! and $2 set to the null string.

```
test "$1" && test "$2"
```

In cases where maximal portability is of concern, replace

```
test expr1 -a expr2
```

with

```
test expr1 && test expr2
```

and replace

```
test expr1 -o expr2
```

with

```
test expr1 || test expr2
```

Note — In test, -a has higher precedence than -o, and && and || have equal precedence in the shell.

You can use parentheses or braces in the shell command language for grouping. You must escape parentheses when using sh; for example,

```
test \( expr1 -a expr2 \) -o expr3
```

This command is not always portable outside XSI-conformant systems. Instead, you can use the following form.

```
( test expr1 && test expr2 ) || test expr3
```

The following two commands could not be used reliably on some historical systems.

```
test "$1"
test ! "$1"
```

Unexpected results occur if such a string condition is used and $1 is expanded to !, (, or a known unary primary. Better constructs are

```
test -n "$1"
test -z "$1"
```

Historical systems have also been unreliable given the common construct

```
test "$response" = "expected string"
```

One of the following is a more reliable form.

```
test "X$response" = "Xexpected string"
test "expected string" = "$response"
```

Note that the second form assumes that "expected string" could not be confused with any unary primary. If "expected string" starts with -, (, ! or even =, use the first form instead. When the preceding rules are used without the marked extensions, any of the three comparison forms is reliable, given any input. Observe, however, that the strings are quoted in all cases.

Because the string-comparison binary primaries = and != have a higher precedence than any unary primary in the >4 argument case, unexpected results can occur if arguments are not properly prepared. For example, in the following construct, if $1 evaluates to a possible directory name of -, the first three arguments are considered a string comparison, and a syntax error is displayed when the second -d is encountered.

```
test -d $1 -o -d $2
```

One of the following forms prevents this problem; the second is preferred.

```
test \( -d "$1" \) -o \( -d "$2" \)
test -d "$1" || test -d "$2"
```

Also in the >4 argument case, syntax errors occur if $1 evaluates to (or !.

```
test "$1" = "bat" -a "$2" = "ball"
```

Syntax errors result if $1 evaluates to (or !. One of the following forms prevents this *New!*
error; the third is preferred.

```
test "X$1" = "Xbat" -a "X$2" = "Xball"
test "$1" = "bat" && test "$2" = "ball"
test "X$1" = "Xbat" && test "X$2" = "Xball"
```

See largefile(5) for the description of the behavior of test when encountering files
greater than or equal to 2 Gbytes (2**31 bytes).

Examples

In the if command examples, three conditions are tested, and if all three evaluate as
true or successful, then their validities are written to the screen.
   The three tests are:

- If a variable set to 1 is greater than 0.
- If a variable set to 2 is equal to 2.
- If the word root is included in the text file /etc/passwd.

/usr/bin/test

The following example performs a mkdir if a directory does not exist.

```
test ! -d tempdir && mkdir tempdir
```

The following example waits for a file to become nonreadable.

```
while test -r thefile
do
  sleep 30
done
echo '"thefile" is no longer readable'
```

The following example performs a command if the argument is one of three strings
(two variations).

```
if [ "$1" = "pear" ] || [ "$1" = "grape" ] || [ "$1" = "apple" ]
then
  command
fi
case "$1" in
  pear|grape|apple) command ; ;
esac
```

For the two forms of the test built-in command, see the Bourne shell if example.

Bourne Shell

The following example uses the `sh` built-in command.

```
ZERO=0 ONE=1 TWO=2 ROOT=root
if  [ $ONE -gt $ZERO ]
[ $TWO -eq 2 ]
grep $ROOT  /etc/passwd >&1 > /dev/null      # discard output
then
   echo "$ONE is greater than 0, $TWO equals 2, and $ROOT
     is a user-name in the password file"
else
   echo "At least one of the three test conditions is false"
fi
```

The following examples use the `test` built-in command.

```
test `grep $ROOT /etc/passwd >&1 /dev/null`  # discard output
echo $?                                       # test for success
[ `grep nosuchname /etc/passwd >&1 /dev/null` ]
echo $?                                       # test for failure
```

C shell

```
@ ZERO = 0; @ ONE = 1; @ TWO = 2;  set ROOT = root
grep $ROOT  /etc/passwd >&1 /dev/null  # discard output
# $status must be tested for immediately following grep
if ( "$status" == "0" && $ONE > $ZERO && $TWO == 2 ) then
   echo "$ONE is greater than 0, $TWO equals 2, and $ROOT
     is a user-name in the password file"
endif
```

Korn Shell

```
ZERO=0 ONE=1 TWO=$((ONE+ONE)) ROOT=root
if  ((ONE > ZERO))                           # arithmetical comparison
[[ $TWO = 2 ]]                               # string comparison
[ `grep $ROOT  /etc/passwd >&1 /dev/null` ] # discard output
then
   echo "$ONE is greater than 0, $TWO equals 2, and $ROOT
 is a user-name in the password file"
else
   echo "At least one of the three test conditions is false"
fi
```

The Korn shell also accepts the syntax of both the `if` command and the `test` command of the Bourne shell.

When using the brackets (`[]`) within `if` commands, you must separate both inside ends of the brackets from the inside characters with a space.

Environment Variables

See `environ`(5) for descriptions of the following environment variables that affect the execution of `test`: LC_CTYPE, LC_MESSAGES, and NLSPATH.

Exit Status

0	Condition evaluated to `true`.
1	Condition evaluated to `false` or condition was missing.
>1	An error occurred.

Attributes

See `attributes`(5) for descriptions of the following attributes:

Attribute Type	Attribute Value
Availability	SUNWcsu

See Also

`csh(1)`, `ksh(1)`, `sh(1)`, `test(1B)`, `attributes(5)`, `environ(5)`, `largefile(5)`

---

tftp — Trivial File Transfer Program

Synopsis

`/usr/bin/tftp` [*host*]

Description

The `tftp` command is the user interface to the Internet TFTP (Trivial File Transfer Protocol) that uses the User Datagram Protocol (UDP) instead of the Transmission Control Protocol (TCP) used by `ftp`. Use `tftp` when you have no login on the remote system and you want to transfer files that are publicly readable. Because `tftp` does not authenticate users, it is insecure. Because there is no user login or validation within the TFTP protocol, many remote sites restrict file access in various ways. Approved methods for file access are specific to each site and therefore cannot be documented here.

`tftp` communicates with the remote system when needed and does not run an interactive session with a remote host.

You can specify the remote host on the command line, in which case `tftp` uses *host* as the default host for future transfers (see the `connect` command).

Note — The default transfer mode is `ascii`. This default differs from pre-SunOS 4.0 and pre-4.3 BSD systems, so you must take explicit action when transferring non-ASCII binary files such as executable commands.

Because the TFTP protocol provides no user login or validation, many remote sites restrict file access in various ways. Approved method for file access are specific to each site and, therefore, cannot be documented here.

New!

Usage

Once `tftp` is running, it issues the `tftp>` prompt and recognizes the following commands.

Commands

`connect` *host-name* [*port*]

> Set the host (and optionally port) for transfers. Unlike FTP, the TFTP protocol does not maintain connections between transfers; thus, the `connect` command does not actually create a connection but merely remembers what host is to be used for transfers. You do not have to use the `connect` command; you can specify the remote host as part of the `get` or `put` commands.

`mode` *transfer-mode*

> Set the mode for transfers; *transfer-mode* can be either `ascii` or `binary`. The default is `ascii`.

`put` *filename*
`put` *localfile remotefile*
`put` *filename1 filename2... filenameN remote-directory*

> Transfer a file or a set of files to the specified remote file or directory. The destination can be in one of two forms: a file name on the remote host if the host has already been specified or a string of the following form to specify both a host and file name at the same time.
>
> *host*: *filename*
>
> If you use the latter form, the specified host becomes the default for future transfers. If you use the *remote-directory* form, the remote host is assumed to be running the UNIX system. Files can be written only if they already exist and are publicly writable (see `in.tftpd`(1M)).
>
> *hostname* can be an IPv4 or IPv6 address string. See `inet`(7P) and `inet6`(7P). Because IPv6 addresses already contain colons, enclose an IPv6 address in a pair of square brackets, as shown in the following example.
>
> `[1080::8:800:200C:417A]:myfile`
>
> Otherwise, the first occurrence of a colon can be interpreted as the separator between *hostname* and *path*.

`get` *filename*
`get` *remotename localname*
`get` *filename1 filename2 filename3... filenameN*

> Get a file or set of files from the specified remote sources. The source can be in one of two forms: a file name on the remote host if the host has already been specified or a string of the following form to specify both a host and file name at the same time.
>
> *host*: *filename*
>
> If you use the latter form, the last host specified becomes the default for future transfers. When using the `get` command to transfer multiple files from a remote host, you must specify three or more files. If you specify two files, the second file is used as a local file.

New!

When using the get command to transfer multiple files from a remote host, you must specify three or more files. If you specify two files, the second file is used as a local file.

New!

quit   Exit tftp. An end-of-file also exits.

verbose   Toggle verbose mode.

trace   Toggle packet tracing.

status   Show current status.

rexmt *retransmission-timeout*

Set the per-packet retransmission timeout in seconds.

timeout *total-transmission-timeout*

Set the total transmission timeout in seconds.

ascii   Shorthand for mode ascii.

binary   Shorthand for mode binary.

? [*command-name*...]

Print help information.

Attributes

See attributes(5) for descriptions of the following attributes:

Attribute Type	Attribute Value
Availability	SUNWtftp

New!

See Also

in.tftpd(1M), hosts(4), ipnodes(4), attributes(5), inet(7P), inet6(7P)

New!

time — Time a Simple Command

Synopsis

/usr/bin/time [-p] *command* [*argument*...]

Description

Use the time command to compute the time it takes a command to execute. time writes a message to standard error that lists timing statistics for *command* and the optional *argument*s. The message includes the following information.

- The elapsed (real) time between invocation of *command* and its termination.
- The user CPU time, equivalent to the sum of the tms_utime and tms_cutime fields returned by the times(2) function for the process in which *command* is executed.

- The system CPU time, equivalent to the sum of the tms_stime and tms_cstime fields returned by the times() function for the process in which *command* is executed.
- When time is used as part of a pipeline, the times reported are unspecified except when it is the sole command within a grouping command in that pipeline. For example, the following commands are unspecified.

```
time a | b | c
a | b | time c
```

- The following commands report on commands a and c.

```
{ time a } | b | c
a | b | (time c)
```

Note — When you run the time command on a multiprocessor system, the total of the values printed for user and sys can exceed real because, on a multiprocessor system, it is possible to divide the task among the various processors.

When the command being timed is interrupted, the timing values displayed may not always be accurate.

Options

-p   Write the timing output to standard error in the following format.

real %f\nuser %f\nsys %f\n real-seconds, user-seconds, system-seconds

Operands

command   The name of the command to be invoked.

argument   Any string to be supplied as an argument when invoking *command*.

Usage

The time command returns exit status 127 if an error occurs so that applications can distinguish "failure to find a command" from "invoked command exited with an error indication." The value 127 was chosen because it is not commonly used for other meanings; most commands use small values for normal error conditions, and the values above 128 can be confused with termination because of receipt of a signal. The value 126 was chosen in a similar manner to indicate that the command could be found but not invoked.

Examples

If you want to apply time to pipelines or lists of commands, you can do so by putting pipelines and command lists in a single file. You can then invoke this file as a command, and the time applies to everything in the file.

Alternatively, you can use the following command to apply time to a complex command.

```
castle% time sh -c 'complex-command-line'
```

The following two examples show the differences between the csh version of time and the version in /usr/bin/time. These examples use the C shell.

```
castle# time find / -name core -print
/export/home/winsor/core
1.0u 13.0s 1:11 19% 0+0k 0+0io 0pf+0w
castle# /usr/bin/time find / -name core -print
/export/home/winsor/core

real      1:10.2
user         1.0
sys         13.5
castle#
```

See csh(1) for an explanation of the format of time output.

Environment Variables

See environ(5) for descriptions of the following environment variables that affect the execution of time: LC_CTYPE, LC_MESSAGES, LC_NUMERIC, NLSPATH, and PATH.

Exit Status

If *command* is invoked, the exit status of time is the exit status of *command*, otherwise, the time command exits with one of the following values.

1-125   An error occurred in the time command.

126   *command* was found but could not be invoked.

127   *command* could not be found.

Attributes

See attributes(5) for descriptions of the following attributes:

Attribute Type	Attribute Value
Availability	SUNWcsu

See Also

csh(1), shell_builtins(1), timex(1), times(2), attributes(5), environ(5)

Bugs

Elapsed time is accurate to the second, whereas the CPU times are measured to the 100th second. Thus, the sum of the CPU times can be up to a second larger than the elapsed time.

timemanp — Front Ends to the mp Text to PDL Pretty Print Filter

New!

Synopsis

/bin/timemanp [*options*] *filename*...

Description

See mailp(1).

---

times — Shell Built-in Function to Report Time Use of the Current Shell

Synopsis

sh

times

ksh

*

times

Description

Bourne Shell

Print the accumulated user and system times for processes run from the shell.

Korn Shell

Print the accumulated user and system times for the shell and for processes run from the shell.

ksh(1) commands that are preceded by one or two asterisks (*) are treated specially in the following ways.

1. Variable assignment lists preceding the command remain in effect when the command completes.
2. I/O redirections are processed after variable assignments.
3. Errors abort a script that contains them.
4. Words following a command preceded by ** that are in the format of a variable assignment are expanded with the same rules as a variable assignment. This means that tilde substitution is performed after the equal sign and that word splitting and file-name generation are not performed.

Attributes

See attributes(5) for descriptions of the following attributes:

Attribute Type	Attribute Value
Availability	SUNWcsu

See Also

ksh(1), sh(1), time(1), attributes(5)

timesysp — Front Ends to the mp Text to PDL Pretty Print Filter New!

Synopsis

/bin/timesysp [*options*] *filename*...

Description

See mailp(1).

timex — Time a Command; Report Process Data and System Activity

Synopsis

/usr/bin/timex [-o] [-p [-fhkmrt]] [-s] *command*

Description

The timex command, provided as part of the sar package, provides better diagnostic information than does the time command, especially for shell scripts that spawn child processes. By default, timex provides the same real, user, and sys times as the time command. In addition, it provides options to display the process accounting data (-p), the disk block use (-o), and total system activity data (-s) if the process accounting software is installed.

The timex command displays its results in seconds to standard error.

Note — Process records associated with *command* are selected from the accounting file /var/adm/pacct by inference because process genealogy is not available. Background processes having the same user ID, terminal ID, and execution time window are spuriously included.

Options

-o   Report the total number of blocks read or written and total characters transferred by *command* and all its children. This option works only if the process accounting software is installed.

-p   List process accounting records for *command* and all its children. This option works only if the process accounting software is installed. Suboptions f, h, k, m, r, and t modify the data items reported.

    -f   Print the fork(2) or exec(2) flag and system exit status columns in the output.

    -h   Instead of mean memory size, show the fraction of total available CPU time consumed by the process during its execution. This "hog factor" is computed as (total CPU time)/(elapsed time).

    -k   Instead of memory size, show total kcore minutes.

-m	Show mean core size (the default).
-r	Show CPU factor (user time/(system time + user time).
-t	Show separate system and user CPU times. Always report the number of blocks read or written and the number of characters transferred.
-s	Report total system activity (not just that because of *command*) that occurred during the execution interval of *command*. Report all the data items listed in sar(1).

Examples

The following is a simple example of using timex.

```
castle% timex -ops sleep 60
```

The following example measures a terminal session of arbitrary complexity by timing a subshell.

```
castle% timex -opskmt sh
session commands
EOT
```

Attributes

See attributes(5) for descriptions of the following attributes:

Attribute Type	Attribute Value
Availability	SUNWaccu

See Also

sar(1), time(1), times(2), attributes(5)

---

tip — Connect to Remote System

Synopsis

/usr/bin/tip [-v] [-*speed-entry*] {*hostname* | *phone-number* | *device*}

Description

Use the tip command to establish a full-duplex terminal connection to a remote host. Once you establish the connection, a remote session using tip behaves like an interactive session on a local terminal.

The /etc/remote file contains entries describing remote systems and line speeds used by tip.

Each host has a default baud rate for the connection, or you can specify a speed with the -*speed-entry* command-line argument.

When you specify *phone-number*, tip looks in the remote file for an entry of the following form.

```
tip -speed-entry
```

When it finds such an entry, tip sets the connection speed accordingly. If it finds no such entry, tip interprets -*speed-entry* as if it is a system name, resulting in an error message.

If you omit -*speed-entry*, tip uses the tip0 entry to set a speed for the connection.

When you specify *device*, tip tries to open that device but does so using the access privileges of the user instead of the usual tip access privileges (setuid uucp). You must have read/write access to the device. The tip command interprets any character string beginning with the slash character (/) as a device name.

When establishing the connection, tip sends a connection message to the remote system. You can find the default value for this message in the remote file.

When tip tries to connect to a remote system, it opens the associated device with an exclusive-open ioctl(2) call. Thus, only one user at a time can access a device. This restriction prevents multiple processes from sampling the terminal line. In addition, tip honors the locking protocol used by uucp(1C).

When tip starts up, it reads commands from the .tiprc file in your home directory.

Options

    -v   Display commands from the .tiprc file as they are executed.

Usage

Typed characters are normally transmitted directly to the remote system (which also does the echoing).

Any time that tip prompts for an argument (for example, during setup of a file transfer) you can edit the typed line with the standard erase and kill characters. A null line in response to a prompt or an interrupt aborts the dialogue and returns you to the remote system.

Commands

A tilde (~) as the first character of a line acts as an escape signal that directs tip to perform some special action. tip recognizes the following escape sequences.

~^D ~.	Drop the connection, and exit (you may still be logged in on the remote system).
~c [*name*]	Change directory to *name*. (No argument implies change to your home directory.)
~!	Escape to an interactive shell on the local system. (Exiting the shell returns you to tip.)
~>	Copy file from local to remote.
~<	Copy file from remote to local.

~p *from* [*to*]

>   Send a file to a remote host running the UNIX system. When you use the put command, the remote system runs the command string cat > *to* while tip sends it the *from* file. If you do not specify the *to* file, use the *from* file name. This command is actually a UNIX-system-specific version of the ~> command.

~t *from* [*to*]

>   Take a file from a remote host running the UNIX system. As in the put command, the *to* file defaults to the *from* file name if you do not specify it. The remote host executes the command string cat *from*; echo ^A to send the file to tip.

~|

>   Pipe the output from a remote command to a local process. The shell processes the command string sent to the local system.

~C

>   Connect a program to the remote system. The shell processes the command string sent to the program. The program inherits file descriptors 0 as remote line input, 1 as remote line output, and 2 as tty standard error.

~$

>   Pipe the output from a local process to the remote host. The shell processes the command string sent to the local system.

~#

>   Send a BREAK to the remote system.

~s

>   Set a variable (see the discussion below).

~^Z

>   Stop tip (only available when run under a shell, such as the C shell, that supports job control).

~^Y

>   Stop only the "local side" of tip (only available when run under a shell, such as the C shell, that supports job control); leave running the "remote side" of tip, the side that displays output from the remote host.

~?

>   Get a summary of the tilde escapes.

   Copying files requires some cooperation on the part of the remote host. When you use a ~> or ~< escape to send a file, tip prompts for a file name (to be transmitted or received) and a command to be sent to the remote system in case the file is being transferred from the remote system. While tip is transferring a file, the number of lines transferred is continuously displayed on the screen. You can abort a file transfer with an interrupt.

Auto-Call Units

You can use tip to dial up remote systems, using a number of auto-call units (ACUs). When the remote system description contains the du capability, tip uses the call unit (cu), ACU type (at), and phone numbers (pn) supplied. Normally, tip displays verbose messages as it dials.

   Depending on the type of auto-dialer being used to establish a connection, the remote host can have garbage characters sent to it on connection. You should never assume that the first characters typed to the foreign host are the first ones presented to it. The recommended practice is to immediately type a kill character on establishing a connection (most UNIX systems support either @ or Control-U as the initial kill character).

tip currently supports the Ventel MD-212+ and DC Hayes-compatible modems.

When tip initializes a Hayes-compatible modem for dialing, it sets the modem to auto-answer. Normally, after the conversation is complete, tip drops DTR, which hangs up the modem.

Most modems can be configured so that when DTR drops, they reinitialize themselves to a preprogrammed state. You can use this feature to reset the modem and disable auto-answer.

Additionally, it is possible to start the phone number with a Hayes S command so that you can configure the modem before dialing. For example, to disable auto-answer, set up all the phone numbers in /etc/remote by using something like pn=S0=0DT5551212. The S0=0 disables auto-answer.

Remote Host Description

Descriptions of remote hosts are normally located in the systemwide file /etc/remote. However, you can maintain personal description files (and phone numbers) by defining and exporting the REMOTE shell variable. The remote file must be readable by tip, but you can maintain a secondary file describing phone numbers readable only by you. This secondary phone number file is /etc/phones unless the shell variable PHONES is defined and exported. The phone number file contains lines of the following form.

system-name phone-number

Each phone number found for a system is tried until either a connection is established or an end-of-file is reached. Phone numbers are constructed from 0123456789-=*, where the = and * indicate to wait for a second dial tone (ACU dependent).

tip Internal Variables

tip maintains a set of variables that are used in normal operation. Some of these variables are read-only to normal users (root is allowed to change anything of interest). You can display and set variables with the ~s escape. The syntax for variables is patterned after vi(1) and mail(1). Supplying all as an argument to the ~s escape displays all variables that you can read. Alternatively, you can request display of a particular variable by attaching a ? to the end. For example, ~s escape? displays the current escape character.

Variables are numeric (num), string (str), character (char), or Boolean (bool) values. You set Boolean variables merely by specifying their name. You can reset them by prepending a ! to the name. You set other variable types by appending an = and the value. The entire assignment must not have any blanks in it. You can use a single set command to interrogate as well as to set a number of variables.

You can initialize variables at runtime by putting set commands (without the ~s prefix) in a .tiprc file in your home directory. The -v option displays the sets as they are made. You can precede comments in the .tiprc file with a #.

Finally, you must either completely specify the variable names or use an abbreviation. The following list details those variables known to tip.

beautify   (bool) Discard unprintable characters when a session is being scripted; abbreviated be. If the nb capability is present, initially set beautify to off; otherwise, initially set beautify to on.

baudrate   (num) The baud rate at which the connection was established; abbreviated ba. If you specified a baud rate on the command line, initially set baudrate to the specified value. If the br capability is present, initially set baudrate to the value of that capability; otherwise, set baudrate to 300 baud. Once tip has been started, only superuser can change baudrate.

dialtimeout (num) When a phone number is dialed, the time (in seconds) to wait for a connection to be established; abbreviated dial. Initially set dialtimeout to 60 seconds. Only superuser can change this value.

disconnect (str) The string to send to the remote host to disconnect from it; abbreviated di. If the di capability is present, initially set disconnect to the value of that capability; otherwise, set disconnect to a null string ("").

echocheck   (bool) Synchronize with the remote host during file transfer by waiting for the echo of the last character transmitted; abbreviated ec. If the ec capability is present, initially set echocheck to on; otherwise, initially set echocheck to off.

eofread   (str) The set of characters that signifies an end-of-transmission during a ~< file transfer command; abbreviated eofr. If the ie capability is present, initially set eofread to the value of that capability; otherwise, set eofread to a null string ("").

eofwrite   (str) The string sent to indicate end-of-transmission during a ~> file transfer command; abbreviated eofw. If the oe capability is present, initially set eofread to the value of that capability; otherwise, set eofread to a null string ("").

eol   (str) The set of characters that indicates an end-of-line. tip recognizes escape characters only after an end-of-line. If the el capability is present, initially set eol to the value of that capability; otherwise, set eol to a null string ("").

escape   (char) The command prefix (escape) character; abbreviated es. If the es capability is present, initially set escape to the value of that capability; otherwise, set escape to ~.

etimeout   (num) The amount of time, in seconds, that tip should wait for the echo-check response when echocheck is set; abbreviated et. If the et capability is present, initially set etimeout to the value of that capability; otherwise, set etimeout to 10 seconds.

exceptions (str) The set of characters that should not be discarded because of the beautification switch; abbreviated ex. If the ex capability is present, initially set exceptions to the value of that capability; otherwise, set exceptions to \t\n\f\b.

force   (char) The character used to force literal data transmission; abbreviated fo. If the fo capability is present, initially set force to the value of that capability; otherwise, set force to \377 (which disables it).

framesize   (num) The amount of data (in bytes) to buffer between file-system writes when receiving files; abbreviated fr. If the fs capability is present, initially set framesize to the value of that capability; otherwise, set framesize to 1024.

halfduplex   (bool) Do local echoing because the host is halfduplex; abbreviated hdx. If the hd capability is present, initially set halfduplex to on; otherwise, initially set halfduplex to off.

hardwareflow

    (bool) Do hardware flow control; abbreviated hf. If the hf capability is present, initially set hardwareflow to on; otherwise, initially set hardwareflow to off.

host   (str) The name of the host to which you are connected; abbreviated ho. Set host permanently to the name given on the command line or in the HOST environment variable.

localecho   (bool) A synonym for halfduplex; abbreviated le.

log   (str) The name of the file used to log information about outgoing phone calls. Initially set log to /var/adm/aculog. log can be inspected or changed only by superuser.

parity   (str) The parity to be generated and checked when talking to the remote host; abbreviated par. The possible values are:

none> zero	Parity is not checked on input and the parity bit is set to 0 on output.
one	Parity is not checked on input and the parity bit is set to 1 on output.
even	Even parity is checked for on input and generated on output.
odd	Odd parity is checked for on input and generated on output.

If the pa capability is present, initially set parity to the value of that capability; otherwise, set parity to none.

phones   The file used to find hidden phone numbers. If the environment variable PHONES is set, set phones to the value of PHONES; otherwise, set phones to /etc/phones. You cannot change the value of phones from within tip.

prompt   (char) The character that indicates an end-of-line on the remote host; abbreviated pr. Use this value to synchronize during data transfers. The count of lines transferred during a file transfer command is based on receipt of this character. If the pr capability is present, initially set prompt to the value of that capability; otherwise, set prompt to \n.

raise   (bool) Uppercase mapping mode; abbreviated ra. When this mode is enabled, map all lowercase letters to upper case for transmission to the remote system. If the ra capability is present, initially set raise to on; otherwise, initially set raise to off.

raisechar   (char) The input character used to toggle uppercase mapping mode; abbreviated rc. If the rc capability is present, initially set raisechar to the value of that capability; otherwise, set raisechar to \377 (which disables it).

rawftp   (bool) Send all characters during file transfers; do not filter nonprintable characters, and do not do translations like \n to \r. Abbreviated raw. If the rw capability is present, initially set rawftp to on; otherwise, initially set rawftp to off.

record   (str) The name of the file used to record a session script; abbreviated rec. If the re capability is present, initially set record to the value of that capability; otherwise, set record to tip.record.

remote   The file used to find descriptions of remote systems. If the environment variable REMOTE is set, set remote to the value of REMOTE; otherwise, set remote to /etc/remote. You cannot change the value of remote from within tip.

script   (bool) Session scripting mode; abbreviated sc. When script is on, record everything transmitted by the remote system in the script record file specified in record. If the beautify switch is on, include only printable ASCII characters in the script file (those characters between 040 and 0177). Use the variable exceptions to indicate characters that are an exception to the normal beautification rules. If the sc capability is present, initially set script to on; otherwise, initially set script to off.

tabexpand   (bool) Expand Tab characters to space characters during file transfers; abbreviated tab. When tabexpand is on, expand each Tab to eight space characters. If the tb capability is present, initially set tabexpand to on; otherwise, initially set tabexpand to off.

tandem   (bool) Use XON/XOFF flow control to limit the rate at which data is sent by the remote host; abbreviated ta. If the nt capability is present, initially set tandem to off; otherwise, initially set tandem to on.

verbose   (bool) Verbose mode; abbreviated verb. When verbose mode is enabled, print messages while dialing, show the current number of lines transferred during a file transfer operations, and more. If the nv capability is present, initially set verbose to off; otherwise, initially set verbose to on.

SHELL   (str) The name of the shell to use for the ~! command; default value is /bin/sh; otherwise, take the value from the environment.

HOME   (str) The home directory to use for the ~c command; take the default value from the environment.

Examples

The following example shows the dialog used to transfer files.

```
castle% tip monet
[connected]
... (assume we are talking to a UNIX system) ...
ucbmonet login: sam
Password:
monet% cat > sylvester.c
~> Filename: sylvester.c
32 lines transferred in 1 minute 3 seconds
monet%
monet% ~< Filename: reply.c
List command for remote host: cat reply.c
65 lines transferred in 2 minutes
monet%
... (or, equivalently) ...
monet% ~p sylvester.c
... (actually echoes as ~[put] sylvester.c) ...
32 lines transferred in 1 minute 3 seconds
monet%
monet% ~t reply.c
... (actually echoes as ~[take] reply.c) ...
65 lines transferred in 2 minutes
monet%
... (to print a file locally) ...
monet% ~|Local command: pr -h sylvester.c | lpr
List command for remote host: cat sylvester.c
monet% ~^D
[EOT]
... (back on the local system) ...
```

Environment Variables

The following environment variables are read by `tip`.

REMOTE	The location of the `remote` file.
PHONES	The location of the file containing private phone numbers.
HOST	A default host to connect to.
HOME	User's login directory (for `chdirs`).
SHELL	The shell to fork on a `~!` escape.

Files

`/etc/phones`

`/etc/remote`

`/var/spool/locks/LCK ..*`

        Lock file to avoid conflicts with UUCP.

`/var/adm/aculog`

        File used to log outgoing calls.

`~/.tiprc`   Initialization file.

Attributes

See `attributes`(5) for descriptions of the following attributes:

Attribute Type	Attribute Value
Availability	SUNWcsu

See Also

`mail(1)`, `vi(1)`, `cu(1C)`, `uucp(1C)`, `ioctl(2)`, `attributes(5)`

Bugs

Two additional variables, `chardelay` and `linedelay`, are currently not implemented.

---

tnfdump — Convert Binary Trace Normal Form (TNF) File to ASCII

Synopsis

New!   `/usr/bin/tnfdump [-r] [-x]` *tnf-file...*

Description

Use the `tnfdump` command to convert the specified binary Trace Normal Form (TNF) trace files to ASCII. You can use the ASCII output to do performance analysis. The default mode (without the -r option) prints all the event records (that were generated by TNF_PROBE(3TNF)) and the event descriptor records only. It also orders the events by time.

Options

`-r`	Do a raw conversion of TNF to ASCII. Translate the output as a literal translation of the binary TNF file and include all the records in the file. This output is useful only if you have a good understanding of TNF.
`-x`	Print all TNF unsigned type argument values in hexadecimal format instead of decimal format. New in the Solaris 9 release.

New! is marked next to the `-x` option.

Examples

The following example converts the file `/tmp/trace-2130` into ASCII use. The output uses very long lines; they are wrapped in this example.

```
castle% tnfdump /tmp/trace-2130
probe       tnf_name: "inloop" tnf_string: "keys cookie main loop;file
   cookie2.c;line 50;sunw%debug in the loop"
probe       tnf_name: "end" tnf_string: "keys cookie main end;file
   cookie2.c;line 41;sunw%debug exiting program"
---------------- ---------------- ----- ----- ---------- ---
Elapsed (ms)      Delta (ms)   PID LWPID    TID    CPU Probe Name
   Data / Description . . .
------ --- ----------------------- -----------------------
0.000000       0.000000  8792     1      0      -    inloop
```

```
   loop_count: 0 total_iterations: 0
0.339000          0.339000  8792     1      0        -    inloop
   loop_count: 1 total_iterations: 1
0.350500          0.011500  8792     1      0        -    inloop
   loop_count: 2 total_iterations: 2
0.359500          0.009000  8792     1      0        -    inloop
   loop_count: 3 total_iterations: 3
0.369500          0.010000  8792     1      0        -    inloop
   loop_count: 4 total_iterations: 4
      7775.969500      7775.600000  8792     1    0      -    inloop
   loop_count: 0 total_iterations: 5
      7776.016000          0.046500  8792     1    0      -    inloop
   loop_count: 1 total_iterations: 6
      7776.025000          0.009000  8792     1    0      -    inloop
   loop_count: 2 total_iterations: 7
      7776.034000          0.009000  8792     1    0      -    inloop
   loop_count: 3 total_iterations: 8
      7776.043000          0.009000  8792     1    0      -    inloop
   loop_count: 4 total_iterations: 9
      7776.052000          0.009000  8792     1    0      -    inloop
   loop_count: 5 total_iterations: 10
      7776.061000          0.009000  8792     1    0      -    inloop
   loop_count: 6 total_iterations: 11
      9475.979500      1699.918500  8792     1    0      -    end
   node_struct: { type: node_tnf cur_sum: 9

max_cnt: 12 }
```

A description is included for all probes that are encountered during execution. The description is one per line prefixed by the keyword `probe`. The name of the probe is in double quotes after the keyword `tnf_name`. The description of this probe is in double quotes after the keyword `tnf_string`.

A heading is printed after all the descriptions of the probes are printed. The first column shows the elapsed time in milliseconds since the first event. The second column shows the elapsed time in milliseconds since the previous event. The next four columns are the process ID, LWP ID, thread ID, and CPU number. The next column is the name of the probe that generated this event. You can match the probe name to the probe description explained above. The last column is the data that the event contains, formatted as `arg_name_n` (see `TNF_PROBE`(3X)) followed by a colon and the value of that argument. The format of the value depends on its type. `tnf_opaque` arguments are printed in hexadecimal; all other integers are printed in decimal. Strings are printed in double quotes and user-defined records are enclosed in braces `{ }`. The first field of a user-defined record indicates its TNF type (see `TNF_DECLARE_RECORD`(3X)), and the rest of the fields are the members of the record.

A – in any column indicates that there is no data for that particular column.

The following example does a raw conversion of the file `/tmp/trace-4000` into ASCII.

```
castle% tnfdump -r /tmp/trace-4000
0x10e00    : {
tnf_tag 0x109c0      tnf_block_header
       generation 1
     bytes_valid 320
          A_lock 0
          B_lock 0
      next_block 0x0
}
```

```
0x10e10   : {
tnf_tag 0x10010    probe1
     tnf_tag_arg 0x10e24    <tnf_sched_rec>
      time_delta 128
      test_ulong 4294967295
       test_long -1
}

0x10e24   : {
tnf_tag 0x10cf4    tnf_sched_rec
            tid 0
          lwpid 1
            pid 13568
       time_base 277077875828500
}
0x10e3c   : {
tnf_tag 0x11010    probe2
     tnf_tag_arg 0x10e24    <tnf_sched_rec>
      time_delta 735500
        test_str 0x10e48    "string1"
}
0x10e48   : {
tnf_tag 0x1072c    tnf_string
   tnf_self_size 16
           chars "string1"
}
     0x10e58   : {
         tnf_tag 0x110ec    probe3
     tnf_tag_arg 0x10e24    <tnf_sched_rec>
      time_delta 868000
   test_ulonglong 18446744073709551615
   test_longlong -1
      test_float 3.142857
}
     ...
     ...
     ...
     0x110ec   : {
         tnf_tag 0x10030    tnf_probe_type
     tnf_tag_code 42
        tnf_name 0x1110c    "probe3"
   tnf_properties 0x1111c    <tnf_properties>
   tnf_slot_types 0x11130    <tnf_slot_types>
    tnf_type_size 32
   tnf_slot_names 0x111c4    <tnf_slot_names>
      tnf_string 0x11268    "keys targdebug main;file targdebug.c;line
   61;"
}
     0x1110c   : {
         tnf_tag 0x10068    tnf_name
   tnf_self_size 16
           chars "probe3"
}
     0x1111c   : {
```

```
            tnf_tag 0x100b4      tnf_properties
    tnf_self_size 20
                0 0x101a0        tnf_tagged
                1 0x101c4        tnf_struct
                2 0x10b84        tnf_tag_arg
}
      0x11130    : {
            tnf_tag 0x10210      tnf_slot_types
    tnf_self_size 28
                0 0x10bd0        tnf_probe_event
                1 0x10c20        tnf_time_delta
                2 0x1114c        tnf_uint64
                3 0x10d54        tnf_int64
                4 0x11188        tnf_float32
}
```

The first number is the file offset of the record. The record is enclosed in braces { }. The first column in a record is the slot name (for records whose fields do not have names, it is the type name). The second column in the record is the value of that slot if it is a scalar (only scalars that are of type tnf_opaque are printed in hexadecimal) or the offset of the record if it is a reference to another record.

The third column in a record is optional. It does not exist for scalar slots of records. If it exists, the third column is a type name with or without angle brackets or a string in double quotes. Unadorned names indicate a reference to the named metatag record (that is, a reference to a record with that name in the tnf_name field). Type names in angle brackets indicate a reference to a record that is an instance of that type (that is, a reference to a record with that name in the tnf_tag field). The content of strings are printed in double quotes at the reference site.

For records that are arrays, their array elements follow the header slots and are numbered 0, 1, 2, ..., except strings where the string is written as the chars (pseudonym) slot.

For records that are events (generated by TNF_PROBE(3X)), the second field has a slot name of tnf_tag_arg, which is a reference to the schedule record. Schedule records describe more information about the event, such as the thread ID, process ID, and the time_base. You can add the time_delta of an event to the time_base of the schedule record of that event reference to give an absolute time. This time is expressed as nanoseconds since some arbitrary time in the past (see gethrtime(3C)).

The following example prints TNF unsigned arguments in hexadecimal for the file /tmp/trace-2192.

```
example% tnfdump -x /tmp/trace-2192
probe        tnf_name: "start" tnf_string: "keys cookie main;
file test17.c;line 20;sunw%debug starting main"
probe        tnf_name: "inloop" tnf_string: "keys cookie main
loop;file test17.c;line 41;sunw%debug in the loop"
probe        tnf_name: "final" tnf_string: "keys cookie main
final;file test17.c;line 32;sunw%debug in the final"
-----------  -----------  ----  -----  ---  ---------  --------------------
Elapsed      Delta        PID   LWPID  TID  CPU Probe  Data/Description ...
  (ms)         (ms)                         Name
-----------  -----------  ----  -----  ---  ---------  --------------------
   0.000000     0.000000  6280    1     1   -   start
2455.211311  2455.211311  6280    1     1   -   inloop  loop_count: 0x0
                                                        total_iterations: 0x0
```

```
2455.215768    0.004457     6280    1    1   - inloop  loop_count: 0x1
                                                       total_iterations: 0x1
2455.217041    0.001273     6280    1    1   - inloop  loop_count: 0x2
                                                       total_iterations: 0x2
2455.218285    0.001244     6280    1    1   - inloop  loop_count: 0x3
                                                       total_iterations: 0x3
2455.219600    0.001315     6280    1    1   - inloop  loop_count: 0x4
                                                       total_iterations: 0x4
4058.815125    1603.595525  6280    1    1   - inloop  loop_count: 0x0
                                                       total_iterations: 0x5
4058.818699    0.003574     6280    1    1   - inloop  loop_count: 0x1
                                                       total_iterations: 0x6
4058.819931    0.001232     6280    1    1   - inloop  loop_count: 0x2
                                                       total_iterations: 0x7
4058.821264    0.001333     6280    1    1   - inloop  loop_count: 0x3
                                                       total_iterations: 0x8
4058.822520    0.001256     6280    1    1   - inloop  loop_count: 0x4
                                                       total_iterations: 0x9
4058.823781    0.001261     6280    1    1   - inloop  loop_count: 0x5
                                                       total_iterations: 0xa
4058.825037    0.001256     6280    1    1   - inloop  loop_count: 0x6
                                                       total_iterations: 0xb
13896.655450   9837.830413  6280    1    1   - final   loop_count16: 0x258
                                                       total_iterations8: 0xb0
::
::
::
example%
```

Notice that the `loop_count` and the `total_iterations` are TNF unsigned arguments. Their values are printed in hexadecimal when requested by option -x.

Exit Status

`tnfdump` returns 0 on successful exit.

Attributes

See `attributes`(5) for descriptions of the following attributes:

Attribute Type	Attribute Value
Availability	SUNWtnfd

See Also

`prex`(1), `gethrtime`(3C), `TNF_DECLARE_RECORD`(3TNF), `TNF_PROBE`(3TNF), `tnf_process_disable`(3TNF), `attributes`(5)

tnfxtract — Extract Kernel Probes Output into a Trace File

Synopsis

`/usr/bin/tnfxtract` [-d *dumpfile* -n *namelist*] *tnf_file*

Description

The `tnfxtract` command collects kernel trace output from an in-core buffer in the Solaris kernel or from the memory image of a crashed system and generates a binary Trace Normal Form (TNF) trace file like those produced directly by user programs being traced.

You must specify both or neither of the -d and -n options. If you specify neither, trace output is extracted from the running kernel. If you specify both, the -d argument names the file containing the (crashed) system memory image, and the -n argument names the file containing the symbol table for the system memory image.

The TNF trace file produced is exactly the same size as the in-core buffer; it is essentially a snapshot of that buffer. It is legal to run `tnfxtract` while kernel tracing is active, that is, while the in-core buffer is being written. `tnfxtract` ensures that the output file it generates is low-level consistent, that is, that only whole probes are written out and that internal data structures in the buffer are not corrupted because the buffer is being concurrently written.

The TNF trace file generated is suitable as input to `tnfdump`(1), which generates an ASCII file.

Options

-d *dumpfile*

Use *dumpfile* as the system memory image instead of using the running kernel image. *dumpfile* is normally the path name of a file generated by the `savecore` command.

-n *namelist*

Use *namelist* as the file containing the symbol table information for the given *dumpfile*.

Operands

tnf-file   Specify the output file generated by `tnfxtract` based on kernel trace output from an in-core buffer in the Solaris kernel.

Examples

The following example probes from the running kernel into `ktrace.out`.

```
castle% tnfxtract ktrace.out
```

The following example probes from a kernel crash dump into `ktrace.out`.

```
castle% tnfxtract -d /var/crash/`uname -n`/vmcore.0 -n /var/crash/`uname
    -n`/unix.0 ktrace.out
```

Exit Status

0   Successful completion.

>0   An error occurred.

Attributes

See attributes(5) for descriptions of the following attributes:

Attribute Type	Attribute Value
Availability	SUNWtnfc

See Also

prex(1), tnfdump(1), savecore(1M), tnf_kernel_probes(4), attributes(5)

touch — Change File Access and Modification Times

Synopsis

```
/usr/bin/touch [-acm] [-r ref-file | -t time] file...
/usr/bin/touch [-acm] date-time] file...
/usr/bin/settime [-f ref-file] [date-time] file...
```
New!

Description

Use the touch command to change access and modification times of files. If the file does not already exist, it is created.

You can specify the time used by -t *time*, by the corresponding time fields of the file referenced by -r *ref-file*, or by the *date-time* operand. If you specify none of these options, touch uses the current time (the value returned by the time(2) function).

If you specify neither the -a nor -m options, touch updates both the modification and access times.

New! A user with write access to a file but who is not either the owner of the file or superuser can change the modification and access times of that file only to the current time. Attempts to set a specific time with touch result in an error.

New! The settime command is equivalent to touch -c [*date-time*] *file*.

> **Note** — Users familiar with the BSD environment should note that, for the touch command, the -f option is accepted but ignored. The -f option is not needed because touch succeeds for all files owned by the user regardless of the permissions on the files.

Options

The touch command has the following options.

-a	Change the access time of *file*. Do not change the modification time unless you also specify -m.
-c	Do not create a specified file if it does not exist. Do not write any diagnostic messages concerning this condition.
-m	Change the modification time of *file*. Do not change the access time unless you also specify -a.
-r *ref-file*	Use the corresponding times of an existing file named by *ref-file* instead of the current time.

-t *time*   Use the specified time instead of the current time. *time* is a decimal number of the form [[*CC*] *YY*] *MMDDhhmm*[. *SS*], where each two-digit pair represents the following:

MM	The month of the year [01-12].
DD	The day of the month [01-31].
hh	The hour of the day [00-23].
mm	The minute of the hour [00-59].
CC	The first two digits of the year.
YY	The second two digits of the year.
SS	The second of the minute [00-61].

The range for *SS* is [00-61] instead of [00-59] because of leap seconds. If *SS* is 60 or 61 and the resulting time, as affected by the TZ environment variable, does not refer to a leap second, the resulting time is one or two seconds after a time where *SS* is 59. If you do not specify *SS*, assume it is 0.

Both *CC* and *YY* are optional. If you specify neither, assume the current year. If you specify *YY* but not *CC*, derive it as follows.

If *YY* is:	*CC* becomes:
69-99	19
00-38	20
39-68	ERROR

The resulting time is affected by the value of the TZ environment variable. If the resulting time value precedes the Epoch, exit immediately with an error status. The range of valid times is the Epoch to January 18, 2038.

The settime command can use the optional -f *ref-time* option to reference the corresponding times from an existing file.

Operands

file   A path name of a file whose times are to be modified.

date-time   Use the specified *date-time* instead of the current time. *date-time* is a decimal number of the following form.

MMDDhhmm[*YY*]

where each two-digit pair represents the following:

MM	The month of the year [01–12].
DD	The day of the month [01–31].
hh	The hour of the day [00–23].
mm	The minute of the hour [00–59].
YY	The second two digits of the year.

YY is optional. If you omit it, assume the current year. If you specify *YY*, derive the year as follows.

YY	Corresponding Year
69-99	1969-1999
00-38	2000-2038
39-68	ERROR

If you specify no -f option, no -t option, at least two operands, and the first operand is an 8- or 10-digit decimal integer, assume the first operand is a *date-time* operand; otherwise, touch assumes the first operand is a *file* operand.

Examples

The following example shows the modification time for the file kookaburra-1 and changes the access and modification times to the current date and time.

```
castle% ls -l kookaburra-1
-rw-r--r--   1 winsor    staff        264 Feb 20 16:12 kookaburra-1
castle% touch kookaburra-1
castle% ls -l kookaburra-1
-rw-r--r--   1 winsor    staff        264 Apr  9 13:59 kookaburra-1
castle%
```

Usage

See largefile(5) for the description of the behavior of touch when encountering files greater than or equal to 2 Gbytes (2**31 bytes).

Environment Variables

See environ(5) for descriptions of the following environment variables that affect the execution of touch: LC_MESSAGES, NLSPATH, and TZ.

Exit Status

0	touch executed successfully, and all requested changes were made.
>0	An error occurred. touch returns the number of files for which it could not successfully modify the times.

Attributes

See attributes(5) for descriptions of the following attributes:

Attribute Type	Attribute Value
Availability	SUNWcsu
CSI	Enabled

See Also

time(2), attributes(5), environ(5), largefile(5)

tplot, t300, t300s, t4014, t450, tek, ver — Graphics Filters for Terminal Output of Various Plotters

Synopsis

```
/usr/bin/tplot [-Tterminal]
```

Description

The `tplot` command reads plotting instructions from the standard input and produces plotting instructions suitable for a particular terminal on the standard output.

If you specify no terminal, the environment variable TERM is used. The default terminal is `tek`.

Environment Variables

Except for `ver`, you can use the following terminal types with `lpr -g` (see `lpr(1B)`) to produce plotted output.

`300`	DASI 300 or GSI terminal (Diablo mechanism).
`300s	300S`	DASI 300s terminal (Diablo mechanism).
`450`	DASI Hyterm 450 terminal (Diablo mechanism).
`4014	tek`	Tektronix 4014 and 4015 storage scope with Enhanced Graphics Module. (Use 4013 for Tektronix 4014 or 4015 without the Enhanced Graphics Module.)
`ver`	Versatec D1200A printer-plotter. The output is scan-converted and suitable input to `lpr -v`.

Files

```
/usr/lib/t300
/usr/lib/t300s
/usr/lib/t4014
/usr/lib/t450
/usr/lib/tek
/usr/lib/vplot
```

Attributes

See `attributes(5)` for descriptions of the following attributes:

Attribute Type	Attribute Value
Availability	SUNWcsu

See Also

`lp(1)`, `vi(1)`, `attributes(5)`

tput — Initialize a Terminal or Query terminfo Database

Synopsis

```
/usr/bin/tput [-Ttype] capname [parm...]
/usr/bin/tput -S <<
```

Description

The tput command uses the terminfo database to make the values of terminal-dependent capabilities and information available to the shell (see sh(1)); to clear, initialize, or reset the terminal; or to return the long name of the requested terminal type. tput outputs a string if the capability attribute (*capname*) is of type string or outputs an integer if the attribute is of type integer. If the attribute is of type boolean, tput simply sets the exit status (0 for true if the terminal has the capability, 1 for false if it does not) and produces no output. Before using a value returned on standard output, you should test the exit status to be sure it is 0 ($?, see sh(1)).

Options

-T*type*   Indicate the type of terminal. Normally, you do not need to use this option because the default is taken from the environment variable TERM. If you specify -T, then do not reference the shell variables LINES and COLUMNS and the layer size.

-S   Allow more than one capability per invocation of tput. You must pass the capabilities to tput from the standard input instead of from the command line. Only one *capname* is allowed per line. The -S option changes the meaning of the 0 and 1 Boolean and string exit statuses.

Operands

capname   Indicate the capability attribute from the terminfo database. See terminfo(4) for a complete list of capabilities and the *capname* associated with each. The following strings are supported as operands by the implementation in the C locale.

clear   Display the clear-screen sequence.

init   If the terminfo database is present and an entry for your terminal exists (see -T*type*), the following occurs.

- If present, output the terminal's initialization strings (is1, is2, is3, if, iprog).

- Set any delays (for instance, newline) specified in the entry in the tty driver.

- Turn on or off Tabs expansion according to the specification in the entry.

- If Tabs are not expanded, set standard Tabs (every 8 spaces).

If an entry does not contain the information needed for any of the above four activities, silently skip that activity.

reset   Instead of putting out initialization strings, output the terminal's reset strings if present (rs1, rs2, rs3, rf). If the reset strings are not present but initialization strings are, output the initialization strings. Otherwise, reset acts identically to init.

longname   If the terminfo database is present and an entry for your terminal exists (see -T*type*), then output the long name of the terminal. The long name is the last name in the first line of the terminal description in the terminfo database (see term(5)).

parm   If the attribute is a string that takes parameters, instantiate the *parm* argument into the string. Pass an all-numeric argument to the attribute as a number.

Examples

The following example initializes the terminal according to the type of terminal in the environment variable TERM.

```
castle% tput init
castle%
```

This command should be included in everyone's .profile after the environment variable TERM has been exported, as illustrated in the profile(4) manual page.

The following example resets an AT&T 5620 terminal, overriding the type of terminal in the environment variable TERM.

```
castle% tput -T5620 reset
castle%
```

The following example sends the sequence to move the cursor to row 0, column 0 (the upper-left corner of the screen, usually known as the home cursor position).

```
castle% tput cup 0 0
castle%
```

The following example echoes the clear-screen sequence for the current terminal.

```
castle% tput clear
castle%
```

The following example prints the number of columns for the current terminal.

```
castle% tput cols
94
castle%
```

The following example prints the number of columns for the 450 terminal.

```
castle% tput -T450 cols
132
castle%
```

The following example sets the shell variables bold (to begin standout mode sequence) and offbold (to end standout mode sequence) for the current terminal, followed by a prompt.

```
$ bold=`tput smso`
$ offbold=`tput rmso`
$ echo "${bold}Please type your name: ${offbold}\c"
```

The following example sets the exit status to indicate whether the current terminal is a hardcopy terminal.

```
castle% tput hc
castle%
```

The following example sends the sequence to move the cursor to row 23, column 4.

```
castle% tput cup 23 4
castle%
```

The following example prints the long name from the terminfo database for the type of terminal specified in the environment variable TERM.

```
castle% tput longname
CDE terminal emulator
castle%
```

The following example shows tput processing several capabilities in one invocation. It clears the screen, moves the cursor to position 10, 10, and turns on bold (extra bright) mode. Terminate the list with an exclamation mark (!) on a line by itself.

```
$ tput -S <<!
> clear
> cup 10 10
> bold
> !
$
```

Environment Variables

See environ(5) for descriptions of the following environment variables that affect the execution of tput: LC_CTYPE, LC_MESSAGES, and NLSPATH.

TERM   Determine the terminal type. If this variable is unset or null and if you did not specify the -T option, use an unspecified default terminal type.

Exit Status

0   If *capname* is of type boolean and you did not specify -S, return true.

               If *capname* is of type string and you did not specify -S, indicate that *capname* is defined for this terminal type.

If *capname* is of type `boolean` or string and you specified -S, indicate that all lines were successful.

If *capname* is of type `integer`.

If the requested string was written successfully.

1   If *capname* is of type `boolean` and you did not specify -S, return `false`.

If *capname* is of type `string` and you did not specify -S, indicate that *capname* is not defined for this terminal type.

2   Usage error.

3   No information is available about the specified terminal type.

4   The specified operand is invalid.

>4   An error occurred.

-1   If *capname* is a numeric variable that is not specified in the `terminfo` database; for instance, `tput -T450 lines` and `tput -T2621 xmc`.

Files

`/usr/include/curses.h`

        `curses`(3X) header.

`/usr/include/term.h`

        `terminfo` header.

`/usr/lib/tabset/*`

        Tab settings for some terminals in a format appropriate to be output to the terminal (escape sequences that set margins and Tabs); for more information, see the "Tabs and Initialization" section of `terminfo`(4).

`/usr/share/lib/terminfo/?/*`

        Compiled terminal description database.

Attributes

See `attributes`(5) for descriptions of the following attributes:

Attribute Type	Attribute Value
Availability	SUNWcsu

See Also

`clear(1)`, `stty(1)`, `tabs(1)`, `profile(4)`, `terminfo(4)`, `attributes(5)`, `environ(5)`

tr — Translate Characters

Synopsis

```
/usr/bin/tr [-cs] string1 string2
/usr/bin/tr -s|-d [-c] string1
/usr/bin/tr -ds [-c] string1 string2
/usr/bin/xpg4/tr [-cs] string1 string2
/usr/bin/xpg4/tr -s|-d [-c] string1
/usr/bin/xpg4/tr -ds [-c] string1 string2
```

Description

Use the tr (translate) command to substitute one set of strings for another in a file or to remove specified characters from a file. The tr command is one of the few common UNIX commands that does not enable you to specify a file name as an argument. Instead, you must use the < redirection symbol.

The tr command can translate any number of characters. Usually, you give tr an input list of characters, specified as *string1*, followed by an output list of characters, specified as *string2*. tr replaces every instance of a character in *string1* with the corresponding character in *string2*.

The options specified and the *string1* and *string2* operands control translations that occur while copying characters and single-character collating elements.

Note — Unlike some previous versions, the tr command correctly processes null characters in its input stream. You can strip null characters by using tr -d '\000'.

Options

-c   Complement the set of characters specified by *string1*.

-d   Delete all occurrences of input characters that are specified by *string1*.

-s   Replace instances of repeated characters with a single character.

When you do not specify the -d option:

- Each input character found in the array specified by *string1* is replaced by the character in the same relative position in the array specified by *string2*. When the array specified by *string2* is shorter that the one specified by *string1*, the results are unspecified.

- If you specify the -c option, the complements of the characters specified by *string1* (the set of all characters in the current character set, as defined by the current setting of LC_CTYPE, except for those actually specified in the *string1* operand) are placed in the array in ascending collation sequence as defined by the current setting of LC_COLLATE.

- Because the order in which characters specified by character class expressions or equivalence class expressions is undefined, you should only use such expressions if you intend to map several characters into one. An exception is case conversion, as described below.

When you specify the -d option:

- Input characters found in the array specified by *string1* are deleted.
- When you specify the -c option with -d, all characters except those specified by *string1* are deleted. The contents of *string2* are ignored unless you also specify the -s option.
- You cannot use the same string for both the -d and the -s options; when you specify both options, both *string1* (used for deletion) and *string2* (used for squeezing) are required.
- When you specify the -s option, then after any deletions or translations have taken place, repeated sequences of the same character are replaced by one occurrence of the same character if the character is found in the array specified by the last operand. If the last operand contains a character class, such as tr -s '[:space:]', the last operand's array contains all of the characters in that character class. However, in a case conversion, as described below, such as tr -s '[:upper:]' '[:lower:]', the last operand's array contains only those characters defined as the second characters in each of the toupper or tolower character pairs, as appropriate. (See toupper(3C) and tolower(3C).)
- An empty string used for *string1* or *string2* produces undefined results.

Operands

string1 *string2*	Translation control strings. Each string represents a set of characters to be converted into an array of characters used for the translation.
	The operands *string1* and *string2* (if specified) define two arrays of characters. You can use the constructs in the following list to specify characters or single-character collating elements. If any of the constructs result in multicharacter collating elements, tr excludes, without a diagnostic, those multicharacter elements from the resulting array.
character	Any character not described by one of the conventions below represents itself.
octal	You can use octal sequences to represent characters with specific coded values. An octal sequence consists of a backslash followed by the longest sequence of one-, two-, or three-octal-digit characters (01234567). The sequence puts the character whose encoding is represented by the one-, two- or three-digit octal integer into the array. Multibyte characters require multiple, concatenated escape sequences of this type, including the leading \\ for each byte.
character	
	The backslash escape sequences \\a, \\b, \\f, \\n, \\r, \\t, and \\v are supported. The results of using any character other than an octal digit following the backslash are unspecified.

c-c (/usr/xpg4/bin/tr)
[*c-c*] (/usr/bin/tr)

> Specify the range of collating elements between the range endpoints, inclusive, as defined by the current setting of the LC_COLLATE locale category. The starting endpoint must precede the second endpoint in the current collation order. Put the characters or collating elements in the range in the array in ascending collation sequence.

[:*class*:] Represent all characters belonging to the defined character *class*, as defined by the current setting of the LC_CTYPE locale category. The following character class names are accepted when specified in *string1*: alnum alpha blank cntrl digit graph lower print punct upper space xdigit.

In addition, character class expressions of the form [:*name*:] are recognized in those locales where the name keyword has been given a charclass definition in the LC_CTYPE category.

When you specify both the -d and -s options, any of the character class names are accepted in *string2*. Otherwise, only character class names lower or upper are valid in *string2* and then only if the corresponding character class upper and lower is specified in the same relative position in *string1*. Such a specification is interpreted as a request for case conversion. When [:lower:] appears in *string1* and [:upper:] appears in *string2*, the arrays contain the characters from the toupper mapping in the LC_CTYPE category of the current locale. When [:upper:] appears in *string1* and [:lower:] appears in *string2*, the arrays contain the characters from the tolower mapping in the LC_CTYPE category of the current locale. The first character from each mapping pair is in the array for *string1*, and the second character from each mapping pair is in the array for *string2* in the same relative position.

Except for case conversion, the characters specified by a character class expression are placed in the array in an unspecified order.

If the name specified for *class* does not define a valid character class in the current locale, the behavior is undefined.

[=*equiv*=] Represent all characters or collating elements belonging to the same equivalence class as *equiv*, as defined by the current setting of the LC_COLLATE locale category. An equivalence class expression is allowed only in *string1* or in *string2* when it is being used by the combined -d and -s options. Put the characters belonging to the equivalence class in the array in an unspecified order.

[*x**n] Represent *n* repeated occurrences of the character *x*. Because this expression is used to map multiple characters to one character, it is valid only when it occurs in *string2*. If you omit *n* or it is 0, interpret it as large enough to extend the *string2*-based sequence to the length of the *string1*-based sequence. If *n* has a leading 0, interpret it as an octal value. Otherwise, interpret it as a decimal value.

Usage

See largefile(5) for the description of the behavior of tr when encountering files greater than or equal to 2 Gbytes (2**31 bytes).

Examples

The following example converts all colons in the `passwd` file to Tabs. Notice that you enclose the Tab character in single quotes to prevent the shell from treating it as white space. In this example, the Tab character is represented as the word `Tab`. When you type the command line, simply press the Tab key. Also notice that you use the < redirection symbol to specify the file name to use as input to the `tr` command.

```
castle% tr : 'Tab' < passwd
root     x      0      1      Super-User        /          /sbin/sh
daemon   x      1      1                 /
bin      x      2      2                 /usr/bin
sys      x      3      3                 /
adm      x      4      4      Admin     /var/adm
lp       x      71     8      Line Printer Admin        /usr/spool/lp
uucp     x      5      5      uucp Admin      /usr/lib/uucp
nuucp    x      9      9      uucp Admin      /var/spool/uucppublic
        /usr/lib/uucp/uucico
listen   x      37     4      Network Admin    /usr/net/nls
nobody   x      60001  60001  Nobody  /
noaccess x      60002  60002  No Access User  /
nobody4  x      65534  65534  SunOS 4.x Nobody          /
winsor   x      1001   10               /export/home/winsor      /bin/csh
ray      x      1002   10               /export/home/ray         /bin/csh
des      x      1003   10               /esport/home/des         /bin/csh
rob      x      1004   10               /export/home/rob         /bin/csh
castle%
```

The following example creates a list of all words in `kookaburra-1`, one per line, in `kook.out`, where a word is taken to be a maximal string of letters.

```
castle% tr -cs "[:alpha:]" "[\n*]" < kookaburra-1 > kook.out
castle% cat kook.out
Kookaburra
sits
in
the
old
gum
tree
Merry
merry
king
of
the
bush
is
he
... (More lines not shown here)
castle%
```

The following example translates all lowercase characters in `file1` to upper case and writes the results to standard output.

```
castle% tr "[:lower:]" "[:upper:]" < kookaburra-1
KOOKABURRA SITS IN THE OLD GUM TREE
```

```
MERRY MERRY KING OF THE BUSH IS HE.
LAUGH, KOOKABURRA, LAUGH, KOOKABURRA
GAY YOUR LIFE MUST BE

KOOKABURRA SITS IN THE OLD GUM TREE
EATING ALL THE GUMDROPS HE CAN SEE.
STOP, KOOKABURRA, STOP, KOOKABURRA
LEAVE SOME THERE FOR ME.
castle%
```

Note — The caveat expressed in the corresponding example in XPG3(5) is no longer in effect. This case conversion is now a special case that uses the `tolower` and `toupper` classifications, ensuring that proper mapping is accomplished when the locale is correctly defined.

The following example uses an equivalence class to identify accented variants of the base character e in file1, which are stripped of diacritical marks and written to file2.

```
castle% tr "[=e=]" e <file1 >file2
castle%
```

Environment Variables

See environ(5) for descriptions of the following environment variables that affect the execution of tr: LC_COLLATE, LC_CTYPE, LC_MESSAGES, and NLSPATH.

Exit Status

| 0 | All input was processed successfully. |
| >0 | An error occurred. |

Attributes

See attributes(5) for descriptions of the following attributes:

/usr/bin/tr

Attribute Type	Attribute Value
Availability	SUNWcsu
CSI	Enabled

/usr/xpg4/bin/tr

Attribute Type	Attribute Value
Availability	SUNWxcu4
CSI	Enabled

See Also

ed(1), sed(1), sh(1), tolower(3C), toupper(3C), ascii(5), attributes(5), environ(5), largefile(5), XPG4(5)

trap, onintr — Shell Built-in Functions to Respond to Hardware Signals

Synopsis

sh

trap [*argument* n [*n2*...]]

csh

onintr [-| *label*]

ksh

*

trap [*arg sig* [*sig2*...]]

Description

Use the built-in shell trap and onintr commands in shell scripts to specify a sequence of commands to be executed when your shell script receives an interrupt signal.

Bourne Shell

The trap command argument is read and executed when the shell receives numeric or symbolic signal(s) (*n*).

Note — *argument* is scanned once when the trap is set and once when the trap is taken.

Trap commands are executed in order of signal number or corresponding symbolic names. Any attempt to set a trap on a signal that was ignored on entry to the current shell is ineffective. An attempt to trap on signal 11 (memory fault) produces an error. If you do not specify *argument*, all trap(s) *n* are reset to their original values. If *argument* is a null string, this signal is ignored by the shell and by the commands it invokes. If *n* is 0, the command *argument* is executed on exit from the shell. The trap command with no arguments prints a list of commands associated with each signal number.

C Shell

The onintr command controls the action of the shell on interrupts. With no arguments, onintr restores the default action of the shell on interrupts. (The shell terminates shell scripts and returns to the terminal command input level.) With the - argument, the shell ignores all interrupts. With a *label* argument, the shell executes a goto label when an interrupt is received or a child process terminates because it was interrupted.

Korn Shell

trap uses *arg* as a command to be read and executed when the shell receives signal(s) *sig*.

Note — *arg* is scanned once when the trap is set and once when the trap is taken.

You can specify each *sig* as a number or as the name of the signal. trap commands are executed in order of signal number. Any attempt to set a trap on a signal that was ignored on entry to the current shell is ineffective. If you omit *arg* or it is -, then the trap(s) for each *sig* are reset to their original values. If *arg* is null (the empty string " "), then this signal is ignored by the shell and by the commands it invokes. If *sig* is ERR, then *arg* is executed whenever a command has a non-zero exit status. If *sig* is DEBUG, then *arg* is executed after each command. If *sig* is 0 or EXIT for a trap set outside any function, then the command *arg* is executed on exit from the shell. The trap command with no arguments prints a list of commands associated with each signal number.

ksh(1) commands that are preceded by one or two asterisks (*) are treated specially in the following ways.

1. Variable assignment lists preceding the command remain in effect when the command completes.
2. I/O redirections are processed after variable assignments.
3. Errors abort a script that contains them.
4. Words following a command preceded by ** that are in the format of a variable assignment are expanded with the same rules as a variable assignment. This means that tilde substitution is performed after the equal sign and that word splitting and file-name generation are not performed.

Attributes

See attributes(5) for descriptions of the following attributes:

Attribute Type	Attribute Value
Availability	SUNWcsu

See Also

csh(1), exit(1), ksh(1), sh(1), attributes(5)

troff — Typeset or Format Documents

Synopsis

/usr/bin/troff [-a] [-f] [-F*dir*] [-i] [-m*name*] [-n*M*] [-o*list*] [-ra*M*]
    [-s*M*] [-T*dest*] [-u*M*] [-z] [*filename*]...

Description

The troff command is a programming language that manipulates text and drives an output device. You create text with a text editor such as vi or emacs, including troff formatting commands and macros within the text to produce an ASCII file that contains both the form and the contents of the document. Then you use the troff command to format or compile the program to produce the final output.

If you specify no *filename* argument, troff reads standard input. A dash (-) as a file name indicates that standard input should be read at that point in the list of input files.

The output of troff is usually piped through dpost(1) to create a printable PostScript file.

Notes

Previous documentation incorrectly described the numeric register yr as being the "Last two digits of current year." yr is, in actuality, the number of years since 1900. To correctly obtain the last two digits of the current year through the year 2099, you can include the following definition of string register yy in a document to display a two-digit year. Note that you can substitute any other available one- or two-character register name for yy.

```
.\" definition of new string register yy--last two digits of year
.\" use yr (# of years since 1900) if it is < 100
.ie \n(yr<100 .ds yy \n(yr
.el \{          .\" else, subtract 100 from yr, store in ny
.nr ny \n(yr-100
.ie \n(ny>9 \{      .\" use ny if it is two digits
.ds yy \n(ny
.\" remove temporary number register ny
.rr ny \}
.el \{.ds yy 0
.\" if ny is one digit, append it to 0
.as yy \n(ny
.rr ny \} \}
```

troff is not 8-bit clean because it is, by design, based on 7-bit ASCII.

Options

You can specify the following options in any order, but they all must appear before the first file name.

-a	Send an ASCII approximation of formatted output to standard output.
-f	Do not print a trailer after the final page of output or relinquish the postprocessor control of the device.
-F*dir*	Search directory *dir* for font width or terminal tables instead of searching the system default directory.
-i	Read standard input after all input files are exhausted.
-m*name*	Prepend the macro file /usr/share/lib/tmac/*name* to the input file names. Note that most references to macro packages include the leading m as part of the name. The man(5) macros reside in /usr/share/lib/tmac/. You can change the macro directory by setting the TROFFMACS environment variable to a specific path. Be certain to include the trailing / at the end of the path.
-n*N*	Number the first generated page *N*.
-o*list*	Print only pages whose page numbers appear in the comma-separated list of numbers and ranges. A range *N*-*M* means pages *N* through *M*, an initial -*N* means from the beginning to page *N*, and a final *N*- means from *N* to the end.
-q	Quiet mode in nroff; ignored in troff.
-ra*N*	Set register a (one-character names only) to *N*.
-s*N*	Stop the phototypesetter every *N* pages. On some devices, troff produces a trailer so you can change cassettes; resume by pressing the typesetter's start button.

-T*dest*   Prepare output for typesetter *dest*. The following values can be
                  supplied for *dest*.

     post   A PostScript printer (the default). You must pipe the
                                    output through dpost(1) before it is sent to the
                                    PostScript printer to get the proper output.

     aps   Autologic APS-5.

-u*N*   Set the bold factor for the font mounted in position 3 to *N*. If *N* is missing,
                  then set the bold factor to 0.

-z   Suppress formatted output. Output only diagnostic messages and
                  messages output using the .tm request.

Operands

  filename   The file containing text to be processed by troff.

Examples

The following example shows how to print an input text file, mytext, coded with
formatting requests and macros. The input file contains equations and tables and must
go through the tbl(1) and eqn(1) preprocessors before it is formatted by troff with ms
macros, processed by dpost(1), and printed by lp(1).

castle% **tbl mytext | eqn | troff -ms | dpost | lp**

Files

  /tmp/trtmp   Temporary file.

  /usr/share/lib/tmac/*

              Standard macro files.

  /usr/lib/font/*

              Font-width tables for alternative mounted troff fonts.

  /usr/share/lib/nterm/*

              Terminal-driving tables for nroff.

Attributes

See attributes(5) for descriptions of the following attributes:

Attribute Type	Attribute Value
Availability	SUNWdoc

See Also

checknr(1), col(1), dpost(1), eqn(1), lp(1), man(1), nroff(1), tbl(1),
attributes(5), man(5), me(5), ms(5)

true, false — Provide Truth Values

Synopsis

```
/usr/bin/true
/usr/bin/false
```

Description

true does nothing, successfully. false does nothing, unsuccessfully. They are typically used in a shell script sh as:

```
while true
  do
    command
  done
```

which executes *command* forever.

Exit Status

true	0.
false	A non-zero value.

Attributes

See attributes(5) for descriptions of the following attributes:

Attribute Type	Attribute Value
Availability	SUNWcsu

See Also

sh(1), attributes(5)

truss — Trace System Calls and Signals

Synopsis

```
/usr/bin/truss [-fcaeildD] [- [tTvx] [!]syscall,...] [-s [!]signal,...]
    [-mM [!]fault,...] [- [rw] [!]fd,...][- [uU] [!] [lib,...:[:]
    [!]func,...] [-o outfile] command | -p pid
```

Description

The truss command executes the specified command and produces a trace of the system calls it performs, the signals it receives, and the system faults it incurs. Each line of the trace output reports either the fault or signal name or the system call name with its arguments and return value(s). System call arguments are displayed symbolically when possible, using defines from relevant system headers; for any path-name pointer argument, the pointed-to string is displayed. Error returns are reported, using the error code names described in intro(2).

Optionally (see the -u option), truss also produces an entry/exit trace of user-level function calls executed by the traced process; that trace indicates nesting.

Notes

Some of the system calls described in Section 2 differ from the actual operating system interfaces. Do not be surprised by minor deviations of the trace output from the descriptions in Section 2.

Every system fault (except a page fault) results in the posting of a signal to the lightweight process that incurred the fault. A report of a received signal immediately follows each report of a system fault (except a page fault) unless that signal is being blocked.

The operating system enforces certain security restrictions on the tracing of processes. In particular, any command whose object file (a.out) cannot be read by a user cannot be traced by that user; setuid and setgid commands can be traced only by superuser. Unless run by superuser, truss loses control of any process that performs an exec() of a set ID or unreadable object file; such processes continue normally, though independently of truss from the point of the exec().

To avoid collisions with other controlling processes, truss does not trace a process that it detects is being controlled by another process through the /proc interface. This allows truss to be applied to proc(4)-based debuggers as well as to another instance of itself.

The trace output contains Tab characters under the assumption that standard Tab stops are set every eight positions.

The trace output for multiple processes or for a multithreaded process (one that contains more than one lightweight process) is not produced in strict time order. For example, a read() on a pipe may be reported before the corresponding write(). For any one lightweight process (a traditional process contains only one), the output is strictly time ordered.

Not all possible structures passed in all possible system calls are displayed under the -v option.

Options

For those options that take a *list* argument, you can use the name all as a shorthand to specify all possible members of the list. If the list begins with a !, the meaning of the option is negated (for example, exclude instead of trace). You can specify multiple occurrences of the same option. For the same name in a list, subsequent options (those to the right) override previous ones (those to the left).

-a   Show the argument strings that are passed in each exec() system call.

-c   Count traced system calls, faults, and signals instead of displaying the trace line-by-line. Produce a summary report after the traced command terminates or when truss is interrupted. If you also specify -f, include all traced system calls, faults, and signals for child processes in the counts.

-d   Include a timestamp on each line of trace output. The timestamp is a field containing *seconds.fraction* at the start of a line. This value represents a time in seconds relative to the beginning of the trace. The first line of the trace output shows the base time from which the individual timestamps are measured, both as seconds since the Epoch (see time(2)) and as a date string (see ctime(3C) and date(1)). Report the times that the event in question occurred. For all system calls, the event is the completion of the system call, not the start of the system call.

-D   Include a time delta on each line of trace output. The value is a field containing *seconds.fraction* that represents the elapsed time for the LWP that incurred the event since the last reported event incurred by that LWP. Specifically, for system calls, this value is not the time spent within the system call.

-e   Show the environment strings that are passed in each exec() system call.

-f   Follow all children created by fork() or vfork(), and include their signals, faults, and system calls in the trace output. Normally, only the first-level command or process is traced. Include the process ID with each line of trace output to indicate which process executed the system call or received the signal.

-i   Do not display interruptible sleeping system calls. Certain system calls, such as open() and read() on terminal devices or pipes can sleep for indefinite periods and are interruptible. Normally, truss reports such sleeping system calls if they remain asleep for more than one second. The system call is reported again a second time when it completes. The -i option reports such system calls only once, when they complete.

-l   Include the ID of the responsible lightweight process with each line of trace output. If you also specify -f, include both the process ID and the lightweight process ID.

-m [!] *fault,...*

     Specify system faults to trace or exclude. Trace those system faults specified in the comma-separated list. You can specify faults by name or number (see <sys/fault.h>). If the list begins with a not symbol (!), exclude the specified faults from the trace output. Default is -mall -m!fltpage.

-M [!] *fault,...*

     Show machine faults that stop the process. Add the specified faults to the set specified by -m. If one of the specified faults is incurred, leave the process stopped and abandoned (see the -T option). Default is -M!all.

-o *outfile*   Specify file to be used for the trace output. By default, the output goes to standard error.

-p *pid*   Interpret the arguments to truss as a list of process IDs for existing processes (see ps(1)) instead of as a command to be executed. truss takes control of each process and begins tracing it, provided that the user ID and group ID of the process match those of the user or that the user is superuser. You can also specify processes by their names in the /proc directory, for example, /proc/12345.

-r [!] *fd*, . . .

Show the full contents of the I/O buffer for each read() on any of the specified file descriptors. Format the output 32 bytes per line, and show each byte as an ASCII character (preceded by one blank) or as a 2-character, C-language escape sequence for control characters such as horizontal Tab (\t) and newline (\n). If ASCII interpretation is not possible, show the byte in 2-character hexadecimal representation. Show the first 12 bytes of the I/O buffer for each traced read() even in the absence of -r. Default is -r!all.

-s [!] *signal*, . . .

Specify signals to trace or exclude. Trace those signals specified in the comma-separated list. Report the receipt of each specified signal even if the signal is being ignored (not blocked). (Blocked signals are not received until they are unblocked.) You can specify signals by name or number (see <sys/signal.h>). If the list begins with a not symbol (!), exclude the specified signals from the trace output. Default is -sall.

-t [!] *syscall*, . . .

Trace those system calls specified in the comma-separated list. If the list begins with a not symbol (!), exclude the specified system calls from the trace output. Default is -tall.

-T [!] *syscall*, . . .

Show system calls that stop the process. Add the specified system calls to the set specified by -t. If one of the specified system calls is encountered, leave the process stopped and abandoned. That is, release the process and exit, but leave the process in the stopped state at completion of the system call in question. You can apply a debugger, other process inspection tool, or truss (with the same or different options to continue tracing) to the stopped process. The default is -T!all.

You cannot restart a process left stopped in this way by using kill -CONT because the process stopped on an event of interest through /proc, not by the default action of a stopping signal. See signal(5). You can use the prun(1) command described in proc(1) to set the stopped process running again.

-u [!]*lib*,...:[:] [!]*func*,...

> Specify user-level function call tracing. Specify *lib*, ... as a comma-separated list of dynamic library names excluding the .so.n suffix. Specify *func*, ... as a comma-separated list of function names. In both cases, the names can include name-matching metacharacters *, ?, [] with the same meanings as those of sh but as applied to the library/function namespaces, not to files. An empty library or function list defaults to *, that is, trace all libraries or functions in a library. A leading ! on either list specifies an exclusion list, names of libraries or functions not to be traced. Excluding a library excludes all functions in that library; ignore any function list following a library exclusion list.

> A single : separating the library list from the function list means trace calls into the libraries from outside the libraries but omit calls made to functions in a library from other functions in the same library. A double :: means trace all calls, regardless of origin.

> Library patterns do not patch either the executable file or the dynamic linker unless there is an exact match (l* does not match ld.so.1). To trace functions in either of these objects, you must specify the names exactly, as in truss -u a.out -u ld.... Use a.out as the literal name for this purpose. It does not stand for the name of the executable file. Tracing a.out function calls implies all calls (default is ::).

> You can specify multiple -u options, and they are honored left to right. If the process is linked with -lthread, the ID of the thread that performed the function call is included in the trace output for the call. truss searches the dynamic symbol table in each library to find function names and also searches the standard symbol table if it has not been stripped.

-U [!]*lib*,...:[:] [!]*func*,...

> Specify user-level function calls that stop the process. Add the specified functions to the set specified by -u. If one of the specified functions is called, leave the process stopped and abandoned (see the -T option).

-v [!]*syscall*,...

> Display the contents of any structures passed by address to the specified system calls (if traced). Show input values as well as values returned by the operating system. For any field used as both input and output, show only the output value. Default is -v!all.

-w [!]*fd*,...

> Show the contents of the I/O buffer for each write() on any of the specified file descriptors (see -r). Default is -w!all.

-x [!]*syscall*,...

> Display the arguments to the specified system calls (if traced) in raw form, usually hexadecimal, instead of symbolically. This option is for unredeemed hackers who must see the raw bits to be happy. Default is -x!all.

See intro(2) for system call names accepted by the -t, -v, and -x options. System call numbers are also accepted.

If you use truss to initiate and trace a specified command and if you use the -o option or if standard error is redirected to a nonterminal file, then truss runs with hangup, interrupt, and quit signals ignored. This behavior facilitates tracing of interactive programs that catch interrupt and quit signals from the terminal.

If the trace output remains directed to the terminal or if existing processes are traced (the -p option), then truss responds to hangup, interrupt, and quit signals by releasing all traced processes and exiting. This behavior enables you to terminate excessive trace output and to release previously existing processes. Released processes continue normally as though they had never been touched.

Usage

See largefile(5) for the description of the behavior of truss when encountering files greater than or equal to 2 Gbytes (2**31 bytes).

Examples

The following example shows the first few lines of a trace of the find(1) command on a terminal.

```
castle% truss find . -print >find.out
execve("/usr/bin/find", 0xEFFFF53C, 0xEFFFF54C)  argc = 3
open("/dev/zero", O_RDONLY)                   = 3
mmap(0x00000000, 4096, PROT_READ|PROT_WRITE|PROT_EXEC, MAP_PRIVATE, 3,
  0) = 0xEF7C0000
open("/usr/lib/libc.so.1", O_RDONLY)          = 4
fstat(4, 0xEFFFF0D4)                          = 0
mmap(0x00000000, 4096, PROT_READ|PROT_EXEC, MAP_PRIVATE, 4, 0) =
  0xEF7B0000
mmap(0x00000000, 761856, PROT_READ|PROT_EXEC, MAP_PRIVATE, 4, 0) =
  0xEF6C0000
munmap(0xEF762000, 61440)                     = 0
mmap(0xEF771000, 29252, PROT_READ|PROT_WRITE|PROT_EXEC,
  MAP_PRIVATE|MAP_FIXED, 4, 659456) = 0xEF771000
mmap(0xEF779000, 2968, PROT_READ|PROT_WRITE|PROT_EXEC,
  MAP_PRIVATE|MAP_FIXED, 3, 0) = 0xEF779000
close(4)                                      = 0
open("/usr/lib/libdl.so.1", O_RDONLY)         = 4
fstat(4, 0xEFFFF0D4)                          = 0
mmap(0xEF7B0000, 4096, PROT_READ|PROT_EXEC, MAP_PRIVATE|MAP_FIXED, 4, 0)
  = 0xEF7B0000
close(4)                                      = 0
... (More information not shown)
```

The following example shows the first few lines of a trace of the open, close, read, and write system calls.

```
castle% truss -t open,close,read,write find . -print >find.out
open("/dev/zero", O_RDONLY)                   = 3
open("/usr/lib/libc.so.1", O_RDONLY)          = 4
close(4)                                      = 0
open("/usr/lib/libdl.so.1", O_RDONLY)         = 4
close(4)                                      = 0
open("/usr/platform/SUNW,SPARCstation-10/lib/libc_psr.so.1", O_RDONLY)
  Err#2 ENOENT
```

```
close(3)                                          = 0
open64("./../", O_RDONLY|O_NDELAY)                = 3
close(3)                                          = 0
```
... (*More information not shown*)

The following example produces a trace of the spell(1) command in the file truss.out.

```
castle% truss -f -o truss.out spell kookaburra-1
Kookaburra
kookaburra
castle% more truss.out
455:    execve("/usr/bin/spell", 0xEFFFF524, 0xEFFFF534)  argc = 3
455:    open("/dev/zero", O_RDONLY)                    = 3
455:    mmap(0x00000000, 4096, PROT_READ|PROT_WRITE|PROT_EXEC,
  MAP_PRIVATE, 3, 0
) = 0xEF7C0000
455:    open("/usr/lib/libsocket.so.1", O_RDONLY)      = 4
455:    fstat(4, 0xEFFFF0BC)                           = 0
455:    mmap(0x00000000, 4096, PROT_READ|PROT_EXEC, MAP_PRIVATE, 4, 0) =
  0xEF7B0
000
455:    mmap(0x00000000, 102400, PROT_READ|PROT_EXEC, MAP_PRIVATE, 4, 0)
  = 0xEF7
90000
455:    munmap(0xEF798000, 61440)                      = 0
455:    mmap(0xEF7A7000, 6977, PROT_READ|PROT_WRITE|PROT_EXEC,
  MAP_PRIVATE|MAP_F
IXED, 4, 28672) = 0xEF7A7000
```
... (*More information not shown*)

spell is a shell script, so you need the -f option to trace not only the shell but also the processes created by the shell. (The spell script runs a pipeline of eight concurrent processes.)

Note — When tracing more than one process, truss runs as one controlling process for each process being traced. In the spell command example, spell itself uses 9 process slots, one for the shell and 8 for the 8-member pipeline, while truss adds another 9 processes, for a total of 18.

In the following (boring) example, 97 percent of the output reports lseek(), read(), and write() system calls.

```
$ truss nroff -mm document >nroff.out
```

You can use the following command to abbreviate the output.

```
$ truss -t !lseek,read,write nroff -mm document >nroff.out
```

The following example traces all user-level calls made to any function in the C library from outside the C library.

```
$ truss -u libc...
```

The following example includes calls made to functions in the C library from within the C library itself.

```
example$ truss -u libc::...
```

The following example traces all user-level calls made to any library other than the C library.

```
$ truss -u '*' -u !libc...
```

The following example traces all user-level calls to functions in the printf and scanf family contained in the C library.

```
$ truss -u 'libc:*printf,*scanf'...
```

The following example traces every user-level function call from anywhere to anywhere.

```
$ truss -u a.out -u ld:: -u ::...
```

The following example verbosely traces the system call activity of process #1, init(1M) (if you are superuser).

```
# truss -p -v all 1
```

Interrupting truss returns init to normal operation.

Files

/proc/*nnnnn*

> Process files.

/proc/*processID*

Attributes

See attributes(5) for descriptions of the following attributes:

Attribute Type	Attribute Value
Availability	SUNWtoo

See Also

intro(2), proc(4), attributes(5), largefile(5)

---

tset, reset — Establish or Restore Terminal Characteristics

Synopsis

```
/usr/ucb/tset [-InQrs] [-ec] [-ic] [-kc] [-m [port -ID
    [baudrate] : type]...] [type]
/usr/ucb/reset [-] [-ec] [-I] [-kc] [-n] [-Q] [-r] [-s] [-m [port -ID]
    [test baudrate]: type]... [type]
```

Description

The `tset` command sets up your terminal, usually when you first log in. It does terminal-dependent processing such as setting erase and kill characters, setting or resetting delays, sending any sequences needed to properly initialize the terminal, and the like. `tset` first determines the type of terminal involved and then does necessary initialization and mode settings. If a port is not wired permanently to a specific terminal (not hardwired), it is given an appropriate generic identifier such as `dialup`.

The `reset` command clears the terminal settings by turning off CBREAK and RAW modes, output delays, and parity checking; turns on newline translation, echo, and Tab expansion; and restores undefined special characters to their default state. It then sets the modes as usual, based on the terminal type (which probably overrides some of the above). See `stty`(1) for more information. You can use all arguments to `tset` with `reset`. `reset` also uses `rs=` and `rf=` to reset the initialization string and file. This feature is useful after a program dies and leaves the terminal in a peculiar state. Often in this situation, characters do not echo as you type them. You may have to type linefeed `reset` linefeed because Return may not work.

When you specify no arguments, `tset` reads the terminal type from the TERM environment variable, reinitializes the terminal, and performs initialization of mode, environment, and other options at login time to determine the terminal type and to set up terminal modes.

When you use `tset` in a startup script (`.profile` for sh(1) users or `.login` for csh(1) users), it is desirable to give information about the type of terminal you usually use on ports that are not hardwired. Any of the alternative generic names given in the file `/etc/termcap` are possible identifiers. Refer to the `-m` option below for more information. If no mapping applies and you specify a final *type* option on the command line not preceded with a `-m`, then that type is used.

It is usually desirable to return the terminal type, as finally determined by `tset`, and information about the terminal's capabilities to a shell's environment. You can do so with the `-`, `-s`, or `-S` options.

For the Bourne shell, put the following command in your `.profile` file.

```
eval `tset -s options...`
```

For the C shell, put the following commands in your `.login` file.

```
set noglob
eval `tset -s options...`
unset noglob
```

With the C shell, it is also convenient to include the following alias in your `.cshrc` file.

```
alias ts 'eval `tset -s \!*`'
```

This alias also allows the following command to be invoked at any time to set the terminal and environment.

```
ts 2621
```

You cannot get this aliasing effect with a Bourne shell script because shell scripts cannot set the environment of their parent. If a process could set its parent's environment, none of this nonsense would be necessary in the first place.

Once the terminal type is known, `tset` sets the terminal driver mode. This process normally involves sending an initialization sequence to the terminal, setting the single character erase (and optionally the line-kill (full line erase)) characters, and setting special character delays. Tab and newline expansion are turned off during transmission of the terminal initialization sequence.

On terminals that can backspace but not overstrike (such as a CRT) and when the erase character is #, the erase character is changed as if you had used -e.

Notes

The tset command is one of the first commands you must master when getting started on a UNIX system. Unfortunately, it is one of the most complex, largely because of the extra effort you must go through to set the environment of the login shell. Something needs to be done to make all this simpler; either the login program should do the setup, a default shell alias should be made, or a way to set the environment of the parent should exist.

This program cannot intuit personal choices for erase, interrupt, and line-kill characters, so it leaves these set to the local system standards.

It could well be argued that the shell should be responsible for ensuring that the terminal remains in a sane state; this would eliminate the need for the reset program.

Options

-
: Output the name of the terminal on the standard output. This information is intended to be captured by the shell and placed in the TERM environment variable.

-e*c*
: Set the erase character to be the named character *c* on all terminals. Default is the backspace key on the keyboard, usually ^H (Control-H). You can either type the character *c* directly or enter it by using the circumflex-character notation used here.

-i*c*
: Set the interrupt character to be the named character *c* on all terminals. Default is ^C (Control-C). You can either type the character *c* directly or enter it by using the circumflex-character notation used here.

-I
: Suppress transmitting terminal-initialization strings.

-k*c*
: Set the line-kill character to be the named character *c* on all terminals. Default is ^U (Control-U). The kill character is left alone if you do not specify -k. You can specify control characters by prefixing the alphabetical character with a circumflex (as in Control-U) instead of entering the actual control key itself. This syntax enables you to specify control keys that are currently assigned.

-m [*port-ID* [*baudrate*] : *type*] . . .
: Specify (map) a terminal type when connected to a generic port (such as dialup or plugboard) identified by *port-ID*. You can use the *baudrate* argument to check the baud rate of the port and set the terminal type accordingly. The target rate is prefixed by any combination of the following operators to specify the conditions under which the mapping is made.

>
: Greater than.

@
: Equal or at.

<
: Less than.

!   It is not the case that. (Negates the above operators.)

?   Prompt for the terminal type. If no response is given, then *type* is selected by default.

In the following example, the terminal type is set to adm3a if the port is a dialup with a speed greater than 300 or to dw2 if the port is a dialup at 300 baud or less. In the third case, the question mark preceding the terminal type means that you are to verify the type desired. A null response indicates that the named type is correct. Otherwise, your response is taken to be the type desired.

```
tset -m 'dialup>300:adm3a' -m
'dialup:dw2' -m \
'plugboard:?adm3a'
```

To prevent interpretation as metacharacters, enclose the entire argument to -m in single quotes. When using the C shell, precede exclamation points by a backslash (\ ).

-n   Specify that the new tty driver modes should be initialized for this terminal. Probably useless because stty new is the default.

-Q   Suppress printing the Erase set to and Kill set to messages.

-r   In addition to other actions, report the terminal type.

-s   Output commands to set and export TERM. This option can be used with

```
set noglob
eval `tset -s...`
unset noglob
```

to bring the terminal information into the environment. Doing so makes programs such as vi(1) start faster. If the SHELL environment variable ends with csh, output C shell commands; otherwise, output Bourne shell commands.

Examples

These examples all use the dash (-) option. A typical use of tset in a .profile or .login also uses the -e and -k options, and often the -n or -Q options as well. These options have been omitted here to keep the examples short.

To select a 2621, you might put the following sequence of commands in your .login file (or .profile for Bourne shell users).

```
set noglob
eval `tset -s 2621`
unset noglob
```

If you have a switch that connects to various ports (making it impractical to identify which port you may be connected to) and use various terminals from time to time, you can select from among those terminals according to the speed or baud rate. In the example below, tset prompts you for a terminal type if the baud rate is greater than 1200 (say, 9600 for a terminal connected by an RS-232 line), and uses a Wyse 50 by default. If the baud rate is less than or equal to 1200, tset selects a 2621. Note the placement of the question mark and the quotes to protect the > and ? from interpretation by the shell.

```
set noglob
eval `tset -s -m 'switch>1200:?wy' -m 'switch<=1200:2621'`
unset noglob
```

The following entry is appropriate if you always dial up, always at the same baud rate, on many different kinds of terminals, and the terminal you use most often is an adm3a.

```
set noglob
eval `tset -s ?adm3a`
unset noglob
```

If you want to make the selection based only on the baud rate, you might use the following settings.

```
set noglob
eval `tset -s -m '>1200:wy' 2621`
unset noglob
```

The following example quietly sets the erase character to backspace and sets kill to Control-U. If the port is switched, tset selects a Concept™ 100 for speeds less than or equal to 1200 and otherwise asks for the terminal type (the default in this case is a Wyse 50). If the port is a direct dialup, tset selects Concept 100 as the terminal type. If login is over the ARPANET, the terminal type selected is a Datamedi 2500 terminal or emulator. Note the backslash escaping the newline at the end of the first line.

```
set noglob
eval `tset -e -k^U -Q -s -m 'switch<=1200:concept100' -m \
  'switch:?wy' -m dialup:concept100 -m arpanet:dm2500`
unset noglob
```

Files

.login

.profile

/etc/termcap

Attributes

See attributes(5) for descriptions of the following attributes:

Attribute Type	Attribute Value
Availability	SUNWscpu

See Also

csh(1), sh(1), stty(1), vi(1), attributes(5), environ(5)

tsort — Topological Sort

Synopsis

```
/usr/ccs/bin/tsort [file]
```

Description

The tsort command produces on the standard output a totally ordered list of items consistent with a partial ordering of items mentioned in the input file.

The input consists of pairs of items (nonempty strings) separated by blanks. Pairs of different items indicate ordering. Pairs of identical items indicate presence, but not ordering.

Operands

file   A path name of a text file to order. If you specify no *file* operand, use the standard input.

Examples

The following command sorts the characters you type between the first and second EOF.

```
castle% tsort <<EOF
a b c c d e
g g
f g e f
EOF
a
b
c
d
e
f
g
castle%
```

Environment Variables

See environ(5) for descriptions of the following environment variables that affect the execution of tsort: LC_CTYPE, LC_MESSAGES, and NLSPATH.

Exit Status

0   Successful completion.

>0   An error occurred.

Attributes

See attributes(5) for descriptions of the following attributes:

Attribute Type	Attribute Value
Availability	SUNWbtool

See Also

lorder(1), attributes(5), environ(5)

Diagnostics

Odd data: The input file contains an odd number of fields.

tty — Return User's Terminal Name

Synopsis

/usr/bin/tty [-l] [-s]

Description

The tty command writes to the standard output the name of the terminal that is open
as standard input. The name that is used is equivalent to the string that would be
returned by the ttyname(3C) function.

Options

-l   Print the synchronous line number to which the user's terminal is
                connected if it is on an active synchronous line.

-s   Inhibit printing of the terminal path name; enables you to test just the
                exit status. The -s option is useful only if you want the exit status. It
                does not rely on the ability to form a valid path name. Portable
                applications should use test -t.

Examples

The following example shows the output of the tty command from two separate
terminal windows.

```
castle% tty
/dev/pts/4
castle% tty
/dev/pts/5
castle%
```

Environment Variables

See environ(5) for descriptions of the following environment variables that affect the
execution of tty: LC_CTYPE, LC_MESSAGES, and NLSPATH.

Exit Status

0	Standard input is a terminal.
1	Standard input is not a terminal.
>1	An error occurred.

Attributes

See attributes(5) for descriptions of the following attributes:

Attribute Type	Attribute Value
Availability	SUNWcsu
CSI	Enabled

See Also

isatty(3C), ttyname(3C), attributes(5), environ(5)

Diagnostics

not on an active synchronous line

> The standard input is not a synchronous terminal, and you specified -1.

not a tty   The standard input is not a terminal, and you did not specify -s.

type — Write a Description of Command Type

Synopsis

/usr/bin/type *name*...

Description

The type command indicates how each *name* operand would be interpreted if used as a command. type displays information about each operand, identifying the operand as a shell built-in, function, alias, hashed command, or keyword, and can display the path name of the operand where applicable.

The shell built-in version of type is similar to the type command.

Operands

name   A name to be interpreted.

Examples

The following example shows the output for the tty, who, and whence commands.

```
castle% type tty
tty is /bin/tty
castle% type who
who is a tracked alias for /bin/who
castle% type whence
```

```
whence is a shell builtin
castle%
```

Environment Variables

See environ(5) for descriptions of the following environment variables that affect the execution of type: LC_CTYPE, LC_MESSAGES, and NLSPATH.

PATH   Determine the location of name.

Exit Status

0   Successful completion.

>0   An error occurred.

Attributes

See attributes(5) for descriptions of the following attributes:

Attribute Type	Attribute Value
Availability	SUNWcsu

See Also

typeset(1), attributes(5), environ(5)

---

typeset, whence — Shell Built-in Command to Get/Set Attributes and Values for Shell Variables and Functions

Synopsis
**
```
typeset [± HLRZfilrtux[n]] [name[=value]]...
whence [-pv] name...
```

Description

The typeset built-in command sets attributes and values for shell variables and functions. When you invoke typeset inside a function, a new instance of the variable's name is created. The variable's value and type are restored when the function completes. You can specify the following attributes.

-f   Specify that names refer to function names instead of variable names. No assignments can be made, and the only other valid options are -t, -u, and -x. The -t option turns on execution tracing for this function. The -u option marks this function undefined. Search the FPATH variable to find the function definition when the function is referenced. The -x option enables the function definition to remain in effect across shell procedures invoked by *name*.

-H   Provide UNIX to host-name file mapping on non-UNIX systems.

-i	Specify *parameter* as an integer to make arithmetic faster. If *n* is non-zero, it defines the output arithmetic base; otherwise, use the first assignment to determine the output base.
-l	Convert all uppercase characters to lowercase characters. Turn off the uppercase -u option.
-L	Left-justify and remove leading blanks from *value*. If *n* is non-zero, it defines the width of the field; otherwise, use the width of the first assignment to determine its value. When the variable is assigned to, it is filled on the right with blanks or truncated, if necessary, to fit into the field. Leading zeros are removed if you also specify the -Z option. The -R option is turned off.
-r	Mark the given names read-only. You cannot change these names by subsequent assignment.
-R	Right-justify and fill with leading blanks. If *n* is non-zero, it defines the width of the field; otherwise, determine it by the width of the value of first assignment. The field is filled on the left with blanks or truncated from the end if the variable is reassigned. The -L option is turned off.
-t	Tag the variables. Tags are user definable and have no special meaning to the shell.
-u	Convert all lowercase characters to uppercase characters. Turn off the lowercase -l option.
-x	Mark the given names for automatic export to the environment of subsequently executed commands.
-Z	Right-justify and fill with leading zeros if the first nonblank character is a digit and you have not specified the -L option. If *n* is non-zero, it defines the width of the field; otherwise, use the width of the first assignment to determine the value.

You cannot specify the -i option along with -R, -L, -Z, or -f.

Using + instead of - turns these options off. If you specify no *name* arguments but do specify options, a list of names (and optionally the values) of the variables that have these options set is printed. (Using + instead of - keeps the values from being printed.) If you specify no names or options, the names and attributes of all variables are printed.

For each name, whence indicates how it would be interpreted if used as a command name.

-p	Do a path search for *name* even if *name* is an alias, a function, or a reserved word.
-v	Produce a more verbose report.

ksh(1) commands that are preceded by one or two asterisks (*) are treated specially in the following ways.

1. Variable assignment lists preceding the command remain in effect when the command completes.
2. I/O redirections are processed after variable assignments.
3. Errors abort a script that contains them.
4. Words following a command preceded by ** that are in the format of a variable

assignment are expanded with the same rules as a variable assignment. This means that tilde substitution is performed after the equal sign and that word splitting and file-name generation are not performed.

Attributes

See attributes(5) for descriptions of the following attributes:

Attribute Type	Attribute Value
Availability	SUNWcsu

See Also

ksh(1), set(1) sh(1), attributes(5)

U

---

u3b, u3b2, u3b5, u3b15, u370 — Get Processor Type Truth Value

Synopsis

```
/usr/bin/u3b
/usr/bin/u3b2
/usr/bin/u3b5
/usr/bin/u3b15
/usr/bin/u370
```

Description

See machid(1).

---

ucblinks — Add /dev Entries for SunOS 4.x Compatibility

Synopsis

```
/usr/ucb/ucblinks [-e rulebase] [-r rootdir]
```

Description

ucblinks creates symbolic links under the /dev directory for devices with SunOS 5.x names that differ from their SunOS 4.x names. Where possible, these symbolic links point to the device's SunOS 5.x name instead of to the actual /devices entry.

ucblinks does not remove unneeded compatibility links; you must remove these by hand.

After any new SunOS 5.x links have been created, you should call ucblinks each time the system is reconfiguration-booted because the reconfiguration may have resulted in more compatibility names being needed.

In releases before SunOS 5.4, ucblinks used a nawk rule-base to construct the SunOS 4.x compatible names. ucblinks no longer uses nawk for the default operation, although you can still specify nawk rule-bases with the -e option. You can find the nawk rule-base equivalent to the SunOS 5.4 default operation in /usr/ucblib/ucblinks.awk.

Options

-e *rulebase*

> Specify *rulebase* as the file containing nawk(1) pattern-action statements.

-r *rootdir*

> Specify *rootdir* as the directory under which dev and devices are found, instead of the standard root directory /.

Files

/usr/ucblib/ucblinks.awk

> Sample rule-base for compatibility links.

Attributes

See attributes(5) for descriptions of the following attributes:

Attribute Type	Attribute Value
Availability	SUNWscpu

See Also

devlinks(1M), disks(1M), ports(1M), tapes(1M), attributes(5)

---

ul — Underline Text on Terminal Display

Synopsis

/usr/bin/ul [-i] [-t *terminal*] [*filename*...]

Description

ul reads the named file names (or the standard input if you specify no file names) and, using the environment variable TERM, determines how to translate underscores to the sequence that indicates underlining for your terminal. ul uses the /usr/share/lib/terminfo entry to determine the appropriate sequences for underlining. If the terminal is incapable of underlining but is capable of a standout mode, that mode is used instead. If the terminal can overstrike or handle underlining automatically, ul degenerates to cat(1). If the terminal cannot underline, underlining is ignored.

Bugs

nroff usually generates a series of backspaces and underlines intermixed with the text to indicate underlining. ul tries to optimize the backward motion.

Options

-i   Indicate underlining by a separate line containing appropriate dashes (-); this option is useful when you want to look at the underlining that is present in an nroff(1) output stream on a CRT-terminal.

-t *terminal*

Override the terminal kind specified in the environment. If the terminal cannot underline, ignore underlining. If the terminal name is not found, do no underlining.

Exit Status

ul returns exit code 1 if the file specified is not found.

Files

/usr/share/lib/terminfo/*

Attributes

See attributes(5) for descriptions of the following attributes:

Attribute Type	Attribute Value
Availability	SUNWdoc

See Also

cat(1), man(1), nroff(1), attributes(5)

ulimit, unlimit — Set or Get Shell Limitations on System Resources

Synopsis

/usr/bin/ulimit [-f] [*blocks*]

sh
ulimit [-[HS] [a | cdfnstv]]
ulimit [-[HS]] c | d | f | n | s | t | v]] *limit*

csh
unlimit [-h] [*resource*]

ksh

```
ulimit [-HSacdfnstv] [limit]
```

Description

See limit(1).

---

umask — Get or Set the File Mode Creation Mask

Synopsis

```
/usr/bin/umask [-S] [mask]
```

sh, csh

```
umask [ooo]
```

ksh

```
umask [-S] [mask]
```

Description

When you create a file or directory, the default file permissions assigned to the file or directory are controlled by the user mask. You set the user mask with the umask command in a user initialization file such as /etc/profile or .cshrc. You can display the current value of the user mask by typing umask and pressing Return.

You set the user mask with a three-digit octal value such as 022. The first digit sets permissions for the user, the second for the group, the third for others. To set the umask to 022, type

umask 022

File permissions of 666 grant read and write permission to the user, group, and others. Directory permissions of 777 grant read, write, and execute permissions to the user, group, and others. The value assigned by umask is subtracted from these values. To determine the umask value you want to set, subtract the value of the permissions you want from 666 (for a file) or 777 (for a directory). The remainder is the value to use with the umask command. For example, suppose you want to change the default mode for files to 644 (rw-r--r--). The difference between 666 and 644 is 022, which is the value to use as an argument to the umask command.

Setting the umask value denies permissions in the same way that the chmod command grants them. For example, while the chmod 022 command grants write permission to group and others, umask 022 denies write permission for group and others.

/usr/bin/umask

The umask command sets the file-mode creation mask of the current shell execution environment to the value specified by the *mask* operand. This mask affects the initial value of the file permission bits of subsequently created files. If umask is called in a subshell or separate command execution environment, such as one of the following,

```
(umask 002)
nohup umask...
find . -exec umask...
```

it does not affect the file-mode creation mask of the caller's environment. For this reason, you cannot use /usr/bin/umask to change the umask in an ongoing session. Its usefulness is limited to checking the caller's umask. To change the umask of an ongoing session, use one of the shell built-ins.

If you do not specify the *mask* operand, the umask command displays to standard output the value of the invoking process file-mode creation mask.

Bourne and C Shells

Set the user file-mode creation mask to *ooo*. The three octal digits refer to read/write/execute permissions for owner, group, and other (see chmod(1), chmod(2), and umask(2)). The value of each specified digit is subtracted from the corresponding digit specified by the system for the creation of a file (see creat(2)). For example, umask 022 removes write permission for group and other (files normally created with mode 777 become mode 755; files created with mode 666 become mode 644).

- If you omit *ooo*, the current value of the mask is displayed.
- umask is recognized and executed by the shell.
- To automatically set the permissions on created files or directories, you can include umask in your .profile for the Bourne shell (see profile(4)) or in your .cshrc file for the C shell. These initialization files are invoked at login.

Korn Shell

Set the user file-mode creation mask to *mask*. *mask* can either be an octal number or a symbolic value as described in chmod(1). If you omit *mask*, the current value of the mask is printed.

Options

    -S   Specify *mask* as a symbolic argument.

The default output style is unspecified but is recognized on a subsequent invocation of umask on the same system as a *mask* operand to restore the previous file-mode creation mask.

Operands

    mask   A string specifying the new file-mode creation mask. The string is treated in the same way as the *mode* operand described in the chmod(1) manual page.

For a *symbolic-mode* value, the new value of the file-mode creation mask is the logical complement of the file permission bits portion of the file mode specified by the *symbolic-mode* string.

In a *symbolic-mode* value, the permissions characters + and – are interpreted relative to the current file-mode creation mask; + clears the indicated permissions in the mask; – sets the bits of the indicated permissions in the mask.

The interpretation of mode values that specify file mode bits other than the file permission bits is unspecified.

The file-mode creation mask is set to the resulting numeric value.

The default output of a prior invocation of umask on the same system with no operand is also recognized as a *mask* operand. The use of an operand obtained in this way is not obsolescent, even if it is an octal number.

Output

When you specify no *mask* arguments, the umask command writes a message to standard output that can later be used as a umask *mask* operand.

If you specify -S for /usr/bin/umask, the output is displayed in symbolic format, as shown in the following example.

```
castle% /usr/bin/umask -S
u=rwx,g=rx,o=rx
castle%
```

The three values are combinations of letters from the set r, w, x; the presence of a letter indicates that the corresponding bit is clear in the file-mode creation mask. The symbolic syntax in the previous example is equivalent to an octal umask of 022.

```
castle% /usr/bin/umask
022
castle%
```

If you specify a *mask* operand, no output is written to standard output.

Examples

Either of the following commands sets the mode mask so that subsequently created files have their S_IWOTH (others) bit cleared.

```
umask a=rx,ug+w
umask 002
```

After setting the mode mask with either of the above commands, you can use the umask command to display the current value of the mode mask.

```
castle% ksh
$ umask 002
$ umask
02
$ umask -S
u=rwx,g=rwx,o=rx
$
```

Note — The output format is unspecified, but historical implementations use the obsolescent octal integer mode format.

You can then use either of these outputs as the mask operand to a subsequent invocation of the umask command.

Assuming the mode mask is set as above, the following command sets the mode mask so that subsequently created files have their S_IWGRP (group) and S_IWOTH (others) bits cleared.

```
$ umask g-w
$ umask
022
$
```

The following command sets the mode mask so that subsequently created files have all their write bits cleared.

```
$ umask -- -w
$ umask
0222
$
```

Note — You must precede mask operands r, w, x, or anything beginning with a dash (-) with two dashes (--) to prevent them from being interpreted as an option.

Environment Variables

See environ(5) for descriptions of the following environment variables that affect the execution of umask: LC_CTYPE, LC_MESSAGES, and NLSPATH.

Exit Status

0	The file-mode creation mask was successfully changed, or no mask operand was supplied.
>0	An error occurred.

Attributes

See attributes(5) for descriptions of the following attributes:

Attribute Type	Attribute Value
Availability	SUNWcsu

See Also

chmod(1), csh(1), ksh(1), sh(1), chmod(2), creat(2), umask(2), profile(4), attributes(5), environ(5)

---

unalias — Remove Command Pseudonyms

Synopsis

```
/usr/bin/unalias alias-name...
/usr/bin/unalias -a
```

csh

```
unalias pattern
```

ksh

```
unalias name...
```

Description

See alias(1).

uname — Print Name of Current System

Synopsis

```
/usr/bin/uname [-aimnprsvX]
/usr/bin/uname [-S system-name]
```

Description

The uname command prints information about the current system on the standard output.

By default, the uname command with no options displays only the name of the current operating system, as shown in the following example.

```
castle% uname
SunOS
castle%
```

When you specify options, symbols representing one or more system characteristics are written to the standard output. The options print selected information returned by uname(2), sysinfo(2), or both.

Independent software vendors (ISVs) and others who need to determine detailed characteristics of the platform on which their software is either being installed or executed should use the uname command.

To determine the operating system name and release level, use uname -sr. To determine only the operating system release level, use uname -r.

Note — Operating system release levels are not guaranteed to be in $x.y$ format (such as 5.5, 5.6, 5.7); future releases could be in the $x.y.z$ format (such as 5.3.1, 5.3.2, 5.4.1).

In SunOS 4.x releases, the arch command was often used to obtain information similar to that obtained with the uname command. The arch command output sun4 was often incorrectly interpreted to signify a SunOS SPARC system. If hardware platform information is desired, use uname -sp.

The arch -k and uname -m commands return equivalent values; however, the use of either of these commands by third-party programs is discouraged, as is the use of the arch command in general. To determine the system's Instruction Set Architecture (ISA or processor type), use uname with the -p option.

Options

-a	Print basic information currently available from the system.
-i	Print the name of the hardware implementation (platform).
-m	Print the system hardware name (class). Use of this option is discouraged; use uname -p instead.
-n	Print the node name (the node name is the name by which the system is known to a communications network).
-p	Print the current host ISA or processor type.
-r	Print the operating system release level.

-s   Print the name of the operating system (the default).

-S *system-name*

Change the node name by specifying a *system-name* argument. The *system-name* argument is restricted to SYS_NMLN characters. SYS_NMLN is an implementation-specific value defined in <sys/utsname.h>. Only superuser can change the node name.

This change does not persist across reboots of the system. To permanently change a host name, use sys-unconfig(1M).   *New!*

-v   Print the operating system version.

-X   Print expanded system information, one information element per line, as expected by SCO UNIX. The displayed information includes:

- System name, node, release, version, system, and number of CPUs.

- BusType, Serial, and Users (set to unknown in Solaris).

- OEM# and Origin# (set to 0 and 1, respectively).

Examples

The following example displays the operating system name and release level, separated by a space.

```
castle% uname -sr
SunOS 5.7
castle%
```

The following example displays basic information currently known about the system.

```
castle% uname -a
SunOS castle 5.7 Generic sun4m sparc SUNW,SPARCstation-10
castle%
```

The seven items listed include the operating system name, node name, operating system release level, kernel ID, system hardware name, current processor type, and platform name.

The following example uses the -X option to display extended system information.

```
castle% uname -X
System = SunOS
Node = castle
Release = 5.7
KernelID = Generic
Machine = sun4m
BusType = <unknown>
Serial = <unknown>
Users = <unknown>
OEM# = 0
Origin# = 1
NumCPU = 1

castle%
```

Environment Variables

SYSV3   Use to override the default behavior of uname to enable some INTERACTIVE UNIX systems and SCO UNIX programs and scripts to work properly. Many scripts use uname to determine the OS type or the version of the OS to ensure that software is compatible with that OS. Setting SYSV3 to an empty string makes uname print the following default values.

nodename nodename 3.2 2 i386

You can also modify the individual elements that uname displays by setting SYSV3 in the following format:

os,sysname,node,rel,ver,mach

os	Operating system (IUS or SCO).
sysname	System name.
node	Node name as displayed by the -n option.
rel	Release level as displayed by the -r option.
ver	Version number as displayed by the -v option.
mach	Machine name as displayed by -m option.

Do not put spaces between the elements. If you omit an element, the current system value is used.

See environ(5) for descriptions of the following environment variables that affect the execution of uname: LC_CTYPE, LC_MESSAGES, and NLSPATH.

Exit Status

0	Successful completion.
>0	An error occurred.

Attributes

See attributes(5) for descriptions of the following attributes:

Attribute Type	Attribute Value
Availability	SUNWcsu

See Also

arch(1), isalist(1), sys-unconfig(1M), sysinfo(2), uname(2), nodename(4), attributes(5), environ(5)

uncompress — Uncompress or Display Expanded Files

Synopsis

```
/usr/bin/uncompress [-cfv] [file...]
```

Description

See compress(1).

unexpand — Convert Space Characters to Tabs

Synopsis

```
/usr/bin/unexpand [-a] [-t tablist] [file...]
```

Description

See expand(1).

unget — Undo a Previous Get of an SCCS File

Synopsis

```
/usr/ccs/bin/unget [-ns] [-rsid] s.filename...
```

Description

See sccs-unget(1).

unhash — Evaluate the Internal Hash Table of the Contents of Directories

Synopsis

csh

unhash

Description

See hash(1).

unifdef — Resolve and Remove ifdef'd Lines from C Program Source

Synopsis

/usr/ccs/bin/unifdef [-clt] [-D*name*] [-U*name*] [-iD*name*] [-iU*name*]...
   [*filename*]

Description

unifdef removes ifdef'd lines from a file while otherwise leaving the file alone. It is smart enough to deal with the nested ifdefs, comments, and the single and double quotes of C syntax, but it does not do any inclusion or interpretation of macros. Neither does it strip out comments, although it recognizes and ignores them. With -D options you specify which symbols you want defined and with -U options those symbols you want undefined. Lines within those ifdefs are copied to the output or removed, as appropriate. Any ifdef, ifndef, else, and endif lines associated with *filename* are also removed.

ifdefs involving symbols you do not specify are untouched and copied out along with their associated ifdef, else, and endif lines.

If an ifdefX is nested inside another ifdefX, the inside ifdef is treated as if it is an unrecognized symbol. If the same symbol appears in more than one argument, only the first occurrence is significant.

unifdef copies its output to the standard output and takes its input from the standard input if you specify no *filename* argument.

Options

-c	Complement the normal operation. Retain lines that would have been removed or blanked, and vice versa.
-l	Replace removed lines with blank lines.
-t	Plain text option. Refrain from attempting to recognize comments and single and double quotes.
-D*name*	Specify which symbols you want defined with *name*.
-U*name*	Specify which symbols you want undefined with *name*.
-iD*name*	Ignore, but print lines associated with the defined symbol *name*. If you use ifdefs to delimit non-C lines, such as comments or code that is under construction, then you must tell unifdef which symbols are used for that purpose so that it does not try to parse for quotes and comments within them.
-iU*name*	Ignore, but print lines associated with the undefined symbol *name*.

Exit Status

0	Success.
1	Problems encountered.

Attributes

See attributes(5) for descriptions of the following attributes:

Attribute Type	Attribute Value
Availability	SUNWbtool

See Also

diff(1), attributes(5)

Diagnostics

Premature EOF

Inappropriate else or endif.

---

uniq — Report or Filter Out Repeated Lines in a File

Synopsis

```
/usr/bin/uniq [-c|-d|-u] [-f fields] [-s chars] [input-file
    [output-file]]
/usr/bin/uniq [-c|-d|-u] [-n] [+m] [input-file [output-file]]
```

Description

The uniq command produces a list of the unique lines in a file by filtering or removing repeated lines. It is usually used with files that have first been sorted with the sort(1) command.

uniq reads an input file, compares adjacent lines, and writes one copy of each input line on the output. The second and succeeding copies of repeated adjacent input lines are not written.

Repeated lines in the input are not detected if they are not adjacent.

Options

-c	Precede each output line with a count of the number of times the line occurred in the input.
-d	Suppress the writing of lines that are not repeated in the input.
-f fields	Ignore the first fields on each input line when doing comparisons, where fields is a positive decimal integer. A field is the maximal string matched by the basic regular expression:

[[:blank:]]*[^[:blank:]]*

If fields specifies more fields than appear on an input line, use a null string for comparison.

-s *chars* Ignore the first *chars* characters when doing comparisons, where *chars* is a positive decimal integer. If specified in conjunction with the -f option, ignore the first *chars* characters after the first *fields*. If *chars* specifies more characters than remain on an input line, use a null string for comparison.

-u Suppress the writing of lines that are repeated in the input.

-*n* Equivalent to -f *fields* with *fields* set to *n*.

+*m* Equivalent to -s *chars* with *chars* set to *m*.

Operands

input-file A path name of the input file. If you do not specify *input-file* or if the *input-file* is -, use the standard input.

output-file

 A path name of the output file. If you do not specify *output-file*, use the standard output. The results are unspecified if the file named by *output-file* is the file named by *input-file*.

Examples

The following example lists the contents of the uniq.test file and outputs a copy of the repeated lines.

```
castle% cat uniq.test
This is a test.
This is a test.
TEST.
Computer.
TEST.
TEST.
Software.
castle% uniq -d uniq.test
This is a test.
TEST.
castle%
```

The following example outputs just those lines that are not repeated in the uniq.test file.

```
castle% uniq -u uniq.test
TEST.
Computer.
Software.
castle%
```

The following example precedes each line with a count of the number of times each line occurred in the file.

```
castle% uniq -c uniq.test
2 This is a test.
1 TEST.
1 Computer.
```

```
2 TEST.
1 Software.
castle%
```

The following example uses the `sort` command to sort the file `kookaburra-1` and pipes the output to the `uniq -c` command. You need to sort the file first because `uniq` does not match discontiguous lines.

```
castle% sort kookaburra-1 | uniq -c
   1
   1 Eating all the gumdrops he can see.
   1 Gay your life must be
   2 Kookaburra sits in the old gum tree
   1 Laugh, kookaburra, laugh, kookaburra
   1 Leave some there for me.
   1 Merry merry king of the bush is he.
   1 Stop, kookaburra, stop, kookaburra
castle%
```

Environment Variables

See `environ`(5) for descriptions of the following environment variables that affect the execution of `uniq`: LC_CTYPE, LC_MESSAGES, and NLSPATH.

Exit Status

0	Successful completion.
>0	An error occurred.

Attributes

See `attributes`(5) for descriptions of the following attributes:

Attribute Type	Attribute Value
Availability	SUNWesu
CSI	Enabled

See Also

`comm`(1), `pack`(1), `pcat`(1), `sort`(1), `uncompress`(1), `attributes`(5), `environ`(5)

---

units — Convert Quantities Expressed in Standard Scales to Other Units

Synopsis

```
/usr/bin/units
```

Description

units converts quantities expressed in various standard scales to their equivalents in other scales. It works interactively in the following way. Type units to start the command. A you have: prompt is displayed. Type the first standard scale and press Return. A you want: prompt is displayed. Type the second standard scale and press Return. The results are displayed as shown in the following examples.

```
castle% units
you have: inch
you want: cm
        * 2.540000e+00
        / 3.937008e-01
you have: 15 lbs force/in2
you want: atm
        * 1.020689e+00
        / 9.797299e-01
you have: 3 teaspoon
you want: tablespoon
        * 1.000000e+00
        / 1.000000e+00
you have: 45 liters
you want: gallons
        * 1.188774e+01
        / 8.412026e-02
you have: 12 gallons
you want: liters
        * 4.542494e+01
        / 2.201434e-02
you have: ^D
castle%
```

To exit, type Control-D or Control-C.

Specify a quantity as a multiplicative combination of units optionally preceded by a numeric multiplier. Indicate powers by suffixed positive integers, division by the usual sign.

units only does multiplicative scale changes; thus, it can convert Kelvin to Rankine, but not Celsius to Fahrenheit. Most familiar units, abbreviations, and metric prefixes are recognized, together with a generous leavening of exotica and a few constants of nature including the following.

pi	Ratio of circumference to diameter.
c	Speed of light.
e	Charge on an electron.
g	Acceleration of gravity.
force	Same as g.
mole	Avogadro's number.
water	Pressure head per unit height of water.
au	Astronomical unit.

Pound is not recognized as a unit of mass, though `lb` is. Compound names are run together (for example, `lightyear`). British units that differ from their U.S. counterparts are prefixed thus: `brgallon`. For a complete list of units, type:

castle% **cat /usr/share/lib/unittab**

Files

/usr/share/lib/unittab

Attributes

See attributes(5) for descriptions of the following attributes:

Attribute Type	Attribute Value
Availability	SUNWesu

See Also

attributes(5)

unix2dos — Convert Text File from ISO Format to DOS Format

Synopsis

/usr/bin/unix2dos [-ascii] [-iso] [-7] [-437 | -850 | -860 | -863 | 865] *New!*
    originalfile convertedfile

Description

unix2dos converts ISO standard characters to the corresponding characters in the DOS extended character set.

You can invoke this command from either DOS or SunOS. However, the file names must conform to the conventions of the environment in which you invoke the command.

If the original file and the converted file are the same, unix2dos rewrites the original file after converting it.

Options

-ascii   Add Returns and convert end-of-file characters in SunOS format text files to conform to DOS requirements.

-iso   Convert ISO standard characters to the corresponding character in the DOS extended character set (the default).

-7   Convert 8-bit SunOS characters to 7-bit DOS characters.

On non-i386 systems, unix2dos tries to get the keyboard type to determine which *New!* code page to use. Otherwise, the default is US. You can override the code page with one of the following options, new in the Solaris 9 release.

-437   Use US code page.

-850   Use multilingual code page.

-860   Use Portuguese code page.

-863   Use French Canadian code page.

-865   Use Danish code page.

New! Operands

originalfile

The original file in ISO format that is being converted to DOS format.

convertedfile

The new file in DOS format that has been converted from the original ISO file format.

Attributes

See attributes(5) for descriptions of the following attributes:

Attribute Type	Attribute Value
Availability	SUNWesu

See Also

dos2unix(1), attributes(5)

Diagnostics

File *filename* not found, or no read permission

The input file you specified does not exist, or you do not have read permission (check with the SunOS command ls -l).

Bad output filename *filename*, or no write permission

The output file you specified is either invalid, or you do not have write permission for that file or the directory that contains it. Check also that the drive or diskette is not write protected.

Error while writing to temporary file

An error occurred while converting your file, possibly because there is not enough space on the current drive.Check the amount of space on the current drive, using the DIR command. Also, be certain that the default diskette or drive is write enabled (not write protected). Note that when this error occurs, the original file remains intact.

Could not rename tmpfile to *filename*.
Translated tmpfile name = *filename*.

The program could not perform the final step in converting your file. Your converted file is stored under the name indicated on the second line of this message.

unlimit — Set or Get Shell System Resource Limitations

Synopsis

csh

unlimit [-h] [*resource*]

Description

See limit(1).

unpack — Compress and Expand Files

Synopsis

/usr/bin/unpack *file*...

Description

See pack(1).

unset, unsetenv — Shell Built-in Functions to Determine Environment Variable Characteristics

Synopsis

sh

unset [*name*...]

csh

unset *pattern*
unsetenv *variable*

ksh

unset [-f] *name*...

Description

See set(1).

unzip — List, Test, and Extract Compressed Files from a Zip Archive

Synopsis

```
/usr/bin/unzip [-A] [-Z] [-cflptTuvz[abBCjnLoMqVX]] file[.zip]
    [file(s)...] [- x xfile(s)...] [-d exdir]
```

Description

unzip lists, tests, or extracts files from a ZIP archive. The default behavior (with no options) is to extract all files from the specified ZIP archive into the current directory (and subdirectories below it). You can use a companion program, zip (available from http://www.cdrom.com/pub/infozip/), to create ZIP archives. Both programs are compatible with archives created by PKWARE's PKZIP and PKUNZIP for MS-DOS, but in many cases the program options or default behaviors differ.

Arguments

file[.zip]   Path of the ZIP archive(s). If you specify a wild-card for file, process each matching file in an order determined by the operating system (or file system). Only the file name can be a wild-card; the path itself cannot. Wild-card expressions are similar to UNIX egrep(1) (regular) expressions and can contain:

        *   Match a sequence of zero or more characters.

        ?   Match exactly one character.

        [...]   Match any single character found inside the brackets; specify ranges with a beginning character, a dash, and an ending character. If an exclamation point (!) or a caret (^) follows the left bracket, then the range of characters within the brackets is complemented (that is, anything except the characters inside the brackets is considered a match).

              Be sure to quote any character that might otherwise be interpreted or modified by the operating system, particularly under UNIX and VMS. If no matches are found, assume a literal file name; if that also fails, append the suffix .zip. Note that self-extracting ZIP files are supported, as with any other ZIP archive; just specify the .exe suffix (if any) explicitly.

[file(s)]   An optional, space-separated list of archive items to be processed. (VMS versions compiled with VMSCLI defined must delimit files with commas instead. See -v.) You can use regular expressions (wild-cards) to match multiple items. Be sure to quote expressions that would otherwise be expanded or modified by the operating system.

[-x *xfile*(s)]

> An optional list of archive items to be excluded from processing. Because wild-card characters match directory separators (/), you can use this option to exclude any files that are in subdirectories. For example,
>
> `unzip foo *.[ch] -x */*`
>
> extracts all C source files in the main directory, but none in any subdirectories. Without the -x option, extract all C source files in all directories within the file.

[-d *exdir*] An optional directory to which to extract files. By default, all files and subdirectories are recreated in the current directory; the -d option enables you to extract into an arbitrary directory (assuming you have permission to write to the directory). This option need not appear at the end of the command line; it is also accepted before the file specification (with the normal options), immediately after the file specification, or between the file(s) and the -x option. You can concatenate the option and directory without any white space between them, but note that this may suppress normal shell behavior. In particular, -d ~ (tilde) is expanded by UNIX C shells into the name of the user's home directory, but -d~ is treated as a literal subdirectory ~ of the current directory.

Options

> **Note** — To support obsolete hardware, the unzip usage screen is limited to 22 or 23 lines. Consider the usage message as a reminder of only the basic unzip syntax instead of as an exhaustive list of all possible options.

The following example shows the unzip usage screen.

```
castle% unzip
UnZip 5.32 of 3 November 1997, by Info-ZIP. Maintained by Greg Roelofs. Send
bug reports to the authors at Zip-Bugs@lists.wku.edu; see README for details.

Usage: unzip [-Z] [-opts[modifiers]] file[.zip] [list] [-x xlist] [-d exdir]
  Default action is to extract files in list, except those in xlist, to exdir;
  file[.zip] may be a wildcard. -Z => ZipInfo mode ("unzip -Z" for usage).

  -p  extract files to pipe, no messages      -l  list files (short format)
  -f  freshen existing files, create none     -t  test compressed archive data
  -u  update files, create if necessary       -z  display archive comment
  -x  exclude files that follow (in xlist)    -d  extract files into exdir

modifiers:                                    -q  quiet mode (-qq => quieter)
  -n  never overwrite existing files          -a  auto-convert any text files
  -o  overwrite files WITHOUT prompting        -aa treat ALL files as text
  -j  junk paths (do not make directories)    -v  be verbose/print version info
  -C  match filenames case-insensitively      -L  make (some) names lowercase
  -X  restore UID/GID info                    -V  retain VMS version numbers
                                              -M  pipe through "more" pager
Examples (see unzip.doc for more info):
  unzip data1 -x joe   => extract all files except joe from zipfile data1.zip
  unzip -p foo | more  => send contents of foo.zip via pipe into program more
```

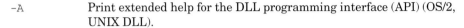

```
unzip -fo foo ReadMe => quietly replace existing ReadMe if archive file newer
castle%
```

The exhaustive list of options is shown below.

-A	Print extended help for the DLL programming interface (API) (OS/2, UNIX DLL).
-c	Extract files to standard output. This option is similar to the -p option, except print the name of each file as it is extracted. Allow the -a option. Automatically perform ASCII-EBCDIC conversion if appropriate. This option is not listed in the unzip usage screen.
-f	Freshen existing files; that is, extract only those files that already exist on disk and that are newer than the disk copies. By default unzip queries before overwriting, but you can use the -o option to suppress the queries. Note that under many operating systems, the TZ (time zone) environment variable must be set correctly for -f and -u to work properly (under UNIX the variable is usually set automatically). TZ must be set to resolve the differences between DOS-format file times (always local time) and UNIX-format times (always in GMT/UTC). A typical TZ value is PST8PDT (U.S. Pacific time with automatic adjustment for standard or daylight saving time).
-l	List archive files (short format). Print the names, uncompressed file sizes, modification dates and times of the specified files, and totals for all files specified. If UnZip was compiled with OS2_EAS defined, the -l option also lists columns for the sizes of stored OS/2 extended attributes (EAs) and OS/2 access control lists (ACLs). In addition, display the zip file comment and individual file comments (if any). If a file was archived from a single-case file system (for example, the old MS-DOS FAT file system) and you specify the -L option, convert the file name to lower case, and prefix it with a caret (^).
-p	Extract files to pipe (standard output). Send nothing but the file data to standard output, and always extract the files in binary format just as they are stored (no conversions).
-t	Test archive files. Extract each specified file in memory, and compare the cyclic redundancy check (CRC, an enhanced checksum) of the expanded file with that of the original file's stored CRC value.
-T	Set the timestamp on the archive(s) to that of the newest file in each one. This option corresponds to the zip -go option except that you can use it on wild-card files (for example, unzip -T *.zip) and it is much faster. (Most operating systems.)
-u	Update existing files, and create new ones if needed. This option performs the same function as the -f option, extracting (with query) files that are newer than those with the same name on disk. In addition, extract those files that do not already exist on disk. See -f for information on setting the time zone properly.
-v	Be verbose, or print diagnostic version information. This option behaves as both an option and a modifier.

As an option, -v has two purposes: when you specify a file with no other options, list archive files verbosely, adding to the basic -l information the compression method, compressed size, compression ratio, and 32-bit CRC. When you specify no file (that is, the complete command is simply unzip -v), print a diagnostic screen. In addition to the normal header with release date and version, list the home Info-ZIP ftp site and where to find a list of other ftp and non-ftp sites, the target operating system for which it was compiled, (possibly) the hardware on which it was compiled, the compiler and version used, and the compilation date. Also list any special compilation options that might affect the program's operation and any options stored in environment variables that might do the same.

As a modifier, the -v option is used with other options (such as -t) to produce more verbose or debugging output. This feature is not yet fully implemented but will be in future releases.

-z   Display only the archive comment.

-Z   If the first option on the command line is -Z, interpret the remaining options as zipinfo(1) options.

Modifiers

-a   Convert text files. Automatically extract files identified by zip as text files (those with the t label in zipinfo listings), converting line endings, end-of-file characters, and the character set itself as necessary. (For example, UNIX files use linefeeds (LFs) for end-of-line (EOL) and have no end-of-file (EOF) marker. Macintosh uses Returns (CRs) for EOLs. Most PC operating systems use CR+LF for EOLs and Control-Z for EOF. IBM mainframes and the Michigan Terminal System use EBCDIC instead of the more common ASCII character set, and NT supports Unicode.) Note that zip identification of text files is by no means perfect; some text files may actually be binary, and vice versa. unzip, therefore, prints [text] or [binary] as a visual check for each file it extracts when you specify the -a option. The -aa double option forces extracting all files as text regardless of the supposed file type.

-b   Treat all files as binary (no text conversions). This option is a shortcut for ---a (non-VMS).

-b   Autoconvert binary files (see -a) to fixed-length, 512-byte record format. Doubling the option (-bb) forces all files to be extracted in this format (VMS).

-B   Save a backup copy of each overwritten file with a tilde appended (for example, rename the old copy of foo to foo~). This option is similar to the default behavior of emacs(1) in many locations. (UNIX only and only if compiled with UNIXBACKUP defined.)

-C   Match file names case insensitively. Because some file systems are fully case sensitive (notably those under the UNIX operating system) and because both ZIP archives and unzip itself are portable across platforms, the default behavior is to match both wild-card and literal file names case sensitively. That is, specifying makefile on the command line only matches makefile in the archive, not Makefile or MAKEFILE (and similarly for wild-card specifications). Because this behavior does not match that of many other operating/file systems (for example, OS/2 HPFS, which preserves mixed case but is not sensitive to it), you can use the -C option to force all file name matches to be case insensitive. In the example above, all three files then match makefile (or make*, or similar form). The -C option affects files in both the normal-file list and the excluded-file list (*xlist*).

-j   Junk paths. Do not recreate the archive's directory structure. Deposit all files in the extraction directory (by default, the current one).

-L   Convert to lower case any file name originating on an uppercase-only operating system or file system. (This was the default behavior in releases before 5.11. The new default behavior is identical to the old behavior with the -U option, which is now obsolete and will be removed in a future release.) Depending on the archiver, store files archived under single-case file systems (such as VMS and old MS-DOS FAT) as all uppercase names. The default behavior can be ugly or inconvenient when extracting to a case-preserving file system such as OS/2 HPFS or a case-sensitive one such as UNIX. By default, unzip lists and extracts file names exactly as they are stored (excepting truncation, conversion of unsupported characters, and so on).

-M   Pipe all output through an internal pager similar to the UNIX more(1) command. At the end of a screen of output, pause with a --More-- prompt. You can view the next screen by pressing the Enter (Return) key or the space bar. You can quit unzip with the q key and, on some systems, the Enter/Return key. Unlike UNIX more(1), unzip does not enable you to search forward or edit. Also, unzip doesn't notice if long lines wrap at the edge of the screen, effectively resulting in the printing of two or more lines or that some text scrolls off the top of the screen before being viewed. On some systems, the number of available lines on the screen is not detected, in which case unzip assumes the height is 24 lines.

-n   Never overwrite existing files. If a file already exists, skip the extraction of that file without prompting. By default, unzip queries before extracting any file that already exists; you can choose to overwrite only the current file, overwrite all files, skip extraction of the current file, skip extraction of all existing files, or rename the current file.

-N   Extract file comments as Amiga file notes. Create file comments with the -c option of zip or with the -N option of the Amiga port of zip, which stores file notes as comments (Amiga).

-o	Overwrite existing files without prompting. This option is dangerous, so use it with care. (Under OS/2, you must often use it with -f as the only way to overwrite directory EAs.)
q	Use quiet mode.
V	Retain VMS version numbers.
X	Restore UID/GID information.

Environment Variables

The default environment variable name is UNZIP for all operating systems except VMS. For VMS systems, the environment variable name is UNZIP_OPTS because the symbol used to install unzip as a foreign command would otherwise be confused with the environment variable. For compatibility with zip, UNZIPOPT is also accepted (don't ask). If both UNZIP and UNZIPOPT are defined, UNZIP takes precedence. You can use the unzip diagnostic option (-v with no file name) to check the values of all possible unzip and zipinfo environment variables, as shown in the following example.

```
castle% unzip -v
UnZip 5.32 of 3 November 1997, by Info-ZIP. Maintained by Greg Roelofs. Send
bug reports to the authors at Zip-Bugs@lists.wku.edu; see README for details.

Latest sources and executables are at ftp://ftp.cdrom.com/pub/infozip/, as of
above date; see http://www.cdrom.com/pub/infozip/UnZip.html for other sites.

Compiled with cc for Unix (Sun SPARC/Solaris) on Sep 10 1998.

UnZip special compilation options:
        COPYRIGHT_CLEAN (PKZIP 0.9x unreducing method not supported)
        LZW_CLEAN (PKZIP/Zip 1.x unshrinking method not supported)
        TIMESTAMP
        USE_EF_UT_TIME

UnZip and ZipInfo environment options:
           UNZIP:  [none]
        UNZIPOPT:  [none]
         ZIPINFO:  [none]
      ZIPINFOOPT:  [none]
castle%
```

Set the time zone variable (TZ) according to the local time zone so that the -f and -u options operate correctly. This variable may also be needed to correctly set timestamps on extracted files. Under Windows 95/NT, unzip should know the correct time zone even if TZ is unset, assuming the time zone is correctly set in the Control Panel.

You can modify the unzip default behavior by putting options in the UNZIP environment variable. You can use any option; however, this feature is probably most useful with the following modifiers to perform the following modifications.

- Autoconvert text files by default (-a).
- Convert file names from uppercase systems to lower case (-L).
- Match names case insensitively (-C).
- Make unzip quieter (-q).
- Always overwrite or never overwrite files as they are extracted (-o or -n).

For example, to make `unzip` act as quietly as possible, reporting only errors, you could use one of the following commands.

`UNZIP=-qq; export UNZIP`	UNIX Bourne shell.
`setenv UNZIP -qq`	UNIX C shell.
`set UNZIP=-qq`	OS/2 or MS-DOS.
`define UNZIP_OPTS "-qq"`	VMS (quotes for lower case).

Environment options are just like any other command-line options except that they are effectively the first options on the command line. To override an environment option, you can use the minus operator to remove it. For example, to override one of the quiet-flags in the example above, use the following command.

`castle% `**`unzip --q[other-options] file`**

The first dash is the normal switch character, and the second is a minus sign acting on the q option. Thus. the effect is to cancel one quantum of quietness. To cancel both quiet options, you can use two (or more) minuses.

`castle% `**`unzip -t--q file`**
`castle% `**`unzip ---qt file`**

The two commands are equivalent. This syntax may seem awkward or confusing, but it is reasonably intuitive. After the first dash, any other dashes signify a negative option. This syntax is consistent with the behavior of the `nice(1)` command.

Decryption

Encrypted archives are fully supported by Info-ZIP software, but because of U.S. export restrictions, the encryption and decryption sources are not packaged with the regular `unzip` and `zip` distributions. Because the sources were written by Europeans, however, they are freely available at sites throughout the world; see

`http://www.cdrom.com/pub/infozip/doc/WHERE`

or the `WHERE` file in any Info-ZIP source or binary distribution for locations both inside and outside the United States.

Because of the separate distribution, not all compiled versions of `unzip` support decryption. To check a version for `crypt` support, either try to test or extract an encrypted archive or check the `unzip` diagnostic screen (see the `-v` option) for `[decryption]` as one of the special compilation options.

You can use the `-P` option to supply a password on the command line, but at a cost in security. The preferred decryption method is simply to extract normally; if a `file` is encrypted, `unzip` prompts for the password without echoing what is typed. `unzip` continues to use the same password as long as it appears to be valid, by testing a 12-byte header on each file. The correct password always checks out against the header, but there is a 1-in-256 chance that an incorrect password may also work. (This is a security feature of the `PKWARE` zipfile format; it helps prevent brute-force attacks that might otherwise gain a speed advantage by testing only the header.) When you give an incorrect password that passes the header test anyway, either an incorrect CRC is generated for the extracted data or `unzip` fails during the extraction because the decrypted bytes do not constitute a valid compressed data stream.

If the first password fails the header check on some file, `unzip` prompts for another password, and so on until all files are extracted. If you do not know the password, press Return or Enter as a signal to skip all further prompting. Thereafter, only unencrypted files in the archive(s) are extracted. (In fact, that's not quite true; older versions of `zip` and `zipcloak` allowed null passwords, so `unzip` checks each encrypted file to see if the null password works. This may result in false positives and extraction errors, as noted above.)

Archives encrypted with 8-bit passwords (for example, passwords with accented European characters) may not be portable across systems and/or other archivers. This problem stems from the use of multiple encoding methods for such characters, including Latin-1 (ISO 8859-1) and OEM code page 850. DOS `PKZIP` 2.04g uses the OEM code page; Windows `PKZIP` 2.50 uses Latin-1 (and is therefore incompatible with DOS `PKZIP`); `Info-ZIP` uses the OEM code page on DOS, OS/2, and Win3.x ports but Latin-1 everywhere else; and Nico Mak's `WinZip` 6.x does not permit 8-bit passwords at all. `UnZip` 5.3 tries to use the default Latin-1 character set first, followed by the alternative one (OEM code page) to test passwords. On EBCDIC systems, if both of these character sets fail, EBCDIC encoding is tested as a last resort. (Because there are no known archivers that encrypt by using EBCDIC encoding, EBCDIC is not tested on non-EBCDIC systems.) ISO character encodings other than Latin-1 are not supported.

Bugs

Multipart archives are not yet supported, except in conjunction with `zip`. To fix the problem, concatenate all parts in order and then perform `zip -F` on the concatenated archive. This problem will definitely be corrected in the next major release.

Archives read from standard input are not yet supported, except with `funzip`, and then you can extract only the first item in the archive.

Archives encrypted with 8-bit passwords (that is, passwords with accented European characters) may not be portable across systems and/or other archivers.

Dates, times, and permissions of stored directories are not restored except under UNIX.

[MS-DOS] When extracting or testing files from an archive on a defective diskette, if you choose the Fail option from the DOS `Abort, Retry, Fail?` message, older versions of `unzip` may hang the system, requiring a reboot. This problem appears to be fixed. You can use Control-C (or Control-Break) to terminate `unzip`.

Under DEC Ultrix, `unzip` sometimes fails on long files (bad CRC, not always reproducible). This problem was apparently because of either a hardware bug (cache memory) or an operating system bug (improper handling of page faults?). Because Ultrix has been abandoned in favor of Digital UNIX (OSF/1), this bug may no longer be an issue.

[UNIX] UNIX special files such as FIFO buffers (named pipes), block devices, and character devices are not restored even if they are somehow represented in the file, nor are hard-linked files relinked. Basically, the only file types restored by `unzip` are regular files, directories, and symbolic (soft) links.

[OS/2] Extended attributes for existing directories are updated only if you specify the `-o` (overwrite all) option. This is a limitation of the operating system; because only directories have a creation time associated with them, `unzip` has no way to determine whether the stored attributes are newer or older than those on disk. In practice, you may need to take a two-pass approach: first unpack the archive normally (with or without freshening/updating existing files), then overwrite just the directory entries (for example, `unzip -o foo */`).

[VMS] When extracting to another directory, only the [.foo] syntax is accepted for the `-d` option; the simple UNIX `foo` syntax is silently ignored (as is the less common VMS `foo.dir` syntax).

[VMS] When the file being extracted already exists, `unzip` queries permit only skipping, overwriting, or renaming. The overwrite choice creates a new version of the file; the old version is not overwritten or deleted.

Examples

The following example extracts all items in the archive `letters.zip` into the current directory and subdirectories below it, creating any subdirectories as necessary.

```
castle% unzip letters
Archive:  letters.zip
  inflating: letters.rtf
castle%
```

The following example extracts all items in `letters.zip` into the current directory.

```
castle% unzip -j letters
Archive:  letters.zip
  inflating: letters.rtf
castle%
```

The following example tests `letters.zip`, printing a summary message indicating whether the archive is OK.

```
castle% unzip -tq letters
No errors detected in compressed data of letters.zip.
castle%
```

The following example tests all zip files in the current directory, printing only the summaries.

```
castle% unzip -tq \*.zip
No errors detected in compressed data of letters.zip.
castle%
```

Note — The backslash before the asterisk is required only if the shell expands wild-cards, as in UNIX. You can use double quotes instead.

The following example extracts to standard output all files in `letters.zip` whose names end in `.rtf`, autoconverting to the local end-of-line convention and piping the output into more(1).

```
castle% unzip -ca letters \*.rtf | more
Archive:  letters.zip
  inflating: letters.rtf          [text]
{\rtf1\mac\ansicpg10000\uc1
  \deff0\deflang1033\deflangfe1033{\upr{\fonttbl{\f0\fn
il\fcharset256\fprq2{\*\panose 02020603050405020304}Times New
  Roman;}{\f6\fnil\fc
harset256\fprq2{\*\panose 02000500000000000000}Courier;}
}{\*\ud{\fonttbl{\f0\fnil\fcharset256\fprq2{\*\panose
  02020603050405020304}Times
New Roman;}{\f6\fnil\fcharset256\fprq2{\*\panose
  02000500000000000000}Courier;}}}
}{\colortbl;\red0\green0\blue0;\red0\green0\blue255;\red0\green255\blue255;
\red0\green255\blue0;\red255\green0\blue255;\red255\green0\blue0;\red255\green2
  55
... (More text not shown)
castle%
```

The following example extracts the binary file `paper1.dvi` to standard output and pipes it to a printing program.

```
castle% unzip -p articles paper1.dvi | lp
request id is seachild-3 (standard input)
castle%
```

The following example extracts all FORTRAN and C source files—`*.f`, `*.c`, `*.h`, and `Makefile`—into the `/tmp` directory.

```
castle% unzip source.zip "*.[fch]" Makefile -d /tmp
```

Note — The double quotes are needed only in UNIX and only if globbing is turned on.

The following example extracts all FORTRAN and C source files, regardless of case (that is, both `*.c` and `*.C`, and any `makefile`, `Makefile`, `MAKEFILE`, or similar capitalization form).

```
castle% unzip -C source.zip "*.[fch]" makefile -d /tmp
```

The following example extracts all FORTRAN and C source files, regardless of case (that is, both `*.c` and `*.C`, and any `makefile`, `Makefile`, `MAKEFILE`, or similar form), converts any uppercase MS-DOS or VMS names to lower case, and converts the line endings of all of the files to the local standard (without respect to any files that might be marked binary).

```
castle% unzip -aaCL source.zip "*.[fch]" makefile -d /tmp
```

The following example extracts only newer versions of the files already in the current directory, without querying.

```
castle% unzip -fo sources
```

Note — Be careful of unzipping in one time zone a file that was created in another time zone. ZIP archives other than those created by `Zip` 2.1 or later contain no time zone information, and a newer file from an Eastern time zone may, in fact, be older.

The following example extracts newer versions of the files already in the current directory and creates any files not already there (same caveat as for the previous example).

```
castle% unzip -uo sources
```

In the following five examples, assume that `UNZIP` or `UNZIP_OPTS` is set to `-q`. The following example does a single quiet listing.

```
castle% setenv UNZIP -qq
castle% unzip -l letters.zip
  20038   02-18-99   08:44    letters.rtf
castle%
```

The following example does a double quiet listing.

```
castle% setenv UNZIP -qq
castle% unzip -ql letters.zip
```

```
   20038  02-18-99  08:44   letters.rtf
castle%
```

> **Note** — You generally don't need to add the `.zip` suffix.

Use any of the following three commands to do a standard listing. The extra dashes are ignored.

```
castle% unzip --ql file.zip
castle% unzip -l-q file.zip
castle% unzip -l--q file.zip
```

To unzip more than one archive file with the asterisk metacharacter, you must escape it by preceding it with a backslash. The following example unzips three archives that start with the characters 085.

```
castle% unzip 085\*
Archive:   085XDOCS.ZIP
  inflating: 085X01.DOC
  inflating: 085X02.DOC
  inflating: 085X03~1.DOC
  inflating: 085X042.DOC
  inflating: 085X08R.DOC
  inflating: 085X09E.RTF

Archive:   085XFILE.ZIP
  inflating: 085X05.DOC

Archive:   085XINTR.ZIP
  inflating: 085X06.DOC
  inflating: 085X07.RTF

3 archives were successfully processed.
castle%
```

Tips

It is worth getting in the habit of testing your `zip` archives. To test them, you may find it useful to define an alias such as the following.

```
alias tt unzip -tq
```

You can then simply type `tt` *file* to test an archive, something that is worth doing. With luck, `unzip` reports `No errors detected in compressed data of zipfile.zip`.

It is also useful to set the `UNZIP` environment variable to `-aLC`. You can set your `ZIPINFO` variable to `-z`.

Exit Status

The exit status (or error level) approximates the exit codes defined by PKWARE and takes on the following values, except under VMS.

0   Normal; no errors or warnings detected.

1	One or more warning errors were encountered, but processing completed successfully. This status includes files where one or more files were skipped because of unsupported compression methods or encryption with an unknown password.
2	A generic error in the file format was detected. Processing may have completed successfully; some broken files created by other archivers have simple workarounds.
3	A severe error in the file format was detected. Processing probably failed immediately.
4	Unable to allocate memory for one or more buffers during program initialization.
5	Unable to allocate memory or unable to obtain a TTY to read the decryption password(s).
6	Unable to allocate memory during decompression to disk.
7	Unable to allocate memory during memory decompression.
8	[Currently not used.]
9	The specified files were not found.
10	Invalid options were specified on the command line.
11	No matching files were found.
50	The disk is (or was) full during extraction.
51	The end of the ZIP archive was encountered prematurely.
80	You aborted unzip prematurely with Control-C (or equivalent).
81	Testing or extraction of one or more files failed because of unsupported compression methods or unsupported decryption.
82	No files were found because of bad decryption password(s). If even one file is successfully processed, however, the exit status is 1.

VMS interprets standard UNIX (or PC) return values as other, scarier-looking things, so unzip instead maps them into VMS-style status codes. The current mapping is as follows:

1 (success)	Normal exit.
0x7fff0001	Warning errors.
(0x7fff000? + 16*normal_unzip_exit_status)	
	All other errors, where the ? is 2 (error) for unzip values 2, 9–11, and 80–82, and 4 (fatal error) for the remaining ones (3–8, 50, 51).

In addition, a compilation option expands on this behavior: defining RETURN_CODES results in a human-readable explanation of what the error status means.

See Also
zipinfo(1)

URL

The Info-ZIP home page is currently at http://www.cdrom.com/pub/infozip/

Copyright

Distributed with permission from Info-ZIP. Please see
http://www.cdrom.com/pub/infozip/doc/COPYING for copyright information.

Authors

The primary Info-ZIP authors (current semiactive members of the Zip-Bugs work group)
are: Greg "Cave Newt" Roelofs (UnZip); Onno van der Linden (Zip); Jean-Loup Gailly
(compression); Mark Adler (decompression, fUnZip); Christian Spieler (VMS, MS-DOS,
Windows 95, NT, shared code, general Zip and UnZip integration and optimization);
Mike White (Windows GUI, Windows DLLs); Kai Uwe Rommel (OS/2); Paul Kienitz
(Amiga, Windows 95); Chris Herborth (BeOS, QNX, Atari); Jonathan Hudson
(SMS/QDOS); Sergio Monesi (Acorn RISC OS); Harald Denker (Atari, MVS); John Bush
(Solaris, Amiga); Hunter Goatley (VMS); Steve Salisbury (Windows 95, NT); Steve
Miller (Windows CE GUI), Johnny Lee (MS-DOS, Windows 95, NT); and Dave Smith
(Tandem NSK).

The author of the original unzip code on which Info-ZIP is based is Samuel H. Smith;
Carl Mascott did the first UNIX port; and David P. Kirschbaum organized and led
Info-ZIP in its early days, with Keith Petersen hosting the original mailing list at
WSMR-SimTel20. The full list of contributors to UnZip has grown quite large; please
refer to the CONTRIBS file in the UnZip source distribution for a relatively complete
version.

Versions

v1.2	15 Mar 89	Samuel H. Smith.
v2.0	9 Sep 89	Samuel H. Smith.
v2.x	Fall 1989	Many Usenet contributors.
v3.0	1 May 90	Info-ZIP (DPK, consolidator).
v3.1	15 Aug 90	Info-ZIP (DPK, consolidator).
v4.0	1 Dec 90	Info-ZIP (GRR, maintainer).
v4.1	12 May 91	Info-ZIP.
v4.2	20 Mar 92	Info-ZIP (Zip-Bugs subgroup, GRR).
v5.0	21 Aug 92	Info-ZIP (Zip-Bugs subgroup, GRR).
v5.01	15 Jan 93	Info-ZIP (Zip-Bugs subgroup, GRR).
v5.1	7 Feb 94	Info-ZIP (Zip-Bugs subgroup, GRR).
v5.11	2 Aug 94	Info-ZIP (Zip-Bugs subgroup, GRR).
v5.12	28 Aug 94	Info-ZIP (Zip-Bugs subgroup, GRR).
v5.2	30 Apr 96	Info-ZIP (Zip-Bugs subgroup, GRR).
v5.3	22 Apr 97	Info-ZIP (Zip-Bugs subgroup, GRR).
v5.31	31 May 97	Info-ZIP (Zip-Bugs subgroup, GRR).
v5.32	3 Nov 97	Info-ZIP (Zip-Bugs subgroup, GRR).

uptime — Show How Long a System Has Been Up

Synopsis

/usr/bin/uptime

Description

The uptime command prints the current time, the length of time the system has been up, and the average number of jobs in the run queue over the last 1, 5, and 15 minutes. It is, essentially, the first line of a w(1) command.

Note — You can use the who -b command to display the time the system was last booted.

Example

The following example shows the output of uptime.

```
castle% uptime
10:47am up 27 day(s), 50 mins, 1 user, load average: 0.18, 0.26, 0.20
castle%
```

Attributes

See attributes(5) for descriptions of the following attributes:

Attribute Type	Attribute Value
Availability	SUNWcsu

See Also

w(1), who(1), whodo(1M), attributes(5)

users — Display a Compact List of Logged-In Users

Synopsis

/usr/ucb/users [*filename*]

Description

users lists the login names of the users currently on the system in a compact, one-line format. Specifying *filename* tells users where to find its information; by default, it checks /var/adm/utmpx.

The users command is equivalent to typing who -q.

Examples

The following example shows that four users are logged in to the system castle.

```
castle% users
winsor ray des rob
castle%
```

Files

/var/adm/utmpx

Attributes

See attributes(5) for descriptions of the following attributes:

Attribute Type	Attribute Value
Availability	SUNWscpu

See Also

who(1), attributes(5)

---

uucp, uulog, uuname — UNIX-to-UNIX System Copy

Synopsis

/usr/bin/uucp [-c | -C] [-d | -f] [-g*grade*] [-jmr] [-n*user*] [-s*file*] [-x*debug-level*]
source-file destination-file
/usr/bin/uulog [-ssys] [-f *system*] [-x] [-*number*] *system*
/usr/bin/uuname [-c|-l]

Description

The uucp (UNIX-to-UNIX copy) suite of commands is part of a data communications
subsystem that enables you to transfer ASCII and binary files between systems, control
execution of commands, queue jobs for later transfer, and automatically retry when
transfer fails. The complete uucp suite of commands includes user commands and
functions, security features, logging and debugging tools, and a number of data transfer
protocols. This section describes the uucp, uulog, and uuname commands.

uucp

uucp copies files named by the *source-file* arguments to the location specified by the
destination-file argument.

uulog

uulog queries a log file of uucp or uuxqt transactions in file
/var/uucp/.Log/uucico/system or /var/uucp/.Log/uuxqt/system.

uuname

uuname lists the names of systems known to uucp.

Notes

For security reasons, the domain of remotely accessible files may be severely restricted. You probably cannot access files by path name; ask a responsible person on the remote system to send them to you. For the same reasons, you probably cannot send files to arbitrary path names. As distributed, the remotely accessible files are those whose names begin /var/spool/uucppublic (equivalent to ~/).

All files received by uucp are owned by uucp.

Protected files and files that are in protected directories that are owned by the requester can be sent by uucp. However, if the requester is root and the directory is not searchable by other or the file is not readable by other, the request fails.

Strings that are passed to remote systems may not be evaluated in the same locale as the one in use by the process that invoked uucp on the local system.

Configuration files must be treated as C- (or POSIX-) locale text files.

Options

uucp

-c	Do not copy local files to the spool directory for transfer to the remote system (default).
-C	Force the copy of local files to the spool directory for transfer.
-d	Make all necessary directories for the file copy (default).
-f	Do not make intermediate directories for the file copy.
-g*grade*	Specify the grade as a single letter, number, or a string of alphanumeric characters defining a service grade. Use the uuglist command to determine whether it is appropriate to use the single letter, number, or a string of alphanumeric characters as a service grade. The output from the uuglist command is a list of service grades that are available or a message that says to use a single letter or number as a grade of service.
-j	Print the uucp job identification string on standard output. This job identification can be used by uustat to obtain the status of a uucp job or to terminate a uucp job. The uucp job is valid as long as the job remains queued on the local system.
-m	Send mail to the requester when the copy is complete. The -m option works only when sending files or receiving a single file. Receiving multiple files specified by special shell characters ?, &, and [...] does not activate the -m option.
-n*user*	Notify user on the remote system that a file was sent.
-r	Do not start the file transfer, just queue the job.
-s*file*	Report status of the transfer to *file*. This option is accepted for compatibility but is ignored because it is insecure.
-x*debug-level*	
	Produce debugging output on standard output. *debug-level* is a number between 0 and 9; as it increases to 9, show more detailed debugging information. This option may not be available on all systems.

uulog

The following options print logging information.

-s*sys*   Print information about file transfer work involving system *sys*.

-f*system*   Do a `tail -f` of the file transfer log for *system*. (You must press the Break key to exit this function.)

Other options you can use in conjunction with the above options are:

-x   Look in the `uuxqt` log file for the given system.

-*number*   Execute a `tail` command of *number* lines.

uuname

-c   Display the names of systems known to `cu`. The two lists are the same unless your system is using different `Systems` files for `cu` and `uucp`. See the `Sysfiles` file.

-l   Display the local system name.

Operands

The source file name may be a path name on your system or may have the form:

system-name!*pathname*

where *system-name* is taken from a list of system names that `uucp` knows about. *source-file* is restricted to no more than one *system-name*. The destination *system-name* can also include a list of system names such as

system-name!*system-name*!...!*system-name*!*pathname*

With this syntax, `uucp` tries to send the file to the destination, using the specified route. Take care to ensure that intermediate nodes in the route are willing to forward information.

Note — The forwarding of files through other systems may not be compatible with the previous version of `uucp`. If you use forwarding, all systems in the route must have compatible versions of `uucp`.

For C shell, surround the ! character with single quotes ('), or precede it with a backslash (\).

The shell metacharacters ?, * and [...] appearing in *pathname* are expanded on the appropriate system.

Path names can be one of the following:

* An absolute path name.
* A path name preceded by ~*user* where *user* is a login name on the specified system and is replaced by that user's login directory.
* A path name preceded by ~/*destination* where *destination* is appended to `/var/spool/uucppublic`.

Note — This destination is treated as a file name unless you are transferring more than one file with this request or the destination is already a directory. To ensure that the destination is a directory, follow it with a slash (/). For example ~/dan/ as the destination creates the directory /var/spool/uucppublic/dan if it does not exist and puts the requested file(s) in that directory. Anything else is prefixed by the current directory.

If the result is an erroneous path name for the remote system, the copy fails. If the *destination-file* is a directory, the last part of the *source-file* name is used.

Invoking uucp with shell wild-card characters as the remote *source-file* invokes the uux(1C) command to execute the uucp command on the remote system. The remote uucp command spools the files on the remote system. After the first session terminates, if the remote system is configured to transfer the spooled files to the local system, the remote system initiates a call and sends the files; otherwise, the user must "call" the remote system to transfer the files from the spool directory to the local system. This call can be done manually with Uutry(1M) or as a side effect of another uux(1C) or uucp call.

Note that the local system must have permission to execute the uucp command on the remote system so that the remote system can send the spooled files.

uucp removes execute permissions across the transmission and gives 0666 read and write permissions (see chmod(2)).

Environment Variables

See environ(5) for descriptions of the following environment variables that affect the execution of uucp: LC_COLLATE, LC_CTYPE, LC_MESSAGES, LC_TIME, TZ, and NLSPATH.

Exit Status

0	Successful completion.
>0	An error occurred.

Files

/bin/uu* uucp commands.

/etc/uucp/* Other data files.

/var/spool/uucp

> Spool directories.

/usr/lib/uucp/*

> Other program files.

/var/spool/uucppublic/*

> Public directory for receiving and sending.

Attributes

See attributes(5) for descriptions of the following attributes:

Attribute Type	Attribute Value
Availability	SUNWbnuu

See Also

mail(1), uuglist(1C), uustat(1C), uux(1C), uutry(1M), uuxqt(1M), chmod(2), attributes(5)

uuencode, uudecode — Encode or Decode a Binary File

Synopsis

/usr/bin/uuencode [*source-file*] *decode-pathname*
/usr/bin/uudecode [-p] *encoded-file*

Description

Use the uuencode/uudecode commands to convert between ASCII and binary data.

Warning — If you run uuencode and then run uudecode on a file in the
same directory, you will overwrite the original file.

uuencode

uuencode converts a binary file into an encoded representation that you can send using
mail(1). It encodes the contents of *source-file* or the standard input if you specify no
source-file argument. The *decode-pathname* argument is required. The
decode-pathname is included in the encoded file header as the name of the file where
uudecode puts the binary (decoded) data. uuencode also includes the permission modes
of *source-file* (except setuid, setgid, and sticky bits) so that *decode-pathname* is
recreated with those same permission modes.

Note — Because the encoded file's size is expanded by 35 percent (3 bytes
become 4, plus control information) it takes longer to transmit than the
equivalent binary file.

uudecode

uudecode reads an *encoded-file*, strips off any leading and trailing lines added by
mailer programs, and recreates the original binary data with the file name and the mode
specified in the header.
   The encoded file is an ordinary, portable, character-set text file; you can edit it with
any text editor. It is best to change only the mode or *decode-pathname* in the header to
avoid corrupting the decoded binary.

Note — The user on the remote system who is invoking uudecode (typically
uucp) must have write permission on the file specified in the
decode-pathname operand.

Options

uudecode

-p   Decode *encoded-file* and send it to standard output. This option
               enables you to use uudecode in a pipeline.

Operands

uuencode

decode-pathname

> The path name of the file where the uudecode command puts the decoded file. If there are characters in *decode-pathname* that are not in the portable file-name character set, the results are unspecified.

source-file

> A path name of the file to be encoded.

uudecode

encoded-file

> The path name of a file containing the output of uuencode.

Usage

See largefile(5) for the description of the behavior of uuencode and uudecode when encountering files greater than or equal to 2 Gbytes (2**31 bytes).

Environment Variables

See environ(5) for descriptions of the following environment variables that affect the execution of uuencode and uudecode: LC_CTYPE, LC_MESSAGES, and NLSPATH.

Output

The standard output is a text file (encoded in the character set of the current locale) that begins with the line

```
"begin%s%s\n", <mode>, decode_pathname
```

and ends with the line

```
end\n
```

In both cases, the lines have no preceding or trailing blank characters.

The algorithm that is used for lines in between begin and end takes three octets as input and writes four characters of output by splitting the input at six-bit intervals into four octets, containing data in the lower six bits only. These octets are converted to characters by addition of a value of 0x20 to each octet so that each octet is in the range 0x20-0x5f. It is then assumed to represent a printable character. Each octet is translated into the corresponding character codes for the codeset in use in the current locale. (For example, the octet 0x41, representing A, is translated to A in the current codeset, such as 0xc1 if it is EBCDIC.)

Where the bits of two octets are combined, the least significant bits of the first octet are shifted left and combined with the most significant bits of the second octet that is shifted right. Thus, the three octets A, B, C are converted into the four octets:

```
0x20 + (( A >> 2) & 0x3F)
0x20 + (((A << 4) ((B >> 4) & 0xF)) & 0x3F)
0x20 + (((B << 2) ((C >> 6) & 0x3)) & 0x3F)
0x20 + (( C) & 0x3F)
```

These octets are then translated into the local character set.

Each encoded line contains a length character, equal to the number of characters to be decoded plus 0x20 translated to the local character set as described above, followed by the encoded characters. The maximum number of octets to be encoded on each line is 45.

Exit Status

0	Successful completion.
>0	An error occurred.

Attributes

See attributes(5) for descriptions of the following attributes:

Attribute Type	Attribute Value
Availability	SUNWesu

See Also

mail(1), mailx(1), uucp(1C), uux(1C), attributes(5), largefile(5)

uuglist — Print the List of Available Service Grades

Synopsis

/usr/bin/uuglist [-u]

Description

A system may provide several grades of service for uucp commands. Each grade receives different priorities from the UUCP system. You can use the uuglist command to display a list of service grades that are available on the system to use with the -g option of uucp(1C) and uux(1C), as shown in the following example.

```
castle% uuglist -u
high
low
medium
castle%
```

Options

-u	List the names of the service grades that can be used with the -g option of the uucp and uux commands.

Files

/etc/uucp/Grades

         Contains the list of service grades.

Attributes

See attributes(5) for descriptions of the following attributes:

Attribute Type	Attribute Value
Availability	SUNWbnuu

See Also

uucp(1C), uux(1C), attributes(5)

---

uulog, uuname — UNIX-to-UNIX System Copy

Synopsis

```
/usr/bin/uulog [-ssys] [-fsystem] [-x] [-number] system
/usr/bin/uuname [-c|-1]
```

Description

See uucp(1).

---

uupick — Public UNIX-to-UNIX System File Copy

Synopsis

```
/usr/bin/uupick [-ssystem]
```

Description

See uuto(1).

---

uustat — uucp Status Inquiry and Job Control

Synopsis

```
/usr/bin/uustat [-m] | [-p] | [-q] | [-kjobid [-n]] | [-rjobid [-n]]
/usr/bin/uustat [-a] [-ssystem [-j]] [-uuser] [-Sqric]
/usr/bin/uustat -tsystem [-c] [-dnumber]
```

Description

uustat functions in the following three areas:

- Displays the general status of, or cancels, previously specified uucp commands.
- Provides remote system performance information, such as average transfer rates or average queue times.

- Provides general, remote-system-specific and user-specific status of uucp connections to other systems.

Note — After the user has issued the uucp request, if the file to be transferred is moved, is deleted, or was not copied to the spool directory (-C option) when the uucp request was made, uustat reports a file size of -99999. This job eventually fails because the file(s) to be transferred cannot be found.

Options

General Status

The following options obtain general status of, or cancel, previously specified uucp commands.

-a	List all jobs in queue.
-j	List the total number of jobs displayed. You can use this option with the -a or the -s option.
-k *jobid*	Kill the uucp request whose job identification is *jobid.* The killed uucp request must belong to the user issuing the uustat command unless the user is the superuser or uucp administrator. If the superuser or the uucp administrator kills the job, send e-mail to the user.
-m	Report the status of accessibility of all systems.
-n	Suppress all standard output, but not standard error. Use this option with the -k and -r options.
-p	Execute the command ps -flp for all the process IDs that are in the lock files.
-q	List the jobs queued for each system. If a status file exists for the system, report its date, time, and status information. If a number appears in parentheses next to the number of C or X files, it is the age in days of the oldest C./X. file for that system. The Retry field represents the number of hours until the next possible call. The Count is the number of failure attempts. Note that for systems with a moderate number of outstanding jobs, this command can take 30 seconds or more of real time to execute. An example of the output produced by the -q option is:

```
eagle 3C 04/07-11:07 NO DEVICES AVAILABLE

mh3bs3 2C 07/07-10:42 SUCCESSFUL
```

This output indicates the number of command files that are waiting for each system. Each command file may have zero or more files to be sent (zero means to call the system and see if work is to be done). The date and time refer to the previous interaction with the system, followed by the status of the interaction.

-r*jobid*   Rejuvenate *jobid.* Touch the files associated with *jobid* so that their modification time is set to the current time. This adjustment prevents the cleanup daemon from deleting the job until the job modification time reaches the limit imposed by the daemon.

Remote System Status

The following options provide remote system performance information such as average transfer rates or average queue times. You can use the -c and -d options only with the -t option.

-c   Calculate average queue time. With no -c option, calculate the average transfer. For example, the command

```
castle% uustat -teagle -d50 -c
```

produces output in the following format:

```
average queue time to eagle for last 50 minutes: 5 seconds
```

The same command without the -c parameter produces output in the following format:

```
average transfer rate with eagle for last 50 minutes:
2000.88 bytes/sec
```

-d*number* Specify *number* in minutes to override the 60-minute default used for calculations. These calculations are based on information contained in the optional performance log and therefore may not be available. Calculations can be made only from the time that the performance log was last cleaned up.

-t*system* Report the average transfer rate or average queue time for the past 60 minutes for the remote system.

User- or System-Specific Status

The following options provide general, remote-system-specific and user-specific status of uucp connections to other systems. You can specify either or both of the following options with uustat. You can use the -j option with the -s option to list the total number of jobs displayed.

-s*system* Report the status of all uucp requests for remote system *system.*

-u*user*   Report the status of all uucp requests issued by *user.*

Output for both the -s and -u options has the following format:

```
eagleN1bd7  4/07-11:07  S  eagle  dan  522     /home/dan/A

eagleC1bd8  4/07-11:07  S  eagle  dan  59      D.3b2a12ce4924
4/07-11:07  S  eagle  dan  rmail  mike
```

The first field is the job ID of the job followed by the date/time. The next field is an S if the job is sending a file or an R if the job is requesting a file. The next field is the system where the file is to be transferred, followed by the user ID of the user who queued the job. The next field contains the size of the file or, in the case of a remote execution, the name of the command. In this example, rmail is the command used for remote mail.

When this field contains the size, the file name is also shown. The file name can either be the name given by the user or an internal name (for example, D.3b2a1ce4924) that is created for data files associated with remote executions (rmail in this example).

-Sqric   Report the job state.

              q   Queued jobs. The transfer has not started.

              r   Running jobs. The transfer has begun.

              i   Interrupted jobs. The transfer began but was terminated before
                      the file was completely transferred.

              c   Completed jobs. The job successfully transferred.

You can use the parameters in any combination, but you must specify at least one parameter. You can also use the -S option with -s and -u options. The output for this option is exactly like the output for -s and -u, except that the job states are appended as the last output word. Output for a completed job has the following format:

eagleC1bd3 completed

When you specify no options, uustat writes to standard output the status of all uucp requests issued by the current user.

Environment Variables

See environ(5) for descriptions of the following environment variables that affect the execution of uustat: LC_CTYPE, LC_MESSAGES, LC_TIME, TZ, and NLSPATH.

Exit Status

0   Successful completion.

>0   An error occurred.

Files

/var/spool/uucp/*

                Spool directories.

/var/uucp/.Admin/account

                Accounting log.

/var/uucp/.Admin/perflog

                Performance log.

Attributes

See attributes(5) for descriptions of the following attributes:

Attribute Type	Attribute Value
Availability	SUNWbnuu

See Also

uucp(1C), attributes(5)

Diagnostics

The -t option produces no message when the data needed for the calculations is not being recorded.

---

uuto, uupick — Public UNIX-to-UNIX System File Copy

Synopsis

```
/usr/bin/uuto [-mp] source-file...destination
/usr/bin/uupick [-s system]
```

Description

uuto

uuto sends *source-file* to *destination*. uuto uses uucp(1C) to send files; it allows the local system to control the file access. A *source-file* name is a path name on your system. Destination has the form:

system[!*system*] ... !*user*

where *system* is taken from a list of system names that uucp knows about. *user* is the login name of someone on the specified system.

The files (or subtrees if you specify directories) are sent to PUBDIR on *system*, where PUBDIR is a public directory defined in the uucp source. By default, this directory is /var/spool/uucppublic. Specifically, the files are sent to

PUBDIR/receive/user/mysystem/files.

The recipient is notified by mail(1) of the arrival of files.

Note — To send files that begin with a dot (for instance, .profile), you must include the dot. For example, the following file names are correct:

.profile.prof* .profil?

The following file names are incorrect:

prof ?profile

---

uupick

uupick accepts or rejects the files transmitted to the user. Specifically, uupick searches PUBDIR for files destined for the user. For each entry (file or directory) found, the following message is printed on standard output:

from *system sysname*: [*file file-name*] [*dir dirname*] ?

uupick then reads a line from standard input to determine the disposition of the file.

newline	Go to next entry.
d	Delete the entry.

m [*dir*]	Move the entry to named directory *dir*. If you do not specify *dir* as a complete path name (in which $HOME is legitimate), assume a destination relative to the current directory. If you specify no destination, the default is the current directory.
a [*dir*]	Same as m above, except move all the files sent from *system*.
p	Print the content of the file.
q	Stop.
EOT (control-d)	
	Same as q.
! *command*	Escape to the shell to run *command*.
*	Print a command summary.

Options

uuto

-m	Send mail to the sender when the copy is complete.
-p	Copy the source file into the spool directory before transmission.

uupick

-s *system*	Search the PUBDIR only for files sent from *system*.

Operands

destination

A string of the form:

system-name! *user*

where *system-name* is taken from a list of system names that uucp knows about; see uuname. The *user* argument is the login name of someone on the specified system. The *system-name* destination can also be a list of names such as

system-name! *system-name*! . . . ! *system-name*! *user*

in which case, try to send the file by the specified route to the destination. Take care to ensure that intermediate nodes in the route are willing to forward information.

source-file

A path name of a file on the local system to be copied to *destination*.

Environment Variables

See environ(5) for descriptions of the following environment variables that affect the execution of uuto and uupick: LC_TYPE, LC_MESSAGES, and NLSPATH.

Exit Status

0	Successful completion.
>0	An error occurred.

Files

PUBDIR   /var/spool/uucppublic public directory.

Attributes

See attributes(5) for descriptions of the following attributes:

Attribute Type	Attribute Value
Availability	SUNWbnuu

See Also

mail(1), uucp(1C), uustat(1C), uux(1C), uucleanup(1M), attributes(5)

---

uux — UNIX-to-UNIX System Command Execution

Synopsis

/usr/bin/uux [-] [-bcCjnprz] [-a*name*] [-g*grade*] [-s*filename*]
    [-x*debug-level*] *command-string*

Description

uux gathers zero or more files from various systems, executes a command on a specified system, and then sends standard output to a file on a specified system.

> **Note —** For security reasons, most installations limit the list of commands executable on behalf of an incoming request from uux, permitting only the receipt of mail (see mail(1)). Remote execution permissions are defined in /etc/uucp/Permissions.

The *command-string* is made up of one or more arguments that look like a shell command line, except that you can prefix the command and file names with *system-name*!. A null *system-name* is interpreted as the local system.
File names can be one of the following:

- An absolute path name.
- A path name preceded by ~*xxx*, where *xxx* is a login name on the specified system and is replaced by that user's login directory.

Anything else is prefixed by the current directory.
For example, the following command gets the filename1 and filename2 files from the sys1 and sys2 systems, executes a diff(1) command, and puts the results in filename.diff in the local PUBDIR/dan/ directory.

```
castle% uux "!diff sys1!/home/dan/filename1sys2!/a4/dan/filename2 >
   !~/dan/filename.diff"
```

PUBDIR is a public directory defined in the uucp source. By default, this directory is /var/spool/uucppublic.

uux tries to get all appropriate files to the specified system where they are processed. For files that are output files, escape the file name by using parentheses. For example, the following command gets /usr/filename from system b and sends it to system a, performs a cut command on that file, and sends the result of the cut command to system c.

```
castle% uux "a!cut -f1 b!/usr/filename >c!/usr/filename"
```

uux notifies you if the requested command on the remote system is disallowed. You can turn off this notification with the -n option. The response comes by mail from the remote system.

The following restrictions apply to the shell pipeline processed by uux.

- Quote any special shell characters, such as <, >, ;, | either by quoting the entire command string or by quoting the special characters as individual arguments.

- In gathering files from different systems, uux does not perform path-name expansion. Thus, a request such as uux "c89 remsys!~/*.c" would try to copy the file named literally *.c to the local system.

- Only the first command of a shell pipeline can have a *system-name*!. All other commands are executed on the system of the first command.

- The use of the shell metacharacter * probably does not do what you want it to do.

- The shell tokens << and >> are not implemented.

- You cannot use the redirection operators >>, <<, >|, or >&.

- You cannot use the reserved word ! at the head of the pipeline to modify the exit status.

- Alias substitution is not performed.

Notes

The execution of commands on remote systems takes place in an execution directory known to the uucp system.

All files required for the execution are put into this directory unless they already reside on that system. Therefore, the simple file name (without path or system reference) must be unique within the uux request. The following command does *not* work.

```
castle% uux "a!diff b!/home/dan/xyz c!/home/dan/xyz >!xyz.diff"
```

But the following command does work if diff is a permitted command.

```
castle% uux "a!diff a!/home/dan/xyz c!/home/dan/xyz > !xyz.diff"
```

Protected files and files that are in protected directories that are owned by the requester can be sent in commands by use of uux. However, the requests fail if the requester is root and the directory is not searchable by other.

Options

–	Specify that *command-string* comes from standard input.
-a*name*	Use *name* as the user job identification replacing the initiator user ID. (Return notification to the user ID name.)
-b	Return whatever standard input was provided to the uux command if the exit status is non-zero.
-c	Do not copy local file to the spool directory for transfer to the remote system (default).
-C	Force the copy of local files to the spool directory for transfer.
-g*grade*	Specify *grade* as a single letter, number, or a string of alphanumeric characters defining a service grade. Use the uuglist(1C) command to determine whether it is appropriate to use the single letter, number, or a string of alphanumeric characters as a service grade. The output from the uuglist command is a list of service grades that are available or a message that says to use a single letter or number as a grade of service.
-j	Output the job ID string on the standard output, which is the job identification. uustat(1C) can use this job identification to obtain the status or terminate a job.
-n	Do not notify the user if the command fails.
-p	Same as –. Specify that *command-string* comes from standard input.
-r	Queue the job but do not start the file transfer.
-s*filename*	Report status of the transfer in *filename*. This option is accepted for compatibility but is ignored because it is insecure.
-x*debug-level*	
	Produce debugging output on the standard output. Specify *debug-level* as a number between 0 and 9; as it increases to 9, show more detailed debugging information.
-z	Send success notification to the user.

Environment Variables

See environ(5) for descriptions of the following environment variables that affect the execution of uux: LC_CTYPE, LC_MESSAGES, and NLSPATH.

Exit Status

0	Successful completion.
>0	An error occurred.

Files

/etc/uucp/*

         Other data and programs.

`/etc/uucp/Permissions`

> Remote execution permissions.

`/usr/lib/uucp/*`

> Other programs.

`/var/spool/uucp`

> Spool directories.

Attributes

See `attributes`(5) for descriptions of the following attributes:

Attribute Type	Attribute Value
Availability	SUNWbnuu

See Also

`cut(1)`, `mail(1)`, `uucp(1C)`, `uuglist(1C)`, `uustat(1C)`, `attributes(5)`

V

vacation — Reply to Mail Automatically

Synopsis

```
/usr/bin/vacation [-I]
/usr/bin/vacation [-a alias] [-f file] [-j] [-m file] [-s sender] [-tN]
    username
```

Description

vacation automatically replies to incoming e-mail. It uses the .forward file in your home directory to automatically forward the message in .vacation.msg to any user who sends you an e-mail message while the vacation program is activated. It also uses the .vacation.pag and .vacation.dir files in your home directory to store a list of senders.

No vacation message is sent in the following cases:

- When the To: or the Cc: line does not list the users to whom the original message was sent or one of a number of aliases for them.
- When the initial From: line includes the string –REQUEST@ or if the header includes a Precedence: bulk or Precedence: junk line.
- When mail is received from postmaster.
- When mail is received from Mailer-Daemon.

Setting Up vacation

vacation provides an interactive program that you can use to set up the basic vacation configuration.

The interactive program automatically creates the following files in your home directory.

`~/.vacation.msg`

>Contains the message that is sent in response to incoming mail.

`~/.forward`   Contains a line of the following form that is used to forward the message in the .vacation.msg file.

>`\`*username*`, "|/usr/bin/vacation` *username*`"`

`~/.vacation.pag`
`~/.vacation.dir`

>Contains a list of senders when `vacation` is enabled.

To set up `vacation`, type the command with no arguments. If there is no .vacation.msg file in your home directory, `vacation` creates it with a default message and starts an editor that you can use to modify the message. If there is an existing .vacation.msg file in your home directory, `vacation` asks you if you want to edit it.

`vacation` uses the VISUAL or EDITOR environment variable to determine which editor to invoke. If neither environment variable is set, `vacation` uses vi(1) as the editor.

The following example sets up `vacation`, using the default .vacation.msg file that already exists in the home directory.

```
castle% vacation
This program can be used to answer your mail automatically
when you go away on vacation.
You have a message file in /export/home/winsor/.vacation.msg.
Would you like to see it? y
From: winsor (via the vacation program)
Subject: away from my mail

I will not be reading my mail for a while.
Your mail regarding "$SUBJECT" will be read when I return.
Would you like to edit it? n
To enable the vacation feature a ".forward" file is created.
Would you like to enable the vacation feature? y
Vacation feature ENABLED. Please remember to turn it off when
you get back from vacation. Bon voyage.
castle%
```

When `vacation` is enabled, the mailer sends a copy of an incoming message to *username* and pipes another copy into `vacation`.

Disabling vacation

The presence of the .forward file determines whether `vacation` is enabled or disabled. To disable `vacation`, remove the .forward file or move it to a new name.

You can use the vacation program to disable `vacation`. If a .forward file is present in your home directory, you are asked whether you want to remove it to disable `vacation` and end the installation.

Existing .vacation.msg, .vacation.pag, and .vacation.dir files are not affected.

The following example uses the `vacation` command to disable `vacation`.

```
castle% vacation
This program can be used to answer your mail automatically
when you go away on vacation.
```

```
You have a message file in /export/home/winsor/.vacation.msg.
Would you like to see it? n
Would you like to edit it? n
You have a .forward file in your home directory containing:
  \winsor, "|/usr/bin/vacation winsor"
Would you like to remove it and disable the vacation feature? y
Back to normal reception of mail.
castle%
```

Additional Configuration

Starting with the Solaris 8 release, vacation provides the -a, -f, -j, -m, -s, and -t configuration options that are not part of the installation. See "Options."

Options

-I   Clear the .vacation.pag and .vacation.dir files. If you do not specify the -I flag and provide a *username* argument, vacation reads the first line from the standard input (for a From: line, no colon). If absent, it produces an error message.

Use the following configuration options in the .forward file, not on the command line. For example, *username*, "|/usr/bin/vacation -t1m *username*" repeats replies to the sender every minute.

-a *alias*   Indicate that *alias* is one of the valid aliases for the user running vacation so that mail addressed to that alias generates a reply.

-f *file*   Use *file* instead of .vacation as the basename for the database file.

-j   Do not check whether the recipient appears in the To: or the Cc: line.

-m *file*   Use *file* instead of .vacation.msg as the message to send for the reply.

-s *sender*   Reply to sender instead of the value read from the UNIX From: line of the incoming message.

-t*N*   Change the interval between repeat replies to the same sender. The default is 1 week. A trailing s, m, h, d, or w scales *N* to seconds, minutes, hours, days, or weeks.

Usage

The ~/.vacation.msg file should include a header with at least a Subject: line. It should not include a From: or a To: line. For example:

```
Subject: I am on vacation
I am on vacation until March 8. If you have an urgent issue, please
  contact my manager.
--Janice
```

If you include the string $SUBJECT in the .vacation.msg file, it is replaced with the subject of the original message when the reply is sent. For example, the following .vacation.msg file includes the subject of the message in the reply.

```
Subject: I am on vacation
I am on vacation until March 8.
```

I will read your mail regarding "$SUBJECT" when I return. If you have an
  urgent issue, please contact my manager.
--Janice

Files

~/.forward

> Contains a line of the following format that is used to forward the
> message in the .vacation.msg file. *username*, "|/usr/bin/vacation
> *username*"

~/.vacation.msg

> Contains the message that is sent in response to incoming mail.

~/.vacation.pag

> Stores a list of senders when vacation is enabled. You cannot view this
> file directly with a text editor.

~/.vacation.dir

> Stores a list of senders when vacation is enabled. You cannot view this
> file directly with a text editor.

Attributes

See attributes(5) for descriptions of the following attributes:

Attribute Type	Attribute Value
Availability	SUNWcsu

See Also

New!

vi(1), sendmail(1M), getusershell(3C), dbm(3UCB), aliases(4), shells(4),
attributes(5)

---

val — Validate an SCCS File

Synopsis

```
/usr/ccs/bin/val -
/usr/ccs/bin/val [-s] [-m name] [-rsid] [-y type] s.filename...
```

Description

See sccs-val(1).

vax — Get Processor Type Truth Value

Synopsis

/usr/bin/vax

Description

See machid(1).

vc — Version Control

Synopsis

/usr/ccs/bin/vc [-a] [-t] [-c*char*] [-s] [*keyword=value... keyword=value*]

Description

Note — This command is obsolete and will be removed in the next release.

The vc command copies lines from the standard input to the standard output, using arguments and control statements from the standard input. In a copy operation, user-declared keywords can be replaced by their string value when they appear in plain text and/or control statements.

The copying of lines from the standard input to the standard output is conditional, based on tests (in control statements) of keyword values specified in control statements or as vc command arguments.

A control statement is a single line beginning with a control character, except as modified by the -t key letter. The default control character is colon (:) except as modified by the -c key letter. Input lines beginning with a backslash (\) followed by a control character are not control lines and are copied to the standard output with the backslash removed. Lines beginning with a backslash followed by a noncontrol character are copied in their entirety.

A keyword is composed of nine or fewer alphanumerics; the first must be alphabetic. A value is any ASCII string that can be created with ed; a numeric value is an unsigned string of digits. Keyword values may not contain blanks or Tabs.

Keywords are replaced by values whenever a keyword surrounded by control characters is encountered on a version control statement. The -a key letter forces replacement of keywords in all lines of text. You can include an uninterpreted control character in a value by preceding it with \. If a literal \ is desired, then you must precede it with \.

Options

-a	Force replacement of keywords surrounded by control characters with their assigned value in all text lines and not just in vc statements.
-c*char*	Specify a control character to be used in place of the colon (:) default.

-s   Silence warning messages (not error) that are normally printed on the diagnostic output.

-t   Ignore all characters from the beginning of a line up to and including the first Tab character for the purpose of detecting a control statement. If a control statement is found, discard all characters up to and including the Tab.

vc recognizes the following version control statements.

:asg *keyword=value*

Assign values to keywords. An asg statement overrides the assignment for the corresponding keyword on the vc command line and all previous asg statements for that keyword. Keywords that are declared but are not assigned values have null values.

:dcl *keyword*[, ..., *keyword*]

Declare keywords. All keywords must be declared.

:if *condition*

. . .

:end   Skip lines of the standard input. If *condition* is true, copy all lines between the if statement and the matching end statement to the standard output. If *condition* is false, discard all intervening lines, including control statements. Note that intervening if statements and matching end statements are recognized solely for the purpose of maintaining the proper if-end matching.

The syntax of a *condition* is:

```
cond   ::= ["not"] <or>
or     ::= <and> | <and> "|" <or>
and    ::= <exp> | <exp> "&" <and>
exp    ::= "(" <or> ")" | <value> <op> <value>
op     ::= "=" | "!=" | "<" | ">"
value  ::= <arbitrary ASCII string> | <numeric string>
```

The available operators and their meanings are:

=   Equal.

!=   Not equal.

&   AND.

| OR.

>   Greater than.

<   Less than.

()   Used for logical groupings.

You can use not only immediately after an if. When not is present, it inverts the value of the entire condition.

> and < operate only on unsigned integer values (for example, : 012 > 12 is false). All other operators take strings as arguments (for example, : 012 != 12 is true).

The precedence of the operators (from highest to lowest) is:

- = != > < All of equal precedence.
- &
- |

You can use parentheses to alter the order of precedence.
Separate values from operators or parentheses by at least one blank or Tab.

:: *text*   Replace keywords on lines that are copied to the standard output. Remove the two leading control characters and replace keywords surrounded by control characters in *text* with their value before copying the line to the output file. This action is independent of the -a key letter.

:on   Turn on or off keyword replacement on all lines.
:off

:ctl *char*   Change the control character to *char*.

:msg *message*

                 Print *message* on the diagnostic output.

:err *message*

                 Print *message* followed by ERROR: err statement on line .. (915) on the diagnostic output. Halt execution, and return an exit code of 1.

Attributes

See attributes(5) for descriptions of the following attributes:

Attribute Type	Attribute Value
Availability	SUNWsprot

See Also

ed(1), attributes(5)

vedit — Screen-Oriented Visual Display Editor Based on ex

Synopsis

```
/usr/bin/vedit [- | -s] [-l] [-L] [-R] [-r [filename]] [-S] [-t tag]
    [-v] [-V] [-x] [-wn] [-C] [+command | -c command] filename...
/usr/xpg4/bin/vedit [  | -o] [-l] [-L] [-R] [-r [filename]] [-S]
    [-t tag] [-v] [-V] [-x] [-wn] [-C] [+command | -c command]
    filename...
/usr/bin/vedit [- | -s] [-l] [-L] [-R] [-r [filename]] [-t tag] [-v]
    [-V] [-x] [-wn] [-C] [+command | -c command] filename...
/usr/xpg4/bin/vedit [- | -s] [-l] [-L] [-R] [-r [filename]] [-t tag]
    [-v] [-V] [-x] [-wn] [-C] [+command | -c command] filename...
```

Description

See vi(1).

---

ver — Graphics Filters for Various Plotters

Synopsis

```
/usr/bin/tplot [-Tterminal]
```

Description

See tplot(1).

---

vgrind — Format Program Listings

Synopsis

New!

```
/usr/bin/vgrind [-2fntwx] [-d defs-file] [-h header] [-l language]
    [-s n] [-opagelist] [-P printer] [-T output-device] filename...
```

Description

vgrind formats the program sources named by the *filename* arguments, using troff(1). Comments are in italics, keywords in bold, and as each function is encountered, its name is listed on the page margin.

vgrind runs in two basic modes, filter mode or regular mode. In filter mode, vgrind acts as a filter in a manner similar to tbl(1). The standard input is passed directly to the standard output except for lines bracketed by the following troff-like macros:

.vS   Start processing.

.vE   End processing.

These lines are formatted as described above. The output from this filter can be passed to troff for output. There need be no particular ordering with eqn(1) or tbl(1).

In regular mode, vgrind accepts input file names, processes them, and passes them to troff for output. If you specify no file name or if you specify - as the argument, vgrind reads from the standard input (default if you specify -f).

New!

In regular mode, if you specify the -t or -P option, the output is:

- Emitted (in troff format) to standard output when you specify the -t option.
- Printed (as PostScript) to the named printer when you specify the -P option.

Otherwise, the output is:

- Printed (as PostScript) on the system default printer if one is defined and if the standard output for the command is a TTY.
- Emitted (as PostScript) to standard output if it is not a TTY, that is, if standard output is a pipe or a redirect to a file.

In both modes, vgrind passes any lines beginning with a decimal point without conversion.

Bugs

vgrind assumes that a certain programming style is followed.

C	Precede function names on a line only with space, Tab, or an asterisk. The parenthesized arguments must also be on the same line.
FORTRAN	Put function names on the same line as the keywords function or subroutine.
MLisp	Do not put function names on the same line as the preceding *defun*.
Model	Put function names on the same line as the keyword *is beginproc*.
Pascal	Put function names on the same line as the keywords function or *procedure*.

If you do not follow these conventions, the indexing and marginal, function-name comment mechanisms fail.

More generally, arbitrary formatting styles for programs mostly look bad. The use of space characters to align source code fails miserably. This result is somewhat inevitable because the fonts vgrind uses are of variable width. Use Tab characters if you plan to use vgrind on your program.

The mechanism of ctags(1) in recognizing functions should be used here.

The -w option is a kludge, but there is no other way to achieve the desired effect.

The macros defined in tmac.vgrind do not coexist gracefully with those of other macro packages, making filter mode difficult to use effectively.

vgrind does not process certain special characters in csh(1) scripts correctly.

The tmac.vgrind formatting macros wire in the page height and width used in two-column mode, effectively making two-column output useless for paper sizes other than the standard American size of 8.5 by 11 inches. For other paper sizes, you need to edit the size values given in tmac.vgrind. A better solution is to create a troff output device specification intended specifically for landscape output and record size information there.

Options

-2	Produce two-column output. Change the default point size to 8 (as if you specified the -s8 option). Arrange for output in landscape mode.
-d *defs-file*	
	Specify an alternative language definitions file (the default is /usr/lib/vgrindefs).
-f	Force filter mode.
-h *header*	Specify a header to appear in the center of every output page. Use quotes to specify headers with embedded spaces.
-l *language*	

Specify the language to use. The languages currently known are:

-lsh	Bourne shell
-lc	C (the default)
-lc++	C++

-lcsh	C shell
-lml	Emacs MLISP
-lf	FORTRAN
-lI	Icon
-li	ISP
-lLDL	LDL
-lm	Model
-lp	Pascal
-lr	Ratfor

-n   Do not make keywords boldface.

-o *pagelist*

      Print only those pages whose page numbers appear in the comma-separated *pagelist* of numbers and ranges. A range *N-M* means pages *N* through *M*, an initial *-N* means from the beginning to page *N*, and a final *N-* means from *N* to the end.

-P *printer*   Send output to the named *printer*.

-s *n*   Specify a point size to use on output (exactly the same as the argument of a troff .ps point size request).

-t   Send formatted text to the standard output. Similar to the same option in troff.

-w   Consider Tab characters to be spaced four columns apart instead of the usual eight.

-x   Output the index file in a pretty format. The index file itself is produced whenever you run vgrind with a file called index present in the current directory. You can then run off the index of function definitions by specifying vgrind -x *index-file*.

      vgrind passes the following options to the formatter specified by the TROFF environment variable.

-T *output-device*

      Format output for the specified *output-device*.

Operands

filename   Name of the program source to be processed by vgrind. Use a dash (-) to specify the standard input.

Environment Variables

      In regular mode, vgrind feeds its intermediate output to the text formatter given by the value of the TROFF environment variable or to troff if the TROFF variable is not defined in the environment. This mechanism allows for local variations in troff's name.

Files

index   File where source for index is created.

/usr/lib/vgrindefs

           Language descriptions.

/usr/lib/vfontedpr

           Preprocessor.

/usr/share/lib/tmac/tmac.vgrind

           Macro package.

Attributes

See attributes(5) for descriptions of the following attributes:

Attribute Type	Attribute Value
Availability	SUNWdoc

See Also

csh(1), ctags(1), eqn(1), tbl(1), troff(1), attributes(5), vgrinddefs(5)

---

vi, view, vedit — Screen-Oriented Visual Display Editor Based on ex

Synopsis

```
/usr/bin/vi [- | -s] [-l] [-L] [-R] [-r [filename]] [-S] [-t tag] [-v]
    [-V] [-x] [-wn] [-C] [+command | -c command] filename...
/usr/bin/view [- | -s] [-l] [-L] [-R] [-r [filename]] [-S] [-t tag] [-v]
    [-V] [-x] [-wn] [-C] [+command | -c command] filename...
/usr/bin/vedit [- | -s] [-l] [-L] [-R] [-r [filename]] [-S] [-t tag]
    [-v] [-V] [-x] [-wn] [-C] [+command | -c command] filename...
/usr/xpg4/bin/vi [- | -s] [-l] [-L] [-R] [-r [filename]] [-S] [-t tag]
    [-v] [-V] [-x] [-wn] [-C] [+command | -c command] filename...
/usr/xpg4/bin/view [- | -s] [-l] [-L] [-R] [-r [filename]] [-S] [-t tag]
    [-v] [-V] [-x] [-wn] [-C] [+command | -c command] filename...
/usr/xpg4/bin/vedit [- | -s] [-l] [-L] [-R] [-r [filename]] [-S]
    [-t tag] [-v] [-V] [-x] [-wn] [-C] [+command | -c command]
    filename...
```

Description

vi (visual) is a display-oriented text editor based on the underlying ex line editor. You can use the command mode of ex from within vi, and you can use the command mode of vi from within ex. The visual commands are described on this manual page. Refer to the ex(1) manual page for information about all ex line editor commands and about how to set options such as automatically numbering lines and automatically starting a new output line when you press Return.

When using vi, changes you make to the file are reflected in what you see on your terminal screen. The position of the cursor on the screen indicates the position within the file.

The view invocation is the same as vi except that the read-only flag is set.

The vedit invocation is intended for beginners. It is the same as vi except that the report flag is set to 1, the showmode and novice flags are set, and magic is turned off. These preset defaults make it easier to learn vi.

Notes

Tampering with entries in /usr/share/lib/terminfo/?/* or /usr/share/lib/terminfo/?/* (for example, changing or removing an entry) can affect programs such as vi that expect the entry to be present and correct. In particular, removing the dumb terminal may cause unexpected problems.

Software Tabs using ^T work only immediately after an autoindent.

Left and right shifts on intelligent terminals do not make use of insert and delete character operations in the terminal.

The standard Solaris version of vi will be replaced by the POSIX.2-conforming version (see standards(5)) in the future. Scripts that use the ex family of addressing and features should use the /usr/xpg4/bin version of these commands.

Options

- | -s
Suppress all interactive user feedback. This option is useful when processing editor scripts.

-C
Same as the -x option except simulate the C command of ex. The C command is like the X command of ex, except that all text read in is assumed to have been encrypted.

-l
Set up for editing LISP programs.

-L
List the name of all files saved as the result of an editor or system crash.

-r *filename*

Edit *filename* after an editor or system crash. (Recover the version of *filename* that was in the buffer when the crash occurred.) The file too large to recover with -r option message that you may see when you load a file indicates that the file can be edited and saved successfully, but if the editing session is lost, recovery of the file is not possible with the -r option.

-R
Set the read-only flag to prevent accidental overwriting of the file.

-S
Use in conjunction with the -t *tag* option to tell vi not to sort the tags file. If the binary search (which relies on a sorted tag file for *tag*) fails to find it, do a much slower, linear search. Because the linear search is slow, for large files, ensure that the tags files are sorted instead of using this option. Creation of tags files normally produces sorted tags files. See ctags(1) for more information on tags files.

-t *tag*
Edit the file containing *tag*, and position the editor at its definition.

-v	Start up in display editing state, using vi. You can achieve the same effect by simply typing the vi command itself.
-V	Echo input to standard error when ex commands are read by means of standard input. This option is useful when processing ex commands within shell scripts.
-w*n*	Set the default window size to *n*. This option is useful when the editor is used over a slow-speed line.
-x	Simulate the X command of ex, and prompt for a key. The key is used to encrypt and decrypt text, using the algorithm of the crypt command. The X command makes an educated guess to determine whether text read in is encrypted. The temporary buffer file is also encrypted, using a transformed version of the key that you type in for the -x option.
+*command* | -c *command*	
	Begin editing by executing the specified editor command (usually a search or positioning command).

Note — Although they continue to be supported, two options have been replaced in the documentation by options that follow the Command Syntax Standard (see intro(1)). A -r option that is not followed by an argument has been replaced by -L, and +*command* has been replaced by -c *command*.

/usr/xpg4/bin/vi

If you use both the -t *tag* and the -c *command* options, the -t *tag* is processed first. That is, the file containing the tag is selected by -t and then the command is executed.

Operands

filename	A file to be edited.

Command Summary

vi Modes

Command	Normal and initial mode. Other modes return to command mode on completion. Use ESC (Escape) to cancel a partial command.
Input	Enter by setting any of the following options: a A i I o O c C s S R. You can then type arbitrary text. You usually exit input mode with an ESC character or, abnormally, with an interrupt.
Last line	Read input for : / ? or !. Terminate by pressing Return. An interrupt cancels termination.

Sample Commands

In the descriptions, CR stands for Return and ESC stands for the escape key.

<- |?v |?^ ->	
	Arrow keys move the cursor.
h j k l	Same as arrow keys.

i *text*ESC	Insert text.
cw*new*ESC	Change word to *new*.
ea*s*ESC	Pluralize word (end of word; append *s*; escape from input state).
x	Delete a character.
dw	Delete a word.
dd	Delete a line.
3dd	Delete three lines.
u	Undo previous change.
ZZ	Save changes and exit.
:q!CR	Discard changes and quit.
/*text*CR	Search for *text*.
^U ^D	Scroll up or down.
:*cmd*CR	Execute the specified ex or ed command.

Counts Before vi Commands

You can type numbers as a prefix to some commands. Numbers are interpreted in one of these ways.

z G |	Line/column number.
^D ^U	Scroll amount.

most of the rest

> Repeat effect.

Interrupting, Canceling

ESC	End insert or incomplete command.
DEL	Delete or rub out interrupts.

Manipulating Files

ZZ	If file modified, write and exit; otherwise, exit.
:wCR	Write back changes.
:w!CR	Force write if permission originally not valid.
:qCR	Quit.
:q!CR	Quit, discard changes.
:e *name*CR	Edit file *name*.
:e!CR	Reedit, discard changes.
:e + *name*CR	
	Edit starting at end of file *name*.
:e +*n*CR	Edit starting at line *n*.

:e #CR	Edit alternate file.
:e! #CR	Edit alternate file, discard changes.
:w *name*CR	Write file *name*.
:w! *name*CR	Overwrite file *name*.
:shCR	Run shell, then return.
:! *cmd*CR	Run *cmd*, then return.
:nCR	Edit next file in *arglist*.
:n *args*CR	Specify new *arglist*.
^G	Show current file and line.
:ta *tag*CR	Position cursor to *tag*.

In general, you can type any ex or ed command (such as substitute or global) preceded by a colon and followed by a Return.

Positioning Within File

^F	Forward screen.
^B	Backward screen.
^D	Scroll down half screen.
^U	Scroll up half screen.
*n*G	Go to the beginning of the specified line (end default), where *n* is a line number.
/*pat*	Display next line matching *pat*.
?*pat*	Display previous line matching *pat*.
n	Repeat last / or ? command.
N	Reverse last / or ? command.
/*pat*/+*n*	Go to *n*-th line after *pat*.
?*pat*?-*n*	Go to *n*-th line before *pat*.
]]	Go to next section/function.
[[	Go to previous section/function.
(	Go to beginning of sentence.
)	Go to end of sentence.
{	Go to beginning of paragraph.
}	Go to end of paragraph.
%	Find matching ( ) or {}.

Adjusting the Screen

| ^L | Clear, and redraw window. |
| ^R | Clear, and redraw window if ^L is -> key. |

zCR	Redraw screen with current line at top of window.
z-CR	Redraw screen with current line at bottom of window.
z.CR	Redraw screen with current line at center of window.
/*pat*/z-CR	Move *pat* line to bottom of window.
z*n*.CR	Use *n*-line window.
^E	Scroll window down one line.
^Y	Scroll window up one line.

Marking and Returning

`` ` `` `` ` ``	Move cursor to previous context.
`' '`	Move cursor to first nonwhite space in line.
m*x*	Mark current position with the ASCII lowercase letter *x*.
`` ` ``*x*	Move cursor to mark *x*.
'*x*	Move cursor to first nonwhite space in line marked by *x*.

Line Positioning

H	Top line on screen.
L	Last line on screen.
M	Middle line on screen.
+	Next line, at first nonwhite.
-	Previous line, at first nonwhite.
CR	Return, same as +.
|?v or j	Next line, same column.
|?^ or k	Previous line, same column.

Character Positioning

^	Find first nonwhite space character.
0	Go to beginning of line.
$	Go to end of line.
l or ->	Move forward.
h or <-	Move backward.
^H	Same as <- (backspace).
space	Same as -> (space).
f*x*	Find next *x*.
F*x*	Find previous *x*.
t*x*	Move to character before next *x*.

Tx	Move to character following previous x.
;	Repeat last f, F, t, or T.
,	Repeat inverse of last f, F, t, or T.
n|	Move to column n.
%	Find matching ( ) or { }.

Words, Sentences, Paragraphs

w	Forward a word.
b	Back a word.
e	End of word.
)	To next sentence.
}	To next paragraph.
(	Back a sentence.
{	Back a paragraph.
W	Forward a blank-delimited word.
B	Back a blank-delimited word.
E	End of a blank-delimited word.

Corrections During Insert

^H	Erase last character (backspace).
^W	Erase last word.
erase	Your erase character, same as ^H (backspace).
kill	Your kill character, erase this line of input.
\	Quote your erase and kill characters.
ESC	End insert, back to command mode.
CTRL-C	Interrupt, suspend insert mode.
^D	Backtab one character. Reset left margin of autoindent.
^^D	Caret (^) followed by Control-D (^D). Backtab to beginning of line; do not reset left margin of autoindent.
0^D	Backtab to beginning of line. Reset left margin of autoindent.
^V	Quote nonprintable character.

Insert and Replace

a	Append after cursor.
A	Append at end of line.
i	Insert before cursor.

I	Insert before first nonblank.
o	Open line below.
O	Open above.
r*x*	Replace single char with *x*.
R*text*ESC	Replace characters.

Operators

Operators are followed by a cursor motion and affect all text that would have been moved over. For example, because w moves over a word, dw deletes the word that would be moved over. Double the operator (for example, dd) to affect entire lines.

d	Delete.
c	Change.
y	Yank lines to buffer.
<	Left-shift.
>	Right-shift.
!	Filter through command.

Miscellaneous Operations

C	Change rest of line (c$).
D	Delete rest of line (d$).
s	Substitute characters (cl).
S	Substitute lines (cc).
J	Join lines.
x	Delete characters (dl).
X	Delete characters before cursor (dh).
Y	Yank lines (yy).

Yank and Put

Put inserts the text most recently deleted or yanked; however, if a buffer is named (using the ASCII lowercase letters a–z), the text in that buffer is inserted instead.

3yy	Yank three lines.
3yl	Yank three characters.
p	Put back text after cursor.
P	Put back text before cursor.
"*x*p	Put from buffer *x*.
"*x*y	Yank to buffer *x*.
"*x*d	Delete into buffer *x*.

Undo, Redo, Retrieve

u	Undo last change.
U	Restore current line.
.	Repeat last change.
"𝑎p	Retrieve 𝑎th last delete.

Usage

See largefile(5) for the description of the behavior of vi and view when encountering files greater than or equal to 2 Gbytes (2**31 bytes).

Environment Variables

See environ(5) for descriptions of the following environment variables that affect the execution of vi: LC_CTYPE, LC_TIME, LC_MESSAGES, and NLSPATH.

The editing environment defaults to certain configuration options. When you initiate an editing session, vi tries to read the EXINIT environment variable. If it exists, the editor uses the values defined in EXINIT; otherwise, it uses the values set in $HOME/.exrc. If $HOME/.exrc does not exist, the default values are used.

To use a copy of .exrc located in the current directory other than $HOME, set the exrc option in EXINIT or $HOME/.exrc. You can turn off options set in EXINIT in a local .exrc only if exrc is set in EXINIT or $HOME/.exrc.

Files

/var/tmp	Default directory in which temporary work files are placed. You can change the default with the directory option (see the ex(1) set command).
/usr/share/lib/terminfo/?/*	
	Compiled terminal description database /usr/lib/.COREterm/?/*. Subset of compiled terminal description database.

Attributes

See attributes(5) for descriptions of the following attributes:

/usr/bin/vi, /usr/bin/view, /usr/bin/vedit

Attribute Type	Attribute Value
Availability	SUNWcsu
CSI	Not enabled

/usr/xpg4/bin/vi, /usr/xpg4/bin/view, /usr/xpg4/bin/vedit

Attribute Type	Attribute Value
Availability	SUNWxcu4
CSI	Enabled

See Also

ctags(1), ed(1), edit(1), ex(1), intro(1), attributes(5), environ(5), largefile(5), standards(5)
   Solaris Advanced User's Guide

Author

vi and ex were developed by The University of California, Berkeley, California, Computer Science Division, Department of Electrical Engineering and Computer Science.

view — Screen-Oriented Visual Display Editor Based on ex

Synopsis

/usr/bin/view [- | -s] [-l] [-L] [-R] [-r [*filename*]] [-S] [-t *tag*] [-v]
   [-V] [-x] [-w*n*] [-C]
/usr/xpg4/bin/view [- | -s] [-l] [-L] [-R] [-r [*filename*]] [-S] [-t *tag*]
   [-v] [-V] [-x] [-w*n*] [-C] [+*command* | -c *command*] *filename*...
/usr/bin/view [- | -s] [-l] [-L] [-R] [-r [*filename*]] [-t *tag*] [-v] [-V]
   [-x] [-w*n*] [-C] [+*command* | -c *command*] *filename*...
/usr/xpg4/bin/view [- | -s] [-l] [-L] [-R] [-r [*filename*]] [-t *tag*] [-v]
   [-V] [-x] [-w*n*] [-C] [+*command* | -c *command*] *filename*...

Description

See vi(1).

vipw — Edit the Password File

Synopsis

/usr/ucb/vipw

Description

vipw edits the passwd file while setting the appropriate locks and does any necessary processing after the password file is unlocked. If the password file is already being edited, you are told to try again later. The vi(1) editor is used unless the environment variable VISUAL or EDITOR indicates an alternative editor.

   vipw performs a number of consistency checks on the password entry for root and does not allow a password file with a "mangled" root entry to be installed. It also checks the /etc/shells file to verify the login shell for root.

Files

/etc/ptmp

/etc/shells

Attributes

See attributes(5) for descriptions of the following attributes:

Attribute Type	Attribute Value
Availability	SUNWscpu

See Also

passwd(1), vi(1), passwd(4), attributes(5)

volcancel — Cancel Request for Removable Medium Not Currently in Drive

Synopsis

/usr/lib/vold/volcancel [-n] [*volume*]

Description

volcancel cancels a request to access a particular diskette or CD-ROM file system. This command is useful when the removable medium containing the file system is not currently in the drive.

Use the path /vol/rdsk/*name_of_volume* to specify the volume. If called without a volume name to cancel, volcancel checks whether Volume Management is running.

Options

-n   Display the nickname to the device name translation table.

Examples

The following example cancels a request to access an unnamed CD-ROM.

castle% **/usr/lib/vold/volcancel vol/rdsk/unnamed_cdrom**

You can use the volcancel command to check if Volume Management is running. In the following example, Volume Management is running.

castle% **/usr/lib/vold/volcancel**
castle%

In the following example, Volume Management is not running and the message volume management is not running is displayed.

castle% **/usr/lib/vold/volcancel**
/usr/lib/vold/volcancel: volume management is not running
castle%

Attributes

See attributes(5) for descriptions of the following attributes:

Attribute Type	Attribute Value
Availability	SUNWvolu

See Also

volcheck(1), volmissing(1), rmmount(1M), vold(1M), rmmount.conf(4),
vold.conf(4), attributes(5), volfs(7FS)

---

volcheck — Check for Medium in a Drive

Synopsis

/usr/bin/volcheck [-v] [-i *secs*] [-t *secs*] *pathname*

Description

The volcheck command tells Volume Management to look at each dev/*pathname* in
sequence and determine if a new medium has been inserted in the drive.
    The default action is for volcheck to run on all checkable media managed by Volume
Management.

Warning — Because of a hardware limitation in many diskette drives,
checking for media results in mechanical action in the diskette drive.
Continuous polling of the diskette drive wears out the drive. It is
recommended that you poll the drive only during periods of high use.

Options

-i *secs*   Set the frequency of device checking to *secs* seconds. The default is 2
seconds. The minimum frequency is 1 second.

-t *secs*   Check the named device(s) for the next *secs* seconds. The maximum
number of seconds allowed is 28800, which is 8 hours. You specify the
frequency of checking with -i. There is no default total time.

-v   Verbose.

Operands

pathname   The path name of a media device.

Examples

The following example asks Volume Management to examine the diskette drive for a
new diskette.

```
castle% volcheck -v /dev/diskette
/dev/diskette has media
castle%
```

The following example asks Volume Management to check in the background for a diskette in the diskette drive every 2 seconds for 600 seconds (10 minutes).

```
castle% volcheck -i 2 -t 600 /dev/diskette1 &
```

Description

/dev/volctl

Volume Management control port.

Attributes

See attributes(5) for descriptions of the following attributes:

Attribute Type	Attribute Value
Availability	SUNWvolu

See Also

eject(1), volcancel(1), volmissing(1) rmmount(1M), vold(1M), rmmount.conf(4), vold.conf(4), attributes(5), volfs(7FS)

---

volmissing — Notify User That Volume Requested Is Not in the CD-ROM or Diskette Drive

Synopsis

/usr/lib/vold/volmissing [-c] [-p] [-s] [-m *alias*]

Description

volmissing informs you when a requested volume is not available. Depending on the specified option, you are notified through your console window, syslogd(1M), or with an e-mail message.

volmissing -p is the default action taken by vold(1M), the Volume Management daemon, when it needs to notify you that the requested volume is not available. If you want to change this default, modify the /etc/vold.conf file. (See vold.conf(4)).

You can change the notification method for your system by editing the vold.conf configuration file and providing a new option for volmissing in the notify entry under the Events category.

Options

-c   Send a message to the console requesting the volume be inserted. To end the notification without inserting the requested volume, use volcancel(1).

-m *alias*   Send an e-mail message to the specified mail alias about the missing volume.

-p   All volmissing events are handled through a GUI, provided a window
            system is running on the console. If you specify this option and no
            window system is running, send all messages to the system console.

-s   Send one message to the syslogd(1M).

Files

/etc/vold.conf

            Volume Management daemon configuration file. Directs the Volume
            Management daemon to control certain devices, and takes action when
            specific criteria are met.

/usr/lib/vold/volmissing_popup

            Pop-up used when the -p option is supplied and a window system is
            running.

Attributes

See attributes(5) for descriptions of the following attributes:

Attribute Type	Attribute Value
Availability	SUNWvolu

See Also

volcancel(1), volcheck(1), rmmount(1M), syslogd(1M), vold(1M),
rmmount.conf(4), vold.conf(4), attributes(5), volfs(7FS)

---

volrmmount — Call rmmount to Mount or Unmount Medium

Synopsis

/usr/bin/volrmmount [-i|-e] [*name* | *nickname*]
/usr/bin/volrmmount [-d]

Description

volrmmount calls rmmount(1M) to simulate insertion (-i) or ejection (-e) of media.
Simulating insertion often means that rmmount mounts the medium. Conversely,
simulating ejection often means that rmmount unmounts the medium. However, these
actions can vary, depending on the rmmount configuration and media type (see
rmmount.conf(4)).

For example, if you use the default /etc/rmmount.conf and insert a music CD, it
won't be mounted. However, you can configure rmmount so that it calls workman
whenever you insert a music CD.

The volrmmount command enables you to override Volume Management's usual
handling of media.

Note — Volume Management (vold) must be running before you can use this command.

Options

-i	Simulate insertion of the specified medium by calling rmmount.
-e	Simulate ejection of the specified medium by calling rmmount.
-d	Display the name of the default device for volrmmount to handle. This device is used if you supply no *name* or *nickname*.

Operands

name The name that Volume Management recognizes as the device's name. See volfs(7FS).

nickname A shortened version of the device's name.

The following list shows the recognized nicknames:

Nickname	Path
fd	/dev/rdiskette
fd0	/dev/rdiskette
fd1	/dev/rdiskette1
diskette	/dev/rdiskette
diskette0	/dev/rdiskette0
diskette1	/dev/rdiskette1
rdiskette	/dev/rdiskette
rdiskette0	/dev/rdiskette0
rdiskette1	/dev/rdiskette1
floppy	/dev/rdiskette
floppy0	/dev/rdiskette0
floppy1	/dev/rdiskette1
cdrom0	/vol/dev/rdsk/cXtYdZ/label
zip0	/vol/dev/rdsk/cXtYdZ/label
jaz0	/vol/dev/rdsk/cXtYdZ/label
rmdisk0	/vol/dev/rdsk/cXtYdZ/label

New!
New!
New!
New!

Examples

When Volume Management finds a diskette that contains a file system, it calls rmmount to mount it. If you want to run tar(1) or cpio(1) on that diskette, it must first be unmounted.

The following example unmounts the diskette.

```
castle% volrmmount -e floppy0
castle%
```

After `volrmmount` unmounts the diskette, if you want to remount it (instead of ejecting it and reinserting it), use the following command.

```
castle% volrmmount -i floppy0
castle%
```

Note — If you are using a named diskette, you can use its name in place of `floppy0`.

Description

/dev/volctl   Volume Management control port.

Attributes

See `attributes`(5) for descriptions of the following attributes:

Attribute Type	Attribute Value
Availability	SUNWvolu

See Also

`cpio(1)`, `eject(1)`, `tar(1)`, `rmmount(1M)`, `vold(1M)`, `rmmount.conf(4)`, `attributes(5)`, `volfs(7FS)`

---

vplot — Graphics Filters for Various Plotters

Synopsis

/usr/ucb/plot [-T*terminal*]

Description

See `plot(1)`.

W

---

w — Display Information About Currently Logged-in Users

Synopsis

```
/usr/bin/w [-hlsuw] [user]
```

Description

The w command displays a summary of the current activity on the system, including what each user is doing. The heading line shows the current time, the length of time the system has been up, the number of users logged in to the system, and the average number of jobs in the run queue over the last 1, 5, and 15 minutes. w is a combination of who, uptime, and ps -a.

The fields displayed are the user's login name, the name of the TTY the user is on, the time of day the user logged in (in hours:minutes), the idle time (that is, the number of minutes since the user last typed anything in hours:minutes), the CPU time used by all processes and their children on that terminal (in minutes:seconds), the CPU time used by the currently active processes (in minutes:seconds), and the name and arguments of the current process.

Notes

The notion of the current process is unclear. The current algorithm is the highest-numbered process on the terminal that is not ignoring interrupts or, if there is none, the highest-numbered process on the terminal. This algorithm fails, for example, in critical sections of programs like the shell and editor or when faulty programs running in the background fork and fail to ignore interrupts. In cases where no process can be found, w prints -.

The CPU time is only an estimate; in particular, if someone leaves a background process running after logging out, the person currently on that terminal is charged with the time.

Background processes are not shown, even though they account for much of the load on the system.

Sometimes processes, typically those in the background, are printed with null or garbled arguments. In these cases, the name of the command is printed in parentheses.

w does not know about the conventions for detecting background jobs. It sometimes finds a background job instead of the right one.

Options

-h	Suppress the heading.
-l	Produce a long form of output (the default).
-s	Produce a short form of output. The short form abbreviates the TTY and omits the login time, CPU times, and the arguments to commands.
-u	Produce the heading line that shows the current time, the length of time the system has been up, the number of users logged in to the system, and the average number of jobs in the run queue over the last 1, 5, and 15 minutes.
-w	Produce a long form of output (same as the default).

Operands

user	Specify the name of a user for whom login information is displayed.

Examples

The following example uses the w command with no option to display a summary of current system activity.

```
castle% w
  2:47pm  up 58 min(s),  1 user,  load average: 0.08, 0.05, 0.04
User      tty          login@  idle   JCPU   PCPU   what
winsor    console      1:52pm    55      3           /usr/dt/bin/sdt_shell
   -c unseten
winsor    pts/3        1:53pm     1                  csh
winsor    pts/4        1:53pm     1                  /bin/csh
winsor    pts/5        1:53pm    54                  /bin/csh
winsor    pts/6        1:53pm            13          w
castle%
```

Environment Variables

See environ(5) for descriptions of the following environment variables that affect the execution of w: LC_CTYPE, LC_MESSAGES and LC_TIME.

Files

/var/adm/utmpx

User and accounting information.

Attributes
See attributes(5) for descriptions of the following attributes:

Attribute Type	Attribute Value
Availability	SUNWcsu

See Also
ps(1), who(1), whodo(1M), utmpx(4), attributes(5), environ(5)

wait — Await Process Completion

Synopsis
sh
wait [*pid*]

/bin/jsh, /bin/ksh, /usr/xpg4/bin/sh
wait [*pid*]
wait [*%job-id*...]

/bin/csh
wait

Description
When writing shell scripts, you will occasionally want to program the script to run simultaneous processes and wait for their conclusion before proceeding with other commands. The wait command provides shells with some of the job control features. It waits for all background processes to complete and reports their exit status.

The shell itself executes wait without creating a new process. If you get the error message cannot fork, too many processes, try using the wait command to clean up your background processes. If this doesn't help, the system process table is probably full or you have too many active foreground processes. (There is a limit to the number of process IDs associated with your login and to the number the system can track.)

Not all the processes of a pipeline with three or more stages are children of the shell and, thus, they cannot be waited for.

Bourne and Job Control Shells
The wait command waits for a background process whose process ID is *pid* and reports its exit status. If you omit *pid*, all the shell's currently active background processes are waited for and the return code is 0. wait accepts a job identifier when job control is enabled (jsh) and you precede the *job-id* argument with a percent sign (%).

If *pid* is not an active process ID, the wait command returns immediately and the exit status is 0.

C Shell
Wait for your background processes.

Korn Shell

When the shell starts an asynchronous list, the process ID of the last command in each element of the asynchronous list becomes known in the current shell execution environment.

If you invoke the `wait` command with no operands, the command waits until all process IDs known to the invoking shell have terminated and have exited with an exit status of 0.

If you specify one or more *pid* operands that represent known process IDs, the `wait` command waits until all of them have terminated. If you specify one or more *pid* operands that represent unknown process IDs, `wait` treats them as if they were known process IDs that exited with exit status 127. The exit status returned by the `wait` command is the exit status of the process requested by the last *pid* or *job-id* operand.

The known process IDs are applicable only for invocations of `wait` in the current shell execution environment.

Operands

    pid   The unsigned decimal integer process ID of a command to be waited for.

    job-id   A job control job ID that identifies a background process group to be waited for. The job ID notation is applicable only for invocations of `wait` in the current shell execution environment and only on systems that support the job control options.

Usage

On most implementations, `wait` is a shell built-in command. If you call `wait` in a subshell or separate command execution environment, such as one of the following, it returns immediately because there are no known process IDs to wait for in those environments.

```
(wait)
nohup wait...
find . -exec wait... \;
```

Examples

Although the exact value used when a process is terminated by a signal is unspecified, if it is known that a signal terminated a process, a script can still reliably figure out which signal is using `kill`. The following example uses a script to identify the exit status.

```
sleep 1000&
pid=$!
kill -kill $pid
wait $pid
echo $pid was terminated by a SIG$(kill -1 $?) signal.
```

For /bin/ksh and /usr/xpg4/bin/sh, if you run the following sequence of commands in less than 31 seconds, `wait` returns the exit status of the second `sleep` in the pipeline.

```
$ sleep 257 | sleep 31 &
[1]     450
$ jobs -l %%
[1] + 450         Running            sleep 257 | sleep 31 &
$ wait %%
```

```
$ [1] -  Done                      sleep 257 | sleep 31 &
$ ksh: wait: no such job
$
```

/bin/csh, however, reports the status of both jobs, as shown below.

```
castle% sleep 257 | sleep 31 &
[2] 442 443
castle% jobs -l
[1]   -    433 Running             sleep 257 |
           434 Done                sleep 31
[2]   +    442 Running             sleep 257 |
           443                      sleep 31
castle% wait
[2]     Done                sleep 257 | sleep 31
[1]   + Done                sleep 257 | sleep 31
castle%
```

Environment Variables

See environ(5) for descriptions of the following environment variables that affect the execution of wait: LC_CTYPE, LC_MESSAGES, and NLSPATH.

Attributes

See attributes(5) for descriptions of the following attributes:

Attribute Type	Attribute Value
Availability	SUNWcsu

See Also

csh(1), jobs(1), ksh(1), sh(1), attributes(5)

wc — Display a Count of Lines, Words, and Characters in a File

Synopsis

/usr/bin/wc [-c | -m | -C] [-lw] [*file*...]

Description

Use the wc command to display a count of the lines, words, and characters in a file. The wc command reads one or more input files and, by default, writes the number of newline characters, words, and bytes contained in each input file to the standard output.

The command also writes a total count for all named files if you specify more than one input file.

wc considers a word to be a non-zero-length string of characters delimited by white space such as space or Tab (see iswspace(3C) or isspace(3C)).

Options

-c	Count bytes.
-C	Same as -m.
-l	Count lines.
-m	Count characters.
-w	Count words delimited by white-space characters or newline characters. Delimiting characters are Extended UNIX Code (EUC) characters from any code set defined by iswspace().

If you specify no option, the default is -lwc (count lines, words, and bytes).

Operands

file   A path name of an input file. If you specify no *file* operands, use the standard input.

Examples

The following example uses the wc command with no options to display the number of lines, words, and characters in the file kookaburra-1.

```
castle% wc kookaburra-1
        9        47       264 kookaburra-1
castle%
```

The kookaburra-1 file contains 9 lines, 47 words, and 264 characters.

The following example uses the wc command to display a count for all of the files in the directory that start with kook.

```
castle% wc kook*
        9        47       264 kookaburra-1
        9        47       264 kookaburra-2
       18        94       528 total
castle%
```

Usage

See largefile(5) for the description of the behavior of wc when encountering files greater than or equal to 2 Gbytes (2**31 bytes).

Environment Variables

See environ(5) for descriptions of the following environment variables that affect the execution of wc: LC_CTYPE, LC_MESSAGES, and NLSPATH.

Exit Status

0	Successful completion.
>0	An error occurred.

Attributes

See attributes(5) for descriptions of the following attributes:

Attribute Type	Attribute Value
Availability	SUNWcsu
CSI	Enabled

See Also

cksum(1), isspace(3C), iswalpha(3C), iswspace(3C), setlocale(3C), attributes(5), environ(5), largefile(5)

what — Extract SCCS Version Information from a File

Synopsis

/usr/ccs/bin/what [-s] *filename*...

Description

Use the what command to print identification strings for Source Code Control System (SCCS) files. The what command searches each file name for occurrences of the pattern @(#) that the SCCS get command (see sccs-get(1)) substitutes for the %Z% ID keyword and prints what follows up to a ", >, newline, \, or null character.

Options

-s   Stop after the first occurrence of the pattern.

Examples

For example, if a C program in file program.c contains the line

char sccsid[] = "@(#)identification information";

and program.c is compiled to yield program.o and a.out, the following command lists the string following the @(#).

```
castle% what program.c program.o a.out
program.c:
        identification information
program.o:
        identification information
a.out:  identification information
castle%
```

Attributes

See attributes(5) for descriptions of the following attributes:

Attribute Type	Attribute Value
Availability	SUNWsprot

See Also

sccs(1), sccs-admin(1), sccs-cdc(1), sccs-comb(1), sccs-delta(1),
sccs-get(1), sccs-help(1), sccs-prs(1), sccs-prt(1), sccs-rmdel(1),
sccs-sact(1), sccs-sccsdiff(1), sccs-unget(1), sccs-val(1), sccsfile(4),
attributes(5)

Diagnostics

Use the SCCS help command for explanations (see sccs-help(1)).

Bugs

There is a remote possibility that what could find a spurious occurrence of the @(#)
pattern.

---

whatis — Display a One-Line Summary About a Command

Synopsis

/usr/bin/whatis *command*...

Description

Some commands are listed in more than one section of the manual pages. You can find
the section number(s) for a manual page with the whatis command. whatis looks up a
given command and displays the header line from the manual section. You can then run
the man(1) command to get more information. If the line starts *name*(*section*) ..., you
can type **man -s *section-number*** to view its documentation.

whatis is actually just the -f option to the man(1) command.

Note — whatis uses the /usr/share/man/windex database that you can
create with the catman(1M) command. If the windex database does not
exist, whatis fails. To use the catman(1M) command to set up manual
pages, become superuser, type catman *n*, and press Return, where *n* is the
number of the section you want to set up.

Examples

The following example lists the header line for the ed manual page.

```
castle% whatis ed
ed               ed (1)             - text editor
```

The following example uses the whatis command to list all of the manual pages for
the chown command.

```
castle% whatis chown
chown          chown (1)        - change file ownership
chown          chown (1b)       - change owner
chown          chown (1m)       - change owner
chown          chown (2)        - change owner and group of a file
castle%
```

To display the manual page for a specific section, type

man -s *section-number command*

Files

/usr/share/man/windex

Table of contents and keyword database.

Attributes

See attributes(5) for descriptions of the following attributes:

Attribute Type	Attribute Value
Availability	SUNWdoc
CSI	Enabled

See Also

apropos(1), man(1), catman(1M), attributes(5)

---

whence — Shell Built-in Function to Get/Set Shell Variable and Function Attributes and Values

Synopsis

whence [-pv] *name*...

Description

See typeset(1).

---

whereis — Locate the Binary, Source, and Manual Page Files for a Command

Synopsis

/usr/ucb/whereis [-bmsu] [-BMS *directory*... -f] *filename*...

Description

whereis locates source binary and manual sections for specified files. The supplied names are first stripped of leading path-name components and any (single) trailing extension of the form .ext, for example, .c. Prefixes of s. resulting from the use of source code control are also stripped. whereis then tries to locate the desired program in a list of standard places:

```
/usr/bin
/usr/bin
/usr/5bin
/usr/games
/usr/hosts
/usr/include
/usr/local
/usr/etc
/usr/lib
/usr/share/man
/usr/src
/usr/ucb
```

Options

-b	Search only for binaries.
-B	Change or otherwise limit the places whereis searches for binaries.
-f	Terminate the last directory list and signal the start of file names. You must use this option with any of the -B, -M, or -S options.
-m	Search only for manual sections.
-M	Change or otherwise limit the places whereis searches for manual sections.
-s	Search only for sources.
-S	Change or otherwise limit the places whereis searches for sources.
-u	Search for unusual sources. A file is unusual if it does not have one entry of each requested type. Thus, whereis -m -u * asks for those files in the current directory that have no documentation.

Examples

The following example finds the location of all files named libc.

```
castle% whereis libc
libc: /usr/lib/libc.so /usr/lib/libc2.so /usr/lib/libc2.a
   /usr/lib/libc.a
castle%
```

The following example finds all files in /usr/ucb with source in /usr/src/cmd that are not documented in /usr/share/man/man1.

```
castle% cd /usr/ucb
castle% whereis -u -M /usr/share/man/man1 -S /usr/src/cmd -f *
Mail: /usr/ucb/Mail
aedplot: /usr/ucb/aedplot
arch: /usr/bin/arch /usr/ucb/arch
```

```
atoplot: /usr/ucb/atoplot
basename: /usr/bin/basename /usr/ucb/basename
bgplot: /usr/ucb/bgplot
biff: /usr/ucb/biff
cc: /usr/ucb/cc
chown: /usr/bin/chown /usr/ucb/chown
clear: /usr/bin/clear /usr/ucb/clear
... (More lines not listed)
castle%
```

Files

/usr/src/*

/usr/{doc,man}/*

/etc, /usr/{lib,bin,ucb,old,new,local}

Attributes

See attributes(5) for descriptions of the following attributes:

Attribute Type	Attribute Value
Availability	SUNWscpu

See Also

chdir(2), attributes(5)

Bugs

Because whereis uses chdir(2) to run faster, you must specify full path names with the -M, -S, or -B options; that is, path names must begin with a slash (/).

---

which — Locate a Command; Display Its Path Name or Alias

Synopsis

/usr/bin/which [*filename*]...

Description

which takes a list of names and looks for the files that would be executed had these names been given as commands. Each argument is expanded if it is aliased and is searched for along the user's path. Both aliases and path are taken from the user's .cshrc file.

> **Note** — which is not a shell built-in command; it is the UNIX command, /usr/bin/which.

Bugs

Only aliases and paths from ~/.cshrc are used; importing from the current environment is not attempted. The which command must be executed by csh(1) because only csh knows about aliases.

To compensate for ~/.cshrc files in which aliases depend on the prompt variable being set, which sets this variable to null. If the ~/.cshrc produces output or prompts for input when the prompt is set, which may produce some strange results.

Examples

In the following example, the which command cannot locate the whence command. Instead, it displays the search path that it used to try to locate the command.

```
castle% which whence
no whence in /usr/openwin/bin /usr/dt/bin /bin /usr/bin /usr/sbin
   /usr/ucb /etc /usr/proc/bin /opt/hpnp/bin /usr/local/games
   /usr/ccs/bin .
castle%
```

In the following examples, the which command displays the location of the which and whereis commands.

```
castle% which which
/bin/which
castle% which whereis
/usr/ucb/whereis
castle%
```

Files

~/.cshrc   Source of aliases and path values.

/bin/which

Attributes

See attributes(5) for descriptions of the following attributes:

Attribute Type	Attribute Value
Availability	SUNWcsu

See Also

csh(1), attributes(5)

Diagnostics

A diagnostic is given for names that are aliased to more than a single word or if an executable file with the argument name was not found in the path.

who — Report Who Is on the System

Synopsis

```
/usr/bin/who [-abdHlmpqrstTu] [file]
/usr/bin/who -q [-n x] [file]
/usr/bin/who am i
/usr/bin/who am I

/usr/xpg4/bin/who [-abdHlmpqrtTu] [file]
/usr/xpg4/bin/who -q [-n x] [file]
/usr/xpg4/bin/who -s [-bdHlmpqrtu] [file]
/usr/xpg4/bin/who am i
/usr/xpg4/bin/who am I
```

Description

The who command displays information about the current status of the system. It can list the user's name, terminal line, login time, elapsed time since activity occurred on the line, and the process ID of the command interpreter (shell) for each current UNIX system user. It examines the /var/adm/utmpx file to obtain its information. If you specify *file*, that file (which must be in utmpx(4) format) is examined. Usually, *file* is /var/adm/wtmpx, which contains a history of all logins since the file was last created.

The general format for output is as follows:

name [*state*] *line time* [*idle*] [*pid*] [*comment*] [*exit*]

where:

name	User's login name.
state	Capability of writing to the terminal.
line	Name of the line found in /dev.
time	Time since user's login.
idle	Time elapsed since the user's last activity.
pid	User's process ID.
comment	Comment line in inittab(4).
exit	Exit status for dead processes.

> **Note —** After a shutdown to the single-user state, who returns a prompt. Because /var/adm/utmpx is updated at login time and there is no login in single-user state, who cannot report accurately on this state. who am i, however, returns the correct information.

Options

-a	Process /var/adm/utmp or the named file with -b, -d, -l, -p, -r, -t, -T, and -u options turned on.
-b	Indicate the time and date of the last reboot.

-d	Display all processes that have expired and that have not been respawned by init. The EXIT field for dead processes contains the termination and exit values (as returned by wait(3UCB)) of the dead process. This information can be useful in determining why a process terminated.
-H	Output column headings above the regular output.
-l	List only those lines on which the system is waiting for someone to log in. The NAME field is LOGIN in such cases. Other fields are the same as for user entries except that the STATE field does not exist.
-m	Output only information about the current terminal.
-n x	Take a numeric argument, x, which specifies the number of users to display per line. x must be at least 1. You can use the -n option only with -q.
-p	List any other process that is currently active and that was previously spawned by init. The NAME field is the name of the program executed by init as found in /sbin/inittab. The STATE, LINE, and IDLE fields have no meaning. The COMMENT field shows the ID field of the line from /sbin/inittab that spawned this process. See inittab(4).
-q	Display only the names and the number of users currently logged in. Ignore all other options.
-r	Indicate the current run level of the init process.
-s	List only the NAME, LINE, and TIME fields (the default).

/usr/bin/who

-T	Same as the -s option, except also write the STATE, IDLE, PID, and COMMENT fields. STATE is one of the following characters:

+	Allow write access to other users.
–	Deny write access to other users.
?	Cannot determine the terminal write access state.

/usr/xpg4/bin/who

-t	Indicate the last change to the system clock (using the date command) by root. See su(1M) and date(1).
-T	Same as the -s option, except also write the STATE field. STATE is one of the characters listed under the /usr/bin/who version of this option. If you use the -u option with -T, add the idle time to the end of the previous format.

-u   List only those users who are currently logged in. The name is the user's login name. The LINE is the name of the line as found in the directory /dev. The TIME is the time that the user logged in. The IDLE column contains the number of hours and minutes since activity last occurred on that particular line. A dot (.) indicates that the terminal has seen activity in the last minute and is therefore current. If more than 24 hours have elapsed or the line has not been used since boot time, mark the entry as old. The IDLE field is useful for determining whether a person is working at the terminal. The PID is the process ID of the user's shell. The COMMENT is the comment field associated with this line as found in /sbin/inittab (see inittab(4)). The COMMENT field can contain information such as the location of the terminal, the telephone number of the data set, and the type of terminal if hardwired.

Operands

am i   In the C locale, limit the output to describing the invoking user,
am I   equivalent to the -m option. You must separate the am and i or I arguments with a space.

file   Specify a path name of a file to substitute for the database of logged-in users that who uses by default.

Environment Variables

See environ(5) for descriptions of the following environment variables that affect the execution of who: LC_CTYPE, LC_MESSAGES, LC_TIME, and NLSPATH.

Exit Status

0   Successful completion.

>0   An error occurred.

Files

/sbin/inittab

Script for init.

/var/adm/utmpx

Current user and accounting information.

/var/adm/wtmpx

Historic user and accounting information.

Attributes

See attributes(5) for descriptions of the following attributes:

/usr/bin/who

Attribute Type	Attribute Value
Availability	SUNWcsu

/usr/xpg4/bin/who

Attribute Type	Attribute Value
Availability	SUNWxcu4

See Also

date(1), login(1), mesg(1), init(1M), su(1M), wait(3UCB), inittab(4), utmpx(4), attributes(5), environ(5), XPG4(5)

whoami — Display the Effective Current User Name

Synopsis

/usr/ucb/whoami

Description

whoami displays the login name corresponding to the current effective user ID. If you have used su to temporarily adopt another user identity, whoami reports the login name associated with that user ID. whoami gets its information from the geteuid and getpwuid library routines (see getuid(2) and getpwnam(3C)).

Examples

The following examples show the current effective user ID. Because root does not have /usr/ucb in the search path, the full path name is required to execute the command as root.

```
castle% whoami
winsor
castle% su
# whoami
whoami: not found
# /usr/ucb/whoami
root
# exit
castle% su ray
castle% whoami
ray
castle%
```

Files

/etc/passwd

User-name database.

Attributes

See attributes(5) for descriptions of the following attributes:

Attribute Type	Attribute Value
Availability	SUNWscpu

See Also

who(1), su(1M), getuid(2), getpwnam(3C), attributes(5)

whocalls — Report on the Calls to a Specific Procedure

Synopsis

```
/usr/ccs/bin/whocalls whocalls [-l wholib] [-s] funcname executable
    [executable arguments...]
```
New!

Description

The whocalls command is based on the Link-Auditing functionality of ld.so.1(1) that *New!*
permits the tracking of a given function call. See *Linker and Libraries Guide* for a
detailed description of the Link-Auditing mechanism. The executable is run as normal
with any associated arguments. Each time the procedure *funcname* is called, both the
arguments to that procedure and a stack trace are displayed on standard output.

Options

-l *wholib*   Specify an alternative who.so Link-Auditing library to use.

-s   When available, examine and use the .symtab symbol table for local   *New!*
                 symbols. Using this option is a little more expensive than using the
                 .dynsym symbol table but can produce more detailed stack trace
                 information. New in the Solaris 9 release.

Examples

This example tracks the calls to printf() made by a simple hello_world program.

```
castle% whocalls printf hello
printf(0x106e4, 0xef625310, 0xef621ba8)
hello:main+0x10
hello:_start+0x5c
hello
castle%
```

Attributes

See attributes(5) for descriptions of the following attributes:

Attribute Type	Attribute Value
Availability	SUNWtoo

See Also

ld.so.1(1), sotruss(1), attributes(5)
Linker and Libraries Guide

---

whois — Internet User Name Directory Service

Synopsis

/usr/bin/whois [-h *host*] *identifier*

Description

whois searches for an Internet directory entry for an *identifier* that is either a name, such as Smith, or a handle, such as SRI-NIC.
The following characters preceding the identifier can modify the search.

.	Force a name-only search.
!	Force a handle-only search.
*	Search for a group or organization entry. The entire membership list of the group is displayed with the record.

You can, of course, use an exclamation point and an asterisk or a period and asterisk together.

Options

-h *host*   Specify the name of the host to search.

Operands

identifier   Specify a name, such as Smith, or a handle, such as SRI-NIC to search for in an Internet directory

Examples

The following command looks for the name or handle Smith.

castle% **whois Smith**

The following command looks only for the handle SRI-NIC.

castle% **whois !SRI-NIC**

The following command looks only for the name John Smith.

castle% **whois .Smith, John**

Adding . . . to the name or handle argument matches anything from that point; that is, ZU. . . matches ZUL, ZUM, and so on.

Attributes

See attributes(5) for descriptions of the following attributes:

Attribute Type	Attribute Value
Availability	SUNWrcmdc

New!

See Also

attributes(5)

write — Write to Another User

Synopsis

/usr/bin/write *user* [*terminal*]

Description

You can use the write command to send a message to the terminal of an individual user. When a windowing system such as CDE or OpenWindows is used, each window is considered a separate login. If the user is logged in more than once, the message is directed to the console window.

The write command reads lines from standard input and writes them to the terminal of another user. When first invoked, it writes the following message to the user.

Message from *sender-login-id* (*sending-terminal*)
[*date*]...

When write has successfully completed the connection, the sender's terminal is alerted twice to indicate that what the sender is typing is being written to the recipient's terminal.

The recipient can reply by typing

write *sender-login-id* [*sending-terminal*]

on receipt of the initial message. Whenever a line of input as delimited by a newline, end-of-file, or end-of-line special character is accumulated while in input mode, the accumulated data is written on the other user's terminal. Characters are processed as follows.

- The alert character writes the alert character to the recipient's terminal.
- The erase and kill characters affect the sender's terminal in the manner described by the termios(3) interface.

- The interrupt or end-of-file characters write an appropriate message (EOT\n in the C locale) to the recipient's terminal and exit.
- Characters from LC_CTYPE classifications are sent to the recipient's terminal.
- Only when the stty iexten local mode is enabled, additional special control characters and multibyte or single-byte characters are processed as printable characters if their wide-character equivalents are printable.
- Other nonprintable characters are written to the recipient's terminal as follows: control characters appear as a ^ followed by the appropriate ASCII character, and characters with the high-order bit set appear in metanotation (M-*char*. For example, \003 is displayed as ^C, and \372 as M-z.

To write to a user who is logged in more than once, you can use the *terminal* argument to indicate which terminal to write to; otherwise, the recipient's terminal is the first writable instance of the user found in /usr/adm/utmp, and the following informational message is written to the sender's standard output, indicating which terminal was chosen:

```
user is logged on more than one place.
You are connected to terminal.
Other locations are: terminal.
```

You can deny or grant permission to be a recipient of a write message with the mesg command. However, a user's privilege may further constrain the domain of accessibility of other users' terminals. The write command fails when the user lacks the appropriate privileges to perform the requested action.

If you use the character ! at the beginning of a line, write calls the shell to execute the rest of the line as a command.

write runs setgid() (see setuid(2)) to the group ID tty to gain write permission on other users' terminals.

The following protocol is suggested for using write: when you first write to another user, wait for him to write back before starting to send. Each person should end a message with a distinctive signal (such as, (o) for over) so that the other person knows when to reply. The signal (oo) (for over and out) is suggested when conversation is to be terminated.

You can also redirect a message from a file with the write command by using the following syntax:

```
write username < filename
```

Operands

user   Login name of the person to whom the message is written. This operand must be of the form returned by the who(1) command.

terminal   Terminal identification in the same format provided by the who command.

Environment Variables

See environ(5) for descriptions of the following environment variables that affect the execution of write: LC_CTYPE, LC_MESSAGES, and NLSPATH.

Exit Status

0	Successful completion.
>0	The addressed user is not logged in or the addressed user denies permission.

Files

`/var/adm/utmpx`

> User and accounting information for `write`.

`/usr/bin/sh`

> Bourne shell executable file.

Attributes

See `attributes`(5) for descriptions of the following attributes:

Attribute Type	Attribute Value
Availability	SUNWcsu
CSI	Enabled

See Also

`mail(1)`, `mesg(1)`, `pr(1)`, `sh(1)`, `talk(1)`, `who(1)`, `setuid(2)`, `termios(3C)`, `attributes(5)`, `environ(5)`

Diagnostics

`user is not logged on`

> The person you are trying to write to is not logged on.

`Permission denied`

> The person you are trying to write to denies that permission (with `mesg`).

`Warning: cannot respond, set mesg -y`

> Your terminal is set to `mesg` n and the recipient cannot respond to you.

`Can no longer write to user`

> The recipient has denied permission (`mesg` n) after you had started writing.

X

xargs — Construct Argument Lists and Invoke Command

Synopsis

```
/usr/bin/xargs [-t] [-p] [-e[eofstr]] [-E eofstr] [-I replstr]
    [-i[replstr]] [-L number] [-l[number]] [-n number [-x]] [-s size]
    [command [argument...]]
```

Description

The xargs command is a shell programming tool that enables you to use the output of one command to define the arguments for another. The xargs command constructs a command line consisting of the specified *command* and *argument* operands followed by as many arguments read in sequence from standard input as fit in the length and number constraints specified by the options. The xargs command then invokes the constructed command line and waits for its completion. This sequence is repeated until an end-of-file condition is detected on standard input or an invocation of a constructed command line returns an exit status of 255.

Separate arguments to the standard input by unquoted blank characters, unescaped blank characters, or newline characters. You can quote a string of zero or more non-double-quote (") and non-newline characters by enclosing them in double quotes. You can quote a string of zero or more nonapostrophe (') and non-newline characters by enclosing them in apostrophes. You can escape any unquoted character by preceding it with a backslash (\). The command is executed one or more times until the end-of-file is reached. If the command tries to read from its standard input, the results are unspecified.

The generated command-line length is the sum of the size in bytes of the command name and each argument treated as a string, including a null byte terminator for each of these strings. The xargs command limits the command-line length so that when the command line is invoked, the combined argument and environment lists do not exceed {ARG_MAX}-2048 bytes. Within this constraint, if you specify neither the -n nor the -s option, the default command-line length is at least {LINE_MAX}.

Options

-e[*eofstr*]   Use *eofstr* as the logical end-of-file string. Underscore (_) is assumed for the logical EOF string if you use neither -e nor -E. When you omit the -*eofstr* option-argument, disable the logical EOF string capability and take underscores literally. Read standard input until either end-of-file or the logical EOF string is encountered.

-E *eofstr*   Specify a logical end-of-file string to replace the default underscore. Read the standard input until either end-of-file or the logical EOF string is encountered.

-i[*replstr*]

Equivalent to -I *replstr*. The string {} is assumed for *replstr* if you omit the option-argument.

-I *replstr*   Execute *command* for each line from standard input, taking the entire line as a single argument, inserting it in argument s for each occurrence of *replstr*. You can use a maximum of five arguments in *argument*, each containing one or more instances of *replstr*. Ignore any blank characters at the beginning of each line. Constructed arguments cannot grow larger than 255 bytes. Option -x is forced on. The -I and -i options are mutually exclusive; the last one specified takes effect.

-l[*number*]   If you omit *number*, 1 is assumed. Option -x is forced on. Equivalent to -L *number*.

-L *number*   Execute the command for each nonempty *number* lines of arguments from standard input. The last invocation of *command* is with fewer lines of arguments if fewer than *number* remain. Consider a line to end with the first newline character unless the last character of the line is a blank character; a trailing blank character signals continuation to the next nonempty line, inclusive. The -L, -l, and -n options are mutually exclusive; the last one specified takes effect.

-n *number*   Invoke *command*, using as many standard input arguments as possible up to a maximum of *number* (a positive decimal integer) arguments. Fewer arguments are used if:

- The command-line length accumulated exceeds the size specified by the -s option (or {LINE_MAX} if there is no -s option).

- The last iteration has fewer than *number*, but not 0, operands remaining.

-p   Prompt whether to execute *command* at each invocation. Turn on trace mode (-t) to write the command instance to be executed, followed by a prompt to standard error. An affirmative response (specific to the user's locale) read from /dev/tty executes the command; otherwise, skip that particular invocation of *command*.

-s *size*   Invoke *command*, using as many standard input arguments as possible and yielding a command-line length less than *size* (a positive decimal integer) bytes. Fewer arguments are used if:

- The total number of arguments exceeds that specified by the -n option.
- The total number of lines exceeds that specified by the -L option.
- End-of-file is encountered on standard input before *size* bytes accumulate.

Support values of *size* up to at least {LINE_MAX} bytes, provided that the specified constraints are met. You can give a value larger than that supported by the implementation or exceeding the specified constraints; xargs uses the largest value it supports within the constraints.

-t   Enable trace mode. Write each generated command line to standard error just before invocation.

-x   Terminate if a command line containing *number* arguments (see the -n option) or number lines (see the -L option) do not fit in the implied or specified *size* (see the -s option above).

Operands

command   The name of the command to be invoked, found by search path with the PATH environment variable; see environ(5). If you omit *command*, the default is the echo(1) command. If the *command* operand names any of the special built-in commands in shell_builtins(1), the results are undefined.

argument   An initial option or operand for the invocation of *command*.

Usage

The 255 exit status enables a command being used by xargs to tell xargs to terminate if it knows that no further invocations using the current data stream will succeed. Thus, *command* should explicitly exit with an appropriate value to avoid accidentally returning with 255.

Input is parsed as lines; blank characters separate arguments. If xargs is used to bundle the output of commands like find *dir* -print or ls into commands to be executed, unexpected results are likely if file names contain any blank characters or newline characters. You can fix this problem by using find to call a script that converts each file found into a quoted string that is then piped to xargs.

Note — The quoting rules used by xargs are not the same as those in the shell. They were not made consistent here because existing applications depend on the current rules and the shell syntax is not fully compatible with it. An easy rule that you can use to transform any string into a quoted form that xargs interprets correctly is to precede each character in the string with a backslash (\).

On implementations with a large value for {ARG_MAX}, xargs may produce command lines longer than {LINE_MAX}. For invocation of commands, this is not a problem. If xargs is being used to create a text file, you should explicitly set the maximum command-line length with the -s option.

The xargs command returns exit status 127 if an error occurs so that applications can distinguish "failure to find a command" from "invoked command exited with an error indication." The value 127 was chosen because it is not commonly used for other meanings; most commands use small values for "normal" error conditions, and the values above 128 can be confused with termination because of receipt of a signal. The value 126 was chosen in a similar manner to indicate that the command could be found, but not invoked.

Examples

The following example moves all files from directory $1 to directory $2 and echoes each mv command just before doing it.

```
ls $1 | xargs -I {} -t mv $1/{} $2/{}
```

The following example combines the output of the parenthesized commands onto one line, which is then written to the end of file log.

```
(logname; date; printf "%s\n" "$0 $*") | xargs >>log
```

The following command invokes diff with successive pairs of arguments originally typed as command-line arguments (assuming there are no embedded blank characters in the elements of the original argument list).

```
printf "%s\n" "$*" | xargs -n 2 -x diff
```

In the following example, the user is asked which files in the current directory are to be archived. The files are archived into arch either one at a time (for the first example) or many at a time (for the second example).

```
castle% ls | xargs -p -L 1 ar -r arch
ar -r arch Mail?...y
ar: creating arch
ar -r arch SOLD515.PKG?...y
ar -r arch catman.man?...y
ar -r arch examples?...y
castle%
```

```
castle% ls | xargs -p -L 1 | xargs ar -r arch
/usr/bin/echo Mail?...y
/usr/bin/echo SOLD515.PKG?...y
/usr/bin/echo arch?...y
/usr/bin/echo catman.man?...y
/usr/bin/echo examples?...y
castle%
```

The following command executes with successive pairs of arguments originally typed as command-line arguments.

```
echo $* | xargs -n 2 diff
```

Environment Variables

See environ(5) for descriptions of the following environment variables that affect the execution of xargs: LC_COLLATE, LC_CTYPE, LC_MESSAGES, NLSPATH, and PATH.

Exit Status

0	All invocations returned exit status 0.
1–125	A command line meeting the specified requirements could not be assembled, one or more of the invocations of the command returned a non-zero exit status, or some other error occurred.
126	The command specified by *command* was found but could not be invoked.
127	The command specified by *command* could not be found.

If a command line meeting the specified requirements cannot be assembled, the command cannot be invoked, an invocation of the command is terminated by a signal, or an invocation of the command exits with exit status 255, then the xargs command writes a diagnostic message and exits without processing any remaining input.

Attributes

See attributes(5) for descriptions of the following attributes:

Attribute Type	Attribute Value
Availability	SUNWcsu
CSI	Enabled

See Also

echo(1), shell_builtins(1), attributes(5), environ(5)

xgettext — Extract gettext Call Strings from C Programs

Synopsis

```
/usr/bin/xgettext [-ns] [-a [-x exclude-file]] [-c comment-tag]
    [-d default-domain] [-j] [-m prefix] [-M suffix] [-p pathname]
    - | filename...
/usr/bin/xgettext -h
```

Description

Use the xgettext command to automate the creation of portable message files (.po). A .po file contains copies of C strings that are found in ANSI C source code in *filename* or the standard input if you specify - on the command line. You can use the .po file as input to the msgfmt(1) command, which produces a binary form of the message file that can be used by an application during runtime.

xgettext writes *msgid* strings from gettext(3C) calls in *filename* to the default output file messages.po. You can change the default output file name with the –d option. *msgid* strings in dgettext() calls are written to the output file *domainname*.po, where *domainname* is the first parameter to the dgettext() call.

By default, xgettext creates a .po file in the current working directory, and each entry is in the same order in which the strings are extracted from *filename*s. When you specify the –p option, the .po file is created in the *pathname* directory. Any existing .po file is overwritten.

Duplicate *msgids* are written to the .po file as comment lines. When you specify the –s option, the .po file is sorted by the *msgid* string and all duplicated *msgids* are removed. All *msgstr* directives in the .po file are empty unless you use the –m option.

Note — xgettext is not able to extract cast strings, for example, ANSI C casts of literal strings to (const char *). This feature is unnecessary anyway because the prototypes in <libintl.h> already specify this type.

New!   In messages and translation notes, lines greater than 2048 characters are truncated to 2048 characters and a warning message is printed to standard error. New in the Solaris 8 release.

Options

–a   Extract all strings, not just those found in gettext(3C) and dgettext() calls. Create only one .po file.

–c *comment-tag*

          Add the comment block beginning with *comment-tag* as the first token of the comment block to the output .po file as # delimited comments. For multiple domains, xgettext directs comments and messages to the prevailing text domain.

–d *default-domain*

          Rename default output file from messages.po to *default-domain*.po.

–h   Print a help message on the standard output.

–j   Join messages with existing message files. If a .po file does not exist, create it. If a .po file exists, append new messages. Comment out any duplicate *msgids* in the resulting .po file. Ignore domain directives in the existing .po file. Results are not guaranteed if the existing message file has been edited.

–m *prefix*   Fill in the *msgstr* with *prefix*. This option is useful for debugging. To make *msgstr* identical to *msgid*, use an empty string (" ") for *prefix*.

–M *suffix*   Fill in the *msgstr* with *suffix*. This option is useful for debugging.

–n   Add comment lines to the output file, indicating file name and line number in the source file in which each extracted string is encountered. These lines appear before each *msgid* in the following format:

```
#
# File: filename, line: line-number
```

-p *pathname*   Specify the directory in which the output files are to be placed. This option overrides the current working directory.

-s   Generate output sorted by *msgids* with all duplicate *msgids* removed.

-x *exclude-file*

          Specify a .po file that contains a list of *msgids* that are not to be extracted from the input files. The format of *exclude-file* is identical to the .po file. However, use only the *msgid* directive line in *exclude-file*. Ignore all other lines. You can use the -x option only with the -a option.

Attributes

See attributes(5) for descriptions of the following attributes:

Attribute Type	Attribute Value
Availability	SUNWloc

See Also

msgfmt(1), gettext(3C), attributes(5)

xstr — Extract Strings from C Programs

Synopsis

```
/usr/bin/xstr -c filename [-v] [-l array]
/usr/bin/xstr [-l array]
/usr/bin/xstr filename [-v] [-l array]
```

Description

xstr maintains a file called strings into which a large program hashes strings in component parts. These strings are replaced with references to this common area. This approach implements shared constant strings, which are most useful if they are also read-only.

The following command extracts the strings from the C source in *filename*, replacing string references by expressions of the form &xstr[*number*] for some number.

castle% **xstr -c *filename***

An appropriate declaration of xstr is prepended to the file. The resulting C text is placed in the file x.c to then be compiled. The strings from this file are placed in the strings database if they are not there already. Repeated strings and strings that are suffixes of existing strings do not change the database.

After all components of a large program have been compiled, you can create a file declaring the common xstr space called xs.c with a command of the following form.

```
castle% xstr
```

You should then compile the resulting xs.c file and load it with the rest of the program. If possible, make the array read-only (shared) to save space and overhead for swapping.

You can also use xstr on a single file. The following command creates files x.c and xs.c as before without using or affecting any strings files in the same directory.

```
castle% xstr filename
```

It can be useful to run xstr after the C preprocessor if any macro definitions yield strings or if there is conditional code that contains strings which may not, in fact, be needed. xstr reads from the standard input when you specify the - argument. The following examples show an appropriate command sequence for running xstr after the C preprocessor.

```
castle% cc -E name.c | xstr -c -
castle% cc -c x.c
castle% mv x.o name.o
```

xstr does not touch the file strings unless new items are added; thus, make(1S) can avoid remaking xs.o unless truly necessary.

Notes

Be aware that xstr indiscriminately replaces all strings with expressions of the form &xstr[*number*] regardless of how the original C code might have used the string. For example, you will encounter a problem with code that uses sizeof() to determine the length of a literal string because xstr replaces the literal string with a pointer that most likely has a different size than the string. To circumvent this problem:

- Use strlen() instead of sizeof(). Note that sizeof() returns the size of the array, including the null byte at the end, whereas strlen() does not count the null byte. The equivalent of sizeof("*xxx*") really is (strlen("*xxx*"))+1.

- Use #define for operands of sizeof() and use the define version. xstr ignores #define statements. Make sure you run xstr on *filename* before you run it on the preprocessor.

You will also encounter a problem when declaring an initialized character array of the following form.

```
char x[] = "xxx";
```

xstr replaces *xxx* with an expression of the following form

```
&xstr[number]
```

which does not compile. To circumvent this problem, use static char *x = "*xxx*" instead of static char x[] = "*xxx*".

Options

-c *filename*

Take C source text from *filename*.

-l *array*

Specify the named array in program references to abstracted strings. The default array name is xstr.

-v   Display a progress report indicating where new or duplicate strings are
                    found.

Files

Strings   Database of strings.

x.c   Massaged C source.

xs.c   C source for definition of array "xstr*(rq.

/tmp/xs*   Temporary file when xstr file name doesn't touch strings.

Attributes

See attributes(5) for descriptions of the following attributes:

Attribute Type	Attribute Value
Availability	SUNWcsu

See Also

make(1S), attributes(5)

Bugs

If a string is a suffix of another string in the database and the shorter string is seen first
by xstr, both strings are placed in the database when just placing the longer one there
would suffice.

Y

yacc — Yet Another Compiler-Compiler

Synopsis

```
/usr/ccs/bin/yacc [-dltVv] [-b file-prefix] [-Q [y|n]] [-P parser]
    [-p sym-prefix] file
```

Description

The yacc command is a fourth-generation development tool that, together with the lex(1) command, enables you to perform lexical analysis and development by describing how an application should act instead of specifying what it should do.

The yacc command converts a context-free grammar into a set of tables for a simple automaton that executes an LALR parsing algorithm. LALR (lookahead LR) parsing is a less powerful variant of LR parsing that produces much smaller parsing tables. The grammar can find LR grammars ambiguous. You can use specified precedence rules to break ambiguities.

You must compile the y.tab.c output file with the C compiler to produce a yyparse() function. You must then load this program with the yylex() lexical analyzer program, as well as with main() and the yyerror() error handling routine. You must supply these routines. The lex(1) command is useful for creating lexical analyzers usable by yacc.

To use the yacc command to generate a parser, specify a grammar file that describes the input data stream and what the parser is to do with the data.

The grammar file includes rules described in the input structure, the code to be invoked when these rules are recognized, and a subroutine to do the basic input.

Two adjacent double percent signs (%%) separate each section of the grammar file. To make the file easier to read, put the %% on a line by themselves. A complete grammar file has the following structure.

```
declarations
%%
rules
%%
programs
```

The declarations section can be empty. If you omit the programs section, also omit the second set of %%. The smallest yacc grammar file has the following structure.

```
%%
rules
```

yacc ignores blanks, Tabs, and newline characters in the grammar files. You can use these characters to make the file easier to read. You should not, however, use blanks, Tabs, or newlines in names or reserved symbols.

yacc uses the information in the grammar file to generate a parser that controls the input process. This parser calls an input subroutine (the lexical analyzer) to pick up the tokens from the input stream. The parser organizes the tokens, using the structure rules from the grammar file. When the parser recognizes one of the grammar rules, it executes the action from the user code supplied for that rule. Actions return values and use the values returned by other actions.

Note — Because file names are fixed, only one yacc process can be active in a given directory at a given time.

Options

-b *file-prefix*

Use *file-prefix* instead of y as the prefix for all output files. The y.tab.c code file, the y.tab.h header file (created when you specify -d), and the y.output description file (created when you specify -v) are changed to *file-prefix*.tab.c, *file-prefix*.tab.h, and *file-prefix*.output.

-d

Generate the y.tab.h file with the #define statements that associate the yacc user-assigned token codes with the user-declared token names. This association enables source files other than y.tab.c to access the token codes.

-l

Specify that the code produced in y.tab.c does not contain any #line constructs. Use this option only after you fully debug the grammar and the associated actions.

-P *parser*

Specify the parser of your choice instead of /usr/ccs/bin/yaccpar. For example, you can specify:

```
castle% yacc -P ~/myparser parser.y
```

-p *sym-prefix*

> Use *sym-prefix* instead of yy as the prefix for all external names produced by yacc. The names affected include the functions yyparse(), yylex(), yyerror(), and the variables yylval, yychar, and yydebug. (In the remainder of this section, the six symbols cited are referenced with their default names only as a notational convenience.) Local names may also be affected by the -p option; however, the -p option does not affect #define symbols generated by yacc.

-Q[y|n]

> Put the version stamping information in y.tab.c. This option enables you to know what version of yacc built the file. The -Qn option (the default) writes no version information.

-t

> Compile runtime debugging code by default. The size and execution time of a program produced without the runtime debugging code is smaller and slightly faster. Runtime debugging code is always generated in y.tab.c under conditional compilation control. By default, this code is not included when y.tab.c is compiled. The runtime debugging code is always under the control of YYDEBUG, a preprocessor symbol. If YYDEBUG has a non-zero value, include the debugging code. If its value is 0, do not include the code.

-v

> Prepare the file y.output, which contains a description of the parsing tables and a report on conflicts generated by ambiguities in the grammar.

-V

> Print on the standard error output the version information for yacc.

Operands

file

> A path name of a file containing instructions for which a parser is to be created.

Examples

Access to the yacc library is obtained with library search operands to cc. The following example uses the yacc library main.

```
castle% cc y.tab.c -ly
```

Both the lex library and the yacc library contain main. The following example accesses the yacc main and ensures that the yacc library is searched first so that its main is used.

```
example% cc y.tab.c lex.yy.c -ly -ll
```

The historical yacc libraries have contained two simple functions that are normally coded by the application programmer. These library functions are similar to the following code.

```
#include <locale.h>
int main(void)
{
    extern int yyparse();
    setlocale(LC_ALL, "");
```

```
    /* If the following parser is one created by lex, the
       application must be careful to ensure that LC_CTYPE
       and LC_COLLATE are set to the POSIX locale.  */
    (void) yyparse();
    return (0);
}

    #include <stdio.h>
    int yyerror(const char *msg)
{

    (void) fprintf(stderr, "%s\n", msg);
    return (0);
}
```

The following example draws yacc rules from the grammar.y file and puts the output in y.tab.c.

castle% **yacc grammar.y**

The following example draws yacc rules from the grammar.y file and puts the output in y.tab.c. It also produces the y.tab.h file, which would contain C-style #define statements for each of the tokens defined in the grammar.y file.

castle% **yacc -d grammar.y**

Environment Variables

See environ(5) for descriptions of the following environment variables that affect the execution of yacc: LC_CTYPE, LC_MESSAGES, and NLSPATH.

yacc can handle characters from Extended UNIX Code (EUC) primary and supplementary code sets as one-token symbols. EUC codes can be only single-character quoted terminal symbols. yacc expects yylex() to return a wide-character (wchar_t) value for these one-token symbols.

Exit Status

0	Successful completion.
>0	An error occurred.

Files

y.output	State transitions of the generated parser.
y.tab.c	Source code of the generated parser.
y.tab.h	Header file for the generated parser.
yacc.acts	Temporary file.
yacc.debug	Temporary file.
yacc.tmp	Temporary file.
yaccpar	Parser prototype for C programs.

Attributes

See attributes(5) for descriptions of the following attributes:

Attribute Type	Attribute Value
Availability	SUNWbtool

See Also

lex(1), cc(1B), attributes(5), environ(5)
Programming Utilities Guide

Diagnostics

The number of reduce-reduce and shift-reduce conflicts is reported on the standard error output. You can find a more detailed report in the y.output file. Similarly, if some rules are not reachable from the start symbol, this instance is also reported.

---

yes — Generate Repetitive Affirmative Output

New!

Synopsis

/bin/yes [*expletive*...]

Description

You can use the yes command, new in the Solaris 9 Operating Environment, to respond programmatically to programs that require an interactive response.

Use the yes command to repeatedly output y, or if you specify *expletive*, it is output repeatedly followed by a newline. Multiple arguments are output separated by spaces and followed by a newline. To terminate, type an interrupt character.

Examples

The following example shows the default output of the yes command.

```
mopoke% yes
y
y
y
...
Ctrl-C
mopoke%
```

The following example shows the output of the yes command when you specify an *expletive* of goodgrief.

```
mopoke% yes goodgrief
goodgrief
goodgrief
goodgrief
...
```

```
Ctrl-C
mopoke%
```

Attributes

See attributes(5) for descriptions of the following attributes.

Attribute Type	Attribute Value
Availability	SUNWesu

See Also

attributes(5)

ypcat — Print Values in an NIS Database

Synopsis

/usr/bin/ypcat [-kx] [-d *ypdomain*] *mname*

Description

The ypcat command prints out values in the NIS name service map specified by *mname*, which may be either a map name or a map nickname. Because ypcat uses the NIS network services, you need not specify an NIS server.

Refer to ypfiles(4) for an overview of the NIS name service.

Options

-d *ypdomain*

Specify a domain other than the default domain.

-k

Display the keys for those maps in which the values are null or the key is not part of the value. None of the maps derived from files that have an ASCII version in /etc fall into this class.

-x

Display map nicknames.

Examples

The following example shows the output of the ypcat -x command on a system that is not on an NIS+ network.

```
castle% ypcat -x
Use "passwd"    for map "passwd.byname"
Use "group"     for map "group.byname"
Use "networks"  for map "networks.byaddr"
Use "hosts"     for map "hosts.byname"
Use "protocols" for map "protocols.bynumber"
Use "services"  for map "services.byname"
Use "aliases"   for map "mail.aliases"
```

```
Use "ethers"      for map "ethers.byname"
castle%
```

Attributes

See attributes(5) for descriptions of the following attributes:

Attribute Type	Attribute Value
Availability	SUNWnisu

See Also

ypmatch(1), ypfiles(4), attributes(5)

ypmatch — Print the Value of Keys from an NIS Map

Synopsis

```
/usr/bin/ypmatch [-k] [-t] [-d domain] key [key...] mname
/usr/bin/ypmatch -x
```

Description

ypmatch prints the values associated with one or more keys from the NIS name services map specified by *mname*, which may be either a map name or a map nickname.

You can specify multiple keys. All keys are searched for in the same map. The keys must be the same case and length. No pattern matching is available. If a key is not matched, a diagnostic message is displayed.

Note — ypmatch fails with an RCP error message on yp operations if enough file descriptors are not available. If this problem occurs, increase the number of file descriptors.

Options

-d *domain*	Specify a domain other than the default domain.
-k	Before printing the value of a key, print the key itself, followed by a colon (:).
-t	Inhibit map nickname translation.
-x	Display the map nickname table. This option lists the nicknames (*mnames*) the command knows and indicates the map name associated with each nickname.

Operands

mname	The NIS name services map.

Exit Status

0	Successful operation.
1	An error occurred.

Attributes

See attributes(5) for descriptions of the following attributes:

Attribute Type	Attribute Value
Availability	SUNWnisu

See Also

ypcat(1), ypfiles(4), attributes(5)

---

yppasswd — Change Your Network Password in the NIS Database

Synopsis

/usr/bin/yppasswd [*username*]

Description

> **Note —** The use of yppasswd is discouraged, as it is now only a link to the passwd(1) command, which you should use instead. Use passwd(1) with the -r nis option to achieve the same results, and be consistent across all available name services.

yppasswd changes the network password associated with the user *username* in the Network Information Service (NIS) database. If the user has done a keylogin(1) and a publickey/secretkey pair exists for the user in the NIS publickey.byname map, yppasswd also reencrypts the secret key with the new password. The NIS password may be different from your local one. Use passwd(1) to change the password information on the local machine, and nispasswd(1) to change the password information stored in Network Information Service Plus, Version 3 (NIS+).

yppasswd prompts for the old NIS password and then for the new one. You must type in the old password correctly for the change to take effect. You must type the new password twice for verification.

New passwords must be at least four characters long if they use a sufficiently rich alphabet, and at least six characters long if monocase. These rules are relaxed if you are insistent enough. Only the owner of the user name or the superuser can change a password; superuser on the root master is not prompted for the old password and does not need to follow password construction requirements.

The NIS password daemon, rpc.yppasswdd, must be running on your NIS server for the new password to take effect.

> **Warning —** Even after you have successfully changed your password using
> this command, the subsequent login(1) using the new password is
> successful only if your password and shadow information is obtained from
> NIS. (See getpwnam(3C), getspnam(3C), and nsswitch.conf(4).)

Attributes

See attributes(5) for descriptions of the following attributes:

Attribute Type	Attribute Value
Availability	SUNWnisu

New!

See Also

keylogin(1), login(1), nispasswd(1), passwd(1), getpwnam(3C),
getspnam(3C), secure_rpc(3NSL), nsswitch.conf(4), attributes(5)

Bugs

The update protocol passes all the information to the server in one RPC call without ever
looking at it. Thus, if you type your old password incorrectly, you are not notified until
after you have entered your new password.

ypwhich — Return Name of NIS Server of Map Master

Synopsis

/usr/bin/ypwhich [-d *domain*] [[-t] -m [*mname*] | [-V*n*] *hostname*]
/usr/bin/ypwhich -x

Description

ypwhich returns the name of the NIS server that supplies the NIS name services to an
NIS client or that is the master for a map. If invoked without arguments, ypwhich gives
the NIS server for the local system. If you specify *hostname*, that system is queried to
find out which NIS master it is using.

Refer to ypfiles(4) for an overview of the NIS name services.

Options

-d *domain*	Use *domain* instead of the default domain.
-m *mname*	Find the master NIS server for a map. You cannot specify a host name with -m. *mname* can be a map name or a nickname for a map. When you omit *mname*, produce a list of available maps.
-t	Inhibit map nickname translation.
-V*n*	Version of ypbind; V3 is the default.
-x	Display the map nickname translation table.

Attributes

See attributes(5) for descriptions of the following attributes:

Attribute Type	Attribute Value
Availability	SUNWnisu

See Also

ypfiles(4), attributes(5)

Z

zcat — Compress, Uncompress Files or Display Expanded Files

Synopsis

```
/usr/bin/zcat [file...]
```

Description

See compress(1).

zip, zipcloak, zipnote, zipsplit — Package and Compress Archive) Files

New!

Synopsis

```
zip [-aABcdDeEfFghjklLmoqrRSTuvVwXyz!@$] [-b path] [-n suffixes]
   [-t mmddyyyy] [-tt mmddyyyy] [zipfile [file1 file2...]] [-xi list]
zipcloak [-dhL] [-b path] zipfile
zipnote [-hwL] [-b path] zipfile
zipsplit [-hiLpst] [-n size [-b path] zipfile
```

1579

Description

The zip command, new in the Solaris 8 release, is a compression and file packaging command for UNIX, VMS, MS-DOS, OS/2, Windows NT, Minix, Atari, Macintosh, Amiga, and Acorn RISC OS.

zip is analogous to a combination of the UNIX commands tar(1) and compress(1) and is compatible with PKZIP (Phil Katz's ZIP for MS-DOS systems).

Note — Source for zip is available in the SUNWzips package.

A companion program, unzip(1), unpacks zip archives. The zip and unzip(1) programs can work with archives produced by PKZIP, and PKZIP and PKUNZIP can work with archives produced by zip. zip version 2.3 is compatible with PKZIP 2.04. Note that PKUNZIP 1.10 cannot extract files produced by PKZIP 2.04 or zip 2.3. You must use PKUNZIP 2.04 or unzip 5.0p1 (or later versions) to extract them.

For brief help on zip and unzip, run each without specifying any parameters on the command line.

zip is useful for packaging a set of files for distribution, for archiving files, and for saving disk space by temporarily compressing unused files or directories.

The zip program puts one or more compressed files into a single zip archive, along with information about the files (name, path, date, time of last modification, protection, and check information to verify file integrity). An entire directory structure can be packed into a zip archive with a single command. Compression ratios of 2:1 to 3:1 are common for text files. zip has one compression method (deflation) and can also store files without compression. zip automatically chooses the better of the two for each file to be compressed.

When given the name of an existing zip archive, zip replaces identically named entries in the zip archive or adds entries for new names. For example, if foo.zip exists and contains foo/file1 and foo/file2, and the directory foo contains the files foo/file1 and foo/file3, then

```
zip -r foo foo
```

replaces foo/file1 in foo.zip and adds foo/file3 to foo.zip. After this, foo.zip contains foo/file1, foo/file2, and foo/file3, with foo/file2 unchanged from before.

If the file list is specified as -@, [Not on MacOS] zip takes the list of input files from standard input. Under UNIX, you can use this option to powerful effect in conjunction with the find(1) command. The following example archives all the C source files in the current directory and its subdirectories.

```
find . -name "*.[ch]" -print | zip source -@
```

Note that you must quote the pattern to keep the shell from expanding it. zip also accepts a single dash (-) as the *zipfile* name, in which case it writes the *zipfile* to standard output, enabling you to pipe the output to another program. The following example writes the zip output directly to a tape with the specified block size to back up the current directory.

```
zip -r - . | dd of=/dev/nrst0 obs=16k
```

zip also accepts a single dash (-) as the name of a file to be compressed. It reads the file from standard input, enabling zip to take input from another program. The following example compresses the output of the tar command to back up the current directory.

```
tar cf - . | zip backup -
```

This command generally produces better compression than the previous example with the -r option because zip can take advantage of redundancy between files. You can restore the backup with the following command.

```
unzip -p backup | tar xf -
```

When you specify no *zipfile* name and standard output is not a terminal, zip acts as a filter, compressing standard input to standard output. The following example

```
tar cf - . | zip | dd of=/dev/nrst0 obs=16k
```

is equivalent to

```
tar cf - . | zip - - | dd of=/dev/nrst0 obs=16k
```

You can extract zip archives that are created in this way with the funzip command, which is provided in the unzip package or by gunzip, which is provided in the gzip package. The following example shows the syntax for extracting a zip archive with funzip.

```
dd if=/dev/nrst0 ibs=16k | funzip | tar xvf -
```

When changing an existing zip archive, zip writes a temporary file with the new contents and replaces the old one only when the process of creating the new version has been completed without error.

If the name of the zip archive does not contain an extension, the extension .zip is added. If the name already contains an extension other than .zip, the existing extension is kept unchanged.

Options

-a	[Systems with EBCDIC] Translate file to ASCII format.
-A	Adjust self-extracting executable archive. Create a self-extracting executable archive by prepending the SFX stub to an existing archive. The -A option tells zip to adjust the entry offsets stored in the archive to take into account this "preamble" data.
	Note: Self-extracting archives for the Amiga are a special case. At present, only the Amiga port of Zip is capable of adjusting or updating these archives without corrupting them. You can use the -J option to remove the SFX stub if you need to make other updates.
-b *path*	Use the specified *path* for the temporary zip archive. The following example puts the temporary zip archive in the directory /tmp, copying stuff.zip to the current directory when done.

```
zip -b /tmp stuff *
```

This option is useful only when updating an existing archive and the file system containing the old archive does not have enough space to hold both old and new archives at the same time.

-B	[VM/CMS and MVS] Force file to be read as binary (default is text).

-B*n*   [TANDEM] Set Edit/Enscribe formatting options with *n* defined as:

Bit 0: Don't add delimiter (Edit/Enscribe).

Bit 1: Use LF rather than CR/LF as delimiter (Edit/Enscribe).

Bit 2: Space fill record to maximum record length (Enscribe).

Bit 3: Trim trailing space (Enscribe).

Bit 8: Force 30K (Expand) large read for unstructured files.

-c   Add one-line comments for each file. File operations (adding, updating) are done first, and you are then prompted for a one-line comment for each file. Enter the comment followed by Return or press Return for no comment.

-d   Remove (delete) entries from a zip archive. The following example removes the entry foo/tom/junk, all of the files that start with foo/harry/, and all of the files that end with .o in any path.

zip -d foo foo/tom/junk foo/harry/* *.o

Note that backslashes inhibit shell path-name expansion so that zip can see the asterisks, enabling zip to match on the contents of the zip archive instead of on the contents of the current directory.

Under MS-DOS, -d is case sensitive when it matches names in the zip archive. This option requires that file names be entered in upper case if they were zipped by PKZIP on an MS-DOS system.

-df   [MacOS] Include only data-fork of files zipped into the archive. Good for exporting files to foreign operating systems. Resource-forks are ignored.

-D   Do not create entries in the zip archive for directories. Directory entries are created by default so that their attributes can be saved in the zip archive. You can use the ZIPOPT environment variable to change the default options. For example under UNIX with sh:

ZIPOPT="-D"; export ZIPOPT

(You can use the ZIPOPT variable with any option except -i and -x, and you can include several options.) The -D option is a shorthand for -x "*/", but you cannot set the latter as default in the ZIPOPT environment variable.

-e   Encrypt the contents of the zip archive with a password that is entered on the terminal in response to a prompt (the password is not echoed; if standard error is not a TTY, zip exits with an error). The password prompt is repeated to minimize typing errors.

-E   [OS/2] Use the .LONGNAME Extended Attribute (if found) as *filename*.

-f   Replace (freshen) an existing entry in the zip archive only if it has been modified more recently than the version already in the zip archive; unlike the update option (-u), this option does not add files that are not already in the zip archive. The following example should be run from the same directory in which the original zip command was run because paths stored in zip archives are always relative.

zip -f foo

Note that you should set the TZ time zone environment variable according to the local time zone for the -f, -u, and -o options to work correctly.

The reasons for this requirement are somewhat subtle but have to do with the differences between the UNIX-format file times (always in GMT) and most of the other operating systems (always local time) and the need to compare the two. A typical TZ value is MET-1MEST (Middle European time with automatic adjustment for summertime or daylight savings time).

-F   Fix the zip archive. You can use this option if some portions of the archive are missing. It is not guaranteed to work, so you *must* make a backup of the original archive first.

When doubled, as in -FF, the compressed sizes given inside the damaged archive are not trusted and zip scans for special signatures to identify the limits between the archive members. The single -F is more reliable if the archive is not too damaged, for example, if it has only been truncated, so try -F first.

Neither option can recover archives that have been incorrectly transferred in ascii mode instead of binary. After the repair, the -t option of unzip may show that some files have a bad CRC. Such files cannot be recovered; you can remove them from the archive with the -d option.

-g   Grow (append to) the specified zip archive, instead of creating a new one. If this operation fails, zip tries to restore the archive to its original state. If the restoration fails, the archive might become corrupted. This option is ignored when there's no existing archive or when at least one archive member must be updated or deleted.

-h   Display the zip help information (this information is also displayed when you run zip with no arguments).

-i *files*   Include only the specified files. The following example includes only the files that end in .c in the current directory and its subdirectories.

zip -r foo . -i *.c

For PKZIP users: the equivalent command is shown below

pkzip -rP foo *.c

PKZIP does not allow recursion in directories other than the current one. The backslash avoids the shell file-name substitution, so that the name matching is performed by zip at all directory levels. The following additional example includes only the files in the current directory and its subdirectories that match the patterns in the file include.1st.

zip -r foo . -i@include.1st

-I   [Acorn RISC OS] Don't scan through Image files. zip does not consider Image files (for example, DOS partitions or Spark archives when SparkFS is loaded) as directories but stores them as single files.

For example, if you have SparkFS loaded, zipping a Spark archive results in a *zipfile* containing a directory (and its content). By contrast, the -I option results in a *zipfile* containing a Spark archive. Obviously you can obtain the second case (without the -I option) if SparkFS isn't loaded.

-j   Store just the name of a saved file (discard the path) and do not store directory names. By default, zip stores the full path (relative to the current path).

-jj   [MacOS] record Fullpath (+ Volname). The complete path, including the volume is stored. By default, the relative path is stored.

-J   Strip any prepended data (for example, an SFX stub) from the archive.

-k   Try to convert the names and paths to conform to MS-DOS, store only the MS-DOS attribute (just the user write attribute from UNIX), and mark the entry as made under MS-DOS (even though it was not). Use this option for compatibility with PKUNZIP under MS-DOS, which cannot handle certain names such as those with two dots.

-l   Translate the UNIX end-of-line character LF into the MS-DOS convention CR LF. Do not use this option on binary files. You can use the -l option on UNIX if the *zipfile* is intended for PKUNZIP under MS-DOS. If the input files already contain CR LF, this option adds an extra CR. This ensures that unzip -a on UNIX gets back an exact copy of the original file, to undo the effect of zip -l.

-ll   Translate the MS-DOS end-of-line CR LF into UNIX LF. Do not use this option on binary files. You can use this option on MS-DOS if the *zipfile* is intended for unzip under UNIX.

-L   Display the zip license.

-m   Move the specified files into the zip archive. This option deletes the target directories/files after making the specified zip archive. If a directory becomes empty after removal of the files, the directory is also removed. No deletions are done until zip has created the archive without error. This option is useful for conserving disk space but is potentially dangerous, so it is recommended that it be used it in combination with -T to test the archive before all input files are removed.

-n *suffixes*

Do not try to compress files named with the given suffixes. Simply store those files (0% compression) in the output *zipfile*, so that zip doesn't waste time trying to compress them. Separate the suffixes by either colons or semicolons. The following example copies everything from foo into foo.zip but stores any files that end in .Z, .zip, .tiff, .gif, or .snd without trying to compress them. (Image and sound files often have their own specialized compression methods.)

zip -rn .Z:.zip:.tiff:.gif:.snd foo foo

By default, zip does not compress files with extensions in the list .Z:.zip:.zoo:.arc:.lzh:.arj. Such files are stored directly in the output archive. You can use the ZIPOPT environment variable to change the default options. For example under UNIX with csh, use

setenv ZIPOPT "-n .gif:.zip"

To attempt compression on all files, use

zip -n : foo

The -9 maximum compression option also tries compression on all files regardless of extension.

On Acorn RISC OS systems, the suffixes are actually file types (3-hex-digit format). By default, zip does not compress files with filetypes in the list DDC:D96:68E (that is, archives, CFS files, and PackDir files).

-N

[Amiga, MacOS] Save Amiga or MacOS file notes as *zipfile* comments. You can restore them with -N option of unzip. If you also specify the -c option, you are prompted for comments only for those files that do not have file notes.

-o

Set the "last modified" time of the zip archive to the latest (oldest) "last modified" time found among the entries in the zip archive. You can use this option without any other operations, if desired. The following example changes the last modified time of foo.zip to the latest time of the entries in foo.zip.

zip -o foo

-P *password*

Use *password* to encrypt *zipfile* entries (if any). *This option is insecure!* Many multiuser operating systems provide ways for any user to see the current command line of any other user. Even on standalone systems, the threat of over-the-shoulder peeking is always possible. Storing the plain-text password as part of a command line in an automated script is even worse. Whenever possible, use the nonechoing, interactive prompt to enter passwords. (And where security is truly important, use strong encryption such as Pretty Good Privacy instead of the relatively weak encryption provided by standard zip command.)

-q   Quiet mode; eliminate informational messages and comment prompts.
            (Useful, for example, in shell scripts and background tasks.)

-Q*n*   [QDOS] Store information about the file in the file header with *n*
            defined as follows: bit 0—Don't add headers for any file; bit 1—Add
            headers for all files; bit 2—Don't wait for interactive key press on exit.

-r   Travel the directory structure recursively. In the following example, all
            the files and directories in foo are saved in a zip archive named
            foo.zip, including files with names starting with . because the
            recursion does not use the shell's file-name substitution mechanism.

            zip -r foo foo

            If you want to include only a specific subset of the files in directory foo
            and its subdirectories, use the -i option to specify the pattern of files to
            be included. Do not use -r with the name ".*" because that matches
            .., which tries to zip the parent directory (probably not what was
            intended).

-R   Travel the directory structure recursively starting at the current
            directory. In the following example, all the files matching *.c in the tree
            starting at the current directory are stored into a zip archive named
            foo.zip.

            zip -R foo '*.c'

            For PKZIP users, the equivalent command is shown below.

            pkzip -rP foo *.c

-S   [MS-DOS, OS/2, WIN32 and ATARI] Include system and hidden files.
            [MacOS] Include finder invisible files, which are ignored otherwise.

-t *mmddyyyy*

            Do not operate on files modified before the specified date, where *mm* is
            the month (0–12), *dd* is the day of the month (1–31), and *yyyy* is the
            year. The ISO 8601 date format *yyyy-mm-dd* is also accepted. The
            following example adds to the infamy.zip archive all the files in foo
            and its subdirectories that were last modified on or after 7 December
            2001.

            zip -rt 12072001 infamy foo

            zip -rt 2001-12-07 infamy foo

-tt *mmddyyyy*

            Do not operate on files modified after or at the specified date, where *mm*
            is the month (0–12), *dd* is the day of the month (1-31), and *yyyy* is the
            year. The ISO 8601 date format *yyyy-mm-dd* is also accepted. The
            following examples add to the infamy.zip archive all the files in foo
            and its subdirectories that were last modified before 10 November
            2001.

            zip -rtt 11102001 infamy foo

            zip -rtt 2001-11-10 infamy foo

-T	Test the integrity of the new *zipfile*. If the check fails, the old *zipfile* is unchanged and (with the -m option) no input files are removed.
-u	Replace (update) an existing entry in the zip archive only if it has been modified more recently than the version already in the zip archive. The following example adds any new files in the current directory and updates any files modified since the archive stuff.zip was last created or modified. Note that zip does not try to pack stuff.zip into itself.

zip -u stuff *

Note that the -u option with no arguments acts like the -f (freshen) option.

-v	Verbose mode or print diagnostic version information. Normally, when applied to real operations, this option enables the display of a progress indicator during compression and requests verbose diagnostic information about *zipfile* structure oddities.

Print a diagnostic screen when -v is the only command-line argument and standard output is not redirected to a file. In addition to the help screen header with program name, version, and release date, some pointers to the Info-ZIP home and distribution sites are displayed. The option shows information about the target environment (compiler type and version, OS version, compilation date, and the enabled optional features used to create the zip executable).

-V	[VMS] Save VMS file attributes. zip archives created with this option generally cannot be used on other systems.
-w	[VMS] Append the version number of the files to the name, including multiple versions of files. (Default: use only the most recent version of a specified file.)
-x *files*	Explicitly exclude the specified files. The following example includes the contents of foo in foo.zip while excluding all the files that end in .o. The backslash avoids the shell file-name substitution, so the name matching is performed by zip at all directory levels.

zip -r foo foo -x *.o

Another use of this option is shown in the following example, which includes the contents of foo in foo.zip while excluding all the files that match the patterns in the file exclude.1st.

zip -r foo foo -x@exclude.1st

-X	Do not save extra file attributes (Extended Attributes on OS/2, UID/GID and file times on UNIX).
-y	Store symbolic links as symbolic links in the zip archive, instead of compressing and storing the file referred to by the link (UNIX only).
-z	Prompt for a multiline comment for the entire zip archive. End the comment with a line containing either just a period or an end-of-file condition (^D on UNIX; ^Z on MS-DOS, OS/2, and VAX/VMS). You can take the comment from a file, as shown in the following example.

```
zip -z foo < foowhat
```

-#   Regulate the speed of compression with the specified digit #, where -0
            means no compression (store all files), -1 means the fastest
            compression method (less compression), and -9 means the slowest
            compression method (optimal compression, ignores the suffix list). The
            default compression level is -6.

-!   [WIN32] Use privileges (if granted) to obtain all aspects of WinNT
            security.

-@   Take the list of input files from standard input. Specify only one file
            name per line.

-$ [MS-DOS, OS/2, WIN32] Include the volume label for the drive holding
            the first file to be compressed. If you want to include only the volume
            label or to force a specific drive, use the drive name as the first file
            name, as shown in the following example.

```
zip -$ foo a: c:bar
```

Examples

The following simple example creates the stuff.zip archive (assuming it does not
exist) and puts into it all of the files in the current directory in compressed form. The
.zip suffix is added automatically unless that archive name contains a dot already. This
feature enables you to explicitly specify other suffixes.

```
zip stuff *
```

In the previous example, because of the way the shell does file-name substitution,
files starting with . are not included. The following example shows how to include the
dot files as well.

```
zip stuff .* *
```

Even this syntax does not include any subdirectories from the current directory. To
zip an entire directory, the following example creates the foo.zip archive containing all
the files and directories in the directory foo that is contained within the current
directory.

```
zip -r foo foo
```

To make a zip archive that contains the files in foo without recording the directory
name foo, you can use the -j option to omit the paths, as shown in the following
example.

```
zip -j foo foo/*
```

If you are short on disk space, you might not have enough room to hold both the
original directory and the corresponding compressed zip archive. In this case, you can
create the archive in steps by using the -m option. If foo contains the subdirectories tom,
dick, and harry, you can use the following set of commands, where the first command
creates foo.zip and the next two add to it. At the completion of each zip command, the
last created archive is deleted, making room for the next zip command to function.

```
zip -rm foo foo/tom
zip -rm foo foo/dick
zip -rm foo foo/harry
```

Pattern Matching

This section applies only to UNIX. Watch this space for details on MS-DOS and VMS operation.

The UNIX shells (sh(1) and csh(1)) do file-name substitution on command arguments. The special characters are listed below.

?	Match any single character.
*	Match any number of characters (including none).
[]	Match any character in the range indicated within the brackets (example: [a-f], [0-9]).

When these characters are encountered (without being escaped with a backslash or quotes), the shell looks for files relative to the current path that match the pattern and replaces the argument with a list of the names that matched.

The zip program can do the same matching on names that are in the zip archive being modified or, in the case of the -x (exclude) or -i (include) options, on the list of files to be operated on, by using backslashes or quotes to tell the shell not to do the name expansion.

In general, when zip encounters a name in the list of files to do, zip first looks for the name in the file system. If it finds the name, the name is added to the list of files. If zip does not find the name, it looks for the name in the zip archive being modified (if the archive exists), using the pattern-matching characters described above if present. For each match, zip adds that name to the list of files to be processed unless this name matches one specified with the -x option or does not match any name specified with the -i option.

The pattern matching includes the path, so patterns like *.o match names that end in .o, no matter what the path prefix is. Note that the backslash must precede every special character (for example, ?*[]), or you must enclose the entire argument in double quotes (""). In general, use backslash to make zip do the pattern matching with the -f (freshen) and -d (delete) options and sometimes after the -x (exclude) option, when used with an appropriate operation (add, -u, -f, or -d).

Environment Variables

ZIPOPT	Contains default options that are used when running zip.
ZIP	[Not on RISC OS and VMS] See ZIPOPT.
Zip$Options	[RISC OS] See ZIPOPT.
Zip$Exts	[RISC OS] Contains extensions separated by a : that add native file names with one of the specified extensions to the zip file with basename and extension swapped.
ZIP_OPTS	[VMS] See ZIPOPT.

See Also

```
compress(1), tar(1), unzip(1), gzip(1)
```

Diagnostics

The exit status (or error level) approximates the exit codes defined by PKWARE and takes on the following values, except under VMS.

0	Normal; no errors or warnings detected.
2	Unexpected end of *zipfile*.
3	A generic error in the *zipfile* format was detected. Processing may have completed successfully anyway; some broken *zipfiles* created by other archivers have simple workarounds.
4	zip was unable to allocate memory for one or more buffers during program initialization.
5	A severe error in the *zipfile* format was detected. Processing probably failed immediately.
6	Entry too large to be split with zipsplit.
7	Invalid comment format.
8	zip -T failed or out of memory.
9	The user aborted zip prematurely with Control-C (or a similar command).
10	zip encountered an error while using a temporary file.
11	Read or seek error.
12	zip has nothing to do.
13	Missing or empty *zipfile*.
14	Error writing to a file.
15	zip was unable to create a file to write to.
16	Bad command-line parameters.
18	zip could not open a specified file to read.

VMS interprets standard UNIX (or PC) return values as other, scarier-looking things, so zip instead maps them into VMS-style status codes. The current mapping is 1 (success) for normal exit, and ($0x7fff000$? $+ 16*normal\_zip\_exit\_status$) for all errors, where the ? is 0 (warning) for zip value 12, 2 (error) for the zip values 3, 6, 7, 9, 13, 16, 18, and 4 (fatal error) for the remaining ones.

Bugs

zip 2.3 is not compatible with PKUNZIP 1.10. Use zip 1.1 to produce *zipfiles* that can be extracted by PKUNZIP 1.10.

zipfiles produced by zip 2.3 must not be updated by zip 1.1 or PKZIP 1.10 if they contain encrypted members or if they have been produced in a pipe or on a nonseekable device. The old versions of zip or PKZIP would create an archive with an incorrect format. The old versions can list the contents of the zip file but cannot extract it anyway (because of the new compression algorithm). If you do not use encryption and use regular disk files, you do not have to care about this problem.

Under VMS, not all of the odd file formats are treated properly. Only stream-LF format *zipfiles* are expected to work with zip. Others can be converted with Rahul Dhesi's BILF program. This version of zip handles some of the conversion internally.

When using Kermit to transfer `zip` files from VAX to MS-DOS, type **"set file type block"** on the VAX. When transferring from MS-DOS to VAX, type **"set file type fixed"** on the VAX. In both cases, type **"set file type binary"** on MS-DOS. Under VMS, `zip` hangs for file specification that uses DECnet syntax `foo::*.*`.

On OS/2, `zip` cannot match some names, such as those including an exclamation mark or a hash sign. This bug is in OS/2 itself: the 32-bit DosFindFirst/Next doesn't find such names. Other programs such as GNUtar are also affected by this bug.

Under OS/2, the amount of Extended Attributes displayed by DIR is (for compatibility) the amount returned by the 16-bit version of DosQueryPathInfo(). Otherwise, OS/2 1.3 and 2.0 would report different EA sizes when using the DIR command on a file. However, the structure layout returned by the 32-bit DosQueryPathInfo() is a bit different; it uses extra padding bytes and link pointers (it's a linked list) to have all fields on 4-byte boundaries for portability to future RISC OS/2 versions. Therefore, the value reported by `zip` (which uses this 32-bit-mode size) differs from that reported by DIR. `zip` stores the 32-bit format for portability and even stores the 16-bit MS-C-compiled version running on OS/2 1.3, so even this one shows the 32-bit-mode size.

Authors

Please send bug reports and comments by e-mail to zip-bugs@lists.wku.edu. For bug reports, please include the version of `zip` (see `zip -h`), the make options used to compile it (see `zip-v`), the machine and operating system in use, and as much additional information as possible.

Acknowledgements

Thanks to R. P. Byrne for his Shrink.Pas program, which inspired this project, and from which the shrink algorithm was stolen; to Phil Katz for placing in the public domain the `zip` file format, compression format, and .ZIP file-name extension and for accepting minor changes to the file format; to Steve Burg for clarifications on the deflate format; to Haruhiko Okumura and Leonid Broukhis for providing some useful ideas for the compression algorithm; to Keith Petersen, Rich Wales, Hunter Goatley, and Mark Adler for providing a mailing list and FTP site for the Info-ZIP group to use; and most importantly, to the Info-ZIP group itself (listed in the file infozip.who) without whose tireless testing and bug-fixing efforts a portable `zip` would not have been possible. Finally we should thank (blame) the first Info-ZIP moderator, David Kirschbaum, for getting us into this mess in the first place. The manual page was rewritten for UNIX by R. P. C. Rodgers.

zipinfo — List Detailed Information About a Zip Archive

Synopsis

```
/usr/bin/zipinfo [-12smlvhMtTz] file[.zip] [file(s)...] [-x xfile(s)...]
/usr/bin/unzip -Z [-12smlvhMtTz] file[.zip] [file(s)...]
   [-x xfile(s)...]
```

Description

> **Note** — zipinfo is the same program as unzip (under UNIX, a link to it);
> on some systems, however, zipinfo support may have been omitted when
> unzip was compiled.

zipinfo lists technical information about files in a ZIP archive. Such information
includes file access permissions, encryption status, type of compression, version, and the
operating or file system of compressing program. The default behavior (specifying *file*
with no options) is to list single-line entries for each file in the archive, with header and
totals lines providing summary information for the entire archive. The format is a cross
between UNIX ls -l and unzip -v output, as shown in the following example.

```
castle% zipinfo 085XDOCS
Archive:  085XDOCS.zip   106272 bytes   4 files
-rw-a--    2.0 fat    76800 t- defN 18-Aug-98 21:55 085X01.DOC
-rw-a--    2.0 fat    67072 b- defN 22-Aug-98 01:39 085X02.DOC
-rw-a--    2.0 fat    95232 t- defN 31-Aug-98 20:29 085X042.DOC
-rw-a--    2.0 fat    63488 t- defN  4-Oct-98 20:24 085X04E.DOC
4 files, 302592 bytes uncompressed, 105858 bytes compressed:  65.0%
castle%
```

> **Note** — You may find it convenient to define an ii alias for zipinfo on
> systems that allow aliases. On other systems you can copy and rename the
> executable, create a link, or create a command file with the name ii. The
> ii usage parallels the common ll alias for long listings in UNIX. The
> similarity between the outputs of the two commands was intentional.

Arguments

file[.zip]   Path of the ZIP archive(s). If you specify a wild-card for *file*, process
each matching file in an order determined by the operating system (or
file system). Only the file name can be a wild-card; the path itself
cannot. Wild-card expressions are similar to UNIX egrep(1) (regular)
expressions and may contain:

    *   Match a sequence of zero or more characters.

    ?   Match exactly one character.

[...] Match any single character found inside the brackets; specify ranges with a beginning character, a hyphen, and an ending character. If an exclamation point (!) or a caret (^) follows the left bracket, then the range of characters within the brackets is complemented (that is, anything except the characters inside the brackets is considered a match).

Be sure to quote any character that might otherwise be interpreted or modified by the operating system, particularly under UNIX and VMS. If no matches are found, assume a literal file name; and if that also fails, append the suffix .zip. Note that self-extracting ZIP files are supported, as with any other ZIP archive; just specify the .exe suffix (if any).

[*file*(s)] An optional, space-separated list of archive members to be processed. (For VMS versions compiled with VMSCLI defined, delimit files with commas instead. See -v.) You can use regular expressions (wild-cards) to match multiple members. Again, be sure to quote expressions that would otherwise be expanded or modified by the operating system.

[-x *xfile*(s)]

An optional list of archive members to be excluded from processing.

Options

-1 List file names only, one per line. This option excludes all others. Never print headers, totals lines, or file comments. This option is intended for use in UNIX shell scripts.

-2 List file names only, one per line, and display headers (-h), totals lines (-t), and file comments (-z). This option can be useful in cases in which the stored file names are particularly long.

-s List file information in short UNIX ls -l format (the default).

-m List file information in medium UNIX ls -l format. Identical to the -s output, except also list the compression factor expressed as a percentage.

-l List file information in long UNIX ls -l format. Identical to the -m output, except express the compressed size (in bytes) instead of the compression ratio.

-v List file information in verbose, multipage format.

-h List header line. Print the archive name, actual size (in bytes), and total number of files.

-M	Pipe all output through an internal pager similar to the UNIX more(1) command. At the end of a screen of output, pause with a --More-- prompt. To view the next screen, you press the Enter (Return) key or the space bar. You can quit zipinfo with the q key and, on some systems, with the Enter/Return key. Unlike UNIX more(1), zipinfo does not allow you to search forward or edit. zipinfo does not notice if long lines wrap at the edge of the screen, effectively resulting in the printing of two or more lines. Some text may scroll off the top of the screen before being viewed.
	On some systems, the number of available lines on the screen is not detected, in which case zipinfo assumes the height is 24 lines.
-t	List the number of files, their uncompressed and compressed total sizes, and their overall compression factor. Alternatively, list the values for the entire archive if only the totals line is printed. Note that the total compressed (data) size never matches the actual file size because the latter includes all of the internal file headers in addition to the compressed data.
-T	Print the file dates and times in a sortable decimal format (*yymmdd.hhmmss*). The default date format is a more standard, human-readable version with abbreviated month names.
-z	Include the archive comment (if any) in the listing.
-Z	If the first option on the command line is -Z, interpret the remaining options as zipinfo(1) options.

Note — When you use the -h or -t options by themselves or with each other, they override any default listings of files in the archive. Only the header and/or totals lines are displayed. This behavior is useful when you use zipinfo with a wild-card file specification; the contents of all files are then summarized with a single command.

Detailed Description

zipinfo has a number of modes, and its behavior can be difficult to fathom if you aren't familiar with the UNIX ls(1) command. The default behavior is to list files in the format shown below.

```
-rw-rws---  1.9 unx    2802 t- defX 11-Aug-91 13:48 perms.2660
```

This example is for a ZIP file generated on a UNIX system. Because it comes from UNIX, the file permissions at the beginning of the line in this example are printed in UNIX format.

The second and third fields indicate that the file was zipped under UNIX with version 1.9 of zip. The fourth field shows the uncompressed file size (2802 in this example).

The fifth field consists of two characters, either of which can have several values. The first character can be either t or b, indicating that zipinfo believes the file to be text or binary. If the file is encrypted, the letters are capitalized. The second character can display four values, depending on whether there is an extended local header and/or an extra field associated with the file. (The values are fully explained in PKWARE's APPNOTE.TXT but are basically analogous to programs in ANSI C—that is, they provide a standard way to include nonstandard information in the archive.)

Values for the second character are summarized below.

-	Neither the header nor the extra field exists.
1	The file has an extended local header but no extra field.
x	The file has an extra field but no extended local header.
X	The file has an extra field and an extended local header.

Thus, the file in this example is (probably) a text file, is not encrypted, and has neither an extra field nor an extended local header associated with it.

The sixth field indicates the compression method and possible submethod used. Six methods are known at present:

- Storing (no compression).
- Reducing.
- Shrinking.
- Imploding.
- Tokenizing (never publicly released).
- Deflating.

In addition, there are four levels of reducing (1 through 4); four types of imploding (4K or 8K sliding dictionary, and 2 or 3 Shannon-Fano trees); and four levels of deflating (superfast, fast, normal, maximum compression). zipinfo represents these methods and their submethods as follows: stor; re:1, re.2, etc.; shrk; i4:2, i8:3, etc.; tokn; and defS, defF, defN, and defX.

The last three fields contain the modification date and time of the file and its name. The case of the file name is respected so that files that come from MS-DOS PKZIP are always capitalized. If the file was zipped with a stored directory name, that name is also displayed as part of the file name.

The following example is an encrypted binary file with an extra field. The file attributes in the first field are listed in VMS format.

```
RWD,R,R     0.9 vms     168 Bx shrk  9-Aug-91 19:15 perms.0644
```

Extra fields are used for various purposes (see the discussion of the -v option), including the storage of VMS file attributes, which is presumably the case here. Some other possibilities for the host file system include OS/2 or NT with High Performance File System (HPFS), MS-DOS, OS/2, or NT with File Allocation Table (FAT) file system, and Macintosh. These are denoted as follows:

```
-rw-a--      1.0 hpf    5358 Tl i4:3  4-Dec-91 11:33 longfilename.hpfs
-r--ahs      1.1 fat    4096 b- i4:2 14-Jul-91 12:58 EA DATA. SF
--w-------   1.0 mac   17357 bx i8:2  4-May-92 04:02 unzip.macr
```

File attributes in the first two cases are indicated in a UNIX-like format, with seven subfields that specify the following information.

1. The file is a directory.
2. The file is readable (always true).
3. The file is writable.
4. The file is executable (guessed on the basis of the extension—.exe, .com, .bat, .cmd, or .btm).
5. The file has its archive bit set.

6. The file is hidden.

7. The file is a system file.

Interpretation of Macintosh file attributes is unreliable because some Macintosh archivers don't store any attributes in the archive.

The medium and long listings are almost identical to the short format except that they add information on file compression. The medium format lists the file compression factor as a percentage, indicating the amount of space that has been removed. In the following example, the file has been compressed by more than a factor of five; the compressed data is only 19 percent of the original size.

```
-rw-rws---  1.5 unx    2802 t- 81% defX 11-Aug-91 13:48 perms.2660
```

The long format shows the compressed file's size in bytes, as shown in the following example.

```
-rw-rws---  1.5 unx    2802 t-     538 defX 11-Aug-91 13:48 perms.2660
```

You can add the -T option to change the file date and time to decimal format, as shown below.

```
-rw-rws---  1.5 unx    2802 t-     538 defX 910811.134804 perms.2660
```

Note that because of limitations in the MS-DOS format used to store file times, the seconds field is always rounded to the nearest even second. For UNIX files, this is expected to change in the next major releases of zip and unzip(1).

In addition to individual file information, a default file listing also includes header and totals lines, as shown in the following example.

```
Archive:  OS2.zip   5453 bytes   5 files
,,rw,       1.0 hpf     730 b- i4:3 26-Jun-92 23:40 Contents
,,rw,       1.0 hpf    3710 b- i4:3 26-Jun-92 23:33 makefile.os2
,,rw,       1.0 hpf    8753 b- i8:3 26-Jun-92 15:29 os2unzip.c
,,rw,       1.0 hpf      98 b- stor 21-Aug-91 15:34 unzip.def
,,rw,       1.0 hpf      95 b- stor 21-Aug-91 17:51 zipinfo.def
5 files, 13386 bytes uncompressed, 4951 bytes compressed: 63.0%
```

The header line shows the name of the archive, its total size, and the total number of files. The totals line shows the number of files listed, their total uncompressed size, and their total compressed size (not including any of zip's internal overhead). If, however, you specify one or more file(s), the header and totals lines are not listed. This behavior is also similar to that of the UNIX ls -l command. You can override this behavior by specifying the -h and -t options. When you specify the -h or -t options, you must also specify the listing format; for example, zipinfo -htl find.zip. If you do not specify a listing format with -h, -t, or -ht, only the specified lines are listed.

The verbose listing is mostly self-explanatory. It also lists file comments, if any, and the type and number of bytes in any stored extra fields. Currently known types of extra fields include PKWARE's authentication (AV) information; OS/2 extended attributes; VMS file system information, both PKWARE and Info-ZIP versions; Macintosh resource forks; Acorn/Archimedes SparkFS information; and so on.

Note — In the case of OS/2 extended attributes—perhaps the most common use of file extra fields—the size of the stored EAs as reported by zipinfo may not match the number given by OS/2's dir command: OS/2 always reports the number of required bytes in 16-bit format, whereas zipinfo always reports the 32-bit storage.

Environment Options

Modifying the zipinfo default behavior with options in an environment variable can be a bit complicated to explain because zipinfo tries to handle various defaults in an intuitive, yet UNIX-like, manner. (Try not to laugh.) zipinfo has three priority levels of options.

- Default options.
- Environment options, which can override or add to the defaults.
- Explicit options specified on the command line, which can override or add to either of the above.

The default variable names are ZIPINFO_OPTS for VMS (where the symbol used to install zipinfo as a foreign command would otherwise be confused with the environment variable) and ZIPINFO for all other operating systems. For compatibility with zip, ZIPINFOOPT is also accepted (don't ask). If you define both ZIPINFO and ZIPINFOOPT, ZIPINFO takes precedence. You can use the unzip diagnostic option (-v with no file name) to check the values of all four possible unzip and zipinfo environment variables.

The default listing format corresponds roughly to the zipinfo -hst command (except when you specify individual files). If you prefer the long format listing (-l), you can change the default by using the ZIPINFO environment variable, as shown below.

```
ZIPINFO=-l; export ZIPINFO
```
> UNIX Bourne shell.

```
setenv ZIPINFO -l
```
> UNIX C shell.

```
set ZIPINFO=-l
```
> OS/2 or MS-DOS.

```
define ZIPINFO_OPTS "-l"
```
> VMS (quotes for lower case).

You can also specify negative options to override defaults. Precede the undesired option with one or more dashes. If, for example, you don't like the totals line, you can specify -l-t or --tl options. The first dash is the regular switch character, but the second one is always interpreted as a minus sign. This dual use of dashes may seem a little awkward, but it's reasonably intuitive. After the first dash, any other dashes signify a negative option. This syntax is consistent with the behavior of the UNIX nice(1) command.

Bugs

As with unzip, the zipinfo -M (more) option is overly simplistic in its handling of screen output. It fails to detect the wrapping of long lines and may scroll lines at the top of the screen before they are read. zipinfo should detect and treat each occurrence of line wrap as one additional line printed, which requires knowledge of both the screen width and height. In addition, zipinfo should detect the true screen geometry on all systems.

The multiple listing formats are unnecessarily complex and should be simplified. (That is not to say that they will be.)

Examples

The following example displays a basic, short-format listing of the complete contents of the 085XDOCS.ZIP archive, with both header and totals lines.

```
castle% zipinfo 085XDOCS
Archive:  085XDOCS.zip   106272 bytes    4 files
-rw-a--    2.0 fat    76800 t- defN 18-Aug-98 21:55 085X01.DOC
-rw-a--    2.0 fat    67072 b- defN 22-Aug-98 01:39 085X02.DOC
-rw-a--    2.0 fat    95232 t- defN 31-Aug-98 20:29 085X042.DOC
-rw-a--    2.0 fat    63488 t- defN  4-Oct-98 20:24 085X04E.DOC
4 files, 302592 bytes uncompressed, 105858 bytes compressed:  65.0%
castle%
```

The following example displays a basic, long-format listing (not verbose), including header and totals lines.

```
castle% zipinfo -l 085XDOCS
Archive:  085XDOCS.ZIP   106272 bytes    4 files
-rw-a--    2.0 fat    76800 t-    28048 defN 18-Aug-98 21:55 085X01.DOC
-rw-a--    2.0 fat    67072 b-    24492 defN 22-Aug-98 01:39 085X02.DOC
-rw-a--    2.0 fat    95232 t-    30592 defN 31-Aug-98 20:29 085X042.DOC
-rw-a--    2.0 fat    63488 t-    22726 defN  4-Oct-98 20:24 085X04E.DOC
4 files, 302592 bytes uncompressed, 105858 bytes compressed:  65.0%
castle%
```

The following example lists the complete contents of the archive without header and totals lines.

```
castle% zipinfo --h-t 085XDOCS
-rw-a--    2.0 fat    76800 t- defN 18-Aug-98 21:55 085X01.DOC
-rw-a--    2.0 fat    67072 b- defN 22-Aug-98 01:39 085X02.DOC
-rw-a--    2.0 fat    95232 t- defN 31-Aug-98 20:29 085X042.DOC
-rw-a--    2.0 fat    63488 t- defN  4-Oct-98 20:24 085X04E.DOC
castle%
```

The following example produces the same result as the previous one, using a different syntax. The backslash is required only if the shell would otherwise expand the * wild-card. Alternatively, you can enclose the * in double quotes.

```
castle% zipinfo 085XDOCS \*
-rw-a--    2.0 fat    76800 t- defN 18-Aug-98 21:55 085X01.DOC
-rw-a--    2.0 fat    67072 b- defN 22-Aug-98 01:39 085X02.DOC
-rw-a--    2.0 fat    95232 t- defN 31-Aug-98 20:29 085X042.DOC
-rw-a--    2.0 fat    63488 t- defN  4-Oct-98 20:24 085X04E.DOC
castle%
```

The following example uses the ZIPINFO environment variable to turn off the totals line.

```
castle% setenv ZIPINFO --t
castle% zipinfo 085XDOCS
Archive:  085XDOCS.zip   106272 bytes    4 files
-rw-a--    2.0 fat    76800 t- defN 18-Aug-98 21:55 085X01.DOC
-rw-a--    2.0 fat    67072 b- defN 22-Aug-98 01:39 085X02.DOC
-rw-a--    2.0 fat    95232 t- defN 31-Aug-98 20:29 085X042.DOC
-rw-a--    2.0 fat    63488 t- defN  4-Oct-98 20:24 085X04E.DOC
castle%
```

The following examples show how to display the full, short-format listing when the
environment variable is set to turn off the totals line. Note that you must explicitly
specify the -s option because the -t option by itself implies that only the totals line is to
be printed.

```
castle% setenv ZIPINFO --t
castle% zipinfo -t 085XDOCS
4 files, 302592 bytes uncompressed, 105858 bytes compressed:  65.0%
castle% zipinfo -st 085XDOCS
Archive:   085XDOCS.zip    106272 bytes    4 files
-rw-a--     2.0 fat    76800 t- defN 18-Aug-98 21:55 085X01.DOC
-rw-a--     2.0 fat    67072 b- defN 22-Aug-98 01:39 085X02.DOC
-rw-a--     2.0 fat    95232 t- defN 31-Aug-98 20:29 085X042.DOC
-rw-a--     2.0 fat    63488 t- defN  4-Oct-98 20:24 085X04E.DOC
4 files, 302592 bytes uncompressed, 105858 bytes compressed:  65.0%
castle%
```

The -s option, like -m and -l, includes header and totals lines by default, unless you
specify otherwise. Because the environment variable specified no totals lines and that
setting has a higher precedence than the default behavior of -s, you must use an explicit
-t option to produce the full listing. Because nothing was indicated about the header,
the -s option is sufficient.

The following example lists information in medium format about a single file within
the archive.

```
castle% zipinfo -m 085XDOCS 085X01.DOC
-rw-a--     2.0 fat    76800 t- 64% defN 18-Aug-98 21:55 085X01.DOC
castle%
```

When you specify any individual file with any of the format options, zipinfo displays
only the single line of information about the requested file, regardless of the default
specifications for header and totals lines. You can, of course, add the t or h option to the
command.

The following example displays the first screen of information about the zip archive,
using the verbose option and piping the output through the more(1) command.

```
castle% zipinfo -v 085XDOCS | more
Archive:  085XDOCS.zip    106272 bytes    4 files

End-of-central-directory record:
-------------------------------

   Actual offset of end-of-central-dir record:      106250 (00019F0Ah)
   Expected offset of end-of-central-dir record:    106250 (00019F0Ah)
   (based on the length of the central directory and its expected offset)

   This zipfile constitutes the sole disk of a single-part archive; its
   central directory contains 4 entries.  The central directory is 226
   (000000E2h) bytes long, and its (expected) offset in bytes from the
   beginning of the zipfile is 106024 (00019E28h).

   There is no zipfile comment.

Central directory entry #0:
---------------------------
```

```
085X01.DOC

  offset of local header from start of archive:       4 (00000004h) bytes
  file system or operating system of origin:          MS-DOS, OS/2 or NT FAT
  version of encoding software:                       2.0
  minimum file system compatibility required:         MS-DOS, OS/2 or NT FAT
  minimum software version required to extract:       2.0
  compression method:                                 deflated
  compression sub-type (deflation):                   normal
  file security status:                               not encrypted
  extended local header:                              no
  file last modified on (DOS date/time):              1998 Aug 18 21:55:14
  32-bit CRC value (hex):                             dcd30c5e
  compressed size:                                    28048 bytes
  uncompressed size:                                  76800 bytes
  length of filename:                                 10 characters
--More--
```

The following example shows the most recently modified files in the archive by using the -T option in conjunction with the sort(1) and tail(1) commands.

```
castle% zipinfo -T 085XDOCS | sort -n +6 | tail -15
Archive:  085XDOCS.zip   106272 bytes    4 files
-rw-a--    2.0 fat     76800 t- defN 19980818.215514 085X01.DOC
-rw-a--    2.0 fat     67072 b- defN 19980822.013946 085X02.DOC
-rw-a--    2.0 fat     95232 t- defN 19980831.202906 085X042.DOC
-rw-a--    2.0 fat     63488 t- defN 19981004.202402 085X04E.DOC
castle%
```

The -n option to sort(1) sorts numerically instead of in ASCII order. The +6 option sorts on the sixth field after the first one (that is, the seventh field). This count assumes the default short-format listing; if you use -m or -l, the proper sort(1) option is +7. The tail(1) command filters out all but the last 15 lines of the listing. Future releases of zipinfo may incorporate date/time and file-name sorting as built-in options.

To display information for a list of files by using the asterisk metacharacter, you must escape it by preceding it with a backslash. The following example shows information about three zip archives.

```
castle% zipinfo \*.ZIP
Archive:  085XDOCS.ZIP   145051 bytes    6 files
-rw-a--    2.0 fat     76800 t- defN 18-Aug-98 21:55 085X01.DOC
-rw-a--    2.0 fat     67072 b- defN 22-Aug-98 01:39 085X02.DOC
-rw-a--    2.0 fat     80384 b- defN 24-Sep-98 18:40 085X03~1.DOC
-rw-a--    2.0 fat     95232 t- defN 31-Aug-98 20:29 085X042.DOC
-rw-a--    2.0 fat     50688 b- defN  8-Jan-99 09:48 085X08R.DOC
-rw-a--    2.0 fat     73238 t- defN 18-Dec-98 14:18 085X09E.RTF
6 files, 443414 bytes uncompressed, 144439 bytes compressed:  67.4%

Archive:  085XFILE.ZIP   30716 bytes    1 file
-rw-a--    2.0 fat     95232 t- defN 31-Aug-98 20:29 085X042.DOC
1 file, 95232 bytes uncompressed, 30592 bytes compressed:  67.9%

Archive:  085XINTR.ZIP   43319 bytes    2 files
-rw-a--    2.0 fat     76800 t- defN 18-Aug-98 21:55 085X01.DOC
-rw-a--    2.0 fat     73238 t- defN 18-Dec-98 14:18 085X09E.RTF
2 files, 150038 bytes uncompressed, 43099 bytes compressed:  71.3%
```

```
3 archives were successfully processed.
castle%
```

See Also

ls(1), unzip(1)

URL

The Info-ZIP home page is currently at http://www.cdrom.com/pub/infozip/

Copyright

Distributed with permission from Info-ZIP. Please see
http://www.cdrom.com/pub/infozip/doc/COPYING for copyright information.

Author

Greg "Cave Newt" Roelofs. ZipInfo contains pattern-matching code by Mark Adler and fixes/improvements by many others. Please refer to the CONTRIBS file in the UnZip source distribution for a more complete list.

GET READY!

Congratulations on taking control of your career! With Sun certification, you can enjoy the benefits of increased job opportunities, greater career advancement potential, and more professional respect.

The first step in preparing for exams is discovering what you need to know. The next step is discovering what you don't. To help you measure your skills and understand any gaps, Sun offers online skills assessments. They'll help you focus your energies on learning the skills that can lead to certification. Online skills assessments are available at: http://suned.sun.com/USA/solutions/assessments.html.

GET SET!

Preparation is the key to success, and this study guide is a good first step. However, our years of experience have taught us that few people learn in exactly the same way. So we've created innovative learning solutions that can augment this guide, including:

Learning Solutions: Delivered via the Sun Web Learning Center, Sun's innovative eLearning solutions include Web-based training, online mentoring, ePractice exams, and the benefits of a community of like-minded people. Available by subscription, eLearning solutions from Sun give you anywhere, anytime learning—providing the flexibility you need to prepare according to your schedule, at your pace. You can visit the Sun Web Learning Center at http://suned.sun.com/WLC.

Practice Exams: Also available through the Sun Web Learning Center, ePractice exams are practice tools that can help you prepare for Sun's Java platform certifications. The questions in the ePractice exams are written in the same format as the certification tests, helping acquaint you with the style of the actual certification exams. You get immediate results and recommendations for further study, helping you prepare and take your certification tests with more confidence. You can register for ePractice exams at http://suned.sun.com/US/wlc/.

Instructor-Led Training: Sun's expert instructors provide unparalleled learning experiences designed to get you up to speed quickly. Available at over 200 Sun locations worldwide or at your facility, instructor-led courses provide learning experiences that will last a lifetime.

Self-Paced CD-ROM-based Training: Using JavaTutor, our CD-ROM-based learning solutions help you prepare for exams on your own terms, at your own pace, in a dynamic environment. After you're certified, they'll serve as perfect reference tools.

GO!

After you take your exams and become certified, go ahead and celebrate. For more information, visit: http://suned.sun.com.

Your road is wide open. Enjoy the journey.